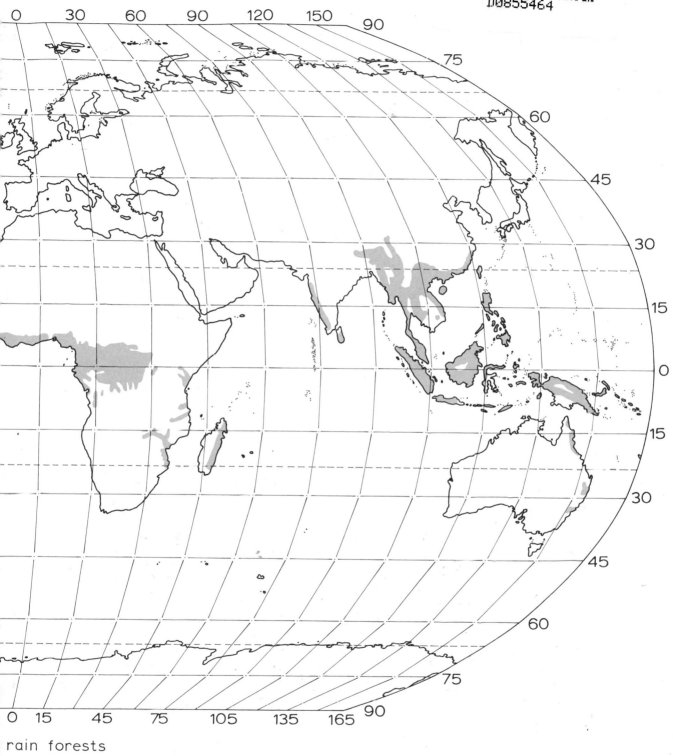

rain forests

ECOSYSTEMS OF THE WORLD 14B

TROPICAL RAIN FOREST ECOSYSTEMS

BIOGEOGRAPHICAL AND ECOLOGICAL STUDIES

ECOSYSTEMS OF THE WORLD

Editor in Chief:

David W. Goodall

CSIRO Division of Land Resources Management, Wembley, W.A. (Australia)

ECOSYSTEMS OF THE WORLD 14B

TROPICAL RAIN FOREST ECOSYSTEMS

BIOGEOGRAPHICAL AND ECOLOGICAL STUDIES

Edited by

H. Lieth

Fachbereich Biologie/Chemie
Universität Osnabrück
Postfach 4469
D-4500 Osnabrück (F.R.G.)

and

M.J.A. Werger

Department of Plant Ecology
State University of Utrecht
Lange Nieuwstraat 106
3512 PN Utrecht (The Netherlands)

ELSEVIER

Amsterdam—Oxford—New York—Tokyo 1989

ELSEVIER SCIENCE PUBLISHERS B.V.
Sara Burgerhartstraat 25
P.O. Box 211, 1000 AE Amsterdam, The Netherlands

Distributors for the United States and Canada:

ELSEVIER SCIENCE PUBLISHING COMPANY INC.
655, Avenue of the Americas
New York, NY 10010, U.S.A.

Library of Congress Cataloging-in-Publication Data

Tropical rain forest ecosystems.

   (Ecosystems of the world ; 14)
   Volume 2 edited by H. Lieth and M.J.A. Werger.
   Includes bibliographies and indexes.
   Contents: A. Structure and function -- B. Biogeograph-
ical and ecological studies.
   1. Rain forest ecology. I. Golley, Frank B.
II. Lieth, Helmut. III. Werger, M. J. A. IV. Series.
QH541.5.R27T76 1983   574.5'2642   81-7861

ISBN 0-444-41986-1 (v. A)
ISBN 0-444-42755-4 (v. B)

ISBN 0-444-42755-4 (Vol. 14B)
ISBN 0-444-41810-5 (Set)

© Elsevier Science Publishers B.V., 1989

Printed in The Netherlands

CORRIGENDUM

A serious printing error has resulted in an exchange of Figs. 2.22 (p. 23), 2.30 (p. 30) and 2.33 (p. 32). The correct figures and their captions are shown below.

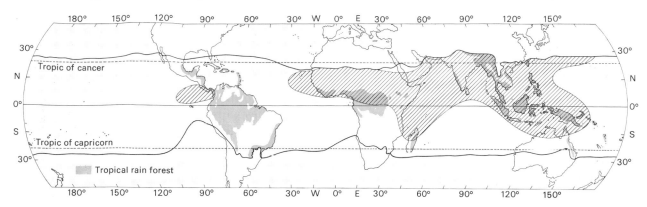

Fig. 2.22. Areas with tropical monsoon circulation. (After various authors.)

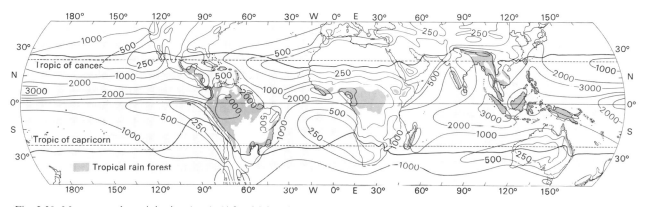

Fig. 2.30. Mean annual precipitation (mm). (After Meinardus, 1933.)

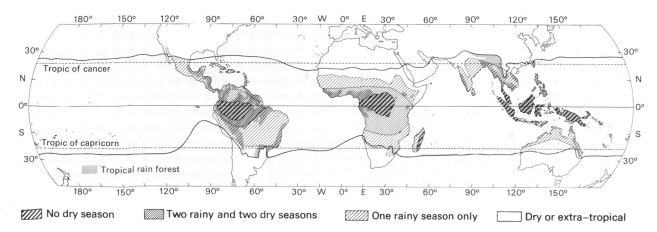

Fig. 2.33. Seasonal rainfall distribution. (After Blüthgen and Weischet, and Nieuwolt, 1982.)

thank Mrs. McCallum, secretary to the senior editor, who kept us in touch with each other and with the authors, and solved many problems for us while both of us were travelling abroad.

We hope we achieved with our volume the most complete coverage of information needed for someone visiting the tropical rain forest areas as an ecologist, or to prepare someone who is interested to work in tropical forest ecosystems in the future.

We also hope that this book can trigger the interest or even the desire of young ecologists to work in the world's most interesting ecosystem, the tropical rain forest.

H. LIETH
Osnabrück
M.J.A. WERGER
Utrecht

LIST OF CONTRIBUTORS TO VOLUME 14

J.M. ANDERSON
Department of Biology
University of Exeter
Exeter (U.K.)

P.S. ASHTON
Arnold Arboretum
22 Divinity Avenue
Cambridge, MA 02138 (U.S.A.)

D.J. BAGYARAJ
Department of Agricultural Microbiology
University of Agricultural Sciences
G.K.V.K. Campus
Bangalore 560 065 (India)

H.G. BAKER
Department of Botany
University of California
Berkeley, CA 94720 (U.S.A.)

K.S. BAWA
Department of Biology
University of Massachusetts
Boston, MA 02125 (U.S.A.)

E.L. BENNETT
World Wildlife Fund
Sarawak Office
7 Jalan Ridgeway
Kuching, Sarawak (Malaysia)

D.H. BENZING
Department of Biology
Oberlin College
Oberlin, OH 44074 (U.S.A.)

P.S. BOURGERON
Natural Resource Ecology Laboratory
Colorado State University
Fort Collins, Colo. (U.S.A.)

F. BOURLIÈRE
15, Avenue de Tourville
75007 Paris (France)

W.L.F. BRINKMANN
FB Geowissenschaften-Hydrologie
Universität Frankfurt
Arndtstr. 11
D-6000 Frankfurt (F.R.G.)

E.F. BRUENIG
Bundesforschungsanstalt für Forst-
und Holzwirtschaft
Leuschnerstr. 91
D-2000 Hamburg 80 (F.R.G.)

J.O. CALDECOTT
World Wildlife Fund
Sarawak Office
7 Jalan Ridgeway
Kuching, Sarawak (Malaysia)

J.M. CHERRETT
School of Animal Biology
University College of North Wales
Bangor, Gwynned LL57 2UW (U.K.)

N.M. COLLINS
International Union for Conservation
of Nature and Natural Resources
219(c) Huntington Road
Cambridge CB3 0DL (U.K.)

F. DIETERLEN
Staatliches Museum für Naturkunde
Schloss Rosenstein
D-7000 Stuttgart 1 (F.R.G.)

J.F. EISENBERG
National Zoological Park
Smithsonian Institution
Washington, DC 20008 (U.S.A.)

G. ESSER
General Ecology Group
FB Biology/Chemistry
University of Osnabrück
P.O. Box 4469
D-4500 Osnabrück (F.R.G.)

J. EWEL
Botany Department
University of Florida
Gainesville, FL 32611 (U.S.A.)

G.W. FRANKIE
Department of Entomology
Texas Agricultural and Mechanical University
College Station, TX 77843 (U.S.A.)

F.B. GOLLEY
Institute of Ecology
University of Georgia
Athens, GA 30602 (U.S.A.)

S.R. GRADSTEIN
Institute of Systematic Botany
State University of Utrecht
Heidelberglaan 2
3584 CS Utrecht (The Netherlands)

A.C. HAMILTON
Department of Biology and Environmental
Sciences
The New University of Ulster
Coleraine, Londonderry (Northern Ireland)

I. HANSKI
Department of Pure and Applied Biology
Imperial College
Silwood Park
Ascot, Berks. SL5 7PY (U.K.)

H. HEATWOLE
Department of Zoology
University of New England
Armidale, N.S.W. 2351 (Australia)

E.E. HEGARTY
Department of Botany
Iniversity of Queensland
St. Lucia, Qld. 4067 (Australia)

J.D. HOLLOWAY
Commonwealth Institute of Entomology
56 Queens Gate
London SW7 5JR (U.K.)

D.H. JANZEN
Department of Biology
University of Pennsylvania
Philadelphia, PA 19104 (U.S.A.)

T.C. JESSUP
Department of Human Ecology
Cook College
Rutgers University
New Brunswick, NJ 08903 (U.S.A.)

D.R. JOHANSSON
VBB AB
Box 5038
10241 Stockholm (Sweden)

C.F. JORDAN
Institute of Ecology
University of Georgia
Athens, GA 30602 (U.S.A.)

J.R. KARR
Department of Biology
Virginia Polytechnic Institute and State University
Blacksburg, VA 20461-0406 (U.S.A.)

K. KARTAWINATA
UNESCO Regional Office for Science and
Technology for Southeast Asia
J1, Thamrin 14
Gromolpos 273/JKT
Jakarta (Indonesia)

T. KIRA
Lake Biwa Research Institute
Uchide-Hama
Otsu, Shiga 520 (Japan)

W. LAUER
Geographisches Institut der Universität Bonn
Franziskanerstr. 2
D-5300 Bonn 1 (F.R.G.)

R. LAURENT
Fundación Lillo
Miguel Lillo 205
4000 Tucuman (Argentina)

R.M. LAWTON
Mulberry House
Stanville Road
Cumnor Hill
Oxford OX2 9JF (U.K.)

H. LIETH
Fachbereich Biologie/Chemie
Universität Osnabrück
Postfach 4469
D-4500 Osnabrück (F.R.G.)

D. McKEY
Zooligisches Institut
University
Universität Basel
Basel (Switzerland)

E. MEDINA
Centro de Ecologia
IVIC
Caracas (Venezuela)

N. MYERS
Upper Meadow
Old Road
Headington, Oxford (U.K.)

P.A. OPLER
Office of Endangered Species
Fish and Wildlife Department
U.S. Department of Interior
Washington, DC 20040 (U.S.A.)

D.F. OWEN
Biology Department
Oxford Polytechnic
Oxford (U.K.)

C. PADOCH
Institute of Environmental Science
University of Wisconsin
Madison, WI 53706 (U.S.A.)

T. POCS
Research Institute for Botany
Hungarian Academy of Sciences
2163 Vácrátót (Hungary)

G.T. PRANCE
The New York Botanical Garden
Bronx, NY 10458 (U.S.A.)

P.A. SANCHEZ
Department of Soil Science
Tropical Soils Research Program
North Carolina State University
Box 7619
Raleigh, NC 27695-7619 (U.S.A.)

M. SCHMID
Muséum National d'Histoire Naturelle
Laboratoire de Phanérogamie
16 Rue Buffon
75005 Paris (France)

H.J.M. SIPMAN
Botanischer Garten und Botanisches Museum
Berlin-Dahlem
Königin Luise Str. 6-8
D-1000 Berlin 33 (F.R.G.)

G.C. STOCKER
CSIRO
P.O. Box 780
Atherton, Qld. 4883 (Australia)

S.L. SUTTON
Department of Pure and Applied Zoology
University of Leeds
Leeds LS2 9JT (U.K.)

J.M. SWIFT
Department of Biological Sciences
University of Zimbabwe
P.O. Box M.P. 167
Mount Pleasant, Harare (Zimbabwe)

P.B. TOMLINSON
Harvard Forest
Petersham, MA 01366 (U.S.A.)

R. TRYON
Harvard University Herbaria
22 Divinity Avenue
Cambridge, MA 02138 (U.S.A.)

A.P. VAYDA
Department of Human Ecology
Cook College
Rutgers University
New Brunswick, NJ 08903 (U.S.A.)

F.H. WADSWORTH
Institute of Tropical Forestry
Southern Forest Experiment Station
Forest Service, U.S. Department of Agriculture
Rio Piedras, PR 00928 (U.S.A.)

B.J. WALLACE
Royal Botanic Gardens
Mrs. Macquarie's Road
Sydney, N.S.W. 2000 (Australia)

M.J.A. WERGER
Department of Plant Ecology
State University of Utrecht
Lange Nieuwstraat 106
3512 PN Utrecht (The Netherlands)

T.C. WHITMORE
Department of Agricultural and Forest Sciences
University of Oxford
South Parks Road
Oxford OX1 3RB (U.K.)

D.E. WILSON
Fish and Wildlife Service
National Museum of Natural History
Washington, DC 20560 (U.S.A.)

G.L. UNWIN
CSIRO
P.O. Box 780
Atherton, Qld. 4883 (Australia)

K. YODA
Department of Biology
Faculty of Science
Osaka City University
Osaka (Japan)

T.M. YUILL
Department of Veterinary Science
University of Wisconsin
Madison, WI 53706 (U.S.A.)

CONTENTS OF VOLUME 14A

CONTENTS OF VOLUME 14B[1]

[1]For short contents of Vol. 14A see p. XII.

Chapter 1

INTRODUCTION

H. LIETH and M.J.A. WERGER

According to prior discussions among the three editors of the Rain Forest volumes, the biogeographical volume should provide a foundation for the discussion of structure and function dealt with in Volume 14A. This volume, 14B, covers also the basic environmental criteria needed to explain the distribution limits of species and the diversity patterns in the rain-forest ecosystems of the tropics.

An introduction to such a volume can be very short if one is able to enlist competent contributors to cover almost all relevant aspects of the biogeography of Tropical Rain Forest Ecosystems. Because of the circumtropical distribution of the rain forest with three strikingly different species compositions, we attempted to get descriptions from all parts of the globe involved. In the course of our work we found it almost necessary to divide this volume again into several books in order to treat every biogeographical province of the tropical rain forests and their various biotic groups adequately. We, however, abandoned this idea.

In many ways we are confronted these days with alarming calls of attention for the rapid decline of and the severe impact by man upon the tropical rain forests. Various sources report rather deviant data on the rates of destruction going on in each of the countries concerned, and it is not always clear on which sources these data are based. In this introduction we like to state some facts as they appear to us in statistics and remote sensing.

SURFACE AREA CHANGE

According to the earlier assessment by Lieth, Whittaker and Likens, both in Lieth and Whit-

taker (1975), stated in their tables that the tropical rain forest must have potentially covered an area of 17×10^6 km^2 worldwide. This area coincides approximately with the green patches shown on the maps of the inside covers of this book. Man's activities have largely diminished the original rain-forest area, as Myers (1983) already pointed out in Volume 14A. In support of some of his statements we can show the facts for South America in a few tables and figures. This region is especially valid, since most of the still untouched rain forest lies here, and species diversity is highest in this area.

Table 1.1 demonstrates the land use changes from forests to non-forested land as we could detect it from Landsat images for most of South America including the extratropical regions. The table shows that during the seventies of this century the rate of forest clearing amounted to 9720 km^2 yr^{-1} for all of South America and to 6889 km^2 yr^{-1} for Brazil where most of the tropical rain forest lies. Figure 1.1 shows where most of the changes occurred and one can see from this figure that very drastic changes occurred, indeed, in areas where we know from vegetation maps that tropical rain forest covers the territory. The figure shows also that the forest clearing occurs uneven over the whole area: some satellite images display almost no change throughout the period of observation — approximately 1972 to 1982 — whereas other images suggest a total destruction over an entire image (about 180×180 km). In Fig. 1.2 we show two examples. Figure 1.2A and B shows the heavy changes in Rondonia, Brazil, and C and D an image along the Manaus–Porto Velho highway with almost no visible human development. These latter two images provide also a fairly good impression of the

TABLE 1.1

Results of the evaluation of 934 Landsat scenes with regard to surface area change of natural or near-natural vegetation in South America during the seventies of this century as compared to statistical assessments by Richards et al. (1983). Taken from Esser and Lieth (1986)

Country	Annual change of forested surface area in $km^2 \, yr^{-1}$			Percentage of countries areas analysed	Annual mean of change between 1958 and 1978 in $km^2 \, yr^{-1}$ assessed from statistical sources by Richards et al. (1983)
	decrease	increase	balance		
Brazil	6889	199	6689	76	7708
Argentina	1533	17	1516	85	1880
Paraguay	791	0.4	790	80	227
Venezuela	360	3	357	65	960
Bolivia	76	0	76	40	713
Chile	69	3	66	90	104
Colombia	3	0	3	30	280
Peru	0	0	0	34	649
Ecuador	0	0	0	6	187
Uruguay	0	0	0	95	−48
Total	9720	223	9497	72	12 660

patchwork land/water which is the real gross structure of the "biotope" one may call tropical rain forest. This enormous change in habitats within a short distance explains why this region is so hostile against human settlement, and therefore requires such enormous and often profound changes, if developments are attempted.

Changes of the dimensions required imply complete destruction of part of the original ecosystems and considerable modification of other parts. Local disappearance of species and also complete extinction are the consequences of such developments. We should realize, however, that in many of the tropical countries harbouring rain forests, destruction of the forest is virtually dictated by the widespread poverty of the people, the rapidly increasing population pressures, the lack of opportunities to make a living, and the absence of adequate knowledge and means to exploit the tropical rain-forest ecosystem without destroying it. These social and economic problems of ever increasing poverty should be solved in order to save the forests (Raven, 1987). An increase in the economic value of the tropical rain forest, for instance by developing and applying ecologically sound ways of logging the forest or exploiting its resources in another way not leading to rapid depletion, will ultimately contribute to

saving some of it. To realize this, a crucial prerequisite is the strict adherence to sound ecological principles as a basis for biologically acceptable land-use practices. Only this will give sustained yields and bring economic profit without leading to ecological degradation and the ultimate waste of land. To achieve this aim much more scientific knowledge is needed and the educational and extension service systems for people living in the tropical forest areas should be improved.

SPECIES DIVERSITY

The high species diversity of the tropical rain forests is well known and discussed in several contributions to this volume. In overall species diversity the tropical rain forest ranks highest in most categories. For individual species groups this may be different, however, since the adaptation to environmental conditions is differently developed among taxa. Furthermore, the evolutionary trends are still poorly understood, such as the presently low percentage of gymnospermous trees in the tropical forest canopy, and the still poorer performance of tree species among ferns. Equally remarkable is the absence of Pinaceae from the tropical rain forest. Whether the epiphytic ferns

Fig. 1.1. Regional distribution of symbols showing a net decrease of natural or near-natural vegetation in South America. The symbols indicate for an average reference time of 6.75 years between the years 1971 and 1982. Circles = area of which the imagery is analysed, crosses = < 20 km², triangles = 20–50 km², and stars = > 50 km². The total area of South America amounts to 17.8×10^6 km² of which 5×10^6 km² are forests according to the definition of Schmithüsen (1976), digitized by Esser (1985).

forests are relatively poor with fewer than 4000 species of phanerogams (Lebrun, 1960; Letouzey, 1978; Gentry, 1982; Whitmore, 1984; and several chapters in this volume).

Apart from high total species diversities for tropical rain-forest areas, local species densities often are impressive. Dodson and Gentry (1978) reported 1025 vascular plant species on 1.7 km² of lowland rain forest in coastal Ecuador, and Hall and Swaine (1981) listed 350 vascular plant species on 0.5 ha in lowland rain forest of Ghana.

Another feature touched upon by many of the authors in this volume is that many species have surprisingly small distribution areas, even in large, more or less continuous areas of forest. Endemism is consequently high in tropical rain-forest regions, though this is not a unique feature of the rain forest. Island ecosystems contain particularly high proportions of endemic species, and several authors in this volume discuss historical and ecological explanations for the strong geographic variation in species diversity, the various types of limited distribution, and for endemism.

Such patterns of variation highly complicate the development of a practical strategy for conservation of a reasonable sample of rain-forest diversity. Much more understanding of the functional relations in the rain-forest ecosystems and of the regulatory processes of evolution and species diversity are urgently needed before such a strategy can be formulated. However, as a result of the present pressure on these systems, leading to a fast disappearance of the forests and extinction of their species, particularly in island nations (Fosberg, 1979; Melville, 1979), some ecologists warned not to wait till sufficient scientific knowledge becomes available. They (Rubinoff, 1983, among others) worked out practical schemes that would conserve sizeable patches of tropical rain forest in a network of parks and reserves all over the globe. These would provide us with a valuable stock of species and important source areas for future research. We should try to realize at least something along these lines.

The authors in this volume have provided a wealth of known facts and often pinpointed future research needs. We hope, therefore, that this volume not only presents the basic facts about the tropical rain-forest ecosystems, their environment,

will stand a chance in the long run against the aggressive evolutionary power of orchids and bromelias remains to be analysed, though Tryon (Ch. 17) reports about their present speciation in the rain-forest ecosystems.

Species diversity seems highest in the South American rain forests: for example, the Amazonian forests alone contain at least 30 000 species of phanerogams; the rain forests of South-East Asia contain some 25 000 species of phanerogams, those of Africa (including Madagascar) about 17 000, while the Australian and Pacific tropical rain

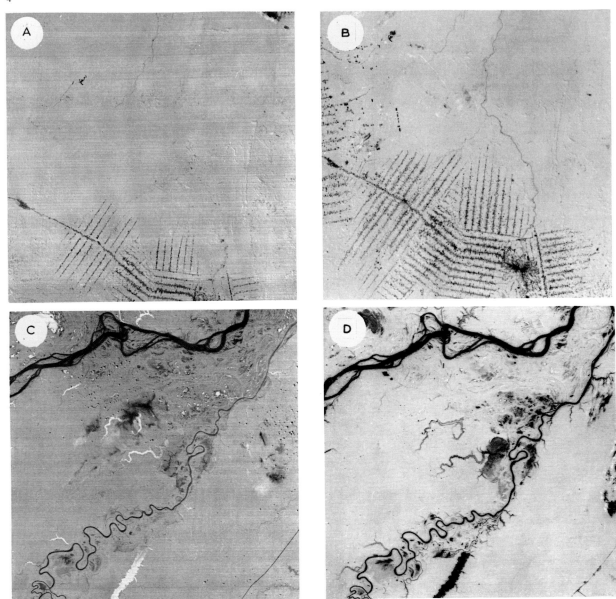

Fig. 1.2. Examples of band 5 (red) satellite images from tropical rain-forest areas in Brazil showing different intensities of visible land use changes, which occurred in the seventies of this century. A, B. Very dramatic visible forest clearance in Rondónia, Brazil, between July 24, 1975, and May 17, 1981. The figures show the systematic opening of forest area along the highway Porto Velho–Cuiaba about 350 km southeast of Porto Velho. Image centers are 10°2′S, 62°6′W for (A) and 10°8′S, 62°4′W for (B). Sources are NASA ERTS for (A) and CNPQ/INPE for (B). C, D. Low visible changes on satellite images from a rain-forest area between July 31, 1972, and December 2, 1981, of the Amazonas district/Brazil, northwest of the highway Manaus–Porto Velho about 300 km southwest of Manaus. The only visible change is a new side road from the main highway on the lower right-hand side of the image. The picture shows the gigantic gross structure of the virgin forest territory between the Rio Solimões (upper river) and the Rio Puru (lower river).

as well as their biota. We hope that it also stimulates new research where it is most urgently needed, to improve our understanding of this most interesting ecosystem, and to provide us with a scientific basis for a sound strategy to maintain the forest for the future.

REFERENCES

Dodson, C.H. and Gentry, A.H., 1978. Flora of the Rio Palenque Science Center. *Selbyana*, 4: 1–6.

Esser, G. and Lieth, H., 1986. *Evaluation of climate relevant land surface characteristics from remote sensing*. Proc. ISLSCP Conf., Rome, ESA SP-248, pp. 205–11.

Fosberg, R.F., 1979. Tropical floristic botany — concepts and status — with special attention to tropical islands. In: K. Larsen and L.B. Holm-Nielsen (Editors), *Tropical Botany*. Academic Press, London, pp. 89–105.

Gentry, A.H., 1982. Patterns of neotropical plant species diversity. *Evol. Biol.*, 15: 1–84.

Hall, J.B. and Swaine, M.D., 1981. *Distribution and Ecology of Vascular Plants in a Tropical Rainforest. Forest Vegetation in Ghana*. Junk, The Hague, 383 pp.

Lebrun, J., 1960. Sur la richesse de la flore de divers territoires africains. *Bull. Séances Acad. R. Sci. Outre-Mer*, 6(4): 669–690.

Letouzey, R., 1978. Floristic composition and typology. In: *Tropical Forest Ecosystems*. UNESCO, Paris, pp. 91–111.

Lieth, H. and Whittaker, R.H. (Editors), 1975. *Primary Productivity of the Biosphere*. Springer, Heidelberg, 339 pp.

Melville, R., 1979. Endangered island floras. In: D. Bramwell (Editor), *Plants and Islands*. Academic Press, London, pp. 361–377.

Myers, N., 1983. Conversion rates in tropical moist forests. In: F.B. Golley (Editor), *Tropical Rain Forest Ecosystems. Structure and Function*. (Ecosystems of the World, 14A) Elsevier, Amsterdam, pp. 289–300.

Raven, P.H., 1988. Tropical floristics tomorrow. *Taxon* (in press).

Richards, J.F., Olson, J.S. and Rotty, R.M., 1983. *Development of a data base for carbon dioxide releases resulting from conversion of land to agricultural uses*. Inst. for Energy Analysis, Oak Ridge Assoc. Univ. ORAU/IEA-82-10 (M), ORNL/TM-8801.

Rubinoff, I., 1983. A strategy for preserving tropical forests. In: S.L. Sutton, T.C. Whitmore and A.C. Chadwick (Editors), *Tropical Rainforest: Ecology and Management*. Blackwell, Oxford, pp. 465–476.

Schmithüsen, J., 1976. *Atlas zur Biogeographie*. (Meyers Großer Physischer Weltatlas 3) Bibl. Inst. Mannheim.

Whitmore, T.C., 1984. *Tropical Forests of the Far East*. Oxford Univ. Press, Oxford, 352 pp.

Chapter 2

CLIMATE AND WEATHER

WILHELM LAUER

INTRODUCTION

In the tropical zone between the Tropics of Cancer and Capricorn warm and cold as well as moist and dry climates occur. Heat decreasing in intensity towards the higher latitudes and with increasing elevation delimits the warm tropics towards the subtropical and tropical cold climates of the high mountain areas. The lack of heat and the occurrence of frost determine the spatial boundaries of the warm tropics (Fig. 2.1).

The water budget determines a division into humid and dry tropics. The humid rain-forest climate mainly occurs immediately north and south of the Equator. However, the spatial combination of favorable elements of climate — particularly on the east coasts of the continents — also provides the preconditions for rain forests even beyond the Tropics of Cancer and Capricorn (Fig. 2.2). Roughly speaking, the rain-forest climates have their boundaries in those areas where they are limited by a negative water budget, unless sufficient groundwater reserves are available to overcome the climatic dryness.

A macroclimatic concept for the entire tropical zone must be taken as a basis to represent the climate and weather of the tropical rain forest, since this is the only means to understand the distribution of rain forests as a function of climate. Climate and weather are determined by the Earth's radiation, heat and water budget, in conjunction with the atmospheric circulation.

RADIATION AND HEAT

Radiation budget of the tropics

The Earth receives 99% of its energy from the Sun. The parameters involved are: rotation, revolution, and the obliquity of the ecliptic, which cause a spatial and temporal differentiation of the Earth's radiation budget. The tropical zone located between the Tropics of Cancer and Capricorn receives the highest amounts of annual radiation (Fig. 2.3). The maximum day length in the tropical zone ranges between 12 h at the Equator and 13.5 h at the tropics. Even at the Earth's farthest point from the Sun, the angle of incidence within this zone is never less than 43° at noon. And yet, distinct differences in radiation are already observable between the inner and outer tropics. While, due to the constant distance of the Sun's transit through the zenith, quite uniform light and radiation conditions prevail in the inner tropics, the Sun's double passage through the zenith occurs at relatively short intervals near the Tropics of Cancer and Capricorn. In the opposite season, the meridian altitude decreases to 43°, which means that differences in day length (up to 3 h) cause the light and radiation conditions near the Tropics of Cancer and Capricorn to assume seasonal characteristics.

The Earth's surface on average receives only 46% of the global radiation. This figure is highest in the tropical zone; thus, this zone shows a clear surplus in comparison to the middle and higher

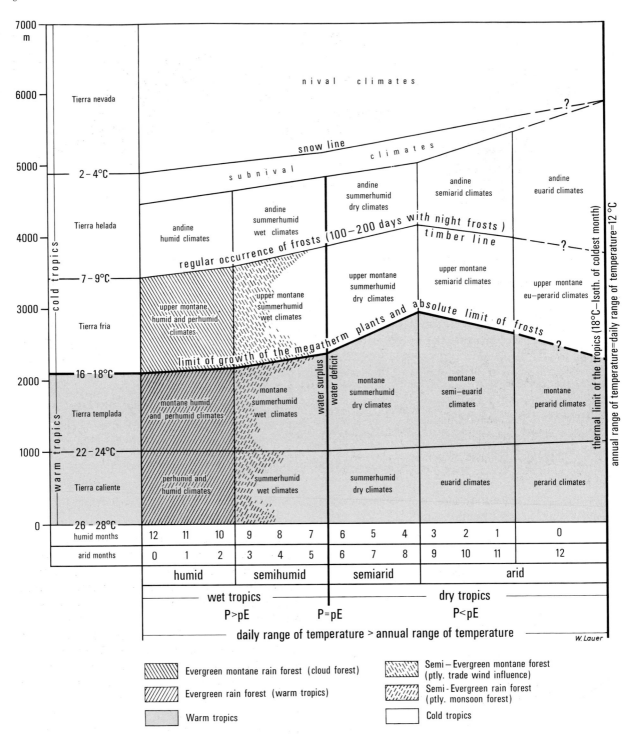

Fig. 2.1. Three-dimensional hygrothermal zones in the tropics (example of Andes).

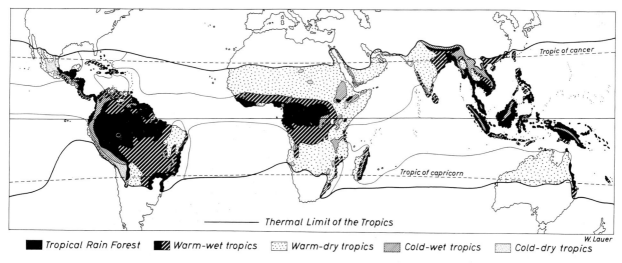

Fig. 2.2. Hygrothermal zonation of the tropics.

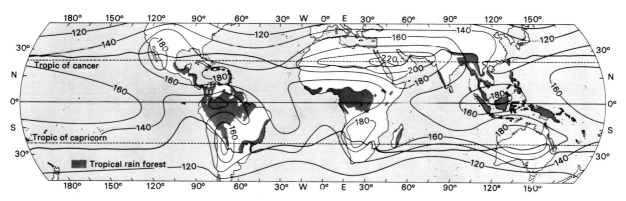

Fig. 2.3. Annual sum of global radiation (kcal cm^{-2}; 1 kcal = 4.18 kJ). (After Budyko, 1958, and Sellers, 1965.)

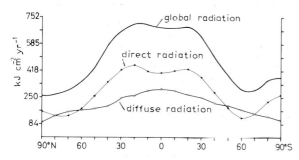

Fig. 2.4. Latitudinal profile of annual sum of global radiation (kJ^{-2}yr^{-1}) and its components. (After Sellers, 1965.)

latitudes. Figure 2.4 shows the annual distribution of global radiation in a meridional profile, from which it can be seen that the inner and outer tropical zones on average receive about the same amount of global radiation, thus representing a surplus area for the entire Earth.

However, the change in the ratio of direct and diffuse solar radiation causes distinct variations in the amount of energy received on the Earth's surface in the tropics. In the equatorial humid tropics the relationship between the direct solar radiation (Q) to the diffuse component (q) is approximately 3:2. The large proportion of diffused radiation results from the frequent occurrence of clouds of great vertical thickness, and a high content of water vapor and aerosols in the inner tropical atmosphere. In the desert areas of the marginal-tropical and subtropical arid regions, the ratio of $Q:q$ is approximately 4:1, which means that these zones receive slightly higher values of gobal radiation. The global radiation ($Q+q$) in the rain forest zone clearly depends on the course, amount and altitude of clouds.

Radiation budget within the rain-forest area

The radiation budget of a specific sector of the Earth's surface and the atmosphere may be expressed by means of the following formula, where the sum of all energy receipts and losses is zero:

$$S + H - R_k - A + G - R_1 \pm V \pm L = 0$$

$S + H - R_k$ represent direct radiation, diffused solar radiation and reflected short-wave radiation (albedo). A is the long-wave reradiation, G the atmospheric back-radiation, and R_1 stands for the reflected long-wave radiation, which is very small. V represents the latent heat (evaporation or condensation), and L the sensible heat. The energy received from the short-wave global radiation (minus albedo) is opposed by an energy loss, which is caused by reradiation, the evaporation of water and the transfer of sensible heat into the atmosphere. A great portion of the long-wave radiation emitted from the surface, however, is returned to the Earth's surface as back-radiation.

Most of the energy gained is received at the Earth's surface. On the other hand, the atmosphere is the source of most of the energy losses to space. Thus, there is a difference in energy levels between the heat source of the Earth's surface and the atmosphere and, consequently, an impulse for the vertical transmisssion of sensible and latent heat. S, H, G, V, and L show high values in the tropical regions, thus resulting in a considerable energy surplus (Figs. 2.5 and 2.6).

The process of radiation absorption is difficult to assess in the rain-forest area. The height and density of the forest vary considerably with time and with the type of plants. Thus, only general

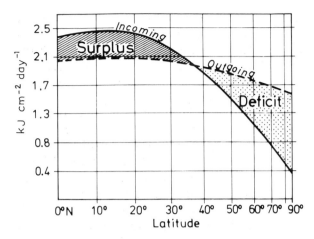

Fig. 2.5. Annual radiation balance of the Northern Hemisphere. (After Houghton, 1954.)

statements can be made regarding the radiation turnover. The main absorption processes — that is, energy transformation — occur in the forest canopy. In the rain forest, only 10% of the incoming insolation reaches the ground. The energy exchange mainly takes place with the air contained in the forest but is extremely slight. The transmission of heat within the forest is also negligible.

Biological regulating mechanisms, such as transpiration, are of much more decisive importance for the temperature than the physical mechanisms of heat transformation. The steady amount of radiation, however, is sufficient to maintain a constant level of sensible heat in the equatorial forest. On the whole, the rain forest has only a poor heat-storing capacity, as it merely keeps the temperature balanced, although it receives energy surpluses.

In the tropical rain forest the effective reradiation emitted is relatively small, since the atmo-

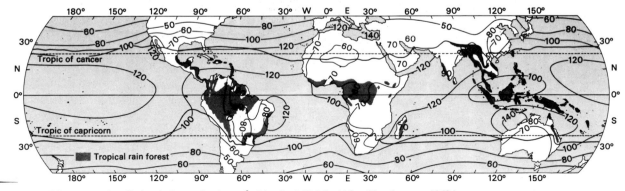

Fig. 2.6. Mean annual radiation balance (kcal cm^{-2}; 1 kcal = 4.18 kJ). (After Kondratyev, 1969.)

sphere has two components — carbon dioxide and water vapor — which absorb the outgoing long-wave radiation more effectively than the short-wave diffuse solar radiation. They are responsible for the greenhouse effect of the atmosphere in the tropical rain forest, which is very great.

Kessler (1973) has shown representative mean daily and annual cycles of the radiation balance in the form of isopleths for various climatic regions of the Earth. The diagram for Yangambi (Fig. 2.7a) in the eastern province of Zaïre may be regarded as representative of the equatorial rain forest. This diagram shows an almost uniform daily cycle throughout the year, with positive values from 06.00 until 18.00 h and negative values during the night. The amount of outgoing energy of 2 to 3 cal cm^{-2} h^{-1} during the whole night is insignificant. From sunrise, the energy balance during the day steadily increases to 40 cal cm^{-2} h^{-1} until noon and decreases just as steadily. Compared with the values of 45 cal cm^{-2} h^{-1} during the equinoxes, the midday maximum values, however, are slightly below 40 cal cm^{-2} h^{-1} in the rainy season from July to October.

In contrast to this, the horizontal course of the isopleths in the diagram for the marginal tropics (Poona station) (Fig.2.7b) indicates a marked diurnal cycle. However, here also a seasonal differentiation can be noticed. In the dry season, during the night, energy losses of -4 and -7 cal cm^{-2} h^{-1} are measured, while in the rainy season these values amount to -2 cal cm^{-2} h^{-1} due to the high water-vapor content of the air. In addition to this, there is the increased amount of energy received at midday during the pre-monsoon period and in the rainy season in the summer (45 and 35 cal cm^{-2} h^{-1}). On the whole, the annual radiation cycle in the tropical rain forest only provides minor impulses for the seasonal growing rhythm of the plants. As tropical short-day plants, they respond very sensitively both to the slightest changes in length of day and to seasonal radiation fluctuations.

Heat budget — sensible and latent heat

The radiation balance Q is converted at the Earth's surface into different heat fluxes which are

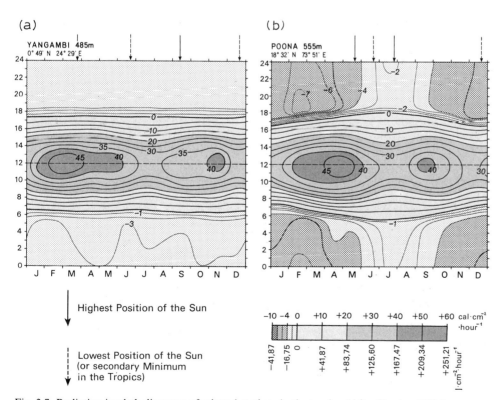

Fig. 2.7. Radiation isopleth diagrams of selected stations in the tropics. (After Kessler, 1973.)

partly directed towards the ground and partly to the atmosphere. The equation may be expressed as follows:

$$Q = B + L + V + U$$

The heat equation is composed of the heat flux into the ground (B), the heat flux for direct heating of the air (L), the heat flux for evaporation (V) as well as other fluxes — for example, biological transformation processes, melting of snow, etc. — which are included in U.

The rain forests of the lower latitudes are areas with a positive radiation balance throughout the year, where the long-wave atmospheric back-radiation represents an essential energy source. Since the tree canopy is the actual conversion surface in the tropical rain forest for the net receipt of energy, the net radiation received during the day is of benefit to the evaporation (V) on the one hand, and to the sensible heat (L) on the other. Both heat currents are directed towards the atmosphere and the ground. However, the ground only receives a small portion of the energy from the heating, as there hardly is any exchange between the canopy and the forest ground (Fig. 2.8).

During the day, the energy received is primarily released again into the atmosphere as latent heat through evapotranspiration. Despite great increase in the water-vapor pressure, the air temperature in the forest itself stays at a relatively constant temperature of 26° to 27°C. Thus, it is typical of the rain forests that the continuous release of water vapor into the air proceeds without disturbance of the atmospheric layers — as is the case over the sea. Energy is released by the forest during the night. Cooling leads to release of heat through condensation. In addition, sensible heat is absorbed from the surrounding air, not only from the atmosphere above the canopy but also to a small extent from the tree bases near the ground. The canopy is the only part that shows greater temperature fluctuations during a diurnal cycle. This variation approximately corresponds to that measured in a properly installed shelter for meteorological instruments (Fig. 2.9).

Table 2.1 shows the energy balance for different tropical latitudes. It is evident that the amount of latent heat is six to eight times higher than the amount of sensible heat during vertical transport into the atmosphere. Only at lat. 15°N or S are these two values nearly balanced. At lat. 25°N, in the arid regions, there is hardly any latent heat. In

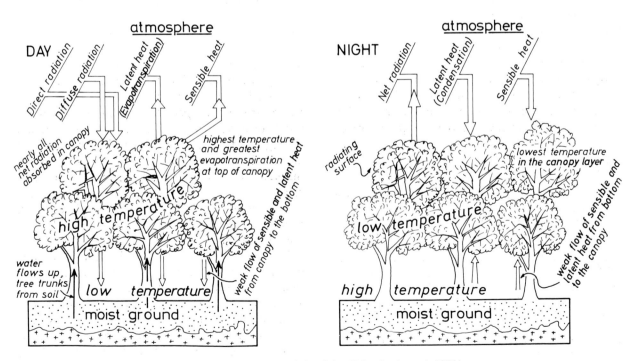

Fig. 2.8. Energy exchange within a forest during the day and the night. (After Lockwood, 1976.)

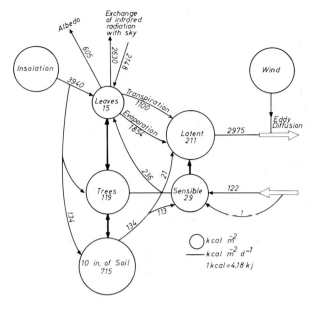

Fig. 2.9. Estimated budget of insolation and heat flow in the forest at El Verde, Puerto Rico, omitting photosynthetic fixation and rain cooling. (After Odum, 1970.)

the Southern Hemisphere, the latent heat is in any case considerably greater, due to the large expanse of the oceans.

Table 2.1 also shows that, as a result of the atmospheric circulation, an advective transport of heat energy occurs, involving both latent and sensible heat. In this connection, the transport of sensible heat plays an increasing role towards the Tropics of Cancer and Capricorn, since the evaporation energy is no longer needed due to increased dryness in the marginal tropics. The surplus of sensible heat in the marginal tropics

TABLE 2.1

Energy-balance terms in tropical regions, land surface only (after Baumgartner and Reichel, 1975)

	Q	H (kJ)	L (cm^2)	$\dfrac{100\,L}{Q}$ (yr)	$\dfrac{100\,H}{L}$ (yr)
25°N	288.4	200.6	87.8	129.6	936.3
15°N	296.8	146.3	150.5	213.2	401.3
5°N	103.0	37.6	263.3	367.8	58.5
5°S	301.0	16.7	284.2	392.9	25.1
15°S	305.1	87.8	217.4	296.8	167.2
25°S	292.6	175.6	117.0	167.2	627.0

Q = net radiation, H = heat flux in the air, L = latent heat flux.

leads to the phenomenon of the mean temperatures in these areas — at least during the summer half-year of the hemisphere — reaching higher values than in the inner tropics, where the process of continuous evaporation keeps the temperatures lower.

Since the proportion of latent heat is extremely high in the rain forest areas, the ratio of sensible to latent heat (L/V) shows a minimum in this region. It can be seen from the maps in Fig. 2.10 that the evaporation increases during the summer of the hemisphere in question, and that the tropical land masses also receive more latent heat at that time.

On average, the smaller land masses of the Southern Hemisphere are favored in terms of latent heat. The annual oscillation of the climatic zones in accordance with the course of the Sun is expressed by the slight seasonal shift of the areas of high latent-heat values with a corresponding delay. It shows in particular the advance of the Intertropical Convergence Zone and, thus, the influence of the equatorial westerlies as well as the tropical monsoons. The increased amounts of latent heat on the east coasts of South America, South Africa, South-East Asia and Australia also show the east-coast effect of the trade winds in their seasonal shift in coastal areas of the marginal tropics.

As a result of the constant high humidity level, the annual cycle of the ratio of sensible to latent heat also remains steady (Fig. 2.11). In the semi-arid and semi-humid tropics, however, the alternating sequence of rainy and dry seasons is expressed in the annual cycle of the ratio, a small value for the rainy period indicating the predominance of latent heat, whereas a high value occurs during the dry period when sensible heat is much greater. In the monsoon-forest areas, a distinctly marked annual cycle becomes apparent. In these regions, during the dry period the latent heat values show a distinct downward trend, whereas, during the monsoon phase, they are as high as in the permanently wet rain forests.

Thanks to the interaction of latent and sensible heat in the rain forest area, the equatorial tropics represent a region of great thermal uniformity. The annual temperature cycle hardly shows any variations; they amount to less than 1°C in the rain forest area. The annual temperature variation steadily increases with the decrease of latent heat, and reaches values of approximately 10°C in the

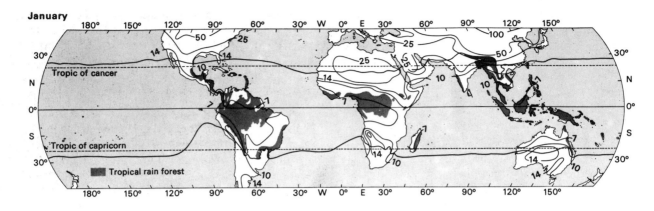

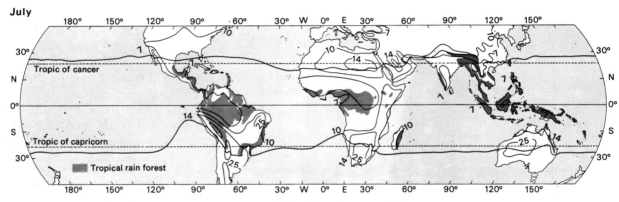

Fig. 2.10. Ratio of sensible (*T*) and latent (*L*) heat (*TK/LK*) (in K) in January and July.

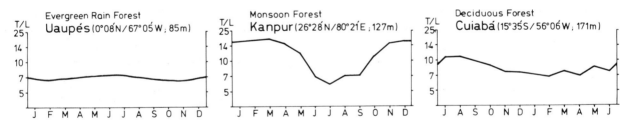

Fig. 2.11. Mean monthly values of the ratio of sensible (*T*) and latent (*L*) heat (*TK/LK*) of selected stations in the tropics.

marginal tropics. The diurnal temperature variations also only amount to a few degrees in the rain
forest, but, due to the radiation emitted during the
night, they are more marked than the annual
variations. Their peaks are at 10°C, particularly in
those cases when the temperatures are measured in
open areas. The fact that the diurnal variations are
higher than the annual variations lead to the
characterization of the tropics as areas governed
by the so-called *Tageszeitenklima* (diurnal variation the only pronounced climatic effect). The
diurnal variations reach maximum values in the

tree canopy — that is, at the surface where the
incoming radiation is transformed. However, the
equatorial rain forests do not show annual variations of more than 5°C, though in the marginal
tropics they may be as high as 10°C.

THERMAL CLIMATE OF THE RAIN-FOREST REGION

The spatial temperature distribution

The horizontal temperature gradients are very
small in the entire tropical zone. They amount to

about 1°C per 1000 km as compared with 5°C per 1000 km in the middle latitudes. This applies in particular to the inner, equatorial tropics, where most of the rain forests are located — that is, between latitudes 10°N and 5°S.

The mean temperature distribution for the months of January and July (Fig. 2.12) shows a range of average temperature in the rain forests from 24° to 27°C. As a result of the asymmetrical distribution of the continents and the resultant asymmetry of the atmospheric circulation, the continental heat maximum — that is, the line of highest mean annual temperature — is shifted on average approximately 3 to 5° of latitude towards the north. Not only the size of the continents, but also the elevated heated areas of the Northern Hemisphere in Central Asia, Iran, Ethiopia and Mexico, are responsible for this effect.

Annual temperature variation

The general uniformity of the tropical climate becomes clearly evident from the types of annual temperature variation seen there. The annual curves for climatological stations located in the rain forests near the Equator only show a limited decrease, often less than 1°C at the time of maximum cloudiness and rainfall (Fig. 2.13). The smallest annual variations in temperature occur on islands of tropical oceans and in tropical high mountains, where they often amount to less than 1°C. These quasi-isothermal conditions may be explained by the days of almost equal length, but particularly by the thermal effect of the proportionally larger expanses of water between the Tropics of Cancer and Capricorn. The sea:land ratio amounts to 3:1 in the tropics, but to 7:3 globally.

Seasonal isothermy particularly applies to the tropical high mountains, where it shows an annual variation of only 0.5°C. Within the rain forest itself, the annual variations also converge towards zero, but immediately above the forest canopy the temperature means show somewhat greater fluctuations (between 2° and 5°C) and thus largely

January

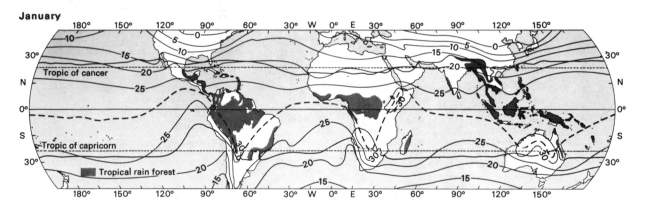

July

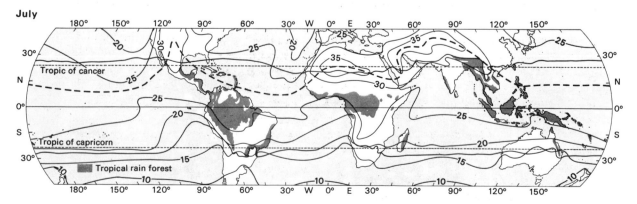

Fig. 2.12. Temperatures at sea level in January and July (°C) and the position of the thermal equator. (After Nieuwolt, 1982.)

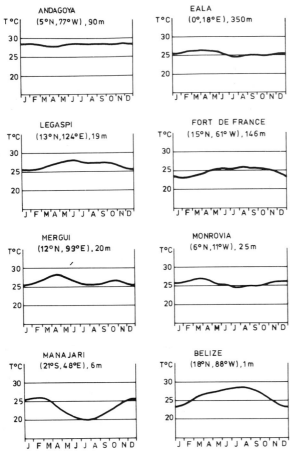

Fig. 2.13. Annual cycle of temperature at various stations in the tropical rain forest.

tropics never drops below 18°C during the winter dry period.

In the inner-tropic rain-forest region, the mean temperature of the coldest month rarely falls below 24°C. In the rain forests of the marginal tropics located within the east-coast climatic zones influenced by the trade winds, as for example in southern Brazil, the Philippines and northeastern Australia, the mean temperature of the coldest month may drop below 18°C. There are days on which the minimum temperatures may fall well below 10°C. This may regularly occur during cold-air influxes from the subarctic or subantarctic regions. Influxes of cold air may even be felt in the central rain-forest areas near the Equator.

Table 2.2 shows mean monthly temperatures of various climatological stations in the tropical rain forest. As a result of the dense cloud cover, the lowest mean monthly values at many stations occur during the rainy period, and the higher values during the relatively dry period. Measurements performed by Schulz (1960) (Fig. 2.14) in the rain forest of Paramaribo show that the mean weekly temperature clearly increases during the two months of the relatively dry period between October and November. The lowest values are measured immediately after the December solstice in January during the short rainy period.

Diurnal temperature cycle

The diurnal temperature cycle is almost balanced, not only over the tropical oceans, but also along the maritime tropical coasts; the central parts of the rain forest, in particular, show only small diurnal temperature variations. Within the continental rain-forest areas, the diurnal temper-

correspond with the values measured in the standard macroclimatic weather instrument shelter standing on the ground without plant cover.

Towards the outer tropics, the times at which the Sun reaches its highest level converge, causing the peaks in the temperature curve to converge as well. Where there is a monsoonal rainfall cycle — as in South-East Asia — the temperature peaks occur before the beginning of the monsoon and, somewhat less, at the end of the monsoon period. A distinctly marked minimum occurs in the dry period of the winter (Ganges type of temperature cycle; Fig. 2.13). In the marginal tropics which are not under the influence of monsoon circulation, the temperature curve shows a peak in the summer and a minimum in the winter. Annual variations of up to 10°C appear regularly in these areas. However, the mean monthly temperature of the marginal

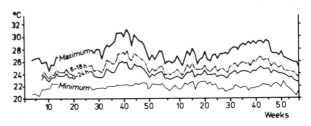

Fig. 2.14. Annual cycle (Jan. 1955 – Jan. 1957) of the weekly means of air temperature. Daily average (for the periods 6–18 and 0–24 h) and daily maximum and minimum, in the tropical rain forest of Surinam. (After Schulz, 1960.)

TABLE 2.2

Temperatures in the tropical rain forest

Locality	Latitude	Temperature (°C)		
		Mean annual	Mean of hottest month	Mean of coldest month
Rain forest				
Singapore	01°18′N	27.2	27.2	26.4
Sandakan, Sabah	05°49′N	27.4	28.1	26.5
Mazaruni Station, Guyana	06°50′N	26.0	27.2	25.1
Manaus, Brazil	03°08′S	27.2	28.2	26.5
Yangambi, Zaïre	0°45′N	24.5	25.2	23.9
Eala, Zaïre	0°03′N	25.6	26.3	24.6
Douala, Cameroon	04°03′N	25.4	26.9	23.8
Rain forest near latitudinal or altitudinal limit				
Apia, Samoa	13°48′S	25.8	26.3	25.1
Cairns, Queensland	16°55′S	24.8	27.2	21.0
Rio de Janeiro, Brazil	22°54′S	22.7	25.6	20.0
Mazindi (1146 m), Uganda	01°35′N	21.8	22.6	20.7

ature curves show considerable differences in their variation values, which, however, always exceed the annual variation. Figure 2.15a shows the diurnal cycle of air temperature at a height of 1.5 m in the rain forest of Surinam. The diurnal minimum occurs shortly before sunrise, then the temperature rises until noon to reach its maximum of approximately 30°C and drops again during the night below the mean value of 27°C. This cycle basically applies to all days of the year. The amplitude is larger during the dry period and smaller in the humid season. A high degree of cloudiness reduces the daily insolation, and also keeps the radiation emitted during the night at a minimum. Consequently, the smallest diurnal variations are recorded not only in the maritime tropics and at high altitudes, but generally also during the rainy period. High-temperature maxima during the day do not prevent generally, but restrict partially plant-physiological activity in the rain forest.

In the central parts of the tropical forests the diurnal heat cycle is balanced, and the turbulent exchange of air minimized due to friction. At noon, the temperature in the undergrowth is a little lower than in the canopy or in clearings (Fig. 2.15B). At night, in contrast to older concepts, the temperature gradient is directed towards the ground, as the nocturnal radiation is emitted from the canopy, and heavy, colder air sinks to the forest ground, where it remains and is warmed up by the flow of ground heat.

Frost and rain forest

As a result of the high humidity, very high temperature values are not reached in the rain forest of the equatorial tropics. On the other hand, there are certain heat deficiency limits (temperature thresholds) that are imposed for plant-physiological reasons. Sporadic spells of frost are lethal for most tropical trees. The absence of frost, therefore, is the limiting and characteristic feature of the evergreen, humid-tropical megathermal rain forest.

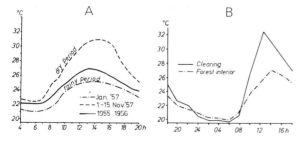

Fig. 2.15A. Diurnal cycle of air temperature during various periods at 1.5 m above ground in the rain forest. (After FAO, Tropical Silviculture I-II, Rome, 1958.) B. Daily cycle of air temperature in an ombrophilous forest in southwest Ghana, in a large clearing and within the closed forest. Both at 10 cm above the ground. (After Longmann and Jenik, 1974.)

Frost definitely represents the factor limiting expansion of the forests towards the Tropics of Cancer and Capricorn. On the western side of the continents where rain forests are only found around the Equator, they may possibly be limited by a certain lack of heat, as is the case in the vicinity of cold ocean currents. In these areas freezing temperatures do not occur. In most cases, hygric threshold conditions prevail that will limit the forests in those regions.

However, frost conditions may occur quite frequently in the forests of the east coasts near the Tropics of Cancer and Capricorn, where cold-air influxes from outside the tropics are familiar phenomena during the winter half-year, thus restricting the expansion of the tropical forests.

Soil temperature

The soil temperature in the tropical rain forest shows even smaller variation than the air in the undergrowth (Fig. 2.15). Although the ground temperature is slightly influenced by the soil type, the air temperature and the soil moisture content, there is no diurnal or annual cycle in rain forests even at a depth of only 30 cm.

Schulz (Fig. 2.16), during a period of two years, recorded a variation range of only 1.5°C at a depth of 5 cm in the rain forest of Paramaribo, which corresponds to the annual variation of the air temperature at this location and follows the annual cycle of mean monthly temperatures with only a slight lag. In the root zone of about 5 to 50 cm, which is of great importance for the rain forest, the temperatures hardly fluctuate.

The heat available throughout the year permits

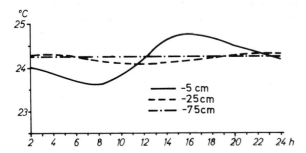

Fig. 2.16. Average daily cycle of soil temperature measured at different depths below the rain forest from Jan. 1955 to Jan. 1957 in northern Surinam. (After Schulz, 1960.)

the plants in the tropical rain forest to be physiologically active without having to rest during cold periods. The daily temperature fluctuation, even though much smaller than in the middle latitudes, represents a specific ecological control of metabolism.

Thermoisopleths

The thermal climates of the Earth can be illustrated quite well with the aid of thermoisopleth diagrams. The diurnal and annual cycles of temperature are entered in a diagram as mean hourly values.

The diagrams for Belém and Quito (Fig. 2.17A and B) show the typical *Tageszeitenklima* of the equatorial humid tropics. The horizontal uniformity of the curve shows an almost isothermic seasonal behavior. At the Belém station, a stronger nocturnal cooling to 24.4°C occurs only during the relatively dry period. Furthermore, the maximum temperature is reached during this period, when it rises to 31.1°C, due to the increased radiation. However, the variations of the mean midday maximum only amount to 2.4° and those of the morning minimum to no more than 1.1°C. Since the annual variations are very small, the diurnal variation of the temperature moulds the isopleth picture, which is expressed by the horizontal course of the curves in the diagram.

The tropical mountains are marked by a very distinct diurnal cycle (Fig. 2.17B). The annual variation differs only slightly from that of the lowlands; it is even smaller, and varies only by 0.4°C in the case of Quito. During the rainy period from March to June, the minimum temperature is low; it is lowest in July. During the relatively dry period from July to September, which, however, is not completely free from precipitation, the maximum temperature shows the highest values, which extend up to November. The annual cycle is almost exclusively determined by the cloud cover and is, thus, completely independent of the Sun's position.

The thermoisopleth diagram for Nagpur (India) represents the tropical monsoon type. The rainy period in the summer is decisive for the annual temperature cycle; the temperature maximum occurs during the hot and still dry month of May, before the summer monsoon causes the temperature to drop slightly. With the abatement of the

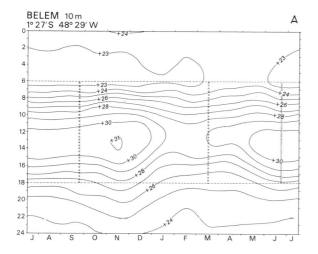

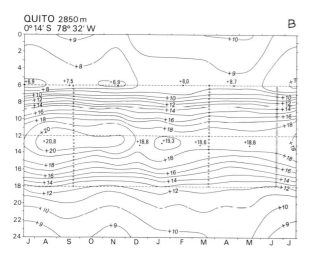

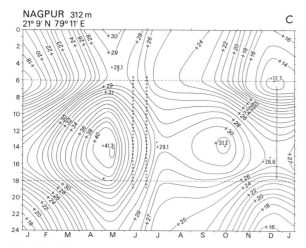

Fig. 2.17. Thermo-isopleth diagrams for some stations in the Tropics. (After Troll, 1943.)

monsoon rain in October, the mean temperatures start to increase again and reach a secondary maximum. During the cool winter period between November and February, the temperature cycle reflects a more extratropical type, as the isarithms partly show a vertical course. On the whole, however, the picture reflects a more tropical course of climate.

Altitudinal zonation of the thermal climates in rain forests

"Warm tropics" and "cold tropics"

In the inner-tropic rain-forest region near the Equator, the mean annual temperature on average decreases by approximately 0.6°C per 100 m of altitude. This decrease occurs in the humid environment of the wooded slopes and is subject to only minor variations.

The temperature-dependent altitudinal belts of tropical landscapes have been described with the Spanish names *tierra caliente*, *tierra templada*, *tierra fria* and *tierra helada*. Tierra caliente and tierra templada denote the warm tropics, tierra fria and tierra helada the cold tropics. As a result of the increased diurnal variations, frost temperatures normally occur at elevations from 2700 to 3300 m upwards, at a mean annual temperature of approximately 18°C (Fig. 2.18).

Climatologically, the tropical mountain areas are to be regarded as real tropics — cold tropics. The minor annual temperature variations give these cold tropical areas a kind of ecological independence, to which the plant formations occurring there have adjusted. Although these plant formations often consist of species from the Holarctic and the Antarctic, due to migrations since the late Tertiary, tropical high-mountain species as well as many endemic species have developed; these occur more frequently in the treeless altitudinal belt of the paramos, but they can also be noticed in the upper forest belt of the upper montane and fog forests.

The forests have adapted themselves to the climatic rhythm of the cold tropics and by no means show the characteristics of extratropical forest formations. Neither can the forest line be equated with that of the extratropical regions. In the tropical mountain areas, frost occurs early in the morning even in the area of the tierra fria and

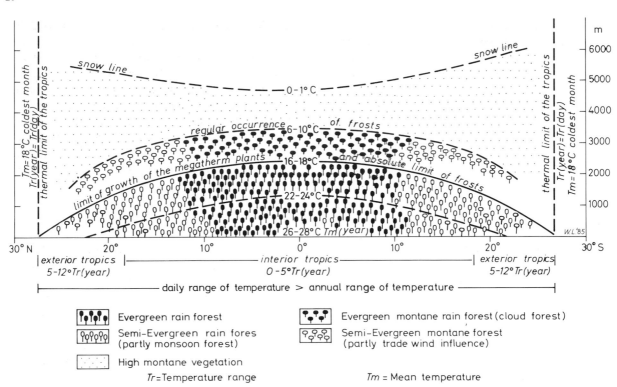

Fig. 2.18. Distribution of climatic types of tropical rain forests.

may occur during any season of the year. Only towards the marginal tropics, a seasonal periodicity of frost occurrence becomes gradually predominant, and leads to a distinct maximum during the winter half-year. The forest line of the humid rain forests is determined less by hygric than by thermal conditions, and runs between the 7° and 9°C isotherms in the zone of the equatorial "Tageszeitenklima". Climatologically, it would not be correct to use for the cool altitudinal belts the names based on latitudinal zonation (for instance, subtropical, temperate, polar, etc.). Since the altitudinal belts of the tropics show temperature features of the tropical climate as well, they can only be characterized by tropical designations (cool tropical, cold tropical, etc.).

THE ATMOSPHERIC CIRCULATION

The trade-wind circulation

Since the equatorial tropical zone, particularly the area of the rain forest, is an intensive source for

heat and water vapor as well as angular momentum, the tropical atmosphere provides an important impulse for the global planetary circulation of the Earth. The initial impetus is the intensive heating of the air masses over the equatorial zone, causing them to rise to the tropopause. As a result of condensation processes at higher altitudes, latent heat is released which triggers an air-pressure gradient from the tropics to the higher latitudes, resulting in a shift of the air masses towards the poles. The resultant cooling, the increased angular momentum, and also the accumulation of air masses between latitudes 25° and 30° in both hemispheres due to the diminishing size of the Earth's surface towards the poles, cause an extensive downward movement of the air masses, which leads to an increased air pressure in the subtropical latitudes. The Coriolis parameter gradually deflects the current into a west to east direction. But since the subtropical high-pressure areas do not form belts encompassing the entire globe, but only individual cells, part of the air is returned to the Equator as a northeast-directed ground current (tropical easterlies), where low pressure prevails due to the generally strong heating. Since air masses from both hemispheres flow together at the Equator, the so-called Intertropical Convergence Zone (ITCZ) is formed, which at the same time provides further impulses. The closed easterly calotte already recognized by Hadley in 1735, which is clapped over the tropical belt, forms the trade-wind circulation and is also called the Hadley Cell (Fig. 2.19).

An undisturbed general trade-wind circulation exists only over the Atlantic and Pacific oceans. In the continental tropics, there is a stronger modification, caused by a different heat balance between the land and the ocean. The release of heat from the ground into the air is two to three times larger in the continental tropics. Since, on the continents, the Intertropical Convergence Zone is shifted seasonally towards the north and/or south due to the strong heating of the tropical–subtropical dry regions, monsoon-like westerly wind components which can be found in all tropical areas with different intensity occur near the Equator. These are of special importance for the occurrence of

rainfall in the equatorial rain forests (Figs. 2.20 and 2.21).

The trade-wind circulation consists of an internal cycle with an easterly current, which is forced by the structure of the subtropical high-pressure cells, and an external cycle located between the extra-tropical west-wind belt and the tropical easterly current, where new air masses of polar origin are incorporated into the easterly current towards the Equator. Since the thermal differences of both hemispheres in the tropics are relatively small, the zone of convergence of both trade-wind belts — the Intertropical Convergence Zone — does not constitute a climatic front.

Near the surface in the trade-wind zone, layers of humid unstable air prevail, since the relatively cool air over the ocean water is heated from below, thus absorbing latent heat. On the other hand, the trade-wind belts diverge towards the Equator — partly because the Earth is of spherical shape, so that the meridians diverge towards the Equator, but above all because the wind component shows a downward trend towards the Equator, due to the Coriolis parameter. These effects normally lead to the sinking of air masses, heating from above and formation of an inversion (trade-wind inversion).

This widely spread inversion to heights between 800 and 2500 m separates the humid cool and unstable lower trade-wind current from the dry warm and stable upper current, which prevents the formation of precipitation. Rainfall does not occur, except in those instances when the trade-wind current near the Equator – particularly over the oceans — is also lifted by confluence. The trade-wind inversion rises to 2500 to 3000 m near the Intertropical Convergence zone, where it is largely destroyed. In this area, due to high-reaching convection, linearly arranged cumulus towers may occur at altitudes of 8 to 12 km without freezing. In this connection, staggered convergences, waves and whirls also occur which are accompanied by rainfall. The trade winds will bring rain also in those cases if an upward movement is caused by the relief. Heavy rains of this type fall on the east coasts of many tropical countries (Philippines, Madagascar, on the eastern slopes of the Caribbean and in Central America, Hawaii, Surinam, southeastern Brazil, Vietnam, India, northeastern Australia and on the eastern slopes of the Andes in South America). Over the

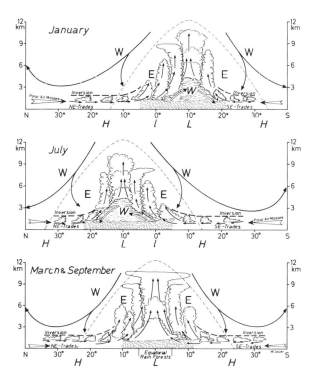

Fig. 2.19. The synoptic structure of the Intertropical Convergence Zone (ITCZ); W = West wind, E = East wind.

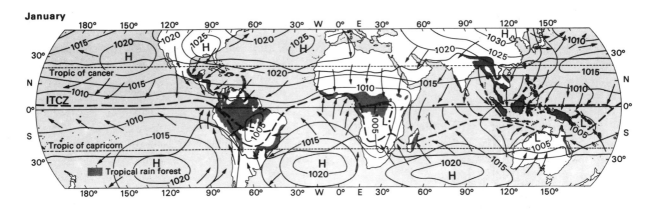

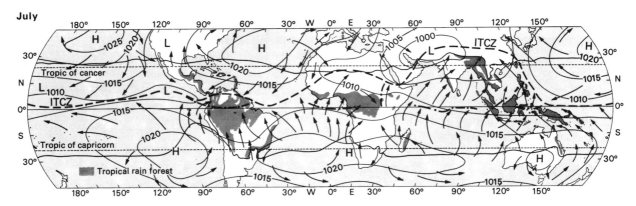

Fig. 2.20. Pressure (hpa) at mean sea level and predominant surface winds in January and July. (After Blüthgen and Weischet, 1980, and Nieuwolt, 1982.)

oceans, however, in the area of convergence of the trade winds, calms often occur which are called "doldrums" or "Mallungen".

The intertropical convergence zone and the monsoon

Over the continents, however, the wind in the equatorial trough primarily blows from a westerly direction, since strong heat lows over the marginal-tropical and subtropical dry areas, in conjunction with the configuration of the continental masses, cause a shift of the ITCZ from the Equator to the marginal-tropical dry areas, and thus favor the monsoon phenomenon. This results in a lower, equatorial westerly current and an upper, easterly current between the shifted ITCZ and the Equator, where humid and unstable cumulonimbus clouds transport the heat of condensation released into the upper troposphere, from which it is trans-

ported poleward. Great amounts of rainfall of the zenithal type frequently occur in the equatorial zone. These westerly winds, with a strong, poleward component and strong friction, have unstable air masses, produce many clouds and high rainfall, and are responsible for most of the rainfall in, for example, western Africa (the Bay of Guinea and the Congo Basin) and over the Indian Ocean towards Indochina and Indonesia as well as on the north coast of Australia. Monsoon-type westerly winds also occur on the west coast of Panama and Columbia (Figs. 2.21 and 2.22).

The Intertropical Convergence Zone, as it is usually shown on maps along the thermal Equator, by no means represents a static line migrating successively and continuously towards the Tropics of Cancer and Capricorn. The migration towards the respective summer hemisphere rather occurs in the form of daily advances and withdrawals. Day-to-day changes in position of several hundreds of

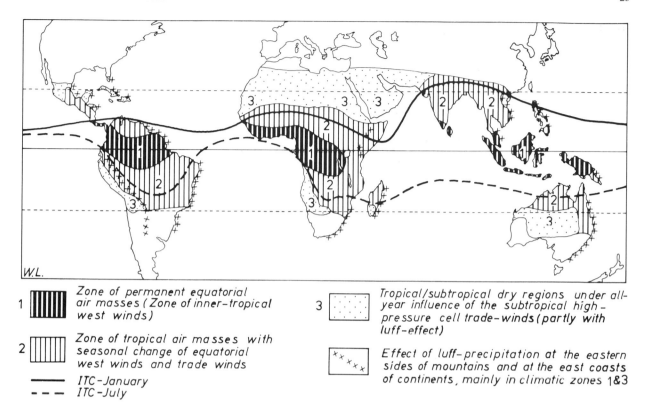

1 ▮▮ Zone of permanent equatorial air masses (Zone of inner-tropical west winds)

2 ▯▯ Zone of tropical air masses with seasonal change of equatorial west winds and trade winds

—— ITC-January

- - - ITC-July

3 ⋯ Tropical/subtropical dry regions under all-year influence of the subtropical high-pressure cell trade-winds (partly with luff-effect)

× × × × Effect of luff-precipitation at the eastern sides of mountains and at the east coasts of continents, mainly in climatic zones 1&3

Fig. 2.21. Distribution of the air masses in the tropics and the position of the ITCZ in January and July.

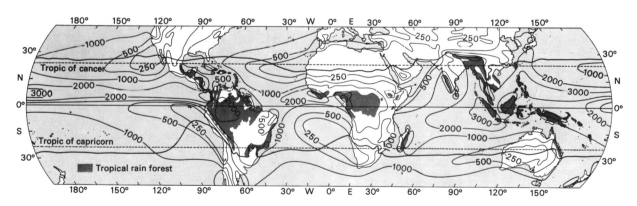

Fig. 2.22. Areas with tropical monsoon circulation. (After various authors.)

kilometers are possible, caused by the energy gradient between the summer and winter hemispheres. The stronger the gradient, the more poleward will the ITCZ advance into the respective summer hemisphere. If in the middle of the period it does not reach the normal poleward summer position, droughts will occur in the respective marginal tropical areas as, for example, in the Sahel zone, India, Zimbabwe, South Africa, Central America, Chaco, etc. Generally, the ratio of sensible and latent heat is of great importance for the actual release and amount of rainfall.

The monsoons in the summer hemisphere must in the final analysis be regarded as trade winds of the winter hemisphere, which cross the Equator and are then deflected by the Coriolis parameter, so that the southeast trade wind of the Southern Hemisphere becomes the southwest monsoon in the Northern Hemisphere and the northeast trade wind of the Northern Hemisphere becomes a northwest monsoon in the Southern Hemisphere (Figs. 2.20 and 2.22).

Weather systems in the equatorial rain-forest region

There is a close relationship between the zonal currents within the tropical circulation and rainfall. The monsoon and trade-wind circulation show a number of dynamic processes that are of decisive importance for the type and intensity of rainfall.

In the equatorial rain-forest areas so-called zenithal rains may often occur. Although this rainfall is not directly a result of the sun's highest position — as is falsely implied by this term — it is linked with the so-called cloud clusters. These phenomena could only be studied and recognized in detail by means of satellite photos. These cloud clusters may be 100 to 1000 km in diameter and reach as high as 14 km. They receive the required water vapor mainly from the "small water cycle" over the ever-humid rain forests, where the continuous supply of water vapor is regenerated from the evaporation processes occurring over these forests (Congo, Amazon, Indonesia).

Apart from the more cellular features over the large rain forest regions producing heavy rainfall, there are a number of "tropical disturbance lines". These disturbance lines extend in a meridional direction, and are accompanied by sporadic thunderstorms occuring in particular in the intertropical trade-wind zone near the Equator. These are not only observable in the Indo-Malayan Archipelago, the western part of the Congo Basin and on the coast of Guinea in West Africa, but also in northeastern Australia and in the Gulf of Panama. They can only develop by a large vertical extension of the intertropical west-wind current, where a convective impulse resulting from slight thermal differences between northern and southern hemispheric air masses initiates upslide processes and leads to heavy rainfall with subsequent cooling, frequently occurring in the afternoon hours and during the night in coastal regions.

In the marginal areas of the inner tropics towards the Tropics of Cancer and Capricorn, "easterly waves" produce greater amounts of rainfall. They occur not only in the maritime tropical regions as, for example, in the Caribbean, the South Pacific and off Madagascar, but also inland — as, for example, at the southern rim of the Sahel zones in Africa. They are connected with waves occurring in the easterly trade-wind current. With falling pressure, the equatorial low-pressure system expands poleward, and with rising pressure the subtropical high-pressure cell will expand towards the Equator (Fig. 2.23). Very often so-called squall lines (lignes des graines) are embedded in these easterly waves. They are separate whirls rotating around a short-lived meridional convergence line, in the trough of which slight cooling will be sufficient to form high-reaching cloud towers and to trigger showers with sleet and hail, lasting 24 h at the most. Very often, they bring the largest proportion of summer rain in many parts of West Africa. They are most frequent prior to a longer dry period, or at its end. Wind velocities may be as high as 20 m s^{-1}. They may

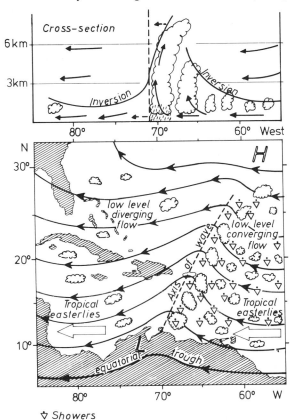

Fig. 2.23. Schematic representation of an easterly wave passing over the West Indies (bottom) and a vertical cross-section (top). (After Riehl, 1954.)

bring rain of up to 100 mm within a very short period of time. Very often the rainfall produced in the easterly waves is intensified or triggered by mountain barriers, as is the case, for example, in many east-coast regions of the tropics. The forced uplifting of the trade-wind belt leads to cumulus clouds producing heavy rain showers with big drops, as is the case, for example, in the Caribbean and on the east coast of Central America (Fig. 2.24), as well as off Madagascar. These easterly waves in many regions contribute to increased rainfall, which is sufficient to convert the normally dry winter half-year into a humid period, thus providing the basis of existence for the rain forests in these areas.

The large amounts of rainfall produced by the monsoons are not only the result of luff effects and uplifting processes caused by the relief. What is more, separate cyclones without real fronts develop, which are accompanied by areas of bad weather with violent storms and heavy rainfall. They are controlled by the upper trade-wind current with the tendency to diverge towards the Equator. The air moisture in the surface air is supplied by the westerlies. Huge nimbostratus clouds develop, and torrential rains occur even over flat terrain. The water content of the monsoon air is extremely high. In equatorial Africa 40 to 50 mm of rain are recorded daily, and in northern India even 60 to 70 mm a day (Fig. 2.25). In combination with luff effects, these cyclones are responsible for the heaviest and often disastrous

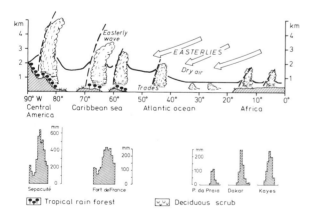

Fig. 2.24. Schematic representation of easterly waves passing over the Atlantic Ocean, the Caribbean Sea and Central America. Rainfall graphs are given for selected stations. (After Boucher, 1975.)

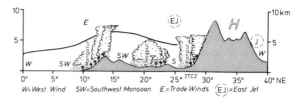

Fig. 2.25. Schematic diagram showing air movements during the summer monsoon (June – October) over India.

rains on the globe. This type of monsoon not only occurs in India, but also in northern Australia, the coast of Guinea in Africa, and in the coastal regions of Colombia and Panama. Temporarily, portions of these cyclones may extend as far as the rim of the dry areas.

Tropical cyclones also often produce the real maximum of rainfall in the marginal tropics, supplementing the annual amounts of rainfall to such an extent that — in conjunction with the normal tropical rains during the summer — they are sufficient for the existence of rain forests. Tropical cyclones develop exclusively over warm tropical oceans from which they receive a great portion of their energy and water vapor. They seldom form in areas located away from the Equator, where the Coriolis force permits the development of whirls. The poleward boundary of tropical cyclones is marked by the subtropical jet stream, whose convergent upper-air currents largely prevent divergence near the surface, and thus the rising of moist air masses from the oceans. Tropical cyclones are concentrated in five clearly defined areas (Fig. 2.26). They occur in the Pacific and Indian Oceans of both hemispheres, and influence the eastern and southern flanks of the respective continents — that is, southern and southeast Asia as well as northern Australia and Madagascar. The Atlantic cyclones only occur in the Northern Hemisphere and primarily affect the Caribbean and Central America. Strangely enough, the east coast of South America is spared from tropical cyclones, for which a final dynamic explanation in terms of circulation is yet to be given. Tropical cyclones mostly occur in the transitional seasons, but may also develop during the summer months.

Rain forests in the marginal tropics often obtain their basis of existence from influxes of extratropical cold air. This applies to the rain forests of the

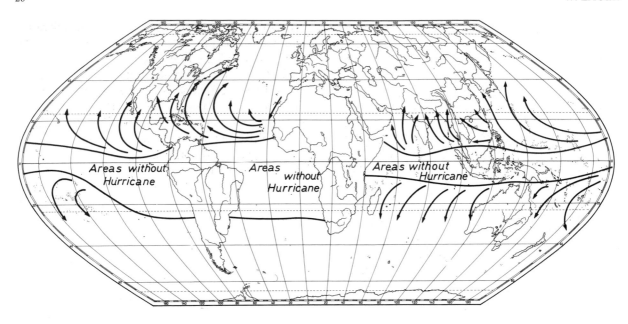

Fig. 2.26. Areas of hurricane formation and their major paths.

marginal tropics located on the east coasts of the continents. They receive their summer rainfall from tropical convectional processes in which the easterly waves are particularly involved. During the winter, however, rainfall from extratropical areas often contributes to the favorable water balance of these forests. Five of twelve classified "Grosswetterlagen" (large-scale weather patterns) occurring over the rain forests on the eastern slopes of Central Mexico were assigned by Klaus (1971) to the extratropical west-wind regime. All of these large-scale weather patterns occur between October and April. The weather patterns producing most rain are those that are linked with the cold-air influxes of the "Northers" (Fig. 2.27). The rain forests located on the eastern slopes between Mexico and Panama owe much of their existence to these extratropical rains. Influxes of extratropi-

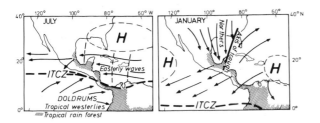

Fig. 2.27. Air flow near the surface over Central America in January and July. (After Boucher, 1975.)

cal cold air have the same effect in East Asia (Philippines), northeastern Australia and particularly on the southeastern coast of Brazil and on the eastern rim of the Andes in Argentina and Bolivia. Influxes of southern-hemispheric cold air are reported on the South American continent as "friagem" even in the upper Amazon forest, with sudden temperature drops of up to 8°.

The circulation belts in the tropics and their rain regimes are indirectly related to the seasonal course of the Sun. Exact analysis of the phenomenon, however, shows that the tropical convectional rains neither fall at the location of the zenithal position of the Sun, nor do they correspond with it in time, but lag behind by 1 to 2 months. The migration of the circulation belts depends rather on the dynamics of the ITCZ and individual weather patterns. It is nevertheless possible to correlate statistically the course of the Sun towards the Tropics of Cancer and Capricorn with the rhythm of the occurrence of rainy and dry periods (Fig. 2.28).

As a result of the sun-dependent migration of the circulation and of the rain zone, so-called steady and alternative climates develop over the respective landscape belts (Fig. 2.21). The superposition of winter and summer circulation patterns produces in the equatorial region a steady climatic zone with rainfall in all seasons, where the ever-

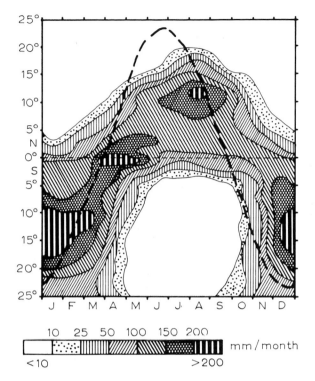

Fig. 2.28. Seasonal rainfall distribution over eastern Africa (32°E), as indicated by monthly mean values: The dashed line represents the Sun's overhead path. (After Flohn, 1964.)

humid rain forests grow. In the outer tropical zone, the course of the Sun induces the development of an alternating climate with a summer rainfall period, and only deciduous forests occur. In the marginal tropical, evergreen rain-forest regions of the east coasts, the winter rain period is caused by disturbances of the easterly waves, influxes of extratropical cold air, and luff effects. It is only in this way that the rain forests can secure the required water balance for the entire year. The forests approach the thermical boundary of the tropics, and gradually change into subtropical rain forests, where frost and lack of heat cause a general change in the composition of the species so that these areas can no longer be regarded as tropical rain forests (Fig. 2.29).

(1) The Meteosat photograph of April 13, 1978 (11.55 GMT, Channel VIS 2; Fig. 2.29A) taken at the time of the Sun's highest position over the Equator (equinoctial position) shows the zone of maximum cloudiness in the equatorial region. Over the Atlantic, the ITCZ is clearly visible as a narrow band of clouds. Over the continent, however, the

inner-tropical low-pressure trough is considerably wider, and extends both southward and northward to the limits of the rain-forest region.

(2) The Meteosat photograph of August 3, 1978 (11.55 GMT, Channel VIS 2; Fig. 2.29B) shows the distribution of clouds in the African tropics during the northern-hemispheric summer. Maximum rainfall is experienced north of the Equator. In the western part of Africa, maximum rainfall occurs in the coastal hinterland, and extends to the dry savannas of the Sahel zone. In the center of the continent, rainfall occurs in the entire region of the equatorial low-pressure trough, particularly north of the Equator and also south of it — that is almost at the southern rim of the rain-forest region.

(3) The convectional clouds on the Meteosat photograph of February 21, 1978 (11.55 GMT, Channel VIS 2; Fig. 2.29C) indicate that the rainfall particularly occurs in the southern-hemispheric tropics of Africa. In other words, the equatorial low-pressure trough extends far into the southern-hemispheric region. But even during this period the central equatorial region of the rain forests still lies within the rainfall area. During the southern-hemispheric summer the intertropical convergence zone over the Atlantic is shifted only slightly southward from its northern-hemispheric position. However, over Liberia, in the area of the coastal rain forests, rainfall occurs in this season as well.

PRECIPITATION IN THE RAIN-FOREST REGION

Spatial distribution of rainfall

In the equatorial tropics, the high water-vapor content of the warm air, in combination with convergent surface air currents and unstable air layers, provides an intensive vertical movement through convection. Therefore, this is the largest area in the world with such a high amount of rainfall (Fig. 2.30). The continental core regions are the Amazon Basin, the Congo Basin and the Indo-Malayan Archipelago.

In the tropical rain forests the mean annual precipitation amounts to 2000 to 3000 mm. While in Africa and South America, towards the Tropics of Cancer and Capricorn, the amount of rainfall

METEOSAT   1978 MONTH 4 DAY 13 TIME 1155 GMT (NORTH) CH. VIS 2
            NOMINAL SCAN/PREPROCESSED SLOT 24 CATALOGUE 1001720100

Fig. 2.29A. METEOSAT photograph of Africa at 11.55 GMT on April 13, 1978.

decreases rapidly due to the shortening rainy period and extended dry season, and the minimum amounts of rainfall of the world occur in fact in the marginal-tropical and subtropical dry belt, the marginal tropics of Southeast Asia are an exception. In this area, even close to the Tropic of Cancer the monsoon phenomenon produces maximum amounts of rainfall during the summer half-year, sometimes exceeding the amounts of equatorial rains equally distributed over the year. The hygric equator — that is, the zone of maximum precipitation — is not located at the astronomic Equator itself. Maximum individual values in most

cases are not reached in equatorial lowlands due to the intensive convectional conditions, but on the western and eastern sides of the continents, as a result of additional relief effects (Fig. 2.31).

In the area of the equatorial tropics, areas with high rainfall are located in the western parts of the continents — for example, in Africa near the coast of Guinea and in the Cameroons, and South America between Panama and Ecuador, concentrated in Columbia. At Mt. Cameroon, a record value of 12 000 mm is reached at the Debunja station. In Columbia as well, the Quibdó station showed values of approximately 10 000 mm as a

METEOSAT   1978 MONTH 8 DAY 3 TIME 1155 GMT (NORTH) CH. VIS 2
LIMITED SCAN/RAW DATA   SLOT 24 CATALOGUE 1005020031

Fig. 2.29B. METEOSAT photograph of Africa at 11.55 GMT on August 3, 1978.

long-term annual mean. In the Indo-Malayan Archipelago the western sides in the equatorial region are generally favored, but peak values with very high mean rainfall also occur in the marginal tropics (Western Ghats in India and west-exposed coastal areas of Indochina, as well as on the southern flank of the Himalaya Mountains).

An annual amount of 11 200 mm, averaged over the period 1851 to 1980, was measured as a record amount of rainfall for the monsoon area at Cherapunji station (1300 m) in the Khasia Mountains of Burma.

In all of these regions the flow of air masses in a western direction within the equatorial trough is of decisive importance for the high amounts of rainfall.

The eastern sides of the continents are considerably drier at the Equator; Africa is the best example. In the marginal tropics, however, the eastern sides are favored by rainfall. In these areas, disturbances of the trade-wind belt and an exposed relief produce record amounts of rainfall (for example, on the eastern flank of Madagascar, the Philippines, eastern Brazil, the Caribbean islands, Central America and the Hawaiian islands). At Mt. Waialeale on Hawaii, an average of 12 547 mm was recorded for the period from 1930 to 1958. On the east coasts generally the

METEOSAT 1978 MONTH 2 DAY 21 TIME 1155 GMT (NORTH) CH. VIS 2
          NOMINAL SCAN/PREPROCESSED SLOT 24 CATALOGUE 1000420028

Fig. 2.29C. METEOSAT photograph of Africa at 11.55 GMT on February 21, 1978.

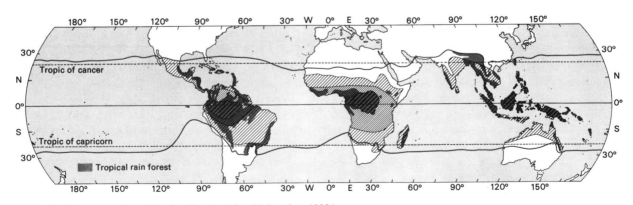

Fig. 2.30. Mean annual precipitation (mm). (After Meinardus, 1933.)

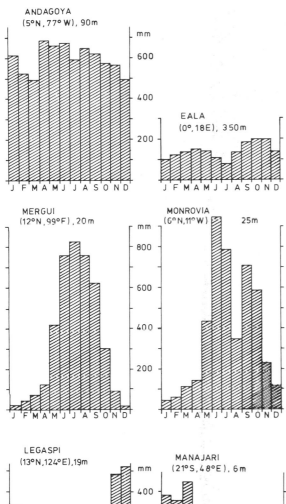

ANDAGOYA
(5°N, 77°W), 90 m

EALA
(0°, 18E), 350 m

MERGUI
(12°N, 99°F), 20 m

MONROVIA
(6°N, 11°W)   25 m

LEGASPI
(13°N, 124°E), 19 m

MANAJARI
(21°S, 48°E), 6 m

Fig. 2.31. Rainfall graphs for several stations in the rain-forest
area.

maximum values range between 4000 and
6000 mm.

Rainfall and altitudinal belts in the equatorial tropics

The rainfall within the tropics shows a characteristic vertical distribution as a function of height
above sea level. As a result of the predominantly
convective type of rainfall, the zone of maximum

precipitation is not located in the tropical lowlands, but at altitudes between 800 and 1500 m.
Exceptions to this rule are known in the monsoon
regions, where maxima can occur even at sea level.
Above this first level of condensation, the amount
of rainfall decreases rapidly. Nevertheless a much
weaker second maximum at a further second level
of condensation is developed, mostly located
between 2700 and 3200 m. Depending on the water
vapor of the air, further insignificant increases may
occur in the high mountains within this rapidly
decreasing tendency (Fig. 2.32). However, the drier
the base of the mountains, the higher are the zones
of maximum rainfall. There is a number of
semihumid foothill areas in the real rain-forest
tropics, where evergreen as well as tropical-
montane rain forests occur only in the altitudinal
belt of the tierra templada — that is, above
1000 m. At higher elevations, these evergreen
forests of the cloud- and fog-forest type mostly
depend on the summer rains and winter fogbanks,
from which the trees absorb the required moisture
during the dry season. Cloud forests of this type
occur in almost all tropical continents.

The seasonal distribution of rainfall in the tropical rain-forest region

The annual course of the Sun between the
Tropics of Cancer and Capricorn results in the fact

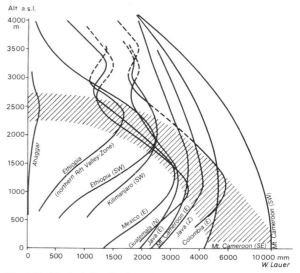

Fig. 2.32. Vertical distribution of precipitation in the rain-forest
area.

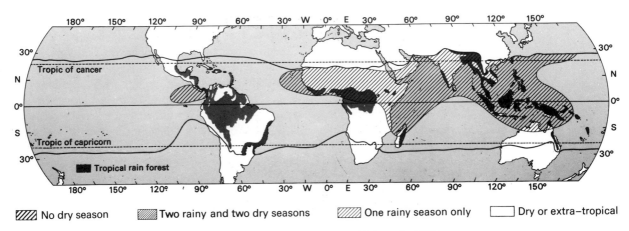

Fig. 2.33. Seasonal rainfall distribution. (After Blüthgen and Weischet, and Nieuwolt, 1982.)

that, in principle, two maxima occur in the annual rainfall cycle at the Equator shortly after the Sun has passed the equinoxes (Fig. 2.28). These two maxima gradually merge into one summer-rain period toward the Tropics of Cancer and Capricorn; this is accompanied by a reduction of the total amount of rainfall and the formation of a more intense and more marked dry period in the winter (Figs. 2.28 and 2.33).

The annual rainfall cycle near the Equator is, in general, relatively balanced and shows two weak maxima and minima (Fig. 2.31). However, the cases in which the occurrence of rainfall in the humid tropics deviates from a regular cycle are quite numerous. They do not only depend on the land/water distribution ratio, the type of relief and the altitude, but also on the exposure and circulation regime (Fig. 2.31). In the rain forests of the monsoon area the amount of summer rainfall is extremely high; however, in most cases, there is a lack of winter rainfall, so that many types of monsoon forests, such as those in southern Asia, can only be regarded as seasonal semi-evergreen, deciduous rain forests (Fig. 2.31). Within the area of the trade-wind climate of the marginal tropics, where rain forests occur, a rainfall period lasting throughout the year is the result of the fact that orographic rain of the trade wind with accompanying disturbances frequently occurs at the time when the Sun is in its lowest position. This winter rainfall, in combination with the solsticial rain in the summer, provides favorable conditions for the existence of evergreen forests (Fig. 2.31). Individual types of rainfall account for different

amounts of the total annual precipitation (Fig. 2.34).

Rain forests in the sense of an evergreen plant formation within the tropics can only exist if the rainfall occurring in the annual cycle provides a continuous positive groundwater balance, so that a permanently humid climate prevails, and dry periods result in negative balances for only a short time. In general, evergreen rain forests are able to survive a period of two months with severe arid conditions without being subject to a lethal water deficiency. Many authors regard an annual total of approximately 2000 mm as the boundary of the Earth's rain-forest areas. However, a precondition is that this rainfall is distributed evenly over the year. Only in this way is it possible that in South America, for example, 1900 mm of rainfall and in

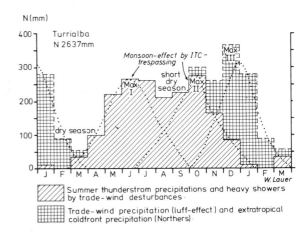

Fig. 2.34. Analysis of the types of precipitation at the Turrialba station (Costa Rica).

TABLE 2.3

Monthly precipitation (mm) at several stations of the tropical rain-forest area

	Latitude	Jan.	Feb.	Mar.	Apr.	May	June	July	Aug.	Sept.	Oct.	Nov.	Dec.	Year
Yangambi, Zaire	0°45'N	80.0	100.0	150.5	150.3	140.7	110.3	120.3	140.2	180.6	200.7	170.4	110.1	1654.1
Eala, Zaire	0°03'N	80.6	130.3	120.1	160.5	160.4	130.5	70.6	160.2	170.6	220.4	190.1	160.5	1754.8
Pontianak, Indonesia	0°06'N	260.9	210.6	240.4	280.2	270.2	220.6	160.5	210.8	210.8	370.3	400.9	330.3	3166.5
Fonte Boa, Brazil	0°32'S	298.3	236.8	278.1	335.9	313.7	238.4	175.0	148.8	149.9	193.8	186.1	246.6	2801.4
Douala, Cameroon	4°05'N	52.0	86.0	198.0	222.0	223.0	510.0	722.0	722.0	530.0	415.0	155.0	67.0	3902.0
Mangalur, India	12°52'N	3.0	3.0	5.0	38.0	157.0	942.0	988.0	597.0	267.0	206.0	74.0	13.0	3293.0
Cherrapunji, India	25°15'N	18.0	53.0	185.0	665.0	1280.0	2695.0	2446.0	1781.0	1100.0	493.0	69.0	13.0	10798.0
Sandakan, Sabah	5°50'N	460.7	240.4	200.3	100.4	150.0	180.5	160.5	200.6	230.9	250.4	370.3	450.0	2995.0
Iloilo, Philippines	10°42'N	59.0	38.0	36.0	52.0	153.0	265.0	390.0	370.0	294.0	263.0	207.0	121.0	2248.0
Legaspi, Philippines	13°08'N	366.0	265.0	218.0	158.0	178.0	194.0	235.9	209.0	252.0	313.0	479.0	503.0	3370.0
Cozumel, Mexico	20°31'N	82.0	67.0	55.0	57.0	150.0	201.0	120.0	162.0	242.0	224.0	110.0	105.0	1575.0
Cairns, Queensland	16°55'N	420.2	390.4	460.0	290.5	100.9	70.1	40.1	40.3	40.3	50.3	90.7	210.8	2204.6
Chinchina, Colombia (1360 m a.s.l.)	4°58'N	147.0	142.0	213.0	312.0	309.0	197.0	173.0	186.0	184.0	326.0	249.0	237.0	2675.0

Africa even only 1600 mm is sufficient for the existence of rain forests (Fig. 2.31 and Table 2.3).

Ashton and Bruenig (1975), using a 71-year observation series, found that months with a negative water balance may occur during all seasons. Overlapping 30-day rainfall totals show that periods of several days without rain occur again and again in the forest areas. In most cases, the dry intervals do not last so long that the existence of a rain forest would be endangered.

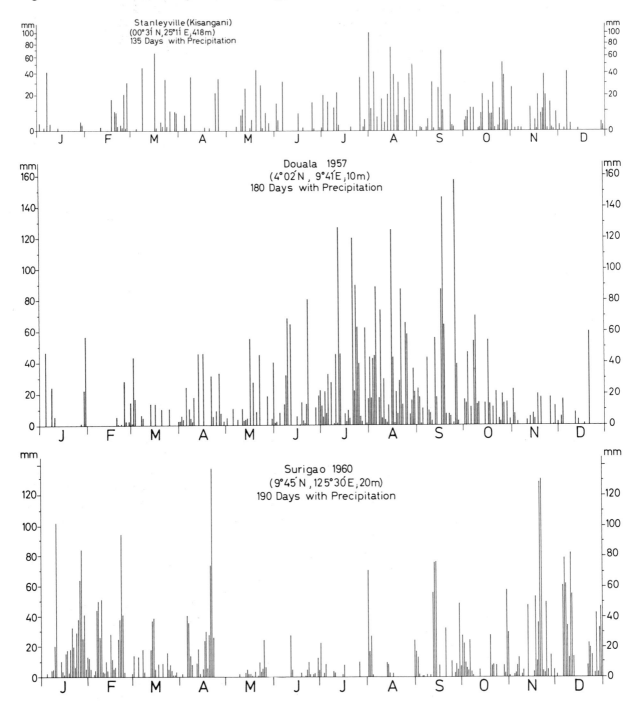

Fig. 2.35. Daily rainfall at three selected stations in the tropical rain-forest area.

However, one must proceed from the assumption that periods without rain are compensated by the formation of ground-water reserves sufficient to enable the vegetation to survive the dry periods. Edaphic humidity often replaces the purely climatic humidity during longer periods without rain. However, the frequency of occurrence and intensity of dry periods will decisively determine the rain forest's physiognomy and ecology (Fig. 2.35).

Diurnal distribution of rainfall

The diurnal rainfall curve shows a high periodicity in some rain-forest areas, which is attributable to the fact that the rains will set in only after the time of daily maximum convection following the Sun's zenithal position; this is the time when they are very heavy, and sometimes continue deep into the night (Fig. 2.36).

In most cases, the mountain slopes and inland regions have their maximum rainfall in the afternoon. Toward the coasts, the maximum of daily convectional rainfall is shifted into the night. The diurnal cycle is distinctly marked only in those areas where convectional rainfall constitutes the predominant type of precipitation. Synoptical processes are of such decisive importance for both monsoons and trade winds that diurnal conditions are unimportant.

THE WATER BUDGET IN THE TROPICAL RAIN-FOREST REGION

Air humidity in the rain forest

In the tropical rain forest, the growth of plants is closely correlated with air humidity. However, the absolute water-vapor content in the air is of less importance for the transpiration, photosynthesis and plant growth than the relative humidity, or the saturation deficit. Despite a permanently humid rain-forest climate, one cannot speak of a uniformly high relative air humidity in the equatorial region. At an almost constant absolute humidity, the relative humidity varies inversely with the temperature, and therefore shows an annual and diurnal variation, particularly in the canopy, which follows that of temperature. However, in the tropical rain forest, the relative humidity remains comparatively high during the day even in open areas, and even during the short dry season. In

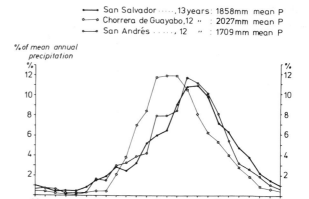

Fig. 2.36. Diurnal rain cycle in percent of the annual mean. (After Lessmann, 1967.)

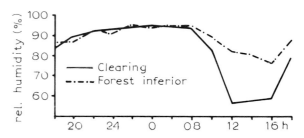

Fig. 2.37. Daily relative humidity cycle in an ombrophilous forest in southwest Ghana on an unusually dry day during a "harmattan" period (5 to 6 Jan., 1967). Both readings at 10 cm above the ground. (After Longmann and Jenik, 1974.)

general, at night the air in the rain forest, with a relative humidity of 95%, is almost saturated (Fig. 2.37). This similarly applies to all forest strata, including the ground layer. It is nevertheless possible, that, during the night, the relative humidity may drop below 65% on days without rain. In the literature, absolute minima below 30% are reported. The average daily maxima amount to 100% (at 06.00 h) and the minima to 60 to 70% (at 14.00 h; Table 2.4).

Water cycle and water budget

The water budget of the continents and the oceans and thus of the entire earth may be expressed by the following water-balance equation:

$$P_L - E_L = R_L = E_M - P_M$$
$$P_W = E_W$$

where L = land areas, M = ocean areas, W = entire Earth, P = precipitation, E = evaporation, and R = runoff.

TABLE 2.4

Relative humidity (%) for selected stations of the tropical rain-forest area

	Local time (h)	Jan.	Feb.	Mar.	Apr.	May	June	July	Aug.	Sep.	Oct.	Nov.	Dec.	Mean of year (%)
Tropical rain forest														
Mazaruni Station, Guyana	07.00	94	93	93	93	93	94	94	94	93	93	93	94	94
	13.00	79	76	73	75	81	82	81	77	73	72	74	81	73
Eala, Zaïre	12.00	74	70	72	73	75	77	76	76	75	74	76	77	75
Douala, Cameroon	07.00	95	96	95	94	95	95	96	96	95	95	95	95	95
	14.00	74	75	76	76	79	82	86	84	85	83	80	78	80
Singapore	09.00	84	83	82	83	85	82	82	82	82	82	83	83	83
	15.00	72	69	75	76	76	74	73	75	75	76	77	77	75
Sandakan, Sabah	06.00	91	91	91	92	92	92	91	91	91	92	93	92	92
	14.00	77	75	74	70	69	69	69	69	67	70	75	76	72
Apia, Samoa	09.00	82	81	81	79	78	77	77	76	75	77	78	79	78
	15.00	79	78	78	76	76	73	75	73	75	76	75	77	76
Tropical rain forest (near climatic limit)														
Port-of-Spain, Trinidad	07.00	92	93	93	92	91	92	93	95	94	94	94	93	93
	15.00	68	63	62	60	60	66	73	73	74	72	74	73	68
Lagos, Nigeria	09.00	84	83	82	81	83	87	87	85	86	86	85	86	85
	15.00	65	69	72	72	76	80	80	76	77	76	72	68	74
Maisindi, Uganda (1146 m a.s.l.)	08.30	70	66	77	80	82	82	88	85	84	81	80	77	79
	14.30	43	42	57	60	66	67	67	65	66	62	56	54	59
Jakarta, Indonesia	08.00	90	92	90	89	89	89	87	84	82	81	84	87	87
	14.00	75	76	73	71	69	68	65	62	62	65	69	73	69

According to this equation, viewed globally, there is a dynamic equilibrium between the continents and the oceans. In other words, the quantity of runoff (R) received by the ocean must be returned to the continents in the form of water surplus in air streams. On the continent, the amount of precipitation (P) is on the average larger than the evaporation (E). The surplus is fed into the ocean as runoff (R). This runoff is equal to the surplus from evaporation over the oceans, which cover 71% of the Earth's total surface. The water-balance equation applies to long periods during which storage processes are negligible.

The water budget and heat budget are closely related with each other through the latent-heat fluxes by means of which the water vapor is released into the atmosphere and horizontally transported. In the rain-forest region, as a result of the high water-vapor content of the atmosphere and the continuous evaporation and condensation processes connected therewith, the sensible/latent heat ratio (Bowen ratio) is strongly shifted in favor of latent heat.

The main area for the supply of water vapor is located in the marginal tropical to subtropical high-pressure regions of both hemispheres (Fig. 2.38). As a result of maximum values of radiation balance occurring in these regions, there is a maximum of evaporation on the oceans in these latitudes (Fig. 2.39). On the continents at the same latitude, however, the evaporation is extremely low, as there is hardly any water in arid regions, although the evaporation power (potential evaporation) is very high in these areas.

The evaporation surplus of the oceans in the marginal tropics is transported into the extratropical westerly trough on the one hand, and to the equatorial regions by the trade winds on the other (Fig. 2.38). The main areas for transportation toward the Equator are located in the eastern Pacific and the eastern Atlantic. However, the transport to the tropical regions is less marked

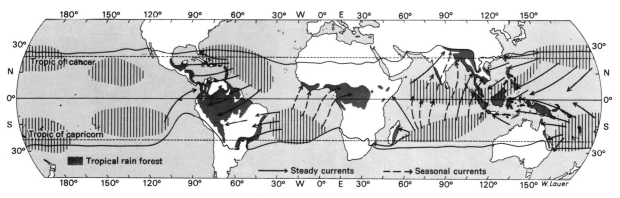

Fig. 2.38. Origins of mean atmospheric water vapor.

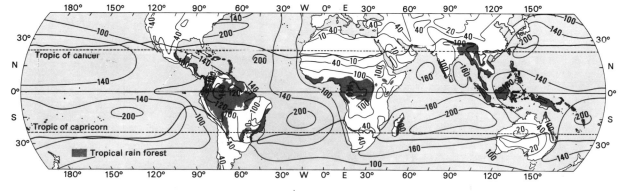

Fig. 2.39. Mean annual actual evaporation (cm). (After **Baumgartner** and **Reichel**, 1975.)

toward higher latitudes, since sufficient water vapor is available over inner-tropical regions due to the high precipitation. The Atlantic circulatory system feeds the African rain-forest regions and to a small extent the Amazon area. The larger Indo-Pacific water cycle comprises South and Southeast Asia, northern Australia, the Indo-Malayan and Pacific archipelagoes as well as the western coasts of Central and South America between Mexico and Ecuador.

The large rain-forest areas in Africa, in the Indo-Malayan Archipelago and particularly in South America receive two-thirds of their water budget from the so-called "small water cycle" over the continents themselves, where the precipitation evaporates over the rain forests, recondenses and is again received as precipitation. The small water cycle has a transfer time of only 1 to 2 days. The remaining one-third of the water budget is, as described above, transported by advection into the rain-forest regions by the monsoons and trade winds in the so-called "large water cycle".

In the area of the equatorial evergreen lowland rain forests, the average annual evapotranspiration amounts to approximately 1000 to 1500 mm yr^{-1} and thus even exceeds the evaporation from the oceans in these latitudes. In the area of the wet savannas and the evergreen wet forests, the annual evaporation drops to about 1000 mm yr^{-1} and less, to converge toward zero in the desert.

On the whole, the equatorial tropics show a surplus of precipitation vis-à-vis evapotranspiration, so that a positive annual water balance is also maintained locally in the rain forests. However, a small deficit may occur in the relatively dry months when the runoff is very high. From the map of mean annual evaporation (Fig. 2.39), it becomes evident that the evaporation values are somewhat higher in the Indo-Malayan Archipelago, and lower in the Congo and Amazon basins. When evenly distributed over the year, the amounts of precipitation exceed the evapotranspiration by approximately one- or two-thirds. The rest is transported to the oceans by the extensive drainage network. Regional differences in the rain-forest areas become evident when the precipitation curves show distinct maxima in their annual cycle. During these perhumid periods, in the monsoon regions the runoff increases in the case of relatively constant evapotranspiration, whereas in the sub-humid to semihumid periods the evapotranspiration exceeds the runoff.

The equatorial region is marked by high amounts of runoff (Fig. 2.40). Tropical mountain areas show higher values than the lowlands; in other words, the highlands of the Indo-Malayan Archipelago, the Himalayan slopes, the eastern Andean slopes of the inner Amazon region, and the western slopes of Columbia have greater runoff than the lowlands of the Congo and Amazon basins.

The problem of evaporation

The most important factor for the water budget and physiological processes in the tropical rain forest is the evapotranspiration (ET) — that is, the total moisture loss of the forest. It is composed of evaporation from open water surfaces (Eo) and transpiration (T) — the moisture loss from plants.

In general, in the rain-forest area, the value of evapotranspiration is smaller than the amount of

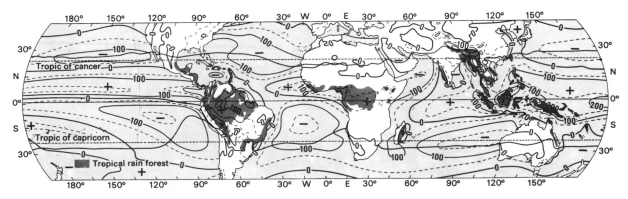

Fig. 2.40. Mean annual runoff (cm). (After Baumgartner and Reichel, 1975.)

precipitation, since sufficient water is available on average through the year. At the same time, actual (*aET*) and potential (*pET*) evapotranspiration are equal. Only during shorter dry periods may the potential evapotranspiration values be higher than those of actual evapotranspiration and of precipitation.

One may proceed from the assumption that in rain-forest areas the transpiration (*T*) will exceed the evaporation from open water surfaces (*Eo*) (Fig. 2.41). Thus, it becomes evident that, in general, the measured evaporation from open water surfaces (*Eo*) will never cover the real value of actual overall evapotranspiration (*ET*) in a rain forest.

In the dry belts of the marginal tropics, potential evapotranspiration will by far exceed precipitation, whereas the actual evapotranspiration will, due to the lack of water, only correspond to the amount of precipitation. In the rain-forest canopy, evapotranspiration may sometimes exceed precipitation, as the canopy often is subject to water stress and, therefore, high transpiration values are reached because of the continuous water flow into the stand.

Figure 2.42 shows maximum values of potential evaporation for the dry belt, where a relatively great portion of solar radiation is absorbed and evaporation is favored by constant winds (trade winds). In the rain-forest area, however, evaporation is reduced to a greater extent by clouds. The maxima of potential evaporation — here mostly identical with the actual evaporation — coincide with the maxima of precipitation and vice versa.

Evapotranspiration in the rain forest is one of the most difficult climatological parameters to

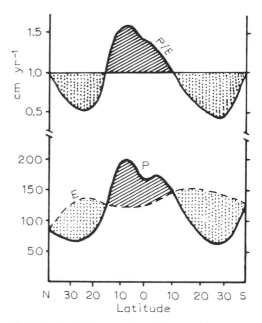

Fig. 2.42. Latitudinal profiles of the precipitation/evaporation ratio and of the annual precipitation and evaporation. (From Riehl, 1979.)

investigate. Generally, rain forests show relatively small amounts of evapotranspiration, as the surrounding air is often almost completely saturated with moisture and winds are lacking in the inner portions of the forest, so that the saturation deficit remains very small. Only the canopy may be regarded as an active transpiration surface. In the inner portions of the stand rates of transpiration drop to less than one-fourth of the values observed in the upper forest stratum. Very often no transpiration is measurable at all during the day in the forest undergrowth. Higher evapotranspiration values, however, are measured during periods without rain.

In a forest reservation in Nigeria (Fig. 2.43), Hopkins (1965a, b) measured the evapotranspiration by means of Piche evaporimeters. During the main rainy period from July to November the evapotranspiration in all strata measured amounted to less then 1 ml day^{-1}. However, during the dry season from January to March it increases to twice that amount. The high humidity on the forest floor remained relatively constant; 40% of the total evapotranspiration occurred during the night. Bruenig (1969) (Fig. 2.44) found for the heath-forest area of Sarawak on Borneo that the evapotranspiration of the rain forest

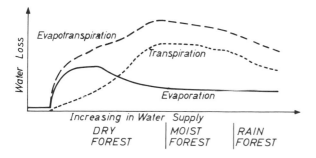

Fig. 2.41. Schematic representation of the relationship between evaporation and transpiration. (After Gentilli, from Keller, 1961.)

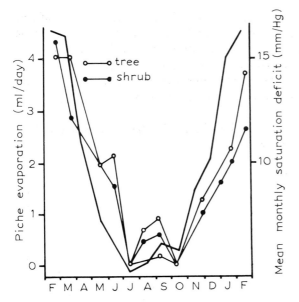

Fig. 2.43. Piche evaporation in trees and shrubs and the mean monthly climatic saturation deficit at 14.30 h from Feb. 1957 to Feb. 1958 in Nigeria. (After Hopkins, 1965a, b.)

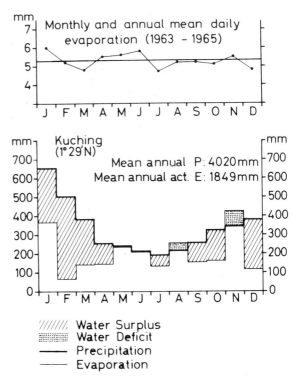

Fig. 2.44. Annual precipitation cycle and monthly mean daily evaporation in Kuching, Borneo. (After Bruenig, 1969.)

almost corresponded with the evaporation of an open water surface. The mean daily values corresponded particularly with the cycle of days with rain and fair-weather periods.

Evapotranspiration measurements in the rain forest particularly suffer from measuring methods. Therefore, evapotranspiration values are again and again estimated by means of calculations. Correlations established between the values obtained by different methods, such as Class A pan, Piche evaporimeter, and the physically determined evapotranspiration formulae showed that the measured values largely correspond within an error range of ±10%. It may be regarded as proven that the curve of evapotranspiration in the rain forest essentially depends upon both solar radiation and the annual cycles of cloud and rain. On the whole, one may say that under average rain-forest conditions the evaporation amounts to between 50 and 80% of the precipitation. Bruenig (1969), for example, has measured for an annual rainfall amount of 2500 mm an evapotranspiration value of 1970 mm (78%), whereas at the Barro Colorado station in Panama, with a precipitation total of 2600 mm, a potential cvapotranspiration of 1680 mm = 65% (after Thornthwaite) or 1464 mm = 56% (after Penman) was computed (Leigh et al., 1983). The relatively great variation between measured and computed

values, using different methods, reveals that the methods of determining evapotranspiration are by no means satisfactory. It is still not possible adequately to distinguish between the contribution of transpiration and that of evaporation within the tropical rain forest.

Measurements conducted on the plant produce similar values to those that are obtained when using an open water surface in a clearing as a device for measuring evaporation. The real evaporation values can probably best be determined by means of physically sound formulae. The integral of evaporation and transpiration was designated by Lauer and Frankenberg (1981) as the potential and/or optimal landscape evapotranspiration (oLET). They have defined it as the optimum evapotranspiration (oLET) of an actual landscape segment by assuming a permanent optimal water supply to the ground. In this connection, the actual landscape with its vegetation cover and the existing typical ecophysiological reaction types is regarded as a surface, where an optimal transpiration of the vegetation is possible.

A map section covering the equatorial area of

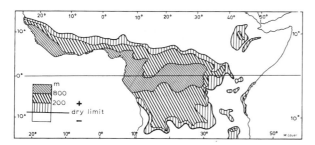

Fig. 2.45. Annual water balance $P - pLET$ in the humid regions of the African tropics.

Africa (Fig. 2.45) shows that the annual balance between precipitation and "potential landscape evaporation" provides a water surplus for the rain-forest region which in this special case does not fall below 800 mm. Furthermore, on the basis of an index, Lauer and Frankenberg (1981) concluded that, in general, a negative water balance must not occur in the rain forest for more than two months, as this would result in a water stress that would basically lead to a change in the vegetation formation.

Soil-moisture content in the tropical rain forest

While the quantity and particularly the seasonal distribution of the precipitation are the determining factors for the tropical rain forests, the soil moisture is of decisive importance for the formation of the forest type. There is a number of locations with restricted, free or excessive drainage. Very often, the water storage capacity of the soil is of decisive importance for the forest vegetation, particularly in those cases when the potential evapotranspiration exceeds the amount of precipitation for a certain period of time, so that the water reserves stored in the soil need to be drawn upon and the plants may be temporarily subject to moisture stress. The soil moisture and its storage capacity are closely correlated with the soil texture. In the case of sandy to loamy humus podzols of medium depth under the heath forest in Sarawak, Bruenig (1969) found field capacities of less than 10 to 15% — which, moreover, were available for only three-fourths of the plants. During extremely dry periods, such as occurred in 1982 and 1983, large portions of the evergreen forest may die, since the critical point of water supply has been exceeded. The critical point will be reached when the capacity of the soil to provide water available for the plants is no longer sufficient to maintain the required transpiration of the forest. In other words, evapotranspiration and the water available for the plants often represent the limiting conditions for tropical rain forests.

Climatic types of the rain forests according to the water budget

In the following, an attempt is made to distinguish climatic types of the tropical rain forest on the basis of the annual cycle of the water budget. Rain forests can only exist if the water budget shows a suitable balance under given megathermal conditions. When optimally developed, they can only bear a short-term water stress. Therefore, the annual cycle of the water budget as a function of the atmospheric circulation will in the last analysis be the decisive factor for the climatic types of the tropical rain-forest area.

With the aid of the monthly water balance it is possible to describe humid and arid phases in terms of duration and intensity, thus permitting a spatial classification of the rain-forest region (Figs. 2.46, 2.47 and Table 2.5).

The equatorial type

Throughout the year, this type is located along the rain equator within the sphere of influence of the intertropical low pressures, where no month will show a negative water balance in the long-term mean. In these areas, arid phases with a negative water balance rarely exceed one to two months. Although they occur at irregular intervals, they are in most cases linked with relative dry periods conditioned by circulation-dynamic processes. The large river systems of the Amazon and Congo as well as the area of the Sunda Islands are examples of the water budget in this rain-forest region.

The Pontianak station may be taken as an example of the Indo-Malayan evergreen rain forest (Fig. 2.46 and Table 2.5). This station, located on the island of Borneo, shows the normal type of equatorial rain climate. The mean annual temperature amounts to approximately 25°C and the annual rainfall 3151 mm. The monthly amounts of rainfall vary between 160 and 300 mm. The optimum evapotranspiration is about 150 mm per month. Runoff reaches peak values during the

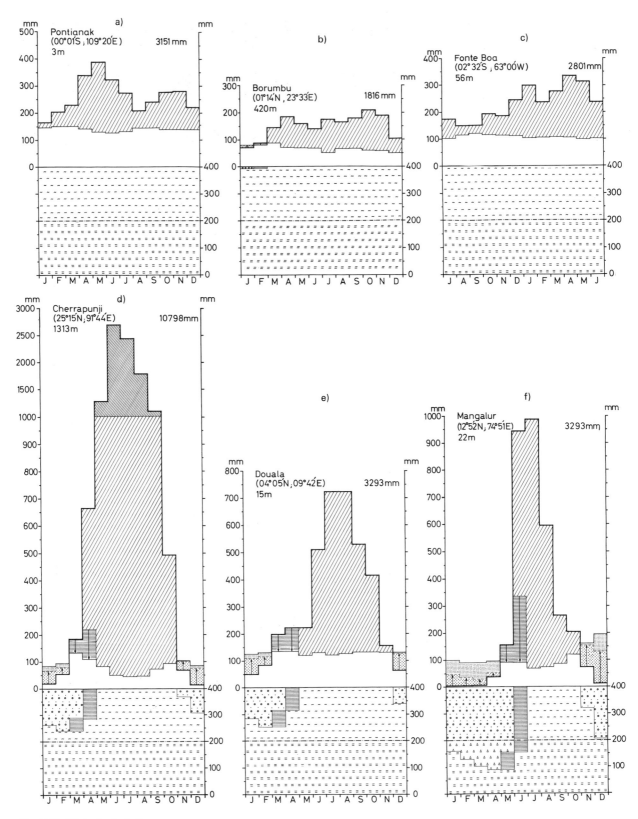

Fig. 2.46. Water budget diagrams.

TABLE 2.5

Water regime at stations within the tropical rain forest (all figures are in mm)

Station	Value	J	F	M	A	M	J	J	A	S	O	N	D	Year
Pontianak (Indonesia) 00°01'S, 109°20'E 3 m	P	274	208	241	277	282	221	165	203	229	339	389	323	3151
	$oLET$	131.0	143.6	143.0	137.4	137.8	137.8	145.2	148.1	148.7	142.9	129.0	126.2	1670.7
	$P{-}oLET$	143.0	64.4	98.0	139.6	144.2	83.2	19.8	54.9	80.3	196.1	260.0	196.8	1480.3
	SWS	400.0	400.0	400.0	400.0	400.0	400.0	400.0	400.0	400.0	400.0	400.0	400.00	400.00
	ΔSWS	0	0	0	0	0	0	0	0	0	0	0	0	0
	R	143.0	64.4	98.0	139.6	144.2	83.2	19.8	54.9	80.3	196.1	260.0	196.8	1480.3
	$aLET$	131.0	143.6	143.0	137.4	137.8	137.8	145.2	148.1	148.7	142.9	129.0	126.2	1670.7
	$aLET{-}oLET$	0	0	0	0	0	0	0	0	0	0	0	0	0
Borumbu (Zaïre) 01°14'S, 23°33'E 420 m	P	72	87	145	185	158	141	175	166	180	210	192	105	1816
	$oLET$	79.1	79.2	87.0	71.1	69.5	67.7	51.5	67.1	67.8	60.0	59.7	51.6	811.3
	$P{-}oLET$	−7.1	7.8	58.0	113.9	88.5	73.3	123.5	98.9	112.2	150.0	132.3	53.4	1004.7
	SWS	393.0	400.0	400.0	400.0	400.0	400.0	400.0	400.0	400.0	400.0	400.0	400.0	
	ΔSWS	−7.0	+7.0	0	0	0	0	0	0	0	0	0	0	
	R	0	0.8	58.0	113.9	88.5	73.3	123.5	98.9	112.2	150.0	132.3	53.4	1004.8
	$aLET$	79.0	79.2	87.0	71.1	69.5	67.7	51.5	67.1	67.8	60.0	59.7	51.6	811.2
	$aLET{-}oLET$	−0.1	0	0	0	0	0	0	0	0	0	0	0	−0.1
Fonte Boa (Brazil) 02°32'S, 63°00'W 56 m	P	298.3	236.8	273.8	335.9	313.7	238.4	175.0	148.8	149.3	193.8	186.1	246.6	2801.4
	$oLET$	102.1	104.2	105.1	103.9	97.2	100.0	101.3	114.7	120.6	113.4	111.6	110.2	1284.3
	$P{-}oLET$	196.2	132.6	173.0	232.0	216.5	138.4	73.7	34.1	29.3	80.4	74.5	136.4	1517.1
	SWS	400.0	400.0	400.0	400.0	400.0	400.0	400.0	400.0	400.0	400.0	400.0	400.0	
	ΔSWS	0	0	0	0	0	0	0	0	0	0	0	0	
	R	196.2	132.6	173.0	232.0	216.5	138.4	73.7	34.1	29.3	80.4	74.5	136.4	1517.1
	$aLET$	102.1	104.2	105.1	103.9	97.2	100.0	101.3	114.7	120.6	113.4	111.6	110.2	1284.3
	$aLET{-}oLET$	0	0	0	0	0	0	0	0	0	0	0	0	0
Cherrapunji (India) 25°15'N, 91°44'E 1313 m	P	18	53	185	665	1280	2695	2446	1781	1100	493	69	13	10798
	$oLET$	83.0	94.4	133.2	109.6	82.2	49.4	44.5	46.6	72.1	93.8	101.4	85.1	995.3
	$P{-}oLET$	−65.0	−41.4	51.8	555.4	1197.6	2645.6	2401.5	1734.4	1027.9	399.2	−32.4	−72.1	9802.7
	SWS	261.9	236.2	288.0	400.0	400.0	400.0	400.0	400.0	400.0	400.0	368.9	308.1	
	ΔSWS	−46.2	−25.7	+51.8	+112.0	0	0	0	0	0	0	−31.1	−60.8	
	R	0	0	0	443.4	1197.8	2645.6	2401.5	1734.4	1027.9	399.2	0	0	9849.8
	$aLET$	64.2	78.7	133.2	109.6	82.2	49.4	44.5	46.6	72.1	93.8	100.1	73.8	948.2
	$aLET{-}oLET$	−18.8	−15.7	0	0	0	0	0	0	0	0	−1.3	−11.3	−47.1

(continued)

TABLE 2.5 (*continued*)

Station	Value	J	F	M	A	M	J	J	A	S	O	N	D	Year
Douala	P	52	86	198	222	223	510	722	722	530	415	155	67	3902
(Cameroon)	oLET	125.0	131.2	136.2	135.7	120.0	128.6	122.0	126.1	132.0	132.8	129.8	130.6	1550.0
04°05'N, 09°42'E	P−oLET	−73.0	−45.2	61.8	86.3	103.0	381.4	600.0	595.9	398.0	282.2	25.2	−63.6	2352.0
15 m	SWS	284.3	253.9	315.7	400.0	400.0	400.0	400.0	400.0	400.0	400.0	400.0	341.2	
	ΔSWS	−56.9	−30.4	+61.8	+84.3	0	0	0	0	0	0	0	−58.8	
	R	0	0	0	2.0	103.0	381.4	600.0	595.9	398.0	282.2	25.2	0	2387.7
	aLET	108.9	116.4	136.2	135.7	120.0	128.6	122.0	126.1	132.0	132.8	129.8	125.8	1514.3
	aLET−oLET	−16.1	−14.8	0	0	0	0	0	0	0	0	0	−4.8	−35.7
Mangalur	P	3	3	5	38	157	942	988	597	267	206	74	13	3293
(India)	oLET	99.8	90.0	90.1	97.3	92.4	90.2	68.2	74.3	86.3	120.1	162.0	195.5	1266.2
12°52'N, 74°51'E	P−oLET	−96.8	−87.0	−85.1	−59.3	64.6	851.8	919.8	522.7	180.7	85.9	−88.0	−182.5	2026.8
22 m	SWS	159.7	128.5	103.9	89.6	154.2	400.0	400.0	400.0	400.0	400.0	321.0	203.4	
	ΔSWS	−43.7	−31.2	−24.6	−14.3	+64.6	+245.8	0	0	0	0	−79.0	−117.6	
	R	0	0	0	0	0	606.0	919.8	522.7	180.7	85.9	0	0	2315.1
	aLET	46.7	34.2	29.6	52.3	92.4	90.2	68.2	74.3	86.3	120.1	153.0	130.0	977.9
	aLET−oLET	−53.1	−55.8	−60.5	−45.0	0	0	0	0	0	0	−9.0	−64.9	−288.3
Legaspi	P	366	265	218	158	178	194	235	209	252	313	479	503	3370
(Philippines)	oLET	108.2	114.0	125.0	136.9	132.1	126.2	115.2	115.2	103.3	108.8	108.2	103.6	1396.7
13°08'N, 123°44'E	P−oLET	257.8	151.0	93.0	21.1	45.9	67.8	119.8	93.8	148.7	204.2	370.8	399.4	1973.3
19 m	SWS	400.0	400.0	400.0	400.0	400.0	400.0	400.0	400.0	400.0	400.0	400.0	400.0	
	ΔSWS	0	0	0	0	0	0	0	0	0	0	0	0	
	R	257.8	151.0	93.0	21.1	45.9	67.8	119.8	93.8	148.7	204.2	370.8	399.4	1973.3
	aLET	108.2	114.0	125.0	136.9	132.1	126.2	115.2	115.2	103.3	108.8	108.2	103.6	1396.7
	aLET−oLET	0	0	0	0	0	0	0	0	0	0	0	0	0
Sandakan	P	483	277	218	114	157	188	170	201	236	259	368	470	3141
(Malaysia)	oLET	104.2	114.2	115.0	132.4	132.4	131.8	137.5	137.5	143.0	129.0	109.2	108.4	1494.6
05°50'N, 118°07'E	P−oLET	378.8	162.8	103.0	−18.4	24.6	56.2	32.5	63.5	93.0	130.0	258.8	361.6	1646.4
46 m	SWS	400.0	400.0	400.0	382.0	400.0	400.0	400.0	400.0	400.0	400.0	400.0	400.0	
	ΔSWS	0	0	0	−18.0	+18.0	0	0	0	0	0	0	0	
	R	378.8	162.8	103.0	0	6.6	56.2	32.5	63.5	93.0	130.0	258.8	361.6	1646.8
	aLET	104.2	114.2	115.0	132.0	132.4	131.8	137.5	137.5	143.0	130.0	109.2	108.4	1494.2
	aLET−oLET	0	0	0	−0.4	0	0	0	0	0	0	0	0	−0.4

Iloilo (Philippines) 10°42'N, 122°34'E, 14 m

	1	2	3	4	5	6	7	8	9	10	11	12	Year
P	59	38	36	52	153	265	390	370	294	263	207	121	2248
oLET	119.2	135.0	151.6	87.6	149.5	131.4	114.8	114.4	109.0	108.6	108.1	109.1	1438.3
P-oLET	-60.2	-97.0	-115.6	-35.6	3.5	133.6	275.2	255.6	185.0	154.4	98.9	11.9	809.7
SWS	344.1	270.0	202.2	185.0	188.5	322.1	400.0	400.0	400.0	400.0	400.0	400.0	
ΔSWS	-55.9	-74.1	-67.8	-17.2	+3.5	+133.6	+77.9	0	0	0	0	0	
R	0	0	0	0	0	0	197.3	255.6	185.0	154.4	98.9	11.9	903.1
aLET	114.9	112.1	103.8	69.2	149.5	131.4	114.8	114.4	109.0	108.6	98.9	11.9	1344.9
aLET-oLET	-4.3	-22.9	-47.8	-18.4	0	0	0	0	0	0	0	0	-93.4

Chinchiná (Colombia) 04°58'N, 75°37'W, 1360 m

	1	2	3	4	5	6	7	8	9	10	11	12	Year
P	147	142	213	312	309	197	173	186	184	326	249	237	2675
oLET	121.7	139.3	122.0	98.8	114.7	110.6	118.7	134.4	120.8	118.3	103.0	124.2	1426.5
P-oLET	25.3	2.7	91.0	213.2	194.3	86.4	54.3	51.6	63.2	207.7	146.0	112.8	1248.5
SWS	400.0	400.0	400.0	400.0	400.0	400.0	400.0	400.0	400.0	400.0	400.0	400.0	
ΔSWS	0	0	0	0	0	0	0	0	0	0	0	0	
R	25.3	2.7	91.0	213.2	194.3	86.4	54.3	51.6	63.2	207.7	146.0	112.8	1248.5
aLET	121.7	139.3	122.0	98.8	114.7	110.6	118.7	134.4	120.8	118.3	103.0	124.2	1426.5
aLET-oLET	0	0	0	0	0	0	0	0	0	0	0	0	0

Cozumel (Mexico) 20°31'N, 86°57'W, 3 m

	1	2	3	4	5	6	7	8	9	10	11	12	Year
P	82	67	55	57	150	201	120	162	242	224	110	105	1575
oLET	80	77	102	132	157	157	162	157	141	126	97	83	1471
P-oLET	2	-10	-47	-75	-7	44	-42	5	101	98	13	22	104
SWS	400.0	390.1	346.9	287.6	282.6	326.6	294.0	299.0	400.0	400.0	400.0	400.0	
ΔSWS	0	-9.9	-43.2	-59.3	-5.0	+44.0	-32.6	+5.0	+101.0	0	0	0	
R	2	0	0	0	0	0	0	0	0	98	13	22	135
aLET	80.0	76.9	98.2	116.3	155.0	157.0	152.6	157.0	141.0	126.0	97.0	83.0	1440.0
aLET-oLET	0	-0.1	-3.8	-15.7	-2.0	0	-9.4	0	0	0	0	0	-31.0

P = precipitation, oLET = optimal landscape evapotranspiration, P-oLET = precipitation – optimal landscape evapotranspiration, SWS = Soil Water Storage, ΔSWS = change in soil water storage, R = runoff, aLET = actual landscape evapotranspiration, aLET-oLET = actual landscape evapotranspiration – optimal landscape evapotranspiration.

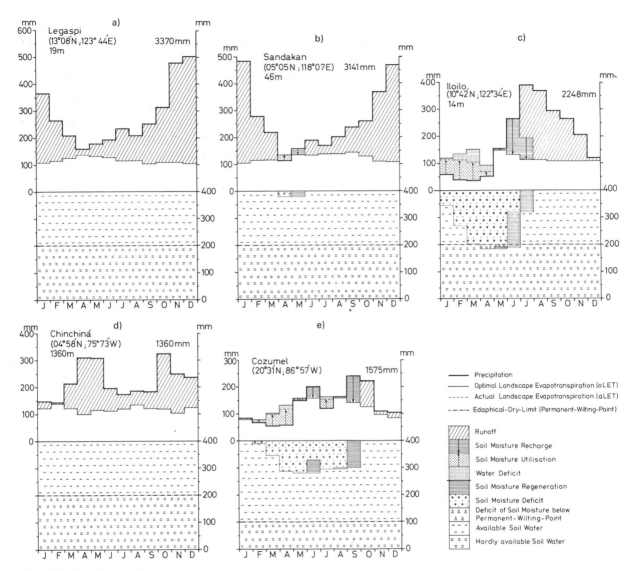

Fig. 2.47. Water budget diagrams.

rainfall maxima. The station, located directly below the Equator, experiences its relative rainfall maxima in the months of April and October/December. The rains involved are delayed equinoctial rains mainly of the convective type, as they normally occur in the area of the inner-tropical trough with partly monsoon-like characteristics. At this time, northeasterly trade winds of the Northern Hemisphere and the southeasterly trades of the Southern Hemisphere are at their lowest intensity and thus provide conditions for zenithal rains. The convection processes, in conjunction with thunderstorms, mainly occur during the afternoon and partly in the night. During the relatively dry period in the months of February and July the station is under the influence of the somewhat stronger trade winds — which, however, are by no means rainless.

Whitmore (1975) described the evergreen tropical lowland rain forest occurring on the island of Borneo as the most luxuriant plant community, which shows a great richness in species, a certain lack of plant individuals, and a clearly marked stratum with giant trees that reach heights of up to 90 m. This type of rain forest can be found at elevations of up to 1200 m above sea level.

The typical evergreen rain forest in Africa may be represented by the water-budget diagram of the Borumbu station in Zaïre (Fig. 2.46 and Table 2.5). In its seasonal cycle, the water budget is very similar to the Pontianak station in Indonesia. However, the diagram shows that the water surplus is considerably smaller in the rainy periods, so that the forest reaches its lowest limit of existence and thus, despite an even distribution of rainfall over the year during the more distinct relatively dry periods, is subject more frequently to water stress. This becomes evident from the one to two arid months recorded, predominantly in January/February.

The rain maxima occur during the equinoctial periods in the spring and fall, the minima between December and February, and in June — in other words at the summer solstice. Also in Borumbu, which is almost constantly under the influence of the equatorial low pressures, convectional rains of monsoon-like character constitute the predominant type of rainfall.

With an annual amount of rainfall of only 1816 mm, the evapotranspiration rate amounts to 45% of this total, the runoff rate to 55%. Evapotranspiration and runoff are inverse — that is, the potential evapotranspiration increases during drier periods whereas runoff decreases, and vice versa.

According to Whitmore (1975), a particularly typical rich lowland rain forest does not exist in the Congo Basin, due to the relatively low amounts of monthly and annual rainfall. It merely owes its formation to the even distribution of rainfall over the year.

In the Amazon Basin, the area of highest rainfall is located in the northwestern and western parts toward the slopes of the Andes. The station of Fonte Bôa (Fig. 2.46 and Table 2.5), which is located immediately south of the Equator in the upper part of the Amazon, clearly reflects the water budget of the evergreen rain forest in the northwestern Amazon region. Evapotranspiration accounts for 50% of the annual rainfall of 2800 mm. The remaining 50% runoff flows into the Amazon river system. The rainfall results from heavy rains and thunderstorms originating from high-altitude cumulus towers which, however, often do not have distinct ice umbrellas. The evaporated water vapor frequently condenses again in the same area, and is returned to the earth within one to two days via the "small water cycle". This circulatory system is subject to a slight shift in a northwesterly direction, caused by the southeast trades. The trade winds themselves produce rainfall originating from the "large water cycle" from the Atlantic. In a strip with less rainfall at the middle portion of the Amazon River, where the annual rainfall does not even reach 2000 mm, a negative water balance occurring during three months causes a striking water stress for the upper tree stratum, which is therefore formed, to the extent of at least 30%, of deciduous species.

The tropical type

The tropical type occurs at a certain distance from the Equator, where the two rainfall maxima of the equinoctial periods converge and merge into a twin and/or single-peak solsticial maximum with heavy, thundery rains by simultaneous shortening of the intervening dry period (small dry period). At the same time, the winter dry period (large dry period) grows longer. In the case of strong monsoonal influence, particularly in the original monsoon region, the small dry period in the summer is generally extinguished and replaced by a marked rainfall maximum. The monsoon period is initiated in the early summer by convectional thunderstorms and disturbances in the trade-wind system, and subsides in a reverse sequence in fall. The monsoonal maxima are excessively developed and bring record amounts of rainfall at many stations.

Since the winter dry period is just as excessive, this climatic type shows a marked seasonality, which leads to the fact that the vegetation is characterized by so-called monsoon forests. A humid type prevails if the winter dry period does not last longer than three to four arid months, and a semihumid type if more than four arid months occur. The very high amounts of summer rainfall can only partly compensate for the negative water balance by means of stored water reserves in the ground. Monsoon forests which may be regarded as part of the evergreen rain-forest region mostly occur in those areas where the varying wind system of monsoons in the summer and trade winds in the winter secure the water supply. Rains resulting from rising trade winds (orographic precipitation) prevent a negative water balance during the winter dry period. This water-budget type occurs not only on the west coasts of the Indo-Malayan Archipelago and in the area of the southern Himalayan mountains, but also in the African Gulf of Guinea near Mount Cameroun, in Liberia, and on the Panamanian and Columbian west coasts.

For the Asian tropics, the Cherrapunji station (Fig. 2.46 and Table 2.5) represents the humid monsoon type with evergreen and semi-evergreen rain forests. The Douala station at the foot of Mt. Cameroun may be regarded as an example for Africa. A distinct maximum of rainfall is recorded at both stations in the summer. During the winter half-year, however, only three arid months occur, which permit the existence of an evergreen to semi-evergreen rain forest. Approximately 80% of the record amount of rainfall of 600 to 1100 mm per month is lost by runoff during the summer. The climatic water stress during the dry months is compensated by water available for the plants in the ground. Even if the differences between potential and actual landscape evaporation show a negative climatic water balance in the dry months from December to February, the critical edaphic dry limit is not reached as a result of sufficient water stored in the ground. However, it is quite clear that the marked seasonality between the rainy and dry periods has an impact on the forest type. Whitmore (1975) has described the semi-evergreen monsoon forest as a type which — compared to the real equatorial rain forest — shows lower tree formations with a reduced diversity of species, and produces less biomass. The considerable proportion of deciduous species in the upper tree stratum amounts to 30 to 40%.

The marginal tropical type

The climatic water budget type of the marginal tropics receives its rainfall during the summer from solstitial rains by the summer location of the Intertropical Convergence Zone. Equatorward it is the tropical westerlies and poleward the tropical easterlies (easterly waves) that contribute to the rainfall. In the winter, the rainfall is received as rains resulting from orographic precipitation by trade winds as well as from extratropical cold waves. Very often the rainfall received is supplemented by rains from tropical cyclones. They occur as hurricanes in the Caribbean and in Central America, as "Mauritius gales" in Madagascar, as typhoons in Indochina and the Philippines, and as cyclones in northeastern Australia.

The rainfall diagram for Turrialba (Costa Rica) (Fig. 2.34) shows the proportions of the various rainfall types in the total annual amount of rainfall. Negative water balances only occur during two to three months prior to the summer rain period. The areas of occurrence mainly comprise the tropical east coasts toward the Tropics of Cancer and Capricorn. A forest type with a marginal tropical water budget occurs along the entire east coast of Central America between Mexico and Panama. The same type can be found on the eastern slopes of the Andes, on the coasts of Guayana and Brazil down to the Tropic of Capricorn. In Africa it occurs at isolated locations on the east coast, particularly the eastern slopes of Madagascar. In the area of the Indo-Malayan Archipelago it is found on the east coasts of almost all islands, particularly in the Philippines, New Guinea and on the northeastern coast of Australia.

The water-balance diagram of Legaspi (Philippines) (Fig. 2.47a and Table 2.5) shows that with a total amount of 3370 mm of rain a distinct winter-rain maximum exists which is attributable to the influence of the northeast trades and cold-air influxes from extratropical regions. The mean monthly evapotranspiration of the forests amounts to between 120 and 150 mm. However, the greatest part of the maximum rainfall in the winter is lost by runoff to the oceans. During the weaker summer-rain period the rainfall totals decrease to the values of potential evapotranspiration, so that a negative water balance may occur for two to three months. At the Sandakan station (Malaysia) (Fig. 2.47b and Table 2.5), the month of April, for example, is climatically arid in the long-term mean. The forest is then forced to use the water reserves in the ground, though without using the whole of the available water up completely.

The tropical montane type

Tropical mountain regions have, like the lowlands, a distinct diurnal climate. However, the water budget shows special characteristic features due to various influences of the relief. Particularly the parameters such as temperature, humidity and wind vary with altitude.

The temperature declines with increased altitude, and the gradient varies, but its mean value amounts to approximately 0.56° per 100 m. The mountains, however, also have a strong impact on air humidity. At constant absolute humidity and decreasing temperature the relative humidity will increase. The potential evapotranspiration decreases, and the amount of rainfall increases up to the level of condensation. On the whole, however, the rainfall decreases from the first level of condensation upwards. Cloud layers in the form of fog banks reduce the incidence of light and restrict assimilation. The vegetation is able to "comb out" fog, and thus supplement precipitation. Seasonal dryness is partly compensated by high frequency of fog. Also the soils in the tropical mountains are different from those in the lowlands, as a result of the climate (Fig. 2.47d and Table 2.5).

Apart from the fact that the megathermal flora only occurs in the lowland rain forests or in frost-free lower mountain forests, the trees of the montane forests are smaller, the foliage becomes darker and sturdier and is mostly hairy. The biomass decreases and plant growth is rather restricted. As a result of these differentiated and mostly microclimatological properties, the water budget shows complicated features, as the amount of water available cannot be covered by the rainfall alone in the water-balance equation.

The edaphic humid type

Independently of the water-budget type which is directly controlled by the rainfall received, there are a number of edaphic variants, whose water budget cannot be represented without difficulty by the diagrams so far shown. In the case of the edaphic water-budget type, soil formation processes, the small-scale relief and the fluctuation of the water level as well as the chemistry of the water bodies are the decisive factors, so that the water budget can only be indirectly determined with the aid of the term "water available for plants".

In many parts, for example in the Indopacific rain-forest area and in the Caribbean, limestone is responsible for the formation of a rough karst relief. The soils in such karst areas receive additional water through underground cave systems and thus make possible the formation of evergreen tropical rain forests even in regions with seasonally dry climates. In Yucatan, for example, there are large regions in which, from the climatic point of view, four to five arid months occur, but which still are occupied by evergreen or semi-evergreen rain forests. Here, the edaphic humidity

as a result of karst water near the surface compensates for at least three to four arid months (Fig. 2.47e and Table 2.5).

In the Amazon and Congo basins, further examples of edaphic-humid flood and swamp forests can be found, whose ecophysiological structure can only be explained by the effects of soil properties and the high groundwater level as well as periodic floods. However, forest types which are poor in species, such as the heath forest in Borneo described by Bruenig (1969), and partly also the thinner rain forests in the Amazon region, also have a soil-controlled water budget which determines the type of vegetation. Intensive podzolization will, under climatically fully humid conditions, often cause periodic water stress and decisively change the composition of the forest and its physiognomic appearance.

Many evergreen gallery forests in the alternating humid tropics can also be regarded as an edaphic variant. They develop particularly well in the mud of river banks which are rich in nutrients, and improve their water budget by ground water near the rivers. They often are the outposts of evergreen rain forests in these areas of alternating humidity.

CLIMATE CHANGES AND TROPICAL RAIN FOREST

Natural climatic changes decisively influence the rain-forest system. Although the assumption has been made that the rain forests had been subject to only minor changes since their formation in the Tertiary, more recent studies have provided evidence that the relatively slight decrease of mean temperature in the Pleistocene has nevertheless caused decisive changes in the forest stand. Basic climatological considerations permit the conclusion that, as a result of the cooler temperatures on the Earth during the cold periods, the water vapor content of the atmosphere would have been smaller, and thus the climate drier than today. The warm periods must, with a higher water vapor content, have been more humid than today. Both geomorphological studies and paleobiological analyses, as well as more recent investigations of deep-sea drill cores, confirm these facts for the tropical regions. Therefore, one will have to give up the opinion that tropical rain forests have been able to develop undisturbed over long geological periods. In the mean time, one has come to realize that even minor and shorter climatic fluctuations have caused reductions and expansions of the tropical-forest regions even in the later Pleistocene.

Arid climatic conditions involving a temperature decrease of about 3 to 4°C in the later Quaternary probably reduced the rain forest between 25 000 and 14 000 B.P. to less than half of its present size (Fig. 2.48). From the distribution patterns of animal groups, several authors have been able to prove the occurrence of drier areas in the present rain-forest region. Pollen analyses partly confirm these theses. The studies apply both to Amazonia and to the Congo Basin. Thus, for the Amazon, the restriction of the forest area to Upper Amazonia and individual coastal locations has been proved (Haffer, 1969; Vuilleumier, 1971). As a result of his studies on forest mammals, Kingdon (1971) was able to prove three forest refuges for Africa: in Guinea, Cameroon/Gabon, and in the Ruwenzori area. Pollen analyses and geomorphological studies [for South America: Van der Hammen (1974), Ab'Sáber (1977) and Salgado-Labouriau (1984); for Africa Van Zinderen-Bakker (1972) and ASEQUA (1978)] have unanimously confirmed the existence of savanna vegetation only in the respective areas of investigation which are occupied by rain forests today. Almost all findings of different disciplines unanimously show that the rain forests in Africa and South America must have been reduced to a considerable extent up until at least 14 000 B.P. However, the forest apparently reacted to the warming of the climate over the entire earth with an equally quick expansion after 10 000 B.P. at the latest. In this case as well, scientists agree that the increase in heat was accompanied by a considerable increase in the water-vapor content

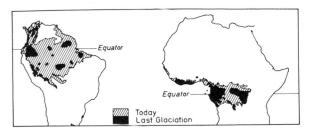

Fig. 2.48. Distribution of the tropical rain forest in Africa and South America during the last glaciation (30 000–12 000 B.P.). (After Haffer, 1969, and Kingdon, 1971.)

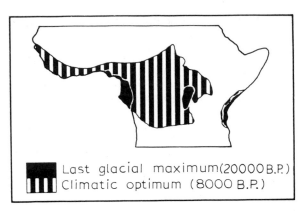

Fig. 2.49. Distribution of the tropical rain forest (lowland forest) during the last glacial maximum (20 000 B.P.) and the warm climatic optimum (8000 B.P.) in Tropical Africa. (After Hamilton, 1976.)

of the atmosphere which favored the quick expansion of the rain-forest regions (Fig. 2.49).

Studies on further developments in the Holocene since 8000 B.P. show that all of the tropical-forest areas started to shrink again after 5500 B.P. at the latest, but to a different extent in the individual regions. As in the period between 14 000 and 10 000 B.P. the more recent development also is marked by short-term, different regional fluctuations of climate and their impact on the landscapes. But since the influence of man on the change of the forest region must also be considered as a result of farming since 5000 B.P., it becomes more and more difficult to distinguish between natural fluctuations and those induced by man. However, it will not be possible any longer to maintain the thesis that the rain forests today represent a real "climax vegetation", since the quick change of climate was accompanied by a continuous change in the soil and vegetation. Thus, the representation of today's climate in the rain forest regions only constitutes an instantaneous picture that merely helps to explain current conditions and processes.

REFERENCES

Ab'Sáber, A.N., 1977. Espaços ocupados pela expansão dos climas secos na América do Sul, por ocasião dos períodos glaciars quaternários. *Palaeoclimas*, 3: 19 pp.

Alayna Street, F., 1981. Tropical palaeoenvironments. *Progr. Phys. Geogr.*, 5(2): 157–186.

ASEQUA, 1978. Extraits de Radiocarbon 1973–1975. *Dakar Juillet*, 52–53: 11–177.

Ashton, P.S. and Bruenig, E.F., 1975. The variation of tropical moist forest in relation to environmental factors and its relevance to land-use planning. *Mitt. Bundesforschungsanst. Forst Holzwirtsch.*, 109: 59–86.

Barry, R.G. and Chorley, R.J., 1976. *Atmosphere, Weather and Climate.* Bungay, Suffolk, 3rd ed., 432 pp.

Baumgartner, A. and Reichel, E., 1975. *The World Water Balance. Mean Annual Global, Continental and Maritime Precipitation, Evaporation, and Runoff.* Oldenburg, München, 179 pp.

Blüthgen, J. and Weischet, W., 1980. *Allgemeine Klimageographie.* De Gruyter, Berlin, 3rd ed., 887 pp.

Boucher, K.B.A., 1975. *Global Climate.* The English Universities Press IX, London, 326 pp.

Brain, C.K., 1981. The evolution of man in Africa: Was it a consequence of Cainozoic cooling? *Geol. Soc. S. Am., Annex. Vol. LXXXIV,* 17: 1–19.

Bruenig, E.F., 1969. On the seasonality of droughts in the lowlands of Sarawak (Borneo). *Erdkunde*, 23: 127–133.

Bruenig, E.F., 1974a. Ökosystem in den Tropen. *Umschau*, 13: 405–410.

Bruenig, E.F., 1974b. *Ecological Studies in the Kerangas Forest of Sarawak und Brunei.* Borneo Lit. Bureau for Sarawak Forest Department, Kuching, 237 pp.

Bruenig, E.F. and Klinge, H., 1975. Structure, functioning and productivity in humid tropical forest ecosystems in part of the neotropics. *Mitt. Bundesforschungsanst. Forst Holzwirtsch.*, 109: 87–116.

Budyko, M.I., 1958. *The Heat Balance of the Earth's Surface* (Leningrad 1956, 236 pp., in Russian) Transl. by N.A. Stephanova, U.S. Weather Bureau, Washington, D.C.

Budyko, M.I., 1974. *Climate and Life.* In: International Geographical Series, 18. Academic Press, New York, N.Y., 508 pp.

Bünning, E., 1956. *Der tropische Regenwald.* Springer, Berlin, 118 pp.

FAO, 1958. *Tropical Silviculture, Vol. I.* FAO For. For. Prod. Stud., 13.

FAO, 1976. *Attempt of a Global Appraisal of Tropical Moist Forest.* Rome.

FAO, 1980. *Forestry Paper.* Rome.

FAO, 1982. *Tropical Forest Resources.* FAO Forestry Paper 30, Rome, 106 pp.

Fletcher, R., 1945. The general circulation of the tropical and equatorial atmosphere. *J. Meteorol.*, 2: 167–174.

Flohn, H., 1964. Über die Ursachen der Aridität Nordost Afrikas. *Würzb. Geogr. Arb.*, 12: 25–41.

Flohn, H., 1965. Studies on the meteorology of tropical Africa. *Bonn. Meteorol. Abh.*, 5: 57 pp.

Flohn, H., 1971. Tropical circulation pattern. *Bonn. Meteorol. Abh.*, 15: 55 pp.

Fosberg, F.R., Garnier, B.J. and Kücher, A.W., 1961. Delimination of the humid tropics. *Geogr. Rev.*, 51: 333–347.

Fournier, F. and Sasson, A., 1983. *Ecosystemes Forestiers Tropicaux d'Afrique.* ORSTOM-UNESCO, Paris, 473 pp.

Haffer, J., 1969. Specification in Amazonian forest birds. *Science*, 165: 131–137.

Hamilton, A.C., 1976. The significance of patterns of distribution shown by forest plants and animals in tropical Africa for the reconstruction of Upper Pleistocene palaeoenvironments: a review. *Palaeoecol. Afr. Surrounding Islands Antarct.*, 9: 63–97.

Hastenrath, S., 1968. Zur Vertikalverteilung der Niederschläge in den Tropen. *Meteorol. Rundsch.*, 21: 113–116.

Hendl, M., 1963. *Einführung in die physikalische Klimatologie.* (Systematische Klimatologie, 2) VEB Deutscher Verlag der Wissenschaften, Berlin, 40 pp.

Heuveldop, J., 1977. Erste Ergebnisse bestandsmeteorolgischer Untersuchungen im Regenwald von San Carlos de Rio Negro. *Mitt. Bundesforschungsanst. Forst Holzwirtsch.*, 115: 101–116.

Hopkins, B., 1965a. Vegetation of the Olokemeji forest reserve, Nigeria II. The climate with special reference to its seasonal changes. *J. Ecol.*, 53: 109–124.

Hopkins, B., 1965b. Vegetation of the Olokemeji forest reserve, Nigeria III. The microclimates with special reference to its seasonal changes. *J. Ecol.*, 53: 125–138.

Houghton, H.G., 1954. On the annual heat balance of the northern hemisphere. *J. Meteorol.*, 11: 1–7.

Jackson, I.J., 1975. Relationship between rainfall parameters and interception by tropical forest. *J. Hydrol.*, 24: 215–238.

Jackson, I.J., 1977. *Climate, Weather and Agriculture in the Tropics.* Longmann, London, 248 pp.

Keller, R., 1961. *Gewässer und Wasserhaushalt des Festlandes Eine Einführung in die Hydrogeographie.* Haude und Spener, Berlin, 520 pp.

Kessler, A., 1968. Globalbilanz von Klimaelementen. Ein Beitrag zur allgemeinen Klimatologie der Erde. *Ber. Inst. Meteorol. Klimatol. Techn. Univ. Hannover*, 3.

Kessler, A., 1973. Zur Klimatologie der Strahlungsbilanz auf der Erdoberfläche. *Erdkunde*, 17: 1–10.

Kingdon, J., 1971. *East African Mammals. An Atlas of Evolution in Africa, Vol. I.* Academic Press, New York, N.Y.

Klaus, D., 1971. Zusammenhänge zwischen Wetterhäufigkeit und Niederschlagsverteilung im zentralmexikanischen Hochland. *Erdkunde*, 25: 81–90.

Klinge, H., 1969. Climatic conditions in lowland tropical podsol areas. *Trop. Ecol.*, 10: 222–239.

Kondratyev, K.Ja., 1969. *Radiation in the Atmosphere.* (Int. Geophys. Ser. Vol. 12) Academic Press, New York, N.Y., 915 pp.

Lamprecht, H., 1972. *Einige Strukturmerkmale natürlicher Tropenwaldtypen.* Forstwissenschaftliches Zentralblatt, 91 (4).

Lauer, W., 1952. Humide und aide Jahreszeiten in Afrika und Südamerika und ihre Beziehung zu den Vegetationsgürteln. *Bonn. Geogr. Abh.*, 9: 1–98.

Lauer, W., 1970. Naturgeschehen und Kulturlandschaft in den Tropen. Beispiel Zentralamerika. In: H. Wilhelmy, H. Blume, K.H. Schröder and A. Karger (Editors), *Beiträge zur Geographie der Tropen und Subtropen.* Tübinger Geogr. Stud., 34(3): 83–105.

Lauer, W., 1973. The altitudinal belts of the vegetation in the central Mexican highlands and their climatic conditions. *Arct. Alpine Res.*, 5(3): 99–113.

Lauer, W., 1975. Vom Wesen der Tropen. Klimaökologische

Studien zum Inhalt und zur Abgrenzung eines irdischen Landschaftsgürtels. *Abh. Math.-Nat. Kl., Akad. Wiss. Lit., Wiesbaden,* 52 pp.

Lauer, W., 1976a. Zur hygrischen Höhenstufung tropischer Gebirge. Neotropische Ökosysteme. In: J. Schmithüsen (Editor), *Biogeographica, Vol. 7.* Junk, The Hague, pp. 169–182.

Lauer, W., 1976b. Klimatische Grundzüge der Höhenstufung tropischer Gebirge. *Proc. Deutschen Geographentages Innsbruck 1975,* Steiner, Wiesbaden, pp. 76–90.

Lauer, W. and Frankenberg, P., 1981. Untersuchungen zur Humidität und Aridität in Afrika. Das Konzept einer potentiellen Landschaftsverdunstung. *Bonn. Geogr. Abh.,* 66: 127 pp.

Lauer, W. and Frankenberg, P., 1982. Weltkarten der Relation von fühlbarer und latenter Wärme. *Erdkunde,* 63: 137–142.

Leigh, E.G., Rand, A.S. and Windsor, D.M., 1983. *The Ecology of a Tropical Forest. Seasonal Rhythms and Long-Term Changes.* Oxford Univ. Press, 468 pp.

Lessmann, H., 1967. *La variatión diurna de lluvia en El Salvador.* Serv. Meteorol. Nac. El Salvador, Publ. Técn., 8.

Lockwood, J.G., 1976. *The Physical Geography of the Tropics.* Oxford Univ. Press, London, 162 pp.

Longman, K.A. and Jenik, J., 1974. *Tropical Forest and its Environment.* Longman, London, 196 pp.

Manshard, W., 1962. Der Ablauf der Regenzeit in Westafrika — dargestellt am Beispiel aus Ghana. *Giess. Geogr. Schrift.,* 2: 47–81.

Meggers, B.J., Ayensu, E.S. and Duckworth, W.D., 1973. *Tropical Forest Ecosystems in Africa and South America: A Comparative Review.* Smithsonian Institution Press, Washington, D.C., 350 pp.

Meinardus, W., 1933. Allgemeine Klimatologie. In: V.F. Klute (Editor), *Handbuch der Geographischen Wissenschaft I. Physikalische Geographie.* Akademische Verlagsgesellschaft Athenaion, Potsdam, pp. 118–226.

METEOSAT-Image Bulletin; February, April, August 1978, issued by: MDMD/Data Service European Space Operation Center (ESOC), Darmstadt.

Messerli, B., 1980. Die afrikanischen Hochgebirge und die Klimageschichte Afrikas in den letzten 20 000 Jahren. In: H. Oeschger, B. Messerli and M. Svilar (Editors), *Das Klima, Analysen und Modelle, Geschichte und Zukunft.* Springer, Berlin, 296 pp.

Nieuwolt, S., 1965. Evaporation and water balance in Malaya. *J. Trop. Geogr.,* 20: 34–53.

Nieuwolt, S., 1982. *Tropical Climatology. An Introduction to the Climates of the Low Latitudes.* Wiley, New York, N.Y., 207 pp.

Odum, H.T., 1970. An emerging view of the ecological system at El Verde. In: H.T. Odum and R.F. Pigeon (Editors), *A Tropical Rain Forest. A Study of Irradiation and Ecology at El Verde, Puerto Rico: I-191 and I-289.* Div. Techn. Inf., U.S. Atomic Energy Commission, Washington, D.C., 1678 pp.

Penman, H.L., 1963. *Vegetation and Hydrology.* Farnham Royal, Bucks., 124 pp.

Richards, P.W., 1939. Ecological studies on the rain forest of southern Nigeria I. *J. Ecol.,* 27: 1–53.

Richards, P.W., 1952. *The Tropical Rain Forest.* Cambridge Univ. Press, Cambridge, 450 pp.

Riehl, H., 1954. *Tropical Meteorology.* McGraw-Hill, New York, N.Y., 392 pp.

Riehl, H., 1962. General atmospheric circulation of the tropics. *Science,* 135(3497): 13–22.

Riehl, H., 1979. *Climate and Weather in the Tropics.* Academic Press, New York, N.Y., 611 pp.

Salgado-Labouriau, M.L., 1984. Late-Quaternary palynological studies in Venezuelan Andes. In: W. Lauer (Editor), *Natural Environment and Man in Tropical Mountain Ecosystems.* (Erdwissenschaftliche Forschung, XVIII) Steiner, Wiesbaden, pp. 279–293.

Salgado-Labouriau, M.L., Schubert, C. and Valastro, S., 1977. Palaeoecological analysis of a Late-Quaternary terrace from Mucubaji, Venezuelan Andes. *J. Biogeogr.,* 4: 313–325.

Schulz, J.P., 1960. Ecological studies on rain forest in northern Suriname. *Verh. Kon. Ned. Akad. Wetensch., Natuurk.,* 2^e reeks, deel 1, LIII, 1:267 pp.

Sellers, W.D., 1965. *Physical Climatology.* Univ. of Chicago Press, Chicago, Ill., 272 pp.

Sioli, H., 1968. Zur Ökologie des Amazonas-Gebietes. In: E.J. Fittkau, J. Illies, H. Klinge, G.H. Schwabe and H. Sioli (Editors), *Biogeography and Ecology in South America.* (Monographiae Biologicae, 18) Junk, The Hague, pp. 137–170.

Sioli, H., 1983. *Amazonien. Grundlagen der Ökologie des größten tropischen Waldlandes.* Wissenschaftliche Verlagsgesellschaft, Wiesbaden, 64 pp.

Sioli, H., 1984. *The Amazon. Limnology and Landscape Ecology of a Mighty Tropical River and its Basin.* (Monographiae Biologicae, 56) Junk, The Hague, 763 pp.

Stott, P.A., 1978. Tropical rain forest in recent ecological thought. *Progr. Phys. Geogr.,* 2: 80–92.

Talbot, M.R., 1980. Environmental response to climatic change in the West African Sahel over the past 20 000 years. In: M.A.J. Williams and H. Faure (Editors), *The Sahara and the Nile.* Balkema, Rotterdam, pp. 36–62.

Tricart, J., 1974. Existence de periodes seches au Quaternaire en Amazonie et dans les régions voisines. *Rev. Geómorphol. Dyn.,* 23: 145–158.

Tricart, J., 1977. Aperçus sur le Quaternaire amazonien. Recherches françaises sur le Quaternaire hors de France. *Bull. Assoc. Fr. Etude Quat., Suppl.,* 1977–1, 50: 265–271.

Troll, C., 1943. Thermische Klimatypen der Erde. *Petermanns Geogr. Mitt.,* 89: 81–89.

Troll, C., 1948. Der asymmetrische Aufbau der Vegetationszonen und Vegetationsstufen auf der Nord- und Südhalbkugel. *Jahresber. Geobot. Forschungsinst. Rübel, 1947,* Zürich, pp. 46–83.

UNESCO, 1958a. *Study of Tropical Vegetation. Proc. Kandy Symp., Ceylon,* 226 pp.

UNESCO, 1958b. *Problem of Humid Tropical Regions.* Paris, 102 pp.

UNESCO, 1961. Tropical Soils and Vegetation. *Proc. Abidjan Symp., Paris,* 115 pp.

UNESCO, UNEP, FAO, 1978. *Tropical Forest Ecosystems.* A State-of-Knowledge-Report, prepared by UNESCO, Paris, 683 pp.

Van der Hammen, T., 1968. Change in vegetation and climate in the Amazon basin and surrounding areas during the Pleistocene. *Geol. Mijnbouw*, 51: 641–643.

Van der Hammen, T., 1974. The Pleistocene change of vegetation and climate in tropical South America. *J. Biogeogr.*, 1: 3–26.

Van Zinderen-Bakker, E.M., 1972. Late Quaternary lacustrine phase in the southern Sahara and East Africa. *Palaeoecol. Afr.*, 6: 15–27.

Van Zinderen-Bakker, E.M. and Coetzee, J.A., 1972. A reappraisal of late-Quaternary climate evidence from tropical Africa. *Palaeoecol. Afr.*, 7: 151–181.

Vuilleumier, B.S., 1971. Pleistocene changes in the Fauna and Flora of South America. *Science*, 173: 771–780.

Walter, H., 1973. *Die Vegetation der Erde in öko-physiologischer Betrachtung, Bd. I: Die tropischen und subtropischen Zonen.* Fischer, Stuttgart, 3rd ed., 743 pp.

Walter, H. and Lieth, H., 1960–1967. *Klimadiagramm-Weltatlas.* Fischer, Jena, 245 pp.

Weischet, W., 1965. Der tropisch konvektive und der außertropisch-advektive Typ der vertikalen Niederschlagsverteilung. *Erdkunde*, 19: 6–14.

Whitmore, T.C., 1975. *Tropical Rain Forest of the Far East.* Clarendon, Oxford, 281 pp.

Chapter 3

VERTICAL STRATIFICATION IN MICROCLIMATE

TATUO KIRA and KYOJI YODA

INTRODUCTION

Information from publications before 1950 on the microclimate in tropical rain forests was well compiled and reviewed by Richards (1952). Summarized accounts have also been given by Walter (1964, 1971), Longman and Jenik (1974), Leigh (1975), Whitmore (1975) and Bazzaz and Pickett (1980), among others. As far as general patterns of the microclimate are concerned, there is little to add to this literature.

However, microclimatology has undergone a fundamental change in recent years with the development of both instruments and theories (see, for instance, Monteith, 1975, 1976). Only a few field studies made in the tropical rain forest have been based on the new approach of microclimatology, in which the observation of vertical gradients of meteorological elements in and above the leaf canopy plays an essential role. Examples are the studies by Odum et al. (1970) in a montane rain forest at El Verde, Puerto Rico; by Chunkao (1971) in a semi-evergreen seasonal forest at Sakaerat, Thailand; by Allen et al. (1972; see also Allen and Lemon, 1976) in an old secondary forest at Turrialba, Costa Rica; and by Aoki et al. (1975) in a lowland rain forest of Pasoh Forest Research Center, Peninsular Malaysia.

In forest communities, particularly in tall tropical forests, the height of trees is the greatest obstacle that must be overcome for ecological studies. This is particularly true of microclimatological studies. Walk-up towers built in several places in the tropical rain-forest zone, such as those at Sakaerat Experiment Station of northeastern Thailand, Ulu Gombak near Kuala Lumpur and Pasoh Forest Research Center of Peninsular Malaysia,

Barro Colorado Island of Panama, and the Forest Experiment Station at Belem in Brazil have been extremely useful, but were not always used for microclimatological observations. The difficulty of maintaining instruments under perhumid conditions also offered a serious handicap for continuous long-term observations.

The material for this article is, therefore, limited both in amount and in quality, especially in the length of observation period. The studies mentioned above were based on observations at a single spot in the forest in question, and often over a very short period from a few to several days. Studies on deciduous seasonal forests are almost absent except for fragmental temperature and light measurements (Ogawa et al., 1961, 1965, among others), so that only evergreen forests containing few seasonally deciduous trees are dealt with here.

LIGHT

Incident radiation

The flux density of incoming solar radiation under tropical rain-forest climate is not much different from that in temperate forest regions. The maximum density of solar radiation flux in November at Pasoh, Peninsular Malaysia (Aoki et al., 1975) and in January to March (dry season) at Chékô, southwestern Khmer (Cambodia) (Hozumi et al., 1969) was 1.1 to 1.2 cal cm^{-2} min^{-1}, a level frequently surpassed during summer in the temperate forest zone. The duration of bright sunshine in tropical rain-forest regions is said to fall within a range of 6 to 7 h day^{-1} (Bazzaz and Pickett, 1980), but the annual mean at Pasoh amounted to only

3.3 to 4.3 h day^{-1}; the observations were, however, made in a forest clearing where surrounding trees intercepted morning and evening sunlight to a certain extent (Soepadmo and Kira, 1977). The annual mean of daily radiation flux at Pasoh was 347 to 359 cal cm^{-2} day^{-1}. These data may represent the prevailing radiational environment in typical equatorial rain-forest areas without a pronounced dry season.

Aoki et al. (1975) obtained the following empirical relation between the total solar radiation (R_s) and the net radiation (R_n) (both in cal cm^{-2} min^{-1}) immediately above the canopy of an undisturbed rain-forest stand in Pasoh forest:

$$R_n = 0.79\, R_s - 0.01$$

The last term corresponds to the net loss of long-wave radiation at night, which was very small — presumably due to the frequent fogs during the period of observation. The R_n/R_s ratio here obtained ($=0.79$) agrees closely with the ratios for temperate forests — for instance, 0.79 in a spruce forest in Germany (Baumgartner, after Tajchman, 1972) and 0.76 in a pine plantation in Australia

(Denmead, 1969). The tropical rain-forest canopy seems to have a similar albedo to temperate forests.

Total interception of light by forest canopy

The light flux density on the ground under typical rain forests is usually less than 1% of that above the canopy surface (Walter, 1971; Leigh, 1975; Alexandre, 1982). Yoda (1974) found that only 1.05 cal cm^{-2} day^{-1} of photosynthetically active radiation (PAR) reached the floor of Pasoh forest on an average of 12 days in February. This value was equal to 0.4% of the amount of PAR received by the canopy surface, though the percentages for individual days varied between 0.12 and 0.99%. Nearly the same percentage (0.3–0.4%) was obtained on the basis of illuminance observed at mid-day (Table 3.1).

The percentage of total light interception tends to decrease slightly in more xerophytic types of tropical evergreen forest, as seen in Table 3.1. The mean relative illuminance at breast height in Pasoh forest is 0.53%, while it amounts to 1.3% in the

TABLE 3.1

Average relative illuminance on or near the ground surface in some tropical and temperate forests

Forest type	Locality	Relative illuminance [%]		Authors
		ground level	1–2 m above the ground	
Undisturbed lowland rain forest	Pasoh, Negri Sembilan, Peninsular Malaysia	0.29	0.52	Yoda (1974)
Regenerating stand of ever-green seasonal forest (wet season)	Khao Chong, southern Thailand	–	1.3	Ogawa et al. (1965)
Undisturbed evergreen seasonal forest (dry season)	Chékô, southwestern Khmer	–	1.3	Hozumi et al. (1969)
Undisturbed semi-evergreen seasonal forest	Sakaerat, northeastern Thailand			Yoda et al. (1983)
Wet season		1.2	2.2	
Dry season		1.7	2.7	
Regenerating stand of ever-green oak forest (summer)	Minamata, Kyushu, Japan	0.57	0.84	Yoda (1978)
Regenerating stand of ever-green oak forest	Yona, Okinawa, Japan	–	2.5	Kawanabe (1977)
Regenerating stand of Japanese beech forest (summer)	Ashiu, Kyoto, Japan	–	2.5	Ogino (1977)

Each value in the table represents the arithmetical mean of 100 to 1000 paired readings of two photo-cells, one exposed to direct daylight and the other moved systematically on the forest floor. The time of observation: 9 a.m.–3 p.m.

evergreen seasonal forests of Thailand and Khmer and 2.2% (wet season) to 2.7% (dry season) in a semi-evergreen seasonal forest (locally called the dry evergreen forest) of northeastern Thailand. For temperate forests it generally ranges from 1.0% to a few percent. However, it is not certain whether or not the reduction in total light interception is caused by decreasing foliar surface of the whole forest from equatorial to more xeric or northern regions. The difference in leaf area index (LAI) between these forest types, if any, may not be so large, in view of the error of LAI estimation.

Table 3.2 shows LAI estimates for tropical evergreen forests, together with some of the most reliable values for temperate broadleaf forests. As far as conventional methods of estimation are concerned, an estimate of LAI in forest cannot be satisfactorily accurate unless the vertical distribution of leaf mass is actually determined by the destructive sampling of a good number of sample trees, and leaf samples for determination of the ratio of area to dry weight (specific leaf area, SLA)

are taken from all height levels, since SLA varies so widely depending on the depth inside the canopy (Table 3.3). Only the data marked with superscripts in Table 3.2 satisfy this condition. A large value for the evergreen seasonal forest of southern Thailand was obtained by inadequate leaf sampling for SLA determination (a single large sample was taken from the mixture of leaves from all height levels). This may presumably be the case with the extremely large values reported from the forests of Panama. It should also be noted that clear-felling a small sample plot tends to result in an overestimation of LAI for the whole forest. In this sort of destructive sampling, one is inclined to choose an area with as few canopy gaps as possible and including at least one tree of the biggest size class, though wind gaps and other disturbed spots are always frequent even in primeval forests. The average LAI on an extensive area of forest may thus be smaller than the value based on the harvest of a small plot for destructive sampling. For instance, the clear-felling of a plot of 0.2 ha in Pasoh forest yielded a LAI of 7.8 (for trees only),

TABLE 3.2

Estimates of leaf area index in some tropical rain forests and temperate forests

Forest type	Locality	LAI			Plot area [ha]	Authors
		trees	undergrowth	total		
Undisturbed lowland rain forest[1]	Pasoh, Negri Sembilan, Peninsular Malaysia	7.8	0.23	8.0	0.2[2]	Kato et al. (1974)
		6.8	–	–	0.8	Kira (1978)
Undisturbed lowland rain forest on laterite	San Carlos, Rio Negro, Venezuela	–	–	5.2	–	Jordan and Uhl (1978)
Undisturbed lower montane rain forest	El Verde, Puerto Rico	6.3	1.0	7.3	0.09	Odum (1970)
Regenerating stand of evergreen seasonal forest	Khao Chong, southern Thailand	10.8	1.5	12.3	0.32[2]	Ogawa et al. (1965)
Undisturbed evergreen seasonal forest[1]	Chékô, Koh Kong, Khmer	5.8	1.6	7.4	0.5	Hozumi et al. (1969)
Semi-deciduous seasonal forest	Darien, Panama	–	–	10.6–22.4	–	Golley et al. (1975)
Regenerating stand of evergreen oak forest[1]	Yona, Okinawa, Japan	–	–	6.0	0.04	Kawanabe (1977)
Regenerating stand of evergreen oak forest[1]	Minamata, Kagoshima (Kyushu), Japan	5.4	1.3	6.6	0.04[2]	Nagano and Kira (1978)
Regenerating stand of Japanese beech forest[1]	Ashiu, Kyoto (Honshu), Japan	3.8	2.3	6.1	0.01[2]	Ogino (1977)

[1]Destructive sampling of trees was made using the stratified clip technique (Monsi and Saeki, 1953), and leaf samples for area determination were taken from all the strata of canopy at different height levels.
[2]Clear-felled.

TABLE 3.3

Mean specific leaf area (SLA) at different height levels of Pasoh forest. Calculated from the original data of Kato et al. (1978)

Range of above-ground height (m)	SLA ($cm^2\ g^{-1}$)	Range of above-ground height (m)	SLA ($cm^2\ g^{-1}$)
57.5–55	82.6	25–20	89.9
55–50	61.5	20–15	103
50–45	57.4	15–10	117
45–40	60.3	10–5	121
40–35	65.1	5–1.3	127
35–30	73.9	1.3–0	166
30–25	91.6		

whereas the estimate for a 0.8 ha plot based on the regression of leaf area per tree on its diameter at breast height (DBH) was smaller (6.8).

In view of these reservations, we may tentatively conclude from Table 3.2 that the total LAI of tree components of tropical rain forests falls within a range of 5.5 to 6.0. The total LAI of the whole forest including the undergrowth layer may be expected to amount to 7.0 to 7.5. Yamakura et al. (1983) recently obtained a similar value in a lowland rain forest of eastern Kalimantan where the maximum tree height reached 64 m. Temperate broadleaf forests tend to have somewhat smaller LAI as suggested by Table 3.2, but it is still premature to draw a definite conclusion because of the scarcity of exact data in both regions.

Low leaf area density (leaf area per unit volume of canopy — LAD) is a remarkable feature of forest canopies (Kira et al., 1969) that strongly affects microclimatological conditions. Forest stands tend to have larger LAI than herbaceous canopies even under the same environment, but the greater height of trees makes the average LAD much smaller in the former than in the latter. If the mean LAD is defined as

$$\overline{LAD} = [\text{total LAI}]/[\text{height of the tallest plant}],$$

the range of $\overline{LAD}$ is generally 2 to 4 $m^2\ m^{-3}$ in herbaceous communities, exceeding 10 $m^2\ m^{-3}$ in certain cases like a densely planted stand of *Gladiolus* with perfectly erect leaves (Kira et al., 1969). In closed forest communities, on the other hand, $\overline{LAD}$ is only one-tenth as large (0.1–0.3 $m^2\ m^{-3}$). For Pasoh forest, $\overline{LAD} = (6.8 + 0.23)/55 = 0.13\ m^2\ m^{-3}$, while the $\overline{LAD}$ for the

beech forest at Ashiu and the evergreen oak forest at Minamata (Table 3.2) are, respectively, 0.25 and 0.28 $m^2\ m^{-3}$. Apparently $\overline{LAD}$ is more or less inversely proportional to the height of forest, so that tall tropical rain forests are characterized by very low $\overline{LAD}$, which lessens the resistance against air flow and results in small vertical gradients of microclimatic elements due to active turbulent diffusion.

Vertical distribution of light flux density and LAD

If LAD is quite uniform throughout the canopy space, the light flux density inside the canopy is expected to decrease more or less exponentially with increasing depth below the canopy surface (Monsi and Saeki, 1953). This is realized in a cultivated stand of young sunflower (*Helianthus annuus*) plants (0.8 m tall) shown in Fig. 3.1B, but not in the other examples illustrated there. In general, the vertical gradient of light flux density differs at different height levels, being steepest in the layer with the maximum LAD. The greater part of light attenuation takes place in the 60 to 110 cm layer at the canopy surface of fully grown stands (1.5–2 m tall) of *H. annuus* and *H. tuberosus* (Jerusalem artichoke) with horizontally oriented leaves, and in the middle 45 to 80 cm layer in a dense stand of *Gladiolus* (1.1 m tall) with its leaves standing almost vertically.

Pasoh forest of Malaysia is the only tropical rain forest where vertical distributions of both light flux density (Fig. 3.1A) and LAD (Fig. 3.2) have actually been measured in the same stand. In the destructive sampling plot (20 × 100 m) of Pasoh forest, stratified clippings of all standing trees revealed the prevalence of a fairly uniform LAD of about 0.2 $m^2\ m^{-3}$ between 10 and 35 m above the ground (Fig. 3.2), corresponding to the moderate and steady exponential decrease of relative illuminance (Fig. 3.1A), while the ground layer (lower than 5 m) consisting of palms, shrubs and tree saplings had the highest LAD and the steepest gradient of light extinction. The density of light flux and that of leaf area are not apparently correlated in the upper-most part of forest profile over 35 m, mainly because the light was measured on a single emergent tree overtopping the surface of the closed main canopy layer at 30 to 35 m (Fig. 3.3). Such tall emergents are usually widely spaced and do not form a continuous crown layer,

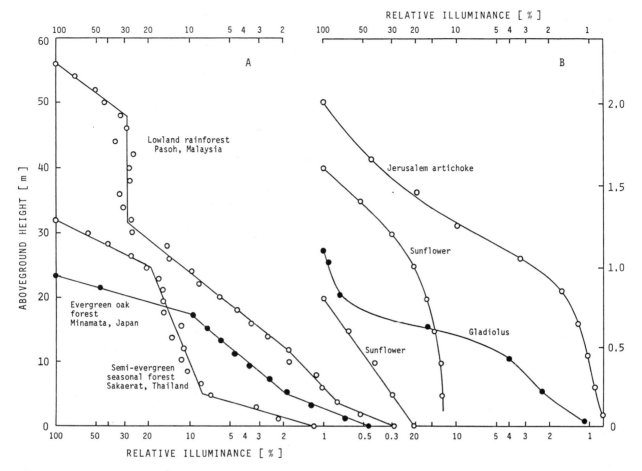

Fig. 3.1. Light profiles in some forest (A) and herbaceous crop (B) communities. B was drawn based on unpublished data from the Laboratory of Plant Ecology, Osaka City University. For the sources of forest data see text.

so that no distinct maximum of LAD appears in the top layer of the forest profile (Fig. 3.2). As far as this particular tree (*Koompassia malaccensis*) was concerned, its crown, 5 to 6 m deep, intercepted about 70% of incident light, and a relative illuminance (RI) of about 30% persisted below the crown between 32 and 48 m, where few leaves existed around the stem. Where emergent trees are absent, however, the surface of the closed canopy layer receives nearly full daylight, so that the light distribution curve of Fig. 3.1A does not represent the *average* light conditions on and above the surface (30–35 m and upwards).

In the semi-evergreen seasonal forest at Sakaerat, where the climate is drier with a dry season of 3 to 4 months per year, the upper surface of the forest is less ragged than in typical rain forests owing to the very infrequent occurrence of tall emergent trees. Since

light observations were made by Yoda et al. (1983) on a tower rising well over the forest surface (Fig.3.4), the RI–height curve in Fig. 3.1A reflects the vertical distribution of LAD more faithfully than that of Pasoh forest throughout the whole forest profile. The RI curve for Sakaerat apparently indicates the existence of three layers, namely the uppermost layer (23–32 m) and the ground layer (0–5 m), both with high LAD, and the mid-layer with relatively low LAD. This type of profile structure seems basically the same as that of the warm-temperate evergreen oak forest of Minamata, Japan (Fig.3.1A).

The extinction of light flux passing through a leaf canopy is often approximated by the De Beer law:

$$I(F)/I_0 = \exp[\ KF]$$ (1)

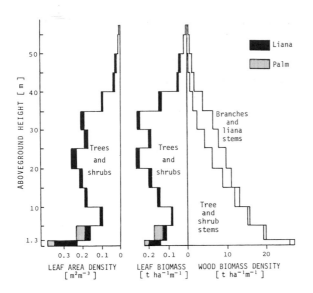

Fig. 3.2. Biomass profiles of the tropical lowland rain forest at Pasoh, Peninsular Malaysia (Kato et al., 1978), based on the clear-felling of a sample plot 20 × 100 m in size.

where I_0 and $I(F)$ are the light flux density on the canopy surface and that at a certain depth from the surface. F stands for the leaf area density accumulated from the canopy surface to the depth concerned, or the LAI through which light has passed. K is the coefficient of light extinction specific to the canopy concerned. This simple model is tested in Fig. 3.5 with the data obtained from the destructive sampling plot in Pasoh forest by plotting ln (I/I_0) against cumulative LAD.

In this plot the illuminance on and above the closed main canopy layer (30–35 m) was measured in and under the crown of a more or less isolated emergent tree, while the open space between neighboring emergent crowns received brighter sunshine even at corresponding height levels, as mentioned above. On the other hand, the cumulative LAD in Fig. 3.5 represents an average for the whole sample plot (20 × 100 m in size) obtained by clear-felling. Therefore, I/I_0 and F for the upper-

Fig. 3.3. Emergent tree crowns overtopping the surface of the closed main canopy layer of Pasoh forest, seen from a height of about 35 m on the *Koompassia* tree on which light observations were made. (Photo by K. Yoda.)

Fig. 3.4. Upper surface of the semi-evergreen seasonal forest at Sakaerat with the observation tower. Only one emergent tree is seen in the upper right corner. (Photo by T. Kira.)

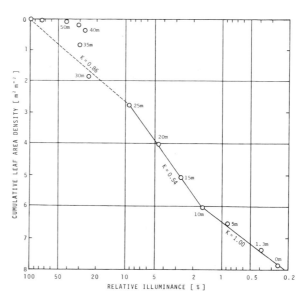

Fig. 3.5. Relationship between the mean relative illuminance at different height levels in Pasoh forest and the cumulative leaf area density above respective levels.

most layer of the forest between 30 and 57.5 m (tree top) cannot be correlated with each other. If the average light extinction in this top layer is assumed to follow the broken line in Fig. 3.5, the relation of $\ln (I/I_0)$ to F in this plot may be approximated by the three segments drawn in the Figure, each representing the exponential attenuation of light flux density with increasing cumulative LAD. The light extinction coefficient is approximately 0.86 for the top layer (25–57.5 m), 0.54 for the middle layer (10–25 m) and 1.00 for the bottom layer (0–10 m).

According to the original interpretation by Monsi and Saeki (1953), K is expected to be equal to 1.0 in a canopy consisting of perfectly horizontal leaves (planophyll canopy) and to decrease with increasing inclination of leaves, as is the case with erectophyll grass communities. A large value of K in the bottom layer (= 1.00) may be caused by the generally horizontal leaf arrangement in ground-layer plants, but there is little evidence to show that middle-layer leaves are more strongly inclined than top-layer leaves. Yoda (1978) also found different K values for the three strata of the Minamata oak forest. Similar data for other forest communities are, however, too scarce for further consideration. In any case, the simple light extinction model initially proposed for mono-layered herbaceous communities is hardly applicable to stratified forest communities. The interception of light by stems and branches should also be taken into consideration in future studies, since leafless shoots alone can intercept 30 to 70% of incident light, as shown by Yim et al. (1969) for some shrub and herb communities.

Horizontal distribution of light flux density at different height levels

Very uneven distribution of light flux density over the forest floor, and its effect on the development of ground vegetation, have attracted the attention of many plant ecologists, especially with reference to the size, frequency and role of sun-flecks. The light reaching the bottom of a leaf canopy consists of the three fractions, direct sunlight, sky-light and the so-called shade light originating from the transmission and reflection of direct sunlight by leaves. The processes involved in the penetration and interception of these light fractions are very complicated and can only be simulated by numerical computation with simplified canopy models (De Wit, 1965; Oikawa, 1977).

An empirical fact found by Ogawa (1967, 1980) may provide a practical and useful approach to the understanding of the pattern of horizontal distribution of light under the forest canopy. He showed that, if the relative illuminance (RI) is measured by simultaneously reading two photo-cells (one placed in the forest and the other exposed to full daylight outside the forest) at a number of spots on a plane at a certain height above the forest floor, the frequency distribution of observed RI values was approximately log-normal. This is a reasonable expectation if the downward attenuation of light inside the canopy follows the De Beers law of eq. 1 and the number of leaves existing along the path of light from the canopy surface to the point of light measurement has a normal frequency distribution.

The log-normality of the frequency distribution of RI can also be confirmed for tropical rain forests, as illustrated in Figs. 3.6 to 3.8.

The skewness of the frequency distribution curve tends to be more pronounced at greater depths from the canopy surface (Fig. 3.6) and on days with brighter sunshine (Fig. 3.8). On the floor of a dense forest, a greater part of the ground surface

receives very weak light, while the area exposed to stronger light is limited.

The relative frequency of a given range of RI in Figs. 3.6 to 3.8 may well be assumed to represent the percentage area on the plane concerned, since the observation points were numerous enough (500–1000 at the levels near the ground) and regularly distributed. Evans (1956, 1966) illustrated the relationship between the brightness of light on the ground and the integrated area

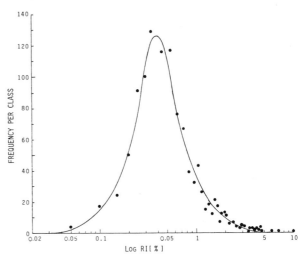

Fig. 3.7. Frequency distribution of the logarithms of relative illuminance (RI) on the 10 m plane in Pasoh forest (July, 1971), drawn from the original data by Yoda (1974). The smooth curve shows the lognormal distribution.

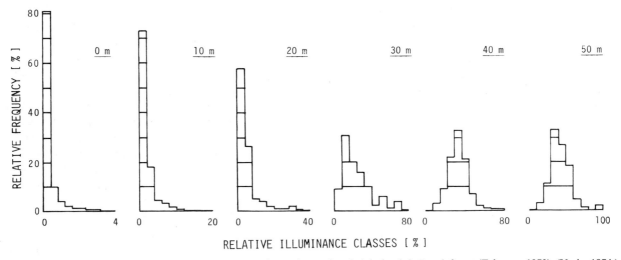

Fig. 3.6. Frequency distribution of relative illuminance observed at various height levels in Pasoh forest (February 1973). (Yoda, 1974.)

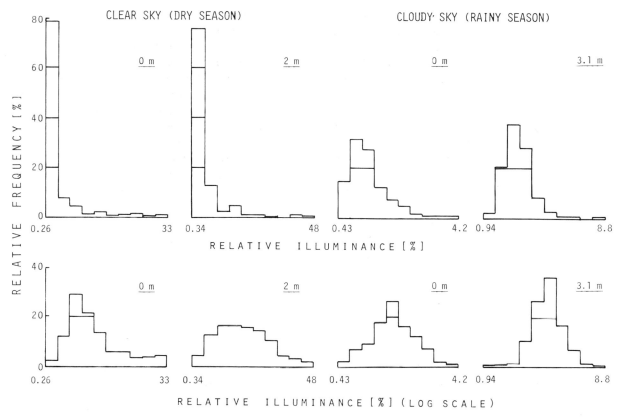

Fig. 3.8. Frequency distribution of relative illuminance (RI) and log (RI) on and immediately above the floor of the semi-evergreen seasonal forest at Sakaerat, northeastern Thailand, under clear (January 1977) and cloudy sky (August 1978). (Yoda et al., 1983.)

exposed to a given range of brightness in the rain forest of Southern Nigeria, suggesting that the area/brightness relationship could be approximated by a negative exponential curve. His curve corresponds fairly well with the frequency distribution curves of RI in the two Southeast Asian rain forests. In fact, the descending arm of a very skewed log-normal curve closely resembles an exponential curve (Koyama and Kira, 1956, their appendix).

To illustrate the three-dimensional heterogeneity of light distribution within a forest community, Yoda (1974) proposed the diagram shown in Fig. 3.9, in which cumulative percentage frequency of RI and aboveground height were taken as abscissa and ordinate respectively, and isopleths were drawn connecting the points where the cumulation reached certain levels of RI such as 0.2%, 0.5%, 1%, etc., based on the smoothed log-normal distribution of RI frequency. On the floor

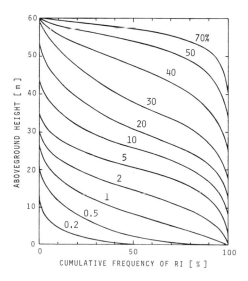

Fig. 3.9. Three-dimensional distribution of relative illuminance in Pasoh forest (February 1973). For further explanation see text. (Yoda, 1974.)

of Pasoh forest, for instance, 50% of ground surface receives dim light less than 0.2% of RI, and the area of bright spots over 1% of RI is only one hundredth of the total area. At a height of 30 m, 55% of the plane area is exposed to a range of RI of 10 to 30%, while the areas corresponding to < 5 and > 40% RI are 7 and 3%, respectively.

The brightest spot on the floor of Pasoh forest under the fine weather of February and July had an RI of only 4 to 6%. Thus there are virtually no sun-flecks on the ground of a typical equatorial rain forest where no appreciable gaps exist in its canopy. In the semi-evergreen forest at Sakaerat, on the other hand, the maximum RI under the clear sky of the dry season amounted to 33% on the ground and to 48% on a plane 2 m above the ground, reaching the level of brightness assigned to a sun-fleck (one-third of full sunlight) by Evans (1966). The LAI of Sakaerat forest is not known, but the forest is likely to have somewhat smaller LAI than Pasoh forest, especially in the dry season when some deciduous tree species growing in the canopy become leafless. However, the difference in light climate near the ground between the two forests may be ascribed more to the difference in canopy structure or in spatial distribution of LAD than to that in total LAI.

The occurrence of 3 to 4 months of dry season at Sakaerat results in the concentration of tree crowns in a single main canopy layer that forms the upper surface of the forest. Tall emergent trees overtopping the surface are rare. The space between the main canopy and the ground layer (lower than 5 m) remains relatively open with low LAD (Fig. 3.1A), so that sunbeams passing through small holes in the main canopy can reach the ground layer unintercepted to produce sun-flecks. The profile structure of Sakaerat forest is thus similar to that of ordinary temperate forests (for instance Minamata forest in Fig. 3.1A), whereas the typical rain forest under an ever-humid equatorial climate such as that of Peninsular Malaysia and Borneo is structurally different. Though the continuous main canopy of typical rain forests tends to be less dense owing to sporadically overtopping emergent trees, the space under the canopy is generally more or less evenly filled with tree crowns of various heights, which intercept sunbeams so efficiently that very few sun-flecks are allowed to reach the forest floor.

Sun-flecks are known to contribute a very large fraction to the total amount of radiant energy received by the forest floor — for instance, up to 70% of visible radiation in a Nigerian forest (Evans, 1956, 1966), and 63% on average in a plantation of *Chamaecyparis obtusa* (Tamai, 1976). They may, therefore, play a significant role in the heat budget of the forest floor, but the relative area they occupy is so small (2% in the Nigerian forest; Evans, 1966) and their duration is so short [7 min on an average day in the Nigerian forest (Evans, 1966); 10–20 min day^{-1} in the montane rain forest of Puerto Rico (Odum et al., 1970)] that there is still room for doubting the substantial effect of sun-flecks on the life of forest-floor plants.

WIND

The main role of wind in microclimate is the acceleration of air turbulence, which controls the rate of vertical transport of heat, water vapor, carbon dioxide, etc. in the atmosphere by eddy diffusion. As is well known, wind speed is drastically reduced inside dense plant communities, owing to the resistance of plant shoots to air flow. Vertical mixing of air within community space is thus generally inactive, and microclimatic conditions under a leaf canopy tend to be less variable over the day than those outside the canopy space.

Tropical rain-forest regions are generally not windy; the prevailing wind speed over the surface of the rain forest does not exceed a few meters per second except during local squalls. The wind profile covering a considerable vertical distance above the surface of tropical rain forests has rarely been observed, but it is unlikely that the profile is different from that above other kinds of plant community, which is commonly formulated by the equation:

$$u(z) = \frac{u^*}{k} \ln\left(\frac{z-d}{z_0}\right) \tag{2}$$

where $u(z)$ denotes wind velocity at an above-ground height z, u^* is the friction velocity, k is Von Karman's constant (= 0.41), and z_0 and d are the roughness length parameter and zero plane displacement, respectively. Chungkao (1971) estimated the average value of d for a profile 14 m deep above the surface of Sakaerat forest at 27 m or 0.84 times the height of the forest surface ($H = 32$ m). The corresponding value for a profile 6 m deep above Pasoh forest was 40 to 45 m or 0.85 to 0.96 H (Aoki et al., 1975; $H = 47$ m). These d values are very large, corresponding to the height of the forests, and the ratios to H are also larger than the normal range met with in herbaceous communities (0.6–0.8; Monteith, 1973). The roughness length z_0 is known to be approximately equal to 0.13 H (Monteith, 1973). However, its estimate for Sakaerat forest was 2.0 m or 0.06 H (Chungkao, 1971).

Wind profiles within different types of plant community are compared in Fig. 3.10, in which both wind speed and above-ground height are normalized by taking the values at the community surface as the standard. In herbaceous crop communities, here represented by paddy fields, the relative wind speed drops sharply in the uppermost layer with the highest LAD, and very low wind speeds prevail in the lower part of the stand. The downward extinction of wind speed is, on the other hand, more gradual in Pasoh rain forest, owing to the low LAD and its even distribution throughout the forest profile. The wind profile in the larch plantation, with a single crown stratum near the

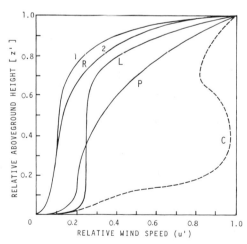

Fig. 3.10. Comparison of wind-speed profiles in different types of plant communities. Both wind speed and above-ground height are normalized by taking the values at the canopy surface as the standard. $R1$ and 2 = paddy fields (Aoki et al., 1975); P = Pasoh forest (Aoki et al., 1975); C = Costa Rican rain forest (Allen et al., 1972); L = Japanese larch plantation in New York (Allen et al., 1972.)

forest surface, is intermediate between those of paddy fields and Pasoh forest. That in the Costa Rican rain forest is different from the other profiles in the very slow reduction of wind speed in the main canopy between 30 and 40 m above the ground and the occurrence of a wind speed maximum in the mid-layer. This forest seems to be less dense than normal rain forests, having a lower LAD in the top layer and lacking mid-story trees.

The wind profiles in Pasoh forest and Japanese paddy fields, except near the ground, can best be fitted by the following exponential equation (Aoki et al., 1975):

$$u'(z') = (1 - \beta)\exp[-\alpha(1 - z')] + \beta \qquad (3)$$

where:

$u'(z') = u/u_H$ = relative wind speed at a relative height z'

z' = relative above-ground height = z/H

$\beta = u_0/u_H$

and where u_H is the wind speed at the height of the community surface (H), and u_0 stands for the extrapolated wind speed at the ground surface ($z' = 0$). The coefficient of wind-speed extinction (α) for Pasoh forest ($\alpha = 2.85$) was nearly half as large as that for the paddy fields.

To summarize, the air inside forests, especially in tall multi-storied rain forests with very low $\overline{LAD}$, is relatively free-moving as compared with the air in lower communities with high $\overline{LAD}$. This favors mixing of inside air with the free atmosphere above the forest canopy due to enhanced turbulent diffusion, and may increase the emission of water vapor from and the uptake of carbon dioxide by leaves. Vertical gradients of microclimatic elements within forests may also be expected to become smaller.

TEMPERATURE AND HUMIDITY

Since much has already been published on the temperature and humidity distribution in tropical rain forests (for instance Richards, 1952; Walter, 1964, 1971), it may suffice here to mention a typical example observed in Pasoh forest by Aoki et al. (1975). The observation was made on a tower 36 m tall constructed around the straight bole of an emergent tree of *Shorea leprosula* 47 m in height. A pole bearing instruments was extended up to the height of 53 m to obtain micrometeorological records above the forest surface. The crown of the *Shorea* tree intercepted about 50% of incident radiation, and the air temperature near the strongly heated crown surface rose to 30 to 32°C during the earlier part of the afternoon, when the air near the forest floor ($z = 0.05$ m) was cooler by about 7°C. (Figs. 3.11 and 3.12). Radiative cooling of the crown surface started at about 17 h to reach a daily minimum of about 21°C at midnight. The whole internal space of the forest remained nearly isothermal at all height levels from 18 to 8 h the next morning, though the lowest temperature of

20.1 to 20.3°C was recorded in the middle story, 20 to 30 m above the ground (Fig. 3.11).

The mean daily range of air temperature in mid-November was 10.4°C at the crown surface and 3.9°C at 5 cm above the ground (Table 3.4). A diurnal range of about 10°C in air temperature at the canopy surface seems common in tropical rain forests under moist sunny weather (for example Richards, 1952; Longman and Jenik, 1974). Although the difference of air temperature between canopy surface and forest floor was fairly large in Pasoh forest, the vertical thermal gradient was very small compared with that in other types of plant communities, owing partly to the very long distance from tree-top to ground level and partly to the fairly active eddy diffusion. There was almost no time lag between the diurnal temper-

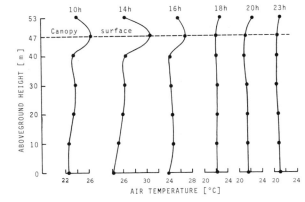

Fig. 3.11. Vertical distribution of air temperature in Pasoh forest on 21 November 1973. (Aoki et al., 1975.)

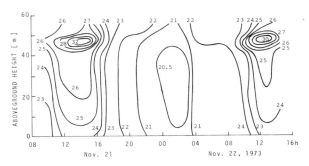

Fig. 3.12. Diurnal change of air temperature [°C] in Pasoh forest shown as isopleths on height and time coordinates. (Aoki et al., 1975.)

TABLE 3.4

Maximum and minimum air temperatures (°C) in and above Pasoh forest (Malaysia) in November, 1973 (Aoki et al., 1975)

Height above ground (m)	Nov. 15		Nov. 22		Mean daily range
	maximum	minimum	maximum	minimum	
53	30.1	21.2	26.1	20.9	7.1
47[1]	32.3	20.9	30.0	20.6	10.4
40	28.2	20.7	25.6	20.3	6.4
30	28.6	20.6	25.8	20.1	6.9
20	28.5	20.3	24.8	20.1	6.5
10	27.4	20.6	24.5	20.4	5.5
0.05	25.4	20.8	23.6	20.5	3.9
>0.00[2]	24.5	22.0	24.0	22.7	1.9

[1]Canopy surface.
[2]Soil temperature.

ature curves at the surface and at the bottom of the forest canopy. This also indicates rapid vertical mixing of air due to the low LAD.

The spatial/temporal distribution of relative humidity (RH) on the same days and at the same place in the Pasoh forest is shown in Fig. 3.13. General patterns of distribution were almost the reverse of those in air temperature (Fig. 3.11), as expected. The RH value corresponding to the afternoon maximum of temperature at the crown surface was as low as 50 to 60%, while the air near the forest floor remained nearly saturated with water vapor (RH 96–100%) throughout the day. The whole forest space was vapor-saturated during the night, but the profile of water vapor pressure (Fig. 3.14) indicated that upward transport of water vapor from the forest to the free atmosphere was taking place even at midnight. The gradient of water vapor pressure was, however, also small.

The remarkable constancy of microclimatic conditions near the floor of tropical rain forests has often been emphasized. The persistence of extremely high humidity is, above all, striking. However, even the most stable rain-forest climates such as those in equatorial districts of Malaysia and Indonesia are not free from long rainless spells that may extend from a few to several months, when the floor of dense rain forests may become completely dried up, with tree seedlings wilted or injured. Such unusual dry periods take place in Peninsular Malaysia at irregular intervals of several years, and are known to give rise to the gregarious flowering and fruiting of forest trees, particularly of the dominant family Dipterocarpaceae, which otherwise rarely flowers (Wycherley, 1973; compare also Whitmore, this volume). It is worthy of special attention that such unusual

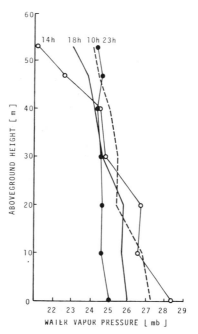

Fig. 3.14. Vertical distribution of water vapor pressure in Pasoh forest on 21 November 1973. (Aoki et al., 1975.)

climatic events are thus imprinted in the life history of dominant tree species of Southeast Asian rain forests, to play an important role in the regeneration and maintenance of this typically pluvial vegetation.

CARBON DIOXIDE CONCENTRATION

Carbon dioxide balance

Carbon dioxide concentration in the air within a plant community represents the balance between consumption by photosynthesis and supply from three sources; the free atmosphere over the leaf canopy; respiration by plant shoots and animals; and emission from the soil surface as soil respiration.

Soil respiration measurements in tropical rain forests are scattered in existing literature (Schulze, 1967; Yoda and Kira, 1969; Wanner, 1970; Ogawa, 1978; Yoda and Nishioka, 1982), and comparisons in terms of absolute values are impossible because of differences in the apparatus used for field measurements. Using the same method as Ogawa (1978), and citing his data obtained in Pasoh

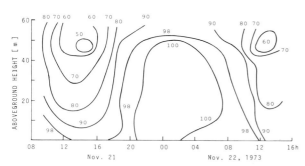

Fig. 3.13. Isopleths of relative humidity in Pasoh forest. (Aoki et al., 1975.)

forest, Nakane (1980) concluded that the rate of carbon-dioxide evolution from a litter-covered forest floor was much higher in the Pasoh forest than in temperate forests on mesic sites in central Japan. Nakane's estimates of annual mean soil respiration rate were 49.7 kg CO_2ha^{-1} day^{-1} in a cool temperate beech/fir forest and 102.3 kg CO_2ha^{-1} day^{-1} in a warm-temperate evergreen oak forest, while it amounted to 143.6 kg CO_2ha^{-1} day^{-1} at Pasoh. In addition, the accumulation of big dead stems on the floor of Pasoh forest, averaging 49 t(dry wt.)ha^{-1} (Yoneda et al., 1977), was estimated to emit carbon dioxide at a rate of 49.5 kg ha^{-1} day^{-1} (Yoneda, 1980). The total flux of carbon dioxide from the forest floor to the air thus amounted to 193 kg ha^{-1} day^{-1} or 8.0 mg CO_2dm^{-2} h^{-1}.

Aoki et al. (1975) used micrometeorological methods to estimate the net canopy photosynthesis rate in Pasoh forest at 43 mg CO_2dm^{-2} h^{-1} at a solar radiation flux of 1.3 cal cm^{-2} min^{-1}. Of this net uptake of carbon dioxide, 8 mg dm^{-2} h^{-1} was contributed by soil respiration, while the rest (35 mg dm^{-2} h^{-1}) was supplied by the downward flux from the free atmosphere. The contribution of soil respiration may be greater if the supply during the night is taken into consideration.

The estimated rates of whole-day carbon dioxide uptake and emissions are given in Table 3.5. The rates estimated by different methods differ widely from each other, but the evolution of carbon dioxide from decomposing organic matter on and in the soil ($\Sigma D = 123$ kg CO_2ha^{-1} day^{-1}) is evidently a very important source of carbon dioxide for canopy photosynthesis, contributing 52 to 92% of the rate of net carbon dioxide uptake. If the net production rate of 25.7 t(dry matter) ha^{-1} yr^{-1}(equivalent to about 134 kg CO_2ha^{-1} day^{-1}) based on study of biomass changes is accepted, the net input of carbon dioxide to this forest ecosystem is nearly balanced by the output from the decomposition of organic matter, leaving little for biomass increment, as might be expected for a steady-state climax forest.

Daily variation of carbon dioxide concentration

Figure 3.15 illustrates an example of the daily variation in the atmospheric concentration of carbon dioxide in and above Pasoh forest as

TABLE 3.5

Estimated rates of CO_2 fluxes in Pasoh forest (kg CO_2 ha^{-1}day^{-1})

	Microclimatologically estimated[1]	Other estimates
Net uptake (A)	238	134[2]
Dark respiration of above-ground shoots (B)	158	279[3]
Gross uptake (root respiration excluded) (A + B)	396	413
Root respiration (C)	–	70[4]
Decomposition of surface litter layer (D_1)	–	36[5]
Decomposition of big dead stems (D_2)	–	50[6]
Decomposition of soil organic matter (D_3)	–	37[4]
Total soil respiration ($C + \Sigma D$)	–	193[5]
Gross uptake (A + B + C)	–	483

[1]By energy balance method. Averages for a few days in mid-November, 1973 (Aoki et al., 1975).
[2]Based on three years' (1971–74) observations of biomass increment and litter fall (Kira, 1982; Kira's 1978 estimate was slightly modified).
[3]Experimentally determined (Yoda, 1982).
[4]Nakane (1981).
[5]Ogawa (1978).
[6]Yoneda (1980); the estimate by Yoneda et al. (1977) was revised.

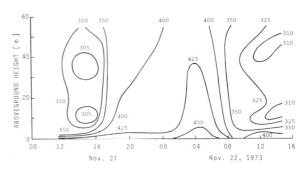

Fig. 3.15. Isopleths of CO_2 concentration (ppm) in Pasoh forest. (Aoki et al., 1975.)

isopleths on time and height coordinates. The ground surface is apparently the most important source of carbon dioxide, the concentration close to the forest floor being always higher than 400 ppm, and amounting to 450 to 500 ppm from midnight to early morning. High concentrations over 400 ppm prevail at all height levels below 53 m almost throughout the night. Since the concentration tended to be lower at higher levels, carbon dioxide emitted from the ground surface is transported upward even at night when the canopy does not operate as a sink for carbon dioxide. Isopleths in the earlier half of the night indicate the progress of accumulation of carbon dioxide originating from soil respiration.

At 8 h in the morning, carbon dioxide concentrations between the levels of 5 and 53 m begin to drop rapidly. A minimum concentration of 305 to 310 ppm is reached around noon and is maintained until 16 h, when the concentration of carbon dioxide increases again. The daytime pattern of carbon dioxide isopleths in Fig. 3.15 suggests that the amount supplied by soil respiration is almost entirely consumed by canopy photosynthesis. The vertical gradient of carbon dioxide concentration between 5 and 53 m is very small, reflecting the even distribution and low density of leaves in this forest, though two minima tended to appear in the carbon dioxide profile at mid-day at the canopy surface (30–40 m) and in the lower stratum (around 10 m) of the forest.

Similarly, two sinks of carbon dioxide were also found by Allen et al. (1972) in the Costa Rican rain forest which consisted of two well-defined tree layers, a main canopy and a dense undergrowth. The structure of the Pasoh forest is more complex, without distinct stratification except for the emergent layer, so that it is not certain whether the two sinks observed there are a general feature of the whole forest or are a result of the specific stand structure around the observation tower.

Aoki et al. (1975) called attention to the fact that the difference in carbon dioxide concentration between the upper surface of canopy and the layer of lowest concentration at mid-day was about 5 ppm in both the Pasoh forest and the Costa Rican forest (Allen et al., 1972) as well as in temperate forests (Yabuki et al., 1978), whereas that in dense crop communities on calm fine days was much greater. For instance, Uchijima et al. (1967) recorded a maximum difference of 27 ppm in a maize field (LAI = 4.2) under strong summer sunshine and low wind. Despite such a contrast in carbon dioxide gradients between forest and herbaceous communities, the daily range of carbon dioxide variation was similar at all height levels

TABLE 3.6

Ranges of atmospheric CO_2 concentration in and above Pasoh forest, Peninsular Malaysia (Aoki et al., 1975)

Height above ground (m)	CO_2 concentration (ppm)[1]		
	minimum	maximum	range
53	310	420	110
30	310	430	120
20	310	430	120
2	340	450	110
0.05	390	510	120

[1]Averages for three days in November, 1973.

of the Pasoh forest (Table 3.6) and in the maize field.

It has sometimes been suggested (Richards, 1952) that the high concentrations of carbon dioxide prevailing near the forest floor are a possible advantage for the photosynthesis and growth of ground-layer plants. However, this is somewhat doubtful, because the real factor controlling the rate of photosynthesis is not the actual concentration of carbon dioxide but the rate of its supply to leaves. In fact, the photosynthesis of a leaf placed in an assimilation chamber can be enhanced by simply increasing the rate of air flow through the chamber without changing the concentration of carbon dioxide. Since the air near the forest floor moves very slowly both horizontally and vertically, the availability of carbon dioxide in the air may not be very high for the plants growing on the ground in a dense forest.

REFERENCES

Alexandre, D.Y., 1982. Étude de l'éclairement du sous-bois d'une fôret dense humide sempervirente (Taï, Côte-d'Ivoire). *Acta Oecol., Oecol. Generales*, 3: 407–447.

Allen. L.H. and Lemon, E.R., 1976. Carbon dioxide exchange and turbulence in a Costa Rican tropical rain forest. In: J.L. Monteith (Editor), *Vegetation and the Atmosphere, Vol. 2, Case Studies*. Academic Press, London, pp. 265–308.

Allen, L.H., Lemon, E.R. and Muller, L., 1972. Environment of a Costa Rican forest. *Ecology*, 53: 102–111.

Aoki, M., Yabuki, K. and Koyama, H., 1975. Micrometeorology and assessment of primary production of a tropical rain forest in West Malaysia. *J. Agric. Meteorol.*, 31: 115–124.

Bazzaz, F.A. and Pickett, S.T.A., 1980. Physiological ecology of tropical succession: a comparative review. *Annu. Rev. Ecol. Syst.*, 11: 287–310.

Chunkao, K., 1971. *An Analysis of Evapotranspiration of Dry–Evergreen Forest at Sakaerat, Thailand.* Forest Research Bull. 16, Kasetsart Univ., Bangkok, 110 pp.

Denmead, O.T., 1969. Comparative micrometeorology of a wheat field and a forest of *Pinus radiata. Agric. Meteorol.*, 6: 357–371.

De Wit, C.T., 1965. *Photosynthesis of Leaf Canopies.* Centre for Agricultural Publications and Documentation, Wageningen, 57 pp.

Evans, G.C., 1956. An area survey method of investigating the distribution of light intensity in woodlands, with particular reference to sunflecks. *J. Ecol.*, 44: 391–428.

Evans, G.C., 1966. Model and measurement in the study of woodland light climates. In: R. Rainbridge, G.C. Evans and O. Rackham (Editors), *Light as an Ecological Factor.* Blackwell, Oxford, pp. 53–76.

Golley, F.B., McGinnes, J.T., Clements, R.G., Child, G.I. and Duever, M.J., 1975. *Mineral Cycling in a Tropical Moist Forest Ecosystem.* Univ. of Georgia Press, Athens, Ga., 248 pp.

Hozumi, K., Yoda, K. and Kira, T., 1969. Production ecology of tropical rain forests of southwestern Cambodia. II. Photosynthetic production in an evergreen seasonal forest. In: T. Kira and K. Iwata (Editors), *Nature and Life in Southeast Asia, Vol. 6.* Japan Society for the Promotion of Science, Tokyo, pp. 57–81.

Jordan, C.F. and Uhl, C., 1978. Biomass of a "tierra firme" forest of the Amazonian basin. *Oecol. Plant.*, 13: 387–400.

Kato, R., Tadaki, Y. and Ogawa, H., 1978. Plant biomass and growth increment studies in Pasoh forest. *Malay. Nat. J.*, 30: 211–224.

Kawanabe, S., 1977. A subtropical broad-leaved forest at Yona, Okinawa. In: T. Shidei and T. Kira (Editors), *Primary Productivity of Japanese Forests.* (JIBP Synthesis Vol. 16) Univ. of Tokyo Press, Tokyo, pp. 268–279.

Kira, T., 1978. Community architecture and organic matter dynamics in tropical lowland rain forests of Southeast Asia with special reference to Pasoh forest, West Malaysia. In: P.B. Tomlinson and M.H. Zimmermann (Editors), *Tropical Trees as Living Systems.* Proc. 4th Cabot Symp. held at Harvard Forest, Petersham, Mass., Cambridge Univ. Press, Cambridge, pp. 561–590.

Kira, T., 1982. Primary production and carbon cycling in a primeval lowland rainforest of Peninsular Malaysia. *Int. Workshop on Special Problems in Physiological Investigations of Tree Crops, Kottayam, Kerala.*

Kira, T., Shinozaki, K. and Hozumi, K., 1969. Structure of forest canopies as related to their primary productivity. *Plant Cell Physiol.*, 10: 129–142.

Koyama, H. and Kira, T., 1956. Intraspecific competition among higher plants. VIII. Frequency distribution of individual plant weight as affected by the interaction between plants. *J. Inst. of Polytechnics, Osaka City Univ., Ser. D*, 7: 73–94.

Leigh, E.G., 1975. Structure and climate in tropical rain forest. *Annu. Rev. Ecol. Syst.*, 6: 67–86.

Longman, K.A. and Jenik, J., 1974. *Tropical Forest and its Environment.* Longman, London, 196 pp.

Monsi, M. and Saeki, T., 1953. Über den Lichtfaktor in den Pflanzengesellschaften und ihre Bedeutung für die Stoffproduktion. *Jpn. J. Bot.*, 14: 22–52.

Monteith, J.L., 1973. *Principles of Environmental Physics.* Arnold, London, 241 pp.

Monteith, J.L. (Editor), 1975. *Vegetation and the Atmosphere, Vol. 1, Principles.* Academic Press, New York, N.Y., 278 pp.

Monteith, J.L. (Editor), 1976. *Vegetation and the Atmosphere, Vol. 2, Case Studies.* Academic Press, New York, N.Y., 439 pp.

Nagano, M. and Kira, T., 1978. Aboveground biomass. In: T. Kira, T. Hosokawa and Y. Ono (Editors), *Biological Production in a Warm-Temperate Evergreen Oak Forest of Japan.* (JIBP Synthesis Vol. 18) Univ. of Tokyo Press, Tokyo, pp. 69–82.

Nakane, K., 1980. Comparative studies of cycling of soil organic carbon in three primeval moist forests. *Jpn. J. Ecol.*, 30: 155–172 (in Japanese with English summary).

Odum, H.T., 1970. Summary: an emerging view of the ecological system at El Verde. In: H.T. Odum and R.F. Pigeon (Editors), *A Tropical Rain Forest — A Study of Irradiation and Ecology at El Verde, Puerto Rico.* Office of Information Services, U.S. Atomic Energy Commission, pp. I191–289.

Odum, H.T., Drewry, G. and Kline, J.R., 1970. Climate at El Verde, 1963–1966. In: H.T. Odum and R.F. Pigeon (Editors), *A Tropical Rain Forest — A Study of Irradiation and Ecology at El Verde, Puerto Rico.* Office of Information Services, U.S. Atomic Energy Commission, pp. B347–418.

Ogawa, H., 1967. Three-dimensional structure of Ashiu beech forest in relation to light distribution. In: T. Kira (Editor), *Progress Report for 1966, JIBP/PT (Studies on the Methods for Assessing Primary Production of Forests).* Osaka, pp. 45–52 (in Japanese, mimeographed).

Ogawa, H., 1978. Litter production and carbon cycling in Pasoh forest. *Malay. Nat. J.*, 30: 367–373.

Ogawa, H., 1980. *Structure and Function of Populations.* (Handbook of Plant Ecology, 5) Asakura Shoten, Tokyo, 221 pp. (in Japanese).

Ogawa, H., Yoda, K. and Kira, T., 1961. A preliminary survey on the vegetation of Thailand. In: T. Kira and T. Umesao (Editors), *Nature and Life in Southeast Asia, Vol. I.* Fauna and Flora Research Society, Kyoto, pp. 21–157.

Ogawa, H., Yoda, K., Ogino, K. and Kira, T., 1965. Comparative ecological studies on three main types of forest vegetation in Thailand. II. Plant biomass. In: T. Kira and K. Iwata (Editors), *Nature and Life in Southeast Asia, Vol. IV.* Fauna and Flora Research Society, Kyoto, pp. 49–80.

Ogino, K., 1977. A beech forest at Ashiu — biomass, its increment and net production. In: T. Shidei and T. Kira (Editors), *Primary Productivity of Japanese Forests.* (JIBP Synthesis, Vol. 16) Univ. of Tokyo Press, Tokyo, pp. 172–186.

Oikawa, T., 1977. Light regime in relation to plant population geometry, I–III. *Bot. Mag. Tokyo*, 90: 1–10, 11–22, 301–311.

Richards, P.W., 1952. *The Tropical Rain Forest — An Ecological Study*. Cambridge Univ. Press, Cambridge, 450 pp.

Schulze, E.D., 1967. Soil respiration of tropical vegetation types. *Ecology*, 48: 652–653.

Soepadmo, E. and Kira, T., 1977. Contribution of the IBP-PT Research Project to the understanding of Malaysian forest ecology. In: C.B. Sastry, P.B.L. Srivastava and A. Manap Ahmad (Editors), *A New Era In Malaysian Forestry*. Univ. Pertanian Malaysia, Serdang (Selangor, Malaysia), pp. 63–90.

Tajchman, S.J., 1972. The radiation and energy balances of coniferous and deciduous forests. *J. Appl. Ecol.*, 9: 359–375.

Tamai, S., 1976. Studies on the stand structure and light climate(II). Methods of investigating the sunfleck on the forest floor(1). *Bull. Kyoto Univ. Forests*, 48: 69–79.

Uchijima, Z., Udagawa, T., Horie, T. and Kobayashi, K., 1967. Studies of energy and gas exchange within crop canopies(1). CO_2-environment in a corn canopy. *J. Agric. Meteorol.*, 23: 99–108 (in Japanese with English summary).

Walter, H., 1964. *Die Vegetation der Erde in öko-physiologischer Betrachtung. Band I: Die tropischen und subtropischen Zonen*. Fischer, Jena, 2nd ed., 592 pp.

Walter, H., 1971. *Ecology of Tropical and Subtropical Vegetation*. Oliver and Boyd, Edinburgh, 539 pp.

Wanner, H., 1970. Soil respiration, litter fall and productivity of tropical rain forest. *J. Ecol.*, 58: 543–547.

Whitmore, T.C., 1975. *Tropical Rain Forest of the Far East*. Clarendon, Oxford, 282 pp.

Wycherley, P.R., 1973. The phenology of plants in the humid tropics. *Micronesica*, 9: 75–96.

Yabuki, K., Aoki, M. and Hamotani, K., 1978. Characteristics of the forest microclimate. In: T. Kira, Y. Ono and T. Hosokawa (Editors), *Biological Production in a Warm-Temperate Evergreen Oak Forest of Japan*. (JIBP Synthesis, Vol. 18) Univ. of Tokyo Press, Tokyo, pp. 55–64.

Yamakura, T., Hagihara, A., Siristeijono, S., 1983. *Plant Biomass of a Tropical Rainforest of East Kalimantan*. Abstracts of Papers, 30th Annual Meeting of the Ecological Society of Japan, Matsumoto, p. 152 (in Japanese, mimeographed).

Yim, Y.-J., Ogawa, H. and Kira, T., 1969. Light interception by stems in plant communities. *Jpn. J. Ecol.*, 19: 233–238.

Yoda, K., 1974. Three-dimensional distribution of light intensity in a tropical rain forest in West Malaysia. *Jpn. J. Ecol.*, 24: 247–254.

Yoda, K., 1978. Light climate within the forest. In: T. Kira, Y. Ono and T. Hosokawa (Editors), *Biological Production in a Warm-Temperate Evergreen Oak Forest of Japan*. (JIBP Synthesis, Vol. 18) Univ. of Tokyo Press, Tokyo, pp. 46–54.

Yoda, K., 1983. Community respiration in a lowland rain forest in Pasoh, Peninsular Malaysia. *Jpn. J. Ecol.*, 33: 183–197.

Yoda, K. and Kira, T., 1969. Comparative ecological studies on three main types of forest vegetation in Thailand. V. Accumulation and turnover of soil organic matter, with notes on the altitudinal sequence on Khao(Mt.) Luang, peninsular Thailand. In: T. Kira and K. Iwata (Editors), *Nature and Life in Southeast Asia, Vol. VI*. Japan Society for the Promotion of Science, Tokyo, pp. 83–109.

Yoda, K. and Nishioka, M., 1982. Soil respiration in dry and wet seasons in a tropical dry-evergreen forest in Sakaerat., NE Thailand. *Jpn. J. Ecol.*, 32: 539–541.

Yoda, K., Nishioka, M. and Dhanmanonda, P., 1983. Vertical and horizontal distribution of relative illuminance in the dry and wet seasons in a tropical dry-evergreen forest in Sakaerat, NE Thailand. *Jpn. J. Ecol.*, 33: 97–100.

Yoneda, T., 1980. *Ecological studies on the processes of fall and decomposition of woody organs in forests*. D. Sci. Thesis, Faculty of Science, Osaka City Univ., Osaka, 164 pp. (in Japanese).

Yoneda, T., Yoda, K. and Kira, T., 1977. Accumulation and decomposition of big wood litter in Pasoh forest, West Malaysia. *Jpn. J. Ecol.*, 27: 53–60.

Chapter 4

SOILS

PEDRO A. SANCHEZ

INTRODUCTION

Soils of the world's humid tropical regions are very variable, ranging from among the youngest to about the oldest, from among the most fertile to the least fertile in the world. Up to a few years ago, it was believed that soils formed in hot humid climates were universally highly weathered, leached and therefore, infertile. Their generally reddish or yellowish colors, indicative of the presence of iron oxides, led to the general assumption that most soils of the humid tropics, if cleared of vegetation, would turn into a laterite, a brick pavement, a red desert or even another Sahel (McNeil, 1964; Goodland and Irwin, 1975; Friedman, 1977; Irion, 1978; Reiss et al., 1980).

Nearly 60 years ago, C.F. Marbut, the father of American soil science, travelled in the Amazon and published an article stating that most of the soils he observed were strikingly similar to those of the southeastern United States where successful and stable agriculture exists (Marbut and Manifold, 1926). Within the last two decades, advances made in the characterization and mapping of soils in the humid tropics, by and large, confirm Marbut's assertions.

A quantitative system for classifying soils, called soil taxonomy, has been developed. It is similar to plant taxonomy in the sense that only properties that can be measured are considered (Soil Survey Staff, 1975). FAO has put together the available soil-survey information into the FAO World Soil Map at the scale of 1:5 million (Dudal, 1980). A common legend for the entire world is now available from FAO and is readily converted into soil taxonomy units (FAO–UNESCO, 1971, 1975, 1977a, b, 1978, 1979).

More detailed surveys have been conducted in parts of the humid tropics using satellite and radar imagery. Most of the Amazon is now mapped at a scale of 1:1 million (Projeto Radambrasil 1972–1978) and a synthesis of the land resources of tropical America is available (Cochrane and Sanchez, 1982; Cochrane, 1984). Detailed soil surveys are available for parts of most countries with humid tropics. Up-to-date information can be obtained at the various soil-resource inventory services of the individual countries.

The purpose of this chapter is to summarize the geographical distribution of soils in the humid tropics, their salient properties and their constraints to plant growth.

SOIL GEOGRAPHY

The humid tropics comprise approximately 1500 million hectares, about 31% of the tropics and 10% of the world's land area (Sanchez, 1976). In soil science terminology, the humid tropics can be defined as areas with high and constant soil temperature regimes (isohyperthermic or isothermic), a udic[1] soil moisture regime characterized by a dry season of less than four consecutive months and an original tropical rain forest or seasonal semi-evergreen tropical forest vegetation. The largest expanse occurs in tropical America with 45% of the world's humid tropics, followed by tropical Africa with 30% and tropical Asia and the Pacific with the remaining 25%. Table 4.1 shows the distribution of soil orders and important subdivisions thereof in the three regions, according

[1]The soil is dry for less than 90 consecutive days per year.

TABLE 4.1

Geographical distribution of soils of the humid tropics based on dominant soil in FAO maps at a scale of 1:5 million

Soil Taxonomy orders and suborders	FAO legend	Humid tropical America[1] (10^6ha)	Humid tropical Africa[2] (10^6ha)	Humid tropical Asia and Pacific[3] (10^6ha)	World's humid tropics total	
					(10^6ha)	%
Oxisols	Ferralsols	332	179	14	525	35
Ultisols	Acrisols[5]	213	69	131	413	28
Inceptisols:						
Aquepts	Gleysols	42	55	23	120	8
Andepts	Andosols	2	1	9	12	1
Tropepts	Cambisols	17	19	58	94	6
Total		61	75	90	226	15
Entisols:						
Fluvents	Fluvisols	6	10	34	50	3
Psamments	Arenosols[6]	6	67	17	90	6
Lithic groups	Lithosols	19	14	39	72	5
Total		31	91	90	212	14
Alfisols	Luvisols[7]	18	20	15	53	4
Histosols	Histosols	4	4	23	31	2
Spodosols	Podzols	10	3	6	19	1
Mollisols	Chernozems[8]	–	–	7	7	–
Vertisols	Vertisols	1	2	2	5	–
Aridisols[4]	Solonchaks	3	1	1	5	–
Total		673	444	379	1496	100

[1]From Sanchez and Cochrane (1980) plus recent adjustments.
[2]From FAO–UNESCO (1975) and Dudal (1980).
[3]From FAO–UNESCO (1977, 1978). Includes 46 million ha of the humid tropics of Australia and Pacific Islands.
[4]Saline soils only (Salorthids).
[5]Plus Dystric Nitosols.
[6]Plus Regosols.
[7]Plus Eutric Nitosols.
[8]Plus Rendzinas.

to soil taxonomy. Table 4.2 shows the nomenclature equivalents in other classification systems used in the humid tropics. The following are general descriptions of the main soil orders and suborders according to soil taxonomy, with their approximate equivalents in the FAO legend in parentheses.

Oxisols (Ferralsols)

The most abundant soils of the humid tropics belong to the order Oxisol, and cover about one-third of the total area. Oxisols or Ferralsols are deep, generally well-drained red or yellowish soils, with excellent granular structure and little contrast between horizon layers. The technical definition (the presence of an oxic horizon of low-activity clays) indicates that these soils are acid and low in available nutrients. Consequently, most of the physical properties of Oxisols are excellent, but their chemical properties are poor. In other classification systems, Oxisols are also known as Latosols and, incorrectly, as lateritic soils. Some properties of widely spread Oxisols of humid tropical areas are shown in Table 4.3.

About two-thirds of the Oxisols of the humid tropics are located in tropical America, mainly in

TABLE 4.2

Translation of soil taxonomy terminology used in the humid tropics into the other soil classification systems

Soil Taxonomy	FAO legend	1938 USDA system	French system	Brazilian system
Oxisols	Ferralsols	Latosols	Sols ferraltiques, fortement désaturés, typiques ou humifères	Latossolos, Terra Roxa Legítima
Ultisols	Acrisols and Dystric Nitosols	Red Yellow Podzolics	Sols ferralitiques, lessivés	Podzólico Vermelho-Amarelo
Inceptisols:	various	various	Sols peu évolués	Solos com horizonte B
Aquepts	Gleysols	Low humic gleys	Sols hydromorphes	Solos hidromórficos
Andepts	Andosols	Andosols	Andosols	–
Tropepts	Cambisols	Brown Forest	Sols brunifiés tropicaux	Solos com hirozonte B, incipiente
Entisols:	Various	Various	Sols minéraux bruts	–
Fluvents	Fluvisols	Alluvials		
Psamments	Arenosols and Regosols	Regosols	Regosols	Regossolos, Areias Quartzisosas
Lithic groups	Lithosols	Lithosols	Sols lithiques	Litossolos
Alfisols	Luvisols, Eutric Nitosols, Planosols	Eutric Red Yellow Podzolics, Terra Roxa, Planosols	Sols ferrigineaux tropicaux lessivés	Podzólico Vermelho-Amarelo equivalente eutrófico, Terra Roxa Estruturada, Planossolos
Histosols	Histosols	Peats and bogs	Sols organiques	Solos orgánicos
Spodosols	Podzols	Podzols	Podzols	Podzols
Mollisols	Rendzinas, Chernozems	Rendzinas Chernozems		Brunizems
Vertisols	Vertisols	Grumusols	Vertisols	Grumusols
Aridisol (saline)	Solonchaks	Solonchaks	Sols halomorphes	Solonchak

the areas geologically affected by the Guyana and Brazilian shields in the Amazon Basin, mostly east of Manaus. Oxisols are also found in the Pacific coast of Colombia, but few Oxisols exist in other humid tropical regions of the Western Hemisphere such as the Atlantic coast of Central America, parts of the Caribbean and the Atlantic coast of Brazil. Oxisols in humid tropical Africa are concentrated in Cameroon, Gabon, central Zaïre, Rwanda, Burundi, eastern Madagascar, Liberia and Sierra Leone. Oxisols are not extensive soils in humid tropical Asia but are found in patches in Kalimantan, Sumatra, Java, Sulawesi, Malaysia, Philippines and Thailand, amounting to about 3% of humid tropical Asia.

Ultisols (Acrisols, dystric Nitosols)

Ultisols of the humid tropics are similar to Oxisols in their morphology but exhibit a marked increase of clay content with depth which is absent in Oxisols. Ultisols are usually deep, well drained, red or yellowish soils, somewhat higher in weatherable minerals than Oxisols but still acid and low in native fertility. They cover about 413 million hectares or 28% of the humid tropics (Table 4.1). Their physical properties are generally not as favorable as those of Oxisols and many of them occupy steep slopes which makes them more susceptible to erosion. Ultisols were formerly known as Red Yellow Podzolics. Properties of representative Ultisols are shown in Table 4.4.

Ultisols are the predominant soils of the Amazon Basin roughly west of Manaus, and in well-drained areas not affected by the two ancient geological shields. They are also the dominant soils of the Atlantic coast of Central America and humid coastal Brazil.

Ultisols are also the most abundant soils of humid tropical Asia, occupying the major part of

TABLE 4.3

Some properties of representative Oxisol profiles in the humid tropics

Horizon depth (cm)	Clay (%)	Silt (%)	Sand (%)	pH[1]	Org.C (%)	Exchangeable				ECEC (c mol kg^{-1})	Al satn.[2] (%)	Olsen P[3] (ppm)
						Al (c mol kg^{-1})	Ca (c mol kg^{-1})	Mg (c mol kg^{-1})	K (c mol kg^{-1})			
Manaus, Brazil. Typic Acrorthox, clayey, kaolinitic, isohyperthermic (FCC=Ceaik)[4]												
0–8	76	9	15	4.6	3.0	1.1	1.7	0.3	0.19	3.29	33	2
8–22	80	8	12	4.4	0.9	1.1	0.2		0.9	1.39	79	1
22–50	84	8	8	4.3	0.7	1.2	0.2		0.7	1.47	82	1
50–125	88	5	7	4.6	0.3	1.0	0.1		0.4	1.14	88	1
125–265	89	6	5	4.9	0.2	0.2	0.1		0.11	3.1	65	–
Sitiung, West Sumatra, Indonesia. Typic Haprorthox, clayey, kaolinitic, isohyperthermic (FCC=Caik)[5]												
0–17	79	18	3	3.9	2.1	4.0	0.2	0.4	0.2	4.8	78	–
17–58	83	14	3	4.1	1.0	3.5	0.1	0.1	0.1	3.8	88	–
58–98	84	14	2	4.2	0.8	3.2	0.1	0.1	0.1	3.5	89	–
98–140	87	10	3	4.6	0.7	2.9	0.1	0.1	0.1	3.2	88	–
140–165	82	15	3	4.7	0.5	1.9	0.1	0.1	0.1	2.2	82	–
165–183	86	12	2	4.9	0.4	1.3	0.1	0.1	0.1	1.6	76	–
Mutobo Series, Burundi. Typic Acrorthox, clayey, oxidic, isothermic (FCC=Ceaik)[6]												
0–20	33	25	42	5.1	1.8	1.5	tr	0.1	0.1	1.7	88	–
20–75	22	27	51	5.2	1.4	1.3	0.1	0.1	tr	1.5	87	–
75–111	21	28	51	5.3	1.0	0.8	tr	0.1	tr	0.9	89	–
111–166	24	20	56	5.3	0.7	0.2	tr	0.1	tr	0.3	67	–
166–200	25	21	54	5.4	0.6	0.2	0.2	0.1	tr	0.2	50	–

[1] pH determined in 1:1 H$_2$O.
[2] Al saturation = Al/Al+Ca+Mg+K × 100.
[3] Olsen P = available phosphorus by the modified Olsen extraction.
[4] Profile SBCS-4, UEPAE de Manaus (Camargo and Rodrigues, 1979).
[5] Pedon SBB3–Block E Sitiung II (Santoso and Sofyan, 1984).
[6] Pedon 84P284, Soil Management Support Services USDA-AID, Washington (unpublished).

TABLE 4.4

Some properties of representative Ultisol profiles of the humid tropics

Horizon depth (cm)	Clay (%)	Silt (%)	Sand (%)	pH (1:1 H_2O)	Org.C (%)	Exchangeable				ECEC (c mol kg^{-1})	Al satn. (%)	Olsen P (ppm)
						Al (c mol kg^{-1})	Ca (c mol kg^{-1})	Mg (c mol kg^{-1})	K (c mol kg^{-1})			
Yurimaguas, Peru. Typic Paleudult fine loamy, siliceous, isohyperthermic (FCC = Leak)[1]												
0–10	6	21	73	4.4	1.7	1.29	1.13	0.60	0.28	3.30	39	9.5
10–30	13	21	66	4.4	0.5	3.31	0.29	0.14	0.8	3.82	87	2.5
30–50	16	24	61	4.6	0.4	3.87	0.29	0.22	0.7	4.45	87	4.1
50–70	16	22	62	4.5	0.3	4.26	0.29	0.16	0.7	4.78	89	1.6
70–100	22	21	56	4.4	0.4	4.80	0.29	0.13	0.14	5.36	90	0.0
100–150	23	19	57	4.3	0.1	6.15	0.16	0.05	0.9	6.45	95	0.0
Sitiung, West Sumatra, Indonesia. Orthoxic Paleudult clayey, kaolinitic, isohyperthermic (FCC = LCeak)[2]												
0–14	27	25	48	4.6	2.8	3.1	0.1	0.1	0.1	3.40	89	—
14–30	46	17	37	4.4	1.0	2.5	0.1	0.1	0.1	2.80	86	—
30–66	55	14	31	4.7	0.5	2.1	0.1	0.1	0.1	2.40	83	—
65–101	60	9	31	4.9	0.3	1.9	0.1	0.1	0.1	1.20	81	—
101–137	57	17	36	4.9	0.3	1.9	0.1	0.1	0.1	1.20	83	—
Florencia, Colombia. Typic Tropudult, clayey, kaolinitic, isohyperthermic (FCC = Cak)[3]												
0–16	37	16	47	4.8	2.0	3.6	0.95	0.80	0.23	5.58	64	14.5
15–85	52	18	30	4.7	0.5	7.76	0.22	0.43	0.3	8.44	92	2.0
85–173	49	21	30	4.9	0.2	6.5	0.1	0.47	0.8	7.15	91	2.0
173–208	28	31	41	4.9	0.1	7.0	0.1	0.41	0.13	7.64	92	—
208–228	20	24	56	4.5	0.1	6.8	0.2	0.56	0.11	7.67	89	—

[1]Tyler et al. (1978).
[2]Santoso and Sofyan (1984).
[3]Benavides (1973).

Malaysia, Sumatra, -Kalimantan, Sulawesi and Mindanao (Dent, 1980). In humid tropical Africa, Ultisols are abundant in the eastern Congo Basin bordering the lake region and in the forested zones of Sierra Leone, parts of Liberia and a thin forested coastal strip from the Ivory Coast through Nigeria. In the temperate region, Ultisols are the dominant soils of the southeastern United States and southeastern China.

For practical purposes, Oxisols and Ultisols can be considered together, encompassing most of the "red" soils of the humid tropics. Their main constraints are chemical: high soil acidity, aluminum toxicity, deficiency of phosphorus, potassium, calcium, magnesium, sulfur, zinc and other micronutrients, and low effective cation exchange capacity which indicates a high leaching potential. Also, Oxisols and Ultisols with clayey topsoils exhibit high capacity to fix phosphorus, but this constraint is less important in those soils with sandy or loamy topsoils. The organic matter contents of Oxisols and Ultisols are adequate and higher than many people expect (Sanchez, 1976). Their physical properties are generally excellent, but some Oxisols have low water-holding capacity and some Ultisols with pronounced increase in clay with depth are very susceptible to erosion.

Inceptisols (Cambisols, Gleysols, Andosols)

The third most widespread soils of the humid tropics are the Inceptisols, which are the dominant soils in 226 million hectares or 15% of the region. These are young soils with sufficient age to have A, B and C horizons. There are three major suborders of Inceptisols in the humid tropics, the poorly drained ones called Aquepts (Gleysols), those of volcanic origin called Andepts (Andosols), and well-drained ones of non-volcanic origin called Tropepts (Cambisols). Some representative Inceptisols are described in Table 4.5.

Aquepts (Gleysols)

Many of the Inceptisols in humid tropical Asia are devoted to lowland rice production. With the exception of acid sulfate soils, most of the wet Inceptisols are of moderate to high native soil fertility and support dense human populations. Acid sulfate soils are classified mainly as Sulfa-

quepts in soil taxonomy and as Thionic Gleysols in the FAO legend.

Aquepts also occur in the older alluvial plains along the major rivers and inland swamps of the Amazon Basin. Of the total of 42 million hectares of Aquepts in tropical America, about half are located on alluvial terraces called "várzeas" or "restingas" with good potential for intensive cultivation. The rest are mainly in palm swamps called "aguajales" in Peru.

In humid tropical Africa, there are considerable areas of wet Inceptisols locally known as hydromorphic soils. They have been traditionally avoided because of human disease hazards, many of which are no longer relevant. Moormann and Greenland (1980) and Sanchez and Buol (1985) have suggested that these soils have a significant rice production potential because Asian lowland rice production technology can be adapted to them.

Andepts (Andosols)

Inceptisols of volcanic origin, called Andepts or Andosols, are important in specific humid tropical regions of the Philippines, Indonesia and Papua New Guinea as well as in parts of Central America, the Caribbean and Ecuador. In humid tropical Africa, these soils are important in Cameroon and in the highlands of Central Africa around the lakes region. In general, Andepts are fertile and have excellent physical properties, but their main constraint is high phosphorus fixation capacity. Andepts are generally densely populated. Their existence in the Amazon is limited to the Coca region of Ecuador where intensive migration is presently taking place.

Tropepts (Cambisols)

Well-drained non-volcanic Inceptisols occupy about 56 million hectares in humid tropical Asia but are less extensive in humid tropical America or Africa. An important distinction must be made at the great group level. Dystropepts are acid Tropepts which often present characteristics very similar to those of Oxisols and Ultisols, including reddish coloration and low native fertility. Such Dystropepts (Dystric Cambisols) are abundant in the Amazon of Peru, Ecuador and Colombia as well as in Indonesia. Dystropepts are usually mixed

TABLE 4.5

Some properties of representative Inceptisols of the humid tropics

Horizon depth (cm)	Clay (%)	Silt (%)	Sand (%)	pH (1:1 H$_2$O)	Org.C (%)	Exchangeable Al (c mol kg⁻¹)	Ca (c mol kg⁻¹)	Mg (c mol kg⁻¹)	K (c mol kg⁻¹)	ECEC (c mol kg⁻¹)	Al sat. (%)	Olsen P (ppm)
Aquept: Malacca, Peninsular Malaysia. Typic Tropaquept, fine, mixed, isohyperthermic (FCC=Cg)[1]												
0–14	55.1	34.0	10.9	4.6	1.99	2.80	5.42	41.1	0.30	12.83	22	—
14–31	57.3	32.3	10.3	4.8	1.12	4.73	3.67	37.4	0.15	12.55	38	—
31–62	62.3	28.3	9.4	4.7	0.47	8.60	1.97	41.1	0.21	15.35	24	—
62–94	51.8	26.0	22.2	4.9	0.34	5.33	2.98	57.5	0.20	14.99	35	—
94–110	45.8	25.3	29.0	5.3	0.43	1.27	2.81	59.1	0.20	11.04	12	—
Andept: Kinigi, Rwanda. Udic Eutrandept, medial, non-acid, isothermic (FCC=Lx)[2]												
0–20	4.2	78.3	17.5	6.9	8.28	0	50.6	11.6	5.0	67.3	0	—
20–75	2.9	62.7	34.4	6.5	5.17	0	24.5	9.0	1.6	35.3	0	—
75–108	0.8	30.8	68.4	6.1	1.60	0	14.1	9.0	1.9	25.1	0	—
108–160	1.8	29.8	68.4	7.0	0.26	0	31.7	11.5	7.3	50.9	0	—
Tropepts: Tingo María, Peru. Fluventic Eutropept, fine loamy, mixed, isohyperthermic (FCC=L)[3]												
0–17	29	40	31	5.7	1.8	0.44	16.61	1.86	0.14	19.05	2	24
17–40	23	43	34	5.7	0.3	0.06	13.81	1.86	0.14	15.87	0	18
40–60	16	48	35	5.5	0.3	0.33	14.58	1.93	0.12	16.96	2	33
60–78	15	50	35	5.5	0.1	0.45	13.81	1.78	0.14	16.18	3	28
78–100	31	50	19	5.5	0.3	0.75	19.15	2.61	0.12	22.63	3	29
Sitiung, West Sumatra, Indonesia. Typic Dystropept, clayey, kaolinitic, isohyperthermic (FCC=Cai)[4]												
0–10	67	25	8	4.8	2.6	3.9	0.5	0.1	0.2	4.7	83	—
10–20	70	22	8	5.1	1.1	3.0	0.2	0.1	0.2	3.5	86	—
20–40	65	27	8	5.1	0.6	2.8	0.1	0.1	0.2	3.2	88	—
40–80	65	28	17	5.2	0.4	2.2	0.2	0.1	0.1	2.7	85	—

[1]Malaysian Society of Soil Science (1977).
[2]Soil Survey No. S84FN-758-010, USDA, SCS, Lincoln, Nebraska (unpublished).
[3]Sanchez and Da Silva (1984).
[4]Santoso and Sofyan (1984).

with Ultisols or Oxisols in those landscapes. An example of a Dystropept is shown in Table 4.5.

Eutropepts (Eutric Cambisols), the non-acid Tropepts, are totally different soils from the chemical and morphological point of view. They seldom exhibit reddish coloration and have high base status and native fertility. Eutropepts are found in valleys of the High Selva of Peru where they are devoted to paddy rice production or intensive cultivation. An example is shown in Table 4.5.

Entisols (Fluvents, Arenosols, Regosols, Lithosols)

The order Entisol is the fourth most extensive in the humid tropics, covering about 212 million hectares or 14% of the ecological zone. Entisols are soils of such slight or recent development that they do not show a significant degree of horizon differentiation. This order includes well-drained alluvial soils (Fluvents or Fluvisols), infertile deep sands (Psamments or Arenosols, Regosols) and many shallow soils on steep slopes or near rock outcrops, called Lithosols in the FAO legend.

Fluvents (Fluvisols)
Young alluvial soils not subject to periodic flooding are among the best soils of the world for agriculture. Humid tropical Asia is blessed with about 34 million hectares of Fluvents along the major river valleys. Most of these soils are under intensive lowland rice production. The extent of such soils in humid tropical America and Africa is unfortunately less, about 6 million hectares in humid tropical America and 10 million hectares in humid tropical Africa, both along river systems. These are excellent soils and deserve high priority in development schemes. Farmers also know they are good, and therefore most Fluvents are already cultivated. The total area of Fluvents, however, accounts for only 3% of the humid tropics. An example of a Fluvent is shown in Table 4.6.

Psamments (Arenosols, Regosols)
Deep sandy Entisols are very different soils, often very acid and of even lower native fertility than the Oxisols and Ultisols. Psamments cover 90 million hectares of the humid tropics. The largest expanses are in the western portion of the Congo Basin of Zaïre, western Central African Republic,

the headwaters of the Tapajós River in Brazil and in scattered areas around the Rio Negro basin in Brazil and Venezuela. In tropical Asia, deep sandy areas occur in Kalimantan and Sumatra. The agricultural potential of these soils is very limited and their erodibility is high. Clearing of Psamments in the humid tropics is generally not recommended.

Lithic Entisols (Lithosols)
Shallow soils over bedrock, called Lithosols in the FAO legend, cover about 72 million hectares of the humid tropics, mostly on steep slopes. They are often classified as lithic subgroups of Entisols in soil taxonomy. Although the native fertility of some of these soils is often high, their limited depth poses major constraints to agricultural development. Shallow soils are common in mountainous regions although they are also found in other areas such as the Cachimbo region of central Amazonia.

Alfisols (Luvisols, Eutric Nitosols, Planosols)

Contrary to common beliefs, there are considerable areas of well-drained soils with moderate to high native fertility in the humid tropics. Soils of the orders Alfisols, Vertisols and Mollisols are high in calcium and magnesium and therefore, of higher native fertility than the dominant Oxisols and Ultisols.

Rhodic Alfisols (Eutric Nitosols)
Many Alfisols look very much like Ultisols and Oxisols in terms of color and other morphological characteristics, but they have high base contents, and are therefore not acid or infertile. Such Alfisols cannot be separated from Oxisols or Ultisols without chemical analysis. Most of them are deep, well-drained and red or yellowish in color. These Alfisols also called Terra Roxa Estruturada in Brazil, and Eutric Nitosols in the FAO legend and many have previously been described as Latosols. In soil taxonomy, they belong to the great groups Rhodustalfs or Rhodudalfs or to Rhodic subgroups. An example is shown in Table 4.6.

Alfisols occur in "spots" among areas dominated by Oxisols and Ultisols in the Amazon Basin. Terra Roxa Estruturada soils and other Alfisols occur near Altamira, Porto Velho and Rio Branco in Brazil, in parts of the High Selva of

TABLE 4.6

Some properties of representative Entisols, Alfisols and Spodosols of the humid tropics

Horizon depth (cm)	Clay (%)	Silt (%)	Sand (%)	pH (1:1 H_2O)	Org.C (%)	Exchangeable				ECEC (c mol kg⁻¹)	Al sat. (%)	Avail. P (ppm)
						Al (c mol kg⁻¹)	Ca (c mol kg⁻¹)	Mg (c mol kg⁻¹)	K (c mol kg⁻¹)			
Entisol: Tundula, Sierra Leone. Fluventic Tropaquent, coarse-loamy, mixed, isohyperthermic (FCC=Seak)[1]												
13–28	2.3	3.6	94.1	4.5	1.08	0.5	0.14	0.07	0.04	8.0	63	–
53–84	18.2	14.4	67.4	5.0	0.28	0.69	0.36	0.30	0.10	15.1	46	–
Alfisol: Altamira, Para, Brazil. Typic Tropudalf, clayey, mixed, isohyperthermic (FCC=C)[2]												
0–8	49	7	44	7.0	2.5	0	25.24	2.28	0.28	291.6	0	8
8–26	49	23	28	7.3	0.8	0.1	5.96	0.70	0.27	89.1	0	2
26–60	50	26	24	6.9	0.5	0	3.22	0.65	0.10	55.5	0	2
60–100	56	21	23	6.4	0.3	0.1	2.47	0.43	0.09	53.4	0	3
100–130+	55	21	24	5.5	0.2	0.1	1.29	0.75	0.06	48.6	0	3
Spodosol: Manaus, Brazil. Arenic Tropaquod, isohyperthermic (FCC=Sgeak)[3]												
0–3	2	9	89	3.8	6.3	5.4	0.30		0.16	58.6	92	–
3–25	2	3	95	4.4	0.5	0.7	0.10		0.04	8.4	83	–
25–50	2	4	94	5.0	0.1	0.1	0.10		0.02	1.2	83	–
50–90	1	1	98	5.1	0.0	–	0.10		0.01	1.1	–	–
90–105	5	2	93	3.7	1.1	3.0	0.10		0.04	31.4	96	–
135–125	9	0	91	4.7	2.2	2.9	0.10		0.03	30.3	96	–
125–165	16	8	76	5.6	0.8	0.4	0		0.03	5.3	75	–

[1] Veldkamp (1980) Keya Profile.
[2] Projeto Radambrasil Vol. 16 (1978) Profile 24.
[3] Camargo and Rodrigues (1979) Profile SBCS 2.

Peru, on the humid coast of Ecuador and in the cacao-growing region of coastal Bahia in Brazil. They are excellent soils, and many of them combine the excellent physical properties of Oxisols with excellent chemical properties. In humid tropical Asia, Alfisols of the Terra Roxa type are found in several areas of the Philippines and Java. In humid tropical Africa they are confined to parts of Cameroon and southern Nigeria, where they are mapped as Eutric Nitosols.

Plinthic Alfisols (Plinthic Luvisols)

It should be emphasized that a completely different kind of Alfisol is very widespread in the subhumid forest zone of West Africa — characterized by a strong dry season. These Alfisols (called Oxic Plinthustalfs or Plinthic Luvisols) have sandy – gravelly surface layers underlaid by gravelly materials or plinthite. Although the chemical properties are favorable, they can become acidic when fertilizers are applied because of their low buffering capacity. These Alfisols therefore, have poor physical properties and poor chemical properties as well. Their management has been well studied by the International Institute of Tropical Agriculture (Lal, 1975; Greenland and Lal, 1977). These Alfisols are the dominant soils of the forested zone of West Africa.

Histosols (Histosols)

Histosols encompass the organic soils which are also known as peats or bogs. Their occurrence is minor in humid tropical America and Africa but they cover 23 million hectares of humid tropical Asia primarily in Sumatra, Kalimantan and peninsular Malaysia. A review about Histosols in Southeast Asia is available (Andriesse, 1974). Organic soils pose management difficulties because of their subsidence upon drainage, difficulties in root anchorage, and the presence of micronutrient deficiencies, particularly copper. Histosols that have a mineral horizon within one meter of the soil surface are less difficult to manage than the deep organics, which pose serious physical management problems (IRRI, 1980).

Spodosols (Podzols)

Another soil order worthy of attention is the Spodosols, also known as Podzols, Ground Water Podzols and Giant Tropical Podzols. These soils are derived from sandy materials and are found in clearly defined locations throughout the Amazon away from the flood plains. Native forest vegetation is often different from the tall rain forests found on Oxisols and Ultisols. An example is shown in Table 4.6. The Radam project identified vast areas of Spodosols along the headwaters of the Rio Negro into the Brazilian Amazon (Projeto Radambrasil 1972–1978). The presence of Spodosols largely accounts for the coffee color of this river as water passing through these soils characteristically carries suspended organic matter.

Spodosols are also abundant in southern Kalimantan, and are the main soils of Bangka and Belitung islands in Indonesia. Being extremely infertile and very susceptible to erosion, Spodosols should be best left in their natural state. Unfortunately the Spodosols have received more scientific attention than they deserve in terms of their areal extent (2.2% of the Amazon, 1% of the humid tropics). Research on tropical Podzols reported in the international literature (Klinge, 1965, 1975; Stark, 1978; Sombroek, 1979) should be kept in perspective; under no circumstances can the results be extrapolated to the dominant Oxisols and Ultisols. An example of this is Stark's (1978) discovery of a phosphorus cycling mechanism that completely bypasses the soil with a direct transfer of phosphorus from the litter to mycorrhiza in Spodosols of Venezuela. The phosphorus cycle in Oxisols and Ultisols does not exclude the soil.

Vertisols (Vertisols)

Vertisols are heavy clay soils that shrink and crack with changes in moisture content. They are generally well supplied with nutrients, except for nitrogen and phosphorus. Vertisols are not abundant in the humid tropics but are found in the High Selva of Peru, the Guayas basin of Ecuador, the lakes region of easternmost Zaïre, and in Java. These soils are also called Grumusols.

Mollisols (Chernozems, Rendzinas)

Mollisols are highly fertile soils typical of the temperate grasslands where they are also known as Chernozems and Rendzinas. They occur in small areas in the humid tropics, usually associated with limestone parent materials. Many of them are located on steep slopes. When found in flat to rolling topography, Mollisols are excellent agricultural soils.

Aridisols (Solonchaks)

The only Aridisols found in the humid tropics are the saline soils classified mainly as Salorthids or Solonchaks. Although their total extent is 0.3% of the humid tropics, saline soils occupy important coastal areas with a potential for rice production. Their constraints, however, are major (Ponnamperuma and Bandypadhya, 1980) and the ecological concerns important.

Comparisons among continents

The previous sections provide a general description of soil distribution and introduce the reader to soil taxonomy and FAO legend terminology. More technical descriptions of soil geography and its constraints in the humid tropics have been reported by Sanchez and Cochrane (1980) and Cochrane (1984) for tropical America, by Dent (1980) for humid tropical Asia, by Moormann and Greenland (1980) for humid tropical Africa, and by Dudal (1980) for the tropics as a whole. In spite of the difference in data base, some broad generalizations can be made in comparing the humid tropics of America, Asia and Africa

(Table 4.7). Acid soils of the orders Oxisols and Ultisols plus Dystropepts cover the largest area in all the humid tropical regions, but their relative importance is greater in Latin America (82%) than in Africa (56%) or Asia (38%). The inverse occurs with moderately fertile to fertile soils of high base status which cover as much as 33% of humid tropical Asia, 12% of humid tropical Africa but only 7% of humid tropical America. Most of these fertile soils in Asia are already under intensive cultivation; therefore, the potential for area expansion into good soils is very limited. This is not the case in humid tropical Africa.

Three broad kinds of problem soils with severe management limitations — the acid sands (Psamments, Spodosols), the shallow soils (Lithosols) and the organics (Histosols) — occur in somewhat similar proportion in the three regions, except for the greater importance of organic soils in Asia and the deep sandy soils in humid tropical Africa.

In summary, the distribution of soils of the humid tropical regions of the world follows a pattern of dominance of acid infertile soils, with the smallest proportion of reasonably fertile, well-drained soils in Latin America and the largest in Asia. On the other hand, the humid tropics of Latin America have the lowest proportion of the "problem soils" (5%) while Asia has the highest (22%). In these broad soil comparisons, humid tropical Africa lies somewhere in between humid tropical America and Asia.

TABLE 4.7

General distribution of main kinds of soils in the humid tropics (calculated from Table 4.1)

General soil grouping	Humid tropical America (%)	Humid tropical Africa (%)	Humid tropical Asia and Pacific (%)	World's humid tropics (%)
Acid, low native fertility soils (Ferralsols, Acrisols, Dystric Nitosols)	81	56	38	63
Moderately fertile, well-drained soils (Luvisols, Vertisols, Chernozems, Andosols, Cambisols, Fluvisols)	7	12	33	15
Poorly drained soils (Gleysols)	6	12	6	8
Very infertile sandy soils (Arenosols, Podzols)	2	16	6	7
Shallow soils (Lithosols)	3	3	10	5
Organic soils (Histosols)	1	1	6	2
Total	100	100	100	100

COMMON MISCONCEPTIONS

Three common misconceptions about soils in the humid tropics deserve clarification at this point. They relate to laterization, organic matter contents and the distribution of nutrients between plant biomass and soil under tropical rain forests.

Laterite formation

The dangers of laterite formation after clearing tropical forests are very limited (Sanchez and Buol, 1975; Moormann and Van Wambeke, 1978; Buol and Sanchez, 1978). In the Amazon, only 6% of the region has soft plinthite in the subsoil, a substance capable of hardening into laterite if this layer is exposed by erosion. These soils are mainly classified as Plinthaquults or Plinthaqualfs (Plinthic Acrisols or Plinthic Luvisols). Since most of these plinthic soils occur in flat, poorly drained topographical positions, the danger of laterite formation is minimal, as it would require massive soil erosion to expose it.

Hardened laterite of geologic origin occurs in scattered areas in the humid tropics, where it serves as excellent road building material. In areas like the Peruvian Amazon, which is essentially devoid of these laterite formations, low-cost roads are definitely inferior in comparison with those of the state of Pará in Brazil where laterite outcrops occur. The laterite hazard, still frequently mentioned in the literature, is therefore of little importance in the humid tropics as a constraint. On the contrary, where laterite outcrops occur they are definitely an asset to development.

It is interesting to note that hardened laterite and plinthic soils are more abundant in the subhumid and semiarid tropics than in the humid tropics. Plinthic soils are also abundant in the southeastern United States, where nobody worries about them.

Organic matter content

Soil organic matter content in soils of the humid tropics compares very favorably to soils of temperate forests. Table 4.8 indicates somewhat higher organic carbon and total nitrogen levels in tropical than temperate region soils. Sanchez et al. (1982b) also found no significant difference in organic

TABLE 4.8

Mean soil organic matter content of soils from the tropical and temperate forests (from Sanchez et al., 1982b)

Parameter	Depth (cm)	Tropical forests	Temperate forests	Significance (P%)
%C	0–15	1.89	1.35	1–5
	0–50	1.14	0.56	< 1
	0–100	0.70	0.33	< 1
%N	0–15	0.182	0.082	5–10
	0–50	0.122	0.046	1–5
	0–100	0.086	0.030	< 1
C/N	0–15	11.3	17.6	5–10
	0–50	10.3	13.2	ns
	0–100	9.0	11.3	ns

matter content between soils of the tropics vs. the temperate region, between Oxisols of the tropics and Mollisols of the temperate region, or between tropical vs. temperate Ultisols. Calculations of fresh organic matter additions and decomposition rates explain the lack of differences (Sanchez and Buol, 1975). In all forested ecosystems, soil organic matter is more concentrated in the topsoil than in the subsoil; this premise holds for tropical forests as well as their temperate counterparts.

Plant nutrient storage in the humid tropics

Another commonly held view is that tropical rain forests essentially feed themselves, since most humid tropical soils are very poor in nutrients (Goodland and Irwin, 1975). Nutrient cycling studies that include the entire soil profile, however, show that most of the ecosystem's nitrogen and phosphorus are located in the soil and not in the biomass (Table 4.9). This is not the case with potassium, calcium and magnesium, the bulk of which remains in the above-ground biomass. An exception to the latter statement occurs on Alfisols of high base status, which also contain the bulk of their bases in the soil. For more details, the readers are referred to a review by Salati and Vose (1984) and Jordan (1985).

SOIL CONSTRAINTS TO PLANT GROWTH

A soil constraint analysis was done using the Fertility Capability Classification System [de-

TABLE 4.9

Proportion of ecosystem nutrient storage in biomass and soil compartments under native humid tropical forests

Location	Soil	N	P	K+	Ca2+	Mg2+
		% of total in the soil				
Manaus, Brazil[1]	Oxisol	73	69	11	0	8
Merida, Venezuela[2]	Inceptisol	81	91	14	31	31
Carare, Colombia[3]	Oxisol	71	85	28	5	21
Kade, Ghana[4]	Alfisol	81	–	56	61	61

[1]Fittkau and Klinge (1973); [2]Fassbender (1977); [3]De las Salas (1978); [4]Greenland and Kowal (1960).

scribed by Buol et al. (1975) and Sanchez et al. (1982a)] to convert the geographical distribution data based on FAO soil maps to constraints for humid tropical Asia, Africa and America. The humid tropics of Australia and the Pacific islands are not included in these calculations.

Topography

The major landscape classes of each region are shown in Table 4.10. Approximately one-third of the humid tropics has flat to gentle topography (<8% slope) and good drainage. Another third has rolling topography (8–30% slopes), one-sixth steep topography and one-sixth flat, poorly drained topography. Among the regions, humid tropical Africa has the least land on steep topography and the most in flat, well-drained areas.

Texture

Soil texture is usually the first parameter used for appraising soils. Data in Table 4.11 show that about half of the soils of the humid tropics have clayey textures throughout the profile, and about 40% have loamy topsoils underlain by either loamy or clayey subsoils. Only 14% of the soils are sandy and 2% organic. Among the regions, humid tropical Africa has the largest proportion of sandy soils.

Chemical and physical constraints

The area distribution of main soil constraints to plant growth in the humid tropics is shown in Table 4.12. The most extensive constraints are chemical (low nutrient reserves: 64%; aluminum toxicity: 56%; high phosphorus fixation: 37%), followed by mild acidity 18%, steep slopes 17%,

TABLE 4.10

Area distribution (in 10^6 ha) of landscape classes in the world humid tropics. Calculated according to Sanchez et al. (1982a)

Landscape and % slope classes	Humid tropical America	Humid tropical Africa	Humid tropical Asia	Humid tropics total	%
Flat (0–8%), poorly drained	90	59	42	191	13
Flat (0–8%), well drained	173	201	49	523	36
Rolling (8–30%)	290	142	59	491	34
Steep (30% +)	144	22	73	239	17
Total	797	424	223	1444	100

TABLE 4.11

Textural class distribution of soils in the humid tropics (in 10^6 ha). Calculated according to Sanchez et al. (1982a)

Textural class	Humid tropical America	Humid tropical Africa	Humid tropical Asia	Humid tropics	
				Total	%
Clayey	453	115	78	646	45
Loamy	144	139	53	337	23
Loamy over clayey	123	51	57	231	16
Sandy	69	105	17	191	13
Sandy over loamy	4	10	4	18	1
Organic	4	4	14	22	2
Total	797	424	223	1444	100

TABLE 4.12

Area distribution of soil constraints in humid tropical regions. Calculated according to Sanchez et al. (1982a)

Soil constraint	Tropical America		Tropical Africa		Tropical Asia		Humid tropics	
	10^6ha	(%)	10^6ha	(%)	10^6ha	(%)	10^6ha	(%)
Low nutrient reserves	543	(66)	285	(67)	101	(45)	929	(64)
Aluminum toxicity	490	(61)	226	(53)	92	(41)	808	(56)
High P fixation	379	(47)	84	(20)	74	(33)	537	(37)
Acid, not Al toxic	88	(11)	92	(22)	74	(33)	255	(18)
Slopes steeper than 30%	145	(18)	22	(5)	73	(33)	241	(17)
Poor drainage	90	(11)	59	(14)	42	(19)	191	(13)
Low ECEC	68	(8)	87	(20)	10	(5)	165	(11)
Shallow depth	54	(7)	17	(4)	27	(12)	98	(7)
No major limitations	28	(3)	7	(2)	5	(2)	40	(3)
Shrink-swell	11	(1)	2	(1)	3	(2)	17	(1)
Allophane	8	(1)	1	(−)	4	(2)	13	(1)
Acid sulfate soils	2	(−)[1]	5	(1)	6	(3)	13	(1)
Gravel	2	(−)	6	(1)	3	(1)	10	(1)
Salinity	3	(−)	1	(−)	4	(2)	8	(−)
Sodic soils	5	(1)	3	(1)	1	(−)	9	(−)

[1] < 1%.

poor drainage 13%, low effective cation exchange capacity 11% and shallow depth 7%. Only 3% of the soils have no major limitations, except for nitrogen deficiency.

These constraints are relevant when appraising developing possibilities. The chemical constraints can be overcome relatively easily with fertilization or with the use of low-input systems for annual crops, pastures or agroforestry. The physical constraints are much harder to overcome, particularly steep slopes and shallow depth. The relative distribution of soil constraints in the humid tropics is rather similar to that of the southeastern United States where agriculture and forestry are both profitable and stable.

Perspective

These constraints are not overwhelming for agricultural production: with judicious soil and crop management practices, sustained production is possible in the humid tropics for annual crops

(Valverde and Bandy, 1982), pastures (Toledo and Morales, 1979; Serrão et al., 1979), and perennial crops (Alvim, 1979, 1982; Chan, 1979). A balance between conservation and development can be achieved in the humid tropics provided sound soil management technology is used, so for each hectare that is cleared and put into sustained production, many hectares will be saved from the shifting cultivator's axe and hopefully remain in its natural state. Without technology, there is little hope for anything but increasingly rampant deforestation, poor yields and subsequent soil degradation.

CONCLUSIONS

Soils of tropical rain forests are so variable that few generalizations can be made. Approximately 35% of the humid tropics is covered by Oxisols, 28% by Ultisols, 15% by Inceptisols and 14% by Entisols, with minor proportions of the remaining soil orders. Approximately one-third of the area has flat to gently sloping, well-drained topography, another third rolling topography with slopes between 8 and 10%, and the rest equally divided between flat poorly drained landscapes and steep ones. Considering both soils and topography, the humid tropics have 63% of its area in acid soils with low native fertility on flat to gently rolling, well-drained landscapes, 15% moderately fertile soils in various landscape positions, 8% of poorly drained soils, 7% of acid very infertile soils, 5% in shallow soils and 2% of organic soils. The proportion of high base status soils is highest in humid tropical Asia. The danger of laterite formation after clearing tropical forest is very limited. Organic matter contents of soils under tropical rain forests are similar to soils under temperate forests. Most of the nitrogen and phosphorus of the rain-forest ecosystem is stored in the soil rather than in the plant biomass, but the reverse is true for calcium, magnesium and potassium in Oxisols and Ultisols. The most widespread soil constraints to plant growth in the humid tropics are chemical rather than physical. The most widespread ones are low nutrient reserves (64%), aluminum toxicity (56%) and high phosphorus fixation (37%). Sound soil management technologies exist for overcoming these constraints and permit sustained production of annual crops, pastures and perennial crops. The judicious use of this technology will promote a balance between conservation and development in the humid tropics.

REFERENCES

Alvim, P.T., 1979. Agricultural production potential of the Amazon region. In: P.A. Sanchez and L.E. Tergas (Editors), *Pasture Production in Acid Soils of the Tropics.* CIAT, Cali, Colombia, pp. 13–23.

Alvim, P.T., 1982. An appraisal of perennial crops in the Amazon Basin. In: S.B. Hecht (Editor), *Amazonia: Agriculture and Land Use Research.* CIAT, Cali, Colombia, pp. 311–328.

Andriesse, J.P., 1974. *Tropical lowland peats of Southeast Asia.* Royal Tropical Institute, Amsterdam, Commun. 63, 63 pp.

Benavides, S.T., 1973. *Mineralogical and chemical characteristics of some soils of the Amazonia of Colombia.* Ph.D. Thesis, North Carolina State Univ., Raleigh, N.C.

Buol, S.W. and Sanchez, P.A., 1978. Rainy tropical climates: Physical, potential, present and improved farming systems. *Proc. 11th Int. Soil Sci. Congress,* Edmonton, Alta., 2: 292–312.

Buol, S.W., Sanchez, P.A., Cate, R.B. and Granger, M.A., 1975. Soil fertility capability classification. In: E. Bornemisza and A. Alvarado (Editors), *Soil Management in Tropical America.* North Carolina State Univ., Raleigh, N.C., pp. 126–141.

Camargo, M.N. and Rodrigues, T.E. (Editors), 1979. Guía de Excursão. *XVII Congreso Brasileiro de Ciencia do Solo (Manaus).* Serviço Nacional de Levantamento e Conservação de Solos. EMBRAPA, Rio de Janeiro, 71 pp.

Chan, H.Y., 1979. *Tropical Tree Crop Requirements and Land Evaluation: a Case Experience in Malaysia.* Rubber Research Institute of Malaysia, Kuala Lumpur, Mimcographed, 34 pp.

Cochrane, T.T., 1984. Amazonia: a computerized overview of its climate, landscape and soil resources. *Interciencia,* 9: 298–306.

Cochrane, T.T. and Sanchez, P.A., 1982. Land resources, soils and their management in the Amazon region: a state of knowledge report. In: S.B. Hecht (Editor), *Amazonia: Agriculture and Land Use Research.* CIAT, Cali, Colombia, pp. 137–209.

De las Salas, G., 1978. *El Sistema Forestal Carare-Upón.* CONIF SER. Tec. 8.

Dent, F.J., 1980. Major production systems and soil-related qualities in humid tropical Asia. In: *Soil-Related Constraints to Food Production in the Tropics.* Int. Rice Res. Inst., Los Baños, Philippines, pp. 79–106.

Dudal, R., 1980. Soil-related constraints to agricultural development in the tropics. In: *Soil-Related Constraints to Food Production in the Tropics.* Int. Rice Res. Int., Los Baños, Philippines, pp. 23–37.

FAO–UNESCO, 1971, 1975, 1977a, b, 1978, 1979. *Soil Map of the World.* Vol. III (Mexico and Central America), Vol. IV (South America), Vol. V (Africa), Vol. VIII (South Asia),

Vol. IX (Southeast Asia), Vol. X (Australia and Oceania). UNESCO, Paris.

Fassbender, H.W., 1977. Ciclos de elementos nutritivos en ecosistema forestales tropicales y su transformación con la agricultura rotativa. In: FAO–SIDA, *Reunión–Taller sobre Ordenación y Conservación de Suelos en América Latina.* Lima, Peru.

Fittkau, E.J. and Klinge, H., 1973. On biomass and trophic structure of the Central Amazonian forest ecosystem. *Biotropica*, 5(1): 2–14.

Friedman, I., 1977. The Amazon basin, another Sahel? *Science*, 197: p. 7.

Goodland, R.J.A. and Irwin, H.S., 1975. *Amazon Jungle: Green Hell to Red Desert?* Elsevier, Amsterdam, 156 pp.

Greenland, D.J. and Kowal, J.M.L., 1960. Nutrient content of a moist tropical forest in Ghana. *Plant Soil*, 12: 154–174.

Greenland, D.J. and Lal, R. (Editors), 1977. *Soil Conservation and Management in the Humid Tropics.* Wiley, New York, N.Y., 283 pp.

Irion, G., 1978. Soil infertility in the Amazonian rain forest. *Naturwissenschaften*, 65: 515–519.

IRRI (Int. Rice Res. Inst.), 1980. Research priorities. In: *Priorities for Alleviating Soil-Related Constraints to Food Production in the Tropics.* Los Baños, Philippines, pp. 451–457.

Jordan, C.F., 1985. *Nutrient Cycling in Tropical Forest Ecosystems.* Wiley, New York, N.Y., 190 pp.

Klinge, H., 1965. Podzol soils in the Amazon basin. *J. Soil Sci.*, 16: 95–103.

Klinge, H., 1975. Root mass estimation in lowland tropical rain forests of central Amazonia, Brazil. III. Nutrients in fine roots from giant humus podzols. *Trop. Ecol.*, 16: 28–39.

Lal, R., 1975. Soil erosion problems on an Alfisol of Western Nigeria and their control. *Int. Inst. Trop. Agric., Monogr., 1*: 159 pp.

Malaysian Society of Soil Science, 1977. Characteristics of some soils in Peninsular Malaysia. *Conf. on Classification and Management of some Tropical Soils.* Kuala Lumpur, Malaysia.

Marbut, C.F. and Manifold, C.B., 1926. The soils of the Amazon basin in relation to agricultural possibilities. *Geogr. Rev.*, 16: 414–442.

McNeil, M., 1964. Lateritic soils. *Sci. Am.*, 211(5): 96–102.

Moormann, F.R. and Greenland, D.J., 1980. Major production systems and soil-related qualities in humid tropical Africa. In: *Priorities for Alleviating Soil-Related Constraints to Food Production in the Tropics.* Int. Rice Res. Inst., Los Baños, Philippines, pp. 55–78.

Moormann, F.R. and Van Wambeke, A., 1978. The soils of the lowland rainy tropical climates, their inherent limitations for food production and related climatic restraints. *Trans. 11th Congress Int. Soc. Soil Sci.*, Edmonton, Alta., 2: 292–312.

Ponnamperuma, F.N. and Bandypadhya, A.K., 1980. Soil salinity as a constraint on food production in the humid tropics. In: *Priorities for Alleviating Soil-Related Constraints to Food Production in the Tropics.* Int. Rice Res. Inst., Los Baños, Philippines, pp. 203–216.

Projeto Radambrasil, 1972–1978. *Levantamento da Região Amazônica.* Vols. 1–12. Ministerio das Minas e Energía,

Dep. Nacional da Produção Mineral, Rio de Janeiro.

Reiss, S., Rother, L., Jensen, H., Came, B., Taylor, J. and Lord, M., 1980. Vanishing Forests. *Newsweek*, 24: 117–122.

Salati, E. and Vose, P.B., 1984. Amazon Basin: A system in equilibrium. *Science*, 225: 129–137.

Sanchez, P.A., 1976. *Properties and Management of Soils in the Tropics.* Wiley, New York, N.Y.

Sanchez, P.A. and Buol, S.W., 1975. Soils of the tropics and the world food crisis. *Science*, 188: 598–603.

Sanchez, P.A. and Buol, S.W., 1985. Agronomic taxonomy for wetland soils. In: *Wetland Soils: Characterization, Classification and Utilization.* Int. Rice Res. Inst., Los Baños, Philippines, pp. 207–227.

Sanchez, P.A. and Cochrane, T.T., 1980. Soil constraints in relation to major farming systems in tropical America. In: *Priorities for Alleviating Soil-Related Constraints to Food Production in the Tropics.* Int. Rice Res. Inst., Los Baños, Philippines, pp. 197–239.

Sanchez, P.A. and Da Silva, L.F., 1984. *Proyecto de Investigación en Suelos.* Red de Investigación Agroecológica para la Amazonía (REDINAA), Lima.

Sanchez, P.A., Couto, W. and Buol, S.W., 1982a. The fertility capability soil classification system: interpretation, applicability and modification. *Geoderma*, 27: 283–309.

Sanchez, P.A., Gichuru, M.P. and Katz, L.B., 1982b. Organic matter in major soils of the tropical and temperate regions. In: *12th Int. Congress of Soil Science*, New Delhi, 1: 99–114.

Santoso, D. and Sofyan, A., 1984. *Penelitian pengelonaan tanak podsolik. Program Tropsoils Laporan Tahunan, 1982–83.* Pusat Penelitan Tanak, Bogor, Indonesia.

Serrão, E.A.S., Falesi, I.C., Veiga, J.B. and Texeira, J.F., 1979. Productivity of cultivated pastures in low fertility soils of the Amazon of Brazil. In: P.A. Sanchez and L.E. Tergas (Editors), *Pasture Production in Acid Soils of the Tropics.* Centro Internacional de Agricultura Tropical, Cali, Colombia, pp. 195–226.

Soil Survey Staff, 1975. *Soil Taxonomy. A Basic System of Soil Classification for Making and Interpreting Soil Surveys.* U.S. Dept. Agric. Handbook 436, Washington, D.C.

Sombroek, W.G., 1979. *Soils of the Amazon Region.* International Soils Museum, Wageningen, Unpubl. Pap., 15 pp.

Stark, N., 1978. Man, tropical forests and the biological life of a soil. *Biotropica*, 10: 1–10.

Toledo, J.M. and Morales, V.A., 1979. Establishment and management of improved pastures in the Peruvian Amazon. In: P.A. Sanchez and L.E. Tergas (Editors), *Pasture Production in Acid Soils of the Tropics.* Centro Internacional de Agricultura Tropical, Cali, Colombia, pp. 177–194.

Tyler, E.J., Buol, S.W. and Sanchez, P.A., 1978. Genetic association of properties of soils of an area in the upper Amazon of Peru. *Soil Sci. Soc. Am., J.*, 42: 771–776.

Valverde, C.S. and Bandy, D.E., 1982. Production of annual food crops in the Amazon. In: S.B. Hecht (Editor), *Amazonia: Agriculture and Land Use Research.* CIAT, Cali, Colombia, pp. 243–280.

Veldkamp, W.J., 1980. *Soil Survey and Land Evaluation in the Mano River Union Area (Eastern Sierra Leone and Western Liberia).* Land Resources Survey Project, Mano River Union, Monrovia (Liberia), Freetown (Sierra Leone).

Chapter 5

HYDROLOGY

W.L.F. BRINKMANN

INTRODUCTION

There are many ways to define the spatial, three-dimensional extension of the Continuously Humid Tropics (CHT), but none of the approaches offers a reasonable solution for all questions raised in tackling the needs of the different fields of research such as climatology, hydrology, soil science, agriculture, forestry and land development.

DEFINITION OF THE AREA

The global distribution of the CHT covered in this chapter (Fig. 5.1) is determined by the complex equatorial circulation patterns, which are represented by the flow dynamics of the Inter-Tropical Convergence Zones (ITCZ) and the monsoon circulation (for more detail see Ch. 2). Up to now, the three-dimensional air-mass exchange mechanisms in the lower troposphere near the equator are insufficiently described only by the interactions of zonal and meridonal circulation dynamics (Walker and Headley circulations). The quasi-stationary position of the double structured ITC Zones (Fig. 1a, b), which are characterized by a strong cloudband at about 6°N the year round and an oscillating, less-structured cloudband distribution between 5° and 10°S (Flohn, 1971) contain the area of the CHT, which coincide fairly well with the areal extension of the tropical rain forests, the distribution patterns of multi-colored, partly bleached latosols and lateritic soils on land never flooded (terra firme), and the area of substantial, mainly convective rainfall (average yearly rainfall above 1700 mm). The CHT areas are coupled with high temperature and a strong evapotranspiration,

derived from the low-latitude and low-altitude rain-forest and wetland systems, which force the bulk of rainwater to be regionally recycled into the tropical atmosphere (recycled water of the combined yearly averages of interception and evapotranspiration being above 1300 mm). Besides the circulation-bound effects on the CHT areas, the three-dimensional distribution of the CHT is elevation-controlled (J. Chang and L. St. Lau, pers. commun., 1983) by the average altitudes of the 18°C isotherm of the monthly average of the coldest month of the year (Fig. 1c). More details about the climate controlled boundaries of the CHT is given in Ch. 2.

LIMITATIONS OF THE APPROACH

There are detailed and thorough studies on the quantitative and/or qualitative hydrology for a number of aquatic and semi-aquatic systems in the CHT. Studying the hydrology of these systems means research on various types of water bodies such as rivers, lakes, man-made lakes, temporarily flooded forests, wetlands, swamps and marshes.

For river systems of the CHT, the availability of information and knowledge on the spatial and temporal distribution patterns of their hydrographs and chemographs is limited as a whole, while non-existent in many tropical regions, even nowadays.

The data-base on the hydrologic conditions, the physicochemical and biological-biochemical properties of the other-than-river aquatic and semi-aquatic systems in the CHT is extremely poor, except for some small-scale studies on individual water bodies.

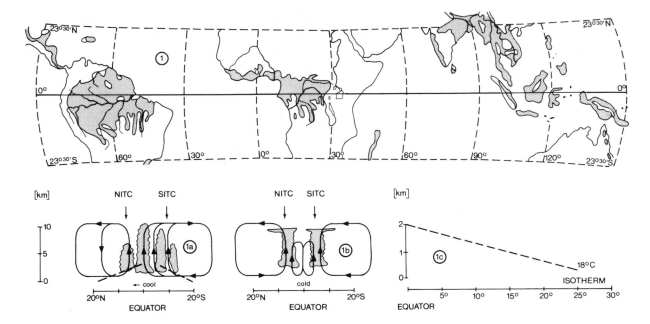

Fig. 5.1. Global distribution patterns of the CHT (*1*); meridional circulation patterns in the tropics* [symmetrical model, warm equator (*1a*); symmetrical model, cold equator (*1b*)] and average altitudes of coldest month isotherm of 18°C in the tropics** (*Flohn, 1971; **Chang and Lau, 1984).

Writing a chapter on the hydrology of the CHT means:

(1) To define the area of the CHT knowing about the limitations of the approach.

(2) To acknowledge the lack of a sound hydrologic data-base in the CHT (frequently available for river systems and lakes in the temperate, mid-latitude zones), which follows from the low-density network of stream gauges and meteorologic stations, the shortness of operation of existing stations, and the operational difficulties in areas difficult to access.

(3) To produce a study, which is (i) selective, non-representative with concern to spatial distribution patterns and for specific features of water bodies such as river systems, lakes, flooded river fringe-forests, swamps, wetlands and marshes; (ii) limited in terms of data-base on the quantitative and/or qualitative hydrologic properties of these water bodies; and (iii) very approximate in the presentation of ways and means for the understanding of the features, dynamics and controls of the aquatic and semi-aquatic systems studied.

OBJECTIVES

The objectives of this chapter are: (i) to review on the quantitative and qualitative hydrology of the CHT being a basic tool for the understanding of the ecology of the tropical environment; (ii) to identify global similarities in water and element cycle-bound mechanisms and properties controlling CHT ecosystems; and (iii) to discriminate on a regional and/or continental scale the specific identities of tropical water bodies.

CHT RIVER REGIMES

The combined hydrograph and chemograph of a river at a specific gaging station is a complex function of land-use and geochemical background of the upstream watershed, the spatial and temporal, integrated output of physical, chemical and biological mechanisms processed in the drainage basin and the climate, mainly the rainfall regime. Small rivers often are fed from homogeneous drainage basins; great river systems, however, may cover partly different climatic zones and various areas of different geochemical background. In fact, the great rivers of the equatorial tropics, — the river systems of the Amazon and the Zaïre — present by no means a characteristic river regime of the CHT. They combine individual flow characteristics of numerous smaller rivers into one composite river system of the typical one-peak (unimodal) or multi-peak (at least bimodal) river regime of the CHT (Fig. 5.2A, B).

The runoff regime (Pardé, 1953) at a specific point along the course of a river, mainly a gaging station, is given by the ratio of the long-term average monthly discharge and the average yearly discharge (MQ_m/MQ_y in m^3 s^{-1}). The great river systems of the CHT, the Amazon (Obidos) and the Zaire (Kinshasa) are characterized by MQ_m/MQ_y ratios close to 1 at their lower gages.

The extensive, continuous rainfall on vast areas of the drainage basins, the basin structure of great parts of the catchments and the composite structure of the flow regimes produced by the numerous tributaries with attachments of one-peak (unimodal) and multi-peak (at least bimodal) runoff regimes are the controls of these particular river regimes (Fig. 5.2C). On the other hand, significant differences occur, primarily affected by the differences of altitude, relief and the distribution of patterns of geochemical units in the catchments. But both river regimes compare even less with the hydrologic features of rivers of the mountainous

Asian CHT (Malaya, Java, Indonesia, Papua New Guinea), where steep slopes and excessive rainfall are the dominant factors controlling the river hydro- and chemographs.

SPECIFIC RUNOFF OF CHT RIVER BASINS

The specific runoff (1 l s^{-1} km^{-2}) of a catchment is given by the ratio of the average yearly runoff (Q) and the surface drainage area of the catchment (A).

The rainfall regime, the relief, the areal water retention capacity of the catchment, the vegetation cover and the river gradients control mainly the yield of a catchment. For the Amazon Basin, the Zaïre Basin and different river catchments in Malaya, Papua New Guinea and Java the calculated average annual yields reveal characteristic distribution patterns (Fig. 5.3), which may be summarized as follows: (i) the "normal" yields of great tropical lowland catchments in the CHT are represented by the Amazon and its great tributaries, of which about ten have a length of more than 1000 km (some African and Asian river systems fit also into this model); (ii) the Zaïre drainage system, mainly the lower parts of the saucer-like basin, produce low yields; and (iii) the steep-slope mountain catchments of many rivers in Java, Indonesia, Malaya and Papua New Guinea generate high to excessive yields, of which the erosion power is fairly controlled by vegetation

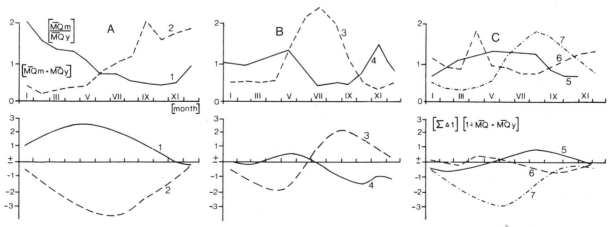

Fig. 5.2. Runoff regimes of CHT rivers. (A) one-peak type (*1* = river Brantas at Pogadjih; *2* = river Sanaga at Edéa); (B) multi-peak type (*3* = river Essequibo at Plantain Island; *4* = river Ogooué at Lambarene); (C) great rivers of the CHT (*5* = river Amazon at Obidos; *6* = river Zaïre at Kinshasa; *7* = river Orinoco at Bolivar). Data sources: Balek, 1977, 1983; UNESCO, 1978; Rodier, 1983.

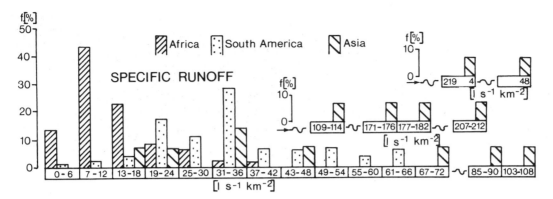

Fig. 5.3. Relative frequency distribution of specific runoff of CHT river basins. Data sources: Bishop, 1973; Balek, 1977; UNESCO, 1978; Németh et al., 1982; Bruijnzeel, 1983; Paolini et al., 1983; Rodier, 1983; Petr, 1983; Pickup, 1983.

cover. The distribution patterns of the specific runoff of CHT river basins point out the latent endanger-potentials in the different drainage basins. Obviously, soil erosion in steep-sloped mountain catchments, but even in tropical lowlands, is considerably buffered by the rain forests. In mountain catchments with very high rainfall changes in land-use practice, even on a local-scale, will cause dramatic soil erosion.

WATER BALANCE OF CHT RIVER SYSTEMS

The water balance of river basins or sub-basins of the CHT in South America, Africa and parts of Asia was calculated as a long-term balance. Data are extracted from various sources (Schmidt, 1972; Bishop, 1973; Balek, 1977, 1983; UNESCO, 1978; Németh et al., 1982; Rodier, 1983; Bruijnzeel, 1983; Pickup, 1983; Salati et al., 1983; Salati and Vose, 1983; Paolini et al., 1983; Brinkmann, 1985).

The water balance is written as:

precipitation (mm) = runoff (mm) + retention (mm)

where the retention contains mainly, but not exclusively, water recycled into the atmosphere (evapotranspiration). For a better comparison, the water balance of CHT catchments was designed (Fig. 5.4) as the ratios of retention/precipitation (%) and runoff/precipitation (%). The results of the water balance estimates presented in Fig. 5.4 are very approximate because of the lack of representative distribution of the meteorologic and hydrologic stations in the catchments.

CHT river catchments are usually intensively covered with rain forests, which are the most important water retention regulatives besides swamps and lakes, the CHT water balance of individual river catchments is controlled by (i) the amount of annual rainfall and its spatial/temporal distribution patterns; (ii) the exposure of the drainage basin to orographic units such as steep-slope mountains, mountain foot-hill zones and lowlands; and (iii) the abundance of swamps, wetlands, seasonally flooded forests and lakes in between the respective orographic units.

Knowing about the limitations of the approach, the water balances composed for a number of CHT river systems (Fig. 5.4) allow for the following conclusions: (i) the retention capacity of CHT catchments in decreasing order of magnitude is: the Zaïre system, the Amazon system and the Asian river systems; (ii) inbetween the South American, the African and the Asian CHT systems, the retention capacity in increasing order of magnitude is mountain land, foothill-zones and lowlands for one-unit, orographically homogenous drainage basins. In most of the cases, the individual water balances display the mixed composition of orographic units in the catchments; (iii) both great river systems, the Amazon and the Zaïre, contain central areas where excessive amounts of water are recycled into the atmosphere, while Asian CHT river systems do not participate on the high evapotranspiration rates, because of steep river gradients; and (iv) primarily the Asian CHT river systems, mentioned in this study, reveal a potential erosion hazard, which immediately is triggered

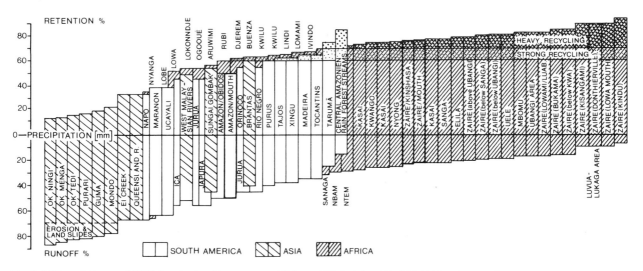

Fig. 5.4. Water balance of CHT river basins. Data sources: Bishop, 1973; Balek, 1977; UNESCO, 1977; Bruijnzeel, 1983; Rodier, 1983; Petr, 1983; Pickup, 1983; Salati and Vose, 1983; Salati et al., 1983; Brinkmann, 1986.

even by local-scale changes of land-use practices (logging, mining, deforestation). In the Amazon and the Zaïre systems, large-scale deforestation is thought to have similar effects.

A considerable amount of short- and long-term water retention in the Amazon and Zaïre systems is brought about by semi-aquatic systems (swamps, flooded fringe-forests and wetlands, mainly in floodplain areas; Balek and Perry, 1973; Beadle, 1974; Serruya and Pollingher, 1983) and lakes.

While the water level of the Zaïre river fluctuates at the gages in the order of about 3.5 m at the most (Marlier, 1973) the floodwaters of the Amazon and of some tributaries inundate the floodplains (var-zéas) and river fringe-forests (Igapós) up to 10 m above the low water level. Although the annual fluctuations of both rivers are significantly differ-ent, its effect on the water balances is a pronounced increase in residence time and areal expansion of open-water surfaces, which contribute additionally to evaporation during the flood seasons. The greatest evapotranspiration rates are obtained from swamps and wetlands (Fig. 5.4). This stands for the varzéa water bodies of the Amazon floodplains, vast areas of Asia (Furtado and Mori, 1982; Serruya and Pollingher, 1983), but in particular for the large depressions in the center of the Zaïre catchment, where lakes and Papyrus swamps extend over thousands of square kilo-meters (Marlier, 1973; Rodier, 1983).

The great CHT river systems, the Amazon and the Zaïre, contain potentials for global fresh-water supply and hydroelectric power generation. Al-though the impact of man on the tropical rain forests is growing, the exploitation of the natural resources such as fresh water and hydroelectric power generation (man-made lakes) are only at the beginning of development.

HYDROGEOCHEMISTRY OF CHT RIVER SYSTEMS

The temporal and areal concentration patterns of total dissolved solids (TDS) and total suspended sediments (TSS) in waters of CHT river systems, which are widely undisturbed by man, produce a thorough overview on the elemental release mech-anisms of rain forests. The elemental composition of river waters produces information on the lithological background of the catchment, the rain regime and climate, the predominant geochemical weathering processes, the retention capacity of forests and soils for specific constituents and the eroding power of flowing water in the drainage basins (Gibbs, 1967; Brinkmann, 1981, 1985, 1986; Emeis and Stoffers, 1982; Richey, 1982; Irion, 1983; Irion and Petr, 1983; Paolini et al., 1983; Stallard and Edmond, 1983). Further on, signifi-cant changes in amount and elemental composi-tion of TDS and TSS along the course of the rivers reveal the hydrologic/hydrodynamic regime of the respective river sections (gradients, deposition, erosion) and provide suggestions and insights about the controls of the exchange mechanisms between river and bed-sediment, river and flood-plain, river and lakes/swamps and last but not least river and inundation forests. Obviously, the geochemical regime of CHT rivers is defined by the temporal and areal distribution patterns of loads ($g\ s^{-1}$) of dissolved and suspended solids (these are calculated from the discharge ($m^3\ s^{-1}$) of the river and the concentration ($mg\ l^{-1}$) of dissolved and suspended constituents in the river waters) and the amount and elemental composition of the loads. There are a number of sophisticated case studies on hydrogeochemistry in the CHT environment, but comparative studies using specific elements for the discrimination of water types are scarce (Sioli, 1950, 1964; Marlier, 1973; Emeis and Stoffers, 1982; Ittekkot et al., 1982; Ittekkot et al., 1983; Irion, 1983).

Reviewing the hydrological and hydrochemical data-base of the CHT, which is available for a very limited number of river basins, the combination of parameters such as the specific runoff (Fig. 5.3), the specific transport of the dissolved solids (TDS), the suspended sediments (TSS), and the TDS/TSS ratio at least allow for an approximate hydrogeochemical classification (Table 5.1) of the Amazonian CHT rivers, if supplemented by the specific transports of humic substances, calcium and bicarbonate.

GEOBIOCHEMICAL CLASSIFICATION OF CHT RIVERS

In fact, loads of TDS and TSS are a complex function of the geobiochemical composition of the CHT river catchments and the particular river itself. CHT river waters may be classified as follows (Table 5.2):

(1) Waters with high contents of dissolved solids and suspended sediment (White waters), the latter being primarily mineral but organic colloids are contained also. Primary production in the main stem of such rivers is low, because of extremely low light transparency (Sioli, 1964, 1965).

(2) Waters with low to moderate contents of dissolved solids and extremely low amounts of suspended sediment mainly composed of mineral and organic materials, which are in the amorphous

TABLE 5.1

Specific runoff ($1\ s^{-1}\ km^{-2}$) and specific transport ($g\ s^{-1}$ km^{-2}) of total dissolved solids (TDS) and total suspended sediment (TSS) in the Amazon Basin (Gibbs, 1967; Schmidt, 1972; UNESCO, 1978; Stallard and Edmont, 1983; Brinkmann, 1986)

River[a]		Specific runoff	Specific transport		
			TDS	TSS	TDS/TSS
Japurá	(1)	63.5	0.35	3.84	0.09
Jutai		32.6	0.16	1.31	0.12
Javari		46.8	0.35	2.18	0.16
Napo		61.3	0.93	5.89	0.16
Ica	(2)	58.2	0.54	1.98	0.27
Madeira		21.9	1.34	5.02	0.27
Maranon		44.6	2.98	8.06	0.37
Jurua	(3)	40.6	1.02	1.57	0.65
Purus		34.5	0.96	1.38	0.69
Araguari	(4)	35.6	0.54	0.22	2.45
Xingu		31.2	0.10	0.03	3.30
Tapajós		31.8	0.13	0.03	4.30
Tefé	(5)	32.3	0.38	0.06	6.30
Coari		30.7	0.42	0.06	7.00
Rio Negro		42.4	0.32	0.02	16.00

[a]The numbers indicate a classification according to the water-type.

and colloidal phase (Clearwaters). Limitations for primary production in these rivers are brought about by the generally low levels of essential plant nutrients, while the light climate is favorable. In some cases, however, the release of nutrients from soils and rocks is sufficiently high to generate a primary production bloom (Marlier, 1973).

(3) Waters with low contents of dissolved solids, very low contents of mineral suspended sediment and high contents of organic colloids (Blackwaters). Primary production is low, because of the lack of essential plant nutrients in solution, while light climate is not a limiting factor (Sioli, 1955; Johnson, 1968; Ziechmann, 1976; Brinkmann, 1981; Paolini et al., 1983; Ertel et al., 1985; Hedges et al., 1985).

(4) Mixed waters of the classified units. There are permanently mixed waters. But on the other hand, rivers are found where the mixed waters undergo seasonal changes in composition and/or in the course of the river. The most favorable conditions for the development of a primary

TABLE 5.2

Dissolved solids of Amazon rivers (Brinkmann, 1981, 1983, 1985, 1986) (CW = Clearwaters, BW = Blackwaters, WW = Whitewaters)

Parameter		CW1	BW1	BW2	BW3	BW4	WW1	WW2
pH		5.1	3.7	4.7	5.4	3.5	6.8	7.1
EC	(μS cm^{-1})	5.7	29.1	8.3	21.0	30.0	13.5	58.7
KMnO$_4$ – d.	(mg l^{-1})	20.7	208.8	58.8	52.0	170.0	39.3	37.9
HS	(mg l^{-1})	8.5	93.1	17.6	25.0	74.0	10.4	?
Ca^{2+}	(μg l^{-1})	tr	tr	340.8	tr	0.0	620.1	7240.0
Mg^{2+}	(μg l^{-1})	130.0	20.0	178.4	128.0	18.0	648.0	1640.0
NH$_4^+$	(μg l^{-1})	90.0	152.8	40.4	626.9	277.0	18.0	14.0
NO$_2^-$	(μg l^{-1})	1.0	0.8	tr	5.8	1.5	1.8	1.8
NO$_3^-$	(μg l^{-1})	4.0	3.9	35.6	72.0	28.0	40.0	47.9
N^t	(μg l^{-1})	320.0	701.4	398.5	2327.0	1099.0	685.0	603.7
N^{org}	(μg l^{-1})	230.0	547.6	357.4	1705.0	822.0	667.1	536.0
P^t	(μg l^{-1})	10.0	57.4	7.6	50.0	53.0	23.0	69.4
Fe^t	(μg l^{-1})	410.0	138.8	430.1	35.0	68.0	653.4	2700.0
Cl$^-$	(μg l^{-1})	700.0	1200.0	1900.0	1300.0	2300.0	700.0	3500.0
SiO$_2$sol.	(μg l^{-1})	1900.0	600.0	2600.0	700.0	400.0	4100.0	3900.0
	n	30	40	40	26	17	18	23

Clearwaters: CW1, rain-forest streams in Central Amazon.
Blackwaters: BW1, rivulet draining a "Campina", Central Amazon. BW2, Rio Negro waters. BW3, near-surface groundwater of hydromorphic latosols adjacent rain forest streams, Central Amazon. BW4, groundwater of giant podzol, "Campina", Central Amazon.
Whitewaters: WW1, Rio Branco waters (Rio Negro Basin). WW2, Rio Solimoes upstream Rio Negro junction.

production bloom and dense stands of aquatic and semi-aquatic macrophytes concentrate in the swamps and the lakes of the nutrient-rich flood-plains.

CLAY MINERALS IN SEDIMENTS OF CHT RIVERS

Amount and composition of clay minerals in the suspended-sediment phase of CHT rivers depend on the geochemical background, the rainfall regime, the slope gradients, the vegetation cover, the erodibility of weathered soils of the drainage basins, and is additionally controlled by the floodwater hydrographs, which trigger the erosion and deposition processes at the river bed, the river banks and on the floodplains. The suspended river sediments are frequently deposited temporarily, of which the residence time at a certain point of the river is controlled by turbulent mixing of water and sediment during the flood wave and the erosional power of the quickflow in the drainage area.

The composition of clay minerals in CHT river sediments allow for at least two groups of rivers (type 1 and 3) to be clearly separated (Table 5.3).

(1) Rivers (type 3), which transport rather exclusively kaolinite in the suspended sediment phase (Gibbs, 1967; Brinkmann, 1981, 1986; Irion, 1983). Kaolinite is a consistant product of deeply weathered, well-drained paleosoils developed on Tertiary deposits and is also leached and/or eroded from the cristalline outcrops of the Shields of Brazil and Guiana as well as from the respective lithologic facies of the Zaïre Basin (Irion, 1983; Kronberg and Fyfe, 1983; Stallard and Edmont, 1983; Brinkmann, 1986).

(2) Rivers (type 1), which contain montmorillonite as the dominant clay mineral of the suspended solids. The suspended materials are as well products of intensive weathering, but of fine-grained, frequently water-logged deposits (Gibbs, 1967; Irion, 1983). The geochemical background of the catchments is also slightly different from the one with kaolinitic dominance.

Both groups of rivers (type 1 and 3) reveal the typical geochemical regimes of the CHT.

The rivers of the groups (type 2 and 4), which classify as Whitewaters receive considerable amounts of suspended materials from the mountainous parts and the foot-hill areas of the

TABLE 5.3

Clay minerals in sediments and suspended sediments of selected CHT rivers (Gibbs, 1967; Eisma et al., 1978; Brinkmann, 1981, 1986; Emeis and Stoffers, 1982; Irion, 1983; Irion and Petr, 1983)

River[a]		Kaolinite/halloysite	Montmorillonite	Chlorite	Illite/Mica	Reference
Rio Purus	(1)	+	XXXXX	−	+	G/I
Rio Javari		XX	XXXXX	−	+	G/I
Rio Jurua		+	XXXXX	−	+	G/I
Amazon*	(2)	+	XXX	X	XX	I
Amazon**		X	XXX	+	XX	G/I
Rio Ucayali		+	XX	+	XXX	G/I
Rio Madeira		XX	+	+	XXXX	I/G
Rio Coari		XX	XX	+	XXX	I/G
Rio Tefé	(3)	XXXX	−	−	XXX	I/G
Orinoco		XXX	X	X	XX	I/EST
Zaire		XXXXX	+	+	X	E
Rio Negro		XXXXX	−	−	−	G/I/B
June River		XXXXX	+	+	X	I
Rio Maués		XXXXX	+	−	+	I
Rio Tapajos		XXXXX	+	−	X	I
Rio Xingu		XXXXX	+	−	X	I
Rio Uatamá		XXXXX	−	−	X	I
Yellow River	(4)	X	XXXX	XX	X	I
Fly River		XX	XXX	X	X	I/IP
Purari		XX	XX	X	X	I/IP

[a]The numbers indicate a classification according to the water type.
*at Iquitos; **at Santarém.
The contents of clay minerals are: XXXXX = extremely high; XXXX = very high; XXX = high; XX = medium; X = low; + = very low; − = not detected.

catchments (Gibbs, 1967; Irion, 1983; Irion and Petr, 1983; Stallard and Edmond, 1983).

The chemical weathering of the lowlands has been substituted by processes of physical weathering of mineral compounds, of which the breakdown products, which include clay minerals, are transported in the suspended sediment phase of the river waters. The erosional power of high rainfall and the steep-sloped environment of the mountainous parts of the catchments control the amount of the eroded materials, while the geochemical background of the rock facies defines the mineral composition.

The Amazon River (type 2), however, being the recipient of the eroded materials from all parts of the vast catchment, produces a composite hydrogeochemical regime, which dilute individual characteristics of tributaries below the limits of discrimination.

COLLOIDAL ORGANIC MATTER IN CHT RIVERS

Tropical river systems, of which the apparent color is dark, are classified as Blackwater rivers. They are found in all parts of the CHT (Sioli, 1955, 1965; Johnson, 1968; Marlier, 1973; Ziechmann, 1976; Brinkmann, 1981, 1986), but the Rio Negro, a tributary of the Amazon, is by far the largest Blackwater river of the tropics.

Blackwater rivers are reasonably characterized by the content and the composition of suspended solids. Blackwaters contain: (1) trace amounts of mineral materials, mainly kaolinite, often some quartz and amorphous silica (Brinkmann, 1981, 1986; Irion, 1983; Paolini et al., 1983; Stallard and Edmond, 1983); and (2) constant but low amounts of colloidal organic materials (Ziechmann, 1976; Brinkmann, 1981; 1986; Ittekkot et al., 1982; Ertel et al., 1985) in the form of non-humic and humic substances [Humic acids (HA), fulvic acids (FA) and humins (H)].

The bulk of the suspended organics in Blackwater rivers is derived from at least three sources (Sioli, 1955; Klinge, 1967; Brinkmann, 1981, 1985, 1986; Hedges et al., 1985): (i) the seasonally flooded fringe-forests of the rivers and swamp-like forests in shallow depressions; (ii) the podzol soils of the CHT lowlands; and (iii) the hydromorphic soils, which accompany the rain forest streams. The organic substances are products of the leaching of life and dead organic standing crop and are generated in the course of the complex processes of biodegradation (the step-by-step breakdown of large and complex organic macromolecules) and biosyntheses (the rapid combination of breakdown products into new molecules) in the CHT environments (Brinkmann, 1983, 1985).

CONCLUSIONS

The data-base for a thorough analysis of the hydrobiogeochemistry of the CHT river basins is unsufficient in general, although for a limited number of areas (case studies) a profound knowledge has been condensed in the CHT environment.

The multi-disciplinary research on hydrobiogeochemistry of the CHT environment has to be intensified, using system analysis as an appropriate tool to balance fluxes of water, mineral and organic compounds as well as energy. Simultaneously, the processes and mechanisms, which control the balances and the network of interactions of terrestrial, semi-aquatic and aquatic systems should be given research priority. The same is true for comparative studies on a regional, continental and global scale (see SCOPE River Carbon Project).

For river basins of low anthropogenic impacts, the amount, and the areal and temporal distribution patterns of loads of dissolved and suspended sediment transported in the river waters, combined with representative sets of data on specific runoff and specific transport of the catchments, provide for a better understanding of the state and ecodynamics of the CHT environment.

The actual research on hydrobiogeochemical balances in the CHT river basins is a basic tool to evaluate the effects of transformation of quasi-natural systems into man-managed land-use schemes in the future.

REFERENCES

Balek, J., 1977. *Hydrology and Water Resources in Tropical Africa.* Elsevier, Amsterdam, 207 pp.

Balek, J., 1983. *Hydrology and Water Resources in Tropical regions.* Elsevier, Amsterdam, 271 pp.

Balek, J. and Perry, J.E., 1973. Hydrology of seasonal inundated African headwater swamps. *J. Hydrol.*, 19: 227–249.

Beadle, L.C., 1974. *The Inland Waters of Tropical Africa.* Longman, London, 365 pp.

Bishop, J.E., 1973. *Limnology of a Small Malayan River Sungai Gombak.* (Monographs in Biology, 22) Junk, The Hague, 485 pp.

Brinkmann, W.L.F., 1981. Zum Chemismus von Schwarzwässern in Zentralamazonien. *Beitr. Hydrol., Sonderh.*, 2: 121–135.

Brinkmann, W.L.F., 1983. Nutrient balance of a cental Amazonian rain forest: comparison of natural and man-managed systems. *Proc. Hamburg Symp., IAHS Publ.* 140: 153–163.

Brinkmann, W.L.F., 1985. Studies on hydrobiogeochemistry of a tropical lowland forest system. *Geo Journal*, 11(1): 89–101.

Brinkmann, W.L.F., 1986. Particulate and dissolved materials in the Rio Negro-Amazon basin. In: P.G. Sly (Editor), *Sediments and Water Interactions.* Springer, New York, N.Y., Part 1, pp. 1–12.

Bruijnzeel, L.A., 1983. *Hydrological and Biogeochemical Aspects of Man-Made Forests in South-Central Java, Indonesia.* Thesis, Kanters, Alblasserdam, 250 pp.

Eisma, D., 1982. Supply and dispersal of suspended matter from the Zaire river. *Mitt. Geol. Paläontol. Inst. Univ. Hamburg, SCOPE/UNEP Sonderb.*, 52: 419–428.

Eisma, D., Kalf, J. and Van der Gaast, S.J., 1978. Suspended matter in the Zaire estuary and the adjacent Atlantic Ocean. *Neth. J. Sea Res.*, 12 (3/4): 382–406.

Emeis, K. and Stoffers, P., 1982. Particulate suspended matter in the major world rivers: EDAX analysis, scanning electron-microscopy and X-ray diffraction study of filters. *Mitt. Geol. Paläontol. Inst. Univ. Hamburg, SCOPE/UNEP Sonderb.*, 52: 529–554.

Ertel, J.R., Hedges, J.I., Devol, A.H. and Richey, J.E., 1986. Dissolved humic substances of the Amazon river system. *Limnol. Oceanogr.*, 31 (4): 739–754.

Flohn, H., 1971. Tropical circulation pattern. *Bonn. Meteorol. Abh.*, 15: 55 pp.

Furtado, J.I. and Mori, S., 1982. *Tasek Bera.* Junk, The Hague, 413 pp.

Gibbs, R.J., 1967. The geochemistry of the Amazon river system: Part 1. The factors that control the salinity and the composition and concentration of the suspended solids. *Geol. Soc. Am. Bull.*, 78: 1203–1232.

Hedges, J.I., Clark, W.C., Quay, P.D., Richey, J.E. and Devol, A.H., 1986. Compositions and fluxes of particulate organic material in the Amazon river. *Limnol. Oceanogr.*, 31 (4): 717–738.

Irion, G., 1983. Clay mineralogy of the suspended load of the Amazon and of rivers in the Purari–New Guinea mainland. *Mitt. Geol. Paläontol. Inst. Univ. Hamburg, SCOPE/UNEP Sonderb.*, 55: 483–504.

Irion, G. and Petr, T., 1983. Clay mineralogy of selected soils and sediments of the Purari river basin. In: T. Petr (Editor), *The Purari*. (Monographs in Biology, 51) Junk, The Hague, pp. 87–107.

Ittekkot, V., Spitzy, A. and Lammers, U., 1982. Data on dissolved carbohydrates and amino acids in the world rivers: a documentation. *Mitt. Geol. Paläontol. Inst. Univ. Hamburg, SCOPE/UNEP Sonderb.*, 52: 575–584.

Ittekkot, V., Martins, O. and Seifert, R., 1983. Nitrogenous organic matter transported by the major world rivers. *Mitt. Geol. Paläontol. Inst. Univ. Hamburg, SCOPE/UNEP Sonderb.*, 55: 119–127.

Johnson, D.S., 1968. Malayan blackwaters. *Proc. Symp. Recent. Adv. Trop. Ecol.*, pp. 303–310.

Klinge, H., 1967. Podzol soils: a source of blackwater rivers in Amazonia. *Atas Symp. Biota Amazonica*, 3: 117–125.

Kronberg, B.J. and Fyfe, W.S., 1983. Geochemical controls in Amazonia on weathering rates. *Mitt. Geol. Paläontol. Inst. Univ. Hamburg, SCOPE/UNEP Sonderb.*, 55: 215–222.

Marlier, G.,1973. Limnology of the Congo and Amazon rivers. In: B.J. Meggers, E.S. Ayesu and W.D. Duckworth (Editors), *Tropical Forest Ecosystems in Africa and South America: A Comparative Review*. Smithsonian Institution Press, City of Washington, pp. 223–238.

Németh, A., Paolini, J. and Herrera, R., 1982. Carbon transport in the Orinoco river: preliminary results. *Mitt. Geol. Paläontol. Inst. Univ. Hamburg, SCOPE/UNEP Sonderb.*, 52: 357–364.

Paolini, J., Herrera, R. and Németh, A., 1983. Hydrochemistry of the Orinoco and Caroni rivers. *Mitt. Geol. Paläontol. Inst. Univ. Hamburg, SCOPE/UNEP Sonderb.*, 55: 223–236.

Pardé, M.,1953. *Fleuves et Rivières*. Colin, Paris, 224 pp.

Petr, T., 1983. *The Purari*. (Monographs in Biology, 51) Junk, The Hague, 624 pp.

Pickup, G., 1983. Sedimentation processes in the Purari river upstream of the delta. In: T. Petr (Editor), *The Purari*. (Monographs in Biology, 51) Junk, The Hague, pp. 205–225.

Richey, J.E., 1982. The Amazon river system: a biogeochemical model. *Mitt. Geol. Paläontol. Inst. Univ. Hamburg, SCOPE/UNEP Sonderb.*, 52: 365–378.

Rodier, J.A., 1983. Aspects scientifiques et techniques de l'hydrologie des zones humides de l'Afrique centrale. *Proc. Hamburg Symp., IAHS Publ.*, 140: 105–126.

Salati, E. and Vose, P.B., 1983. Analysis of Amazon hydrology in relation to the geoclimatic factors and increased deforestation. *Beitr. Hydrol.*, (1): 11–22.

Salati, E., Lovejoy, E. and Vose, P.B., 1983. Precipitation and water recycling in tropical rain forests with special reference to the Amazon basin. *Environmentalist*, 3(1): 67–72.

Schmidt, G.W., 1972. Amounts of suspended solids and dissolved substances in the middle reaches of the Amazon over the course of one year (August, 1969–July, 1970). *Amazoniana*, 111(2): 208–223.

Serruya, C. and Pollingher, U., 1983. *Lakes of the Warm Belt*. Cambridge Univ. Press, Cambridge, 569 pp.

Sioli, H., 1950. Das Wasser im Amazonasgebiet. *Forsch. Fortschr.*, 26: 274–280.

Sioli, H., 1955. Beiträge zur regionalen Limnologie des Amazonasgebietes. III. Über einige Gewässer des oberen Rio Negro-Gebietes. *Arch. Hydrobiol.*, 50: 1–32.

Sioli, H., 1964. General features of the limnology of Amazonia. *Verh. Int. Verein. Limnol.*, 15: 1053–1058.

Sioli, H., 1965. Bemerkungen zur Typologie amazonischer Flüsse. *Amazoniana*, 1(1): 74–83.

Stallard, R.F. and Edmond, J.M., 1983. Geochemistry of the Amazon. 2. The influence of geology and weathering environment on the dissolved load. *J. Geophys. Res.*, 88(C14): 9671–9688.

UNESCO, 1978. World water balance and water resources of the earth. *Stud. Rep. Hydrol.*, 25: 663 pp.

Ziechmann, W., 1976. Huminstoffe in südamerikanischen Flußsystemen. *Amazoniana*, 1(19): 135–144.

Chapter 6

AMERICAN TROPICAL FORESTS

G.T. PRANCE

INTRODUCTION

To cover the neotropical forests and their phytogeography in the limited space available is almost impossible because of the diversity of species, of forest types and of the various approaches which could be taken to such a subject. Since some of the classical works on these forests, such as Beard (1944) and Richards (1952), were published, many new ideas have been gathered which give us a much better idea of the structure, species composition, diversity and succession of the neotropical forests. There have been many different approaches to define tropical forest types based on the background of the authors. For example, Richards (1952) stressed the physiognomy and structure of the forests, whereas Holdridge et al. (1971) in their life-zone system stress climatic factors, rainfall and temperature as well as altitude. Other authors have taken a more ecological or physiological approach, and yet others such as Projeto Radambrasil (1973–1983) have stressed edaphic factors.

In this account I have separated the different types and regions largely from a floristic or phytogeographic point of view, together with the consideration of the different vegetation types based on their physiognomy and structure. I have also concentrated more on data about tree species rather than the extensive literature on lianas, herbs and epiphytes. There is naturally a close correlation between species distribution and vegetation type, because the majority of tropical forest species are of restricted ecological range and may occur in only one forest type. This can best be illustrated by Fig. 6.1 which shows the spatial distribution of two species on 10.5 ha of forest in the Mocambo

Reserve in Belém, Brazil. The central part is *terra firme* and the corner areas flooded *várzea* forests[1]. The two species concerned, *Virola surinamensis* (várzea) and *Goupia glabra* (terra firme), occur only in one forest type.

Together with a definition of the major forest types of the neotropics I have used the term phytochorion, which had been little applied to the neotropics but has been used extensively for Africa (Werger and Van Gils, 1976; Werger, 1978; White, 1979) where both phytochorion and the associated terminology have been well defined. Phytochoria are based on the distribution of species rather than on the vegetation types which are based mainly on physiognomy. Phytochoria are not necessarily mutually exclusive areas further subdivided hierarchically such as Regions, Domains or other phytogeographic divisions. Phytochoria effectively reflect the predominant distribution patterns of species. Different parts of the neotropics differ considerably in the number of endemic species and in the types of distribution patterns which occur, which are also linked closely to the different speciation patterns involved. The phytochoria given in Fig. 6.2 are based on the mapping of a large number of neotropical species as well as the study of distribution maps in the volumes of *Flora Neotropica*. The four different types of phytochoria are explained in the legend of the figure, and further details will be given in Prance (in press). As would be expected, the boundaries of the various phytochoria correspond closely to those of the major vegetation types as

---

[1]The terms terra firme and várzea forests are the most used terms in Brazil for upland non-flooded forests and for seasonally inundated forests and are described in further detail below.

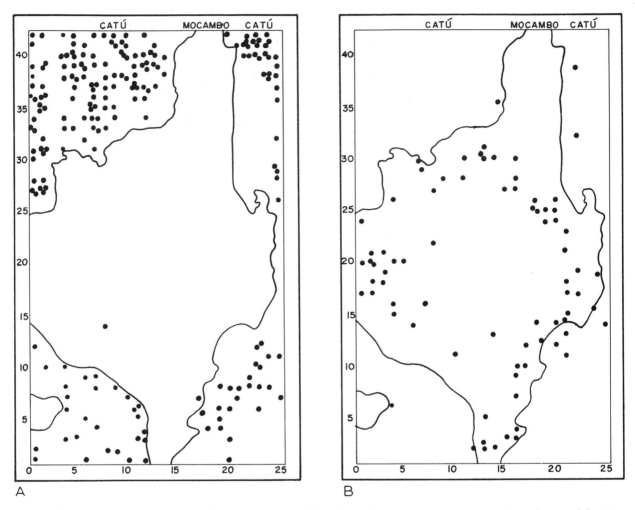

Fig. 6.1. Distribution of two species in the Mocambo Reserve in Belém, Brazil. The central area is non-flooded terra firme, and the area around the four corners is tidally flooded várzea. (A) *Virola surinamensis*, a species of inundated forest; (B) *Goupia glabra*, a species of terra firme. (Adapted from Pires and Prance, 1977.)

Fig. 6.2. The phytochoria or floristic provinces of South America as defined by the author. These are divided into four types following the categories of White (1976, 1979):

A. Regional centers of endemism with a high percentage of endemism, which are general areas rather than local pockets of endemism such as exist within some of the regional centers; the regional centers are: *1* = Panama – Chocó; *2* = Magdalena – Venezuela Gulf; *3* = northern Andean submontane; *3a* = southern Andean submontane; *9* = Guiana – eastern Amazonia; *10* = Amazonia; *12* = northeastern Brazil; *13* = Planalto; *14* = Atlantic coastal region; *15* = southern Pacific; *16* = Chaco; *17* = southern Brazil.

B. Archipelago-like centers (▲) of endemism differ from regional centers in their discontinuous distribution, because of their occurrence on isolated mountain tops. The South American centers are: *4* = north Andean montane; *4a* = southern Andean montane; *5* = Central Cordillera Venezuela; *7* = Guayana Highland.

C. Regional transition zones (■) are regions where there is a gradual transition between two centers, with elements from both types and low endemism. In South America the single such zone of significance is: *11* = Amazon Transition Zone, around the south of Amazonia.

D. Regional mosaics (●) are areas that are not well categorized as centers of endemism or as transition zones. They may or may not be rich in endemic species. In South America the Pantanal mosaic (*17*) is not rich in endemism, but the other areas are: *6* = Catatumbo – Llanos mosaic; *8* = Venezuelan Amazonas – savannas mosaic.

found on such vegetation maps as those of Hueck and Seibert (1972), UNESCO, (1981) and Projeto Radambrasil (1973–1983).

The phytochoria are considered as roughly equivalent to regions in the sense of Engler (1964, and previous versions of his Syllabus). They are, therefore, generally large areas with a set of species that characterize them. The phytochoria of Africa were defined by White (1979) as areas with 50% or more of the species confined to them or with a total of more than 1000 endemic species. This would also apply to the phytochoria proposed here, although further distribution maps are needed to confirm the number of endemic species. Table 6.1

TABLE 6.1

The tropical South American phytochoria

Region	Forest types predominating (+ other vegetation)
1. Panama – Chocó regional center *Licania* 13, *Parinari* 2, *Maranthes* 1, *Hirtella* 4	Tropical moist forest
2. Magdalena – Venezuela Gulf regional center *Licania* 1	Tropical dry deciduous forest (+non-forest arid formations)
3. Northern Andean submontane regional center *Licania* 5, *Couepia* 3, *Hirtella* 3 + 1 var.	Montane and lower montane moist forest Dry forest in isolated valleys
3a. Southern Andean submontane regional center	Montane and lower montane moist forest (eastern slopes) Dry deciduous forest (slopes)
4. Andean Montane regional center (archipelago)	(páramo, puna, etc.)
4a. Southern Andean Montane regional center (archipelago)	(puna)
5. Coastal cordillera region (archipelago) *Licania* 2	Tropical moist forest (isolated patches) Montane and lower montane forest (arid formations)
6. Catatumbo–Llanos mosaic *Licania* 1	Tropical moist forest Gallery forest (savanna)
7. Guayana Highland Region (archipelago) *Licania* 10, *Parinari* 1, *Couepia* 2, *Hirtella* 3	Tropical forest (lowlands) Lower montane forest (savanna and other open formations)
8. Venezuelan Amazonas Savannas mosaic *Licania* 3, *Hirtella* 4	(predominantly savanna) Gallery forest White-sand forests
9. Guianas – Eastern Amazonian regional center *Licania* 27, *Parinari* 2, *Couepia* 5, *Hirtella* 11, *Acioa* 1	Tropical moist forest White-sand forests (savanna)
10. Amazonian regional center	Tropical moist forest
10a. Northwestern Amazonia *Licania* 3, *Hirtella* 5, *Acioa* 1	Inundated forests White-sand forests (savanna islands)
10b. North Central Amazonia *Licania* 3, *Couepia* 5, *Hirtella* 2	
10c. Southwestern Amazonia *Licania* 12, *Parinari* 3, *Couepia* 3, *Hirtella* 11	
10d. South-central Amazonia *Licania* 2, *Couepia* 3, *Hirtella* 1	

TABLE 6.1 (*continued*)

Region	Forest types predominating (+ other vegetation)
11. Southern Amazonian transition region *Couepia* 1	Transition forests, palm forest, liana forest, bamboo forest, etc. (cerrado)
12. Northeastern Brazil regional center *Licania* 1	Dry deciduous forest (caatinga and scrub)
13. Planalto regional center *Licania* 6, *Parinari* 1, *Exellodendron* 2, *Couepia* 3, *Hirtella* 3	Predominantly cerrado Tropical moist forest (in isolated patches) Gallery forest
14. Atlantic coastal regional center *Licania* 13, *Parinari* 4, *Exellodendron* 1, *Couepia* 12, *Hirtella* 10	Tropical moist forest
15. Southern Pacific coastal regional center	(Predominantly desert and lomas) Dry deciduous forest
16. Chaco regional center	Dry deciduous forest
17. Pantanal mosaic	Gallery forest Cerradão Semideciduous forest (swamp, cerrado, dry chaco)
18. Southern Brazil regional center	*Araucaria* forest

Endemic species of Chrysobalanaceae are shown in the first column for each Region.

gives the number of Chrysobalanaceae found in each phytochorion. That family is a lowland group mostly confined to wetter areas, and therefore would be expected to be absent or nearly absent from the montane and especially the most arid phytochoria, but it is present in most of the forest phytochoria considered here. Werger and Van Gils (1976) did not use the 50% limit to define their phytochoria.

The data for neotropical Chrysobalanaceae show that 61% of 349 species studied have distributions that are almost confined to a single phytochorion, and another 22% that occur only within the Guiana-Amazonian phytochoria. Only 16.6% of the Chrysobalanaceae are widespread over the boundaries of phytochoria, and are thus *chorological transgressors* in the terminology of White (1979). These percentages are approximated in the other families studied, which would indicate that, at least for the lowland areas which are the focus of this study, the phytochoria as defined here meet the conditions of White (1979).

Some of the neotropical phytochoria, such as that of the Planalto of central Brazil, contain little forest; these are not considered further here, since only the forests and the forest-containing phytochoria will be discussed.

The different major categories of forest which are considered are given in Table 6.2. I have taken the term "tropical forest" to include all evergreen, and semi-deciduous tree formations including the Amazonian transition forests, but have excluded the deciduous tree formations such as thorn forests and cerradões and scrub formations and woody savannas, which are treated in the volume on savannas (Bourlière, 1983).

LOWLAND TROPICAL MOIST FORESTS

Included under this heading are the tall evergreen forests, high in biomass and diverse in species, which have been subdivided by some authors (e.g. Holdridge, 1967) into moist forests,

TABLE 6.2

Major categories of neotropical forest

1. Lowland tropical moist forest
2. Montane and lower montane moist forest
    Lower montane forest
    Upper montane forest
    Subalpine forest
    Podocarpus forest
3. Inundated forest
    a. Permanent swamp forest
    b. Periodically flooded forest
        1. Mangrove
        2. Tidal swamp forest
        3. Seasonal swamp forest
            a. with associated grassland
            b. without grassland
        4. Seasonal igapó
        5. Floodplain forest
    c. Gallery forest
4. Transition forest
    a. Open evergreen forest without palms
    b. Open evergreen forest with palms
    c. Liana forest
    d. Bamboo forest
    e. Dry semideciduous forest
5. Tropical and subtropical evergreen seasonal conifer forest
6. Forest on white-sand soil

wet forests and rain forests depending on variation in seasonality and rainfall. Richards (1952) regarded such forests as lowland rain forests. Figure 6.3 shows the area in which the tree species of tropical moist forests can occur in the neotropics. This area is not continuous moist forest, as is evident from the descriptions of other formations given below as well as from the considerable areas of savanna which occur within Amazonia (area *D* on Fig. 6.3). However, it is the area in which species characteristic of moist forests may be found. It is connected by a large number of widespread species which occur in all or most of the areas, and sometimes beyond in gallery forest and forest islands in savanna regions. Figure 6.4 gives the distribution of six such widepread species. There are also a large number of moist-forest species which are endemic to one of the five regions, and others which are disjunct between two or more of these regions.

The best summary of the general details of tropical moist forest is still that of Richards (1952). Although intended to cover the neotropics, it was based largely on work in the Guianas rather than

throughout the six phytochoria concerned. Many more recent data about the structure and species diversity of these forests are now known, but in the short space available I can do little more than point to some of the most important works with details relating to the neotropical moist forests.

Figure 6.2 gives the floristic provinces (phytochoria in the sense of White, 1979) into which I divide South America. It can be seen from this that the tropical moist forest falls into four different provinces, plus two additional ones not on the map, which are Mexico – Central America and the Caribbean. The six moist-forest provinces represent areas of considerable local endemism, and the distribution of a few moist-forest endemics is shown in Fig. 6.5. A few of the common disjunctions between rain-forest phytochoria are shown in Fig. 6.6. The division of the region into phytochoria will facilitate the discussion of the various forest types considered below. A similar subdivision of the neotropical region was made by Gentry (1982b), who recognized ten phytogeographic regions in tropical America: one for Mexico and Central America, one for the Caribbean and eight within tropical South America.

The six principal areas in which moist forest occurs are:

(1) Mexico and Central America (Fig. 6.3,*A*), from the southern part of Veracruz in discontinuous patches to Panama. More rain forest exists on the Caribbean side of the region, but some areas of rain forest occur near the Pacific, such as on the Osa Peninsula in Costa Rica. The species in this forest are a mixture of local endemics and widespread moist-forest species (see Figs. 6.4 and 6.5). Recent collections in moist-forest areas are constantly increasing the number of South American moist-forest species found in Central America, for example in 1982 the collection (by B. Hammel) of two common Guianian species, *Licania affinis* and *L. glabriflora* (Fig. 6.6A), in La Selva, Costa Rica. Good descriptions of rain forest in Central America are given in Allen (1956), Holdridge et al. (1971) and Gentry (1978), and for Mexico by Rzedowski (1962).

(2) Various Caribbean Islands, especially Cuba, Jamaica, Hispaniola and Puerto Rico (Fig. 6.3,*C*), but also some of the Lesser Antilles where the mountainous topography is responsible for the rainfall patterns resulting in the occurrence of

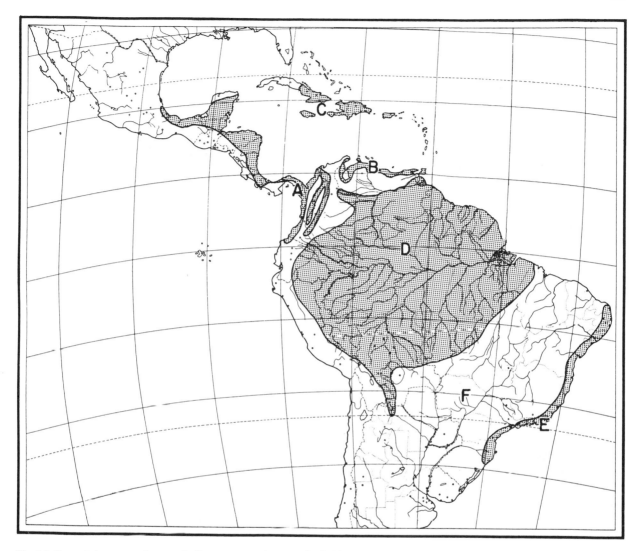

Fig. 6.3. Present-day areas where moist forest tree species occur in the Neotropics. *A* = Mexico, Central American/northwestern South America; *B* = Coastal Venezuela; *C* = Caribbean; *D* = Amazonia, including the basins of the Amazon and the southern Orinoco river and the Guianas; *E* = Atlantic coastal forest of Brazil; *F* = the Planalto of Brazil and similar areas in adjacent countries — within this region *cerrado* and *caatinga* prevail but moist forest species are found where conditions are favorable, as in gallery forests. (Adapted from Mori et al., 1981.)

moist forest. These forests also contain a mixture of endemic species and widespread species. An excellent summary of the vegetation types and distribution patterns within the Antilles is that of Howard (1973).

(3) The Pacific coastal region of South America from northern Colombia to northern Ecuador (Fig. 6.3,*A*), which also extends north into Panama. This region is extremely high in endemics at the species level; some are widespread throughout the region, but more occur either in the northern part

in Chocó and El Valle or in the southern part of Nariño, Colombia and northern Ecuador. Cuatrecasas (1947) gave an early account of the vegetation of this region together with lists of species. This region and its phytogeography has been discussed in some detail by Forero (1982) and Gentry (1977, 1978, 1982a). Gentry (1982b) discussed the link between the Central American and South American floras. The endemic tree species are predominantly of Amazonian genera, and the effect of isolation by the uplift of the Andes is the

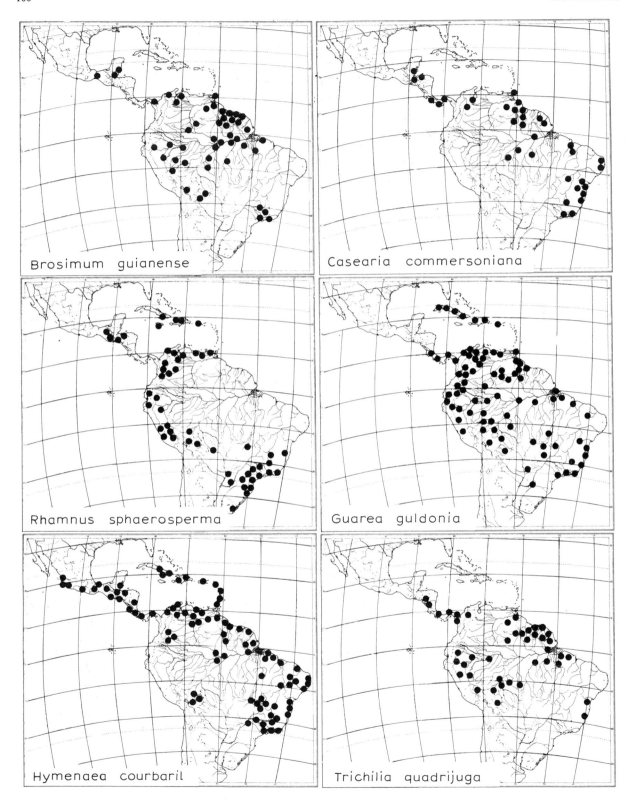

Fig. 6.4. Selected tree species widespread in the neotropics. (From Mori et al., 1981.)

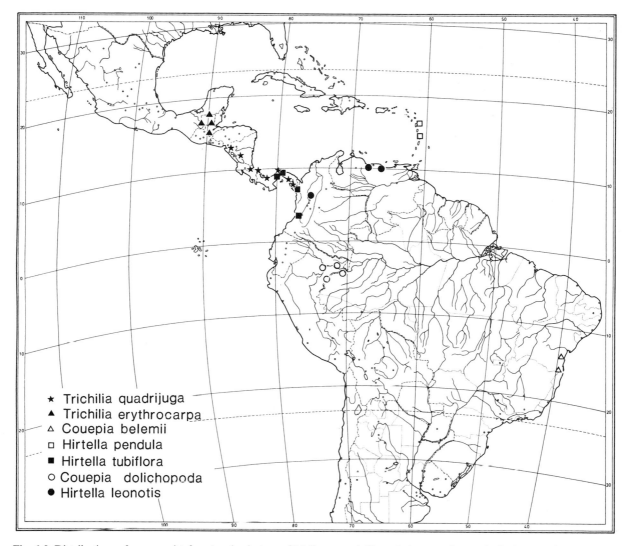

Fig. 6.5. Distributions of some moist-forest endemic taxa of Meliaceae and Chrysobalanaceae from principal areas of moist forest.

cause of such a high species endemism. Another important forest area which lies between the Pacific coastal region and Area 4 below (northern Venezuela) is the Magdalena River valley of Colombia. The tall rain forest of this area has many endemic species, but is now largely destroyed. *Cariniana pyriformis* is a species of the Magdalena valley and the northern Chocó region, and *Caryocar amygdaliferum* is an example of a Magdalena valley endemic. The forests of this region are an interesting mixture of Central American and Amazonian species together with local endemics. An inventory of forests of this region is given in Vega (1968).

(4) The northern part of Venezuela (Fig. 6.3,*B*),

in the shadow of both the Andes around the Catatumbo region and the Coastal Cordillera. This area, which is broken into many small patches by the drier forest and montane forests, also possesses a high degree of endemism. It was discussed in some detail by Steyermark (1974, 1979b, 1982) who provided many examples of endemic species, as well as species disjunct with other moist forest areas, as exemplified by the genus *Froesia* (Fig. 6.6C).

(5) The largest area of continuous moist forest is that of Amazonia and the Guianas (Figs. 6.3,*D*, 6.7 and 6.8), here treated together because of their floristic and structural similarity. Many species are

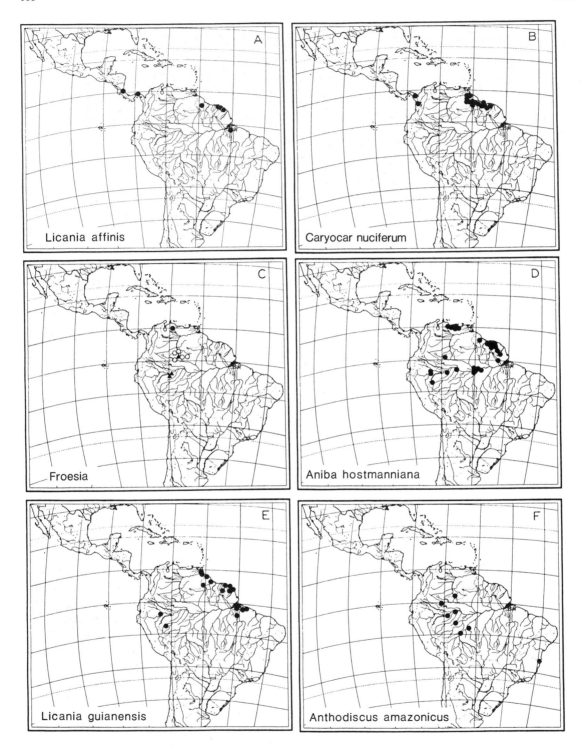

Fig. 6.6. Some common disjunctions found in rain-forest species illustrated by six distribution maps. (A) *Licania affinis*, a Central America – Guiana disjunct; (B) *Caryocar nuciferum*, a Chocó – Guiana disjunct; (C) The genus *Froesia* (●, *F. venezuelensis*; ○, *F. tricarpa*; ▲, *F. crassiflora*), a coastal Cordillera – Amazonian disjunct; (D) *Aniba hostmanniana*, disjunct within Amazonia; (E) *Licania guianensis*, a Guiana – western Amazonia disjunct; (F) *Anthodiscus amazonicus*, an Amazonian – eastern Brazilian coast disjunct.

Fig. 6.7. Tropical moist forest in French Guiana with strong presence of large woody vines.

common to both the Guianas and Amazonia, while others, confined to smaller regions, are treated below in the discussion on endemism. Numerous accounts of the Amazonian forest are available. Some which give considerable details concerning the structure and composition of the vegetation include the classical work on Amazonian phytogeography by Ducke and Black (1953); analyses of small areas of forest by Black et al. (1950), Takeuchi (1961, 1962b, 1973), Grubb et al. (1963), Rodrigues (1967), Prance et al. (1976), Pires and Prance (1977), and Campbell et al. (1986); discussions of the forests of the Guianas by Davis and Richards (1933, 1934), Fanshawe (1952), Schulz (1960) and De Granville (1978); a more general account by Aubréville (1961); and descriptions of phytogeographic regions by Ducke and Black (1953), Rizzini (1963) and Prance (1977).

(6) The Atlantic coastal forest of Brazil (Fig. 6.3,E), like the Pacific region, is quite isolated from other moist forest regions and consequently has a high percentage of endemism. In a study of 127 tree species of this forest Mori et al. (1981) found that 53.5% are endemic to the coastal forest (see examples, Fig. 6.9), 11.8% to the coastal forest plus some part of the adjacent Planalto of central Brazil, 7.8% disjunct with the Amazon region (for instance *Anthodiscus amazonicus*; Fig. 6.6F), and only 26% are widespread species. Another similarity to the Pacific moist forest region is the tendency for the endemic species to be segregated into separate northern and southern groups. An excellent review and forest inventory of a part of this forest in southern Bahia is that of Mori et al. (1983); some phenological details were reported by De Andrade-Lima (1957b), who later (1966) published a discussion of the Amazon – eastern Brazil disjuncts. An inventory of this forest was published by Da Vinha et al. (1976).

Diversity

The moist forests are characterized by their enormous species diversity. Studies throughout

Fig. 6.8. Large buttressed tree of the Bombacaceae in tropical moist forest near Lábrea, in Brazilian Amazonia.

different moist-forest regions indicate this to be typical. For example, Tschirley et al. (1970) found 105 tree species (over 2.5 cm diameter) in an area of 1 ha in Puerto Rico, Holdridge et al. (1971) 106 in 1 ha in Costa Rica, Knight (1975) 118 (over 2.5 cm diameter) in Barro Colorado Island, Panama, Maas (1971) 125 in Surinam, Prance et al. (1976) 179 (over 15 cm diameter) near Manaus, Brazil, Cain et al. (1956) and Pires et al. (1953) 144 in Belém, Brazil, and Mori et al. (1983) 178 species in 0.67 ha in Bahia, Brazil (all figures for trees over 10 cm diameter unless stated). Gentry (1982c) reviewed the work on species diversity in moist forests, and presented data from his analysis of several 1000 m² plots of both moist and dry forest; data from more plots of the same size in Peru were given in a subsequent paper by Gentry (1984). His work showed a close correlation between increasing forest diversity and higher rainfall. The extremely wet seasonal forests near Tutunendó, Chocó, Colombia in the Pacific coastal region (rainfall 9000 mm), were found to be most diverse, with 258 species of trees and lianas as compared with 167 species in the Pipeline Road in Panama (rainfall 3000 mm) or 110 at Manaus, Brazil (rainfall 1995 mm). This conclusion is backed up by my own quantitative forest inventories in different parts of the Amazon moist-forest region, and confirms the earlier conclusions of Holdridge et al. (1971) on correlations between rainfall and diversity. The most recent data of Gentry (pers. commun., 1984) show an asymptote in diversity at about 4000 mm of rainfall.

Recent data have also shown an enormous diversity in non-tree groups of plants within the tropical rain forest. Fewer inventories exist for non-trees, but the indications are that much of the total species richness is accounted for by herbs, lianas and shrubs and epiphytes. Gentry (1982c) included lianas in his inventory data, and Emmons and Gentry (1983) stressed the importance of liana diversity. They found that the neotropical rain forests are richer in lianas than tropical Asia, but fewer than the African forests. Gentry and Dodson (1985) have given comparative species-richness data for three sites in western Ecuador and showed the diversity of the herbs, shrubs and epiphytes. There is a great need for future inventory data to include more analysis of the species richness of plants other than trees.

Many causes of diversity in tropical moist forest and many theories to explain it have been proposed, but cannot be reviewed in detail here. Richards (1969) and Ashton (1969) emphasized niche specialization, and Connell (1978) and Anderson and Benson (1980) stressed the import-ance of habitat disturbance to maintain species diversity in tropical forests. Others such as Haffer (1969), Brown (1975) and Prance (1973, 1982) have emphasized speciation in refugia when the forests were splintered by Pleistocene climate changes. Each of the above factors has probably contrib-uted to the complexity of the tropical moist forests of the neotropics.

Centers of endemism

Botanists who have discussed Pleistocene forest refugia have based much of their work on the localization of centers of endemism within the moist-forest areas. They have found that within

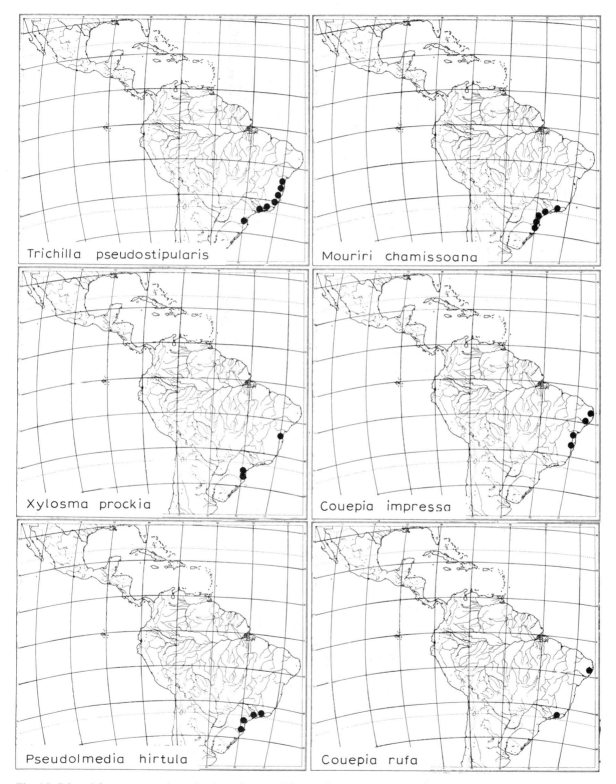

Fig. 6.9. Selected forest tree species endemic to the coastal forest of eastern Brazil. (From Mori et al., 1981.)

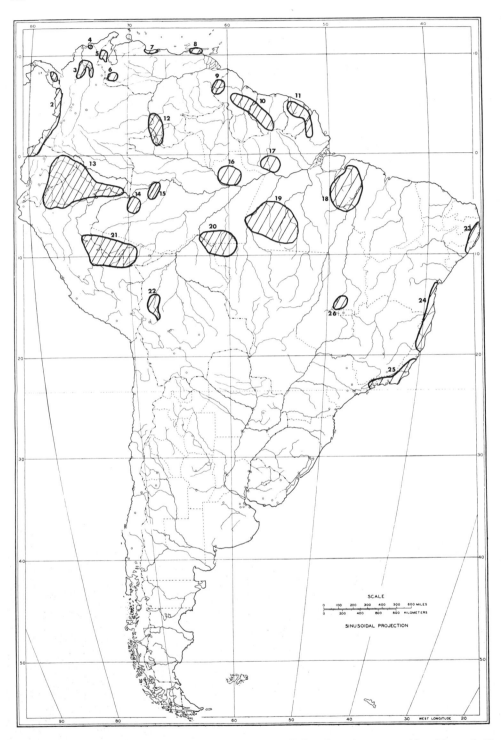

Fig. 6.10. Pleistocene forest refugia proposed by Prance (1982), based on phytogeographic evidence. *1* = Panama – Darién; *2* = Chocó; *3* = Rio Magdalena; *4* = Santa Marta; *5* = Catatumbo; *6* = Apure; *7* = Rancho Grande; *8* = Paria; *9* = Imataca; *10* = western Guiana; *11* = eastern Guiana; *12* = Imeri; *13* = Napo; *14* = São Paulo de Olivença; *15* = Tefé; *16* = Manaus; *17* = Trombetas; *18* = Belém; *19* = Tapajós; *20* = Aripuanã; *21* = eastern Peru – Acre; *22* = Beni; *23* = Pernambuco; *24* = Bahia; *25* = Rio – Espírito Santo; *26* = Araguaia.

each of the major moist-forest areas there is a large amount of local endemism. Centers of forest endemism have been discussed by Toledo (1976, 1982) for Mexico, Gentry (1982c) for the Chocó region, Steyermark (1979b, 1982) for Venezuela, De Granville (1982) for French Guiana, Prance (1973, 1982) for Amazonia, and Mori et al. (1981) for eastern Brazil. Each author has pointed out a number of local centers of endemism within each major moist-forest phytochorion. Figure 6.10 shows the centers of endemism suggested by Prance (1982), based mainly on the distribution of four woody plant families: Caryocaraceae, Chrysobalanaceae, Dichapetalaceae and Lecythidaceae. In each area of the areas marked there is a much higher number of endemic species than in the intervening areas. This local endemism also accounts for some of the species diversity and the large total number of species of the neotropical rain forests.

Particularly helpful to knowledge of the tropical moist forests has been the preparation of a few local florulas of small areas, especially the Flora of Barro Colorado Island (Croat, 1978), the Flora of the Río Palenque Science Center in Ecuador (Dodson and Gentry, 1978), and the Flora of Jauneche (Dodson et al., 1985). The first work described 1321 species from an area of 15.6 km², the second 1025 species from just 1.7 km², of which only 0.8 km² is natural vegetation and the rest a palm plantation, and the third 728 species from 130 ha.

MONTANE AND LOWER MONTANE MOIST FORESTS

Since extensive mountain ranges occur in the American tropics, there are many types of montane forests throughout the region (Fig. 6.11). The mountains vary from ancient Precambrian forma-

Fig. 6.11. View from ridge of Serra Parima, Brazil, showing the boundary between the plateau's open vegetation and the lower montane forest which covers the slopes.

tions of the Guiana and Brazilian shields to the recently formed Andes. The mountains occur in both humid and arid areas, and consequently the forests range from dry lower montane forest to extremely humid cloud forests. Small changes in altitude can have extremely important changes on vegetation type, physiognomy, species composition and climate. For example, small low hills in the arid northeast of Brazil tend to accumulate cloud and therefore are covered by tall moist forest. These forest islands, termed *brejos* were described in some detail by De Andrade-Lima (1982). The differences between larger and smaller mountains, or the *Massenerhebung* effect (Grubb and Whitmore, 1966), as well as the effect of latitude on vegetation type, is quite striking in the neotropics. Consequently, there are many small patches of typically montane or cloud forests on small outcrops throughout the lowland region. Also the altitudinal limits of the different forest types vary considerably, depending on the effects of local climate, soil, latitude, etc. It is therefore not possible to separate different categories of forest solely on altitude as has been done by Projeto Radambrasil (1973–1983), although the distinction made between the lowland forest on flat plains and the forest on more undulating terrain over 200 m altitude is important in terms of species differences. Figure 6.9 gives distribution maps of a few upland forest species.

The Andes

In the more extensive mountain areas, such as those of the Central American Cordilleras, the Andes and the Guayana Highland, the lowland forest types tend to extend up the mountains to between 700 and 1000 m, above which they are replaced first by lower montane followed by montane vegetation types. A useful subdivision of montane forests, which applies well through much of the higher mountain ranges of Andean South America, is that of Grubb (1974). He recognized three distinct forest types which occur between the lowland rain forest and the tree line: (1) lower montane forest; (2) upper montane forest; and (3) subalpine forest (which Grubb divides into two zones).

Lower montane forest begins between 700 and 1200 m. It is quite similar to lowland rain forest, but a large number of species drop out and are replaced by more upland species. This forest tends to be lower than that of the surrounding lowland area, with fewer woody vines and less-buttressed trees. Vascular epiphytes are of common occurrence, and mesophyll leaf types are still predominant. Many of the lowland taxa still persist in this zone, such as species of *Licania* (Chrysobalanaceae) and *Eschweilera* (Lecythidaceae), but a number of distinctly highland elements also enter the lower montane forest, for example in the Colombian Andes: *Alchornea bogotensis*, *Brunellia comocladifolia*, and *Cinchona cuatreca-sasii*. Palms such as *Euterpe purpurea* and *Wettiniicarpus cladospadix* are still quite abundant, and woody vines include *Anomospermum chloranthum* and species of *Passiflora* and *Paullinia*. This zone typically extends upwards to anywhere between 1800 and 2400 m, depending on latitude and local conditions. The forest studied in detail by Grubb et al. (1963), and Grubb and Whitmore (1966) was of the lower montane forest type.

The **upper montane forest** which begins at 1800 to 2400 m may extend in places up to 3400 m. It is usually less tall than the lower montane forest, with a predominance of microphyllous trees. Vascular epiphytes are still common, but woody lianas rarer. An increasing number of species characteristic of higher altitude enter the flora, for example *Brunellia occidentalis*, *Symplocos pichindensis* and *Weinmannia balbisiana*, and the vines include *Hydrangea peruviana* and *Liabum megacephalum*. Good descriptions of the upper montane forests of Peru were given by Weberbauer (1911, 1945).

The **subalpine forest**, including the dwarf elfin forests of frequent occurrence in the Andes and locally in Central America, is microphyllous or, at its altitudinal extreme, nanophyllous. Few vascular epiphytes and climbers occur, but there are abundant bryophytes and lichens. This formation may extend up to 3800 m in some places, above which it is replaced by the herbaceous alpine formations such as páramo and puna. The subalpine forest has few predominantly lowland genera, but many characteristic of the highland, for example, many species of *Befaria* (Ericaceae), *Brunellia* (Brunelliaceae), *Clusia* (Clusiaceae), *Gynoxys* (Asteraceae), *Miconia* (Melastomataceae), *Rhamnus* (Rhamnaceae) and *Weinmannia* (Cunoniaceae).

A list of species and genera which occur in the montane forest of the Colombian Andes was given by Cuatrecasas (1957, 1958).

Other writers who have described the Andean forest vegetation in some detail include Weberbauer (1911), Herzog (1923), Diels (1937), Ellenberg (1959), Troll (1959), Ferreyra (1960), Koepcke (1961), and Van der Hammen et al. (1983).

In the Andean region a marked difference is found between the forests north and south of the Huancabamba deflection or the Piura divide (Vuilleumier, 1969). At this low altitudinal point in Andes chain, noteworthy changes occur in species composition in both the cloud forest and the herbaceous alpine formations. This was well documented for species of *Fuchsia* by Berry (1982).

Podocarpus forest

A separate category is needed for this forest which remains today mainly in the lower montane region of the department of Cajamarca in northern Peru. Naturally it occurs scattered along the Andes of Colombia and Peru and in the Coastal Cordillera of Venezuela, but little of this forest type still stands today. In the Cajamarca region *Podocarpus oleifolius* is dominant in mixed forest, where *Drimys winteri* and *Weinmannia* are also common trees.

Isolated cloud forests on low mountains

In some places, especially near the sea, the zones of montane forest are compressed into a lower and smaller range of altitude. For example, in the classic studies of Beard (1946) in Trinidad, three zones are recognized: but lower montane forest occurs from 250 to 760 m, montane rain forest from 760 to 880 m and elfin woodland above 880 m. These zones are distinct both physiognomically and in species composition from those of the Andes, which extend over a much greater altitudinal range. For example, *Byrsonima spicata* and *Licania ternatensis* dominate the lower montane forest while *Eschweilera trinitensis* and *Richeria grandis* dominate the montane forest. *Clusia intertexta* is the commonest tree in the elfin woodland. The predominance of particular species

in each formation suggests another difference between the montane formations and those of the lowland forest, namely, a tendency towards dominance accompanied by a loss of species diversity. Hence, in the montane regions many attempts have been made to classify the vegetation of local areas in terms of Braun-Blanquet associations such as the *Cordietum lanatae*, *Hesperomeletum ferruginae*, *Weinmannietum tolimense* and *Weinmannietum tomentosae* of Cuatrecasas (1934). In the elfin forests of Trinidad the entire woody flora amounts to only eleven species. As in the Andes vascular epiphytes are absent or rare, but are replaced by an extremely rich epiphyte synusia of bryophytes and lichens. This compression of the montane zones into only 1000 m in Trinidad serves to illustrate the inadequacy of depending exclusively on altitude in an attempt to classify the montane formations. The physiognomy, leaf types, and species composition are much better criteria.

Another area of montane formations which has been the subject of a detailed analysis is the Serrania de Macuira, Guajira, Colombia also located at a comparatively low altitude. This has been studied by Sugden (1982a, b), and is typical of several small isolated mountains in northern Colombia and Venezuela (Fig.6.12F). Although Serrania de Macuira only reaches 865 m, and the rainfall of the surrounding area is less than 1000 mm, the mountain top is covered by typical cloud forest with low gnarled stunted trees and an abundance of vascular epiphytes (see Sugden and Robbins, 1979). In the latter respect this forest is similar to the lower montane rain forest of Grubb (1974), but in physiognomy and leaf structure it is much more similar to that of the upper montane forest. This illustrates the inadequacy of any simple treatment of the montane vegetation types of South America. In this brief space only generalities can be given rather than full local details. Sugden gave full species lists as well as phytogeographical details of the species present, showing that they are not endemic to this small cloud-forest area. Similar areas of cloud forest include mountains in Panama (Myers, 1969; Gentry, 1978), the Peninsula de Paraguana, Venezuela (Tamayo, 1941), the island of Margarita (Johnston, 1909), and Jamaica (Tanner, 1980). Lewis (1971) pointed out the high number of endemics in the low-altitude cloud forests of

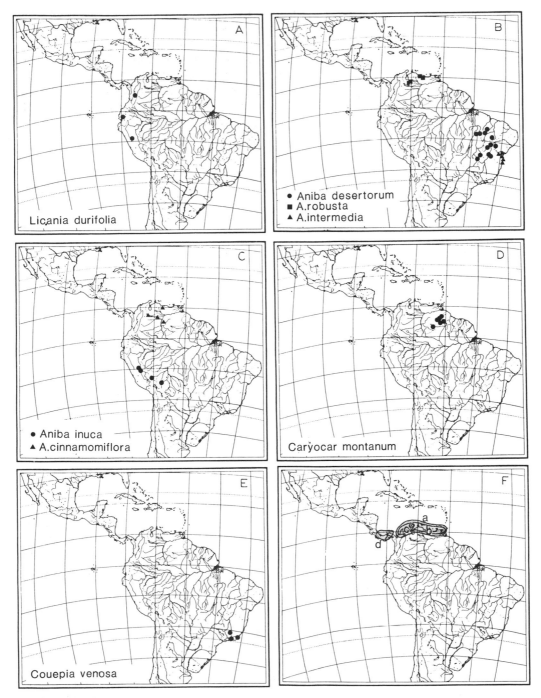

Fig. 6.12. Distribution of some montane forest species: (A) *Licania durifolia*; (B) *Aniba robusta*; (C) *Aniba muca* and *A. cinnamomiflora*; (D) *Caryocar montanum*; (E) *Couepia venosa*; (F) distribution of groups of upland species adapted from Sugden (1982a): *a* = *Anthurium crassinervium, Coccoloba coronata, Guettarda divaricata, Machaerium humboldtianum, Philodendron erubescens, Ruellia macrophylla*; *b* = *Actinostemon concolor, Croton margaritensis, Elleanthus arpophyllostachys, Epidendrum agathosmicum, Guzmania cylindrica, Hillia costanensis, Mandevilla bella, Maxillaria sophronitis, Mouriri rhizophoraefolia, Vriesea splendens, Zamia muricata*; *c* = *Cynanchum atrovirens, Rudgea marginata, Scutellaria verecunda*; *d* = *Schlegelia fuscata, Stemmadenia minima*.

Panama on Cerro Jefe and the Santa Rita ridge. He cited examples of many endemic species.

Atlantic coastal Brazil

The mountains of the coastal range of Brazil in Rio de Janeiro and São Paulo states, for example Serra dos Orgãos, Serra Itatiáia and Serra do Mar, which in places range up to 2000 m, are mainly covered by lower montane forest, with a higher percentage of endemics that do not occur in other distant montane forests. Toward the summits, compressed into the smaller altitudinal range available, forests of lower stature occur, similar to the cloud forests described for Venezuela and Panama and the elfin forests of the Andes. The montane forests of eastern Brazil are particularly rich in Myrtaceae (*Eugenia* spp.), and other common genera are *Roupala* (Proteaceae), *Alsophila* and *Dicksonia* (tree ferns), and many Malpighiaceae. Above 1600 m stands of the gymnosperms *Araucaria angustifolia* and *Podocarpus lambertii* are frequent.

The Guayana Highland

An area with an extremely complex mixture of vegetation types is the Guayana Highland. Mountain slopes covered by lower and upper montane forest are common. In many cases there is an abrupt change to open savanna and swamp formations on the summits of the mountains, because of the sheer sandstone cliff faces. On the summits of the highest mountains there is more open vegetation and less forest, except for gallery forest along the streams. The lower mountains have considerable quantities of forest on their summits. For example, Cerro Guaiquinima, one of the largest sandstone *tepuis*[1], has 40% of the summit covered by forest (Steyermark and Dunsterville, 1980), both tall forest and relatively low dense forest, as well as intermediate types. Steyermark and Dunsterville emphasized the relationship between the forest on the summit of this and other Guayana mountains with the forest of the low-

---

[1]*Tepui* is the Venezuelan term for the characteristic table mountains of the Guayana Highland with more or less flat surfaces formed of sandstone from the Roraima Formation.

lands. A good review of the history of the flora of this region was published by Maguire (1970).

A series of papers by Steyermark (1968, 1974, 1979a, b, 1982) provides information concerning the flora and distributions of species in the Guayana Highland, including data on forest as well as herbaceous formations. Disjunctions of species such as *Graeffenrieda weddellii* (Melastomataceae) in the coastal Cordillera and the Guayana Highland, and many local centers of endemism of forest species, are also discussed by Steyermark (1982).

Life zones

Montane forests have also been divided into life zones summarized by Holdridge (1967) and Holdridge et al. (1971). In this system premontane, lower montane, montane and subalpine forests are recognized, as well as forests having different levels of humidity, resulting in categories designated as dry, moist, wet and rain forests. This system is applicable in Central America where there are extreme variations in altitude and climate over short distances, and is useful for ecological studies. A good summary of the vegetation of Costa Rica using the life zones of the Holdridge system is given by Hartshorn (1983), where nine categories of montane and premontane forest are recognized. Since the forest types discussed in this Chapter are defined more in terms of phytogeography, the life-zone system is not discussed in further detail here. In the larger areas of Amazonian South America where edaphic factors are major vegetational determinants, and in small mountain ranges where the *Massenerhebung* effect is particularly apparent, it is less applicable.

INUNDATED FOREST TYPES

The larger river basins, and the periodic heavy rainy seasons responsible for the rise and fall of the river level, create substantial areas of inundated forest types in South America. Consequently, these forests are distinct due to edaphic reasons rather than local climate differences. Because of the stress caused by waterlogging of the root systems, inundated forest types are generally less diverse in species than well-drained upland forest and there is

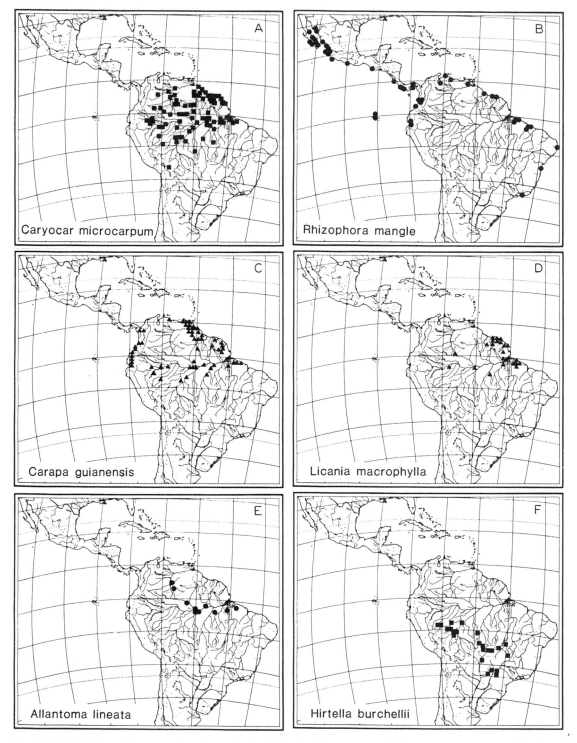

Fig. 6.13. Distribution of some species characteristic of inundated forest types. (A) *Caryocar microcarpum*; (B) *Rhizophora mangle*, mangrove species; (C) *Carapa guianensis*; (D) *Licania macrophylla*; (E) *Allantoma lineata*; (F) *Hirtella burchellii*, riverside in Amazonia extending into gallery forest of cerrado region.

TABLE 6.3

Summary of inundated forest types

1. Permanent swamp forest
   a.   Pemanent white-water swamp forests
   b.   Permanent igapó (black or clear water)
2. Periodically flooded forest
   a.   Mangrove
   b.   Tidal swamp or várzea forest
   c.   Seasonal várzea
   d.   Seasonal igapó
   e.   Floodplain forest
3. Gallery forest

also less regional endemism. The inundated forest types of Amazonia were defined and described in detail by Prance (1979) and were also discussed in Junk (1983). There is relatively little permanent swamp forest in South America, but a large amount of seasonal swamp. The various inundated forest types are defined in Table 6.3, and some typical distributions of inundated forest species are shown in Fig. 6.13.

Permanent swamp forest

This occurs in a few regions especially in low ground behind natural levees. It is most common in white-water regions although a few black-water swamps occur. Species diversity is low, and the soil under the forest is a eutrophic gley, or dystrophic humic gley in some palm swamps. Most permanent swamp areas are dominated by palms, especially species of *Mauritia* and *Euterpe*. Both genera are widely distributed and have species in most of the major phytogeographic regions.

Periodically flooded forest

There are two types of periodic flooding, those caused twice daily by tidal movements and those caused by the seasonal rise and fall of the river levels. It is important to distinguish these types because of the differences in forest composition. Mangrove and tidal várzea are flooded daily, the others seasonally.

Mangrove forests

Mangrove forests owe their existence to salt water, and are adapted to the daily flooding by

tide, hence the elaborate root structure to anchor the trees in the muddy waterlogged soil, and the presence of pneumatophores on the roots of most species. On the Atlantic side of South America mangroves occur along parts of the coasts of Colombia and Venezuela, especially in the Orinoco Delta and the Gulf of Paria, the Puerto Cabello region and the west coast of Lake Maracaibo, the coast of the Guianas and along the Brazilian coast to 28°S. On the Pacific coast, mangroves occur along the entire coast of Colombia, to the San Lorenzo region of Ecuador, and in northern Peru in the Tumbes Delta. They do not extend farther south because of the cool Humboldt current of the western coast. In the Caribbean, mangroves occur in limited coastal areas and in some extensive swamp formations. *Avicennia germinans* is the species most tolerant of low temperatures, and usually marks the northern and southern extremes of mangrove (West, 1977).

The Brazilian mangrove forests are dominated by *Rhizophora mangle* (Fig. 6.13B) which occurs nearest the sea, *Avicennia tomentosa* and *A. germinans* farther inland into the estuary of the Amazon, while *Laguncularia racemosa* occurs in the higher slightly brackish, sandy terrain. *Conocarpus erectus* is another common species. Species which are often found on the fringes of these mangroves include *Annona glabra*, *Hibiscus tiliaceus*, *Pithecellobium cochleatum* and *Pterocarpus officinalis*.

The Pacific coastal mangrove forests are much richer in species (see Gentry, 1982a), and typical ones include: *Ardisia granatensis*, *Avicennia germinans*, *Conocarpus erectus*, *Conostegia polyandra*, *Laguncularia racemosa*, *Mora megistosperma*, *Pelliciera rhizophorae*, *Rhizophora harrisonii*, and *Tabebuia palustris*. Characteristic of the margins of Pacific mangrove forests is *Hirtella carbonaria*, a species much sought-after as a source of charcoal. *Avicennia*, *Conocarpus*, *Laguncularia* and *Rhizophora* all extend as far south as northern Peru. The mangroves of Ecuador were discussed by Acosta-Solís (1959).

In the West Indies one species each of *Avicennia*, *Conocarpus*, *Laguncularia* and *Rhizophora* occur. *Rhizophora mangle* often occurs in pure stands, and is by far the most abundant species. Various legumes characterize the margins of the mangrove forests such as species of *Caesalpinia*, *Dalbergia*, *Piscidia* and *Pterocarpus*.

A good comparative review of the structure of several American mangrove forests is that of Pool et al. (1977). The Brazilian mangrove forests were discussed in some detail by Huber (1909a) and a good review of the American mangroves was given by West (1977) where distribution maps of the principal species are given. More recently mangrove forests were reviewed by Tomlinson (1986).

Tidal swamp forest (tidal várzea)

This is a forest of the delta regions on muddy soil formed by back-up of fresh water caused by tidal movements. The largest area is in the Amazon delta region, where it extends at least 100 km inland; but such flooding also occurs in the delta regions of several other major South American rivers, such as the Orinoco and the rivers of the west coast of Colombia. Tidal swamp tends to have an extraordinary abundance of palms, for example in Amazonia: *Astrocaryum murumuru*, *Euterpe oleracea*, *Jessenia bataua*, *Manicaria saccifera*, *Mauritia flexuosa*, *Maximiliana regia*, *Oenocarpus* sp., and *Raphia taedigera*. Other common species are *Calophyllum brasiliense*, *Ficus* sp., *Macrolobium acaciifolium*, *Pachira aquatica*, *Symphonia globulifera*, and *Triplaris surinamensis*. Some of the estuarine swamp forests have an extremely high biomass and are consequently subject to much timber exploitation, especially on Marajó Island in the Amazon delta.

Buttresses and stilt roots are particularly common in this formation. The Pacific coastal swamp forests were described by Cuatrecasas (1958), who listed as characteristic species *Brosimum utile*, *Dussia lehmannii*, *Iryanthera ulei*, *Mora oleifera*, *Pachira aquatica*, *Pterocarpus officinalis*, *Symphonia globulifera* and *Tovomita rhizophoroides*. Stilt-root palms include *Euterpe cuatrecasana*, *E. rhodoxyla* and *Mauritiella pacifica*. In the Orinoco swamp forest *Carapa guianensis*, *Ceiba pentandra*, *Mora excelsa*, *Hirtella triandra*, *Pentaclethra filamentosa* and *Terminalia obovata* are common species, as well as the following palms: *Astrocaryum* sp., *Manicaria saccifera* and *Mauritia flexuosa*. Anderson and Mori (1967) described a swamp forest in Puerto Viejo, Costa Rica, which is dominated by *Raphia taedigera*. This forest occurs both in tidal areas and other permanently waterlogged areas beyond the tidal influence.

Seasonal swamp forest (Amazonian várzea)

This forest is flooded periodically by muddy or white water from rivers. It is tall and physiognomically quite similar to upland forest, but has fewer species. This formation, known as *várzea* in Brazil and *tahuampa* in Peru, occurs on sedimentary ground. In flooded areas of clay soil there is a tendency towards high river banks or natural levees. There are several different types of seasonal swamp forest. In the lower Amazon it tends to be associated with large expanses of robust grassland (*canarana*), while in the upper Amazon and other river basins this is absent.

Swamp forest (várzea) with associated grassland. These canarana grassland várzeas are typical of the lower Amazon, especially in the region between Monte Alegre in Pará and Itacoatiara in Amazonas where the river tends to be broad, and they also occur in the lower Rio Madeira region and were discussed by Junk (1983). The forest occurs as narrow stretches on higher ground beside the rivers, and behind are meadows of robust grasses including *Echinochloa polystachya*, *E. spectabilis*, *Hymenachne amplexicaulis*, *H. donacifolia*, *Leersia hexandra*, *Luziola spruceana*, *Panicum elephantipes*, *P. fasciculatum* and *Paspalum platyaxis*. The grass meadows stretch from the várzea forest to the margin of the terra firme forest, and in the lowest parts lakes are formed. Some characteristic tree species of the lower Amazon várzea are *Pseudobombax munguba*, *Calycophyllum spruceanum*, *Cecropia paraensis*, *Crateva tapia*, *Cordia tetrandra*, *Hura crepitans*, *Muntingia calabura*, *Pithecellobium multiflorum* and *Trichilia singularis*. *Salix humboldtiana* occurs mainly on muddy beaches that are in the process of formation, and is thus an important colonizer species.

Swamp forest (várzea) without canarana. In Amazonia these várzeas are found along all muddy or white water rivers above Manaus. The forest is continuous up to the terra firme, or is broken up by lakes, but without large areas of grass. The understory vegetation is rich, especially in the upper Amazon and in Amazonian Peru, where abundant species of *Heliconia*, Cyclanthaceae, Marantaceae and Zingiberaceae occur. Buttressed trees are common, such as *Ceiba pentandra*, one of the most characteristic trees of the várzea. Other common trees are *Astrocaryum jauari, Calycophyllum spruceanum, Carapa guianensis, Caryocar microcarpum, Hevea brasiliensis, Hura crepitans, Macrolobium acaciifolium* and several species of *Eschweilera*.

In some places the várzea forest has a rather different physiognomy, and is much lower in stature with few big trees. Characteristic of these forests are *Hevea benthamiana, Pachira aquatica, Symphonia globulifera* and *Virola surinamensis*.

Other areas outside Amazonia where seasonal swamp forest occurs in significant quantities include the lower Orinoco and some of its tributaries (where palms are particularly common), the lower Río Magdalena in Colombia, and a few small patches along the rivers of the lowland Pacific coastal region of Colombia and Ecuador.

Seasonal igapó

This is a seasonally flooded forest (Fig. 6.14) along black-water and clear-water rivers, and occurs mainly within Amazonia. Physiognomically and in species content it is quite different from the várzea. It also has fewer species and generally a lower biomass, associated with the poor sandy soil and lack of nutrients in the water. The white sand margins of these rivers are covered by trees, which in the dry season grow on pure sand but in the flood season are immersed. Because of the lack of sediments and the sandy soil, natural levees do not form in this vegetation type. Large black-water rivers of Brazil include the Rio Negro and the Rio Ipixuna, and the principal clear-water rivers are the Tapajós, Xingu and Tocantins. The Atabapo on the Colombia – Venezuela border and the Nanay in Peru are other important black-water rivers. Further details of the black-water habitats were given in Huber (1909), Takeuchi (1962c) and Junk (1983).

The most common trees are various members of the Myrtaceae, such as *Eugenia inundata*; species in other families include *Alchornea castaneifolia, Allantoma lineata* (Fig. 6.13E), *Copaifera martii*,

Fig. 6.14. Interior of igapó forest seasonally inundated by the black-water Rio Negro in Brazil.

Couepia paraensis, *Licania apetala*, *Piranhea trifoli-ata*, *Tabebuia barbata* and *Triplaris surinamensis*. The largest area of this type of forest, recently discovered by the Radambrasil project, occurs in the lower Rio Branco region, the area linking the Rios Xeriuini, Catrimani, Univini, and the igapós of the Rios Anaua and Jauaperi. This vast area is connected by water during the crest of the flood season and the vegetation is characteristic of igapó, but is rather more diverse in species than in other areas.

A study of the igapó forest on the Rio Negro near to Manaus by Keel and Prance (1979) found 54 species of trees and shrubs in the area studied. There is a distinct zonation along the moisture gradient from heavily to lightly flooded, but the boundaries of the zones are not abrupt. For example, near the river in heavily flooded areas *Myrciaria dubia* is the commonest species, while farther up the beach it is replaced by *Eugenia cachoeirensis* and *E. chrysobalanoides*, whereas *Schistostemon macrophyllus* grows in less flooded areas and the palm *Leopoldinia pulchra* occurs only in lightly flooded areas.

Floodplain forest

This forest (Fig. 6.15) occurs mainly in the upper parts of the various river basins, and in small rivers flooded at irregular intervals by quickly draining flash floods. Since flooding is generally for short periods only, stress is minimal, and there is consequently a greater diversity of species. Many but not all of the species of terra firme forest can tolerate short periods of inundation. The inundated forests, as well as the gallery forests (see below), are important historically because they persisted, although with decreased area, under the drier climate regimes of the Pleistocene. Although many species of the terra firme do not survive prolonged flooding, they can exist on the fringe of sporadically inundated flood-plain forest, in the same way that forest species survive today at the outer edge of the gallery forests of savanna regions.

Gallery forest

I have separated gallery forests from the flooded forests of predominantly forested areas such as Amazonia, on the basis of important differences. Not only is the species composition often consider-

Fig. 6.15. Floodplain forest on the Rio Curuá in Pará, Brazil. This area is subject to irregular flash floods. The stilt roots are of the palm *Socratea exorrhiza*.

ably different, but the flooding patterns are much less regular or drastic. All major savanna areas, such as the Colombian *llanos*, the Gran Sabana of Venezuela, the Roraima – Rupununi savanna, and the *cerrado* of central Brazil, have gallery forests along the watercourses. Gallery forest exists within a drier vegetation type because of the availability of water. This forest type is usually flooded for short periods. Species of the gallery forest of the cerrado region include: *Cariniana estrellensis*, *Chlorophora tinctoria*, *Hirtella martiana*, *Ilex para-guariensis*, *Licania gardneri*, *Dulacia singularis*, *Qualea ingens*, *Tabebuia caraiba*, *Ternstroemia candolleana*, and *Xylosma venosum*. *Mauritia* palms are frequent in gallery forests. In the caatinga region of northeastern Brazil the gallery forest is often a pure stand of the Carnauba-wax palm, *Copernicia prunifera*. The gallery forest of the llanos has various endemic species such as *Licania subarachnophylla*. Common species include

Allophylus amazonicus, *Bauhinia tarapotensis*, *Casearia javitensis*, *Jacaranda obtusifolia*, *Palicourea condensata*, *Pterocarpus ulei* and the palm, *Mauritia minor*.

The central part of some gallery forests, nearest to the watercourse, is subject to inundation or waterlogging, the outer part usually not being flooded, but the forest occurs because the roots of the trees are able to obtain water.

Gallery forests of the cerrado region were discussed by Eiten (1972, 1975), and Ratter et al. (1973, 1978). A quantitative survey of an area of gallery forest farther south in cerrado region of Mogi Guaçu, São Paulo, was made by Gibbs and Leitão Filho (1978). The most frequent species were *Cyclolobium vecchii* and *Sebastiana klotzschiana* and other common species were *Alchornea triplinervia*, *Duguetia lanceolata*, *Genipa americana* and *Guarea trichilioides*. A total of 59 species of trees occurred in the 7200 m² studied.

TRANSITION FORESTS

I have separated this category for Amazonia because of the large quantities of transition forests that have become apparent since the Projeto Radambrasil (1973–1983) survey of Amazonia. Transition forests are intermediate between the tall rain forest characteristic of much of Amazonia and the open areas of savanna and cerrado. There are several types of transition forest, and they vary from evergreen to semideciduous. They tend to occur in areas with a medium (2000 mm) and highly seasonal rainfall. The largest area of transition forests occurs in the broad belt between the cerrado of the Planalto of central Brazil and the Amazon rain forest, although there are also areas of transition forest types to the north, especially bordering the Roraima – Rupununi savannas. Some types of transition forest, especially *babaçu* forest, have been expanded by human activity. Transition forests are taller and have a more closed canopy and greater biomass than *cerradão* (see below), but are considerably lower in biomass than typical Amazonian rain forest on terra firme. A few scattered patches of similar forest types occur for edaphic reasons within the central part of Amazonia rather than around the perimeter. The lowland transition forests can be

generally grouped into five principal types: open forest without palms, palm forest, liana forest, bamboo forest and dry semideciduous forest.

Open forest without palms

In open forest the cover is considerably lower than in rain forest, usually around 20 m² basal area per hectare, and the trees are generally lower, although occasional individual large trees occur scattered throughout the open forest. Since the canopy is rather open, shrub and liana species are abundant. This open forest is not confined to the periphery of Amazonia, but occurs under various edaphic conditions such as lower water table, impermeable soil, poor soil drainage, and in areas with longer dry seasons and lower relative humidity. Open forest of this type is evergreen and is not affected by fire.

Palm forest

This forest differs from the last type by the abundance of palms, and it is much more widespread than forest without palms. Much of the palm forest is dominated by the *babaçu* palm, *Orbignya* sp. (Fig. 6.16); but other palms may also dominate or occur mixed together, especially bacaba (*Oenocarpus distichus* and other species of *Oenocarpus*), patua or ungarahui (*Jessenia bataua*), açaí da mata (*Euterpe precatoria*) and inajá (*Maximiliana regia*). The largest area of babaçu-dominated forest occurs in Maranhão. This area of pure stands of babaçu is largely man-made. It occurs where open transition forest with babaçu has been felled and the babaçu has regenerated rapidly because of its fire-resistant qualities. The palm forests have a relatively low species diversity and few endemics. There are frequently present a large number of Brazil-nut trees (*Bertholletia excelsa*) and sometimes there are concentrations of the banana-like *Phenakospermum guyannense*.

Liana forest

This is a type of open forest with an exceptional abundance of lianas. In Brazil it is termed *cipoal* or *mata de cipó*. The trees are well spaced and often completely entwined by lianas. In many areas it also contains both the babaçu palm and Brazil-nut

Fig. 6.16. Transition forests dominated by the babassu palm (*Orbignya* sp.) in Maranhão, Brazil.

trees, and the tree species are some of those typical of Amazonian rain forest. It is of low species diversity, and only some Amazonian rain-forest species seem to thrive in liana forest. Liana forests cover a vast area, but tend to be intermeshed with dense forests rather than forming continuous bands. The areas where they occur are therefore complex mosaics of dense and open forest. Liana forest is most abundant between the Xingu and Tocantins rivers, but occurs as far west as the Tapajós. The TransAmazon highway between Marabá and Itaituba cuts right through the area of the most abundant liana forest. It is the dominant forest type in the region of the Rio Itacaiuna and the region of Serra Norte and Serra dos Carajás.

Liana forests occur mainly on the elevated terrain of the Brazilian crystalline shield rather than in the more recently formed alluvial areas of Amazonia. Although they are mostly in southern Amazonia, there are also patches north of the Amazon River — for example, in the Rio Jarí basin and especially in Roraima territory. The Juaneche forest in western Ecuador may be a similar formation (A. Gentry, pers. commun., 1984).

The liana families which predominate are Bignoniaceae, Dilleniaceae, Malpighiaceae, Menispermaceae, and Mimosaceae. Some of the common tree species of liana forest are *Acacia polyphylla*, *Apuleia molaris*, *Astronium gracile*, *Bagassa guianensis*, *Bertholletia excelsa*, *Castilla ulei*, *Hymenaea parvifolia*, *Myrocarpus frondosus*, *Sapium marmieri*, and *Tetragastris altissima*. In low humid areas near streams the mahogany (*Swietenia macrophylla*) is common.

A study by Falesi (1972) of soils along the TransAmazon Highway did not encounter any correlation between soil type and vegetation. At the gross level of his study, liana forest was found to occur both on the richer terra roxa soils and the poorer latosols.

Bamboo forest

This is an open forest type which is abundant from the southern part of Amazonian Peru across Acre, Brazil into Bolivia. It dominates large parts of Acre, and is characterized by the presence of large clumps of bamboo which reach up into the canopy at 30 m and spread over the trees. Some preliminary details of bamboo forest were given by Huber (1906), and it was also described in Projeto Radambrasil (1976). It is an open forest with characteristic tree species of terra firme, and the understory dominated by bamboos. The bamboos rarely form pure stands, and the interspersed trees support the long branches of the bamboos. Three species of bamboo abound (T.R. Soderstrom, pers. commun., 1981), two of *Bambusa* subgenus *Guadua* and one of *Merostachys*. One *Bambusa* species grows along the river edges, and the other two are distributed through the terra firme. In southern Peru this forest type seems to occur in areas with poor soil drainage (A. Gentry, pers. commun., 1984).

Dry semideciduous forest

This is a semideciduous formation found in scattered places in southern Amazonia. It occurs in the region with a more seasonal and much drier climate. In the dry season the trees lose some of their leaves. There are few large expanses of this forest, and it usually occurs in small clusters except for the large amount at the eastern and southern edge of the Amazon forest. Like the liana forest a similar dry forest also occurs to the north in Roraima territory near Caracaraí. The dry-forest region does not have endemic species and contains both Amazonian and drier regional elements from the cerrado and chaco. Some common species of the southern dry forest are: *Bowdichia virgilioides*, *Cenostigma macrophyllum*, *Combretum leprosum*, *Erythrina ulei*, *Geissospermum sericeum*, *Lafoensia pacari*, *Magonia glabrata*, *Orbignya barbosiana*, *Physocalymma scaberrimum*, *Sterculia striata*, *Vochysia haenkeana* and *V. pyramidalis*. In the territory of Roraima, where the forest is physiognomically similar, the species composition is quite different — for example, *Cassia moschata*, *Centrolobium paraense*, *Mimosa schomburgkii* and *Richardella surumuensis*.

The dry forests should not be confused with *cerradão* which also occurs in the same region. Cerradão is tall woody cerrado with typical cerrado species and cerrado physiognomy, and with a great amount of xeromorphism and fire adaptations, such as thick bark and tortuous branches with short internodes.

Ratter et al. (1973, 1978) studied some examples of dry forest in Mato Grosso between Serra Roncador and the headwaters of the Xingu river. In the area studied by Ratter et al. the canopy was at 18 to 23 m, and some of the common canopy trees included *Aspidosperma nitidum*, *Enterolobium schomburgkii*, *Jacaranda copaia*, *Sacoglottis guianensis*, *Sloanea eichleri*, *Vochysia ferruginea* and *Xylopia amazonica*. There is little stratification in this forest except for a few tall emergents such as *Copaifera langsdorffii* and *Hymenaea stilbocarpa*. Lianas are abundant in this forest, but much less so than in liana forest. Ratter et al. (1978) and Eiten (1975) both discussed the distribution of transition forest in Serra do Roncador. Ratter used the presence of *Pterodon pubescens* in dry forest as an indicator of areas that were previously covered by cerrado, but Eiten regarded it simply as a species that can grow in dry forests if they are dry enough. Eiten (1975) gave details of the gradual transition from open cerrado through cerradão with 30 to 40% tree cover to tall forest. The tall tree species of the cerradão gradually drop out and are replaced by elements typical of the Amazon forest. Further details of the cerrado – Amazonian transition vegetation types are given by Eiten (1972).

TROPICAL (AND SUBTROPICAL) EVERGREEN SEASONAL CONIFER FOREST

This tall dense forest, which extends well into the subtropics, is characterized by the presence of the conifer *Araucaria angustifolia*. *Podocarpus lambertii* and *P. sellowii* are also present. It is mainly in Brazil from 20° to 29°30'S, but extends into the province of Missiones in Argentina. This distinct region has many endemic species and must be regarded as a separate phytochorion (see Fig. 6.4). Most of the area has been destroyed, and only a few patches of original vegetation remain in reserves. Some characteristic species include the tree fern *Dicksonia sellowiana*, *Aspidosperma poly-*

neuron, *Cedrela fissilis*, *Drimys brasiliensis*, *Ilex paraguariensis*, *Tabebuia ipe*, and the palm *Arecastrum romanzoffianum* which often occurs in large stands.

FOREST ON WHITE-SAND SOIL

In addition to the igapó or black-water flooded areas with white-sand soils, within Amazonia there are some quite large areas of oligotrophic seral vegetation on leached white-sand soils (spodosols), as well as many smaller islands of similar vegetation. The largest white-sand areas occur in the upper Rio Negro region of Venezuela and Brazil, the Guianas, and Serra do Cachimbo in Pará, Brazil. However, patches of white-sand vegetation occur scattered throughout the region even into Amazonian Peru.

Within Amazonia there has been much confusion in terminology for these areas, for example, in the Rio Negro region it is called Amazonian caatinga, but this can be confused with the entirely different arid caatinga formation in northeastern Brazil. In central Amazonia the word *campina* is used for open areas and *campinarana* for forest, and in Roraima *chavascal* and *charravascal* are applied. In Guyana the vegetation on white sand is known as muri bush and wallaba forest, the latter after the local name of the dominant species, *Eperua falcata*. In the Rio Negro region of Venezuela the term for open scrub on white sands is *bana* and in Peru white-sand forest is termed *varillal* (Revilla, 1978). Other terms are given by Anderson (1981).

The white sands have a variety of origins. In the Guianas the belts of white sand are former sea beaches. Many areas in central Amazonia are uplifted former river beaches or beaches created by inland embayment at the time of higher sea level. Other sandy areas are derived from the weathering of sandstone rocks. In all cases the effect on the vegetation is the same, giving a characteristic form adapted to the nutrient-poor and excessively well drained soil conditions. White-sand formations develop in a climate suitable for rain forest, but limiting factors restrict the vegetation cover, and the species have adapted to the various stress factors of nutrient scarcity and the drainage properties of the soil. There are a reduced number of species and a tendency towards dominance, as for example, in the white-sand often dominated by *Humiria balsamifera*. Physiognomically the vegetation is distinct because of the tendency to have gnarled trunks and small scleromorphic leaves. In some white-sand areas, especially the larger ones, there is a considerable amount of local endemism. This is especially true in the caatinga of the upper Rio Negro, the wallaba forest of Guyana and the cachimbo formation. The vegetation cover varies from open areas with exposed patches of white sand, through scrub, to medium tall forest up to 30 m in height.

The Amazonian caatinga of the upper Rio Negro was first described in detail by Spruce (1908), who was fascinated by it. A quantitative inventory was made by Rodrigues (1961), and terminology was defined by Lisboa (1975), Klinge and Medina (1979) and Anderson (1981). Here I have adopted the terminology of Anderson (1981), and use the term Amazonian caatinga for the forests on white sand. Anderson recognized the following structural phases of Amazonian caatinga: caatinga savanna, caatinga scrub, caatinga woodland and caatinga forest. The latter two categories should be included among the forest types of Amazonia and are referred to below.

Caatinga woodland is more open than the forest type, and has a patchy canopy with trees usually between 5 and 15 m in height, and emergents at 20 m. Caatinga forest has a uniformly closed canopy at 20 to 30 m.

Many other publications have described caatinga vegetation under one or more names. Among the most important are Ducke and Black (1953), Ferri (1960), and Takeuchi (1960 and 1962a, the first treating low caatinga woodland and the second caatinga forest), Aubréville (1961), Rodrigues (1961), Vieira and Oliveira Filho (1962) and Klinge (1967). Descriptions of white-sand vegetation in the Guianas are given by Davis and Richards (1933, 1934), Richards (1952), Fanshawe (1952), Schulz, (1960) and Heyligers (1963).

Certain genera of plants are characteristic of Amazonian caatinga in the Rio Negro region, such as *Byrsonima*, *Clusia*, various Ericaceae, *Henriquezia*, *Lissocarpa*, *Pagamea*, *Platycarpum*, *Retiniphyllum*, *Sipapoa* and *Tovomita*, also many terrestrial Bromeliaceae, Haemodoraceae, Rapateaceae and Xyridaceae. Characteristic species include

Caryocar gracile, Compsoneura debilis, Hevea camporum, H. rigidifolia, Phyllanthus atabapoensis and the palm *Barcella odora*. Grasses and sedges are absent from some Amazonian caatingas such as those of the Rio Vaupés (see Ferri, 1960; Rodrigues, 1961; Vieira and Oliveira Filho, 1962; Pires and Rodrigues, 1964), whereas other caatingas which are lightly flooded, such as those of the Rio Anaua, are rich in grasses and sedges.

The small patches of caatinga (locally called campinas) which occur around Manaus are dominated by such species as *Aldina heterophylla, Glycoxylon inophyllum* and *Humiria balsamifera*. The gnarled, tortuous trees are loaded with epiphytes of Araceae, Bromeliaceae, Gesneriaceae, Orchidaceae and pteridophytes. The open areas of sand are covered by the blue-green alga *Stigonema tomentosum*, and clumps of shrubs and low trees occur with abundant lichens (especially *Cladonia* spp.) around their perimeters. Prance and Schubart (1978) presented evidence that some of these areas were opened up by Indian activity about 800 years ago. The open white-sand vegetation of the lower Rio Negro has been described in some detail by Anderson et al. (1975), and Klinge and Medina (1979) related these areas to the heath forests of Asia.

Anderson (1981) estimated that 54.5% of the vascular flora of the central Amazonian caatingas are species endemic to white-sand vegetation. The other species generally occur in different types of vegetation, especially in igapó and sandstone mountain regions. Of these species 23.6% also occur in upland forest on terra firme oxisols.

Macedo and Prance (1978) studied the dispersal of the species of a small white-sand area, and showed that 75.5% of the species have diaspores adapted to long-distance dispersal by bats, birds or wind. This enables dispersal from one isolated island of white sand to another, and explains the distribution of the species.

An important and large area of open caatinga vegetation on sandy soil occurs in Serra do Cachimbo and the adjacent Rio Cururú region on the Pará – Mato Grosso border in Brazil (Fig. 6.17). Although frequently classified as cerrado or savanna vegetation (by, for example, Projeto Radambrasil, 1975), the dominant vegetation of the entire area is actually similar in physiognomy and structure to that of the caatingas

of the lower Rio Negro, but most of the species are different. This caatinga was described and illustrated in some detail by Lleras and Kirkbride (1978). The Cachimbo caatinga has a mixture of species characteristic of Amazonian white-sand areas and of cerrado species, such as *Caryocar brasiliensis* and *Parinari obtusifolia*. Scrub formations are predominant, but arboreal and woodland caatinga also occur on Serra do Cachimbo.

Caatinga also occurs in other isolated areas of sandy soil scattered throughout Amazonia. Each area has a similar physiognomy, but a rather different species content. Some of the more important areas include the large patches of white sand in the Chapada dos Parecis in Rondônia, where such characteristic caatinga genera as *Abolboda, Clusia, Humiria, Paepalanthus, Retiniphyllum, Syngonanthus, Ternstroemia, Tovomita* and *Xyris* abound. There is also an area of caatinga northwest of Cruzeiro do Sul in Acre, between the Rios Moa and Ipixuna, which are described in Projeto Radambrasil (1977). There are also isolated caatinga areas in the region of the Rios Trombetas and Mapuera, the region of Vigia, and near to Tucuruí, all situated in Pará. The area of these white-sand formations is much larger than was previously believed.

Revilla (1978) and Kinsey and Gentry (1979) described the caatinga of Amazonian Peru. In this wetter region it is more arborescent, and many endemics occur, such as *Hirtella revillae*.

The most detailed study of any caatinga area has been made in the Venezuelan caatinga and bana, where an interdisciplinary group of scientists have made an extensive study of the caatinga ecosystem (see, for example, Herrera, 1977; Herrera et al., 1978; Klinge and Medina, 1979; Uhl and Murphy, 1981).

Two associated formations should be briefly mentioned, *campo rupestre* and *restinga*. Both tend to be open vegetation types, but, as in the case of white-sand formations, closed forest also occurs.

Campo rupestre is caatinga-like vegetation which occurs on open rocky sandstone areas. It is physiognomically similar in species composition to campina. It occurs in Serra do Cachimbo and the Rio Cururu region, in some places in the Campos de Ariranha, and in a few other scattered locations, especially in Bahia and Minas Gerais. Various species of Theaceae, *Clusia, Cyrtopodium,*

Fig. 6.17. Low caatinga forest in sand at Serra do Cachimbo, Pará, Brazil.

Furcraea, Retiniphyllum and several Cactaceae are typical plants of this formation. It is usually rather open, but in some places a forest cover has developed quite similar to some of the transition-forest types.

Restinga is a low scrub or low forest which occurs along the coast of Brazil, on sand-dune areas beyond the influence of salt water. This narrow belt of vegetation occurs as an interrupted belt from Amapá south to Santa Catarina. It is forest-like, especially in Bahia where there are a large number of endemics. More typical thicket-type restinga is characterized by the presence of *Byrsonima crassifolia, Chrysobalanus icaco, Hibiscus tiliaceus, Ipomoea asarifolia, I. pes-caprae, Manilkara triflora* and *Senna uniflora*; Cactaceae are interspersed, such as *Cereus variabilis, Melocactus violacea* and *Opuntia brasiliensis*. A good description of restinga vegetation is given by Morawetz (1983).

Less woody deciduous scrub occurs on the coastal sands and dunes of Colombia and Venezuela.

ACKNOWLEDGMENTS

I thank Drs. G. Eiten, A. Gentry, S.A. Mori, J.A. Steyermark and Douglas Daly for critical reading of this paper, and Rosemary Lawlor for typing the various drafts. Field work that has enabled my study of the different forest areas of South America was financed in major part by the National Science Foundation. I also thank my many friends at the Instituto Nacional de Pesquisas da Amazônia, Manaus and the Museu Paraense Emílio Goeldi for their assistance, especially Drs. João Murça Pires and William A. Rodrigues.

REFERENCES

Allen, P.H., 1956. *The Rain Forests of Golfo Dulce*. Univ. of Florida Press, Gainesville, Fla., 417 pp.

Anderson, A.B., 1981. White-sand vegetation of Brazilian Amazonia. *Biotropica*, 13: 199–210.

Anderson, A.B. and Benson, W.W., 1980. On the number of tree species in Amazonian forests. *Biotropica*, 12: 235–237.

Anderson, A.B., Prance, G.T. and De Albuquerque, B.W.P., 1975. Estudos sobre a vegetação lenhosa da Campina da Reserva Biologica INPA-SUFRAMA. Acta Amazonica, 5(3): 225–246.

Anderson, R.C. and Mori, S.A., 1967. A preliminary investigation of Raphia swamps, Puerto Viejo, Costa Rica. Turrialba, 17(2): 221–224.

Ashton, P., 1969. Speciation among tropical forest trees: Some deductions in the light of recent evidence. Biol. J. Linn. Soc., 1: 155–196.

Aubréville, A., 1961. Etude Écologique des Principales Formations Végétales du Brésil et Contribution à la Connaissance des forêts de l'Amazonie Brésilienne. Centre Technique Forestier, Nogent-sur-Marne, 268 pp.

Beard, J.S., 1944. Climax vegetation in tropical America. Ecology, 25: 127–158.

Beard, J.S., 1946. The Natural Vegetation of Trinidad. Oxford. For. Mem. No. 20, Clarendon, Oxford.

Berry, P.E., 1982. The systematics and evolution of Fuchsia sect Fuchsia (Onagraceae). Ann. Mo. Bot. Gard., 69: 1–237.

Black, G.A., Dobzhansky, T. and Pavan, C. 1950. Some attempts to estimate species diversity and population density of trees in Amazonian forests. Bot. Gaz., 111: 413–425.

Brown Jr., K.S., 1975. Geographical patterns of evolution in Neotropical Lepidoptera: Systematics and derivation of known and new Heliconiini (Nymphalidae: Nymphalinae). J. Entomol., Ser. B, 44(3): 201–242.

Bourlière, F. (Editor), 1983. Tropical Savannas. (Ecosystems of the World, 13) Elsevier, Amsterdam, 730 pp.

Cain, S.A., Castro, G.M. de O., Pires, J.M. and Da Silva, N.T., 1956. Application of some phytosociological techniques to Brazilian rain forest. Am. J. Bot., 43: 911–941.

Campbell, D.G., Daly, D.C., Prance, G.T. and Maciel, V.N., 1986. Quantitative ecological inventory of terra firme and várzea tropical forest on the Rio Xingu, Brazilian Amazon. Brittonia, 38: 369–393.

Connell, J.H., 1978. Diversity in tropical rain forests and coral reefs. Science, 199: 1302–1310.

Croat, T.B., 1978. Flora of Barro Colorado Island. Stanford Univ. Press, Stanford, Calif.

Cuatrecasas, J., 1934. Observaciones geobotánicas en Colombia. Trab. Mus. Nac. Cienc. Nat., Ser. Bot., 27: 1–144.

Cuatrecasas, J., 1947. Vistazo a la vegetación natural del Bajo Calima. Rev. Acad. Colomb. Cienc. Exact. Fís-Quím. Nat., 7(27): 306–312.

Cuatrecasas, J., 1957. A sketch of the vegetation of the North-Andean province. Proc. 8th Pacific Science Congress, 1953, Univ. of Philippines, Diliman, Quezon City, 4: 167–173.

Cuatrecasas, J., 1958. Aspectos de la vegetación natural de Colombia. Rev. Acad. Col. Cienc. Exact. Fís. Nat., 10(40): 221–268.

Davis, T.A.W. and Richards. P.W., 1933. The vegetation of Moraballi Creek, British Guiana. An Ecological study of a limited area of tropical rain forest I. J. Ecol., 21: 350–384.

Davis, T.A.W. and Richards, P.W., 1934. The vegetation of Moraballi Creek, British Guiana: An ecological study of a limited area of tropical rain forest II. J. Ecol., 22: 106–155.

Da Vinha, S.G. and Ramos, T. de J., 1976. Inventário florestal. In: Diagnóstico Socioeconômico da Região Cacaueira,

Recursos Florestais. Vol. 7. Commissão Executiva do Plano du Lavoura Cacaueira and the Instituto Interamericani de Ciências Agrícolas. O.E.A. Ilheus, Bahia, pp. 20–212.

De Andrade-Lima, D., 1957a. Notas para a fenologia da zona da mata de Pernambuco. Rev. Biol. (Lisboa), 1: 125–135.

De Andrade-Lima, D., 1957b. Estudos fitogeograficos de Pernambuco. Inst. Pesq. Agron. Pernambuco, 2.

De Andrade-Lima, D., 1966. Contribuição ao estudo de paralelismo da flora Amazônica-nordestina. Bol. Tecn. Inst. Pesq. Agron. Pernambuco, New. Ser., 19: 1–30.

De Andrade-Lima, D., 1982. Present-day forest refugia in Northeastern Brazil. In: G.T. Prance (Editor), Biological Diversification in the Tropics. Columbia Univ. Press, New York, N.Y., pp. 245–254.

De Granville, J.J., 1978. Recherches sur la flore et la végétation guyanaises. Thesis, Univ. des Sciences et Techniques du Languedoc, Montpellier.

Diels, L., 1937. Beitrage zur Kenntnis der Vegetation und Flora von Ecuador. Bibl. Bot., 116: 1–190.

Dodson, C.H. and Gentry, A.H., 1978. Flora of the Río Palenque Science Center, Los Ríos Province, Ecuador. Selbyana, 4: 1–628.

Dodson, C.H., Gentry, A.H. and Valverde, F.M., 1985. La Flora de Jauneche, Los Ríos, Ecuador. Banco Central de Ecuador, Quito, 512 pp.

Ducke, A. and Black, G.A., 1953. Phytogeographical notes on the Brazilian Amazon. Ann. Acad. Bras. Sci., 25: 1–46.

Eiten, G., 1972. The cerrado vegetation of Brazil. Bot. Rev., 38: 201–341.

Eiten, G., 1975. The vegetation of the Serra do Roncador. Biotropica, 7(2): 112–135.

Ellenberg, H., 1959. Typen tropischer Urwälder in Peru. Schweiz. Z. Forstw., 110: 109–187.

Emmons, L.H. and Gentry, A.H., 1983. Tropical forest structure and the distribution of gliding and prehensile-tailed vertebrates. Am. Nat., 121: 513–524.

Engler, A., 1964. Syllabus der Pflanzenfamilien. Bornträger, Berlin, 12th ed.

Falesi, I.C., 1972. Solos da rodovia Transamazônica. Bol. Tecn. IPEAN, 55: 1–196.

Fanshawe, D., 1952. The vegetation of British Guiana: a preliminary review. Inst. Pap. Commonw. For. Inst. 29, Oxford.

Ferreyra, R., 1960. Algunos aspectos fitogeográficos de Perú. Rev. Inst. Geogr., 6: 41–88.

Ferri, M.G., 1960. Contribution to the knowledge of the Rio Negro "caatinga" (Amazon). Bull. Res. Counc. Israel, Sect. D, 8(3–4): 195–208.

Forero, E., 1982. La flora e la vegetación del Chocó e sus relaciones fitogeograficas. Colomb. Geogr., 10: 77–90.

Gentry, A.H., 1977. Endangered plant species and habitats of Ecuador and Amazonian Peru. In: G.T. Prance and T.S. Elias (Editors), Extinction is Forever. New York Botanical Garden, N.Y., pp. 136–149.

Gentry, A.H., 1978. Floristic knowledge and needs in Pacific Tropical America. Brittonia, 30: 134–153.

Gentry, A.H., 1982a. Phytogeographic patterns as evidence for a Chocó refuge. In: G.T. Prance (Editor), Biological Diversification in the Tropics. Columbia Univ. Press, New York, N.Y., pp. 112–136.

Gentry, A.H., 1982b. Neotropical floristic diversity: Phytogeo-graphical connections between Central and South America, Pleistocene climatic fluctuations, or an accident of the Andean orogeny? *Ann. Mo. Bot. Gard.*, 69: 557–593.

Gentry, A.H., 1982c. Patterns of Neotropical plant species diversity. *Evol. Biol.*, 15: 1–84.

Gentry, A.H., 1984. Some preliminary results of botanical studies in Manu Park. In: *Estudios Biologicas de Parque Nacional de Manu.* Ministerio de Agricultura, Lima.

Gentry, A.H. and Dodson, C., 1988. Tropical rain forests without trees: still the world's most species-rich plant communities. *Biotropica* (in press).

Gibbs, P.E. and Leitão Filho, H.F., 1978. Floristic composition of an area of gallery forest near Mogi Guaçu, State of São Paulo, S.E. Brazil. *Rev. Bras. Bot.*, 1: 151–156.

Grubb, P.J., 1974. Factors controlling the distribution of forest types on tropical mountains: New facts and new perspec-tive. In: J.R. Flenley (Editor), *Altitudinal Zonation in Malaysia.* Trans. 3rd Aberdeen–Hull Symp. on Malaysian Ecology, Univ. Hall, Dept. Geogr., Miscell. Ser., 16: 13–46.

Grubb, P.J. and Whitmore, T.C., 1966. A comparison of montane and lowland rain forest in Ecuador II. The climate and its effects on the distribution and physiognomy of the forests. *J. Ecol.*, 54: 303–333.

Grubb, P.J., Lloyd, J.R., Pennington, T.D. and Whitmore, T.C., 1963. A comparison of montane and lowland rain forest in Ecuador I. The forest structure, physiognomy, and floristics. *J. Ecol.*, 51: 567–601.

Haffer, J., 1969. Speciation in Amazonian forest birds. Science, 165: 131–137.

Hartshorn, G.S., 1983. Introduction to plants. In: D.H. Janzen, (Editor), *Costa Rican Natural History.* Univ. Chicago Press, Chicago, Ill., pp. 118–157.

Herrera, R., 1977. Soil and terrain conditions in the Interna-tional Amazon Project at San Carlos de Rio Negro, Venezuela: Correlation with vegetation types. In: E.F. Brunig (Editor), *Transactions of the Int. MAS-IUFRO Workshop on Tropical Rainforest Ecosystem Research.* Univ. Hamburg, Hamburg, pp. 182–188.

Herrera, R., Jordan, C.F., Klinge, H. and Medina, E., 1978. Amazon ecosystems. Their structure and functioning with particular emphasis on nutrients. *Interciencia*, 3: 223–232.

Herzog, T., 1923. *Die Pflanzenwelt der bolivischen Andean und ihres östlichen Vorlandes.* (Vegetation der Erde, 15) Engelmann, Leipzig, 258 pp.

Heyligers, P.C., 1963. *Vegetation and Soil of a White-Sand Savanna in Suriname.* Elsevier, Amsterdam, 148 pp.

Holdridge, L.R., 1967. *Life Zone Ecology.* Tropical Science Center, San José, Costa Rica.

Holdridge, L.R., Grenke, W.C., Hatheway, W.H., Liang, T. and Tosi Jr., J.A., 1971. *Forest Environments in Tropical Life Zones. A Pilot Study.* Pergamon, Oxford.

Howard, R.A., 1973. The vegetation of the Antilles. In: A. Graham (Editor), *Vegetation and Vegetational History of Northern Latin America.* Elsevier, Amsterdam, pp. 1–38.

Huber, J., 1906. La végétation de la vallée de Rio Purus (Amazone). *Bull. Herb. Boissier*, 4: 249–276.

Huber, J., 1909a. Materiaes para a flora Amazônica. *Bol. Mus. Goeldi Pará*, 5: p. 368.

Hueck, K. and Seibert, P., 1972. *Vegetationskarte von Südamer-ika.* Fischer, Stuttgart.

Johnston, J.R., 1909. Flora of the islands of Margarita and Coche, Venezuela. *Contrib. Gray Herb. Harv. Univ.*, 37: 1–149.

Junk, W., 1983. Ecology of swamps on the middle Amazon. In: A.J.P. Gore (Editor), *Mires: Swamp, Bog, Fen and Moor.* (Ecosystems of the World, 4) Elsevier, Amsterdam, pp. 269–294.

Keel, S.H.K. and Prance, G.T., 1979. Studies of the vegetation of a white-sand black water igapó (Rio Negro, Brazil). *Acta Amazonica*, 9: 645–655.

Kinsey, W.G. and Gentry, A.H., 1979. Habitat utilization in two species of *Callicebus.* In: R.W. Sussman (Editor), *Primate Ecology: Problem-Oriented Field Studies.* Wiley, New York, N.Y., pp. 89–100.

Klinge, H., 1967. Podzol soils: A source of black water rivers in Amazonia. In: H. Lent (Editor), *Atas Simp. Biota Amazônica, Belém 1966*, 3: 117–125.

Klinge, H. and Medina, E., 1979. Rio Negro caatingas and campinas, Amazonas states of Venezuela and Brazil. In: R.L. Specht (Editor), *Heathlands and Related Shrublands.* (Ecosystems of the World, 9) Elsevier, Amsterdam, pp. 483–488.

Klinge, H., Medina, E. and Herrera, R., 1978. Studies on the ecology of the Amazon caatinga forest in Southern Venez-uela: General features. *Acta. Cient. Venez.*, 28: 270–276.

Knight, D.H., 1975. A phytosociological analysis of species-rich tropical forest on Barro Colorado Island, Panama. *Ecol. Monogr.*, 45: 259–284.

Koepcke, H.W., 1961. Synökologische Studien an der Westseite der peruanischen Anden. *Bonn. Geogr. Abh.*, 29.

Lewis, W.H., 1971. High floristic endemism in low cloud forests of Panama. *Biotropica*, 3: 78–80.

Lisboa, P.L., 1975. Observações gerais e revisão bibliográfica sobre as campinas amazonicas de areia branca. *Acta Amazonica*, 5: 211–233.

Lleras, E. and Kirkbride, J.H., 1978. Alguns aspectos da vegetaçao da serra do Cachimbo. *Acta Amazonica*, 8(1): 51–65.

Maas, P.J.M., 1971. Floristic observations on forest types in western Surinam I. *Verh. Kon. Ned. Akad. Wet.*, 74: 269–302.

Macedo, M. and Prance, G.T., 1978. Notes on the vegetation of Amazonia II. The dispersal of plants in Amazonia white sand campinas: The campinas as functional islands. *Brittonia*, 30: 203–215.

Maguire, B., 1970. On the flora of the Guayana Highland. *Biotropica*, 2: 85–100.

Morawetz, W., 1983. Dispersal and succession in an extreme tropical habitat: Coastal sands and xeric woodland in Bahia (Brazil). In: K. Kubitzki (Editor), *Dispersal and Distribution.* Sonderb. Naturwissensch. Verh. Hamburg, Parey, Hamberg, 7: 359–380.

Mori, S.A., Boom, B.M. and Prance, G.T., 1981. Distribution patterns and conservation of Eastern Brazilian coastal forest tree species. *Brittonia*, 33: 233–245.

Mori, S.A., Boom, B.M., De Carvalho, A.M. and Dos Santos, T.S., 1983. Southern Bahian Moist Forests. *Bot. Rev.*, 49: 155–232.

Myers, C.W., 1969. The ecological geography of cloud forest in Panama. *Am. Mus. Novit.*, 2396: 1–52.

Pires, J.M. and Prance, G.T., 1977. The Amazon forest: A natural heritage to be preserved. In: G.T. Prance and T.S. Elias (Editors), *Extinction is Forever*. New York Botanical Garden, N.Y., pp. 158–194.

Pires, J.M. and Rodrigues, J.S., 1964. Sobre a flora das caatingas do Rio Negro. *Anais do XIII Congr. Soc. Bot. Bras.*, pp. 242–262.

Pires, J.M., Dobzhansky, T. and Black, G.A., 1953. An estimate of the number of species of trees in an Amazonian forest community. *Bot. Gaz.*, 114: 467–477.

Pool, D.J., Snedaker, S.C. and Logo, A.E., 1977. Structure of mangrove forests in Florida, Puerto Rico, Mexico and Costa Rica. *Biotropica*, 9: 195–212.

Prance, G.T., 1973. Phytogeographic support for the theory of Pleistocene forest refuges in the Amazon Basin based on evidence from distribution patterns in Caryocaraceae, Chrysobalanaceae, Dichapetalaceae, and Lecythidaceae. *Acta Amazonica*, 3: 5–28.

Prance, G.T., 1977. The phytogeographic subdivisions of Amazonia and their influence on the selection of biological reserves. In: G.T. Prance and T.S. Elias (Editors), *Extinction is Forever*. New York Botanical Garden, N.Y., pp. 195–213.

Prance, G.T., 1979. Notes on the vegetation of Amazonia III. The terminology of Amazonia forest types subject to inundation. *Brittonia*, 31: 26–38.

Prance, G.T., 1982. Forest refuges: Evidence from woody angiosperms. In: G.T. Prance (Editor), *Biological Diversification in the Tropics*. Columbia Univ. Press, New York, N.Y., pp. 137–156.

Prance, G.T. and Schubart, H.O.R., 1978. Notes on the vegetation of Amazonia I. A preliminary note on the origin of the open white sand campinas of the lower Rio Negro. *Brittonia*, 30: 60–63.

Prance, G.T., Rodrigues, W.A. and Da Silva, M.F., 1976. Inventário florestal de um hectare de mata de terra firme Km 30 da Estrada Manaus-Itacoatiara. *Acta Amazonica*, 6: 9–25.

Projeto Radambrasil, 1973–1983. *Levantamento de Recursos Naturais Vols. 1–22*. Ministério das Minas e Energia, Rio de Janeiro.

Projeto Radambrasil, 1975. *Levantamento de Recursos Naturais Vol. 7*. Ministério das Minas e Energia, Rio de Janeiro.

Projeto Radambrasil, 1976. *Levantamento de Recursos Naturais Vol. 12*. Ministério das Minas e Energia, Rio de Janeiro.

Projeto Radambrasil, 1977. *Levantamento de Recursos Naturais Vol. 13*. Ministério das Minas e Energia, Rio de Janeiro.

Ratter, J.A., Richards, P.W., Argent, G. and Gifford, D.R., 1973. Observations on the vegetation of northeastern Mato Grosso I. The woody vegetation types of the Xavantina–Cachimbo expedition area. *Philos. Trans. R. Soc. London, Ser. B*, 266: 449–492.

Ratter, J.A., Askew, G.P., Montgomery, R.F. and Gifford, D.R., 1978. Observations on the vegetation of northeastern Mato Grosso II. Forests and soils of the Rio Suiá–Missu area. *Proc. R. Soc. London, Ser. B*, 203: 191–209.

Revilla, J., 1978. *Comunidades vegetales de Mishima, Río Nanay, Loreto, Peru*. Tese de Grad., Univ. Nacional Mayor de San Marcos, Lima.

Richards, P.W., 1952. *The Tropical Rain Forest: An Ecological Study*. Cambridge Univ. Press, Cambridge, 450 pp.

Richards, P.W., 1969. Speciation in the tropical rain forest and the concept of the niche. *Biol. J. Linn. Soc. London*, 1: 149–154.

Rizzini, C.T., 1963. Nota prévia sobre a divisão fitogeografica do Brasil. *Rev. Bras. Geogr.*, 25: 1–64.

Rodrigues, W.A., 1961. Aspectos fitssociológicos das catingas do Rio Negro. *Bol. Mus. Para. Emílio Goeldi. Nova Ser. Bot.*, 15: 1–41.

Rodrigues, W.A., 1967. Inventário florestal pilôto ao longo da estrada Manaus–Itacoatiara, Estado do Amazonas: Dados preliminares. *Atas do Simpósio Sobre a Biota Amazônica*, 7: 257–267.

Rzedowski, J., 1962. *Vegetación de México*. Editorial Limusa, Mexico City, 432 pp.

Schulz, J.P., 1960. *Ecological Studies on Rain Forest in Northern Suriname*. Noord-Hollandsche, Amsterdam, 267 pp.

Spruce, R., 1908. *Notes of a Botanist on the Amazon and Andes*. Macmillan, London, 2 Vols.

Steyermark, J.A., 1968. Contribuciones a la flora de la Sierra de Imataca, Altiplanicie de Nuria y region adyacente del Territorio Federal Amacuro al sur del río Orinoco. *Acta. Bot. Venez.*, 3: 49–175.

Steyermark, J.A., 1974. Relación floristica entre la cordillera de la costa y la zona de Guayana y Amazonas. *Acta. Bot. Venez.*, 9: 248–249.

Steyermark, J.A., 1979a. Flora of the Guayana Highland: Endemicity of the generic flora of the summits of the Venezuelan tepuis. *Taxon*, 28: 45–54.

Steyermark, J.A., 1979b. Plant refuge and dispersal centres in Venezuela: Their relict and endemic element. Pages 183–221. In: K. Larsen and L.B. Holm-Nielsen (Editors), *Tropical Botany*. Academic Press, London, pp. 183–221.

Steyermark, J.A., 1982. Relationships of some Venezuelan forest refuges with lowland tropical floras. In: G.T. Prance (Editor), *Biological Diversification in the Tropics*. Columbia Univ. Press, New York, N.Y., pp. 182–220.

Steyermark, J.A. and Dunsterville, G.C.K., 1980. The lowland floral element on the summit of Cerro Guaiquinima and other cerros of the Guayana Highland of Venezuela. *J. Biogeogr.*, 7: 285–303.

Sugden, A.M., 1982a. The vegetation of Serranía de Macuira, Guajira, Colombia: a contrast of arid lowlands and an isolated cloud forest. *J. Arnold Arb.*, 63: 1–30.

Sugden, A.M., 1982b. The ecological, geographical, and taxonomic relationships of the Flora of an isolated Colombian cloud forest, with some implications for island biogeography. *J. Arnold Arb.*, 63: 31–61.

Sugden, A.M. and Robbins, R.J., 1979. Aspects of the ecology of vascular epiphytes in Colombian cloud forests 1. The distribution of the epiphytic flora. *Biotropica*, 11: 173–188.

Takeuchi, M., 1960. A estrutura de vegetação na Amazonia III. A mata de campina na região do Rio Negro. *Bol. Mus. Para. Emilio Goeldi Nova Ser. Bot.*, 8: 1–13.

Takeuchi, M., 1961. The structure of the Amazonian vegetation II. Tropical rain forest. *J. Fac. Sci. Univ. Tokyo, Sect. III, Bot.*, 8: 1–26.

Takeuchi, M., 1962a. The structure of the Amazonian vegetation IV. High campina forest in the Upper Rio Negro. *J. Fac. Sci. Univ. Tokyo, Sect. III, Bot.*, 8: 279–288.

Takeuchi, M., 1962b. The structure of the Amazonian vegetation V. Tropical rain forest near Uapés. *J. Fac. Sci. Univ. Tokyo, Sect. III, Bot.*, 8: 289–296.

Takeuchi, M., 1962c. The structure of the Amazonian vegetation VI. Igapó. *J. Fac. Sci. Univ. Tokyo, Sect. III, Bot.*, 8: 297–304.

Takeuchi, M., 1973. The structure of the Amazonian vegetation VII. Tropical rain forest near Leticia in Colombia. *Rep. Inst. Breeding Res., Tokyo Univ. Agric.*, 4: 11–18.

Tamayo, F., 1941. Exploraciones botánicas en la Península de Paraguaná, Estado Falcón. *Bol. Soc. Venez. Ci. Nat.*, 7: 1–90.

Tanner, E.V.J., 1980. Studies on the biomass and productivity of a series of montane rain forests in Jamaica. *J. Ecol.*, 68: 573–588.

Toledo, V.M., 1976. *Los cambios climáticos del Pleistoceno y sus efectos sobre la vegetación tropical cálida y húmeda de México*. Ms. thesis, Fac. de Ciencias, Univ. Nac. Autómoba de México.

Toledo, V.M., 1982. Pleistocene changes of vegetation in Tropical Mexico. In: G.T. Prance (Editor), *Biological Diversification in the Tropics*. Columbia Univ. Press, New York, N.Y., pp. 93–111.

Tomlinson, P.B., 1986. *The Botany of Mangroves*. Cambridge Univ. Press, Cambridge, 413 pp.

Troll, C., 1959. Die Tropischen Gebirge. Ihre dreidimensionale klimatische und pflanzengeographische Zonierung. *Bonn. Geogr. Abh.*, 25.

Tschirley, F.N., Dowler, C.C. and Duke, J.A., 1970. Species diversity in two plant communities of Puerto Rico. In: H.T. Odum (Editor), *Tropical Rain Forest*. U.S. Atomic Energy Commission, Oak Ridge, Tenn., pp. B91–B96.

Uhl, C. and Murphy, P., 1981. Composition, structure, and regeneration of a terra firme forest in the Amazon Basin of Venezuela. *Trop. Ecol.*, 22: 219–237.

UNESCO, 1981. *Vegetation Map of South America*. Natural Resources Research Publ. 17.

Van der Hammen, T., Perez Preciado, A. and Pinto, E.P., (Editors), 1983. *La Cordillera Central Colombiana, Transecto Parque Los Nevados*. (Studies on Tropical Andean Ecosystems 1). Cramer, Vaduz, 345 pp.

Vega, L., 1968. La estructura de los bosques húmedos tropicales del carare, Colombia. *Turrialba*, 18: 416–436.

Vieira, L.S. and Oliveira Filho, S.P., 1962. As caatingas do Rio Negro. *Bol. Téc. Inst. Agron. N.*, 42: 7–32.

Vuilleumier, F., 1969. Pleistocene speciation in birds living in the high Andes. *Nature*, 223: 1179–1180.

Weberbauer, A., 1911. *Die Pflanzenwelt der peruanischen Anden*. (Vegetation der Erde, 12) Engelmann, Leipzig, 352 pp.

Weberbauer, A., 1945. *El Mundo Vegetal de los Andes Peruanos*. Ministerio de Agricultura, Lima.

Werger, M.J.A., 1978. Biogeographical division of Southern Africa. In: M.J.A. Werger (Editor), *Biography and Ecology of Southern Africa*. Junk, The Hague, pp. 145–170.

Werger, M.J.A. and Van Gils, H., 1976. Phytosociological classification in chorological borderline areas. *J. Biogeogr.*, 3: 49–54.

West, R.C., 1977. Tidal salt-marsh and mangal formations of Middle and South America. In: V.J. Chapman (Editor), *Wet Coastal Ecosystems*. (Ecosystems of the World, 1) Elsevier, Amsterdam, pp. 193–213.

White, F., 1976. The vegetation map of Africa: the history of a completed project. *Boissiera*, 24: 659–666.

White, F., 1979. The Guineo–Congolian region and its relationships to other phytochoria. *Bull. Jard. Bot. Natl. Belg.*, 49: 11–55.

Chapter 7

VASCULAR EPIPHYTISM IN AMERICA

DAVID H. BENZING

INTRODUCTION

The distinguished 19th century biogeographer A.F.W. Schimper studied vegetation the world over, but nowhere was he more impressed by floristic diversity than in tropical America. So striking were contributions of the epiphyte synusia to complexity in Brazilian, Venezuelan and Caribbean humid forests that an entire volume (1888) was devoted to describing the canopy-based plant life he observed there. Schimper's judgments on variety and botanical novelty have indeed proven accurate. A little more than half of all vascular epiphytes are American (Madison, 1977) and these exhibit many of the most specialized features known in the group. Yet despite their impressive numbers and uniqueness, and Schimper's provision of a sound formation for further investigation, neotropical epiphytes have attracted little beyond horticultural, anatomical, and taxonomic interest until quite recently. Biologists are just now becoming aware of the myriad influences epiphytes have on the structure and dynamics of tropical forest ecosystems (Strong, 1977; Benzing and Seemann, 1978; Nadkarni, 1981, 1985; Benzing, 1983, 1984). Central themes of this chapter are: (1) species diversity and the possible reasons why epiphytes are so well represented in neotropical compared to Old World rain forests; (2) adaptations American epiphytes exhibit for dispersal and the gain and processing of resources; and (3) the impact these organisms exert on arborescent supports and other nearby vegetation and animals. No description of neotropical epiphytism is complete without considering this third item, even though similar influences may prevail in the occasional paleotropical forest where the canopy-dependent flora is also unusually well developed.

THE EPIPHYTE SYNUSIA

Categories of epiphytes

Plants that routinely spend at least part of their existence anchored in forest canopies are divisible into four categories:

(1) Holoepiphytes germinate in tree crowns and remain free for life of vascular contact with either phorophyte (supporting tree) or ground (Fig. 7.1); growth on bark is obligate. Essential ions and moisture are usually secured from decomposing litter and rainfall, supplemented by leachates from overhead vegetation.

(2) Facultative epiphytes grow interchangeably on bark and ground; when terrestrial in relatively dry forests, they are restricted to such substrata as rocks and well-drained sand (e.g. many cacti; *Aechmea recurvata* and *Tillandsia capitata* of Bromeliaceae). Most facultative epiphytes are more mesic, preferring pluvial conditions where rooting media in canopy and understory alike are wetted continuously. Bark and soil covered with thick, moist mantles of debris and living thallophytes indiscriminately support numerous aroids, bromeliads, ferns, orchids and gesneriads in neotropical cloud forests. Fresh road cuts throughout much of lower and midmontane tropical America are rapidly colonized by orchids, bromeliads and particularly ferns recruited from adjacent trees. These are eventually displaced by taller vegetation, a sign that epiphytism — at least in cool, humid, neotropical sites — has a decidedly weedy charac-

Fig. 7.1. Fruiting *Tillandsia paucifolia* specimen growing on *Taxodium distichum* in southern Florida. Note sparse rooting.

ter, in the sense that competitive ability is poor and new substrata are preferred. There is evidence that adventitiousness also occurs on drier sites. Claver et al. (1983) reported that xerophytic *Tillandsia aëranthos* and *T. recurvata* were spreading rapidly through crowns of exotic conifers and broad-leaf trees in and around La Plata, Argentina. The authors labelled these species "epiphytic weeds". (On the basis of preliminary experiments, they suspected that the heliophilic *T. recurvata* may hasten the death of its supports by producing a chemical defoliant).

(3) Hemiepiphytes include all species that root in soil at some point in the life cycle. American aroids (especially species of *Anthurium* and *Philoden-dron*), many Cyclanthaceae and Marcgraviaceae exemplify a group known as secondary hemiepi-phytes whose members begin life as vines but become epiphytic later. Primary hemiepiphytes germinate in tree crowns, but eventually anchor in

the forest floor. Roots of stranglers, a small aggregation of the primary hemiepiphytes, expand and fuse upon reaching the ground, and can kill the host by preventing further trunk growth. Palms with persistent leaf bases are especially good supports for stranglers but, in the absence of a cambium, they escape the fate experienced by many dicotyledonous woody hosts. *Ficus* spp. are the most conspicuous neotropical stranglers (Fig. 7.2). *Clusia* and *Griselinia* spp. may also become free-standing trees (Madison, 1977), but rarely, if ever, kill their supports.

(4) Technically, species which produce haustoria constitute a fourth type of epiphyte; unlike the others, these plants draw upon host vasculature and exhibit no other obvious means of taking up mineral ions and moisture. Occasionally, hemi-parasites are quite abundant in neotropical forests:

Fig. 7.2. *Ficus aurea* growing on *Sabal palmetto* in southern Florida.

Tanner (1980) found that these plants comprised up to 25% of the total epiphyte biomass in several moist montane canopies in Jamaica. However, they might have done even better, were it not for a relatively narrow host preference: 80 to 90% of the loranthaceous biomass recorded by Tanner at one site was harvested from crowns of a single *Lyonia* (cf. *octandra*) species. As a whole, Loranthaceae (*sensu lato*) is the largest group of neotropical shoot parasites. Gómez (1983) reported that 38 Costa Rican species in 9 genera parasitize 42 families of dicotyledons. Impressive as this host range may be, it is probably not as great as equal numbers of bromeliads or orchids with comparable geographic distributions would exploit. Should epiparasitism via fungal intermediates indeed exist between some orchids and their hosts, as several reports contend (Ruinen, 1953; Johannson, 1977), category (4) will have to be expanded.

Geographic occurrence

Neotropical epiphytes (hereafter, the term "epiphyte" will designate holoepiphyte unless otherwise qualified) experience a wide range of moisture regimes — their habitats range from rain forests to cactus savannas. Both numbers of individuals and diversity of species vary greatly across this gradient, showing the expected increases at higher humidity. Shrubby epiphytes, like most hemiepiphytes, prefer wet canopies; herbaceous epiphytes are much more versatile. The most arid localities harbor only bromeliads and orchids, and very few of those. In a dry forest in Santa Rosa National Park, Costa Rica, epiphytes constitute only 2% of all species (Janzen and Liesner, 1980). Under somewhat more humid conditions at Juaneche in extreme western Ecuador, that percentage rises to 7%; here, individual plants were counted: 4% of the flora was epiphytic (C.O. Dodson and A.H. Gentry, pers. commun., 1983). In rain forest at Río Palenque, Ecuador (elevation 150–200 m), these same authors noted that 35% of the vascular species and 49% of all individuals were canopy dwellers. Kelly (1985) identified 24.9% of all vascular taxa as "habitual" epiphytes in a Jamaican lower montane rain forest. When the definition was expanded to include every canopy-dependent species, the figure exceeded 38%. Smith (1970) reported that epiphytes constituted 23.4% of the

vascular species in a wet location at 480 m in Puerto Rico. As much as 50% of the flora roots on bark in certain pluvial Ecuadorian montane forests (C.O. Dodson, pers. commun., 1987).

A great abundance of precipitation is not necessarily conducive to epiphytism; in fact, the heavy rainfall characteristic of many hot regions may explain the unexpected scarcity of epiphytes there. Sugden and Robins (1979) concluded that such sites subjected to frequent torrential storms offer poor colonizing opportunities for these plants. Propagules are dislodged before anchorage can take place, and canopies dry out rapidly between storms at high temperatures, rendering exposed bark surfaces too droughty. Epiphytism is best developed where moisture supply is continuous but not necessarily plentiful. This condition obtains in cool cloud forests; here trees are most heavily laden and their foliage often correspondingly diminished. However, relatively few species may account for most of the biomass (Nadkarni, 1983). A preference for relatively cool, humid

Fig. 7.3. Distribution in South America of five genera of Bromeliaceae in the largely epiphytic subfamily Tillandsioideae. Degree of stippling illustrates amount of generic overlap. Note that only the genus *Tillandsia* occurs over most of Amazonia. (After Smith and Downs, 1977.)

conditions is illustrated by the subfamily Tilland-sioideae of Bromeliaceae (Fig. 7.3). Five South American genera range over much of the highlands rimming Amazonia, with greatest diversities in the Andean foothills (Smith and Downs, 1977). Only *Tillandsia* extends through the vast area between. Within this single genus the pattern is repeated (Fig. 7.4): all but one of its six South American subgenera are essentially upland. *Tillandsia* and closely related *Vriesea* are also well represented in Mexico and Central America, respectively, where they show similar geographic affinities. Montane sites are heavily exploited, but *subgenus Tillandsia* once again expresses the most pronounced prefer-ence for warm and, in this case, often arid lowlands (for instance, *T. concolor*, *T. ionantha*, *T. pauci-folia*).

Edaphic occurrence

No systematic effort has been made to document the effects of soil type or fertility on epiphyte

development in neotropical forests. Judging by the heliophilic nature of so many species, opaque canopies promoted by fertile substrata should limit population densities, while heavily leached or acidic soils, if they increase canopy transparency, should allow bark fuller exposure to light and precipitation. Oligotrophic forests over white sands may harbor substantial epiphyte communi-ties (Anderson, 1981), suggesting that shade, more than a meager nutrient supply, limits epiphyte growth in some cases. Dwarf oaks dominating infertile coastal strand communities in southwest-ern Florida (Fig. 7.5) and old, nutrient-stressed specimens of *Taxodium distichum* on thin soils within the Big Cypress Swamp support some of the densest and most diverse *Tillandsia* colonies in the state (Benzing and Renfrow, 1974; Benzing and Seemann, 1978). Bromeliad colonies in crowns of vigorous, denser-canopied *Taxodium* individuals on deeper, richer soils nearby are far fewer, although individual epiphytes can be unusually robust. Janzen (1977) has offered an interesting but as yet untested hypothesis: that epiphytes are, in effect, "starved off" dipterocarps and other trees in certain oligotrophic Malaysian forests. He sug-gested that neotropical counterparts, because they

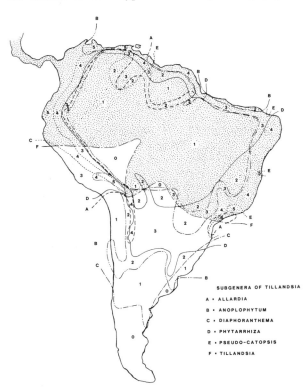

Fig. 7.4. Distribution of *Tillandsia* subgenera in South America. Numbers illustrate degrees of subgeneric overlap. Stippling depicts the range of *Tillandsia*, the only subgenus to have extensively penetrated Amazonia. (After Smith and Downs, 1977.)

Fig. 7.5. An isolated dwarf specimen of *Quercus virginiana* in southwestern Florida heavily infested with *Tillandsia recurvata*. Height <2 m.

most often grow on richer soils, produce much more harvestable food. The resulting better-developed avifauna sustained by this largesse create a "rain of nutrients" that presumably promotes luxuriant epiphyte growth.

Vertical stratification

Epiphytes in dry, open, neotropical forests exhibit little or no vertical segregation, probably because atmospheric humidity and exposure to light are much the same throughout the short canopy. Particular taxa may prefer twigs to thicker axes, and knot-holes or crotches to less penetrable surfaces, but these choices are probably dictated by moisture rather than light requirements. Microclimates vary in denser-foliated, taller, neotropical forests on moister sites; here canopy floras are diverse and stratified, as shown by Pittendrigh's (1948) investigation of bromeliad distribution in cacao plantations and adjacent native forest in humid northern Trinidad. He discovered that these canopy-dwellers could be categorized into three groups based on adaptation for water balance and capacity to tolerate deep shade. Occupying upper, well-illuminated perches in dense wet forest or drier, more open woodlands were members of his "exposure" group (Table 7.1). These were either xeromorphic tankless taxa without absorbing roots — the so-called atmospherics (Fig. 7.1) — or species with deep interfoliar catchments capable of creating large impoundments relative to overall shoot size (Fig. 7.6D). Bromeliad impoundments qualify as phytotelmata, a term which describes all natural water-filled cavities produced by plants. "Sun" group members, most of which possessed sizable tank rosettes, were located deeper in the canopy. At the base of dense, humid forest were the "shade-tolerant" populations, the most hygrophytic of all examined species. Their shallow catchments fashioned of lax rosulate shoots were usually filled with moisture and fallen debris (Fig. 7.6A).

A number of studies have been conducted as follow-ups to Pittendrigh's bromeliad survey, aimed at detecting the physiological concomitants of his three light-related categories (Benzing and Renfrow, 1971; Griffiths and Smith, 1983; Smith et al., 1986a,b; Lüttge et al., 1986; Griffiths et al., 1986). Contrary to Pittendrigh's proposal that members of this group are heliophiles forced to inhabit shady microsites in order to satisfy high humidity requirements, these plants in reality showed adaptation for efficient use of shade light (Benzing and Renfrow, 1971). Nevertheless, Pittendrigh's impression that neotropical epiphytes partition dense forests along ecoclimatic gradients is certainly correct; his proportionalities are probably representative of other humid sites as well. The Trinidad bromeliads were segregated into groups of 14, 21 and 6 taxa in order of increasing shade tolerance (Table 7.1); the vascular rain-forest epiphytes at Río Palenque were divided by Dodson (in Gentry, 1982a) into 111 "canopy-top", 120 "mid-canopy", and 17 "understory" species. Kelly (1985) also observed the greatest diversity of vascular epiphytes in a Jamaican lower montane rain forest at mid-canopy level.

Occasionally, a population's position in a humid forest profile is even more narrowly circumscribed. At Río Palenque, *Peperomia tropaeolifolia* (Fig. 7.7) almost always grows on tree trunks in deep shade within a meter or two of the ground. This same well-defined niche is occupied by distinct bryophyte assemblages in some other forests (Pócs, 1982). In contrast, microsite choices are unusually varied in certain taxa — on occasion, enough to change an epiphyte's category. Several *Tillandsia* species in Florida that root exclusively in tree crowns over much of the state also thrive as terrestrials if substrata are dry enough. Conversely, a number of ferns and flowering plants which are confined to soil at certain locations in tropical America will also root in canopies at other moister sites. Kelly (1985) observed *Philodendron lacerum* growing as a holoepiphyte, secondary hemiepiphyte and terrestrial plant in different Jamaican locations.

MAJOR ADAPTATIONS

Water balance and photosynthesis

An epiphyte's ability to resist desiccation ranges from low for the most hygrophytic hymenophyllous ferns to high in atmospheric bromeliads and many orchids. No neotropical epiphyte beyond some poikilohydrous ferns (e.g. *Polypodium polypodioides*) is fully desiccation-tolerant. Pitten-

TABLE 7.1

Trinidad Bromeliaceae photosynthetic pathway[1], habit[1] exposure and humidity preferences[2]

Category/species	Photo-synthetic pathway	Habit	Relative abundance[3] in humidity zones (maximum rainfall in mm yr^{-1})						
			A 6500	B 5000	C 3200	D 2800	E 2300	F 1800	G 1300
I. EXPOSURE GROUP									
Tillandsia didistichoides	C3	tank	+++						
Catopsis berteroniana	C3	tank		+++	++				
Vriesea amazonica	C3	tank		++	+++	+			
Catopsis sessiliflora	C3	tank		++	+++	++	++	++	
Vriesea procera var. *procera*	C3	tank		++	+++	+++	+++	++	
Catopsis floribunda	C3	tank			++	++	++	++	
Tillandsia gardneri	CAM	atmospheric					++	++	
Tillandsia tenuifolia	CAM	atmospheric					++	++	
Tillandsia stricta var. *stricta*	CAM	atmospheric					++	++	
Tillandsia usneoides	CAM	atmospheric					++	++	
Tillandsia juncea	CAM	atmospheric					++	+++	
Tillandsia utriculata	CAM	tank			+	+	+++	+++	
Tillandsia elongata var. *elongata*	C3/CAM	tank (little impoundment)					++	+++	
Tillandsia flexuosa	CAM	tank						++	+++
II. SUN GROUP									
Vriesea johnstonii	C3	tank	+++						
Glomeropitcairnia erectiflora	C3	tank	+++						
Vriesea broadwayi	C3	tank	+++						
Tillandsia spiculosa var. *micrantha*	C3	tank	+++						
Aechmea aripensis	C3	tank	+++	++					
Vriesea capituligera	C3	tank		+++					
Vriesea rubra	C3	tank		+++					
Tillandsia complanata	C3	tank		+++					
Aechmea fendleri	CAM	tank		+++	++				
Guzmania sanguinea var. *sanguinea*	C3	tank	+	+++	++				
Vriesea splitgerberi	C3	tank	+	+++	++				
Vriesea platynema var. *platynema*	C3	tank		+++	++				
Araeococcus micranthus	CAM	absorptive roots, common ant nest inhabitant			+++				
Aechmea dichlamydea	CAM	tank		++	+++	+++	+++	++	
Guzmania monostachia var. *monostachia*	C3/CAM	tank		++	++	+++	+++	++	+
Aechmea aquilega	CAM	tank			++	++	++	+++	

Tillandsia fasciculata var. *fasciculata*	CAM	tank (little impoundment)	++	++	++	+++	
Tillandsia bulbosa	CAM	atmospheric myrmecophyte	+++	++++	+++	+++	+++
Hohenbergia stellata	CAM	tank	+++	++++	++++		
Aechmea lingulata	CAM	tank	++	++++	++++	++	
Aechmea nudicaulis	CAM	tank	++	++	++++	++++	++

III. SHADE-TOLERANT GROUP

Tillandsia anceps	C3	tank (little impoundment)	+++	+++	+++	+++
Tillandsia monadelpha	C3	tank (little impoundment)	+++	+++	+++	+++
Vriesea simplex	C3	tank	+++	+++	+++	
Vriesea rubra	C3	tank	+++	++	++	
Guzmania lingulata var. *lingulata*	C3	tank	+++	+++	+++	++
Vriesea splendens var. *formosa*	C3	tank	+++	++	++	++

[1] Griffiths and Smith, 1983.
[2] **Pittendrigh**, 1948.
[3] + + + : abundant.
+ + : intermediate.
+ : scarce.

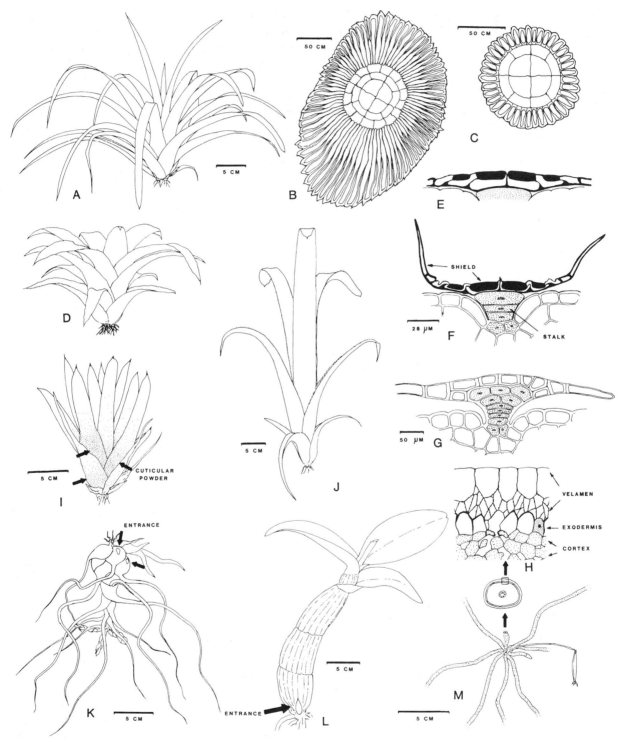

Fig. 7.6. Habits and anatomical details of neotropical epiphytes. (A) Habit of typical shade-tolerant bromeliad; (B) foliar trichome shield of heliophilic *Tillandsia paucifolia*; (C) foliar trichome shield of shade-tolerant *Catopsis nutans*; (D) habit of exposure-type tank bromeliad with an impounding shoot; (E) configuration of central portion of trichome shield of an atmospheric bromeliad when wet; (F) same trichome while leaf surface is dry; (G) foliar trichome of the fern *Polypodium hirsutissimum* (after Müller et al., 1981); (H) velamen and exodermis tissue of *Polyradicion lindenii*; (I) habit of *Catopsis berteroniana*; (J) habit of *Billbergia zebrina*; (K) habit of myrmecophytic *Tillandsia bulbosa* showing entrances created by ants; (L) habit of *Schomburgkia* sp. showing naturally formed entrance for ants; (M) habit of fruiting *Polyradicion lindenii*.

Fig. 7.7. *Peperomia tropaeolifolia* (with the lanceolate, simple leaves).

drigh's bromeliads exemplify the range of humidity requirements and associated adaptations among homoiohydrous epiphytes about as well as any American group. These plants are able to cope with various degrees of drought by adaptations involving shoot habit and leaf physiology/anatomy, including type of photosynthetic pathway.

Forest canopies are relatively arid habitats supplied with water only in pulses; the substrata may be thoroughly soaked during a heavy storm, but are often air-dry within hours. Some epiphytes counter drought by a tank-forming shoot, others make sure that their absorbing organs are in contact with moisture-retaining mats of debris and vegetation. Those canopy dwellers that have neither type of external reservoir face the most rigorous conditions and must rely on tissue capacitance to survive prolonged dry spells. If moisture stores become depleted, they must be replenished quickly. These services are provided to the nonimpounding, essentially rootless, atmospheric bromeliads of Pittendrigh's exposure group by succulent leaves bearing absorbing trichomes

(Fig. 7.1 and 7.6B, C, E, F). Similar epidermal appendages (Fig. 7.6G), characterize at least two South American epiphytic species of *Polypodium* and *Pleopeltis angusta* (Müller et al., 1981). Thick stems may also provide capacitance (e.g. some ferns, Cactaceae and Orchidaceae), as can tubers that serve a variety of New World epiphytes, including *Markea* (Solanaceae), young *Ficus* and several Ericaceae and Melastomataceae. In some aroids (*Anthurium, Hedychium*) and many orchids, particularly those without well-developed vegetative shoots (e.g. *Polyradicion*, Fig. 7.6M), roots, not leaves, are the most succulent parts.

A third mechanism beyond succulence and absorbing trichomes helps to maintain adequate hydrature in many neotropical epiphytes: crassulacean acid metabolism. CAM promotes high water-use efficiency and great flexibility in the face of fluctuating moisture supplies, a major impediment to canopy life. Very likely, switching between CAM and C_3 photosynthesis, as is exhibited by several bromeliads (Table 7.1) in transitions between wet and dry weather, may also occur in many other epiphytes. CAM idling would also be adaptive under prolonged drought, but neither capacity is apparent in published $\delta^{13}C$ values (e.g. Medina et al., 1977). The presence of CAM in Bromeliaceae as a means of countering drought is probably symptomatic of an even wider existence; one may consider the prevalence of CAM in Orchidaceae (Arditti, 1979; Avadhani et al., 1982), a family that surpasses Bromeliaceae in ecological variety and contains fully two-thirds of the world's vascular epiphytes (Madison, 1977).

The habitat preferences of Bromeliaceae identified by Pittendrigh as shade-tolerant in Trinidad are, as he opined, actually imposed by humidity requirements. These plants employ C_3 photosynthesis which, while allowing vigorous carbon gain, imposes high moisture demands. Over streams where water-vapor deficits are low, plants of the same species grow profusely in full sun. The usual association of CAM with high light demands may account for its absence or weak development in deep-forest species. Furthermore, the foliar trichomes associated with CAM bromeliads of the subfamily Tillandsioideae prohibit success in overly humid circumstances (Fig. 7.6B, E, F; Mez, 1904; Benzing and Renfrow, 1971). While these structures allow rapid uptake during transitory contact with canopy fluids, they become detrimental to photosynthesis when their confluent shields hold suffocating films of moisture over stomata for extended periods. Additionally, the reflective qualities of dry shields are counterproductive in dim light. Shade-tolerant bromeliads, in response to these complications, possess thinner, water-repellent leaves bearing fewer trichomes with reduced caps (Fig. 7.6C). Accompanying light compensation and saturation intensities are lower than those of atmospherics (Benzing and Renfrow, 1971). For occasional species, the harvest of weak, red-enriched, shade light is promoted by cyanic abaxial leaf surfaces (e.g. *Nidularium bruchellii* and *Vriesea simplex*; Lee et al., 1979; Benzing and Friedman, 1981). Photon recycling is probably encouraged by similar epidermal mirrors in a number of New World epiphytic Araceae and Gesneriaceae.

Mineral nutrition

Tropical American mistletoes, like relatives elsewhere, are mostly strict xylem-feeders. Nutrient ions are concentrated to levels above those in hosts by diverting disproportionate amounts of the xylem stream through the parasite. Relatively insensitive stomata are required to maintain the necessary conductivity. Nutritional mechanisms are more divergent among free-living canopy associates. High shoot/root ratios, specialized morphology, and associations with ants indicate that varied mechanisms centered in stem and foliage are used by many American epiphytes to acquire essential ions, but absorptive functions remain largely confined to roots in most species. The only data available on the relative importance of roots and shoots in absorption among neotropical epiphytes pertains to bromeliads, orchids and a few myrmecophytes in other families (Benzing et al., 1976; Huxley, 1978, 1980; Benzing and Pridgeon, 1983). The foliar trichomes which are so important for water uptake in atmospheric bromeliads serve equally well to acquire solutes (Mez, 1904; Benzing et al., 1976). Root systems constitute virtually the entire vegetative body of shootless orchids (Benzing and Ott, 1981; Fig. 7.6M) and, like those of leafy relatives, are conspicuously modified for aerial service, the more so the drier the habitat. Araceae and Orchidaceae with velamen have spongy mantles that allow absorption

of a considerable volume of the first, and probably most mineral-charged, fluid moving through the canopy at the onset of a storm (Benzing et al., 1983; Fig. 7.6H). Held against an underlying hypodermis equipped with transfer cells, nutrient ions in the engorged velamen are less likely to be washed away than if uptake into living tissue were confined to the outer root surface.

Certain epiphytic Bromeliaceae and Orchidaceae exhibit disproportional diminutions in root or shoot systems, accompanied by the merging of functions that are normally performed separately by these two body parts (Benzing and Renfrow, 1980; Benzing and Ott, 1981). Economies achieved through the production of multipurpose vegetative tissue make scarce resources available for reproductive purposes. Presumably, selection arising from the combination of high physical stress, disturbance and patchiness in canopy habitats have favored this type of morphological reduction.

Litter, precipitation and animal life that collect in phytotelmata serve as soil substitutes for numerous species of *Anthurium*, ferns and especially bromeliads, the most important of the three groups by reason of both numbers and tank capacity. Bromeliads comprise more than half of all phytotelm-plant species (Fish, 1983), and some impound more material than any other epiphyte. Picado (1913) found approximately 20 l of material in a single *Glomeropitcairnia erectiflora* shoot; something less than a liter is probably the average for all species. Bromeliad tanks assume many shapes that correlate with habitat preference and nutritional mode (Benzing, 1986). *Billbergia zebrina* and species forming similar deep funnels (Fig. 7.6J) occur in seasonally dry, exposed locations, and often serve as daytime havens for frogs. Pittendrigh's shade-tolerant species have small, open axils that intercept considerable litter, and attract the detritivores needed to process this vegetable matter (Benzing, 1986; Fig. 7.6A).

Experiments have demonstrated nutrient flux from the fluid in a bromeliad tank to the shoot containing it (Benzing, 1970), but impoundment has additional implications for the community as a whole. The capacity of many neotropical forests to support canopy fauna must be greatly increased by the foodstuffs, water and cover provided by epiphyte phytotelmata, especially where bromeliads are abundant. Sugden and Robins (1979) reported an average density of 17.5 mature tank bromeliads per square meter of ground area in a Colombian cloud forest, and Fish (1983) estimated conservatively that a population of this magnitude would provide 50 000 l of water per hectare for direct exploitation by canopy fauna. Accompanying nutritional gains by epiphytes must be comparably impressive. A recent account of fauna in bromeliad tanks has been provided by Frank (1983). Impoundment epiphytes are limited in the paleotropics to *Astelia* (Liliaceae), a few other monocotyledons, and ferns.

Mineral-nutrient demands are probably modest for the more stress-tolerant neotropical epiphytes, in part because of slow growth. Harris (1918) reported unusually low osmotic pressures in the cell sap of some Jamaican and Florida epiphytes; values for the supporting trees were at least twice as great. Perhaps these dilutions are part of an "early warning system" designed to promote stomatal closure while moisture deficits are still small, so as to mitigate the effects of possible prolonged droughts later. Unfortunately, individual solutes have not been assayed. Mistletoes are direct opposites: solute potentials are routinely much lower and foliar conductance usually exceeds that of hosts especially during drought (Ehleringer et al., 1985). Concentrations of nitrogen, potassium and phosphorus in healthy foliage of atmospheric bromeliads are quite modest, which does indeed suggest that nutritional economies are operative in some epiphytes. However, this pattern is not consistent, even among taxa which occur together (Benzing and Renfrow, 1971, 1974; Benzing and Davidson, 1979). The orchid *Encyclia tampensis* is richer in nitrogen, phosphorus and potassium than is *Tillandsia paucifolia* (Fig. 7.1) with which it shares *Taxodium* hosts in Florida.

Ant-fed plants are almost exclusively epiphytic (Thompson, 1981). Three New World families have used three different organs in evolving habits that accommodate ant colonies: leafy stems (e.g. *Schomburgkia* of the Orchidaceae, Fig. 7.6L); leaf bases (e.g. *Tillandsia* of the Bromeliaceae, Fig. 7.6K); and rhizomes (e.g. *Solenopteris* of the Polypodiaceae). Huxley (1978) has demonstrated nutrient transfer from insect to plant in paleotropical *Myrmecodia* (Rubiaceae). Other investigations (Benzing, 1970; Rickson, 1979; Huxley, 1980)

point to similar fluxes in other putative trophic myrmecophytes, including American forms.

Canopy gardens based on ant-nests, a largely neotropical phenomenon, are common in many warm, humid, American forests, especially those over nutrient-impoverished white sands; each may weigh several kilograms (Fig. 7.8). Thirty-four were recorded on a single plot measuring 1 × 10 m in an Amazonian caatinga forest (Madison, 1979). Individual citrus trees in a northern Trinidad grove supported 3 to 10 nests (pers. observ., 1972). Exposed sites are favored, perhaps because the plants involved are heliophilic (Kleinfeldt, 1978), or because the ants cannot tolerate nests that would become rain-sodden in the absence of drying sunlight. Several families with a propensity for epiphytism combine with numerous ant genera to create these microcosms in tropical America. Among Gesneriaceae, *Codonanthe* is the most faithful genus in many locations. *Aechmea* and *Streptocalyx* are common nest-garden bromeliads. *Anthurium* and *Philodendron* represent the Araceae. Other genera frequently encountered are

Fig. 7.8. Partially dissected arboreal ant-nest at Río Palenque, Ecuador, reinforced with roots of bromeliads, cacti and ferns.

Epidendrum, Epiphyllum (Cactaceae), *Ficus, Markea* and *Peperomia* (Piperaceae). The nest-builders include *Anochetus, Azteca, Camponotus, Crematogaster, Dolichoderus* and *Solenopsis*. Nest-gardens in Central America are rather simple, comprising one or a few plant species, especially the wide-ranging *Codonanthe crassifolia*, and a single ant colony. South American systems often harbor several ant taxa and a more diverse flora (D. Davidson, pers. commun., 1986).

Nest-garden ants are versatile; they raise broods in rotting wood and other protected canopy sites as well. Nest plants appear rigid in their requirements; a number of *Coryanthes* and several species of *Epidendrum* reject all rooting media other than ant-cartons. According to Ule (1901), Kleinfeldt (1978) and Madison (1979) ants create their gardens by carrying seeds into nests prior to consuming attached edible appendages. Wheeler (1942) and Weber (1943) disagree, asserting that nest colonization by plants is fortuitous. Apparently the relationship has additional mutualistic qualities. Several common nest-plants produce extrafloral nectar, for instance, *Codonanthe uleana, Codonanthopsis ulei* and *Philodendron myrmecophyllum* (Madison, 1979). Ants have been noted tending aphid colonies on garden plants (Kleinfeldt, 1978), but even the rewards offered by animals and plants combined seem too meager to support the number of insects present in a single large colony — foraging must extend well beyond the nest-garden. Plants undoubtedly gain nutrients and sometimes protection from aggressive nest builders, but to what extent remains undetermined. At Río Palenque, I witnessed small, pugnacious ants swarming over an undisturbed *Aechmea angustifolia* inflorescence in a citrus-tree ant-nest. Following agitation of the supporting branch, these insects literally launched themselves into the air in a successful attempt to attack their tormentor. Carton enclosures, in turn, are greatly strengthened by epiphyte roots (Fig. 7.8). Nest-plants may also provide a service by regulating humidity in brood chambers. Roots could release water vapor into overly dry ant colonies or hasten the dissipation of excess moisture when the weather turns wetter.

Determining that ants sow seeds in their nests is only the first step toward understanding the dynamics of these microcosms and the broader ramifications of their presence in tropical American forest ecosystems. Kleinfeldt (1978) observed high densities of nest-gardens created by the single ant *Crematogaster longispina* and the plant *Codonanthe crassifolia* at La Selva, Costa Rica; those gardens occupying clustered trees constituted single colonies whose parts — the individual nests — were interconnected by trails. She also discovered that nest-gardens can turn over rapidly, in part through displacement of the original builder by more aggressive but less industrious ants — *Solanopteris picta* in this study. Within months, neglected gardens deteriorate and plant roots are bared. Should this phenomenon be widespread, mineral cycling at the ecosystem level could be affected significantly.

Carnivory, a more direct way to acquire animal nutrients, is rare among the epiphytes of forest canopies, supposedly because the moisture supplies required to make this strategy cost-effective are not reliably available to most epiphytes (Thompson, 1981; Givnish et al., 1984). However, *Utricularia* (Lentibulariaceae) manages to inhabit tree crowns in humid forests of both the Old and the New World by rooting in continuously wet moss, debris or bromeliad tanks where its tiny traps presumably harvest small invertebrates. The heliophilic, tank-forming plant *Catopsis berteroniana* (Bromeliaceae) is reputedly carnivorous (Fish, 1976). Its upright, densely glaucous leaves (Fig. 7.6I) seem to attract flying insects seeking sky light in order to avoid obstructions as they negotiate forest canopies. Lubricating qualities of the loose, UV-reflecting, cuticular powder responsible for this visual response impede escape after insects blunder into tanks. In southern Florida, the leaf axils of *C. berteroniana* contain abundant exoskeletal remains of nonaquatic animals, but more definitive study is required to determine whether the mineral economy of this epiphyte differs substantially from that of hundreds of epiphytic relatives whose preference for shadier sites promotes impoundment of more vegetable than animal material.

PHYTOGEOGRAPHY AND DIVERSITY

Refuge theory

Vascular plant diversity in tropical America is about 2.5 and 3.0 times greater (in total number of species) respectively than that in equivalent Australasian and African regions (Raven, 1976; Gentry, 1982b). Efforts to explain these disparities have most recently focused on Pleistocene climatology and humid refuges (Haffer, 1969, 1978; Richards, 1973; Van der Hammen, 1974; Simpson and Haffer, 1978). Pockets of tropical forest isolated by aridification during glacial advances at higher latitudes were most numerous in the New World, particularly on the periphery of Amazonia. Hence, their purported dual effect on biotic diversity was especially marked in the neotropics where mesic plant taxa were most often (1) conserved, and (2) encouraged to undergo allopatric speciation. However, Gentry's (1982b) appraisal of South and Central American floristics, combined with paleontological data, indicates that less neotropical diversity is explained by shifting paleoclimate than authorities have suggested. Moreover, humid-refuge theory does not offer much insight into the current status of some neotropical synusiae.

Amazonian-centered taxa, a subset of the tropical American flora identified by Gentry as composed predominantly of canopy trees and lianas, show the most convincing evidence of refuge influences among New World Gondwanan plant groups. Closely related populations tend to be geographically distinct, and genera are relatively small. Humid lowlands are common habitats. Andean-centered taxa — the other Gondwanan group — exhibit a different profile. Genera are larger, and frequently contain sympatric species. Shrub, palmetto and epiphyte habits characterize much of its membership, and ranges are concentrated in premontane and low montane wet Andean forests.

Laurasian lineages (few of which contain epiphytes; Table 7.2), have made only minor contributions to neotropical diversity in South America, except at relatively high elevations beyond the range of lowland refuges. Almost half the Laurasian species are wind-pollinated or otherwise poorly suited for sympatric speciation (Gentry, 1982b). Also contributing to the limited panneotropical distribution and size of this group is its recent southward penetration. Most Laurasian taxa were probably denied access to South America prior to the Pliocene closure of the Isthmus of Panama, an event that produced the first continuous post-Cretaceous land bridge between the two New World continents (Keigwin, 1978). Whatever the reason, Amazonian- and Andean-centered groups together still constitute more than 70% of all tropical South American species (Gentry, 1982b).

Epiphytes, more than most soil-rooted flora, challenge the humid refuge model. The fact that members of this synusia are usually drought-tolerant, not particularly fastidious in phorophyte choice, and quite dispersible suggests that at least the more xeric forms were less subject than trees to isolation by changes in rainfall patterns. Dry rather than moist refuges quite possibly had the most telling effect on such types as atmospheric bromeliads. Several *Tillandsia* subgenera whose members cannot tolerate extreme humidity exhibit distinct centers of diversity in South America (Smith and Downs, 1977) that may reflect historical distributions of arid forest. De Granville (1982) proposed that localized arid zones provided sanctuary for certain epiphytes in French Guiana during the wettest parts of glacial interphases. *Aechmea setigera* (Bromeliaceae), *Epidendrum nocturnum* and *Topobea parasitica* (Melastomataceae) are cited as probable beneficiaries of xeric refuges.

Dispersal

Statistics on seed dispersal by neotropical epiphytes are strongly skewed by Orchidaceae. Most of the more than 800 genera in this family produce dust-sized seeds containing minute, poorly differentiated embryos and no endosperm. Somewhat more substantial dust seeds occur in various epiphytic Melastomataceae, Bignoniaceae, Rapataceae and Lentibulariaceae. Fern spores, of course, also fit the dust-size category. Members of Asclepiadaceae, Bromeliaceae–Tillandsioideae, Ericaceae and Rubiaceae utilize air currents to carry appendaged diaspores. A majority of families containing American epiphytes (Madison, 1977) ripen rather small seeds in fleshy fruits; birds are major dispersal agents for these diaspores. Bats feed on the large berries of certain *Billbergia* species, perhaps explaining an occasional preference for knot-holes in this genus. Insects disperse seeds of *Vanilla* and (possibly) certain *Peperomia* species. Seeds of some nest-dwelling species of *Coryanthes* are among the myrmecochores. All but the very small mistletoes are disseminated by birds.

TABLE 7.2

Abundance and ranges of epiphytic species among angiosperm and pteridophyte families [after Madison (1977) and Gentry (1982b)]

I. ANGIOSPERMS

Neotropical Family	Number of epiphytic species	Range assignment[1]	Pantropical Family	Number of epiphytic species[2]	Range assignment[1]	Paleotropical Family	Number of epiphytic species
Agavaceae	1	U	Araceae	684/166	NA	Amaryllidaceae	1
Asteraceae	3	NA	Araliaceae	5/8 (60)	NA	Aquifoliaceae	1
Bromeliaceae	919	NA	Asclepiadaceae	2/133	U	Celastraceae	2
Cactaceae	133	GO	Balsaminaceae	(5)	L	Costaceae	4
Campanulaceae	18	NA	Begoniaceae	(10)	NA	Cunoniaceae	2
Commelinaceae	3	U	Bignoniaceae	2/1	A	Elaeocarpaceae	1
Cyclanthaceae	31	NA	Burmanniaceae	1/1	GU	Myrtaceae	7
Dulongiaceae	1	U	Clusiaceae	7/0	U	Nepenthaceae	6
Gentianaceae	1	L	Crassulaceae	2/2 (85)	L	Pandanaceae	4
Marcgraviaceae	94	NA	Ericaceae	263/193	NA	Pittosporaceae	5
Onagraceae	3	SA	Gesneriaceae	430/126 (23)	NA	Poaceae	2
Rapateaceae	6	GU	Griseliniaceae	(3)	U	Potaliaceae	20
			Lentibulariaceae	(12)	U	Ranunculaceae	1
			Liliaceae	4/13	L	Rosaceae	3
			Melastomataceae	137/346	NA	Vitaceae	4
			Moraceae	20/1 (500)	A	Winteraceae	1
			Myrsinaceae	11/5 (12)	NA		
			Orchidaceae	15 000	NA		
			Philesiaceae	1/1	U		
			Piperaceae	700/0 (10)	NA		
			Rubiaceae	52/157 (7)	NA		
			Scrophulariaceae	3/3	L		
			Solanaceae	15/2 (15)	SA		
			Urticaceae	1/20 (20)	NA		

II. PTERIDOPHYTES

Pantropical Family	Number of epiphytic species[2]	Paleotropical Family	Number of epiphytic species
Aspidiaceae	254	Schizeaceae	2
Aspleniaceae	400		
Davalliaceae	185		
Hymenophyllaceae	500		
Lycopodiaceae	175		
Ophioglossaceae	2		
Polypodiaceae	1027		
Psilotaceae	8		
Selaginellaceae	10		
Vittariaceae	142		

[1] A: Amazonian-centered, Gu: Guayanan, NA: northern Andean-centered, U: unassigned, Go: Gondwanan, L: Laurasian. SA: southern Andean-centered
[2] Ratios are of the number of neotropical species/number of paleotropical species. Numbers in parentheses are species in genera whose neotropical/paleotropical ratios are not given by Madison (1977).

Here as in many Old World forests a guild of specialized avians is responsible. Some of these same frugivors feed on *Anthurium*, *Ripsalis* and possibly other epiphyte fruits.

Accounts of breeding systems in American epiphytes are few. Many bromeliads and orchids are outcrossers. The Mexican *Catopsis nutans* is dioecious, but flowers are perfect in outlying, smaller populations in Florida and Caribbean islands. Myrmecophytes and nest epiphytes tend to be autogamous, possibly in deference to the aggressive behavior of their insect associates (Madison, 1979), although bees visiting flowers of *Markea ulei* and *Codonanthe uleana* were ignored by ants at a Peruvian site (D. Davidson, pers. commun., 1986). Virtually all chasmogamous epiphytes are animal-pollinated, as are the trees that support them, but probably not by the same vectors. Bats pollinate a number of bromeliads, including some Central American species of *Vriesea*. The importance of euglossine bees and birds is considered shortly.

Epiphyte diversity

Epiphytes occur in 53 angiosperm and at least 9 pteridophyte families (Table 7.2). Major angiosperm taxa containing canopy dwellers are, on the whole, mostly cosmopolitan, but the epiphytic members of 12 families are strictly neotropical, those of 17 others are wholly paleotropical (Madison, 1977). The Orchidaceae are surprisingly insular, considering the family's buoyant seeds: only about 5% of the 500 or so epiphytic genera are pantropical. Just 8 other genera in Magnoliophyta contain both New and Old World epiphytes. Of the 86 fern genera listed by Madison as having canopy-adapted members, about two-thirds are pantropical. The remainder are almost equally divided between genera with exclusively neotropical (16) or paleotropical (14) ranges. The relatively broad distributions characterizing most pteridophyte families (Table 7.2) may be attributable to high dispersibility or substantial evolutionary stasis through the Cenozoic.

The study of tropical American floristics leads to an unavoidable conclusion: a number of New World epiphytic taxa have undergone unusually broad expansions. An estimated 17% of all neotropical species fit into one of the first three categories (p. 133) of canopy dwellers (Gentry, 1982b) compared to about 10% for the world's flora as a whole (Madison, 1977). Coincidence may, in part, explain this disparity. Bromeliaceae and Cactaceae — the two largest among essentially New World families — contain many epiphytic members (Table 7.2). One could argue that both taxa were especially well predisposed to succeed in tree crowns, by such preadaptive features as xeromorphy and CAM, and they just happened to have neotropical origins. But several pantropical families point to the existence of other area-specific reasons for this neotropical bias. More than a third of all American epiphytes are represented by three orchid subtribes exclusive to the New World: Maxillariinae, Oncidiinae and Pleurothallidinae. Concentrations of closely related taxa are, on the whole, less pronounced in paleotropical forests. The New World genera *Anthurium* and *Philodendron* have many more species than any of seven African and Australasian aroid genera containing canopy dwellers. Among the Gesneriaceae, epiphytism is best developed in the Americas. Only the Ericaceae, of the families containing sizable numbers of epiphytes, are about equally represented in forest canopies of the New and Old World. While the Asclepiadaceae have exploited the Paleotropics far more extensively than the Neotropics, numbers of species are modest. Among the larger groups of epiphytes, Rubiaceae and Melastomataceae exhibit the strongest paleotropical bias.

Radiation of neotropical epiphytes on humid sites has been exceptional compared to that of associated trees and lianas. The previously quoted figures for two Ecuadoran forests of differing moisture status are a case in point: while the total number of taxa at the wetter of the two sites (Río Palenque) was about twice that at Juaneche, the percentage of epiphytic species was five times as great (35 vs. 7%). Another peculiar statistic may be revealing. Epiphytes tend to form sizeable assemblages of closely related species, a fact that lends credence to Gentry's (1982b) impression that evolution remains exceptionally active in this synusia. At Río Palenque, there are 21 flowering-plant genera containing 7 or more species; of these genera, 11 are fully or largely epiphytic; only one contains trees. At Barro Colorado Island, 12 genera include at least 10 species; 5 are mostly epiphytic and none is arborescent (Gentry, 1982a).

In drier sites, too, genera may be represented by several species. Seven species of *Tillandsia* grow on stunted cypress in southwestern Florida, where their only canopy associates are *Catopsis berteroniana*, a *Psilotum* and one orchid from each of three genera.

ORIGINS OF NEOTROPICAL EPIPHYTE DIVERSITY

Gentry's observation that the neotropical epiphyte synusia continues to expand, while associated woody communities appear to have approached more closely to a taxonomic steady state, prompts the question: Are there any characteristics of tree-crown habitats in general that make them especially conducive to speciation? If so, what additional phenomena might explain why this potential has been more fully realised in tropical America than anywhere else? First, one may consider features of tree crowns that probably account for their ability to support high epiphyte diversity. One can then move on to identify factors that helped to pack certain neotropical forests with so many canopy-dependent species.

The substratum

Reproductive isolation alone cannot engender exceptional diversity in any group of plants: there must also be some means of apportioning living space among populations, especially if they coexist. Recent studies indicate that variety within communities of sessile organisms is promoted by intermediate-level disturbance and its frequent product — patchiness (Connell, 1978). Disturbance, if appropriately timed and spatially limited, creates a kaleidoscope of regenerative gaps that allow opportunists, regardless of competitive prowess, to find space for colonization. Aggregations as disparate as intertidal algae and barnacles, coral-reef fishes, and moist tropical forest trees are increasingly viewed as maintaining continuity and diversity by a lottery-like rotation whereby no resident species excludes another by competitive exclusion. Diversity persists as long as no one population becomes so dominant that it can preempt enough of the community's gaps to exclude another.

Forest canopies provide an unstable substratum for epiphytes. Bark exfoliates, twigs and branches are shed, and eventually entire trees die, creating a shifting mosaic of unevenly-aged sites for anchorage. A constant rain of dislodged epiphytes betokens a steady progression of small-scale disturbances, even in what appear to be the most stable forests. Nowhere is patch life long enough to allow even the most aggressive epiphyte to match the capacity of many terrestrial species to spread continuously over large spaces by either seed or clonal expansion. Thus epiphyte synusiae are, perhaps more than most, shaped by disturbance and patchiness rather than by competition. Statistical evidence for this hypothesis is admittedly scanty. Hazen (1966) failed to demonstrate spatial patterns among canopy associates inhabiting dense, mixed bromeliad colonies in wet forest near Turrialba, Costa Rica; but more extensive observations are needed for confirmation. At present, it seems that conditions in many humid neotropical forests — namely, the presence of diverse epiphyte populations comprising many taxa with apparently interchangeable microsites (e.g. 49 orchid species in a single Venezuelan tree; Dunsterville, 1961) — fit the intermediate disturbance model.

Tree crowns on drier sites feature even less crowding, as indicated by the larger areas of exposed bark (Benzing, 1978, 1981). This fact probably reflects low vigor among canopy residents there, adding another dimension — low interference — to the disturbance/patchiness factor. Growth-suppressing aridity and substratum infertility seem to promote exceptionally rich shrub floras in certain highly seasonal sites in Australia and South Africa (Milewski, 1983). With few exceptions, forest canopies may prove to be a parallel since they too are stressful habitats, judging by the elaborate adaptations for obtaining nutrient ions and the xeromorphic nature of so many epiphytes. Very likely, much of the epiphyte synusia is not saturated with either biomass or taxa, even in tropical America. Exploitation of forest canopies by epiphytes seem to be limited the world over, particularly in the more arid areas, by the small number of major evolutionary lines which can counter scarcities of key nutrients, and moisture and still maintain enough regenerative capacity to succeed, despite heavy mortality imposed by disturbance and habitat patchiness and by climatic stress (Benzing, 1978).

Ethological factors

Neotropical fauna that foster reproductive isolation among plants have been major contributors to radiation of numerous large taxa, including several with a strong propensity for epiphytism. Canopy-dwelling Bromeliaceae commonly exhibit floral displays to attract hummingbirds, as do many co-occurring Gesneriaceae and Ericaceae. Nowhere else are avian pollinators as numerous as in northern Andean forests (Stiles, 1975). Euglossine bees, an exclusively neotropical group whose foraging behavior has become almost legendary, maintain sexual isolation within many, but not all, American Orchidaceae (Dressler, 1981, pp. 102–104; Williams and Whitten, 1983). The orchid subtribe Pleurothallidinae (about 3800 spp.) is perhaps the best example of a neotropical taxon which belies the widely held view that pollinators are the most important reason why the family Orchidaceae is so large. Fetid rather than pleasant odors characterize the blossoms of many species, and flowers are often too small to attract strong fliers. There is also no basis for believing that the *Diptera* suspected of pollinating Pleurothallidinae are as constant as male euglossines and therefore as effective in ensuring either isolation between populations of different species occurring together, or fruit-set in widely dispersed conspecific populations. Quite likely, *Anthurium* and *Peperomia* also have been less affected than some other groups by ethological factors, and instead owe their large size to aspects of substratum type and topography. Pollinators have played no role in pteridophyte evolution, yet the large fern flora of climatically diverse Costa Rica includes approximately 70% of epiphytes (Wagner and Gomez, 1983) as compared with only 20 to 30% for the Pteridophyta as a whole.

History and topography

The mesic epiphytes exhibit narrowly defined ranges. Populations growing along roads through montane regions in the Americas, for instance, appear and disappear abruptly when patterns of temperature, and especially of rainfall, change. Mountains separated by lowlands offer unusual opportunity for allopatric speciation to a climatic specialist with widely dispersed diaspores. Moist montane habitats conducive to this type of cladogenesis occur in the New and Old World tropics, but less widely in the latter. The Andes is by far the most extensive low-latitude mountain range in the world (Gentry, 1982b). In its northern reaches, forest canopies support large epiphyte communities; most neotropical angiosperm families containing epiphytes are well represented there (Table 7.2). Only two, Onagraceae and Solanaceae, with less than 20 epiphytic species between them, exhibit a southerly bias. Geological history may provide an explanation. Southern and central Andean areas achieved their current altitude (Zeil, 1979) in the mid-Tertiary, perhaps before resident neotropical families had evolved a capacity for canopy life, or their current associations with specialized pollinators. Most of the uplift of the northern Andes has taken place during the past 5 m.y., allowing more than enough time to generate the numerous species that so densely populate forest canopies in this region.

Summarizing briefly: Very likely, many factors have contributed to the great expansion of neotropical epiphytes. One — permissive habitats — is not a region-specific phenomenon, but is nevertheless indispensable to accommodation of dense canopy-dependent floras. The others, including chance occurrences of key taxa in the New World as opposed to the Old World tropics, are more localized. A uniquely complex neotropical topography has enhanced epiphyte evolution by providing exceptional opportunities for creating founder populations through extensive breakup of climatic zones, past and present. South and Central American land forms promoted unparalleled formation of refugia during the Pleistocene, but consequences in the epiphyte synusia remain unclear. An unmatched abundance of specialized pollinators has undoubtedly fostered much cladogenesis in Orchidaceae and several other predominantly canopy-based groups. Additional inquiry will be necessary to determine possible synergisms among factors responsible for the diversity of neotropical epiphytes, and which agencies have been particularly important in shaping the systematic profiles of specific higher taxa.

EPIPHYTES VIS-À-VIS OTHER VEGETATION

Discussing the many ways in which epiphytes can interact with associated biota and thereby influence broader aspects of ecosystem structure and function is appropriate in a neotropical context for several reasons. First, research opportunities have been especially favorable in Central and South America, and indeed most of the pertinent literature centers on these regions. Second, epiphytic vegetation is often denser and more diverse in tropical forests of the New as opposed to the Old World. Finally, various sorts of catchment structures, which greatly heighten the epiphyte's interaction with nearby plants and animals, are best developed in neotropical taxa, especially in the Bromeliaceae. The contribution of epiphytes to the welfare of canopy faunas, especially that of those producing large phytotelmata, has been noted previously. Also of considerable import are the effects that these plants have on phorophyte performance, whole-system productivity, water relations, mineral use efficiency, mineral interception and storage capacity. The effects vary in kind and intensity with the densities, habits and physiological attributes of the epiphytes involved, and, less directly, with the factors of climate, soil condition and disturbance in the particular habitat.

On those few occasions when vascular epiphytes have been treated as separate components in biomass surveys, their contribution to total aboveground standing crops has been recorded as no more than a few percent (for example, Fittkau and Klinge, 1973). Accepted uncritically, these figures signal no major role for the canopy dweller in whole-community phenomena. But even if nonvascular forms are excluded, epiphytes still generate a fourth to a third of the green tissue present in many tropical forests. Edwards and Grubb (1977) calculated the mass of vascular epiphytes at about 50% of that for tree leaf biomass in a New Guinea lower montane rain forest. Tanner (1977) observed values as great as 35% in surveys of several humid montane sites in Jamaica. Bromeliad foliage alone must outweigh that of hosts in many neotropical sites (pers. observ.).

Also revealing are the fractions of a community's mineral nutrient capital that can be tied up in the largely herbaceous bodies of epiphytes; these elements are more actively engaged in community metabolism than are those in a good deal of the remaining biomass, most of which is wood. In a coastal strand community in southwestern Florida, nitrogen and phosphorus were about evenly appor-

tioned between dense colonies of *Tillandsia recurvata* and *T. usneoides*, and the foliage plus twigs of supporting *Quercus virginiana* (Benzing and Seemann, 1978). Nadkarni (1983, and in press) demonstrated that, depending on the element, vascular and nonvascular epiphytes in a Costa Rican cloud forest contained up to 45% of the nutrients committed to total photosynthetic tissue.

Epiphytes can improve whole-community nutrient status. Nadkarni (1981) made the point that epiphytic vegetation increases nutrient storage capacity, and captures atmospheric inputs that could be lost from communities lacking an equally well-developed epiphyte component. Tank-formers seem to be especially effective in this role. Epiphytes must be especially important in communities on weathered or heavily leached soils where the atmosphere is the sole source of nutrient supply. Jordan et al. (1980) reported considerable scavenging of nutrient ions from rainfall by tree crowns in an Amazonian rain forest, but no information was provided on the loads of epiphytes or epiphylls. If present, these plants will intercept nutrient fluxes traversing the space between host crown and root system by "nutritional piracy" (Benzing and Seemann, 1978; Benzing, 1983, 1984). Even if not caught in this manner, atmospheric ions that reach the ground on entry may still end up in epiphyte biomass later during the recycling process.

Humidification of the surrounding atmosphere through evaporation of moisture trapped by epiphytes must be conducive to biological activity, including that of nitrogen fixers on canopy surfaces. Sengupta et al. (1981) demonstrated extraordinary amounts of nitrogenase activity specifically associated with the leaf surfaces of certain epiphytes, notably orchids. Enough nitrogen fixation was accomplished by epiphylls on the fronds of a palm at La Selva, Costa Rica, to account for 10 to 25% of its foliar nitrogen (Bentley and Carpenter, 1984). Canopy-dependent plants (epiphytes or parasites), especially the impounding type so prevalent in tropical America, may reduce an ecosystem's losses of mobile ions in wet regions through reduction of stem-flow and fall-through. In addition, relatively dry detritus lodged around epiphytes must retain nutrients more effectively than does moist litter on soil; the latter is more vulnerable to leaching and detritivores. Some neotropical trees have responded to stores of moisture and nutrients suspended in their crowns by developing canopy roots that tap these rich resources (Nadkarni, 1981).

To fully appreciate how plants perched in tree crowns might wield much influence on forest dynamics, one must consider how material resources move through, and are utilized by, epiphyte communities. Epiphytic foliage is rather long-lived — several years, as opposed to about 12 months for the typical evergreen leaf in a humid forest canopy (Medina, 1984). In effect, epiphytes not only exhibit high avidities for certain nutrients passing through the canopy, but they hold on tenaciously to those they do garner, perhaps even imposing nutritional stress on phorophytes, that must efficiently recycle lost ions to avoid deficits. Epiphytic piracy and tenacity may be partly responsible for dwarfing in the coastal strand community of southern Florida previously mentioned (Benzing and Seemann, 1978). Where soils are richer, trees must still contend with the weight and shade cast by crown inhabitants, but ample nutrient supplies are more likely to be available for all. The effect of piracy on supporting trees depends on nutrient abundance, interception coefficients, turnover rates and maturity of the epiphyte biomass. Where epiphyte loads have reached mature status, something approaching a nutritional steady state should develop: nutrients captured from passing sources will evenly balance outputs lost in litterfall, dislodged plants and those decomposing in place.

The presence of a massive epiphyte flora also has direct implications for community-wide energetics, especially where it comprises a goodly fraction of the canopy leaf surface. Epiphyte colonies increase genetic diversity and promote partitioning and diverse use of resources in tree crowns. Under certain conditions, total aboveground vegetation might produce larger and/or more competent foliar biomass than would be possible were epiphytes and epiphylls absent. In other circumstances, the effects would be quite different. Humidity is probably the decisive factor. Trees have access to more continuous moisture supplies than do their crown inhabitants; consequently the material resources they allot to foliage should, in theory, produce relatively high yields. Epiphytes in humid canopies are apt to have the C3 types of photosynthesis, and their production and patterns of mineral use are comparable to those of their supports. In drier crowns, epiphytes are less vigorous producers. Here, many are CAM plants; adapted for drought, they probably achieve higher water-use efficiencies, but less impressive instantaneous energy return on nutrient investments. Indeed, analyses have shown far greater photosynthetic rates in C3 than in CAM green-plant tissues, although the former often contain only fractionally more foliar nitrogen (Larcher, 1980). Instantaneous values of nitrogen-use efficiency in terms of carbon gain are lower in CAM forms; however, given their propensity for long-lived foliage, these plants receive a better cumulative return on investment.

In relatively stable wet forests, sizable epiphyte loads (particularly of phytotelm-species) could substantially increase nutrient and moisture interception and storage (and possibly nitrogen fixation) to the point where canopy productivity would be greater than that achievable in their absence. Even if carbon gain were slower among epiphytes on a leaf area or biomass basis, that shortfall would be cancelled if aggregate foliar mass were large enough to ensure that the combined outputs of both canopy-dependent and other plants exceeded the maximum attainable by soil-rooted vegetation alone. Conversely, epiphytes in dry and/or oligotrophic forests should have a negative influence on the community's productivity and instantaneous mineral-use efficiency. Here, scarce mineral ions would be committed to CAM epiphytes and poikilohydrous thallophytes at the expense of a synusia (trees and lianas) with superior photosynthetic capacity. Disturbance would have still another effect. Communities that experience frequent losses of nutrient capital through destruction of phytomass could never achieve a nutritional steady state: epiphyte loads would be constantly engaged in mineral accumulation and biomass regeneration at the expense of supporting trees. Long-term research will be required to elucidate the nature of epiphyte involvement in the ecosystems where they grow. Many of the more appropriate sites for such enquiries are in the New World.

REFERENCES

Anderson, A.B., 1981. White sand vegetation of Brazilian Amazonia. *Biotropica*, 13: 199–210.

Arditti, J., 1979. Aspects of the physiology of orchids. In: H.W. Woolhouse (Editor), *Advances in Botanical Research, V. 7.* Academic Press, London, pp. 422–655.

Avadhani, P.N., Goh, C.J., Rao, A.N. and Arditti, J., 1982. Carbon fixation in orchids. In: J. Arditti (Editor), *Orchid Biology Reviews and Perspectives II.* Cornell Univ. Press, Ithaca, N.Y., pp. 173–194.

Bentley, B.L. and Carpenter, E.J., 1984. Direct transfer of newly-fixed nitrogen from free-living epiphyllous micro-organisms to their host plant. *Oecologia*, 63: 52–56.

Benzing, D.H., 1970. Foliar permeability and the absorption of minerals and organic nitrogen by certain tank bromeliads. *Bot. Gaz.*, 131: 23–31.

Benzing, D.H., 1978. The life history profile of *Tillandsia circinnata* (Bromeliaceae) and the rarity of extreme epiphytism among the angiosperms. *Selbyana*, 2: 325–337.

Benzing, D.H., 1981. Bark surfaces and the origin and maintenance of diversity among angiosperm epiphytes: A hypothesis. *Selbyana*, 5: 248–255.

Benzing, D.H., 1983. Vascular epiphytes: A survey with special reference to their interactions with other organisms. In: S.L. Hutton, T.C. Whitmore and A.C. Chadwick (Editors), *Tropical Rain Forest: Ecology and Management.* British Ecological Soc., Oxford, pp. 11–24.

Benzing, D.H., 1984. Epiphytic vegetation: A profile and suggestions for future inquiries. In: E. Medina, H.A. Mooney and C. Vázquez-Yánes (Editors), *Physiological Ecology of Plants of the Wet Tropics.* Proc. Int. Symp., Mexico, Junk, The Hague, pp. 155–172.

Benzing, D.H., 1986. Foliar specializations designed to promote animal-assisted nutrition in Bromeliaceae. In: T.R.E. Southwood and B.E. Juniper (Editors), *Proc. Symp. The Plant Surface and Insects.* The Linnean Society of London, London, pp. 235–256.

Benzing, D.H. and Davidson, E., 1979. Oligotrophic *Tillandsia circinnata* Schlecht (Bromeliaceae): An assessment of its patterns of mineral allocation and reproduction. *Am. J. Bot.*, 66: 386–397.

Benzing, D.H. and Friedman, W.E., 1981. Patterns of foliar pigmentation in Bromeliaceae and their adaptive significance. *Selbyana*, 5: 224–240.

Benzing, D.H. and Ott, D.W., 1981. Vegetative reduction in epiphytic Bromeliaceae and Orchidaceae: its origin and significance. *Biotropica*, 13: 131–140.

Benzing, D.H. and Pridgeon, A., 1983. Foliar trichomes of Pleurothallidinae (Orchidaceae): Functional significance. *Am. J. Bot.*, 70: 173–180.

Benzing, D.H. and Renfrow, A., 1971. The significance of photosynthetic efficiency to habitat preference and phylogeny among tillandsioid bromeliads. *Bot. Gaz.*, 132: 19–30.

Benzing, D.H. and Renfrow, A., 1974. The nutritional status of *Encyclia tampensis* and *Tillandsia circinnata* on *Taxodium ascendens* and the availability of nutrients to epiphytes on this host in South Florida. *Bull. Torrey Bot. Club*, 101: 191–197.

Benzing, D.H. and Renfrow, A., 1980. The nutritional dynamics of *Tillandsia circinnata* in southern Florida and the origin of the "air plant" strategy. *Bot. Gaz.*, 141: 165–172.

Benzing, D.H. and Seemann, J., 1978. Nutritional piracy and host decline: A new perspective on the epiphyte–host relationship. *Selbyana*, 2: 133–148.

Benzing, D.H., Henderson, K., Kessel, B. and Sulak, J., 1976. The absorptive capacities of bromeliad trichomes. *Am. J. Bot.*, 63: 1009–1014.

Benzing, D.H., Friedman, W.E., Peterson, G. and Renfrow, A., 1983. Shootlessness, velamentous roots, and the pre-eminence of Orchidaceae in the epiphytic biotope. *Am. J. Bot.*, 70: 121–133.

Claver, F.K., Alaniz, J.R. and Caldíz, D.O., 1983. *Tillandsia* spp.: Epiphytic weeds of trees and bushes. *Forest Ecol. Manage.*, 6: 367–372.

Connell, J.H., 1978. Diversity in tropical rain forests and coral reefs. *Science*, 199: 1302–1310.

De Granville, J.J., 1982. Rain forest and xeric flora refuges in French Guiana. In: G.T. Prance (Editor), *Biological Diversification in the Tropics.* Columbia Univ. Press, New York, N.Y., pp. 159–181.

Dressler, R.L., 1981. *The Orchids.* Harvard Univ. Press, London.

Dunsterville, G.C.K., 1961. How many orchids on a tree? *Am. Orchid Soc. Bull.*, 30: 362–363.

Edwards, P.J. and Grubb, P.J., 1977. Studies of mineral cycling in a montane rain forest in New Guinea. I. The distribution of organic matter in the vegetation and soil. *J. Ecol.*, 65: 943–969.

Ehleringer, J.R., Schulze, E.D., Ziegler, H., Lange, O.L., Fahrguhar, G.D. and Cowen, I.R., 1985. Xylem-tapping mistletoes: Water or nutrient parasites? *Science*, 227: 1479–1481.

Fish, D., 1976. *Structure and composition of the aquatic invertebrate community inhabiting bromeliads in south Florida and the discovery of an insectivorous bromeliad.* Ph.D. Thesis, Univ. of Florida, Gainesville, Fla.

Fish, D., 1983. Phytotelmata: flora and fauna. In: J.H. Frank and L.P. Lounibos (Editors), *Phytotelmata: Terrestrial Plants as Hosts for Aquatic Insect Communities.* Plexus, Medford, N.J., pp. 1–28.

Fittkau, E.J. and Klinge, H., 1973. On biomass and trophic structure of the central Amazonian rain forest ecosystem. *Biotropica*, 5: 2–14.

Frank, J.H., 1983. Bromeliad phytotelmata and their biota, especially mosquitoes. In: J.H. Frank and L.P. Lounibos (Editors), *Phytotelmata: Terrestrial Plants as Hosts for Aquatic Insect Communities.* Plexus, Medford, N.J., pp. 101–128.

Gentry, A.H., 1982a. Patterns of neotropical plant species diversity. In: M.K. Hecht, B. Wallace and G.T. Prance (Editors), *Evolutionary Biology, V. 15.* Plenum, New York, N.Y., pp. 1–84.

Gentry, A.H., 1982b. Neotropical floristic diversity: Phytogeographical connections between Central and South America, Pleistocene climatic fluctuations, or an accident of the Andean orogeny? *Ann. Mo. Bot. Gard.*, 69: 557–593.

Givnish, T.J., Burkhardt, E., Happel, R. and Weintraub, J., 1985. Carnivory in the bromeliad *Brocchinia reducta*, with a cost/benefit model for the general restriction of carnivorous plants to sunny, moist, nutrient-poor habitats. *Am. Nat.*, 124: 479–497.

Gómez, L.D., 1983. Parasitic plants. In: D.H. Jenzen (Editor), *Costa Rican Natural History*. Univ. Chicago Press, Chicago, Ill., pp. 292–298.

Griffiths, H. and Smith, J.A.C., 1983. Photosynthetic pathways in the Bromeliaceae of Trinidad: Relations between lifeforms, habitat preference and the occurrence of CAM. *Oecologia*, 60: 176–184.

Griffiths, H., Lüttge, U., Stimmel, K.H., Crook, C.E., Griffiths, M.N. and Smith, J.A.C., 1986. Comparative ecophysiology of CAM and C_3 bromeliads. III. Environmental influences on CO_2 assimilation and transpiration. *Plant Cell Environ.*, 9: 385–393.

Haffer, J., 1969. Speciation in Amazonian forest birds. *Science*, 165: 131–137.

Haffer, J., 1978. Distribution of Amazon forest birds. *Bonn. Zool. Beitr.*, 29: 38–78.

Harris, J.A., 1918. On the osmotic concentration of tissue fluids of phanerogamic epiphytes. *Am. J. Bot.*, 5: 490–506.

Hazen, W.E., 1966. Analysis of spatial pattern in epiphytes. *Ecology*, 47: 634–635.

Huxley, C.R., 1978. The ant-plants *Myrmecodia* and *Hydnophytum* (Rubiaceae), and the relationships between their morphology, ant occupants, physiology and ecology. *New Phytol.*, 80: 231–268.

Huxley, C.R., 1980. Symbiosis between ants and epiphytes. *Biol. Rev.*, 55: 321–340.

Janzen, D.H., 1977. Promising directions of study in tropical animal–plant interactions. *Ann. Mo. Bot. Gard.*, 64: 706–736.

Janzen, D.H. and Liesner, R., 1980. Annotated checklist of lowland Guanacaste Province, Costa Rica, exclusive of grasses and nonvascular cryptograms. *Brenesia*, 18: 15–90.

Jordan, C.F. and Herrera, R., 1981. Tropical rain forests: Are nutrients really critical? *Am. Nat.*, 117: 167–180.

Jordan, C.F., Golley, F.B. and Hall. J.B., 1980. Nutrient scavenging of rainfall by the canopy of an Amazonian rain forest. *Biotropica*, 12: 61–66.

Keigwin, Jr., L.D., 1978. Pliocene closing of the Isthmus of Panama, based on biostratigraphic evidence from nearby Pacific Ocean and Caribbean Sea cores. *Geology*, 6: 630–634.

Kelly, D.L., 1985. Epiphytes and climbers of a Jamacian rain forest: verticle distribution, life forms and life histories. *J. Biogeogr.*, 12: 223–241.

Kleinfeldt, S.E., 1978. Ant-gardens: The interaction of *Codonanthe crassifolia* (Gesneriaceae) and *Crematogaster longispina* (Formicidae). *Ecology*, 59: 449–456.

Larcher, W., 1980. *Physiological Plant Ecology*. Springer, New York, N.Y., 2nd ed., 252 pp.

Lee, D.W., Lowry, J.B. and Stone, B.C., 1979. Abaxial anthocyanin layer in leaves of tropical rain forest plants: Enhancer of light capture in deep shade. *Biotropica*, 11: 70–77.

Lüttge, U., Stimmel, K.H., Smith, J.A.C. and Griffiths, H., 1986. Comparative ecophysiology of CAM and C_3 bromeliads. II. Field measurements of gas exchange of CAM bromeliads in the humid tropics. *Plant Cell Environ.*, 9: 377–383.

Madison, M., 1977. Vascular epiphytes: Their systematic occurrence and salient features. *Selbyana*, 2: 1–13.

Madison, M., 1979. Additional observations on ant-gardens in Amazonas. *Selbyana*, 5: 107–115.

Medina, E., 1984. Nutrient balance and physiological processes at the leaf level. In: E. Medina, H.A. Mooney and C. Vásquez-Yánes (Editors), *Physiological Ecology of Plants of the Wet Tropics*. Junk, The Hague, pp. 139–154.

Medina, E., Delgado, M., Troughton, J.H. and Medina, J.D., 1977. Physiological ecology of CO_2 fixation in Bromeliaceae. *Flora*, 166: 137–152.

Mez, C., 1904. Physiologische Bromeliaceen-Studien I. Die Wasser-Ökonomie der extrem atmosphärischen Tillandsien. *Jahrb. Wissensch. Bot.*, 40: 157–229.

Milewski, A.V., 1983. A comparison of ecosystems in Mediterranean Australia and southern Africa: nutrient-poor sites at the Barrens and the Caledon Coast. *Annu. Rev. Ecol. Syst.*, 14: 57–76.

Müller, L., Starnecker, G. and Winkler, S., 1981. Zur Ökologie epiphytischer Farne in Südbrasilien. I. Saugschuppen. *Flora*, 171: 55–63.

Nadkarni, N.M., 1981. Canopy roots: Convergent evolution in rainforest nutrient cycles. *Science*, 214: 1023–1024.

Nadkarni, N.M., 1983. *The effects of epiphytes on nutrient cycles within temperate and tropical rainforest tree canopies*. Part of Ph.D. Thesis, Univ. of Washington, Seattle, Wash.

Nadkarni, N.M., 1985. Epiphyte biomass and nutrient capital of a neotropical cloud forest. *Biotropica*, 16: 249–256.

Picado, C., 1913. Les Bromeliacées epiphytes considérée comme milieu biologique. *Bull. Sci. Fr. Belg.*, 47: 215–360.

Pittendrigh, C.S., 1948. The bromeliad–Anopheles–malaria complex in Trinidad. I. The bromeliad flora. *Evolution*, 2: 58–89.

Pócs, T., 1982. Tropical forest bryophytes. In: A.J.E. Smith (Editor), *Bryophyte Ecology*, Chapman and Hall, London, pp. 59–104.

Raven, P.H., 1976. Ethics and attitudes. In: J. Simmons et al. (Editors), *Conservation of Threatened Plants*. Plenum, New York, N.Y., pp. 155–179.

Richards, P.W., 1973. Africa, the "odd man out". In: Meggers et al. (Editors), *Tropical Forest Ecosystems in Africa and S. America: a Comparative Review*. Smithsonian Inst. Press, Washington, D.C., pp. 21–26.

Rickson, F.R., 1979. Ultrastructural development of the beetle food tissue of *Calycanthus* flowers. *Am. J. Bot.*, 66: 80–86.

Ruinen, J., 1953. Epiphytosis: A second view on epiphytism. *Ann. Bogor.*, 1: 101–157.

Schimper, A.F.W., 1888. *Die epiphytische Vegetation Amerikas*. (Bott. Mitt. Tropen, II) Fischer, Jena, 162 pp.

Sengupta, B., Nandi, A.S., Samanta, R.K., Pal, D., Sengupta, D.N. and Sen, S.P., 1981. Nitrogen fixation in the phyllosphere of tropical plants: Occurrence of phyllosphere nitrogen-fixing microorganisms in eastern India and their utility for the growth and nitrogen nutrition of host plants. *Ann. Bot.*, 48: 705–716.

Simpson, B.B. and Haffer, J., 1978. Speciation patterns in the Amazonian forest biota. *Annu. Rev. Ecol. Syst.*, 9: 497–518.

Smith, J.A.C., Griffiths, H. and Lüttge, U., 1986a. Comparative ecophysiology of CAM and C₃ bromeliads. I. The ecology of Bromeliaceae in Trinidad. *Plant Cell Environ.*, 9: 359–376.

Smith, J.A.C., Griffiths, H., Lüttge, U., Crook, C.E., Griffiths, N.M. and Stimmel, K.H., 1986b. Comparative ecophysiology of CAM and C₃ bromeliads. IV. Plant water relations. *Plant Cell Environ.*, 9: 395–410.

Smith, R.F., 1970. The vegetation structure of a Puerto Rican rain forest before and after short-term gamma irradiation. In: H. Odum (Editor), *A Tropical Rain Forest*. U.S. Atomic Energy Commission, Oak Ridge, Tenn., pp. D-103–140.

Smith, L.B. and Downs, R.J., 1977. *Tillandsioideae (Bromeliaceae)*. (Flora Neotropica, Monogr. 14, Pt. 2). Hafner, New York, N.Y., 1492 pp.

Stiles, G., 1975. Ecology, flowering phenology and pollination of some Costa Rican *Heliconia* species. *Ecology*, 56: 285–301.

Strong, Jr. D.R., 1977. Epiphyte loads, tree falls, and perennial forest disruption: a mechanism for maintaining higher tree species richness in the tropics without animals. *J. Biogeogr.*, 4: 215–218.

Sugden, A.M. and Robins, R.J., 1979. Aspects of the ecology of vascular epiphytes in Colombian cloud forests, I. The distribution of the epiphytic flora. *Biotropica*, 11: 173–188.

Tanner, E.V.J., 1977. Four montane rain forests of Jamaica: A quantitative characterization of the floristics, the soils and the foliar mineral levels, and a discussion of the interrelations. *J. Ecol.*, 65: 883–918.

Tanner, E.V.J., 1980. Studies on the biomass and productivity in a series of montane rain forests in Jamaica. *J. Ecol.*, 68: 573–588.

Thompson, J.N., 1981. Reversed animal–plant interactions: The evolution of insectivorous and ant-fed plants. *Biol. J. Linn. Soc.*, 16: 147–155.

Ule, E., 1901. Ameisengärten in Amazonasgebiet. *Bot. Jahrb. Syst.*, 30: 45–52.

Van der Hammen, T., 1974. The Pleistocene changes of vegetation and climate in tropical South America. *Am. J. Biogeogr.*, 1: 3–26.

Vitousek, P.M., 1984. Litterfall, nutrient cycling, and nutrient limitation in tropical forests. *Ecology*, 65: 285–298.

Wagner, W.H. and Gómez, L.D., 1983. Pteridophytes. In: D.H. Janzen (Editor), *Costa Rican Natural History*. Univ. of Chicago Press, Chicago, Ill., pp. 311–318.

Weber, N.A., 1943. Parabiosis in neotropical "ant-gardens". *Ecology*, 24: 400–404.

Wheeler, W.M., 1942. Studies of neotropical ant-plants and their ants. *Bull. Mus. Comp. Zool.*, 90: 1–262.

Williams, N.H. and Whitten, W.M., 1983. Orchid floral fragrances and male euglossine bees: Methods and advances in the last sesquidecade. *Biol. Bull.*, 164: 355–395.

Zeil, W., 1979. *The Andes: A Geological Review*. Bornträger, Berlin, 260 pp.

Chapter 8

AFRICAN FORESTS

ALAN HAMILTON

INTRODUCTION

Despite a rapid recent rate of deforestation, rain forest still covers vast areas of tropical Africa. Yet our knowledge of this important ecosystem remains very poor. Access to many areas is difficult and the large and unfamiliar flora is a handicap to many workers. It is a matter for concern that, while the pressure of agriculture within the forest zone is rising, the amount of scientific work carried out on forest or forest-derived systems in Africa has been declining during the last one or two decades (Léonard, 1975).

The distribution of vegetation in Africa south of the Tropic of Cancer has been mapped by AETFAT (1959) and a new map of African vegetation has recently been published by UNESCO (White, 1983). Vegetational types containing forest appearing on the AETFAT map are shown on Fig. 8.1, on which it may be seen that forest is concentrated in an equatorial belt, a region of relatively high precipitation. The forest climate is not, however, uniform everywhere in Africa. Nearer the Equator, there tend to be two annual rainy periods and higher total rainfall, while to the north and south rainfall becomes less and is increasingly concentrated into only part of the year with the development of a long dry season. There are two gaps in the forest belt, in East Africa and in Togo–Benin, both associated with climatic dryness. Among the interesting features of the AETFAT map are the major division recognized between lowland and montane forests, with the latter descending to sea level in southern Africa (type 2 on the map), and the peripheral forest–savanna mosaic bordering regions of denser forest vegetation. The forest–savanna mosaic is a zone of relatively low rainfall and fertile soils in which forest is the climax vegetation, but where a long history of human disturbance has resulted in the replacement of large areas of forest with derived savanna and agricultural land.

The forests of Africa have a general physiognomic similarity to tropical forests in other parts of the world (Richards, 1939), but a number of floristic peculiarities serve as a reminder that they have evolved in virtual isolation for a very long period of time. Schnell (1967) has made an interesting comparison with South America, pointing out that *Symphonia globulifera* is almost the only species of forest tree common to both land masses and that there are several families which are well represented in South America but which are absent or virtually so from Africa. The Bromeliaceae, with many American species, has only a single species in Africa, *Pitcairnia feliciana*. Another contrast with South America is in the rarity of palms: those that do occur tend to be specialists, such as climbers (*Calamus*), swamp forest trees (*Raphia*) or light-demanders (*Elaeis*). African forests are, however, similar to the South American in their richness in legumes and in the absence of Dipterocarpaceae, a family so typical of Southeast Asia (Ashton, Ch. 11 and Whitmore, Ch. 10, this volume). Major families shared with South America include Euphorbiaceae, Meliaceae, Moraceae, and Sapotaceae: these probably represent old families which were present on both continents before rifting.

The relative poverty of African forests in numbers of tree species has been commented on by a number of workers (Richards, 1939, for example). Huttel (1975) has shown that the density of tree species in various lowland evergreen forests in

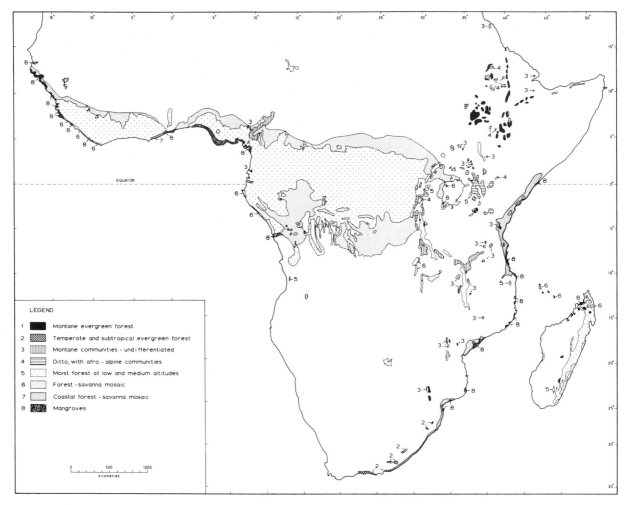

Fig. 8.1. Occurrence of forests in Africa south of the Tropic of Cancer. (After AETFAT, 1959.)

LEGEND

1 ■ Montane evergreen forest
2 ▨ Temperate and subtropical evergreen forest
3 ▤ Montane communities - undifferentiated
4 ▦ Ditto, with afro - alpine communities
5 ∴ Moist forest at low and medium altitudes
6 ░ Forest - savanna mosaic
7 ▒ Coastal forest - savanna mosaic
8 ▨ Mangroves

the Ivory Coast is much lower than has been recorded for forests in Malaysia and Surinam. By African standards these Ivory Coast forests are floristically rather rich, yet they contain only about a quarter of the number of tree species per unit area found in Malaysia. The reason for the poverty of the African forest flora is still very much a matter of speculation. One problem is uncertainty as to whether the flora has always been poorer or whether it has become so relatively recently. Unfortunately, there are few plant fossil floras described for Africa dating to the Cretaceous or Tertiary periods. It has sometimes been suggested (Axelrod and Raven, 1978; among others) that the forest flora was once much richer than today, but has been reduced by progressive aridity since the Miocene, and especially by a series of severe dry

episodes during the Quaternary. Various lines of evidence suggest that some world ice maxima during the Pleistocene were marked by a cold dry climate in much of tropical Africa, with forest concentrated in a number of refugia, two of the most important of which were in Cameroon – Gabon and eastern Zaïre (Hamilton, 1982). The extinction of thermophilous species would be expected to have been particularly marked in the eastern Zaïre refuge because of the high minimum altitude (Hall and Bada, 1979).

African forests can be developed on a variety of rock and soil types, but typically the rocks tend to be rather poor in nutrients and the soils deep and very well weathered. Soils in wetter areas (ferralitic soils) are even poorer than those in drier parts (ferruginous soils). Production and nutrient studies carried out under the International Biological Programme in the Ivory Coast (Lemée, 1975a, b) support the well-known generalization that nutrient levels in the soil are low and that a large part of the nutrient stock is contained within the plant biomass (but see Sanchez, Ch. 4, this volume). Nutrient turnover rates are high. These often tall, dense forests can, therefore, give a deceptive picture of the potential productivity of the soils for agriculture. They are highly efficient systems for utilizing the available resources of energy, water and nutrients, and forest destruction is liable to lead to an irreversible loss in fertility.

Any short account of forest types in tropical Africa is bound to be highly selective. An *entrée* into the literature is provided by the references given here, among which Knapp (1973), Lind and Morrison (1974), Monod (1957), Schnell (1976–77), Richards (1979) and White (1983) are especially noteworthy as sources of further references.

MAJOR FLORISTIC DIVISIONS

There is general agreement that most species of plants found in African rain forests are virtually confined to this type of vegetation, a fact which led Monod (1957), among others, to place all tropical African forests in one major phytochorion, the Guineo-Congolian Region (*Région Guineo-Congolaise*). This region was further divided by Monod into two domains, a *Domaine atlantico-congolais* comprising the main blocks of forest in West and Central Africa and a *Domaine oriental* to include the isolated forests found near the Indian Ocean. The floristic distinctiveness of the East Coast forests has also been emphasized by Léonard (1965), Moll and White (1978) and White (1979, 1983). White (1979) has shown that the East Coast forests are very distinctive at the specific level, and believed that they should not be included within the Guineo-Congolian Region. He also recognized an important north–south divide within these eastern forests, and preferred to place them into either a Zanzibar–Inhambane Regional Mosaic if to the north of the River Limpopo or in a Pongaland–Pondoland Regional Mosaic if to the south.

Monod (1957), again in common with some other workers, has distinguished between two phytochoria within the main Guineo-Congolian block, a more equatorial *Sous-domaine central* and an outer *Sous-domaine périphérique*. The latter zone is sometimes referred to as a transition zone between forest and savanna (refer to Fig. 8.1 for the corresponding vegetational transition zone). This zone contains few forest endemics.

Despite a shortage of detailed studies, there is nevertheless a considerable body of evidence that African forests show a pattern of local centres of relatively high numbers of species and endemism separated by intervals of more impoverished vegetation (Hamilton, 1976, 1982; White, 1978a). The centres also form the foci of the isolated populations of those many species which show disjunct distributions. The pattern is shared by various groups of forest animals in addition to the plants [see, for instance, Diamond and Hamilton (1980) and Rodgers et al. (1982)] and is found in both lowland and montane species. Further work is needed to fill in the details but it is thought that major species-rich centres are situated in Cameroon – Gabon, eastern Zaïre, eastern Ivory Coast – western Ghana, Sierra Leone – Liberia and near the East African coast, especially around the Usambara – Uluguru area (Fig. 8.2). The central Congo basin has a rather impoverished biota. Recent work gives no support to the hypothesis, at one time in favour, that there is a major phytogeographical divide within eastern Nigeria; rather, the savanna barrier in Togo and Benin is now believed to mark a major floristic boundary (White, 1979, 1983). Nigerian forests become poorer in species from east to west.

A study on Uganda may be taken as an illustration of the pattern of distribution shown by forest tree species within a relatively small area (Hamilton, 1974, 1975b). Uganda, a country in which the distribution of forest trees is rather well known, lies to the east of the important species-rich centre, in eastern Zaïre, which indeed might be said to just penetrate over its western border. Distributions were analysed in relation to the four areas distinguished in the Flora of Tropical East Africa (1952 et seq.). Trees found in lowland and moist lower montane forests share a similar pattern of distribution to each other, that for lowland forest species being illustrated on Table 8.1. It may be observed that the northern and

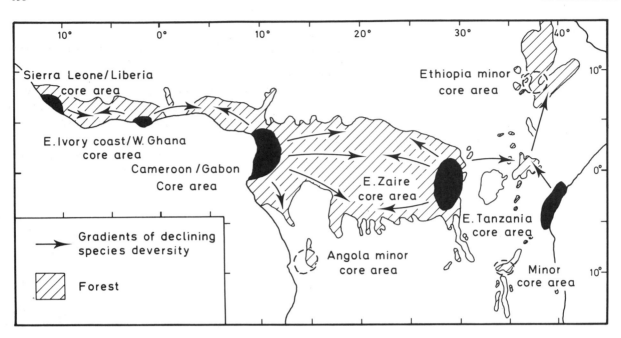

Fig. 8.2. Equatorial Africa showing the main endemic and species-rich centres (core areas) and gradients of declining species diversity extending away from these. (Modified from Hamilton, 1982.)

south-eastern parts of the country each have fewer than half the numbers of forest tree species found in either the southwest or south-centre. This in itself might not be regarded as surprising in that the climate becomes generally less favourable for forest (that is, drier) to the north and east, but less explicable in terms of the modern environment is the total absence of species confined to the impoverished areas. After all, not all species are expected to respond to an environmental gradient in the same way. The southwestern and south-central flora areas are not floristically uniform. There are two main centres of species concentration in the southwest, Bwindi–Kayonza and Bwamba, both close to the border with Zaïre, while in the south-centre the forests around Sango Bay are relatively species-rich.

A few other investigations of the large-scale patterns of distribution of species within African forests may be briefly mentioned. In a study of Euphorbiaceae in the Guineo-Congolian Region, Léonard (1965) emphasized the richness in endemic species of the region between eastern Nigeria and Mayoumba particularly the basin of the Oggooué River in Gabon, and also of forests between about 700 and 1400 m altitude on the eastern side of the Congo basin to the west of Lake Kivu. The central

Congo basin is poor in species and endemics of Euphorbiaceae. Another person who has mentioned the floristic richness of the Cameroon–Gabon region is White (1962) in a study of the distribution of *Diospyros*. White (1962) went on to analyse the distribution of a sample of 288 forest tree species found in the Atlantic–Congolian Domain of the Guineo-Congolian Region and has confirmed the presence of three important endemic centres, these being situated to the west of the Togo–Benin savanna gap, in the Cameroon – Gabon region and in eastern Zaïre. Finally may be mentioned some comments of Friis et al. (1982) on the forest vegetation of Ethiopia. Ethiopia is a long way removed from the forest centres of Africa rich in species and endemics and, perhaps not surprisingly, Ethiopia is impoverished in its number of forest tree species and has very few forest endemics.

Why are there centres rich in species and endemics? They generally occur in places of particularly high rainfall, and it is likely that to some degree this is a causal relationship. However, for several reasons this is widely regarded as inadequate as a complete explanation. For example, it is difficult to envisage how many of the disjunct distributions could have arisen if the environment has always remained the same as it is

TABLE 8.1

The numbers of lowland forest tree species recorded from different combinations of flora areas in Uganda (data from Hamilton, 1981; flora-areas after Flora and Tropical East Africa, 1952 et seq.)

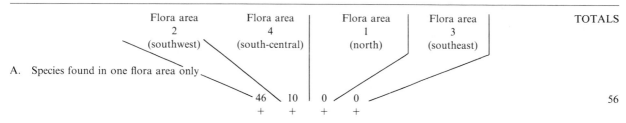

	Flora area 2 (southwest)	Flora area 4 (south-central)	Flora area 1 (north)	Flora area 3 (southeast)	TOTALS
A. Species found in one flora area only	46	10	0	0	56

B. Species found in two flora areas only

```
               87
            + ───── +
                 7
            + ───────── +
               3
            + ─────────────── +
                   0
               + ───── +
                     0
               + ───────── +
                   0
               + ───── +
```
97

C. Species found in three flora areas only

```
             43
        + ─── + ─── +
             39
        + ─── + ───────── +
           1
        + ─────────── + ─── +
             1
        + ───── + ───── +
```
84

D. Species found in all four flora areas

```
             56
        + ─── + ─── + ─── +
```

| TOTALS | 282 | 236 | 108 | 100 | 293 |

now; and why, it may be asked, are endemics so rare in forests in the intervals between the species-rich centres? Today, there is general acceptance that the pattern has been brought about partly by major changes in the environment in the past. In particular, climatic change is believed to have been responsible for widespread movements and local extinctions of species. Change is likely to have been a fact of the African climate over many millions of years, but Quaternary climatic fluctuations were particularly severe, and the species-rich centres are identified as places which retained a mesic climate during general ice age aridity (Hamilton, 1982; Rodgers et al., 1982). It is envisaged that substantial tracts of forest outside the centres were destroyed during dry periods, and that some species were able to expand their ranges quickly when the climate improved. The identification of high-rainfall areas with Quaternary refugia is not surprising, given the view widely held by meteorologists that the pattern of air-mass movement over tropical Africa during glacial periods differed from modern circulation in intensity and position but not greatly in overall pattern. Air masses moving off the Atlantic onto equatorial Africa during Quaternary arid episodes are believed to have had a reduced water content, but the rising ground of Cameroon–Gabon and eastern Zaïre would still have attracted relatively high precipitation.

Montane forests occur scattered throughout tropical Africa in an archipelago-like fashion. These forests, together with other types of montane vegetation, have been regarded as floristically sufficiently distinct to be worthy of classification in their own major phytochorion, the Afromontane Region (White, 1978b, 1983). However, it would be mistaken to regard montane forests as homogeneous; like species of lowland forests, some montane forest plants are widely distributed, while others are local. Eastern Zaïre and its environs is a rich area, and there is impoverishment from here both northwards towards Ethiopia and to the south (Hamilton, 1976). There is no simple correlation between degree of modern geographical isolation and species richness and, as with lowland forests, sites of species richness and high endemism are identified as sites of relative long-term climatic stability (Hamilton, 1982). An important and as yet unresearched difference between the lowland and montane patterns is in the numbers of species and endemics of forest trees concentrated in the Cameroon area of West Africa. This is a major centre of endemism for lowland, but not montane forest trees.

LOWLAND FORESTS

While the great majority of understorey trees in African forests are evergreen, a substantial proportion of the taller trees can be deciduous. The categorization of particular species as evergreen or deciduous can be problematical, but nevertheless degree of deciduousness provides a much used means of classifying the lower-altitude forests of Africa into major categories (Fig. 8.3). Broadly, the percentage contribution of deciduous trees rises as the climate becomes drier and, according to Lebrun and Gilbert (1954), is relatively high in secondary forest and on poorer soils within the evergreen forest zone.

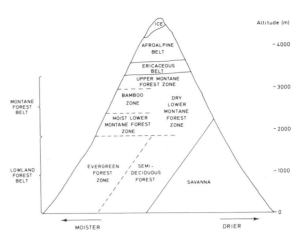

Fig. 8.3. Forest belts and zones in tropical Africa. Based partly on Hamilton (1982).

Recognition of the importance of deciduousness is demonstrated by the terminology used in a number of systems of classification proposed for extensive areas of tropical forest in Africa and elsewhere. Burtt Davy (1938) divided lowland tropical forest globally into three formations: (1) tropical lowland evergreen rain forest (found typically in areas with over 2000 mm annual rainfall); (2) tropical semi-evergreen rain forest (intermediate); and (3) tropical moist deciduous forest (rainfall typically 1000–2000 mm). Another tripartite scheme, this time proposed for African forests specifically, is that of Aubréville, discussed by Chevalier (1948). The types are *Forêts denses humides sempervirentes, Forêts denses humides semi-décidues* and *Forêts denses sèches semi-décidues*. Lebrun and Gilbert (1954) give a two-category scheme for Zaïre, *Forêts ombrophiles sempervirentes* and *Fôrets mésophiles semi-caducifoliées*. These are equivalent to *Forêts ombrophytes* and *Forêts tropophytes* of Léonard (1955). (Confusingly, the term *Forêts tropophiles* is used for a type of savanna woodland by Lebrun and Gilbert.)

A study of leaf fall in various types of semi-deciduous forest in the Ivory Coast has indicated that deciduousness is influenced by both internal rhythms and the external environment (Fig. 8.4; Devineau, 1976b). Upper-strata trees on well-drained sites are characteristically deciduous, while upper-strata trees in wetter valley bottoms, as well as lower strata trees generally, are typically evergreen. Investigations of the periodicity of leaf fall form part of the study of forest seasonality,

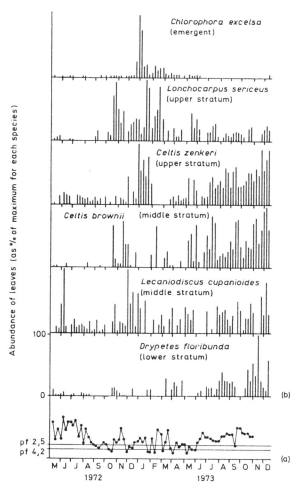

Fig. 8.4. (a) Variation in soil moisture suction at a depth of 40 to 50 cm beneath old secondary semi-deciduous forest on a well-drained site in the Ivory Coast. *pf* is the logarithm of the negative head of water in cm: higher figures mean drier soils.

(b) Leaf fall of various species expressed as percentages of the maximum recorded for each species. Emergents and upper storey trees show greatest seasonality and there is also a considerable difference between the behaviour of species between the two years related to climatic variation. (After Devineau, 1976b.)

and it is appropriate to mention that a study of the seasonality of growth in Olokemeji Forest in Nigeria has emphasized the individuality of the pattern shown by each species (Hopkins, 1970). Hopkins believed that, despite a general relationship between the time of maximum plant growth and the rainy season, the onset of a rainy period may not be the actual factor which triggers growth and suggested that changes in photoperiod may be important. Earlier, Nkoju (1963) had proposed

that both photoperiod and temperature are major factors controlling the seasonal periodicity of growth and development of some forest trees in Nigeria.

The classificatory schemes mentioned above are the work of widely experienced botanists and foresters. However, none is based on information from plots disposed according to some reasonably objective sampling procedure. The vast scale and the great variability shown by African forests pose great challenges to phytogeographers. A major study of forest types in Ghana by Hall and Swaine (1976, 1981), based on a large number of samples arranged to give a good coverage of the entire forested zone of the country, is thus to be warmly welcomed. Only more mature forests were included. The study was based on a set of samples consisting of 155 25×25 m plots in which all species of plant, whether trees or not, were recorded. Structural and environmental, as well as floristic, information was collected.

Figure 8.5 shows an ordination and classification of the samples of Hall and Swaine. Seven forest types are recognized, and rainfall is identified as the most important single environmental variable related to floristic composition; indeed, axis 1 of the ordination, which is the main direction of variation in floristic composition (accounting for 52% of the total variance), corresponds closely to variation in climatic moistness. The moist end of the rainfall spectrum is on the left-hand side of Fig. 8.5 and the dry end on the right. Hall and Swaine pointed out that all forest types are subject to great seasonality in rainfall, and that the main rainfall differentiation between the types is in the amount of precipitation received during the rainy seasons.

This finding of a strong relationship between rainfall and floristic variation in lowland forest supports the views of many earlier workers. The work also demonstrates the continuous nature of vegetational variation within the forests. For example, the proportion of deciduous trees varies continuously and there is no sharp divide between evergreen and deciduous forests. Hall and Swaine believed that this continuum of variation was characteristic of African forests generally, adding that it was unlikely that any African forest was either completely evergreen or completely deciduous. The systematic nature of this study of

the area today consists of patches of semi-deciduous forest with many Moraceae, Sapotaceae and Ulmaceae, scattered in a general landscape of derived savanna and cultivation. The pollen diagram, which is very well dated by radiocarbon determinations, shows that lowland forest was absent from the area from at least 14 500 until 12 200 years B.P., that is during the final part of the period containing the last major world glaciation, which was marked by aridity throughout much of tropical Africa (Hamilton, 1982). The spread of lowland forest trees after 12 200 B.P. soon resulted in a general covering of forest. Kendall (1969) has interpreted some of the changes in the diagram after 6000 B.P. as being due to a drier climate favouring semi-deciduous trees. In particular, he noted a decrease in the abundance of the pollen of a number of trees found in both evergreen and semi-deciduous forest, including *Alchornea*, Moraceae, Myrtaceae and *Tetrorchidium*, and an increase in the pollen of *Celtis* and *Holoptelea*, both taken to be particularly characteristic of semi-deciduous forest.

Dominance of the canopy by a single species is common in lowland African forests. It is especially a feature of evergreen forests, with the dominants being one or another of a number of caesalpinaceous trees including *Brachystegia laurentii*, *Gilbertiodendron dewevrei* and *Cynometra alexandri*. Several authors have noted the abundance of Caesalpinaceae in wetter forests in Africa, for example in Ghana, Nigeria, Cameroon and Gabon (Richards, 1963a; Aubréville, 1968; Hall and Swaine, 1976). *Cynometra* is particularly characteristic of altitudes of about 1000 m in northeastern Zaïre and neighbouring parts of Uganda (Langdale-Brown et al., 1964). The local dominance of *Gilbertiodendron* at c. 500 m near Yangambi in Zaïre led Léonard (1955) to recognize two forest types for the area, one with much *Gilbertiodendron* and the other richer in species and lacking dominance by a single species (*Forêt à Scorodophleus zenkeri*). *Gilbertiodendron* constitutes 80% of the canopy in the former type and the lower vegetational strata are relatively open; regeneration of *Gilbertiodendron* is active and the forests appear stable. Charcoal and pottery are absent from the soils beneath *Gilbertiodendron* forests, but present in those under *Scorodophleus* forests, leading Léonard to postulate that *Scorodophleus*

forests are of secondary origin. *Brachystegia*-dominated forests near Yangambi have been described by Germain and Evrard (1956) who commented on their great height (45–50 m), continuous canopy, almost complete absence of lianes and rather open lower tree strata. The seeds of *Brachystegia* are heavy and germinate rapidly, and the forests are believed to be similar to the *Gilbertiodendron* forests in that they are stable, mature ecosystems.

Many relatively local classifications of lowland forest in Africa have been proposed, among which may be mentioned that of Letouzey (1968) for Cameroon. A primary division between evergreen and semi-deciduous forests is recognized and the evergreen category is further broken down into the following three types: (1) *Forêt littorale*, extending inland from the sea for up to 100 km and characterized by an abundance of *Lophira alata* and *Sacoglottis gabonensis*; the soils tend to be sandy and there has been much human influence; (2) *Forêt biafréene*, reaching to about 200 km inland and very rich in, often gregarious, Caesalpinaceae; and (3) *Forêt congolaise*, in the southeast of the country and extending across the borders into the Congo Basin. There is local dominance by *Gilbertiodendron dewevrei*, but otherwise Caesalpinaceae are much rarer. An interest of Letouzey's study is the various evidence which he presents for local replacement of *Forêt congolaise* by semi-deciduous forest. In particular, some evergreen forests rich in *Baillonella toxisperma* are believed to be in the process of replacement by semi-deciduous forests rich in Sterculiaceae and Ulmaceae. He speculated that this might be due to a move towards a drier climate.

Another nationally based survey is Hall's (1977) classification of forest types in Nigeria based on pre-exploitation data from 46 forests widely scattered throughout the forest zone. Forests were found to fall into two main groups, associated with ferralitic and ferruginous soils, respectively. Ferralitic soils are found in wetter areas and ferruginous soils in drier, as is usual, and Hall reported the presence of a zone of overlap from 1800 to 2400 mm annual rainfall where ferralitic soils occur on Cenozoic sands and ferruginous soils on rocks of the Basement Complex. Forests in southeastern Nigeria are floristically similar to those in nearby Cameroon and Gabon, and were believed by Hall to have formed part of a refuge area for forest during Quaternary arid episodes.

There have been few investigations of variation with position on slope within African forests. Swamp forests, both seasonal and permanent, are vegetatively distinct, as is shown by their classification by phytosociologists in quite different categories from forests on well-drained sites (see Tables 8.3 to 8.5). The degree of distinction between forests on different well-drained parts of catenas, whether lowland or montane, varies greatly. For example, catenary zonation, while existing, was found not to be particularly well marked along a catena which Lawson et al. (1970) studied near Kade in Nigeria. On the other hand, there are very great differences in the vegetation of different parts of the catena on the rugged topography of the moist montane forest of Bwindi in Uganda (Hamilton, 1969).

It is probable that several factors influence catenary variation in forest vegetation, but the availability of water is probably of particular importance. A study of floristic variation on the borderline between raised and swamp forest in Rugege Forest, Rwanda, has shown soil moisture to be the single most important environmental variable related to vegetational composition (Bouxin, 1976). The position of species on the catena can vary with climate. For example, *Carapa procera* and *Symphonia globulifera* are typical of swamp forest and stream valleys in western Nigeria, but grow on well-drained sites in southeastern Nigeria and Cameroon (Richards, 1963a). In Uganda there are many species (for instance *Ilex mitis*, *Podocarpus latifolius*, *Xymalos monospora*) which are found on well-drained soils at higher altitudes (climatically wetter) and in swamp forest at lower altitudes (climatically drier). Finally, it may be mentioned that there are floristic similarities between lower-slope sites in western Uganda, which is climatically wet and topographically rugged, and the forests of the wetter western side of Mt. Elgon (which has much gentler slopes) and between upper-slope sites in western Uganda and the drier eastern forests of Elgon (Hamilton, 1972).

MONTANE FORESTS

The distribution of higher land in tropical Africa is such as to result in a widely scattered distribu-

tion for montane forest (Fig. 8.1). The majority of highlands are associated with the rift valleys of central and eastern Africa, occurring most notably in Ethiopia, the Kivu – Ruwenzori – Rwanda area of central Africa, Kenya, northern Tanzania and to the north and west of Lake Malawi. In terms of area, Ethiopia is by far the most mountainous country in Africa. In addition to these rift-related highlands, further important montane areas include the Usambaras, Ulugurus and other mountains near the East African coast and the various highlands in Cameroon, including Mt. Cameroon itself. There are also highlands further west in West Africa, though these are not very high and the fact that their vegetation has sometimes been classified as montane serves as a useful reminder of the relative nature of the concepts of "lowland" and "montane". The degree of climatic moistness varies greatly between different highlands, as usually within single highlands as well, but all highlands show declines in temperature with altitude, and the similarities between the vegetation of the various montane areas have resulted in their incorporation into a single phytogeographical region, the Afromontane, by White (1978b).

Similarities between the vegetation of different highlands in East Africa led Hedberg (1951) to propose a general zonal scheme, a more recent variant of which is shown on Fig. 8.3. It may be seen that variation in forest vegetation occurs both with increasing altitude (related to reduction in temperature and other factors) and also, particularly at lower altitudes, along a moist–dry spectrum. Lower-altitude forests in wet and dry places are vegetatively quite distinct and may conveniently be placed in different zones, but the forests become increasingly similar at higher altitudes and a single zone suffices for the highest-altitude forest type (Hamilton and Perrott, 1981). The relative homogeneity of high-altitude forests is believed to be largely the result of the decrease in water stress in climatically drier areas as altitude increases and may also result from a widening of the niche-width of species where the flora is greatly reduced.

White (1978b) has classified montane forests into two categories, Afromontane rain forest and Undifferentiated montane forest (equivalent, respectively, to Submontane forest and Montane forest sensu strictu of Chapman and White, 1970).

Afromontane rain forest is equivalent to Moist lower montane forest and Undifferentiated montane forest to all the other montane forest categories of Hamilton (1982). White's classification emphasizes the peculiarities of moist lower-altitude montane forest, which is the most similar montane forest type to lowland forest, but it underemphasizes the wide range of other types of montane forest.

The names of some taxa have sometimes been employed in the designation of montane forest zones. Langdale-Brown et al. (1964) proposed a classification of the montane forests of Uganda into four zones, the *Hagenia – Rapanea* Moist Montane Forest, *Arundinaria* Montane Bamboo Forest, *Prunus* (*Pygeum*) Moist Montane Forest and *Juniperus – Podocarpus* Dry Montane Forest. These are equivalent to the Upper montane, Bamboo, Moist lower montane and Dry lower montane forest zones shown on Fig. 8.3. There seems little to be gained from the use of generic names in this context, especially since some of the plants used (*Prunus*, among others) are common in a number of forest types, and also because a genus can sometimes be absent from "its" forest type, for example for historical reasons.

The montane bamboo in tropical Africa is *Arundinaria alpina*, which can form very extensive and conspicuous patches, especially between the altitudes of 2450 and 3050 m. *Arundinaria* is believed sometimes to play a colonizing role, among other situations in drier forests and outside the altitudinal range given above, but its frequent great abundance in moist areas is believed to be a natural feature and not due to human disturbance. Its abundance can probably be regarded in part as a reflection of the difficulties of tree establishment in higher-altitude forests (see later).

There are very few species of conifers in tropical Africa, but some of those that are found can be common in montane forest and have figured in classificatory schemes. Logan (1946) classified the montane forests of Ethiopia into Tropical montane bamboo forest, Tropical upper montane rain forest and Tropical high montane conifer forest. Tropical upper montane rain forest was further divided into two associations, a *Pouteria* (*Chrysophyllum*) – *Albizia* association in wetter places and a *Podocarpus* association, characterized by the presence of *Podocarpus falcatus*, in drier areas. Tropical high

montane conifer forest, with much *Juniperus procera*, was said to occur under an even drier climate than *Podocarpus* forest. The same general distribution of these two conifers in respect of rainfall is also found further south in Africa, and here a third conifer, *Podocarpus latifolius*, can also be conspicuous, growing typically in wetter places than *Podocarpus falcatus* (Hamilton and Perrott, 1981). *Juniperus* requires open conditions for regeneration and can be favoured by fires (Lind and Morrison, 1974). A further genus of gymnosperm, *Widdringtonia*, grows in montane forests from Malawi southwards (White, 1978b).

Moreau (1966), and a number of other workers such as White (1978b), have advanced the opinion that lowland and montane forests are fundamentally rather distinct from one another, lacking the continuum of biotic intergradation in respect of a steady environmental gradient which might be expected. A criticism of this view has been given by Hamilton and Perrott (1981) and Hamilton (1982). It is possible that those who hold to a clear-cut lowland/montane divide have been influenced by the fact that surviving patches of forest in some parts of Africa are often altitudinally well separated. This is because forest passes down into non-forest vegetation in drier areas frequently at *c.* 2000 m, while in wetter districts the altitudinal band of 1500 to 2000 m has proved attractive to cultivators and has been largely cleared of forest.

Central Africa, especially the Kivu district of Zaïre and neighbouring parts of Burundi, Rwanda and Uganda, might be considered to be the "best" part of Africa to examine altitudinal change in forest vegetation, since this is a climatically wet area and only here is forest a common vegetation type over a wide range of altitude, extending from Guineo-Congolian type lowland forests up to the altitudinal forest limit of about 3300 m. One student of zonation in this area was Lebrun (1960), who studied altitudinal change in vegetation on Ruwenzori and the Virunga Volcanoes. These two highland areas display contrasting geological conditions, Ruwenzori being an upthrust block of Precambrian rocks while the Virungas are Quaternary volcanoes with soils and vegetation generally at an early stage of development (Lebrun, 1942). The analysis was based on altitudinal ranges for species given by Robyns (1947–55), 54% of the total flora being used in the case of Ruwenzori and a slightly lower proportion in the case of the Virunga Volcanoes. Taxa were classified into "ecological groups" — for example the Ericaceae and Myrsinaceae were classified as sclerophylls — and then the proportion of each "ecological group" present in each 100 m altitudinal band was calculated. A number of stages (fr. *étage* — Lebrun preferred the term "zone" to be reserved for latitudinal changes in vegetation) were then recognized on the basis of the changing representation of different "ecological groups". For example, on Ruwenzori Lebrun recognized an Afroalpine stage above 3750 m, an Afro-subalpine stage from 2600 to 3750 m, a Montane stage from 1750 to 2600 m and a Submontane stage found up to 1750 m. An obvious problem with this method is that the final classification depends heavily on the initial classification of species into "ecological groups", which itself is based largely on a preconception of the ecology of the species. The classification has little objective basis.

A description of altitudinal changes in the vegetation of western Burundi by Lewalle (1972) is notable for its use of well-recorded *relevés* in the phytosociological tradition. He recognized four vegetational belts, and within the latter a number of stages, some based on earlier suggestions by Lebrun (1935). Excluding the Bamboo stage (*Arundinaria* does not form extensive stands in Burundi which is a relatively low-altitude country) and various pre-forest types, Lewalle recognized the following three horizons within the submontane and montane forest stages. According to Lewalle, these various horizons pass gradually into one another.

(1) Lower horizon (1600–1900 m). The upper tree layer can attain 25 m and includes *Anthonotha pynaertii*, *Albizia gummifera*, *Parinari excelsa*, *Prunus africana* and *Syzygium staudtii*.

(2) Middle horizon (1900–2250 m). The upper stratum can reach 30 m and sometimes even 40 m, and includes *Entandrophragma excelsum*, *Parinari excelsa*, *Polyscias fulva* and *Prunus africana*.

(3) Upper horizon (2250–2450 m). Trees attain 15 m (exceptionally 20 m) and include *Monanthotaxis orophila*, *Maytenus acuminata*, *Podocarpus latifolius* and *Rapanea melanophloeos*.

One of the most comprehensive studies of altitudinal zonation in central Africa was made by Pierlot (1966), based on 25 exceptionally large plots (mostly 4 ha or more) placed in apparently undisturbed forests at altitudes ranging between 450 and 2400 m in eastern Zaïre. The five altitudinal types of forest recognized by Pierlot are shown in Table 8.2. The two most critical altitudes according to Pierlot are 1200 and 2000 m, with species typical of the lowland forests of the Congo basin present below 1200 m and trees characteristic of higher montane forest, such as *Cassipourea gummiflua*, *Ilex mitis*, *Podocarpus* spp. and *Prunus africana*, becoming prominent above 2000 m. Unfortunately, despite the excellence of the data in some other respects, only one sample was taken between 1400 and 2200 m, so that caution is needed in accepting the existence of these critical altitudes.

Pierlot's study provides some firm information about some of the ways in which forests change with altitude. For example, as altitude increases, the number of species declines, tree density at first rises and then falls, with a maximum at about 1000 m, and basal area remains rather constant at about 35 m^2 ha^{-1} (Fig. 8.9). The combination of constancy in basal area and considerable variation in density is partly due to the distribution of very large trees, which tend to be few between 1200 and 1600 m.

TABLE 8.2

Forest types of eastern Zaïre (after Pierlot, 1966).

2000–2400 m. *La forêt de haute montagne.* Poor in species, with many tall light-lovers. Rather open lower tree strata. Typical species include *Carapa grandiflora*, *Symphonia globulifera* and *Podocarpus latifolius*. Bamboo is present above 2350 m.

1600–2000 m. *La forêt de montagne.* Rather rich in tree species, with some tall light-lovers and rather open lower tree strata. Typical species include *Beilschmiedia oblongifolia*, *Carapa grandiflora*, *Drypetes* spp. and *Newtonia buchananii*.

1200–1600 m. *La forêt de basse montagne.* Rather rich in tree species, except for the upper stratum which contains some light-lovers. Lower strata very dense. Typical species include *Beilschmiedia oblongifolia*, *Cleistanthus pierlotii* and *Pentadesma lebrunii*.

750–1200 m. *La forêt de piedmont.* Very rich in species and with very dense lower tree strata. Typical species include *Celtis mildbraedii* and *Cynometra alexandri*.

450–750 m. *La forêt de cuvette.* This includes a number of types, some dominated by single species, notably *Gilbertiodendron dewevrei* (which ascends to 1000 m), *Michelsonia microphylla* and *Scorodophloeus zenkeri*.

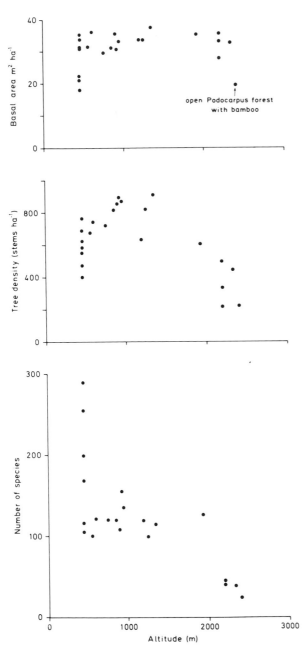

Fig. 8.9. Basal area, tree density and species diversity plotted against altitude for central African forests, mainly in Kivu (Zaïre). Only individuals over 20 cm circumference at a height of 1.5 m above the ground are included. (Constructed from data in Pierlot, 1966.)

Decline in number of tree species with altitude is a well-known feature of tropical forest (Richards, 1979). Some comparative data regarding density and basal area are available from a study on Mt. Elgon, though based on much smaller sample plots (Hamilton and Perrott, 1981). Considering only a transect which was relatively little disturbed by man, basal area was also found to be rather constant and tree density to vary greatly. Basal area averaged about 55 m² ha⁻¹, which is considerably higher than Pierlot's figures, while tree density declined to a minimum at 2650 m and thereafter rose. The higher figures of basal area on Elgon are partly, but certainly not entirely, due to a lower minimum circumference used for deciding whether a tree should be included in the survey (15 cm rather than 20 cm at breast height).

A study of altitudinal zonation in Uganda by Hamilton (1975a) employed methods similar in some regards to those of Lebrun, but was more broadly based. An objective method was used for selecting a sample of the better-known forest trees (comprising 35% of the forest tree flora). Taking the entire country, which includes several major highland areas, all altitudinal records for these species available in Uganda from herbarium specimens and publications were collated and the occurrence of each species in 305 m wide altitudinal bands ascertained. The results of this study show that the forest changes in its floristic composition in a regular way with increasing altitude, without any critical altitudes, and that the numbers of both species and families decline gradually (Fig. 8.10). The distribution of some physiognomic characters was also studied, and it was shown that average leaf size and the percentages of species which have compound leaves, which are deciduous, which have thorns or which are buttressed all decline with altitude. All these are well-known features of the altitudinal gradient in tropical forest (Richards, 1979).

Cameroon is the only place in West Africa with a sufficient range of altitude to allow studies which may be compared with the findings of Pierlot and

Fig. 8.10. Altitudinal changes in Ugandan forests based on a 35% sample of the forest tree flora. The sample includes tree species of denser type of Ericacecous and Afroalpine vegetation. Figures for mean lamina area are calculated excluding *Dendrosenecio* spp. The similarity values refer to the similarities in species composition of adjacent altitudinal bands. (Adapted from Hamilton, 1975.)

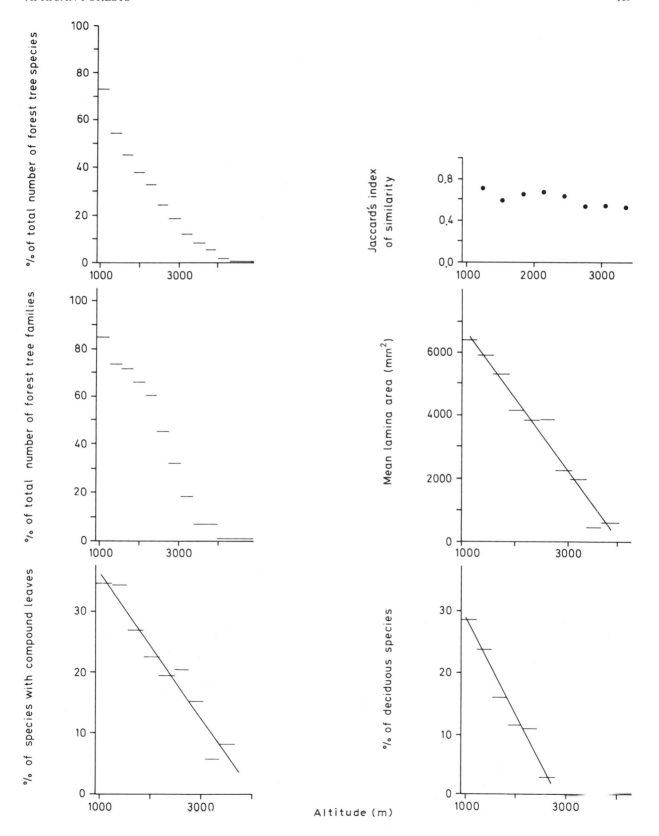

others in central Africa, but no detailed work has yet been undertaken. A notable feature of the highland forests at rather low altitudes further west in West Africa is the common occurrence of *Parinari excelsa* at altitudes above 1000 m (Schnell, 1976–77). This is a well-known species of moist montane forests at slightly higher altitudes in central Africa (Lind and Morrison, 1974). Returning to Cameroon, according to Richards (1963b), Letouzey (1968) and Hall (1973), there are similarities between forest zonation on Mt. Cameroon and in central Africa. Letouzey identified a submontane forest zone between 1000/1200 and 1600/1800 m and a montane forest zone between 1600/1800 and 2200/2500 m. Forest reaches up to an altitude of only 2650 m on Mt. Cameroon, and Richards (1963b) believed that much of the grassland present at higher altitudes has been derived from forest through the action of fire.

More is known about the Upper Quaternary history of montane forest than other African vegetational types, thanks to the relatively favourable conditions for pollen preservation found in wetter montane areas. The evidence is summarized by Hamilton (1982). Pollen diagrams show that montane forests have been subject to much climatically induced vegetational change during the past 40 000 years; instability of this type should be regarded as a normal feature of these forests over a very long period of time. One aspect of climatic change has been rises and falls in temperature; these are known to have been responsible for causing vertical movements in montane taxa. Such altitudinal movements of vegetation are most clearly recorded in pollen diagrams from places which have remained relatively moist during episodes of temperature fluctuation, for example Mt. Kenya, Ruwenzori and southwestern Uganda. In all of these places, vegetational belts were displaced downwards by about 1000 m, equivalent to a temperature lowering of about 6°C, during the height of the last glaciation at *c*. 21 000 to 14 000 years B.P. (Coetzee, 1967; Livingstone, 1967; Morrison, 1968; Hamilton, 1982). The change-over from *Hagenia* forest to forest with a wider diversity of species shown at the base of the Butongo pollen diagram (Fig. 8.11) is believed to have been caused partly by a rise in temperature at the beginning of the Postglacial. This event is also known from other

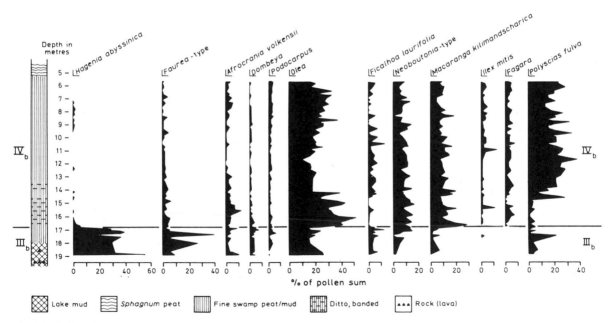

Fig. 8.11. Pollen diagram from Butongo Swamp at 2050 m in the moist lower montane forest zone of western Uganda. Only tree pollen types are shown here. The sum used for calculating pollen percentages consists of the above pollen types plus *Isoglossa* and *Mimulopsis* (not shown) minus *Podocarpus*. The decline in *Hagenia* near the base of the diagram is believed to be due to a rise in temperature at the beginning of the postglacial. The length of time covered by the diagram is not known exactly, but will be in the order of 10 000 to 11 000 years.

sites in the vicinity. In places where rainfall has varied greatly, changes in vegetation associated with a shift along the moist–arid axis have been so great as largely to mask any changes due to fluctuations in temperature which might have occurred. For example, at the height of the last glaciation on Mt. Elgon, the pollen of grasses completely dominate the pollen spectra and little can be said about the downward movement of montane forest, which in any case appears to have been very much reduced in extent (Hamilton, 1982).

One intriguing feature of pollen diagrams from widely scattered sites in Ethiopia, Kenya and Uganda is a rise in *Podocarpus* pollen soon after 2000 B.C. More than one species of *Podocarpus* must have been involved in this population expansion, the cause of which was probably a shift to a drier climate. Clearance of montane forest by man can be seen in pollen diagrams from Ethiopia and southwestern Uganda (Morrison and Hamilton, 1974; Hamilton, 1982).

THE FOREST CYCLE

Pollen analysis, while still at a very young stage in tropical Africa, does provide some insight into the behaviour of forest systems on a time-scale of hundreds to thousands of years. Two examples are shown here, one being from a small basin (Butongo) in highland Uganda and believed to give a relatively good picture of the changes in abundance of species growing close to the sample site (Fig. 8.11; Morrison and Hamilton, 1974), and the other being from Lake Victoria and believed to be heavily biased in favour of anemophilous taxa (Fig. 8.8; Kendall, 1969). The feature which is stressed is the impression of orderliness which these diagrams provide. Pollen types fluctuate within rather well-defined limits or rise and fall in a regular way, for example due to changes in climate. The Lake Victoria pollen diagram covers 14 500 years and the Butongo diagram, while not well dated, certainly extends over several thousand years. One can be certain that many generations of trees have replaced one another during the time periods recorded in these two diagrams. It is concluded that the sizes of the populations of individual tree species must be under a high degree

of control, and accordingly that the forest ecosystems are strongly regulated and, to a large extent at least, intrinsically understandable.

Climatic, edaphic and other variables of the physical environment certainly serve as controls over forest composition, as has been demonstrated elsewhere in this chapter, but there seems to be much variation in floristic composition on a relatively small geographical scale which is not determined by such factors (Bouxin, 1976; Hall and Swaine, 1976). There is widespread agreement that some of this unexplained variation is related to biotic interactions, about which very little is known.

The mechanism of forest renewal, more specifically the method by which the site of a dead individual tree becomes occupied by another, is one of the keys to an understanding of tropical forest ecology (Grubb, 1977; Hartshorn, 1978; Whitmore, 1978). A useful concept when considering the workings of the forest system is that of the forest cycle (Fig. 8.12; Whitmore, 1978). A forest may be regarded as an intricate mosaic of patches in different stages of development, ranging from a gap phase created on the death of a tree to a building phase marked by high net production, and a rather stagnant mature phase. It is advisable to distinguish clearly between this series of phases and the succession of forest types (early secondary, late secondary, climax) which may succeed one another with forest spread onto, for example, abandoned agricultural land. However, there are clearly similarities between the forest stages associated with the two processes.

Forest renewal begins with the creation of a gap, which can vary in size from the space left by one tree rotting in situ to a clearing of several hectares created by the occasional severe storm (Whitmore, 1978). Although studies of gaps are widely thought to be important, there have been few such studies in tropical forest in Africa. According to Oldeman

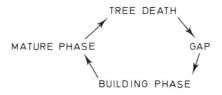

Fig. 8.12. The four phases of the forest cycle. (After Whitmore, 1978.)

(1978), gaps in tropical forest are typically 200 to 800 m² in area, though measurements in Costa Rica give a smaller average size of only about 100 m² (Hartshorn, 1978). If a gap is fairly large (over 500 m² according to Hartshorn, 1978), then pioneer species such as *Musanga cecropioides* and *Trema orientalis* are able to become established in its central portion, but otherwise and more frequently forest growth continues by the expansion of existing crowns and by the growth of shade-tolerant seedlings and saplings already in existence. Available evidence indicates that the incidence of gap formation is rather frequent (a mean gap occurrence of 118 ± 27 years for any given spot in the forest has been determined in Costa Rica by Hartshorn, 1978), which may account for the paucity of really large trees in many forests. Gap formation is also rather unpredictable, which may be a major factor maintaining species diversity.

When a gap is formed, a prerequesite for the success of a tree is that it must either be already established as a young individual, or be present as a viable seed in the soil, or be able to invade rapidly from elsewhere. Clearly, investigations of all the intricacies of reproductive biology should form a major element in the analysis of forest ecosystems. Seeds vary greatly in their methods of dispersal and dormancy. Studies in both Ghana and Nigeria have shown that the soil beneath even dense primary forest generally contains large numbers of viable seeds belonging to such pioneer trees as *Musanga* and *Trema* (Keay, 1960; Hall and Swaine, 1980). The seeds of these and other very early colonizers are typically small, bird-dispersed and have long viability. This is a strategy evolved to utilize a niche which is rare in space and short in duration in natural forest. Studies of forest soils have also demonstrated the rarity of viable seeds belonging to species of more mature forest stages (Keay, 1960; Hall and Swaine, 1980). Such species typically have large seeds and seedlings, and rapid germination (Ng, 1978). The large seeds of these species help their seedlings and saplings to become sufficiently well established to persist in the forest undergrowth with minimal growth for a very long period of time (Oldeman, 1978). The sudden creation of a gap can create the opportunity for rapid expansion, but competition is fierce and those species which are already relatively well established have a vital advantage.

Forest trees can be classified according to their positions on a spectrum ranging from pioneers to primary forest species. One method of placing species along this spectrum is to determine the numbers of individuals in different size classes in a given area (Jones, 1955–56; Germain and Evrard, 1956; Sarukhan, 1978). Only stable (climax) forests should be used in such analyses — these can of course be difficult to recognize. Pierlot (1966) analysed such data for twenty-five large (often 4–10 ha) plots placed in apparently primary forest in Zaïre. Size was determined as circumference at breast height, as is usual in such studies, and species were grouped into three categories according to their number/size relationships (Fig. 8.13). These groups are: (1) sciaphytes (plants tolerant of shade) which have a large number of small individuals and fewer and fewer specimens in progressively larger size classes, the relationships being very well described by hyperbolic expressions (it is more normal to compare such data with exponential curves); (2) hemisciaphytes; and (3) heliophytes (light-loving plants), which have either irregular number/size distributions, or relationships approaching gaussian in form. One species singled out as unusual was *Parinari excelsa* which had a particularly disproportionate number of large stems; this plant was held to be a relict — that is, the forest was not in equilibrium and the species was a remnant from a previous forest type. The species shows a similar type of number/size relationship in some Ugandan forests (Langdale-Brown et al., 1964).

An interesting finding of Pierlot was that the number of light-loving species tends to become higher with altitude, especially above 2000 m. This is a general phenomenon in tropical African forests. There are many forest tree species which are generally common at high altitudes but which become more and more confined to marginal roles as altitude diminishes. *Hagenia* and *Prunus* may be cited as examples. One cause is believed to be that high-altitude forests in the tropics are naturally fragile and tend to suffer much from disturbance, leading to a high incidence of gaps (Oldeman, 1978). The causes of this enhanced instability are little known, but could include greater substrate instability with steeper slopes and higher rainfall, a high incidence of large herbivores, higher epiphyte loads and more frequent strong winds. The more

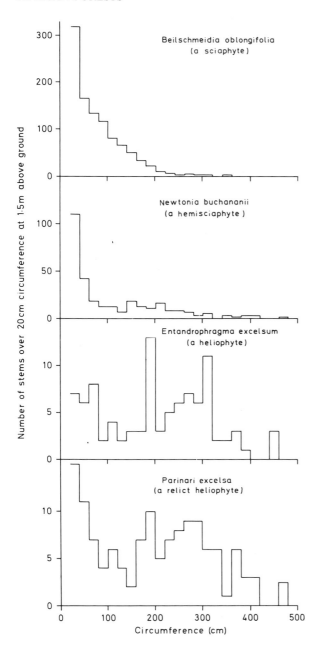

Fig. 8.13. The number of individuals in various size classes for four species in a moist montane forest in eastern Zaïre (*Forêt de la Tschinganda* at 1950 m). Total area sampled = 28 ha. (Drawn from data in Pierlot, 1966.)

open understorey of higher-altitude forests may also encourage heliophytes. On Mt. Elgon, for example a well-developed understorey tree stratum is absent above 2600 m (Hamilton and Perrott, 1981).

THE FOREST BOUNDARY

Forest was once much more extensive in tropical Africa than it is today, having been destroyed by man over thousands of years through cutting and burning, principally with the intention of opening up new land for agriculture. The adjective "derived" is sometimes used for savanna which is believed to have replaced forest through human actions (Keay, 1960); derived savanna is particularly extensive in relatively dry areas (Hopkins, 1962). The boundary between forest and savanna is often sharp, with an almost complete change in biota as one steps from one ecosystem type to the other, but this may not always have been the case. Certainly, the distinctness of the boundary is much enhanced by the burning of savanna, which is a process in which man plays a major part. Could it have been that before man became a major influence on ecosystems in Africa there was a gradual transition between forest and savanna?

Keay (1959) has listed criteria for deciding the status of savanna vegetation.

(1) Climate. Aubréville (1949) had earlier concluded that savanna occurs extensively in Africa in places which are climatically capable of supporting forest. Thus, maps of former forest distribution can be drawn from climatic parameters, though care must be exercised in weighing up the influence of variations in soil. The latter complication may be illustrated with reference to Ghana where forest is present under a drier climate on base-rich rocks than on sandstones and shales (Swaine et al., 1976).

(2) Remnant forests. Farmers prefer better soils and thus may leave forest on poorer sites. Such a distribution of forest indicates that forest once occurred on the better soils as well. Forests are sometimes protected for religious reasons.

(3) Odd specimens of forest trees may be found in savanna; these may have been left behind on forest contraction. However, such individuals may also be associated with especially favourable microenvironments; for example, termite mounds can offer better soils and protection from burning. In the latter instances, forest retreat may not have occurred.

(4) Derived savanna tends to have a poorer grass flora than neighbouring natural savanna. Among the common grasses of derived savanna are

Pennisetum purpureum and *Imperata cylindrica*, typically associated with better and poorer soils, respectively.

(5) Fire protection experiments. Three famous examples are at Olokemeji and Akpaka in Nigeria and at Ndola in Zambia where a long period of fire protection has resulted in the invasion of forest trees into former savanna vegetation.

These considerations led Keay (1959) to postulate that forest was once considerably more extensive in Nigeria than it is today and that an intermediate type of vegetation, which he called transition woodland, existed extensively between "true" forest and savanna. Transition woodland is envisaged to have been very susceptible to burning and survives today only as a narrow strip on some forest edges and very rarely on a more extensive scale. Keay envisaged that transition woodland in Nigeria contained such trees as *Afzelia africana*, *Albizia coriaria*, *A. zygia*, *Daniellia oliveri*, *Khaya senegalensis*, *Terminalia glaucescens* and *Vitex doniana*, forming a single tree stratum over a shrub layer of *Coffea rupestris*, *Tricalysia sudanica* and others.

Vegetation intermediate between forest and savanna woodland has been described as occurring very locally over a band 500 km wide on the southern fringes of the Congo forest in northern Angola, southern Zaïre and northern and western Zambia (Lebrun and Gilbert, 1954; Devred, 1958; Werger and Coetzee, 1978; White and Werger, 1978). This mixed forest–savanna vegetation, which is sometimes referred to in the scientific literature by one of its vernacular names "muhulu", is readily destroyed by burning and is regarded as relictual. The canopy is typically 25 to 30 m tall, with the canopy trees tending to have coriaceous leaves which are either evergreen or only briefly deciduous. A dense layer of mainly evergreen shrubs sometimes grows below. Characteristic species include *Brachystegia spiciformis*, *B. taxifolia*, *Diospyros hoyleana*, *Entandrophragma delevoyi*, *Marquesia acuminata*, *M. macroura*, *Parinari excelsa*, *Podocarpus latifolius* and *Syzygium guineense*.

Fire is clearly a major factor clarifying and maintaining the forest boundary. The characteristics of fires on the margin of semi-deciduous forest in the Ivory Coast have been studied by Devineau (1976a), who found that fires occasionally penetrated up to 10 m into the forest,

sometimes destroying a few trees and shrubs. The ability of fires to extend into the forest was determined by the dryness of the litter, which itself depended on the amount of rainfall in the period preceding the burn.

In addition to fire, inadequate seed supply and especially soil degradation resulting from agricultural practices are major factors which prevent forest re-establishment in derived savanna (Juo and Lal, 1977; Jordan and Herrera, 1981). Climatic alterations resulting from forest destruction also have an influence (Ross, 1954). A number of authors have noted that the soils of neighbouring areas of forest and savanna are often different, but the extent to which the vegetational boundary is due to the soil boundary or vice versa is difficult to determine. An example of a soil study across the forest/savanna boundary is that of Markham and Babbedge (1979) based on two catenas in Ghana. Here forest occurs in valleys and on hilltops, with savanna on the slopes between. A clear difference between forest and savanna soils emerged, with pH and the levels of total phosphorus and exchangeable calcium and potassium all being higher under the forest. However, all these edaphic characteristics are believed to be secondary, the primary factors separating the soil types being the greater effective depth, higher clay content and more readily available water of the forest soils. The forest/savanna boundary appears stable in this area today and the authors did not speculate as to whether the savanna was derived.

While the overall current trend is certainly for forest retreat, there are instances where forest has spread recently over substantial areas of savanna or abandoned cultivated land. The example shown on Fig. 8.14 is from the Ivory Coast (Devineau, 1976a). The former presence of savanna where forest now stands is indicated by the incorporation of the savanna species *Borassus aethiopum* and *Crossopteryx febrifuga* within the forest. In Uganda, forest has grown up over extensive areas close to the northern Lake Victoria shoreline following a sleeping sickness epidemic at the beginning of the century (Lind and Morrison, 1974). The three forest types depicted on Fig. 8.15 were recorded in Budongo Forest, Uganda, by Eggeling (1947), who believed that they stood in a successionary series, starting with *Maesopsis* forest invading non-forest vegetation.

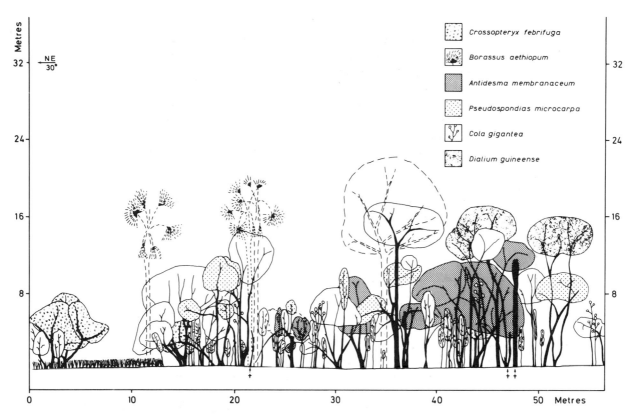

Fig. 8.14. Forest advancing over savanna near Lamto, Ivory Coast. Some individuals of the savanna palm tree *Borassus aethiopum* and *Crossopteryx febrifuga* have become incorporated into the forest. Savanna on the left, early seral forest in the centre and older forest on the right. *Antidesma membranaceum* is a characteristic species of the first stages of forest spread at Lamto. Trees marked with a cross are dead. (From Devineau, 1976.)

The forest/savanna boundary has fluctuated to and fro with the repeated climatic changes which have characterized the Quaternary Period. The beginning of the present relatively warm and wet postglacial phase was marked by a big expansion of forest, which is well documented in the pollen contained in lake muds close to the northern shore of Lake Victoria (Fig. 8.8; Kendall, 1969). The following stages may be noted:

(1) An early period (14 500–14 000 B.P.) marked by much grass pollen and other indications of aridity. *Podocarpus* pollen is the most common tree pollen type, possible reasons being differential preservation, efficient long-distance transport by wind or water or a downward extension of montane forest (the latter was probably not a major feature in this area which appears to have been climatically rather arid).

(2) A major influx of tree pollen began at 12 200 B.P. and a substantial amount of semi-deciduous forest occurred by 11 000 B.P. Initially the most abundant tree-pollen type was *Olea*, with *Diospyros*, *Myrica*, Rhamnaceae, Rutaceae (especially *Fagara*) and *Trema* also being conspicuous. *Celtis*, Moraceae and Urticaceae start to rise.

(3) There was a brief, probably climatically determined, forest recession at about 10 000 B.P.

(4) *Celtis*, Moraceae and Oleaceae are abundant between 9500 and 2000 B.P. and new pollen types appearing here, and not present in significant amounts in earlier levels, include *Alchornea*, *Bosqueia*, *Mallotus*, *Musanga* and *Tetrorchidium*.

An early abundance of *Olea* followed by a rise in *Celtis* is also shown in a postglacial pollen diagram from Ruwenzori (Livingstone, 1967). *Olea* and *Celtis* pollen on Ruwenzori are believed to be largely of long-distance origin, originating from lowland forest at the foot of the mountain, and the early pollen peak of *Olea* in Lake Victoria and on Ruwenzori fits in with Eggeling's (1947) view that

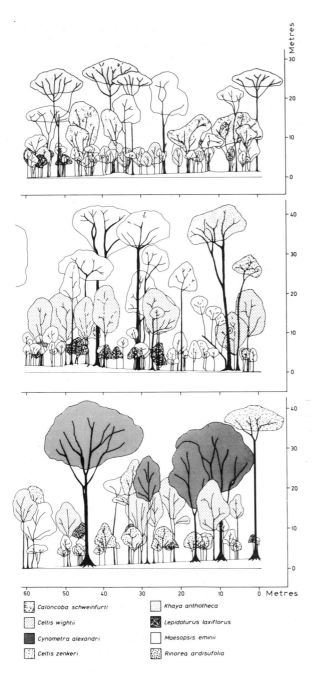

O. capensis (likely to be the main species of *Olea* represented in the pollen diagrams in these cases) is characteristic of colonizing forest in parts of Uganda. The early presence of *Trema* in the Lake Victoria pollen diagram is also not unexpected, given the abundance of *Trema* in early successional forest types today. The rise in *Musanga* occurs later than that of *Trema*, possibly either because the genus dispersed relatively slowly from its arid-period refugia (rather unlikely) or because the early forest soils were too poor for this species to flourish.

AGRICULTURE AND THE FOREST FALLOW

Man can influence the forest ecosystem in various ways and on various scales. A widespread activity, but one which probably has relatively little general impact, is the selective removal of occasional specimens of valuable timber trees by hand felling. A much more dramatic type of intervention is wholesale tree destruction to make way for a phase of cultivation. The traditional pattern in many areas involves the alternation of a phase of cultivation with a phase of fallow during which the ground may become reforested (Fig. 8.16; Aubréville, 1947; see also Lawton, Ch. 33, this volume). Repeated clearing generally occurs after a period of only a few decades, so that forest may never reach the primary state. There is said to be sometimes a stage of short-lived nitrophilous herbs following on immediately after the cessation of agriculture (Lebrun and Gilbert, 1954).

The extent of forest which has been influenced by man in Africa is certainly very great, though difficult to quantify. Chevalier (1948) estimated that at least two-thirds of forest in the Ivory Coast had been modified by man, while Hall and Swaine (1981) go further in stating that it is unlikely that there is any forest in Africa which has not been subject to human interference. Certainly, it is striking, in account after account of particular forests by ecologists, who have often attempted to choose primary forests for their studies, that mention is made of signs of former human presence. The difficulty of distinguishing between primary and late secondary forest has been noted by many authors.

Fig. 8.15. Three forest types in Budongo Forest, Uganda. Each profile represents a strip of forest 7.6 m wide. After Eggeling (1947), who believed that the upper type (*Maesopsis* forest) represents early secondary forest, the central type (Mixed forest) late secondary forest and the lower type (Ironwood forest) the climax. The upper type would be accepted as an early type on recently forested land by other workers, but the relationship between the lower two types is not well established. There is some evidence that Ironwood forest is found on poor soils and also that it is encouraged by elephant pressure.

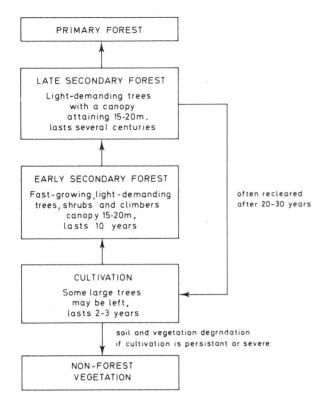

```
                    ┌─────────────────────────┐
                    │     PRIMARY FOREST       │
                    └─────────────────────────┘
                                 ▲
                    ┌─────────────────────────┐
                    │  LATE SECONDARY FOREST   │
                    │  Light-demanding trees   │
                    │      with a canopy       │
                    │    attaining 15-20m.     │
                    │   lasts several centuries│
                    └─────────────────────────┘
                                 ▲
                    ┌─────────────────────────┐        often recleared
                    │  EARLY SECONDARY FOREST  │        after 20-30 years
                    │ Fast-growing,light-demand│
                    │ trees, shrubs and climbers│
                    │      canopy 15-20m.      │
                    │      lasts 10 years      │
                    └─────────────────────────┘
                                 ▲
                    ┌─────────────────────────┐
                    │       CULTIVATION        │
                    │    Some large trees      │
                    │      may be left.        │
                    │     lasts 2-3 years      │
                    └─────────────────────────┘
                                 │   soil and vegetation degradation
                                 ▼   if cultivation is persistant or severe
                    ┌─────────────────────────┐
                    │      NON-FOREST          │
                    │      VEGETATION          │
                    └─────────────────────────┘
```

Fig. 8.16. Agriculture and the forest fallow. (Based on Aubréville, 1947.)

Early forest succession on a patch of cleared land in Ghana has been studied in detail by Swaine and Hall (1983), who classified trees into three categories according to their seral position. The first group consists of small (to 30 m), short-lived, secondary forest species such as *Musanga cecropioides* and *Trema orientalis* which require a gap for germination and establishment. The second group comprises large secondary forest trees such as *Alstonia boonei* and *Chlorophora* spp., which are similar to the first group in their requirement for light, but which differ in that they persist to form part of the mature forest canopy. Finally, there are the primary trees, capable of germination and establishment under at least partial shade and which also persist into mature forest. Swaine and Hall emphasized that the Clementsian model of succession, which could be said to be implied by Aubréville's scheme shown on Fig. 8.16, does not apply in this case. According to this widely held model, one clearly defined forest type should replace another, the earlier types providing necessary preparation for the invasion of later species.

Swaine and Hall saw succession at their site more as a competitive hierarchy in which there is a large initial population of pioneers and a much smaller population of primary species. The progressive elimination of pioneers is compensated by slow and persistent accretion of primary species. A similar conclusion based on forest succession on abandoned agricultural land in eastern Nigeria had earlier been reached by Ross (1954).

The site studied by Swaine and Hall in Ghana appears to have been relatively fertile, despite severe disturbance and possibly even removal of the topsoil. This may be deduced from the luxuriant growth of *Musanga*, which is characteristic of high rainfall (over 1500 mm yr^{-1}) areas where soil fertility has not been drastically reduced through intensive farming (Coombe and Hadfield, 1962; Hall and Okali, 1979). The type of vegetation which occurs after man has ceased to cultivate on land within the forest zone is actually very variable and often much less vigorous than in Swaine and Hall's example (Ross, 1954; Nye and Greenland, 1960). Determining factors include geology, soil type, topography and previous land-use (Hall and Okali, 1979). It may be seen under the section "The forest boundary" that large areas of savanna are believed to have been derived from forest.

Aweto (1981a–c) has studied the soil and vegetation of fallow within the forest zone of southwestern Nigeria. The approach involved the careful positioning of sample sites within fallow of known ages. Regrowth following the cessation of cultivation was found to be much less luxuriant than that seen at Swaine and Hall's site in Ghana, and *Musanga* was absent. Instead, the succession was characterized by a gradual change from forb-rich vegetation with much *Eupatorium odoratum* after 1 year to 6 m tall vegetation dominated by the small trees *Allophylus africanus*, *Harungana madagascariensis* and *Rauvolfia vomitoria* after 10 years. This type of succession is quite typical of fallow vegetation in many parts of tropical Africa, and its presence must surely often be due to soil degradation resulting from man's activities. Aweto found increase in the fertility of the topsoil during the fallow to be strongly correlated with tree size and the amount of vegetational cover. Low-growing fallow vegetation is very inefficient in restoring soil fertility. Aweto stresses the widespread problem of depletion of natural resources in tropical Africa,

involving an increasing population, a fallow vegetation which is declining in luxuriance and in
length of establishment before reclearing and a
progressive deterioration in the quality of the soil.

PHYTOSOCIOLOGY

There have been a number of publications
dealing with the description and classification of
forest vegetation according to the phytosociological tradition in the French-speaking parts of
Africa. Three examples of classificatory schemes
are shown in Tables 8.3 to 8.5: one for forests on
well-drained land in the Congo basin by Lebrun
and Gilbert (1954) [with some additions and
modifications after Devred (1958)], one by Mangenot (1955) for primary forest types in the Ivory
Coast, and one by Schmitz (1963) for swamp
forests in Katanga.

An attraction of phytosociology is that it rests
(or should rest) on a more or less standardized
method of vegetational description and classification, easing the problem of comparison between
different areas and potentially allowing the systematic build-up of knowledge. Phytosociology can
also serve as an excellent generator of hypotheses
about the relationships between vegetation and its
determining factors, whether physical, biotic or
historical. These hypotheses can later be tested
experimentally or studied in greater detail in the
field.

Criticisms of phytosociological work in African
forests stem both from general methodological
considerations and from the more particular
inadequacies of individual studies. In the former
category may be mentioned the problems of
working in species-rich, tall vegetation — this
might be regarded as more of a difficulty with
phytosociology than in a study based on a more
objective sampling strategy such as that used by
Hall and Swaine (1976), since the choice of a site
for a traditional phytosociological *relevé* depends
on initial recognition of pattern in the vegetation.
Another major point is that a hierarchical system
of classification such as that used in phytosociology can give a false impression of the complexity
and multi-dimensional variation of African forests
(Aubréville, 1950–51). In this context it may be
noted that phytosociology has probably met with

TABLE 8.3

Phytosociological classification of primary forests on well-
drained soils in Zaïre [after Lebrun and Gilbert (1954), with a
few additions and modifications after Devred (1958) noted]

1. Order: Gilbertiodendretalia dewevrei Lebrun and Gilbert
(1954). (Lowland evergreen forests.) This is divided into two
alliances by Devred, viz.:
    Alliance: Gilbertiodendron Devred (1958). (Forests in which
either *Gilbertiodendron dewevrei* or *Julbernardia seretii* is
abundant.)
    Alliance: Brachystegion laurentii Devred (1958). (Forests
with abundant *Brachystegia laurentii*. These are said to be
common on damp sandy soils.)

2. Order: Ficalhoeto–Podocarpetalia Lebrun and Gilbert
(1954). (Moist evergreen montane forests at 1600–2400 m
altitude.)
    Alliance: Galiniero–Parinarion holstii Devred (1958).

3. Order: Piptadenio–Celtidetalia Lebrun and Gilbert (1954).
(Semi-deciduous forests.) The alliances recognized in this order
differ somewhat between Lebrun and Gilbert, and Devred.
Devred gives the following:
    Alliance: Oxystigmo–Scorodophleion Lebrun and Gilbert
(1954). (Includes types with abundant *Cynometra alexandri*.)
    Alliance: Albizia–Chrysophyllion Devred (1958). (In some-
what wetter areas than above.)
    Alliance: Beilschmiedion Devred 1958. (Submontane semi-
deciduous forests at *c*. 1150–1800 m.)
    Alliance: Diospyro–Entandrophragmion delevoyi Devred
(1958). (Found in the driest places; now relictual, having been
largely destroyed by fire and the axe.)

4. Order: Olea–Jasminetalia Lebrun and Gilbert (1954). (Dry
montane forests.)
    Alliance: Grewio–Carission edulis Lebrun and Gilbert
(1954). (Densely bushy, liane-rich forests found on lava and in
other dry places.)
    Alliance: Oleo-Juniperion Devred (1954).
    Alliance: Agaurio–Myricion Lebrun and Gilbert (1954).
(Includes bamboo, *Hagenia*, Ericaceae and *Dendrosenecio*
associations.)

5. Order: Musangetalia Lebrun and Gilbert (1954). (Found in
gaps and clearings.)
    Alliance: Caloncobo–Tremion Lebrun and Gilbert (1954).
(Includes a type with much *Trema*.)
    Alliance: Musangion cecropioidis Lebrun and Gilbert (1954).
(With much *Musanga*.)

6. Order: Fagaro–Terminalietalia Lebrun and Gilbert (1954).
(Secondary forests.)
    Alliance: Pycnantho–Fagarion Lebrun and Gilbert (1954).
(Within the moist lowland evergreen area.)
    Alliance: Triplochito–Terminalion Lebrun and Gilbert
(1954). (Within the semi-deciduous area.)

7. Order: Polyscietalia fulvae Lebrun and Gilbert (1954).
(Secondary montane forest vegetation.)
    Alliance: Lobelion gibberoae Lebrun and Gilbert (1954). (An
early seral stage rich in giant herbs.)
    Alliance: Polyscion fulvae Lebrun and Gilbert (1954). (A
later stage, with more trees.)

TABLE 8.4

Phytosociological classification of primary forests in the Ivory Coast (after Mangenot, 1955)

A. Class Pycnanthetea Schnell (1950). (Forests on well-drained soils.)

1. Order: Uapacetalia Mangenot (1950). (In areas with over 1700 mm rainfall.)
    Association: *Diospyro–Mapanietum* Mangenot 1955. (On clay-rich soils.)
    Alliance: Conopharyngion Mangenot 1955. (On more sandy soils.)
    Association: *Turraeantho–Heisterietum* Mangenot (1955). (In more humid areas.)
    Association: *Eremospatho–Mabetum* Mangenot (1955). (In less humid areas.)

2. Order: Celtidetalia Mangenot (1955). (In areas with 1100/1300–1700 mm rainfall.)
    (This contains three divisions related to climate.)

B. Class: Mitragyno–Raphietea Schnell (1952). (Swamp forests.)
    Association: *Mitragyno-Symphonietum* Mangenot (1955). (Primary swamp forests.)

TABLE 8.5

Phytosociological classification of swamp forests in Katanga (after Schmitz, 1963)

Class: Mitragynetea Schmitz (1962). (This includes all edaphically wet forest types in central Africa except mangrove forests. There is much variability within this class, but common and widely distributed species include *Ficus mucuso*, *Phoenix reclinata*, *Syzygium guineense* and *Xylopia rubescens*.)

1. Order: Alchorneetalia cordiofolia Lebrun (1947). (Riparian colonizing forests in central Africa. Three alliances are described.)

2. Order: Pterygotetalia Lebrun and Gilbert (1954). (On drier alluvial soils. Contains a single alliance only.)

3. Order: Mitragyno–Raphietalia (Schnell, 1952) Lebrun and Gilbert (1954). (Periodically inundated swamp forests.) Contains two alliances, as follows:
    Alliance: Mitragyno–Symphonion Devred (1958). (This contains a number of different types associated mainly with substrate variation.)
    Alliance: Raphion Devred (1958). (A palm-rich type, playing a pioneer role to the former.)

its greatest successes in African forests when it has been applied to specialized and impoverished types such as swamp forest and early secondary forest. Finally, and this is a very general criticism of phytosociology, the use of statistics to define vegetational types by character species is problematical given the highly subjective sampling procedure.

The particular problems of individual studies should not be overstressed given the general difficulties mentioned above and the early date of some of the work. In several investigations there has been a tendency to identify and name forest categories after prominent taxa in the canopy stratum — a practice reminiscent of the naming of vegetational types by "dominant" species in the Tansleyian tradition of vegetation classification; it is certainly not correct phytosociological procedure. Aubréville (1950–51) has criticized Mangenot's (1955) study in the Ivory Coast on a number of grounds, such as his use of a plot size $(10 \times 10$ m$)$ too small to give a good picture of the vegetation from a phytosociological viewpoint (less than the minimal area) and also for naming the class used for primary forest vegetation after a genus (*Pycnanthus*) which is actually characteristic of secondary rather than primary forest. According to White and Werger (1978) the classification of Zaïre forests by Lebrun and Gilbert (1954) was not based on detailed *relevé* data.

ACKNOWLEDGEMENTS

I am very grateful to Professor R. Schnell and Dr. M. Swaine for help in the preparation of this chapter. My work has been supported financially by the Natural Environment Research Council (U.K.), the Royal Society and the University of Ulster.

REFERENCES

AETFAT (L'Association pour l'Étude Taxonomique de la Flore d'Afrique Tropicale) 1959. *Vegetation Map of Africa South of the Tropic of Cancer (1:10 000 000) with Explanatory Notes by R.W.J. Keay*. Oxford Univ. Press, London, 24 pp.

Aubréville, A., 1947. Les brousses secondaires en Afrique équatoriale. *Bois Forêts Trop.*, 2: 24–49.

Aubréville, A., 1949. *Climats, Forêts et Désertification de l'Afrique Tropicale*. Larose, Paris, 351 pp.

Aubréville, A., 1950–51. Le concept d'association dans la forêt dense équatoriale de basse Côte d'Ivoire. *Mém. Soc. Bot. Fr.*, pp. 145–158.

Aubréville, A., 1968. Les Césalpinioidées de la flore camerouno-congolaise. Considérations taxonomiques, chorologiques, écologiques, historiques et évolutives. *Adansonia*, 8: 147–175.

Aweto, A.O., 1981a. Secondary succession and soil fertility restoration in south-western Nigeria, I. Succession. *J. Ecol.*, 69: 601–607.

Aweto, A.O., 1981b. Secondary succession and soil fertility restoration in south-western Nigeria, II. Soil fertility restoration. *J. Ecol.*, 69: 609–614.

Aweto, A.O., 1981c. Secondary succession and soil fertility restoration in south-western Nigeria, III. Soil and vegetation interrelationships. *J. Ecol.*, 69: 957–963.

Axelrod, D.I. and Raven, P.H., 1978. Late Cretaceous and Tertiary vegetation history of Africa. In: M.J.A. Werger (Editor), *Biogeography and Ecology of Southern Africa*. Junk, The Hague, pp. 77–130.

Bouxin, G., 1976. Ordination and classification in the upland Rugege Forest (Rwanda, Central Africa). *Vegetatio*, 32: 97–115.

Burtt Davy, J., 1938. *The Classification of Tropical Woody Vegetation Types*. Imperial Forestry Institute, Oxford, Pap. 13, 85 pp.

Chapman, J.D. and White, F., 1970. *The Evergreen Forests of Malawi*. Commonwealth Forestry Institute, Univ. of Oxford, Oxford, 190 pp.

Chevalier, A., 1948. Biogéographie et écologie de la forêt dense ombrophile de la Côte d'Ivoire. *Rev. Bot. Appl.*, 28: 101–115.

Coetzee, J.A., 1967. Pollen analytical studies in East and Southern Africa. *Palaeoecol. Afr.*, 3: 1–146.

Coombe, D.E. and Hadfield, W., 1962. An analysis of the growth of *Musanga cecropioides. J. Ecol.*, 50: 221–234.

Devineau, J.-L., 1976a. Principales caractéristiques, physionomiques et floristiques des formations forestières de Lamto (Moyenne Côte d'Ivoire). *Ann. Univ. Abidjan, Sér. E*, 9.

Devineau, J.-L., 1976b. Données préliminaires sur la litière et la chute des feuilles dans quelques formations forestières semi-décidues de moyenne Côte d'Ivoire. *Oecol. Plant.*, 11: 375–395.

Devred, R., 1958. La végétation forestière du Congo belge et du Ruanda-Urundi. *Bull. Soc. R. For. Belg.*, 65: 409–468.

Diamond, A.W. and Hamilton, A.C., 1980. The distribution of forest passerine birds and Quaternary climatic change in tropical Africa. *J. Zool. London*, 191: 379–402.

Eggeling, W.J., 1947. Observations on the ecology of Budongo rain forest, Uganda. *J. Ecol.*, 34: 20–87.

Flora of Tropical East Africa, 1952 et seq. Crown Agents, London; later Balkema, Rotterdam.

Friis, I., Rasmussen, F.N. and Vollesen, K., 1982. Studies in the flora and vegetation of southwest Ethiopia. *Opera Bot.*, 63: 1–70.

Germain, R. and Evrard, C., 1956. Étude écologique et phytosociologique de la forêt à *Brachystegia laurentii*. *Publ. Inst. Natl. Etude Agron. Congo Belge, Sér. Sci.*, 67: 105 pp.

Grubb, P.J., 1977. The maintenance of species-richness in plant communities: the importance of the regeneration niche. *Biol. Rev.*, 52: 107–145.

Hall, J.B., 1973. Vegetational zones on the southern slopes of Mount Cameroon. *Vegetatio*, 27: 49–69.

Hall, J.B., 1977. Forest-types in Nigeria: an analysis of pre-exploitation forest enumeration data. *J. Ecol.*, 65: 187–199.

Hall, J.B. and Bada, S.O., 1979. The distribution and ecology of obeche (*Triplochiton scleroxylon*). *J. Ecol.*, 69: 543–564.

Hall, J.B. and Okali, D.U.U., 1979. A structural and floristic analysis of woody fallow vegetation near Ibadan, Nigeria. *J. Ecol.*, 67: 321–346.

Hall, J.B. and Swaine, M.D., 1976. Classification and ecology of closed-canopy forest in Ghana. *J. Ecol.*, 64: 913–951.

Hall, J.B. and Swaine, M.D., 1980. Seed stocks in Ghanaian forest soils. *Biotropica*, 12: 256–263.

Hall, J.B. and Swaine, M.D., 1981. *Distribution and Ecology of Vascular Plants in a Tropical Rain Forest: Forest Vegetation in Ghana*. (Geobotany 1) Junk, The Hague, 383 pp.

Hamilton, A.C., 1969. The vegetation of southwest Kigezi. *Uganda J.*, 33: 175–199.

Hamilton, A.C., 1972. The interpretation of pollen diagrams from highland Uganda. *Palaeoecol. Afr.*, 7: 45–149.

Hamilton, A.C., 1974. Distribution patterns of forest trees in Uganda and their historical significance. *Vegetatio*, 29: 21–35.

Hamilton, A.C., 1975a. A quantitative analysis of altitudinal zonation in Uganda forests. *Vegetatio*, 30: 99–106.

Hamilton, A.C., 1975b. The dispersal of forest tree species in Uganda during the Upper Pleistocene. *Boissiera*, 24: 29–32.

Hamilton, A.C., 1976. The significance of patterns of distribution shown by forest plants and animals in tropical Africa for the reconstruction of Upper Pleistocene palaeoenvironments: a review. *Palaeoecol. Afr.*, 9: 63–97.

Hamilton, A.C., 1981. A field guide to Uganda forest trees. Privately published.

Hamilton, A.C., 1982. *Environmental History of East Africa*. Academic Press, New York, N.Y., 328 pp.

Hamilton, A.C. and Perrott, R.A., 1981. A study of altitudinal zonation in the montane forest belt of Mt. Elgon, Kenya/Uganda. *Vegetatio*, 45: 107–125.

Hartshorn, G.S., 1978. Tree falls and tropical forest dynamics. In: P.B. Tomlinson and M.H. Zimmermann (Editors), *Tropical Trees as Living Systems*. Cambridge Univ. Press, Cambridge, pp. 617–638.

Hedberg, O., 1951. Vegetation belts of the East African mountains. *Sven. Bot. Tidskr.*, 45: 140–202.

Hopkins, B., 1962. Vegetation of the Olokemeji Forest Reserve, Nigeria, I. General features of the reserve and the research sites. *J. Ecol.*, 50: 559–598.

Hopkins, B., 1970. Vegetation of the Olokemeji Forest Reserve, Nigeria, VI. The plants of the forest site with special reference to their seasonal growth. *J. Ecol.*, 58: 765–793.

Huttel, C., 1975. Recherches sur l'ecosystème de la forêt subéquatoriale de basse Côte d'Ivoire, III. Inventaire et structure de la végétation ligneuse. Programme ORSTOM–Forêt dense (P.B.I.). *Terre Vie, Rev. Ecol. Appl.*, 29: 178–191.

Jones, E.W., 1955–56. Ecological studies on the rain forest of Southern Nigeria, IV. The plateau forest of the Okomu Forest Reserve. Parts 1 and 2. *J. Ecol.*, 43: 564–594 and 44: 83–117.

Jordan, C.F. and Herrara, R., 1981. Tropical rain forests: are nutrients really critical? *Am. Nat.*, 117: 167–180.

Juo, A.S.R. and Lal, R., 1977. The effect of fallow and continuous cultivation on the chemical and physical properties of an Alfisol in Western Nigeria. *Plant Soil*, 47: 567–584.

Keay, R.W.J., 1957. Wind-dispersed species in a Nigerian forest. *J. Ecol.*, 45: 471–478.

Keay, R.W.J., 1960. Derived savanna — derived from what? *Bull. Inst. Fr. Afr. Noire*, 21: 427–438.

Kendall, R.L., 1969. An ecological history of the Lake Victoria basin. *Ecol. Monogr.*, 39: 121–176.

Knapp, R., 1973. *Die Vegetation von Afrika.* Fischer, Stuttgart, 626 pp.

Langdale-Brown, I., Osmaston, H.A. and Wilson, J.G., 1964. *The Vegetation of Uganda.* Govt. Printer, Uganda, 159 pp.

Lawson, G.W., Armstrong-Mensah, K.O. and Hall, J.B., 1970. A catena in tropical moist semi-deciduous forest near Kade, Ghana. *J. Ecol.*, 58: 371–398.

Lebrun, J., 1935. Les essences forestières du Congo belge, II. Les essences forestières des régions montagneuses du Congo oriental. *Publ. INEAC, Sér. Sci.*, 1: 264 pp.

Lebrun, J., 1942. La végétation du Nyiragongo. *Inst. Parcs Nationaux Congo Belge, Aspects Végét., Sér. 1*, 3–5: 121 pp.

Lebrun, J., 1960. Sur une methode de delimitation des horizons et étages de végétation des montagnes du Congo oriental. *Bull. Jard. Bot. Etat. Brux.*, 30: 75–94.

Lebrun, J. and Gilbert, G., 1954. Une classification écologique des forêts du Congo. *Publ. Inst. Natl. Étude Agron. Congo Belge, Sér. Sci.*, 63: 89 pp.

Lemée, G., 1975a. Recherches sur l'écosystème de la forêt subéquatoriale de basse Côte d'Ivoire, 1. Introduction. Programme ORSTOM–Forêt Dense (P.B.I.). *Terre Vie, Rev. Écol. Appl.*, 29: 169–170.

Lemée, G., 1975b. Recherches sur l'écosystème de la forêt subéquatoriale de basse Côte d'Ivoire, VII. Conclusions générales. Programme ORSTOM–Forêt Dense (P.B.I.). *Terre Vie, Rev. Écol. Appl.*, 29· 255–264.

Léonard, J., 1955. Les divers types de forêts du Congo belge. *Lejeunia*, 16: 81–93.

Léonard, J., 1965. Contribution à la subdivision phytogéographique de la région guineo-congolaise après la répartition géographique d'Euphorbiacées d'Afrique tropicale. *Webbia*, 19: 627–649.

Léonard, J., 1975. Statistiques des progrès accomplis en 21 ans dans la connaissance de la flore phanérogamique africaine et malgache (1953–1973). *Boissiera*, 24: 15–19.

Letouzey, R., 1968. *Étude Phytogéographique du Cameroun.* (Encyclopédie Biologique, 69) Lechevalier, Paris, 511 pp.

Lewalle, J., 1972. Les étages de végétation du Burundi occidental. *Bull. Jard. Bot. Natl. Belg.*, 42: 1–247.

Lind, E.M. and Morrison, M.E.S.M., 1974. *East African Vegetation.* Longman, London, 257 pp.

Livingstone, D.A., 1967. Postglacial vegetation of the Ruwenzori Mountains in Equatorial Africa. *Ecol. Monogr.*, 37: 25–52.

Logan, W.E.M., 1946. *An Introduction to the Forest of Central and Southern Ethiopia.* Imperial Forestry Inst., Univ. of Oxford, Pap. 24.

Mangenot, G., 1955. Étude sur les forêts des plaines et plateau de la Côte d'Ivoire. *Étud. Éburn*, 4: 5–61.

Markham, R.H. and Babbedge, A.J., 1979. Soil and vegetation catenas on the forest-savanna boundary in Ghana. *Biotropica*, 11: 224–234.

Moll, E.J. and White, F., 1978. The Indian Ocean coastal belt. In: M.J.A. Werger (Editor), *Biogeography and Ecology of Southern Africa.* Junk, The Hague, pp. 561–598.

Monod, T., 1957. Les grandes divisions chorologiques de l'Afrique. *Cons. Sci. Afr. Sud Sahara*, 24: 146 pp.

Moreau, M.E.S., 1966. *The Bird Faunas of Africa and its Islands.* Academic Press, New York, N.Y., 424 pp.

Morrison, M.E.S., 1968. Vegetation and climate in the uplands of south-western Uganda during the Later Pleistocene Period, I. Muchoya Swamp, Kigezi District. *J. Ecol.*, 56: 363–384.

Morrison, M.E.S. and Hamilton, A.C., 1974. Vegetation and climate in the uplands of south-western Uganda during the Later Pleistocene Period, II. Forest clearance and other vegetational changes in the Rukiga Highlands during the past 8000 years. *J. Ecol.*, 62: 1–31.

Ng, F.S.P., 1978. Strategies of establishment in Malayan forest trees. In: P.B. Tomlinson and Zimmermann (Editors), *Tropical Trees as Living Systems.* Cambridge Univ. Press, Cambridge, pp. 129–162.

Nkoju, E., 1963. Seasonal periodicity in the growth and development of some forest trees in Nigeria, I. Observations on mature trees. *J. Ecol.*, 51: 617–624.

Nye, P.H. and Greenland, D.J., 1960. *The Soil under Shifting Cultivation.* Techn. Comm. 51, Commonwealth Bureau of Soils, Harpenden, 156 pp.

Oldeman, R.A.A., 1978. Architecture and energy exchange of dicotyledonous trees in the forest. In: P.B. Tomlinson and M.H. Zimmermann (Editors), *Tropical Trees as Living Systems.* Cambridge Univ. Press, Cambridge, pp. 535–560.

Pierlot, R., 1966. Structure et composition des forêts denses d'Afrique Centrale, spécialement celles du Kivu. *Acad. R. Sci. Outre-Mer, Classe Sci. Nat. Médic., n.s.*, 16: 367 pp.

Richards, P.W., 1939. Ecological studies on the rain forest of Southern Nigeria, I. The structure and floristic composition of the primary forest. *J. Ecol.*, 27: 1–61.

Richards, P.W., 1963a. Ecological notes on West African vegetation, II. Lowland forest of the Southern Bakundu Forest Reserve. *J. Ecol.*, 51: 123–149.

Richards, P.W., 1963b. Ecological notes on West African vegetation, III. The upland forests of Cameroons Mountains. *J. Ecol.*, 51: 529–554.

Richards, P.W., 1979. *The Tropical Rain Forest.* Cambridge Univ. Press, Cambridge, 450 pp.

Robyns, W., 1947–55. *Flore des Spermatophytes du Parc National Albert. Vols. I–III.* Inst. Parcs Natl. Congo Belge, 745, 626 and 571 pp.

Rodgers, W.A., Owen, C.F. and Homewood, K.M., 1982. Biogeography of East African forest mammals. *J. Biogeogr.*, 9: 41–54.

Ross, R., 1954. Ecological studies on the rain forest of southern Nigeria, III. Secondary succession in the Shasha Forest Reserve. *J. Ecol.*, 42: 259–282.

Sarukhan, J., 1978. Studies on the demography of tropical trees.

In: P.B. Tomlinson and M.H. Zimmermann (Editors), *Tropical Trees as Living Systems.* Cambridge Univ. Press, Cambridge, pp. 163–184.

Schmitz, A., 1963. Aperçu sur les groupements végétaux du Katanga. *Bull. Soc. R. Bot. Belg.*, 96: 233–447.

Schnell, R., 1967. Problèmes biogéographiques comparés de l'hylaea amazonienne et de la forêt dense tropicale d'afrique. *Atas Simp. Sôbre a Biota Amazôn.*, 4: 229–239.

Schnell, R., 1976–77. *La Flore et la Végétation de l'Afrique Tropicale. Vols. 3 and 4.* Gauthier-Villars, Paris, 459 and 378 pp.

Swaine, M.D. and Hall, J.B., 1974. Ecology and conservation of upland forests in Ghana. In: *Proc. Ghana Scope's Conf. on Environment and Development in West Africa.* GAAS, UNESCO, EPC., Accra, pp. 151–157.

Swaine, M.D. and Hall, J.B., 1983. Early succession on cleared forest land in Ghana. *J. Ecol.*, 71: 601–627.

Swaine, M.D., Hall, J.B. and Lock, J.M., 1976. The forest–savanna boundary in west-central Ghana. *Ghana J. Sci.*, 16: 35–52.

Werger, M.J.A. and Coetzee, B.J., 1978. The Sudano-Zambezian Region. In: M.J.A. Werger (Editor), *Biogeography and Ecology of Southern Africa.* Junk, The Hague, pp. 301–422.

White, F., 1962. Geographic variation and speciation in Africa with particular reference to *Diospyros.* In: *Taxonomy and Geography.* Syst. Assoc. Publ., 4: 71–103.

White, F., 1978a. The taxonomy, ecology and chorology of African Ebenaceae, I. The guineo-Congolian species. *Bull. Jard. Bot. Natl. Belg.*, 48: 245–358.

White, F., 1978b. The Afromontane Region. In: M.J.A. Werger (Editor), *Biogeography and Ecology of Southern Africa.* Junk, The Hague, pp. 463–513.

White, F., 1979. The Guineo-Congolian Region and its relationships to other phytochoria. *Bull. Jard. Bot. Natl. Belg.*, 49: 11–55.

White, F., 1983. *The Vegetation Map of Africa.* UNESCO, Paris, 356 pp.

White, F. and Werger, M.J.A., 1978. The Guineo-Congolian transition to southern Africa. In: M.J.A. Werger (Editor), *Biogeography and Ecology of Southern Africa.* Junk, The Hague, pp. 599–620.

Whitmore, T.C., 1978. Gaps in the forest canopy. In: P.B. Tomlinson and M.H. Zimmermann (Editors), *Tropical Trees as Living Systems.* Cambridge Univ. Press, Cambridge, pp. 639–655.

Chapter 9

VASCULAR EPIPHYTISM IN AFRICA

DICK R. JOHANSSON

HOW COMMON ARE VASCULAR EPIPHYTES IN AFRICA?

The whole palaeotropical region exhibits a paucity of epiphytes[1] when compared to the Neotropics. This is particularly evident for mainland Africa, where the epiphytic flora consists almost solely of pteridophytes and orchids.

The reason for an impoverished epiphytic flora in Africa where, for instance, only 243 species of angraecoid orchids occur on the whole continent (Stewart, 1976), has been related to bouts of aridity and the lack of refugia during the late Pleistocene.

In Zaïre there are 414 species of orchids (Nihoul et al., 1969), compared with an estimated 3000 species in Colombia and an estimated 5000 in Malaysia (Van Steenis, 1938; Stewart, 1970).

The American and Indo-Malayan rain-forest formations are thus generally much richer in orchids, especially epiphytic ones; but in addition they have floristic elements which are almost absent in Africa. For instance, species of Bromeliaceae, Cactaceae and Gesneriaceae form an important part of the epiphytic flora in the Neotropics, while Africa lacks epiphytic bromeliads and has only one, pan-tropical, species of epiphytic cactus. The Indo-Malayan rain forest is much richer in epiphytic species in, for instance, the Asclepiadaceae, Ericaceae and Rubiaceae.

The richness of epiphytes in a particular region can be expressed in several ways: (1) the total number of epiphytic species in the region, as documented from floras or extensive collections; (2) the percentage of trees of a certain minimum

height that carry epiphytes; or (3) the number of epiphytes on one tree.

Total number of epiphytic species in a region

In the Budongo rain forest in Uganda, Eggeling (1947) recorded nearly one hundred species of epiphytes, while Johansson (1974) reported 153 species (101 orchids, 39 pteridophytes and 13 others) from the Nimba region in Liberia.

The African epiphytic orchids are generally better known than the rest of the epiphytes (Sanford, 1969, 1974; Johansson, 1977). West Tropical Africa has 232 species of epiphytic orchids (Hepper, 1968) and Kenya 113 (Stewart, 1973). Morris (1970) mentioned 70 species of epiphytic orchids in Malawi and Harrison (1972) listed 41 species for South Africa, while Van Ede (1976) reported 30 species in twelve genera for the Transvaal.

Percentage of trees carrying epiphytes

Available data of this kind refer to investigations made on felled trees. The minimum height of the trees included in the count is of great importance, since the smaller the trees included the lower will be the percentage of trees with epiphytes.

Results are available from several places in Africa and other tropical regions. Comparison is difficult, however, since the minimum height of trees included often varies considerably. For instance, in a Nigerian lowland rain forest, Richards (1939) found that 15 to 24% of the trees 5 m or higher carried epiphytes, while in a Liberian rain forest, at 500 m altitude, on the border with the Ivory Coast and Guinea, 40 to 62% of the trees

---

[1]When nothing else is stated the term epiphyte refers to vascular epiphytes.

10 m or higher were reported to carry epiphytes (Johansson, 1974).

The successional stage of the forest is also important. In a young secondary forest in Uganda, approximately 12% of the trees bore epiphytes, while in an older forest the number of trees with epiphytes had increased to 16%, compared to 23% in a climax forest (Eggeling, 1947).

Number of epiphytes on one tree

Tall trees in the Nimba region in Liberia seldom carry more than 20 species of epiphytes but occasionally there may be up to 30. Somewhat surprisingly, this is approximately 20% of the total epiphytic flora of the region. The maximum number of epiphyte species on tall trees in sample plots in the Budongo rain forest in Uganda is reported to be 26, and on especially suitable host trees (phorophytes) elsewhere, 40 to 45 species have been counted (Eggeling, 1947).

Records of this nature are of limited use in assessing the epiphytic flora in various regions. Comparisons should be made on host trees of the same species and size, due to the strong correlation of these factors with the abundance of epiphytes. Certain species of trees may harbour very high numbers of epiphytes; for instance, in the Nimba region a total of 1857 individuals, representing 23 different species, were counted on a rather small Whismore tree (*Heritiera utilis*).

Distribution of epiphytes on the host tree

The exact habitat conditions of epiphytes on a tree are poorly known both in Africa and elsewhere in the tropics. This often is due to the inaccessible sites where the epiphytes grow. Under ordinary circumstances in a tropical rain forest it is difficult to get even a limited view of the crowns of the highest trees from ground level. This means that most studies have to be performed on felled or fallen trees.

The results from the use of three different methods, presented below, give a general view of the distribution pattern of some African epiphytes.

Zonal distribution

In order to map the zonal distribution there is a need for some kind of subdivision of the host tree.

Richards (1939) used the height above the ground as a way to describe the distribution of epiphytes, and an arbitrary division of the host tree into 5-m zones from the ground and upwards was employed by Grubb et al. (1963). It is, however, more common to subdivide the trees into broad ecological units. Van Oye (1924), recognized five zones on the trunks of oilpalms. Hosokawa (1954), Tixier (1966) and Johansson (1974) used varying numbers of zones in their division of the trees. A general tendency to divide the basal parts of the host tree into a large number of zones is evident. The crowns of the trees have often been regarded as one unit or rarely two, although the crown as a rule displays a far wider variety of habitats for the epiphytes than does the trunk (Fig. 9.1).

A study of the zonal distribution pattern of epiphytes on 463 individual trees divided into five zones (Fig. 9.2) is available from Liberia (Johans-

Fig. 9.1. Epiphytic growth on *Parinari excelsa*, a tree exceptionally attractive to epiphytes.

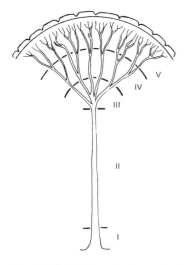

Fig. 9.2. Subdivision of a large rain-forest tree. *I*: the basal parts of the trunk (0–3 m); *II*: the trunk from 3 m to the first major ramification; *III–V*: each section is 1/3 of the total length of the major branches.

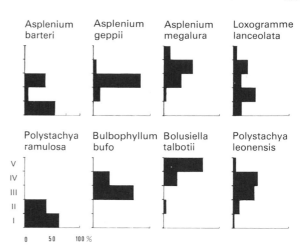

Fig. 9.3. Distribution of some epiphytes over the five sections recognized (Fig. 2), expressed as a percentage of the total number of records for each species.

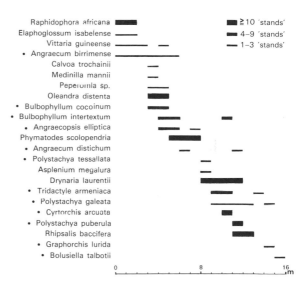

Fig. 9.4. Distribution of epiphytes along a large branch of a rain-forest tree (*Parinari excelsa*). The stretch examined starts at the main ramification of the trunk, 18 m above the ground. The abundance of the different species, of which the orchids are marked by a dot, is given by "stands" since the actual numbers of individuals are difficult to determine due to long rhizomes and intermingled growth habits (see Sanford, 1968).

son, 1974). It showed that most species of epiphytes are more or less restricted to one, or two, particular section(s), of the host tree, while a few occur more evenly in more sections (Fig. 9.3).

Distribution along a large branch

The occurrence of epiphytes on the large branches of the crowns may be mapped by the use of a "transect". Since neither the trunks nor the branches represent straight lines, one may simply follow the twistings and bends of the stretch to be examined and present this as if it were a straight line. From the point of ramification onwards, the transect covers an ever smaller area as the branches get thinner. This should be considered when interpreting the results (Fig. 9.4). The transect method is useful to show the sequential distribution pattern for the various species.

Distribution in relation to the circumference of the trunk or branch

Many epiphytes seem to have a distribution related to the age of the substrate to which they attach. In a study of the epiphytic orchids of East Africa, Moreau and Moreau (1943) stated: "A few small pieces e.g. *Angraecum viride* are found always on twigs rather than branches".

By measuring the circumference of the trunk, branch or twig at the point of attachment of each epiphyte it is possible to obtain information on this variable (Johansson, 1978). Results from the examination of a large rain-forest tree by this method appear in Fig. 9.5. It can be seen that the statement given above concerning *Angraecum*

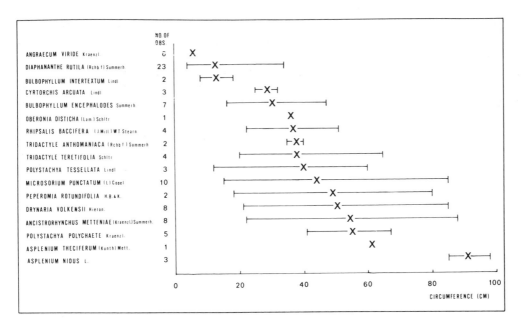

Fig. 9.5. Distribution of epiphytes on a major branch of a rain-forest tree (*Chlorophora excelsa*), Usambara Mts., Tanzania. The mean branch circumference for each species is marked by a cross and the range of occurrence by a thin line.

viride is supported by these measurements. The mean circumference of the twigs carrying the six specimens was 5.7 cm, corresponding to a diameter of only 1.8 cm.

Another epiphytic orchid, *Microcoelia exilis*, also is conspicuously often confined to small twigs. The use of the "circumference method" in the analyses of a small tree confirmed the very narrow range of distribution for this species (Fig. 9.6).

SPECIES, COMMUNITIES AND SUCCESSIONS

Species in virgin forest

The humid environment of the rain forest favours the epiphytic way of life. It is particularly evident with respect to the pteridophytes, which here reach their greatest diversity. Light often is a limiting factor, and epiphytes are thus rather scarce in the lower strata of the forest. On trunks near the ground one very seldom finds epiphytic orchids, and even pteridophytes are rare. However, where the direct light penetrates the canopy — for instance, through a gap — one may find a luxuriant epiphytic flora near the ground.

The epiphytic species occurring on a large rain-forest tree in the Usambara Mountains in Tanza-

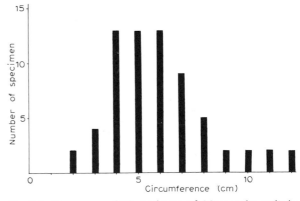

Fig. 9.6. Occurrence of 69 specimens of *Microcoelia exilis* in relation to the circumference of the branch at their attachment.

nia are listed in Table 9.1, while some details on West African epiphytes follow below.

Asplenium barteri and *Tectaria angelicifolia* may exemplify pteridophytes which occur on the lowest parts of the trunks in heavy shade. Higher up the trunks of the large trees one finds *Asplenium africanum* in West Africa, and *Asplenium nidus* in East Africa, on sites where few other epiphytes thrive.

A suitable habitat for many epiphytes is found at the ramification of the main trunk. Here the light intensity may be described as open shade, and a

TABLE 9.1

Epiphytes in different sections of a 32 m tall *Parinari excelsa*, Amani 950 m, Usambara Mountains, Tanzania (Johansson, 1974)

Section	Species of epiphyte
I	No epiphytes present
II	*Asplenium nidus*
III	**Pteridophytes**
	Asplenium pellucidum
	Asplenium megalura
	Drynaria volkensii
	Elaphoglossum acrostichoides
	Elaphoglossum lastii
	Lycopodium warneckei
	Microgramma owariensis
	Oleandra distenta
	Vittaria ensiformis
	Orchids
	Ancistrorhynchus refractus
	Bulbophyllum plathyrachis
	Cirrhopetalum umbellatum
	Oberonia disticha
	Polystachya adansoniae
	Rangaëris muscicola
	Tridactyle anthomaniaca
	Tridactyle bicaudata
IV	**Pteridophytes**
	Drynaria volkensii
	Microgramma owariensis
	Orchids
	Ancistrorhynchus refractus
	Bulbophyllum bequaertii
	Bulbophyllum encephalodes
	Bulbophyllum plathyrachis
	Diaphananthe subsimplex
	Polystachya adansoniae
	Tridactyle teretifolia
	Other vascular epiphytes
	Rhipsalis baccifera
V	**Orchids**
	Bolusiella iridifolia
	Tridactyle anthomaniaca

substantial amount of humus with good water-holding capacity and sufficient nutrients accumulates, which can support epiphytes sensitive to drought. Many species of pteridophytes thus have their main distribution here — for instance, *Nephrolepis biserrata* and *Oleandra distenta*. Among the orchids *Diaphananthe pellucida* and *Polystachya polychaete* are typical of this site.

Epiphytic begonias and various species of the genera *Calvoa*, *Medinilla* and *Preussiella* of the Melastomataceae are also common here. Facultative epiphytes and climbers are also richly represented in these humus accumulations, such as species in the araceous genera *Culcasia*, *Raphidophora* and *Remusatia*.

The middle section of the large branches is, generally speaking, less rich in humus deposits and more exposed to direct sun. Correspondingly, the epiphytes of this section are better adapted to desiccation. Among the pteridophytes *Drynaria* and *Platycerium* spp. are often very prominent, but as a whole rather few pteridophytes can withstand the climatic conditions in this section. Orchids are however most abundant here, such as many species of the genera *Bulbophyllum*, *Chamaeangis*, *Cyrtorchis*, *Diaphananthe*, *Polystachya*, *Rangaëris* and *Tridactyle*. The epiphytic cactus *Rhipsalis baccifera* (Fig. 9.7), which is widespread in Africa, also is typical of this section.

Fig. 9.7. *Drynaria volkensii* and *Rhipsalis baccifera*.

Fig. 9.8. Xeromorphic epiphytes on the outer part of a branch of a rain-forest tree (*Lophira alata*). **A**: *Bulbophyllum schimperanum;* **B**: *Nephrangis filiformis*; **C**: *Chamaeangis vesicata*; **D**: *Tridactyle anthomaniaca*; **E**: *Bulbophyllum linderi.*

The outermost parts of the branches usually carry a sparse epiphytic flora. When vascular epiphytes occur in this section their sizes are much smaller than further down the branches, indicating the more severe living conditions (Fig. 9.8). However, non-vascular epiphytes, such as sun-demanding lichens, are abundant.

Species in degraded forest

Through interference by man the dense rain forest has been replaced over vast areas by farmlands or tree plantations. Reminders of the virgin forest appear as patches of regenerating forest and small relicts of mature trees. This rather open environment differs very much from that of the rain forest proper. Sun-demanding and drought-resistant orchids here form a very promi-

nent part of the epiphytic flora, while pteridophytes are proportionally less common than in the dense forest. In forest clearings there often are a number of dead or dying trees. During the dying process, many epiphytes take advantage of the increased light intensities caused by the fall of leaves, and also of the incipient decomposition of the bark (Went, 1940). Such exposure of the habitat will soon exert a strong influence on the composition of the epiphytic flora, favouring the drought-resistant species. Within a few years, the altered environmental conditions, combined with exhaustion of the substrate, will result in an impoverished epiphytic flora, even though certain species will occur in large numbers.

Under high light intensities in open habitats, epiphytes occur on branches and trunks near the ground, and often in a haphazard way, which creates an impression of randomness. Old but rather small trees in rubber and cacao plantations may harbour a rich epiphytic flora, sometimes easily reached by hand.

Community building

Epiphytes often are aggregated in limited areas on the host tree in what can be called epiphyte communities (Fig. 9.9). The terminology used in the classification of epiphyte aggregations is confusing (Johansson, 1974). Like epiphytes in general, epiphyte communities are most abundant on older trees. The communities provide information on the common environmental requirements for various species, and can be used to analyse the gradual development of the epiphytic flora on a host tree.

The substrate-building capacity of certain pteridophytes seems to form the basis for many epiphyte communities. Several ferns are pioneers on smooth surfaces — for instance *Drynaria* and *Platycerium* spp. *Drynaria* spp. have two kinds of fronds. The fertile fronds are long with pinnately arranged lobes, while the sterile fronds are papery and held in an upright position. Between the sterile fronds and the substratum a space is formed, in which materials of various kinds are collected. The sterile leaves remain in function as "humus collectors" even after they have died, since their veins persist forming a delicate net. *Platycerium* spp. also have leaves of different shape and

Fig. 9.9. An epiphytic community on *Parinari excelsa* dominated by the fern *Oleandra distenta* and the orchid *Tridactyle armeniaca*. Orchids are rather common in the early development of this community but as more and more debris is accumulated they decline.

functions. The fertile leaves are long and pendulous, while the sterile leaves are shorter and upright. They collect the falling debris which slowly builds up to a considerable mass of humus. In or near the substrate gathered by the pteridophytes other epiphytes establish themselves.

Succession

As the host tree grows it will pass through several "environmental stages" — for instance, its position in the forest canopy shifts, the size and shape of the crown and the morphology of the bark alter. These are primary changes which will affect the epiphytes. Secondary changes, such as the establishment of new species of epiphytes, may lead to competition between the epiphytes or to successional processes through active or passive contributions to the formation of humus.

Analyses of humus deposits may reveal traces of an earlier flora — for instance, rhizomes or pseudobulbs from ferns and orchids. Sometimes the remains of dead plants are so abundant that it is possible to follow the successional phases. In the bottom layer one finds species which are able to colonize clean bark surfaces, pioneer epiphytes like *Drynaria* and *Bulbophyllum*. Above the bottom layer humus-demanding species are commonly encountered, while the surface layer often consists entirely of ferns or non-orchid epiphytes.

The changes during a period of two years in the epiphytic flora on a branch fallen down from a large tree may serve as an example of developments which may occur when the environment becomes darker and more humid. The branch was lying about 2 m above the ground, across a small stream. A length of 6 m was examined after one and two years.

Initially it carried 13 species of sun-demanding epiphytes. After some months only, the leaves of the orchids turned yellow and after one year only three species out of the seven original ones were still alive, all in rather poor condition. Two species out of six pteridophytes were still alive, and two new species had appeared.

After two years the branch was completely overgrown by epiphytes. *Nephrolepis undulata* and *Raphidophora africana* were in total dominance. Only one species of the original group of orchids and two of the pteridophytes were still alive. However, the total number of epiphytic species had grown to 14.

ENVIRONMENTAL INFLUENCE

Light

Light is probably the most difficult factor to record, or assess, among all environmental influences on the epiphytes. Existing knowledge of light conditions in the crowns of trees in the tropics is very scanty (see Ch.3). The need for the erection of large structures to reach the upper parts or above the canopy has been difficult to overcome and investigations of this nature are rare in Africa.

The decrease in light intensity from the canopy downwards is not gradual; rather abrupt changes occur at various levels depending on the structure of the forest.

For instance, 10 m below the upper levels of the canopy of a rain forest in the Ivory Coast, a 90% reduction has been recorded (Cachan, 1963). At ground level, light intensity seldom reaches more than 1% of that above the canopy.

Rainfall

The dry periods which occur in the rain-forest climate are of critical importance for the survival of many epiphytes, particularly those in the upper parts of the canopy. Their drought resistance shows a wide range of variation, from the poorly adapted filmy ferns such as *Hymenophyllum* and *Trichomanes*, to the extremely resistant epiphytic Cactaceae.

One may divide the epiphytes into two major groups, the drought-tolerant and the drought-avoiding. The shape and texture of the leaves often indicate to which group a species belongs. Drought-avoiding epiphytes are deciduous in the "dry season". Many species in the fern genera *Davallia*, *Drynaria* and *Nephrolepis* and several species of *Polystachya* (*Orchidaceae*) belong to this group. The drought-tolerant species often have a small number of leaves, or possess succulent or terete leaves. The combination of few and succulent leaves is, for instance, common among the *Bulbophyllum* orchids.

Two of the largest orchid genera in Africa, *Bulbophyllum* and *Polystachya*, have sympodial growth — that is, the plants develop a shoot which is limited in apical growth. Development of new pseudobulbs and leaves takes place during the wet season, each shoot terminating in an inflorescence. Orchids with monopodial growth, where each stem has an indefinite apical growth, are subject to possible desiccation in the dry season since they keep their leaves.

In the high-rainfall type of *Brachystegia* woodland in northwestern Zambia there are about forty species of epiphytic orchids. However, in the dry *mopane* woodland of the Luangwa valley, Zambia, only two species of epiphytes occur, the orchids *Acampe pachyglossa* and *Ansellia gigantea* var. *nilotica* (Williamson, 1977).

The orchid *Tridactyle tricuspis* is common in *Brachystegia* woodlands in southern Tanzania where the rainfall is approximately 800 to 1000 mm yr^{-1}. An examination of fifty randomly selected trees revealed its presence on all but one of the trees and often in a surprisingly high number of individuals (Johansson, 1974).

In central Tanzania, the huge orchid *Ansellia gigantea* may locally occur in areas with a yearly rainfall as low a 600 to 800 mm; apparently it is well adapted to dry conditions, since it occurs in very exposed locations on the trees. Its root system is composed of "normal" aerial roots attached to the substrate, from which numerous negatively geotropic roots arise (Fig. 9.10). There erect roots, which are covered with velamen, form a dense "tussock" which greatly increases the surface area of the root system exposed to the air. It is very probable that these roots have a special absorptive function (Sanford and Adanlawo, 1973). Water vapour may condense on the roots during the night and then be transferred into the plant.

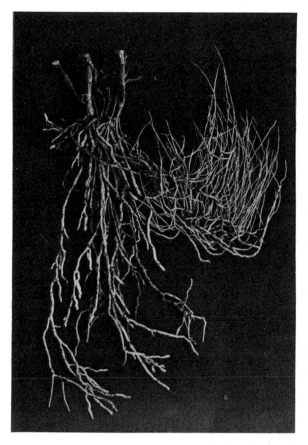

Fig. 9.10. Root system of *Ansellia africana*.

Epiphytes, particularly orchids, seem able to utilize the microclimatic advantages of special environments, such as the relatively humid riparian environment in the woodlands of East and Central Africa which harbour orchids such as *Aërangis flabellifolia*, *A. kotschyana*, *Cyrtorchis arcuata* subsp. *whytei* and *Microcoelia exilis*; but pteridophytes are rare in this environment.

Altitude

The epiphyte flora changes with altitude. Generally speaking, orchid species outnumber pteridophytes in the lowlands of the equatorial zone. However, with increasing altitude pteridophytes become more common, while the number of orchids decreases. In the Nimba Mountains, the ratio of pteridophytes to orchids is 1:3 in the foothills (5–700 m) but 1:1 at the crest (1000–1300 m).

On Mount Kenya, epiphytic orchids seem to be absent from trees near the forest boundary at approximately 3200 m altitude. Epiphytic ferns such as *Asplenium kassnerii*, *Pleopeltis excavata* and *Xiphopteris flabelliformis* are present, however. Further down slope, at 2600 m, several species of epiphytic orchids occur, such as *Polystachya campyloglossa*, *P. cultriformis* and *Tridactyle scottelii*. At a similar altitude on the eastern slope of Mount Meru in Tanzania epiphytic orchids are very rare, the commonest being *Polystachya campyloglossa*, while several epiphytic pteridophytes are abundant, such as *Asplenium aethiopicum*, *A. friesiorum* and *A. loxoscapoides*. Below 2000 m the orchids become successively commoner on this mountain.

Sometimes the relation with altitude has been interpreted in terms of greater drought at higher altitudes, or as a result of lower temperatures. As regards the pteridophytes the increased-drought hypothesis seems an unlikely explanation for their dominance at higher altitudes, since they usually are less drought resistant than epiphytic orchids. Opinions differ on whether or not orchids are able to survive frost. Piers (1968) stated that epiphytic orchids cannot survive frost, while Stewart (1970) reported that *Bolusiella iridifolia* "may even withstand frost on the coldest night of the year".

Substrate

The substrate and nutrients available to the epiphytes come from a variety of sources (Fig. 9.11). The bark seems to be particularly important.

The properties of the bark affect epiphytes in several ways, — through its method of growth, relief, structure or porosity and chemical composition. Which properties ultimately make a certain tree suitable as a host for epiphytes is poorly understood.

There often is a striking difference in the abundance and floristic composition of the epiphyte load in relation to the species of host tree. *Heritiera utilis*, *Lophira alata*, *Mitragyna ciliata* and *Parinari excelsa* (Fig. 9.1) are good examples of large trees with a rich epiphyte growth. The cola tree, *Cola nitida*, which is cultivated near villages, is also, almost without exception, extraordinary rich in epiphytes. Some other tree species seldom or

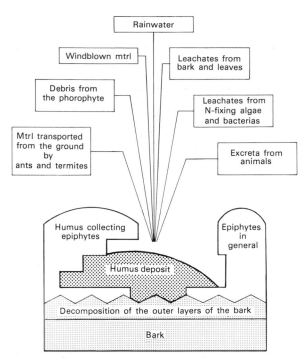

Fig. 9.11. Components of the substrate.

never carry epiphytes. *Albizzia glaberrima, A. zygia, Fagara tessmannii, Terminalia ivorensis* and *T. superba* are examples of large rain-forest trees with a very scarce load of epiphytes. *Acacia* and *Ficus* trees are avoided by most epiphytic orchids. The same applies to the tree euphorbias, many exotic conifers and *Eucalyptus* trees. The absence of epiphytic orchids on the trunks of the oil palm, *Elaeis guineensis*, is conspicuous, though it supports a rich flora of pteridophytes.

Some trees which exhibit a poor presence of epiphytes, such as *Terminalia ivorensis*, frequently carry a large number of epiphytes after death. The cause for this is unknown, but one may speculate that it results from a cessation in the production of phytotoxins by the host tree.

There are several reports of a relationship between a particular species of host tree and a particular species of epiphyte. Whether such a relation exists in reality is doubtful, and the occurrence of an epiphyte on a particular host tree might be just a matter of chance. It can be assumed that an increased knowledge of the occurrence of epiphytes will decrease the number of reported "specific relationships" between epiphyte and host tree. Epiphytes are not confined to trees only, but

may occur on perennial herbs as well — for instance, on the curious-looking *Afrotrilepis pilosa* (Cyperaceae), which has stems covered with closely packed persistent old leaf sheaths. Eleven species of epiphytic orchids are reported to occur on *Afrotrilepis* in Nigeria (Richards, 1957). In East and Central Africa, *Vellozia splendens* (Velloziaceae) plays a similar role for the epiphytic orchids (Moreau and Moreau, 1943; Morris, 1968).

Epiphytes on rocks and soils

In seasonally dry areas of East Africa, for instance, one may find a wide range of epiphytic orchids growing on rocks, and sometimes even on the naked soil where competition from terrestrial plants is weak or absent. In humid areas strong competition from terrestrial plants reduces the available habitat for epiphytes on the ground or on rocks. Here, on the other hand, terrestrial plants live as facultative epiphytes in humus accumulations on the trees.

Occasionally epiphytes may grow on rocks or directly on the soil even in humid rain-forest environments; steep banks on newly built roads may be colonized. In these sites epiphytes gradually are overgrown by habitually terrestrial plants, and disappear.

EFFECTS OF EPIPHYTES ON THEIR HOST TREES

Vascular epiphytes are generally considered harmless to their host trees, or at most damaging when they occur in large masses that can cause branches to break after rainfall.

A rich epiphytic growth may contribute to a higher humidity in the bark. This would favour the development of bacteria and fungi, which saprophytically or parasitically could affect the host tree. The interaction between epiphytes and the host tree is more complex than that (Benzing, 1983; see also Ch.7). Nutritional piracy — the immobilization by epiphytes of nutrient resources which would otherwise be recycled — is one way in which the epiphytes could deprive the host tree of scarce nutrient resources (Benzing and Seeman, 1978).

There are even a number of cases where there are strong reasons to believe that plants which in fact are epiphytes may indirectly function as parasites. Cook (1926) reported that two different species of

Fig. 9.12. The leafless orchid *Microcoelia exilis*.

orchids were found to be active agents in killing branches of citrus trees in Puerto Rico. Sometimes branches as much as 8 cm in diameter were killed. Planters in Java clear their coffee and citrus trees of epiphytes because these plants were felt to kill "the finest branches of the trees" (Went, 1940). These observations by the planters were confirmed by Ruinen (1953), who also reported that trees cleared of epiphytes become healthier.

Johansson (1977) found that *Microcoelia exilis*, a leafless epiphytic orchid, was more common on dead sections of branches than on living ones (Fig. 9.12). Although this could indicate merely that this type of substrate is most suited for this species, it was evident that several branches and twigs with *Microcoelia* showed signs of a gradual deterioration, carrying only a few half-wilted leaves, while the ones without the epiphyte remained healthy. The alleged "parasitism" of *Microcoelia* was questioned by Jonsson (1981), on the grounds that no morphological adaptations for parasitism was found in the root system and that the adult plants apparently are well sustained by their own photosynthetic activity, although he acknowledged that the mycorrhizal symbiont could be expected to be more or less deleterious to the host tree. Functionally, epiphytes act as parasites if they, through a fungal intermediary, receive nutrients from the vessels of their host. At the moment this is a matter that still needs experimental research.

REFERENCES

Benzing, D.H., 1983. Vascular epiphytes: a survey with special reference to their interactions with other organisms. In: S.L. Sutton, T.C. Whitmore and A.C. Chadwick (Editors), *Tropical Rain Forest: Ecology and Management*. Spec. Publ. Ser. Br. Ecol. Soc., 2: 11–24.

Benzing, D.H. and Seemann, J., 1978. Nutritional piracy and host decline: a new perspective on the epiphyte–host relationship. *Selbyana*, 2: 133–148.

Cachan, P., 1963. Signification écologique des variations microclimatiques verticales dans la forêt sempervirante du basse Côte d'Ivoire. *Ann. Fac. Sci. Univ. Dakar*, 8: 89–155.

Cook, M.T., 1926. Epiphytic orchids as an epiphytic pest on citrus trees. *J. Dept. Agric. P.R.*, 10: 5–9.

Eggeling, W.J., 1947. Observations on the ecology of the Budongo rain forest, Uganda. *J. Ecol.*, 34: 20–87.

Grubb, P.J., Lloyd, J.R., Pennington, T.D. and Whitmore, T.C., 1963. A comparison of montane and lowland rain forests in Equador. *J. Ecol.*, 51: 567–601.

Harrison, E.R., 1972. *Epiphytic Orchids of southern Africa — A Field Guide to the Indigenous Species*. The Natal Branch of the Wildlife Protection and Conservation Society of South Africa, 107 pp.

Hepper, F.N. (Editor), 1968. *Flora of West Tropical Africa. Vol. III, Part I*. Crown Agents, London, 2nd ed., 276 pp.

Hosokawa, T., 1954. On the structure and composition of the Campnosperma forests in Palau, Micronesia. *Mem. Fac. Sci., Kyushu Univ.*, E(1): 199–218.

Johansson, D., 1974. Ecology of vascular epiphytes in West African rain forest. *Acta Phytogeogr. Suec.*, 59: 129 pp.

Johansson, D., 1976. African epiphytic orchids. — An annotated guide to the literature. *Am. Orchid. Soc. Bull.*, 45: 889–891.

Johansson, D., 1977. Epiphytic orchids as parasites of their host trees. *Am. Orchid. Soc. Bull.*, 46: 703–707.

Johansson, D., 1978. A method to register the distribution of epiphytes on the host tree. *Am. Orchid. Soc. Bull.*, 47: 901–904.

Jonsson, L., 1981. A monograph of the genus Microcoelia (Orchidaceae). *Symb. Bot. Ups.*, 23(4): 151 pp.

Moreau, W.M. and Moreau, R.E., 1943. *An Introduction to the Epiphytic Orchids of East Africa*. East Africa Natl. Hist. Soc., Nairobi, 27 pp.

Morris, B., 1968. The epiphytic orchids of the Shire highlands, Malawi. *Proc. Linn. Soc.*, 179(1): 51–66.

Morris, B., 1970. *The Epiphytic Orchids of Malawi*. The Society of Malawi, Blantyre, 136 pp.

Nihoul, E., Schelpe, E.A. and Hunt, P.F., 1969. A provisional checklist of the orchids in the Congo–Kinshasa. *Am. Orchid. Soc. Bull.*, 38: 578–584.

Piers, F., 1968. *Orchids of East Africa*. Cramer, Lehre, 304 pp.

Richards, P.W., 1939. Ecological studies of the rain forest of Southern Nigeria, I. The structure and floristic composition of the primary forest. *J. Ecol.*, 27: 1–61.

Richards, P.W., 1957. Ecological notes on West African vegetation. *J. Ecol.*, 45: 563–577.

Ruinen, J., 1953. Epiphytosis. A second view on epiphytism. *Ann. Bogor.*, 1: 101–157.

Sanford, W.W., 1968. Distribution of epiphytic orchids in semi-deciduous tropical forest in Southern Nigeria. *J. Ecol.*, 56: 697–705.

Sanford, W.W., 1969. The distribution of epiphytic orchids in Nigeria in relation to each other and to geographic location and climate, type of vegetation and tree species. *Biol. J. Linn. Soc.*, 1: 247–285.

Sanford, W.W., 1974. The ecology of orchids. In: C.L. Withner (Editor), *The Orchids, Scientific Studies.* Wiley, New York, N.Y., pp. 1–100.

Sanford, W.W. and Adanlawo, I., 1973. Velamen and exodermis characters of West African epiphytic orchids in relation to taxonomic grouping and habitat tolerance. *Bot. J. Linn. Soc.*, 666: 307–321.

Stewart, J., 1970. *Orchids of Tropical Africa.* Allen, London, 117 pp.

Stewart, J., 1973. A second checklist of the orchids of Kenya. *Am. Orchid. Soc. Bull.*, 42: 525–531.

Stewart, J., 1976. The Vandaceous group in Africa and Madagascar. In: K. Senghas (Editor), *Proc. 8th World Orchid Conf., Frankfurt 1975*, pp. 239–248.

Tixier, P., 1966. *Flore et Végétation Orophiles de l'Asie Tropicale.* Soc. d'Édition d'Enseignement Supérieur, Paris, 240 pp.

Van Ede, G., 1976. The orchids of Transvaal. In: K. Senghas (Editor), *Proc. 8th World Orchid Conf., Frankfurt 1975*, pp. 230–234.

Van Oye, P., 1924. Ecologie des épiphytes des troncs d'arbres au Congo Belge. *Rev. Gen. Bot.*, 36: 481–498.

Van Steenis, C.G.G.J., 1938. Recent progress and prospects in the study of the Malaysian flora. *Chron. Bot.*, 4: 392–397.

Went, F.W., 1940. Soziologie der Epiphyten eines tropischen Urwaldes. *Ann. Jard. Bot. Buitenz.*, 50: 1–98.

Williamson, G., 1977. *The Orchids of South Central Africa.* Dent, London, 237 pp.

Chapter 10

SOUTHEAST ASIAN TROPICAL FORESTS

T.C. WHITMORE

INTRODUCTION

More ecological studies have been published on the tropical rain forests of the Far East than on those of either Africa or America. A recent detailed regional account (Whitmore, 1984a) refers to some 1200 publications, half of them issued since 1973. Here I attempt a bird's eye view to give access to the copious literature by way of citing key references. The opportunity is taken to pinpoint areas of ignorance and topics for further research.

EXTENT OF THE SOUTHEAST ASIAN TROPICAL RAIN FORESTS

The eastern tropical rain forests, variously called Indo-Malayan or southeast Asian, stretch from India through to Polynesia. These forests are the second largest in extent amongst the world's rain forests, after the American block, as is discussed by Lieth and Werger (Ch. 1).

The limits

These rain forests are centred on the Malay archipelago, which primevally was nearly all forest-clad. They extend as a finger protruding southwards down the east coast of Australia in Queensland (Webb et al., 1984) and continue eastwards and southwards beyond the archipelago into Melanesia (the Solomon Islands, Santa Cruz Islands, Vanuatu and Fiji), Micronesia and Polynesia (Ch. 14). In continental Asia tropical rain forests clothe the Malay peninsula about as far as Chumphon (11°N) north of the Isthmus of Kra, then continue up the west coast in Burma into the

Pegu Yoma east of the Irrawaddy river. West of the Irrawaddy a detached block follows the Arakan Yoma in Burma, north through the Chittagong Hill Tracts of Bangladesh to Nagaland and Assam in northeastern India. There are outlying pockets on the Western Ghats of peninsular India and in perhumid southwestern Sri Lanka. In the Indo-China peninsula (Thailand, Kampuchea, Vietnam and Laos) scattered patches of tropical rain forest exist where perhumid conditions obtain, though these have now been much reduced in area. One such is the Chanthaburi pocket, 12°45'E, 102°N (Whitmore, 1984a), which lies on the coastal, rain relief, slopes of the Cardamomes mountains on the Kampuchea–Thailand border and in which live disjunct populations of typically Malayan rain-forest plants, for example *Diospyros hermaphroditica* and hygrophilic undergrowth palms. There are scattered patches of rain forest also in southern China from Xishuangbanna in Yunnan eastwards to Hai-nan Tao (Academia Sinica, 1979; Wu, 1979). Indeed, it is in China and northeastern India, along the south slopes and at the eastern end of the great wall of the Himalaya, that tropical rain forests extend further from the Equator, 26°, than anywhere else on earth (Whitmore, 1982).

In continental Asia north of the Isthmus of Kra, tropical rain forests lie in a complex mosaic with the monsoon and savanna forests (sensu Schimper, 1903) of seasonal climates. The disposition of the different forests depends much on local climate, and on soil depth, texture and fertility, and is made more complex by fire, and also by other human activities. Over the centuries there has been much destruction and degradation, often taking the form of alteration to a forest type characteristic (in floristics and structure) of a more drought-prone habitat. These pockets of tropical rain forest, occupying as they do only part of the potential area, have not been comprehensively mapped. Local maps for different countries were listed by De Rosayro (1974) and Legris (1974), but there is likely to be less forest remaining now. It would be possible to make a regional map from satellite imagery, especially from images made during the dry season, and to trace the recent rates of attrition. There are no detailed regional accounts of rain forests on the Asian continent. Legris (1974) gave a summary, based on the many local and national studies. There are problems of nomenclature between different countries, though less than with forests of seasonal climates. An early comprehensive account for Greater India (India, Pakistan, Burma, Bangladesh, Sri Lanka) which is still useful is that of Champion (1936). The remaining rain forests of Sri Lanka, at Sinharaja and Kottawa in the southeast, have been described by Peeris (1975) and Gunatilleke and Gunatilleke (1981). Vidal (1979) updated the account of Legris for Indo-China.

At the northern limit tropical rain forest only occurs on the warmest (south-facing) and moistest sites. In this "tension zone" it must be especially vulnerable to climatic change, and it would therefore be of interest to establish plots for long-term observation of species reproduction and to follow any changes in composition. Would this be affected by the slight progressive warming or the alterations in rainfall that increasing atmospheric carbon dioxide may be causing?

Wolfe (1979) considered that the northernmost lowland tropical rain forests have close similarities in structure and flora with lower montane rain forest at more equatorial latitudes. He believed these two kinds should jointly be renamed "para-tropical" rain forest. He described the northern belt of this forest type in southern China, interpreting and amplifying the important study of Wang (1961), which was derived from surveys in the 1930s. Wolfe's conclusion was based on perceived similarities in the overall annual temperature regime in perhumid climates between the lowland subtropics and middle mountain elevations within the tropics. He believed the big differences between a tropical mountain, with its strong diurnal temperature fluctuation but little change through the year, and the subtropics, with diurnal plus annual rhythm, to be unimportant. It would be interesting to extend Wolfe's approach to cover the annual moisture regime and to perform studies of ecosystem processes, for example decomposition, nutrient cycling and biomass production. At present the similarities and differences within different parts of "paratropical" rain forest remain incompletely explored. Chang (1981) gave a useful descriptive account of the sector of these forests which lies in southeastern Tibet. Comparisons of structure and habitat were made between rain forests at a number of sites on the northern and southern fringes in Thailand and Australia, respectively, by Smitinand et al. (1982).

The heartland

The Malay archipelago, originally nearly all forest-covered, is the heartland of the eastern tropical rain forests. These forests are currently suffering rapid attrition. They are at the present day the main world source of tropical hardwood timbers. After logging, much of the forest is left to regenerate; but extensive areas are changed to agricultural land for food crops (Fig. 10.1) and for plantation crops (principally oil palm and rubber) (Lanly, 1982) which produce food or, by export, hard currency for national development, to meet the rising aspirations of rapidly increasing human populations. Figure 10.2 shows the extent remaining in the early 1980s.

The tropical rain forests are partially divided into western and eastern blocks by two wedges of monsoon forest in the middle of the archipelago (Fig. 10.2). The northern wedge of seasonal climates lies in the western Philippines. The southern wedge occupies much of Java, the whole of the Lesser Sunda Islands (Nusa Tenggara) and parts of southern Celebes (Sulawesi) and of the Moluccas (Maluku). In the southern wedge it is very dry in the middle months of the year when hot, desiccating winds blow north off Australia.

There has been much more extensive forest destruction in the monsoon forest wedges than in the rain-forest blocks, and monsoon forest has disappeared from Java and Madura. Seasonal drought permits annual burning. Also, as on the Asian continent, some rain forests near the boundary and in pockets within the wedges have

Fig. 10.1. A patchwork of primary lowland evergreen dipterocarp rain forest (grey crowns *Shorea curtisii*), shifting cultivators' fields and "bush fallow" of various ages. Pahang, central Malaya. The numbers of shifting cultivators is increasing, and so therefore is their impact on the forest.

been degraded to monsoon forest by human activities.

The monsoon forests and savanna forests, as well as the woodlands and savanna grasslands of southernmost New Guinea, are outside the scope of this volume. As on the continent, the boundary with rain forest is a complex, little understood mosaic. The ecotone between these two great classes of vegetation has been little studied. The exact position of the boundary with rain forest remains a matter of subjective choice. Monsoon forests contain the commercially valuable species *Tectona grandis* (teak), extensively planted on Java, and also found on Bali, Muna and Kangean. It is not known if it is indigenous or whether it was introduced in the seventh century by Hindu settlers. *Tectona philippinensis*, a wild relative of no commercial interest, occurs on Luzon near Batangas and on Iling Island off Mindoro (Hedegart,

1976). The monsoon forests have a strong Australian floristic element which includes several *Eucalyptus* species, and these are of forestry interest. On Luzon and Mindoro in the Philippines two subtropical pines, *Pinus kesiya* and *P. merkusii*, reach into the tropics from centres in Indo-China. The latter species, which is very widely planted in Indonesia, also occurs in three separate seasonally dry enclaves in Sumatra, one of which is the only place where the genus occurs naturally south of the Equator.

FLORISTICS OF THE ASIAN TROPICAL RAIN FORESTS

Malesia

Malesia is the phytogeographical region which stretches from Sumatra and Malaya eastwards to

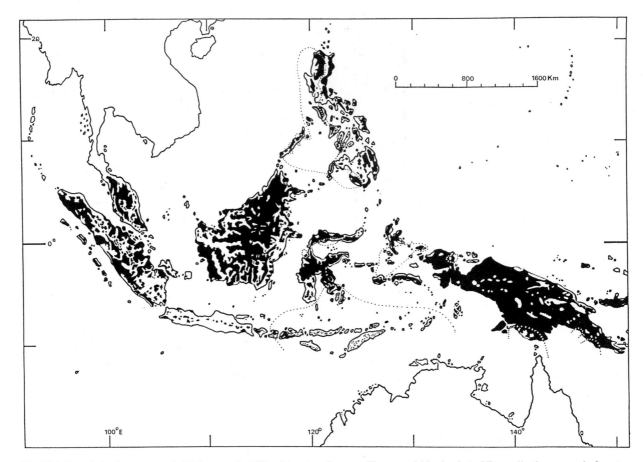

Fig. 10.2. Remaining forest cover in Malaya, early 1980s. Monsoon forests still occur within the dotted lines, all others are rain forests. Areas shown white were primevally mostly forested but have been lost in decreasing order of importance to permanent agriculture (including tree plantation crops), shifting agriculture, mining and towns. Note that more monsoon forests have disappeared, they are annually inflammable. Remaining forests, the black areas, include both virgin forest and places logged but then left to regrow (this is forest *sensu* FAO, see Lanly, 1982). (Based on Whitmore, 1984b.)

the Bismarck Archipelago. It is coterminous with the heartland of the eastern rain forests. Where these terminate sharply there is a strong floristic change because monsoon forests of different floristic composition come to occupy much of the land surface. Malesia has been defined by Van Steenis (1950) and is not to be confused with the political state of Malaysia. On the Asian continent the Malesian boundary lies approximately at the frontier of Malaysia and Thailand at the Kangar–Pattani line of Whitmore (1975). There is a second sharp boundary north of the Philippines and a third one at Torres Strait between New Guinea and Australia. To the east, where rain forest continues to cover the landscape, Malesia is not sharply bounded.

Outliers and extensions

Outside Malesia the rain-forest flora embraces the same families, mostly the same genera and many of the same species as the heartland itself. Overall it is probably slightly less rich both on small plots (α diversity, sensu Whittaker, 1972) and on a local scale (β diversity) though there seem to be no comparable hard data.

To the south of Malesia in Australia the predominantly Malesian flora is supplemented by a local element some of which extends northwards into the heartland. In Australia the rain-forest flora contrasts strongly with that of the contiguous sclerophyll forests (Webb et al., 1984) which is very strongly centred in Australia, though the sclerophyll element does extend into the seasonal climatic area of New Guinea, tailing off westwards along the Lesser Sunda Islands, where the climate is also seasonal. Within the aseasonal part of Malesia, clothed by rain forest, the Australian taxa are especially common in heath forest (see Specht and Womersley, 1979), as was first pointed out by Richards (1943) and has been thoroughly expounded by Van Steenis (1979). A notable species of Australian affinity is the only rain-forest eucalypt, *Eucalyptus deglupta* Bl., a pioneer found in New Britain, New Guinea, the Moluccas, Celebes and Mindanao (Whitmore, 1984a), which is of considerable forestry importance.

To the north of Malesia, in continental Asia, the Dipterocarpaceae, so prolifically developed in western Malesia, have fewer genera and species (Ch. 11) and become very sparse and patchy in the northern fringe rain forests of southern China. Towards this fringe, in Vietnam, Laos and southern China, a substantial temperate floristic element occurs amongst the trees, listed by Wolfe (1979). Detailed ecological studies of these forests have yet to be published.

The flora of the rain-forest outliers to the west in Greater India is reported in many local studies, conveniently summarized by Legris (1974); the regional surveys of Champion (1936) and Champion and Seth (1968) also give general accounts.

Eastwards of Malesia into the islands of the Pacific there is gradual floristic impoverishment (Van Balgooy, 1971; see also Ch. 14) which becomes abruptly sharper at the "andesite line" marking the boundary between continental and oceanic islands, which can be explained in terms of ocean-floor spreading and the migration into the Pacific of island arcs (Whitmore, 1973a). A detailed survey of the flora of the Solomon Islands showed that this whole archipelago has few endemics, and is monotonously uniform from island to island with very little local endemism. Lower montane rain forests and taxa which typify it, such as Araucariaceae and especially Fagaceae, are absent (Whitmore, 1969).

Floristics within Malesia

The flora of Malesia itself is not homogeneous. There are marked differences from island to island.

Richness

The Malesian flora is very rich and diverse. Over half (220) of the world's flowering plant families are represented, as well as about one-quarter of the genera (2400), of which about 40% are endemic; there are between 25 000 and 30 000 species, of which about one-third are trees more than 10 cm in diameter (Jacobs, 1974).

There is great, but varied, endemism. For example, in New Guinea *Rhododendron* has 155 endemics out of a total of 158 species (Sleumer, 1966); and Borneo has 9 endemic species of *Gonystylus*, while the whole region has only 19 species in that genus (Airy Shaw, 1953).

Malaya (Peninsular Malaysia plus Singapore), has been explored most thoroughly, and its flora described in more publications than for anywhere else. This small region of 132 100 km² has about 7900 species of flowering plants in 1500 genera. Eighty-two tree families recently critically investigated (Whitmore, 1972, 1973b; Ng, 1978), which comprise 388 genera, have 27% of their species endemic (Ng and Low, 1982). This richness may be contrasted with the poverty of the British Isles (311 100 km²) which have a native flora of 1430 species (18%) and 628 genera (42%), in an area 2.3 times greater. It would be interesting to compare this Malayan countrywide diversity (δ-diversity: Whittaker, 1972) with similar areas elsewhere in the tropics.

Species richness on small plots (α-diversity of Whittaker), amongst trees $\geqslant 10$ cm in diameter (1 ft girth) is greater in Malaya (164 and 176 species in 1.0 ha: Wyatt-Smith, 1966) and Kalimantan (239 in 1.6 ha at Wanariset: Kartawinata et al., 1981) than in any other rain forest recorded, though similar or greater richness probably does occur in parts of tropical America (177 species $\geqslant 15$ cm diameter in 1 ha; Prance et al., 1976). Over a larger area (β diversity), Ashton (1969) recorded 711 species $\geqslant 10$ cm diameter on non-contiguous plots of total area 8.8 ha at Bukit Raya, western Sarawak. This figure lies on an extrapolation of the species/area curves which may be drawn from the smaller Malayan and Kalimantan plots. By contrast, Whitmore (1974) found only 184 species $\geqslant 10$ cm diameter in 13.7 ha (sum of 22 non-contiguous plots each of 0.625 ha) on Kolombangara in the Solomon Islands.

There are as yet no complete counts of *all* plant

species on plots from anywhere in the eastern rain forests.

Sunda and Sahul

Some plant groups are more or less evenly represented throughout Malesia, for example *Eugenia* s.l. (Myrtaceae). Some others are centred either on the lands of the Sunda Shelf (principally Sumatra, Malaya, Borneo, Palawan, Java), which extends out from the Asian continent, or on the lands of the Sahul Shelf (New Guinea and adjacent islands), which reaches out from Australia. Groups centred on the Sunda Shelf include Dipterocarpaceae (Ashton, Ch.11), the climbing palms (known as rattans: subfamily Calamoideae), Magnoliaceae and *Artocarpus* [figs. 6.7 and 8.4 of Whitmore (1981) and fig. 1.8b of Whitmore (1984a)]. Groups with an eastern focus, on the Sahul Shelf, extend there from a centre in Australasia and Melanesia and include Araucariaceae, *Styphelia* (Epacridaceae) and Winteraceae [figs. 8.7–8.9 of Whitmore (1981)]. Some genera which are well represented throughout Malesia have been revealed on critical taxonomic study to have western and eastern subgroups — for example *Chisocheton* [Meliaceae (Mabberley, 1979); see fig. 8.2 of Whitmore (1981)] and *Horsfieldia* [Myristicaceae (De Wilde, 1983)].

A few genera are known which are strongly represented at both ends of Malesia but poorly in the middle, for example the bamboo *Nastus* and the palms *Licuala* and *Livistona* (Dransfield, 1981). The family Proteaceae is centred on the Sahul Shelf except for *Heliciopsis* which has a Sundaic focus [fig. 8.11 of Whitmore (1981)].

Tertiary history

These various patterns are believed to reflect the geological history of Malesia during the Tertiary. In brief, Laurasia and Gondwanaland were far apart at the start of that period, and came progressively closer by movement of the continental plates to collide with each other in mid-Miocene, about 15 Ma ago, either at Celebes or just east of it (Audley Charles et al., 1981; Audley Charles, 1981). Both Laurasia and Gondwanaland had angiosperms on board. The Australasian fringe of east Gondwanaland carried southern New Guinea on its margin and travelled northwards from south temperate latitudes, probably undergoing strong desiccation on the way. At about 15 Ma it reached and underthrust an island arc, which was thereby elevated and now forms the north coast ranges of present-day New Guinea. The New Guinea fragment was isolated to its south by a continental sea. Due to this isolation, and probably desiccation too, far fewer Gondwanic flowering plants entered what became Malesia and the flora of New Guinea is overwhelmingly of Laurasian groups which immigrated after the mid-Miocene collision. The mountains of New Guinea are the biggest in the region. They were uplifted 2000 m during the Pliocene and Pleistocene epochs. Fresh habitats were created, and in these explosive speciation occurred in the new warm-temperate environment. Evolution took place on the grand scale, for example in *Columnea* (Gesneriaceae), *Psychotria* (Rubiaceae), *Rhododendron* (Ericaceae) and *Schefflera* (Araliaceae) (Axelrod and Raven, 1982). There is massive endemism, but this can only be specified in groups where there has been a modern critical taxonomic revision. An example is Ericaceae, which in New Guinea have 6 genera and 403 species, of which 400 are endemic (Stevens, 1982).

Wallace's Line

The Tertiary geological history is much more closely reflected in the ranges of animals than plants. A very strong zoogeographical boundary runs through the Malay archipelago. This is Wallace's Line, dividing the faunas of the Sunda and Sahul regions. Its exact position has been a matter of controversy. Its strength as a boundary varies with the ease with which the animal group under consideration disperses over salt water (Cranbrook, 1981; George, 1981).

Pleistocene climates

The eastern tropical rain-forest region is much more mountainous than is either the African or American. Climatic deterioration during the Pleistocene associated with high-latitude Ice Ages depressed the tree line several times by as much as 1500 m, and compressed all altitudinal forest zones downwards throughout Malesia. Lowland climates became cooler, drier and more seasonal. At times of glacial maxima large areas of the Sunda and Sahul continental shelves were exposed by falling sea levels. Currently we live in an interglacial, and the mountain forest belts are at, or near, their maximum vertical extent. During the Pleistocene many species have had their altitudinal ranges alternately contracted and expanded. Species ranges at the present time, and perhaps local floristic composition of areas of forest, may reflect these repeated vicissitudes. It has been argued that different species associations on different mountains in New Guinea reflect the vagaries in upward migration of species since the last glacial maximum (Walker and Flenley, 1979; Walker and Hope, 1982). Van Steenis (1979) has described the increasing disjunctions in range of species which grow in areas with increasing degrees of seasonal drought. He has argued that those species with range-gaps beyond dispersal distance of their diaspores must have attained their current distributions when the climate was more seasonal in the past and the gaps in range shorter.

Dipterocarpaceae

Probably the most important single distinction between the forests west and east of Wallace's Line is the very strong concentration of dipterocarps in the lands of the Sunda Shelf. This is discussed further by Ashton (Ch. 11) so here brief mention of the most salient features suffices.

The rain forests in Malesia west of Wallace's Line are like no others anywhere in the world because of their unique dominance by a single family. Dipterocarpaceae are extremely diverse in genera and species and extremely abundant in most lowland forest formations. They also contribute many (Sumatra, Malaya), most (Borneo) or all (Philippines) of the top-of-canopy giant trees. There are important consequences.

Big dipterocarps are very tall trees, and the forests where they are common are the grandest of all tropical rain forests, of greater stature than others elsewhere. The tallest trees occur, not as isolated single emergents about 60 m tall, but as groups. The top of the forest canopy is therefore very rough, with groups of giant billowing crowns of characteristic cauliflower-like construction, separated by deep holes. From an aeroplane the traveller can easily see a difference as he flies from dipterocarp-rich Borneo to dipterocarp-poor Celebes or the Moluccas, where the forest canopy top is much more even.

All big dipterocarps (and most smaller ones) have useful timber. The combination of dense stocking and very big trees gives dipterocarp forests an extremely high timber volume and hence commercial value per hectare.

Many dipterocarps share a "strategy" for regeneration scarcely found in other rain-forest tree families. Fruits are produced in gargantuan quantities at intervals a few years apart (although annually by the gregarious *Anisoptera thurifera* of New Guinea). The seeds germinate immediately. The gloomy, humid forest floor becomes carpeted with seedlings which persist for a few years. If a canopy gap occurs, those seedlings underneath it immediately grow up fast to fill it. There is a remarkable change in these young plants from shade-tolerant to light-demanding, the physiology of which remains uninvestigated. In the absence of gap-formation the seedling population dwindles. There have been very few critical studies of this facet of dipterocarp ecology, and of how different species differ. In Malaya, typically, seedlings disappear before the next gregarious flowering; but in Sabah successive seedling cohorts characteristically overlap. However, this warrants further investigation, and the observations need to be extended to Brunei, Sarawak, Indonesia and the Philippines. These various autecological features make silviculture of dipterocarp rain forests easy. The forester needs only to ensure that at the time of felling a seedling carpet is present, that during log extraction he does not destroy it, and that he does not open up the canopy so much that the microclimate favours invasive secondary-forest pioneers (mainly trees of *Macaranga* and *Trema*, with many woody climbers, notably *Merremia* and *Mezoneuron*). If these provisos are followed a new forest of valuable timber will grow. Estimates show that new trees grown from seedlings will reach commercial size in about 70 years. In the dipterocarp rain forests of western Malesia biology is on the forester's side, and silvicultural success depends largely on enforcement of simple regulations. A review of the historical development of silviculture, current practices, and how these are based on dipterocarp autecology, was given by Whitmore (1984a).

The high-mountain flora

Within the Malesian flora it is possible to distinguish megatherm and microtherm families. Megatherms are confined, or nearly confined, to elevations below about 1000 m. These include Anacardiaceae, Burseraceae, Capparidaceae, Combretaceae, Connaraceae, Dilleniaceae, Dipterocarpaceae, Flacourtiaceae, Marantaceae, Myristicaceae and Rhizophoraceae. Their geographical distribution is predominantly tropical.

Conversely, microtherms have predominantly temperate distribution areas. There are several families and numerous genera, found mostly above 1000 m. Tree families in this group include Aceraceae, Cunoniaceae, Fagaceae, Podocarpaceae, Symplocaceae and Theaceae.

The origins and affinities of the Malesian mountain flora have been thoroughly explored in a long series of papers by Van Steenis (for instance Van Steenis 1964, 1972). Taxa occur of both northern (e.g. *Primula*) and southern (e.g. *Gunnera*) affinity. Resemblances to the flora of the lowland forests of southern China have already been described above.

Even at Pleistocene glacial maxima, when cool mountain climates were more extensive than today, there were almost certainly still considerable distances between adjacent areas of suitable montane habitat. It seems probable that mountain plants have arrived by long-distance dispersal using intermediate mountains as stepping stones, not via continuous "bridges" of high country. Entry from Asia could have been through Indo-China to Sumatra, and Taiwan to the Philippines, with a third track entering New Guinea from Australia (Van Steenis, 1964). A detailed analysis of the New Guinea high-mountain flora has been made by Smith (1982).

Conifers

The eastern tropical rain forests differ from others in the abundance in genera and species of conifers (De Laubenfels, 1969; Whitmore, 1980). By contrast, the African and American rain forests have only a few species each. Conifers occur principally but not entirely in the mountain forests, where *Dacrydium* (Fig. 10.12) and *Podocarpus* are the main genera, each with several species. These two genera also grow, mostly scattered, in lowland rain forests (Fig. 10.3), where locally *Agathis* and *Araucaria* also occur, sometimes as dense, extensive stands covering many square kilometres, of very high commercial value, and in consequence

Fig. 10.3. *Podocarpus neriifolius*, a giant conifer which reaches the canopy top and occurs from east India to south China and Japan and throughout Malesia to Fiji in Melanesia. It is found as scattered single trees in lowland evergreen rain forest, usually in hilly country above 300 m elevation, as here in Kedah, Malaya. Conifers are common in the Asian rain forests.

now much depleted by logging. These conifers all belong to the two families, Araucariaceae and Podocarpaceae, which today are almost confined to the Southern Hemisphere. There has been considerable ecological study of *Agathis* and *Araucaria*. This and other work on conifers has been reviewed by Whitmore (1984a). No northern conifer actually enters the eastern rain forests, though *Pinus* extends south into monsoon forest enclaves in western Malesia as described above. If fire is excluded from pine forests in Sumatra long enough, big old relict *P. merkusii* come to stand as veterans in a matrix of broadleaf rain-forest species. Veteran *Araucaria cunninghamii* in the Queensland rain forest are believed likewise to have relict status (Webb and Tracey, 1967).

THE TROPICAL RAIN-FOREST FORMATIONS

The eastern rain forests may be divided into thirteen different formations, major kinds, with distinctive structure and physiognomy. The formations occupy different habitats, and because these are usually sharply bounded so are the formations. Species are restricted to one formation to various degrees. Some are strictly endemic to a single formation; for example, *Gonystylus bancanus* (source of the important export timber ramin) is confined to peat swamp forest. Others are of wider ecological amplitude; for example *Koompassia malaccensis* (which produces the timber kempas) occurs in tropical lowland evergreen rain forest, as well as in peat and fresh-water swamp forests. So far as is known, animals are less strongly confined within particular forest formations than are plants and this is markedly so amongst vertebrates (see discussion by Whitmore, 1984a). The formations are of wide geographical range. Within them there are both regional and local differences in floristic composition.

The forest formations have been fully defined and described and their floristic composition discussed in earlier publications (Whitmore, 1975, 1984a), where there are also notes on their occurrence in Africa and America, and on their economic importance. This full information is not repeated here. Instead I present a general introduction and indicate points of interest for further scrutiny. The occurrence of the forest formations within the Malesian heartland has recently been depicted on a wall map at a scale of 1:5 million, which incorporates all published information including that derived from satellite imagery (Whitmore, 1984b). The maps accompanying this chapter are derived from that compilation.

Tropical lowland evergreen rain forest and semi-evergreen rain forest (Figs. 10.4–10.8)

These are the two rain-forest formations of mesic lowland sites, constituting the climatic climax. Their remaining extent within Malesia is shown on Fig. 10.4. Semi-evergreen rain forest occurs where there is a modest annual dry season. Evergreen rain forest occurs where the climate is perhumid, and parts of Malesia (for example, Singapore) have a more continually humid climate

than anywhere else in the humid tropics. In discussing climate it must always be remembered that differences from year to year in rainfall total and its distribution, with occasional markedly drier years, are of indubitable biological importance even for evergreen rain forest and are not revealed in the great majority of published climatic diagrams which show instead long-term averages (see below, and for further discussion Whitmore, 1984a).

The structural and physiognomic differences between the evergreen and semi-evergreen rain-forest formations, which are rather subtle but quite clear, were first pointed out by Baur (1968). One distinctive feature is the presence of deciduous trees in the top of the canopy. Most of the Malesian heartland bears evergreen rain forest. The semi-evergreen formation has been observed in southernmost Thailand at the northern fringe of the rain-forest block of the western Sunda Shelf, where the climate becomes slightly seasonal. It probably occurs elsewhere as a narrow belt along the border between rain and monsoon forests. The extensions and outliers of the eastern rain forests in continental Asia are probably mostly the semi-evergreen formation. The Australian finger certainly is. To the east, the tropical oceanic climate of most of the Solomon Islands, with heavy continual rainfall, suggests that evergreen rain forest occurs. The other Pacific islands are perhumid to variously seasonal, and correspondingly bear one formation or the other.

The boundary between these two formations has never been precisely mapped anywhere in the region. They are now both so substantially disturbed or destroyed, especially at the fringes where they probably once co-existed, that delimitation is no longer possible. It would aid precision, however, if rain-forest researchers were to say to which of these formations the forest they are studying belongs.

An important factor, which locally determines details of forest flora and canopy structure, is catastrophic disturbance by cyclones (typhoons, hurricanes). Within the tropical Far East the areas which lie in cyclone belts are, in the Northern Hemisphere, Bangladesh and the northern and eastern Philippines south as far as northern Mindanao, and, the same distance (10–20°) from the Equator in the Southern Hemisphere, the

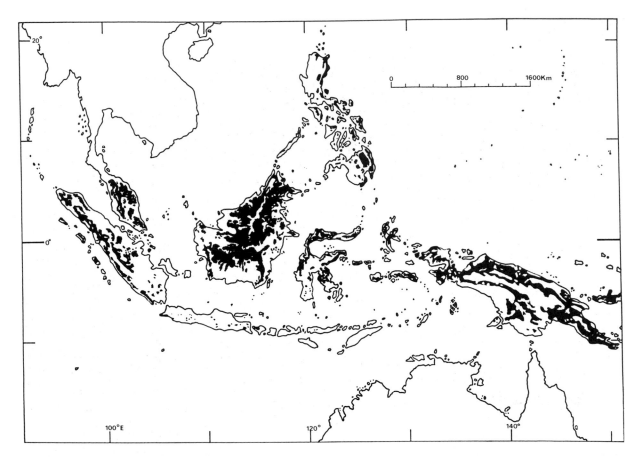

Fig. 10.4. Remaining lowland evergreen rain forest (the bulk) and lowland semi-evergreen rain forest (a little) in Malesia, early 1980s. These are the "climatic climax" forests of low elevations. (Based on Whitmore, 1984b.)

Melanesian archipelagos and Queensland. Much of New Guinea is also prone to catastrophic disturbance, though from earthquakes, landslides and volcanic eruptions rather than cyclones (White, 1973). The forests which regrow after wide-scale destruction are characteristically dominated by fast-growing, light-demanding tree species, often as pure stands or mixtures of only a few species. Canopy structure is in consequence rather simple. Only after many years, perhaps a century or more, are these forests replaced by one containing shade-tolerant species of many different ages, and usually in richer mixture. Canopy structure is in consequence more complex. In the Solomon Islands there were large tracts (now largely logged out) of post-cyclone forests dominated mainly by *Campnosperma brevipetiolatum*, *Endospermum medullosum* and *Terminalia calamansanai*. Foresters there have capitalized on the

resurgence after logging of these and other ecologically similar species to establish a similar and equally valuable replacement forest. In New Guinea the apparently ubiquitous abundance of *Pometia pinnata* is probably an indicator of catastrophic disturbance.

Thus, quite apart from considerations of historical plant geography, such as the abundance of Dipterocarpaceae only to the west of Wallace's Line, there are other regional factors which determine the floristic composition of an area of forest.

It is widely believed, and supported by many observations, that primary lowland rain forest in the Far East is not usually inflammable. (Observations, however, are needed to see if this is true of the semi-evergreen forest formation). Catastrophic destruction by fire is, however, now known to occur, albeit very rarely. In February 1983 fires

Fig. 10.5. Lowland evergreen dipterocarp rain forest. Slopes of Main Range, Malaya, *c.* 800 m. The domed emergent crowns are mostly species of Dipterocarpaceae (the grey crowns are of *Shorea curtisii*, frequently gregarious on ridge crests). Note the very uneven, billowing canopy and rather open crowns of many of the trees (contrast Fig. 10.13).

broke out in eastern Kalimantan. By the time they had burned out in July, drought and fire had destroyed over 3×10^6 ha of lowland dry-land rain forest, including much primary forest as well as areas which had been logged or converted to tree plantation. The approximate area destroyed (which is nearly that of The Netherlands) is shown on Fig. 10.9. There were also fires in northern Sabah (P.F. Burgess, pers. commun., 1984), east Sumatra (R. Blouch, pers. commun., 1984) and the interior of Halmahera (M.G. Audley Charles, pers. commun., 1984). These fires occurred after a drought which had lasted for over twelve months, itself a consequence of an exceptional perturbation in the atmospheric pressure patterns over the tropical part of the Pacific Ocean (Gill and Rasmusson, 1983), which also caused heavy flooding in South America and drought in southern Africa. A strong drought in 1915 in Sabah was followed by fire which destroyed the forest in an area still largely grass-covered, the 80 000 ha Sook Plain (Cockburn, 1974). Big primary rain-forest trees probably live for several hundred years. Thus, even rare catastrophic fires can have very long-term consequences on forest composition. There are unexplained differences between Malaya and eastern Borneo in the abundance and gregariousness of the big dipterocarps. Could rare catastrophes be a determining factor? Is there charcoal to be found in the soil profile indicative of past

Fig. 10.6. *Dialium platysepalum* in lowland evergreen rain forest, central Malaya, showing its characteristic steep, branching plank buttresses; these are a common feature of this forest formation. The bark is smooth.

Fig. 10.7. *Myristica maingayi* showing its characteristic flying buttresses. Lowland evergreen rain forest, northeast Malaya. This is one of the few timber-size, canopy-top Myristacaceae in the Asian rain forests. It can reach 45 m tall. The bark is black and closely fissured with rugose ridges; it belies the frequently repeated myth that rain forest trees all have smooth bark.

fires? Can it be dated? The 1983 fires emphasize how profoundly ignorant one still remains about the eastern rain forests.

As this chapter is being written, information about the 1983 "Great Fire of Borneo" is still being pieced together (Asiaweek, 13 July 1984; IUCN, 1984). Since it occurred folk memories have been probed and earlier droughts vaguely recalled. Of the 3×10^6 ha destroyed by the 1983 catastrophe, it is estimated that 40% were in logged forest and only 23% in primary forest, where moreover the flames were shorter-lived and less hot so that destruction was less and the recovery potential of the forest better. The piles of dead wood in logged forest became tinder-dry in the drought and highly inflammable. The logging industry in Kalimantan began in the late 1960s. The year 1983 was the first big drought since that time. It might be the case that man's activities as

commercial logger meant that a rare (but not unique) climatic perturbation was followed, when it came, by a more catastrophic fire than had ever previously occurred.

Lowland evergreen and semi-evergreen rain forests are still the most extensive formations. They are, however, under greatest pressure from the logging industry, and for conversion to agricultural land. Nowadays there are vast areas of logged forest, destroyed to varying extents depending on the intensity and date of logging, and also of secondary forest where forest destruction by logging or agriculture was complete (Figs. 10.1 and 10.10).

Fig. 10.8. *Koompassia excelsa* is the tallest broad-leaf tree ever recorded from the tropics (83.82 m in Sarawak). It occurs in the west Malesian lowland evergreen rain-forest block, in Sumatra, Malaya and Borneo. Here it is seen in central Malaya having just exchanged a complete flush of new leaves for old. Such leaf-exchange is a common feature of this forest formation. Deciduousness, which means a bare period before the new leaves flush, is rare and restricted to a few species, though some species which exchange leaves in perhumid climates may be briefly bare in more seasonal ones.

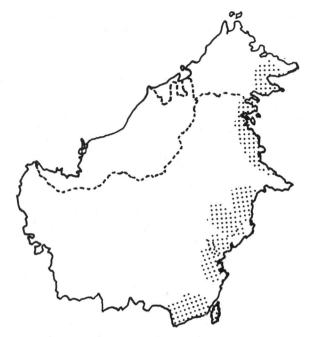

Fig. 10.9. "Extremes are more important than means". An exceptional drought which lasted most of 1982, was followed by fires in 1983. Drought and fire destroyed 3.1×10^6 ha of natural (mainly) and plantation (a little) rain forest in Kalimantan, shown here. A further burned area in north Sabah has not been mapped (IUCN, 1984). This catastrophe will profoundly affect forest structure and floristics for centuries to come and raises the question whether such freak events are, unknown to ecologists, determinant factors in these forests.

The montane rain forests (Figs. 10.11–10.14)

Lower montane, upper montane, and, on a few of the very tallest mountains, subalpine rain forests are distinct in structure, physiognomy and flora. The tree line is reached at 3720 to 3840 m on only a few scattered peaks. Above it occurs alpine grassland. Permanent snow lies on parts of the central cordillera of western New Guinea. These montane forest formations have been described very fully by Whitmore (1984a). Here attention is drawn only to a few key issues.

There is a marked *Massenerhebung* effect, with the formations occurring at much higher elevations on the giant mountains of Sumatra and New Guinea than elsewhere. On the smallest mountains the transition is from lowland to upper montane rain forest. The lower montane formation is missing.

Upper montane rain forest has structural and physiognomic similarities with heath forest and with the forest found at the centre of the best-developed domed peat bogs. There are also similarities with forest over peat on parts of limestone hills. Some species are common to these various formations. Upper montane forest may clothe the whole landscape at higher elevations, but at lower elevations occurs on ridge crests and knolls. Its lower boundary is commonly sharp, where peat accumulation on the soil surface commences, and occurs at the lower limit of prevalent cloud, which, it is believed, creates waterlogged anaerobic conditions in the humus layer and hence triggers peat development. There has been much discussion as to whether the occurrence of this highly distinctive formation is determined by nutrient deficiency, to which peat accumulation contributes, or instead to periodic drought, which certainly occurs in some upper montane forests. The various locations of other similar forests support either hypothesis. Experi-

Fig. 10.10. *Macaranga gigantifolia* growing by a logging road in east Kalimantan. This is perhaps the most spectacular species of the biggest genus of pioneer trees in the tropics (280 species, west Africa to Polynesia, 44 in Borneo, 73 in New Guinea). In west Malesia many *Macaranga* species belong to sect. *Pachystemon* with big palmately lobed leaves reminiscent of the common pioneers *Cecropia* of America and *Musanga* of Africa, but elsewhere *Macaranga* species have "normal" elliptic, pinnately nerved leaves.

mental evidence is very scanty. It seems likely that both explanations may hold, but as alternatives in different places. For example, the island of Kolombangara (1662 m) in the Solomons is exceedingly wet and has very leached soils; oligotrophy is likely. By contrast, the high volcanoes of Java have young, nutrient-rich soils but an annual dry season; periodic drought is probable.

Montane forests are fine laboratories for detailed ecophysiological studies of the relationships between trees and their environment, and rich rewards await the investigator. It would be especially interesting, for example, to study the autecology of species which occur in both lower and upper montane forests, or to see whether the litter of upper montane species really does decay slowly, and thereby locks up nutrients and contributes to oligotrophy.

Montane rain forests occur mostly on steep, broken country. They contain timber of less commercial value than lowland rain forest (the timbers of the abundant Fagaceae, for example, tend to degrade excessively on seasoning, are difficult to work, and in consequence have little commercial value). Overall, therefore, montane forests are under less threat of destruction or depletion than lowland formations, except locally, as for example at Genting Highlands, Malaysia, where a new hill station is continually expanding. It is tempting for hard-pressed land-planners to set aside areas of montane forest for the conservation of all those actual and potential economic products and cultural values of rain forest which are currently so well publicized. This is a mistake. Most of the distinctive animals of rain forest live only in the lowlands, and so do most of the many plants which provide resins, latexes, spices, fruits and rattans. There is a real fear for the survival of the orang outang and elephant in northern Sumatra if the few flattish parts of the proposed National Park there at Gunung Leuser are deforested, although the Sumatran rhinoceros has already moved into the hilly interior. Many of the conservation values of tropical rain forest are not met by the montane formations. Just as valuable timber mainly occurs in the lowlands, so do most of the animals and other useful plants (Fig. 10.14).

Heath forest (Fig. 10.15)

The heath-forest formation is found on podzolized siliceous sands (spodosols), drained by characteristic black-water streams, bearing humic acids in suspension and foaming from saponins in solution. It varies greatly in stature, as is shown by the exhaustive descriptions for Sarawak by Bruenig (1974). Its main occurrence is in Borneo. Small areas remain in Malaya (though much has now been degraded to open grassland with scattered trees) and on lesser islands of the Sunda Shelf. Forests of similar structure and physiognomy are very extensive in South America where they are called campina (forest) or Amazonian caatinga.

It has long been believed that the occurrence of

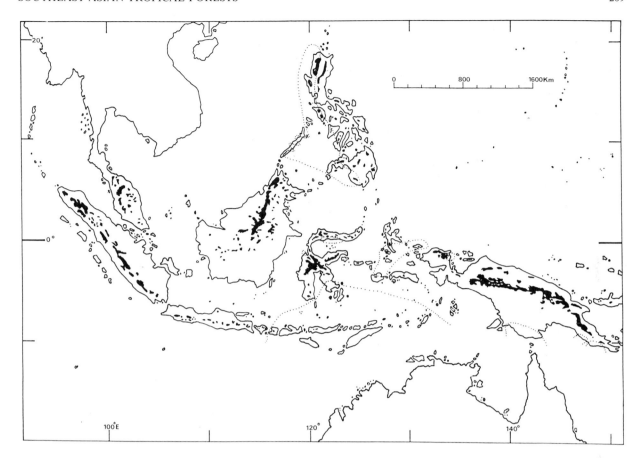

Fig. 10.11. The montane forests. Monsoon forests occur within the dotted lines, all other are rain forests. Different formations not distinguished, nor are the small areas above the tree line on highest peaks (mainly in New Guinea). Mapped simply by including areas known still to bear forests above 1500 m (Sumatra and New Guinea), 1000 m (Borneo), 900 m (elsewhere); this makes some allowance for the *Massenerhebung* effect. (Based on Whitmore, 1984b.)

heath forest in Asia is linked to extreme nutrient deficiency, though periodic water shortage has been demonstrated [see Bruenig (1969) and Baillie (1976) for Sarawak] and this too could help mould its highly distinctive structure and xeromorphic physiognomy. Recent studies in Borneo have shown, surprisingly, that the soil under virgin heath forest has mineral nutrient concentrations comparable to those under evergreen rain forest, but the soils are extremely acid (pH <4) and have a low clay concentration (Riswan, 1982; Proctor et al., 1983). Just as for upper montane forest, the different factors of periodic water stress and lack of available nutrients may both be important in this formation, and need to be disentangled for individual forests. The following scenario has been suggested (Whitmore, 1984a). Firstly, the physiog-

nomic features of uniform crown, small clustered leaves (microphylls), upturned twigs and high albedo are considered to minimize heat load at times of water shortage, thus preventing leaves from over-heating and dying. Secondly, the soils are so acid that hydrogen-ion toxicity occurs, and the low concentrations of iron and aluminium sesquioxides mean that buffering is minimal. Phenols are abundant in leaves and litter, and these too may be toxic or inhibit uptake when they leach into the soil. Fallen litter contains only small amounts of nutrients, especially nitrogen. All these factors imply a deficiency of nutrients available to the plants, even though amounts in the soil are not usually low.

Heath-forest sites are notorious for their inability to sustain agriculture. Thus, the discovery that

Fig. 10.12. Upper montane rain forest with the conifer *Dacrydium* dominant; 1700 m elevation, summit plateau of Gunung Ulu Kali, Malaya. Note that gully forest is taller than the ridge facies.

under primary forest their soil is not unduly short of mineral nutrients is surprising. Apart from the possible low availability of nutrients just considered, there is another factor. These soils are naturally low in clay (and what clay there is soon moves down the profile after felling; Riswan, 1982); the cation exchange capacity is provided mainly by humus, and this very quickly oxidizes on exposure to the sun. These soils degrade very quickly to bleached sand once the forest cover is removed. Thus they then have little ability to retain nutrients, and their surface layer gets extremely hot. It may be for these reasons that agriculture and forest renewal are very difficult.

Further investigations are needed into the water relations and nutrient economy of heath forests of different natural stature. Different samples range in height from 40 to 50 m down to low thickets (Bruenig, 1974). There seems to be a genuine difference from the apparently similar forests of southern Venezuela which have been recently described as growing on naturally nutrient-poor soils (Herrera et al., 1978).

Fig. 10.13. Upper montane rain forest with dominant *Dacrydium*, in profile, 1750 m, Gunung Ulu Kali, Malaya. Note the uniform canopy top, predominance of microphylls, dense crowns made up of dense sub-crowns (contrast Fig. 10.5) and peat accumulation on the soil surface.

Fig. 10.14. Upper and lower montane rain forest, Malayan Main Range looking northeast to Gunung Benom in the distance. Forests on steep mountains, such as these, are under much less threat of destruction than lowland forests but contain fewer animals and different, less valuable plants. It will not be sufficient to confine conservation areas to the mountains.

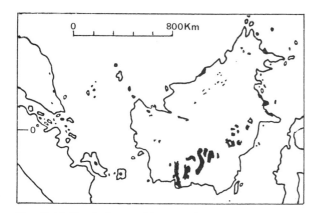

Fig. 10.15. Heath forest. This formation is found mainly in Borneo, lesser areas occur in Malaya and some of the small islands of the Sunda Shelf. Small patches occur also in west New Guinea and perhaps in north Sumatra but these have never been mapped. Places where heath forest has been replaced by grassland, or grassland with scattered tree clumps (for example, east coast Malaya) not shown. (Based on Whitmore, 1984b.)

Heath forest can support careful selective timber removal, on a polycyclic system, whereby the forest canopy is only locally broken. This is shown at Menchali forest, Malaya. Clear felling quickly leads to irreversible soil deterioration and growth of a low scrub or grassland. These forests are truly fragile.

Rain forest over limestone (Figs. 10.16 and 10.17)

Spectacular karst limestone hills are conspicuous in the landscape in various parts of Malesia. The Sarawak and Papua New Guinea limestones have the world's biggest cave systems. Coastal coralline limestone is very extensive in southwestern New Britain, and occurs throughout the Pacific islands in rain-forest climates and in the monsoon-forest climates of the Lesser Sunda Islands and Moluccas in southern Indonesia. Limestone dries out easily,

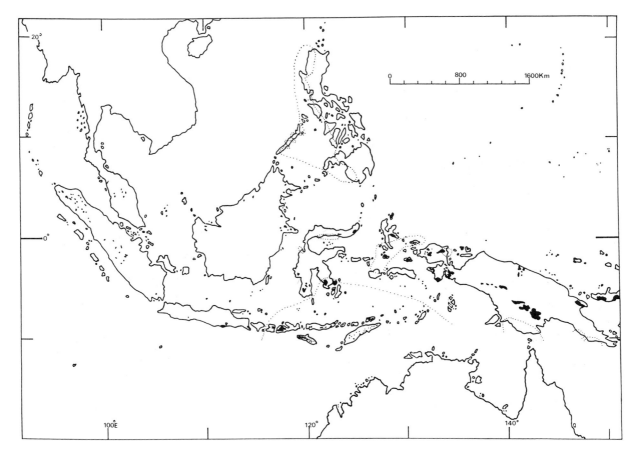

Fig. 10.16. Limestone outcrops which still carry their distinctive forest formation; in many places this has been altered by fire (often started by mineral prospectors). Rain-forest and monsoon-forest limestone are distinguished by the latter being enclosed by dotted lines. (Based on Whitmore, 1984b.)

and in many places the forest has been burned, for example by prospectors for gold, tin or guano. In monsoon climates forest over limestone has been extensively destroyed by fire; Fig. 10.16 shows how scattered are the remaining fragments. The forest on limestone in peninsular Thailand and the Indo-China peninsula is mostly monsoon forest rather than rain forest, and has been very much damaged or destroyed by burning.

The limestone hills of Malaya and Sarawak have received much attention, others less. There are many different habitats on a limestone hill. Lower talus slopes bear tall forest [studied at Gunung Mulu, Sarawak, by Proctor et al. (1983)]. There are moist ravines, dry exposed summit slopes, and areas of acid peat (referred to above) in which calcifuge plants thrive. Anderson (1965) gave a description for Sarawak (see also Whitmore, 1984a). The many habitat niches support a rich

flora with high endemism. Gesneriaceae are well developed. The continental limestone hills from Malaya north to southern China (Kweilin) support a group of extremely primitive endemic palm genera. The limestone flora of Malaya has 1210 species, of which 11% (143 species) are endemic (Chin, 1977, 1979).

The most extensive limestone area is in Papua New Guinea (Fig. 10.16). These considerable tracts are uninhabited, and extremely difficult to penetrate or to survive in. Their forests and flora remain completely undescribed. Although they have been mapped by geomorphologists (Löffler, 1974; Maire, 1983), the various maps and vegetation descriptions of the country make no mention of them. This is clearly a large gap in our knowledge.

In the species-poor Solomon Islands there are, so far as is known, no endemic species in the many

Fig. 10.17. Pulau Dayang Bunting, one of the Langkawi islands, northwest Malaya. Karst limestone with forest characteristically rich in endemic species, including the primitive palm *Maxburrettia gracilis* confined to these islands.

tracts of pericoastal coral limestone (Whitmore, 1984a).

Limestone hill forests have little commercially valuable timber. They are not under threat from logging, but damage from fire is a constant risk. Their many showy herbs, especially Balsaminaceae, Begoniaceae and Gesneriaceae, have horticultural potential, largely unexplored. In a few places in Sumatra and in Malaya limestone is much visited by hikers and naturalists, who without care can easily degrade the natural beauty. Batu Caves and Bukit Takun north of Kuala Lumpur are a *cause célèbre* in this respect. The former site also suffers from quarrying.

Forest over ultrabasic rocks

In the Solomon Islands the most distinctive lowland forest is that which occurs over ultra-basics, and these areas have been mapped by geologists from aerial photographs of the vegetation. *Casuarina papuana* and *Dillenia crenata* are dominant in many stands. At the other extreme the only outcrop of ultrabasic rocks in Malaya, near Raub, has a forest of the same structure and physiognomy as lowland evergreen rain forest. The same is true of an outcrop near Ranau, Sabah, which in fact was enumerated as an example of evergreen rain forest before study of the soil revealed the ultrabasic substrate (Fox and Tan, 1971). Several dipterocarps confined to ultrabasics in Sabah are more widely distributed in Sarawak (Meijer, 1965). In Papua New Guinea the patches of tall lowland forest along the Sepik Valley in which *Agathis labillardieri* is dominant occur on ultrabasic outcrops.

In summary, the scattered published studies indicate great diversity in the degree of distinction in forest over ultrabasic rocks within Malesia and the Solomon Islands. This may reflect a great diversity in the soils, presumably significantly in the amounts of heavy metals they contain. Outside Malesia and the Solomon Islands there are no reports of rain forest over ultrabasics from the tropical Far East. The well-known very high endemism and distinctive fire-climax "maquis" of ultrabasics in subtropical New Caledonia (Ch. 14) is different from anything else in the eastern tropics.

Beach vegetation

Beach vegetation has two facies (Van Steenis, 1957, 1961; Whitmore, 1984a). Along accreting coasts the initial vegetation is the *pes-caprae* association, a low, herbaceous plant cover of which most members are creepers and include,

prominently, *Ipomoea pes-caprae*. The species are mostly pan-tropical. The second facies is the beach forest, most of whose species in the eastern rain forests range from the east coast of Africa eastwards and right across the Pacific Ocean. This is the so-called Indo-Pacific strand flora. Species are either wind-dispersed (e.g. *Casuarina equisetifolia*) or water-dispersed (e.g. *Barringtonia asiatica*, *Calophyllum inophyllum*). The coconut *Cocos nucifera*, found wild along the strand-line of many Pacific islands, may be in origin a member of this flora. Many shrubs have big peltate or cordate, vertically held leaves, typically grey below from felted hairs or wax. Examples are *Hernandia nymphaeifolia* (*peltata*), *Hibiscus tiliaceus* and *Thespesia populnea*. The ecophysiology of these features would be interesting to investigate. The beach-forest formation is found in both perhumid and seasonally dry climates. It has been massively

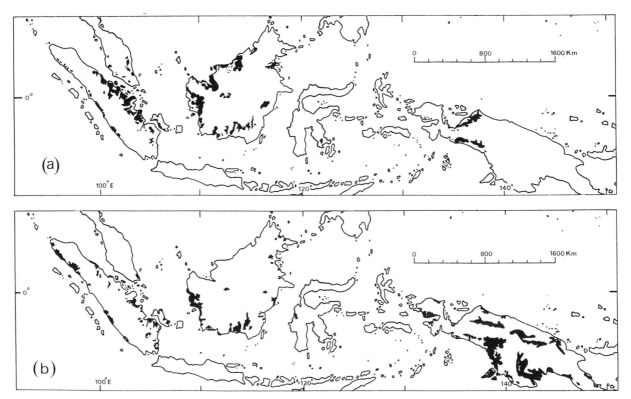

Fig. 10.18. (a) Peat swamp forest. The western stands, in Sumatra, Malaya and Borneo, have long been known but the full extent of those in west New Guinea was only discovered in 1982/83. Shallow peat lands are being developed for agriculture. Deep peat is likely to remain under forest, it is a valuable timber producing resource and has been heavily exploited in west Malesia, especially in Sarawak.

(b) Freshwater swamp forest and seasonal swamp forest formations. The extent in Sumatra, Kalimantan and west New Guinea has recently been accurately surveyed for the first time. Very substantial areas in the west have been converted to agricultural lands, especially wetland rice. Similar changes are planned for New Guinea.

destroyed, and is rarely found now in its primeval glory except on remote uninhabited islands, such as some of the Solomons. Conversion to coconut plantations has been a common fate.

Peat swamp forest (Fig. 10.18)

This formation has been described by Anderson (1983). Since then the true extent of peat swamp forest (c. 1.5×10^6 ha) in Irian Jaya and occurrences in Sumatra and Kalimantan have been accurately mapped from satellite imagery backed up by ground survey. These new findings are shown on the map.

Fresh-water swamp forest and seasonal swamp forest (Fig. 10.19)

These forest formations are very diverse in structure and floristics, partly reflecting diversity in substratum and water regime. There is, for example, a facies flooded daily, or for a few days a month at times when high tides cause river water to back up (Whitmore, 1984a). The map shows the extent of these formations which remains. It is planned that much of the huge areas in Irian Jaya will be converted to wetland rice fields over the next decade. Thereby, this extensive, sparsely populated wilderness of eastern Indonesia, still largely in its pristine state, is to be tamed, and its population to be almost doubled by transmigration from overpopulated Java and Madura. In western Malesia most of the areas of swamp forest were long ago converted — for example, the western side of the Malay peninsula.

Mangrove forest and brackish-water forest

These two contiguous forest formations are outside the scope of this volume. They have

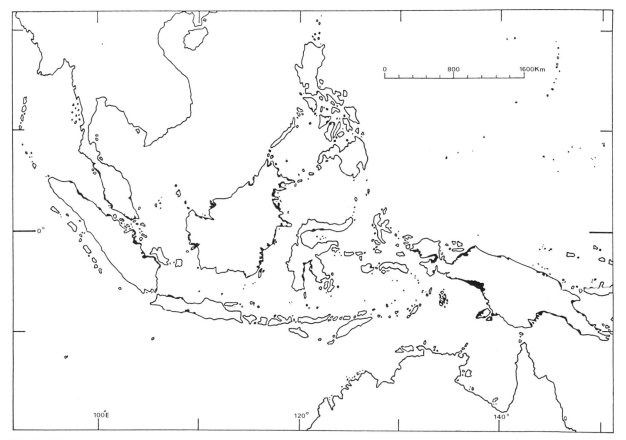

Fig. 10.19. Mangrove forests. The huge areas in West New Guinea have only recently been accurately mapped for the first time. (Based on Whitmore, 1984b.)

recently been fully described in another volume of this series (Chapman, 1977) and elsewhere (Chapman, 1975). Suffice it to say that the Sunderbans mangrove forests of the Ganges Delta (8000 km^2; Blasco, 1975) and those of western New Guinea are by far the most extensive in the world, and that the mangroves of the heartland of the eastern rain forests are richer in species than those anywhere else in the world (Hou, 1958).

During the last two decades mangroves have come under strong threat from total felling for wood chips (western New Guinea, Sabah) and conversion to industrial land, agricultural land or prawn and fish ponds (Peninsular Malaysia, Singapore). They have also begun to receive much-needed study of productivity and nutrient cycling, and of their role as nurseries for maintaining fish and shellfish stocks. A discussion of these modern developments has been given by Whitmore (1984a).

CONCLUSIONS

The climate of the eastern rain forests is more universally perhumid (or aseasonal) than that of either the African or American rain-forest regions; strong seasonality only pertains at the fringes. Probably this is the reason that a simple scheme containing thirteen formations suffices for the description of these forests.

This chapter has been limited in scope to a discussion of vegetation and plant geography. In recent years the attention of ecologists had swung away to investigations of ecosystem functioning on which many papers are now being published. It has been hoped to show here that this current trend should not be taken to suggest that the older kind of investigation has nothing more to discover. We may have a general comprehension of the tropical rain forests of the Far East, but there is still much for the well-informed biologist to contribute to human understanding of these grand places.

REFERENCES

Academia Sinica, 1979. *The Vegetation of China.* Map Publisher of the People's Republic of China, Beijing (in Chinese).
Airy Shaw, H.K., 1953. Thymelaeaceae–Gonystyloideae. *Flora Malesiana, Ser. 1,* 4: 349–365.
Anderson, J.A.R., 1965. Limestone habitat in Sarawak. In: *Proc. Symp. on Ecological Research into Humid Tropics Vegetation.* UNESCO, Kuching.
Anderson, J.A.R., 1983. The tropical peat swamps of western Malesia. In: A.J.P. Gore (Editor) *Mires: Swamp, Bog, Fen and Moor. B. Regional Studies.* (Ecosystems of the World, 4) Elsevier, Amsterdam, pp. 181–200.
Ashton, P.S., 1969. Speciation amongst tropical trees: some deductions in the light of recent evidence. *Biol. J. Linn. Soc.,* 1: 155–196.
Audley Charles, M.G., 1981. Geological history of the region of Wallace's Line. In: T.C. Whitmore (Editor), *Wallace's Line and Plate Tectonics.* Clarendon, Oxford, pp. 24–35.
Audley Charles, M.G., Hurley, A.M. and Smith, A.G., 1981. Continental movements in the Mesozoic and Cenozoic. In: T.C. Whitmore (Editor), *Wallace's Line and Plate Tectonics.* Clarendon, Oxford, pp. 9–23.
Axelrod, D.I. and Raven, P.H., 1982. Palaeobiogeography and origin of the New Guinea Flora. In: J.L. Gressitt (Editor), *Biogeography and Ecology of New Guinea.* Junk, The Hague, pp. 919–944.
Baillie, I.C., 1976. Further studies on drought in Sarawak, East Malaysia. *J. Trop. Geogr.,* 43: 20–29.
Baur, G.N., 1968. *The Ecological Basis of Rain Forest Management.* New South Wales Forestry Commission, Sydney, N.S.W.
Blasco, F., 1975. Les mangroves l'Inde. *Pondichery Inst. Fr., Trav. Sect. Sci. Tech.,* 14.
Bruenig, E.F., 1969. On the seasonality of drought in the lowlands of Sarawak (Borneo). *Erdkunde,* 23: 127–133.
Bruenig, E.F., 1974. *Ecological Studies in the Kerangas Forests of Sarawak and Brunei.* Bornes Literature Bureau, Kuching.
Champion, H.G., 1936. A preliminary survey of the vegetation types of India and Burma. *Indian For. Rec., New Ser.,* 1: 1–286.
Champion, H.G. and Seth, S.K., 1968. *A Revised Survey of the Forest Types of India.* Manager of Publications, Delhi.
Chang, D.H.S., 1981. The vegetation zonation of the Tibetan plateau. *Mount. Res. Dev.,* 1: 29–48.
Chapman, V.J., 1975. *Mangrove Vegetation.* Cramer, Vaduz.
Chapman, V.J. (Editor), 1977. *Wet Coastal Ecosystems.* (Ecosystems of the World, 1) Elsevier, Amsterdam, 440 pp.
Chin, S.C., 1977. The limestone hill flora of Malaya. I. *Gard. Bull. Singapore,* 30: 165–219.
Chin, S.C., 1979. The limestone hill flora of Malaya. II. *Gard. Bull. Singapore,* 32: 64–203.
Cockburn, P.S., 1974. The origin of the Sook Plain, Sabah. *Malay. For.,* 37: 61–63.
Cranbrook, Lord, 1981. The vertebrate faunas. In: T.C. Whitmore (Editor), *Wallace's Line and Plate Tectonics.* Clarendon, Oxford, pp. 57–69.
De Laubenfels, J., 1969. A revision of the Malesian and Pacific rainforest conifers. I. Podocarpaceae. *J. Arn. Arbor., Harvard Univ.,* 50: 274–314, 315–369.
De Rosayro, R.A., 1974. Vegetation of humid tropical Asia. In: *Natural Resources of Humid Tropical Asia.* UNESCO, Paris.
De Wilde, W.J.J.O., 1983. *Horsfieldia* inside and outside Malesia. *Acta Bot. Neerl.,* 32: p. 117.
Dransfield, J., 1981. Palms and Wallace's Line. In: T.C.

Whitmore (Editor), *Wallace's Line and Plate Tectonics.* Clarendon, Oxford, pp. 43–57.

Fox, J.E.D. and Tan, H., 1971. Soils and forest on an ultrabasic hill north-east of Ranau, Sabah. *J. Trop. Geogr.,* 32: 38–48.

George, W., 1981. Wallace and his line. In: T.C. Whitmore (Editor), *Wallace's Line and Plate Tectonics.* Clarendon, Oxford, pp. 3–8.

Gill, A.E. and Rasmusson, E.M., 1983. The 1982–83 climate anomaly in the equatorial Pacific. *Nature,* 306: 229–234.

Gunatilleke, C.V.S. and Gunatilleke, I.A.U.N., 1981. The floristic composition of Sinharaja — a rain forest in Sri Lanka with special references to endemics and diptero-carps. *Malay. For.,* 44: 386–396.

Hedegart, T., 1976. Breeding systems, variation and genetic improvement of teak (*Tectona grandis* L.F.). In: J. Burley and B.T. Styles (Editors), *Tropical Trees, Variation, Breeding and Conservation.* Academic Press, London, pp. 109–124.

Herrera, R., Jordon, C.F., Klinge, H. and Medina, E., 1978. Amazon ecosystems, their structure and functioning with particular emphasis on nutrients. *Interciencia,* 3: 223–231.

Hou, D., 1958. Rhizophoraceae. *Flora Malesiana, Ser. I,* 5: 429–493.

I.U.C.N., 1984. Kalimantan — biggest fire ever? *I.U.C.N. Bull.* 15(7).

Jacobs, M., 1974. Botanical panorama of the Malesian archipelago (vascular plants). In: *Natural Resources of Humid Tropical Asia.* UNESCO, Paris.

Kartawinata, K., Abdulhadi, T. and Partomihardjo, T., 1981. Composition and structure of a lowland dipterocarp forest at Wanariset, East Kalimantan. *Malay. For.,* 44: 397–406.

Lanly, J.P., 1982. Tropical forest resources. *F.A.O. For. Pap.* 30: 1–106.

Legris, P., 1974. Vegetation and floristic composition of humid tropical continental Asia. In: *Natural Resources of Humid Tropical Asia.* UNESCO, Paris.

Löffler, E., 1974. Geomorphological map of New Guinea (1.1 million) plus explanatory notes. *Land Res. Ser. C.S.I.R.O.,* 33.

Mabberley, D.J., 1979. The species of *Chisocheton* (Meliaceae). *Bull. Br. Mus. Nat. Hist.,* 6: 301–386.

Maire, R., 1983. Les Karsts de haute montagne et la notion d'étagement des karsts en Nouvelle Guinée. *Rev. Géomorphol. Dyn.,* 32: 49–68.

Meijer, W., 1965. Forest types in North Borneo and their economic aspects. In: *Proc. Symp. on Ecological Research into Humid Tropics Vegetation.* UNESCO, Kuching.

Ng, F.S.P. (Editor), 1978. *Tree Flora of Malaya 3.* Longman, Kuala Lumpur.

Ng, F.S.P. and Low, C.M., 1982. Check list of endemic tree of the Malay peninsula. *Malay. For. Dept. Research Pamphlet* 88.

Peeris, C.V.S., 1975. *The Ecology of the Endemic Tree Species of Sri Lanka in Relation to their Conservation.* Ph.D. thesis, Aberdeen Univ., Aberdeen.

Prance, G.T., Rodrigues, W.A. and De Silva, M.F., 1976. Inventario florestal de um hectare de mata de terra firme km 30 da estrada Manaus–Itacoatiara. *Acta Amazon.,* 6: 9–35.

Proctor, J., Anderson, J.M., Chai, P. and Vallack, H.W., 1983.

Ecological studies in four contrasting rain forests in Gunung Mulu National Park, Sarawak. I. Forest environment. *J. Ecol.,* 71: 237–260.

Richards, P.W., 1943. The ecological segregation of the Indo-Malayan and Australian elements in the vegetation of Borneo. *Proc. Linn. Soc. N.S.W.,* 154: 154–156.

Riswan, S., 1982. *Ecological Studies on Primary, Secondary and Experimentally Cleared Mixed Dipterocarp Forest and Kerangas Forest in East Kalimantan, Indonesia.* Ph.D. thesis, Aberdeen Univ., Aberdeen.

Schimper, A.F.W., 1903. *Plant-Geography upon a Physiological Basis.* Oxford Univ. Press, Oxford.

Sleumer, H., 1966. Ericaceae. *Flora Malesiana, Ser. I,* 6: 469–668.

Smith, J.M.B., 1982. Origins of the tropicalpine flora. In: J.L. Gressitt (Editor), *Biogeography and Ecology of New Guinea.* Junk, The Hague, pp. 287–308.

Smitinand, T., Webb, L.J., Santisuk, T. and Tracey, J.G., 1982. A cooperative attempt to compare the habitats of primary forest in Thailand and northern Australia. In: *Ecological Basis for Rational Resource Utilization in the Humid Tropics of South East Asia.* Univ. Pertanian Malaysia, Serdang, pp. 77–107.

Stevens, P.F., 1982. Phytogeography and evolution of the Ericaceae of New Guinea. In: J.L. Gressitt (Editor), *Biogeography and Ecology of New Guinea.* Junk, The Hague, pp. 331–354.

Van Balgooy, M.M.J., 1971. Plant geography in the Pacific. *Blumea (Suppl.),* 6: 1–122.

Van Steenis, C.G.G.J., 1950. The delimitation of Malaysia and its main plant geographical divisions. *Flora Malesiana, Ser. I,* 1: IXX–IXXV.

Van Steenis, C.G.G.J., 1957. Outline of vegetation types in Indonesia and some adjacent regions. *Proc. Pac. Sci. Congress* 8(4): 61–97.

Van Steenis, C.G.G.J., 1961. Discrimination of tropical shore formations. In: *Proc. Symp. on Humid Tropics Vegetation.* UNESCO, Tjiawi.

Van Steenis, C.G.G.J., 1964. Plant geography of the mountain flora of Mt. Kinabalu. *Proc. R. Soc. London, Ser. B,* 161: 7–37.

Van Steenis, C.G.G.J., 1972. *The Mountain Flora of Java.* Brill, Leiden.

Van Steenis, C.G.G.J., 1979. Plant geography of east Malesia. *Bot. J. Linn. Soc.,* 79: 97–178.

Vidal, J.E., 1979. Outline of ecology and vegetation of the Indo-Chinese Peninsula. In: K. Larsen and L.B. Holm Nielsen (Editors), *Tropical Botany.* Academic Press, London.

Walker, D. and Flenley, J.R., 1979. Late Quaternary vegetational history of the Enga Province of upland Papua New Guinea. *Philos. Trans. R. Soc. London, Ser. B,* 286: 265–344.

Walker, D. and Hope, G.S., 1982. Late Quaternary vegetation history. In: J.L. Gressitt (Editor), *Biogeography and Ecology of New Guinea.* Junk, The Hague, pp. 263–286.

Wang, C.W., 1961. *The Forests of China.* Maria Moor Cabots Foundation, Boston, Mass., Publ. 5.

Webb, L.J. and Tracey, J.G., 1967. An ecological guide to new planting areas and site potential for hoop pine. *Aust. For.,* 31: 224–239.

Webb, L.J., Tracey, J.G. and Williams, W.T., 1984. A floristic framework of Australian rain forests. *Aust. J. Ecol.*, 9: 169–198.

White, K.J., 1973. The lowland rain forest in Papua New Guinea. *Pacific Sci. Assoc. Precongress conf. in Indonesia: Planned Utilization of the Lowland Tropical Forests.* Pacific Science Association, Bogor.

Whitmore, T.C., 1969. The vegetation of the Solomon Islands. *Philos. Trans. R. Soc. London, Ser. B*, 255: 259–270.

Whitmore, T.C. (Editor), 1972. *Tree Flora of Malaya 1.* Longman, Kuala Lumpur.

Whitmore, T.C., 1973a. Plate tectonics and some aspects of Pacific plant geography. *New Phytol.*, 72: 1185–1190.

Whitmore, T.C. (Editor), 1973b. *Tree Flora of Malaya 2.* Longman, Kuala Lumpur.

Whitmore, T.C., 1974. Change with time and the role of cyclones in tropical rain forest on Kolombangara, Solomon Islands. *Commonw. For. Inst., Pap.* 46.

Whitmore, T.C., 1975. *Tropical Rain Forests of the Far East.* Clarendon, Oxford.

Whitmore, T.C., 1980. A monograph of *Agathis. Plant Syst. Evol.*, 135: 41–69.

Whitmore, T.C. (Editor), 1981. *Wallace's Line and Plate Tectonics.* Clarendon, Oxford.

Whitmore, T.C., 1982. Fleeting glimpses of some Chinese rain forests. *Commonw. For. Rev.*, 61: 51–58.

Whitmore, T.C., 1984a. *Tropical Rain Forests of the Far East.* Clarendon, Oxford (2nd ed.).

Whitmore, T.C., 1984b. A vegetation map of Malesia at scale 1:5 million. *J. Biogeogr.*, 11: 461–471.

Whittaker, T.H., 1972. Evolution and measurement of species diversity. *Taxon*, 21: 213–251.

Wolfe, J.A., 1979. Temperature parameters of humid to mesic forests of eastern Asia and relation to forests of other regions of the northern hemisphere and Australasia. *U.S. Geol. Surv., Prof. Pap.*, 1106.

Wu, Z., 1979. *The Vegetation of China.* Academica Sinica, Beijing (in Chinese).

Wyatt-Smith, J., 1966. Ecological studies on Malayan forests 1. *Malay. For. Dept. Res. Pamphlet* 52.

Chapter 11

DIPTEROCARP REPRODUCTIVE BIOLOGY

PETER S. ASHTON

INTRODUCTION

Though the exclusively tropical tree family Dipterocarpaceae is now known to have a world-wide distribution, it is only in Asia that anything is known concerning the reproductive biology of the species. This is because in Asia alone the family achieves ecological dominance. Also, the timbers of certain sections of the mainly emergent genus *Shorea*, known as meranti, currently supply almost half of the volume of hardwoods in world trade. The dipterocarps of Asia, Africa and South America belong to three distinct subfamilies, Dipterocarpoideae, Monotoideae and Pakaraimoideae, the first of which Maury (1978, 1979) has suggested should be raised to a family. Though there are a number of shared characteristics which link the three, there is ample justification for discussing the Dipterocarpoidcae in isolation, as must be done here.

The biology of the dipterocarpoids has been reviewed by Ashton (1982). They occur from the Seychelles and Sri Lanka where there are more than forty species of which all but one are endemic, through southern and eastern India to Hainan, southeast to Sundaland where their species diversity reaches its zenith, and east to New Guinea and the Louisiades. Most abundant at low altitudes, they can occur to 2000 m as scattered groups, and in Sri Lanka as gregarious stands (Ashton, 1980).

The subfamily occurs in three principal forest formations, mainly climatically defined. Its species are generally, though by no means always, dominant in the canopy where they occur. These formations are medium-stature evergreen or semi-evergreen savanna woodland, in which the canopy is closed if undisturbed, but in which the under-storey is periodically burned; and two types of more or less tall evergreen forest within which fire is a rare event. The first of the two types prevails where there is a predictable dry season though, as shall be described, more or less severe droughts occur supra-annually (once every few years) through prolongation of the dry season. Though overall forest structure does not differ between these two types, and there is considerable and parallel variation with site conditions within them the forest communities in regions lacking a season in which evapotranspiration predictably exceeds precipitation, here called on this account aseasonal regions, are of the order of 2 to 5 times richer in species. Also, dipterocarps differ substantially and consistently in thcir reproductive biology and demography between the two types, so they will be treated separately here.

DRY EVERGREEN FORESTS

These forests are generally of medium stature, with an even canopy lacking emergents. They are frequently dominated by a single species. They are maintained by periodic fire. Nowadays, they are often open-canopied as a result of felling, or the effects of browsing and burning on regeneration over many decades.

After teak, more publications on the biology and silviculture of the dipterocarp heavy hardwood Sal (*Shorea robusta*) exist than on any other tropical timber tree (see Joshi et al., 1980, for a comprehensive review). Sal occurs in the Himalayan foothills from northwestern Himachal Pradesh to central Assam and south to Tripura, and in the east of the peninsula south to Andhra, on soils of moderate to high acidity generally overlying sediments, including alluvium and acid igneous rocks. It is the only dipterocarp in the forests in which it occurs.

The species extends over a considerable range of climates, with dry seasons of from four to seven months. Throughout, Sal is a gregarious tree. Nowadays, it most often comprises more than half of the canopy cover, although this is the result of management at least towards the extremes of its range. At its wettest, northeastern limits, during periods without fire the regeneration competes unfavourably with other, fire-sensitive, evergreen species which ultimately will replace it (Milroy, 1930).

Sal is a diploid ($2n = 14$; Roy and Jha, 1965). Embryogenesis is normal and of the *Polygonum* type (Rao, 1956). Sal flowers towards the beginning of the hot dry season; and the fruit falls at the commencement of the following monsoon. Sal trees, when grown in the open, fruit for the first time at 15 years (Champion and Seth, 1968). At flowering, the trees have lost most of their leaves, a new flush appearing with the ripening fruits. The degree of deciduousness increases with the mean length of the dry season. The dry season begins in November. The buds open in late January or in February, and flowering continues for about five weeks (Krishnaswamy and Mathauda, 1954). The trees are broadly synchronized, but individual trees can flower for less than half the period of the whole stand. The pollinator is unknown.

The flowers are copiously borne on spreading axillary and terminal panicles up to 23 cm in length. The buds are *c.* 1.5 cm long and fusiform; the open corolla is *c.* 2.5 cm diameter. The open flower is pendant and very delicate, easily falling if handled. The petals are cream to deep pink on different trees (Davidson, 1938; De, 1938); they are contorted and fall, usually as a loosely connate corona, with the *c.* 30 stamens adnate at their bases. The anthers are four-locular. They are surmounted by a bristled club-shaped connectival appendage which, with the anthers, becomes somewhat reflexed at anthesis so that the urn-shaped base of the corolla is closed by a palisade. The pollen is released into this cage. Though the flower is pendant, the chances of accidental self-pollination are slight, for the small stigmatic pad caps a style which projects well beyond the

appendages. The pollen grains, which are similar in gross morphology throughout the subfamily (Maury et al., 1975; Muller, 1979, 1982) are spherical, smooth and slightly sticky.

Though no quantitative studies of post-anthesis mortality have been published, the majority of the flowers initially set young fruits. The calyx, which is imbricate in flower, is persistent in dipterocarps. In *Shorea*, three of the five sepals expand into wings. The 3-celled ovary contains six ovules at first, but only one develops. This embryo expands to its full size within the seed after the wings have developed. By the time the fruit are ripe, they are much reduced in number. Though weevils predate the developing embryo, the principal cause of mortality at this stage is unknown.

Fruit production occurs almost annually, but varies much between years; heavy fruiting occurs at intervals of 3 to 5 years (Champion and Seth, 1968). At Dehra Dun, between 1926 and 1954, these authors recorded 5 good, 16 moderate and 7 poor years. It is unclear, from the literature, whether poor flowering is the main cause of poor fruiting. Storms during flowering and early fruiting can destroy the crop, but flowering intensity does vary greatly between years (Krishnaswamy and Mathauda, 1954; Champion and Seth, 1968).

Seed dispersal of dipterocarps is said to be by wind but, once the fruit has penetrated the canopy, most lateral movement will be effected through gyration on account of the slightly twisted wings. The embryos are rich in fats. Though ground squirrels transport the fruits and store them in caches, they likely do not carry them far.

A mature sal will drop *c.* 4000 viable seeds in a good year (Champion and Pant, 1931). The seeds have little dormancy, and germinate within a few days of falling. The cotyledons of the mature embryo are fleshy and unequal, one enfolding the other. At germination, the radicle protrudes through the apex of the pericarp, which thereby splits, irregularly and longitudinally. Extension proceeds rapidly. The apex penetrates the litter if successful establishment is to occur, and anchors before the cotyledons expand and become freed from the husk. Thick litter is inimical to successful establishment. Behind the root apex, a collar of slime is secreted into which the root hairs expand. Later, the first adventitious roots appear.

Seedling establishment is variable, and has been

the subject of much research. Though seed size is variable, both within and between trees, there is no relation between size and germinability (Shaukat Husain, 1927, 1928; Champion, 1927, 1928; Champion and Pant, 1931). Champion and Pant found the crown size and vigor of the parent to be positively correlated with germination percentage, establishment percentage, and initial height growth. Delayed rains can be catastrophic (Bailey and Champion, 1927; Ford Robertson, 1927). Smythies (1918) noted that, though 85% of the season's crop can die back during their first dry season, most recover. Even frost (in the Himalayan foothills) affects regeneration less than it does older trees (Osmaston, 1928). Though soil water-retaining capacity can affect seedling mortality during the first dry season under some circumstances (Seth and Bhatnagar, 1959), it is generally agreed that early seedling mortality is greatest during the first two wet seasons (Smythies, 1918), when at least three-quarters of initially established seedlings die. Makins (1920) noted that, though sal seedlings are shade-tolerant, establishment is greater under the crowns of other species than their own. This has been ascribed to the soggy conditions which persist during the monsoon under the litter of the parent tree (Makins, 1920; Smythies, 1926, 1936; Bailey and Champion, 1927; Ford Robertson, 1927; Osmaston, 1928; Chaturvedi, 1929; Champion, 1933; Mobbs, 1936; Anon., 1940; De, 1941; Jacob, 1941; Sahay, 1955; Raynor, 1960). On this account, light ground fires before fruit-fall, and ground-working if compaction exists, have been used as standard regeneration procedures following the now classical experiments conducted by Smythies in Uttar Pradesh during the twenties, with modifications at the two climatic extremes and where extraneous factors such as browsing and trampling intervene.

Once established, however, the species has a strong capacity to coppice (De, 1925, 1941; Howard, 1925; Nicholson, 1925). Year after year, the sapling may be killed to the ground by fire, and, if nothing more palatable is around, browsed by deer or cattle. But a stout deep taproot is meanwhile developing, and can ultimately descend for more than three meters. Eventually, following the favorable combination of some short dry seasons without fire and low browsing pressures, a strong leader is established which thereafter per-

sists (Chaturvedi, 1929). Thick fissured fire-resistant bark develops. As the tree grows larger, its capacity to coppice and shoot epicormically declines, but is never completely lost. Howard (1925) claimed, though, that the epicormic branches seen so abundantly on mature trees, especially when open-grown, arise in youth and persist.

Sal is extraordinarily variable, both within stands and regionally, in form, phenology, leaf and fruit size. Bearing in mind also its gregariousness and roughly synchronous flowering, it appears that the tree is an outbreeder.

This description of sal, to the extent that knowledge is available, broadly applies to other dipterocarpoids of this forest formation. There are five others, all confined to Indo-Burma in the community to which Champion (1961) restricted the name Dry Dipterocarp forest. No details of their phenology are published though only one, *Shorea siamensis*, is completely deciduous. All flower during the dry season, and fruit at the onset of the wet. In the three species of *Dipterocarpus* the seed is enclosed by, but free from, the fused base of the calyx. In *D. tuberculatus* and *S. siamensis* at least, regeneration is overwhelmingly by coppicing, and seedling establishment rare in nature (Blanford, 1915; Nixon, 1929; Unwin, 1931), though Blanford found that a light ground fire before seed-fall encouraged seedling establishment in the former.

The species in this community are variable too, notably in the distribution and density of tomentum. Interestingly, though hybridization is uncommon among dipterocarps, there are several records of morphological hybrids in seasonal forests, particularly in *Dipterocarpus* (Kerr, 1914; Parker, 1927; Parkinson, 1932). Hybrids among the dry evergreen species are unknown, but there are several records, in *Shorea* as well as *Dipterocarpus*, of the occurrence of mature trees morphologically intermediate between species of dry and seasonal evergreen forest, presumably in the ecotone which frequently separates them. This suggests close genetic similarity, and likely recent common ancestry, of dry evergreen and evergreen forest species.

SEASONAL EVERGREEN DIPTEROCARP FOREST

This forest type occurs in the intermediate zone of western and southern Sri Lanka and the

Western Ghats of Peninsular India, the Andaman Islands, and widely from Assam and Chittagong eastwards to southernmost Yunnan and Hainan, then south to Perlis in northwest peninsular Malaysia; also in parts of Sulawesi, the Moluccas and New Guinea, Bali and Lombok. Altogether, about sixty dipterocarps species occur in this formation. They are, without exception, members of the mature phase of the forest, though in New Guinea *Anisoptera thurifera* is said to re-establish early following cultivation.

Information on the reproductive biology of these species is scant, though Indian and Indochinese foresters have long recognized difficulties in managing them through natural regeneration (Chengappa, 1934, 1937, 1944; Seth and Dabral, 1960; Joshi et al., 1980). The absence of fire notwithstanding, in most other respects the species of *Anisoptera*, *Dipterocarpus*, *Hopea* and *Shorea* occurring in these forests appear to resemble sal in their reproductive biology (Joshi et al., 1980). About *Vatica*, though, nothing is known. These dipterocarps flower during the dry season, but are evergreen or only very briefly deciduous. Populations flower over a relatively short period, the individuals being tightly synchronized (personal observation). In *Dipterocarpus*, flowering is annual but seedlings rare except following occasional unusually heavy fruiting (Chengappa, 1934, 1937, 1944; Kadambi, 1954a, b; Seth and Dabral, 1960). In *D. indicus* abundant fruiting only occurs at long intervals (Kadambi, 1954), in the riparian *D. alatus* about every two years (Chengappa, 1934, 1937, 1944; Joshi et al., 1980). In South India *Hopea parviflora* is said to fruit prolifically every 4 to 6 years, followed by up to two years of "comparative sterility"; stands of *H. utilis* alternate between 2 to 3 heavy, and 2 to 3 light fruiting years; while *H. wightiana* fruits heavily "at frequent intervals" (Kadambi, 1954a, b). In northeastern India, *Shorea assamica* fruits heavily every 3 to 4 years; there is much pre-fall damage by insects, and post-fall predation is also heavy (Chowdhuri, 1960). Though *Vateria indica* flowers annually, copious fruiting occurs only every 4 to 5 years (Kadambi, 1954a, b). It is clear that heavy fruitings cannot coincide among sympatric species, but it has not been recorded whether heavy flowerings do so.

Predation of the very young fruit of *Dipterocarpus* by insects and sometimes parakeets is excep-

tionally severe, and the large seed are commonly predated after falling by scolytid beetles, deer and pigs. Late rains prevent any successful establishment in many years (Chengappa, 1934, 1937, 1944).

Evergreen forest dipterocarps lose their capacity to coppice soon after the sapling stage (Joshi et al., 1980). These forests differ notably from those of sal and other savanna species in the rarity of pole-sized trees, especially of *Dipterocarpus*, in nature; though some of the *Hopea* species in the Western Ghats and Indo-Burma are in this respect exceptional (Kadambi, 1954b; Joshi et al., 1980; Ashton, pers. observ.). This, combined with the generally low seedling survival, *Hopea* excepted, and in some cases low establishment rates also, explains the great difficulty of regenerating the forests after exploitation. In view of the abundance of these refractory species in the primary forest canopy, it must be assumed that sufficient regeneration does get through over the years in nature. Chengappa (1944) found that understorey clearing, and raising of the canopy, achieved successful *Dipterocarpus* regeneration in the Andamans, but that easy access by the seedling radicle to mineral soil was also essential, as in sal.

A notable respect in which these forests differ from dry evergreen woodlands is in the general absence of single-species dominance in the canopy, which here is structurally heterogeneous, the larger dipterocarps and some legumes and others becoming emergent. The dipterocarps rarely comprise half the canopy as a whole, though more than half of the emergents often belong to the family. Though the species population densities of the sexually mature individuals is therefore lower, the individuals are generally more or less strongly clumped. The possible reasons for this will be discussed in the next section.

In marked contrast with dry evergreen species, and in spite of the frequent records of hybridization, species of seasonal evergreen forest are on the whole morphologically extraordinarily constant. Even *Dipterocarpus turbinatus* and *Shorea roxburghii* whose populations, disjunct in peninsular India and Indo-Burma, have likely been so divided for millions of years, differ only in certain trivial quantitative respects. The *Hopea* species in this formation are of particular interest: With a few exceptions species in other genera are wide-ranging, but *Hopea* species are often highly local and frequently endemic. This will also be discussed later.

ASEASONAL EVERGREEN DIPTEROCARP FORESTS

These forests prevail through southwestern Sri Lanka, in Peninsular Malaysia, Sumatra, Borneo and the Philippines, and probably originally in lowland west Java. Analogous forests, though poor in dipterocarp species which are generally subordinate in the canopy there, occur in eastern Indonesia especially Irian (New Guinea). Altogether, about 400 dipterocarp species occur in these forests. It is remarkable that the increase in the number of species through the sequence of the three forest formations is almost an order of magnitude in each case. As will be seen, the reproductive biology of dipterocarps in the evergreen, so-called Mixed Dipterocarp, forests differs from that of the preceding two formations more than they differ from one another.

Regional species richness of the family, and degree of single species dominance in this formation is correlated both to local endemism, habitat diversity, and island biogeographic factors. In northwestern Borneo for instance, a region of exceptional soils diversity, there are 242 described species, of which 89 are unknown elsewhere on the island notwithstanding its position on the Sunda shelf. In the whole of Borneo, 155 of the 267 species are endemic (Ashton, 1982). Ashton (1964, 1969) found single species dominance to increase on both the least and also on the most fertile soils in northwestern Borneo. In the Moluccas, an archipelago sandwiched between the Sunda and the Sahul shelves and east of Wallace's line, only one of the six species is endemic and *Shorea selanica* widely dominates the emergent canopy (Ashton, 1982). It seems generally to be true that Dry Evergreen forest species such as sal have wider edaphic amplitudes than those of Evergreen Dipterocarp forests, and this seems also to be true for species of Seasonal versus Evergreen Aseasonal forests though *Hopea dyeri*, for instance, appears to be strictly confined to podzolic soils in Indochina.

There is, too, a distinct high-altitude element, generally confined above 1000 m, with high ende-

mism in Sri Lanka, and some also in Malaya and Borneo but no species, interestingly, in New Guinea in spite of the extensiveness and height of its mountains.

Though the major islands and island groups of the Far East, notably Borneo, the Philippines and New Guinea, each possess a distinct endemic element whose members are nevertheless widespread within their distributional limits, certain more local regions are rich in endemics. These are southwestern Sri Lanka, northwestern Borneo, northeastern Borneo, western and southwestern, and southeastern New Guinea, northwestern and eastern peninsular Malaysia, and northern Luzon, in that order. The possible significance of dipterocarp reproductive biology in this regard will be discussed.

The most striking reproductive characteristic of the dipterocarps in this formation is their supra-annual flowering phenology. First noted among the dipterocarps of peninsular Malaysia (Ridley, 1901; Foxworthy, 1932), and later northeastern Borneo (Wood, 1956), it is neither confined to dipterocarps, nor do all dipterocarps or regions manifest it in like manner. Though records of annual flowering are fortunately fairly complete for the State of Selangor in western peninsular Malaysia over the last fifty years (the Second World War excepted), they are more patchy elsewhere in the peninsula, in Sabah and Sarawak (Wood, 1956; Smythies, 1958; Burgess, 1972; Cockburn, 1975), and also Sri Lanka (Holmes, 1942; Koelmeyer, 1959), but non-existent elsewhere.

In peninsular Malaysia many mature-phase tree species, including most dipterocarps, flower more heavily at intervals of 3 to 5 years. Among those that do not habitually flower in the intervals, there may be a lesser flowering in the year preceding or following the mass-flowering year. Besides Dipterocarpaceae, families as diverse as the legumes (notably Caesalpiniaceae), Polygalaceae and Bombacaceae in the canopy, and Myristicaceae and Euphorbiaceae in the understorey, possess genera in which flowering may be rigidly supra-annual, and in many canopy taxa is synchronized with the dipterocarps (Medway, 1972; Appanah, 1979; Yap, 1982). Others flower annually, or supra-annually but more frequently than dipterocarps, but particularly profusely in dipterocarp years (Appanah). Yet others, such as the understorey tree *Xerospermum noronhianum* (Sapindaceae), flower annually, but with periodic heavy flowering years which are not synchronized with those of the dipterocarps (Appanah, 1979, 1982).

Gregarious flowering (Fig. 11.1) may be confined to a single district, or spread throughout the whole region (Burgess, 1972; Sasaki et al., 1979); adjacent districts may flower in the same season, but up to several months apart (Wood, 1956; Sasaki et al., 1979; Chan and Appanah, 1980). Both Ridley (1901) and Burgess (1972) commented that it is possible to find wild dipterocarps in flower somewhere in peninsular Malaysia every year. This notwithstanding, several years can pass without a single flowering *Shorea* being observed within a particular forest, and a flowering year is an unforgettable experience (Wood, 1956).

Certain species, notably *Neobalanocarpus heimii* species of *Dryobalanops* and some of *Dipterocarpus* flower more frequently, sometimes heavily, outside the principal flowering years, though even then not annually at any one site (Chan, 1977; Appanah, 1979).

In Sri Lanka there appears to be some flowering every year, though varying greatly in intensity and between species (Holmes, 1942; Koelmeyer, 1959). *Shorea* and *Hopea* species there generally do not flower annually, except in *Shorea* section *Doona* where some individuals in perhaps all species can be found in flower every year. Koelmeyer found numbered trees of *S. (Doona) congestiflora* to flower five times, and to fruit 3 to 4 times, over the ten years 1942/1951. In a *Dipterocarpus zeylanicus* population, he found at least one tree in flower every year, though the number in flower varied. Over the same decade, two heavy flowerings were noted, in 1948 and 1951. Trees in a *D. hispidus* population flowered at most four years during the decade, and fruited heavily as a population only in 1947, though some fruiting occurred also in 1949. Lowland understorey species of the endemic genus *Stemonoporus* appear to flower annually, and over periods which can exceed one month. Unlike other dipterocarps, they present few flowers daily (pers. observ.). In this they resemble the curious peninsular Malaysian local endemic *Dipterocarpus concavus* which presents a few flowers continuously in

Fig. 11.1. In Sri Lanka, different dipterocarp species may flower in different years. Here, synchronous gregarious flowering exposes two "drifts", at left middle distance and mid-right background, of *Shorea trapezifolia*, section *Doona*.

the Kepong Arboretum, but whose phenology in the wild is unknown. Koelmeyer did not recognize a definite familial flowering cycle in Sri Lanka.

Interestingly, planted individuals of many species will flower outside the main flowering years more frequently than they do in primary forest, where such instances are rather rare in many species (Ng, 1977, 1981; see also Sasaki et al., 1979). Riparian species also flower more frequently (Ridley, 1901; pers. observ.). Also, the canopy species as a rule flower for the first time only after their crowns have emerged. When planted as isolated individuals some can even flower precociously in their second year, though onset is generally 10 to 20 years (Kochummen, 1961; Ng, 1966, 1980; Srivastava, 1977; Tang, 1978; Lee, 1980), which is still earlier than in nature. Viable seed have been recorded in trees six years old (Lee, 1980; Tang, 1978). In *Vatica* where, alone among Far Eastern genera, the flowers are in most species presented in the understorey, flowering is still in my experience gregarious, highly synchronized and occasional, but often outside the mass-flowering years.

The cause of the synchronized flowering in the forest canopy in the Far East remains unknown. An internal mechanism cannot be discounted as partial controller of flowering intensity, and also periodicity. I reason thus because mast years seem to be universal in the subfamily irrespective of climate, and because, in the extraordinarily equable climate of southwestern Sri Lanka, the different canopy species populations manifest flowering cycles that are out of phase with one another. Against this argument, though, is the fact that individuals of some species of all formations, including *Shorea robusta* and *S. trapezifolia*, can flower in successive years and even, in the latter, twice annually (C.V.S. and I.A.U.N. Gunatileke, pers. commun., 1985). Dipterocarp inflorescences, which in the majority of species are both terminal and axillary (though all axillary in *Dipterocarpus* and some *Hopea*) arise from buds which, in non-flowering seasons, produce leafy shoots. These buds therefore arise subsequent to the previous leaf flush, which in the aseasonal tropics is generally within the previous seven months. There is therefore no appreciable period of bud dormancy, and the trigger to formation of the reproductive shoot primordium cannot be separated from that respon-

sible for its expansion. Following flowering, and as the fruits ripen, a new leaf flush arises, principally from residual axillary buds. The trigger for the synchronous flowering of many species must be climatic. Because the forest comes into flower synchronously independently of local topography, factors such as water stress and diurnal maximum leaf temperature, which will be affected by topographic shading as well as transpiration rates, can be eliminated (Palmer, 1979). The causative factor must be one which can act on a regional scale, yet which can explain why species in the coastal peat swamps flower in different years (Wood, 1956), while the hill forest species flower more frequently, or in different years (Burgess, 1972), or at different times (Wood, 1956; Sasaki et al., 1979; Chan, 1979) from the lowland inland species. These facts, plus the fact that flowering of sal in Dehra Dun at 30°N and the main dipterocarp flowering season in peninsular Malaysia at 2° to 7°N almost coincide in the first half of the year, while the main season in northwestern Borneo, due east of the latter, is in August, rule out day length as the cause.

It is therefore no surprise that the obvious broad correlation between mass flowerings and droughts shows many exceptions. The severe regional drought of 1982/1983 was associated, though, with heavy fruiting in eastern and northeastern Borneo and to a lesser extent in peninsular Malaysia, but not in northwestern Borneo where there was no drought that year. In peninsular Malaysia, heavy flowerings were only definitely recorded following the first of the two drier seasons, which occurs in January to February (see, for instance, Burgess, 1972), though a substantial flowering followed the second dry season (July to August) in 1982 (S. Appanah, pers. commun., 1984). Wycherley (1973) pointed out that there is no consistent difference between these two "drier" seasons in total rainfall or in length in peninsular Malaysia, but that the second is generally cloudy while the first is characterized by prolonged periods of clear sky. Wycherley concluded that unusually prolonged insolation could allow build-up of photosynthate and thus provide the cause, but he also pointed out that periods of cloudless skies both increase surface temperatures by day, and decrease them through black-body radiation at night. He favored, on balance, the view that increase in daily temperature range, or unusually low night temperatures, are the trigger. Taking into consideration the relationships observed between altitude and onset of flowering, and the fact that surface temperatures will closely follow ambient temperatures at night, Ashton et al. (in press) examined the phenological and daily temperature records in western peninsular Malaysia between 1975 and 1982. There were two flowerings in March to May, and one in August during this period. Extrapolating the probable date for primordium initiation from comparisons of the phenology of sequentially flowering congeners, they found a very close coincidence between the dates identified and the three times during this period that night temperatures dropped below 20°C on more than four consecutive days.

To resolve this problem, so important in the silviculture of the dipterocarp forests which currently yield so much of the world's timber, one needs prolonged and detailed phenological and climatic measurements. It should be possible to test this hypothesis experimentally on specimen trees. A practical method of inducing flowering among dipterocarps could revolutionize their silviculture and contribute to the survival of their biome.

There is growing evidence that the supra-annual mass flowerings of Far Eastern forests, which have never been noted elsewhere, are correlated to the El Niño weather phenomenon across the Pacific (Ashton et al., in press). The periodicity broadly coincides.

The reproductive biology is best known among certain species in *Shorea*, section *Mutica*, thanks to the work of Foxworthy (1932), Symington (1943), Burgess (1969a), Chan (1977, 1980, 1981), Kaur (1977), Kaur et al., (1978) and Appanah (1979, 1981). As this section contributes most of the meranti timber of peninsular Malaysia, more is known also concerning the demography of species in this section.

In studies spanning the 1976 mass flowering at Pasoh forest, peninsular Malaysia, one hundred tagged mature individuals in six species all came into flower (Chan, 1977; Chan and Appanah, 1980). Flowering was highly synchronized within species, individuals flowering over 11 to 30 days, populations 14 to 30 days according to the species. These six ecologically sympatric species flowered sequentially, with overlap; the sequence was non-random at 0.01 significance (Ashton et al., in press). With one exception, each species was the only one in its section in flower when at peak bloom.

The panicles of the species studied are 8 to 14 cm long. In *S. leprosula*, Chan found an average of 84 buds per inflorescence. The flowers of the individual species are not reliably distinguishable from one another. The flower structure at anthesis is similar to that of *Shorea robusta* (section *Shorea*), the principal differences being that they are smaller, 4 to 8 mm long and 8 to 15 mm diameter; that there are only 15 stamens; that each stamen bears a filiform appendage but otherwise lacks bristles, and that anthers with appendages become completely reflexed during anthesis to form the cage into which the pollen is released. The spherical pollens range between 2.5 and 3 μm in diameter. Pollen production ranges between 3000 and 5500 grains in flowers of different species. Petals are cream with a median pink stripe, or entirely pink, or even deep crimson. *S. curtisii* bears cream petals in Malaya, dark crimson in Borneo.

Dipterocarp crowns in flower appear cream and contrast conspicuously against the surrounding canopy from a distance, though different species are usually indistinguishable. The flowers scent the air heavily with orange blossom. Chan and Appanah (1980) found thrips (*Thrips* sp., some *Thrips hawaiensis*, and *Megalurothrips* sp.) to comprise 95% of floral visitors, along with a few unidentified Diptera, Hemiptera and Coleoptera. The flowers are well adapted to thrips pollination. Thrips and their larvae are present in the spaces between the flower buds and the inflorescence bracts. Examination of the buds of *S. macroptera*, the first in the sequence to come into flower, revealed thrips eggs imbedded in the petals and, in some buds, on the bracts and even the ovary and style. Larval thrips were seen to rasp on the soft petal tissue. Some buds, recognizably shorter and stouter, showed damage: they failed to open and, instead, numerous thrips larvae emerged. In *S. lepidota* 18% of buds were so damaged. As a rule, though, thrips appeared not to damage the reproductive parts. Sticky traps confirmed that the thrips involved occur in low numbers in all stages, and at all seasons in the air in the forest canopy, but increase dramatically when the dipterocarps flower. Larval stages were found feeding in the flowers of certain continuous-flowering under-storey species, notably *Randia scortechinii* (Rubiaceae). Counts on dipterocarp flowers indicated that numbers on branches within the crown varied greatly from day to day. On average, three adults per flower were found, with a maximum of sixteen. The adult insects feed on both petal tissue and pollen, puncturing the grains with their styluses and sucking out the contents. Nevertheless, thrips were seen bearing the smooth but slightly sticky grains on the back of their thoraces where, it seemed, they had difficulty in dislodging them during their frequent cleaning activities. An average of 2.5 grains per thrips were found, a maximum of 27. At anthesis, pollen grains were seen abundantly both within and outside the floral cage, but flowers with abundant thrips were noticeably depleted. Thrips were seen to both land on, and take off from, the protruding style and stigma. Thrips fly slowly, and apparently haphazardly, being easily deflected even by convectional wind movements (Lewis, 1970, 1973). Thrips pollination differs from wind pollination, though, in that the insect can land directionally.

Trees of *S. leprosula* were found by Chan to produce between 63 000 and 4 000 000 flowers in a season, and present up to one-fifth of this number daily at peak bloom. The flowers open in acropetal succession. The pendant flowers open, and the anthers dehisce, in the evening at which time they already contain thrips at all stages within. During the following morning the loosely adhering petals, with stamens attached, spiral to the ground, often with thrips on board. Thrips larvae were found by Appanah to continue to feed on the fallen petals for up to five days; the full life cycle of *Thrips* sp. he found to be accomplished in eight days. Sticky traps indicated that thrips are concentrated at all times in the forest canopy. In the early evening, Appanah observed adult thrips taking off from the carpet of corollas on the forest floor, apparently making their way haphazardly back to the canopy. He surmised that the oblique spiral trajectory of the falling corollas combines with the returning upward flight of the adult thrips to facilitate cross-pollination.

The female *Thrips* sp. lays slightly under thirty eggs. It is not known what time interval elapses between the first opportunity for thrips to oviposit on the developing bud, and anthesis; but it is likely to be at least three weeks. This will allow at least two generations and a substantial increase in thrip numbers before the flowering of the first species in the sequence, *S. macroptera*. It may be significant that Foxworthy (1932) described multiple seedlings to arise from seeds of this species, which Kaur (Kaur, 1977; Kaur et al., 1978) inferentially attributed to adventive embryony. I suggest that this form of apomixis, which appears to be rare in the five species which follow in the flowering sequence, allows *S. macroptera* to maintain fecundity when thrips numbers fail to build up adequately.

Chan (1981) failed to obtain viable seed from bagged or selfed flowers of seven species of *Shorea* section *Mutica* tested, and concluded that they are highly self-incompatible.

Thrips are found abundantly in flowers of many dipterocarp species. They were the only insects seen in a cursory inspection of *Shorea maxima*, section *Richetioides*, in which the petals are lemon yellow (Appanah, 1979), and in *Hopea utilis* in which they are cream (pers. observ.). The former is curious, because Ashton (1969) and Chan (1977) observed sequential flowering in that section also, while Chan found that the flowering sequences of the two sections almost completely overlapped. How sequential flowering is maintained within, but not between sections sharing a common pollinator (if indeed they do), is unexplained.

Most dipterocarps examined in Malaysia have been found to be visited by flower thrips, but other visitors in substantial numbers may occur in addition. In Section *Shorea*, Subsection *Shorea*, bugs are thought to be the principal visitors (Appanah, in press). In *S. stenoptera*, Section *Pachycarpae*, Thysanoptera, Hemiptera, Coleoptera and Diptera were found, in that order of abundance, though the last two were uncommon (Appanah, 1979). So far, thrips have been found to be the most abundant visitors in *Dipterocarpus costulatus*, with a small number of Coleoptera also. The large flowers in this genus, often with numerous stamens bearing large anthers, would suggest that another pollinator awaits discovery.

Shorea ovalis ssp. *sericea* was found to be visited by bees of the genera *Apis* and *Trigona*; also a *Nomia* species (Xylocopidae) (Chan, 1977; Appanah, 1979). Visits were observed on only four of the eleven days of observation. No thrips were seen. The flowers are almost scentless. The corolla is pale yellow, tinged pink at the base. It opens fully to the base, forming a saucer within which the more than fifty stamens, whose anthers on slender filaments protrude far beyond the stigma, are displayed. The anthers lack connectival appendages. The pollen, unlike all other dipterocarp pollen examined, is powdery and non-adherent. Here, the flowers open between 1530 and 1600 h, the anthers dehiscing somewhat before opening. The corolla falls the following morning, but the stigma, which becomes receptive at anthesis, remains so for some hours after the anthers fall.

Neobalanocarpus heimii has also been studied by Chan (1977) and Appanah (1979). Here the petals, which are yellow and elliptic, also open fully to the base so that the bright yellow cylindrical anthers are conspicuously displayed. The flowers open in the early morning, and the petals fall separately, generally by noon. Chan (1977) and Appanah (1979, 1981) observed *Apis dorsata* to be the principal visitor, with some *A. cerana*, but on one occasion the bee *Trigona canifrons* invaded a tree and dislodged other visitors. Visitation occurred between 0630 and 1500 h, and peaked between 0900 and 1000 h.

I have seen a swarm of *Trigona* visiting the flowers of *Shorea ovalifolia*, section *Doona*. The eleven species of this section are endemic to Sri Lanka. The flower is broadly similar in structure to that of *Neobalanocarpus*, though the petals are cream. In *Stemonoporus*, also endemic to Sri Lanka, the stamens remain closely appressed to the gynoecium, while the corolla of the nodding flower becomes patent. In *S. gracilis* [*S. lancifolius* (Thw.) Ashton var. sensu Ashton] I observed *Trigona* bees to land on the flower by clasping the style, then gnaw at the apices of the apparently indehiscent anthers. Any pollen already on the lower surface of the thorax would thereby easily be transferred to the stigma.

In *Dryobalanops oblongifolia* ssp. *occidentalis*, in which the flowers resemble *Shorea* section *Doona* in gross morphology at anthesis, Appanah (1979) found the same visitors as in *Neobalanocarpus*.

Species in these three groups, as stated earlier, flower more frequently than the majority of species in the aseasonal tropics. With the exception of some lowland species of *Stemonoporus*, they are also generally locally gregarious. It may not be an accident that these properties are associated with pollinators whose life cycles are relatively long.

Among dipterocarps examined by Chan (1981), only the gregarious riparian species *Dipterocarpus oblongifolius* was found to be both fully self compatible and with normal embryogenesis (Kaur, 1977). This discovery was in conflict with the predictions of Corner (1954), Catinot (1976) and others who reasoned that rain forest trees of the mature phase, on account of their low population densities yet frequently enormous flower production, would likely be self-pollinated. Nevertheless, self-incompatibility has been found to prevail in other Far Eastern rain forest trees of both mature (Yap, 1976) and gap (Taylor, 1982) phases, and also in a majority of Central American species (Bawa, 1979; Baker et al., 1983).

Apomixis, through adventive embryony, is now well established among dipterocarpoids (Kaur, 1977; Kaur et al., 1978, 1986; Jong and Kaur, 1979; Jong, 1982). Kaur confirmed nucellar embryogeny in two species, inferred it on the basis of triploidy in a further 6 out of 68 examined cytologically, and tentatively suggested that it occurs in a further 16 on the basis of multiple seedlings. Multiple seedlings have been found in at least some seed from all four polyploids which have been examined; one of these was a tetraploid, the others triploid. As several of these species were selected for embryological or cytological examination on account of their known production of multiple seedlings, the proportion of facultative apomicts observed may be higher than in the subfamily as a whole. On the other hand, it is also possible that many single embryos are of adventive origin.

Embryogenesis in the Dipterocarpoideae is of the *Polygonum* type (Rao, 1953, 1955a, b, 1956, 1962). In *S. ovalis* ssp. *sericea* and *S. agami*, Kaur observed that a zygote was formed, but failed to divide. Instead, a number of cell clusters began forming within the nucellar tissue. Bagged flowers of *S. ovalis* set fruit, but failed to do so after emasculation, implying that the species is pseudogamous. Alone among the species studied by Chan, though clumps of *S. ovalis* trees flowered synchronously over 21 days, there was asynchrony between clumps of up to 12 days. This implies that the pollinators do not act as a selecting agent for high flowering synchrony within populations. Such asynchrony concentrates pollen exchange among the most genetically similar individuals between which incompatibility, if it exists, would be highest.

Jong and Kaur (1979) and Kaur et al. (1986) have shown that the well-known correlation between apomixis and polyploidy occurs in this family. Subfamily Dipterocarpoideae is divided into two tribes which differ in basic chromosome number: Dipterocarpeae, $n = 11$, and Shoreae, $n = 7$ (Ashton, 1982; Jong, 1982 on the basis of Roy and Jha, 1965; Jong and Lethbridge, 1967; Jong, 1976; Somego, 1978; Jong and Kaur, 1979). Polyploidy and multiple seedlings are known from both, but apomixis has only been confirmed in the latter. Triploidy occurs in several species of *Hopea*, and in *Shorea resinosa* which is well known for its multiple seedlings (Kaur et al., 1978; Jong, 1982). Triploidy has been found in root squashes in all seedlings examined from single trees, and it is difficult in those cases to avoid concluding that they are apomictic. In species such as *S. ovalis* and *S. resinosa* the limited evidence available suggests that most embryogenesis is apomictic. In *S. macroptera* though, Kaur found individuals within one population to vary between 0 and 70% in the proportion of their seeds which yielded multiple seedlings.

Ripe fruit-fall of six ecologically sympatric species of *Shorea* section *Mutica* starts roughly synchronously, over a period of about two weeks (Chan, 1977, 1980). In *S. macroptera* and *S. dasyphylla*, the first two species to flower in sequence, there were eighteen weeks between the end of anthesis and the onset of fruit-fall, while in *S. leprosula*, the last to flower, there were twelve. Burkill (1917) and Ng and Loh (1974) found species in four different genera to vary in this respect between 2 and 6 months. In fact, the onset of fruit-fall is roughly synchronized among all members of the subfamily which flower in the same season, including *S. ovalis* which fails to flower synchronously. The remarkable fact, that relative rates of floral and fruit morphogenesis are inversely proportional among dipterocarps, argues for strong selection for synchronous mast fruiting, supporting the supposition of Janzen (1974) and others that seed predation of the fat- and starch-rich seeds is thus reduced through predator saturation.

Following anthesis, Chan (1977) found high but declining abortion rates through to ripening in *S. leprosula*. The young sepals rapidly expand into full-sized wings. As they begin they turn brilliant anthocyanin crimson, but in many species they turn to green after expansion. Only then does the embryo start to swell. By maturity, only 0.7 to 3.5% of the original flower buds had survived on different trees. This still represents between 5000 and 115 000 viable seeds per tree. By contrast, Chan (unpublished) failed to find any viable seed resulting from an out-of-season fruiting by several individuals of *Dipterocarpus grandiflorus*. This seems to be a general occurrence, and again supports Janzen's (1974) hypothesis for the maintenance of mast fruiting among dipterocarps. Chan, who traced floral events from the young bud to fruit ripening on tagged inflorescences, found no discernible spatial patterns in survivorship within them. Aborted fruit in Chan's fruit traps accounted for only 18 to 62% of mortality between anthesis and ripe fruit-fall, suggesting that most mortality occurs immediately following anthesis, and before the sepals begin to expand.

As in other dipterocarps, curculionid beetles (*Alcidodes*, *Nanophyes* spp.) and Lepidopteran larvae (Pyralidae, Tortricidae) early infect the seed, devouring the cotyledons. No host specificity has been observed. It is not known to what extent seed predation, failed pollination, climatic damage or some form of physiological self-thinning contribute towards this post-anthesis, pre-fruiting mortality. There was no significant difference between isolated and clumped trees, however, in abortion percentage of young or mature fruit nor between trees of *S. leprosula* and the apomict *S. ovalis*. Fruit set among six species of *Shorea* section *Mutica* in 1976 occurred among 57 to 100% of the individuals that flowered except in one species, *S. dasyphylla*, in which only one of the four trees in its very low density population fruited. In this case, failed cross-pollination might have been the cause.

The mature dipterocarp embryo bears more or less unequal cotyledons, one enfolding the other, but otherwise manifests considerable variation whose ecological significance is unknown, but which provides valuable characters for establishing intergeneric relationships and intrageneric groupings (Maury, 1978, 1979). The radicle emerges by bursting through the woody or corky pericarp, which splits irregularly or along loculicidal suture lines. In *Anisoptera* and *Dipterocarpus* the embryo is cryptocotylar, the cotyledons being non-photosynthetic and remaining within the pericarp, while the plumule is released through elongation of the cotyledonary petioles.

Ripe dipterocarp fruits vary greatly in size between species. They may or may not bear wing-like sepals. Sepal length varies among closely related species (Symington, 1934, 1943; Ashton, 1963). In *Shorea*, many of the largest fruit bear vestigial wings. In *Shorea*, section *Richetioides*, Ashton (1969) showed that emergent species were predominantly winged-fruited, main canopy species wingless, implying either that the wings aid dispersal only of those species whose crowns are emergent, or that the winged condition, presumably ancestral in *Shorea*, is only positively disadvantageous in main canopy species. Fruit size is large among many riparian species, whose fruit are known to be dispersed through flotation. Many bear corky pericarps, though all dipterocarp fruit float in water.

Webber (1934) observed *Shorea* fruit to be carried several hundred meters in a gust of wind, and J. Muller (pers. commun., 1984) saw the fallen fruit of *S. albida* up to 1 km from the edge of the forest in the Brunei oilfields; but this appears to be unusual. Kochummen and Ng (1977) and Kochummen (1977) found *S. leprosula* saplings in secondary forest 200 m from the parent butt; but Chan observed that fruit of forest-grown trees fall within 30 m of the butt, and mostly within 15 m as Ridley (1930) originally indicated. This may largely explain the clumping that occurs among conspecifics in the forest (Ashton, 1969).

As in other regions, dipterocarp seeds lack natural dormancy, and attempts to induce it have met with limited success (Jansen, 1971; Tang, 1971; Tang and Tamari, 1973; Tamari, 1976; Sasaki, 1980; Maury et al., 1981; Yap, 1981).

The period of successful seedling establishment is one of high mortality also. Post-fall seed predation by *Poecileps* spp. (Scolytidae) is well known (Browne, 1939, 1961; Daljeet Singh, 1974). Chan (1980) found scolytid infestation to account for 90 and 49% failure in seed germination in individuals of *S. ovalis* and *S. leprosula*, respectively, which had flowered out of season. One month after establishment, further scolytid attack had caused 100 and 89% further mortality among

those seedlings that had established. In contrast, during the 1976 flowering year successful germination among four trees of *S. macroptera* and *S. leprosula* varied between 78 and 90%, and of these successfully established seedlings 46 to 64% survived after one month. This again is evidence in favor of the predator saturation hypothesis.

Singh (1966) first observed the presence of ectotrophic mycorrhizae on dipterocarp roots, in several genera in peninsular Malaysia. Smits (1983) had preliminary evidence that some dipterocarp mycorrhizae may be host-specific, and that dipterocarps are obligately mycorrhizal. If correct, it adds to the syndrome of characteristics associated with the clumping of the trees, particularly if the fungal spores lack dormancy in the equable climate of the rain-forest understorey and if infection is therefore principally through root contact (Ashton, 1982; Smits, 1983).

Once fully established, seedling mortality proceeds more gradually. Causes of mortality remain unclear, though periodic drought as well as adverse light conditions are thought to play a part (see, for instance, Chai, 1973; Fox, 1973; Gong, 1981; Burgess, in Ashton, 1982). Herbivory does not seem to be a major factor (Becker, 1983). Daljeet Singh (1975) found that, though infestation by shoot borers does not vary between seedlings of different species, some species generate several, others only one new leader. Ng (1976, 1981) found that such reiterated shoots can arise from accessory axillary buds in some *Shorea*. The capacity for such reiteration seems to decline as the tree grows larger. Similarly, coppicing capacity is very limited among dipterocarps of the aseasonal tropics, and rarely persists beyond the pole stage, though wind-thrown canopy individuals of *Shorea albida* of the northwest Borneo swamps can send out epicormic shoots (pers. observ.).

Seedlings can be found at most times on the ground between flowering years (Fig. 11.2). Little growth occurs, however, unless the plants are exposed to direct sunlight (Fox, 1973; Liew and Wong, 1973; Sasaki and Mori, 1981). Different taxonomic groups as well as different species are known to foresters to have different light requirements (Nicholson, 1960; among others). The species of *Dipterocarpus*, and *Shorea* section *Mutica*, are mostly considered to be "light demanders", whereas *Shorea* section *Shorea* species, and

Fig. 11.2. Owing to poor seed dispersal dipterocarp seedlings form single-species stands, as here in *Shorea laxa*, section *Richetioides*.

Neobalanocarpus heimii, arc "shade tolerant". Among *Shorea* section *Mutica*, *S. leprosula* is well known to be less shade tolerant than other species. Whether the differences in sunlight requirements that exist among congenerics are fortuitous inherited traits, or the result of interspecific competition, is not known.

The population density of sapling- and pole-size dipterocarp trees is generally low in Mixed Dipterocarp forest, though the forests of the Philippines are reported generally to be exceptional in this respect. Declining populations of successively larger size classes suggests that mortality continues, though specific causes are again unknown. In all immature size classes variation in growth rates is great, and Nicholson (1963) has suggested that all but the fast growing minority in each class may already be senescent. If correct, the time to

reproductive maturity in nature can only be calculated through extrapolation from growth measurement of those faster growing individuals, and may not be greatly longer than among specimen trees.

Closely related emergent species, particularly of *Shorea*, usually differ principally in leaf characters at maturity, and can always be identified when sterile. These diagnostic characters become fully manifest after the crown has begun to emerge from the canopy. This suggests that, whereas intraspecific competition is clearly prevalent among seedlings, as the tree grows up towards the canopy and towards the end of the period of intense competition, this competition becomes increasingly interspecific (Ashton, 1969).

The predominant pattern of morphological variation among mature trees within species in Mixed Dipterocarp forests is of striking uniformity, but sometimes of small but constant geographical discontinuity. Nevertheless, though Gan (1976) and Gan et al. (1977) found little isozyme variation among seedlings and mature trees of the apomict *S. ovalis* ssp. *sericea* (which may nevertheless have been due to its tetraploidy), the diploid *S. leprosula* manifested 56% between-tree variation in rF value of the band positions in a sampled population. She found some evidence that genetic similarity between seedling population samples decreases with distance. Between-tree variation in leaf blade and petiole length was found to increase with distance up to 100 m (Chan, 1977), after which it reached a plateau. This might indicate the normal distance of pollen or seed dispersal.

In view of the observed pattern of overlapping sequential flowering, at least within some sections of *Shorea*, it is hardly surprising that morphological evidence of hybridization is rare. In species which co-occur in the same habitat, among the many thousands of specimens of *Shorea* section *Mutica* examined by me I have only once seen morphological hybrids, between *S. parvifolia* and *S. acuminata* from a Sumatran locality. Small hybrid populations of the hillside species *S. leprosula* and the ridge-top *S. curtisii* are known from several localities in peninsular Malaysia, where the ecological ranges overlap — though even there it is unusual for the ranges overlap throughout their peninsular distribution. In one example examined, all seed produced by a mature hybrid individual lacked embryos. A notable exception, though, is in *Shorea* section *Pachycarpae*, consisting of ten species all endemic to Borneo, which is curious as the island has frequently been connected to Sumatra and the Peninsula during the Pleistocene. Here *S. mecistopteryx* alone is uniform and consistently definable. The others show marked and often quite local variation, and in every case manifest populations of morphological hybrids with at least one other species, generally in one restricted part of their range. Chan (1981) successfully hybridized *S. stenoptera* with *S. splendida* but the resultant fruit were gathered by an assistant when still unripe, and seed viability was therefore indeterminable.

Jong and Kaur (1979) has suggested that the magnificent monotypic tree *Neobalanocarpus heimii*, endemic to peninsular Malaysia, may be an intergeneric hybrid on the basis of abnormal chromosome pairing at metaphase I and high pollen sterility. The species shares the characters of *Shorea* section *Pentacme* and *Hopea* section *Hopea*.

Occasional among dipterocarps of this formation, and particularly among *Shorea* section *Pachycarpae*, is the occurrence of highly localized populations which differ in a minor but distinct way from those of a more widespread species, and sometimes even co-occur with the latter. The form described as *S. rotundifolia*, known from three localities in Sarawak, East Malaysia, in each of which it manifests further minor, but constant, differences, clearly bears such a relationship with *S. amplexicaulis* with which it co-occurs, as does *S. praestans* with *S. macrophylla*. A series of populations close to the podzol species *S. stenoptera*, but not to any other known species and each distinct from the others, occurs northeast of the range of the latter and on the same soils. Though adventive embryony is inferred in the gregarious riparian species *Hopea odorata* and *Dipterocarpus obtusifolius* of Dry Dipterocarp forest, other inferred or confirmed examples are from taxa with distinct geographic forms. Thus, within *S. ovalis* three, and within *S. macroptera* four, geographical subspecies respectively have been described. *S. parvifolia*, which Maury (1970) found to occasionally bear twin embryos apparently derived from a single ovule, also manifests regional variation. The apomictic triploid *S. resinosa*, endemic to peninsu-

lar Malaysia, differs only in minor characters of the leaf and fruit base from *S. agami*, endemic to Borneo, which itself occurs as two geographical subspecies. The apomictic triploid *Hopea subalata*, known only from one restricted location in Peninsular Malaysia where it is nevertheless rather abundant, differs only in trivial respects, though constantly, from *H. mesuoides* which is endemic to but widespread in northwestern Borneo.

Ashton (1969) reported the presence of two so-called subspecies of *S. macroptera* in mixed populations in Sarawak. No morphological hybrids were found in an enumeration and, whereas one was an emergent at maturity the other never exceeded the main canopy. They seem therefore to behave as biological species, though it would be difficult to raise their formal status to that level in the absence of data from other similar taxa.

DISCUSSION

Arguments still rage whether the extraordinarily rich species composition of tropical rain forest can be explained in terms of the evolution, over time, of increasingly narrow niche specifity (Ashton, 1969; Connell, 1978), known to Hubbell (1979) and Hubbell and Foster (1983) as the equilibrium theory; or through random aggregation owing to the opportunities afforded for immigration, which in time become balanced by equally fortuitous hazards of extinction, known to Hubbell, its proponent in the present context, as the non-equilibrium theory. Hubbell based his reasoning on the analysis of community structure, arguing that a species whose population distribution within a uniform site is random, and neither positively or negatively associated with any other species population, must be free of interspecific selective mortality. He found that the majority of tree species mapped in a 50 ha plot in Panama were randomly dispersed at all size classes, and is now seeking to strengthen this evidence by monitoring patterns of mortality over time.

Hubbell's theory does not of course imply that natural selection does not operate in species-rich tropical forest, but that it operates in a generalized manner common to groups of species which, as a consequence, can be recognized as sharing a guild. The search for differentials in the ecology of species which systematic study has determined to be closely related yet which, contrary to Gause's Law, appear to be interchangeable in space within a common community can provide a poignant means of testing Hubbell's hypothesis. In the case of the six *Shorea* species studied by Chan, there was evidence of positive spatial association (Chan, 1977).

Gan's (1976) and Gan et al.'s (1977) evidence of high heterosis in *Shorea leprosula*, and Chan's (1977, 1981) that it is an outbreeder, argue indirectly but strongly for high niche specificity in a biotically ever-changing environment, for this common and widespread species (Ashton, 1969; Levin, 1975; Solbrig, 1976; Lloyd, 1980a, b). On the other hand, the common and apparently genetically uniform tetraploid *S. ovalis* may have retained a high level of apomixis as a means of maintaining fecundity in a genotype of high fitness but with mating difficulties occasioned by hybrid origin (Gustafson, 1946–1947); while in the early flowering *S. macroptera* periodic pollinator shortages maintain a fluctuating balance between outbreeding and agamospermy (Williams, 1970). In both, it must be assumed that their capacity to survive is impaired by inevitable loss of genetic variability, unless they occupy exceptional niches (Lloyd, 1980b).

In *Shorea* section *Mutica*, Ashton et al. (1985) suggest that the closest related geographically sympatric species as a rule occupy different habitats. The commonly allopatric distribution of morphological subspecies suggests that speciation is allopatric, and that Chan's six species came together through subsequent immigration. Once together, the phenological evidence suggests that competition for pollinators exists and, as in the case of *Shorea dasyphylla*, may locally influence mortality. The dispersal distance of pollinators such as thrips, which are presumably lured from a distance by a visual cue and from the vicinity by scent, may not be greater than wind. But their capacity to search out flowers enables them to be effective in mixed forest. This could be a further factor indirectly favoring clumping of individuals.

Hubbell cited the occurrence of site-independent clumping, which occurs among many rain forest tree species, in support of the non-equilibrium theory, arguing that restrictions on dispersal in this case reduce the opportunities for seed to find specialized sites. If Smits' (1983) hypothesis that some mycorrhizae are both obligate and host-specific is correct, the possibility arises that allelopathic effects between the fungal symbionts may favor either persistence of clumps, or gradual replacement of one species clump with another. Either would support the equilibrium theory, and the latter would also explain why heterosis is so unexpectedly high in *S. leprosula*. Why should it be necessary, in the savanna woodlands of eastern Asia, to maintain the dominance of the sal by burning its litter? Why does the single-species dominant *S. albida*, of the lowland peat swamps of Borneo, so rarely regenerate (Anderson, 1961)? Could these be for the same reason? The suspected, but so far inadequately documented, existence of site-independent aggregations of consectional species suggests that some mycorrhizae may be host-specific at the sectional level. If the latter proves to be the case, and bearing in mind the abundant and synchronous fruiting of dipterocarps, the possibility of direct interspecific competition, even of seedlings, among consectional species in a species-rich forest cannot be discounted. Physiological ecological studies could test whether, as in the case of flowering phenology, differentials between sympatric species in light responses, for instance, are random. The comparative physiology of the sympatric subspecies of *S. macroptera* would be of particular interest.

Why should the single-dominant species sal flower over a period of six weeks, while in Peninsular Malaysia the sequential flowering of at least three related species is crammed into the same period? It is difficult to conceive of a testable hypothesis to explain this. Unpredictable environmental variability, notably in length of the dry season, and periodic catastrophic drought would appear likely explanations why such intricate phenological sequences among conspecifics do not develop in sal forests. In support of this supposition, even mature sal does suffer periodic major mortality from drought (Troup, 1921; Seth et al., 1960), and this has been observed also in the locally dominant Malaysian ridge-top species *S. curtisii* (Tang and Chong, 1979). Ashton (1984) has pointed out the high endemicity and species richness of ecological islands in northwestern Borneo compared with the same habitats in eastern Borneo, a region exposed to periodic severe drought. Also, the unusual morphological variability of sal and other Dry Evergreen forest dipterocarps suggests a high capacity for adjustment of the species as a whole in the face of environmental change.

Plant species richness in tropical forest is due though to the extraordinary number of species with low population densities. It is these whose mortality must be interpreted (Ashton, 1984). Among dipterocarps, there seem to be examples to support both equilibrium and non-equilibrium hypotheses: the example of the presumed outbreeder *Shorea dasyphylla* provides the case of a species in process of local extinction, apparently through species-specific natural selection. The facultative apomict *Hopea subalata* is a species which is rare because it is highly localized, in this case to a soil type rare in its region. Here, it appears that apomixis has maintained high fecundity in a favorably preadapted genotype [See Lloyd (1980b) for a full discussion]. So long as the habitat persists, and no better adapted species invades, *H. subalata* may persist. But it has little capacity to adapt to change.

The case of *Shorea rotundifolia* suggests the survival and reproduction of a fertile mutant. This may be a species *in statu nascendi*, in which case its origin hardly suggests gradual evolution through specific natural selection. It may merely be an ephemeral morph, or it may vindicate the non-equilibrium theory (Ashton, 1984). The lowland species of *Stemonoporus* provide an extreme example of this form of variation, unparalleled elsewhere in the subfamily. Most lowland species are extremely local, and still further divided into distinct morphs which are in several cases known only from a single plant. Variation is complex and apparently reticulate, and the concept of the morphological species seems as arbitrary as in the entire-leaved *Sorbus* or North American *Crataegus*. These are trees of the equable rain-forest understorey whose wingless fruits, sparsely produced, appear to be poorly dispersed. Unfortunately, nothing is yet known of their breeding systems.

The existence of a remarkable number of mature-phase species, of highly uniform morphology, which are widespread in the Mixed Dipterocarp forests of Sundaland provides another challenge to equilibrium theory, for the species with which they are associated vary substantially throughout their range. Nevertheless at least one, *S. leprosula*, is known to be a genetically variable outbreeder.

Ashton (1979) has indicated an overall evolutionary trend towards smaller flowers with fewer stamens and smaller anthers, from the seasonal to the aseasonal regions, from the canopy to the understorey, and from wide ranging to local species among dipterocarps. The trend occurs both when genera with relatively large, many-stamened flowers (*Shorea*, for instance) are compared with others, such as the related *Hopea* with smaller flowers and generally fewer stamens; and also within such large genera. Also, species that flower within the canopy present fewer flowers per inflorescence (Fig. 11.3). Among emergents there is apparently a commensurate increase in the number of flowers simultaneously presented, but the number is always relatively low in understorey species. High pollen/ovule ratios allow both maximum opportunity for cross pollination, and for selection among male gametes. The almost universal persistence of six ovules in the dipterocarpoid flower, only one of which normally survives to form a seed, similarly promotes selection among female gametes and among developing embryos. The latter may serve to further reduce the level of selfing (Ledig, 1986). High self-compatibility is generally associated with low pollen/ovule ratios (Cruden, 1976). Does this overall decrease in pollen/ovule ratios, in an environment where pollen transfer is so particularly difficult, indicate that self-compatibility is more widespread among dipterocarps than current evidence suggests? In *Stemonoporus*, there is a reduction in ovule number from six to four, as well as a reduction in stamen number from fifteen to five, in three species which are endemic to the wettest, lowland to mid-altitude, region around Adam's Peak in southwestern Sri Lanka. Here, the reduction in the ratio noted in many wet-zone dipterocarps, and occasioned by reduction in pollen number, is partially offset. Could the reduction of both floral pollen and ovules be an indication of widespread apomixis and lowered selection, particularly among local species and those with low-density populations?

The morphological patterns described do not appear to be unique to dipterocarps. That of

Fig. 11.3. Species which present their flowers outside the forest canopy, such as *Stemonoporus zeylanicus* (left), usually bear more, and larger, inflorescences and present more flowers simultaneously than species which present their flowers within the canopy, such as *Stemonoporus petiolaris* (right).

Stemonoporus, for instance, resembles some species groups in *Garcinia* (Clusiaceae) and *Syzygium* (Myrtaceae), genera in which apomixis is known to occur (Treub, 1911; Ha, 1979). Patterns in the species-rich genera *Diospyros* (Ebenaceae), *Knema* (Myristicaceae) and *Baccaurea* (Euphorbiaceae) resemble those described in *Shorea* section *Mutica*. Hubbell and Foster (1983) have recognized the existence of selection at the level of ecological guilds. The evidence from *Shorea* suggests that one should expect selection to operate also at various levels of the phylogenetic hierarchy. Specialization among different sections of *Shorea*, each containing several sequentially flowering species, to different pollinators could provide a means whereby a considerable number of related species could coexist, but in a manner that need not be manifested in spatial patterns (Ashton, 1984). Among alkaloid-producing families much seed-predator specificity may operate at generic, even familial level. In this case spatial patterns may be expected (Janzen, 1971), but at supraspecific systematic levels.

If competition for pollinators, as in the example of *Shorea* section *Mutica* and thrips, or specificity among mycorrhizae, or perhaps even specificity in light response among related congeners, provides the basis for niche specifity, it is possible that species are interchangeable in the congeneric sequences that occur within individual forests, and that relatively minor shifts in gene frequencies can allow widespread species to adjust, within limits, to the changing array of co-occurring congeners with which each local population is associated. The extraordinary precision of the flowering sequence demonstrated in *Shorea* section *Mutica* by Chan can provide a test of this, for the species array in this section does differ from one forest to another, though some members are ubiquitous. Do the flowering times of those ubiquitous species, such as *S. leprosula* or *S. parvifolia*, differ to some degree according to the congeners with which they occur? An additional intriguing explanation for the existence of morphologically uniform widespread species, which is compatible with the equilibrium theory, is that of Smits (1983), who has suggested that the geographic uniformity of these species may reflect uniformity of their mycorrhizal symbionts which are nevertheless highly specific in their edaphic and micro-organismic interactions.

It may finally be asked what evolutionary trends in reproductive biology might have occurred among dipterocarpoids. Ashton (1982, and in Maguire and Ashton, 1977) has argued that the family has a seasonal tropical origin, and that the multistaminate condition is primitive. The synchronized presentation of many visually conspicuous flowers over a short period, called by Gentry (1974) big-bang flowering, is characteristic of canopy species which flower during the dry season in the seasonal tropics, but is less dependable in climates lacking a predictable dry season. Hermaphroditism, however, may have allowed the family to maintain maximum flexibility: In particular, pollen/ovule ratios at whole-tree level can vary through variation in post-anthesis seed mortality, whereby a variable number of flowers are effectively males [see Bawa and Webb (1984) for a fuller discussion]. If it is assumed that dipterocarps are outbreeders, and that they bear many more flowers than the number of fruits that their physiology can sustain to maturity, then their variability may be of selective advantage in maximizing fruit set in mast years, particularly in the seasonal tropics where flowering is annual.

Among dipterocarps the fruit sepals, which are photosynthetic, fully enlarge before the embryo expands. This occurs in most flowers following anthesis even though most will abort without embryogenesis. Thus, the energistic cost of such post-anthesis culling is likely offset as has been shown in some temperate trees (Bazzaz et al., 1979), and effective male flowers may even subsidize those that ripen seed. The evolutionary trend towards increase in flower number per tree with concomitant decrease in stamen number per flower, which appears to have occurred at least among emergent *Shorea* in the aseasonal tropics has further increased potential versatility in this respect, for stamen number is remarkably constant within the flowers of each species. This trend seems to have been possible owing to the versatility of the fecund, rapidly multiplying pollinators in the species-rich genera such as *Shorea* and *Hopea*. They have also allowed accumulation of ecologically sympatric species, surviving in mixture through subtle, fragile, competitive interactions made possible by a predictable climate in spite of their infrequent opportunities for reproduction.

REFERENCES

Anderson, J.A.R., 1961. *The ecology and forest types of the peat swamp forests of Sarawak and Brunei in relation to their silviculture.* Ph.D. thesis, Univ. of Edinburgh, Edinburgh.

Anon., 1940. Sal regeneration de novo. *Indian For.*, 66: 525–529.

Appanah, S., 1979. *The ecology of insect pollination of some tropical rain forest trees.* Ph.D. thesis, Univ. of Malaya.

Appanah, S., 1981. Pollination in Malaysian primary forests. *Malays. For.*, 44: 37–42.

Appanah, S., 1982. Pollination of androdioecious *Xerospermum intermedium* Radlk. (Sapindaceae) in a rain forest. *Bot. J. Linn. Soc.*, 18: 11–34.

Appanah, S., 1985. General flowering in the climax rain forests of South-East Asia. *J. Trop. Ecol.*, 1: 225–240.

Appanah, S. and Chan, H.T., 1981. Thrips: The pollinators of some dipterocarps. *Malays. For.*, 44: 234–252.

Ashton, P.S., 1963. Taxonomic notes on Bornean Dipterocarpaceae. *Gard. Bull. Singapore*, 20: 229–284.

Ashton, P.S., 1964. Ecological studies in the Mixed dipterocarp forests of Brunei State. *Oxford For. Mem.*, 25: 75 pp.

Ashton, P.S., 1969. Speciation among tropical forest trees: Some deductions in the light of recent evidence. *Biol. J. Linn. Soc.*, 1: 155–196.

Ashton, P.S., 1977. A contribution of rain forest research to evolutionary theory. *Ann. Mo. Bot. Gard.*, 64: 694–705.

Ashton, P.S., 1979. Some geographic trends in morphological variation in the Asian tropics and their possible significance. In: K. Larsen and L.B. Holm-Nielson (Editors), *Tropical Botany*. Academic Press, New York, N.Y., pp. 35–48.

Ashton, P.S., 1980. Dipterocarpaceae. In: D.S. Dassanayake and F.R. Fosberg (Editors), *Handbook to the Flora of Ceylon, I.* Amerind, Ceylon, pp. 364–423.

Ashton, P.S., 1982. Dipterocarpaceae. *Flora Malesiana, Ser. I.* 9: 251–552.

Ashton, P.S., 1984. Biosystematics of tropical forest plants: A problem of rare species. In: W.F. Grant (Editor), *Plant Biosystematics*. Academic Press, New York, N.Y., pp. 497–518.

Ashton, P.S., Gan, Y.Y. and Robertson, F.W., 1985. Electrophoretic and morphological comparisons in ten rain forest species of Shorea (Dipterocarpaceae). *Bot. J. Linn. Soc.*, 89 (4): 293–304.

Ashton, P.S., Givnish, T.J. and Appanah, S., 1988. Staggered flowering in the Dipterocarpaceae: New insights into floral induction and the evolution of mast flowering in the aseasonal tropics. *Am. Nat.* (in press).

Bailey, W.A. and Champion, H.G., 1927. Sal germination in the United Provinces. *Indian For.*, 53: 190–194.

Baker, H.G., Bawa, K.S., Frankie, G.W. and Opler, P.A., 1983. Reproductive biology of plants in tropical forests. In: F.B. Golley (Editor), *Tropical Rain Forest Ecosystems.* (Ecosystems of the World, 14A) Elsevier, Amsterdam, pp. 183–215.

Bawa, K.S., 1979. Breeding systems of trees in a tropical lowland wet forest. *N.Z. J. Bot.*, 17: 521–524.

Bawa, K.S. and Webb, C.J., 1984. Flower, fruit and seed abortion in tropical forest trees: Implications for the evolution of paternal and maternal reproductive patterns. *Am. J. Bot.*, 71: 736–751.

Bazzaz, F.A., Carlson, R.W. and Harper, J.L., 1979. Contribution to reproductive effort by photosynthesis of flowers and fruits. *Nature*, 279: 552–553.

Becker, P., 1983. Effects of insect herbivory and artificial defoliation on survival of *Shorea* seedlings. In: S.L. Sutton, T.C. Whitmore and A.C. Chadwick (Editors), *Tropical Rain Forest: Ecology and Management*. Blackwell, London, pp. 241–252.

Blanford, H.R., 1915. Some notes on the regeneration of In and Kanyin in an Upper Burma Division. *Indian For.*, 41: 78–81.

Borchert, R., 1983. Phenology and control of flowering in tropical trees. *Biotropica*, 15: 81–89.

Browne, F.G., 1939. The Chengal beetle, *Coccotypes graniceps* Erch. (Coleoptera: Scolytidae). *Malay. For.*, 7: 107–115.

Browne, F.G., 1961. The zoology of Malayan Scolytidae and Platypodidae. *Malay. For. Rec.*, 22: 255 pp.

Burgess, P.F., 1969a. Preliminary observations on the autecology of *Shorea curtisii* Dyer ex King in the Malay Peninsular. *Malay. For.*, 24: 66–80.

Burgess, P.F., 1969b. Ecological factors in hill and mountain forests of the states of Malaya. *Malay. Nat. J.*, 22: 119–128.

Burgess, P.F., 1970. An approach towards a silvicultural system for the hill forests of the Malay Peninsular. *Malay. For.*, 33: 126–134.

Burgess, P.F., 1972. Studies on the regeneration of hill forests of the Malay Peninsular: The phenology of dipterocarps. *Malay. For.*, 35: 103–123.

Burgess, P.F., 1975. *Silviculture in the hill forests of the Malay Peninsular*. Forest Res. Inst. Kepong, Res. Pamph., 66.

Burkill, I.H., 1917. Notes on dipterocarps, 2. The seedling and seed-production in some specis of Shorea. *J. Straits Branch R. As. Soc.*, 76: 161–167.

Catinot, R., 1976. The present and the future of tropical rain forests. Biological and economic possibilities of tropical forest ecosystems. Limitations on their conversion, with special reference to tropical Africa. *Proc. 7th World Forestry Congress, Argentina*, pp. 2432–2441.

Chai, N.P.C., 1973. A note on *Parashorea tomentella* (Urat mata beledu) seed and its germination. *Malay. For.*, 36: 202–204.

Champion, H.G., 1927. Sal germination. *Indian For.*, 53: 616–617.

Champion, H.G., 1928. The effect of size on germination and development of seed of Sal. *Indian For.*, 54: 93–96.

Champion, H.G., 1933. Regeneration and management of Sal (*Shorea robusta*). *Indian For. Rec. (O.S.) Silvic.*, 19(3): 159 pp.

Champion, H.G., 1961. A preliminary survey of the forest types of India. *Indian For. Rec. (N.S.) Silvic.*, 1: 204 pp.

Champion, H.G. and Pant, B.D., 1931. Investigation on the seed and seedlings of *Shorea robusta* Gaertn. f. *Indian For. Rec. (O.S.) Silvic.*, 16(5): 33 pp.

Champion, H.G. and Seth, S.K., 1968. *A Revised Survey of the Forest Types of India*. Manager of Publications, Delhi, 404 pp.

Chan, H.T., 1977. *Reproductive biology of some Malaysian dipterocarps*. Ph.D. thesis, Univ. of Aberdeen, Aberdeen.

Chan, H.T., 1980. Reproductive biology of some Malaysian dipterocarps II. Fruiting biology and seedling studies. *Malay. For.*, 43: 438–451.

Chan, H.T., 1981. Reproductive biology of some Malaysian dipterocarps. III. Breeding systems. *Malay. For.*, 44: 28–36.

Chan, H.T. and Appanah, S., 1980. Reproductive biology of some Malaysian dipterocarps. I. Flowering biology. *Malay. For.*, 43: 132–143.

Chaturvedi, M.D., 1929. Resistance of seedlings of Sal to burning. *United Provinces For. Bull.*, 2: 276–281.

Chengappa, B.S., 1934. Andaman forests and their reproduction. *Indian For.*, 60: 117–119, 185–198.

Chengappa, B.S., 1937. Reproduction of the Andaman forests. *Indian For.*, 63: 16–29.

Chengappa, B.S., 1944. Andaman forests and their regeneration. *Indian For.*, 70: 297–304, 339–351, 380–385, 421–430.

Chowdhuri, A.K., 1960. A short note on *Shorea assamica* (Makai). *Indian For.*, 86: 205–206.

Cockburn, P.S., 1975. Phenology of dipterocarps in Sabah. *Malay. For.*, 38: 160–170.

Connell, J.H., 1978. Diversity in tropical rain forests and coral reefs. *Science*, 199: 1302–1310.

Corner, E.J.H., 1954. The evolution of tropical forests. In: J. Huxley, A.C. Hardy and E.B. Ford (Editors), *Evolution as a Process*. Allen and Unwin, London, pp. 34–46.

Cruden, R.W., 1976. Intraspecific variation in pollen–ovule ratios and nectar secretion — preliminary evidence of ecotypic adaptation. *Ann. Mo. Bot. Gard.*, 63: 277–289.

Daljeet-Singh, K., 1974. Some pests of some dipterocarps. *Malay. For.*, 37: 24–28.

Daljeet-Singh, K., 1975. A preliminary survey of insect attack on seedlings and saplings in Bukit Belata Forest Reserve. *Malay. For.*, 38: 14–16.

Daljeet-Singh, K., 1976. The influence of seed predators on the development and yield of dipterocarps. *Paper presented at 5th Malaysian Forestry Conf., Kuching*.

Davidson, D.A.E., 1938. Sal inflorescence. *Indian For.*, 64: p. 300.

De, R.N., 1925. Coppicing power of Sal. *Indian For.*, 51: p. 423.

De, R.N., 1938. Sal inflorescence. *Indian For.*, 64: 5–2.

De, R.N., 1941. Sal regeneration de novo. *Indian For.*, 67: 283–292.

Divekar, Y.R., 1941. Sal regeneration de novo. *Indian For.*, 67: 506–507; 68(1942): 339–340.

Ford Robertson, F.C., 1927. The problem of Sal regeneration with special reference to the "moist" forests of the United Provinces. *Indian For.*, 53: 500–511, 560–565.

Fox, J.E.D., 1973. Dipterocarp seedlings behaviour in Sabah. *Malay. For.*, 36: 205–214.

Foxworthy, F.W., 1911. Philippine Dipterocarpaceae. *Philipp. J. Sci. Sect. C*, 6: 231–280.

Foxworthy, F.W., 1932. Dipterocarpaceae of the Malay peninsula. *Malay. For. Rec.*, 10: 289 pp.

Gan, Y.Y., 1976. *Population and phylogenetic studies on species of Malaysian rainforest trees*. Ph.D. thesis, Univ. of Aberdeen, Aberdeen.

Gan, Y.Y., Robertson, F.W. and Ashton, P.S., 1977. Genetic variation in wild populations of rain forest trees. *Nature*, 269: 323–324.

Gentry, A.H., 1974. Flowering phenology and diversity in tropical Bignoniaceae. *Biotropica*, 6: 64–68.

Gong, W.K., 1981. Studies of the natural regeneration of a hill dipterocarp species. *Hopea pedicellata. Malay. For.*, 44: 357–369.

Gustafson, A., 1946–1947. Apomixis in higher plants I–III. *Lunds Univ. Arsskr.*, 42: 1–67; 43: 68–179, 181–371.

Ha, C.O., 1979. *Embryological and cytological aspects of the reproductive biology of some understorey rain forest trees.* Ph.D. thesis, Univ. of Malaya.

Holmes, C.H., 1942. Flowering and fruiting of forest trees of Ceylon. *Indian For.*, 68: 411–420(I); 498–499(II).

Howard, S.H., 1925. Epicormic branches in Sal. *Indian For.*, 51: 160–163.

Hubbell, S.P., 1979. Tree dispersion, abundance, and diversity in a tropical dry forest. *Science*, 213: 1299–1309.

Hubbell, S.P. and Foster, R.B., 1983. Diversity of canopy trees in a neotropical forest and implications for conservation. In: S.L. Sutton, T.C. Whitmore and A.C. Chadwick (Editors), *Tropical Rain Forest: Ecology and Management.* Blackwell, London, pp. 25–41.

Jacob, M.C., 1941. Sal regeneration de novo. A rejoinder. *Indian For.*, 66: 337–346.

Jansen, L.A., 1971. Observations on the viability of Borneo camphor *Dryobalanops aromatica* Gaertn. *Proc. Int. Seed Test Assoc.*, 36: 141–146.

Janzen, D.H., 1970. Herbivores and the number of tree species in tropical forests. *Am. Nat.*, 104: 501–528.

Janzen, D.H., 1974. Tropical blackwater rivers, animals and mast fruiting by the Dipterocarpaceae. *Biotropica*, 4: 69–103.

Jong, K., 1976. Cytology of the Dipterocarpaceae. In: J. Burley and B.T. Styles (Editors), *Tropical Trees, Variation, Breeding and Conservation.* Academic Press, New York, N.Y., pp. 79–84.

Jong, K., 1982. Cytotaxonomy. In: P.S. Ashton (Editor), *Dipterocarpaceae. J. Flora Malesiana, Ser. I*, 9: 268–273.

Jong, K. and Kaur, A., 1979. A cytotaxonomic view of the Dipterocarpaceae with some comments on polyploidy and apomixis. *Mem. Mus. Natl. Hist. Nat. N.S., Ser. B*, 26: 41–49.

Jong, K. and Lethbridge A., 1967. Cytological studies in the Dipterocarpaceae, I. Chromosome numbers of certain Malaysian genera. *Notes R. Bot. Gard. Edinburgh*, 27: 175–184.

Joshi, H.B. and editorial board, 1980. *Troup's The Silviculture of Indian Trees.* Delhi.

Kadambi, K., 1954a. *Dipterocarpus indicus* Bedd. (Syn. D. turbinatus Gaertn. f.) — its silviculture and management. *Indian For.*, 80: 264–276.

Kadambi, K., 1954b. *Hopea parviflora* Bedd. Its Silviculture and management. *Indian For.*, 80: 390–408.

Kadambi, K., 1957a. *Vateria indica* Linn. *Indian For.*, 83: 317–323.

Kadambi, K., 1957b. *Balanacarpus utilis* Bedd. (*Hopea longifolia* Ayer). *Indian For.*, 83: 465–468.

Kaur, A., 1977. *Embryological and cytological studies on some members of the Dipterocarpaceae.* Ph.D. thesis, Univ. of Aberdeen, Aberdeen.

Kaur, A., Ha, C.O., Jong, K., Sands, V.E., Chan, H.T., Soepadmo, E. and Ashton, P.S., 1978. Apomixis may be widespread among trees of the climax rain forest. *Nature*, 271: 440–442.

Kaur, A., Jong, K., Sands, V.E. and Soepadmo, E., 1986. Cytoembryology of some Malaysian dipterocarps, with some evidence of apomixis. *Bot. J. Linn. Soc.*, 92 (2): 75–88.

Kerr, A.F.G., 1914. Hybrid dipterocarps. *J. Siam. Soc.*, 2: p. 9.

Kochummen, K.M., 1961. Precocious flowering in Dipterocarpaceae. *Malay. For.*, 24: 236–237.

Kochummen, K.M., 1977. Natural plant succession after farming at Kepong. *Malay. For.*, 41: p. 76.

Kochummen, K.M. and Ng, F.S.P., 1977. Natural plant succession after farming in Kepong. *Malay. For.*, 40: 61–78.

Koelmeyer, K.O., 1959. The periodicity of leaf change and flowering in the principal forest communities in Ceylon. *Ceylon For.*, 4: 157–189.

Krishnaswamy, V.S. and Mathauda, G.S., 1954. Phenological behaviour of a few forest species at New Forest, Dehra Dun. *Indian For.*, 80: 124–153, 187–206.

Ledig, F.T., 1986. Heterozygosity, heterosis, and fitness in outbreeding plants. In: M.E. Soulé (Editor), *Conservation Biology. The Science of Scarcity and Diversity.* Sinauer, Sunderland, Mass., pp. 77–104.

Lee, H.S., 1980. *Shorea pinanga* flowers 6 years after planting in Research Plot No. 76. *Malay. For.*, 43: 126–127.

Levin, D.A., 1975. Pest pressure and recombination systems in plants. *Am. Nat.*, 109: 437–541.

Lewis, T., 1970. Patterns of distribution of insects near a windbreak of tall trees. *Ann. Appl. Biol.*, 65: 213–220.

Lewis, T., 1973. *Thrips, their Biology, Ecology and Economic Importance.* Academic Press, New York, N.Y., 349 pp.

Liew, T.C. and Wong, F.O., 1973. Density, recruitment, mortality and growth of dipterocarp seedlings in virgin and logged-over forests in Sabah. *Malay. For.*, 36: 3–15.

Lloyd, D.G., 1980a. Demographic factors and mating patterns in angiosperms. In: O.T. Solbrig (Editor), *Demography and Evolution in Plant Populations.* Blackwell, Oxford, pp. 67–88.

Lloyd, D.G., 1980b. Benefits and handicaps of sexual reproduction. *Evol. Biol.*, 13: 69–111.

Maguire, B. and Ashton, P.S., 1977. *Pakaraimoideae*, Dipterocarpaceae of the Western Hemisphere. II. Systematic, geographic and phyletic considerations. *Taxon*, 26: 359–368.

Makins, F.K., 1920. Natural reproduction of Sal in Singhbhum. *Indian For.*, 20: 292–296.

Maury, G., 1968. Germinations anormales chez les Diptérocarpacées de Malaisie. *Bull. Soc. Hist. Nat., Toulouse*, 104: 183–202.

Maury, G., 1970. Différents types de polyembryonie chez quelques Diptérocarpacées Asiatiques. *Bull. Soc. Hist. Nat., Toulouse*, 106: 282–288.

Maury, G., 1978. *Diptérocarpacées, du fruit à la plantule.* Thesis, Univ. of Toulouse, Toulouse.

Maury, G., 1979. Conséquences taxonomiques de l'étude des caractères des fruits-germinations, embryons et plantules de Diptérocarpacées. *Mem. Mus. Natl. Hist. Nat., N.S., Ser. B*, 26: 81–106.

Maury, G., Muller, J. and Lugardon, B., 1975. Notes on the morphology and fine structure of the exine of some pollen types in Dipterocarpaceae. *Rev. Palaeobot. Palynol.*, 19: 241–289.

Maury, G., Hassan, A.M. and Bravo, D.R., 1981. Seed storage of *Shorea parvifolia* and *Dipterocarpus humeratus*. *Malay. For.*, 44: 267–280.

Medway, Lord, 1972. Phenology of a tropical rain forest in Malaya. *Biol. J. Linn. Soc.*, 4: 146–177.

Milroy, A.J.W., 1930. The relation between Sal forests and fire. *Indian For.*, 56: 442–447.

Mobbs, E.C., 1936. Sal natural regeneration experiments in the United Provinces. *Indian For.*, 62: 260–267.

Muller, J., 1979. Pollen size in Dipterocarpaceae. *Mem. Mus. Natl. Hist. Nat., N.S., Ser. B*, 26: 35–40.

Muller, J., 1982. Palynology. In: P.S. Ashton (Editor), Dipterocarpaceae. *Flora Malesiana, Ser. I*, 9: p. 268.

Ng, F.S.P., 1966. Age at first flowering of dipterocarps. *Malay. For.*, 29: 290–295.

Ng, F.S.P., 1973. Germination of fresh seeds of Malaysian trees. *Malay. For.*, 36: 129–140.

Ng, F.S.P., 1975. Germination of fresh seeds of Malaysian trees. *Malay. For.*, 38: 171–176(II); 40(1977): 160–163(III).

Ng, F.S.P., 1976. Responses to leader-shoot injury in *Shorea platyclados*. *Malay. For.*, 39: 91–100.

Ng, F.S.P., 1977. Gregarious flowering of dipterocarps in Kepong, 1976. *Malay. For.*, 40: 126–137.

Ng, F.S.P., 1980. Flowering of *Vatica wallichii* at 5 years. *Malay. For.*, 43: 393–394.

Ng, F.S.P., 1981. Vegetative and reproductive phenology of dipterocarps. *Malay. For.*, 44: 197–221.

Ng, F.S.P. and Loh, H.S., 1974. Flowering to fruiting periods of Malaysian trees. *Malay. For.*, 37: 127–132.

Ng, F.S.P. and Mat. Asri bin Ngah Sanah. 1979. Germination of fresh seeds of Malaysian trees. IV. *Malay. For.*, 42: 221–227.

Nicholson, D.I., 1960. Light requirements of seedlings of five species of Dipterocarpaceae. *Malay. For.*, 23: 344–356.

Nicholson, D.I., 1963. A study of a virgin forest near Sandakan, North Borneo. *Symp. on Ecological Research in Humid Tropics Vegetation*, UNESCO, Paris, pp. 67–87.

Nicholson, J.W., 1925. Epicormic branches in Sal. *Indian For.*, 51: p. 283.

Nixon, A.B., 1929. The uniform compartment system in the Yinke reserve, Burma. *Indian For.*, 55: 293–297.

Osmaston, F.C., 1928. Sal and its regeneration. *Indian For.*, 54: 567–577; 639–655.

Palmer, J.R., 1979. Gregarious flowering of dipterocarps in Kepong, 1976. *Malay. For.*, 43: 74–75.

Parker, R.N., 1927. Illustrations of Indian forest plants, I–V. Species of *Dipterocarpus*. *Indian For. Rec.*, 13: p. 1; 16: p. 1.

Parkinson, C.E., 1932. A note on the Burmese species of *Dipterocarpus*. *Burma For. Bull.*, 27: 35 pp.

Rao, A.N., 1953. The embryology of *Shorea talura* Roxb. *Phytomorphology*, 3: 476–484.

Rao, A.N., 1955a. Development of gametophyte in *Hopea wightiana*. *J. Mysore. Univ.*, 15: 7–15.

Rao, A.N., 1955b. A contribution to the embryology of *Vateria indica*. *Proc. Natl. Inst. Sci. India*, 21: 247–255.

Rao, A.N., 1956. Life history of *Shorea robusta* Gaertn. *Curr. Sci.*, 25: 128–129.

Rao, A.N., 1962. Floral anatomy and gametogenesis in *Hopea racophloea* *J. Indian Bot. Soc.*, 41: 551–562.

Raynor, E.W., 1960. Sal regeneration de novo. *Indian For.*, 66: 525–529.

Ridley, H.N., 1901. The Timbers of the Malay Peninsular (cont.). *Agric. Bull. Straits Settl. Fed. Malay. States*, 1: p. 53.

Ridley, H.N., 1930. *The Dispersal of Plants Throughout the World*. Reeve, Ashford.

Roy, R.P. and Jha, R.P., 1965. Cytological studies in the Dipterocarpaceae. *J. Indian Bot. Soc.*, 44: 387–397.

Sahay, B.K., 1955. The problem of Sal (*Shorea robusta* Gaertn.) regeneration in a dry peninsular Sal forest of Bihar. *Indian For.*, 81: 668–676.

Sasaki, S., 1980. Storage and germination of dipterocarp seeds. *Malay. For.*, 43: 290–308.

Sasaki, S. and Mori, T., 1981. Growth responses of dipterocarp seedlings to light. *Malay. For.*, 44: 319–345.

Sasaki, S., Tan, C.H. and Zulfatah, A.R., 1979. Some observations of unusual flowering and fruiting of dipterocarps. *Malay. For.*, 42: 38–45.

Seth, S.K. and Bhatnagar, H.P., 1959. Soil suitability index for Sal (*Shorea robusta*) natural regeneration. *Indian For.*, 86: 590–601.

Seth, S.K. and Dabral, S.N., 1960. Characteristic features of natural regeneration under various tending schedules in Holong–Nahor (*Dipterocarpus-Mesua*) forests of Assam. *Indian For.*, 86: 355–373.

Seth, S.K., Khan, M.A.W. and Yadav, J.S.P., 1960. Sal mortality in Bihar. *Indian For.*, 86: 645–679.

Shaukat Husain, M., 1927. Sal germination. *Indian For.*, 53: 476–477.

Shaukat Husain, M., 1928. Sal germination from *Sakhu* and *Sakhui* seed. *Indian For.*, 54: p. 67.

Singh, K.G., 1966. Ectotropic myccorhiza in equatorial rain forests. *Malay. For.*, 29: 13–19.

Smits, W. Th. M., 1983. Dipterocarps and mycorrhiza. An ecological adaptation and a factor in forest regeneration. *Flora Malay. Bull.*, 36: 3926–3937.

Smythies, B.E., 1958. The illipe-nut. *Sarawak Gaz.*, 31: 146–148.

Smythies, E.A., 1918. Note on the dying back of Sal seedlings. *Indian For.*, 44: 420–422.

Smythies, E.A., 1924. The evolution of a Sal seedling. *Indian For.*, 50: 57–67.

Smythies, E.A., 1926. The problem of Sal regeneration. *Indian For.*, 52: 395–400.

Smythies, E.A., 1936. Seedling regeneration in B-3 Sal. *Indian For.*, 42: 186–204.

Solbrig, O.T., 1976. On the relative advantages of cross and self fertilization. *Ann. Mo. Bot. Gard.*, 63: 262–275.

Somego, M., 1978. Cytogenetical study of Dipterocarpaceae. *Malay. For.*, 41: 358–366.

Srivastava, P.B.L., 1977. Precocious flowering in Dipterocarpaceae. *Malay. For.*, 40: 251–253.

Symington, C.F., 1934. Notes on Malayan Dipterocarpaceae. *Gard. Bull. Straits Settl.*, 8: 1–40.

Symington, C.F., 1943. Forester's manual of Dipterocarps. *Malay. For. Rec.*, 16.

Tamari, C., 1976. Phenology and seed storage trials of dipterocarps. *Forest Research Institute, Malaysia, Res. Pamph.* 69.

Tang, H.T., 1971. Preliminary tests on the storage and collection of some *Shorea* species seeds. *Malay. For.*, 34: 84–98.

Tang, H.T., 1978. Age of first fruiting in *Shorea leprosula*. *Malay. For.*, 41: 294–295.

Tang, H.T. and Chong, P.F., 1979. "Sudden" mortality in a regenerated stand of *Shorea curtisii* in Senaling Inas Forest Reserve, Negri Sembilan. *Malay. For.*, 42: 240–254.

Tang, H.T. and Tamari, C., 1973. Seed description and storage tests of some dipterocarps. *Malay. For.*, 36: 113–128.

Taylor, C.E., 1982. *Reproductive Biology and Ecology of Some Tropical Pioneer Trees*. Ph.D. thesis, Univ. of Aberdeen, Aberdeen.

Treub, M., 1911. Le sac embryonnaire et l'embryon dans les Angiospermes. *Ann. Jard. Bot. Buitenzorg*, 24: 1–27.

Troup, R.S., 1921. *The Silviculture of Indian Trees. I.* Clarendon, Oxford, 336 pp.

Unwin, R., 1931. Regeneration of "In" (*Dipterocarpus tubercu-*

latus), Yinke Reserve, Katha Division. *Indian For.*, 57: 149–153.

Webber, M.L., 1934. Fruit dispersal. *Malay. For.*, 3: 18–19.

Williams, R.R., 1970. Factors affecting pollination in fruit trees. In: L.C. Luckwill and C.V. Cutting (Editors), *Physiology of Tree Crops*. Academic Press, London, pp. 193–207.

Wood, G.H.S., 1956. The dipterocarp flowering season in North Borneo, 1955. *Malay. For.*, 19: 193–201.

Wycherley, P.R., 1973. The phenology of plants in the humid tropics. *Micronesica*, 9: 75–96.

Yap, S.K., 1976. *The reproductive biology of some understorey fruit tree species in the lowland dipterocarp forest of West Malaysia*. Ph.D. thesis, Univ. of Malaya.

Yap, S.K., 1981. Germination and storage of dipterocarp seeds. *Malay. For.*, 44: 281–300.

Yap, S.K., 1982. The phenology of some fruit tree species in a lowland dipterocarp forest. *Malay. For.*, 45: 21–35.

Chapter 12

THE RAIN FORESTS OF NORTHEASTERN AUSTRALIA — THEIR ENVIRONMENT, EVOLUTIONARY HISTORY AND DYNAMICS

G.C. STOCKER and G.L. UNWIN

INTRODUCTION

Tropical rain forests constitute an interesting but small proportion (< 1%) of Australia's tropical vegetation. The present distribution of rain forests in this region (Fig. 12.1) is reportedly influenced by climate, soil fertility and water regimes (see, for instance, Tracey, 1969; Webb, 1969), by historical factors — especially Pleistocene climatic change — (Webb and Tracey, 1981), and by fire regimes established by the Aborigines (Stocker and Mott, 1981). Rain forests are found from sea level to almost the top of the highest mountain in the region (Mt. Bartle Frere, 1622 m). It has been estimated that at the time Europeans arrived there were about 1.2 million ha of rain forest in this region. About 80% remains, either as selectively logged forest or virtually untouched in National Parks and inaccessible portions of State Forests (Winter et al., 1984).

Features of the region's rain forests include their apparent floristic relationships with both South-East Asian and Gondwanaland floras; the great contrast between their structural, floristic and dynamic features and those of the widespread open eucalypt dominated forests and woodlands; the general lack of frugivorous mammals (especially the primates); and the absence of an Aboriginal population which practiced shifting cultivation. The following account reviews research into aspects of the history and dynamics of these forests.

ENVIRONMENTAL FEATURES

Climate

The climate of the region has been generally described by the Australian Bureau of Meteoro-

logy (Anon., 1965, 1971, 1977a) and by Lauer in Ch. 2 of this volume. The following notes concentrate on those aspects relevant to rain forests of the region. Climatic influences which occasionally have a catastrophic impact on rain forest (drought, strong winds, frost, etc.) are described in further detail later.

Temperature

Mean monthly temperature data (Table 12.1) for selected sites indicate predictable drops in winter temperatures at higher latitudes and elevations. However, summer temperatures are influenced more by elevation than by latitude. While winter temperatures are low enough to have a measurable effect on plant growth in areas above about 500 m elevation, a more important aspect of the temperature regime is the occurrence of frost (see below).

Rainfall

Although the region contains the wettest part of Australia, the rainfall distribution exhibits a marked summer maximum. Rainfall is generated by three general synoptic patterns:

(1) Convectional storms — These mostly occur during November, December and January. They are of greater frequency on the western edge of the Atherton Tablelands than elsewhere (Anon., 1971). Storm rains are often heavy but isolated and of short duration. They occur late in the year when rain from other sources is infrequent.

(2) Tropical interconvergence zone — This feature usually moves far enough south to bring heavy rain lasting one or two weeks, several times each year, in the period January to March. Associated winds are usually southeasterly and rainfall is heaviest along the eastern coast and on

TABLE 12.1

Meteorological data for selected localities within or near the rain forest region of northeastern Australia (data from Anon., 1965, 1971)

	Jan.	Feb.	Mar.	Apr.	May	Jun.	Jul.	Aug.	Sep.	Oct.	Nov.	Dec.	Year
THURSDAY ISLAND (10°36'S, 142°12'E; 8 m)													
Mean monthly rainfall (mm)	441	409	345	202	48	16	11	6	3	9	46	193	1729
Temperature (°C) mean max.	30.5	30.0	29.5	29.5	29.0	28.5	27.5	27.5	28.5	29.5	31.0	31.5	29.5
mean min.	25.0	25.0	25.0	25.0	24.5	23.5	22.5	22.5	23.0	24.0	25.0	25.5	24.0
Humidity (%) 0900 h	82	83	82	80	79	79	80	77	74	72	71	74	78
1500 h	77	78	76	74	72	71	71	68	68	66	67	69	71
COOKTOWN (15°28'S, 145°15'E; 2 m)													
Mean monthly rainfall (mm)	368	367	396	208	75	52	27	29	16	23	64	159	1784
Temperature (°C) mean max.	31.5	31.0	30.5	29.0	27.5	26.5	26.0	26.5	28.0	29.5	31.0	32.0	29.0
mean min.	24.0	24.0	23.5	23.0	21.5	20.0	19.0	19.5	21.0	22.5	23.5	24.0	22.0
Humidity (%) 0900 h	79	81	80	77	76	77	76	72	71	69	70	73	75
1500 h	72	72	73	73	72	71	69	65	65	64	65	69	69
CAIRNS (16°55'S, 145°46'E; 2 m)													
Mean monthly rainfall (mm)	421	422	460	264	110	72	39	42	43	50	98	203	2224
Temperature (°C) mean max.	32.0	31.5	30.5	29.5	27.5	26.0	25.5	26.5	28.0	30.0	31.0	32.0	29.0
mean min.	23.0	23.0	22.5	21.0	19.0	17.5	16.0	16.0	17.5	19.5	21.0	22.5	20.0
Humidity (%) 0900 h	74	76	78	78	77	77	75	72	69	67	68	69	73
1500 h	69	68	70	68	68	67	63	61	61	62	63	66	66
ATHERTON (17°16'S, 145°29'E; 760 m)													
Mean monthly rainfall (mm)	287	305	268	105	60	46	30	25	22	28	76	173	1425
Temperature (°C) mean max.	28.5	28.0	27.0	25.0	23.0	22.0	21.5	22.5	25.0	27.5	29.0	29.5	26.0
mean min.	18.0	18.0	17.5	15.0	13.0	10.5	10.0	10.0	11.0	13.5	16.0	17.0	14.0
Humidity (%) 0900 h	78	83	82	83	83	82	80	75	67	62	65	68	75
INNISFAIL (17°31'S, 146°2'E; 7 m)													
Mean monthly rainfall (mm)	530	606	706	470	309	190	126	113	92	81	153	265	3641
Temperature (°C) mean max.	31.0	30.5	29.5	28.0	26.5	24.5	24.0	25.0	27.0	2.5	30.0	31.0	28.0
mean min.	22.0	22.0	21.5	19.5	17.5	15.5	14.0	14.0	16.0	18.0	19.5	21.0	18.5
Humidity (%) 0900 h	80	84	86	86	87	87	85	83	80	77	77	76	82
1500 h	73	72	72	70	70	69	69	65	64	63	66	68	68
INGHAM (18°42'S, 146°12'E; 13 m)													
Mean monthly rainfall (mm)	421	457	418	181	93	57	38	34	36	47	87	165	2034
MACKAY (21°6'S, 149°6'E; 11 m)													
Mean monthly rainfall (mm)	335	321	306	152	94	67	41	26	40	46	74	164	1666
Temperature (°C) mean max.	30.0	29.5	28.5	27.0	24.5	22.0	21.5	23.0	25.0	27.5	29.0	30.0	26.5
mean min.	23.0	23.0	21.5	19.5	16.0	13.5	12.0	12.5	15.0	18.5	21.0	22.5	18.0
Humidity (%) 0900 h	75	76	78	77	77	78	76	73	69	67	67	69	73
1500 h	68	71	72	69	67	68	64	64	64	65	65	67	67

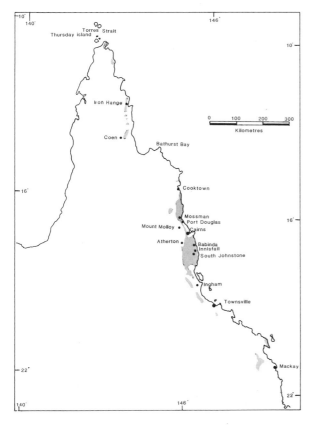

Fig. 12.1. The shaded portions show the limits of tropical rain forests in northeastern Australia at the time of first settlement by people of European origin. Towns and localities mentioned in the text are superimposed.

the slopes of the coastal ranges. This influence often causes minor flooding and may bring persistent rains to the drier areas west of the Great Dividing Range. Sometimes a tropical low-pressure system will form in the monsoonal trough, causing continuous heavy rain and high winds for as long as a week. These tropical lows frequently develop into hurricanes, or cyclones as they are called in this region (see below).

(3) Southeasterly trades — As anti-cyclones move across southern Australia during winter they generate a southeasterly air stream which, though shallow, is often sufficiently moist to produce showers in coastal areas and rain and drizzle on the mountains and eastern parts of the tablelands. Rain from the trades can occur at almost any time of the year but it is most prominent in the period from March to August when the main path of the southern anti-cyclones is further south and the

trades blow over longer stretches of ocean. Falls are generally persistent but light with predictable variations according to aspect and elevation. Instability of the upper atmosphere may increase rain intensity and falls are then more widespread.

Annual rainfall isohyets for the region are shown in Fig. 12.2. Mean monthly falls for selected localities (Table 12.1 and Fig. 12.3) illustrate the strong rainfall seasonality, especially when compared to Lae (Papua New Guinea) or Brisbane (southern Queensland). Monthly rainfall variability for sites listed in Table 12.1 ranges from 29% for Thursday Island to 43% for Cairns (Anon., 1971). Average annual frequency of days with rain varies from 101 days (Barrine) to 178 days (South Johnstone).

Evaporation

There are few records of evaporation (E) for the region. By applying the Waite formula, $E = 21.2$ (saturation vapour deficit), evaporation in the eastern part of the region was estimated to be between 1270 and 1397 mm yr^{-1} (Anon., 1971). It was greatest during November and December with average monthly values for coastal areas of about 152 mm.

Humidity

Humidity records are only available for a few localities in the region. Those for Cairns (Table 12.1) are probably reasonably representative of most of the coastal lowlands within the region.

Geology, geomorphology and soils

The landscapes of the region began to evolve into their present form during the latter part of the Tertiary. De Keyser (1972) noted that during the Pliocene strong block faulting broke up an ancient peneplain, uplifting the tablelands but causing subsidence of the coastal plain and continental shelf. These movements were accompanied by sporadic volcanism. The rain forest soils of the region can be divided into three broad groups which reflect these events. The groups are: (1) the granitic soils on some of the foothills but more characteristically of the mountains; (2) the metamorphic soils derived from ancient shales which underlay the old peneplain; and (3) the basaltic soils mainly of the tablelands.

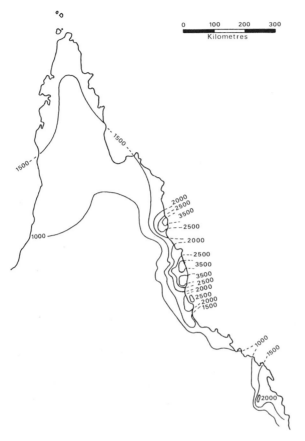

Fig. 12.2. Annual rainfall isohyets (mm) within the northeastern Australian region. (Data from Anon., 1965, 1971.)

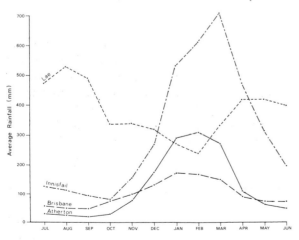

Fig. 12.3. Monthly rainfall averages are plotted for some northeastern Australian sites and compared with those for Lae (Papua New Guinea) and Brisbane (southern Queensland) to illustrate the seasonality of rainfall in the former region. (Data from Anon., 1977a; McAlpine et al., 1975.)

Disturbances

The role of natural disturbances in initiating changes in rain-forest structure and floristics is widely appreciated. Those affecting rain forests in northeastern Australia are described, with some emphasis placed on their intensity, extent, frequency and predictability.

Wind

Convectional storms appear to be the main source of destructive winds in the equatorial zone within 5° latitude of the Equator. Further north and south the incidence of forest disturbance due to convectional storms declines and the effects of tropical cyclones are more significant.

Unfortunately, there is little information on the frequency and extent of damage from convectional storms to tropical forests in this region. The record of thunder-days (the average annual number of days on which thunder is heard at a given locality) provides the only regular statistic of any value. The number of these events in the rain forest belt of this region (20–40) is low compared with many other tropical localities — for instance, in Borneo, Anderson (1964) noted that three localities, Kuching, Bintulu and Miri, had annual averages of 163, 96 and 109 thunder-days, respectively. In northeastern Australia, storm damage is usually confined to narrow strips of vegetation no more than a few hundred metres wide. Typically branches are torn off and trees are occasionally uprooted.

The extent of forest disturbance resulting from a cyclone may be several orders of magnitude greater than that from a convectional storm. Because cyclones may affect large numbers of people adversely, their influences on forests are better (if sometimes incidentally) recorded. The typical extent of severe forest disturbance in this region has not been estimated, however it is thought that the individual areas of damage measure tens or hundreds of square kilometres rather than the 2000 km² observed following the 1956 cyclone in Puerto Rico (Wadsworth and Englerth, 1959).

Records indicate that a cyclone affects the rain forests of part of this region about once a year (Dobson and Stewart, 1974; Lourensz, 1977). The peak in seasonal frequency corresponds with the summer wet season (Table 12.2). Differences in

TABLE 12.2

Number of cyclones influencing at least a part of the northeastern Australian region for the
50-year period 1911 to 1960 (adapted from Anon., 1971)

Month	J	F	M	A	M	J	J	A	S	O	N	D	Total
No. cyclones	18	17	13	4	–	–	–	–	–	–	–	3	55

frequency for various parts of the region are shown
in Fig. 12.4. The highest wind velocity ever
recorded for this region was near Innisfail during a
1986 cyclone when maximum gusts were estimated
at 176 km h^{-1} (Anon., 1986). Estimates of extreme
gusts over the region for various return periods are
given in Table 12.3.

The landfall of some cyclones in this region is
sometimes accompanied by tidal surges (up to
12 m in Bathurst Bay in 1899; Anon., 1971), which
may have catastrophic effects on low-lying coastal
vegetation.

Webb (1958) seems to have been the first to
appreciate the wider ecological effects of cyclones
on the rain-forest vegetation of this region. He
described the damage to rain forests caused by the
severe cyclone of 1956 and some cyclone-related
phenomena such as the vine tangles which are
locally called "cyclone scrub" (Figs. 12.5 and
12.6). He estimated that none of the rain forests of
the lowlands and foothills of north Queensland has
escaped severe or general cyclone damage for more
than 40 years and he thought it unlikely that any

TABLE 12.3

Return periods for estimated extreme wind gusts in northeastern Australia (adapted from Anon., 1971)

Return period (years)	10	20	50	100
Extreme gusts (m s^{-1})	33	36	41	46

rain-forest area in Queensland could remain
unaffected by cyclones for as long as 500 years. In
this study Webb also recognized the potential
effects of fire in cyclone debris and attributed some
of the grassland tongues on ascending spurs in the
Babinda area to the combined effects of both types
of disturbance.

A few large rain-forest tree species may have
structural features which enable them to react to
high winds in a similar manner to the eucalypts
(Stocker, unpublished). These species (for instance,
Backhousia bancroftii[1] and *Lindsayomyrtus bra-
chyandrus*) often dominate the rain forests of some
lowland areas where the frequency of hurricane
force winds appears higher than elsewhere.

Droughts

Droughts severe enough to affect the structure
and floristics of rain forest assemblages do not
appear to be at all frequent in northeastern
Australia. The most severe drought recorded in
this region appears to have been that of 1915.
During this year the Atherton Tableland and
associated region received less than half its normal
rainfall. The Queensland Department of Forestry
annual report for 1915 noted that "As a result (of
the drought) moist evergreen scrubs were rendered
leafless, while the underwood and much of the
overwood was killed, this allowing fires to spread
in reserves which are usually considered quite safe
from fire danger". The report for the following
year observed that inkweed (*Phytolacca octandra*)

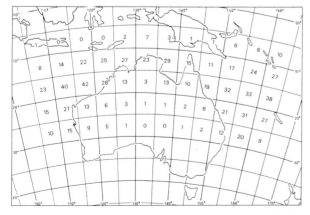

Fig. 12.4. The average frequency of cyclones recorded for 5°
latitude/longitude squares over 10-year periods show those
areas most vulnerable to cyclone disturbance. (From Lorensz,
1977.)

---

[1]Tree species nomenclature follows Hyland (1982).

Fig. 12.5. Severe disturbance to lowland rain forest near Innisfail due to cyclone Winifred, February 1986.

and stinging trees (*Dendrocnide* spp.), both short-lived shrubby weed species, had invaded forest damaged by drought.

The year of 1923 was also very dry in some parts of north Queensland and Herbert (1935) reported the death of many rain-forest epiphytes during that year.

Frost

Although frost is not usually considered to be an influence on tropical rain forests, but in this region frost is a significant part of the environment above 700 m. Frost effects on forest vegetation are mainly observed on artificially maintained forest edges but there are records of severe frost damaging undisturbed forest. For example the Queensland Forestry Department Annual Report for 1932 observed that severe frosts in June of that year had "burnt jungle trees to a height of 70 feet and killed lantana (*Lantana camara*) outright."

It is also suspected that fires lit by Aborigines in frost damaged vegetation may have once been a significant factor in converting some areas of rainforest to eucalypt forest and in maintaining and extending the eucalypt forest (see below).

Fire

Fire is not normally considered to be a factor causing either local or widespread disturbance to rain forests. Although most rain-forest species are relatively fire sensitive (but not as fire sensitive as often thought) the litter on the forest floor is usually too moist and sparse to support a fire (Stocker and Mott, 1981). However, as noted above, there are two situations (following cyclones or severe droughts) where extensive fires can readily occur in rain forests. Fires of limited extent also seem possible in areas defoliated by severe frost.

Before the arrival of man in the region the ignition of droughted or wind damaged forest would have occurred very infrequently for lightning would have been the only reliable ignition source.

Fig. 12.6. Patches of rain forest which have been severely disturbed by past cyclones have characteristic features such as vine tangles and climber towers. The dominant vine species here is *Merrima peltata*.

Geomorphological disturbance

Several relatively small, if conspicuous, landslips occurred during January 1979 in undisturbed forest on the slopes of Mt. Bartle Frere and Mt. Bellenden Ker after several weeks of heavy rain (4.8 times the monthly mean). However, the frequency and extent of these events and similar catastrophic changes in landform suggest that they are relatively insignificant in forest dynamics. This is in marked contrast with neighbouring New Guinea where successions of landslips, recent alluvial deposits and fresh volcanic landscapes are commonplace (White, 1975).

Human occupation

The arrival of man on the continent created new disturbance possibilities. The time of his arrival in Australia is still very much a matter of debate. Man was certainly well established in southern Australia at 32 000 B.P. (Barbetti and Allen, 1972). More debatable evidence led Merrilees (1979) to suggest that man could have arrived 200 000 years

ago. All researchers agree that he came from the north and most (except for Abbie, 1975) accept that at least two successive waves of invasion were involved. The lower sea levels during most of the Quaternary would have allowed easy movements into the continent with minimal boating skills.

Views of the effects of man's arrival on the vegetation of Australia vary enormously. For example Specht (1975) saw Aborigines as model conservationists lacking the technology to make any impact. Horton (1980) had similar views. Jones (1975), Merrilees (1979), Jones and Bowler (1980) and Tindale (1981) saw their impact mainly as a new predator and an efficient hunter although they were also aware that his use of fire may have been important. Stocker and Mott (1981) examined the role of fire in the ecology of the tropical forests and woodlands of northern Australia and postulated that the introduction of a new fire regime by Aborigines would have a profound effect on the vegetation of that part of Australia.

Fires in the grasslands and woodlands would

have changed with habitation by Aborigines, from periodic catastrophes to regular and usually seasonal features of the environment.

It has been suggested (Stocker, 1980; Stocker and Mott, 1981) that the change in fire ignition regime would have resulted in the breaking up of the ancient rain-forest/closed thicket continuum which appears to have existed over a wide range of annual rainfall (500–4000 mm) on free-draining soils in northern Australia. While the rain forests, characteristic of the high rainfall end of this continuum, may have been reduced in area they have not suffered the fragmentation typical of the closed woodlands and thickets of drier areas. Remnants of this closed-forest continuum are now only found on some sites naturally protected from fire. The balance has been replaced by open forests and woodlands which are composed of fire-adapted species and usually dominated by eucalypts. The local retreat and reinvasion of the more mesic rain-forest elements, to and from refugia, in response to climatic change, would have been much more difficult (in some cases virtually impossible) after this disruption. This is because eucalypt dominated assemblages are easily maintained by fire, even in high rainfall environments, provided there is a short dry season and a reliable ignition of grass fuels.

The other significant feature of Aboriginal culture in Australia is that they never practiced shifting cultivation, except on some of the northern Torres Strait Islands between the continent and New Guinea. If shifting agriculture had found its way further south into the main rain-forest block, the climate and soils are such that it could have been very successful. However, studies of the dynamics of hillside vegetation near Cairns (Stocker and Mott, 1981) suggested that under the present climate, repeated fires in abandoned gardens would have resulted in the development of extensive areas of grassland and eventually, of open eucalypt forest.

In northern Australia there are, in many areas, indications that closed forests have expanded since the breakdown 50–100 years ago of traditional Aboriginal lifestyles (and associated patterns of fire use) (Stocker, 1981). Blake (1939) noted recent increase in rain forests in this region but does not seem to have appreciated the role of fire in the dynamics of the eucalypt/rain-forest boundary.

Phytogeography

The hypothesis of an Indo-Malaysia origin for the Australian rain-forest flora was first formalized by Hooker (1860). At the time it would have been readily accepted, as the closed tropical forests were seen to resemble those of the Indian and Malaysian regions, whereas open eucalypt forests and woodlands were conceived as the characteristic Australian vegetation. Initially there was little to argue about for the regional floristics were poorly known. It is now realised that many of the northern rain-forest plants have affinities with those normally considered to be typically Australian.

The notion that there were at least some Australian elements in the rain forest is, however, not new. In one of the earliest studies of Queensland's vegetation Domin (1911) saw the wet tropics of this region as having a truly Malayan–Papuan flora. He also noted that there were many endemic Australian genera and species in this flora and concluded that it must have separated at an early epoch to enable numerous endemics to develop independently. Swain (1928) viewed the "Malayan flora" as having displaced *Eucalyptus* and *Araucaria* species from more favourable sites. Herbert (1960) suggested that Australia was the co-inheritor of an ancient and widespread flora and although he was the first really to emphasize the endemic nature of many rainforest plant species, he still saw the rain forests of this region as being basically Indo-Malayan. Burbidge (1960) extended these thoughts by recognizing that "there are plants both in the tropic zone and the 'Eremaea' which though not sclerophyllous are genuinely endemic elements in a floristic and phytogeographic sense". She also noted the close affinity of the flora of the region first with New Guinea but also that there was a long-standing, but lesser, relationship with the floras of Malaysia, New Caledonia and New Zealand.

Thorne (1963) placed the tropical and subtropical rain-forest areas of coastal eastern Queensland and the adjacent Torres Strait Islands in the Torresian Province of the Papuan Subregion of the Oriental Region, even though he saw this area as a zone of heavy overlap with the Australian Region. Although mainly concerned with the phytogeography of the Pacific Islands, Van Balgooy (1971) considered Thorne's subdivision to be one of the most acceptable biogeographically. Aubréville (1975) considered the vegetation of the Western Pacific to have been derived from two old floras which were now well mixed. He also suggested that this region might be the cradle of the angiosperms.

Beadle (1981) analysed the rain-forest flora of tropical and subtropical eastern Australia, and also detected an Asian–Australian relationship. He noted that 120 genera of dicotyledons were represented in Australia by a single species and in Asia by several to many (up to 200) species. Another 100 genera were represented in Australia by a few species and in Asia by several to many species. The typical rain-forest families Meliaceae and Lauraceae provide many examples of genera which are represented in Australia but have many more species in Malaysia. Webb and Tracey (1981) listed eight rain-forest families (Akaniaceae, Austrobaileyaceae, Baueraceae, Davidsoniaceae, Gyrostemonaceae, Idiospermaceae, Petermanniaceae and Tetracarpaeaceae) as being endemic to Australia. It has, however, been suggested that one, the Idiospermaceae, more properly belongs in the Calycanthaceae and no others, except the Austrobaileyaceae, are strictly endemic to the rain forests of the northeast region.

Within Australian rain forests Webb and Tracey (1981) recognized three floristic regions and nine provinces. Most of the tropical rain forests discussed in this chapter are found in their Region B. The rain forests of subtropical and temperate Australia are included in Region A, while the rain forests (sensu Webb 1959) of drier areas of eastern and northern Australia are contained in Region C. Webb and Tracey claimed that the floras of A and C developed separately from B. A degree of overlap does, however, seem apparent when generic and family occurrences are compared amongst these regions.

Webb and Tracey (1981) divided their Region B into three floristic provinces. Province B1 was described as a scattered province of tropical moist seasonal forest extending from Cape York to south of Gladstone with outliers interwoven with B2 and A1 on drier coastal sites. The main areas are Bamaga–Lockerbie at Cape York, the riverine alluvia of the Iron Range area (for instance, Claudie, Pascoe and Lockhart Rivers), and the alluvia, upper slopes and gorges of the McIlwraith

Range. Province B2 is found in the humid tropical region between Cooktown and Cairns, north Queensland, from near sea level to highlands approximately 1600 m altitude and inland to a mean annual rainfall of approximately 1300 mm. Several outliers near Mackay in central Queensland were recognized. This province contains by far the largest proportion of this region's rain forests. Province B3 was described as containing forests restricted to a few special niches on the sand dunes of northeastern Cape York Peninsula, and some sandstone areas of Arnhem Land.

Although the early supposition of Hooker (1860) that this flora had a strong Indo-Malaysian element, might still be correct, it is now difficult to agree with Richards (1952) when he noted that "In tropical Queensland this forest closely resembles the rainforest of Indo-Malaysia in general aspect and except for the complete absence of Dipterocarpaceae in floristic composition". The similarities in structure may be there, but floristically the forests differ in much more than the presence or absence of the dipterocarps. The north Queensland rain forests have a significant upper canopy component of the following endemic or near-endemic genera: *Backhousia*, *Blepharocarya*, *Buckinghamia*, *Cardwellia*, *Castanospermum*, *Ceratopetalum*, *Darlingia*, *Doryphora*, *Flindersia*, *Musgravea* and *Placospermum*. The presence of other primitive and restricted Angiosperm genera — *Austrobaileya*, *Bubbia*, *Eupomatia*, *Galbulimima*, *Idiospermum*, *Neostrearia*, *Ostrearia* and *Sphenostemon* — adds a further distinctive character to the rain forest of this region.

Floral history

Specific information relating to the origins of the flora of northeastern Australia is not currently available for epochs earlier than the Pleistocene. However, this epoch is a convenient time to begin a consideration of the origins of this flora, as the characteristic landscape of the region did not commence to develop until late in the Tertiary. The early Tertiary habitat seems to have been relatively uniform, with little opportunity for significant refugia until the end of this period when block faulting provided some relief. However, it should be observed that the highlands of New Guinea began to develop much earlier (during the late

Eocene). Furthermore, New Guinea cannot be considered separately from this region, as it has, more often than not, been contiguous with the Australian continent.

A first glimpse of the origins of the flora came from a small coal seam of either early Quaternary or late Pliocene age, on the eastern edge of the Atherton Tableland. Kershaw and Sluiter (1982) reported that these deposits contained large proportions of pollen of Casuarinaceae, Cunoniaceae, *Elaeocarpus*, Myrtaceae, *Nothofagus*, *Podocarpus* and *Symplocos* as dryland taxa. All the taxa recognized, except for *Nothofagus* and *Dacrydium*, have extant species in or near the present-day rain forests of north Queensland.

Craters formed by Quaternary volcanism have provided suitable sites for long pollen sequences extensively studied by Kershaw, Walker and associates (for a useful summary see Kershaw, 1981). The longest sequence was that for Lynch's Crater (*c.* 120 000 years).

Kershaw's analyses have indicated great changes in the composition of the pollen rain during this period. Several pollen types (for instance, those attributed to *Nothofagus* and *Dacrydium*) were absent from the upper levels of the deposits and these genera are not present in the forests of the present day. *Araucaria* pollen also became less apparent in the upper portion of the record but two species may still be found in isolated pockets within the region's rain forests. The presumed decline of *Araucaria* has been linked to the suggestion that fire frequencies would have increased with the arrival of man on the continent. The density of charcoal particles in these deposits tended to support this hypothesis.

Kershaw also suggested that changes in the relative quantities of various pollen types, especially the "*Eucalyptus*" component, indicated changes in the floristics and structure of the plant assemblages dominating the site and that these changes were a reflection of a changing climate. For example he envisaged open eucalypt forest as replacing rainforest during dry intervals. Indeed he postulated that the mean annual rainfall at Lynch's Crater (now about 2600 mm) was generally less than 1500 mm and sometimes as low as 600 mm during the period from 8000 to 75 000 years B.P. There are, however, some alternative explanations to account for the changes in the proportions of different pollen types in the sediment profile and further evidence is required before postulated changes in regional vegetation patterns during the Pleistocene and Recent can be accepted with any confidence.

From the viewpoint of rain-forest floristics and dynamics, the studies reviewed above and others in related fields are not particularly conclusive [for example, biogeography — Burbridge (1960), Cogger and Heatwole (1981), Kikkawa et al. (1981); geomorphology — Hoply (1973), Bowler et al. (1976), Coventry et al. (1980); climatology — Nix and Kalma (1972), Oliver (1980)]. One cannot really determine whether rain-forest assemblages in this region have been fluctuating in extent in only a relatively minor way since the Tertiary or whether they are on relatively new ground after recent expansion from local refugia (as postulated by Webb and Tracey, 1981). Perhaps their component species have only recently come from refugia as far away as the foothills of the Owen Stanley Range in Papua New Guinea. If their species have been restricted to refugia then it is very likely that some present-day assemblages might not contain species with slow dispersal rates. Indeed it seems possible that some may be so recent that the entrance of slowly dispersing species is in itself a major source of floristic change.

The only contemporary evidence that species may have recently expanded from refugia is some rather tentative information from an examination of the chemistry of the volatile oils of *Flindersia bourjotiana* (Wiffin, 1978). Studies of the distribution of isozymes within selected plant species appear to offer some new possibilities for a closer look at these interesting problems.

Ecological studies

One may begin a review of ecological research in the region's rain forests with the visit of Dr. Karel Domin of Prague during 1909 to 1910. His paper on Queensland's plant associations (Domin, 1911) showed remarkable insight. Domin referred to the rain forests as "vine scrubs". He was the first to observe that in northeastern Australia these assemblages are found on a variety of soils, noting that "They prefer, of course, always a rich, deep soil, especially alluvial and basaltic, but in those portions where the rainfall reaches a very high range, we find them on a very poor, almost innutritious soil, as on Bellenden Ker or Bartle Frere, on a poor granitic soil". Domin recognized five different types of rain forest; one on lowland alluvials, three on "non basalts" and one on the basalts of the Atherton Tablelands as well as other types he calls "coastal scrubs". Unfortunately he provided few other details of his types.

Domin was also impressed by the sharp boundary between open eucalypt forests and rain forests. He noted that "*The line of demarcation between them is most distinct*, a phenomenon which is unique in the whole world". Domin explained many of the boundaries in terms of soil-water and nutrient regimes and appeared close to understanding the role of fire in preventing rain-forest species from invading the eucalypt forest. He was, however, unable to explain some of the other boundaries he saw, especially those on the Atherton Tablelands.

Local interest in the relationships between structural and floristic features of the rain forests and their environment developed with the publication of papers by Francis (1928, 1939) and Swain (1928). Francis (1928) had examined the rain forests of the Eungella Range west of Mackay. As well as noting the favourable climatic conditions for rain forests in this region he observed that "As the equator is approached the relative importance of soil is not so evident, because the increasing temperature and humidity in combination with heavy rainfall appear to be sufficient to maintain rain forest growth on comparatively poor soils". This observation paralleled that of Domin 18 years earlier. Francis (1939) thought that the diversity of the rain forests of the Atherton Tableland might be due to the fertile basaltic soil.

Swain (1928) attempted to resolve the problem of what to call the closed forests of this region: "jungles", "rain forests" or "scrubs". He decided that none of these terms was really suitable as the word "jungles" came from a Sanskrit word meaning open woodland; "rain forest" he thought could not exist in a seasonally dry climate; while "scrub", a local name still extensively used, implied an assemblage of much lower stature than the forests in question.

Although Swain seemed to have assumed that rain-forest soils were all of high fertility, he had a relatively good appreciation of the role of fire in

the dynamics of the rain-forest edge. He also seems to have been the first to attempt to divide, along traditional lines, the northern rain forests into floristic associations, naming three major and six minor units. In the light of present-day experience, these associations seem to reflect more the limited accessibility of these rain forests to Swain rather than natural species groupings.

While Jack (1921) provided some information on the vegetation of the more isolated northern part of this region, little was known of its biology until the 1948 Archbold expedition (Brass, 1953). It is interesting to observe the occasional problems L.J. Brass, the leader of this expedition, had in distinguishing monsoon forests from rain forests and also his prediction that the dry area between Cooktown and Coen would be an important break in the distribution of many rain-forest plants and mammals.

Herbert (1960) suggested that while the tropical and subtropical rain forests of Australia were the "climatic climax" on the most favourable soils, they also formed an "edaphic climax" in those regions where high temperature, humidity and rainfall showed little variation throughout the year. Herbert, like Swain before him, took care to point to the seasonality of the northeast environment and the effects of fire.

From the late 1950's to the present, L.J. Webb and his co-workers (primarily J.G. Tracey and W.T. Williams) have dominated ecological research in the rain forests of this region. To a large degree this group pioneered the use of numerical methods for studies in rain-forest synecology, and their influence on ecological research in Australian rain forests has been considerable.

In one of his early papers, Webb (1959) attempted to overcome some of the problems of using floristics as a starting point for subdividing rain forests into more manageable units. Instead he chose physiognomic features, especially the average size of the leaves of the larger trees, as a basis for characterization. He described most of the rain forests of northeastern Australia as either complex notophyll vine forests or complex mesophyll vine forests. In its revised form, Webb's classification recognizes 23 rain-forest types (Webb, 1968, 1978).

Webb and his co-authors also explored the possibilities for using numerical analysis of stand floristics to divide rain forests into types and, in the first (Webb et al., 1967a) of two related papers, compared methods applicable to site/species data. They found that the 18×0.5 ha sites could be classified into six groups each of three sites.

In the second study (Webb et al., 1967b) the species were divided into ten subsets on the basis of their life form (big trees, shrubs, etc). They concluded that species of the big tree group carried the whole of classificatory information reproducing the original classification of the first paper down to the ultimate division of the hierarchy. No other subset possessed this property. They also noted that there was a tendency for big tree species to be confined to a single site or at least be very restricted in their distribution. The authors concluded that some form of physiognomic structural classification would be essential for typing the region's rain forests.

The value of a physiognomic–structural classification in mapping rain-forest types was put to test when Tracey and Webb (1975) used a modification of the system initially described by Webb (1959). These maps, at a scale of 1:100 000, cover that part of the region's rain forests from Cooktown to Ingham. While the major types are primarily based on physiognomic features, soils and/or soil parent materials are often used to delineate subdivisions. Despite some inaccuracies in the typing (possibly due to the variable quality of the aerial photographs used) these maps have proved most useful to those concerned with broad aspects of land-use planning, particularly for the delineation of conservation areas. Tracey (1982) provided useful supplementary material examining some of the environmental relationships among the forest types recognized on this series of maps.

Further developments to forest-typing techniques based on physiognomic features were made when Webb et al. (1976) collected detailed structural data from 45 sites in the Bloomfield–Mareeba area of northeastern Australia. A classificatory analysis of this data revealed that structural information was in general unsatisfactory for the classification of simple forests, regrowth rain forests, forests under extremely limiting conditions and eucalypt woodlands and that under these circumstances the use of supplementary floristic information seemed inevitable. Their approach, however, seemed useful in complex rain forest where floristic information is much harder to

obtain. The authors claimed that in these complex assemblages their use of structural features produced ecologically meaningful divisions below the subformation level.

Studies elsewhere in the tropics (Dolph and Dilcher, 1980, among others) and some preliminary data from this region, have suggested that the use of leaf-size characteristics at such a high level in a forest-type classification could present some problems. Trends in leaf size may not follow expected patterns (for instance, a decrease in average leaf size with increasing elevation). A cursory assessment of the dominant leaf size of an assemblage can be deceptively difficult and quantitative checks have sometimes yielded very different results (Stocker et al., unpublished).

Webb (1968) endeavoured to relate his structural types to environmental parameters. His 400 study sites covered a wide latitudinal and altitudinal range along the east Australian coast. In summary he claimed that the following relationships exist between physiognomic features and environmental parameters:

(1) **Deciduousness**: (a) deciduous species became fewer with increasing latitude; (b) they were more numerous on eutrophic soils; (c) they were more numerous with lower rainfall, especially on eutrophic soils; and (d) they became fewer with increasing altitude.

(2) **Leaf size**: the proportion of species with microphyll leaf sizes generally increases, while those with mesophyll sizes decrease, with (a) increasing altitude; (b) increasing latitude; (c) decreasing rainfall; and (d) decreasing mineral nutrient status of the soil.

(3) **Special life forms** (robust woody lianes, palms, plank buttresses and tree ferns): the number of species in these categories generally decreases with (a) increasing latitude; (b) increasing altitude; and (c) decreasing annual rainfall.

Webb suggested that, in the higher-rainfall areas in this region, eucalypt forest is the climatic type only on oligotrophic soils and nowhere else.

In a subsequent study Webb (1969) examined the relationships among some forest types in eastern Australia and soil chemical characteristics, on 27 different sites using numerical classification and ordination techniques. Although he concluded that the distribution of different structural types of vegetation along the wet coast of eastern Australia is broadly correlated with different soil nutrient levels, this conclusion may have rested on the inclusion of four sites which were clearly not rain forest. These four sites were all on Frazer Island which originated as a large mass of wind-deposited sand and is separated from the northern rain-forest sites by over 1400 km.

Tracey (1969) did not use the same sites in his "parallel" study of soil physical properties. However, Tracey's 49 sites covered a similar geographic range and again most of the sites were in rain forest with only 17 in assemblages of other affinity. He concluded that the forest vegetation patterns in eastern Australia were not generally correlated, except under extreme conditions, with soil physical properties such as moisture availability and aeration. However, some complex types of rain forest were, in the wet tropics and subtropics, restricted to soils with favourable aeration at field capacity.

Williams et al. (1969) studied a small patch (0.4 ha) of unlogged rain forest in North Queensland and detected what they saw as a striking spatial pattern, which they ascribed largely to environmental discontinuity or gradients. However, it seems possible that such patterns could arise from the characteristics of regeneration in tree-fall gaps (for instance the availability of seed of a certain species at the right time; Nicholson, 1965).

In recent years Stocker, Unwin, West and associates, based mainly at the Atherton laboratory of the CSIRO, have examined several aspects of the dynamics of the region's rain forests. This work commenced with the establishment throughout the region of a series of 0.5 ha plots in unlogged rain forest. These plots provide basic information on forest structure, floristics, regeneration, mortality and the growth rates of individual trees. Some of their features are summarized in Tables 12.4 and 12.5.

Within these plots the number of tree species (Table 12.5) illustrate the relatively low species richness of these rain forests in comparison with many of those within the nearby Malesian region. For example species richness in the rain forests of the northeastern Australian region was only about half that of the alluvial and dipterocarp forests of Sarawak (Proctor et al., 1983). They did, however, appear to be a little richer than the isolated forests of the Solomon Islands (Whitmore, 1974, 1975).

It was also observed that the average canopy heights of these rain forests (Table 12.5) appeared to be lower than those elsewhere, particularly the dipterocarp forests of Malesia (Ashton, 1964; and others). Although maximum height growth could be restricted by the effect of hurricane-force winds associated with periodic cyclones, height limitations imposed by water stress during the dry season may be significant. Trees over 45 m high are certainly extremely rare in the rain forests of northeastern Australia.

The average basal area of the plots (48.1 m^2 ha^{-1}) was somewhat higher than the pantropic mean (36 m^2 ha^{-1}) given by Dawkins (1958, 1959). This finding is consistent with observations of Baur (1964) and Whitmore (1975). Although the range of stem densities was large (486–1104 ha^{-1}), the mean (869 ha^{-1}) was above the range observed for plots studied by Proctor et al. (1983) in Sarawak, even though the mean tree basal area was about the same for both sets of plots. The high basal area of rain forests in northeastern Queensland is difficult to explain, but could be related to the large proportion of "small gap" species (see below) in these forests (Stocker et al., unpublished).

Preliminary analysis of the plot data has suggested that there are few relationships between parameters of the vegetation and those of the environment. Among those detected were an

TABLE 12.4

Annual mortality of trees in the rain forests of northeastern Australia (adapted from Stocker et al., unpublished)

	Size class (dbh, cm)									
	10–20	20–30	30–40	40–50	50–60	60–70	70–80	80–90	90–100	100+
Deaths ha^{-1} yr^{-1}	4.21	1.41	0.55	0.43	0.22	0.09	0.05	0.06	0.03	0.03
% size class total	0.83	0.86	0.75	0.95	1.1	0.83	0.71	1.8	1.1	0.83

TABLE 12.5

Some environmental characteristics of the rain-forest sites examined by Stocker et al. (unpublished) in northeastern Australia

Plot no.	Location		Elevation (m)	Estimated Mean Annual Rainfall (mm)	Parent material	Topography	Slope/aspect	Distance from sea (km)
1	Downfall L.A.	S.F.185	720	1200	Granite	Tableland foothill	<5°SE	36
2	Emerald L.A.	S.F.607	1120	2400	Granite	Highland slope	10°–15°NE	34
3	Little Pine L.A.	S.F.933	80	2500	Granite	Coastal foothill	<5°SW	2
4	Robson L.A.	S.F.185	800	2000	Granite	Dissected upland	15°–20°E	30
5	North Mary L.A.	S.F.143	1100	2500	Granite	Exposed highland	<5°W	16
6	Burgoo L.A.	Garrawalt	620	2000	Granite	Exposed upland	5°–8°SE	45
7	Mt. Fisher	S.F.650	1200	2700	Rhyolite	Exposed highland	10°–12°SE	57
8	Agapetes L.A.	S.F.144	980	1500	Granite	Upland	5°W	45
9	Barong L.A.	S.F.755	80	4000	?Metamorphic	Coastal valley	5°S	25
10	McIlwraith Ra.	T.R.14	450	2000	Metamorphic	Upland	<5°SW	23
11	Curtain Fig	S.F.452	720	1400	Basalt	Flat stony tableland	–	43
12	Gosschalk L.A.	S.F.755	380	4000	Granitic alluvium	River terrace	<5°SW	32
13	Chinaman L.A.	T.R.55	230	2900	Metamorphic	Low coastal range	5°–10°SE	8
14	Clarke Ra.	S.F.679	920	2400	Basalt	Upland plateau	3°–5°SE	70
15	The Crater	S.F.194	1000	1800	Rhyolite	Upland	5°–8°SE	58
16	Agapetes L.A.	S.F.144	800	1300	Granite	Upland ridge	0°–8°N	40
17	Arsenic Creek	N.P.	15	3500	Granitic alluvium	Coastal riverine lowland	<5°SE	1
18	West Claudie R.	Iron Ra.	30	2200	Alluvium	Coastal riverine backwater	0–10°SE	13
19	Compartment 59	S.F.194	1120	2000	Rhyolite	Highland slope	15°–20°S	60

L.A. = logging area, S.F. = state forest, T.R. = timber reserve, N.P. = national park, MAR = mean annual rainfall.

TABLE 12.6

Some structural and floristic features of the northeastern Australian rain forests examined by Stocker et al. (unpublished)

Plot no.	Numbers of vascular plant species							Diversity indices[4]		Basal area (m² ha⁻¹)	Canopy height range (m)
	Total	large tree[1]	plot tree >10 cm dbh	small tree[2] and shrub	liane[3]	epiphyte[3]	other[3]	stem numbers	basal areas		
1	92	56	35	10	14	3	9	13	10	28.2	15–23
2	149	105	67	12	14	11	7	26	23	63.4	25–40
3	163	112	68	14	24	5	8	11	21	36.0	16–25
4	184	135	89	14	19	9	7	17	22	37.8	26–38
5	184	127	83	13	20	24	0	30	28	60.8	23–34
6	145	105	64	9	19	5	7	20	13	40.6	22–38
7	121	84	49	16	10	5	6	20	18	40.0	18–34
8	149	105	65	13	17	9	5	12	19	58.8	22–37
9	137	93	46	20	15	2	7	9	2	41.2	21–44
10	114	70	50	8	15	12	9	17	11	29.6	19–30
11	108	75	46	12	15	1	5	15	13	63.0	32–43
12	164	99	64	25	20	5	15	33	19	48.0	27–50
13	111	87	67	15	4	0	5	26	21	38.8	17–35
14	88	52	32	5	12	8	11	7	5	60.2	32–41
15	144	94	61	12	23	4	11	21	14	45.2	27–39
16	121	80	47	18	14	4	5	10	5	55.6	30–42
17	116	83	56	14	11	7	1	6	5	43.8	25–34
18	108	80	58	6	13	2	7	27	12	43.0	24–38
19	153	112	59	12	15	5	11	10	11	64.6	27–42

[1] All tree species capable of reaching the upper canopy.
[2] Tree species which are very rarely, if ever, found in the upper canopy. These species seldom grow beyond 10 cm dbh.
[3] Species counts in these categories are based on a preliminary assessment. Many may prove to be underestimates with further study.
[4] Based on data for trees >10 cm dbh using the reciprocal of Simpson's index (Simpson, 1949).

inverse relationship between exchangeable soil calcium and stem density and a direct relationship between this soil feature and the height of dominants. More intriguing was the increase in stand basal area with elevation. This phenomenon has often been observed by foresters and is now thought to reflect the effects of increased cyclone frequency and intensity on the floristics of coastal lowland forests. The data did not appear, however, to support the "intermediate disturbance" hypothesis established by Connell (1978) to explain the establishment and maintenance of the high floristic diversity characteristic of rain forests.

Studies of the role of the cassowary (*Casuarius casuarius*) in dispersing the seeds of rain-forest plants (Stocker and Irvine, 1984) highlighted both the importance of these birds for the spread of plants with large diaspores, and the general absence of specialized mammalian frugivores (except fruit bats) from this and adjacent regions. Seed stores in the soils from beneath a range of natural and successional assemblages in this region were examined by Hopkins and Graham (1983). In soils from undisturbed rain forests they found seeds of many "secondary" species but few of "primary" species which had not recently been observed fruiting.

Stocker (1981) examined the regeneration mode within a rain-forest patch of one hectare which had been felled and burnt. It was found that of the 82 tree species on the site 23 months after the fire, 74 had coppiced, 10 had produced root suckers and 34 had developed from seed. Those species developing mainly from seed appeared to have the highest growth rates. These results suggested that on this site a catastrophe of this nature might not deflect the floristics of the regenerating stand as much as might be expected. Stocker (1984) also examined regeneration processes in small artificially created gaps in rain forests. These studies illustrated the influence that gap size has upon the growth and survival of tree species. "Shade tolerant" or "small gap" species, although growing taller in the larger gaps than in the smaller gaps, survived in gaps of all sizes. While "intolerant" or "large gap" species did not survive in small gaps, they grew much faster than "small gap" species in the biggest gaps. It was suggested that these results and associated gap regeneration theory may go some way towards explaining the establishment and maintainance of the high diversity usually observed in tropical rain forests. They also appear relevant to the refinement of silvicultural systems for rain-forest management.

The Atherton group also investigated aspects of the dynamics of the rain forest/eucalypt forest ecotone (Unwin et al., 1984). These studies highlighted the role of established fire regimes and topography in determining the stability and position of the ecotone. Soil and climatic characteristics appeared to exert a secondary influence through their effects on the floristics and thus on the flammability of the vegetation where the ecotone has been disturbed.

Aspects of nutrient accession within rain forests and adjacent plantations, examined by Brasell et al. (1980), indicated site rather than forest type can have the most influence on flux rates. This study also illustrated strong seasonal patterns in phenological processes in these forests.

Mention must also be made of the silvicultural research which has been carried out over the past 70 years by Atherton based personnel of the Queensland Department of Forestry. While much of the data obtained is still to be published, papers by Volck (1968, 1975), Nicholson (1972), Anon. (1983) and various Research Reports (especially Anon., 1977b, 1979) provide some insights. Of special interest are the data relating to yield from rain forests subject to logging with or without various forms of silvicultural treatment. Volck (1975) produced some early results indicating that yield might be highest from the granitic soils but subsequent data suggested that this was not always so (Anon., 1979). From the point of view of forest dynamics one of the most important findings (M. Higgins, pers. commun., 1981) was that although the growth of trees in areas silviculturally treated[1] increased initially they were back to their predisturbance levels within ten years. On the other hand, the effects on growth of a much heavier disturbance — the selective logging of about 25% of the original basal area of the stand — lasted almost twenty years.

In conclusion it is observed that the rain forests of northeastern Australia have some environmental, floristic and structural features which seem to

---

[1]Useless trees killed, some understorey shrubs and vines removed — see Baur (1964) for details of these treatments.

set them apart from those of the equatorial zone. However, their relatively undisturbed nature and accessibility, together with the prevailing social and political circumstances of the region, create an environment where the basic mechanisms controlling rain-forest functioning can be further explored.

REFERENCES

Abbie, A.A., 1975. *Studies in Physical Anthropology.* Aust. Inst. Aboriginal Stud., Canberra, A.C.T.

Anderson, J.A.R., 1964. Observation on climatic damage in peat swamp forest in Sarawak. *Comm. For. Rev.*, 43: 145–158.

Anderson, J.A.R., 1966. A note on two tree fires caused by lightning in Sarawak. *Malay. For.*, 29: 18–20.

Anonymous, 1965. *Climate of Pioneer — Region 13 — Queensland.* Aust. Bur. Meteorology, Melbourne, Vict.

Anonymous, 1971. *Climate Survey — Northern Region 16 — Queensland.* Aust. Bur. Meteorology, Maribyrong, Vict.

Anonymous, 1977a. *Climatic Averages — Australia.* Aust. Bur. Meteorology, Canberra, A.C.T.

Anonymous, 1977b. *Report on Research Activities.* Div. Tech. Serv., Queensland Dep. of Forestry, Brisbane, Qld.

Anonymous, 1979. *Report of Research Activities for 1978/1979.* Div. Tech. Serv., Queensland Dept. of Forestry, Brisbane, Qld.

Anonymous, 1983. *Rainforest Research in North Queensland.* Queensland Dept. of Forestry, Brisbane, Qld.

Anonymous, 1986. *Report on Cyclone Winifred — February 1986.* Aust. Bur. Meteorol., Canberra, A.C.T.

Ashton, P.S., 1964. Ecological studies in mixed dipterocarp forest of Brunei State. *Oxford For. Mem.*, 25: 75 pp.

Aubréville, A., 1975. La flore Australe-Papoue. Origine et distribution. *Adamsonia*, 15: 159–170.

Barbetti, M. and Allen, H., 1972. Prehistoric man at Lake Mungo, Australia by 32 000 years B.P. *Nature*, 240: 46–48.

Baur, G.N., 1964. *The Ecological Basis of Rainforest Management.* Government Printer, Canberra, A.C.T., 499 pp.

Beadle, N.C.W., 1981. *The Vegetation of Australia.* Fischer, Stuttgart, 690 pp.

Blake, S.T., 1939. The interrelationships of the plant communities of Queensland. *Proc. R. Soc. Qld.*, 51: 24–51.

Bowler, J.M., Hope, G.S., Jennings, J.N., Singh, G. and Walker, D., 1976. Late Quaternary climate of Australia and New Guinea. *Quat. Res.*, 6: 359–394.

Brasell, H.M., Unwin, G.L. and Stocker, G.C., 1980. The quantity, temporal distribution and mineral element composition of litter fall in two forest types at two sites in tropical Australia. *J. Ecol.*, 68: 123–139.

Brass, L.J., 1953. Results of the Archbold Expeditions, No. 68. Summary of the 1948 Cape York (Australia) Expedition. *Bull. Am. Mus. Nat. Hist.*, 102: 139–205.

Burbidge, N.T., 1960. The phytogeography of the Australian region. *Aust. J. Bot.*, 8: 74–209.

Cogger, H.G. and Heatwole, H., 1981. The Australian reptiles:

Origins, biogeography, distribution patterns and island evolution. In: A. Keast (Editor), *Ecological Biogeography of Australia.* Junk, The Hague, pp. 1331–1373.

Connell, J.H., 1978. Diversity in tropical rain forests and coral reefs. *Science*, 199: 1302–1310.

Coventry, R.J., Hopley, D., Campbell, J.B., Douglas, I., Harvey, N., Kershaw, A.P., Oliver, J., Phipps, C.V.G. and Pye, K., 1980. The Quaternary of northeastern Australia. In: R.A. Henderson and P.J. Stephenson (Editors), *The Geology and Geophysics of Northeastern Australia.* Geol. Soc. Aust., Qld., Div., Brisbane, Qld., pp. 375–417.

Dawkins, H.C., 1958. *The Management of Natural Tropical High Forests with Special Reference to Uganda.* Imperial Forestry Inst., Oxford, Inst. Pap. 34, 155 pp.

Dawkins, H.C., 1959. The volume increment of natural tropical high forest and limitations on its improvement. *Emp. For. Rev.*, 38: 175–180.

De Keyser, F., 1972. *Explanatory Notes, Innisfail, Queensland, 1:250 000, Geological Series.* Bur. Miner. Res., Canberra, A.C.T.

Denmead, A.K., 1947. *Re Coal, Malanda.* Memo to Chief Govt. Geologist, Brisbane, Qld.

Dobson, A.J. and Stewart, J., 1974. Frequencies of tropical cyclones in the north eastern Australia area. *Aust. Meteorol. Mag.*, 22: 27–36.

Dolph, G.E. and Dilcher, D.L., 1980. Variation in leaf size with respect to climate in Costa Rica. *Biotropica*, 12: 91–99.

Domin, K., 1911. Queensland's plant associations. *Proc. R. Soc. Qld.*, 23: 57–74.

Francis, W.D., 1928. Rain forest of the Eungella Range. *Proc. R. Soc. Qld.*, 39: 107–114.

Francis, W.D., 1939. Field notes on some rain forests and rain forest trees of tropical Queensland. *Qld. Agric. J.*, 51: 250–279.

Fuguay, D.M., Baughman, R.G. and Latham, D.J., 1979. *A Model for Predicting Lightning Fire Ignition in Wildland Fuels.* U.S. Dept. Agric. For. Serv., Res. Pap. INT-217.

Gillman, G.P., 1976. Red basaltic soils in north Queensland. 2. Chemistry. *CSIRO Aust. Div. Soils, Tech. Pap.*, 28: 23–42.

Hall, J.B. and Swaine, M.D., 1976. Classification and ecology of closed-canopy forest in Ghana. *J. Ecol.*, 64: 913–951.

Herbert, D.A., 1935. *The Climatic Sifting of Australian Vegetation.* Rep. Melbourne Meeting, Aust. and N.Z. Assoc. Adv. Sci., pp. 349–370.

Herbert, D.A., 1960. Tropical and subtropical rain forest in Australia. *Aust. J. Sci.*, 22: 283–290.

Hooker, J.D., 1860. *Introductory Essay to the Flora of Tasmania.* Lovell Reeve, London.

Hopkins, M.S. and Graham, A.W., 1983. The species composition of soil banks beneath lowland tropical rainforests in north Queensland, Australia. *Biotropica*, 15: 90–99.

Hopley, D., 1973. Geomorphic evidence for climatic change in the late Quaternary of north east Queensland Australia. *J. Trop. Geogr.*, 36: 20–30.

Horton, D.R., 1980. A review of the extinction question: man, climate and megafauna. *Archaeol. Phys. Anthropol. Oceania*, 15: 86–97.

Hughes, P.J. and Sullivan, M.E., 1981. Aboriginal burning and late Holocene geomorphic events in eastern N.S.W. *Search*, 12: 217–278.

Hyland, B.P.M., 1982. *A Revised Card Key to the Rainforest Trees of North Queensland*. CSIRO, Canberra, A.C.T.

Isbell, R.F., Stephenson, P.J., Murtha, G.C. and Gillman, G.P., 1976. Red basaltic soils in north Queensland. *CSIRO, Aust. Div. Soils, Tech. Pap.* 28: 1–22.

Jack, R.L., 1921. *North most Australia*. Simpkin, London.

Jones, R., 1975. The neolithic, palaeolithic and the hunting gardeners: man and land in the antipodes. In: R.P. Suggate and M.M. Cresswell (Editors), *Quaternary Studies*. R. Soc. N.Z., Wellington, pp. 21–34.

Jones, R. and Bowler, J., 1980. Struggle for the savanna: northern Australia in ecological and prehistoric perspective. In: R. Jones (Editor), *Northern Australia: Options and Implications*. ANU Press, Canberra, A.C.T.

Kershaw, A.P., 1981. Quaternary vegetation and environments. In: A. Keast (Editor), *Ecological Biogeography of Australia*. Junk, The Hague, pp. 83–101.

Kershaw, A.P. and Sluiter, I.R., 1982. Late Cenozoic pollen spectra from the Atherton Tableland. *Aust. J. Bot.*, 30: 279–295.

Kikkawa, J., Monteith, G.B. and Ingram, G., 1981. Cape York Peninsula: Major region of faunal interchange. In: A. Keast (Editor), *Ecological Biogeography of Australia*. Junk, The Hague, pp. 1695–1742.

Lourensz, R.S., 1977. *Tropical Cyclones in the Australian Region*. July 1909 to June 1975. Aust. Govt. Publ. Serv., Canberra, A.C.T.

McAlpine, J.R., Keig, G. and Short, K., 1975. Climatic tables for Papua New Guinea. *CSIRO Div. Land Use Research, Tech. Pap.* 37.

Merrilees, D., 1979. The prehistoric environment in Western Australia. *J. R. Soc. W.A.*, 62: 109–128.

Nicholson, D.I., 1965. A study of virgin forest near Sandakan, North Borneo. In: *Proc. Sympon. Ecological Research in Humid Tropics Vegetation*. UNESCO, Paris, pp. 67–87.

Nicholson, D.I., 1972. Compartment sampling in north Queensland rainforests as a basis for silvicultural treatment. *Comm. For. Rev.*, 51: 314–326.

Nix, H.A. and Kalma, J.D., 1972. Climate as a dominant control in the biogeography of northern Australia and New Guinea. In: D. Walker (Editor), *Bridge and Barrier: the Natural and Cultural History of Torres Strait*. Australian National Univ., Canberra, A.C.T., Publ. BG/3.

Oliver, J., 1980. Considerations affecting palaeoclimatic models of northeastern Australia. In: R.A. Henderson and P.J. Stephenson (Editors), *The Geology and Geophysics of Northeastern Australia*. Geol. Soc. Aust., Qld. Div., Brisbane, Qld., pp. 395–398.

Probert, M.E., 1977. The distribution of sulphur and carbon – nitrogen – sulphur relationships in some north Queensland soils. *CSIRO Aust. Div. Soils, Tech. Pap.*, 31: 1–20.

Proctor, J., Anderson, J.M., Chai, P. and Vallack, H.W., 1983. Ecological studies in four contrasting lowland rain forests in Gunung Mulu National Park, Sarawak. 1. Forest environment, structure and floristics. *J. Ecol.*, 71: 237–260.

Reid, J.H., 1926. Limestone deposit, Mulgrave River near Gordonvale. *Qld. Govt. Min. J.*, 27: 341–342.

Richards, P.W., 1952. *The Tropical Rain Forest: An Ecological Study*. Cambridge Univ. Press, Cambridge, 450 pp.

Simpson, E.H., 1949. Measurement of diversity. *Nature*, 163: p. 688.

Specht, R.L., 1975. A heritage inverted: our flora endangered. *Search*, 6: 472–477.

Stocker, G.C., 1976. *Report on Damage to the Natural Vegetation after Cyclone Tracey*, Darwin Area, December 1974. Forestry and Timber Bureau, Leaflet 127.

Stocker, G.C., 1980. Fire in the forests and woodlands of north Queensland. In: B. Roberts (Editor), *Proc. Qld. Fire Res. Workshop*. Darling Downs Inst. Adv. Ed., Toowwoomba, Qld.

Stocker, G.C., 1981. The regeneration of a north Queensland rainforest following felling and burning. *Biotropica*, 13: 86–92.

Stocker, G.C., 1984. Aspects of gap regeneration theory and the management of tropical forests. In: K. Shepherd (Editor), *Proc. Tropical Forest Management Workshop, Gympie 1983*. ANU, Canberra, A.C.T.

Stocker, G.C. and Irvine, A.K., 1984. The role of cassowaries in dispersing plants in north Queensland's rainforests. *Biotropica*, 15: 170–176.

Stocker, G.C. and Mott, J.J., 1981. Fire in the tropical forests and woodlands of northern Australia. In: A.M. Gill, R.H. Groves and I.R. Noble (Editors), *Fire and the Australian Biota*. Aust. Acad. Sci., Canberra, A.C.T., pp. 425–439.

Stocker, G.C. and Unwin, G.L., 1986. Fire. In: H.T. Clifford and R.L. Specht (Editors), *Tropical Plant Communities — Their Resilience, Functioning and Management in Northern Australia*. Univ. of Queensland, St. Lucia, Qld., pp. 91–104.

Swain, E.H.F., 1928. *The Forest Condition of Queensland*. Govt. Printer, Brisbane, Qld.

Thorne, R.F., 1963. Biotic distribution patterns in the tropical Pacific. In: J.L. Gressitt (Editor), *Pacific Basin Biogeography*. Bishop Museum Press, Honolulu, Hawaii, pp. 311–354.

Tindale, N.B., 1981. Prehistory of the Aborigines. Some interesting considerations. In: A. Keast (Editor), *Ecological Biogeography of Australia*. Junk, The Hague, pp. 1761–1797.

Tracey, J.G., 1969. Edaphic differentiation of some forest types in eastern Australia. 1. Soil physical factors. *J. Ecol.*, 57: 805–816.

Tracey, J.G., 1982. *The Vegetation of the Humid Tropic Region of North Queensland*. CSIRO, Melbourne, Vic.

Tracey, J.G. and Webb, L.J., 1975. *Vegetation of the Humid Tropical Region of North Queensland*. (15 maps at 1:100 000 plus key) CSIRO, Indooroopilly, Qld.

Unwin, G.L., Stocker, G.C. and Sanderson, K.D., 1984. Fire and the forest ecotone in the Herberton Highlands, north Queensland. *Proc. Ecol. Soc. Aust.*, 13: 215–224.

Van Balgooy, M.M.J., 1971. Plant geography of the Pacific. *Blumea* (suppl), 6: 1–222.

Volck, H.E., 1968. *Silvicultural Research and Management in North Queensland Rainforests*. Queensland Department of Forestry, Brisbane, Qld.

Volck, H.E., 1975. *Problems in the Silvicultural Treatment of the Tropical Rainforests of Queensland*. Queensland Department of Forestry, Brisbane, Qld.

Wadsworth, F.H. and Englerth, G.H., 1959. Effects of the 1956 hurricane on forest in Puerto Rico. *Caribb. For.*, 20: 38–51.

Webb, L.J., 1958. Cyclones as an ecological factor in tropical lowland rainforest, north Queensland. *Aust. J. Bot.*, 6: 220–228.

Webb, L.J., 1959. A physiognomic classification of Australian rainforest. *J. Ecol.*, 47: 551–570.

Webb, L.J., 1968. Environmental relationships of the structural types of Australian rainforest vegetation. *Ecology*, 49: 296–311.

Webb, L.J., 1969. Edaphic differentiation of some forest types in eastern Australia. II. Soil chemical factors. *J. Ecol.*, 57: 817–830.

Webb, L.J., 1978. A general classification of Australian rainforest. *Aust. Plants*, 9: 349–363.

Webb, L.J. and Tracey, J.G., 1981. Australian rainforest: patterns and change. In: A. Keast (Editor), *Ecological Biogeography of Australia*. Junk, The Hague, pp. 605–694.

Webb, L.J., Tracey, J.G., Williams, W.T. and Lance, G.N., 1967a. Studies in the numerical analysis of complex rainforest communities. I. A comparison of methods applicable to site/species data. *J. Ecol.*, 55: 171–191.

Webb, L.J., Tracey, J.G., Williams, W.T. and Lance, G.N., 1967b. Studies in the numerical analysis of complex rainforest communities II. The problem of species sampling. *J. Ecol.*, 55: 525–578.

White, K.J., 1975. *The Effects of Natural Phenomenon on the Forest Environment*. Pres. address, Papua New Guinea, Sci. Soc., Port Moresby.

Whitmore, T.C., 1974. Change with time and the role of cyclones in tropical rainforest on Kolombangara, Solomon Islands. *Common, For. Inst.*, Pap. 46.

Whitmore, T.C., 1975. *Tropical Rain Forest of the Far East*. Clarendon, Oxford, 282 pp.

Wiffin, T., 1978. Geographic variation in tropical tree species. In: P.B. Tomlinson and M.H. Zimmermann (Editors), *Tropical Trees as Living Systems*. Cambridge Univ. Press, Cambridge, pp. 31–54.

Williams, W.T., Lance, G.N., Webb, L.J., Tracey, J.G. and Connell, J.H., 1969. Studies in the numerical analysis of complex rain forest communities. IV. A method for the elucidation of small scale forest pattern. *J. Ecol.*, 57: 635–654.

Winter, J.W., Bell, F.C., Pahl, L.I. and Atherton, R.G., 1984. *The Specific Habitats of Selected Northeastern Australian Rainforest Mammals*. Report to World Wildlife Fund, Australia.

Chapter 13

VASCULAR EPIPHYTISM IN AUSTRALO-ASIA

B.J. WALLACE

INTRODUCTION

A broad concept is followed in this chapter on the definition of "vascular epiphyte" and the scope of forms encompassed by it. Included are those species of vascular plants which during any phase of their life cycle typically gain all, or a substantial part of their water and mineral nutrients from sources outside of terrestrial soil, without being parasitic.

In this broad sense, epiphytes tend to form a continuum from typical terrestrial plants through to the most extreme, totally obligate, aerial epiphytes, particularly so in the lusher, more complex tropical rain forests where the most extensive range of possible epiphytic niches and plant growth opportunities is to be found. The main groupings include casual or facultative epiphytes, typical or holoepiphytes, hemi-cpiphytes, semi-epiphytic climbers and lithophytes; this is basically the approach taken in recent works on vascular epiphytes (for instance, Johansson, 1974; Madison, 1977; Wallace, 1981; Kress, 1987; Benzing, Ch. 7).

The geographical area reviewed is bounded by the two Tropics and by India and Sri Lanka in the west and the Pacific Islands as far east as Tahiti.

FLORA AND PHYTOGEOGRAPHY

Taking the above-defined approach, the total number of Australo-Asian vascular epiphytes is in the vicinity of 11 000 species in 320 genera. These represent 47 families and span 4 Divisions of vascular plants. Appendix 1 delineates this flora to generic level (data are derived in large part from

Madison, 1977) and Table 13.1 presents a summary of this. Numbers of species and genera, and even families are rather dependent on the taxonomic system followed for each group — here quite varied, in some cases specified. Also numbers of epiphytic species per genus are often more or less estimates, thus the data on species are not of a high degree of precision.

On the basis of apparent phytogeographic origin and dispersal, the region appears to be a fairly coherent unit. The Australian epiphytes are quite few — c. 350 spp. in all — with low endemism (Wallace, 1981) and whereas other elements of the Australian flora may be either autochthonous or have changed little since the times of Gondwana and thus related to Asian relatives via rafting on the Indian block (Webb, 1981), the epiphytic taxa are apparently relatively recent arrivals from Malesia or derivatives of these.

Although hard data are not readily available, the geographic centre of diversity of the epiphytic groups appears to the Borneo, Java, Sumatra, Malay Peninsula region, with a secondary complex radiation in New Guinea. These appear to be areas

TABLE 1

Synopsis of numbers and groupings of Australo-Asian vascular epiphytes (see Appendix 1 for full data)

Taxonomic grouping	No. families	No. genera	No. species
Pteridophytes	14	70	2200
Dicotyledons	23	72	2300
Monocotyledons	10	187	5800
non-orchid	9	17	300
orchids	1	170	5500

that have enjoyed warm, mesic climates during much of the Tertiary Period and at least in the Neogene apparently have had mountains high enough for marked altitudinal zonation, thus presenting greater opportunity for speciation.

The origins of the forebears of this primary centre of diversity are related to such matters as continental drift, the origins of the angiosperms, etc. There is, however, a closer affinity to the African/Madagascan flora than to the Neotropics; even so, this may rather be a reflection of greater opportunity for long-distance dispersal between Africa/Madagascar and India and Sri Lanka.

Rather than attempting to comment on all of the epiphytes of the region, a number of groups, important on the basis of distinctiveness from endemism, diversity and ecological specialization, will be selected for closer review.

Ferns

Among the Australo-Asian pteridophytes are many hundreds of species that are typically epiphytic (Table 1). Most of these, however, appear to be relatively unspecialized ecologically, particularly with regard to environmental water deficiency. Only a few groups have developed highly effective mechanisms to cope with the persistent and severe water stress of the more xeric epiphytic microhabitats. Also, from a phyletic/ phytogeographic viewpoint, few groups above generic rank are restricted to the Australo-Asian region — no family is endemic unless *Tmesipteris* is accorded that status. The other epiphytic fern allies, *Psilotum* and *Lycopodium* are pantropical and subtropical. They are all rather low-grade, nest-invading epiphytes.

In five of the larger fern families a majority of species is epiphytic. These are the Vittariaceae, Hymenophyllaceae, Davalliaceae, Grammitidaceae and Polypodiaceae, and they are all pantropical, extending to the subtropics and some temperate areas. In two of them, however, there are significant developments restricted to the Australo-Asian region.

The subfamily Davallioideae is endemic here except for a few species of *Davallia* and *Rumohra* in Africa and Southwest Europe, and South America (one species *Rumohra*). Most of the groups are medium-creeping, nest-invading epiphytes some of which have fleshy rhizomes for the storage of starch and water.

In the scheme of Crabbe et al. (1975) the family Polypodiaceae is divided into five subfamilies, two of which, Microsoroideae and Drynarioideae, are largely confined to the region, each with a few species reaching Africa. The former group is relatively large and diverse, having nineteen genera and about 200 species, though generally, the species are not highly specialized. Exceptions are the myrmecophilous *Microsorum* relatives, genus *Lecanopteris*, which will be further discussed in the section on antplant epiphytes.

The Drynarioideae appear to have arisen from a *Microsorum*-like ancestor, perhaps resembling *M. musaefolium* (Copeland, 1947; etc.). The subfamily comprises about thirty species in eight genera and was considered sufficiently cohesive and distinctive by Ching (1978) to merit family status. However, it appears to contain two separate phylogenetic lines (Chandra, 1981, 1982) which have converged in adapting to various, but somewhat similar environmental needs.

They are all rather large, moderately heliophilous and xerophytic, typical epiphytes with medium-creeping, thick, fleshy rhizomes. Most commonly they inhabit mid-strata in various grades of rain forest and related communities from complex, tall, wet, lowland rain forest to small refugia of simple deciduous vine thicket in monsoonal woodland. In such stressed environments as the latter they are often lithophytic or even terrestrial on sand and are themselves deciduous.

One line is represented by *Drynaria* and *Photinopteris* which are distinctive in having fronds arranged in two rows on the rhizome. *Photinopteris* is monotypic and is widespread in Southeast Asia and Malesia. It represents a relatively unspecialized state regarding litter-impounding adaptation — it develops neither special "basket" fronds, nor a broadened, non-deciduous frond lamina base for litter retention. It does, however, retain the frond axis even when the lamina disarticulates from it in response to drought, thus some litter retention occurs. *Drynaria* comprises about twenty species, three endemic in Africa with the remainder distributed from India to southern China, through Malesia to Tonga and northern Australia. They all produce two markedly different types of fronds (Fig. 13.1). The sterile basket fronds are short,

Fig. 13.1. *Drynaria rigidula*, showing short, broad sterile nest, or basket fronds at base and tall, strongly divided spore-bearing type above.

broad, and shallowly lobed, soon drying off to become stiffly papery but long-persistent and arranged in such a manner as to efficiently catch and retain falling debris. The spore-bearing type is much taller, narrower and more deeply dissected; a variant of this form is sterile but otherwise similar. Their general shape and disposition tends to direct falling litter and water into the nest but they appear principally adapted to raise the fertile parts above the "boundary layer" of relatively still air near the nest and substrate. Thus air movement around them will be maximized, facilitating drying and dehiscence of the ripe sporangia as well as dispersal of spores so released.

A variation in growth habit occurs in relation to the arrangement of fronds, basically resulting from direction of growth of the rhizome. In the case of, for instance, *D. rigidula*, the rhizome most often grows horizontally such that characteristically, it

encircles tree trunks and branches, forming a full, typical basket shape (Fig. 13.2). In some other species, such as *D. sparsisora*, on vertical surfaces the rhizome tends to grow upwards, often obliquely, so that each basket frond acts individually rather than in concert (see Fig. 13.3). This pattern may make more effective use of thin tree trunks as well as giving the plant the opportunity to "shift" vertically, in relation to possible changes in microhabitat factors.

The second drynarioid line is typified by *Aglaomorpha* which itself has three species. Their geographic distribution is centred on the Philippine Islands. *A. pilosa* is endemic, *A. meyeniana* reaches Taiwan and *A. splendens* extends to New Guinea, Borneo and the Malay Peninsula. There are five other monotypic genera (the number of both genera and species vary according to author) closely related to *Aglaomorpha*. They differ mainly in soral arrangement but are similar in the possession of only one basic type of frond which has a persistent, broad, papery lamina base that acts to impound litter. These are *Drynariopsis heraclea* widespread in Malesia, *Pseudodrynaria coronans*, India to Taiwan, *Merinthosorus drynarioides*, Malesia excluding the Philippines, *Holostachyum buchananii* of New Guinea and *Thayeria cornucopia* of the Philippines (Fig. 13.4). Two variations in nest-forming habit are noteworthy. *Holostachyum* and *Aglaomorpha pilosa*, like *Photinopteris* in the *Drynaria* line, lack the litter-impounding specialization of the broad, persistent papery base of the frond lamina. But again, the frond axis is persistent while the lamina segments are deciduous. *Thayeria* appears to be the most specialized of the whole alliance. Here, frond production is restricted to a single one at the apex of each of short lateral branches of the rhizome. The frond is a typical *Aglaomorpha* type except that the papery, persistent, lamina base is wrapped around in a funnel shape, thus forming an individual catchment unit. The roots arising from most of the rhizome are relatively scant and apparently function mainly as holdfasts; a special batch of densely furry roots grows from the apex of each of the lateral rhizome branches, up into the cornucopia and its impounded debris, giving access to the water and dissolved minerals held in the decaying humus.

In all of the drynarioid ferns, roots of the latter

Fig. 13.2. *Drynaria rigidula* forming typical basket-like nest. Goroka, New Guinea.

type are produced in association with the litter reservoir. These roots not only function in water and mineral uptake, but themselves form a substantial part of the spongy peat mass in the lower, decomposing parts of the nest. Thus, they contribute to the water and mineral-holding capacity of the plant itself.

Another drought-resisting adaptation featured in the drynarioid ferns is the thick, fleshy rhizome possessed by most species which is important in the storage of water and starch. Thus, during times of prolonged water stress, the water-expensive foliage can be shed leaving the perennating buds and the reserves of the rhizome buried, dormant in the nest, ready to resume new growth after the next rains.

The Platycerioideae are almost exclusively Old World but with a single species known from the Neotropics. Neither their phyletic nor geographic origins are clear but the majority of species and the greatest diversity occurs in Australo-Asia.

Pyrrosia and *Drymoglossum* species have been

shown to exhibit a type of Crassulacean Acid Metabolism (CAM), a physiological water conserving device and as such, appear to be unique among pteridophytes (see the section below on CAM in the Australian epiphytes).

The Staghorn Ferns, genus *Platycerium* form the most spectacular group of epiphytes in the Polypodiaceae and are perhaps the most highly adapted of the nest-forming ferns. There are about seventeen species (fourteen according to Hennipman and Roos, 1982), twelve of which occur in the Australo-Asian region, four in Madagascar, three in Africa and one in the northern Andes. They have strongly dimorphic frond types. The vegetative, litter-impounding, shield fronds are erect, broad, more or less appressed and entire or variously lobed above. The fertile, strap fronds are narrow and divided, either hanging, or standing free to facilitate spore dispersal. They are shed with age whereas the shield fronds are persistent. The basal parts of the latter are thick and fleshy when young and function, with the rhizome, to store starch and

Fig. 13.3. *Drynaria sparsisora*, at base, with nest fronds arranged in vertical series. *Hoya* sp. above, left and *Pyrrosia lanceolata* on right. Cape York, Australia.

water. After completing growth they die, becoming quite spongy in the lower section and papery in the upper parts. The vasculature is sclerified forming a stiff framework to retain the frond shape in some species, while in others, the upper parts, on drying, curl inwards over the nest. Trapped litter works its way down between the shield fronds and as it decays, is invaded by masses of furry roots. Like those of the drynarioid ferns, these roots not only take up water and dissolved minerals, but also form an integral part of the nest. Thus the nest becomes a compact, spongy mass of peat-like material consisting of frond bases, roots and humus from impounded litter, which absorbs and retains water and mineral nutrients, the whole being trapped in, and appressed to the tree by the outer shield fronds. As with typical peat, the nest material resists rapid decay, probably due to high acidity. Boyer (1964) made an eco-physiological

study of two drought-tolerant African species *P. stemaria* and *P. elephantotis* (syn. *P. angolense*) noting, interalia, how the growth cycles correlated with the wet and dry seasons. Gametophytes germinated and produced young sporophytes during the 3 to 4 month wet season following the main dry period. These displayed some poikilohydric ability, desiccating during the subsequent short dry season, then rehydrating and returning to normal growth with the next rains. A number of other species have adapted to seasonally dry climates and presumably have evolved similar adaptations. Perhaps the most extremely adapted xerophyte of the genus is *P. veitchii* of Queensland, which is a lithophyte of open, monsoonal eucalypt woodlands.

Myrmecophilous epiphytes

A notable feature of the Australo-Asian tropical rain forests and related ecosystems is the large number and diversity of epiphytes that have developed specialized cavernous organs for the accommodation of nesting colonies of arboreal ants.

Plant parts modified for this function include rhizomes, stems and leaves. The taxonomic groupings include a genus of ferns and at least nine genera from three different families of flowering plants totalling more than 200 species. As well as these there are a number of accessory species which commonly establish in antplant microcommunities but do not contribute substantially to ant accommodation.

Antplants have long fascinated scientists and a considerable literature has built up over the last century or so dealing with their morphology, anatomy, physiology, ecology, evolution and ant relations. Key early works relevant to the Australo-Asian region include Beccari (1884–86), Treub (1883a, b, 1888), Scott and Sargant (1893), Groom (1893), Heim (1898), Yapp (1902), Ridley (1910), Miehe (1911a, b), and Bequaert (1922). Important contributions have also been made by several workers in the last decade — Janzen (1974), Jermy and Walker (1975), Rickson (1979) and, particularly, Huxley (1978, 1980, 1982).

The adaptive strategy involved in this form of myrmecophily is basically a mutalism in which the plants gain extra mineral nutrients as a result of the

Fig. 13.4. *Thayeria cornucopia* showing rhizome and funnel-shaped frond base. In cultivation, Royal Botanic Gardens, Sydney, and Mt. Apo, Philippines.

ant activities and perhaps also some defence against predation and disturbance. The ants benefit from the provision by the plant of a ready-made, well-constructed home.

Various organic products are carried by the ants into their nests, and fall basically into three categories, nest-building material, food, and products of the ants themselves. Nesting materials include fragments of leaf, twig, bark, etc., and are placed either inside the antplant or added around the base of the plant to build extra chamber space or runways. Mineral salts from the breakdown of this material are taken up by the roots when dissolved in rainwater. Products placed inside the chambers of the antplant, nesting materials, food remains, excretory products, dead ants, etc., break down by microbial activity, releasing mineral decomposition products and are either taken up by intrusive adventious roots or absorbed through specialized wall linings (see under myrmecophilous

groups below). The water content and concentrations of salts appear problematical in this circumstance. The general system has been described as the "feeding of plants by ants" (Janzen, 1974; Huxley, 1978, 1980; Rickson, 1979), and Janzen likens the ants to auxiliary extensive, mobile root systems for the plants, a rather apt simile.

Protection from predation by grazing invertebrates may also be afforded by the ants — slugs have shown considerable predilection and preference for young *Lecanopteris mirabilis* (Jermy and Walker, 1975). More research is required to establish the extent and importance of such effects, especially in the field.

Some protection against disturbance by climbing animals may also be a benefit to the antplants. The effect of bumping, even lightly tapping (for example *Myrmecodia platytyrea*) is usually to cause hordes of small black ants to swarm out all over the surroundings including the hand of an observer or collector. Such ants may not have an actual sting but the combined effect of dozens of simultaneous bites is immediate withdrawal of the hand, and beware in future! Similar reactions in arboreal animals may occur and this must decrease the likelihood of damage to soft-bodied plants. Again, more research here is desirable.

The fern genus *Lecanopteris* (Polypodiaceae) as circumscribed by Jermy and Walker (1975), includes eleven species (four of these are split off into *Myrmecophila* by some authors). They are restricted to Malesia, most having a rather limited range within this region, though one, *L. carnosa* (Fig. 13.5), is widespread. Typically they inhabit relatively exposed mid- to upper-level microhabitats in rain forests and equally exposed sites in lower, more open communities such as heath forests or kerangas.

All have swollen, fleshy, cavernous rhizomes which are almost invariably inhabited by small ants, mostly of the genera *Crematogaster* and *Iridomyrmex*. The "ant-houses" appear to be formed in two ways: (a) by the collapse and disintegration of parenchymatous tissue, forming individual, interconnected chambers within rhizome growth units, as in *L. spinosa* and *L. carnosa* (Jermy and Walker, 1975); or (b) as in *L. mirabilis* Fig. 13.6), the rhizome is very wide and rather laminar, but arched up, providing a sheltered space beneath, where the ants nest among the roots.

The greatest numbers and diversity of antplants occurs in the angiosperm family Rubiaceae, tribe Psychotrieae. These are the ones with massive, chambered, tuberous stem bases (Fig. 13.7). Five genera have been delineated, containing more than 150 species. *Hydnophytum* is the largest and most widespread with *c.* 80 species, ranging from Indochina through Malesia to the Southwest Pacific

Fig. 13.5. *Lecanopteris carnosa* in crown of *Podocarpus* sp. Mt. Kinabalu, Sabah, *c.* 1800 m altitude.

Fig. 13.6. *Lecanopteris mirabilis*, view of upper and under side of rhizome. Bulolo, New Guinea.

Fig. 13.7. Rubiaceous tuberous antplants; *Myrmecodia platy-tyrea* above, in front, *M.* sp. behind, *Hydnophytum papuanum* below; *Dendrobium wassellii* at base; all on *Araucaria cunninghamii* in Semi-evergreen Notophyll Vine Forest, Cape York, Australia.

and Cape York, Australia. It also has two satellite genera, each with a couple of species, *Myrmephytum* from the Philippines and Sulawesi and *Squamellaria* of Fiji. Generic separation of these is based mainly on floral and inflorescence characters. They differ from *Myrmecodia* and its offshoot *Myrmedoma* in that the leaf-bearing stems are "normal", that is, more or less terete with internodes several to many times stem width; also the leafstalk bases are unspecialized. In the latter two genera, the stems are relatively thick and contracted and largely covered by clypeoles — specialized, persistent, flattened, phyllopodia-like shields which are often armed with marginal spines. *Myrmecodia* has *c*. 50 species spread throughout Malesia and the Southwest Pacific islands with about five species in

northern Australia, mostly restricted to Cape York. *Myrmedoma* is endemic in New Guinea, having but two species, which differ from *Myrmecodia* in having six- rather than four-merous flowers and having a prominently leathery bracteolate inflorescence.

The ontogeny, morphology, anatomy and physiology of the tubers of the rubiaceous antplants have been reasonably well studied (for instance, Treub, 1883a, b; Miehe, 1911a, b; Spanner, 1938; Janzen, 1974; Huxley, 1978, 1980). The tuber begins with the swelling of the seedling hypocotyl and the cavities are formed later when cork-generating meristems arise in the inner parenchymatous tissue forming a corky wall, cutting off various shaped and sized enclosures (Treub, 1883b) (Fig. 13.8). The contents of these then die and dry off, leaving the chambers empty. The ants may clean out remnant dead tissue but do not primarily excavate — this has been shown by the production of chambers in plants to which ants never had access (Forbes, 1880; among others).

Myrmecodia species appear to be the most specialized in regard to chamber form and function. There are two distinct types according to the lining: (a) smooth-walled ones which are used by the ants as brood nurseries; and (b) those with warty, fissured walls which are storage and/or waste disposal areas for insect prey remains, dead ants, faecal matter, etc. The walls of this latter type are absorbent (Miehe, 1911a, b) and both Huxley (1978) and Rickson (1979) have demonstrated uptake of radioactive tracers from material deposited by the ants in these chambers, into the living tissue of the tuber and then more distant translocation to other parts of the plant.

A further interesting point, which needs more investigation relates to two different fungi commonly found in *Myrmecodia* chambers. One species is apparently parasitic in the walls of the smooth chambers and the other saprophytic on the debris in the rough-walled type. It is suspected that the ants eat the fertile bodies of these as they are often found to have been removed from the fungi and also, there is some coincidence in the geographic ranges of the commonest ant species and those of the fungi (Miehe, 1911a, b; Huxley, 1978), that is, the ants probably disperse the spores.

In *Hydnophytum* the chamber wall texture differences are not so clear but warty areas are still

Fig. 13.8. *Myrmecodia muelleri* with tuber sectioned showing internal cavities.

present (Huxley, 1980) and probably also function in absorption. The situation regarding the satellite genera is unknown but is presumably somewhat similar.

The main other family containing myrmecophilous epiphytes in Australo-Asia is the Asclepiadaceae. In three genera, *Dischidia*, *Dischidiopsis*, and *Hoya*, the majority of species are twining rootclimbers, obligately or facultatively epiphytic and as many as forty or more have hooded, appressedcupped, or bladder-like leaves specifically adapted for mutualistic ant-housing.

The general method of operation of the nutrient acquisition system of this group is not as thoroughly investigated as for example in *Myrmecodia*, but appears to differ from the latter in that adventitious roots enter each ant-chamber, proliferating in those containing nesting debris (Fig. 13.8). This suggests that it may be the main mode of uptake of mineral nutrients although Yapp (1902) found that the inner walls of antleaves

of *Dischidia major* (syn. *D. rafflesiana*) were absorbent.

Another notable feature of antleaf anatomy and physiology is the preponderance of stomates on their inner surface (Huxley, 1980). This would enable gas exchange to take place in an atmosphere of high humidity and minimal air movement, reducing transpirational waterloss greatly. Ant respiration and nest material decay may also yield an enriched CO_2 concentration. All species of *Hoya* and *Dischidia* tested by Winter et al. (1983) showed ^{13}C values indicative of moderate to strong CAM. Such factors together give clues to the possession of considerable tolerance of water deficiency by these plants.

Hoya is the largest genus, with *c.* 200 species, ranging from Southeast Asia through Malesia to the Southwest Pacific and Australia. It is the most diverse in plant habit and ecology but perhaps only half to two-thirds of the total species are epiphytic. As few as ten or so are specialized antplants but again, they show a range of stages of adaptation of the antleaves. As with *Dischidia*, most species display two distinct vegetative growth types, viz. a compact, shrubby type which produces long-internoded runners that eventually again produce shrubby growth, and so on. Roots may be produced at most, if not all nodes and usually are so at those which firmly contact the substrate, enabling a climbing and also an epiphytic mode of life. Such prolific adventitious root production could also be seen as a "preadaptation" to antleaf evolution. *Hoya mitrata* shows an early stage of such development. Leaves of its short-growth stages are horizontal, short-petioled and convex, or more or less hooded and together form an effective roof under which ants construct their carton nests. The adventitious roots grow into this and are also useful to the ants as structural framing members for nest construction. A slight advance on this is seen in *Hoya imbricata* in which the cupped leaves are appressed to the substrate, forming bubble-like cavities in which the ants nest

and into which the *Hoya* roots grow. An elaboration from these conditions has developed in *Hoya darwinii* in which some of the leaves form into a domed shape with the central lamina bulging while the margins contract rather in the manner of a small cloth bag with draw-string, but leaving a large opening. Sometimes only one leaf of a pair forms thus, in which case it may appress against the substrate, or, both may form into antleaves and appress against one another making a closed unit.

Dischidia comprises about eighty species and has a geographical range similar to *Hoya*. They are almost all obligate epiphytes, usually having smaller, more succulent leaves than *Hoya* and are taxonomically distinguished from it by having much smaller, urn-shaped, scarcely opening flowers with a different pollination ecology. Some thirty species are specialized in myrmecophily and many of these have advanced one or two stages beyond those described above for *Hoya*. The bladder-leaves of some, such as *D. major* (Fig. 13.9) are more exaggerated than *H. darwinii*

Fig. 13.9. *Dischidia major* showing unspecialized and bladder antleaves, one in section showing ant entry at base of leaf, ant nesting material and adventitious root ramifying in leaf cavity. Cape York, Australia.

with greater enclosed volume and a smaller, more concealed entrance tunnel formed from the leaf tip. In the most modified condition of all, such as in *D. pectenoides*, this tip itself forms a second chamber enclosed within the main one (Pearson, 1902); the function and adaptive value of this arrangement is not clear.

Dischidiopsis has about ten species which are distributed in the Philippines and New Guinea; they differ little from *Dischidia* and the bladder-bearing species are similar in specialization to species of *Dischidia*.

The third angiosperm family with antplant representatives in Australo-Asia is the Melastomataceae, though the number, diversity and degree of development in myrmecophytism is meagre when compared with the previous two families, or with its own representation in other regions and in non-epiphytic plants (like *Tococa*, *Ossaea*, *Maieta* spp. of the Neotropics — Whiffin, 1972). The genus *Pachycentria* consists of about a dozen species spread from Burma to Indonesia. A number of epiphytic species produce fleshy root tubers and some of these are hollow and become ant-inhabited (Beccari, 1884–86), however, little is known of their biology.

It would seem that, in many cases, the contribution of *Pachycentria* in any apparent myrmecophilous mutualism amounts to one of minimal importance by, for example, providing with its roots structural members around which the ants construct carton chambers and runways. As with other secondary antplants such as orchids and non-bladder-leaved *Dischidia*, the seeds are attractive to ants and are carried by them to the nest and built into it, where they germinate, establish and take advantage of the mineral nutrients therein. Janzen (1974) refers to such epiphytes as parasites but this is incorrect and confusing usage; perhaps a term like "nutritional piracy" (see Benzing and Seeman, 1978, and Ch. 7) would be appropriate here. Orchids in this group include several species of *Dendrochilum, Dendrobium* and *Liparis*, amongst others; of the asclepiads, *Dischidia nummularia* (syn. *D. gaudichaudii*) is the most widespread.

The common development of antplant microcommunities can be attributed to the seed-collecting habit of ants. This may also help explain why *Myrmecodia* species are often found growing on the underside of branches. On Cape York, Australia, primary dispersal of both *Myrmecodia* and *Hydnophytum* is by *Dicaeum hirundinaceum*, the Mistletoe-bird, a flower-pecker of the family Dicaeidae. The red berries are similar to those of various mistletoes, are taken by the birds in a very similar manner, and are presumably deposited by defaecation in the same effective way.

Orchids

Finally, some comment is made on the group of epiphytes which by a glance at Table 13.1 is seen to be considerably the largest and most diverse, the orchids.

Judging from the frequency with which new species are discovered and described — from, for instance, Malaysia and New Guinea — the figure of 6000 epiphytic orchid species may be conservative. It is also an indication of the extreme plasticity of the group, not only in floral morphology and pollination ecology, leading to breeding barriers and speciation but also in vegetative structure and function and in physiology and biochemistry, enabling colonization of the full spectrum of epiphytic microhabitats. The development of CAM as discussed in the following section is an example of the latter.

The leafless epiphytic orchids, numbering about 200 species in at least four genera form distinct, adaptive lines. *Taeniophyllum, Microtatorchis* and *Chiloschista* (Fig. 13.10) are monopodials species and appear to be adapted to brighter, somewhat exposed microhabitats, in the case of the former two, and the latter to shaded, lower microhabitats in drier communities. Some species do have small photosynthetic leaves, often temporarily, but in most the photosynthetic function resides in the roots (which, incidentally, lack stomates). Two Australian sympodial species, *Bulbophyllum minutissimum* (Fig. 13.11) and *B. globuliforme* are aphyllous but the roots do not photosynthesize; this has been taken over by the pseudobulbs. In the case of *B. minutissimum*, stomates are restricted to the lining of a crypt in the pseudobulb apex and it has been shown to be a CAM plant, as also have *Chiloschista* and *Taeniophyllum* species (Winter et al., 1983).

Numerous epiphytic orchids have developed special litter-retaining devices with the same gen-

Fig. 13.10. *Chiloschista phyllorhiza*, leafless monopodial orchid; roots *c.* 5 mm wide. Cape York, Australia, in low shaded microhabitat in monsoonal vine thicket in hind-dune swale.

Fig. 13.11. *Bulbophyllum minutissimum* among lichens, pseudo-bulbs are *c.* 2–3 mm diameter, North Coast, N.S.W.

eral function as other nest-forming epiphytes, that is, as moisture and mineral reservoirs. In the commonest form, masses of upward-growing heavily velamentous aerial roots form a catchment to trap falling litter, growing through this, and then dying off, the whole forming a spongy peat-ball. Examples are *Grammatophyllum* species, some *Cymbidium* species and *Dendrobium speciosum*. A remarkable and different example is *Bulbophyllum beccarii* (Fig. 13.12) of Borneo in which the large (to 30 × 20 cm) leaves are scoop-shaped and obliquely projected from the substrate to catch litter. A special batch of roots grows up from the pseudobulb base and into the trapped litter.

Regarding large radiations in response to the various factors of pollination ecology, three instances are notable in the Australo-Asian region. These are the subtribes Sarcanthinae with *c.* 1000 species in 86 genera, Dendrobiinae with 1500 + species, in 6 genera (plus 40 sections in *Dendrobium* itself) and Bulbophyllinae, 1500 or so species in 7 genera, and again, with about 40 sections in the genus *Bulbophyllum*. The anthecology of these groups has not been closely studied but reports and pollination syndromes indicate that the former two may be pollinated by Hymenoptera and the latter by Diptera. In various respects these groups parallel the Oncidiinae, Laeliinae and Pleurothallidinae, respectively, of the Neotropics.

Bulbophyllum and *Dendrobium* are also good illustrations of the secondary, New Guinea centre of diversity in the Australo-Asian epiphyte flora. Each has around 500 species there, with a high degree of endemism especially in some sections, such as *Calyptrochilus* and *Oxyglossum* in *Dendrobium*. These two sections appear to be derived from section *Pedilonum*, a group widespread in Malesian

Fig. 13.12. *Bulbophyllum beccarii* with spirally arranged, scoop-shaped, 30 cm long leaves. In tall Kerangas, nutrient-poor forest.

rain forests, and have radiated concomitantly with New Guinea honey-eating bird groups, their apparent pollinators.

Somewhat similar, if less spectacular examples may be found in other orchid subtribes, such as the Glomerinae, Podochilinae and Thelasiinae, also among the ferns and in all probability, numerous other groups as well.

CRASSULACEAN ACID METABOLISM (CAM) IN THE AUSTRALIAN VASCULAR EPIPHYTES

In the last three decades or so the adaptive value of CAM as an important water-conserving device in plants of semi-arid biomes has been increasingly investigated and understood. Kluge and Ting (1978), Osmond (1978), and Winter (1985) have amply reviewed the literature covering this topic.

Only quite recently has the physiological and ecological relevance of CAM in epiphytes been appreciated (for instance, McWilliams, 1970; Medina, 1975; Medina et al., 1977; Winter et al., 1983; Benzing, Ch. 7).

Epiphyte microhabitats vary greatly in their physical attributes, especially those which bear on plant–water relations, such as temperature, relative humidity and movement of air. Epiphytes on the trunk base of a rain-forest tree will be subject to much less water stress than those in the exposed upper branches. Thermohygrographs clearly show the higher temperatures and lower humidities of the upper zone when compared with the lower, especially during midday to early afternoon. Air movement will also be greater in the upper zones, and more so at such times. So it is that even in a relatively lush rain forest, some epiphyte microhabitats will be, at least periodically, quite xeric. Therefore, owing to the nature and operation of the CAM pathway, epiphytes thus adapted will be at a considerable advantage in maintaining favourable water relations while assimilating sufficient carbon to sustain growth.

Figure 13.13 (Wallace, 1981) records the simultaneous fluctuation through 24 h of physiological attributes of an epiphytic CAM orchid, *Dendrobium speciosum*, as well as those of some pertinent physical factors of the microhabitat. The interrelation between these, particularly the relationship between leaf diffusive resistance ($\simeq$ stomatal aperture) and atmospheric evaporative strength as measured by vapour pressure deficit, gives a clear insight into the water-conserving value of CAM. That is, stomates open when air-evaporative strength is low, minimizing evapotranspirational waterloss. (At the same time however, lack of cooling effect from such waterloss may mean that CAM is not adaptive in very hot, dry sites.)

In the same work, but on a particularly "aerial" species, *Plectorrhiza tridentata*, data gave some indication that air-drying power exerted a secondary, "trimming" control on stomatal aperture, that is, after the primary effect of CO_2 concentration inside the leaf. Other data (Wallace, 1981) also indicated that this species may be capable of "idling" during prolonged drought, keeping stomates largely closed for extended periods.

The study of Winter et al. (1983) appears to be the first investigation of a major proportion of a

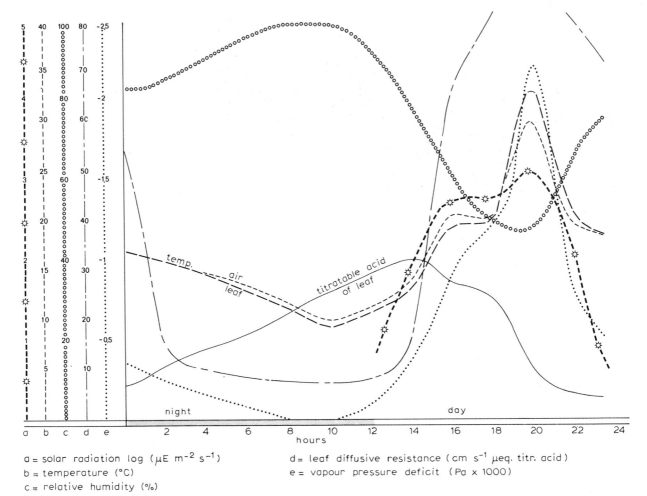

a = solar radiation log (µE m⁻² s⁻¹)   d= leaf diffusive resistance (cm s⁻¹ µeq. titr. acid)
b = temperature (°C)   e = vapour pressure deficit (Pa x 1000)
c = relative humidity (%)

Fig. 13.13. Ecological and physiological factors related to CAM in *Dendrobium speciosum*; autumn 1980, Long Point (Wallace, 1981).

significant epiphyte flora. 136 species were tested for $\delta^{13}C$ value (see Fig. 13.14) and 60 of these returned values of $-22‰$ or less negative, indicating significant CAM activity. Fifteen were tested for daily leaf acidity fluctuation and in each case the results concurred with those derived from $\delta^{13}C$ determinations.

The three species of fern allies tested — one *Psilotum* and two *Lycopodium* — yielded results typical for C_3 plants. This is not unexpected as they frequent lower, less water-stressed microhabitats and are generally thought of as archaic in both form and function.

Fig. 13.14. Distribution of 136 species of Australian epiphytes in regard to ^{13}C relative ratio of leaf tissue. The block on the left shows ^{13}C contents typical of CAM-plants, on the right of C_3 plants.

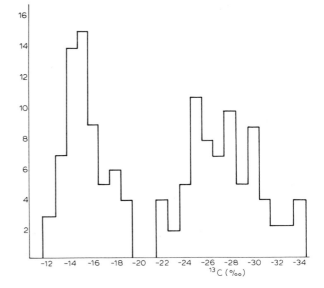

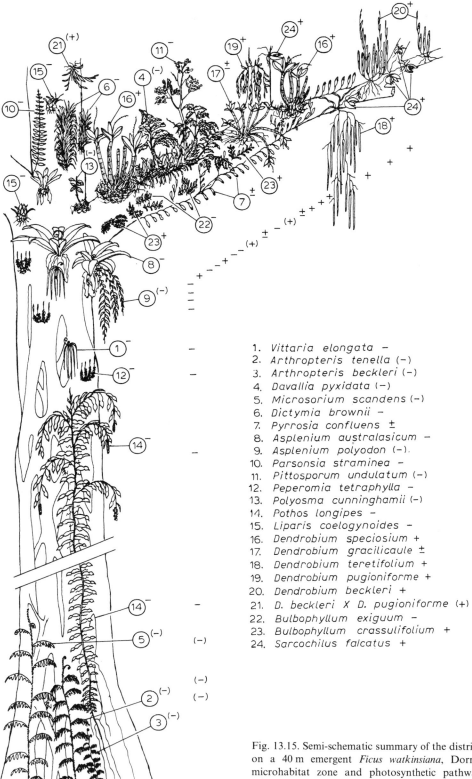

1. *Vittaria elongata* −
2. *Arthropteris tenella* (−)
3. *Arthropteris beckleri* (−)
4. *Davallia pyxidata* (−)
5. *Microsorium scandens* (−)
6. *Dictymia brownii* −
7. *Pyrrosia confluens* ±
8. *Asplenium australasicum* −
9. *Asplenium polyodon* (−)
10. *Parsonsia straminea* −
11. *Pittosporum undulatum* (−)
12. *Peperomia tetraphylla* −
13. *Polyosma cunninghamii* (−)
14. *Pothos longipes* −
15. *Liparis coelogynoides* −
16. *Dendrobium speciosum* +
17. *Dendrobium gracilicaule* ±
18. *Dendrobium teretifolium* +
19. *Dendrobium pugioniforme* +
20. *Dendrobium beckleri* +
21. *D. beckleri* X *D. pugioniforme* (+)
22. *Bulbophyllum exiguum* −
23. *Bulbophyllum crassulifolium* +
24. *Sarcochilus falcatus* +

Fig. 13.15. Semi-schematic summary of the distribution of vascular epiphytes on a 40 m emergent *Ficus watkinsiana*, Dorrigo, N.S.W., according to microhabitat zone and photosynthetic pathway. +sign indicates CAM photosynthetic CO_2 fixation. Parentheses indicate suspected conditions on the basis of leaf succulence type.

Of the nineteen true ferns investigated, only three species of *Pyrrosia* gave results clearly indicating CAM activity. Ecophysiological and evolutionary inferences can be drawn here. These species, particularly *P. confluens* and *P. dielsii*, occupy the most xeric microhabitats of all epiphytic ferns, often growing among lichens and xerophytic orchids on upper, exposed small branches. Phyletically they belong to a highly derived group, the subfamily Platycerioideae of Polypodiaceae.

Representatives of eleven flowering plant families were assayed. In the dicots only rubiaceous antplants and asclepiads gave indications of CAM activity. *Myrmecodia beccarii* yielded "borderline" $\delta^{13}C$ results but leaf acidity values (unpublished) confirmed some CAM. Its leaves are noticeably more succulent than its congeners and typically it inhabits brighter, somewhat more exposed microhabitats. *Hydnophytum papuanum* (*H. formicarium* of Winter et al., 1983) is a very similar case.

The two closely related asclepiad genera *Hoya* and *Dischidia* exhibited moderately strong CAM. They are somewhat, to considerably succulent and generally occupy relatively exposed microhabitats.

The herbs *Boea* (Gesnericeae) and *Peperomia* (Piperaceae) both gave typical C_3 results. The former, usually a lithophyte, has well-developed "resurrection ability" and can thus evade drought. *Peperomia* is often very fleshy and can store considerable water but even so usually inhabits more mesic microhabitats.

All the woody dicots tested, *Schefflera*, *Ficus*, *Fagraea*, *Timonius*, *Procris* and *Agapetes* are non-succulent hemi-epiphytes and predictably yielded C_3 results. The non-orchid monocots included in the survey, *Pothos longipes* and *Rhaphidophora pachyphylla*, were both found to be non-CAM. As with other semi-epiphytic climbing aroids they occupy low, sheltered microhabitats in wetter grades of rain forest; *R. pachyphylla* does however have slightly succulent-textured leaves.

Of the epiphytic and lithophytic orchids, 87 species were tested, 53 giving values of moderately strong to pronounced CAM, two were marginal and the remainder clearly C_3, ranging from -23 to -34‰. Generally, the orchid results were in accord with the hypothesis that CAM species tend to occupy more exposed, xeric microhabitats than do C_3 species. Figure 13.15 depicts this; it is a semi-schematic trunk/branch transect of an actual tree. Visual perspective proportions and numbers of plants are not accurate but positions of the species in relation to one another and to approximate tree zone, are as they occurred. On this tree the epiphyte flora was rich and the epiphytic vegetation well developed which is in part a reflection of the maturity and richness of the whole community there. Less well developed, species-poorer examples rarely show the ecological zoning/phytosynthetic pathway correlation with such clarity.

From the evidence presented and cited above, fundamental implications are that: (a) the epiphytic life form/biotope is a major area of CAM development and evolution; and (b) this physiological device is of considerable importance in the ecology of many epiphytes, particularly those of the xeric, outer microhabitats.

APPENDIX 1

Systematic list of Australo-Asian vascular epiphytes

	Epiphytic spp. (generic total)	Epiphytic spp. total shared with	Dissemimule type	Epiphytic life form
PTERIDOPHYTA				
Psilotaceae				
Psilotum	2(2)	Af, Am	D	T
Tmesipteris	9(9)		D	T
Lycopodiaceae				
Lycopodium	100(450)	Af, Am	D	T, SEC
Selaginellaceae				
Selaginella	20(700)	Af, Am	D	T, F

APPENDIX 1 (*continued*)

	Epiphytic spp. (generic total)	Epiphytic spp. total shared with	Dissemimule type	Epiphytic life form
Ophioglossaceae				
Ophioglossum	2(40)	Am	D	T
Hymenophyllaceae				
Hymenophyllum s.l.	250(300)	Af, Am	D	T
Trichomanes s.l.	250(300)	Af, Am	D	T
Schizaeaceae				
Schizaea	2(30)		D	T, F
Vittariaceae				
Antrophyum	40(40)	Af	D	T
Monogramma	2(2)	Masc	D	T
Vaginularia	6(6)		D	T
Vittaria	80(90)	Af, Am	D	T
Lindsaeaceae				
Lindsaea	20(200)		D	SEC
Davalliaceae				
Araiostegia	12(12)		D	T
Arthropteris	20(20)	Af	D	SEC
Davallia	40(40)	Madag	D	T
Davallodes	11(11)		D	T
Humata	50(50)	Madag	D	T
Nephrolepis	20(30)	Af, Am	D	T, F
Oleandra	20(40)	Af, Am	D	T, F
Parasorus	1(1)		D	T
Scyphularia	8(8)		D	T
Trogostolon	2(2)		D	
Grammitidaceae				
Acrosorus	5(5)		D	T
Calymmodon	25(25)		D	T
Ctenopteris	200(200)	Af, Am	D	T
Grammitis	150(150)	Af, Am	D	T
Nematopteris	1(1)		D	T
Scleroglossum	6(6)		D	T
Xiphopteris	50(50)		D	T
Polypodiaceae				
Aglaomorpha	3(3)		D	T, N
Anarthropteris	1(1)		D	T
Arthromeris	69(69)		D	T
Belvisia	15(15)	Af	D	T
Christiopteris	4(4)		D	T
Crypsinus	40(40)		D	T
Dendroconche	2(2)		D	T, N
Diblemma	1(1)		D	T
Dictymia	3(3)		D	T
Drymotaenium	2(2)		D	T
Drynaria	20(20)	Af	D	T, N
Drynariopsis	1(1)		D	T, N
Goniophlebium	20(20)		D	T
Grammatopteridium	2(2)		D	T
Holcosorus	2(2)	D	T
Holostachyum	1(1)		D	T, N

APPENDIX 1 (*continued*)

	Epiphytic spp. (generic total)	Epiphytic spp. total shared with	Dissemimule type	Epiphytic life form
Lecanopteris	11(11)		D	T, A
Lemmaphyllum	4(4)		D	T
Leptochilus	1(1)		D	T
Loxogramme	40(40)		D	T
Merinthosorus	2(2)		D	T, N
Microsorum	40(40)		D	T
Neocheiropteris	5(5)		D	T
Oleandropsis	1(1)		D	T
Paragramma	2(2)		D	T
Paraleptochilus	2(2)		D	T
Photinopteris	1(1)		D	T, N
Platycerium	17(17)	Af, Am	D	T, N
Pleopeltis	40(40)	Af, Am	D	T
Polypodiopsis	3(3)		D	T
Polypodium	70(70)	Af, Am	D	T
Pteropsis	6(6)	Madag	D	T
Pycnoloma	3(3)		D	T
Selliguea	4(5)		D	T
Thayeria	1(1)		D	T, N
Thylacopteris	1(1)		D	T, N
Aspidiaceae				
Polystichum	1(135)		D	T
Blechnaceae				
Stenochlaena	1(5)	Af	D	SEC
Lomariopsidaceae				
Elaphoglossum	250(400)	Af, Am	D	T
Teratophyllum	9(9)		D	SEC
Lomariopsis	40(40)	Af, Am	D	SEC

MAGNOLIOPHYTA

MAGNOLIOPSIDA (DICOTYLEDONES)

Winteraceae				
Tasmannia	1(70)		S	F
Piperaceae				
Peperomia	700(1000)	Af, Am	Small Adhesive	T
Piper	10(2000)	Am	S	T, SEC
Elaeocarpaceae				
Sericolea	1(20)		S	F
Escalloniaceae				
Quintinia	3(20)		Small	SEC, H
Urticaceae				
Elatostema	10(200)		S	T, F
Pilea	20(400)	Am	S	T, F
Procris	10(20)		S	T, F
Moraceae				
Antiaris	1(1)		S	T
Ficus	500(800)	Af, Am	S	H
Rosaceae				
Pyrus	3(30)		S	F

APPENDIX 1 (*continued*)

	Epiphytic spp. (generic total)	Epiphytic spp. total shared with	Dissemimule type	Epiphytic life form
Myrtaceae				
Mearnsia	4(7)		W	F
Metrosideros	3(60)	(Pacific)	Small	H
Melastomataceae				
Catanthera	5(5)		S	T, F
Creochiton	4(6)		S	T, F
Hypenanthe	4(4)		S	T, F
Kendrickia	1(1)		D	T
Medinilla	300(400)	Af	S	T, F, SEC
Medinillopsis	2(2)		S	T, F
Memecylon	1(300)		S	F
Pachycentria	7(8)		S	T, F
Pogonanthera	6(6)		S	T, F
Cornaceae	3(6)	(NZ)	S	H
Vitaceae				
Pterisanthes	2(20)		S	F, SEC
Tetrastigma	2(90)		S	F, SEC
Nepenthaceae				
Nepenthes	6(70)		W	T, F, SEC
Begoniaceae				
Begonia	10(900)	Af, Am	S, W	T, SEC, F
Balsaminaceae				
Impatiens	5(500)	Am	Small (explos.)	F
Araliaceae				
Pentapanax	2(15)		S	H
Polyscias	5(80)		S	H, F
Schefflera	60(200)	Af, Am	S	H
Ericaceae				
Agapetes	6(80)		S	T, H
Costera	8(8)		S	T
Dimorphanthera	10(60)		S	T, F, H
Diplycosia	25(60)		S	T, F
Gaultheria	8(200)		S	T, F
Rhododendron	100(500)		W	T, H, F
Vaccinium	15(350)	Af, Am	S	T, F
Potaliaceae				
Fagraea	20(35)		S	H
Myrsinaceae				
Embelia	3(130)	Af	S	H, F
Rapanea	10(200)	Af, Am	S	F, T
Rubiaceae				
Amaracarpus	3(60)		S	F
Coprosma	6(90)		S	F
Hydnophytum	75(80)		S	T
Lecananthus	1(2)		S	F
Lucinaea	15(25)		S	T, F
Myrmecodia	40(45)		S	T
Myrmedoma	2(2)		S	T
Myrmephytum	2(2)		S	T

APPENDIX 1 (*continued*)

	Epiphytic spp. (generic total)	Epiphytic spp. total shared with	Dissemimule type	Epiphytic life form
Nertera	6(12)		S	T, F
Ophiorrhiza	5(150)		D	F
Procephaleium	1(1)		S	F/T
Psychotria	7(700)		S	F, T
Squamellaria	2(2)		S	T
Gesneriaceae				
Aeschynanthus	80(80)		W	T, SEC
Agalmyla	15(15)		W	T
Boea	2(25)		W	F
Crytandra	10(600)		S	F, T, SEC
Dichrotricum	4(4)		W	T, SEC
Loxostigma	3(4)		W	F, T
Lysionotus	2(2)		W	T
Asclepiadaceae				
Ceropegia	3(160)		W	F, SEC
Dischidia	80(90)		W	T
Dischidiopsis	9(9)		W	T
Heynella	1(1)		W	T
Hoya	100(200)		W	T, F, SEC
Solanaceae				
Lycianthes	2(200)		S	F
Solanum	15/1700	Am	S	F
Scrophulariaceae				
Wightea	3(3)		W	T, F
LILIOPSIDA (MONOCOTYLEDONES)				
Amaryllidaceae				
Curculigo	1(10)		S	F
Liliaceae				
Dianella	2(30)		S	F
Pandanaceae				
Pandanus	4(600)		S	T, F
Freycinetia	*c.* 80(100)		S	SEC
Araceae				
Amydrium	4(4)		S	SEC
Epipremnum	15(15)		S	SEC
Pedicellarum	1(1)		S	SEC
Pothos	25(75)		S	SEC
Rhaphidophora	100(100)		S	SEC
Scindapsus	20(30)		S	SEC
Zingiberaceae				
Brachychilum	2(2)		S	T, F
Hedychium	12(50)		S	T, F
Riedelia	*c.* 20(50)		S	T, F
Burmanniaceae				
Burmannia	2(57)	Am	D	F
Apostasiaceae				
Apostasia	1(10)		D	F
Neuwiedia	1(10)		D	F

APPENDIX 1 (*continued*)

	Epiphytic spp. (generic total)	Epiphytic spp. total shared with	Dissemimule type	Epiphytic life form
Cypripediaceae				
Paphiopedilum	10(100)		D	T, F
Orchidaceae				
Spiranthoideae				
Goodycrinae	*c.* 20(450)	Am	D	F
Orchidoideae				
Pterostylidinae	2(70)		D	F
Acianthinae	*c.* 20(100)		D	F
Epidendroideae				
Bletiinae	*c.* 100(380)	Af	D	T, F
Coelogyninae	*c.* 350(440)		D	T
Adrorhizinae	3(3)		D	T
Eriinae	500(500)	Af	D	T
Podochilinae	230(230)		D	T
Thelasiinae	270(270)		D	T
Glomerinae	130(130)		D	T
Dendrobiinae	1645(1650)		D	T
Bulbophyllinae	1500(1500)	Af, Am	D	T
Sunipiinae	25(25)		D	T
Sarcanthinae	1000(1000)	Af	D	T
Cyrtopodiinae	*c.* 300(450)	Af, Am	D	T
Thecostelinae	5(5)		D	T
Acriopsidinae	12(12)		D	T

Abbreviations:

Af = Africa	F = facultative	S = succulent
Am = the Americas	H = hemi-epiphyte	SEC = semi-epiphytic climber
D = dustseed or spores	N = nest-former	T = typical
		W = winged

REFERENCES

Beccari, O. 1884–86. *Pianti Opsitatrici. Malesia vol. 2.* Tipogr. Ist. Sordo Muti Genoa.

Benzing, D.H. and Ott, D.W., 1981. Vegetative reduction in epiphytic Bromeliaceae and Orchidaceae: its origin and significance. *Biotropica*, 13(2): 131–140.

Benzing, D.H. and Seemann, J., 1978. Nutritional piracy and host decline: a new perspective on the epiphyte–host relationships. *Selbyana*, 2: 133–148.

Bequaert, J., 1922. Ants in their diverse relationships to the plant world. *Bull. Am. Mus. Nat. Hist.*, 45: 333–358.

Boyer, Y., 1964. Contribution a l'étude de l'écophysiologie de deux fougères épiphytes, Platycerium stemaria (Beauv.) Desv. et P. angolense Wellwitsch. *Ann. Sci. Nat. Bot. Sér.*, 12(5): 87–228.

Chandra, S., 1981. Some aspects of interrelationships among the drynarioid ferns. *Gard. Bull. Singapore*, 34(2): 229–238.

Chandra, S., 1982. Notes on some ecological adaptations in Drynarioid ferns. *Malay. Nat. J.*, 35: 133–148.

Ching, R.C., 1940. On the natural classification of the Polypodiaceae. *Sunyatsenia*, 5: 201–268.

Ching, R.C., 1978. The Chinese fern families and genera: Systematic arrangement and historical origin. Acta Phytotax. Sin., 16: 1–37.

Copeland, E.B., 1947. *Genera Filicum.* Waltham, Mass.

Crabbe, S.A., Jermy, A.C. and Mickel, J.T., 1975. A new generic sequence for the pteridophyte herbarium. *Fern Gaz.*, 11: 141–162.

Forbes, H.O., 1880. Notes from Java. *Nature*, 22: p. 148.

Groom, P., 1893. *On Dischidia rafflesiana* (Wal.). *Ann. Bot.*, 7: 223–242.

Heim, D.R., 1898. The biologic relations between plants and ants. *Smithsonian Report* for 1896, pp. 411–455.

Hennipman, E. and Roos, M.C., 1982. *A Monograph of the Fern Genus Platycerium.* Elsevier, Amsterdam, 126 pp.

Huxley, C.R., 1978. The antplants Myrmecodia and Hydnophytum (Rubiaceae) and the relationship between their morphology, ant occupants, physiology and ecology. *New Phytol.*, 80: 231–268.

Huxley, C.R., 1980. Symbiosis between ants and epiphytes. *Biol. Rev.*, 55:321–340.

Huxley, C.R., 1982. Ant epiphytes of Australia. In: R.C. Buckley (Editor), *Ant–Plant Interactions in Australia*. Junk, The Hague, pp. 63–73

Janzen, D.H., 1974. Epiphytic myrmecophytes in Sarawak:

mutualism through the feeding of plants by ants. *Biotropica*, 6(4): 237–259.

Jermy, A.C. and Walker, T.G., 1975. Lecanopteris spinosa — a new ant-fern from Indonesia. *Fern Gaz.*, 11: 165–176.

Johansson, D., 1974. Ecology of vascular epiphytes in West African rainforest. *Acta Phytogeogr. Sin.*, 59: 1–136.

Kluge, M. and Ting, I.P., 1978. *Crassulacean Acid Metabolism — Analysis of an Ecological Adaptation.* Springer, Berlin, 209 pp.

Kress, W.J., 1987. The systematic distribution of vascular epiphytes: an update. *Selbyana*, 9: 2–22.

Madison, M., 1977. Vascular epiphytes: their systematic occurrence and salient features. *Selbyana*, 2(1): 1–13.

McWilliams, E.L., 1970. Comparative rates of CO_2 uptake and acidification in the Bromeliaceae, Orchidaceae and Euphorbiaceae. *Bot. Gaz.*, 13(14): 285–290.

Medina, E., 1975. Dark CO_2 fixation, habitat preference and evolution within the Bromeliaceae. *Evolution*, 28(4): 677–686.

Medina, E., Delgado, M., Troughton, J.H. and Medina, J.D., 1977. Physiological ecology of CO_2 fixation in Bromeliaceae. *Flora*, 166: 137–152.

Miehe, H., 1911a. Untersuchungen über die javanische Myrmecodia. In: Javanische Studien 2. *Abh. Sächs. Akad. Wiss. Math. Phys. Kl.*, 32: 312–361.

Miehe, H., 1911b. Uber die javanische Myrmecodia und die Beziehung zu ihren Ameisen. *Biol. Zentralbl.*, 31: p. 733.

Osmond, C.B., 1978. Crassulacean acid metabolism: a curiosity in context. *Ann. Rev. Plant Physiol.*, 29: 379–414.

Pearson, H.H., 1902. On some Dischidia with double pitchers. *J. Linn. Soc.*, 35: 375–390.

Rickson, F.R., 1979. Absorption of animal tissue breakdown products into a plant stem — the feeding of a plant by ants. *Am. J. Bot.*, 66(1): 87–90.

Ridley, H.N., 1910. Symbiosis of ants and plants. *Ann. Bot.*, 24(114): 457–483.

Scott, D.H. and Sargant, E., 1893. On the pitchers of Dischidia rafflesiana (Wall.). *Ann. Bot.*, 26: 243–268.

Spanner, L., 1938. Ein Beitrag zur Morphologie einiger Myrmecodien. *Beih. Bot. Zentralbl.*, 58: 267–290.

Treub, M., 1883a. Sur le urnes dei Dischidia rafflesiana. *Ann. Jard. Bot. Buitenzorg*, 3: 13–34.

Treub, M., 1883b. Sur le Myrmecodia echinata Gaudich. *Ann. Jard. Bot. Buitenzorg*, 3: 129–159.

Treub, M., 1888. Nouvelles researches sur le Myrmecodia de Java. *Ann. Jard. Bot. Buitenzorg*, 7: 191–212.

Wallace, B.J., 1981. *The Australian vascular epiphytes: Flora and ecology.* Ph.D. Thesis, Univ. of New England, Armidale, N.S.W.

Webb, L.J. and Tracey, J.G., 1981. The rainforests of northern Australia. In: R.H. Groves (Editor), *Australian Vegetation.* Cambridge Univ. Press, Melbourne, Vict.

Whiffin, T., 1972. Observations on some upper Amazonian formicarial Melastomataceae. *Sida*, 5(1): 33–41.

Winter, K., 1985. Crassulacean acid metabolism. In: J. Barber (Editor), *Topics in Photosynthesis, Vol. 6.* Elsevier, Amsterdam.

Winter, K., Wallace, B.J., Stocker, G.C. and Roksandic, Z., 1983. Crassulacean acid metabolism in Australian vascular epiphytes and some related species. *Oecologia*, 57: 129–141.

Yapp, R.H., 1902. Two Malayan "myrmecophilous" ferns, Polypodium (Lecanopteris) carnosum (Blume) and Polypodium sinuosum, Wall. *Ann. Bot.*, 62: 185–231.

Chapter 14

THE FORESTS IN THE TROPICAL PACIFIC ARCHIPELAGOES

M. SCHMID

INTRODUCTION

The tropical Pacific is dotted in its central and western part with numerous islands, a few relatively isolated, many clustered in archipelagoes which are situated on anticlinal ridges separated by deep submarine troughs (Fig. 14.1). Except for New Guinea and the Bismarck Archipelago connected with the Malay Archipelago, and for Taiwan and Hai-Nan, which may be considered as dependencies of the Asian continent, the total area of the emerged lands is less than 125 000 km². The more important groups are to the south, from 150° to 180°E, the Solomon Islands (37 000 km²), New Caledonia and the Iles Loyauté (19 100 km²), Vanuatu (New Hebrides) (13 000 km²) and lastly Fiji (18 000 km²), the four archipelagoes being Melanesian; from 180° to 135°W, Samoa (3150 km²), Tonga (700 km²), the Society Islands (1680 km²) and the Marquesas Islands (1275 km²), which are Polynesian. To the east of 135°W there are only the Galapagos Islands (7850 km²) at the Equator, 1000 km from the American coast. To the north, the numerous Micronesian Islands, the Mariana, Caroline and Marshall Islands (altogether less than 2500 km²), are scattered over 5000 km between 135° and 180°E, and the Hawaiian Islands (16 400 km²), particularly isolated, are located between 160° and 155°W.

Vegetation varies with the climatic and edaphic conditions, the latter, while being linked to the climate, depending for a large part on the rock types and the geomorphology. But the composition and, to some degree, the structure of the vegetation are also linked to the conditions under which local flora evolved. As most of the islands are small and scattered throughout an immense oceanic area, it appears important to discuss

phytogeographical aspects. Finally, the effects of human activities on the evolution of the natural ecosystems have also to be taken into account, these ecosystems being all the more fragile the more isolated they are.

ENVIRONMENT

Climatic factors

Except for western Micronesia, situated within the influence of the Asian monsoon, trade winds dominate the climate everywhere. They blow with intensity varying with the season, from the south-east in the Southern Hemisphere, and from the northeast in the Northern Hemisphere. These winds take up moisture over the ocean, and most of the Pacific islands have ample precipitation. Save in the Galapagos Islands, where the climate is semi-arid with rains concentrated from February to April, and in the low coral islands at the Equator, the average annual precipitation generally varies between 1500 and 4000 mm, and the dry season is not very severe. This is compatible with evergreen forest vegetation. However, abundance of rains depends on the relief, and, in the case of relatively high islands, conditions on the leeward side may be fairly dry. Thus, in New Caledonia, the annual precipitation, which varies from 2500 to 8000 mm on the slopes facing east, is only 600 mm on some parts of the western coast. In Hawaii, up to 15 000 mm have been registered at an altitude of 1600 m on the mountain of Waialeale, and less than 600 mm in the driest places. In Vanuatu, even in relatively small islands such as Aneityum (165 km²), parts to the northwest have a fairly low

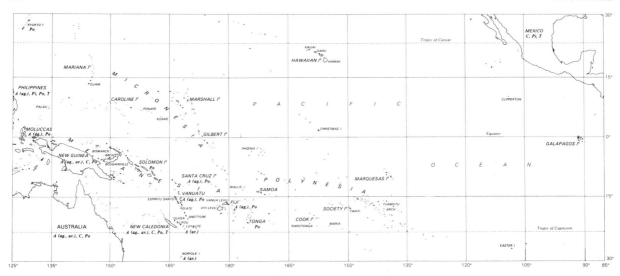

Fig. 14.1. Map of the tropical Pacific region showing the distribution of the coniferae. *A* = Araucariaceae; *ag.* = *Agathis*; *ar.* = *Araucaria*; *C* = Cupressaceae; *Pi* = Pinaceae; *Po* = Podocarpaceae; *T* = Taxaceae.

humidity and are colonized by *Leucaena leucocephala*; but in Samoa the extent of such dry areas is very limited, owing to the orientation of the main relief lines parallel to the prevailing winds.

Diminution of annual precipitation is accompanied by an increase in irregularity of rains and strengthening of seasonal contrasts. The differentiation between leeward and windward vegetation is stronger where shortage of moisture makes the effects of human activities, especially fire damage, more severe. Nevertheless, though fairly dry areas have often been more extensively deforested (New Caledonia, Fiji), the tallest forests are often located in zones of medium rain intensity rather than on the wettest slopes (New Caledonia, Vanuatu).

Humidity generally increases with altitude up to a certain level, rarely over 2000 m, corresponding to the maximum of cloud density. It decreases above this altitude. The comparative dryness near the summits of the highest islands (Hawaii: 600 mm at about 3400 m on Mauna Loa; Tahiti), together with a decrease in temperature, intense insolation and wind action, impede forest establishment. At the level where the cloud sheet is generally located, vegetation appears very peculiar. "Cloud forest" or "mossy forest", a low-branching formation where lianas are rare and epiphytes very abundant, occurs at about 1100 m in New Caledonia, but may be found under 500 m in southern

Vanuatu. Its appearance is related to the frequency of mist rather than to the abundance of rain; in New Caledonia, it might be favoured by ultrabasic outcrops.

Cyclonic disturbances, occurring generally at about the end of the warm season, mainly affect the western Pacific archipelagoes (Melanesia, western Micronesia). They may have strong effects on forest dynamics. Thus, the powerful tap-root system of the Araucariaceae gives them an unquestionable advantage in competition with other species on slopes exposed to strong winds. In the Iles Loyauté, *Araucaria columnaris*, besides benefiting from its special architecture, grows on sublittoral cliffs facing the prevailing winds (Fig. 14.2).

Mean temperature at sea level is about 23°C near the Tropics, and 27.5°C at the Equator. It may be more than 1°C lower in the wettest sites. The difference in temperature between the hottest and the coolest month is small owing to the oceanic environment, varying from 1 to 6°C from the Equator to the Tropics. The amplitude of diurnal variations, which is about 5°C in the low islands, rises to 15°C during the dry season on the western plains of New Caledonia, owing to the mountainous hinterland. The decrease in temperature with altitude is 0.5 to 0.6°C for every 100 m up to 800 to 1000 m. In Tahiti, the gradient may be steeper at higher altitudes, reaching 0.8°C per

Fig. 14.2. Stand of *Araucaria columnaris* on a low coral islet close to the south of New Caledonia. In the foreground *Casuarina equisetifolia*.

100 m between 1500 and 2000 m (Papy, 1955). In Hawaii, at a latitude of 20°N, slopes over 4000 m may be snow-covered for several months, and cloud forest is replaced over 2000 m by an open woodland, which continues up to about 3200 m. Everywhere else, woody vegetation reaches the summits, but, owing either to climatic or edaphic conditions, the formations observed above the cloud forest are generally low and more or less open, and show certain xeric features (Hawaii, Tahiti, New Caledonia).

Geology, relief and soils

The Melanesian archipelagoes are situated on the margin of Gondwanaland. New Caledonia is supposed by some authors (Van Steenis, 1979) also to have been a part of it which has been isolated for a long time. The shifting of the Gondwana Plate produced deformations of the ocean floor accompanied by volcanic eruptions, and involved the emergence of Fiji, the Solomon Islands and Vanuatu. It also led to the intrusion of ultrabasic rocks, outcrops of which have played an important role in the evolution of the New Caledonian flora. The other tropical Pacific islands may be considered as entirely oceanic.

With the exception of New Caledonia, where varied sedimentary rocks are found, the oldest dating from the Permian, the Pacific lands are relatively recent and almost entirely composed of volcanic rocks of basaltic or andesitic composition, dating from the Miocene to the present for the Hawaiian Islands and Melanesia, and from the Pliocene to the present for the Galapagos Islands and Polynesia. Lava flows have been partly covered by coral limestone during the period when the volcanic deposits were below the ocean waters; subsequently, coral-reef terraces may have been raised to different levels by relative vertical movement of land and sea.

Among the entirely coralline islands, the atolls,

which are ring-shaped islands encircling a lagoon, have to be distinguished from the raised atolls with a central plateau surrounded by cliffs. The land surface of the emergent part of the atolls is small and the prevailing ecological conditions do not favour forest settlement; their flora is very poor and specialized. The surface area of the raised atolls may be large (Lifou: 1200 km^2), and their soils, often enriched superficially by volcanic deposits, are suitable for forest development.

Most of the high islands have a rugged relief which involves great heterogeneity of the microclimatological and edaphic conditions. At the same elevation, slopes are steeper in relatively small or narrow islands; relief is also more abrupt with narrower ridges in the older islands, where erosion, though it has shaped the mountain slopes, has not yet substantially reduced their altitude (contrast between Kauai and Hawaii in the Hawaiian archipelago).

Under the hot and humid conditions prevailing in the tropical Pacific, neutral or weakly acid volcanic rocks break down into ferrallitic soils which rapidly grow deeper and poorer, where the slope is not too steep. In Fiji, the Santa Cruz Islands, and some islands of Vanuatu, tall *Agathis* forests are found on leached ferrallitic soils. However, there are well-saturated fersiallitic or vertic brown soils in the relatively dry parts, and brown soils or immature soils formed by erosion on fairly steep slopes. Around active or recently extinct volcanoes (Hawaiian Islands, Samoa, Vanuatu), there are raw mineral soils and andosoils, the latter in the wet highlands being generally very leached (cloud–forest zone). Volcanic ashes, which may fall far from the crater, enrich the soils in mineral nutrients; but that does not necessarily favour the rain forest. Piedmont or valley soils, enriched by leaching down the hillsides and well supplied with water, often support luxuriant forests where alluvial deposits are not too heavy.

Vegetation colonizes scoriaceous lava flows (aa) more rapidly than ropy ones (pahoehoe). In Vanuatu, flora associated with juvenile volcanic soils is rather poor, including palms and tree ferns as distinctive elements.

Soils on old coral terraces are often partly derived from volcanic material. They are generally ferrallitic but not very deep and somewhat unsaturated owing to the calcareous substratum. Some floristic groups are missing in the vegetation associated with them: Coniferae (except for *Araucaria columnaris* in New Caledonia), Cunoniaceae, *Campnosperma*, etc.

On the low coral islands and calcareous cliffs, rendzinas are commonly found. On the atolls, the presence of limestone in the soil and the proximity of saline ground water have a very severe selective action upon the flora.

In New Caledonia, where the rocks are of varied and very contrasted types, forest mainly occurs on unsaturated fersiallitic or ferrallitic soils derived from sandstones or schists, sometimes slightly calcareous, sometimes highly siliceous, and on ferruginous ferrallitic soils derived from ultrabasic material. In the latter case, the presence of indurated horizons, more or less thick, more or less continuous, and often fossilliferous, may restrain vegetation development. The forest flora on ultrabasic terrain contains very peculiar elements, but it appears poorer than those on neutral or on acid terrain. This does not apply to the flora of the shrubby formations ("maquis").

FLORISTIC RESOURCES

The distinction between continental islands such as New Caledonia, semi-continental ones such as Fiji, and oceanic ones such as the Hawaiian Islands, appears to be very significant in the genesis of the present-day floras. However, authors who have dealt with this question do not agree on all points. Undoubtedly, the notion of oceanic islands does not completely explain evolutionary processes which have led to the differentiation of floras as dissimilar as those of the Hawaiian Islands and Samoa, both island groups emerged directly from the ocean floor.

The New Caledonian flora is noteworthy for its richness and its peculiarity. The rate of endemism is about 75%, and there are about twice as many native species as in the floras of the Hawaiian Islands or Fiji, each of which is comparable in area. Besides, the New Caledonian flora, with 680 genera of phanerogams (14% endemic), appears more diversified than the Fijian flora, numbering 476 genera (2% endemic), or the Hawaiian flora, which comprises only 210 genera (14.3% endemic).

At the species level, the rate of endemism is also very high in Fiji (66%), and above all in the Hawaiian Islands (95%).

It seems that the New Caledonian flora evolved in the course of a long period of isolation from a floristic stock already well diversified at the time of separation from Gondwanaland. The exposure of peridotites, linked to the Tertiary orogenesis, favoured speciation within certain groups; for other groups, whose evolutionary capability was almost exhausted, it might have resulted in the conservation of relictual forms.

In the Hawaiian Islands, the flora originated in isolated elements from distant continents, established in an environment where competition was greatly reduced. According to Fosberg (1961), the present phanerogamic flora could have originated from only 272 species of seed plants. These ancestor species most probably were not from forest communities.

In Fiji, the genesis of the flora has been related to terrestrial connexions with the Malesian region during certain periods of the Tertiary. It has been disturbed by volcanic phenomena. Evolution has not been as active as in New Caledonia, the environment being less contrasted and the time of isolation having been shorter. The floristic stock consists mainly of forest elements with a few relictual forms (*Degeneria*).

The strand flora, whose composition generally varies little from one archipelago to another, is distinguished in the Hawaiian Islands by the presence of numerous endemics and, even more, by the absence of species widespread elsewhere (*Pisonia grandis*, *Guettarda speciosa*, *Pemphis acidula*, etc). That of New Caledonia, which is relatively rich, includes a few endemics (*Acropogon bullatus*, etc.) and species with a restricted regional distribution (*Rottboellia*, *Nicotiana*, *Wedelia*, etc.), in addition to most of those widespread throughout the tropical Pacific.

The Solomon Islands, Vanuatu and Tonga have, like Fiji, semi-continental floras which originated from the Malesian region either directly (Solomon Islands) or, at least partly, through Fiji.

Amongst the truly oceanic islands, the flora of Samoa has close affinities with that of Fiji, but does not contain Coniferae. Micronesia, which forms a fairly continuous chain extending 5000 km from the Moluccas to Kiribati (Gilbert Islands),

also has a Malesian flora. However, the distances between the high volcanic islands, which are the only ones where conditions are suitable for rain forest, are generally great; consequently, the flora is rather poor, with a high rate of endemism at the species level considering the small area of the islands and the brevity of the evolutionary period. Finally, in eastern Polynesia, Hawaiian and Austral elements are found in addition to the Malesian elements which still predominate. As in the Hawaiian Islands, the low forests or thickets contain woody species belonging to families which are represented within continental areas mainly by herbaceous plants (Amaranthaceae, Asteraceae, Campanulaceae–Lobelioideae). Evolutionary processes leading to the origin of these peculiar forms, considered primitive by some authors, might be linked to extreme isolation. However, speciation phenomena associated with adaptive radiation are less noteworthy here than in the Hawaiian Islands, owing to the more restricted diversification of the ecological conditions.

The Galapagos Islands belong to the American zone (Cactaceae, *Bursera*, etc.). A dry climate and active volcanism did not favour the establishment of a closed forest flora. An endemic genus of the Asteraceae, *Scalesia*, is found, which includes some species of fairly big trees. Endemism at the species level is about 36%.

The relations between the flora, environment, geological events and the geographic situation appear clearly in the distribution of certain groups of plants.

The pteridophytes, diaspores of which may be transported over long distances, are known as pioneers on bare lands under relatively humid conditions and as "healing plants" — gap colonizers — in forest communities. Throughout the Pacific their importance in the vegetation is much above the normal, especially in islands which are more recent, more isolated, or moister. The rate of endemism for the group is generally inferior to that of the phanerogams. However, that does not apply to the Cyatheaceae, which abound in the forests of the Southern Hemisphere, some species being more than 20 m high. In New Caledonia, endemism for the Cyatheaceae reaches 90%, against 46% for the pteridophytes as a whole.

The Coniferae, which are numerous in the forests of New Caledonia and Fiji, are not represented in the oceanic islands. They are not found further east than Tonga.

The paucity of native Asteraceae and Poaceae, generally associated with open vegetation, is striking in Melanesia, except in the strand flora, whereas in the Hawaiian Islands the Asteraceae include several endemic genera and many endemic species, and the Poaceae are fairly well represented in the highlands.

Palms are generally associated with forest environments, and many species have very restricted areas. They abound in the western Pacific. One group, including 15 endemic genera, is peculiar to New Caledonia; another is common to Fiji, Vanuatu and Samoa; a third group with more affinities to New Guinea is found in the Solomon Islands. There is only one genus in the Hawaiian Islands, with more than 30 species. Palms are present, but infrequent, in eastern Polynesia.

There are no epiphytic Orchidaceae in the Hawaiian Islands, where the family is only represented by four terrestrial species, growing within open formations. This absence might be related to conditions initially unsuitable to forest. Orchids are numerous in the other archipelagoes, especially in the western Pacific.

The presence of the genus *Vaccinium* on many high islands, but not in New Caledonia, shows the deep penetration to the east of certain orophilous elements of the Malesian flora. The montane floras also include species of subantarctic affinities (such as *Astelia*). In New Caledonia, the montane flora mainly originated from the local floristic stock, either by adaptive radiation or by redistribution of pre-existent elements.

The data gathered in Table 14.1 give a general idea of the distinctiveness of the floras throughout the tropical Pacific.

The principal families of the dominant forest strata are:

Araucariaceae (in Melanesia)
Caesalpiniaceae (*Intsia, Maniltoa*)
Clusiaceae (*Calophyllum* and, in New Caledonia, *Montrouziera*)
Cunioniaceae (in the Southern Hemisphere)
Euphorbiaceae (*Bischofia, Endospermum*, etc.)
Hernandiaceae
Lauraceae
Mimosaceae (*Serianthes*)
Moraceae (*Antiaris, Ficus* and, in Micronesia, *Artocarpus*)
Myrtaceae (*Metrosideros, Syzygium* and related genera)
Papilionaceae (*Inocarpus*)

Podocarpaceae (in Melanesia)
Proteaceae (in New Caledonia)
Rosaceae (*Parinari* and, in the Solomon Islands, *Maranthes*)
Sapindaceae (*Pometia*, etc.)
Sapotaceae

In the Solomon Islands, according to Whitmore (1969) about 60 species of big trees are common.

THE DIFFERENT TYPES OF FORESTS

The forests of the tropical Pacific are generally evergreen. Their structure is comparable to that of the Malesian forests, with several synusiae, but the flora of the dominant strata is often relatively poor.

Formations associated with the marine environment

Along the low coasts mangrove vegetation occupies areas of active sedimentation which are permanently or periodically flooded by the sea. It covers rather large areas in the Melanesian archipelagoes and in the Caroline Islands. East of Samoa, it disappears, but it is found again in the Galapagos Islands.

In the Solomon Islands, the mangroves are commonly 25 m high. In New Caledonia, almost on the southern margin of its area, mangrove forest is rarely over 10 m high, but its flora is still fairly rich (about 15 tree species).

The main constituents of mangrove forest are Rhizophoraceae together with the genera *Avicennia, Lumnitzera, Sonneratia*, and *Xylocarpus. Nipa fruticans* is found only in the Solomon Islands and in western Micronesia. In the Galapagos Islands, the mangrove species belong to the same families but are of American origin.

Forests along non-muddy coasts are generally rather low, though they may reach 30 m in well-protected places. Often they have been replaced by coconut plantations. Where the littoral is exposed to constant winds carrying salt spray, trees branch horizontally at low levels and, at the seaside, the vegetation is reduced to a low thicket.

Many woody species of these formations have widespread distribution, Indo-Pacific (*Argusia, Cordia, Pemphis, Pisonia, Scaevola*), or pantropical (*Guettarda, Sophora, Suriana, Thespesia, Ximenia*),

TABLE 14.1

Floristics of Pacific islands and archipelagoes (species considered as native)

	New Caledonia	Lifou	Solomon Islands	Vanuatu	Fiji	Micronesia (Caroline Islands) Palau Islands	Micronesia (Caroline Islands) Ponape	Hawaiian Islands	Society Islands (incl. Makatea)	Galapagos Islands	Maria Island
Average latitude	21°S	21°S	8°S	16°S	17°S	7°5N	6°5N	20°5N	17°S	0.5°S	21°5S
Average longitude	165°E	167°E	158°E	167°E	179°E	135°E	158°E	160°W	150°W	91°W	154.4°W
Area (km²)	16 750	1200	37 000	13 000	18 000	500	380	16 640	1680	7855	1.5
Highest point (m)	1640	105	2765	1880	1323	240	791	4205	2240	1707	3
Pteridophytes (species)	245	30	310	249	290	135	104	180	250	89	4
Coniferae (species)	42	1	5	3	9	0	0	0	0	0	0
Angiosperms (genera)*	680(98)	280(0)	654(0)	451(1?)	476(10)	370(1)	212(0)	210(30)	186(1)	309(2)	21(0)
Angiosperms (species)	3200	430	2100	900	1550	635	340	1400	450	553	21
Palms (genera)**	16(33)	1(1)	14-16	8-9	10(26)	6(6)	4(5)	1(33)	1(1)(?)	0	0
Phanerogam genera comprising from 9 to 19 species **	53(618)	0	10	8-10	20(225)	6	1	17(230)	7(85)	3(31)	0
Phanerogam genera comprising 20 species or more **	122(700)	0	2	1-2	7(240)	0	0	17(730)	0	0	0
Raunkiaer's pteridophyte quotient ***	2.2	1.8	3.8	7.0	4.7	5.2	5.7	3.2	13.8	4.0	5.0

* In brackets, number of genera peculiar to the territory.

** In brackets, number of species in the territory.

***Calculated on a supposedly normal proportion of 25 species of phanerogams to every species of pteridophytes for the world as a whole.

N.B. Data approximate for the genera and above all for the species. Particularly, the inventories of the flora of the Solomon Islands and of Vanuatu are still very incomplete.

but few are found in the Hawaiian Islands (*Pandanus, Scaevola*). Strand vegetation includes also some endemic species, especially in the Hawaiian Islands and in the New Caledonian region (*Araucaria columnaris*).

The flora is rather poor and very specialized, and monospecific stands of vegetation are rather frequently observed (e.g. *Neisosperma oppositifolia*). Vines (Leguminosae, Convolvulaceae), and at times epiphytes (ferns, orchids), may abound.

Pisonia grandis is one of the most characteristic constituents of these formations. Under particularly favourable conditions it may be over 30 m high, and is one of the few big tree species native to eastern Polynesia. *Barringtonia asiatica, Calophyllum inophyllum, Intsia bijuga, Terminalia catappa, T. samoensis* and certain Sapotaceae (*Manilkara, Planchonella*) also reach quite large dimensions, and in New Caledonia *Araucaria columnaris*

(Fig. 14.2), which grows on ultrabasic terrains as well as on limestone, may be 50 m tall. *Casuarina equisetifolia* (Fig. 14.3) and *Hibiscus tiliaceus*, which are very common, do not reach such a height. Both are also found inland in secondary vegetation: *Casuarina*, though not fire-tolerant, may be observed in savannas, especially on ridges; *Hibiscus* behaves as a pioneer in forest areas, where it can multiply by natural layering (Hallé, 1978).

The tallest forests are generally observed on rocky soils. Among the trees commonly found on sandy soils, *Hernandia nymphaeifolia*, distributed throughout the Pacific, and *Acacia simplex*, occurring from New Caledonia to Samoa, may be mentioned.

Inland forests at low and medium altitudes

The extent of these forests remains considerable, at least at medium altitude in the Melanesian

Fig. 14.3. *Casuarina equisetifolia* on fringing coral terraces on Aneityum, Vanuatu.

archipelagoes and in western Polynesia (Samoa). They are more localized in the Hawaiian Islands, and, especially, in the Galapagos Islands. They are still represented on the largest islands of Micronesia. In eastern Polynesia, *Inocarpus fagiferus*, the main constituent of the inland forest, might have been introduced by man.

Changes in ecological conditions, which are often pronounced over short distances owing to the rugged relief, are associated with changes in the vegetation. Furthermore, climax communities are often replaced by secondary formations, which are lower and structurally less homogeneous. In many cases these transitional vegetation types occupy land which was formerly cultivated, but hurricanes, landslides or volcanic phenomena may also be the cause of their appearance.

The flora of the climax communities, contrary to that of the secondary formations, contains many species peculiar to one archipelago or even to one island; but generally, except for many of those in the Hawaiian Islands and New Caledonia, these endemics belong to genera which have widespread distribution areas.

Hardwood forests with several dominant tree species in the upper stratum

On volcanic rocks. The tallest formations are found on deep volcanic soils, with a great water-holding capacity but rather poor in mineral nutrients.

The forests which are most similar to those of the Malesian region, as regards complexity of structure and composition, are found in the Solomon Islands, but they are less high and not so floristically rich as the Malesian forests.

The height of the formation ranges from 30 to 45 m. About a dozen big tree species (*Calophyllum, Campnosperma, Dillenia, Elaeocarpus, Endospermum, Gmelina, Maranthes, Parinari, Schizomeria, Terminalia*) are the main constituents of the dominant stratum, overtopped at long intervals by banyan figs (for instance, *Ficus prolixa*) and by *Terminalia calamansanay* (Whitmore, 1969). Trees with large buttresses are frequent, especially in the alluvial areas where the flora differs from that on the slopes (Papilionaceae Mimosaceae, Sapotaceae, *Dracontomelon, Kleinhovia*, etc., in Bougainville *Octomeles sumatranus*). Vines and semi-

epiphytes (Araceae, *Calamus, Freycinetia, Piper* and ferns) abound, but in the climax communities the understorey is rather open. Epiphytes are present everywhere and become more luxuriant as altitude increases. In the lower strata pachycaulous species (Araliaceae, *Cyrtandra, Ficus, Tapeinosperma*) and palms, among which some species have stilt roots, are conspicuous.

On poorly drained soils gregarious species such as *Terminalia brassii* and *Campnosperma brevipetiolata* predominate, and semi-epiphytes (mainly ferns) are especially abundant.

In Vanuatu, Fiji and Samoa the forest is somewhat lower (about 30 m). The dominant stratum is mainly composed of species belonging to the genera *Calophyllum, Endospermum, Hernandia, Myristica*, and to the Lauraceae, Moraceae, Myrtaceae and Sapotaceae. Very large dome-shaped banyan figs stand out in the landscape, often marking the sites of villages that are still inhabited or have been deserted for a long time. The lower strata are rich in Myrsinaceae, Rubiaceae, Urticaceae and ferns, and, along the valley bottoms, *Cyrtandra* and *Cyathea*. Palms and Zingiberales (*Alpinia, Heliconia*) occur in patches. Vine palms (*Calamus*) abound in certain biotopes.

In dry areas, semi-deciduous forests (*Garuga floribunda, Gyrocarpus americanus*) may be observed.

In Micronesia the most characteristic big tree species of the rain forest belong to the genera *Calophyllum, Campnosperma, Eugenia* and *Manilkara* (Fosberg, 1960). Palms are common in the western and central Caroline Islands.

In the Marquesas Islands the inlands forest is comparatively low (less than 20 m). The presence at medium altitude of *Thespesia populnea*, elsewhere considered as strictly littoral, is noteworthy (Hallé, 1978).

On sandstones, schists or mica-schists. The New Caledonia hardwood forests are found mainly on terrains of this type. Soils may vary with the silica content of the substratum, but generally they do not differ much in physicochemical properties from those on fairly old volcanic terrains under humid conditions. However, the flora is totally distinct from that of the forests in other parts of Melanesia. Clusiaceae (*Calophyllum, Montrouziera*), Cunoniaceae, Myrtaceae Myrtoideae, Proteaceae, and

Sapotaceae, less frequently Araliaceae, Lauraceae (*Cryptocarya*), Meliaceae (*Dysoxylum*), Mimosaceae (*Archidendropsis*) and Rhizophoraceae (*Crossostylis*) predominate in the upper stratum (Fig. 14.4). Trees with large buttresses are rare (*Sloanea*, some Sapotaceae). As in the Solomon Islands, pachycaulous species are frequent in the understorey (*Dysoxylum*, *Ficus*, *Meryta*, *Acropogon*; Fig. 14.5); Palms abound, especially on the slopes. Tree ferns, mainly along the valley bottoms, may be over 20 m high, just as in the southern part of Vanuatu. Lianas are not very numerous (*Hugonia*, *Oxera*). Urticaceae are uncommon, and Zingiberales and vine palms are missing.

On ultrabasic rocks. In New Caledonia, where these terrains cover very large areas, Coniferae generally predominate. However, especially in the southern part of the island, forest formations are found with Casuarinaceae or Myrtaceae (*Arillastrum gummiferum*) as the main constituents. The upper stratum of these formations is more or less open, and the understorey contains species of the "maquis" peculiar to the ultrabasic areas (Apocynaceae, Clusiaceae, Cunoniaceae, Cyperaceae, Dilleniaceae, Epacridaceae, Myrtaceae, Rutaceae).

In the Solomon Islands, where ultrabasic outcrops are fairly restricted, the flora is poorer and not so distinctive. *Gymnostoma papuanum* and *Dillenia crenata* are the major constituents of the dominant stratum, and there are only four species which are peculiar to the vegetation associated with these outcrops, *Gulubia hombronii* (a palm), *Pandanus lamprocephalus*, and two shrub species,

Fig. 14.4. Hardwood forest (Myrtaceae, Lauraceae, Araliaceae) at medium altitude on the windward slopes of Colnett, a micaschistous massif in the northeast of New Caledonia. The tree ferns are *Cyathea intermedia*.

Fig. 14.5. A pachycaulous *Ficus otophora* in the understorey of the hardwood forest on siliceous terrains in central New Caledonia.

Myrtella beccarii and *Xanthostemon* sp. (Whitmore, 1969).

On limestone. The forests of the Iles Loyauté (2100 km²), raised atolls which emerged relatively recently and lie close to New Caledonia, are fairly well known. The flora is relatively poor and varies in its composition according to the altitude of the central plateau — that is, according to the depth of the ground water.

On Lifou, where this altitude varies from 15 to 40 m, the forest is 15 to 25 m tall with some emergents. The most distinctive species is *Schefflera golip* (Araliaceae); *Canarium balansae*, *Cryptocarya schmidii*, *Elaeocarpus angustifolius* and *E. rotundifolius*, *Elaeodendron curtipendulum* and *Serianthes lifouensis*, as well as two banyan figs and a few Myrtaceae (*Syzygium*) and Sapotaceae

are associated with it. In the lower strata, Ebenaceae, Euphorbiaceae, Rubiaceae, Sapindaceae, *Hybanthus caledonicus*, and a species of *Pandanus* are frequent. Terrestrial ferns abound, but there are few species (*Microsorum punctatum*). Lianas are mainly Menispermaceae, Moraceae and Smilacaceae. The epiphytes include ferns and about 15 species of orchids. The understorey is normally rather open, except on the cliffs where the flora differs from that on the plateau (*Arytera*, *Eugenia*, *Ixora*, *Manilkara*, and Euphorbiaceae).

On Ouvéa, where a great part of the lagoon is still covered by the sea and where the altitude of the plateau varies from 5 to 10 m, the forest flora behind the cliff contains species of the littoral zone, such as *Intsia bijuga* and *Guettarda speciosa*, which in well-protected sites may attain rather a large size.

The Iles Loyauté belong to the New Caledonian region. It is significant that the Cunoniaceae, Cyatheaceae, Proteaceae, and Myrtaceae–Leptospermoideae, which play such an important role in the forests of the "Grande Terre", are not represented here.

In western Micronesia, the dominant species on the raised coral-reef terraces belong to the Moraceae (*Artocarpus*, *Ficus*), the Myrtaceae–Myrtoideae, the Sapotaceae and the genera *Elaeocarpus* and *Hernandia*. In the Mariana Islands there is an endemic genus of Annonaceae, *Guamia*, in the understorey.

With the exception of the coconut palm, which is probably not native, palms are not commonly found on limestone. Those that occur belong to the genera *Gulubia*, *Pritchardia* and *Cyphophoenix* (*C. nucele* narrowly localized in Lifou).

Hardwood and softwood mixed forests

In these forests, the Coniferae associated with the angiosperms belong to the Araucariaceae, Cupressaceae, Podocarpaceae and Taxaceae.

Cupressaceae and Taxaceae (*Austrotaxus*, a monotypic genus) are found only in New Caledonia, where they are fairly rare and localized. The Podocarpaceae are represented throughout Melanasia and in Tonga, but it is only in Fiji, and to a lesser extent in New Caledonia, that they play an important role. The distribution areas of some species which do not occur in New Caledonia are fairly extensive. The Araucariaceae are represented in New Caledonia and, by the genus *Agathis* only, in Fiji, Vanuatu and the Santa Cruz Islands, a small archipelago to the south of the Solomon Islands.

Most of the Araucariaceae are semi-heliophilous. Their establishment may be favoured by natural catastrophes (landslides, extensive windfalls), but they do not appear normally as constituents of the secondary vegetation. Thanks to their powerful tap-roots, they are resistant to cyclones. They grow scattered or more often in groups, generally emerging above the broad-leaved trees.

In Fiji, mixed communities of softwood and hardwood species are found from sea level up to 1000 or 1200 m. *Agathis macrophylla* is the biggest tree of the Fijian forest; it may reach a height of 35 or even 45 m, with a trunk of 1.5 to 3 m in diameter at breast height (DBH). Several species of Podocarpaceae are commonly associated with *Agathis*.

In Vanuatu (Aneityum, Eromanga, Espiritu, Santo) and in the Santa Cruz Islands, *Agathis macrophylla*, with similar habit and ecological requirements, is also found in fairly large stands. In the Santa Cruz Islands, *Campnosperma brevipetiolata* is the main broad-leaved constituent of the dominant stratum.

In New Caledonia, there are five species of *Agathis* and about a dozen of *Araucaria*, all endemic. The *Araucaria* species, except for two or three, grow mainly in more or less open formations on ultrabasics, often on steep slopes or narrow ridges, at rather high altitudes. Three species of *Agathis* are found in closed forest at medium altitude, *A. lanceolata* being peculiar to ultrabasics, while *A. corbassonii* and *A. moorei* grow on siliceous schists. These three species may reach 40 m in height, with trunks of more than 2 m DBH. Some species of *Araucaria* grow higher (up to 60 m), but their trunks rarely exceed 1 m in diameter. Among the broad-leaved trees commonly associated with *Agathis*, certain Clusiaceae are found on siliceous as well as on ultrabasic substrata; six species of palms appear specific to the ultrabasic terrains and a dozen to the siliceous ones.

Broad-leaved forests with a single species predominating in the upper stratum

Many forest trees are rather frequently observed in small stands, but there are few which, like

Nothofagus in New Caledonia, are manifestly gregarious. Some species which normally grow scattered tend to form fairly pure stands in a special environment (*Campnosperma brevipetiolata* on peaty soils). Forests with a monospecific or almost monospecific uppermost stratum are often found close to the upper altitudinal margin of the tall forest area (*Metrosideros* forest).

Nothofagus forests in New Caledonia. These are stands of limited area, generally linked to ultrabasics and mainly found at medium or fairly high altitudes, but sometimes descending to less than 200 m. Shrub species associated with *Nothofagus* are few. The trees completely renew their foliage every year within a short time. The New Caledonian species of *Nothofagus* are related to those of New Guinea. There are five species, but stands are rarely mixed.

Metrosideros collina forests. *Metrosideros collina* is a very polymorphic species, including many subspecies or varieties, and varies in habit from a low shrub to a tall tree, according to the environment. It is spread throughout the tropical Pacific, except in Micronesia and the Galapagos Islands, where the genus does not exist, and in New Caledonia, where several endemic species of *Metrosideros* are found, most of them in forests or thickets at fairly high altitudes. In the Hawaiian Islands, *M. collina* is a pioneer on lava flows. It also occurs as an epiphyte, especially on tree-fern trunks. Under the best conditions on deep soils it may be over 30 m high (Fosberg, 1961).

Hawaiian *Metrosideros* forests have certain characteristics of montane formations (canopy shaped like an umbel, leaves rather small, sclerophyllous). A few other big trees — *Bobea*, *Cheirodendron*, *Elaeocarpus* and *Eugenia* s.l. — occur scattered through these forests. In the lower tree strata, Araliaceae, Rubiaceae and Rutaceae (*Pelea*), and, in the understorey, *Cyrtandra*, woody Lobelioideae, tree ferns (*Cibotium*) and palms (*Pritchardia*, in patches) predominate. Epiphytes (ferns) abound, but there are not many lianas (*Alyxia*, *Freycinetia*, *Smilax*). Normally in the Hawaiian Islands the *Metrosideros* forest occurs on slopes above the *Acacia koa* forest which grows under drier conditions. At its upper limit it gives way to cloud forest.

In Melanesia, the *Metrosideros collina* forest replaces those with a plurispecific dominant stratum as altitude increases. Higher up the slope it is progressively replaced by the lower formations of the cloud zone. The altitude at which it is most distinctive varies with topography. In Vanuatu, it is found at about 500 m in Efate, the highest point of which is 650 m; it is located between 800 and 1200 m in Espiritu Santo Island, which rises to 1888 m. In Tahiti (eastern Polynesia) it is found between 300 and 1000 m on the leeward slopes but it may descend below 300 m on the wettest slopes. Its height does not exceed 15 m. The associated species in the upper stratum belong to the genera *Celtis*, *Dodonaea*, *Fagraea* and *Neonauclea* (Florence, 1984).

In New Caledonia some *Metrosideros* species are found scattered, often as stranglers, in moist forest at medium altitudes. Others play a major role in the forests, thickets or maquis of the cloud zone.

The *Acacia koa* forest of the Hawaiian Islands. *Acacia koa*, an endemic species, is related to the Australian group of *Acacia* with phyllodes. It is found in more or less dense stands on fairly deeply weathered lavas. The species associated with *Acacia* in the upper stratum are all endemic, and belong to the genera *Bobea*, *Charpentiera* (an arborescent genus of Amaranthaceae), *Dodonaea*, *Osmanthus* and *Pisonia*. In the shrub stratum *Scaevola*, *Wikstroemia* and tree ferns (*Cibotium*, *Sadleria*) occur. The herbaceous layer is poorly developed (ferns) and there are few lianas and epiphytes (Fosberg, 1961).

The *Scalesia pedunculata* forest of the Galapagos Islands. There is no closed forest at low altitudes in the Galapagos Islands because of the dry climate. The *Scalesia* forest occurs between 180 and 550 m on the wettest slopes. The formation is 15 to 20 m high. In its umbel-shaped canopies and foliage it resembles the *Metrosideros* forest. *Scalesia pedunculata* may be associated with *S. microcephala* and also with *Pisonia floribunda* and *Psidium galapageium*, both endemic. Epiphytes (Orchidaceae, *Tillandsia*, ferns) and vines (legumes, Cucurbitaceae) are not common, and the shrub understorey (*Psychotria*, *Tournefortia*) is rather open (Wiggins and Porter, 1971).

Montane forests

Changes in the moisture and edaphic conditions near the ridges or summits have a pronounced effect upon the vegetation independently of that of the fall in temperature. This effect is felt at lower altitudes in relatively small islands.

The cloud forest, which may appear from 400 or 500 m upwards, replaces formations which include many species of the forests at low altitudes but in which elements that are more or less regularly associated with the montane environment (*Ascarina*, *Astronidium*, *Metrosideros*, *Weinmannia*, certain palms) tend to become important. At higher altitudes, depending on the topography, it gives way to thickets, maquis or heath formations which have some xeromorphic features.

Compared with the flora at lower altitudes, the montane flora may be either relatively rich (eastern Polynesia) or relatively poor (Solomon Islands). It contains many narrowly localized species which are often peculiar to one island or even to one massif. In Tahiti, the rate of endemism of the montane flora is 75%, in New Caledonia and the Hawaiian Islands nearly 100%. A few species however are common to summits which are very distant from one another (*Coriaria ruscifolia*), and several montane genera have very broad distribution areas (*Vaccinium*). Taxa which are almost everywhere well represented in the cloud forest include the bryophytes, the pteridophytes (Cyatheaceae, Hymenophyllaceae), *Astelia* s.l. (epiphytic Liliaceae) and *Freycinetia* (vine Pandanaceae).

The montane woody formations generally occupy areas difficult of access, where conditions are unsuitable for agriculture and where the climate is very humid (except close to the summits in the highest islands), so that the spread of fire is prevented. Consequently, they are on the whole rather well preserved.

Melanesia

In the Solomon Islands the montane flora is especially rich in Myrtaceae. The presence of four epiphytic species of *Rhododendron* is explained by the proximity of New Guinea, but otherwise very few characteristic elements of the montane flora of that island occur (Whitmore, 1969).

In Vanuatu the mossy forest is generally composed of small trees or shrubs, among them various Myrtaceae and Urticaceae, and species belonging to the genera *Ascarina, Balanops, Coprosma, Geniostoma, Quintinia.*

In Fiji the tall forest of Coniferae and broad-leaved trees nearly reaches the highest points. On the high ridges two species of *Podocarpus* of small size, *Coriaria ruscifolia* and *Crossostylis parksii* are found; *Freycinetia* often forms impenetrable thickets.

In New Caledonia there are various types of montane vegetation. Between about 1100 and 1300 m, on ultrabasic terrain, the cloud forest presents very typical features. The soil consists of a deep layer of organic matter directly in contact with almost unweathered bedrock. There are some formations with thick very short trunks and wide-spreading branches; the main constituents are various Myrtaceae (*Mearnsia, Metrosideros*), Cunoniaceae (*Cunonia*), Epacridaceae, (*Dracophyllum*) and Podocarpaceae. Formations of small trees or shrubs also occur; they are apparently richer in flora and include some palms. Still on ultrabasic terrains, stands of *Araucaria humboldtensis*, a low-growing species, occur in the southern part of the island (Fig. 14.6); the shrub layer contains Coniferae (Cupressaceae, Podocarpaceae), Cunoniaceae, Epacridaceae and Escalloniaceae (*Quintinia*). On micaschists, from 1200 m up to the highest point (1640 m), in the north-eastern part of the island, there are forests of *Agathis montana*, a rather mighty tree though not over 15 to 20 m high, with an understorey of palms and tree ferns. Epiphytes are less abundant in the formations where Coniferae are dominant than in the broad-leaved formations, though the former often occupy very moist sites. The commonest tree ferns on ultrabasic terrains belong to the genus *Dicksonia*, and on schists to the genus *Cyathea* (Fig. 14.7).

Some of the most noteworthy elements of the New Caledonian flora are peculiar to the montane vegetation (the endemic families Paracryphiaceae and Strasburgeriaceae, the endemic genera *Apiopetalum, Canacomyrica*, etc.).

Micronesia
In Micronesia, cloud forest is only found in the eastern Caroline Islands, on Ponape and Kusaie, which do not rise over 800 m. On the slopes at medium altitude palms tend to be dominant.

Fig. 14.6. Coniferae forest at about 900 m altitude, on the windward slopes of Kuakue, an ultrabasic massif in the southeast of New Caledonia. The picture shows *Callitris neocaledonica, Araucaria humboldtensis,* and *A. subulata* (in the background).

Higher up, typical constituents of the vegetation include the genera *Astronidium, Clinostigma, Cyathea, Elaeocarpus, Eurya* and *Pandanus*; among the lianas, *Freycinetia*; and among the epiphytes, orchids and Hymenophyllaceae. *Lepinia ponapensii*, a genus elsewhere only represented in Tahiti and the Solomon Islands, is peculiar to the formation (Fosberg, 1960).

Hawaiian Islands
On the highest Hawaiian mountains, above the *Metrosideros* forest, cloud-belt formations are found which are fairly tall in well-protected places, but reduced to more or less open thickets or heaths on especially exposed ridges.

The flora is rich, containing many species belonging to endemic genera (Asteraceae, Campanulaceae–Lobelioideae, Rutaceae, Hydrangeaceae) or to genera represented only in a few archipelagoes of the Pacific (*Cheirodendron*). Spe-

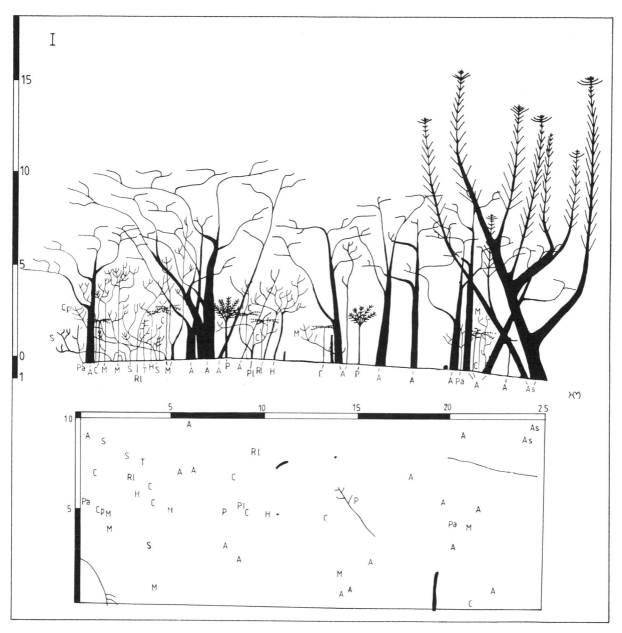

Fig. 14.7. Profile diagrams of the vegetation of Mt Panié, in northeastern New Caledonia. The scale is in m. (By courtesy of Michel Hoff.) I. Vegetation on the top of Mt. Panié (1628 m) in New Caledonia. *A* = *Agathis montana*; *As* = *Araucaria schmidii*; *C* = *Cyathea vieillardii*; *Cp* = *Cunonia pulchella*; *H* = *Hedycarya chrysophylla*; *M* = *Metrosideros dolichandra*; *P* = palms; *Pa* = *Paracryphia* sp.; *Pl* = *Polyosma* sp.; *Rl* = *Rapanea* sp.; *S* = *Styphelia cymbulae*; *T* = *Tapeinosperma* sp.

cies of *Coprosma, Metrosideros, Vaccinium,* palms (*Pritchardia*) and tree ferns (*Cibotium*) are also important constituents (Fosberg, 1961).

Polynesia

In Samoa, the montane flora is closely related to that of Fiji, but there are no Coniferae. The most

characteristic species belong to the genera *Ascarina, Coprosma, Coriaria, Pittosporum, Rapanea, Vaccinium* (on very exposed ridges) and, among the epiphytes, to *Collospermum* (a genus close to *Astelia*).

In Rarotonga (67 km² in area, 652 m in altitude, latitude 21°S), the largest of the Cook Islands, the

Fig. 14.7 (*continued*). II. Vegetation on the east slope of Mount Panié at about 950 m. *A* = Araliaceae; *Ac* = *Apodytes clusiifolia*; *B* = *Belliolum* sp.; *C* = *Cupaniopsis macrocarpa*; *Cc* = *Coronanthera* sp.; *D* = *Dutaillyea* sp.; *Dl* = *Diospyros* sp.; *E* = *Elattostachys apetala*; *F* = ferns; *Fa* = *Falcatifolium taxoides*; *G* = *Guioa glauca*; *Gd* = *Geniostoma* sp.; *H* = *Hedycarya cupulata*; *J* = *Joinvillea* sp.; *K* = *Kibaropsis caledonica*; *L* = *Litsea triflora*; *Lb* = *Lethedon* sp.; *M* = *Meryta* sp.; *P* = *Pandanus* sp.; *Pa* = palms; *Pg* = *Pycnandra* sp.; *Ph* = *Phyllanthus* sp.; *Pl* = *Piliocalyx* sp.; *Pb, Pd, Pt* = *Psychotria* spp.; *Rm, Rs* = *Rapanea* spp.; *S* = *Syzygium tripetalum*; *Sa* = Sapindaceae; *Sv* = *Schefflera* sp.; *T, Tp, Tk* = *Tapeinosperma* spp.; *Ti* = *Polyscias (Tieghemopanax)* sp.; *Z* = *Zygogynum* sp.

"montane" vegetation appears above 300 m. Slopes are very steep, soils are very shallow, and there is much cloud. The flora consists mainly of shrubby species including *Ascarina*, *Coprosma*, *Metrosideros*, *Vaccinium* and *Weinmannia*. Particularly noteworthy taxa are *Fitchia speciosa*, a woody composite with stilt roots which enable it to resist buffeting winds, and *Sclerotheca viridiflora*, a ligneous member of the Campanulaceae; elsewhere, these two genera are found only in eastern Polynesia (Sykes, 1980).

In Tahiti (1042 km² in area, and attaining an altitude of 2240 m, latitude 17°S) the cloud forest occupies the wettest slopes between 500 and 1500 m; in less humid parts it occurs only above 900 m. In well-protected sites, the formation is 12 to 15 m tall. The dominant constituents of the upper stratum are *Alstonia costata* and *Weinmannia parviflora*, the latter being more abundant on windy slopes or ridges. *Metrosideros collina*, *Ilex tahitensis*, *Reynoldsia tahitensis* (a genus of Araliaceae peculiar to Polynesia including the Hawaiian Islands), *Streblus tahitensis*, and several species of Euphorbiaceae are associated with these two species. The shrub stratum, which is rather rich floristically (*Cyathea*, *Cyrtandra*, *Psychotria*, *Rapanea*), contains *Sclerotheca arborea*, *S. jayorum* and, on the leeward, drier slopes, *Fitchia nutans*, *F. tahitensis* and *Fuchsia cyrtandroides*. *Freycinetia impavida*, a vine, is especially abundant, and pteridophytes with some orchids compose the epiphytic flora. Close to the summits, where the wind becomes more violent and humidity and temperature decrease, the vegetation is sub-shrubby and includes *Vaccinium cereum*, a few Epacridaceae and *Coriaria ruscifolia* (Florence, 1984).

In the Marquesas (1275 km² in area, and rising to an altitude of 1250 m, latitude 9°S) the montane vegetation above 900 m, which is less than 10 m high and reduced to a heath on the ridges, has a relatively rich flora with, as its most distinctive elements, woody species belonging to the genera *Alstonia*, *Bidens*, *Cheirodendron*, *Crossostylis*, *Reynoldsia*, *Sclerotheca*, *Styphelia*, *Trimenia*, *Vaccinium*, and *Weinmannia* (Hallé, 1978). The floristic affinities with the Hawaiian Islands are clear.

FORESTS, FAUNA AND HUMAN ACTIVITIES

While many islands have a rich fauna of invertebrates with a high degree of endemism (Arthropoda, Mollusca in New Caledonia), the native terrestrial fauna of vertebrates essentially consists of birds and reptiles. Amphibians are found in the Solomon Islands and Fiji. Except for one phalanger in the Solomon Islands, the only native mammals are bats.

Many species are endemic to one archipelago or to one island. Adapted to very protected habitats, they have suffered much from the damage caused to their environment by man and the animals he has introduced.

The rapid multiplication of allochthonous mammals, often originating from domesticated strains, has been favoured by the absence of predators. This may be harmful to the vegetation, but the recession of the forests results above all from direct human intervention.

Man arrived in the tropical Pacific a few thousand years ago, and most of the large islands have been occupied. The Galapagos Islands, however, were still uninhabited when the Europeans discovered them in the sixteenth century.

The soils have been extensively cultivated, except for the steepest slopes and the highest parts, where the soils are too poor or the climate less favourable. In the interior of many islands the population has probably been more numerous in the past than today, as indicated by traces of earthworks in areas now under forest (Solomons, Vanuatu, Samoa, etc.). Since the arrival of the Europeans the islanders have tended to settle along the coasts, and native vegetation has been able to recover on the lands thus deserted; but the development of mining (New Caledonia), of forest exploitation or of tourism may increase the threat to remote places of special interest until now difficult of access.

The extent, often considerable, of relatively low woody formations, dominated by species normally absent from the climax communities (Euphorbiaceae, Sapindaceae, *Hibiscus*, *Zizyphus*, etc.), provides evidence of former occupation by man, as also does the presence of even-aged stands of light-tolerant species (*Campnosperma*, *Endospermum*, etc.) or of tree species commonly cultivated ("orchard forests" of *Artocarpus*, *Barringtonia*, *Mangifera*, etc., or almost pure stands of *Aleurites*, *Inocarpus*, etc. especially in valleys and along streams). Under relatively dry conditions, savannas of *Heteropogon* and *Miscanthus* and, on leached soil and under relatively humid conditions, ferns heaths with Gleicheniaceae have often replaced the forests. Bush fires play an important part in their maintenance and spread. In the driest parts, the soils of which, though shallow, are not too poor in mineral nutrients, destruction of the native vegetation has often favoured the propagation of exotic legumes, forming thickets (*Leucaena*) or low, fairly open, forests (*Prosopis* in the Hawaiian Islands). The secondary nature of the savannas is confirmed by the absence of fire-tolerant species in the tree-layer, *Melaleuca quinquenervia* in New Caledonia being the only exception.

When the flora is more or less disharmonic (taxonomically unbalanced — see Carlquist, 1974), as is often the case in oceanic islands, plant species introduced by man may become established in the climax communities and eventually replace the native species (*Miconia* in Tahiti, *Psidium* in the Hawaiian Islands). This does not seem to be the case in Melanesia, where the floristic stock appears well balanced (New Caledonia) or where it is composed of elements that remain sufficiently competitive as they are less isolated from their mainland ancestors. Besides, exotic species generally do not have the capacity to grow on ultrabasic soils, even where the native vegetation has been partly destroyed (New Caledonia).

CONCLUSIONS

With the exception of the Galapagos Islands, the highest parts of the Hawaiian Islands, and the drier ultrabasic parts of New Caledonia, and of atolls that are too small or too low, the lands of the tropical Pacific originally have probably been almost entirely covered with forests, very locally deciduous, but usually evergreen.

The effects of insular isolation on the evolution of the floristic stock cannot be accurately interpreted without referring to geological and geographical data. The ecological conditions, often especially contrasted in mountainous islands, have entailed a great diversification of plant communities; the presence of endemic species, together with the major structural features developed in response to the environment, confer a peculiar physiognomy on each community.

The comparative paucity of the tree flora, owing to the isolation and the relative shortness of evolution of the ecosystems, may cause pronounced predominance of certain species in the upper stratum, whereas the lower strata have a rather rich flora. However, speciation has been, and probably is still today, very active, particularly in the Hawaiian Islands and New Caledonia. It has led to the differentiation of peculiar forms, so that the tropical Pacific appears to be a prime field for studying evolutionary processes.

When man arrived, relatively recently, he found conditions favourable to his settlement in most of the archipelagoes. Besides, he introduced various plant and animal species, some of which proved to be aggressive competitors in biotopes which had long been isolated from the exterior.

The consequences of the disturbing or destructive interventions of man have been all the more severe wherever the available space was more restricted, the soils more fragile and the flora and the fauna more disharmonic.

On the deep and leached soils so widespread under humid and hot climates, outside the areas of active volcanism, climax communities regenerate very slowly; their reappearance is still more belated and uncertain within areas of steep relief and on ultrabasic substrates. Where the native vegetation disappeared a long time ago and existing conditions make its regeneration problematical, colonization by exotic species may be beneficial to the environment (*Leucaena* thickets, *Aleurites* forests).

In some territories (the Hawaiian Islands, New Caledonia), measures to protect native vegetation and fauna have been adopted, but their application may raise difficulties owing to economic development.

REFERENCES

Braithwaite, A.F., 1975. The phytogeographical relationships and origin of the New Hebrides fern flora. *Philos. Trans. R. Soc. London, Ser. B*, 272: 293–313.

Carlquist, S., 1974. *Island Biology. Columbia Univ. Press*, Columbia, S.C., 660 pp.

Florence, J., 1984. *Les Forêts de Polynésie*. ORSTOM, Papeete, 15 pp.

Fosberg, F.R., 1960. The vegetation of Micronesia. *Bull. Am. Mus. Nat. Hist.*, 119(1): 75 pp.

Fosberg, F.R., 1961. Guide to Excursion (on the Vegetation of Hawaii). *10th Pacific Sci. Congress, Univ. of Hawaii, Honolulu, Hawaii*, 207 pp.

Fosberg, F.R. and St. John, H., 1951. Végétation et flore de l'atoll Maria. *Rev. Sci. Bourbonnais Cent. Fr.*, 7 pp.

Fosberg, F.R., Sachet, M.H. and Oliver, R., 1979. A geographical checklist of the Micronesian Dicotyledonae. *Micronesica*, 15: 41–295.

Fosberg, F.R., Sachet, M.H. et al., 1980. *Vascular Plants of Palau*. Smithsonian Inst. Oceanogr., La Jolla, Calif., 43 pp.

Glassman, S.F., 1952. The flora of Ponape. *Bernice P. Bishop Mus. Bull.*, 209: 152 pp.

Hallé, F., 1978. Arbres et forêts des îles Marquises. *Cah. Pac.*, 21: 315–357.

Jaffré, T., 1980. *Végétation des Roches Ultrabasiques en Nouvelle-Calédonie*. ORSTOM, Paris, 273 pp.

Morat, P. and Veillon, J.M., 1985. Conribution à la connaissance de la végétation et de la flore de Wallis et Futuna. *Bull. Mus. Hist. Nat., 4ème sér., B, Adansonia*, 3: 259–329.

Papy, H.R., 1955. La végétation des îles de la Société et de Makatea. *Trav. Lab. For. Toulouse*, V, 2(1,3): 385 pp.

Quantin, P., 1975. Soils of the New Hebrides islands. *Philos. Trans. R. Soc. London, Ser. B*, 272: 287–292.

Schmid, M., 1978. The Melanesian forest ecosystems. In: *Tropical Forest Ecosystems*. UNESCO, Paris, pp. 654–683.

Schmid, M., 1981. *Fleurs et Plantes de Nouvelle-Calédonie*. Ed. du Pac. Papeete, 164 pp.

Smith, A. C., 1951. The vegetation and flora of Fiji. *Sci. Mon.*, 73(1): 3–15.

Smith, A.C., 1979, 1985. *Flora Vitiensis*. Pac. Trop. Bot. Garden, Lawai, Vol. 1, 495 pp.; Vol. 2, 810 pp; Vol. 3, 758 pp.

St. John, H., 1973. *List and Summary of the Flowering Plants in the Hawaiian Islands*. Pac. Trop. Bot. Garden, Lawai, Mem., 1: 519 pp.

Sykes, W.R., 1980. *Bibliography of Research on the Cook Islands — Botanical Science*. N.Z. Comm. UNESCO, pp. 11–67.

Val Balgooy, M.M., 1971. Plant geography of the Pacific. *Blumea*, suppl. 6: 222 pp.

Van Steenis, C.G.G.J., 1979. Plant-geography of east Malesia. *Bot. J. Linn. Soc.*, 79(2): 97–178.

Whistler, W.A., 1980. The vegetation of Eastern Samoa. *Allertonia*, 2: 45–190.

Whitmore, T.C., 1969. The vegetation of the Solomon islands. *Philos. Trans. R. Soc. London, Ser. B*, 255: 259–270.

Wiggins, I.L. and Porter, D.M., 1971. *Flora of the Galapagos Islands*. Stanford Univ. Press, Stanford, Calif., 998 pp.

Wright, A.C.S., 1963. *Soils and Land Use of Western Samoa*. N.Z. Dep. Sci. Indust. Res., 191 pp.

Yuncker, T.G., 1959. Plants of Tonga. *Bernice P. Bishop Mus. Bull.*, 220: 283 pp.

Chapter 15

LICHENS

H.J.M. SIPMAN and R.C. HARRIS

INTRODUCTION

Lichens are not among the most striking elements of a tropical rain forest. They are absent from the forest floor, and on the tree trunks bryophytes are generally more conspicuous, especially in the lower layers of the forest. In the higher light levels of the canopy lichens are better represented, but here their presence cannot easily be observed. Moreover, the species are mostly crustose, not very conspicuous, and often scarcely distinguishable from tree bark. It is evident also that, in terms of biomass, lichens play a less important role in lowland rain forests than in montane cloud forests, for example, which may be festooned with lichen beards.

Nevertheless lichens are not only very common in most rain forests, but also represented by many species. They cover not only the bark of many trees, saplings and lianas, especially in the lighter levels of the forest, but are even more frequent as inhabitants of leaf surfaces.

AVAILABLE KNOWLEDGE

No complete inventories of the lichen flora of tropical rain forests have ever been published. The only study that approaches this in scope is an inventory by Schomburgk (1848, "Region des Urwaldes"). His lichen lists are unfortunately very outdated, and no doubt also very incomplete. Another source of information on rain-forest lichens is Wainio's (1890, 1909–1923) important works on the lichen flora of Brazil and the Philippines. However, his works do not specify habitats in such a way that the rain-forest elements can be properly selected.

The main explanation for this lack of information on the lichens of tropical rain forests is the fact that they are taxonomically very poorly known. Thirty years ago Mattick (1954) depicted this lack of knowledge in an account on the state of lichenology of the tropics, and although much work has been done since, much more still remains to be done. Many groups have had virtually no attention since the last century, when the taxonomic tools for classification of lichens were still highly inadequate. Consequently, the delimitation of most taxa is still unclear, and many new species remain to be discovered. Such a stage of knowledge makes investigations of distribution and ecology in many groups of lichens impossible. Only some widespread species are better known, probably because they had a better chance of being recognized early.

Due to this lack of taxonomic knowledge the following discussion of ecological aspects and phytogeography must be concentrated on a few groups for which recent revisions are available. The general outlines and several of the notes on special aspects are based mainly on unpublished observations by the authors.

GENERAL OUTLINES OF LICHEN VEGETATION IN TROPICAL RAIN FORESTS

Dominant among the lichens in the rain forest are members of the crustose, mainly corticolous families Arthoniaceae, Graphidaceae, Lecideaceae s.l. (for instance, the groups of *Crocynia*, *Lecidea piperis* and *Phyllopsora*), Letrouitiaceae, Thelotremataceae, Trichotheliaceae, Trypetheliaceae, various families of foliicolous lichens, and quite a few taxa in which fruitbodies are extremely rare and which are consequently of uncertain taxonomic position. Less dominant, but not less characteristic, is the good representation of the foliose genera *Coccocarpia* and *Coenogonium*.

With increasing altitude the number of foliose and fruticose lichens increases, by, for instance, representatives of the families Collemataceae, Pannariaceae and Usneaceae, which show a significant increase already around 1000 m elevation, and Lobariaceae and Parmeliaceae, which show an optimal distribution at about 2000 m elevation. Crustose families which become more conspicuous in forests of higher elevations include Phyllopsoraceae, and, above 1000 to 2000 m, Megalosporaceae, Pertusariaceae and Pyrenulaceae.

Comparison with more open tropical vegetation, including drier forest types, shows that the following groups are less well represented in rain forests: Arthoniaceae, Lecanoraceae, Pertusariaceae, Pyxinaceae, Ramalinaceae and Trypetheliaceae. The epiphyllous lichen flora also shows differences between the rain forest and more open vegetation types. Comparison with epiphytic vegetation in temperate areas shows that the tropical rain forest is poor, for instance, in Caliciaceae, Nephromataceae and Teloschistaceae.

Most rain-forest lichens are epiphytes on tree trunks, branches, twigs, saplings or lianas. In general living phorophytes are preferred. Upright dead tree-trunks may bear a specialized lichen vegetation with, for instance, Caliciaceae. The frequency of foliicolous lichens in tropical rain forests is remarkable, though unlike foliicolous bryophytes, which are largely restricted to tropical forests, foliicolous lichens are found also in humid temperate areas. Terrestrial lichens are extremely rare in tropical rain forests. The light and humidity requirements of terrestrial groups like Cladoniaceae are evidently not provided inside closed tropical lowland forests, though they occur in some open places. Epilithic lichens are equally unusual, probably as a result of the scarcity of free rock faces in tropical forests.

Inside the forest there is a distinct zonation from base to crown. This is no doubt due to the sensitivity of lichens to excessive shade and moisture. In the lowest, almost permanently moist and very shady levels bryophytes usually compete successfully with lichens, and predominate in corticolous and foliicolous habitats. At this level *Coenogonium*, *Leptogium* and *Porina* are among the better represented lichen genera. With improving light conditions the Thelotremataceae become an important family, together with, for instance, *Chiodecton*, *Crocynia*, *Phyllopsora* and large sterile crustose lichens. Foliicolous lichens also are common at this level. In the canopy layer Graphidaceae and Trypetheliaceae take over the dominance, and are accompanied by foliose Parmeliaceae such as *Parmotrema* and *Relicina*.

This zonation is best investigated for Thelotremataceae, where different species have been shown to frequent different levels (Hale, 1974, 1978, 1981). Some *Relicina* species are mainly found in the canopy (Hale, 1975).

In more open forests the zonation tends to move downward, and in very humid situations the mosses may extend into the canopy.

Since lichen taxonomy is based on the fungal partner, the zonation patterns described above apply to the fungal partners. The question can be raised whether the algal partners show the same patterns. Unfortunately, the taxonomy of the algal partners is much less known than that of the fungal partners. Modern techniques (cf. Tschermak-Woess, 1978) have made the available identifications of algal partners of tropical rain-forest lichens, based on study of herbarium specimens only, obsolete. Consequently, the traditional division of the algal partners into a few conspicuous groups has to be considered here. Of these groups, the following seem to be represented in the rain forest: *Trentepohlia* and protococcoid algae, belonging to the Chlorophyceae, and *Nostoc*, belonging to the Cyanobacteria. *Trentepohlia* is much more frequent as an algal partner in tropical rain forests than in any other vegetation in the world. *Nostoc*-containing lichens seem to prefer the more sheltered and humid situations in the forest, and protococcoid algae the more exposed sites. This latter group, however, is very heterogeneous.

PHYTOGEOGRAPHY

General

At the family level it appears that most, if not all, families of tropical rain-forest lichens are pantropical. All twenty families mentioned above, either as such or by representatives, show a pantropical distribution. Seven families are largely restricted to the tropics and occur only scattered in oceanic sites of the warm-temperate zone. Nine families penetrate rather far into the temperate zones, and four may be regularly encountered even in arctic habitats. Strictly tropical families are evidently less common in lichens than in phanerogams.

In contrast with phanerogams (cf. Good, 1974), the pantropical character of the lichen flora of the tropical rain forest is also found at the generic level: Out of 32 recently revised genera, only two appear to be restricted to the Neotropics; all others are pantropical. They may be represented in different areas by very unequal numbers, and endemic infrageneric groups may occur.

The picture changes when distribution patterns are investigated at species level. For this purpose some recent revisions have been studied (Santesson, 1952; Hale, 1975, 1976a, b, c; Hafellner, 1981; Arvidsson, 1982; Harris, 1986). Thus the distribution of some 250 supposed rain-forest species has been checked. This procedure is not very accurate, because in many cases it is not clearly indicated whether a species occurs in tropical rain forest. Moreover, the known areas may still be incomplete. Truly pantropical species, found in various parts of both the Neotropics and the Palaeotropics, appear to be well represented, and may constitute about one-third of all species. Sometimes they have a more or less weedy character, and extend into the humid temperate regions. About two-thirds of all species are distinctly centered in either the Neotropics or the Palaeotropics, both patterns occurring in about equal numbers. It is noteworthy that several species which have been collected commonly in one of these regions are known from only a few collections in the other region.

Neotropical distribution patterns

Neotropical taxa are usually centered in the rain-forest areas of northern South America. Better-known species often show extensions into the West Indies and Central America. Not uncommon also is an extension into Africa, especially the East African islands, but more rarely also into continental Africa.

Indications for the existence of restricted ranges for tropical rain-forest lichens in the Neotropics are still weak, due to the poor state of collecting in most areas. Possible endemism is documented for the Guiana Shield (*Coccocarpia filiformis*, *Mazosia tumidula*), the Amazon basin (13 species of Trypetheliaceae), the West Indies (*Parmelina antillensis*), and Trinidad (*Phyllobathelium thaxteri*). Other areas renowned for their endemism, like various parts of the Andes and southern Brazil, are of no importance here because tropical rain forests are scarce or absent in these areas.

Insufficient collecting also prevents an understanding of the influence of the climatic shifts of the Glacial Period on the distribution of rain-forest lichens. It seems unlikely that new species have evolved in the refugia, but relict occurrences could have resulted.

The distribution of *Coccocarpia domingensis* is remarkable. It occurs widely in the Neotropics, but has been found also on the Fiji Islands. Such a completely unexpected distribution suggests the possibility of introduction by man.

Palaeotropical distribution patterns

Palaeotropical taxa are generally centered in Indomalaysia. Their ranges may show extensions into New Guinea and Oceania eastward, into Queensland southward, into India, Sri Lanka, the East African islands and mainland Africa westward, and into Taiwan northward. A number of species, however, seem restricted to the core, or even a part of it — for instance, *Relicina luteoviridis*, known only from Sabah, and *R. precircumnodata* and *Calenia leptocarpa*, only known from the Philippines. The genus *Laurera* has 20 to 30 species restricted to Indomalaysia and the Philippines, many known from only a single island. Indications of further centers of endemism are *Pseudoparmelia dahlii* from Sri Lanka, *Coccocarpia fulva* from New Caledonia, and *Letrouitia coralloidea* from Queensland.

Coccocarpia pruinosa has a remarkable distribution, suggesting a relictual status: it is known only from Madagascar and New Caledonia.

Conclusions

The lichens of tropical rain forests appear to have wider ranges than phanerogams. Only at species level is the differentiation between Paleo-tropics and Neotropics pronounced. Few species are restricted to a minor phytogeographical unit. Otherwise their distribution patterns parallel those observed in other plant groups; consequently the same theories concerning the origin of these distribution patterns can be applied — for instance, the division of Gondwanaland (cf. Arvidsson, 1982). The wide ranges of most species could be explained by the assumption that they have good dispersal capacities. However, we doubt this, and are inclined to see a better explanation in the great age of lichen taxa and their very slow rates of evolution (cf. the note on dispersal below). Probably many lichen species are older than most other phanerogram species in the forest in which they live. This hypothesis is supported by the occurrence of disjunct ranges like that of *Coccocarpia pruinosa* (see above).

VARIOUS BIOLOGICAL ASPECTS

This section treats a series of remarkable aspects of lichens with the intention to bring them to wider attention. It is based in part on recent literature, in part on our personal experience.

Size and habit

The large size of many crustose lichens, which often spread over adjacent roots, lianas or bryophytes, suggests that some species grow fast and have an unusual competitive power.

As already mentioned, the crustose thallus form predominates in the tropical rain forest. Besides this compact crustose growth form, which is a widespread type, several forms occur which are much less frequent outside tropical rain forests. These are, for instance, thalli with a crustose shape but a loose, felty texture, as in *Crocynia*. Perhaps this growth form is an adaptation to high air humidity. Another unusual growth form is shown by the genus *Coenogonium*, of which many species form flat, shelf-like structures, again of a loose, felty texture. The true foliose lichens are often strongly appressed to the substrate, so as to avoid disadvantages of their foliose growth form. A remarkable squamulose growth form is shown by the genus *Phyllopsora*; the thallus squamules

are scattered on an often felty layer of fungal hyphae.

Algal partners and nitrogen fixation

As has already been indicated above, *Trentepohlia* is the dominant algal partner in tropical rain-forest lichens. For this feature two explanations seem possible. Firstly, non-lichenized *Trentepohlia* is ubiquitous in moist, shaded habitats, and thus readily available to form lichen associations in rain forests. Secondly, associations with *Trentepohlia* may be more stable under rain-forest conditions than those with *Trebouxia*, which is more frequent elsewhere (see below). In view of their importance in tropical ecosystems, physiological and ultra-structural studies on *Trentepohlia*-containing lichens are urgently required.

Forman (1975) in his study of nitrogen fixation by *Nostoc*-containing lichens in a Colombian montane rain forest concluded that they provide a significant portion of the total annual nitrogen input to the ecosystem. His visual estimates in a lowland rain forest in Costa Rica suggested that the quantity of potential nitrogen-fixing lichen was of the same order of magnitude as in Colombia. The lichens involved occurred mainly in the canopy (none below 4 m) and were macrolichens, mainly *Sticta* and *Leptogium*. It is clear that future studies of nutrient cycling in tropical rain forests must consider this role played by lichens.

Reproduction and dispersal

The ascospores of rain-forest lichens show some features which, though not absent outside the rain forest, are more frequent here. One such feature is large size. The significance of such large spores is unclear (cf. Hafellner and Bellemère, 1983).

Several observations are available of the production of conidia by such large spores while still in the ascus (Santesson, 1952, p. 25; Henssen, 1981; Hafellner and Bellemère, 1983). This phenomenon has been observed in Asterothyriaceae, Brigantiaeaceae, and *Lopadium* sensu lato. It would be of interest to investigate whether it occurs normally in liberated ascospores also.

Another frequent feature in lichens of the tropical rain forest is the occurrence of thick-walled spores — for instance, in Graphidaceae,

Pyrenulaceae, Thelotremataceae, and Trypetheliaceae. Unpublished observations on Graphidaceae,
Pyrenulaceae and Trypetheliaceae suggest a storage function for the extra wall material. In
contrast, such thick spore walls are absent in
foliicolous lichens. Santesson (1952) discussed this
feature and supposed that it enhances rapid
germination, needed for the rapid colonization of
the ephemeral leaf surfaces.

The distribution patterns of many lichens in a
forest seem to reflect a weak dispersal capacity.
Often they show local dominance: a given species
may be dominant on one tree, whereas it is
completely absent from seemingly identical trees
nearby.

Little is known about dispersal mechanisms. The
normal mechanism for (lichenized) ascomycetes
would be the production of ascospores, which are
subsequently dispersed by wind. This would open
possibilities for long-distance dispersal, as has been
made probable for bryophytes, for instance (Van
Zanten and Pócs, 1981). Indeed, the usual sizes of
lichen ascospores, under 20 µm long, suggest that
they are suited for wind dispersal. However, inside
the tropical rain forest winds are generally very
weak, and cannot be a very effective means of
dispersal. Moreover, many lichen species in the
rain forest produce large ascospores, which are
unlikely to be spread by wind. Dispersal of such
spores by animals is postulated by Sipman (1983,
p. 186).

Vegetative reproduction may be more important
for the distribution of lichens, as is suggested by
the wide range of specialized structures for this
purpose that can be found in tropical rain-forest
lichens. However, they also do not seem very
suitable for long-distance dispersal.

Environmental relations

Seasonal effects are a poorly known feature even
for lichens of the northern temperate zone. For
certain *Opegrapha* species from temperate regions
it is known that they produce their spores in
autumn or in spring. Likewise thallus growth may
show seasonal fluctuations. In rain forests with
marked dry and wet seasons it can be imagined
that one season is better suited for ascospore
production. Certain lichens may suffer from extreme humidity in the wet season and recover in
the dry season.

Numerous studies of temperate lichens have
shown that alternating periods of wet and dry are
necessary for resynthesis of the separated partners
and maintenance of the association. Since *Trebouxia* is the dominant algal partner in the
temperate zone, the conclusion could be drawn
from these experiments that the absence of lichens
containing *Trebouxia*, or their restriction to the
canopy, may be due to the constancy of the
humidity rather than to its amount.

As has been demonstrated for temperate forests
(Rose, 1976; among others) lichens of natural
forests are often very sensitive to disturbance.
Reestablishment of the natural lichen vegetation in
a clear-felled forest area does not occur within
about 500 years of continuous forest cover.

This phenomenon has not yet been investigated
for lichens from the tropical rain forest, but field
experience shows that the lichen flora of secondary
or strongly influenced forest is very different from
that in undisturbed forest, and lacks the rich flora
of Thelotremataceae, for instance. Evidently the
lichen vegetation of the tropical rain forest is
sensitive to disturbance.

Interactions with other biota

Interactions between epiphytic lichens and the
surrounding flora and fauna, including nutrient
flux, shelter function, influence on the supporting
bark, are still very poorly known. One of the few
rather established facts is that lichens do not
extract nutrients out of living host tissue.

Observations of lichen habitats in tropical rain
forests suggest some peculiarities. The rich concentration of botanical and zoological life in the
crown layer of the tropical rain forest, which
causes a "nutrient rain", may influence the lichen
vegetation on the lower branches and trunks, for
instance by leachates of excrements, which run
down with rainwater.

Some lichens (like Pyrenulaceae and Trypetheliaceae) influence bark formation and cause the bark
to develop cancer-like swellings (in all phorophytes?). Both families were already noted in the
Ceylon Administrative Report for 1921 as causing
galls on tea plants; this has been confirmed by our
observations in neotropical rain forests.

As in temperate forests, thick and old tree trunks
are the main habitat of certain lichen species in the

tropical rain forest. Probably the age of such trunks is more important than their size, and the occurrence of the lichen may be primarily associated with bark that has undergone a certain degree of weathering. On such a substrate Caliciaceae, *Lecanactis* and some pyrenocarpous lichens can be encountered.

Apparently lichens show little preference among phorophytes. This has been demonstrated for foliicolous species by Santesson (1952). The physical properties of the habitat are probably more important. And even in this respect the rain-forest lichens appear to be rather insensitive, as species from thick trunks may spread over adjacent thin epiphyte stems. Often very smooth bark is preferred — for instance, certain lianas, and saplings.

Foliicolous lichens have already attained much attention, results of which are found in the fundamental work of Santesson (1952). Their most remarkable aspect perhaps is the short life cycle required by their habitat. Wide distributions predominate, endemism seems to be the exception. Different associations can be found in shady conditions near the forest floor and in well-illuminated parts of the crown. A number of species have developed peculiar structures for vegetative reproduction.

Epizoic occurrence has been found in forests which do not belong to the tropical rain forest sensu stricto, but the feature is remarkable enough to mention here. Members of the weevil genus *Gymnopholus* in the mountain forests of Papua New Guinea possess special features which enable a range of organisms to grow on their back, including lichens (Gressit, 1966). The lichens observed include *Hypotrachyna crenulata, Parmotrema reticulatum* and unidentified species of *Heterodermia, Parmelia* and *Physcia* (see Gradstein and Pocs, Ch. 16).

A still largely virgin field of research is the (fungal) parasites on tropical lichens. Preliminary observations show that tropical rain-forest lichens form no exception in this respect, and house a range of parasitic fungi (Hafellner, 1985).

REFERENCES

Arvidsson, L., 1982. A monograph of the lichen genus *Coccocarpia. Opera Bot.*, 67: 96 pp.
Forman, R.T.T., 1975. Canopy lichens with blue-green algae: a nitrogen source in a Colombian rainforest. *Ecology*, 56: 1176–1184.
Good, A., 1974. *The Geography of the Flowering Plants.* Longman, London, 518 pp.
Gressitt, J.L., 1966. Epizoic symbiosis: the papuan weevil genus *Gymnopholus* (Leptopiinae) symbiotic with cryptogamic plants, oribatid mites, rotifers and nematodes. *Pac. Insects*, 8(1): 221–280.
Hafellner, J., 1981. Monographie der Flechtengattung *Letrouitia* (Lecanorales, Teloschistineae). *Nova Hedwigia*, 35: 645–729.
Hafellner, J., 1985. Studien über lichenicole Pilze und Flechten IV. Die auf *Brigantiaea*-Arten beobachteten Ascomyceten. *Herzogia*, 7: 163–180.
Hafellner, J. and Bellemère, A., 1983. Über die Bildung phialidischer Konidien in den mauerförmigen, einzeln im Ascus liegenden Sporen von *Brigantiaea leucoxantha* (lichenisierte Ascomycetes, Lecanorales). *Nova Hedwigia*, 38: 169–186.
Hale, M.E., 1974. Morden-Smithsonian expedition to Dominica: The lichens (Thelotremataceae). *Smithson. Contrib. Bot.*, 16: 46 pp.
Hale, M.E., 1975. A monograph of the lichen genus *Relicina* (Parmeliaceae). *Smithson. Contrib. Bot.*, 26: 32 pp.
Hale, M.E., 1976a. A monograph of the lichen genus *Pseudoparmelia* Lynge (Parmeliaceae). *Smithson. Contrib. Bot.*, 31: 62 pp.
Hale, M.E., 1976b. A monograph of the lichen genus *Bulbothrix* Hale (Parmeliaceae). *Smithson. Contrib. Bot.*, 32: 29 pp.
Hale, M.E., 1976c. A monograph of the lichen genus *Parmelina* Hale (Parmeliaceae). *Smithson. Contrib. Bot.*, 33: 60 pp.
Hale, M.E., 1978. A revision of the lichen family Thelotremataceae in Panama. *Smithson. Contrib. Bot.*, 38: 60 pp.
Hale, M.E., 1981. A revision of the lichen family Thelotremataceae in Sri Lanka. *Bull. Br. Mus. Nat. Hist., Bot. Ser.*, 8(3): 227–332.
Harris, A.C., 1986. The family Trypetheliaceae (Loculoascomycetes: lichenized Melanommatales) in Amazonian Brazil. *Acta Amazon. (suppl.)*, 14: 55–80.
Henssen, A., 1981. A corticolous species of *Gyalectidium* from Costa Rica. *Lichenologist*, 13: 155–160.
Mattick, F., 1954. Lichenologische Notizen 6–7. *Ber. Dtsch. Bot. Ges.*, 67(4): 133–145.
Rose, F., 1976. Lichenological indicators of age and environmental continuity in woodlands. In: D.H. Brown, D.L. Hawksworth and R.H. Bailey (Editors), *Lichenology: Progress and Problems.* Academic Press, London, pp. 1–551.
Santesson, R., 1952. Foliicolous lichens I, a revision of the taxonomy of the obligately foliicolous, lichenized fungi. *Symb. Bot. Ups.*, XII: 590 pp.
Schomburgk, R., 1848. Versuch einer Fauna und Flora von British-Guiana. In: R. Schomburgk (Editor), *Reisen in British-Guiana 3.* Weber, Leipzig, pp. 533–1260.
Sipman, H.J.M., 1983. A monograph of the lichen family Megalosporaceae. *Bibl. Lichenol.*, 18: 241 pp.
Tschermak-Woess, E., 1978. Myrmecia reticulata as a phycobiont and free-living — Free-living Trebouxia — The problem of Stenocybe septata. *Lichenologist*, 10: 69–79.

Van Zanten, B.O. and Pócs, T., 1981. Distribution and dispersal of bryophytes. Adv. Bryol., 1: 479–562.

Wainio, A.E., 1890. Étude sur la classification naturelle et la morphologie des lichens du Brésil. *Acta Soc. Fauna Flora Fenn.*, 7(1): 1–246; 7(2): 1–256.

Wainio, E.A., 1909–1923. Lichenes Insularum Philippinarum, Part 1. *Philipp. J. Sci., Sect. C*, 4: 651–662; Part 2, 8: 99–137; Part 3, Ann. Acad. Sci. Fenn., Ser. A, 15(6): 1–368; Part 4, 19(15): 1–84.

Wirth, M. and Hale, M.E., 1978. Morden-Smithsonian expedition to Dominica: The lichens (Graphidaceae). *Smithson. Contrib. Bot.*, 40: 64 pp.

Chapter 16

BRYOPHYTES

S.R. GRADSTEIN and T. POCS

INTRODUCTION

Tropical rain forests (including montane forests) probably harbour more bryophyte species than any other of the world's major ecosystems. Our rough estimate, based on recent catalogues and taking into account the discrepancy between published and accepted names (Touw, 1974), would arrive at about 1500 to 2000 species of mosses and a similar number of liverworts, hence totalling about 25 to 30% of all bryophytes. The number of synonyms among names of tropical bryophyte species is very high, as taxonomists have pointed out repeatedly. For example, Edwards (1980) could recognize only 6 instead of 93 described species in West African *Calymperes* and Bischler (1984) found 9 good species and 60 synonyms in New World *Marchantia*.

Why are there so many unnecessary names in tropical bryophytes? Reasons may be their relatively large areas of distribution, the serious lack of floras, keys and monographs, and ignorance of the variation patterns and phenotypic plasticity of the species. Mostly they were described by people who were not familiar with the species in the field. In Pterobryaceae and other tropical mosses, for example, male plants are often smaller than females. This type of sexual dimorphy is rare in temperate bryophytes and, when not properly understood, may lead to the description of different species (Argent, 1979). In tropical liverworts, habitat-induced plant size variation and leaf character modifications have often led to the unnecessary description of new taxa (Van Reenen, 1982; among others).

How well has the tropical rain forest been explored for bryophytes? As compared to angio-sperms (Prance, 1977), the inventory has certainly been less detailed for bryophytes, but a precise answer to the question cannot be given at this stage. However, some useful information can be obtained from Geissler and Greene's (1982) world review of the extent of bryological exploration. It appears that in Malesia bryophyte exploration has been more intensive in the western than in the eastern portion of the area — possibly with the exception of Papua New Guinea where much recent fieldwork was done — and that very little is known about the bryoflora of the rain-forest remnants of northern Australia. As to tropical America, the better explored areas include the Caribbean and portions of the northern Andes, while vast other areas including large parts of the Amazon Basin remain virtually unexplored. In tropical Africa, a good deal of collecting has been done (Greene and Harrington, 1979; Pócs, 1982), and probably this continent is now bryologically better known than other tropical regions, at least for liverworts. This seems to be true for angio-sperms as well (Prance, 1977). Nevertheless, also in Africa much basic collecting remains to be done, as Richards (1984b) has recently pointed out.

TROPICAL RAIN FORESTS OF AMERICA, ASIA AND AFRICA — A BRYOGEOGRAPHICAL COMPARISON

About 90% of the bryophytes of the tropical rain forest belong to only 15 families: Calympera-ceae, Dicranaceae, Fissidentaceae, Hookeriaceae, Hyphaceae, Meteoriacea, Neckeraceae, Orthotri-chaceae, Pterobryaceae and Sematophyllaceae (mosses); Frullaniaceae, Lejeuneaceae, Lepodizia-ceae, Plachiogilaceae and Radulaceae (Liverworts). Yet, characteristic assemblages of bryophytes may be found in each of the three main regions America, Asia, Africa, as the following abbreviated survey indicates.

The American rain forest is characterized by the almost exclusive presence of Pilotrichaceae (mainly Caribbean), Phyllogoniaceae, the Hookeriaceous genera *Crossomitrium, Hypnella* and *Lepidopilum, Porotrichodendron* (Lembophyllaceae), *Chorisodontium* (Dicranaceae), *Phyllodrepanium* (Phyllodrepaniaceae), and, among the liverworts, the robust thalloid Monocleales (also southern temperate) and a large number of Lejeuneaceous genera: *Brachiolejeunea, Bryopteris, Cyclolejeunea, Odontolejeunea, Omphalanthus, Symbiezidium,* etc. (Grolle, 1969). The richness in *Ceratolejeunea* and *Octoblepharum* species in lowland forests is also notable.

The Asiatic tropical rain forest holds a bryoflora quite different from that of tropical America. Very characteristic are the robust Dawsoniaceae, Hypnodendraceae, Spiridentaceae and Garovaglioideae. The region furthermore holds the centres of evolution for *Mitthyridium* (Calymperaceae), *Dicranoloma* and *Braunfelsia* (Dicranaceae), *Macrothamnium* (Hylocomiaceae), *Cyathophorella* (Hypopterygiaceae), *Aerobryum* (Meteoriaceae), *Homaliodendron* (Neckeraceae), several Pterobryoideae (*Pterobryella, Symphysodontella, Trachyloma*), *Acroporium, Trismegistia* and *Mastopoma* (Sematophyllaceae) and Trachypodaceae. Among the liverworts *Podomitrium, Psiloclada, Wettsteinia,* and Treubiales — all four groups also in Australasia and presumably of southern temperate origin — and the Lejeuneaceae *Spruceanthus, Stenolejeunea* and *Tuyamaella* are characteristic. The peculiar neotenic epiphylls *Ephemeropsis* and *Metzgeriopsis* are also typical Asiatic rain-forest elements.

To characterize the African rain forest bryologically is more difficult as it has fewer elements of its own, which concurs with the overall relative poverty of the flora of this continent (Richards, 1973). Typical African rain-forest elements are *Leucoloma* (Dicranaceae), some Cryphaeaceae, Rutenbergiaceae, certain Fabroniaceae (especially *Rhizofabronia*), the Pterobryaceous genera *Hildenbrandtiella* and *Renauldia*, and the liverwort *Sprucella*. The species richness in *Fissidens*, both in the lowlands and in the mountains, also is notable.

More striking are the various bryophyte links between the African rain forest and the two other regions. With tropical America it shares the richness in species of *Pilotrichella, Schlotheimia* and *Zygodon,* as well as the presence of *Jaegerina, Leptoscyphus, Marchesinia, Mittenothamnium, Porothamnium, Porotrichum* and *Squamidium,* which are lacking in Asia. At the species level, numerous examples of Afro-American links have recently become known (Gradstein et al., 1984a; Buck and Griffin, 1984). Characteristic Afro-Asiatic links are *Chaetomitrium, Cyathophorella, Ectropothecium, Leucophanes* and *Macrohymenium* among the mosses, and *Mastigophora, Ptychanthus,* and Schistochilaceae (also southern pan-temperate but lacking in tropical America) in liverworts. Among epiphylls, *Cololejeunea* is much richer in species in the palaeotropics than in the neotropics. Numerous bryophyte species with an Afro-Asiatic distribution area are known (Pócs, 1976).

Summing up, it appears that tropical Asia holds the most diversified rain-forest bryoflora in terms of generic and familial diversity, with a great number of moss groups restricted to that region. Rain forests of tropical America hold fewer unique moss groups but have a somewhat more diversified liverwort flora, especially regarding Lejeuneaceae. In montane rain forests of this continent, liverwort cover values may exceed those for mosses by far (Fig. 16.4). The African rain forest, finally, has few bryophyte groups of its own and holds a bryogeographical position somewhat intermediate between Asia and America.

ALTITUDINAL DIVERSIFICATION

A characteristic feature of the lowland tropical rain forest is the increase in abundance and species richness of bryophytes with increasing elevation up to the forest limit (Fig. 16.1). At family level about 60% are chiefly montane whereas less than 5% (Pilotrichaceae, Calymperaceae, Leucobryaceae) are predominantly lowland groups. In terms of biomass, montane forests may yield at least ten times more bryophyte weight than lowland forests (see below: bryophyte habitats).

It is generally assumed that climatic factors, especially the more favourable moisture conditions in the mountains, due to clouds and fog, and the prevailing lower temperatures, are responsible for

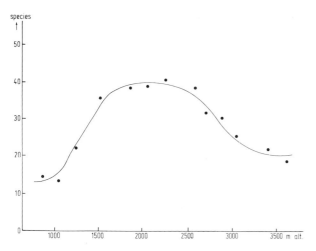

Fig. 16.1. Bryophyte species richness in relation to altitude in rain forests of the Sierra Nevada de Santa Marta, Colombia. Data taken in forest plots, 0 to 3 m above ground level. Epiphylls excluded. (After Van Reenen and Gradstein, 1983, and unpubl.)

the higher bryophyte diversity in the montane forests. The importance of the temperature factor has recently been emphasized by Richards (1984, p. 1238): "The increase in the abundance and species-richness of bryophyte vegetation with increasing elevation suggests that it may be high temperature which is unfavourable for the development of a rich and varied bryophyte flora. It is interesting that, though the bryophytes of the montane forest at El Yunque, Puerto Rico, were tolerant of very cold conditions..., most of them could not survive temperatures above 35°C (Biebl, 1964). The lack of tolerance of high temperatures might be because of high rates of respiration and because bryophytes are unable to maintain sufficiently high values of net assimilation at high temperatures and relatively low light intensity."

Laboratory measurements of assimilation and respiration rates under varying temperatures and light intensities in selected montane rain-forest bryophytes by Frahm (1987), show that these plants are not able to photosynthesize under tropical lowland rain-forest conditions (high temperatures together with low light intensity). Apparently these species are ecophysiologically not well adapted to life in lowland rain forests. It should be interesting to investigate lowland species in a similar manner.

Parallel to an elevational increase, species rich-

ness increases with latitude. A cursory inventory of a Vietnamese evergreen rain forest near sea level (Cuc Phuong National Park) yielded over 125 bryophyte species within a radius of not more than 4 km (Pócs, unpubl.). This type of forest lacks prolonged dry periods, and has a misty, cool winter monsoon instead. In temperate lowland forests bryophyte species richness may also be higher than in the equatorial lowland forest (Richards, 1984).

The bryoflora of the lowland rain forest is largely made up of members of pantropical families, such as Calymperaceae, Hookeriaceae and Lejeuneaceae. The montane bryoflora is much more heterogeneous and contains a mixture of tropical elements and cool-adapted elements of southern or northern temperate origins (Schuster, 1983). In the tropical Andes, for example, the Laurasian *Scapania portoricensis* and the Gondwanalandic *Lepicolea pruinosa* are very conspicuous components of the bryophyte layer of high montane cloud forests (Gradstein et al., 1977). Parallels are found among the dominant trees of these forests, viz. *Quercus* and *Weinmannia* spp. Presumably these groups could migrate into the cold Tropics since the upheaval of the Andes in the late Tertiary (Van der Hammen and Van Dommelen, 1973; Griffin et al., 1982).

The *Nothofagus*-dominated montane rain forests of New Guinea hold a characteristic mixture of Malesian elements and of putatively Gondwanalandic elements such as Dawsoniaceae, Hypnodendraceae and Schistochilaceae. The Gondwanalandic groups are often quite abundant and may determine the aspect of the bryophyte vegetation of these forests. Presumably they migrated northwards to New Guinea during the Tertiary step-by-step overland or via short-range aerial dispersal by way of mountain hopping, at times when the island was still evolving and attached to the Australian landmass (Van Zanten and Pócs, 1981).

SPECIES RANGES

In the early 19th century there was a common belief that in many cases bryophyte species distribution was world-wide. Influenced by the evolution theory, the idea that bryophytes are normally restricted to single continents or smaller regions became more widely accepted and initially resulted in an enormous increase in the number of described species. Recent monographic studies show that this "geographic species concept" was ill-founded and gradually the true ranges of species are now becoming known.

For brevity, this short review of species ranges will focus mainly on the endemic and on the transoceanic rain-forest species. It should be pointed out that the species concept in tropical bryophytes is still mainly morphological-anatomical. Genetic and chemical information is becoming increasingly important in the systematics and biogeography of temperate bryophytes (Szweykowski, 1982; Mues et al., 1984), but in tropical bryology these fields remain largely unexplored. A first attempt to apply these modern techniques to the problem of species definition in rain-forest bryophytes is the paper by De Vries et al. (1983) on genetic variability and population dispersal in two species of *Racopilum* from the Philippines.

Endemism

Distribution areas in bryophytes, as well as other spore plants, are usually larger than in seed plants, and endemism therefore is comparatively rare. The geologically young Galapagos Islands have an endemism of about 50% among native phanerogams, whereas in ferns and bryophytes only *c.* 10% of the species are considered endemic (Gradstein and Weber, 1982). It is generally assumed that the relatively slow process of evolution at the morphological level, in addition to the obvious advantage of the possession of wind-carried diaspores for long-distance dispersal, are main reasons why endemism in bryophytes is rare (Van Zanten and Pócs, 1981).

In the Tropics, rates of endemism are probably higher in the mountains than in lowland areas (Schuster, 1983). Especially isolated mountains, such as the African massifs, may act as "biotic islands", enhancing speciation. The African genus *Renauldia*, for instance, has several species of apparently very restricted distribution, including *R. lycopodioides* known only from montane forest of the Usambara Mts. in Tanzania and *R. dusenii*, which is restricted to Mt. Cameroun. They are very conspicuous, robust epiphytes, which could hardly be overlooked. In tropical America, along the

Andean chain, the montane rain forest is less discontinuous and most species tend to spread almost continuously from Bolivia to Mexico, as for example the pendulous *Phyllogonium* species (Lin, 1983).

Endemism is also somewhat more pronounced in island regions than on the continent. In the Neotropical genus *Pilotrichum*, 50% of the species are restricted to rain forests of the Caribbean Islands (Crosby, 1969). Some are found only in the Greater Antilles, others are confined to the Lesser Antilles, but none of the species are restricted to one single island. During (1977) found good examples of island endemism at the infraspecific level in Indo-Pacific Garovaglioideae. His study shows that speciation can only be dealt with when large amounts of material are available for variation analysis. In many groups of rain-forest bryophytes, collections sufficient for that purpose are still wanting.

Probably the highest rates of endemism among rain-forest bryophytes are found in New Guinea, New Caledonia and Madagascar. According to Inoue (1982), 47 out of 59 species of *Plagiochila* from New Guinea are endemic. More than 65% of the species of Frullaniaceae are endemic to New Caledonia (Hattori, 1984) and Madagascar holds speciation centres for the epiphyllous *Colura* and *Diplasiolejeunea* and for the moss genus *Leucoloma*. The Madagascar flora holds close links to the flora of the old crystalline mountain massifs of Tanzania, however, and Pócs (1975) could record several examples of putative Madagascar endemics from the adjacent African mainland.

Rates of endemism are very low among tropical lowland bryophytes. For instance, members of the Calymperaceae are widespread in lowland rain-forest formations of America, Africa and Asia, and are usually epiphytic though sometimes found on the ground. They are usually dioecious, hence have unisexual spores, but in addition produce numerous gemmae from leaf tips, which may enhance dispersal over short distances. Reese (1978) reviewed the American species of the genus *Syrrhopodon* and found only 4 endemics among 35 species (*S. theriotii* from Costa Rica, *S. steyermarkii* from Venezuela and *S. annotinus* and *S. rupestris* from limited areas in the Amazon Basin). Most other species proved to be rather wide-ranging, occurring throughout large parts of South America and often penetrating into Central America and the West Indies.

Even larger distribution areas are seen in West African *Calymperes*. According to Edwards (1980), 50% of the species are Afro-American. One species proved to be pantropical, although an exhaustive comparison with Asiatic collections was not made.

Transoceanic ranges

Transoceanic ranges, as in *Calymperes* (see above), have been the subject of several papers (Pócs, 1976; Frahm, 1982; Buck and Griffin, 1984; Gradstein et al., 1984a) and appear to be more common among rain-forest bryophytes than previously believed. Most transoceanic species dwell in the warmer lowland and submontane regions, which is in clear contrast to the endemics. They seem to be rare in the montane forests, but are again more common in the tropical alpine zone where temperate, peregrine taxa abound (Van Zanten and Pócs, 1981). A reason for the higher ratio of transoceanic species in the tropical lowlands may be the younger age and greater isolation of upland regions; but, in addition, it may be assumed that lower speciation rates in the lowlands enhanced wider ranges.

Among liverworts, the greater part of the transoceanic species are members of the family Lejeuneaceae, whereas among mosses *Fissidens asplenioides*, *Floribundaria floribunda* and *Neckeropsis disticha* are characteristic and well-known examples.

There are different approaches to explain these intercontinental disjunctions. Some authors underline the importance of the geological events, especially plate tectonics, and step-by-step dispersal overland or short-range air dispersal. Others advocate the possibility of long-range air dispersal, using the floras of young oceanic islands as proof. The subject has been discussed at length by Van Zanten and Pócs (1981). For the long-range dispersal hypothesis, experimental studies by Van Zanten (1978, 1984) and Van Zanten and Gradstein (1987) are particularly relevant. Van Zanten tested spore survival following exposure to conditions simulating those experienced during long-distance transport. For New Zealand mosses, he demonstrated that wide-ranging species in general

have more resistant spores than endemic species. He furthermore established that spores of tropical moss species, especially those of the lowland rain forests, are less resistant to drought than temperate species (see also Egunyomi, 1978), but survive wet-freezing at $-30°C$. These results may imply that tropical mosses could migrate over longer distances via typhoons or heavy showers. Tests on tropical liverworts yielded comparable results, although in general spores were less viable under extreme conditions (Van Zanten and Gradstein, 1987).

In addition to good spore resistance several other conditions may determine successful long-range dispersal, such as: (1) whether or not spores are small and bisexual and plants monoecious; and (2) whether or not migrating species are able to compete successfully with autochthonous species after arrival in suitable habitats. Furthermore, spores should have good opportunities for take-off.

Competitive vigour: transoceanic species meeting this requirement would include the common, "weedy" ones, which may grow in primary as well as secondary habitats. Examples are *Cololejeunea cardiocarpa*, *Lophocolea martiana*, *Octoblepharum albidum* and *Rhizogonium spiniforme*. However, other weedy rain-forest species are presumably not transoceanic, such as the Neotropical *Frullania brasiliensis*, *Groutiella mucronifolia*, *Leptolejeunea elliptica*, *Meteoriopsis remotifolia* and *Plagiochila guilleminiana*. They may be "chance endemics" (Van Zanten, 1978), if their spores are apt for long-range dispersal.

Sexuality and spore size: although one would assume that bisexuality prevails in the transoceanic species, this is not true for mosses, where most transoceanic species are dioecious (Van Zanten and Pócs, 1981). However, in Neotropical liverworts about 2/3 of the transoceanic species are monoecious. Almost all of them are members of the family Lejeuneaceae and, except for *Rectolejeunea brittoniae*, no dioecious transoceanic taxa are known in this family. This would suggest that sex distribution, sometimes considered of little value as a taxonomic character in this family, is of considerable biogeographic significance in Lejeuneaceae. In the rain-forest genus *Stictolejeunea*, for instance, *S. balfourii* is pantropical and monoecious whereas *S. squamata* is Neotropical and dioecious (Gradstein, 1985). The genus consists of only three species and the third one, *S. iwatsukii*, is endemic to Japan (Fig. 16.2). Known from the three continents among different names, *S. balfourii* is a highly skiophilous element of sheltered habitats in lowland rain forests, where it grows close to the ground on tree bases and roots. These locations can hardly be considered as suitable for long-range dispersal, as against forest margins and tree crowns, where many other transoceanic rain-forest species grow (Gradstein et al., 1984a). In the case of *Stictolejeunea balfourii*, one might therefore assume that the species is very old and became widespread by the ancient migration of land masses, but such explanations remain purely speculative.

Spore-size data for Neotropical transoceanic liverworts (Gradstein et al., 1984) indicate that dioecious species usually have small spores (< 25 μm in diameter), hence by their size well-suited for air transport. In the Lejeuneaceae, however, spores are larger and multicellular (40–60 μm in diameter). This would suggest that in Lejeuneaceae the disadvantage of having large spores is compensated by bisexuality, which would increase their chances for successful establishment after transoceanic spore migration.

EPIPHYTISM AND GROWTH FORMS

A characteristic feature of the tropical rain forest is the enormous development and diversification of epiphytism (see Benzing, Ch. 7, Johansson, Ch. 9, and Wallace, Ch. 13). Very important in this respect is the constantly high atmospheric humidity in the lower levels of the forest.

Among the 15 main bryophyte families of the tropical rain forest, 14 are predominantly epiphytic; the Fissidentaceae are the exception. Epiphytic bryophytes are sometimes classified as microepiphytes, as opposed to the vascular macroepiphytes (Tixier, 1966). In a phylogenetic sense, most of them are on the branch tips of bryophyte evolution (Vitt, 1984, p. 717, fig. 34) and presumably coevolved with the rain forest since the late Cretaceous. Their evolution parallels that of the main macroepiphytic groups of the rain forest, such as the Orchidaceae and Bromeliaceae.

Most epiphytic bryophytes inhabit the trunks, branches and twigs of trees, but some, the epiphylls, have adapted to growth on living leaves. Various structural adaptations, aimed at survival in the hazardous epiphytic environment, are seen among epiphytic bryophytes:

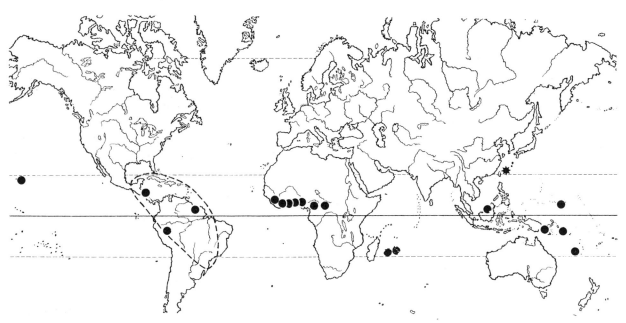

Fig. 16.2. The distribution of *Stictolejeunea* (Lejeuneaceae). Dots: *S. balfourii*, star: *S. iwatsukii*, broken line: *S. squamata*. (After Gradstein, 1984.)

(1) Development of green, multicellular spores containing endosporous protonema which may germinate within the spore wall before or upon spore release from the capsule. Examples are Dicnemonaceae and Lejeuneaceae (Nehira, 1983).

(2) Sexual dimorphism and development of phyllodioecy in various mosses, possibly enhancing gene flow.

(3) Development of numerous devices for asexual reproduction, monoecious condition, and retention of juvenile characters in the adult stage (neoteny) in response to ephemeral environments such as fine twigs and living leaves (Schuster, 1984; Richards, 1984a). Examples are found especially in Lejeuneaceae.

(4) Development of rhizoid discs for anchoring and adhesion on smooth surfaces, especially in epiphylls (Winkler, 1967).

(5) Development of devices for absorption and retention of atmospheric water, such as the water sacs (lobules) in Frullaniaceae and Lejeuneaceae and hyaline leaf margins in epiphylls. Particularly sophisticated are the water sacs of *Colura*, which possess a complicated closing apparatus at the entrance of the sac (Jovet-Ast, 1953). Water retention is probably also enhanced by the hyaline cells of the leaves in many Calymperaceae (Richards, 1984a).

(6) Occurrence of cushion-form growth types which promote humus and water accumulation. These growth forms are characteristic for the branching system of rather open, montane forests, where nutrients and water are available in limited amounts for the epiphytes (Pócs, 1982).

Attempts to classify the different ecological adaptations of rain-forest bryophytes have resulted in the recognition of a considerable number of growth forms (Fig. 16.3). Several of these growth forms occur almost exclusively in the tropical rain forest, including the feather type, the bracket type and the hanging, pendulous type (Fig. 16.6d). Only very few representatives of these three types are known from temperate forests, — *Leucodon sciuroides* and *Neckera pennata* in Europe, *Leucodon pendulus* in the East Siberian taiga and *Leucodon immersus* and *Pseudoleskiella laxiramea* in the South Caspian lowland forest (Frey and Probst, 1974).

In contrast to growth forms, which are static morphological features each with presumed adap-

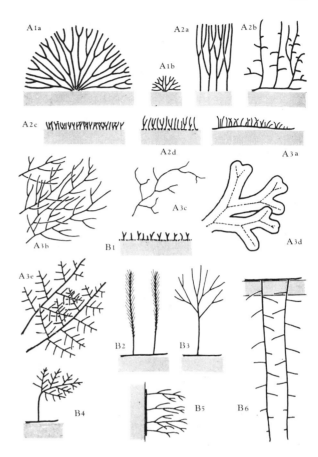

Fig. 16.3. Classification of growth forms of tropical forest bryophytes (from Richards, 1984). A1 a: large cushions; A1 b: small cushions; A2 a: tall turfs; A2 b: tall turfs with divergent and creeping branches; A2 c: short turfs; A2 d: open turfs; A3 a: rough mats; A3 b: smooth mats; A3 c: thread-like forms; A3 d: thallose mats; A3 e: wefts; B1: protonematal bryophytes; B2: unbranched dendroid forms; B3: branched not dorsiventral dendroid forms; B4: feather forms; B5: bracket mosses; B6: hanging bryophytes.

tations to the environment, the life strategy system elaborated for bryophytes by During (1979) reflects a dynamic approach which mirrors ecologically relevant life-history characteristics of the bryophytes. Six different bryophyte life strategies were established for temperate bryophytes, based on ways of sexual and a-sexual reproduction, size and number of spores, annual production, standing crop and life expectancy. Their correlation with growth forms was also established. Evidently, life strategies should be a workable tool for a better understanding of the ecology of tropical rain-forest bryophytes, but no comprehensive attempts have been made as yet to study these in the tropics.

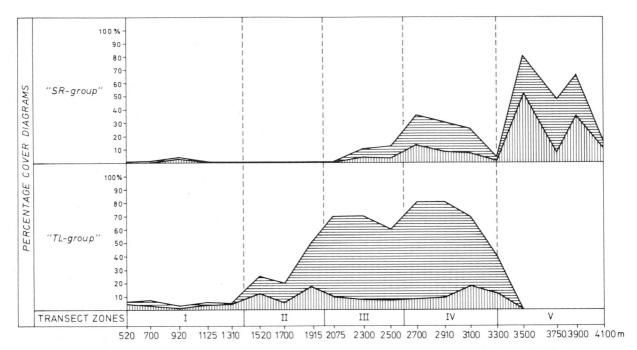

Fig. 16.4. Bryophyte cover values in relation to altitude in the Sierra Nevada de Santa Marta, Colombia (after Van Reenen and Gradstein, 1983). Zone I: lowland rain forest; zone II: submontane rain forest; zone III: lower montane rain forest; zone IV: upper montane rain forest (condensation zone); zone V: paramo. TL group: epiphytes; SR group: terrestrial and saxicolous species. Vertical lines: mosses; horizontal lines: liverworts.

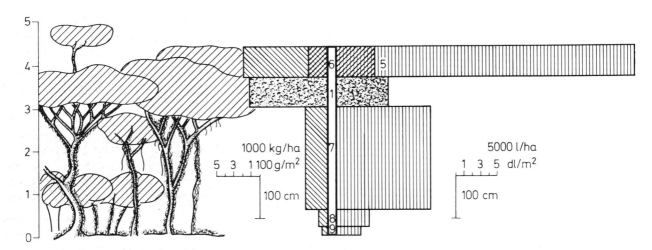

Fig. 16.5. The biomass and water interception of epiphytes and phorophyte leaves in a mossy elfin forest in Tanzania, Uluguru Mts. at 2140 m alt. (after Pócs, 1980). On the left side the dry weight of different layers in 1000 kg ha^{-1}. On the right side the water interception capacity in l ha^{-1} according to the different layers, as: 1, Leaves of phorophyte trees forming the canopy; 5, humus and detritus among the canopy epiphytes (the darker part); 6, canopy microepiphytes including small orchids; 7, microepiphytes (bryophytes and filmy ferns) on the trunk; 8, microepiphytes (bryophytes) on the roots; 9, bryophyte cover on the ground.

Fig. 16.6. (a) Lowland rain forest in Vietnam with bryophyte-covered buttressed tree bases; (b) epiphyllous liverworts (mostly *Radula acuminata*) on leaves of shrubs in Vietnamese lowland rain forest; (c) ramicolous *Plagiochila floridana* in the lower layer of a montane rain forest in Cuba; (d) hanging *Zelometeorium patulum* in submontane forests of the Galapagos Islands. (Photographs by the authors.)

BRYOPHYTE HABITATS

Lowland rain forests

The bryophytes of lowland and lower submontane rain forests — which are ranging up to 1500 m near the Equator and up to 600 m near the northern and southern boundaries of the Tropics — may be divided into two groups, separated spatially by the morphological inversion surface of the forest (Hallé et al., 1978). This surface runs practically at the lower surface of the closed canopy of the B layer (below the emergents), joining the lower branches. According to Richards (1983) this imaginary plane, which is undulating from place to place, separates the exposed "euphotic" zone from the shaded region below it, called "oligophotic" zone. Sun epiphytes are characteristic for the euphotic zone, whereas shade epiphytes and terrestrial species are mainly in the oligophotic zone.

Euphotic habitats

Main habitats in the euphotic zone are the twigs and main branches of the canopy. Twigs in the canopy are inhabited only in the most humid types of lowland rain forest. A dense, rain-absorbing bryophyte vegetation may develop in full light, consisting of feathery or hanging mosses and liverworts or tiny species adherent to the twigs. These species are not easily detected due to the inaccessibility of the canopy, and their geographical distribution is therefore poorly known. Examples are *Mastigolejeunea turgida* and *Pycnolejeunea contigua* in West Africa (Jones and Harrington, 1983). In drier types of forest, if not mist-affected, this vegetation cannot develop, as the habitat is too much exposed to temporary droughts.

The inner part of the canopy, where the main branches are, is more protected against direct irradiation and desiccation than the outer part but still receives a considerable amount of light. Usually a rich bryophyte vegetation of dense, mat- or cushion-forming, more or less drought-tolerant species develops here, belonging, for instance, to the genera *Frullania* and *Macromitrium*. Under very humid conditions pendulous bryophytes are present and epiphyllous lichens and liverworts establish themselves on the inner crown leaves.

Oligophotic habitats

The oligophotic zone includes tree trunks, small trees and shrubs, living leaves, decaying wood and the ground surface. The upper part of tree trunks is inhabited by shade-tolerant and more or less drought-tolerant species, which usually cover the bark only partly and not in large masses. Patches of crustose lichens, small turfs of mosses (such as Orthotrichaceae) and appressed mats of liverworts (mainly Lejeuneaceae) are common here. This habitat is also characterized by the occurrence of bracket mosses, including several Pterobryaceae (Pócs, 1982).

Tree bases offer the most shady habitats in tropical rain forests (Fig. 16.6a). Due to the steadily high degree of humidity, bryophyte diversity reaches peak values here, both in cover and in species richness (Richards, 1954). Mat-, weft- and turf-forming mosses, and to a lesser extent liverworts, form an almost continuous, often thick carpet, which is usually intermixed with creeping Hymenophyllaceae. Perhaps the most typical bryophyte growth form here is the feather type which may occur in great masses. The upper limit of this moss carpet is called the "moss line" (Richards, 1984a) which in ever-wet rain forests may be 5 to 8 m up the trunk. In less humid, seasonal rain forests this moss line may be as low as 50 cm above the ground. Above the moss line, air humidity values are more variable and may sink to 60% during dry periods (Pócs, 1974), causing the scantiness of the bryophyte vegetation at higher trunk levels.

Narrow stems of small trees and branches of shrubs in this zone are inhabited by ramicolous bryophytes which usually include other species than the bark-inhabiting corticolous group (Pócs, 1982). Many dendroid, feather or bracket-type mosses and liverworts, belonging to Neckeraceae, Hookeriaceae, Pterobryaceae, Plagiochilaceae and Lejeuneaceae, are specialists of this habitat.

Fig. 16.7. (a) Large cushions of *Dicranoloma billardieri* and *Lepidozia cupressina* in the montane mossy forests on Mt. Kilimanjaro, at 2700 m alt.; (b) epizoic *Daltonia angustifolia* in the montane mossy forests of New Guinea. (Photographs by the authors.)

The upper surface of the living, evergreen leaves in this zone are often covered by epiphylls (Fig. 16.6b). The majority of the obligatory epiphyllous bryophyte species are liverworts of the family Lejeuneaceae. They show interesting adaptations to their habitat (see above). In a sufficiently humid and not too shady environment, large amounts of epiphyllous bryophytes may develop during the 2 to 4 years' life-span of an evergreen leaf, which eventually becomes fully covered. Species diversity increases with leaf age, and a well-developed epiphyllous community may consist of 8 to 15 (seldomly up to 30) species on one leaf (Pócs, 1978).

Epiphyllous communities are a special feature of tropical rain forests and only very rarely have they been recorded outside the tropical belt (Richards, 1984a). Presence of well-developed epiphyllous communities always indicates high atmospheric humidity. It has been shown that the epiphyllous community promotes nitrogen uptake by the host plant through the leaf surface, probably due to blue-green algae living in the community (Harrelson, 1969; Edmisten, 1970). On the other hand, extensive epiphyllous growth can be harmful for the host, because too dense a cover may presumably prohibit leaf assimilation and can promote fungal infection (Thorold, 1952). Epiphylls in general seem to behave as epiphytes, not taking nutrients from the host leaves nor causing mechanical damage, although some exceptions were noted (Winkler, 1967; Berrie and Eze, 1975).

Decaying logs, stumps and branches on the forest floor are also important bryophyte habitats. They may be fully covered by mats of species belonging to Hookeriaceae, Hypnaceae, Lepidoziaceae, Lophocoleaceae, Sematophyllaceae, as well as by cushions of Leucobryum. The floor of the lowland rain forest is very poor in bryophytes, probably due to the smothering effect of leaves covering the ground (Richards, 1954). Terrestrial species are mainly found on exposed patches of disturbed soil, such as road cuts and termite mounds, and include many species of Fissidens.

There are several other special bryophyte habitats in rain forests, such as palm, bamboo and tree-fern stems, each of which may be inhabited by characteristic bryophyte communities. For a discussion we refer to Pócs (1982).

Montane rain forests

Montane rain forests — ranging from 1500 to 3000 or 4000 m near the Equator, but lower in elevation at increasing latitudes, on islands and in coastal regions — are cooler and wetter than lowland rain forests. Mean annual temperatures are usually between 20 and 10°C, decreasing gradually with altitude and latitude. Frosts are very rare. Annual rainfall is usually over 2000 mm and, in addition, clouds and mist precipitation may supply extra liquid water to the forest. These climatic conditions are more or less even throughout the year, and are thus favourable for bryophyte growth.

While the montane rain forest is structurally simpler than the lowland forest and woody species diversity is lower, the epiphytic vegetation including the bryophyte component is perplexingly more diversified, both in terms of species richness and of biomass. Van Reenen and Gradstein (1983) measured the total bryophyte cover in rain-forest plots along an altitudinal gradient in the Andes of Colombia, and found epiphytic bryophyte cover values in the montane forests up to ten times higher than in the lowland forests (Fig. 16.4). Bryomass measurements taken from selected rain-forest trees along an altitudinal gradient in Peru yielded similar results (Frahm, 1987). Van Reenen and Gradstein found highest cover values in the condensation zones where cloud formation was maximal. These cloud forests are usually called "mossy forests" and include the mossy dwarf forests or elfin forests, which develop near the forest line and on exposed mountain ridges, as well as in summit areas of low tropical islands. Not only tree stems but often all branches, canopy twigs and shrubs in mossy forests are covered by a bryophytic "fur" often much thicker than the branches themselves (Fig. 16.7a). The bryophyte biomass of a Tanzanian elfin forest (Fig. 16.5) can be as much as $11\,000\,\text{kg ha}^{-1}$ dry weight as compared to 1773 kg in lower submontane rain forest in the same area (Pócs, 1982), 355 kg in an oak forest in Atlantic Europe (Schnock, 1972) and 41 kg in a continental European oak forest (Simon, 1974).

Pócs (1980) established that montane rain-forest bryophytes are very effective rainfall interceptors. Comparative measurements in Tanzania showed that rainfall interception in the elfin forest was about 2,5 times higher than in the submontane rain forest. Total interception in the elfin forest was over 50% of the annual rainfall, due largely to the dense carpet of bryophytes in the canopy layer which made up about 80% of the total canopy biomass (Fig. 16.5). The liverworts *Bazzania* and *Plagiochila* (Fig. 16.6c), as well as *Frullania*, *Lepidozia* and *Trichocolea* proved to be the most effective rain interceptors.

After interception part of the rainwater re-evaporates and another part is retained by the epiphyte. The surplus rainwater slowly drips down, keeping the environment moist even in periods when there is no rain or mist. Apparently, suitable conditions are thus created for terrestrial bryophyte growth. The continuous supply of humus provided by the epiphytic bryophytes, and the relatively small size of the leaves of trees at these altitudes, are other factors which are favourable for terrestrial growth (Pócs, 1980).

The richness of the bryophytic ground cover of the mossy montane rain forest as opposed to its virtual absence in lowland rain forest is perhaps one of the most striking differences between the two forest types (Fig. 16.4). Also characteristic is the diminution of substrate preference of individual species in mossy forest. Thus, epiphytic species may establish themselves on the ground or on fallen logs, whereas terrestrial species may be found on the trees (Van Reenen and Gradstein, 1983). Some species invade unusual substrates, such as the moss *Daltonia angustifolia*, which in New Guinean mossy forest may colonize the back of slow-moving weevils (Fig. 16.7b). The ability of this moss to mature rapidly, its growth on a soft substrate (such as bark) and its ramicolous habit on very small branches, are presumably attributes that allow its epizoic growth (Gressitt et al., 1968; Gradstein et al., 1984b).

In terms of bryophyte habitat diversification, montane rain forests are only partly similar to lowland forests. The simpler forest stratification, the lower canopy height and the more favourable moisture conditions allow the moss line to go up higher and even reach the canopy (Fig. 16.7a), (Richards, 1984). The oligophotic zone is strongly reduced or absent and the entire tree trunk may be covered by the community of the tree base. Feathery, dendroid, large cushion and pendulous growth forms are much more common than in the lowland forests, and often dominant. Horizontal branches of small trees and shrubs are the usual substrates of the pendulous Meteoriaceae (Fig. 16.6d), Phyllogoniaceae, *Frullania* and *Taxilejeunea*. Epiphyllous communities occur in the montane rain forest up to about 3000 m (Pócs, 1982). The upper limit of their existence seems to be determined by the occurrence of night frosts.

ACKNOWLEDGEMENTS

We are grateful to Dr. P.W. Richards and G.B.A. van Reenen for their comments on the manuscript.

Preparation of this chapter was made possible through a grant of the Netherlands Organization for the Advancement of Pure Research to S.R.G.

REFERENCES

Argent, G.C.G., 1979. The systematics of tropical mosses. In: G.C.S. Clarke and J.G. Duckett (Editors), *Bryophyte Systematics*. Academic Press, London, pp. 185–193.

Berrie, G.K. and Eze, J.M.O., 1975. The relationship between an epiphyllous liverwort and host leaves. *Ann. Bot.*, 39: 953–963.

Biebl, R., 1964. Temperaturresistenz tropischer Pflanzen auf Puerto Rico. *Protoplasma*, 59: 133–156.

Bischler, H., 1984. *Marchantia* L. The New World Species. *Bryophyt. Bibl.*, 26: 1–228.

Buck, W.R. and Griffin, D., 1984. *Trachyphyllum*, a moss genus new to South America with notes on African–South American bryogeography. *J. Nat. Hist.*, 18: 63–69.

Crosby, M.R., 1969. Distribution patterns of West Indian mosses. *Ann. Mo. Bot. Gard.*, 56: 409–416.

De Vries, A., Van Zanten, B.O. and Van Dijk, H., 1983. Genetic variability within and between populations of two species of *Racopilum* (Racopilaceae, Bryopsida). *Lindbergia*, 9: 73–80.

During, H.J., 1977. A taxonomical revision of the Garovaglioideae (Pterobryaceae, Musci.) *Bryophyt. Bibl.*, 12: 1–244.

During, H.J., 1979. Life strategies of bryophytes: a preliminary review. *Lindbergia*, 5: 2–18.

Edmisten, J., 1970. Preliminary studies of the nitrogen budget of a tropical rain forest. In: H.T. Odum (Editor), *A Tropical Rain Forest, a Study of Irradiation and Ecology at El Verde, Puerto Rico*. U.S. Atomic Energy Commission, Washington, D.C., pp. 211–215.

Edwards, S.R., 1980. A revision of West Tropical African Calymperaceae I. *J. Bryol.*, 11: 49–93.

Egunyomi, A., 1978. The viability of spores of some tropical moss species after long-time storage and their survival chances in nature. *J. Hattori Bot. Lab.*, 45: 167–171.

Frahm, J.P., 1982. Grossdisjunktionen in Artarealen südamerikanischer und afrikanischer *Campylopus*-Arten. *Lindbergia*, 8: 45–52.

Frahm, J.-P., 1987. Ökologische Studien an der epiphytische Moosvegetation in Regenwäldern NE-Perus. In: Ergebnisse der BRYOTROP Expedition nach Peru 1982. *Beih. Nova Hedwigia*, 88.

Frey, W. and Probst, W., 1974. Hangeformen von *Pseudoleskeella laxiramea* (Schiffn.) Broth. und *Leucodon immersus* Lindb. (Musci) im südkaspischen Waldgebiet (Iran). *Bot. Jahrb. Syst.*, 94: 267–282.

Geissler, P. and Greene, S., 1982. Bryophyte taxonomy: methods, practices and floristic exploration. *Beih. Nov. Hedwigia*, 71: 1–558.

Giesenhagen, K., 1910. Moostypen der Regenwälder. *Ann. Jard. Bot. Buitenzorg (Suppl.)*, 3: 711–790.

Gradstein, S.R., 1985. A revision of the genus *Stictolejeunea* (Spruce) Schiffn. *Beih. Nov. Hedwigia*, 80: 209–232.

Gradstein, S.R. and Weber, W.A., 1982. Bryogeography of the Galapagos Islands. *J. Hattori Bot. Lab.*, 52: 127–152.

Gradstein, S.R., Cleef, A.M. and Fulford, M.H., 1977. Oil body structure and ecological distribution of selected species of tropical Andean Jungermanniales. *Proc. K. Ned. Akad. Wet., Ser. C*, 80: 377–420.

Gradstein, S.R., Pócs, T. and Vána, J., 1984a. Disjunct Hepaticae in tropical America and Africa. *Acta Bot. Hung.*, 29: 127–171.

Gradstein, S.R., Vitt, D.H. and Anderson, R.S., 1984b. The epizoic occurrence of *Daltonia angustifolia* (Musci) in Papua New Guinea. *Cryptog. Bryol. Lichén.*, 5: 47–50.

Greene, S.W. and Harrington, A., 1979. *The Bryological Literature of Africa*. Nature Conservation Research Council, Penicuik, 141 pp.

Gressitt, J.L., Samuelson, G.A. and Vitt, D.H., 1968. Moss growing on living Papuan moss forest weevils. *Nature*, 217: 765–767.

Griffin, D., Gradstein, S.R. and Aguirre, J., 1982. On a new antipodal element in the Neotropical páramos — *Dendrocryphaea latifolia* sp. nov. (Musci). *Acta Bot. Neerl.*, 31: 175–184.

Grolle, R., 1969. Grossdisjunktionen in Artarealen Lateinamerikanischer Lebermoose. In: E.J. Fittkau, J. Illies, H. Klinge, G.H. Schwabe and H. Sioli (Editors), *Biogeography and Ecology in South America, Vol. 2*. Junk, The Hague, pp. 562–582.

Hallé, F., Oldeman, R.A.A. and Tomlinson, P.B., 1978. *Tropical Trees and Forests*. Springer, Berlin, 441 pp.

Harrelson, M.A., 1969. *Nitrogen fixation in the epiphyllae*. Ph.D. Diss., Univ. of Georgia, Athens, Ga., 103 pp.

Hattori, S., 1984. New Caledonian Frullaniaceae. *J. Hattori Bot. Lab.*, 57: 405–426.

Inoue, H., 1982. Speciation and distribution of *Plagiochila* in Australasia and the Pacific. *J. Hattori Bot. Lab.*, 52: 45–56.

Jones, E.W. and Harrington, A.J., 1983. The hepatics of Sierra Leone and Ghana. *Bull. Br. Mus. Nat. Hist. Bot.*, 11: 215–289.

Jovet-Ast, S., 1953. Le genre *Colura*. *Rev. Bryol. Lichén.*, 22: 206–312.

Lin, S.H., 1983. A taxonomic revision of Phyllogoniaceae (Bryopsida), Part. I. *J. Taiwan Mus.*, 36: 37–86.

Mägdefrau, K., 1982. Life-forms of bryophytes. In: A.J.E. Smith (Editor), *Bryophyte Ecology*. Chapman and Hall, London, pp. 45–58.

Mues, R., Hattori, S., Asakawa, Y. and Grolle, R., 1984. Biosystematic studies on *Frullania jackii* and *F. davurica*. *J. Hattori Bot. Lab.*, 56: 227–240.

Nehira, K., 1983. Spore germination, protonema development and sporeling development. In: R.M. Schuster (Editor), *New Manual of Bryology, Vol. 1*. The Hattori Botanical Laboratory, Nichinan, pp. 343–385.

Pócs, T., 1974. Bioclimatic studies in the Uluguru Mountains (Tanzania, East Africa) I. *Acta Bot. Hung.*, 20: 115–135.

Pócs, T., 1975. Affinities between the bryoflora of East Africa and Madagascar. *Boissiera*, 24: 125–128.

Pócs, T., 1976. Correlations between the tropical African and Asian bryofloras, I. *J. Hattori Bot. Lab.*, 41: 95–106.

Pócs, T., 1978. Epiphyllous communities and their distribution in East Africa. *Bryophyt. Bibl.*, 13: 681–713.

Pócs, T., 1980. The epiphytic biomass and its effect on the water balance of two rain forest types in the Uluguru Mountains (Tanzania, East Africa). *Acta Bot. Hung.*, 26: 143–167.

Pócs, T., 1982. Tropical forest bryophytes. In: A.J.E. Smith (Editor), *Bryophyte Ecology*. Chapman and Hall, London, pp. 59–104.

Prance, G.T., 1977. Floristic inventory of the Tropics: where do we stand? *Ann. Mo. Bot. Gard.*, 64: 659–684.

Reese, W.D., 1978. The genus *Syrrhopodon* in the Americas II. The limbate species. *Bryologist*, 81: 189–225.

Richards, P.W., 1954. Notes on the bryophyte communities of lowland tropical rain forest, with special reference to Moraballi Creek, British Guiana. *Vegetatio*, 6: 319–328.

Richards, P.W., 1973. Africa, the "odd man out". In: B.J. Meggers, E.S. Ayensu and W.D. Duckworth (Editors), *Tropical Forest Ecosystems in Africa and South America*. Smithsonian Institution, Washington, D.C., pp. 21–26.

Richards, P.W., 1983. The three-dimensional structure of tropical rain forest. In: S.L. Sutton, T.C. Whitmore and A.C. Chadwick (Editors), *Tropical Rain Forest: Ecology and Management*. Blackwell, Oxford, pp. 3–24.

Richards, P.W., 1984a. The ecology of tropical forest bryophytes. In: R.M. Schuster (Editor), *New Manual of Bryology, Vol. 2*. The Hattori Botanical Laboratory, Nichinan, pp. 1233–1270.

Richards, P.W., 1984b. The bryologically underworked regions of the world, with special reference to West Africa. *J. Hattori Bot. Lab.*, 55: 165–172.

Schnock, G., 1972. Evapotranspiration de la végétation épiphytique de la base des troncs de chêne et d'érable champètre. *Bull. Soc. R. Bot. Belg.*, 105: 143–150.

Schuster, R.M., 1983. Phytogeography of the Bryophyta. In: R.M. Schuster (Editor), *New Manual of Bryology, Vol. 1*. The Hattori Botanical Laboratory, Nichinan, pp. 463–626.

Schuster, R.M., 1984. Evolution, phylogeny and classification of the Hepaticae. In: R.M. Schuster (Editor), *New Manual of Bryology, Vol. 2*. The Hattori Botanical Laboratory, Nichinan, pp. 892–1070.

Simon, T., 1974. Estimation of phytomass dry-weight of epiphytic mosses at Sikfókut (near Eger, N. Hungary). *Acta Bot. Hung.*, 21: 117–136.

Szweykowski, J., 1982. Genetic differentiation of liverwort

populations and its significance for bryotaxonomy and bryogeography. *J. Hattori Bot. Lab.*, 53: 21–28.

Thorold, C.A., 1952. The epiphytes of *Theobroma cacao* in Nigeria in relation to the incidence of black pod disease *(Phytophtora palmivora)*. *J. Ecol.*, 40: 125–142.

Tixier, P., 1966. *Flore et végétation orophiles de l'Asie tropicale. Les épiphytes du flanc méridional du Massif Sud Annamitique.* Thesis, Univ. of Aix-Marseille, pp. 1–240.

Touw, A., 1974. Some notes on taxonomic and floristic research on exotic mosses. *J. Hattori Bot. Lab.*, 38: 123–128.

Van der Hammen, T. and Van Dommelen, H., 1973. Palynological record of the upheaval of the northern Andes. *Palaeogeogr., Palaeoclimatol., Palaeoecol.*, 16: 1–24.

Van Reenen, G.B.A., 1982. High Andean species of *Herbertus* S.F. Gray (Hepaticae). *Lindbergia*, 8: 110–120.

Van Reenen, G.B.A. and Gradstein, S.R., 1983. A transect analysis of the bryophyte vegetation along an altitudinal gradient on the Sierra Nevada de Santa Marta, Colombia. *Acta Bot. Neerl.*, 32: 163–175.

Van Zanten, B.O., 1978. Experimental studies on transoceanic long-range dispersal of moss spores in the Southern Hemisphere. *J. Hattori Bot. Lab.*, 44: 455–482.

Van Zanten, B.O., 1984. Some considerations on the feasibility of long-distance transport in bryophytes. *Acta Bot. Neerl.*, 33: 231–232.

Van Zanten, B.O. and Gradstein, S.R., 1987. Experimental dispersal geography of neotropical Liverworts. *Beih. Nova Hedwigia*, 89.

Van Zanten, B.O. and Pócs, T., 1981. Distribution and dispersal of bryophytes. In: W. Schultze-Motel (Editor), *Advances in Bryology, Vol. 1.* Cramer, Vaduz, pp. 479–562.

Vitt, D.H., 1984. Classification of the Bryopsida. In: R.M. Schuster (Editor), *New Manual of Bryology, Vol. 2.* The Hattori Botanical Laboratory, Nichinan, pp. 696–759.

Winkler, S., 1967. Die epiphyllen Moose der Nebelwälder von El Salvador, C.A. *Rev. Bryol. Lichén.*, 35: 303–369.

Chapter 17

PTERIDOPHYTES

R. TRYON

INTRODUCTION

Pteridophytes are often a significant element in the vegetation of the tropical rain forests, especially montane rain forests and cloud forests. In the lowland rain forest, pteridophytes are often less prominent except in naturally disturbed sites. This is especially true for regions between the Tropic of Cancer and the Tropic of Capricorn.

Most ferns are evolutionary opportunists, since their genetic systems promote variation, and they have the capacity for speciation and exploiting new environments. The lack of secondary tissues, and the water-dependent life-cycle usually limit them to a subsidiary ecological role within the vegetation. They are adapted to occupy natural openings within primary vegetation. The copious production and wide dispersal of spores have a vital role in the occupancy of suitable sites. This chapter will focus on the diversity of tropical rain-forest pteridophytes, their endemism, their ecology, and historical considerations.

For the purpose of this chapter, three types of tropical rain forest can be distinguished, based on altitude and correlated floristic composition. Near the equator lowland rain forest occurs mostly from 0 to 1000 m, montane rain forest centers on 1500 to 2500 m, and cloud (elfin or mossy) forest, centers on 2500 to 3000 m. These elevations are lowered toward 20°N and 20°S of the Equator (Troll, 1968). Lowland rain forest is characterized by a tall forest with a closed canopy, relatively high temperatures, deep shade on the forest floor, and a pronounced humidity gradient from ground level to the canopy. Montane rain forest (Figs. 17.1 and 17.2) is usually not as tall and the canopy is often somewhat open. There is more light at ground level

and the zone of high humidity extends further above the ground due to lower temperatures combined with a higher rainfall. The cloud forest is dominated by cool and foggy conditions. The canopy is low and broken, allowing light to enter the forest on sunny days. It is often disjunct and of local distribution compared to the continuity of the other forest types.

A biogeographic discussion is dependent upon the taxonomy and in order to provide uniformity the classification of Tryon and Tryon (1982) is adopted, with few exceptions, for families and genera. Species taxonomy is taken from current floristic and monographic literature. The pteridophytes include 33 families, 300 genera and about 10 000 species. These numbers represent a conservative classification that does not include subfamilies or tribes which some taxonomists recognize as families, or subgenera and sections which may be recognized as genera. Nevertheless, it is adequate to present the basic aspects of biogeography.

The American and Malesian rain forests have the highest diversity of genera and species, and are central to a discussion of tropical rain-forest pteridophytes. Africa has an uncertain position with respect to many aspects of biogeography because its role is undoubtedly obscured by the depletion of its flora during the fluctuations of climate during the Pleistocene (Van Zinderen Bakker, 1967; Raven and Axelrod, 1974; Mayr and O'Hara, 1986).

Pteridophytes of tropical rain forests are those that occur either within primary forest or in naturally disturbed (or man-disturbed) sites within it that will eventually return to forest if permitted to do so. Taxa which occur in special edaphic situations, or which are not associated with the original forest vegetation are excluded.

Fig. 17.1. *Alsophila manniana* (Cyatheaceae) in montane rain forest, The Cameroon Mountain, Federal Republic of Cameroon. (Photo Alice F. Tryon.)

Most pteridophyte taxa occur in the tropical rain forest. These include 32 of the 33 families, 250 of the 300 genera, and about 5800 of the 10 000 species (Table 17.1). Genera and species that grow only outside of the rain forest are mostly those of high altitudes on tropical mountains, such as *Jamesonia* and species of *Lycopodium* in the high Andes, and *Grammitis* species at high elevations in New Guinea, as well as those of xeric and semi-xeric regions such as species of *Cheilanthes, Pellaea,* and *Notholaena*. In addition, there are perhaps as many as 2500 mesic temperate species primarily of China and Japan.

Other accounts of the pteridophytes of tropical rain forests have been provided by Holttum (1938, 1954), Iwatsuki (1972), and Page (1979).

DIVERSITY

Families, genera and species

Most families of the Pteridophyta are widely distributed and there is no great difference in their diversity among the major regions of tropical rain forest (Table 17.1). Only the family Stromatopteridaceae, which grows on serpentine or rarely on iron soils of New Caledonia, is not in the rain forest. A few families with only one or two genera have restricted distributions. These include Lopho-

TABLE 17.1

Numbers of families, genera, and species of Pteridophyta in the tropical rain forest of major regions. The taxa grow in the rain forest, but are not necessarily confined to it

	Families	Genera	Species
America	29	120	2100
Africa/Madagascar	23	80	500
Malesia	28	190	3200
Total	32 of 33	250 of 300	5800 of 10 000

Fig. 17.2. *Nephelea polystichoides* (Cyatheaceae) in montane rain forest, Tapanti, Costa Rica. (Photo Alice F. Tryon.)

soriaceae, Metaxyaceae and Hymenophyllopsidaceae, which are only in America, and Cheiropleuriaceae and Matoniaceae only in Malesia. The Loxomataceae occur in New Zealand and America, Dipteridaceae in Malesia and the western Pacific (to Fiji), and Plagiogyriaceae in eastern and southeastern Asia, Malesia and America.

Generic diversity is highest in Malesia, somewhat less in America, and low in Africa/ Madagascar (Table 17.1). The lower number in the latter region is probably due to the rather small area of rain forest in Madagascar and the depletion of the tropical African flora in the Pleistocene. The high diversity in Malesia may partly relate to the proximity of the rich pteridophyte flora of China and the eastern Himalayas, which may have served as a source for the tropics to the southeast. A similar source was not available to supplement the flora of the American tropics.

The primary interest in diversity is at the species level since the ranges of both genera and families are based on species. The diversity of species in the major regions of rain forest is shown in Table 17.1. Species diversity correlates with that of genera, except that the proportion of species occurring in rain forests is lower. Species diversity is highest in relatively cool and moist areas which represent optimal conditions for the pteridophyte life-cycle. It is also highest in regions of high ecological diversity. These features are prominent in tropical mountains of the world and especially in the montane rain forests. New Guinea, for example, has about 2000 species of pteridophytes, Ecuador 1000, Peru 1000, and smaller regions such as Chiapas, Mexico, over 600, and Malaya 500. These regions have pronounced physiographic relief, which provides for ecological diversity. They are regions where the opportunities for geographic speciation and for alloploid speciation are maximal. They provide for geographic isolation and also for an environmental mosaic allowing species of different habitats to grow in sufficient proximity for hybridization to be possible. In contrast, some areas have low diversity — for example Surinam with 260 species and the state of Falcon, Venezuela with 215. While these are relatively small areas, it is notable that the very large Amazon Basin of Brazil also has low diversity with only 280 pteridophytes (Tryon and Conant, 1975). The few species in this large region of rain forest reflect the low ecological diversity and few opportunities for pteridophyte speciation.

Distribution and diversity

Several aspects of the distribution of species within a region relate to diversity. One is the local or wide distribution of species within a region. Many species occur in only one or a few smaller areas within a region and, following a hollow curve, few species occur in all of them. In the Amazon Basin of Brazil, for example, of 280 species, 135 are known in only one of the States, 54 in two of them, 45 in three, 31 in four and 15 in all five states. Among the 30 species of *Cyathea* in South America 15 occur in only one of 10 countries, 6 in two countries, 3 in three, 1 in four, 3 in five, and 1 in eight countries. Among the 66 species of *Adiantum*, *Pteris* and *Lindsaea* in Peru, primarily in the rain forest, 35 of them occur in one to three of the Departments, 22 in four or five Departments, and 9 in six to twelve Departments.

The distribution of species within the range of a genus is another feature of diversity. The species may be concentrated within one area of the range, or rather equally distributed throughout its range. In *Mesophlebion* for example, among the 17 species, 13 occur in Borneo, 7 in Sumatra and others are represented by 1 or 2 species elsewhere in Malesia (Holttum, 1982). Among the 40 American species of the genus *Cyathea*, 19 occur in Colombia, 10 to 13 in Venezuela and Peru, 9 in Mexico and Central America, 8 in the Greater Antilles, and fewer elsewhere (Tryon, 1976). In contrast, both *Bolbitis* (Hennipman, 1977) and *Ophioglossum* (Clausen, 1938) have nearly equal numbers of species in America, Africa/Madagascar, India/Sri Lanka, and Malesia.

The species diversity within a region frequently correlates with altitude, although there are differences among genera. Table 17.2 presents information on the altitudinal occurrence of the species of one family, and two genera. In New Guinea, *Grammitis* species occur mostly between 1500 and 3900 m, with definitely fewer above and below (Parris, 1983). The Cyatheaceae of both the Andes and New Guinea are strongly represented at altitudes of 500 to 2900 m, with a decline in species at lower and higher elevations (Tryon and Gastony, 1975). The occurrence of *Thelypteris* in Chiapas, Mexico, contrasts with these other groups as the species grow primarily from 500 to 1900 m, with only a single species above 3000 m (Smith, 1981). The species included in Table 17.2 occur most frequently between 500 and 2400 m, which places them within the montane rain forest.

TABLE 17.2

Altitudinal occurrence of species of tropical rain-forest pteridophytes in selected groups and regions. The range for a species is recorded for all altitudes between its minimum and maximum

	Grammitis in New Guinea	Cyatheaceae in		*Thelypteris* in Chiapas, Mexico	Total
		Andes	New Guinea		
4000–4500	5	2	0	0	7
3500–4000	22	4	8	0	34
3000–3500	25	11	17	1	54
2500–3000	25	21	23	7	76
2000–2500	23	38	31	16	108
1500–2000	23	43	30	23	119
1000–1500	15	43	29	33	120
500–1000	16	34	22	31	103
0–500	7	12	13	17	49
Total	61	75	79	50	265

TABLE 17.3

Comparison of species diversity of Pteridophyta at local sites in forests of Peru and Massachusetts

	Tingo María, Peru	Massachusetts
Local sites	A B C D	a b c d
Number of species	10 17 15 8	20 16 21 20
At only one site	42	8
At only two sites	4	4
At only three sites	0	3
At all four sites	0	13
Total	46	28

Data by Johns (1985) on the distribution of genera in New Guinea is in close agreement, with most genera occurring between 700 and 1800 m, the part he designates as the lower montane forest.

A final aspect of species distribution is the relation between their local occurrence and regional diversity. As an example, Table 17.3 provides data from collections made at Tingo María in Peru, within the montane forest zone, and in the forests of Massachusetts. Each of the sites were c. 10 000 m^2 in area. The sites at Tingo María occurred in a small region of c. 4 km^2, while those in Massachusetts were c. 10 to 40 km apart. It is notable that while the total number of species is relatively high at Tingo María, those growing at any one of the four sites are relatively few. Nearly all of the species at Tingo María occur at only one site, with little replication of species from one site to another. This phenomenon may be the basis for the high diversity of pteridophytes in the tropical rain forest. In contrast, four sites of similar size in Massachusetts forests show a larger number of species at each one but also much replication between sites, so that the total number of species is rather low. The difference in species diversity is especially significant since the sites in Massachusetts are distributed over a much larger area than those at Tingo María.

ENDEMISM

Endemism is often a significant factor in the species diversity of a region. For example, Borneo and the Philippine Islands each have about 1000 species, and the endemism is 33 and 44%, respectively. New Guinea has some 2000 species and an endemism of probably 50% or more. An area with low diversity such as Surinam with 260 species has about 2% endemism, and Amazonian Brazil with a similar number of species has none. Species endemism relates to the opportunities for speciation within a region, which involve both ecological diversity and size. The former feature seems to be the more important, since the very large Brazilian Amazon has low ecological diversity, while small Costa Rica with high ecological diversity has about 700 species and at least 35% endemism. Speciation, whether by geographic isolation or by alloploidy, is promoted by ecological diversity, in the first case with respect to isolating mechanisms, and in the latter by a strongly developed environmental mosaic permitting those species that can hybridize to grow in proximity.

Endemics are often referred to as paleo-endemics or neo-endemics although the distinction is often unclear. Species of monotypic genera may confidently be recognized as paleo-endemics, and those with close relatives in adjacent regions as neo-endemics. Among paleo-endemics are *Cystodium sorbifolium*, *Macroglossum alidae*, *Stenolepia tristis* and *Trogostolon falcinellus* of Malesia, and *Anetium citrifolium*, *Hecistopteris pumila*, *Hemidictyum marginatum*, *Lophosoria quadripinnata* and *Metaxya rostrata* of America. These paleo-endemics may well have had wider ranges in the past, since they must have persisted through periods of changing environments. Among neo-endemics are the American *Adiantum oyapokense*, *Cyathea furfuracea*, *Pteris horizontalis* and *Thelypteris pavoniana*, and the Malesian *Bolbitis sinuata*, *Gleichenia alstonii*, *Grammitis sumatrana*, *Grammitis impressa* and *Lindsaea media*.

The significance of endemism in a region is difficult to assess if there has been extensive environmental change in the recent past. This does not seem to be true, however, of the Amazon region of Brazil, where species endemism in angiosperm groups is high, but absent in pteridophytes. Although there is evidence of changing climates, these were evidently not of sufficient severity to deplete the flora. The cause of the lack of endemism among the pteridophytes of the Amazonian region seems to be the lack of opportunities for speciation within the region, rather than extinction.

Local endemics are of special interest because their restricted ranges seem to contrast with their high spore-dispersal capacity. They are distributed nearly throughout the World, except in regions strongly affected by Pleistocene climatic changes, very arid regions, and the Amazon Basin (Tryon, 1985). Some examples are *Alsophila rupestris*, Río Margua, near Sarare, Norte de Santander, Colombia; *Oleandra ejurana*, Ejara scarp, Mampong District, Ghana; *Grammitis trogophylla*, Mt. Saraket, New Guinea; and *Tapeinidium acuminatum*, Palanan Bay, Isabela Prov., Luzon, Philippine Islands. In spite of high dispersal capacity these species maintain a very small range. They perhaps have special ecological requirements which confine them to a small region of suitable environment.

One line of evidence for ecological specialization comes from the local distribution of species which indicates that they have different ecological requirements. In the Amazon region of Manaus (Tryon and Conant, 1975), this was shown by plants of the epiphytic *Polypodium nanum*, which were especially abundant on tree trunks up to 60 cm above the ground, while plants of *Elaphoglossum glabellum* occurred abundantly up to 180 cm above the ground. In an open white sand area with scattered clumps of shrubs and small trees, the distribution of *Schizaea* species showed local preferences. *Schizaea pennula* grew mostly in the shade of the woody plants, only rarely at the periphery of the small canopies, while *Schizeae stricta* did not occur in the shade but nearly always at the periphery of the canopies, and more rarely in the openings between clumps of shrubs. Other evidence of ecological specialization comes from paleo-endemics. Genera such as *Dicranopteris*, *Matonia* and *Dipteris* have fossil records at sites far beyond their present distribution (Seward, 1922). It is evident that the environmental conditions under which these genera grow had a much wider range in the earlier times, and that the ranges of the genera were subsequently restricted concomitantly with environmental changes. Obviously the same relations between environment and distribution apply today and in most cases the past ranges of species are unknown.

In comparison to the local endemics, species with wider ranges are considered to have (a) a series of ecotypes, (b) phenotypic plasticity, or (c) a broadly adapted genotype. Each of these attributes would permit a broad range to be established.

ECOLOGICAL ASPECTS

The diverse forest environment

The ground floor of the *lowland rain forest* is usually deeply shaded, except for patches where trees have fallen, and supports few terrestrial pteridophytes. Among these the species of *Adiantum*, *Angiopteris*, *Danaea*, *Selaginella* and *Trichomanes* occurring there are adapted to low light intensities. Epiphytic species on the trunks of trees or in the canopy are more frequent. Groups of epiphytes especially well represented are *Asplenium*, *Drynaria*, *Polypodium* and allies, *Pyrrosia*, Vittariaceae, and the Hymenophyllaceae. Species of *Lomagramma*, *Polybotrya* and *Teratophyllum* with a climbing stem which carries the leaves to levels of increased light are less common. Species of *Lygodium* and also *Salpichlaena volubilis*, with high climbing leaves which may reach nearly to the canopy, also occur in lowland rain forest.

Natural tree falls and stream and river erosion create habitats where there is greater diversity of pteridophytes than in the forest. In these natural openings species of Cyatheaceae, Thelypteridaceae and Dryopteridaceae may be frequent (Fig. 17.3). River slumps provide areas favoured by species of the Gleicheniaceae, which often form dense tangled thickets with their branched, scrambling leaves. In open sites of somewhat greater soil stability, *Dennstaedtia*, *Hypolepis* and *Pteridium*, which have extensive rhizome systems, often form large colonies. Near major waterways, the role of submergence for extended periods needs study. Annual flooding may be a decisive factor in the assemblage of species present in this habitat. At the borders of lakes and estuaries, *Acrostichum* may grow in permanently aquatic sites.

The *montane forest* is more diverse in species than lowland rain forest, largely because of greater ecological diversity created by the varied topography, landslides, and stream erosion. The forest on mountain sides has a more open and lower canopy than the lowland rain forest. There is more light and often more moisture due to the higher precipitation and cooler temperatures. Tree ferns

Fig. 17.3. *Thelypteris kunthii* (Thelypteridaceae), stream side in lowland rain forest, Veracruz, Mexico, (Photo Alice F. Tryon.)

(Cyatheaceae), with crowns of leaves occupying spaces between canopies of the larger trees, are often a prominent feature. The variety of pteridophytes in the montane forest is too great to mention or even characterize. Many species, especially in the Dryopteridaceae, Hymenophyllaceae, Polypodiaceae, Pteridaceae (Fig. 17.4), and Thelypteridaceae are frequent on the forest floor or as epiphytes. The Polypodiaceae and *Asplenium* especially contribute to the epiphytic flora. Here, as well as in the lowland rain forest, low epiphytes with higher moisture requirements include species of *Asplenium*, *Hymenophyllum*, *Polypodium* and *Trichomanes*, while species of *Crypsinus*, *Elaphoglossum*, *Lepisorus*, *Lycopodium* and *Pyrrosia* are often high epiphytes. In constantly wet habitats, such as waterfalls, rocky coves, and narrow stream channels, there is an assemblage of species similar to that of the cloud forest.

Landslides are of special interest in this forest. In

central Puerto Rico it was observed that *Cyathea arborea*, *Gleichenia bifida*, *Lycopodium reflexum*, *Odontosoria aculeata* and *Pityrogramma tartarea* are among the initial colonizers, while later invaders are *Blechnum occidentale*, *Dicranopteris pectinata*, *Lycopodium cernuum*, *Pityrogramma calomelanos* and *Thelypteris opposita*. The invading species and the sequence of invasion may differ at other sites. The species are all heliophiles, which must frequently establish new colonies in other sites in order to survive. Similar sets of species occur in the Old World tropics, including *Dicranopteris linearis*, *Lycopodium cernuum* and *Lygodium* species as well as *Nephrolepis* and some species of Cyatheaceae.

Rheophytes are species growing on rocks in a stream or river or along the banks where they are covered by swift water during periods of flooding (Van Steenis, 1981; Iwatsuki et al., 1983). They present an especially interesting ecological adaptation which is only poorly understood. Most species are evidently not obligate rheophytes as they also occur in constantly wet areas not subject to flooding. Some of the rheophytes are *Asplenium repandulum*, *Thelypteris aspidioides* and *fluminalis* in the American tropics, *Bolbitis heudelotii* in Africa, and *Asplenium subaquatile*, *Dipteris lobbiana*, *Osmunda angustifolia* and *Thelypteris salicifolia* in Malesia.

The *cloud forest* is the most constantly cool and moist type of rain forest. The canopy is often open and low and epiphytes are abundant on the trunks and branches of the small trees. Pteridophytes are often a prominent element of this vegetation, including epiphytic species of *Lycopodium* especially the pendent ones, *Asplenium*, *Elaphoglossum*, *Grammitis* and *Polypodium*. Species of many genera such as *Ctenitis*, *Dicksonia*, *Loxsomopsis*, *Plagiogyria*, *Selaginella*, and often Cyatheaceae are terrestrial among the tangled growth. In spite of locally high species diversity, the cloud forest as a whole has fewer species than the montane forest; it is smaller in area and has lower ecological diversity.

Habitat and life-form

Pteridophyte species are usually obligately terrestrial, rupestral or epiphytic in the rain forest, although, especially in the genus *Asplenium*, they

Fig. 17.4. Ferns in montane rain forest. The Cameroon Mountain, Federal Republic of Cameroon. The large species (Pteridaceae) are *Pteris togoensis* (left and right) and *Adiantum poiretii* (center). (Photo Alice F. Tryon.)

may be facultatively rupestral or epiphytic. The terrestrial habit is presumably more primitive and ecological specialization has occurred in the rupestral and epiphytic species. It is uncertain how often this basic evolution has occurred within the rain forest. Rupestral and epiphytic species usually occupy local sites where there are few other plants. However, some epiphytes may be crowded among many plants when light and water resources are abundant, as in the canopy of the cloud forest. High epiphytes are adapted to a dry season of usually short duration and also to possible desiccation during the day. Leaves of these species usually have a thick cuticle and often disarticulate if the dry period is seasonal. The most specialized of the epiphytes are those with the stem highly modified and often inhabited by ants. These ant-ferns are represented in America by the small genus *Solanopteris*, which has tuber-like, hollow stems borne along a creeping stem, and in the paleotropics

particularly by the genus *Lecanopteris* with indurated stems often forming large masses (Tryon, 1985). The role of ants with respect to the modification of the stem is uncertain. They may protect the plant from insect herbivory, serve as a source of additional nutrients, or the indurated stems may even serve for water storage (see also Benzing, Ch. 7, and Wallace, Ch. 13). A few pteridophytes are aquatic including *Acrostichum* (Fig. 17.5) in swamps and marshes and *Isoetes* in ephemeral pools or submerged in permanent water bodies. *Azolla* and *Salvinia* are floating aquatics, and *Ceratopteris* often is, although it may also be rooted in wet mud.

Among the variety of life-forms of pteridophytes two are most common. In one, species have a short erect or decumbent stem and a crown of leaves, as in *Diplazium*, *Dryopteris* and *Polystichum*. In the other common form the stem is long-creeping and frequently branched and bears rather widely

Fig. 17.5. *Acrostichum danaeifolium* (Pteridaceae) in aquatic border of lowland rain forest, Barro Colorado Island, Panama. (Photo Alice F. Tryon.)

spaced leaves. It may be epigeal as in *Microgramma*, *Pleopeltis* and *Polypodium loriceum*, or subterraean as in *Dennstaedtia*, *Hypolepis* and *Pteridium*. More unusual is the liana form with a high climbing leaf in *Lygodium* and *Salpichlaena*. Several genera have leaves which are scrambling, supported by other vegetation, rather than climbing. Examples are *Dicranopteris linearis*, *Eriosorus flexuosus* and *Odontosoria jenmanii*. A high climbing stem occurs in *Alsophila biformis*, *Bolbitis* species, *Lomagramma*, *Polybotrya* and *Teratophyllum*. Trees are the predominent life-form in the Cyatheaceae, with a single erect stem to 10 m or more tall and a crown of large leaves. The tree form also occurs, rarely, in *Ctenitis* and in *Thelypteris*. The least common is the shrub form developed especially by *Oleandra* species with an erect, short, branched stem and often tufted leaves.

Another aspect of life-form relates to the part of a plant — roots, stem, leaves — exposed to a particular environment. All of these major organs may be in essentially the same micro-environment, or some may be in a quite different micro-environment. Species of the cloud forest often have all parts of the plant in the same wet environment, such as small species of *Elaphoglossum*, *Grammitis*, *Hymenophyllum* and *Trichomanes*. Species of *Asplenium* and *Pleopeltis* that have creeping stems on wet rocks are other examples. Canopy epiphytes usually also have the basic organs in a similar environment. Most ferns, as in *Diplazium*, *Dryopteris* and Cyatheaceae have roots in the soil while the stem and leaves are above the substrate in a different environment. Species with high climbing stems as in *Polybotrya*, *Blechnum* and *Bolbitis* are of this type. Other ferns such as *Pteridium*, *Dennstadetia*, *Hypolepis* and *Pteris grandifolia* have the roots and stem below ground and the leaves in quite a different aerial environment.

HISTORY

Evolution of the living pteridophytes and geographic changes in their ranges are critical to a consideration of the biogeographic history of the group. The genus is the most appropriate taxonomic level for this discussion. The usually extensive range of families, and species ranges which are often small are not as useful for a biogeographic analysis involving a long period of time.

Analysis of the present ranges of genera in the tropical rain-forest regions suggests that several processes were instrumental in development of the present distributions. Fifty of the tropical rain-forest genera occur in all three major regions — America, Africa/Madagascar and Malesia — and an additional 40 occur in two of the three. These 90 widespread genera suggest a history related to continental drift or to migration. Endemic genera, however, suggest that ranges may be determined by other processes. The 115 genera endemic to one region include 45 in America, 5 in Africa/Madagascar, and 65 in Malesia. These endemics, as well as 45 other genera which occur in only one rain-forest region, but are not confined to it, suggest a history of evolution within one region or extinction in others. Four processes will be considered in relation to the history of the rain-forest pteridophytes: continental drift, migration, evolution and extinction.

Continental drift could be the primary factor determining generic ranges which include more than one of the major regions of tropical rain forest. These genera would necessarily be old, and persistent on the continental masses as they were displaced. The few fossil records and the uncertain association of fossils with living genera severely limit the utility of this source of data. Nevertheless, some pteridophyte families such as the Gleicheniaceae, Lycopodiaceae, Marattiaceae, Ophioglossaceae, Osmundaceae, Schizaeaceae and Selaginellaceae surely represent primitive groups of sufficient age to be represented on Pangea. Extant genera of these families may also be old and their present ranges may reflect the displacement of continents. However, other widespread tropical rain-forest genera such as *Antrophyum*, *Ctenitis*, *Diplazium*, *Elaphoglossum*, *Platycerium*, *Polystichum* and *Vittaria* are usually considered to represent younger,

derived groups. Concepts of fern evolution will need revision if these genera are considered to be Pangean elements.

Migration of a genus by gradual expansion of its range could lead to representation in more than one region. This requires the previous existence of suitable environmental conditions beyond the present rain-forest regions. There is evidence that both northern and southern routes were available in the early Tertiary, via Antarctica (Raven and Axelrod, 1974), via the Bering Straits (Wolfe, 1972; Tiffney, 1985a), and via the North Atlantic (Tiffney, 1985b). Genera that may have migrated by one of these routes include *Cibotium*, *Dicksonia* and *Plagiogyria* now with somewhat restricted ranges. Many of the pan-tropical genera also might have migrated in this manner.

Migration can also occur by long-distance dispersal of spores. There is ample evidence of the high dispersal and migration capacity of ferns from their occurrence on isolated oceanic islands. The importance of long-distance dispersal between continents is difficult to assess. Dispersal of spores is a continuous process that is most effective over short distances and becomes less frequent with increased distance. Recent dispersal between continents is suggested by the presence of at least 40 species or vicarious pairs in tropical America and tropical Africa (Tryon, 1986). These amphi-Atlantic disjunct ranges as in *Pleopeltis macrocarpa* and *Microgramma lycopodioides* in America and in Africa, were probably established rather recently because of the morphological similarities of the geographically distant populations.

Evolution within one area must be considered in relation to the genera endemic to a single tropical forest region. Some of the endemic genera, such as *Campyloneurum* and *Dicranoglossum* in America, and *Arcypteris*, *Pleocnemia* and *Pteridrys* centering in Malesia, are closely related to others in the same region and these may be assumed to have evolved in situ. Other genera may also have persisted within the region of their origin. However, these are difficult to identify without evidence of their close affinity to others of the region.

Extinction as a process is not well understood since an adequate fossil record is required as well as details of the paleo-environments. However, it may be decisive in the history of endemics. The fossil records of *Dipteris* and *Matonia* clearly document cases of extinction. Highly distinctive genera such as *Cystodium* and *Phanerosorus* undoubtedly have had their ranges molded through time by climatic changes and extinction.

The following sequence of historical events, which could account for the biogeography of tropical rain-forest pteridophytes, provides a framework for further investigations.

Most of the pteridophyte genera on Pangea had broad ranges which were disrupted with the separation of the continents. Some of them undoubtedly became extinct but others persisted in or near the present three major rain-forest regions. As new genera evolved they had the potential for range expansion into other regions, either by long-distance dispersal or by gradual migration at a time of suitable environment to the north or south. Long-distance dispersal would be most effective while the land masses were close and less effective as they came to their present positions. Evolution of genera and also extinction continued over time. Finally, late in biogeographical history, the extreme climates of the Pleistocene might have greatly altered previous ranges. The present distributions of the rain-forest genera have been molded by changing environments, restricting and reducing their range, and also by the inherent capacity of ferns to disperse and thereby extend their range.

ACKNOWLEDGEMENTS

I am indebted to Dr. Alice F. Tryon for the photographs and for critically reading the manuscript.

REFERENCES

Much of the data for this contribution has been obtained from a wide variety of floristic treatments. Only some of the general accounts of tropical rain forest Pteridophyta and special sources are included here.

Clausen, R.T., 1938. A monograph of the Ophioglossaceae. *Mem. Torrey Bot. Club*, 19: 1–177.

Hennipman, E., 1977. A monograph of the fern genus *Bolbitis*. *Leiden Bot. Ser.*, 2: 1–331.

Holttum, R.E., 1938. The ecology of tropical pteridophytes. In: F. Verdoorn (Editor), *Manual of Pteridology*. Nijhoff, The Hague, pp. 420–450.

Holttum, R.E., 1954. *Ferns of Malaya. A Revised Flora of Malaya, Vol. 2*. Govt. Printing Office, Singapore, pp. 1–643.

Holttum, R.E., 1982. Thelypteridaceae. *Flora Malesiana, Ser. II*, 1(5): 331–599.

Iwatsuki, K., 1972. Phytogeography of the pteridophytes in northern Thailand. *Acta Phytotaxon. Geobot.*, 25: 69–78.

Iwatsuki, K., Kato, M., Okamoto, M., Ueda, K. and Darnaedi, D., 1983. Botanical expedition to East Kalimantan during 15th June and 15th September 1981. In: T. Hidaka (Editor), *Taxonomical and Evolutionary Studies on the Biota in Humid Tropical Malesia, with Reference to Diversity of Species*. Dept. of Zoology, Kyoto Univ., pp. 31–69.

Johns, R.J., 1985. Altitudinal zonation of pteridophytes in Papuasia. *Proc. R. Soc. Edinburgh, Sect. B*, 86: 381–389.

Mayr, E. and O'Hara, R.J., 1986. The biogeographic evidence supporting the Pleistocene forest refugium hypothesis. *Evolution*, 40: 55–66.

Page, C.N., 1979. The diversity of ferns: an ecological perspective. In: A.F. Dyer (Editor), *The Experimental Biology of Ferns*. Academic Press, London, pp. 9–56.

Parris, B.S., 1983. A taxonomic revision of the genus *Grammitis* Swartz (Grammitidaceae: Filicales) in New Guinea. *Blumea*, 29: 13–222.

Raven, P.H. and Axelrod, D.I., 1974. Angiosperm biogeography and past continental movements. *Ann. Mo. Bot. Gard.*, 61: 539–673.

Seward, A.C., 1922. A study in contrasts: the present and past distribution of certain ferns. *J. Linn. Soc. Bot.*, 46: 219–240.

Smith, A.R., 1981. Pteridophytes. In: D.E. Breedlove (Editor), *Flora of Chiapas, part 2*. California Academy of Sciences, San Francisco, Calif., pp. 1–370.

Tiffney, B.H., 1985a. Perspectives on the origin of the floristic similarity between eastern Asia and eastern North America. *J. Arnold Arb.*, 66: 73–94.

Tiffney, B.H., 1985b. The Eocene North Atlantic land bridge: its importance in Tertiary and modern phytogeography of the northern hemisphere. *J. Arnold Arb.*, 66: 243–273.

Troll, C., 1968. Geo-ecology of the mountainous regions of the tropical Americas. *Colloq. Geogr.*, 9: 1–221.

Tryon, A.F., 1985. Spores of myrmecophytic ferns. *Proc. R. Soc. Edinburgh, Sect. B*, 86: 105–110.

Tryon, R., 1976. A revision of the genus *Cyathea*. *Contrib. Gray Herb. Harv. Univ.*, 206: 19–98.

Tryon, R., 1985. Fern speciation and biogeography. *Proc. R. Soc. Edinburgh, Sect. B*, 86: 353–360.

Tryon, R., 1986. The biogeography of species, with special reference to ferns. *Bot. Rev.*, 52(2): 118–156.

Tryon, R. and Conant, D.S., 1975. The ferns of Brazilian Amazonia. *Acta Amazon.*, 5: 23–34.

Tryon, R. and Gastony, G.J., 1975. The biogeography of endemism in the Cyatheaceae. *Br. Fern Gaz.*, 11: 73–79.

Tryon, R. and Tryon, A.F., 1982. *Ferns and Allied Plants*. Springer, New York, N.Y., 857 pp.

Van Steenis, C.G.G.J., 1981. *Rheophytes of the World*. Sijthoff and Noordhoff, Groningen, 405 pp.

Van Zinderen Bakker, E.M., 1967. Upper Pleistocene and

Holocene stratigraphy and ecology on the basis of vegetation changes in Sub-Saharan Africa. In: W.W. Bishop and J.D. Clark (Editors), *Background to Evolution in Africa*. Univ. of Chicago, Chicago, Ill., pp. 125–147.

Wolfe, J.A., 1972. An interpretation of Alaskan Tertiary floras. In: A. Graham (Editor), *Floristics and Paleofloristics of Asia and Eastern North America*. Elsevier, Amsterdam, pp. 201–233.

Chapter 18

THE CLIMBERS — LIANES AND VINES

ELWYN E. HEGARTY

INTRODUCTION

Most rain forests contain at least some climbers, but it is tempting to make both physical and mental detours around them when observing how a rain forest is constructed. Quantitative studies are made with considerable discomfort, and contain more inherent sources of error than is usual with studies of tree populations. It is therefore understandable that much of the published material concerning climbers as a group deals with the useful or ornamental species (for instance, Menninger, 1970; Herklots, 1976; Beekman, 1982; Beckett, 1983). There is also an increasing volume of literature on how climbers detract from the efficiency of timber production, and what can be done to control them before, during and after logging (Fox, 1968; Liew, 1973a; among others).

Even though they are regarded with a lack of enthusiasm, if not hostility, the climbers are of interest as the most abundant minority group in many tropical rain forests. They contribute up to half as much leaf to canopy biomass as the trees, and so are important in the maintenance of an enclosed environment at sub-canopy level, as well as in the processes of succession and cyclic renewal.

Though climbing plants may be found almost everywhere there is something to climb — even in xeric and arctic regions — they are largest, and most diverse, in the humid tropical lowlands. Gentry (1982) sampled a set of dry, moist and wet forests and found that liana diversity increased directly with precipitation (though remaining at about 20% of total species); liana density was relatively constant for all the tropical communities sampled.

Jacobs (1976) described practical aspects of studying lianes in field conditions, also summarising some of their striking features as a group. But it is still difficult to decide where many of the rambling species belong in forest succession, especially if single plants persist for long periods by cloning. It is symptomatic of the difficulty of studying climbers as a group that the works of Darwin (1875) and Schenck (1892–93) describing variously the behaviour of climbers, and their anatomy and distribution in families, are still among the more useful references.

This chapter will outline some of the methods used to classify climbers, and their distribution, form and behaviour when co-existing and competing with rain-forest trees.

CLASSIFICATION OF CLIMBERS

By general form

There are strong regional differences in use of the terms liane or liana. As well, the word "vine" is understood in Europe to mean *Vitis* spp., usually grapes, whereas elsewhere it is variously applied, and a "vine" may become a liane as its stems extend and become virtually leafless for great lengths. The term "climber" is used here as far as possible (following Whitmore, 1975) to include climbing vines, lianes, palms, bamboos and ferns, but not epiphytes (considered elsewhere in Ch. 7, 9, 13 and 16) or stranglers which descend rather than climb.

By method of climbing

Four main techniques are usually distinguished. Plants may be (1) scandent (scramblers), often possessing thorns or hooks; (2) they may climb by tendrils (tendrillar climbers), or (3) by adhesive organs such as roots (root or bole climbers); (4) most usually, they twine (twiners), using either the apical portions of the shoot, or twisting branches or petioles/petiolules. Many species exhibit several techniques at once or in sequence. Twiners may be further subdivided according to the direction of climbing. While the great majority of twining species climb anti-clockwise, wherever found, a few always twine clockwise. Genera such as *Dioscorea* may contain species of both kinds, but usually all species of a genus twine similarly. The climbing direction of many genera is given by Baillaud (1957). Other forms of climber do not conspicuously twine, and even the "water" shoots of twiners grow vertically at first, but twine later.

By size

Richards (1952, p. 104) stated that "from the ecological point of view, the method of climbing is less important than the size of the climber and the mean height which it reaches". He recognized two groups, not always distinct — large, almost always woody, lianes reaching the lower tree crowns, and smaller, mainly herbaceous climbers of shaded undergrowth. Each of these groups, as well as the groups of the following sections, contains scramblers, twiners, root climbers and tendrillar plants.

By light – shade preference

The evident differences in distribution of climbing species attributable to a light requirement were acknowledged by Grubb et al. (1963), who proposed the terms photophytic and skiophytic respectively for climbers of the upper canopy and of the zone below the bases of the upper tree crowns.

By climatically linked characters

Many climbers are deciduous. Box (1981, pp. 41 and 168–169) has classified climbers as: (1) tropical broad-evergreen lianas; (2) broad-evergreen vines; (3) broad-raingreen vines; and (4) broad-summergreen vines, and defined climatic tolerances for each.

By taxonomic affiliation

There are climbers in about half the angiosperm families, but estimates vary because of the many scandent forms which may be included with trees and shrubs. The climbing habit is a derived one — the trees, in developmental terms, being older than the climbers (Hutchinson, 1970, p. 10). Although climbers are present early in the fossil record, they are more characteristic of later and "advanced" families. Most belong to only a dozen or so dicotyledonous families (Menninger, 1970; Jacobs, 1976), some closely related. There are also some climbing gymnosperms, ferns and monocotyledons like palms, bamboos, lilies and orchids. The ferns and orchids include many epiphytic forms outside the scope of this chapter.

DISTRIBUTION IN FLORAS OF THE WORLD

The climbing habit has developed independently in many taxa, but the number of climbing species within families is very unevenly distributed. For example, most of the 350 species of Menispermaceae are climbers, but there are very few in the Myrtaceae, which contains over eight times as many species. Over 90% of climbers are tropical (often extending into the subtropics), and the families with most climbers are all pantropical. Their present distribution reflects past climates, water barriers and tectonic movements. For example, most of the Asian rattans do not extend beyond Malaysia and Indonesia (Whitmore, 1975, pp. 8–9, and Ch. 10). Climbing forms of *Piper* (Piperaceae) and Annonaceae abound in Southeast Asia, but are much outnumbered by shrubby and tree forms in tropical America.

The locations of some genera with substantial numbers of climbing species are shown in Table 18.1, but it must be stressed that this table gives no indication of abundance or breadth of distribution. Littoral species, especially, have fairly wide distribution areas (for instance, *Caesalpinia*, *Entada*, *Mucuna* spp.), whereas montane species may include many rather narrow endemics. Some widespread species, such as *Flagellaria indica* (Flagellariaceae) and *Malaisia scandens* (Moraceae) have few, or no close relatives — climbing or erect.

TABLE 18.1

Distribution of some genera with many tropical and subtropical climbing species (excluding aroids, ferns, orchids, parasites, and most smaller herbaceous climbers and epiphytes)

Family	America (north and south)	Africa, Mediterranean region	Asia, western Pacific region
Acanthaceae	+	*Thunbergia*	*Thunbergia*
Alstroemeriaceae	*Bomarea*	0	0
Annonaceae	+	*Artabotrys, Uvaria*	*Artabotrys, Uvaria*
Apocynaceae	*Mandevilla, Odontadenia*	*Landolphia, Strophanthus*	*Melodinus, Parsonsia*
Arecaceae	*Desmoncus*	+	*Calamus, Daemonorops, Korthalsia*
Aristolochiaceae	*Aristolochia*	+	*Aristolochia*
Asclepiadaceae	*Gonolobus, Oxypetalum*	*Ceropegia*	*Ceropegia, Hoya, Marsdenia*
Asteraceae	*Mikania, Mutisia*	*Gynura, Senecio*	*Gynura*
Bignoniaceae	*Arribidaea, Schlegelia,* etc.	+	*Pandorea, Tecomanthe*
Caesalpiniaceae	*Bauhinia*	+	*Bauhinia, Caesalpinia/Mezoneuron*
Cactaceae	*Hylocereus, Selenicereus*	0	0
Combretaceae	+	*Combretum*	+
Connaraceae	*Connarus, Rourea*	*Agelaea, Cnestis, Connarus*	*Agelaea, Connarus, Rourea*
Convolvulaceae	*Ipomoea, Jacquemontia, Merremia*	*Ipomoea, Jacquemontia, Merremia*	*Argyreia, Ipomoea, Jacquemontia, Merremia, Porana*
Cucurbitaceae	+ + + + +; *Gurania*	+ + + + +	+ + + + +
Cyclanthaceae	*Asplundia*	0	0
Dioscoreaceae	*Dioscorea, Rajania*	*Dioscorea*	*Dioscorea*
Fabaceae	*Dioclea, Machaerium*	*Rhynchosia*	*Dalbergia, Derris, Millettia, Pueraria*
Gnetaceae	*Gnetum*	+	*Gnetum*
Hippocrateaceae	*Hippocratea, Salacia*	*Salacia*	*Salacia*
Loganiaceae	*Strychnos*	*Strychnos*	*Strychnos*
Malpighiaceae	*Heteropteris, Stigmaphyllon*	*Tristellateia*	+
Marcgraviaceae	*Norantea, Souroubea*	0	0
Menispermaceae	+ + + +	+ + + + +	+ + + +
Mimosaceae	+	*Entada*	+
Moraceae	+	+	*Ficus*
Oleaceae	+	*Jasminum*	*Jasminum*
Pandanaceae	0	0	*Freycinetia*
Passifloraceae	*Passiflora*	*Adenia*	*Adenia, Passiflora*
Piperaceae	+	+	*Piper*
Poaceae (bamboos only)	*Arthrostylidium, Chusquea*	0	*Dinochloa, Schizostachyum*
Polygalaceae	*Securidaca*	+	+
Ranunculaceae	*Clematis*	*Clematis*	*Clematis*
Rhamnaceae	*Gouania*	*Gouania, Ventilago*	*Gouania, Ventilago*
Rosaceae	+	+	*Rosa, Rubus*
Rubiaceae	*Manettia, Sabicea*	*Canthium, Sabicea*	*Mussaenda, Uncaria*
Sapindaceae	*Paullinia, Serjania*	+	+
Smilacaceae	*Smilax*	*Smilax*	*Smilax*
Solanaceae	*Solandra, Solanum*	+	+
Tropaeolaceae	*Tropaeolum*	0	0
Verbenaceae	*Lantana, Petrea*	*Clerodendrum*	*Clerodendrum, Faradaya*
Vitaceae	*Cissus*	*Cissus*	*Cissus, Vitis, Tetrastigma*

Key: +   Present, but relatively few.
     + + + + +   Numerous genera, mostly small.
     0   Climbing forms absent.

In subtropical and montane areas, there are relatively few species of climber, and drought, cold and wind may be limiting factors here. In seasonally dry or sub-humid areas, such families as Asclepiadaceae, Convolvulaceae, Cucurbitaceae, Fabaceae, and Vitaceae are frequently well represented [including many "stragglers of open spaces rather than climbers in the bush" — Bews (1925), of South African climbers]. Climbing palms, bamboos and most semi-epiphytic species are usually absent in these areas. Climate-induced contraction of suitable habitats has presumably limited the number of climbing species in Africa and Australia.

THE CLIMBING FORM

Leaf and branching architecture

Leaves of rain-forest climbers tend to be similar in texture and size to those of the tree stratum they reach, but different in shape (Richards, 1952, p. 107). Such an observation is reinforced by the theoretical models of Givnish and Vermeij (1976) for energy-efficient liane leaves: cordate bases for sun-exposed sites, small area, short petioles and narrow bases for deep shade, and compound or deeply lobed leaves of the smallest effective size in the most exposed situations. The leaf architecture and size may vary greatly within a single plant, especially when leafy shoots are used in climbing, as in *Triphyophyllum peltatum* (Menninger, 1970).

When the climbers have reached their optimum height in relation to the forest canopy, and expand their foliage within that stratum, their branching architecture often approximates that of trees. Cremers (1973, 1974) has related the branching pattern of some climbing species to existing models for trees, and developed further models unique to climbers.

A feature of many woody climbers is the sharp differentiation between the short-internodal, often descending, flowering or vegetative branches, and the long-internodal, leaflessly extending canopy branches (sometimes called canes or sarments, both terms rather inexactly applied). Thus shade-intolerant climbers often fruit abundantly at the edges of gaps, while extensions from the upper canopy increase the area within which foliage may be placed.

The production of vigorous "water" shoots from positions near the base is often noted in woody and herbaceous climbers. Often there is "no obvious reason but maturity" when it occurs under closed forest, as in Apocynaceae, Bignoniaceae, Celastraceae or Fabaceae (Beekman, 1981a); such

reiterations are plagiotropic at first (that is, horizontally directed or suberect) — in contrast to the orthotropic (that is, erect) reiterations of climbers following disturbance (Beekman, 1981a) (Fig. 18.1). Reiteration is equated by Tomlinson (1983) with growth response to environmental circumstances.

Stems

Internal structure

The most obvious differences between the internal structure of stems of climbers and of trees are the vessel diameters and length, the vertical and tangential extent of medullary rays, and the arrangement of vascular and supporting tissues — histological features which have been described by Carlquist (1985). The width of vessels is unusually small in young stems (Haberlandt, 1914, p. 694). An abrupt change to production of larger vessels, which allow rapid rates of flow, takes place when leaf expansion begins; xylem parenchyma development greatly increases at the same time (Obaton, 1960).

The "anomalous" forms of secondary growth in climbers are often noted in stem sections. A number of common types of variation have been recognized and classified by Schenck (1892–93), Obaton (1960) and Metcalfe and Chalk (1983). In large climbers, a "ropey" profile may reflect an unusual vascular arrangement; for instance, in some Sapindaceae where detached sections of cambium may form separate units of secondary tissue. Tensile strength and flexibility are increased by partial or complete separation of vascular tissues into loosely twining strands.

External appearance

For identification of species, bark characters are useful, but cannot be relied on (Jacobs, 1976). They change as the plant grows, and there may be local differences related to site. Some useful key characters include bark colour, texture, odour, fissuring, slash characters, lenticel shape and arrangement, internodal and nodal profiles, stem flexibility and weight, and frequency of aerial roots and lichens. Climbers found in exposed situations are sometimes clothed in remarkably thick or laminated corky bark.

Fig. 18.1. Shoots from ground-level stem of *Legnephora moorei* (Menispermaceae) following bulldozing (Mt. Glorious, Australia).

Roots and tubers

While tubers are not characteristic of mature rain-forest vines (Janzen, 1975, p. 11), they are relatively common in species of seasonally dry areas, where complete loss of foliage by browsing or fire is likely (especially common in Asclepiadaceae, Dioscoreaceae, Menispermaceae and Vitaceae). The potential size and depth varies with species, and they may form under deeply buried rocks, on or near the surface, or even as bulbils on stems. The ability of many tall rain-forest climbers to form occasional "sinker" roots from stems in contact with the soil enables their indefinite presence in a area even if the original stem decays. Stolons with numerous roots are characteristic of herbaceous twining Convolvulaceae and Fabaceae,

and of young shade-demanding bole climbers. Peñalosa (1984) discussed the methods of vegetative spread, and stem architecture, of two tropical climbers.

Free-hanging aerial roots are common in Marcgraviaceae, Moraceae and Vitaceae. Van den Honert (1941) reported that diurnal changes in the foliar environment of *Cissus sicyoides* (Vitaceae) led swiftly to variation in the thickness and growth rate of its aerial roots.

Ecophysiological adaptations

The distinctive morphological and behavioural characters described above also entail physiological adaptations to a lianescent form which have been little investigated in mature plants — except for some species of economic importance such as grapevines, for which extensive data exist (see, for example, Smart and Coombe, 1983).

Climbers typically have high water conductivity, and are particularly vulnerable to drought, frost and nutrient deficiency (Beekman, 1981a). The maximum rates of photosynthesis in (cultivated) *Vitis vinifera* (grape) leaves are among the higher values reported for C_3 plants (Smart and Coombe, 1983). From data so far published (for instance, Krenzfer et al., 1975), climbers are usually C_3 plants; however, some of the succulent Asclepiadaceae (*Hoya* spp.) are CAM climbers (Winter et al., 1983).

Climbers of forest margins, typically tendrillar plants or twiners, with most of their leaves in full sun, must survive periodic desiccation. They are usually assisted by deep primary and sinker roots, and often develop stolons and tubers; they readily coppice and sucker following setbacks. They are likely to have pulvinar (compound or peltate) leaves, with high cuticular resistance, and stomata mostly on abaxial surfaces — and to be wholly or partially deciduous at times.

Inside humid closed rain forest, the predominantly evergreen, herbaceous climbing species are not adapted to exposure, and so are vulnerable to sudden opening of the canopy.

Climbers and scramblers contain an impressive array of phytotoxins. These include picrotoxins, saponins, alkaloids and cardiac glycosides. The poisonous (to humans) qualities of various parts of climbers of the Apocynaceae, Aristolochiaceae, Asclepiadaceae, Dioscoreaceae, Fabaceae, Menispermaceae and Solanaceae are well known [Jacobs (1976), and many individual references and herbarium notes]. Sometimes toxicities are lower in cultivated populations than in wild plants (such as *Dioscorea alata*, *D. bulbifera*; Verdcourt and Trump, 1969).

Perhaps the relatively high leaf area required by a climber in proportion to the rest of the plant (Table 18.2) puts the individual at high risk if much is lost to predators, fires, or by stem breakage. This

TABLE 18.2

Biomass of climbing species associated with tropical forest

Region (reference)	Plant community	Biomass (t ha^{-1})					
		total above-ground			leaf only		
		climbers	total	(%)	climbers	total	(%)
SOUTH AMERICA							
Brazil (Fittkau and Klinge, 1973)	Central Amazonian rain forest	46(fw)	731(fw)	6	–	–	–
French Guiana (Beekman, 1981a, b)	Evergreen tropical rain forest	13	458	3	1	8	11
Venezuela (Klinge and Herrera, 1983)	Tall caatinga forest	2	277	1	–	–	–
(Putz, 1983)	Tierre firme evergreen rain forest	15	351	4	1	n.d.	–
AFRICA							
Gabon (Hladik, 1974)	Moist evergreen forest	–	–	–	1.6[1]	4.4[1]	33–39
Ghana (Greenland and Kowal, 1960)	Moist semi-deciduous forest	14	308	4	–	–	–
ASIA							
Malaysia (Kato et al., 1978)	High dipterocarp forest	9	475	2	0.5	8	6
South Thailand (Ogawa et al., 1965)	Seasonal evergreen forest	20	404	5	2	8	25

[1]Fresh weight of litter.

may have resulted in selective development of phytotoxins noxious to animals, insects, nematodes, fungi and bacteria, appropriate to the risk, and placed equally selectively within the plant. The frequency with which roots of climbers are reported to be toxic suggests that the specialized risks of a climbing form may necessitate a high level of chemical protection of below-ground resources.

CLIMBERS IN RAIN-FOREST STRUCTURE

Biomass and abundance

Some values for biomass of climbers are given in Table 18.2. While the results are at least comparable for widely separated areas, there are many sources of potential error in this type of quantitative study. For example, perhaps 30% of the material may be blown away or buried during destructive sampling (Ogawa et al., 1965); the distinction between epiphytes and climbers is variously drawn; and seasonal variation due to herbivores and leaf shedding is unknown. As well, the distribution of climbers in rain forest is normally patchy, and little indication can be given of whether high values are related to canopy gaps or genuine abundance.

The leaf area index of climbers is often relatively high — about 10, 20 and 30% of the total value for the canopy in studies mentioned by Putz (1983). But the ratio of leaf-to-stem biomass in climbers is intrinsically higher than in trees (Gentry, 1983), so it is not surprising that the total above-ground biomass of climbers is only of the order of 1 to 4% of the total stand value. The total leaf biomass of a stand is little influenced by presence of lianes; where a tree supports a heavy mass of climber leaf, its own leaf mass is correspondingly reduced (Ogawa et al., 1965; Kira and Ogawa, 1971).

Allometric relationships for climbers depend strongly on species involved. The total dry weight of leaf increases much more rapidly with stem basal area in lianes than in trees (Putz, 1983). The proportion of leaf to total stem biomass of individual climbers decreases as stems thicken, yet 36% of the total liane leaf biomass in an area of 0.25 ha was contributed by the three largest individuals (Beekman, 1981a).

Canopy trees do not all carry lianes or vines, the crowns of taller trees being often clear of climbers (Richards, 1952, p. 70). Various studies have estimated the percentage of canopy trees carrying lianes at up to 50%. Beekman (1981a), in Venezuela, found that seventeen trees, accounting for 35% of tree leaf biomass, supported 89% of the liane leaf biomass.

Some records of numbers of climbing stems (usually not defining numbers of plants) are given in references listed in Table 18.3. While larger diameter size-classes have a close to Poissonian distribution (Rollet, 1971), there are remarkably few climbers in intermediate height-classes of 4 to 24 m, except at gap edges (Putz, 1984a).

Climbing species vary considerably in gregariousness. While juvenile plants, and many herbaceous species, may be locally very abundant, the larger woody climbers are often widely separated within the rain forest. Individual plants of families such as Cucurbitaceae, Menispermaceae and Passifloraceae are often widely spaced (Gilbert, 1975), with local species diversity strikingly and consistently low.

Analysis of mineral composition of climbers, compared with that of associated trees, suggests

TABLE 18.3

References dealing with floristic and numerical abundance of climbers associated with tropical forest

AMERICA, WEST INDIES	
Brazil	Cain et al. (1956)
Puerto Rico	Smith (1970)
Ecuador	Grubb et al. (1963)
French Guiana	Beekman (1981a, 1981b)
Panama	Croat (1978)
	Putz (1984a)
Venezuela	Rollet (1971)
+ various areas	Gentry (1982, 1983)
	Emmons and Gentry (1983)
AFRICA	
Ghana	Hall and Swaine (1981)
Gabon; Nigeria	Caballé (1984)
	Emmons and Gentry (1983)
ASIA	
Malaysia	Fox (1968, 1969)
	Gentry (1982)
	Kochummen and Ng (1977)
	Proctor et al. (1983)
Thailand; Kampuchea	
	Kira and Ogawa (1971)

that a general similarity exists (Greenland and Kowal, 1960; Grubb and Edwards, 1982). The latter authors reported a rather high calcium content of stems, but not leaves, of some New Guinea climbers.

Stratification and the effects of disturbance

The stratification of climbing synusiae in rain forest is inextricably bound up with successional processes. Eggeling (1947) observed three synusiae in Ugandan rain forest: (a) a layer at 20 to 24 m or more; (b) a layer of tall strong, but not woody, climbers mostly 9 to 15 m tall; and (c) a layer of small, mostly herbaceous climbers, seldom taller than 7 to 9 m.

Stratum (a) is absent from colonizing forest, reaches a peak during intermediate successional

stages, and then declines in the mature stage. Only the middle layer (b) is reliably present, with the lowest synusia gradually disappearing from the forest. Whitmore (1975) distinguished three vertically stratified synusiae of bole-climbers (that is, climbers adhering by roots), which increase in number and diversity with age of the forest. Vareschi (1980) depicted four ways in which climbers place their foliage upon host trees: (a) clinging on the bole; (b) in the inner crown; (c) above and on the crown; and (d) as hanging curtains, linking crowns and sides of two or more trees. Beekman (1981a) also illustrated the liane – tree relationship with emphasis on architectural interaction. Some of the above features of stratification of climbers in and near rain forest are shown in Fig. 18.2.

Both Budowski (1970) and Hall and Swaine

Fig. 18.2. Schematic profile of tropical rain forest to show distribution of foliage and seedlings of climbers.

(1981) related the successional status of forest to the size (and height) of climbers present. Gentry (1982) also suggested that liane density and stand maturity were negatively correlated, while observing that lianes are not always characteristic of disturbed areas. It must be assumed that the usual effects of chance, competition and site character apply to climbers as well as to trees, but the presence of climbers following disturbance is more often commented upon than their absence.

CLIMBERS AS COMPETITORS WITH RAIN-FOREST TREES

Ways of climbing

In rain forests of comparable structure, a similar array of climbing techniques is found, often having evolved in different families but fulfilling the same roles in succession. While both twiners and tendrillar plants are usually present within rain forest, twiners are better suited to the interior of humid tropical forest than tendrillar plants (Darwin, 1875). Twiners climb the thin bare vertical stems, up to 10 cm diameter, which are abundant in tropical rain forest, with great facility. The growing tip of the twiner is always close to the stem being climbed. In contrast, tendrillar plants tend to grow obliquely, with tendrils attaching in various planes, often to highly temporary supports (Fig. 18.3). However, such a method is ideal for traversing the sides and tops of shrubs and trees, and allows some measure of freedom from breaking as the supports sway in winds.

Climbers with branch attachments close to their main axis ascend vertical stems almost as well as twiners (*Bauhinia*, *Strychnos*, *Rauwenhoffia* spp., with attachments variously derived). Woody scramblers, often armed with spines or thorns, are common in sunny patches of seasonally dry forests, but may persist in deepening shade if their

Fig. 18.3. Expanding shoot of *Cissus sterculiifolia* (Vitaceae) moving through rain-forest understorey (Mt. Glorious, Australia).

foliage remains in the sun (like *Cudrania conchin-chinensis*). Scandent climbers without such modifications lean on shrubs and small trees, with which they are sometimes classified. Semi-epiphytes and other bole-climbers are characteristic of areas of tall trees and deep shade, and seldom move easily from tree to tree.

Special relationships of climbers with palms and buttressed trees

It is occasionally observed that few climbers are associated with palms or buttressed trees, and there has been some recent interest in whether this is true, and if so, why (Strong, 1977; Black and Harper, 1979; Putz, 1980, 1984b; Boom and Mori, 1982). Figures abstracted from the survey by Emmons and Gentry (1983) giving numbers of palms and lianes in many areas of rain forest suggest that some inverse relationship is usual (but climbing palms complicate the argument). While climbers may experience difficulty in climbing, and staying up on various kinds of tree and palm stems (Putz, 1980, 1984b), further studies may consider more particularly the relative diversity of both trees and lianes in areas where palms and/or buttressed trees are abundant, and the possible effects of poor soil aeration (waterlogging vs. temporary inundation) which may allow monocotyledonous species to compete more favourably than usual with dicotyledonous species (Walter, 1964, p. 165). Woody species, including climbers, although abundant nearby, regenerate very poorly in areas where there are many palms (pers. obs., 1983).

Climber tangles

In most tropical rain forest, early succession is marked by an abundance of climbing stems, those derived from existing plants being at some competitive advantage over seedlings. Small gaps, created when only one or two trees fall, are not as likely to be overrun by climber tangles as are the large swathes cut by cyclones, cultivation or logging. Jacobs (1976), supporting Fox (1968), and Kochummen and Ng (1977) observed that the end result of such radical damage is a lower species diversity of climbers, not added species richness. The same authors suggested that the damping effect of climbers on succession is temporary, as

only pioneer tree species of limited life expectancy are shaded out by climbers — not later successional species, which tolerate shade better. However, climbing bamboos, or naturalized scramblers such as *Lantana camara*, may seriously delay succession (Willis, 1949; Liew, 1973b). Other references to papers dealing with climber tangles and liane forests are listed by Rollet (1971, p. 65; see also Prance, Ch. 6, and Hamilton, Ch. 8).

Physical interactions between stems

When twiners ascend growing saplings, the resulting stem contact may affect both, but infrequently proves fatal to either. A twiner may constrict the growth of a sapling, by interfering with downward translocation; the sapling stem bulges over the twiner and encloses it from above, meanwhile changing from vertical to oblique translocation paths parallel to the stem of the twiner (Lutz, 1943). Meanwhile the twiner, whose enclosed shoot will die as a result, (with possible exceptions involving strangling figs), develops one or more new climbing shoots from lower axillary buds, which may, if reserves permit, retrace the path of the enclosed stem rather more easily because of the rougher profile (Fig. 18.4). In the alternative case, where the growing sapling snaps the twining stem (because of its inextensibility) axillary buds are also called into use. Compared with trees, vines have a disproportionately higher tendency to produce supernumerary buds — that is, extra reserve meristems (Tomlinson, 1983, p. 18) — which may facilitate recovery.

Mortality of trees and shrubs following shading or weighting by foliage of climbers is commonly observed, especially following disturbance. But lianes show a higher mortality than trees, when suppressed, in later stages of succession (Beekman, 1981a). Bole climbers are not subject to enclosure or snapping, as they do not encircle boles, and may even detach on reaching the canopy. But, unlike twiners, they are frequently associated with only a single large tree, whose suitability is critical to the survival of the climber. The skototropic (dark-seeking) juvenile behaviour described by Strong and Ray (1975) for *Monstera gigantea* seedlings appears common in rain-forest bole climbers (Jones and Gray, 1977 p. 45; Hegarty and Clifford, 1984).

Fig. 18.4. Enclosure of a twiner by a sapling, with subsequent recovery of the climber from axillary buds. Ulu Gombak Field Station, University of Malaysia.

The value to trees of resident ant populations in repelling vines in Central America is described by Janzen (1966).

FLOWERING, DISPERSAL, GERMINATION AND PERSISTENCE

From studies on Barro Colorado Island, Croat (1978) indicated that the onset of the dry season precipitates flowering in many lianes and herbaceous vines, and that as a group the climbing species reach their peak of flowering a little earlier than the arboreal plants. Though some largely climbing families (such as Dioscoreaceae, Menispermaceae, and Smilacaceae) contain many dioecious climbers, dioecism in climbers is not normally high. Where it does occur, a male-biased sex ratio is sometimes observed, with extended flowering seasons in male plants. Croat (1979) listed species with unisexual flowers in the Barro Colorado flora. They included 21 dioecious, 31 monoecious climbers (mostly vines) and 23 polygamous species (all of them lianes, and including 21 species of Sapindaceae) out of a total of 265 climbers.

The fruits and seeds of climbers have been reported to be dispersed in similar ways to those of other life forms of the same strata — with a bias towards wind dispersal in the upper canopy (Keay, 1957). But Gentry (1982) found that wind dispersal was substantially commoner for climbers than for canopy trees in dry to moist Central and South American forests, and was still (but to a lesser extent) the commonest way in wet forests of Ecuador and Colombia. Bird dispersal was similar for lianes and canopy trees, but mammal dispersal less common for climbers than trees.

Wind-dispersed species in general bear fruit in the dry season, and their seeds are dispersed en masse on days with low humidity (Gómez-Pompa and Vázquez-Yanes, 1981). Plumed seeds (as in Asclepiadaceae) travel further than winged seeds (as in Dipterocarpaceae) (Ridley, 1930).

Bats, reptiles and water are among other reported vectors of dispersal of seeds of climbers. Garwood (1983) found that seed dispersal of climbers reached a peak when dispersal of seeds of canopy trees was temporarily declining. Foster (1982) found that while canopy trees had seeds of a broad range of weights, over half of 80 liane species collected had seeds of between 0.01 and 0.1 g. While seeds in this range will often germinate in darkness (pers. obs., 1983), they are seldom successful in the deep shade of rain forest because of such problems as litter-fall, predation and shading of the shoot. The mean dormancy for seeds of 42 species of liane in Panama was similar to that of canopy trees, although the peak was a little more extended (Garwood, 1983).

Viable germination of lianes in rain forest is commonly hypogeal or cryptogeal, with fast elevation of the shoot tip to 10 cm or so, and subsequent leisurely growth until the sudden onset of climbing.

Estimates of the proportion of seedlings in wet lowland forest which are climbers range from 11 to 18% (Putz, 1984a). Some monocotyledonous species germinate ubiquitously (such as *Calamus*:

Wang, 1961; Whitmore, 1974), but once established may grow very slowly. Similarly in woody dicotyledonous climbers, climbing may not commence for a period of years (for instance, *Embelia australiana*, Myrsinaceae, pers. obs. 1972–1984). Very low seedling survival rates are quoted by Young (1984) for *Mucuna urens* in Costa Rica. Predation of the single shoot tip of juvenile climbers is potentially lethal (Janzen, 1971).

Three germination-survival patterns for climbers have been defined (UNESCO, 1978, p. 124): (a) light-demanding species which do not regenerate in closed forest and have a very sporadic distribution; (b) relatively shade-tolerant species with a weak regeneration but rather high survival; and (c) shade-tolerant species with abundant regeneration but relatively low survival (illustrated in Fig. 2).

Longevity of individuals is difficult to estimate, but in Central America Budowski (1970) identified forest climbers of 20 cm diameter with a late phase of succession. Many tendrillar and twining species persist for extended periods by suckering and cloning, with no effective regeneration from seeds in their vicinity — for instance, two twiners observed by Peñalosa (1984).

NATURALIZED CLIMBERS

It is impossible to ignore the success of exotic climbers in tropical and subtropical areas close to settlements. On islands with a limited flora, either local or introduced species may be troublesome. Instances are given by Willis (1949, pp. 406–410), Mueller-Dombois (1975, p. 360), Monsi and Ogawa (1977), UNESCO (1978) and Haridasan et al. (1981).

Some of the numerous species which flourish as introductions in many areas of the tropics and subtropics include *Anredera cordifolia* (Madeira vine), *Cryptostegia grandiflora* (rubber vine), *Pueraria* spp. (including kudzu), and several species of *Cardiospermum*, *Doxantha/Macfadyena*, *Ipomoea*, *Lantana*, and *Passiflora*. The identification of such species is often somewhat difficult. Each can form a curtain of foliage over disturbed areas and forest edges, and suppress competing native species. Nearly all such species are heliophytes (sun plants) and an impressive number have spread when introduced to gardens from Central and South America. The absence of natural restraints on such climbers in humid areas may often result from their distastefulness to local predators.

DISCUSSION

Climbers depend on the involuntary support and protection of the trees with which they are associated. The integrity of the forest is maintained in an uneasy truce, as the result of a long period of co-evolution of trees and climbers. Some of the more obvious similarities between trees and climbers are:

> taxonomic origins, succession of species (with increasing woodiness and longevity), stratification, vulnerability to habitat change, and many aspects of regeneration.

Differences between trees and climbers include: size and population structure; foliar arrangement and deployment; allometric relationships — such as leaf : stem biomass, surface : volume ratio; stem structure, and readiness to coppice, sucker and clone; some aspects of phenology and dispersal.

There is still a very limited understanding of the less visible aspects of competition between climbers and trees. As climbers are essentially opportunists, it may be expected that a high degree of plasticity enhances their prospects of colonizing habitats which are less than ideal. Such morphological plastic characters — size of vegetative parts; number of shoots, leaves and flowers; elongation of stems, and hairiness (from those listed by Bradshaw, 1965) — may be highly variable in climbing species. Their range of physiological plasticity, when investigated, may often be found to be just as wide.

The various forms of climber — twiners, scramblers, tendrillar and root-climbers — occupy somewhat different niches in rain-forest succession, but there are many areas of overlap because of variable environmental tolerances and life expectancy, and the versatility of climbers in employing more than one method of climbing at once, or in sequence.

Climbers are difficult to study in natural conditions, but the more interesting and virtually unexplored aspects of their relationship to other components of rain-forest ecosystems include the physiological adaptations which a climbing form requires, and the protective mechanisms, especially phytotoxins, which assist the survival of plants whose foliage and root systems are rather distantly and insecurely related.

REFERENCES

Baillaud, L., 1957. *Recherches sur les mouvements spontanes des plantes grimpantes*. Thesis 1, Faculté des Sciences de Besançon. Carrère, Rodez, 235 pp.

Beckett, K.A., 1983. *Climbing Plants*. Croom Helm, London, 178 pp.

Beekman, F., 1981a. *Structural and Dynamic Aspects of the Occurrence and Development of Lianes in the Tropical Rain Forest*. Agricultural Univ., Wageningen, 45 pp.

Beekman, F., 1981b. Biomasse des lianes en forêt primaire dans la region de la piste de St. Elie. *Bull. de Liaison du Groupe de Travail — L'Ecosystème forestier Guyanais (étude et mise en valeur) C.T.F.T./I.N.R.A./Muséum/O.R.S.T.O.M.*, 3: 38–39.

Beekman, F., 1982. *Bibliography on Rattans*. Rijksinstituut voor Onderzoek in de Bos- en Landschapsbouw "de Dorchkamp", Wageningen, 286: 5–26.

Bews, J.W., 1925. *Plant Forms and their Evolution in South Africa*. Longmans Green, London, 199 pp.

Black, H.L. and Harper, K.T., 1979. The adaptive value of buttresses to tropical trees; additional hypotheses. *Biotropica*, 11: p. 240.

Boom, B.M. and Mori, S.A., 1982. Falsification of two hypotheses on liana exclusion from tropical trees possessing buttresses and smooth bark. *Bull. Torrey Bot. Club*, 109: 447–450.

Box, E.O., 1981. *Macroclimate and Plant Forms: an Introduction to Predictive Modelling in Phytogeography*. (Tasks for Vegetation Science, 1) Junk, The Hague, 258 pp.

Bradshaw, A.D., 1965. Evolutionary significance of phenotypic plasticity in plants. *Adv. Genet.*, 13: 115–155.

Budowski, G., 1970. The distinction between old secondary and climax species in tropical Central American lowland forests. *Trop. Ecol.*, 11: 44–48.

Caballé, G., 1984. Essai sur la dynamique des peuplements de lianes ligneuses d'une forêt du nord-est du Gabon. *Rev. Ecol. (Terre Vie)*, 39: 3–35.

Cain, S.A., Castro, G.M. de O., Murça Pires, J. and Da Silva, N.T., 1956. Application of some phytosociological techniques to Brazilian rain forest. *Am. J. Bot.*, 43: 911–941.

Carlquist, S., 1985. Observations on functional wood histology of vines and lianas: vessel dimorphism, tracheids, vasicentric tracheids, narrow vessels, and parenchyma. *Aliso*, 11: 139–157.

Cremers, G., 1973. Architecture de quelques lianes d'Afrique tropicale. 1. *Candollea*, 28: 249–280.

Cremers, G., 1974. Architecture de quelques lianes d'Afrique tropicale. 2. *Candollea*, 29: 57–110.

Croat, T.B., 1978. *Flora of Barro Colorado Island*. Stanford Univ. Press, Stanford, Calif., 943 pp.

Croat, T.B., 1979. The sexuality of the Barro Colorado Island flora (Panama). *Phytologia*, 42: 319–348.

Darwin, C., 1875. *The Movements and Habits of Climbing Plants*. Murray, London, 208 pp.

Eggeling, W.J., 1947. Observations on the ecology of the Budongo rain forest, Uganda. *J. Ecol.*, 34: 20–87.

Emmons, L.H. and Gentry, A.H., 1983. Tropical forest structure and the distribution of gliding and prehensile-tailed vertebrates. *Am. Nat.*, 121: 513–524.

Fittkau, E.J. and Klinge, H., 1973. On biomass and trophic structure of the Central Amazonian rain forest ecosystem. *Biotropica*, 5: 2–14.

Foster, R.B., 1982. The seasonal rhythm of fruitfall on Barro Colorado Island. In: E.C. Leigh, A.S. Rand and D.M. Windsor (Editors), *The Ecology of a Tropical Forest*. Smithsonian Inst. Press, Washington, D.C., pp. 151–172.

Fox, J.E.D., 1968. Logging Damage and the influence of climber cutting prior to logging in the lowland dipterocarp forest of Sabah. *Malay. For.*, 31: 326–347.

Fox, J.E.D., 1969. Climbers in the lowland dipterocarp forest. *Commonw. For. Rev.*, 48: 196–198.

Garwood, N.C., 1983. Seed germination in a seasonal tropical forest in Panama: a community study. *Ecol. Monogr.*, 53: 159–181.

Gentry, A.H., 1982. Patterns of neotropical plant species diversity. *Ecol. Biol.*, 15: 1–84.

Gentry, A.H., 1983. Lianas and the "paradox" of contrasting latitudinal gradients in wood and litter production. *Trop. Ecol.*, 24: 63–67.

Gilbert, L.E., 1975. Ecological consequences of a coevolved mutualism between butterflies and plants. In: L.E. Gilbert and P.H. Raven (Editors), *Coevolution of Animals and Plants*. Univ. of Texas Press, Austin, Tex., pp. 210–240.

Givnish, T.J. and Vermeij, G.J., 1976. Sizes and shapes of liane leaves. *Am. Nat.*, 110: 743–778.

Gómez-Pompa, A. and Vázquez-Yanes, C., 1981. Successional studies of a rainforest in Mexico. In: D.C. West, H.H. Shugart and D.B. Botkin (Editors), *Forest Succession: Concepts and Applications*. Springer, New York, N.Y., pp. 246–266.

Greenland, D.J. and Kowal, J.M.L., 1960. Nutrient content of the moist tropical forest of Ghana. *Plant Soil*, 12: 154–174.

Grubb, P.J. and Edwards, P.J., 1982. Studies of mineral cycling in a montane rain forest in New Guinea, 3. *J. Ecol.*, 70: 623–648.

Grubb, P.J., Lloyd, J.R., Pennington, T.D. and Whitmore, T.C., 1963. A comparison of montane and lowland rainforest in Ecuador. 1. The forest structure, physiognomy and floristics. *J. Ecol.*, 51: 567–601.

Haberlandt, G., 1914. *Physiological Plant Anatomy*. Macmillan, London, 777 pp.

Hall, J.B. and Swaine, M.D., 1981. *Distribution and Ecology of Vascular Plants in a Tropical Rain Forest. Forest Vegetation in Ghana*. (Geobotany, 1) Junk, The Hague, 383 pp.

Haridasan, K., Kumar, Y. and Rao, R.R., 1981. Enumeration of some important forest weeds of Meghalaya with special emphasis on their role and distribution. *J. Econ. Tax. Bot.*, 2: 161–171.

Hegarty, E.E. and Clifford, H.T., 1984. Climbing angiosperms in the Australian flora. In: G.L. Werren and A.P. Kershaw

(Editors), *Australian National Rainforest Study Report to the World Wildlife Fund (Australia) Volume 1. Proc. Workshop on the Past, Present and Future of Australian Rainforests, Griffith University (1983)*. Dept. Geography, Monash Univ., Melbourne, for Australian Conservation Foundation, pp. 238–250.

Herklots, G., 1976. *Flowering Tropical Climbers*. Dawson Science History Publ., Folkestone, 194 pp.

Hladik, A., 1974. Importance des lianes dans la production foliare de la forêt équatoriale du nord-est du Gabon. *C.R. Acad. Sci. Paris, Sér. D*, 278: 2527–2530.

Hutchinson, J., 1970. *The Genera of Flowering Plants. 1.* Clarendon, Oxford, 516 pp.

Jacobs, M., 1976. The study of lianas. *Flora Malesiana Bull.*, 29: 2610–2618.

Janzen, D.H., 1966. Coevolution of mutualism between ants and acacias in Central America. *Evolution*, 20: 249–275.

Janzen, D.H., 1971. Escape of juvenile *Dioclea megacarpa* (Leguminosae) vines from predators in a deciduous tropical forest. *Am. Nat.*, 103: 97–112.

Janzen, D.H., 1975. *Ecology of Plants in the Tropics.* (Studies in Biology 58) Edward Arnold, London, 66 pp.

Jones, D.L. and Gray, B., 1977. *Australian Climbing Plants.* Reed, Sydney, N.S.W., 166 pp.

Kato, R., Tadaki, Y. and Ogawa, H., 1978. Plant biomass and growth increment studies in Pasoh forest. *Malay. Nat. J.*, 30: 211–224.

Keay, R.W.J., 1957. Wind dispersed species in a Nigerian forest. *J. Ecol.*, 45: 471–478.

Kira, T. and Ogawa, H., 1971. Assessment of primary productivity in tropical and equatorial forests. In: *Proc. Brussels Symposium (1969): Productivity of Forest Ecosystems*. UNESCO, Paris, pp. 309–321.

Klinge, H. and Herrera, R., 1983. Phytomass structure of natural plant communities on spodosols in southern Venezuela: the tall Amazon caatinga forest. *Vegetatio*, 53: 65–84.

Kochummen, K.M. and Ng, F.S.P., 1977. Natural plant succession after farming in Kepong. *Malay. For.*, 40: 61–78.

Krenzfer, E.G., Moss, D.N. and Crookston, R.K., 1975. Carbon dioxide compensation points of flowering plants. *Plant Physiol.*, 56: 194–206.

Liew, T.C., 1973a. The practicability of climber cutting and tree marking prior to logging as a silvicultural tool in the management of Dipterocarp forests in Sabah. *Malay. For.*, 36: 5–19.

Liew, T.C., 1973b. Eradication of climbing bamboo in dipterocarp forests of Sabah. *Malay. For.*, 36: 243–246.

Lutz, H.J., 1943. Injuries to trees caused by Celastrus and Vitis. *Bull. Torrey Bot. Club*, 70: 436–439.

Menninger, E.A., 1970. *Flowering Vines of the World*. Hearthside, New York, N.Y., 410 pp.

Metcalfe, J.R. and Chalk, L., 1983. *Anatomy of the Dicotyledons Vol. 2.* Clarendon, Oxford, 297 pp.

Monsi, M. and Ogawa, K., 1977. Ecological considerations of some characteristics of liana communities. In: A. Miyawaki and R. Tüxen (Editors), *Vegetation Science and Environmental Protection*. Meruzen, Tokyo, pp. 325–336.

Mueller-Dombois, D., 1975. Some aspects of island ecosystem

analysis. In: F.B. Golley and E. Medina (Editors), *Tropical Ecological Systems*. Springer, Berlin, pp. 353–366.

Obaton, M., 1960. Les lianes ligneuses à structure anormale des forêts denses d'Afrique occidentale. *Ann. Sci. Nat. Bot. Ser.*, 12(1): 1–220.

Ogawa, H., Yoda, K., Ogino, K. and Kira, T., 1965. Comparative ecological studies of three main types of forest vegetation in Thailand, 2: Plant biomass. *Nature Life S.E. Asia*, 4: 49–80.

Peñalosa, J., 1984. Basal branching and vegetative spread in two tropical rain forest lianas. *Biotropica*, 16: 1–9.

Proctor, J., Anderson, J.L., Chai, P. and Vallack, H.W., 1983. Ecological studies in four contrasting lowland rain forests in Gunung Mulu National Park, Sarawak. 1. Forest environment, structure and floristics. *J. Ecol.*, 71: 237–260.

Putz, F.E., 1980. Lianas vs trees. *Biotropica*, 12: 224–225.

Putz, F.E., 1983. Liana biomass and leaf area of a "tierra firme" forest in the Rio Negro basin, Venezuela. *Biotropica*, 15: 185–189.

Putz, F.E., 1984a. The natural history of lianas on Barro Colorado Island, Panama. *Ecology*, 65: 1713–1724.

Putz, F.E., 1984b. How trees avoid and shed lianas. *Biotropica*, 16: 19–23.

Richards, P.W., 1952. *The Tropical Rain Forest*. Cambridge Univ. Press, Cambridge, 450 pp.

Ridley, H.N., 1930. *The Dispersal of Plants Throughout the World*. Reeve, Ashford, 744 pp.

Rollet, B., 1971. La regeneración natural en bosque denso siempreverde de llanura de al Guayana Venezolana. *Bol. Inst. For. Lat. -Am. Invest. Capacit.* (Merida, Venez.), 35: 39–73. (Transl. from French, *Bois For. Trop.*, (1969), 124: 19–38.)

Schenck, H., 1982–93. Beiträge zur Biologie und Anatomie der Lianen im besonderen der in Brasillien einheimischen Arten: 1. Beiträge zur Biologie der Lianen; 2. Beiträge zur Anatomie der Lianen. In: A.F.W. Schimper (Editor), *Botanische Mitteilungen aus den Tropen*. Fischer, Jena, 4: 1–253 and 5: 1–271.

Smart, R.E. and Coombe, B.G., 1983. Water relations of grape vines. In: T.T. Kozlowski (Editor), *Water Deficits and Plant Growth. 7.* Academic Press, New York, N.Y., pp. 137–196.

Smith, R.F., 1970. The vegetation structure of a Puerto Rican rain forest before and after short term γ irradiation. In: H.T. Odum (Editor), *A Tropical Rain Forest*. Dept. Tech. Inf. USAEC, Washington, D.C., pp. D103–D140.

Strong Jr., D.R., 1977. Epiphyte loads, treefalls and perennial forest disruption; a mechanism for maintaining higher tree species richness in the tropics without animals. *J. Biogeogr.*, 4: 215–218.

Strong Jr., D.R. and Ray, T.S., 1975. Host tree location behaviour of a tropical vine (*Monstera gigantea*) by skototropism. *Science*, 190: 804–806.

Tomlinson, P.B., 1983. Structural elements of the rain forest. In: F.B. Golley (Editor), *Tropical Rain Forest Ecosystems. Structure and Function.* (Ecosystems of the World, 14A) Elsevier, Amsterdam, pp. 9–28.

UNESCO, 1978. *Tropical Forest Ecosystems. A State of Knowledge Report. Nat. Resour. Res.*, 14: 683 pp.

Van den Honert, T.H., 1941. Experimentation on the water

household of tropical plants. 1. Water balance of *Cissus sicyoides* L. *Ann. Bot. Gard. Buitenzorg*, 51: 58–82.

Vareschi, V., 1980. *Vegetationsökologie der Tropen.* Ulmer, Stuttgart, 293 pp.

Verdcourt, B. and Trump, E.C., 1969. *Common Poisonous Plants of East Africa.* Collins, London, 254 pp.

Walter, H., 1964. *Die Vegetation der Erde in öko-physiologischer Betrachtung. 1.* Fischer, Stuttgart, 592 pp.

Wang, C.W., 1961. *The Forests of China.* (Marie Moors Cabot Found. Publ. 5) Harvard Univ., Cambridge, Mass., 312 pp.

Whitmore, T.C., 1974. Change with time and the role of cyclones in tropical rain forest on Kolombangara, Solomon Islands. *Commonw. For. Inst.*, Oxford, 46: 1–78.

Whitmore, T.C., 1975. *Tropical Rain Forests of the Far East.* Clarendon, Oxford, 281 pp.

Willis, J.H., 1949. The birth and spread of plants. *Boissiera*, 8: 1–561.

Winter, K., Wallace, B.J., Stocker, G.C. and Roksandic, Z., 1983. Crassulacean acid metabolism in Australian vascular epiphytes and some related species. *Oecologia*, 57: 129–141.

Young, A.M., 1984. Seed mortality and recruitment in the forest canopy vine *Mucuna urens* (Leguminosae) in the central highlands of Costa Rica. *Brenesia*, 21: 13–25.

Chapter 19

PRIMATES OF PENINSULAR MALAYSIA

ELIZABETH L. BENNETT and JULIAN O. CALDECOTT

INTRODUCTION

Peninsular Malaysia or Malaya lies roughly between 1°30′ and 6°30′ north of the Equator (Fig. 19.1). Its climate is moist and equatorial, and its natural vegetation is tropical evergreen rain forest (Whitmore, 1975). Ten species of primate occur in Malaya; these have been the subject of much study in recent years, so there is now a wealth of data on the behaviour and ecology of most species. These data can only be understood in the light of the anatomical adaptations of individual species, especially those of their gastro-intestinal tract, as they limit the type of food which the animals can obtain and process. In turn, this has wide repercussions on most aspects of their life-style. This chapter attempts to synthesize information on the habitat and distribution of potential foods with that on the primates' gastro-intestinal anatomy and physiology. The aim of this is to produce an explanation of observed patterns of behaviour and ecology in the different species.

The Malayan primate fauna comprises three gibbons (*Hylobates* spp.), three macaques (*Macaca* spp.), three langurs (*Presbytis* spp.) and one prosimian (*Nycticebus coucang*) (Table 19.1). The slow loris (*N. coucang*) is small-bodied and nocturnal (Medway, 1978; Barrett, 1981), and thus differs in its ecological associations from the larger-bodied, diurnal primates. In view of this, and the paucity of knowledge of its ecology, it is not considered further in this chapter.

Generally, no more than six simian primates occur sympatrically in Malaya. The silvered langur (*P. cristata*) has a restricted distribution in Malaya, and occurs only in the mangrove, riverine and freshwater swamp forests of the west coast

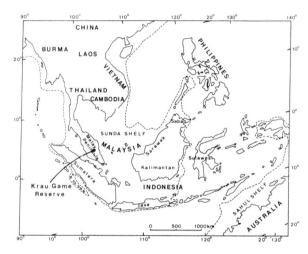

Fig. 19.1. South-East Asia showing the continental shelf, major geographical regions and location of the Krau Game Reserve.

(Medway, 1978; Marsh and Wilson, 1981). The banded and dusky langurs (*P. melalophos* and *P. obscura*) are generally syntopic in primary and secondary forest throughout the rest of the country, although *P. melalophos* tends to be numerically dominant in the south and *P. obscura* in the north (Marsh and Wilson, 1981). *P. melalophos* is the only langur occurring in hill forest (Caldecott, 1980; Marsh and Wilson, 1981).

Of the macaques, *M. arctoides* is a non-Sundaic species which mainly lives north of the Isthmus of Kra and occurs only marginally in northern Malaya (Marsh and Wilson, 1981; Fooden, 1982; Caldecott, 1986). Both of the other macaque species occur throughout Malaya, although *M. fascicularis* is generally much more abundant than is *M. nemestrina*. This is because the former typically lives in the productive riverine and secondary forests of the lowlands, while the latter

TABLE 19.1

Primates of Peninsular Malaysia

Family	Species	Common name	male:female body weight (kg)	Distribution within Malaya	Forest type	Altitude
Cercopithecidae (Colobinae)	*Presbytis cristata*	Silvered langur	?:6.2[2]	West coast	Coastal and swamp	Lowland
	Presbytis melalophos	Banded langur	5.9:5.8[3]	General	Primary and secondary	Lowland and hill
	Presbytis obscura	Dusky langur	7.4:5.5[4]	General	Primary and secondary	Lowland
(Cercopithecinae)	*Macaca arctoides*	Stump-tailed or bear macaque	?:?	Extreme north	Primary and secondary	Lowland and hill
	Macaca fascicularis	Long-tailed macaque	5.9:4.1[5]	General	Riverine, secondary and swamp	Lowland
	Macaca nemestrina	Pig-tailed macaque	14.0:7.5[6]	General	Primary and secondary	Lowland, hill and montane
Hylobatidae	*Hylobates agilis*	Agile gibbon	6.1:5.7[7]	Northwest	Primary and secondary	Lowland and hill
	Hylobates lar	Lar gibbon	5.7:4.8[8]	General except northwest	Primary and secondary	Lowland and hill
	Hylobates syndactylus	Siamang	10.9:10.6[8]	North and central	Primary and secondary	Lowland, hill and lower montane
Lorisidae	*Nycticebus coucang*	Slow loris	0.7:0.6[1]	General	Primary and secondary	Lowland and hill

[1] E. Barrett, in prep.
[2] Chivers and Hladik, 1980.
[3] Bennett, 1983.
[4] Burton, 1983.
[5] Napier and Napier, 1967.
[6] Robertson, 1986.
[7] Medway, 1978.
[8] Schultz, 1973.

lives at low density in other forest types, including montane forest (Marsh and Wilson, 1981; Caldecott, 1986). The two species are often syntopic in the lowlands, however, since *M. nemestrina* ranges very widely, and its home range may embrace areas locally occupied by *M. fascicularis*.

Hylobates agilis and *H. lar* are very similar ecologically and are almost entirely allopatric, although both coexist with the larger siamang (*H. syndactylus*) in certain lowland areas (Chivers, 1974; Gittins and Raemaekers, 1980). The siamang, however, is the only gibbon to be found in the montane forest (Chivers, 1974; Caldecott, 1980).

In the lowland forests of central Malaya, therefore, a "typical" primate community would comprise *Hylobates lar*, *H. syndactylus*, *Presbytis melalophos* and *P. obscura*, with *Macaca fascicularis* along the rivers and *M. nemestrina* ranging widely throughout the area. Such a community is found at Kuala Lompat in the Krau Game Reserve (Fig. 19.1) where many of the data on Malayan primates have been collected [see papers cited by

Chivers (1980) and Nordin et al. (1981)] and to which this chapter refers unless otherwise specified.

THE HABITAT

The tropical rain forests of Peninsular Malaysia are extremely diverse in structure and species composition. The main canopy is up to about 40 m high, overtopped by occasional giant emergents up to 70 m tall. The canopy comprises a deep layer of interlocking crowns, many bearing epiphytes, and it is entwined with large numbers of rattans and other climbing plants. Frequent tree falls create a mosaic of forest patches, each at a different stage of regeneration, and hence with a structure different from that of the surrounding forest (Whitmore, 1975).

The species composition of the forest varies between areas, depending on soil type as well as historical factors (Whitmore, 1975). Although their relative proportions vary, the same tree families generally occur in all areas of lowland forest throughout the Peninsula. Common emergents at most sites include members of the Anacardiaceae, Caesalpiniaceae, Dipterocarpaceae, and Mimosaceae: a significant proportion of the trees in the middle canopy are usually of the Euphorbiaceae (Poore, 1968; Whitmore, 1975; Raemaekers et al., 1980). The abundance of dipterocarps in Sundaic forests is of significance to the primates because, even though they are such large, common trees, their value as food sources is minimal (Chivers, 1974; Marsh and Wilson, 1981). Thus, there often seems to be a negative correlation between the proportion of dipterocarps and that of good food trees in a forest (Marsh and Wilson, 1981; Bennett, 1983; Davies, 1984; Caldecott, 1986).

The species diversity of Malayan forests is among the greatest in the world (Richards, 1952; Whitmore, 1975). At Kuala Lompat, for example, the study area of about 1.25 km^2 contains a minimum of 400 tree and 100 liana species (Bennett, 1983). Dense aggregations of any one species are uncommon (Whitmore, 1975); individuals of most species usually occur singly, and rarely with more than three stems in any one hectare of forest (Wyatt-Smith, 1966; Kaur et al., 1978; Raemaekers et al., 1980).

A primate feeding in such a forest not only has to select its foods from a great diversity of different plant species, but also faces an enormous array of chemical compounds. Compounds of particular relevance to a primate are of two main types: those which it must obtain in order to survive and reproduce, and those which are potentially harmful if ingested. The nutrients likely to have the greatest influence on primate feeding strategies are protein, sources of digestible energy, and minerals. There are two main types of potentially deleterious compounds: toxins, and digestion inhibitors, the latter mostly comprising tannins and fibre (Waterman, 1984; see also Ch. 29). A primate must select its foods to maximize the intake of vital nutrients while minimizing that of deleterious compounds (Freeland and Janzen, 1974; Westoby, 1974; Pulliam, 1975).

Leaves, especially young leaves, are generally the richest sources of protein and minerals in a plant (Hladik, 1978; Oates et al., 1980; Waterman et al., 1980; McKey et al., 1981; Vellayan, 1982). How-ever, leaves contain high proportions of digestion inhibitors (Waterman, 1984). Mature leaves generally have higher levels of digestion inhibitors, especially fibre, than do young leaves (Milton, 1979; Coley, 1980; Choo et al., 1981), although concentrations of alkaloids and other toxins are generally higher in the young leaves (McKey, 1979).

Fruits and seeds tend to contain the highest levels of easily digested energy in the form of sugars and starch, respectively (Waterman, 1984), although they may also contain many toxins. Species whose fruits are dispersed by animals often protect their unripe fruits with toxic steroidal alkaloids which are withdrawn as the fruit ripens (McKey, 1979). Other species may retain alkaloids in the ripe fruits, so that they can only be dispersed by specially adapted frugivores (Janzen, 1978). Similarly, many unripe fruits contain high levels of tannin (McKey, 1979; Swain, 1979) although the pulp of ripe, fleshy fruits is generally low in digestion inhibitors.

Food availability to primates is influenced not only by the phytochemistry but also the seasonality of potential foods. Although there are usually leaves, flowers and fruit in the forest at all times of year, there are marked seasonal trends (McClure, 1966; Medway, 1972; Raemaekers et al., 1980). Duration and frequency of production cycles are species-specific and highly variable, and this often results in any one type of food being available only for a short period each year. The food availability may vary greatly between years because of the tendency of many trees within dipterocarp forests to produce their fruit every few years in sporadic and synchronized bursts known as "mast fruiting" (Janzen, 1974; Whitmore, 1975).

DIGESTIVE SYSTEMS AND DIET

The Malayan primates can be divided into two groups according to their gastro-intestinal anatomy and physiology: those which are polygastric (the langurs) and those which are monogastric (the gibbons and macaques). This division is crucial since the form and function of the gut determines the animal's dietary demands (Davies et al., 1983).

Langurs

The Malayan langurs, like all other colobines, possess a complex stomach comprising four parts (Kuhn, 1964; Bauchop, 1978). The fore-stomach is greatly enlarged to form a chamber in which a diverse array of microflora, including cellulose-digesting bacteria, ferment the food (Kuhn, 1964; Bauchop and Martucci, 1968; Moir, 1968; Ohwaki et al., 1974). In order for the microflora to survive, the fore-stomach is maintained at or around neutral pH, and it is separated from the acidic pyloric region (Bauchop and Martucci, 1968; Bauchop, 1978). In colobines, the fermentation process and its end products appear extremely similar to those of all ruminants studied (Kuhn, 1964; Bauchop and Martucci, 1968; Kay et al., 1976). Carbohydrates are converted by the microflora into short-chain volatile fatty acids which pass through the stomach wall and are used by the animal as an energy source (Bauchop and Martucci, 1968; Bauchop, 1978; Parra, 1978), and the bacterial flora are used together with the fermentation end products for nutrition by the host.

This system has many advantages for the monkeys, including:

(1) The bacteria may deactivate many plant toxins before they can be absorbed by the host. This allows the colobine to eat plants containing toxins which would otherwise be harmful (Freeland and Janzen, 1974; Oates et al., 1977; Waterman, 1984).

(2) The bacteria can assist in the breakdown of plant cell walls, thereby releasing the cell contents so that the host can digest and absorb them. This allows the monkey to use the protein bound up inside leaf cells.

(3) The bacteria may be able to break down cellulose to release volatile fatty acids from which the monkey can obtain energy. The extent to which this occurs in small colobines such as the Malayan langurs is unknown.

(4) Synthesis of vitamins by the bacteria may make the animal independent of all dietary sources of vitamins except A and D (Bauchop, 1978).

(5) Preliminary studies and inferences drawn from a knowledge of ruminants indicate that the bacteria can use non-protein nitrogen for growth. Urea from protein catabolism in the colobine diffuses into the stomach, where it is converted to microbial protein. Many of the microbes then pass into the acidic, distal part of the stomach where they are digested, allowing the colobine to obtain adequate high-quality protein even though the dietary supply is limited (Bauchop, 1978).

In spite of these advantages, langurs cannot feed indiscriminately as their fermentative digestion imposes constraints on the types of food eaten. First, polygastric animals can only tolerate a certain maximum amount of fibre in their diet. This proportion decreases with decreasing body size (Janis, 1976; Parra, 1978). Thus, a relatively small colobine cannot utilize mature leaves with a high fibre content. Second, it seems that colobines cannot eat pulpy or sugary fruits. The reasons for this are not altogether clear, but it is possibly due to the simple sugars being fermented more rapidly than the acids and methane produced can be absorbed into the body or processed by other microflora (Davies, 1984; Davies et al., 1983). This leads to hyper-acidity of the stomach (Goltenboth, 1976), which would be deleterious to the microflora (Bauchop and Martucci, 1968), and to "bloat", which has led to death in captive colobines (Collins and Roberts, 1978).

Langurs obtain protein by eating leaves, as the bacteria can break down the cell walls and also synthesize high-quality protein from a low-quality diet. Eating leaves also provides them with minerals (Golley et al., 1980a, b). The langurs tend to eat more young leaves than mature ones, because the former contain both more nutrients and less fibre than the latter. *P. obscura* is slightly heavier than *P. melalophos* (Table 19.1), and also has a relatively larger stomach (Chivers and Hladik, 1980). This is likely to enable *P. obscura* to eat foods with a lower ratio of nutrients to fibre, and consequently to eat more mature leaves than can *P. melalophos* (Table 19.2).

Small animals require foods with a relatively higher energy content than do large ones (Kleiber, 1961), and the release of volatile fatty acids from the fermentation of cellulose is probably too slow to supply all of the energy requirements of these relatively small colobines. Thus, they need to obtain energy from sources other than leaves. Since they do not eat fleshy fruits, they mostly obtain that energy by eating seeds from Caesalpiniaceae, Celastraceae, Mimosaceae, Myristicaceae, Papilionaceae (Bennett, 1983).

TABLE 19.2

Percentage of time spent feeding on different foods by Malayan primates

Species	Young leaves	Mature leaves	Flowers	Fruits and seeds	Insects	Reference
Hylobates lar	25	4	7	50	13	Gittins and Raemaekers,
H. syndactylus	38	5	6	36	15	1980
Macaca fascicularis	13	3	5	52	23	Aldrich-Blake, 1980
M. nemestrina	6	3	1	74	12	Caldecott, 1986
Presbytis melalophos	28	9	12	50	1	Bennett, 1983
P. obscura	36	22	7	35	0	Curtin, 1980

All data were from Kuala Lompat except for those on *M. nemestrina* which were from Lima Belas.

The foods selected by the langurs are relatively common in Malayan forests. Their ability to cope with items containing toxins means that the langurs can eat quite a wide variety of young leaves and seeds. Some of their most favoured foods come from *Intsia palembanica* (Caesalpiniaceae) and *Parkia javanica* (Mimosaceae), which are large trees and common in many lowland forests.

Gibbons and macaques

Gibbons and macaques have a simple, globular stomach, the contents of which are maintained at an acid pH (Chivers and Hladik, 1980). Within the gut, the animal's own enzymes digest proteins to polypeptides, and complex sugars to monosaccharides (Schmidt-Nielson, 1975). Such a digestive system allows the animal to obtain energy from succulent fruits which are easily and quickly digested. However, it limits food selection in two main ways. First, any toxins may be absorbed directly into the bloodstream, so foods containing such toxins must be avoided (review in Waterman, 1984). The lar gibbon, for example, apparently only eats foods which contain no alkaloids (Vellayan, 1982). Second, these primates have few microbes capable of digesting cellulose. Thus, the cellulose in leaves, one of the most abundant and ubiquitous sources of carbohydrates in the forest, is denied to them. Moreover, the animals' inability to break down the cellulose of plant cell walls efficiently means that it is difficult for them to have access to the protein contained within those cells.

None of the monogastric primates eat many mature leaves, although *Hylobates agilis* and *H. lar*

eat appreciable quantities of young leaves, which are more digestible and nutritious (Table 19.2). This is most pronounced in *H. syndactylus*, which is larger than *H. lar* (Table 19.1) and also has a relatively large gut, in which some midgut fermentation may occur (Chivers and Hladik, 1980). However, the monogastric primates cannot obtain as much protein from leaves as can the colobines, nor do they possess bacteria capable of converting urea into high-quality microbial protein. Thus, both gibbons and macaques eat significant quantities of insects to obtain protein (Table 19.2).

All the monogastric primates obtain most of their energy from pulpy, fleshy fruits such as *Sapium baccatum* and *Ficus* spp. Except in the riverine forest, many of the fruits and young leaves eaten come from relatively small, rare trees (Gittins and Raemaekers, 1980; Caldecott, 1986). This is presumably because the plant parts of many of the larger trees contain alkaloids or other toxins.

Dietary overlap

Even though the diets of the monogastric and polygastric primates may be superficially similar (compare, for example, the diets of *P. melalophos* and *H. lar* in Table 19.2), the physiological constraints on feeding result in their selecting foods from different plant species. Moreover, most of the fruit/seed component of the langurs' diet consists of seeds, and while that of the gibbons and macaques consists of fruits and fruit pulp. Thus, there is only about 2% of overlap between the diets of *P. melalophos* and *H. lar* at Kuala Lompat (Bennett, 1983). By contrast, the diets of the two gibbon species superficially appear rather different (Table 19.2), but the dietary overlap between them is about 41% (Raemaekers, 1977).

RANGING AND SOCIAL BEHAVIOUR

The distribution of a primate's food directly influences its ranging behaviour and the size of social group in which it lives, both of which are aimed at exploiting the food efficiently (Clutton-Brock and Harvey, 1977a, b; Wrangham, 1979). Predation pressure is also likely to play a role in determining primate social systems (Van Schaik and Van Hoof, 1983), but the levels of predation on all Malayan primates are similarly low (papers in Chivers, 1980). Thus, differences in ranging and social behaviour of the different species are unlikely to be due to differences in predation pressure.

The langurs' food trees are large and quite common, so groups do not have to travel far each day to obtain enough food (Table 19.3). Home ranges are relatively small and neither species exhibits pronounced territoriality; indeed, groups of *P. melalophos* are extremely tolerant of each other and home ranges overlap extensively (Bennett, 1983). Moreover, the food sources are large enough to support social groups comprising about 15 monkeys (Table 19.3).

The monogastric primates, with their much sparser and more scattered food, are severely restricted in their options for survival. Indeed, *M. fascicularis* seems unable to live in primary dipterocarp forest away from rivers (Caldecott, 1986). Instead, it occupies riverine and disturbed habitats where productivity, especially of fruits, is greater and more constant than in non-riverine forest (Wheatley, 1980). In its restricted habitats, food is abundant, so *M. fascicularis* live in large groups in small home ranges and do not need to travel far each day to obtain enough food (Table 19.3).

M. nemestrina manage to survive in dipterocarp forest primarily because it is anatomically suited to long-distance terrestrial travel. It obtains its food by travelling over enormous distances, and during the day social groups may fragment and rejoin or even join other conspecific groups, so the monkeys constantly adjust the size of their feeding group to that of their food sources in a highly opportunistic manner (Caldecott, 1986).

The gibbons adopt an alternative strategy — that of living in very small, monogamous family groups. Each group occupies an area of forest large enough to contain food for themselves throughout the year, provided they do not have to share it with others: thus, each group is strictly territorial (Chivers, 1974; Gittins and Raemaekers, 1980). Even though the social groups are small, they have to travel quite far each day, exploiting small, scattered sources of high-quality food. *H. lar*

TABLE 19.3

Parameters of ranging and social behaviour of primates in Peninsular Malaysia

Species	Mean day range length (m)	Home range area at Kuala Lompat (ha)	Social system	Mean size of social group	Reference
Hylobates lar	1490	54	Monogamous pair + offspring	4	Gittins and Raemaekers, 1980
H. syndactylus	738	41	Monogamous pair + offspring	4	Chivers, 1974; Gittins and Raemaekers, 1980
Macaca fascicularis	760	35	Multi-male groups	23	Aldrich-Blake, 1980
M. nemestrina	2960	828	Multi-male groups	30	Caldecott, 1986
Presbytis melalophos	680	29	Predominantly 1-male groups	15	Bennett, 1983
P. obscura	560	33	Predominantly 1-male groups	15	Curtin, 1980; MacKinnon and MacKinnon, 1980; Marsh and Wilson, 1981

All data refer to Kuala Lompat except for those on *M. nemestrina* which were from Pasoh.

travels even further than do *H. syndactylus* due to its smaller body size, higher metabolic requirements and consequent frugivorous diet — fruits being more sparsely distributed than are leaves (Raemaekers, 1977).

BIOMASS

Features which limit the biomass of a species in any given habitat include overall food levels, predation, disease, parasitism and irregular catastrophic events such as severe weather (Bradbury and Vehrencamp, 1976). Although many such factors combine to influence biomass, much of the variation is likely to be due to differences in food availability limiting the number of animals which can be supported (Schoener, 1971; Clutton-Brock and Harvey, 1977b; Marsh and Wilson, 1981).

The food in the forest which is available to a primate is highly dependent on that animal's gastro-intestinal physiology, so the habitat is likely to have a very different carrying capacity for monogastric and polygastric herbivores. At Kuala Lompat, the biomass of the two langurs is very much greater than that of any of the monogastric species, and comprises 78% of the total (Table 19.4). There is a general tendency for polygastric primates to live at higher biomasses than sympatric monogastric ones, in both Africa and Asia (Struhsaker and Leland, 1979; Marsh and Wilson, 1981).

TABLE 19.4

Density and biomass of diurnal primates at Kuala Lompat (after Marsh and Wilson, 1981)

	Groups (km^{-2})	Biomass (kg km^{-2})	% of total biomass of diurnal primates
Hylobates lar	2.1	34	3
H. syndactylus	1.0	31	3
Macaca fascicularis	2.6	189	16
Presbytis melalophos	7.2	486	42
P. obscura	6.2	419	36
Total	19.1	1159	100

M. nemestrina are occasionally present but were not seen during censuses. Mean individual weights are taken to be: *P. melalophos* and *P. obscura*: 4.5 kg (Davies, 1984); *M. fascicularis*: 3.2 kg; *H. lar*: 4.0 kg; *H. syndactylus*: 7.7 kg (Marsh and Wilson, 1981).

This is likely to result from their ability to deactivate plant toxins and possibly also to synthesize vitamins and recycle nitrogen. This allows polygastric primates to subsist on a much greater proportion of available plant parts at all times than can monogastric species, and this difference is likely to be particularly important when favoured foods are scarce (Chivers, 1974; Marsh and Wilson, 1981).

CONCLUSION

A primate living in a South-East Asian dipterocarp forest is in an extremely diverse habitat in terms of structure, composition and the countless combinations of nutrients and plant-defence compounds which the vegetation contains. Out of this variety, the primate must select its foods, and the gastro-intestinal physiology of each species largely determines what constitutes "acceptable" food. Thus, food sources are distributed differently for the different primate species. This affects every aspect of their lives, from immediate effects on their feeding and ranging behaviour through to their social organization and population density.

ACKNOWLEDGEMENTS

Research on primates in Peninsular Malaysia has been supported in many ways over the years by the Malaysian Department of Wildlife and National Parks, the Socio-Economic Research Unit of the Prime Minister's Department, Universiti Malaya, Universiti Kebangsaan Malaysia, Universiti Pertanian Malaysia and the University of Cambridge. Financial support has been provided by many funding agencies which are acknowledged in the individual reports referred to herein. The authors' work in Peninsular Malaysia was supported by the Leverhulme Trust, the L.S.B. Leakey Foundation and the Boise Fund Oxford (E.L.B.), and the United States National Cancer Institute (grant no. NO1-CO-85409) via the University of Cambridge and the L.S.B. Leakey Foundation (J.O.C.), within the context of the Malaysian Primates Research Programme 1978–1981.

We would like to thank David Chivers for everything that he has contributed towards the work on Peninsular Malaysian primates, Peter Waterman for all his help on the phytochemistry, and also Eamonn Barrett, Glyn Davies and Michael Kavanagh for their comments on a previous draft of this chapter.

REFERENCES

Aldrich-Blake, F.P.G., 1980. Long-tailed macaques. In: D.J. Chivers (Editor), *Malayan Forest Primates*. Plenum, New York, N.Y., pp. 147–165.

Barrett, E., 1981. The present distribution and status of the slow loris in Peninsular Malaysia. *Malays. Appl. Biol.*, 10: 205–211.

Barrett, E., 1984. *The ecology of some nocturnal arboreal mammals in the rain forest of Peninsular Malaysia*. Ph.D. Thesis, Univ. of Cambridge, Cambridge.

Bauchop, T., 1978. Digestion of leaves in vertebrate arboreal folivores. In: G.G. Montgomery (Editor), *The Ecology of Arboreal Folivores*. Smithsonian Institution Press, Washington, D.C., pp. 193–204.

Bauchop, T. and Martucci, R.W., 1968. Ruminant-like digestion of the langur monkey. *Science*, 161: 698–700.

Bennett, E.L., 1983. *The banded langur: ecology of a colobine in West Malaysian rain-forest*. Ph.D. Thesis, Univ. of Cambridge, Cambridge.

Bennett, E.L., 1986. Environmental correlates of ranging behaviour in the banded langur, *Presbytis melalophos*. *Folia Primatol.*, 47: 26–38.

Bradbury, J.W. and Vehrencamp, S.L., 1976. Social organization and foraging in Emballonurid bats. II. A model for the determination of group size. *Behav. Ecol. Sociobiol.*, 1: 383–404.

Burton, G.J., 1983. Aspects of the reproductive anatomy of the dusky leaf monkey (*Presbytis obscura*). *Malay. Nat. J.*, 36: 285–288.

Caldecott, J.O., 1980. Habitat quality and populations of two sympatric gibbons (Hylobatidae) on a mountain in Malaya. *Folia Primatol.*, 33: 291–309.

Caldecott, J.O., 1986. An ecological and behavioural study of the pig-tailed macaque. *Contrib. Primatol.*, 21: 1–259.

Chivers, D.J., 1974. The siamang in Malaya: a field study of a primate in a tropical rain forest. *Contrib. Primatol.*, 4: 1–335.

Chivers, D.J. (Editor), 1980. *Malayan Forest Primates*. Plenum, New York, N.Y., 364 pp.

Chivers, D.J. and Hladik, C.M., 1980. Morphology of the gastrointestinal tract in primates: comparisons with other mammals in relation to diet. *J. Morphol.*, 166: 337–386.

Choo, G.M., Waterman, P.G., McKey, D.B. and Gartlan, J.S., 1981. A simple enzyme assay for dry matter digestibility and its value in studying food selection by generalist herbivores. *Oecologia*, 49: 170–178.

Clutton-Brock, T.H. and Harvey, P.H., 1977a. Primate ecology and social organization. *J. Zool. London*, 183: 1–39.

Clutton-Brock, T.H. and Harvey, P.H., 1977b. Species differences in feeding and ranging behaviour in primates. In:

T.H. Clutton-Brock (Editor), *Primate Ecology*. Academic Press, London, pp. 557–584.

Coley, P.D., 1980. *Ecological and evolutionary responses of tropical trees to herbivory: a quantitative analysis of grazing damage, plant defenses and growth rates*. Ph.D. Thesis, Univ. of Chicago, Chicago, Ill.

Collins, L. and Roberts, M., 1978. Arboreal folivores in captivity — maintenance of a delicate minority. In: G.G. Montgomery (Editor), *The Ecology of Arboreal Folivores*. Smithsonian Institution Press, Washington, D.C., pp. 5–12.

Curtin, S.H., 1980. Dusky and banded leaf monkeys. In: D.J. Chivers (Editor), *Malayan Forest Primates*. Plenum, New York, N.Y., pp. 107–145.

Davies, A.G., 1984. *An ecological study of the red leaf monkey (Presbytis rubicunda) in the dipterocarp forest of northern Borneo*. Ph.D. Thesis, Univ. of Cambridge, Cambridge.

Davies, A.G., Caldecott, J.O. and Chivers, D.J., 1983. Natural foods as a guide to the nutrition of Old World primates. In: J. Remfry (Editor), *Standards in Laboratory Management*. U.F.A.W., Potters Bar, pp. 225–244.

Fooden, J., 1982. Ecogeographic segregation of macaque species. *Primates*, 23: 574–579.

Freeland, W.J. and Janzen, D.H., 1974. Strategies of herbivory in mammals and the role of plant secondary compounds. *Am. Nat.*, 108: 269–289.

Gittins, S.P. and Raemaekers, J.J., 1980. Siamang, lar and agile gibbons. In: D.J. Chivers (Editor), *Malayan Forest Primates*. Plenum, New York, N.Y., pp. 63–105.

Golley, F.B., Yantko, J. and Jordan, C., 1980a. Biogeochemistry of tropical forests: 2. The frequency distribution and mean concentration of selected elements near San Carlos de Rio Negro, Venezuela. *Trop. Ecol.*, 21: 71–80.

Golley, F.B., Yantko, J., Richardson, T. and Klinge, H., 1980b. Biogeochemistry of tropical forests: 1. The frequency distribution and mean concentrations of selected elements in a forest near Manaus, Brazil. *Trop. Ecol.*, 21: 59–70.

Hladik, C.M., 1978. Adaptive strategies of primates in relation to leaf-eating. In: G.G. Montgomery (Editor), *The Ecology of Arboreal Folivores*. Smithsonian Institution Press, Washington, D.C., pp. 373–395.

Janis, C., 1976. The evolutionary strategy of the Equidae and the origins of rumen and caecal digestion. *Evolution*, 30: 757–774.

Janzen, D.H., 1974. Tropical blackwater rivers, animals and mast fruiting by the Dipterocarpaceae. *Biotropica*, 6: 69–103.

Janzen, D.H., 1978. Complications of interpreting the chemical defenses of trees against tropical arboreal plant-eating vertebrates. In: G.G. Montgomery (Editor), *The Ecology of Arboreal Folivores*. Smithsonian Institution Press, Washington, D.C., pp. 73–84.

Kaur, A., Ha, C.O., Jong, K., Sands, V.E., Chan, H.T., Soepadmo, E. and Ashton, P.S., 1978. Apomixis may be widespread among trees of the climax rain forest. *Nature*, 271: 440–442.

Kay, R.N.B., Hoppe, P. and Maloiy, G.M.O., 1976. Fermentative digestion of food in the colobus monkey, *Colobus polykomos*. *Experentia*, 32: 485–487.

Kleiber, N., 1961. *The Fire of Life*. Wiley, New York, N.Y.

Kuhn, H.-J., 1964. Zur Kenntnis von Bau und Funktion des Magens der Sclankaffen (Colobinae). *Folia Primatol.*, 2: 193–221.

MacKinnon, J.R. and MacKinnon, K.S., 1980. Niche differentiation in a primate community. In: D.J. Chivers (Editor), *Malayan Forest Primates*. Plenum, New York, N.Y., pp. 167–190.

Marsh, C.W. and Wilson, W.L., 1981. *A Survey of Primates in Peninsular Malaysian Forests*. Univ. Kebangsaan Malaysia, Kuala Lumpur.

McClure, H.E., 1966. Flowering, fruiting and animals in the canopy of a tropical rain forest. *Malay. Forest.*, 29: 182–203.

McKey, D.B., 1979. The distribution of secondary compounds within plants. In: G.A. Rosenthal and D.H. Janzen (Editors), *Herbivores, their Interactions with Secondary Plant Metabolites*. Academic Press, New York, N.Y., pp. 55–133.

McKey, D.B., Gartlan, J.S., Waterman, P.G. and Choo, G.M., 1981. Food selection by black colobus monkeys (*Colobus satanas*) in relation to plant chemistry. *Biol. J. Linn. Soc.*, 16: 115–146.

Medway, Lord, 1972. Phenology of a tropical rain forest in Malaya. *Biol. J. Linn. Soc.*, 4: 117–146.

Medway, Lord, 1978. *The Wild Mammals of Malaya (Peninsular Malaysia) and Singapore*. Oxford Univ. Press, Kuala Lumpur.

Milton, K., 1979. Factors influencing leaf choice by howler monkeys: a test of some hypotheses of food selection by generalist herbivores. *Am. Nat.*, 114: 362–378.

Moir, R.J., 1968. Ruminant digestion and evolution. In: C.F. Code (Editor), *Handbook of Physiology, Section 6-V*. American Physiological Society, Washington, D.C., pp. 2673–2694.

Napier, J.R. and Napier, P.H., 1967. *A Handbook of Living Primates*. Academic Press, London.

Nordin, M., Kavanagh, M. and Vidyadaran, M.K. (Editors), 1981. Proceedings of the symposium on the biology of Peninsular Malaysian primates. *Malays. Appl. Biol.*, 10(2).

Oates, J.F., Swain, T. and Zantovska, J., 1977. Secondary compounds and food selection by colobus monkeys. *Biochem. System. Ecol.*, 5: 317–321.

Oates, J.F., Waterman, P.G. and Choo, G.M., 1980. Food selection by the South Indian leaf monkey, *Presbytis johnii*, in relation to leaf chemistry. *Oecologia*, 45: 45–56.

Ohwaki, H., Hungate, R.E., Lotter, L., Hofmann, R.R. and Maloiy, G.M.O., 1974. Stomach fermentation in East African *Colobus* monkeys in their natural state. *Appl. Microbiol.*, 27: 713–723.

Parra, R. 1978. Comparison of foregut and hindgut fermentation in herbivores. In: G.G. Montgomery (Editor), *The Ecology of Arboreal Folivores*. Smithsonian Institution Press, Washington, D.C., pp. 205–229.

Poore, M.E.D., 1968. Studies in Malaysian rain forest. 1. The forest on the Triassic sediments in Jengka Forest Reserve. *J. Ecol.*, 56: 143–196.

Pulliam, H.R., 1975. Diet optimization with nutrient constraints. *Am. Nat.*, 109: 765–768.

Raemaekers, J.J., 1977. *Gibbons and trees: comparative ecology of the siamang and lar gibbons*. Ph.D. Thesis, Univ. of Cambridge, Cambridge.

Raemaekers, J.J., Aldrich-Blake, F.P.G. and Payne, J.B., 1980. The forest. In: D.J. Chivers (Editor), *Malayan Forest Primates*. Plenum, New York, N.Y., pp. 29–61.

Richards, P.W., 1952. *The Tropical Rain Forest: An Ecological Study*. Cambridge Univ. Press, Cambridge, 450 pp.

Robertson, J.M.Y., 1986. *On the evolution of pig-tailed macaque societies*. Ph.D. Thesis, Univ. of Cambridge, Cambridge.

Schmidt-Nielson, K., 1975. *Animal Physiology*. Cambridge Univ. Press, Cambridge.

Schoener, T.W., 1971. Theory of feeding strategies. *Annu. Rev. Ecol. Syst.*, 2: 369–403.

Schultz, A.H., 1973. The skeleton of the Hylobatidae and other observations on their morphology. In: D.M. Rumbaugh (Editor), *Gibbon and Siamang, Vol. 2*. Karger, Basel, pp. 1–54.

Struhsaker, T.T. and Leland, L., 1979. Socioecology of five sympatric monkey species in the Kibale Forest, Uganda. In: J.S. Rosenblatt, R.A. Hinde, C. Beer and M.C. Busnel (Editors), *Advances in the Study of Behavior, Vol. 9*. Academic Press, New York, N.Y., pp. 159–228.

Swain. T., 1979. Tannins and lignins. In: G.A. Rosenthal and D.H. Janzen (Editors), *Herbivores, their Interactions with Secondary Plant Metabolites*. Academic Press, New York, N.Y., pp. 637–682.

Van Schaik, C.P. and Van Hoof, J.A.R.A.M., 1983. On the ultimate causes of primate social systems. *Behaviour*, 85: 91–117.

Vellayan, S., 1982. *Chemistry and digestibility of foods of the lar gibbon (Hylobates lar)*. M.Sc. Thesis, Univ. Pertanian Malaysia.

Waterman, P.G., 1984. Food acquisition and processing by primates as a function of plant chemistry. In: D.J. Chivers (Editor), *Food Acquisition and Processing in Primates*. Plenum, New York, N.Y., pp. 177–211.

Waterman, P.G., Mbi, C.N., McKey, D.B. and Gartlan, J.S., 1980. African rainforest vegetation and rumen microbes: phenolic compounds and nutrients as correlates of digestibility. *Oecologia*. 47: 22–33.

Westoby, M., 1974. The analysis of diet selection by large generalist herbivores. *Am. Nat.*, 6: 290–304.

Wheatley, B.P., 1980. Feeding and ranging of East Bornean *Macaca fascicularis*. In: D.G. Lindburg (Editor), *The Macaques*. Van Nostrand Reinhold, New York, N.Y., pp. 215–246.

Whitmore, T.C., 1975. *Tropical Rain Forests of the Far East*. Clarendon, Oxford, 281 pp.

Wrangham, R.W., 1979. On the evolution of ape social systems. *Soc. Sci. Inf.*, 18: 335–368.

Wyatt-Smith, J., 1966. *Ecological Studies on Malayan Forests, 1*. Malayan Forestry Department Research Pamphlet 52.

Chapter 20

BATS

D.E. WILSON

INTRODUCTION

Bats are a frequently neglected but critically important component of most ecosystems. This is particularly true in the tropics, where the diversity and sheer biomass of bats is staggering. Because of their almost completely nocturnal habits, bats tend to be overlooked by the one primate capable of studying them, the almost completely diurnal *Homo sapiens*.

Tropical rain forests are the epitome of richness for many taxonomic groups, but bats play a critical role in shaping both pattern and process of this diversity. Bats serve rain-forest ecosystems by pollinating many plants and dispersing the seeds of many others. Other bat species play an important role as predators of rain-forest insects, and perhaps a lesser role as predators of other vertebrates.

This co-evolutionary theme of the food habits of bats is an important and recurring one, regardless of the aspect of their biology under consideration. It permeates the classification of bats and lends congruence to taxonomic and trophic categories. A major factor in the distribution of bats is availability of food resources. Bat morphology, the basis for most phylogenetic schemes, is affected distinctly by the food habits of the taxon under consideration (Findley, 1969, 1973, 1976; Eisenberg and Wilson, 1978; Freeman, 1979, 1981; Baron and Jolicoeur, 1980; Findley and Wilson, 1982). Critically important attributes of bats such as flight (Findley et al., 1972; Norberg, 1981a, b), and unusual ones such as echo location (Fenton, 1982), are influenced by feeding patterns.

This review of rain-forest bats will center on the importance of food habits and feeding patterns in ordering the composition and density of bat faunas

in tropical ecosystems. In spite of a wealth of data on the natural history of bats gathered mainly during the last 100 years, much of current understanding of the role of bats in rain-forest ecosystems remains as speculation (Janzen and Wilson, 1983). Although the rudiments of the trophic roles of most species of bats are known, the natural history data needed to define adequately their role in tropical ecosystems is lacking. Data on roosting habits (Allen, 1939; Wilson, 1970; Kunz, 1982) and foraging territory (Dwyer, 1970; Wilson and Findley, 1972; Fleming, 1982), for example, are scarce for rain-forest species. Fortunately, a talented and ever-increasing group of young students is beginning to replace such speculation with empirical data.

Although the systematics of bats is not as well known as it is for some other groups, and although undoubtedly there remain undescribed species in tropical rain forests, the basic distribution patterns are well enough understood to make possible some useful generalizations. Knowledge of the origin and dispersal of the major groups of bats throughout the world remains woefully inadequate, owing primarily to a paucity of fossil remains from the transition period before bats attained their present morphology (Hill and Smith, 1984). Unfortunately, many available faunal studies are constrained by political boundaries rather than by natural ones (Cabrera, 1958; Rosevear, 1965; Gardner et al., 1970; Lekagul and McNeely, 1977; Mok et al., 1982; Strahan, 1983).

Early attempts at describing bat faunas based on studies in museums, often located halfway around the world from where specimens had been collected in the field, sometimes led to misinformation, but on the whole they were enormously helpful in advancing our knowledge. Early German natural-ists of the last century alleged blood-sucking habits in a variety of rather innocuous fruit-eating species in South America. Thus there are the genera *Vampyrops*, *Vampyressa*, *Vampyrum* and *Vampy-rodes*, none of which are vampires (Fig. 20.1).

During the last two decades or so, biologists have expanded their research on tropical bats to include a variety of ecological topics, such as reproductive patterns (Baker, 1938; Carter, 1970; Wilson and Findley, 1970; Fleming, 1971; Mares and Wilson, 1971; Wilson and Findley, 1971; Medway, 1972; Wilson, 1973a, 1979; Racey, 1982), as well as the more traditional systematic and distributional studies. Community ecology has stressed the interactions of various components of the fauna, and more importantly, interactions with the plants that form the dominant stratum of the habitat of every species of tropical bat (Fleming, 1982). It is in these studies that the extraordinary reliance of many tropical plants on bats for pollination and dispersal has been documented.

Fig. 20.1. *Vampyressa pusilla*, an inappropriately named Neotropical frugivore. (Photo by R.K. LaVal.)

Actually, the groundwork for these develop-ments was well laid in the 1950s by the Dutch biologist L. van der Pijl (1956) in a series of papers describing the syndrome of chiropterophily. More recently, efforts have been made to understand the role of bats in a variety of tropical ecosystems (Wilson, 1971a; Fleming et al., 1972; Heithaus et al., 1975; Fenton, 1975, 1982; Erkert et al., 1980), and to understand the often complex physiological devices they use to accommodate a life style dominated by flight and echolocation (McNab, 1969, 1982; Studier and Wilson, 1970, 1979, 1983; Gardner and Wilson, 1971; Geluso, 1980; Studier et al., 1983a, b). Bats are also exceptionally long-lived for small mammals, and even tropical rain-forest species may live for ten years or more (Wilson and Tyson, 1970; Tuttle and Stephenson, 1982).

To date, very little effort has been devoted to careful comparisons of tropical ecosystems, especi-ally between those located on different continents. Neotropical ecosystems have been studied prim-arily by North American scientists (Fig. 20.2), whereas Paleotropical ecosystems have been stud-ied by European biologists. A promising trend in all of these tropical areas, most of which are located in developing nations, is the development of a new cohort of local biologists who are now adding steadily to our knowledge of these areas.

Current efforts at synthesizing this blossoming of knowledge lean towards trying to understand individual adaptations in an evolutionary context, and towards unifying those individual adaptations into a robust theory of ecosystem structure and function. This particular synopsis of rain-forest bats will examine briefly where they occur, their species diversity, and how they affect the ecosys-tem, each subject being couched within a frame-work of trophic structure (Wilson, 1973b).

ZOOGEOGRAPHY

The zoogeography of bats on a worldwide basis was essentially neglected until 1970, when Koop-man (1970) provided a most useful summary of the worldwide distribution of bat genera. I used this information (Wilson, 1973b) to compare the distribution of bats based on their food habits and feeding strategies. The distribution of bats based

Fig. 20.2. The rain forest on Barro Colorado Island, Panama, where bats have been studied intensively for the past 20 years.

on traditional taxonomic treatments yields useful information on the evolution and potential dispersal of groups throughout the world. An analysis based on trophic structure yields information about how bats affect ecosystems in different areas, regardless of their taxonomic affinity. Convergent evolution and parallelism in the floras of tropical rain forests have led to similar states in the faunas they support.

The two basic lineages of bats, the suborders Megachiroptera and Microchiroptera, also reflect the two basic feeding types known for the order Chiroptera. The suborder Megachiroptera, limited to the Old World, is essentially a group of bats feeding on fruit and nectar, with a preponderance of large-bodied forms. Microchiroptera are distributed worldwide, and include species representing all of the known feeding types, but they are predominantly insectivorous (Fig. 20.3).

Frugivory is probably a derived trait in Chiroptera, insectivory being the primitive condition [but see Hill and Smith (1984) for a discussion of

alternatives]. The two suborders are sufficiently distinct for it to seem likely that frugivory arose independently in the New and Old World tropics. The abundant fruit resources of tropical forests, and the ability of a highly mobile, nocturnal animal to exploit them, were ideally suited for broad radiations in both parts of the world.

SPECIES RICHNESS

Tropical rain forests contain more species of bats than any other habitat on earth. This phenomenon is by no means limited to bats, and biologists have been drawn to these areas at an increasing rate for more than a century. Documentation and description of this richness were begun by early naturalists and have been continued by present-day ecologists. Early comparisons were simply faunal lists, and species numbers were the units of comparison. Later, diversity indices of various sorts were used, so as to include consider-

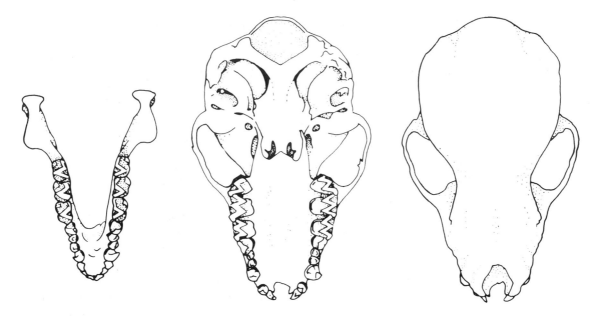

Fig. 20.3. Skull of a typical insectivorous bat, *Myotis nigricans*.

ation of abundance and, in some cases, breadth of distribution to allow more precise comparisons.

Latitudinal gradients of species richness have been described by a number of workers in the New World (Simpson, 1964; Wilson, 1974). Comparisons between New and Old World areas are complicated by differences in data sets gathered by different investigators, but some attempts have been made (Wilson, 1973b; Findley and Wilson, 1983).

Findley and Wilson were impressed by the seemingly lower species richness of bats in African rain forests in comparison to that of the Neotropics. In terms of overall number of species, the Neotropical region clearly exceeds Africa about 215 to 160. In Africa, only 27 species (17%) are frugivorous, whereas in the Neotropics 86 species (40%) are frugivorous. This indicates that the difference in number of species is due to there being fewer frugivores in Africa.

Keast (1972) estimated that 32% of the Neotropical Region is rain forest, and that only 10% of Africa and 5% of Australia are rain forest. Fenton and Kunz (1977) suggested that these smaller areas had more highly seasonal habitats, leading to migratory patterns in many species of pteropodids, and an overall inability to support as many species of frugivores.

Africa has only about half as many species of plants as the Neotropics (25–30 000 versus 50–60 000; Thorne, 1973), but, even so, the number of frugivorous bat species per 1000 species of plants is 1.6 in the Neotropics and 1.0 in Africa. In addition, Africa has fewer species of other arboreal frugivores, which may competitively inhibit bats (Findley and Wilson, 1983).

Total area of rain forest seems to be correlated with diversity of frugivorous bats, with a relationship of about one species of frugivorous bat per 70 000 km^2 of rain forest. Using data from eight neotropical localities, four from Africa, West Malaysia, Sumatra, Borneo, and New Guinea, Findley and Wilson (1983) developed a predictive equation

$$S = 4.94 + 0.000013A$$

where S is the number of species and A the area in km^2, which describes the relationship remarkably well ($r = 0.99$).

Although total available area of rain forest is clearly an important determinant in patterns of species richness, two other factors may complicate the pattern. In temperate zones, where species richness is lower than in the tropics, the overall abundance of individuals of many species is greater. This phenomenon of numerical density compensation (MacArthur, 1972) does not seem to be a factor when comparing data across tropical rain-forest areas (Findley and Wilson, 1983). The second factor, biomass compensation, may be more important. African pteropodids are considerably heavier on the average than are Neotropical phyllostomids (52 vs. 18 g), and the limited available data suggest that, even though there are fewer individuals and fewer species in Africa, the overall biomass may be close to comparable figures for the Neotropics.

It is possible to calculate similarity indices for the various rain-forest regions (Table 20.1). The generic importance value was obtained by weighting the relative importance of a genus to a region by the number of species in the genus as a proportion of the total species number for the region (Wilson, 1973b). Shared values between regions for each genus that occupies a given pair of regions were summed to provide the common generic importance values that indicate degree of similarity between regions.

These values indicate that distance is the primary determinant of similarity in this type of taxonomic comparison. The Neotropical Region is farthest from all of the Old World regions, and the similarity values between it and the other three are consistently low (Table 20.1). The greatest similarity is between Asia and Africa and the lowest is between the Neotropical and Australian (including New Guinea) regions, presumably reflecting dispersal patterns of various taxa through time. The only genera shared by the Neotropical and Australian regions are the five cosmopolitan genera *Eptesicus*, *Myotis*, *Nycticeius*, *Pipistrellus* and *Tadarida*.

TROPHIC STRUCTURE

It is possible to do the same kind of numerical comparisons between regions using importance values for the major feeding types (Table 20.2). Aerial insectivory is clearly the major trophic role in all rain forests. Interestingly, frugivory is the second most important in all but Africa, lending further support to the notion that it is a paucity of fruit-eating species that causes the low diversity figures for African rain forests. In all of the Old World areas, foliage-gleaning of insects is more important than nectar feeding, but this is not the case in the Neotropics, where a significant radiation of two subfamilies has contributed numerous species. Carnivores are an almost negligible component of all areas.

Recalculating the common generic importance values on the basis of trophic role yields far higher similarity values (Table 20.3). Presumably these values are more a reflection of current ecological

TABLE 20.2

Relative frequency values for the seven trophic roles in the four major rain-forest regions

Trophic role	Neotropics	Asia	Africa	Australia
Fish-eating	0.9	0.9	0.3	0.3
Blood-feeding	1.4	0	0	0
Other carnivores	1.8	0.6	0.3	1.0
Foliage-gleaning of insects	10.1	15.6	14.3	9.3
Aerial insectivory	43.6	60.5	65.8	48.4
Nectar-feeding	13.3	3.5	5.5	6.4
Frugivory	30.2	19.5	13.8	35.1

TABLE 20.1

Taxonomic comparison of the four major rain-forest regions. The upper figure is the common generic importance, and a value of 100 would indicate complete overlap; the lower figure is the number of shared genera

Region	Asian	African	Australian
Neotropical	9.8	9.7	7.6
	5	6	5
Asian		46.9	45.2
		15	12
African			38.3
			15

TABLE 20.3

Trophic comparison of the four major rain-forest regions. The numbers are the common trophic role frequencies, and a value of 100 would indicate complete overlap. The lower figure is the number of shared genera

Region	Asian	African	Australian
Neotropical	78.2	73.6	90.8
	5	6	5
Asian		92.7	81.6
		15	12
African			77.6
			15

conditions than of historic or phylogenetic relationships. Asia and Africa are the most similar in both the taxonomic and trophic analyses. Africa and the Neotropics are the least similar in the trophic analysis. This analysis points out the importance of convergence in trophic roles, where taxonomically unrelated groups use identical feeding strategies. Such ecological equivalence is common in a variety of rain-forest organisms. With these generalizations in mind, it is possible to examine the contribution of these various feeding types to each region in more detail.

Neotropics

Neotropical rain forests contain the greatest diversity of bats in the world (Table 20.4). Of the 75 genera occurring in the region, almost two-thirds (48) belong to the family Phyllostomidae. In addition, there are five small families endemic to the region. Apparently, bats reached the rain forests of the New World at an early evolutionary stage and radiated extensively. The Neotropical region is the only one to contain representatives of all seven of the trophic roles ascribed to bats (Wilson, 1973b), and six of the seven are found in the family Phyllostomidae (Gardner, 1977).

Fish-eating bats

The family Noctilionidae is endemic to the Neotropical Region. There are only two species in the single genus *Noctilio*, and only one, *Noctilio leporinus*, specializes on fish. This rather bizarre feeding habit for a flying animal probably developed from an ancestor that gleaned insects from the surface of streams, a habit which the other species, *N. albiventris*, may still follow. *Noctilio leporinus* uses its remarkably well-developed hind claws to scoop small fish from the surface or from just below the surface after echolocating them. This species occurs from Mexico and the Caribbean islands southwards to Argentina. Although these bats occupy a variety of habitats, they are conspicuous members of most rain forests, where they can be seen foraging over large rivers and lakes, as well as coastal lagoons and estuaries.

Other carnivores

In the New World, four phyllostomid bats, *Chrotopterus auritus*, *Phyllostomus hastatus*, *Tra-*

TABLE 20.4

Number of genera per family in each of the four major rain-forest regions. Australian includes New Guinea

Family	Neotropics	Asia	Africa	Australia
Craseonycteridae	0	1	0	0
Emballonuridae	8	2	3	2
Furipteridae	2	0	0	0
Megadermatidae	0	1	2	1
Molossidae	7	2	5	2
Mormoopidae	2	0	0	0
Myzopodidae	0	0	1	0
Natalidae	1	0	0	0
Noctilionidae	1	0	0	0
Nycteridae	0	1	1	0
Phyllostomidae	48	0	0	0
Pteropodidae	0	27	13	10
Rhinolophidae	0	7	5	5
Thyropteridae	1	0	0	0
Vespertilionidae	6	17	11	11
Total	75	59	41	31

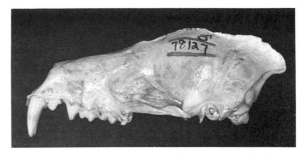

Fig. 20.4. Skull of the largest carnivorous bat, *Vampyrum spectrum*.

chops cirrhosus and *Vampyrum spectrum*, are carnivorous (Wilson, 1973b). *Vampyrum spectrum* (Fig. 20.4), the largest New World bat, eats a variety of small vertebrates (Navarro L. and Wilson, 1982), as does *Chrotopterus auritus*. *Phyllostomus hastatus* apparently includes vertebrates in its omnivorous diet (Gardner, 1977). Unique among carnivorous bats, *Trachops cirrhosus* (Fig. 20.5) preys heavily on frogs, which are located by their breeding calls (Tuttle and Ryan, 1981). Although this is the first known occurrence of bats locating prey by sounds the prey makes rather than by echolocation, it is likely that other species will prove to do the same. This might be especially useful to foliage-gleaners. All of the known carnivores in the New World are inhabi-

Fig. 20.5. *Trachops cirrhosus*, a carnivore which locates frogs by their courtship calls. (Photo by J. Scott Altenbach.)

tants of primary rain forest, and most occur at low densities. Thus, carnivorous bats are not an important component of the region as a whole.

Carnivory may have arisen in two ways in tropical rain forests. The family Megadermatidae contains several members that are carnivorous on at least two continents, and would seem to be an example of a successful, but limited, radiation of carnivorous forms. The family Phyllostomidae, endemic to the New World, also experienced a minor radiation of carnivorous forms within the subfamily Phyllostominae. Fish-eating bats, on the other hand, seem to have arisen independently in the New and Old World with little or no radiation in either hemisphere.

Vampires

Although feeding on blood can be considered a specialized form of carnivory, it is sufficiently unusual to warrant a separate category. In spite of their notoriety, there are only three species of vampires, *Desmodus rotundus*, *Diphylla ecaudata* and *Diaemus youngi*, all limited to the New World. They belong to the phyllostomid subfamily Desmodontinae, sometimes considered a separate family. Although it represents an extreme specialization, blood-feeding has allowed at least one

species, *Desmodus rotundus*, to expand its range both north and south of the tropical rain-forest zone, probably due to the introduction of domestic livestock by humans (Janzen and Wilson, 1983). Even *Desmodus* is rare in primary rain forest. This trophic role is also not very important to the region as a whole.

Foliage-gleaning

Insectivores may be easily divided into two groups: those that feed on flying insects, and those that pick, or glean, resting insects from surfaces such as the ground or vegetation. Foliage-gleaning has independently evolved on every continent, and is particularly common in rain forests, where the abundant vegetation provides an equally abundant food resource of large insects moving about on the vegetation at night.

In the New World, the phyllostomid subfamily Phyllostominae has undergone a radiation similar to that of the Old World Megadermatidae. There are several species that specialize in foliage-gleaning of insects, and some that combine this habit with gleaning small vertebrates as well. There are six genera that are at least partially foliage-gleaners in neotropical rain forests. Probably the most significant is the genus *Micronycteris* with ten

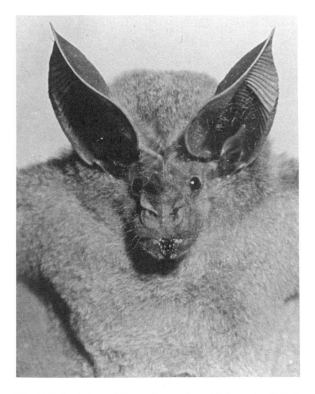

Fig. 20.6. Some large foliage-gleaners like this *Tonatia silvicola* may also eat small vertebrates on occasion.

species, all of which foliage in rain forest (Medellin et al., 1985). These bats specialize in picking large insects off the surface of the vegetation at night, and some augment this diet with fruit during certain seasons (Wilson, 1971b). The genus *Tonatia* with six species is also an important member of this group (Fig. 20.6). Averaging somewhat larger in size than *Micronycteris*, some *Tonatia* species may prove to be carnivorous as well. Three species of the genus *Mimon* are also likely all foliage-gleaners. All of the genera mentioned so far are members of the phyllostomid subfamily Phyllostominae. Two vespertilionid genera, *Myotis* and *Bauerus* (Engstrom and Wilson, 1981), also have foliage-gleaning species in Neotropical rain forests. This trophic role is moderately important in the region, but less important than it is in other tropical regions (Wilson, 1973b).

Aerial insectivory

As noted earlier, aerial insectivores dominate every tropical rain-forest area. Three cosmopolitan families, Emballonuridae, Vespertilionidae and

Molossidae provide most of the species in this category. However, in the Neotropical region, several endemic families are also in this group. These include the Furipteridae, Mormoopidae, Natalidae, Noctilionidae and Thyropteridae. In general, these families contain few species, but many are widespread within the region.

With eight genera in the Neotropical region, the family Emballonuridae has obviously undergone a major radiation in the New World (Table 20.4). These bats are common in primary rain forest, and often begin their foraging activities well before dark (Fig. 20.7). Many roost in essentially open areas, such as between the buttresses of large trees, or on tree trunks overhanging water. Such species frequently exhibit complicated social systems such as harems (Bradbury and Vehrencamp, 1976; Bradbury, 1977a).

The six Neotropical genera of Vespertilionidae include only four occurring in rain forest: the cosmopolitan genera *Eptesicus*, *Myotis*; and *Lasiurus*, which includes migratory temperate-zone forms as well (Wilson, 1980); and *Rhogeessa*, which also extends northward well out of the rain-

Fig. 20.7. A foraging emballonurid, *Rhynchonycteris naso*. (Photo by J.S. Altenbach.)

forest area. Two South American endemics, *Histiotis* and *Tomopeas*, are found in highland areas rather than in rain forests. *Myotis* has the largest number of species in the region — twelve, seven of which are endemic (LaVal, 1973; Wilson and LaVal, 1974).

There are seven genera of molossids in the region, more than in any other region (Table 20.4). Members of this family are probably the most numerous aerial insectivores in the region. They tend to be fast flyers, foraging over large bodies of water or over the forest canopy itself (Vaughan and Bateman, 1980). As a consequence of their high-flying habits, they are rarely captured in mist nets set at ground level. Hence our knowledge of their natural history is poor in spite of their abundance and importance.

Noctilio albiventris, the only congener of the fishing bat *Noctilio leporinus*, is widespread and abundant in neotropical rain forests. Although known to be insectivorous, the amount of time spent catching insects from the air or from the surface is unknown. I have watched individuals of this species foraging on flying insects above water surfaces, and have also seen them taking something (presumably insects) from the water surface in Panama.

Of the two genera of mormoopids, *Pteronotus* (Fig. 20.8) is more widespread and abundant, and has more species than *Mormoops* (Smith, 1972).

These bats are also fast-flying aerial insectivores, but are much more likely to forage within the forest than are molossids. The single genus of the family Natalidae, *Natalus*, contains two rain-forest species, both of which are slow-flying, highly maneuverable aerial insectivores, fragile in appearance. The two genera of Furipteridae, *Amorphochilus* and *Furipterus*, are both monotypic and rare, and little is known about them. *Amorphochilus* sometimes occurs in dry forest areas as well.

The Neotropical endemic family Thyropteridae contains the single genus *Thyroptera*, with two species, both occurring in rain forest (Fig. 20.9). These unique bats have suction cups on the wrists and ankles, which allows them to attach themselves to the insides of rolled leaves of plants of the genus *Heliconia* (Findley and Wilson, 1974). Ecological equivalents of these bats may be found in *Myzopoda* of Malagasy and *Tylonycteris* of Southeast Asia, although those genera have much

Fig. 20.8. *Pteronotus parnellii*, a member of the New World endemic family Mormoopidae.

Fig. 20.9. Suction cups on the wrists and ankles allow *Thyroptera tricolor* to hang from surfaces as slick as glass. (Photo by J.S. Findley.)

less well-developed suction cups (Schliemann and Mags, 1978; Schliemann and Hoeber, 1978; Kunz, 1982).

Nectar-feeders

The habit of feeding on flowers and nectar is a specialized offshoot of frugivory. It has arisen independently in both the Megachiroptera in the Old World and the Microchiroptera in the New World. Nectar feeding is an important trophic role in the Neotropical region — more so than elsewhere. A dozen genera of the phyllostomid subfamily Glossophaginae are nectar-feeders (Griffiths, 1982), and three genera of the West Indian endemic subfamily Phyllonycterinae also feed on flowers or nectar. *Glossophaga*, with five species, is the only genus that is both widespread and abundant. Several are monotypic and rare.

These bats pollinate more than 500 species of neotropical plants, in 27 families (Heithaus, 1982). More than 30 species of plants were identified from pollen grains in the stomachs of a single species (*Glossophaga soricina*) in Mexico (Alvarez and Gonzalez Q., 1970). Many of the plants pollinated by bats are commercially valuable, and tropical forest conservation schemes must consider these co-evolved relationships between plants and bats.

Frugivores

The situation in frugivores exactly parallels that in nectar-feeding bats. Fruit-eating is limited to pteropodids in the Old World and phyllostomids in the New World.

Frugivory is second only to aerial insectivory in importance in the Neotropical region. The phyllostomid subfamily Stenodermatinae includes 19 genera of fruit-eating bats. Several, such as *Artibeus* (Fig. 20.10), *Carollia* and *Sturnira* are widespread, abundant, and rich in species. Some members of the subfamilies Glossophaginae and Phyllostominae also eat fruit on occasion.

Fruit-eating bats disperse a wide variety of fruits. Gardner (1977) listed more than 175 species of plants used as food by phyllostomid bats. Some of these bats move large numbers of seeds. A single *Artibeus jamaicensis* may eat more than 2000 figs per year, spreading tens of thousands of seeds in the process (Morrison, 1978). A single *Carollia perspicillata* may disperse over 2500 seeds of certain kinds of fruit per night (Heithaus, 1982).

Fig. 20.10. *Artibeus jamaicensis*, a widespread and abundant Neotropical frugivore. Note the small metal identification band placed on a necklace on this individual.

The effects of such major seed dispersers on the composition and diversity of the forest are apparent. As with the nectar-feeders, many of these dispersal systems are highly co-evolved, and the loss of one of the members of the pair may result in the loss of the other, triggering a series of changes throughout the rain-forest ecosystem (Fig. 20.11).

Southeast Asia

With 59 genera in 8 families, Asia ranks second to the Neotropical region in diversity of bats. The family Pteropodidae is largest with 27 genera although Vespertilionidae are well represented with 17 genera. The only endemic family is the monotypic Craseonycteridae, limited so far as is known to Thailand (Lekagul and McNeeley, 1977). This region may be at the center of several major radiations that involved dispersal to Africa and Australia.

Fish-eating bats

Fish-eating is uncommon among bats in the Old World tropics. In Southeast Asia, *Megaderma lyra* of the family Megadermatidae occurs from Pakistan, India, and Sri Lanka eastwards to southeastern China and the Malay Peninsula. An opportunistic consumer of large insects and small vertebrates, this species also has been reported to eat fish (Wilson, 1973b).

The only other known fish-eating bats belong to

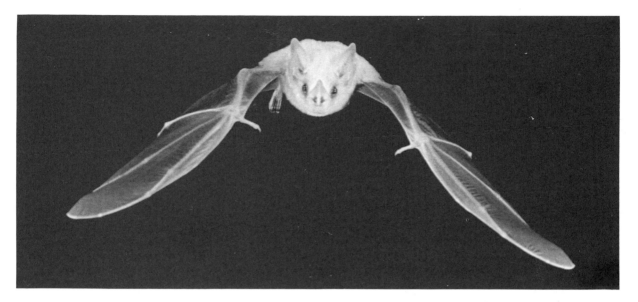

Fig. 20.11. *Ectophylla alba*, a small frugivore that is almost totally white in color. (Photo by J.S. Altenbach.)

the genus *Myotis* of the family Vespertilionidae. This family is almost entirely insectivorous, as is the genus, which includes about 90 species distributed more widely than any other genus of bat. In fact, members of the genus *Myotis* (Fig. 20.12) probably are distributed more widely than any other mammal, save *Homo*. The fishing bat, *Myotis vivesi*, is not a rain-forest inhabitant, but the morphologically similar *M. hasseltii* of southeast Asia and *M. macrotarsus* of Borneo and the

Fig. 20.12. Small insectivorous bats of the genus *Myotis* are more widely distributed than any other genus of mammal except for human beings.

Philippines are both rain-forest species which may catch fish (Wilson, 1973b).

Other carnivores

The other species of *Megaderma*, *M. spasma*, is less carnivorous than *M. lyra*, but both species at least occasionally eat small vertebrates. Both species are widespread within the region.

Foliage-gleaners

Foliage-gleaning is important in Asian rain forests (Table 20.2). The bulk of the species that use this feeding strategy are members of the genera *Rhinolophus* and *Hipposideros* (family Rhinolophidae — *Hipposideros* is accorded familial rank by some workers). Both genera are diverse (68 and 45 species respectively), and both occur in all three Old World tropical regions. Many species in both groups are aerial insectivores, and many may well practice both aerial insectivory and foliage-gleaning. Some species of *Nycteris* (Family Nycteridae) and *Myotis* (Vespertilionidae) also are foliage-gleaners in Asian rain forests. Megadermatids of several species are foliage-gleaners, and are represented in all rain forests of the Old World. Many species combine foliage-gleaning for insects with feeding on small vertebrates, which might be thought of as a specialized form of foliage-gleaning.

Aerial insectivores

As in the other regions, aerial insectivores are in the majority in Asian rain forests. Seventeen genera of vespertilionids feed on flying insects in this region. The cosmopolitan genera *Myotis* and *Pipistrellus* are particularly widespread and have numerous species in southeast Asia. Most members of this family are agile flyers, likely to forage at all levels within primary rain forest.

The rhinolophids are also well represented in this category with seven genera and numerous widespread species. As noted earlier, many may practice both aerial insectivory and foliage-gleaning. Two genera of emballonurids are wide ranging tropical genera shared with the African region.

Two genera of molossids (Fig. 20.13). *Tadarida* and *Otomops*, are high-flying aerial insectivores occurring in all Old World rain-forest regions. *Cheiromeles* is an Asian endemic with two species. This genus is remarkable for several anatomical peculiarities. To begin, they are nearly hairless, and the skin is tough and elastic. The wings are attached along the midline of the back, and the

Fig. 20.13. Free-tailed bats of the family Molossidae are distributed throughout tropical areas in both New and Old World rain forests.

ears are well separated, unlike most molossids. There is a pouch along each side into which the bat can tuck its wings when folded, apparently enabling it to move about on all fours much more adroitly than most other bats.

The most distinctive component of this feeding type in Asian rain forest is the endemic family Craseonycteridae. The single known species, *Craseonycteris thonglongyai*, is known only from Thailand. This bat is probably the world's smallest mammal with a body about the size of a large bumblebee; it was described only recently (Hill, 1974), and little is known about its natural history.

Nectar-feeding bats

The family Pteropodidae has traditionally been divided into two subfamilies, the Macroglossinae, which are primarily nectar-feeding forms, and the Pteropinae, which are mainly frugivores. Five genera of pteropodids are at least partially nectarivorous in Asian rain forests. *Rousettus*, a wide-ranging genus of ten species scattered throughout Asia, Africa, and into New Guinea, has five species in the Asian region. They feed on nectar from a variety of flowers, and eat a substantial amount of fruit as well. Many species of the huge genus *Pteropus* also occasionally feed on flowers, although most are predominantly frugivores. The same is true for some species of *Dobsonia*.

The true nectar-feeding specialists in Asian rain forests are five species of *Eonycteris* and four of *Macroglossus*. These bats have elongated rostra and tongues specialized for lapping up nectar and pollen from flowers. They are important pollinators for a variety of Asian plant species (Dobat and Peikert-Holle, 1985; Marshall, 1985).

Frugivores

Asian frugivores all belong to the megachiropteran family Pteropodidae, 27 genera of which are known from the region (Table 20.4). The subfamily Pteropinae has radiated widely throughout the Old World tropics. These animals, called flying foxes, are the largest bats known, and many are widespread and conspicuous. Some members of the genus *Pteropus* have wing-spans greater than 1.5 m, and weigh more than 1.5 kg (Nowak and Paradiso, 1983). Although mainly crepuscular and nocturnal, some have been observed flying during daylight. They shift around forming huge camps in forested areas, following seasonal fruiting patterns of a wide variety of plants. They are important seed dispersal agents for numerous rain-forest trees.

The genus *Pteropus* contains 63 species, about a third of which occur in the Asian region, mostly on southeast Asian islands. Some form huge colonies, and are considered pests on some fruit crops, although damage estimates appear to be exaggerated in many instances. These animals are also frequently harvested for food or medicinal purposes. Their numbers are declining at an alarming rate in many areas, and many insular forms may become extinct in the near future unless drastic conservation measures are implemented.

Africa

African rain forests contain 41 genera of bats in 8 families. The Pteropodidae are the most diverse with 13 genera, but there arc 11 genera of vespertilionids as well. Rhinolophids and molossids are also well represented with five genera each. The only endemic family is the Myzopodidae, a monotypic family limited to the Malagasy Republic (Madagascar). The African rain forests share many genera with those of Asia, and in many cases, with those of Australia as well.

Carnivores

Bats that feed on small terrestrial vertebrates are known from Asia, Australia, and the Neotropical Region. Curiously, carnivorous bats are almost unknown in Africa. *Cardioderma cor*, a megadermatid, occasionally eats other bats, but feeds mainly on insects (Vaughan, 1976). The other African megadermatid, *Lavia frons*, is apparently wholly insectivorous. There is a report of an African pteropodid, *Hypsignathus monstrosus*, eating chickens (Van Deusen, 1968). Lacking subsequent confirmation, this would be a strange departure from the otherwise fruit- and nectar-feeding habits of the Megachiroptera.

Foliage-gleaners

The family Nycteridae is essentially endemic to Africa and contains several species of foliage-gleaners which inhabit the rain forests of West Africa (Rosevear, 1965). Both African megadermatids are foliage-gleaners, taking large insects

from vegetation or the ground surface. Probably some species of *Myotis* (Vespertilionidae) practice foliage-gleaning in this region as well.

The largest group of foliage-gleaners in Africa are rhinolophids in the genera *Rhinolophus* and *Hipposideros*. Both of these genera have radiated extensively in Africa, as well as in other Old World tropical regions.

Aerial insectivores

Bats which catch flying insects are most familiar to people living in the temperate zones of the world, and also occur throughout the tropics. The ubiquitous family Vespertilionidae contains species on each of the continents with rain forests, probably representing the largest radiation of aerial insectivores (Fig. 20.14). The pantropical families Emballonuridae and Molossidae have members in all of the rain-forest regions. The family Rhinolophidae has aerial insectivores distributed throughout the Old World tropics.

The Old World sucker-footed bat, *Myzopoda aurita*, is in thc family Myzopodidae endemic to Malagasy. Its ecological equivalent in the New World is *Thyroptera* of the endemic family Thy-

Fig. 20.14. Vespertilionids such as these *Myotis* are the most common aerial insectivores in almost all rain-forest areas. Note the identification bands placed on the wrists of these individuals.

ropteridae (Findley and Wilson, 1974; Wilson, 1976, 1978; Wilson and Findley, 1977).

Three genera of emballonurids and five of rhinolophids provide many of the species of aerial insectivores in the region. Eleven genera of vespertilionids contribute the most diversity to this feeding type in the region. Molossids are also well represented, with five genera in Africa.

Little is known of the specific food habits and foraging patterns of Africa rain-forest bats. The diversity and abundance of insectivorous forms is comparable to those in the other areas of the Old World tropics.

Nectar-feeding bats

Generalist frugivores in the genera *Epomophorus*, *Micropteropus*, *Pteropus* and *Rousettus* occasionally feed on nectar and pollen, and several species of both *Epomophorus* and *Rousettus* occur in the region. *Pteropus* is basically a South Pacific genus, but has mainland representatives in both Asia and Australia. Curiously enough, this genus does not occur on the mainland of Africa, being limited to Malagasy and nearby islands.

The true nectar-feeding specialists in Africa are in the genera *Megaloglossus* and *Nanonycteris*. Both are monotypic, and limited in distribution to West African rain forests. They are probably the most effective pollinators of *Parkia* trees, although the blossoms attract other species of bats as well (Baker, 1973).

Frugivores

Thirteen genera of pteropodids occur in Africa, and all but the two nectar feeders mentioned above are frugivorous. Important genera include *Eidolon*, *Epomophorus*, *Epomops* and *Rousettus*. Five species of *Rousettus*, three of *Epomops* and seven of *Epomophorus* are widespread and locally abundant. *Eidolon helvum* is the most broadly distributed of all African fruit bats.

An African endemic, the hammer-headed bat, *Hypsignathus monstrosus*, has curious behavioural habits to match its rather bizarre appearance. Males have an enlarged, truncate head adorned with enormous lips, nose ruffles, and a split chin. They have an enlarged larynx that allows them to make loud and continual cries to attract females. Males gather on traditional calling grounds or "leks", frequently arranged linearly along rivers,

and try to attract females to their own small territory within the calling grounds (Bradbury, 1977a, b).

Australia

The Australian Region has 31 genera in 6 families, most of which are represented in rainforest communities (Strahan, 1983). Vespertilionidae with 11 genera and Pteropodidae with 10 are the most diverse. There are 2 genera each of emballonurids and molossids, 5 of rhinolophids, and 1 megadermatid. Curiously, there are no bat families endemic to Australia, although New Zealand harbours one, the Mystacinidae. Most of the Australian bat fauna appears to have been developed through island-hopping colonists from Southeast Asia.

Carnivores

Macroderma gigas (Megadermatidae), the Australian false vampire, or ghost bat, is the only truly carnivorous species in Australia (Fig. 20.15). Although now limited to the northern two-thirds of the continent, it apparently enjoyed a much wider distribution in the Pleistocene, when rain forests extended much farther south than they do today (Hudson and Wilson, 1986). Recent evidence has

Fig. 20.15. *Macroderma gigas*, an Australian carnivore. (Photo by F. Greenwell.)

suggested that *Nycticeius rueppellii*, a vespertilionid, also may feed on small vertebrates occasionally.

Foliage-gleaners

The family Rhinolophidae (including *Hipposideros*) has undergone a major radiation throughout the Paleotropical Region, producing foliage-gleaning species in rain forests on each Old World continent. Four species of *Hipposideros* and three of *Rhinolophus* (both Rhinolophidae) probably are capable of gleaning insects from the foliage or ground surface. An additional rhinolophid, *Rhinonicteris aurantius*, is one of Australia's only two endemic bats.

The family Vespertilionidae is worldwide in distribution, and contains many species of foliage-gleaners. Curiously enough, most vespertilionids that practice foliage-gleaning are inhabitants of the temperate zone, rather than tropical forests. The only exceptions are found in New Guinea and Australia, where a few species occur in rain forests.

Several vespertilionids probably include foliage-gleaning in their feeding habits, most notably the six species of long-eared bats in the genus *Nyctophilus*. The single species of *Myotis* in Australia, *M. adversus*, forages over water surfaces, gleaning insects and other arthropods in the same way as fishing bats catch small fish from the water surface. *Phoniscus papuensis*, a strikingly colored inhabitant of coastal rain forests, was thought to be extinct but has recently been taken in several areas, as far south as New South Wales. The extremely rare *Murina florius* may also be a foliage-gleaner in mountainous rain forests.

Aerial insectivores

Seven species of the emballonurid genus *Taphozous* are inhabitants of Australian rain forests. Molossids are represented by six species in three genera — the ubiquitous *Tadarida*, together with *Chaerophon* and *Mormopterus*.

Vespertilionids include two species of a widespread Old World genus, *Miniopterus*. *Chalinolobus*, a genus centered in the Australia–New Guinea region, has five species in the area. *Nycticeius*, a cosmopolitan genus, also has five species in Australia. Two species of *Pipistrellus* and three of *Eptesicus* complete the Australian vespertilionid aerial insectivores.

Nectar-feeding bats

In both the New and Old World, radiations of nectar-feeding forms have been sufficiently extensive to result in occupation of all rain-forest regions. As in the other paleotropical rain forests, many Australian pteropodids feed on both fruit and nectar. The true nectar-feeding specialists in Australia are *Macroglossus lagochilus* and *Syconycteris australis*. Both are important pollinators of a variety of tropical Australian plants.

Frugivores

The family Pteropodidae has nearly 150 species, and although a third of them occur in New Guinea, only 8 are found in Australia. Four of these are species of *Pteropus*, all of which are probably both frugivorous and nectarivorous. Many Australian frugivores feed on *Eucalyptus* flowers as well as fruit. Although commercial fruit growers complain of losses to fruit bats in this region, almost all species prefer native fruits when available. Camps of *Pteropus scapulatus* have been estimated at over 100 000 individuals, and these bats frequently wander over large distances in search of food.

Dobsonia is another genus of naked-backed bats, with the wings joining at mid-body instead of along the flanks. Easily the most spectacular of the Australian fruit bats, however, is *Nyctimene robinsoni*, the tube-nosed bat. These bats have rolled nostrils that protrude about 5 mm from the rostrum, and greenish-yellow spots scattered along the wings and ears, presumably an adaptation for roosting in sun-dappled foliage.

CONCLUSION

The bat faunas of tropical rain forests are quite variable and distinctive, with the New World rain forests harbouring a greater variety than any comparable areas in the Old World tropics. In the Old World, although Asia, Africa and Australia all have distinctive faunas, many of the genera are shared between two or even all three regions, and endemism is less apparent than in the New World. All tropical areas are richer in bat species than the temperate zones in either hemisphere.

Many of the differences detailed by taxonomic and traditional zoogeographic analyses disappear when these faunas are compared ecologically. Numerical zoogeographic analyses based on trophic structure point out many similarities among all regions in basic foraging patterns and food habits of their contained faunas. Aerial insectivory is the predominant trophic role for bats in all regions, and frugivory is second in all except Africa, where foliage-gleaning is slightly more important. Nectar-feeding is practiced by a wider variety of bats in the Neotropics than in the Old World regions. Carnivory, including fish-eating and blood-feeding, is relatively unimportant overall, and more common in the New than in the Old World.

One unfortunate similarity shared by all rainforest bats is their uncertain future (Johns et al., 1985). The widespread effects of habitat disturbance and the wholesale destruction of tropical forests threaten the existence of many of these species of bats. The importance of bats to pollination and dispersal systems of hundreds of species of tropical plants has been well documented. The loss of these key links could cause reverberations throughout the ecosystem. Clearly, conservation efforts directed at tropical rain forests should strive to include the faunas they support.

REFERENCES

Allen, G.M., 1939. *Bats*. Harvard Univ. Press, Cambridge, Mass., 368 pp.

Alvarez, T. and Gonzalez Q., L., 1970. Analisis polinico del contenido gastrico de murcielagos Glossophaginae de Mexico. *An. Esc. Nacl. Cienc. Biol.*, 18: 137–165.

Baker, H.G., 1973. Evolutionary relationships between flowering plants and animals in American and African forests. In: B.J. Meggers, E.S. Ayensu and W.D. Duckworth (Editors), *Tropical Forest Ecosystems in Africa and South America: A Comparative Review*. Smithsonian Institution Press, Washington, D.C., pp. 145–159.

Baker, J.R., 1938. Evolution of breeding seasons. In: G.R. de Beer (Editor), *Evolution. Essays on Aspects of Evolutionary Biology. Presented to Professor E.S. Goodrich*. Clarendon, Oxford, pp. 161–177.

Baron, G. and Jolicoeur, P., 1980. Brain structure in Chiroptera: some multivariate trends. *Evolution*, 34: 386–393.

Bradbury, J.W., 1977a. Social organization and communication. In: W.A. Wimsatt (Editor), *Biology of Bats*. Academic Press, New York, N.Y., pp. 1–72.

Bradbury, J.W., 1977b. Lek mating behavior in the hammerheaded bat. *Z. Tierpsychol.*, 45: 225–255.

Bradbury, J.W. and Vehrencamp, S.L., 1976. Social organiza-

tion and foraging in emballonurid bats. I. Field studies. *Behav. Ecol. Sociobiol.*, 1: 337–381.

Cabrera, A., 1958. Catalogo de los mamiferos de America del Sur. *Rev. Mus. Argent. Cienc. Nat. "Bernardino Rivadavia"*, 4: 1–307.

Carter, D.C., 1970. Chiropteran reproduction. In: B.H. Slaughter and D.W. Walton (Editors), *About Bats*. Southern Methodist Univ. Press, Dallas, Tex., pp. 233–246.

Dobat, K. and Peikert-Holle, T., 1985. *Bluten und Fledermaus. Bestaubung durch Fledermaus und Flughundt (Chiropterophilie)*. Waldemar Kramer, Frankfurt, 370 pp.

Dwyer, P.D., 1970. Foraging behaviour of the Australian large-footed *Myotis* (Chiroptera). *Mammalia*, 34: 76–80.

Eisenberg, J.F. and Wilson, D.E., 1978. Relative brain size and feeding strategies in the Chiroptera. *Evolution*, 32: 740–751.

Engstrom. M.D. and Wilson, D.E., 1981. Systematics of *Antrozous dubiaquercus* (Chiroptera: Vespertilionidae), with comments on the status of *Bauerus* Van Gelder. *Ann. Carnegie Mus.*, 50: 371–383.

Erkhert, H.G., Kracht, S. and Haussler, U,. 1980. Characteristics of circadian activity systems in Neotropical bats. In: D.E. Wilson and A.L. Gardner (Editors), *Proc. 5th Int. Bat Research Conf.* Texas Tech Press, Lubbock, Tex. pp. 95–104.

Fenton, M.B., 1975. Observations on the biology of some Rhodesian bats, including a key to the Chiroptera of Rhodesia. *Life Sci. Contrib., R. Ont. Mus.*, 104: 1–27.

Fenton, M.B., 1982. Echolocation, insect hearing, and feeding ecology of insectivorous bats. In: T.H. Kunz (Editor), *Ecology of Bats*. Plenum, New York, N.Y., pp. 261–285.

Fenton, M.B. and Kunz, T.H., 1977. Movements and Behaviour. In: R.J. Baker, J.K. Jones, Jr. and D.C. Carter (Editors), *Biology of Bats of the New World Family Phyllostomatidae. Part II*. Spec. Publ., Museum Texas Tech Univ., Lubbock, Tex., pp. 351–364.

Findley, J.S., 1969. Brain size in bats. *J. Mammal.*, 50: 340–344.

Findley, J.S., 1973. Phenetic packing as a measure of faunal diversity. *Am. Nat.*, 107: 580–584.

Findley, J.S., 1976. The structure of bat communities. *Am. Nat.*, 110: 129–139.

Findley, J.S. and Wilson, D.E., 1974. Observations on the Neotropical disk-winged bat, *Thyroptera tricolor* Spix. *J. Mammal.*, 55: 562–571.

Findley, J.S. and Wilson, D.E., 1982. Ecological significance of chiropteran morphology. In: T.H. Kunz (Editor), *Ecology of Bats*. Plenum, New York, N.Y., pp. 243–260.

Findley, J.S. and Wilson, D.E., 1983. Are bats rare in tropical Africa? *Biotropica*, 15: 299–303.

Findley, J.S., Studier, E.H. and Wilson, D.E., 1972. Morphologic properties of bat wings. *J. Mammal.*, 53: 429–444.

Fleming, T.H., 1971. *Artibeus jamaicensis*: delayed embryonic development in a Neotropical bat. *Science*, 171: 402–404.

Fleming, T.H., 1982. Foraging strategies of plant-visiting bats. In: T.H. Kunz (Editor), *Ecology of Bats*. Plenum, New York, N.Y., pp. 287–325.

Fleming, T.H., Hooper, E.T. and Wilson, D.E., 1972. Three Central American bat communities: structure, reproductive cycles, and movement patterns. *Ecology*, 53: 653–670.

Freeman, P.W., 1979. Specialized insectivory: beetle-eating and moth-eating molossid bats. *J. Mammal.*, 60: 467–479.

Freeman, P.W., 1981. Correspondence of food habits and morphology in insectivorous bats. *J. Mammal.*, 62: 166–173.

Gardner, A.L., 1977. Feeding habits. In: R.J. Baker, J.K. Jones, Jr. and D.C. Carter (Editors), *Biology of Bats of the New World Family Phyllostomatidae*. Part II. Spec. Publ., Museum Texas Tech Univ., Lubbock, Tex., pp. 351–364.

Gardner, A.L. and Wilson, D.E., 1971. A melanized subcutaneous covering of the cranial musculature in the phyllostomid bat, *Ectophylla alba*. *J. Mammal.*, 52: 854–855.

Gardner, A.L., LaVal, R.K. and Wilson, D.E., 1970. The distributional status of some Costa Rican bats. *J. Mammal.*, 51: 712–729.

Geluso, K.N., 1980. Renal form and function in bats: an ecophysiological appraisal. In: D.E. Wilson and A.L. Gardner (Editors), *Proc. 5th Int. Bat Research Conf*. Texas Tech Press, Lubbock, Tex., pp. 403–414.

Griffiths, T.A., 1982. Systematics of the New World nectar-feeding bats (Mammalia, Phyllostomidae), based on the morphology of the hyoid and lingual regions. *Am. Mus. Novit.*, 2742: 1–45.

Heithaus, E.R., 1982. Coevolution between bats and plants. In: T.H. Kunz (Editor), *Ecology of Bats*. Plenum, New York, N.Y., pp. 327–367.

Heithaus, E.R., Fleming, T.H. and Opler, P.A., 1975. Foraging patterns and resource utilization in seven species of bats in a seasonal tropical forest. *Ecology*, 56: 841–854.

Hill, J.E., 1974. A new family, genus and species of bat (Mammalia: Chiroptera) from Thailand. *Bull. Br. Mus. (Nat. Hist.), Zool.*, 30: 1–28.

Hill, J.E. and Smith, J.D., 1984. *Bats: a Natural History*. Univ of Texas Press, Austin, Tex., 243 pp.

Hudson, W.S. and Wilson, D.E., 1986. *Macroderma gigas*. *Mammal. Species*, 260: 1–4.

Janzen, D.H. and Wilson, D.E., 1983. Mammals. In: D.H. Janzen (Editor), *Costa Rican Natural History*. Univ. of Chicago Press, Chicago, Ill., pp. 426–442.

Johns, A.D., Pine, R.H. and Wilson, D.E., 1985. Rain forest bats — an uncertain future. *Bat News*, Fauna and Flora Preservation Society, London, 5: 4–5.

Keast, A., 1972. Comparisons of contemporary mammal faunas of southern continents. In: A. Keast, F.C. Erk and B. Glass (Editors), *Evolution, Mammals, and Southern Continents*. State Univ. of New York Press, New York, N.Y., pp. 433–501.

Koopman, K.F., 1970. Zoogeography of bats. In: B.H. Slaughter and D.W. Walton (Editors), *About Bats*. Southern Methodist Univ. Press, Dallas, Tex., pp. 29–50.

Kunz, T.H., 1982. Roosting ecology. In: T.H. Kunz (Editor), *Ecology of Bats*. Plenum, New York, N.Y., pp. 1–56.

LaVal, R.K., 1973. A revision of the neotropical bats of the genus *Myotis*. *Sci. Bull., Los Angeles County Mus.*, 15: 1–54.

Lekagul, B. and McNeely, J.A., 1977. *Mammals of Thailand*. Association for the Conservation of Nature, Bangkok, Thailand, 758 pp.

MacArthur, R.H., 1972. *Geographical Ecology*. Harper and Row, New York, N.Y., 269 pp.

Mares, M.A. and Wilson, D.E., 1971. Bat reproduction during the Costa Rican dry season. *Bioscience*, 21: 471–477.

Marshall, A.G., 1985. Old World phytophagous bats (Megachiroptera) and their food plants: A survey. *Zool. J. Linn. Soc.*, 83: 351–369.

McNab, B.K., 1969. The economics of temperature regulation in Neotropical bats. *Compar. Biochem. Physiol.*, 31: 227–268.

McNab, B.K., 1982. Evolutionary alternatives in the physiological ecology of bats. In: T.H. Kunz (Editor), *Ecology of Bats*. Plenum, New York, N.Y., pp. 151–200.

Medellin, R.A., Wilson, D.E. and Navarro L., D., 1985. *Micronycteris brachyotis*. *Mammal. species*, 251: 1–4.

Medway, Lord, 1972. Reproductive cycles of the flat-headed bats *Tylonycteris pachypus* and *T. robustula* (Chiroptera: Vespertilionidae) in a humid equatorial environment. *J. Linn. Soc. London, Zool.*, 51: 33–61.

Mok, W.Y., Wilson, D.E., Lacey, L.A. and Luizao, R.C., 1982. Lista atualizada de quiropteros da Amazonia Brasileira. *Acta Amazon.*, 12: 817–823.

Morrison, D.W., 1978. Foraging ecology and energetics of the frugivorous bat *Artibeus jamaicensis*. *Ecology*, 59: 716–723.

Navarro L., D. and Wilson, D.E., 1982. *Vampyrum spectrum*. *Mammal. Species*, 184: 1–4.

Norberg, U.M., 1981a. Allometry of bat wings and legs and comparison with bird wings. *Philos. Trans. R. Soc. London, Ser. B*, 292: 359–398.

Norberg, U.M., 1981b. Flight, morphology and the ecological niche in some birds and bats. In: M.H. Day (Editor), *Vertebrate Locomotion*. Symp. Zoological Society London, 48: 173–196.

Nowak, R.M. and Paradiso, J.L., 1983. *Walker's Mammals of the World*. Johns Hopkins Univ. Press, Baltimore, Md., 4th ed., 1: 1–568.

Racey, P.A., 1982. Ecology of bat reproduction. In: T.H. Kunz (Editor), *Ecology of Bats*. Plenum, New York, N.Y., pp. 57–104.

Rosevear, D.R., 1965. *The Bats of West Africa*. British Museum of Natural History, London, 418 pp.

Schliemann, H. and Hoeber, M., 1978. The structure and function of the pads on the thumb and foot *Tylonycteris*. In: R.J. Olimbo, J.B. Castelino and F.A. Mutere (Editors), *Proc. 4th Int. Bat Research Conf*. Kenya Literature Bureau, Nairobi, pp. 39–50.

Schliemann, H. and Mags, B., 1978. *Myzopoda aurita*. *Mammal. Species*, 116: 1–2.

Simpson, G.G., 1964. Species density of North American recent mammals. *Syst. Zool.*, 13: 57–73.

Smith, J.D., 1972. Systematics of the chiropteran family Mormoopidae. *Univ. Kansas Mus. Nat. Hist., Misc. Publ.*, 56: 1–132.

Strahan, R. (Editor), 1983. *Complete Book of Australian Mammals*. Angus and Robertson, Sydney, N.S.W., 472 pp.

Studier, E.H. and Wilson, D.E., 1970. Thermoregulation in some Neotropical bats. *Compar. Biochem. Physiol.*, 34: 251–262.

Studier, E.H. and Wilson, D.E., 1979. Effects of captivity on thermoregulation and metabolism in *Artibeus jamaicensis* (Chiroptera: Phyllostomatidae). *Compar. Biochem. Physiol.*, 62B: 347–350.

Studier, E.H. and Wilson, D.E., 1983. Natural urine concentrations and composition in Neotropical bats. *J. Mammal.*, 64: 445–452.

Studier, E.H., Boyd, B.C., Felman, A.T., Dapson, R.W. and Wilson, D.E., 1983a. Renal function in the Neotropical bat, *Artibeus jamaicensis. Compar. Biochem. Physiol.*, 75A: 509–515.

Studier, E.H., Wisniewski, S.J., Feldman, A.T., Dapson, R.W., Boyd, B.C. and Wilson, D.E., 1983b. Kidney structure in Neotropical bats. *J. Mammal.*, 64: 445–452.

Thorne, R.F., 1973. Floristic relationships between tropical Africa and tropical America. In: B.J. Meggers, E.S. Ayensu and W.D. Duckworth (Editors), *Tropical Forest Ecosystems in Africa and South America: a Comparative Review.* Smithsonian Institution Press, Washington, D.C., pp. 27–47.

Tuttle, M.D. and Ryan, M.J., 1981. Bat predation and evolution of frog vocalizations in the Neotropics. *Science*, 214: 677–678.

Tuttle, M.D. and Stephenson, D., 1982. Growth and survival of bats. In: T.H. Kunz (Editor), *Ecology of Bats.* Plenum, New York, N.Y., pp. 105–150.

Van der Piji, L., 1956. Remarks on pollination by bats in the genera *Freycinetia, Duabanga*, and *Haplophragma*, and on chiropterophily in general. *Acta Bot. Neerl.*, 5: 135–144.

Van Deusen, H.M., 1968. Carnivorous habits of *Hypsignathus monstrosus. J. Mammal.*, 49: 335–336.

Vaughan, T.A., 1976. Nocturnal behavior of the African false vampire bat (*Cardioderma cor*). *J. Mammal.*, 57: 227–248.

Vaughan, T.A. and Bateman, M.M., 1980. The molossid wing: some adaptations for rapid flight. In: D.E. Wilson and A.L. Gardner (Editors), *Proc. 5th Int. Bat Research Conf.* Texas Tech Press, Lubbock, Tex., pp. 69–78.

Wilson, D.E., 1970. An unusual roost of *Artibeus cinereus watsoni. J. Mammal.*, 51: 204–205.

Wilson, D.E., 1971a. Ecology of *Myotis nigricans* (Mammalia: Chiroptera) on Barro Colorado Island, Panama Canal Zone. *J. Zool.*, 163: 1–13.

Wilson, D.E., 1971b. Food habits of *Micronycteris hirsuta* (Chiroptera: Phyllostomidae). *Mammalia*, 35: 107–110.

Wilson, D.E., 1973a. Reproduction in Neotropical bats. *Period. Biol.*, 75: 215–217.

Wilson, D.E., 1973b, Bat faunas: a trophic comparison. *Syst. Zool.*, 22: 14–29.

Wilson, D.E., 1976. The subspecies of *Thyroptera discifera* (Lichtenstein and Peters). *Proc. Biol. Soc. Wash.*, 89: 305–312.

Wilson, D.E., 1978. *Thyroptera discifera. Mammal. Species*, 104: 1–3.

Wilson, D.E., 1979. Reproductive patterns. In: R.J. Baker, J.K. Jones, Jr. and D.C. Carter (Editors), *Biology of Bats of the New World Family Phyllostomatidae. Part III.* Spec. Publ., Museum Texas Tech Univ., Lubbock, Tex., pp. 317–378.

Wilson, D.E., 1980. Murcielagos migratorios en el continente Americano. *Organizacion de los Estados Americanos*, Reunion tecnica sobre conservacion de animales migratorios del hemisferio occidental y sus ecosistemas, SG/Series P/III, 3: 62–63.

Wilson, D.E. and Findley, J.S., 1970. Reproductive cycle of a Neotropical insectivorous bat, *Myotis nigricans. Nature*, 225: p. 1155.

Wilson, D.E. and Findley, J.S., 1971. Spermatogenesis in some Neotropical species of *Myotis. J. Mammal.*, 52: 420–426.

Wilson, D.E. and Findley, J.S., 1972. Randomness in bat homing. *Am. Nat.*, 106: 418–424.

Wilson, D.E. and Findley, J.S., 1977. *Thyroptera tricolor. Mammal. Species*, 71: 1–3.

Wilson, D.E. and LaVal, R.K., 1974. *Myotis nigricans. Mammal. Species*, 39: 1–3.

Wilson, D.E. and Tyson, E.L., 1970. Longevity records for *Artibeus jamaicensis* and *Myotis nigricans. J. Mammal.*, 51: 203.

Wilson III, J.W., 1974. Analytical zoogeography of North American mammals. *Evolution*, 28: 124–140.

Chapter 21

RODENTS

F. DIETERLEN

INTRODUCTION

Of all the orders of vertebrates, the Rodentia are among the richest in species; and they are far the richest among the orders of mammals, containing 40% of the total species in that class. They have an important role in almost all ecosystems of the world, and particularly in the tropical rain forest, which is a center of rodent occurrence (Fig. 21.1). About 400 species, that is 25% of all rodents, inhabit that biome, either exclusively or as part of their range. Due to their wealth of niches and habitats, tropical lowland and montane rain forests are of outstanding importance for speciation and other evolutionary processes in rodents. Many groups, such as the Muridae, have evolved there and have their main distribution in that biome.

Knowledge of rodent ecology and taxonomy is still limited. Little is known about their ecological requirements, their exact habitat needs, their feeding habits, their role in seed consumption and seed distribution, and in insect predation. Their dependence on seasonal events like food availability, and along with this their breeding habits and population dynamics, are not yet fully understood. Therefore, an inventory of the species occurring in the tropical rain forest and of the state of knowledge of their ecology will be useful. Such a compilation has not previously been undertaken.

Rodents of the African and South-East Asian (especially Malayan) rain forests are relatively well known, whereas the other parts of the Oriental region and the Australian region are not well enough investigated. The Neotropics, clearly the richest region in rain-forest rodents, is the least known. For this reason, this chapter pays most attention to the better-known African fauna and its ecology.

THE ORIENTAL REGION

The Oriental region consists of four subregions: Indian, Indo-Chinese, Sundaic and Wallacea. This chapter considers the area in two parts: (a) the Indomalayan region in South-East Asia from India to Borneo; and (b) the Wallacean region from the Philippines and Sulawesi (Celebes) to the Sunda Islands from Lombok to Timor.

The Indomalayan region

General aspects

Within this region, the ecology of rodents in rain forests has been relatively well investigated in continental Malaysia and Thailand. These regions are the richest in species number; fewer rain-forest species inhabit the Sunda Islands, and the Indian subregion must be considered as impoverished. Rain forest in the whole region includes the categories of tropical evergreen forest and hill evergreen forest (Lekagul and McNeeley, 1977).

The rodent fauna

Representatives of three rodent sub-orders and four families inhabit the rain forest: Sciuromorpha with Sciuridae (squirrels), Myomorpha with Muridae (murid rats and mice) and Rhizomyidae (bamboo rats), and Hystricomorpha with Hystricidae (Old World porcupines). There are some 95 species belonging to about 40 genera (Table 21.1).

Sciuridae, with two subfamilies: Sciurinae (diurnal squirrels) and Petauristinae (nocturnal flying

TABLE 21.1

Rodents occurring in rain forests of the Indo-Malayan region (after Harrison and Traub, 1950; Harrison, 1957; Ellerman, 1961; Medway, 1969; Lim, 1970; Walker, 1975; Lekagul and McNeeley, 1977; Muul and Lim, 1978; Corbet and Hill, 1980; Musser and Newcomb, 1983; and others).

SCIURIDAE	*Reithrosciurus macrotis*	*Pteromyscus pulverulentus*	*Lenothrix*[1] *canus*
Sciurinae (diurnal squirrels)	*Rhinosciurus laticaudatus*	RHIZOMYIDAE	*Leopoldamys*[1] *edwardsi*
Callosciurus adamsi	*Sundasciurus brookei*	(bamboo rats)	*L. sabanus*
C. *baluensis*	S. *hippurus*		*Maxomys*[1] *alticola*
C. *caniceps*	S. *jentinki*	*Rhizomys sumatrensis*	M. *inas*
C. *finlaysoni*	S. *lowi*		M. *ochraceiventer*
C. *flavimanus*	S. *tenuis*	MURIDAE (murid rats	M. *rajah*
C. *melanogaster*	*Tamiops macclellandi*	and mice)	M. *surifer*
C. *nigrovittatus*	T. *rodolphi*		M. *whiteheadi*
C. *notatus*		*Chiropodomys gliroides*	*Niviventer*[1] *bukit*
C. *prevosti*	Petauristinae (flying squirrels)	C. *major*	N. *cremoriventer*
Dremomys everetti	*Aeromys tephromelas*	C. *muroides*	N. *fulvescens*
D. *lokriah*	A. *thomasi*	*Dacnomys millardi*	N. *langbianis*
D. *rufigenys*	*Belomys pearsoni*	*Haeromys margarettae*	N. *rapit*
Exilisciurus exilis	*Hylopetes lepidus*	H. *pusillus*	*Srilankamys*[1] *ohiensis*
E. *whiteheadi*	H. *platyurus*	*Hapalomys longicaudatus*	*Sundamys*[1] *infraluteus*
Funambulus layardi	*Iomys horsfieldi*	*Mus crociduroides*	S. *maxi*
F. *sublineatus*	*Petaurillus emiliae*	M. *famulus*	S. *muelleri*
F. *tristriatus*	P. *hosei*	M. *fernandoni*	*Vernaya fulva*
Glyphotes canalvus	P. *kinlochi*	M. *mayori*	
G. *simus*	*Petaurista elegans*	M. *vulcani*	HYSTRICIDAE
Lariscus hosei	P. *petaurista*	*Pitecheir melanurus*	(Old World porcupines)
L. *insignis*	*Petinomys fuscocapillus*	*Rattus koratensis*	
L. *niobe*	P. *genibarbis*	R. *rattus*	*Atherurus macrourus*
Menetes berdmorei	P. *hageni*	R. *tiomanicus*	*Hystrix brachyura*
Ratufa affinis	P. *setosus*	*Berylmys*[1] *berdmorei*	H. *hodgsoni*
R. *bicolor*	P. *vordermanni*	B. *bowersii*	H. *javanicum*
		Kadarsanomys[1] *sodyi*	*Trichys lipura*

[1]These genera were formerly included in *Rattus*, but now are accorded generic status (Musser and Newcomb, 1983).

squirrels). There is in no part of the world such a concentration of squirrels as in the Indomalayan rain forests. Here, myomorph rodents (36 species) are outnumbered by far by sciurids (51 species). All flying squirrels are arboreal and also the majority of diurnal squirrels. *Lariscus insignis* inhabiting the forest floor is one of the exceptions. Most of the diurnal squirrels live in the middle and upper storey of the forest. They are active only by day, whereas flying squirrels are nocturnal. These latter are not only excellent climbers but also able to glide between trees over long distances up to 60 m. A furred flying membrane (patagium) along the flanks, joining fore and hind limb enables them to use this remarkable type of locomotion. The frequency of arboreality and of gliding are a peculiar South-East Asian phenomenon, occurring in several taxonomic groups of rain-forest vertebrates. Most of the sciurids are primarily vegetarians, but many also eat insects and other invertebrates.

Muridae and **Rhizomyidae**. In the absence of Cricetidae, dormice (Gliridae) and others, some 38 murids and one rhizomyid are the only myomorphs inhabiting the rain forest. Because many ecological niches of this biome are occupied by squirrels, the number of forest-dwelling murids is relatively small. And due to arboreality of squirrels, arboreal murids are even fewer. *Pitecheir melanurus*, *Lenothrix canus* and *Niviventer cremoriventer* are examples of the few arboreal species. *Chiropodomys gliroides* is a specialized form, generally common in bamboo thickets and often nesting in the internodes of large bamboos (Medway, 1967). The remaining species are mostly forest-floor dwellers, in spite of the fact that most are excellent climbers. The majority belong to the genus *Rattus*, which is extremely rich in species (including the house rat *Rattus rattus* with a world-wide distribution and the Norway rat *Rattus norvegicus*), or to other genera with astonishing convergent trends to *Rattus* (Musser, 1981; Musser and Newcomb, 1983).

Hystricidae. All Old World porcupines are terrestrial. Five species inhabit the South-East Asian rain forest in different distribution patterns. *Hystrix hodgsoni* is continental. *H. brachyura* is found in some areas of the continent and in Sumatra and Borneo. *H. javanicus* inhabits Java and Sulawesi. Hystricids are vegetarians, mostly feeding on roots, tubers, bark, fallen fruits, etc.

Feeding ecology

As in other parts of the world, fruits and seeds of the trees, together with insects, form the major part of the rodent's food. But it is noteworthy that most species of flying squirrels are specialized for folivory and herbivory (Muul and Lim, 1978). The most folivorous genus is *Petaurista*, its cecum being long and folded, and the large intestine also very long. Tree fruits and seeds constitute the major food of the diurnal squirrels, and of many murid species. Harrison (1954) has shown that most arboreal species of squirrels and rats are more or less vegetarian, while others, such as *Dremomys everetti*, a ground-dwelling squirrel, are predominantly insectivorous. Nevertheless the most surprising fact in Harrison's results was the high amount of insect material in the diet of Malaysian rodents. In several rats (*Rattus r. jalorensis*, *Leopoldamys sabanus*, *Maxomys rajah*) insects, such as termites and ants, form a major food source. According to Lim (1970), some ground-dwelling rats feed on molluscs, and *Sundamys muelleri* is partially crab-eating, corresponding with its preference for wetter habitats in the rain forest.

Reproduction and population dynamics

Data on breeding of forest-dwelling rodents from South-East Asia were published by Harrison (1951, 1952, 1955) from continental Malaysia and by Wade (1958) from Borneo. In the Bornean rain forest, reproduction of many species starts almost abruptly, shortly after the beginning of a period of decreasing rains (which cannot be called a dry season). The reproduction peak is attained within this period. This is a proof that near to the Equator breeding periodicity really can exist. On the Malayan Peninsula there are no evident reproductive peaks, and only slight relations between

breeding and precipitation. From his results Harrison (1955) deduced "the virtual elimination of the breeding season", due to the comparatively uniform climate near the Equator. But Medway (1972), working on the phenology of the rain forest of that region has shown from Harrison's results that at least *Leopoldamys sabanus* and *Sundamys muelleri* had seasonally elevated pregnancy rates: "These rats are probably dependent for food to a great extent on fallen fruit, and it is notable that the peak in their reproductive cycle coincided with the seasonal peak of fruiting".

Generally, rodents of tropical rain forests have litters with relatively few young compared with species occurring in open tropical habitats or in forests of the temperate regions. In Malaysia three species of the sciurid *Callosciurus* had only 2.2 young per litter, *Chiropodomys gliroides* had 2.2, and the average litter size of nine rat species of seven genera varied between 3.0 and 4.3 (Harrison, 1955).

The Wallacean sub-region

General aspects

According to Groves (1975) there is no evidence of any significant exchange of mammalian fauna between Sulawesi and the Philippines. This view was strongly confirmed for murid rodents by Musser (1977), who wrote "each area has its unique assemblage of endemic species of rats and mice; these are mostly restricted to primary forest". Thus the sub-regional identity of the Wallacea sub-region is questionable. But on grounds of simplification and clearness the two island complexes are treated here together. Tropical rain forest in this region is composed of lowland forest, and moss forest at higher altitudes.

The rodent fauna

From Table 21.2 it can be seen that only the genus *Rattus* has species in the rain forests of both the Philippines and Sulawesi. The whole fauna has an extraordinarily great number of endemics, due to geological and other isolating events in the past. Sulawesi alone harbours at least 10 endemic rodent genera in its rain forests. Its rain-forest rodent fauna is at least twice as rich in species number as that of the Philippines. About 50% of the murids

TABLE 21.2

Rodents occurring in rain forests of the Philippines (P) and of Sulawesi (S) (after Musser 1969, 1977, 1981, 1982; and others)

SCIURIDAE	MURIDAE (murid rats and mice)
Sciurinae (diurnal squirrels)	
Callosciurus leucomus (S)	*Archboldomys luzonensis* (P)
C. mowewensis (S)	*Bunomys penitus* (S)
C. prevosti (S)	*Crunomys fallax* (P)
C. sarasinorum (S)	*C. melanius* (P)
Hyosciurus heinrichi (S)	*Echiothrix leucura* (S)
Nannosciurus concinnus (P)	*Eropeplus canus* (S)
N. luncefordi (P)	*Haeromys minahassae* (S)
N. samaricus (P)	*Lenomys meyeri* (S)
N. surrtilus (P)	*Margaretamys beccarii* (S)
Prosciurillus abstrusus (S)	*M. elegans* (S)
P. leucomus (S)	*M. parvus* (S)
P. murinus (S)	*Maxomys dollmani* (S)
Rubrisciurus rubriventer (S)	*M. hellwaldi* (S)
Sundasciurus hoogstraali (P)	*M. musschenbroeki* (S)
S. mindanensis (P)	*Melasmothrix naso* (S)
S. mollendorffi (P)	*Paruromys dominator* (S)
S. philippensis (P)	*Rattus*[1] *hoffmani* (S)
S. samarensis (P)	*R. marmosurus* (S)
	Taeromys callitrichus (S)
Petauristinae (flying squirrels)	*T. hamatus* (S)
Hylopetes mindanensis (P)	*Tateomys macrocercus* (S)
H. nigripes (P)	*T. rhinogradoides* (S)
Petinomys crinitus (P)	

HYSTRICIDAE (Old World porcupines)

Hystrix javanicus (S)

[1]There are at least 15 other species of *Rattus* living in rain-forest habitats in the Philippines and Sulawesi.

inhabiting rain forests of the Wallacea belong to the genus *Rattus*.

The ecological requirements of many rodent species are uncertain or unknown. Many of them seem not to belong to the rain-forest habitat — for instance in the Philippines, *Batomys*, *Carpomys*, *Celaenomys*, *Chrotomys*, *Crateromys*, *Lenomys*, *Mindanaomys*, *Phloeomys*, *Rhynchomys* and *Tryphomys*. Those which are known to occur in rain forests are listed in Table 21.2. In all, about 20 genera and 60 species of rodents inhabit the rain forests of the Wallacea sub-region.

Ecology

Very little is known on the habitats and habits of Wallacean rodents. Musser (1982) has studied the strange group of "shrew rats", containing similar, but not very closely related, genera: *Melasmothrix*,

Tateomys and *Echiothrix* in Sulawesi, and *Archboldomys* and *Rhynchomys* in the Philippines. They all have an elongated shrew-like snout, and are specialized to eat animal food like insects, snails and earthworms. Most of them live in the upper montane forest of central Sulawesi as ground-dwelling rodents. This moss forest, lying above 2000 m, is humid and cool. Most other rodent genera (*Bunomys*, *Eropeplus*, *Haeromys*, *Margaretamys*, *Maxomys*, *Rattus*, *Taeromys*) eat fruit, seeds or leaves, or have a mixed diet of plant and animal material. Because leaf-eating species are very rare among rodents, the two Philippine genera *Crateromys* and *Phloeomys* should be mentioned here, although their habitat is not the rain forest (Eisenberg, 1978).

THE AUSTRALIAN REGION

General aspects and rodent fauna

Only one rodent family, the Muridae, has reached the Australian region and evolved there. Marsupials and murids form the endemic and widely radiating Australian and New Guinean fauna of non-flying mammals. The rodent fauna of New Guinea (Tate, 1951; Menzies and Dennis, 1979; Ziegler, 1982) includes about 60 species, of which at least 45 inhabit rain forests which here consist of lowland forest up to 1500 m, and upper montane forest, so-called moss forest, between 1500 and 3200 m (Table 21.3). Australian rain forests contain only five rodent species (three of which are also found in New Guinea), this small number being evidently due to the restricted area of rain forest, which occurs only as a narrow fringe along the northeastern coast of Queensland. In New Guinea, in contrast, the wealth of regions bearing rain forests and availability of a large number of unfilled niches — due to the absence of mammalian orders other than rodents and marsupials — has led to an extensive adaptive radiation in both groups.

Ecology

Data on habitats and habits are very scarce, and have mostly been obtained during the last 20 years (Brass, 1964; Lidicker and Ziegler, 1968; Dwyer, 1975; Lee et al., 1981).

TABLE 21.3

Rodents occurring in Lowland rain forests (L) and Montane "Moss" forests (M) of New Guinea (Papua N.G. and Irian Jaya) and Australia (after Menzies and Dennies 1979; Lee et al., 1981; Kikkawa et al., 1981; Ziegler, 1982)

New Guinea

MURIDAE (murid rats and mice)

Murinae
Anisomys imitator (L,M)
Hyomys goliath (M)
Lorentzimys nouhuysi (M,L)
Macruromys elegans (L,M)
  M. major (L)
Mallomys rothschildi (M)
Melomys fellowsi (M)
  M. leucogaster (L)
  M. levipes (L,M)
  M. lorentzi (L,M)
  M. moncktoni (L,M)
  M. platyops (L)
  M. rubex (M)
  M. rufescens (L,M)
Pogonomelomys bruijni (L)
  P. sevia (L,M)
Pogonomys forbesi (L)
  P. kagi (L)
  P. lamia (L)
  P. loriae (L,M)
  P. macrourus (L)
  P. mollipilosus (L,M)
  P. sylvestris (M)
  P. vates (L)

Rattus leucopus (L)
  R. niobe (M)
  R. obiensis (L)

R. verecundus (L)
Uromys anak (L,M)
  U. caudimaculatus (L,M)
Xenuromys barbatus (L)

Hydromyinae (water rats and shrew-mice)
Crossomys moncktoni (L,M)
Hydromys chrysogaster (L)
  H. habbema (M)
  H. spec. (L)
Leptomys elegans (L)
Mayermys ellermani (M)
Microhydromys richardsoni (L)
Neohydromys fuscus (M)
Parahydromys asper (L,M)
Paraleptomys rufilatus (L)
  P. wilhelmina (M)
Pseudohydromys murinus (M)
  P. occidentalis (M)
  P. spec. (L)

Australia

MURIDAE

Murinae
Melomys cervinipes (L)
Pogonomys spec. (L)
Rattus leucopus (L)
Uromys caudimaculatus (L)

Hydromyinae
Hydromys chrysogaster (L)

Preferred habitat and locomotion are well correlated with taxonomy — for instance, all species of *Pogonomys* are arboreal; *Macruromys*, *Melomys* and *Rattus* are more or less ground-dwelling; and the shrew-mice (*Mayermys*, *Microhydromys*, *Neohydromys* and *Pseudohydromys*) are mostly subfossorial. There are relatively many species (*c.* 50%), inhabiting the montane moss forest. Particularly members of the Hydromyinae live in that habitat — for instance the shrew-mice showing evolutionary convergence with the shrew-rats of Sulawesi and the Philippines. *Hydromys* and *Crossomys* are well adapted to life near or in water habitats. *Crossomys moncktoni*, the "earless water rat", is the most specialized of the hydromy-ines, and perhaps of all myomorphs. The large paddle-shaped hind feet and the very short ears, its small eyes, its aquatic habitats, and its food, including aquatic insects and small aquatic vertebrates, are some of its outstanding characters. Among the Murinae most species are found in the lower rain forest. Some inhabiting the moss forest are remarkably large (300–400 mm head and body length, 1–2 kg weight): *Hyomys goliath*, *Mallomys rothschildi* and *Uromys anak*. Australian rain-forest rodents have been discussed by Harrison (1962) and Lee et al. (1981).

Ecological studies of food and reproduction are still in an initial phase. From observations on the breeding biology of ten murid species made by Dwyer (1975), one notes that all show seasonal breeding, with reduced or no breeding through the drier months of the year. This was most striking in such rain-forest species as *Melomys levipes*, *M. rubex*, *Rattus niobe* and *R. verecundus*, in which periods of high breeding activity were at least one month shorter than in species occurring outside the rain forest.

As in other rain forests of the world, litter size is relatively low in all species of murids. Mean embryo counts in eight species varied between 2.64 in *Pogonomys sylvestris* and 1.00 in *Pogonomelomys sevia* (Dwyer, 1975).

ETHIOPIAN REGION

General aspects

On a continental basis, most research on rain-forest rodents has been done in Africa. But they are far from being well-known. From the ecological point of view the major part of the Central African rain forest — that is, the central Congo basin, covering a great part of Zaïre and the People's Republic of Congo — is completely unknown.

According to Lebrun and Gilbert (1954) and Richards (1966), the following main zones of African rain forest may be distinguished:

(1) Tropical rain-forest zone (Forêts ombrophiles sempervirentes équatoriales) — upper limit 1100 to 1300 m.

(2) Transition forest zone (Forêt de transition) — from 1100/1300 to 1650/1750 m.

(3) Montane rain-forest zone (Forêts ombrophiles sempervirentes de montagne) — from 1650/1750 up to about 2400 m.

Above 2400 m the rain forest passes into a bamboo zone followed by an Ericacean zone and finally an Afroalpine zone. These three zones do not bear rain forest, and are inhabited by montane rodent elements of the African savanna. The African rain forest may be divided into seven "blocks" (Liberian, Ghanaian, western Nigerian, eastern Nigerian, Gabon, Congo and Central African), each of which has its own distinctive mammalian and rodent fauna (Delany and Happold, 1979).

The rodent fauna

Members of six rodent families inhabit the African rain forest (see Table 21.4). In all there are 69 species belonging to 29 genera. Of these, 38 are species of the lowland rain forest, 11 are confined to montane forest, and 20 species are common to both biomes.

In Table 21.4 only those species are listed which can occur in rain-forest habitats, including species from the edge of the forest, such as the murids *Oenomys hypoxanthus* and *Lophuromys flavopunctatus*, and the cricetid *Otomys denti*. These species are mainly found in moist (montane) savanna habitats, but also occur at the edge of rain forests and — in smaller numbers — inside them. Not included in Table 21.4 are true savanna species which never enter true primary rain forests, but occur immediately outside in secondary forest, cultivated land, grassy habitats, along roads and rivers, and in villages. The forest species seem surprisingly incapable of exploiting these situations fully, probably because each has a narrow range of ecological requirements (Delany, 1972). These "exclusive" forest species are, however, relatively rare — for instance, *Deomys ferrugineus* and *Malacomys longipes*. Nevertheless, if the primary forests disappear and are replaced by farmland and plantations most of their typical rodent fauna are unable to survive (Happold, 1975).

Concerning species numbers of rodents, the richest rain forests are: (a) The Central African block in which, in the single locality of Irangi in eastern Zaïre 26 rodents were found (Rahm, 1966,

TABLE 21.4

Rodents occurring in African lowland (L) and montane (M) rain forests (Misonne, 1963; Rahm, 1966, 1972; Dieterlen, 1968, 1976, 1985a; Dubost, 1968a; Eisentraut, 1973; Happold, 1975, 1977; Delany and Happold, 1979; and others)

SCIURIDAE (squirrels)	MURIDAE (murid rats and mice)
Epixerus ebii (L)	
E. wilsoni (L)	*Colomys goslingi* (L,M)
Funisciurus anerythrus (L)	*Hybomys trivirgatus* (L)
F. bayonii (L)	*H. univittatus* (L,M)
F. carruthersi (M)	*Hylomyscus alleni* (L,M)
F. isabella (L,M)	*H. baeri* (L)
F. lemniscatus (L)	*H. carillus* (L)
F. pyrrhopus (L)	*H. denniae* (M)
F. substriatus (L)	*H. fumosus* (L)
Heliosciurus rufobrachium (L)	*H. parvus* (L)
H. ruwenzorii (M)	*H. stella* (L,M)
Myosciurus pumilio (L)	*Lophuromys flavopunctatus* (M)
Paraxerus alexandri (L)	*L. luteogaster* (L)
P. boehmi (L,M)	*L. medicaudatus* (M)
P. cooperi (M)	*L. nudicaudus* (L)
P. poensis (L)	*L. rahmi* (M)
Protoxerus aubinnii (L)	*L. sikapusi* (L)
P. stangeri (L,M)	*L. woosnami* (M)
	Malacomys edwardsi (L)
ANOMALURIDAE	*M. longipes* (L,M)
(scaly-tailed squirrels)	*M. verschureni* (L)
	Oenomys hypoxanthus (L,M)
Anomalurus beecrofti (L,M)	*Praomys hartwigi* (M)
A. derbianus (L,M)	*P. jacksoni* (L,M)
A. peli (L)	*P. morio* (L,M)
A. pusillus (L,M)	*P. tullbergi* (L)
Idiurus macrotis (L)	*Stochomys defua* (L)
I. zenkeri (L)	*S. longicaudatus* (L)
Zenkerella insignis (L)	*Thamnomys rutilans* (L,M)
	T. venustus (M)
CRICETIDAE (cricetid rats and mice)	
	GLIRIDAE (dormice)
Cricetomyinae	
Cricetomys emini (L)	*Graphiurus christyi* (L)
C. gambianus (L,M)	*G. crassicaudatus* (L)
Dendromurinae	*G. hueti* (L)
Dendromus kahuziensis (M)	*G. lorraineus* (L)
Dendroprionomys rousseloti (L)	*G. murinus* (L,M)
	G. surdus (L)
Deomys ferrugineus (L,M)	
Prionomys batesi (L)	HYSTRICIDAE (Old World porcupines)
Otomyinae	
Otomys denti (M)	*Atherurus africanus* (L,M)

and Dieterlen, unpubl.); and (b) the Gabon forest block including West Cameroon; for this area Eisentraut (1973) has listed 31 rain-forest species. West from Cameroon the rodent fauna of rain forests is decidedly poorer: in the Gambari forest in western Nigeria, Happold (1977) found only nine rodent species. Adam (1977) listed 15 species in the Basse Côte d'Ivoire in the Ghanaian forest block; and Misonne and Verschuren (1976), working on Mount Nimba in Liberia (Liberian forest block), have recorded 14 species. Abundant or dominant species in undisturbed primary forests belong consistently to the murid genera *Hybomys*, *Hylomyscus* and *Praomys*. *Praomys tullbergi* is often the dominant species in West Africa. In southern Nigeria it forms up to 83% of the small terrestrial rodent population (Happold, 1975). In the Central African forest of Irangi, *Praomys jacksoni* and *Hybomys univittatus* outnumber by far the other rodent species. A unique endemicity of rain-forest rodents occurs in the Kivu mountains along the Central African rift valley from Ruwenzori southwards to the Itombwe Plateau. Seven endemics were found in rain forests (*Dendromus kahuziensis*, *Funisciurus carruthersi*, *Heliosciurus ruwenzorii*, *Lophuromys medicaudatus*, *L. rahmi*, *L. woosnami*, *Thamnomys venustus*) and two outside the forests (Dieterlen, unpubl.).

Sciuridae. Nineteen species — that is, about two thirds of the African squirrels — are confined to rain-forest areas. In size they range from the pigmy form *Myosciurus* (head and body 70 mm, tail 60 mm) to the giant *Protoxerus stangeri* (250 mm/330 mm). Rahm (1972) noted that their biology was very poorly known. Regarding the preferred biotopes, the observations of Eisentraut (1973) from Cameroun and of Rahm (1972) from eastern Zaïre agree well. In both regions the giant squirrel (*Protoxerus stangeri*) is known as an inhabitant of the canopy, whereas the sun squirrel *Heliosciurus rufobrachium* prefers the middle stratum and *Funisciurus isabella*, *F. pyrrhopus* and *Paraxerus poensis* are found in the lower stratum between the ground and up to 5 m. *Funisciurus leucogenys* can be considered as almost terrestrial (Eisentraut, 1963). Other species are specially linked with edge situations, such as secondary forests or abandoned plantations in rain forests. In eastern Zaïre, this applies to *Funisciurus aneryth-rus, Paraxerus alexandri* and *P. boehmi* (Rahm, 1972).

Anomaluridae. Taxonomically the scaly-tailed flying squirrels belong to an isolated endemic group of African rodents. They are not related to other flying squirrels, such as the Petauristinae of South-East Asia, but show remarkable convergent evolutionary trends. All are rain-forest dwellers, and all but one species (*Zenkerella insignis*) have flying membranes between hindlimbs and tail, enabling them to glide from tree to tree over distances up to 100 m. Their name comes from a row of sharp, horny scales on the underside of the tail which aid the animals in running up tree trunks. In size they vary from pigmy forms (*Idiurus*) to large squirrels (*Anomalurus*). Most species are nocturnal, spending the daytime in hollow trees. Little is known of their habits. Their food consists of fruits, bark, leaves and — in small proportion — of insects. Their reproductive biology is almost unknown.

Cricetidae. Most of the members of this family are specialized, particularly when compared with murids. This is one of the arguments that these forms are relicts of a former abundant fauna of Mio-Pliocene cricetid rodents, occupying large regions and biomes of Africa before immigration of Muridae from Asia took place. All recent cricetids are well adapted to particular ecological niches. Only a few species, most of them belonging to the heterogeneous subfamily of Dendromurinae, have occupied the African rain forest, or have survived in it. This is an astonishing fact in view of the relatively recent penetration of murids into rain-forest habitats, and their slight radiation there, which is still in an initial phase. No explanation has been advanced for this vacuum between a small and well-adapted but evidently declining cricetid fauna, and the advancing but not yet very specialized group of rain-forest murids.

Of the giant pouched rats (*Cricetomys*), *C. emini* is a true rain-forest species (Genest-Villard, 1967), while *C. gambianus* is a savanna species and only an occasional visitor to forest habitats. *Otomys denti*, feeding on grass and herbs, is the only species of the Otomyinae which has penetrated the montane primary forest (Dieterlen, 1968); but its main habitats lie outside the forest in bamboo stands and marshes. *Deomys ferrugineus* is very specialized in characters of skull, dentition and diet, thus resembling the shrew-rats of Sulawesi and New Guinea.

Muridae. Twenty-nine species from 9 genera have been shown to occur in the African rain forest. At least 50% of them can also be met outside, in secondary forests, clearings, gallery forests and moist savannas in the vicinity of rain forests.

Regarding radiation in forest biomes and adaptation to forest habitats, Bigalke (1968) has presumed that several tree-dwelling mouse-sized mammals of the families Galagidae (primates), Anomaluridae and Sciuridae (rodents) have occupied the habitats above the ground, thus filling the "mouse-niche" there and preventing the murids evolving in this direction. He also stated that "the murids have not radiated to any extent in the forest biomes of Africa probably because they arrived late (Misonne, 1963)[1]. Those few species that are found in forests have evolved relatively recently from savanna lines". And Misonne (1969) wrote "only two African genera are normally found in true rain forest..." As is shown in the present chapter, Bigalke and Misonne were wrong in many respects, because the forest species in Africa are relatively numerous, and because signs of radiation are already visible.

Arboreal species showing some morphological and biological adaptations are *Thamnomys rutilans* and *T. venustus*, the former being "considered as a model of a murid highly specialized for tropical forest conditions". (Genest-Villard, 1972). *Colomys goslingi* is well adapted to semi-aquatic rain-forest habitats, and is specialized in respect of morphology and feeding (Dieterlen and Statzner, 1981; Dieterlen, 1983). *Malacomys longipes* shows similar evolutionary trends. All species of *Lophuromys* can be considered as more or less specialized in morphology, feeding and breeding, and some in adaptation to rain-forest habitats (Dieterlen, 1976). *Hylomyscus* and *Praomys* appear to be generalized, but show strong trends to arboreal life.

Gliridae. In tropical Africa — and nowhere else in the tropics — the dormice are represented by one single arboreal genus: *Graphiurus*. Six species occur in rain-forest habitats, but some, such as the widespread *G. murinus*, are widely distributed outside rain forests as well. Most species are the size of a small mouse, but squirrel-like. The tail is thick and bushy, and the feet are relatively short and broad, as is common in many arboreal

rodents. Their feeding habits are indicated as omnivorous.

Hystricidae. The only porcupine living in the rain forest is *Atherurus africanus*, the brush-tailed porcupine. It is the smallest African hystricid, but at the same time the largest rodent in the rain forest: head and body length 500 mm, weight *c.* 2 kg. The pelage is almost entirely spiny. Normally these porcupines are ground-dwellers, but able to climb trees fairly well (Rahm, 1962).

Feeding ecology

Sciuridae. Rahm (1972) has analysed the stomach contents of some hundreds of specimens of *Funisciurus anerythrus* and *Paraxerus boehmi*. Both species eat mainly fruits of bananas, oil palms, etc., but also include a certain amount of insects in their diet. In the food of *P. boehmi*, ants and termites are preferred, the former seasonally making up to 70% of the total. It is interesting that, among at least a dozen ant species, the very aggressive ants such as *Dorylus* and *Oecophylla* are not represented.

Emmons (1980), working on nine squirrel species in the Gabon rain forest, observed complex patterns of resource partitioning. Generally it can be said that all African rain-forest squirrels eat insects in varying amounts, but that fruits and other plant material constitute their major food. Each species has a relatively wide "feeding spectrum", which minimizes competition for a particular food.

Cricetidae and Muridae. The most comprehensive study on the feeding of murids and cricetids was that of Genest-Villard (1980) in the Central African Republic. This author pointed out that most rodents of the dense forest seemed to be more or less insectivorous. Only a few species, such as *Oenomys hypoxanthus*, *Stochomys longicaudatus* and *Thamnomys rutilans*, were vegetarians. To this group the strict herbivores *Stochomys defua* and *T. venustus* can be added. The cricetid *Otomys denti* also eats only herbs and grass (Dieterlen, 1968). Other mainly vegetarian species belong to the *Praomys–Hylomyscus* group, although some species can be entirely insectivorous, such as *Praomys jacksoni (lukolelae)* in the Central African Republic, but not in eastern Zaïre. Between 60 and 100% of the food of the cricetid

---

[1]Pliocene immigration of murids into Africa from South-East Asia is very probable.

Deomys ferrugineus consists of insects and other invertebrates. *Prionomys batesi* is apparently a pure insectivore (Genest-Villard, 1980). *Hybomys trivirgatus* and *H. univittatus* have a very mixed diet, but seem to consume insects whenever possible. All the seven species of *Lophuromys* are carnivorous/insectivorous to an extent varying from 40 to 100%. *L. luteogaster* lives almost entirely on animal food (Dieterlen, 1976). Animal food items, in which slugs and earthworms play an important part, are found in stomachs of *Malacomys longipes*, which also feeds on fallen fruit and other plant material (Cole, 1975). *Colomys goslingi* is an almost purely carnivorous rodent, its habitat being confined to limnetic ecosystems; invertebrates of running water heavily predominate in the stomach contents. *Colomys* is also able to feed on fishes and tadpoles, which are detected and hunted with the aid of its extremely sensitive vibrissae (Dieterlen and Statzner, 1981). Thus, in feeding biology *Colomys* seems to be the most specialized rodent of the African rain forest. But its specialization is exceptional; as has been seen, most rodents have a very varied diet. Some may have a selective diet, but according to Genest-Villard (1980) the small myomorph rodents "do not compete to any extent with each other or with other vertebrates. This enables them to avoid extensive journeys to find food whatever the season of the year".

Reproduction and population dynamics

From various parts of the African rain forest, some limited studies or occasional observations on the breeding of rodents are available, most of them showing or indicating a relationship between tropical seasons and reproduction. In many savanna species, and in some forest species also occurring in moist savanna, this relationship was already pointed out by Dieterlen (1967a), Delany and Neal (1969) and Delany (1972). But regarding rain-forest rodents there are only a few investigations dealing with more abundant material, with many species and over longer periods, which could give an idea of the particular problems of reproduction and population dynamics in that biome.

One precondition for a better understanding of the (lowland) rain-forest ecosystems is the fact that the environment is not truly stable and nonseasonal, with abundant non-fluctuating resources.

Several ecological studies, even in rain forests near the Equator, have revealed that various seasonal changes occur. The availability of ripe fruits, which may strongly influence the ecosystem, can serve as an example (see for instance, Hladik, 1973; Dieterlen, 1978). Regarding rodent reproduction, Dieterlen (1967b) in a preliminary note considered the seasonal relationships between precipitation, the fruiting periods of the trees, and the reproduction, and population dynamics of rain-forest rodents, as very important. This view was confirmed by the results of Rahm (1970), working on sciurids and murids in the same region of eastern Zaïre. Dubost (1968a) studied the seasonal distribution of pregnant females in the rain forest of Makokou in Gabon. Like the former authors, he noted that there was breeding activity all the year round, but with three maxima and three minima corresponding with higher and lower precipitation, respectively. In the Nigerian rain forest, Happold (1974, 1977, 1978) observed a bimodal peak of breeding activity in three murid species, corresponding, but not synchronized, with the bimodal pattern of precipitation. This means that breeding activity has started already in the late dry season but reached its peak in the rainy season. A releasing factor could be the greater amount of fruit falling in the dry season (Happold, 1977), and the consequent availability of more food. Dieterlen (1978, 1985a, b, 1986) and Genest-Villard (1980) have shown that, in spite of their partly insectivorous diet, most rain-forest rodents are strongly dependent on fallen fruit, and in consequence on seasonal events that cause flowering and fruiting of the trees. Both authors, working respectively at 03°55′N and 01°54′S in the great Central African forest, found a clear periodicity of fruiting, and that the highest availability of fruits occurs 5 to 6 months after the beginning of the nine-month rainy season. These fruiting peaks are attained north of the equator in August and south of it in February. Dieterlen (1985b, 1986) has found that the annual curve of reproductive activity runs almost parallel to the curve of availability of fruits and seeds of trees.

Litter sizes of African rain-forest rodents have been reported by Dubost (1968a), Rahm (1970), Delany (1971), Happold (1974), Dieterlen (1976, 1985a, 1986) and Cross (1977). The average litter size is generally very small. In squirrels three species of *Funisciurus* had 1.0 to 1.7 young per litter, *Paraxerus boehmi* only 1.1. *Heliosciurus* and *Protoxerus* may have young numbering between 2 and 3. In cricetids the average litter size of *Deomys ferrugineus* is reported as 1.69, that of *Otomys denti* 1.02. Murids: in two species of *Hybomys* litter size is between 2.02 and 2.80. Two *Hylomyscus* species have 2.9 to 3.4 young per litter; *H. denniae* has the maximum litter size reported till now: 4.55. In six *Lophuromys* species, litters range between 1.83 and 3.00; two *Malacomys* species have litters of 2.50 and 3.19; in *Oenomys* they range between 2.27 and 2.61; three species of *Praomys* range from 3.19 to 3.80. *Stochomys longicaudatus* has 2.4 to 2.5 young per litter, and in two species of *Thamnomys* litter size varies between 1.3 and 2.1.

THE NEOTROPICAL REGION

General aspects

The rodent fauna of the neotropical rain forest is one of the richest and most diverse in the world, but information on habitats and habits is very scarce. Most species are known only from taxonomic and biogeographic studies, but even knowledge of systematics and distribution patterns is very incomplete. Thus, besides more collecting and more taxonomic revisions, broad investigations on ecology and behaviour are urgently needed. Few studies have sought to gather ecological data at particular localities and for periods of several months or more. In this respect the early work of Enders (1935) and Davis (1945) must be quoted. After the sixties, an increasing number of ecological and biological studies were published, mainly from Panama and Costa Rica.

The zoogeographic regions in which rain-forest rodents occur are, according to Hershkovitz (1958, 1969): (a) the Brazilian subregion, of which the southern province has, firstly, lowland rain forest covering the Amazon basin and its adjacent regions, including eastern Colombia, southern Venezuela and the Guianas; and secondly, upland rain forest on the eastern slopes of the Andes from Bolivia to Colombia, and on the mountains along the Atlantic coast of eastern Brazil. In the northern province, lowland and upland forest are distributed from north-western

Colombia to southern Mexico. (b) The West Indian Subregion, with some lowland and upland forest relicts on the Caribbean islands.

Important habitats in the Amazon basin are (a) Igapó: permanently inundated lowland, with swamps and forests; (b) Várzea: higher forested land, seasonally flooded by the Amazon; and (c) Terra Firme: unflooded lowland forest.

The higher uplands of the eastern slopes of the Andes and the Brazilian highlands are long-established faunal centers, having been forested nearly continuously throughout history and so forming refugia and centres of speciation over long periods (Cerqueira, 1982). Accordingly, the diversity of rain-forest rodents inhabiting the Amazon valley of today originated from the upland refugia.

The rodent fauna

The neotropical rain forest is inhabited by about 130 rodent species belonging to 41 genera and to 10 families.

Sciuridae. Of this worldwide family only the tree squirrels spread into Central and South America. The four genera are almost entirely arboreal, and are distributed in a varying number of species in lowland and montane forests. A pigmy tree-squirrel is *Sciurillus*. Relatively large forms are the Amazonian *Sciurus igniventris* and *S. spadiceus*.

Heteromyidae. Three species of *Heteromys* are distributed in the forests of Central America. One (*H. desmarestianus*) is found in extreme northwestern Colombia. All other representatives of this very rich family occur outside the rain forest, mostly in dry habitats.

Cricetidae. All rain-forest species are endemics of the Neotropical region. Their body size ranges from that of a mouse to that of a giant rat. Diversity and radiation is very high. According to Hershkovitz (1969) there are several monophyletic "clusters" of radiating species, and some aberrant species: "Each species (or sibling species group) of a cluster differs from other members of the same cluster by a complex of adaptive characters which fit it for a particular ecological niche".

There are remarkably many arboreal forms, as for example *Rhipidomys* (climbing mice) and *Nyctomys* (vesper rats) with broad feet, adapted for arboreal life and with long tufted tails. Similar characters are found in *Tylomys* (climbing rats). Tails of some forms, as in *Oecomys* (subgenus of *Oryzomys*), are long and semi-prehensile. Arboreal rats of several species build large nests of twigs and fibres, similar to those of squirrels.

Other groups, as the genus *Thomasomys*, have mainly terrestrial-scansorial species. *Daptomys*, *Ichthyomys*, *Nectomys* and *Rheomys* are adapted to palustrine, semi-aquatic and aquatic life. Generally they have small ears, long tails and a water-shedding coat. Their diet is based on freshwater invertebrates and vertebrates.

The following rodents belong to the New World suborder, the Caviomorpha.

Erethizontidae: These New World porcupines are well adapted to arboreal life, and their tails are strongly prehensile. All species are relatively large forms.

Hydrochoeridae: The capybara is the largest living rodent. It is a semi-aquatic grass-feeder, and is always found near water-courses and swamps, mostly outside the rain forests. Its swimming ability is excellent.

Dinomyidae: The pakarana (*Dinomys branickii*) is a large terrestrial rodent occurring in the rain-forest valleys of the Andes. Very little is known about the ecology and biology of this rare species.

Agoutidae: The paca (*Agouti paca*) is also a large caviomorph with a wide distribution. It lives on the forest floor, often near water, and feeds mainly on fallen fruits and seeds.

Dasyproctidae: Agoutis (*Dasyprocta*) and acouchys (*Myoprocta*) occur often sympatrically in rain forests. Morphologically and by their habits they are well adapted to terrestrial life. They depend strongly on fallen fruits and seeds. Seeds are buried in large quantities, and recovered in times of scarcity. This burying behaviour plays an important role in seed dispersal (Smythe, 1978). Agoutis keep their mates for their entire lifetime.

Capromyidae: The hutias range in size from that of a Guinea pig to that of a large domestic cat. They inhabit the rain-forest relicts of the Caribbean islands, to which they are endemic. Hutias are exclusively arboreal, with partially or fully prehensile tails, and are strongly adapted to folivory and frugivory. Some of their interesting behaviour was observed in captivity by Mohr (1939). Most species are seriously threatened with extinction.

Echimyidae: These "spiny rats" form the most diversified group of caviomorphs. All rain-forest genera (except *Proechimys* and *Hoplomys*) are completely or partly arboreal. Species of *Kannaba-teomys* and *Dactylomys* are morphologically highly adapted to life in bamboo thickets. *Echimys* is an inhabitant of trees on river-banks and in flooded areas, nesting in tree trunks and in holes in trees. *Proechimys* is mainly ground-dwelling beneath tree roots and among rocks in the rain forest, and can be very numerous in this habitat.

Feeding ecology

Fruits and seeds of the trees make up the major part of the diet of rain-forest rodents, most of which are sedentary and dependent on the regular availability of that food. Glanz (1982) found 95% of fruit and seeds in the diets of several rodents in Panama. Thus, reproductive rates and mortality of these species are highly dependent on food availability.

In two rodent communities studied by Fleming (1970, 1971) in Panama, all Sciuridae, Heteromyidae and Caviomorpha were frugivorous or granivorous, while Cricetidae were partly omnivorous with some percentage of insect food, but there were no species specialized for insect-eating. Whether any rain-forest rodents in the Neotropics eat insects or other invertebrates to any extent is not known. But many rodent species occurring outside rain forests are known to be insect-eating. There is, however, strong indication that possible competition by the small insectivorous marsupials could be responsible for the rodent associations including only fruit and seed-eating species, as was shown by Charles-Dominique et al. (1981) in French Guiana. The most frequent arboreal species (*Coendu prehensilis*, *Makalata armata* and *Oryzomys concolor*) were predominantly granivorous against five species of carnivorous and frugivorous marsupials. The rain-forest water rats (*Daptomys*, *Ichthyomys*, *Nectomys* and *Rheomys*), however, appear clearly specialized to eat insects and other carnivorous food. Among seed-eating rodents some specialists seem to have developed — for instance, for very hard seeds, such as the nuts of some palms. According to Smythe (1970), Janzen (1971) and Glanz (1982), *Sciurus granatensis* and *Dasyprocta punctata* are the only rodents able to open the nuts and eat the endosperm. Sixty-five percent of the annual food of *Sciurus granatensis* consists of these hard-shelled palm nuts. By its nut-burying behaviour *Dasyprocta* plays an important role in the dispersal and germination of the nuts. Exploiting those trophic niches certainly has clear selective advantages.

Reproduction and population dynamics

The most continuous reproductive data available for neotropical rain-forest rodents were collected in Panama (and Costa Rica) by Fleming (1970, 1971, 1973); but unfortunately the monthly numbers of adult females collected per species were too small to give a clear picture. Fleming supposed that 10 of 15 species were year-round polyoestrous breeders, most of them belonging to the families Cricetidae and Echimyidae. Concerning the Echimyidae there have been several confirmations from other parts of the region (e.g. Davis, 1945). *Agouti paca* and *Dasyprocta punctata* are seasonally breeding, and it is assumed for them and for other species that the cessation of heavy rains could be a stimulus for the onset of reproductive activity. Sciuridae are seasonally monestrous breeders. Most species probably produce their young when availability of food is highest.

In the rain forest along the Brazilian coast near Rio de Janeiro the breeding season of rodents begins in July/August, at the end of the cool and dry season. But they reach full reproductive activity in October after the onset of the warm and rainy season. Breeding continues for several months till April, when the dry and cool period starts again (Davis, 1945). At this latitude near to the southern tropic, cooler temperature (combined with dryness) seem to have an important effect upon reproduction. Flowering (and fruiting) phenology of trees and other plants is here also strongly dependent on periods of higher temperature.

The annual reproduction cycle of the forest-dwelling species *Oryzomys capito* and *Proechimys semispinosus* was studied by Fleming (1971). Although numbers of animals observed were not sufficient at all times, it seems that both species are year-round breeders, and that the dry and rainy seasons have no important influence on reproduction. Other species showed similar patterns, but Fleming (1970) himself admitted that "more data

are needed before it is known whether the intensity of reproduction in species breeding year-around remains the same throughout the year."

CONCLUSIONS

Adding up the number of rodent species occurring in the rain forests of the world (Fig. 21.1 and Tables 21.1–21.5), one obtains 399, say 400 species. Compared with the total number of recent rodents in the world, amounting to *c.* 1600 species (Corbet and Hill, 1980), rain-forest rodents make up almost exactly 25%. Considering the fact, that less than 10% of the land surface of the world is covered with rain forest, 25% of rodents is an extraordinary high percentage, although not all species are "exclusive" rain-forest dwellers.

This striking wealth of species is also observed in other mammalian orders. The main reason for this is the stratification of the rain forest, extending 40 to 50 m between the floor and the high canopy, and providing a diversity of niches and habitats, most of which have been exploited by rodents. Moreover, rain forests harbour a wealth of food resources, based on the number and diversity of plant species whose leaves, fruits, seeds and bark constitute food, not only for the rodents themselves, but also for countless invertebrates which constitute an exclusive or additional food for them. These food resources are mostly abundant and many remain available throughout the year. Often they can be utilized by several rodent species, but mostly in different ways in respect of time and space, thus avoiding competition.

All the continents, and most of the greater tropical islands, have their own endemic rodent faunas, with a few exceptions in South-East Asia. Comparing the rodent faunas of the different zoogeographical regions, it can be said that the Indomalayan region is very rich in rain-forest species (*c.* 95). This richness is still high in the relatively small Wallacean subregion (including the Philippines), which contains some 62 rain-forest rodents. A similar high species number (46) is present in New Guinea, whereas the neighbouring Australian rain forest appears to be impoverished (5). Sixty-nine rodent species occur in the African rain forest, a relatively low number compared to the island faunas mentioned above. But consider-

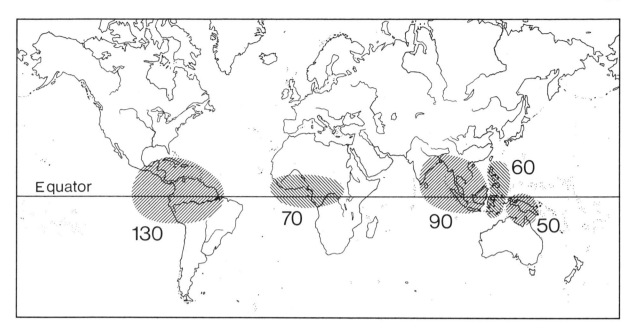

Fig. 21.1. Approximate species numbers of rodents occurring in tropical rain forests of zoogeographic regions: Neotropics (130), Ethiopian region (70), Indomalayan sub-region (90), Wallacean sub-region (60), Australian region (50).

ing the fact that only 9% of the African continent is covered with rain forest, the species number seems not to be particularly low. Of the whole rodent fauna of Africa (c. 280 species) the proportion of rain-forest species amounts to 25%. Although data on the neotropical rodent fauna must be regarded with reservation, the proportion occurring in that region is certainly very high: c. 132 species.

The higher taxonomic groups of rodents (suborders and families) participate in the rain-forest faunas in very different ways. For example, squirrel-like forms (flying and non-flying), most of them occupying niches above the ground, are unevenly distributed. In the Indomalayan forest they make up to 54% of the total fauna, in Africa c. 29%, but in the New World only 10%. On the other hand, many rat-like forms of the suborders Caviomorpha and Myomorpha, and even caviomorph porcupines and hutias, combine to fill all the arboreal niches of the neotropical rain forest. In Africa there exist a good number of squirrel-like forms, in two families, but it appears that many additional arboreal niches are still available or not fully occupied by the cohort of mostly terrestrial rodents. In New Guinea, where the rodents are represented only by murids, the arboreal niches —

in the absence of squirrels, monkeys, etc. — were exploited by this family, together with marsupials.

The flying squirrels and similar forms are distributed only in South-East Asia (c. 20 rain-forest species of Petauristinae) and in Africa (seven species of the convergent family of Anomaluridae). There are only a few large forms among the terrestrial rodents of rain forest; most of them — agoutis, paca, capybaras, etc. — live in the Neotropics. In the Old World the same niches were filled not only by rodents but also by ungulates (Dubost, 1968b). Smaller terrestrial and arboreal forms — normally known as rats and mice — constitute the majority of rain-forest rodents. Those species belong to different groups such as the caviomorph Echimyidae, the Old and the New World Cricetidae and the Muridae.

Comparing the exploitation of rain-forest niches in the different continents, and between taxonomic groups, one finds very different degrees of radiation. Apart from squirrel-like forms, exploitation of arboreal habitats by rat and mouse-sized rodents is extraordinarily strong in the Neotropics (genera of Cricetidae and Echimyidae), a fact which cannot be explained only by the relatively small representation of squirrels. In contrast, in African rain forests few of the murid rodents

TABLE 21.5

Rodent species occurring in rain forests of South and Central America (after Walker, 1975; Corbet and Hill, 1980; Hall, 1981; Alho, 1982; Honacki et al., 1982; Mares and Ojeda, 1982; and others). Due to the unsatisfactory taxonomical and ecological investigation of this fauna exact occurrence and habitat of many taxa is poorly known. Therefore in many cases listing of names or number of species should be regarded with reservation

SCIURIDAE (squirrels)	*N. spinosus*	**ERETHIZONTIDAE**	*C. pilorides*
	N. tenuipes	(new world porcupines)	*C. prehensilis*
Microsciurus alfari	*Nectomys parvipes*		*C. sanfelipensis*
M. flaviventer	*N. squamipes*	*Coendu bicolor*	and perhaps some more
M. mimulus	*Oryzomys alfaroi*	*C. prehensilis*	*Plagiodontia aedium*
M. santanderensis	*O. bicolor*	*C. rothschildi*	*P. hylaeum*
Sciurillus pusillus	*O. capito*	*Echinoprocta rufescens*	
Sciurus aestuans	*O. concolor*	*Sphiggurus vestitus*	**ECHIMYIDAE** (spiny rats)
S. gilvigularis	*O. delicatus*		
S. granatensis	*O. fulvescens*		*Dactylomys dactylinus*
S. ignitus	*O. utiaritensis*	**HYDROCHAERIDAE**	*Diplomys caniceps*
S. igniventris	and *c.* 5–10 further species	(Capybaras)	*D. labilis*
S. pucheranii	*Otonyctomys hatti*		*Echimys chrysurus*
S. pyrrhinus	*Peromyscus mexicanus*	*Hydrochaeris hydrochaeris*	*E. grandis*
S. spadiceus	*P. oaxacensis*		*E. macrurus*
Syntheosciurus brochus	and some further species		*E. nigrispinus*
	Reithrodontomys probably	**DINOMYIDAE** (pacaranas)	*E. saturus*
	some species		*Hoplomys gymnurus*
HETEROMYIDAE	*Rheomys hartmanni*	*Dinomys branickii*	*Isothrix bistriatus*
(heteromyids)	*R. mexicanus*		*I. pictus*
	R. raptor	**AGOUTIDAE** (pacas)	*I. villosus*
Heteromys anomalus	*R. thomasi*		*Kannabateomys amblyonyx*
H. desmarestianus	*R. underwoodi*	*Agouti paca*	*Lonchothrix emiliae*
H. goldmani	*Rhipidomys leucodactylus*		*Makalata armata*
	R. macconnelli	**DASYPROCTIDAE** (agoutis)	*Mesomys didelphoides*
CRICETIDAE (cricetid rats	*R. mastacalis*		*M. hispidus*
and mice)	*R. scandens*	*Dasyprocta cristata*	*M. obscurus*
	R. sclateri	*D. fuliginosa*	*M. stimulax*
Blarinomys breviceps	and some further species	*D. leporina*	*Proechimys amphichoricus*
Bolomys lasiurus	*Thomasomys* some 5–10	*D. prymnolopha*	*P. brevicauda*
Daptomys oyapocki	species	*D. punctata*	*P. canicollis*
D. peruviensis	*Tylomys fulviventer*	*Myoprocta acouchy*	*P. cuvieri*
D. venezuelae	*T. mirae*	*M. exilis*	*P. goeldii*
Holochilus brasiliensis	*T. nudicaudus*		*P. guayannensis*
H. sciureus	*T. panamensis*	**CAPROMYIDAE** (hutias)	*P. hendeei*
Ichthyomys hydrobates	and perhaps two further		*P. longicaudatus*
I. pittieri	species	*Capromys angelcabrerai*	*P. quadruplicatus*
I. stolzmanni		*C. arboricolus*	*P. semispinosus*
Neacomys guaianae		*C. auritus*	
		C. melanius	
		C. nanus	

exploit the niches above ground, probably due to their relatively late immigration into the biome. For the Indomalayan and Australian region these relations have already been mentioned above. Special arboreal forms adapted to stem-climbing in bamboo forests occur in Indomalaya (*Chiropodomys gliroides*) and in South America (species of *Dactylomys* and *Kannabateomys*).

Cricetidae and Muridae, morphologically often highly specialized, have also occupied niches in aquatic environments which are normally taken by Insectivora, Carnivora and others: four genera (and still more outside the rain forest) in the Neotropics, at least two in the Australian region, and one in Africa.

Another radiating group is the shrew-mice, relatively long-snouted and predominantly insect-eating rodents, of which several occur in Sulawesi, the Philippines and in New Guinea, evidently due to the rarity or absence of Insectivora (shrews and others) in those regions. In Africa the shrew-mouse type is realized in *Deomys* and *Lophuromys*, both largely insect-eating genera. It appears that this type of rodent is not represented in the neotropical rain forest (except *Blarinomys*?), and that, in the absence also of Insectivora, this niche is entirely filled by small insect-eating marsupials.

Apart from this special groups of "shrew-mice", numerous other rain-forest rodents (squirrels, rats, mice, dormice) feed in an opportunistic manner on insects and other invertebrates to a varying degree, as reported from all continents.

But the main food of the majority of rodents is plant material, and particularly, mostly preferred and available over longer periods, the fruits and seeds of the trees, which are harvested ripe or unripe on the trees or after falling on to the ground. Other plant materials consumed by rodents are bark, leaves, herbs and — rarely in rain forests — grasses. As already shown, folivore species are not numerous and very few are exclusively leaf-eating.

Reproduction and population dynamics are largely dependent on the food supply. Several examples from various rain-forest regions showed that even slight seasonal variations — that is, changes between rainy seasons and periods of decreased precipitation — influence the vegetation by causing flowering and fruiting rhythms in the trees. In most cases fruiting maxima run parallel with precipitation maxima. Thus, the annual course is an unequal, mostly periodic, distribution of fruit production, influencing in turn the reproduction and population dynamics of many rodent species.

Considerable seasonality, with combined periodicity in flowering and fruiting, has been observed even in close proximity to the Equator. But seasonal contrasts here are nowhere so distinct as in savannas or other drier biomes. Consequently, a total absence of food (from the trees) and a complete cessation of breeding activity is rarely met with. Nevertheless, there are pronounced annual changes in population dynamics among rain-forest rodents. The annual curves of food availability and of breeding activity run synchronously or with only a slight time-shift. Although food other than fruits, particularly insect food, plays an important role, it appears that its influence on breeding and population dynamics is similar to that of the fruiting of the trees. Exceptions to this rule were observed: cessation of

heavy rains, or even dry-season influence may act as releasing factors for breeding. These studies, however, were not based upon sufficient field data.

It can be considered as probable that the meteorological Equator generally constitutes a zone of inversion, not only for seasons but also for fruiting patterns and periodicity, and consequently for breeding patterns of rain-forest rodents.

It has been seen that fruit (food) availability seems to be the primary determinant of rodent population dynamics. Other factors, however, may be equally important, as for example predation, because rodents are typical animals of prey, constituting a main food resource for snakes, birds, Viverridae, Felidae, etc. But compared with savanna species the litter sizes in rain forests are very limited, averaging about 2 to 3 young per litter. Litter sizes of more than four young are almost exceptional, while 1 to 2 young per litter occur very frequently. Relations between litter size of rain-forest rodents and conditions of predation have not been investigated.

Due to the strong attachment to their biome, rain-forest rodents never or rarely become "pests" in forest plantations or other human environments. In these cases savanna species are more likely to play the part of "pests". On the other hand, some typical montane species in Africa and other regions are increasingly endangered by human activities, and will disappear if destruction of montane rain forests continues.

REFERENCES

Adam, F., 1977. Données préliminaires sur l'habitat et la stratification des rongeurs en forêt de Basse Côte d'Ivoire. *Mammalia*, 41: 283–290.

Alho, C.J.R., 1982. Brazilian rodents: their habitats and habits. In: M.A. Mares and H.H. Genoways (Editors), *Mammalian Biology in South America*. Special Publication Series, Pymatuning Laboratory of Ecology, Univ. of Pittsburgh, Pittsburgh, Pa., Vol. 6, pp. 143–166.

Bigalke, R.C., 1968. Evolution of mammals on southern continents. III. The contemporary mammal fauna of Africa. *Quart. Rev. Biol.*, 43: 265–300.

Brass, L.J., 1964. Results of the Archbold Expeditions. No. 86. Summary of the sixth Archbold expedition to New Guinea (1959). *Bull. Am. Mus. Nat. Hist.*, 127: 145–216.

Cerqueira, R., 1982. South American landscapes and their mammals. In: M.A. Mares and H.H. Genoways (Editors), *Mammalian Biology in South America*. Special Publication Series, Pymatuning Laboratory of Ecology, Univ. of Pittsburgh, Pittsburgh, Pa., Vol. 6, pp. 53–73.

Charles-Dominique, P., Atramentowicz, M., Charles-Dominique, M., Gérard, H., Hladik, A., Hladik, C.M. and Prévost, M.F., 1981. Les mammifères frugivores arboricoles nocturnes d'une forêt guayanaise: inter-relations plantes-animaux. *Rev. Ecol.*, 35: 341–435.

Cole, L.R., 1975. Foods and foraging places of rats (Rodentia; Muridae) in the lowland evergreen forest of Ghana. *J. Zool.*, 175: 453–471.

Corbet, G.B. and Hill, J.E., 1980. *A World List of Mammalian Species*. British Museum (Natural History) Comstock Publishing Assoc. (a division of Cornell Univ. Press) London, 226 pp.

Cross, R.M., 1977. Population studies on Praomys tullbergi (Thomas) and other rats of forest regions of Sierra Leone. *Rev. Zool. Afr.*, 91: 345–367.

Davis, D.E., 1945. The annual cycle of plants, mosquitoes, birds and mammals in two Brazilian forests. *Ecol. Monogr.*, 15: 243–295.

Delany, M.J., 1971. The biology of small rodents in Mayanja forest, Uganda. *J. Zool.*, 165: 85–129.

Delany, M.J., 1972. The ecology of small rodents in tropical Africa. *Mammal Rev.*, 2: 1–42.

Delany, M.J. and Happold, D.C.D., 1979. *Ecology of African Mammals*. Longman, London, 434 pp.

Delany, M.J. and Neal, B.R., 1969. Breeding seasons in rodents in Uganda. *J. Reprod. Fert., Suppl.*, 6: 229–235.

Dieterlen, F., 1967a. Jahreszeiten und Fortpflanzungsperioden bei den Muriden des Kivusee-Gebietes (Congo). Ein Beitrag zum Problem der Populationsdynamik in den Tropen. *Z. Säugetierk.*, 32: 1–44.

Dieterlen, F., 1967b. La dynamique des populations des Muridés dans les forêts centrafricaines (région du Kivu). *Chron. IRSAC*, 2: 33–34.

Dieterlen, F., 1968. Zur Kenntnis der Gattung Otomys (Otomyinae; Muridae; Rodentia). Beiträge zur Systematik, Ökologie und Biologie zentralafrikanischer Formen. *Z. Säugetierk.*, 33: 321–352.

Dieterlen, F., 1976. Die afrikanische Muridengattung Lophuromys PETERS, 1874. Vergleiche an Hand neuer Daten zur Morphologie, Ökologie und Biologie. *Stuttg. Beitr. Naturk., Ser. A*, 285: 1–96.

Dieterlen, F., 1978. *Zur Phänologie des äquatorialen Regenwaldes im Ost-Zaire (Kivu), nebst Pflanzenliste und Klimadaten*. Diss. Botanicae No. 47, Cramer, Lehre, 132 pp.

Dieterlen, F., 1983. Zur Systematik, Verbreitung und Ökologie von Colomys goslingi Thomas & Wroughton, 1907 (Muridae; Rodentia). *Bonn. Zool. Beitr.*, 34: 73–106.

Dieterlen, F., 1985a. Daten zur Fortpflanzungs- und Populations-struktur der myomorphen Nager eines afrikanischen Tieflandsregenwaldes (Ost-Zaïre). *Z. Säugetierk.*, 50: 68–88.

Dieterlen, F., 1985b. Beziehungen zwischen Umweltfaktoren und Fortpflanzungsperiodik myomorpher Nager eines afrikanischen Tieflandsregenwaldes (Ost-Zaïre). *Z. Säugetierk.*, 50: 152–166.

Dieterlen, F., 1986. Seasonal reproduction and population dynamics in rodents of the African rain forest. *Cimbebasia, Ser. A*, 8, H 1: 1–7.

Dieterlen, F. and Statzner, B., 1981. The African rodent Colomys goslingi Thomas and Wroughton, 1907 (Rodentia: Muridae) — a predator in limnetic ecosystems. *Z. Säugetierk.*, 46: 369–383.

Dubost, G., 1968a. Aperçu sur le rhythme annuel de reproduction des Muridés du Nord-Est du Gabon. *Biol. Gabonica*, 4: 227–239.

Dubost, G., 1968b. Les niches écologiques des forêts tropicales sud-américaines et africaines, sources de convergences remarquables entre rongeurs et artiodactyles. *Terre Vie, Rev. Écol. Appl.*, 32: 3–28.

Dwyer, P.D., 1975. Observations on the breeding biology of some New Guinea murid rodents. *Aust. Wildlife Res.*, 2: 33–45.

Eisenberg, J.F., 1978. The evolution of arboreal herbivores in the class Mammalia. In: G.G. Montgomery (Editor), *The Ecology of Arboreal Folivores*. Symposia of the National Zoological Park, Smithsonian Inst. Press, Washington, D.C., pp. 135–152.

Eisentraut, M., 1963. *Die Wirbeltiere des Kamerungebirges*. Parey, Hamburg, 353 pp.

Eisentraut, M., 1973. Die Wirbeltierfauna von Fernando Poo und Westkamerun. *Bonn. Zool. Monogr.*, 3: 1–428.

Ellerman, J.R., 1961. Rodentia. In: M.L. Roonwal (Editor), *The Fauna of India Including Pakistan, Burma and Ceylon*. (Mammalia, Vol. 3) Zoological Survey of India, Calcutta, 884 pp.

Emmons, L.H., 1980. Ecology and resource partitioning among nine species of African rain forest squirrels. *Ecol. Monogr.*, 50: 31–54.

Enders, R.K., 1935. Mammalian life histories on Barro Colorado Island. *Bull. Mus. Comp. Zool.*, 78: 383–502.

Fleming, T.H., 1970. Notes on the rodent faunas of two Panamanian forests. *J. Mammal.*, 51: 473–490.

Fleming, T.H., 1971. Population ecology of three species of Neotropical rodents. *Misc. Publ. Mus. Zool. Univ. Michigan*, 143: 1–77.

Fleming, T.H., 1973. The reproductive cycles of three species of opossums and other mammals in the Panama canal zone. *J. Mammal.*, 54: 439–455.

Genest-Villard, H., 1967. Revision du genre Cricetomys (Rongeurs, Cricetidae). *Mammalia*, 31: 390–455.

Genest-Villard, H., 1972. Contribution à l'écologie et l'éthologie d'un petit rongeur arboricole. Thamnomys rutilans, en République Centrafricaine. *Mammalia*, 36: 543–578.

Genest-Villard, H., 1980. Régime alimentaire des rongeurs myomorphes de forêt équatoriale (région de M'Baiki, République Centrafricaine). *Mammalia*, 44: 423–484.

Glanz, W.E., 1982. Adaptive zones of neotropical mammals: a comparison of some temperate and tropical patterns. In: M.A. Mares and H.H. Genoways (Editors), *Mammalian Biology in South America*. Special Publication Series, Pymatuning Laboratory of Ecology, Univ. of Pittsburgh, Pittsburgh, Pa., Vol. 6, pp. 95–110.

Groves C.P., 1976. The origin of the mammalian fauna of Sulawesi (Celebes). *Z. Säugetierk.*, 41: 201–216.

Hall, E.R., 1981. *The Mammals of North America*. Wiley, New York, N.Y., 1181 pp.

Happold, D.C.D., 1974. The small rodents of the forest–savanna–farmland association near Ibadan, Nigeria, with observations on reproduction biology. *Rev. Zool. Afr.*, 88: 814–836.

Happold, D.C.D., 1975. The effects of climate and vegetation on the distribution of small rodents in Western Nigeria. *Z. Säugetierk.*, 40: 221–242.

Happold, D.C.D., 1977. A population study of small rodents in the tropical rain forest of Nigeria. *Terre Vie*, 31: 385–458.

Happold, D.C.D., 1978. Reproduction, growth and development of a West African forest mouse, Praomys tullbergi (Thomas). *Mammalia*, 42: 73–95.

Harrison, J.L., 1951. Reproduction of rats of the subgenus Rattus. *Proc. Zool. Soc. London*, 121: 673–694.

Harrison, J.L., 1952. Breeding rhythms of Selangor rodents. *Bull. Raffles Mus.*, 24: 109–131.

Harrison, J.L., 1954. The natural food of some rats and other mammals. *Bull. Raffles Mus.*, 25: 157–165.

Harrison, J.L., 1955. Data on the reproduction of some Malayan mammals. *Proc. Zool. Soc. London*, 125: 445–460.

Harrison, J.L., 1957. Habitat of some Malayan rats. *Proc. Zool. Soc. London*, 128: 1–21.

Harrison, J.L., 1962. The distribution of feeding habits in a tropical rain forest. *J. Anim. Ecol.*, 31: 53–63.

Harrison, J.L. and Traub, R., 1950. Rodents and insectivores from Selangor, Malaya. *J. Mammal.*, 31: 337–346.

Hershkovitz, P.H., 1958. A geographical classification of neotropical mammals. *Fieldiana Zool.*, 36: 581–620.

Hershkovitz, P.H., 1969. The evolution of mammals on southern continents. VI. The recent mammals of the Neotropical region: a zoogeographic and ecological review. *Quart. Rev. Biol.*, 44: 1–70.

Hladik, C.M., 1973. Alimentation et activité d'un groupe de Chimpanzés réintroduits en forêt gabonaise. *Terre Vie*, 27: 343–413.

Honacki, J.H., Kinman, K.E. and Koeppl, J.W., 1982. *Mammal Species of the World: A Taxonomic and Geographic Reference*. Allen, and The Association of Systematics Collections, Lawrence, Kans., 694 pp.

Janzen, D.H., 1971. Seed predation by animals. *Annu. Rev. Ecol. Syst.*, 2: 465–492.

Kikkawa, J., Monteith, G.B. and Ingram, G., 1981. Cape York Peninsula: Major region of faunal interchange. In: A. Keast (Editor), *Ecological Biogeography of Australia*. Vol. 3. Junk, The Hague, 1695–1742.

Kingdon, J., 1974. *East African Mammals. An Atlas of Evolution in Africa*. Vol. 1. Academic Press, London, 446 pp.

Lebrun, J. and Gilbert, G., 1954. Une classification écologique des forêts du Congo. *Publ. de l'I.N.E.A.C., Sér. Sci.*, 63: 1–89.

Lee, A.K., Baverstock, P.R. and Watts, C.H.S., 1981. Rodents — The late invaders. In: A. Keast (Editor), *Ecological Biogeography of Australia*. Vol. 3. Junk, The Hague, 1521–1553.

Lekagul, B. and McNeeley, J.A., 1977. *Mammals of Thailand*. Association for the Conservation of Wildlife, Bangkok, 758 pp.

Lidicker Jr., W.Z. and Ziegler, A.C., 1968. Report on a collection of mammals from Eastern New Guinea, includ-

ing species keys for fourteen genera. *Publ. Zool. Univ. Calif.*, 87: 1–60.

Lim, B.L., 1970. Distribution, relative abundance, food habits, and parasite patterns of Giant rats (Rattus) in West Malaysia. *J. Mammal.*, 51: 730–740.

Mares, M.A. and Ojeda, R.A., 1982. Patterns of diversity and adaptation in South American hystricognath rodents. In: M.A. Mares and H.H. Genoways (Editors), *Mammalian Biology in South America*. Special Publication Series, Pymatuning Laboratory of Ecology, Univ. of Pittsburgh, Pittsburgh, Pa., Vol. 6, pp. 393–432.

Medway, Lord, 1967. Observations on breeding of the pencil-tailed tree mouse, Chiropodomys gliroides. *J. Mammal.*, 48: 20–26.

Medway, L., 1969. *The Wild Mammals of Malayan and Offshore Islands Including Singapore*. Oxford Univ. Press, London, 127 pp.

Medway, L., 1972. Phenology of a tropical rain forest in Malaya. *Biol. J. Linn. Soc.*, 4: 117–146.

Menzies, J.I. and Dennis, E., 1979. *Handbook of New Guinea Rodents*, Wau Ecology Institute, Handbook No. 6, 68 pp.

Misonne, X., 1963. Les rongeurs du Ruwenzori et des Régions voisines. *Inst. Parcs Nat. Congo, Explor. Parc Nat. Albert*, 2, 14: 1–164.

Misonne, X., 1969. African and Indo-Australian Muridae. Evolutionary trends. *Ann. Mus. R. Afr. Centr., Tervuren, Sci. Zool.*, 172: 1–220.

Misonne, X. and Verschuren, J., 1976. Les rongeurs du Nimba Libérien. *Acta Zool. Pathol. Antverpsiana*, 66: 199–220.

Mohr, E., 1939. Die Baum- und Ferkelratten-Gattungen Capromys DESMAREST (sens ampl.) und Plagiodontia CUVIER. *Mitt. Hamburg. Zool. Mus. Inst.*, 48: 48–118.

Musser, G.G., 1969. Results of the Archbold Expeditions. No. 89. Notes on the Taxonomic Status of Rattus aspinatus Tate and Archbold and Mus callitrichus Jentink (Rodentia, Muridae). *Am. Mus. Novit.*, 2365: 1–9.

Musser, G.G., 1977. Epimys benguetensis, a composite, and one zoogeographic view of rat and mouse faunas in the Philippines and Celebes. *Am. Mus. Novit.*, 2624: 1–15.

Musser, G.G., 1981. The giant rat of Flores and its relatives east of Borneo and Bali. *Bull. Am. Mus. Nat. Hist.*, 169: 67–175.

Musser, G.G., 1982. Results of the Archbold Expeditions No. 110. Crunomys and the small-bodied shrew rats native to the Philippines islands and Sulawesi (Celebes). *Bull. Am. Mus. Nat. Hist.*, 174: 1–95.

Musser, G.G. and Newcomb, C., 1983. Malaysian murids and the Giant Rat of Sumatra. *Bull. Am. Mus. Nat. Hist.*, 174: 329–598.

Muul, I. and Lim, B.L., 1978. Comparative morphology, food habits, and ecology of some Malaysian arboreal rodents. In: G.G. Montgomery (Editor), *The Ecology of Arboreal Folivores*. Symposia of the National Zoological Park, Smithsonian Inst. Press, Washington, D.C., pp. 361–368.

Rahm, U., 1962. Biologie und Verbreitung des afrikanischen Quastenstachlers, Atherurus africanus Gray (Hystricomorpha). *Rev. Suisse Zool.*, 69: 344–358.

Rahm, U., 1966. Les mammifères de la forêt équatoriale de l'Est du Congo. *Ann. Mus. R. Afr. Centr. Tervuren, Sér. in-8, Sci. Zool.*, 149: 1–121.

Rahm, U., 1970. Note sur la réproduction des Sciuridés et Muridés dans la forêt équatoriale au Congo. *Rev. Suisse Zool.*, 77: 635–646.

Rahm, U., 1972. Note sur la répartition, l'écologie et le régime alimentaire des Sciuridés au Kivu (Zaire). *Rev. Zool. Bot. Afr.*, 85: 321–339.

Rahm, U. and Christiaensen, A., 1963. Les mammifères de la région occidentale du lac Kivu. *Ann. Mus. R. Afr. Centr., Tervuren, Série in-8, Sci. Zool.*, 118: 1–83.

Richards, P.W., 1966. *The Tropical Rain Forest. An Ecological Study.* Cambridge Univ. Press, Cambridge, 450 pp.

Smythe, N., 1970. Relationships between fruiting seasons and seed dispersal methods in a neotropical forest. *Am. Nat.*, 104: 25–35.

Smythe, N., 1978. The natural history of the Central American agouti (*Dasyprocta punctata*). *Smithson. Contrib. Zool.*, 257: 1–52.

Tate, G.H.H., 1951. Results of the Archbold Expeditions No. 65. The rodents of Australia and New Guinea. *Bull. Am. Mus. Nat. Hist.*, 97: 183–430.

Wade, P., 1958. Breeding season among mammals in the lowland rain-forest of North Borneo. *J. Mammal.*, 39: 429–433.

Wagner, H.O., 1961. Die Nagetiere einer Gebirgsabdachung in Südmexiko und ihre Beziehungen zur Umwelt. *Zool. Jahrb. (Syst.)*, 89: 177–242.

Walker, E.P., 1975. *Mammals of the World.* The Johns Hopkins Univ. Press, Baltimore, Md., 1500 pp.

Ziegler, A.C., 1982. An ecological checklist of New Guinea recent mammals. In: J.L. Gressitt, (Editor), *Biogeography and Ecology of New Guinea. Vol. 2.* Junk, The Hague, pp. 863–894.

Chapter 22

BIRDS

JAMES R. KARR

INTRODUCTION

The dominant theme of a review paper on birds of tropical forests written thirty years ago would have been systematic and distributional. Further, a static perspective would have dominated, except perhaps for consideration of paleontological evidence (and speculation) on the origin and dispersal of higher taxa. The data base for such analyses was species lists and distributional information for selected, usually politically defined, areas.

During the 1960s ecological research in the tropics expanded and work on birds contributed significantly to that growth. Most research was directed toward untangling the reasons for latitudinal diversity gradients. Evidence for high species richness relative to temperate areas was convincing, but evidence for other conclusions (for instance, narrow niches, high species packing, stability begets diversity) was at best elusive and often nonexistent. During this period several pioneers (Snow, 1966, 1981; Moreau, 1966; Skutch, 1972; among others) pursued other research avenues as well.

As the 1970s arrived, attention focused on comparative ecological studies within and between tropical regions. Researchers were concerned both with patterns general to all tropical regions, and with differences among regions. Others pursued more detailed analyses of the natural history of certain species and groups of species. Coevolutionary interactions among taxa were (and are) a special focus in many recent research programs. With expanding knowledge and perspective, the simplicity and elegance of early 'robust' conclusions were undermined.

Two major approaches to the study of the ecology of tropical-forest birds occurred more or less simultaneously. In one, the avian community was the primary focus with attributes measured through synthetic indexes of structure and function (for instance, species diversity). The other emphasized the basic biology (natural history) of individual species and the interactions of a few species.

A growing awareness of the need to integrate knowledge of basic natural history with a multispecies perspective seems to dominate the study of tropical-forest birds in the 1980s. As a result, some reorientation of approach by community ecologists is needed, as is a more sophisticated approach to data collection and interpretation in "natural history" studies. Descriptive natural histories are being replaced by more integrative examination of the ecological and evolutionary pressures responsible for the natural histories of tropical birds. Rigorous integration of knowledge about physical and biological environments as well as the reciprocal influences of birds with their environments is necessary.

I now selectively review three major topics: zoogeography, species richness, and trophic structure of tropical-forest avifaunas. Comprehensive treatment of these subjects is impossible here. I have, in general, been descriptive while reluctantly restraining myself from exploring the "why?" question about pattern in nature.

ZOOGEOGRAPHY — AN ECO-TAXONOMIC ANALYSIS

The extraordinary species richness of the avifaunas of wet lowland tropical forest results from the radiation of selected major taxa (generally different taxa on each continent) and the presence of numerous families with a few species. In this section, I present a summary of the distribution of major taxa among the tropical forests of the world. For illustrative purposes, I limit consideration to terrestrial birds in four major ecotaxonomic groups (Moreau, 1966): (1) carnivores (raptors); (2) nonpasserine ground birds; (3) other nonpasserines; and (4) passerines. Within each group, taxa with similar food habits are grouped. I note the major families and their relative representation in each major geographic region: Neotropics, Africa, Southeast Asia and Australia–New Guinea. In addition, endemic families for each region are mentioned. Some areas are excluded with this approach (the Caribbean and most of the East Indies and Indian Subcontinent). However, those exclusions are not critical as this is intended only as a general comparative survey. Finally, I have used avian systematics at the familial level of a decade ago rather than adopt more recent taxonomies. For example, the numerous "families" that have been merged into the Muscicapidae are more reflective of the broad ecological groups I consider.

Carnivores

Throughout the tropics the Accipitridae is the largest family among birds that consume vertebrates. The size range in this family is tremendous. In Panama, the smallest member of the family is the tiny hawk (*Accipiter superciliosus*) with a weight of 75 g (male) while the magnificent harpy eagle (*Harpia harpyja*) weighs over 4000 g. The other major family of diurnal raptors (Falconidae) contains many fewer forest species. The falcons are most diverse in the Neotropical region, where bird hawks in the genus *Micrastur* apparently replace the more diverse Old World *Accipiter*. In addition, several New World caracaras (*Daptrius*) occur without an obvious Old World analog. New World vultures (Cathartidae) are an important radiation of carrion feeders. Among the nocturnal carnivores, the Strigidae are well represented in tropical forest throughout the world, including specialized fish-eating forms in Africa.

Nonpasserine ground birds

The Phasianidae occur worldwide but are especially diverse in Southeast Asian forests where they are represented by a variety of partridge, pheasant and peacock allies. In Africa the taxonomic diversity is lower and *Francolinus* is the primary forest group. Australia–New Guinea support two especially interesting groups, the very large cassowary (Casuariidae) and the smaller but no less interesting brush-turkeys (Megapodidae). In the New World, large Cracidae (*Crax*) may be similar ecologically to the cassowary. Two additional endemic Neotropical groups include the tinamous (Tinamidae) which are important in forest habitats and the trumpeters (Psophidae), a small and geographically restricted family with only three species. Terrestrial cuckoos occur in forest in the Neotropics (*Neomorphus* — ground cuckoo) and in Madagascar (several species of *Coua*). Finally, a number of specialized pigeons (Columbidae) occupy the ground layer in virtually all tropical forests. *Geotrygon* and *Leptotila* are important Neotropical pigeons while *Aplopelia* occurs in Africa and *Chalcophaps* in Asia. The spectacular crowned pigeons (*Goura*) of New Guinea are an extreme group of terrestrial columbids.

Other nonpasserines

Large-insect feeders

Of the 30 families in this "other nonpasserine" group, most feed primarily on large insects. Among the four nocturnal families in this group, only one is distributed throughout the world (Caprimulgidae). A few species can be found on the ground in mature forest or forest openings, and in some regions a species that roosts and forages in the canopy may occur (Africa — *Caprimulgus binotatus*; Neotropics — *Lurocalis*). The potoos (Nyctibiidae) are endemic to the Neotropics while the smaller owlet frogmouths (Aegothlidae) are endemic to New Guinea and Australia. The frogmouths (Podargidae) are restricted to forests of Southeast Asia, the East Indies and Australia. None of these families are represented by more than a few species in any forest area and all forage from a relatively exposed perch such as a dead branch.

Many families are represented in the diurnal large-insect feeders. Only the cuckoos (Cuculidae) are found in all regions, and they are especially diverse in Southeast Asia and New Guinea with fewer forest species occurring in African and, especially, Neotropical regions. Although the kingfishers (Alcedinidae) occur throughout the tropics, none of the species are found away from streams in the Neotropics, perhaps because of the diversity of puffbirds, motmots, and other similar groups. Insectivorous kingfishers are especially diverse in the forests of New Guinea. A number of bee-eaters (Meropidae) occupy African forest, but fewer species from this family occur in Southeast Asia and New Guinea. Like the Meropidae, the rollers (Coraciidae) are restricted to the Old World. They are represented by only a few species in forest in each region. Three endemic New World families occur in this group: puffbirds (Bucconidae), motmots (Momotidae) and jacamars (Galbulidae). None of these families are rich in forest species but, in the aggregate, they add appreciably to the diversity of tropical-forest avifaunas and include some of the more striking examples of ecological convergence between continents.

Bark-insect feeders

Two nonpasserine families seem to be primarily associated with feeding on insects associated with bark: woodpeckers (Picidae) and wood hoopoes (Phoeniculidae). Both include species that feed on fruits as well, and ants are a common food for many woodpecker species. The Picidae occur everywhere except New Guinea, and are especially diverse in Southeast Asian forests. African forests contain relatively few woodpeckers. The endemic African wood hoopoes are a small group of species with exceedingly interesting social systems (Ligon and Ligon, 1978). A passeriform family of the Neotropics (Dendrocolaptidae) feeds primarily on bark insects and will be discussed later.

Frugivores

Among the nonpasserines that feed primarily on fruits, two families occur worldwide — pigeons (Columbidae) and parrots (Psittacidae). Both have undergone a tremendous radiation in New Guinea where many species occupy forest. In the case of Columbidae they typically occupy either the canopy or ground levels and range widely in size. Parrots tend to occupy forest canopy and also represent a wide size range. Strictly speaking, most of the parrots (psittacids, cacatuids) feed on the seeds of a variety of fruiting trees. In addition, a number of species (lories) in New Guinea exploit

non-fruit resources such as nectar and pollen, as do a number of the smaller neotropical parakeets. Relatively few parrots occur in African and Southeast Asian forests when compared to their radiation in Neotropical and especially New Guinea forests.

Pigeons, on the other hand, have their greatest radiation in Southeast Asia with fewer forest species in both African and Neotropical regions. One family of large frugivores is endemic to Africa (touracos–Musophagidae). Arboreal cracids (*Penelope, Pipile*) occur in forest throughout the Neotropics, usually in groups of 2 to 20 individuals exploiting fruits and arthropods. One additional Neotropical family, the endemic oilbird (Steatornithidae), apparently feeds primarily on palm nuts where it has been studied.

Insectivore–frugivores

A mixed fruit and insect diet is consumed by five families: Ramphastidae (toucans), Opisthocomidae (hoatzin), Bucerotidae (hornbills), Capitonidae (barbets) and Trogonidae (trogons). Many members of several of these families also prey on lizards and nestling birds. The hoatzin is an aberrant form which frequents forest edge and open woodland in northern South America. Toucans of the Neotropics generally travel in search of food in flocks of a few to twenty or more individuals. The Old World hornbills (Bucerotidae) seem to be ecological analogs of the toucans. The hornbills vary from exclusively petty predators on large insects, lizards, and similar prey to exclusively frugivores, while most toucans seem to be mixed feeders.

Two nearly pantropical groups (not found on New Guinea) are the barbets (Capitonidae) and the trogons (Trogonidae). The barbets are well represented in Africa and Southeast Asia but not in the Neotropics, while the trogons are by far the richest in Latin America and barely represented in Africa.

Nectarivores

Two nonpasserine groups specialize in exploitation of nectar resources — hummingbirds (Trochilidae) and lories (Loriidae). Hummingbirds, a very diverse group of mostly small, long-billed species, are restricted to the New World and feed on flower nectars and, to a lesser extent, insects. The lories are restricted to New Guinea and Australia.

Other foods

Three other specialized families should be mentioned. The pantropical swifts (Apodidae) feed on insects above the forest canopy as do the crested swifts (Hemiprocnidae) of Southeast Asia and New Guinea. Finally, the honeyguides (Indicatoridae) of Africa (one Southeast Asian species) include a number of forest species with the peculiar habit of brood parasitism and, in one African species, a propensity for leading mammals to the nests of bees.

Passerines

Passerines dominate tropical-forest avifaunas throughout the world. Suboscines are dominant in the Neotropics, but are poorly represented in other regions. Major insectivorous suboscine families include antbirds (Formicariidae), ovenbirds (Furnariidae), and woodcreepers (Dendrocolaptidae). The New World flycatchers (Tyrannidae) are mostly insectivorous, but a number of species are more opportunistic in their consumption of fruits and insects, and a few even specialize on fruits. Manakins (Pipridae) and cotingids (Cotingidae) are mostly frugivorous with a few insectivores. These six families make up the majority of passerines in Neotropical forest, especially in forest undergrowth.

Important oscine families include the insectivorous wrens (Troglodytidae) and vireos (Vireonidae). Mixed feeders include the species-rich tanagers (Thraupidae) and wood-warblers (Parulidae) and a smaller number of honeycreepers (Coerebidae), thrushes (Turdidae), and icterids (Icteridae). A few fringillids (Fringillidae) occur in Neotropical lowland forest. Several oscine groups are more important in highland than in lowland forest, especially in Middle America (for instance, Parulidae, Turdidae, Vireonidae, Thraupidae, Turdidae, and Fringillidae).

The dominant passerine nectar-feeders in Old World forest are the sunbirds (Nectariniidae) in Africa and Asia, and honeyeaters (Meliphagidae) in New Guinea. (One may recall the importance of lories as nectar feeders in New Guinea and the hummingbirds in the Neotropics. Some of the Coerebidae in the Neotropics feed extensively on nectar resources. Most passerine nectar feeders also consume arthropods.)

African forest undergrowth is dominated by three families: bulbuls (Pycnonotidae), thrushes (Turdidae), and Old-World flycatchers (Muscicapidae). Babblers (Timaliidae) are also common in forest undergrowth. Several important families are more common at intermediate to canopy heights: shrikes (Laniidae), sunbirds (Nectariniidae), old-world warblers (Sylviidae), and starlings (Sturnidae). Families represented by only a few species include drongoes (Dicruridae), tits (Paridae), broadbills (Eurylamidae), orioles (Oriolidae), cuckoo-shrikes (Campephagidae) and several groups of Old World finches and weaver birds (Ploceidae).

Southeast Asian forest generally supports more species of cuckoo-shrikes, drongoes, broadbills, and pittas (Pittidae) than does African forest. Babblers are especially rich in Southeast Asia, whereas forest bulbuls are less well represented than in Africa. Taxa present in Southeast Asia but generally not in Africa include the flowerpeckers (Dicaeidae), fairy bluebirds (Irenidae), and nuthatches (Sittidae).

Because of its relative isolation and complex topography, several major radiations are endemic to Australia–New Guinea. These include the often spectacular birds of paradise (Paradisaeidae), bowerbirds (Ptilorhynchidae), whistlers (Pachycephalidae), and wren-warblers (Maluridae). Many species of cuckoo-shrikes, flowerpeckers, Old-World flycatchers, and Old-World warblers occur in forests of Southeast Asia. The white-eyes (Zosteropidae) are abundant especially in disturbed and island forest. Another family, the wood-swallows (Artamidae), occurs from India to Australia.

While this analysis briefly summarizes the zoogeography of tropical forest birds from an ecological perspective, it does little to aid insight into ecological patterns and the processes that generate them.

SPECIES RICHNESS

Without doubt, the high species richness of tropical-forest avifaunas is their most striking attribute. That richness and its origin have fascinated biologists since before Charles Darwin.

Species richness can be examined at three major scales in the present context: (1) regional/continental; (2) habitat type; and (3) habitat patch. At the first level (regional/continental), one deals with a geographically defined mosaic of habitats. Since this chapter deals with tropical-forest birds, this scale will not be considered further.

When one focuses more narrowly on forest habitat, the primary factors at continental scales that determine the number of species (or proportion of a fauna) found in forest habitats are the extent of forest habitat and, secondarily, the history of forest distribution in the region (Karr, 1976a; Pearson, 1977, 1982). Africa, an area of 20×10^6 km², supports only about 400 species of forest birds (wet, dry and montane forest; Moreau, 1966), while the much smaller New Guinea $(0.3 \times 10^6$ km²) supports 380 species of rain-forest birds (Bell, 1982a). Most of New Guinea (86%) is forested, but only a relatively small porportion of sub-Saharan Africa is forested (9%; Myers, 1979). The diverse New Guinea avifauna developed through a diversification of a limited founder stock (Cracraft, 1976). About 2/3 (800 spp.) of the fauna of Southeast Asia (total area 2.5×10^6 km², 75% forested) occurs in a variety of forest habitats. Of the awesome 3300 Neotropical species (total area 20.0×10^6 km², 24% forested), perhaps 40% (1300) are forest birds. Temperate-tropical migrants are a minority of species in all major geographic areas, ranging from 4.5 to 11.9% of the total faunas (Karr, 1980b).

Smaller-sized areas on the order of 40 to 600×10^3 km² are less variable in species richness of tropical-forest birds when one selects areas dominated by forest habitats (Karr, 1980b). Even then, an area such as Liberia in West Africa $(111 \times 10^3$ km²) has only half the total number of species (381) not associated with aquatic environments as Panama with 727 species in only 75×10^3 km². The richest tropical-forest avifauna occurs in western Amazonia, where from one small area John Terborgh of Princeton University and colleagues (pers. commun., 1984) have recorded about 540 species near their primary research site in Manú National Park. A local diversity of habitat types contributes to the high species richness in the Manú fauna (wet forest, flooded forest, bamboo, palm swamp, etc.).

Broad geographic comparisons emphasize the importance of habitat area and long-term evolutionary dynamics, especially since the Pleistocene,

in structuring avian communities (Haffer, 1969; Karr, 1976a; Pearson, 1982). They certainly do not provide insight about the details of variation in avian communities within and among regions.

Two ecologists have attempted pantropical comparisons (Karr, 1976a, 1980a, b; Pearson, 1977, 1982). Pearson surveyed birds in six tropical areas at two spatial scales (Table 22.1) and found that South American forests were richest, Africa was intermediate, and island sites on Borneo and New Guinea were lowest. Evaluation of two additional sites from Central America (Pipeline Road, Panama; La Selva, Costa Rica) shows Central America to be at the low end of the South American range but well above other geographic regions. I used nets to sample the undergrowth avifaunas of a number of tropical-forest areas. As with Pearson's conclusions, Neotropical forest was the richest in the world, with forest in mainland Malaysia, Africa, and on islands, following in that order (Fig. 22.1).

But these general patterns of species richness are a function of more subtle local and regional dynamics in the avifaunas of tropical forest. For example, Karr et al. (1982), working in Panama, found that movements of birds in response to rainfall seasonality altered local and regional species richness. In that study a site with moderate

TABLE 22.1

Species richness at two spatial scales for related tropical-forest areas throughout the world

Region/country	Total number of species in primary forest		Source
	12–15 km²	15 ha	
South America			
Ecuador	478	232	Pearson (1982)
Peru	415	204	Pearson (1982)
Bolivia	385	181	Pearson (1982)
Middle America			
Panama	383	225	Karr (pers.observ.)
Costa Rica	382	–	Stiles (1983)
Africa			
Gabon	365	158	Pearson (1982)
East Indies			
Borneo	220	142	Pearson (1982)
New Guinea	191	114	Pearson (1982)

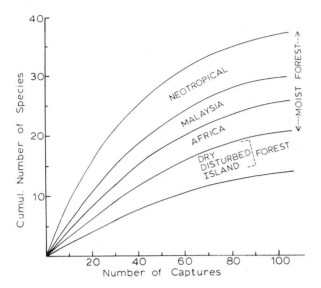

Fig. 22.1. Generalized diagram showing relative ranges of species accumulation curves for avifaunas of tropical forest undergrowth for several geographic regions. (From Karr 1980a.)

moisture regime varied in species richness in standard 100-capture mist-net samples from 28 to 38 species. During wet years birds were not concentrated in moist valley sites, while in dry years species richness increased at moist and intermediate sites while dry sites were avoided (Karr, 1981; Karr and Freemark, 1983).

However, not all species survive seasonal variation in their environment by movements. Some species simply switch the resource types used; many insectivorous species that face seasonal resource shortages during the dry season survive on nectar (for instance of *Erythrina, Balsa* and *Combretum*) and fruits (like figs), much like the primates in Peru studied intensively by Terborgh (1983).

Recently, research in tropical forest as well as other habitats has concentrated on the role of disturbance in organizing biological communities (Pickett and White, 1985). For birds, it is clear that species richness is determined by a variety of forces acting probabilistically, especially those that vary in space and/or time. A greater understanding of how patchiness affects species and community attributes will likely be a central problem in community ecology in the next decade (Karr and Freemark, 1983, 1985).

TROPHIC STRUCTURE

Sympatry of species is possible only if they are sufficiently different that they do not compete over the long term for the same limiting resource(s) (Schoener, 1974, 1982). Three major axes of separation that involve foraging have been studied: food type, foraging behavior, and foraging site. In this section, I focus on the food resources and patterns of food resource exploitation in tropical-forest avifaunas.

Lein (1972) compared the avifaunas of the six major faunal regions with respect to their major food resources. At these continent-wide scales, tropical regions were more similar among themselves than they were to temperate regions. More detailed comparisons among the tropical regions showed that the differences that did exist were due to the relative areas of major vegetation types. For example, faunal regions dominated by grassland and/or dry open forest supported a higher proportion of their fauna as granivores than did faunal regions dominated by moist forest.

More recently, several researchers have taken more narrowly defined geographical areas as the basis for comparison of the trophic structure of tropical forest avifaunas. Again, tropical forests support avifaunas that are more similar among themselves than is any tropical forest to the trophic structure of temperate-forest avifaunas. Further, within tropical areas, geographic proximity seems to be the primary factor producing similar trophic grouping among samples (Fig. 22.2).

Although a number of ecologists have classified species according to trophic status, classification

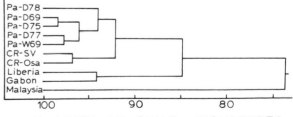

SIMILARITY OF GUILD SIGNATURES

Fig. 22.2. Dendrogram of similarity (ecological-overlap) indices for guild signatures (trophic structure) based on undergrowth mist-net samples from tropical-forest areas. *Pa* = Limbo Hunt Club, Panama; *CR-SV* = San Vito, Costa Rica; *CR-Osa* = Osa Peninsula, Costa Rica; *D78* = dry season 1978; *W69* = wet season 1969; etc. (From Karr, 1980a.)

systems vary considerably. Careful comparison allowing for those differences demonstrates detailed differences among tropical regions. Peru (and by inference the Neotropics more generally) has specialized raptors, woodpeckers, and vine gleaners which are unrepresented in other regions, especially New Guinea (Beehler, 1981). But New Guinea has lichen gleaners and arboreal-to-ground insect feeders (several kingfishers; Beehler, 1981), groups that are not well represented in the Neotropics. Pearson (1982) noted that New Guinea was high in frugivore species but low in omnivores relative to primary forest in other areas. Africa has honeyguides (Malaysia has one), and both Africa and the Neotropical region have professional ant-followers. Neotropical forests have more species that glean arthropods from dead leaves suspended above the ground, omnivores, and bark gleaners, but fewer mast-eaters, frugivores, and nectar feeders than New Guinea (Beehler, 1981; Pearson, 1982). The undergrowth of Malaysian forest supports very few frugivores (Janzen, 1977, 1980; Karr, 1980a; Wong, 1983) while forest on Borneo supports few frugivores, and hover-gleaning insectivores (Pearson, 1982).

The number of species using a specific food resource is likely related to the number of ways that the resource can be divided (Karr, 1975) and the general stability of the resource (Karr, 1976b), while the number of individuals (biomass) that can be supported in a guild probably reflects the availability of that resource. Of course, resources that are superabundant for short periods, such as fig fruits or termites during major emergences, may temporarily support a rich bird and mammal fauna. More stable resources, such as undergrowth insects, usually support many species with a diverse array of foraging strategies and locations. In contrast, fruits are generally advertised and the richness of species that can be supported is much lower where a single resource dimension (fruit size) is being exploited (Karr, 1980a; Wong, 1983). Thiollay (1973) found that the number of frugivorous species in a West African forest was only 15, while 49 species were insectivorous and 12 had mixed diets. However, frugivorous birds made up nearly as great a proportion of the consuming biomass (41%) as did the more species-rich insectivores (46%). This attempted generality, of course, minimizes variation in mass, nutrient and

energy content, density, and temporal availability of fruits.

As food resource abundance varies among continents, of course, the precise nature of this pattern varies. Avian trophic organization in the fruit-poor Malaysian rain-forest understory conforms to the species richness pattern noted above (2 frugivorous species, 50 insectivorous species, 20 species with mixed diet) but differs in its low biomass of frugivores (4%) and high biomass (75%) and per-species abundance of insectivores (Wong, 1983).

General comparisons of the trophic structure of tropical and north temperate forest-bird communities (Terborgh, 1980) invariably demonstrate that tropical forests support:

(1) Specialists that exploit resources not reliably available throughout the year in temperate forest (like, for instance, fruits, nectar, large insects, arthropods living in dead leaf clumps or flushed by army ants from other hiding places).

(2) Tighter species packing relative to total number of species, especially among insectivorous groups of forest undergrowth. This pattern is often associated with low density for each species. Densities per species for the rich foliage insectivore fauna of Peru seem to be lower than for the less rich fauna of forest in central Panama (S. Robinson and J. Karr, unpublished observations).

(3) Guilds with few species and narrowly defined diets (for example, raptors specializing on reptiles, homopteran specialists, lichen-feeding parrots, honeyguides).

(4) Broad guild niches as reflected by wider ranges of sizes of birds in a guild.

(5) A great variety of microhabitats within forest due to floristic and structural diversity (Medway and Wells, 1976; Terborgh, 1980; Greenburg and Gradwohl, 1980; Pearson, 1982).

These tropical-temperate differences were attributed to the general pattern of increased specialization (on all niche dimensions) among tropical birds; but that view should not be too widely generalized (Terborgh, 1980). Indeed, studies in tropical lowland forest often conclude that habitat specialization (vegetation structure) is high while food specialization seems to be relatively lower for many species (Karr, 1971; Beehler, 1981). River-edge (Remsen and Parker, 1983) and bamboo habitats often contain an avifauna that is very specialized in its habitat requirements.

Variation among species and geographic areas emphasizes multivariate influences on the structure and function of tropical-forest avifaunas. As one climbs mountains in New Guinea, dietary specialization increases (Beehler, 1981). Clearly, careful documentation of many related variables is necessary before broad generalizations on niche breadth at the faunal level should be attempted. Overall, assemblage attributes are the product of many forces acting probabilistically, the cumulative effects of which are large but the individual effects are minor, interactive and uncertain (McNaughton, 1983; Karr and Freemark, 1983, 1985).

Nectarivores

Although nectarivorous birds occur in tropical forest throughout the world, only the Neotropical hummingbirds are well studied. Among the hummingbirds, the primary mechanisms of resource segregation are bill length (associated with corolla length) and the defensibility of food resources (Feinsinger and Colwell, 1978). Six ecological and behavioral groups were recognized:

Some species (the long-billed hermits) visit but do not defend nectar-rich flowers with long corollas. These are referred to as high-reward trapliners. Territorialists are smaller species that defend dense clumps of short flowers. Low-reward trapliners exploit dispersed and nectar-poor flowers. Territory parasites tend to be either large species that aggressively steal territorial resources or small and more secretive nectar thiefs. Finally, a group of generalists also occurs. High-reward trapliners are resident in forest undergrowth while the others tend to be more sporadic in their presence, mostly in canopy of forest and/or in edge and/or tree-fall sites. Sporadic nectar resources and highly mobile species are characteristic of these other groups.

Gill and Wolf (1977) provide insight about resource use and territoriality in savanna sunbirds in East Africa, but no detailed studies have been conducted on nectarivorous birds in Old-World tropical forest. I am not familiar with any detailed studies of the ecology of nectarivores in the brush-tongued parrots, meliphagids, and certain marsupial mammals in forests of Australia and New Guinea. Carpenter (1978) compared nectarivore communities in Australian meliphagids, mountain hummingbirds, and Hawaiian drepanidids. Although not all her research areas were in forest, she demonstrated the importance of nectar limitation on hummingbirds but not in the other two communities. Nectar is limiting in the Hawaiian system in some years but apparently not at all in Australian heath. Partitioning and community structure likewise vary along the nectar-limitation gradient; meliphagid communities are diverse and partitioning is subtle. Carpenter speculated that partitioning occurred on the insect aspect of their foods. Drepanidid communities are simple, the number of true nectar-feeding species being reduced in times of nectar limitation, and partitioning occurs through aggressive exclusion of species at different flower densities. Montane hummingbird communities are even simpler due to dramatic temporal partitioning of nectar resources. Even in lowland forest (for instance in Panama) seasonal increases in nectar abundance are important for many bird species. Plants evolve with highly specialized bird-pollination relationships in the hummingbird system, but plants are less tied to birds in the other systems where mammals (Australia) and insects (Hawaii) are more important to the plants.

These examples illustrate the complex interaction of physical climate, food resource reliability, and complex coevolutionary relationships among taxa for a single resource type. As one final caution, I point out that most work on these groups of birds overlooks the importance of insects and perhaps pollen to many species that are assumed to be narrowly nectarivorous. Clarification of evolutionary pattern in these birds should explicitly incorporate studies of consumption of resources other than nectar.

Frugivores

Specialized frugivores in tropical forest may be grouped into one of four classes:

Large species that feed in the canopy — These species travel extensively (often in flocks) as they exploit widely dispersed fruiting trees. Important taxa here include pigeons, toucans, hornbills, and large barbets. Often, especially among the pigeons (for instance in New Guinea), a fairly clear-cut series of species of varying weight is involved in exploitation of a series of fruit sizes (Diamond, 1973; Crome, 1975).

Small species that feed in the canopy — Many of these species are mobile but apparently use smaller areas than the preceding group. Many join mixed species groups that travel together. Often these birds are less specialized as frugivores than the preceding group. They may even consume other foods associated with fruits and flowers. Examples include many tanagers found in the canopy of Neotropical forest and the smaller barbets, starlings, fairy bluebirds and other groups in other regions.

Small species that feed in the undergrowth — This group generally involves only a few species at any site but each species is generally very common. Manakins dominate this group in the Neotropics while bulbuls prevail in Africa. Only one or two species of this type are present in Malaysian forest and they are very rare (Karr, 1980a; Wong, 1983). In Africa and in Latin America, a group of three to four species constitutes 25 to 35% of the individuals captured in mist nets in forest undergrowth (Karr, 1976a, 1980a). Among the manakins high mobility, especially among juveniles and adult females, exaggerates their densities so they do not constitute a high proportion of the local avifauna (Karr, 1971; Karr et al., 1982; Graves et al., 1983). Invariably the size range of species in this group is small, mostly between 10 and 20 g.

Terrestrial — Commonly from two to five species of terrestrial birds consume fruits that have fallen from above. Generally larger (60–200 g) than undergrowth species, these species may be from several taxa but pigeons dominate nearly everywhere.

Snow (1966, 1981) and Snow and Snow (1971) pioneered analysis of the ecology of frugivory in tropical forest birds from an evolutionary perspective. McKey (1975) and Howe and Estabrook (1977) theorized two major fruiting strategies: "high investment" and "low investment". They further speculated that high-investment fruits are used primarily by specialist frugivores, while low-quality fruits are used more by opportunistic feeders. Expansion and refinements of this model (Howe and Smallwood, 1982; Wheelwright and Orians, 1982; Martin, 1985) emphasize that frugivore function does not really separate as specialist

versus opportunist, and that frugivory is more complex than this simple dichotomy because a myriad of factors are active in design of fruits and their dispersers. These include the role of predation on frugivores (Howe, 1977; Howe and Smallwood, 1982; Martin, 1985), the influence of behavioral interference (Martin, 1985), timing of fruit production (range and peak), rates of fruit ripening, consumption, and decomposition, the array of dispersers competing for fruits (Janzen, 1983), fruit size (Martin, 1985), and display pattern and fruit density (Denslow and Moermond, 1982; Moermond and Denslow, 1983; Martin, 1985).

The timing of fruit production and bird activity is often strikingly concordant. Availability of some fruits (for instance *Guarea glabra* in Panamanian forest) is concentrated during the northward migration of migrant frugivores (Howe and De Steven, 1979; Greenberg, 1981a). Other species mature fruit during the southward migration. Similarly, many primarily insectivorous birds increase consumption of fruits during periods of low insect abundance; loss of the tree *Casearia* from forest in Costa Rica would likely result in loss of several bird species (Howe, 1977). As noted earlier, figs may play a similar role in lean times in many tropical-forest areas.

Further, the role of birds in affecting forest structure and species composition, reproductive strategies of plants, and related phenomena deserves more careful study. At Rio Palenque in Ecuador, 48% of large trees, 46% of lianas, and 72% of small trees have birds as their primary dispersal agents (Gentry, 1982).

Insectivores

The extreme radiation of insectivorous birds in tropical forests relative to most temperate forests results from three factors: (1) exploitation of an array of large insects consumed by both specialists and opportunists (Orians, 1969; Schoener, 1971; Karr, 1971, 1975); (2) higher species-packing on complex food-resource bases (Karr and James, 1975; Sherry, 1984); and (3) numerous specialized insectivores [dead-leaf-clump gleaners (Remson and Parker, 1984), bamboo gleaners, ant-followers (Willis and Oniki, 1978)] occupy tropical forest. However, not all insectivore guilds in tropical forest support many species relative to temperate forests (for instance, bark excavators — Karr, 1971, 1976a; Askins, 1983).

The key to accounting for specific patterns of species richness in insectivores (as in other groups) is careful documentation of connections between the abundance of resources and their seasonal reliability.

In addition, the extent of avian opportunism during periods of low insect abundance must also be clarified. The low number of frugivores in the undergrowth of Malaysian forest is clearly tied to lack of fruits (Wong, 1983). The small number of hover-gleaning species in Borneo relative to other regions (Pearson, 1982) probably reflects lower densities of insects on undersides of leaves. Alternatively, perhaps there is a critical but short period of resource depression that precludes specialization on this food resource, except for species that can opportunistically shift to other resources.

Recently, several researchers have begun to document connections between resource availability and dynamics of tropical forest insectivores. First, sampling of insect populations by Wolda (1978a, b), Greenberg and Gradwohl (1980), Levings and Windsor (1982) and Karr (unpubl.) in Panama, and Wong (1983) in Malaysia, demonstrates the complex dynamics of the insect resource. In forest undergrowth most insect activity seems to occur at night, with many insects resting on the lower surface of leaves during the day. Greenberg and Gradwohl (1980) considered that this propensity for the undersurface of leaves might result from physiological factors: Larger insects seem to be less restricted to lower surfaces, brightly colored insects prefer lower surfaces, lower surfaces are used more in dry than wet season, and the upper surface is used more at high-elevation sites. Karr (unpubl.) found similar seasonal and insect-size patterns and also showed that these patterns were repeated along a moisture gradient within and between dry seasons.

This knowledge, when coupled with detailed foraging observations and analysis of gut contents (Greenberg and Gradwohl, 1980; Wong, 1983; Sherry, 1984), yields considerable insight about assemblages of insectivorous birds. Insectivorous birds of forest undergrowth concentrate their feeding (75–92%) on lower surface of leaves while canopy birds are less specialized (51%) (Greenberg

and Gradwohl, 1980). Climatic variability in the forest canopy apparently produces a less stable food resource that requires more opportunistic foraging, as well as seasonal shifts in species richness and abundances (Karr, 1976; Greenberg, 1981a).

In New Guinea lowland forest, birds tend to be habitat specialists but food generalists (Beehler, 1981). However, dietary specialization increases with elevation, perhaps due to truncation of selected resources and thus reduced survivorship of opportunistic species. Only specialists on reliable food resources can persist. Further, bird size declines with increased elevation in New Guinea as both insect and fruit size distributions are truncated. Again, marginal resources (fruits, large insects, nectar; Karr, 1975) become less available, much as they do when one moves from tropical to temperate areas. Perhaps this factor drives altitudinal migration in many birds (Stiles, 1983).

Throughout the tropics, canopy species are more likely to be generalists (mixed herbivore–insectivores) while undergrowth avifaunas are more dominated by specialist insectivores (Bell, 1979; Greenberg, 1981a; Frith, 1984). The seasonal instability of the forest canopy (Karr, 1976b; Greenberg, 1981a; Bell, 1982b) may require species to exploit a more opportunistic set of food resources than is required for the species of the more stable (but *not absolutely stable*: Karr and Freemark, 1983) forest undergrowth. Similar opportunism also may drive vertical and horizontal shifts in birds of all strata (Pearson, 1971; Karr, 1971; Greenberg, 1981a; Bell, 1982c; Karr and Freemark, 1983; Frith, 1984). The extent of these shifts may be quite variable among taxa, depending on the seasonality of their food supply. As noted above, some of the most extreme movements may come among the nectarivores.

Schoener (1971) called attention to the larger bills of tropical insectivores and concluded that this was due to abundance of larger insects. Indeed, experiments suggest that small differences in bill size may significantly influence prey selection and thus produce diverging diets under natural conditions (Paszkowski and Moermond, 1984). Recently, Greenberg (1981b) noted that neotropical gleaners have longer, narrower bills than temperate species. He attributed this to the higher frequency of Orthoptera in the diets of tropical-forest birds, especially in food provided to nest-lings. Many temperate birds with their shorter bills exploit caterpillars as their major food. Longer bills may be better for handling larger and more mobile orthopteran prey (Beecher, 1962; Ashmole, 1968; Lederer, 1975). M. Wong (pers. commun., 1984) indicates that Orthoptera are rare in Malaysian forest. Are bird bills shorter there?

Subtle patterns of bird use of habitat are now well documented. In forest in central Panama, Karr and Freemark (1983) showed that birds concentrated their activities at dry sites and sites with intermediate shrub density. However, considerable variation in habitat selection was exhibited among species on both moisture and vegetation gradients. For example, ruddy quail-doves (*Geotrygon montana*) preferred sites at the wet end of the moisture gradient, whereas song wrens (*Cyphorhinus phaeocephalus*) preferred dry sites (Fig. 22.3a). For some species, preferred habitat changed as macroclimatic conditions changed. Ochre-bellied flycatchers (*Mionectes oleagineus*) preferred sites with lower shrub density during dry periods more than during wet periods (Fig. 22.3b). Overall, avian activity reflected a dynamic process of habitat selection in both space and time. Each species had a preferred habitat condition in space (Fig. 22.3a), but that preferred position changed over time as a function of macroclimatic, and thus

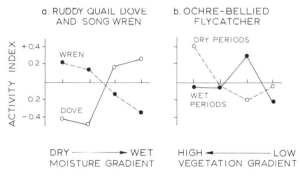

Fig. 22.3. Activity patterns for selected bird species when sampling sites are classed according to position along environmental gradients. The activity index is an assessment of capture rates in mist nets for sites having a specific gradient position relative to sample effort (mist-net hours) at that gradient position. (a) Avian activity along a moisture gradient that integrates undergrowth microclimatic conditions from dry to wet. (b) Avian activity along a gradient of vegetation structure (low to high shrub density). All patterns shown are significantly different from random by a χ^2 test ($p < .05$). (Modified from Karr and Freemark, 1985.)

microclimatic, conditions (Fig. 22.3b). Differential shifts in distribution of manakins and ochre-bellied flycatchers in Panama apparently reflect their different abilities to respond to changing food availabilities (Karr, 1982). Normally, both feed primarily on fruits, but in a recent period of fruit shortage the flycatchers consumed mostly insects while the manakins moved to other areas in search of fruit (Karr, 1982). The subtlety of resource patterns that may be important to birds is demonstrated by *Dacnis cayana* (blue dacnis); foraging adults may rely on brown spots on leaves to detect presence of small herbivorous insects (Greenberg and Gradwohl, 1980).

Seed-eaters

Seed-eaters in tropical forests are relatively rare, especially in undergrowth, in contrast to the rich seed-eater assemblages that characterize grassland and shrubland avifaunas. However, one group of birds (parrots and allies) seem to be specialized on the seeds of tropical forest trees. While a number of psittaciforms consume nectar and/or pollen, and one is reputed to glean lichens and insects from tree bark, most are seed predators (Janzen, 1983).

Mixed feeders

Many tropical species exploit two or three major food types (nectar, insects, and/or fruit). Perhaps 25 to 35% of the increased species richness of tropical over temperate-forest avifaunas is due to mixed feeders (Karr, 1975). Consumption of two or more resources results in more complicated population dynamics and mobility. One may recall for example the relatively high density per species of frugivores relative to insectivores of tropical forest (for birds of similar size). In a study of 14 species of tanagers, all of which ate some combination of insects and fruits, the most frugivorous species had higher numerical abundances than species that were more insectivorous (Snow and Snow, 1971).

General comments

The primary purpose of this set of examples is to show that simple univariate explanations are insufficient to account for pattern in tropical forest avifaunas. A commonly cited example of a relatively simple pattern is the sequence of species of frugivores with doubling of weights between species (Diamond, 1973). For sets of ecologically similar species segregated on a single resource axis, species sequences may indeed approximate the 2× ratio of weights discussed by Diamond (1973) or 1.4× ratio of linear dimensions (Hutchinson, 1957). However, when two or more resource axes interact (for instance, fruit size and type of fruit display), some divergense from those theoretical distributions predicated on single axis system might be expected (Fig. 22.4b). As a result, weight ratios may diverge from the theoretical 2× expectation. In contrast, resource complexes with two (or more) axes that cannot be simply apportioned on a single axis (Fig. 22.4c), would not yield simple sequences of species. Frugivory in birds is more like the situation in Fig. 22.4a and b, while 22.4c illustrates the situation that produces rich insectivorous assemblages.

Finally, as Brown and Davidson (1977) have demonstrated for desert communities, other taxa may also affect the evolution of avian assemblages. Several groups of large frugivorous birds in New Guinea (cassowaries, megapodes and fruit pigeons) may have developed in the absence of a rich mammal fauna attuned to consumption of fruits (Beehler, 1981). Pearson (1982) discussed the relationship between primates and birds in tropical forest, and Karr (1976a) suggested that the rich squirrel fauna of Africa may have limited development of frugivorous birds, due to altered selection pressures on fruiting plants (that is, hard seeds instead of soft fleshy fruits). Also, evolutionary interactions of birds and bats (Fenton and Fleming, 1976) and birds and lizards (Wright, 1979) constrain these groups.

DISCUSSION

The pattern of avian natural-history attributes and species-assemblage characteristics as well as the processes that produce that pattern are exceedingly complex. Comprehension of such patterns and processes requires sophisticated observational and experimental studies over extended periods. Snapshots of a few weeks to a year typically fail to convey the subtle dynamics of

a SINGLE AXIS RESOURCE VARIATION

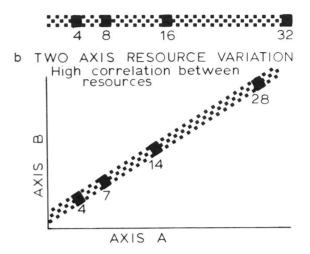

b TWO AXIS RESOURCE VARIATION

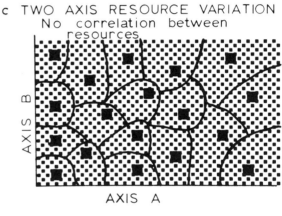

c TWO AXIS RESOURCE VARIATION

Fig. 22.4. Distribution of available resources and species centers in subdivision of single and two-dimensional resource systems. Numbers indicate sequential weights of birds along the axis of exploitable resources in a and b. In c no simple single axis sequences exist and the situation would be even more complex in situation with three or more dimensions.

tropical avifaunas (and their causes) when compared to temperate-zone summer–winter changes. Elucidation of the complex of factors responsible for both temporal and spatial dynamics is essential.

In one summary of that complexity, I developed a conceptual model (Karr, 1980a) showing the primary variables (and their interactions) that govern the development of avian assemblages (Fig. 22.5). The challenge is first to sort out the variables and their interactions at species and guild

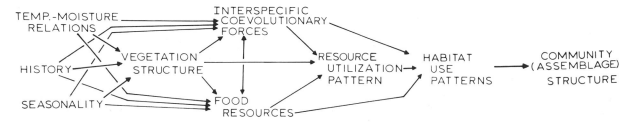

Fig. 22.5. Conceptual model showing the primary variables (and their interactions) that govern the development of avian community structure. (Modified from Karr, 1980a.)

levels, then how these interactions in the aggregate have produced specific assemblages composed of differing guild combinations among geographic regions. Without doubt, the linkages involved vary in relative importance from place to place, even over time at the same place.

Explanations that account for patterns of avifaunal richness vary significantly with the geographical scale considered. When continental areas are considered, habitat distribution and total area dominate as causes of variation. However, when smaller areas are compared among regions, historical factors such as Pleistocene refuges [Haffer (1969), Pearson (1982), but also see Beven et al. (1984)] and island biogeography theories are more pertinent to the explanation of pattern (Karr, 1976a; Pearson, 1982). Ecological factors such as competition were poor predictors of rank order in species richness in comparisons of six major tropical areas (Pearson, 1982).

However, as one moves to consideration of pattern within a geographic region, aspects of macro- and microclimatic variation, foliage complexity, degree of seasonality, species packing, niche replacement, and presence of potential nonavian competition seem to be of greater significance. Further, ornithologists have concentrated on food as the dominant factor of importance. Perhaps more effort should be made to clarify the role of predation and nest-site availability and selection.

Elevational gradients provide an excellent example of the complex of factors producing pattern in avian assemblages. Invariably, species richness declines from lowlands to high mountains, although some evidence of a minor peak at about 1000 m exists (Chapman, 1926; Moreau, 1966; Terborgh, 1971, 1977; Diamond, 1973; Medway and Wells, 1976; Beehler, 1981; Wells et al.,

undated). This general pattern is likely due to several factors: monotonic decline in both available land area and mean temperature, increase in cloud cover (reduced light and photosynthesis), and increase in frequency of physical disturbance (landslips, frosts, etc.: Beehler, 1981). In addition to the general pattern of decreased species richness, birds exhibit increased dietary specialization and reduced habitat specialization with increasing elevation (Beehler, 1981).

SUMMARY

Existing avian assemblages in tropical forest vary considerably among regions. Different taxa have colonized and diversified in each geographic area. Tropical-forest avifaunas seem to be richer than temperate-forest avifaunas due to higher rates of tropical speciation. In addition, among tropical-forest faunas greater evolutionary age of habitats and habitat patch size and distributional effects are important factors among continents. On ecological scales, a complex array of within- and between-habitat specializations have added to the complexity of tropical avifaunas. Increased structural complexity of habitats, broader tropical resource spectra, varying abundances and seasonal and between year reliability of resources varies among tropical regions. Biological pressures (for instance, competition and predation) from other organisms are also important in accounting for differences among areas. Finally, the presence of relative climatic stability without severe seasonal (especially temperature) extremes that cause most organisms to become dormant, but with some seasonal variation (for example in moisture availability), keeps systems from attaining a simple competitive equilibrium. These dynamics interact to produce avian assemblages that are complex. Despite considerable growth in research programs in the last twenty years, much remains to be learned.

ACKNOWLEDGMENTS

This paper was made possible by research support from Earthwatch, National Science Foundation (DEB 82–06672), National Geographic Society, and Smithsonian Tropical Research Institute. J. Blake, K. Freemark, T. Martin, B. Maurer, M. Moynihan, D. Pearson, S. Robinson, N. Smith and M. Wong commented constructively on an early draft of this paper.

REFERENCES

Ashmole, N.P., 1968. Body size, prey size and ecological segregation in five sympotic tropical terns (Aves: Laridae). *Syst. Zool.*, 17: 292–304.

Askins, R.A., 1983. Foraging ecology of temperate-zone and tropical woodpeckers. *Ecology*, 64: 945–956.

Beecher, W.J., 1962. The bio-mechanics of the bird skull. *Bull. Chicago Acad. Sci.*, 11: 10–33.

Beehler, B., 1981. Ecological structuring of forest bird communities in New Guinea. In: J.L. Gressitt (Editor), *Biogeography and Ecology of New Guinea*. Monogr. Biol., 42: 837–861.

Bell, H.L., 1979. The effects on rain-forest birds of plantings of Teak, *Tectona grandis*, in Papua, New Guinea. *Aust. Wildlife Res.*, 6: 305–318.

Bell, H.L., 1982a. A bird community of lowland rainforest in New Guinea. 1. Composition and density of the avifauna. *Emu*, 82: 24–41.

Bell, H.L., 1982b. A bird community of lowland rainforest in New Guinea. 4. Use of secondary vegetation. *Emu*, 82: 217–224.

Bell, H.L., 1982c. A bird community of New Guinean lowland rainforest. 3. Vertical distribution of the avifauna. *Emu*, 82: 143–162.

Beven, S., Connor, E.F. and Beven, K., 1984. Avian biogeography in the Amazon basin and the biological model of diversification. *J. Biogeogr.*, 11: 383–399.

Brown, J.H. and Davidson, D.W., 1977. Competition between seed-eating rodents and ants in desert ecosystems. *Science*, 196: 880–882.

Carpenter, F.L., 1978. A spectrum of nectar-eater communities. *Am. Zool.*, 18: 809–819.

Chapman, F.M., 1926. The distribution of bird-life in Ecuador. *Bull. Am. Mus. Nat. Hist.*, 55: 1–784.

Cracraft, J., 1976. Avian evolution on southern continents: influences of the paleogeography and paleoclimatology. In: H.J. Frith and J.H. Calaby (Editors), *Proc. 16th Int. Ornithological Congress*. Australian Academy of Science, Canberra, A.C.T., pp. 40–52.

Crome, F.H.J., 1975. The ecology of fruit pigeons in tropical Northern Queensland. *Aust. Wildlife Res.*, 2: 155–185.

Denslow, J.S. and Moermond, T.C., 1982. The effect of accessibility on removal rate of fruits from tropical shrubs: an experimental study. *Oecologia*, 54: 170–176.

Diamond, J.M., 1973. Distributional ecology of New Guinea birds. *Science*, 179: 759–769.

Feinsinger, P. and Colwell, R.K., 1978. Community organization among Neotropical nectar-feeding birds. *Am. Zool.*, 18: 779–795.

Fenton, M.B. and Fleming, T.H., 1976. Ecological interactions between bats and nocturnal birds. *Biotropica*, 8: 104–110.

Frith, D.W., 1984. Foraging ecology of birds in an upland tropical rainforest in North Queensland. *Aust. Wildlife Res.*, 11: 325–347.

Gentry, A.H., 1982. Pattern of Neotropical plant species diversity. In: M.K. Hecht, B. Wallace and G.T. Prance (Editors), *Evolutionary Biology, Vol. 15*. Plenum, New York, N.Y., pp. 1–84.

Gill, F.B. and Wolf, L.L., 1977. Nonrandom foraging by sunbirds in a patchy environment. *Ecology*, 58: 1284–1296.

Graves, G.R., Robbins, M.B. and Remsen Jr., J.V., 1983. Age and sexual difference in spatial distribution and mobility in manakins (Pipridae): Inferences from mist-netting. *J. Field Ornithol.*, 54: 407–412.

Greenberg, R., 1981a. The abundance and seasonality of forest canopy birds on Barro Colorado Island, Panama. *Biotropica*, 13: 241–251.

Greenberg, R., 1981b. Dissimilar bill shapes in New World tropical versus temperate forest foliage-gleaning birds. *Oecologia*, 49: 143–147.

Greenberg, R. and Gradwohl, J., 1980. Leaf surface specializations of birds and arthropods in a Panamanian forest. *Oecologia*, 46: 115–124.

Haffer, J., 1969. Speciation in Amazonian forest birds. *Science*, 165: 131–137.

Howe, H.F., 1977. Bird activity and seed dispersal of a tropical wet forest tree. *Ecology*, 58: 539–550.

Howe, H.F., 1979. Fear and frugivory. *Am. Nat.*, 114: 925–931.

Howe, H.F. and De Steven, D., 1979. Fruit production, migrant bird visitation, and seed dispersal of *Guarea glabra* in Panama. *Oecologia*, 39: 185–196.

Howe, H.F. and Estabrook, G.F., 1977. On intraspecific competition for avian dispersers in tropical trees. *Am. Nat.*, 111: 817 832.

Howe, H.F. and Smallwood, J., 1982. Ecology of seed dispersal. *Annu. Rev. Ecol. Syst.*, 13: 201–228.

Hutchinson, G.E., 1957. Concluding remarks. *Cold Spring Harbor Symp. Quant. Biol.*, 22: 415–427.

Janzen, D.H., 1977. Promising directions of study in tropical-plant interactions. *Ann. Mo. Bot. Gard.*, 64: 706–736.

Janzen, D.H., 1980. Heterogeneity of potential food abundance for tropical small land birds. In: A. Keast and E.S. Morton (Editors), *Migrant Birds in the Neotropics*. Smithsonian Institution Press, Washington, D.C., pp. 545–552.

Janzen, D.H., 1983. Dispersal of seeds by vertebrate guts. In: D.J. Futuyma and M. Slatkin (Editors), *Coevolution*. Sinauer Assoc., Sunderland, Mass., pp. 232–262.

Karr, J.R., 1971. Structure of avian communities in selected Panama and Illinois habitats. *Ecol. Monogr.*, 41: 207–233.

Karr, J.R., 1975. Production, energy pathways, and community diversity in forest birds. In: F.B. Golley and E. Medina (Editors), *Tropical Ecological Systems: Trends in Terrestrial and Aquatic Research*. Springer, New York, N.Y., pp. 161–176.

Karr, J.R., 1976a. Within- and between-habitat avian diversity in African and Neotropical lowland habitats. *Ecol. Monogr.*, 46: 457–481.

Karr, J.R., 1976b. Seasonality, resource availability, and community diversity in tropical bird communities. *Am. Nat.*, 110: 973–994.

Karr, J.R., 1980a. Geographical variation in the avifaunas of tropical forest undergrowth. *Auk*, 97: 283–298.

Karr, J.R., 1980b. Patterns in the migration systems between the north temperate zone and the tropics. In: A. Keast and E.S. Morton (Editors), *Migrant Birds in the Neotropics: Ecology, Behavior, Distribution and Conservation*. Smithsonian Institution Press, Washington, D.C., pp. 519–543.

Karr, J.R., 1981. Surveying birds with mist nets. In: C.J. Ralph and J.M. Scott (Editors), *Estimating Numbers of Terrestrial Birds*. (Studies in Avian Biology, 6) Cooper Ornithological Society, Las Cruces, N.M., pp. 62–67.

Karr, J.R., 1982. Population variability and extinction in the avifauna of a tropical land bridge island. *Ecology*, 63: 1975–1978.

Karr, J.R. and Freemark, K.E., 1983. Habitat selection and environmental gradients: Dynamics in the "stable" tropics. *Ecology*, 64: 1481–1494.

Karr, J.R. and Freemark, K.E., 1985. Disturbance, perturbation, and vertebrates: An integrative perspective. In: S.T.A. Pickett and P.S. White (Editors), *Natural Disturbance: An Evolutionary Perspective*. Academic Press, New York, N.Y., in press.

Karr, J.R. and James, F.C., 1975. Eco-morphological configurations and convergent evolution in species and communities. In: M.L. Cody and J.M. Diamond (Editors), *Ecology and Evolution of Communities*. Harvard Univ. Press, Cambridge, Mass., pp. 258–291.

Karr, J.R., Schemske, D.W. and Brokaw, N., 1982. Temporal variation in the understory bird community of a tropical forest. In: E.G. Leigh, Jr., A.S. Rand and D.M. Windsor (Editors), *The Ecology of a Tropical Forest: Seasonal Rhythms and Long-Term Changes*. Smithsonian Institution Press, Washington, D.C., pp. 441–453.

Lederer, R., 1975. Bill size, food size, and jaw forces of insectivorous birds. *Auk*, 92: 385–387.

Lein, M.R., 1972. A trophic comparison of avifaunas. *Syst. Zool.*, 21: 135–150.

Levings, S. and Windsor, D.M., 1982. Seasonal and annual variation in litter anthropod populations. In: E.G. Leigh, Jr., A.S. Rand and D.M. Windsor (Editors), *The Ecology of a Tropical Forest: Seasonal Rhythms and Long-Term Changes*. Smithsonian Institution Press, Washington, D.C., pp. 355–387.

Ligon, J.D. and Ligon, S.H., 1978. The communal social system of the Green Woodhoopoe in Kenya. *Living Bird*, 17: 159–197.

Martin, T.E., 1985. Resource selection by tropical frugivorous birds: Integrating multiple interactions. *Oecologia*, in press.

McKey, D., 1975. The ecology of coevolved seed dispersal systems. In: L.E. Gilbert and P.H. Raven (Editors), *Coevolution of Animals and Plants*. Univ. of Texas Press, Austin, Tex., pp. 159–191.

McNaughton, S.J., 1983. Serengeti grassland ecology: The role of composite environmental factors and contingency in community organization. *Ecol. Monogr.*, 53: 291–320.

Medway, Lord and Wells, D.R., 1976. *The Birds of the Malay Peninsula. V. Conclusion, and Survey of Every Species*. Withenby, London, 448 pp.

Moermond, T.C. and Denslow, J.S., 1983. Fruit choice in Neotropical frugivorous birds: Effects of fruit type and accessibility on selectivity. *J. Anim. Ecol.*, 52: 407–420.

Moreau, R.E., 1966. *The Bird Faunas of Africa and its Island*. Academic Press, New York, N.Y., 424 pp.

Myers, N., 1979. *The Sinking Ark*. Pergamon, New York, N.Y., 307 pp.

Orians, G.H., 1969. The number of bird species in some tropical forests. *Ecology*, 50: 783–801.

Paszkowski, C.A. and Moermond, T.C., 1984. Prey handling relationships in captive ovenbirds. *Condor*, 86: 410–415.

Pearson, D.L., 1971. Vertical stratification of birds in a tropical dry forest. *Condor*, 73: 46–55.

Pearson, D.L., 1977. Ecological relationships of small antbirds in Amazonian bird communities. *Auk*, 94: 283–292.

Pearson, D.L., 1982. Historical factors and bird species richness. In: G.T. Prance (Editor), *Biological Diversification in the Tropics*. Columbia Univ. Press, New York, N.Y., pp. 441–452.

Pickett, S.T.A. and White, P.S., 1985. *Natural Disturbance: The Patch Dynamics Perspective*. Academic Press, New York, N.Y., 472 pp.

Remsen Jr., J.V. and Parker III, T.A., 1983. Contribution of river habitats to bird species richness in Amazonia. *Biotropica*, 15: 223–231.

Remsen Jr., J.V. and Parker III, T.A., 1984. Arboreal dead-leaf-searching birds of the Neotropics. *Condor*, 86: 36–41.

Schoener, T.W., 1971. Large-billed insectivorous birds: A precipitous diversity gradient. *Condor*, 73: 154–161.

Schoener, T.W., 1974. Resource partitioning in ecological communities. *Science*, 185: 27–39.

Schoener, T.W., 1982. The controversy over interspecific competition. *Am. Sci.*, 70: 586–595.

Sherry, T.W., 1984. Comparative dietary ecology of sympatric, insectivorous Neotropical flycatchers (Tyrannidae). *Ecol. Monogr.*, 54: 313–338.

Skutch, A., 1972. *Studies of Tropical American Birds*. Publ. Nuttall Ornithological Club, No. 10.

Snow, B.K. and Snow, D.W., 1971. The feeding ecology of tanagers and honeycreepers in Trinidad. *Auk*, 88: 291–322.

Snow, D.W., 1966. A possible selective factor in the evolution of fruiting seasons in a tropical forest. *Oikos*, 15: 274–281.

Snow, D.W., 1981. Tropical frugivorous birds and their food plants: A world survey. *Biotropica*, 13: 1–14.

Stiles, F.G., 1983. Checklist of birds. In: D.H. Janzen (Editor), *Costa Rican Natural History*. Univ. of Chicago Press, Chicago, Ill., pp. 530–544.

Terborgh, J., 1971. Distribution of elevation gradients: Theory and a preliminary interpretation of distributional patterns in the avifauna of the Cordillera Vilcabamba, Peru. *Ecology*, 52: 23–40.

Terborgh, J., 1977. Bird species diversity on an Andean elevational gradient. *Ecology*, 58: 1007–1019.

Terborgh, J., 1980. Causes of tropical species diversity. *Proc. 17th Int. Ornithological Congress*, 17: 955–961.

Terborgh, J., 1983. *Five New World Primates: A Study in Comparative Ecology*. Princeton Univ. Press, Princeton, N.J., 260 pp.

Thiollay, J.M., 1973. Place des oiseaux dans les chaînes trophiques d'une zone pré forestière en Côte-d'Ivoire. *Alauda*, 41: 273–300.

Wells, D.R., Hails, C.J. and Hails, A.J., undated. *A Study of the Birds of the Gunung Mulu National Park, Sarawak, with Special Emphasis on Those of Lowland Forests*. Report of Royal Geographical Society, Gunung Mulu Expedition, 61 pp.

Wheelwright, N.T. and Orians, G.H., 1982. Seed dispersal by animals: contrasts with pollen dispersal, problems of terminology, and constraints on coevolution. *Am. Nat.*, 119: 402–413.

Willis, E.O. and Oniki, Y., 1978. Birds and Army Outs. *Annu. Rev. Ecol. Syst.*, 9: 243–263.

Wolda, H., 1978a. Fluctuations in abundance of tropical insects. *Am. Nat.*, 112: 1017–1044.

Wolda, H., 1978b. Seasonal fluctuation in rainfall, food and abundance of tropical insects. *J. Anim. Ecol.*, 47: 369–481.

Wong, M., 1983. *Patterns of food availability and understory bird community structure in a Malaysian rain forest*. Ph.D. Thesis, Univ. of Michigan, Ann Arbor, Mich.

Wright, J.J., 1979. Competition between insectivorous lizards and birds in central Panama. *Am. Zool.*, 19: 1145–1156.

Chapter 23

HERPETOFAUNA OF TROPICAL AMERICA AND AFRICA

R.F. LAURENT

INTRODUCTION

Amphibians and reptiles are the two smallest classes of vertebrates. The contrast is even sharper in cold countries because they are the only ones which are not well protected against low temperatures. Fishes are generally living in a buffered environment whereas birds and mammals have their thermic regulation.

However, in tropical countries, frogs, lizards, snakes, turtles, crocodiles are diverse and constitute a significant part of the communities. The adaptive zones are not numerous. The most generalized is just terrestrial and accordingly it is abundantly, although not densely populated. Others are the fossorial, arboreal and aquatic zones.

ZONAL DISTRIBUTION

Terrestrial zone

The basic zone for tetrapods is of course the terrestrial one: many amphibians and reptiles indeed content themselves with wandering on the soil, occasionally hiding between small plants or rocks or under dead leaves. Most terrestrial amphibians spend a good part of their life in water as well, specially at breeding time. Few reptiles do so, for the obvious reason that they do not need water for their reproduction. Some amphibians emulated reptiles in this respect, however, by resorting to a variety of devices which all amount to shortening or avoiding the free-swimming tadpole stage.

The list of merely terrestrial tropical amphibians and reptiles is large indeed.

Amphibians

First of all, a striking difference between Africa and South America must be stressed: salamanders are conspicuous by their absence in equatorial Africa, whereas they successfully invaded and radiated in Tropical America. The lungless salamanders (Plethodontidae) are represented in Brazilian forests by the genus *Bolitoglossa* which is basically terrestrial but needs a very humid environment since its breathing is exclusively cutaneous.

Prominent in Africa as well as in South America are the true toads or bufonids. The family, presumably an early offshoot of South American leptodactylids, is said (Laurent, 1979a) to have dispersed into the Old World through Africa, where it radiated almost as widely as in the neotropical realm. Some primitive smooth-skinned forest species living in northern South America (*Bufo blombergi*, *B. guttatus*, *B. haematiticus*) still have closely related forms in western Africa: *B. superciliaris* and the genus *Werneria*. The bulk of *Bufo* species, however, belongs to two different groups: the Neotropical forms (*B. crucifer*, *B. typhonius*, *B. marinus*, etc.) have cranial ridges and 22 chromosomes, whereas the African species (*B. maculatus*, *B. camerunensis*, *B. funereus*, etc.) have no cranial ridges and only 20 chromosomes. Other bufonid or bufonoid genera have a slightly different ecology, because of their generally small size: they tend to hide below and between dead leaves. In both continents, there seem to be specialized derivates of the primitive species of the genus *Bufo*: in Africa, the genera *Wolterstorffina* and *Didynamipus* are examples, whereas in America a similar niche is occupied by the derived brachycephalid frogs (*Brachycephalus*, *Psyllo-*

phryne). *Atelopus* includes aposematic Neotropical species (Fig. 23.1) that are not small, do not hide so much, and have no counterpart in Africa.

The Neotropical Dendrobatidae, a late offshoot of leptodactylids, are also aposematic and their skin poisons are in many cases so virulent that the Indians use them to make their arrows deadlier. Their reproductive specialization is worth mentioning: the eggs are laid in some humid place on the ground, guarded by the mother or the father, and the tadpoles climb upon the back of the guardian who wanders with them for a while and finally releases them into water. Among the leptodactylids, many are purely terrestrial. The very numerous species of the genus *Eleutherodactylus* are also ground dwellers of Neotropical forests. Their terrestrial adaptation is completed by their direct development. The genera *Arthroleptis* and *Schoutedenella* are their counterpart in Africa; but the genus *Cardioglossa*, of the same subfamily Arthroleptinae, has kept a tadpole which makes it more dependent on water. The convergence between *Eleutherodactylus* which is a leptodactylid and the Arthroleptinae is specially striking, because they also have the same appearance, except that in the Arthroleptinae the males have an elongated, sometimes enormously elongated, third finger which is, at least in some species, hooked on the corner of the mouth of the female during amplexus.

In both continents, however, most terrestrial frogs are only partly so. Even the true toads (Bufonidae) as we have seen are slaves of the water for breeding, but this dependence is more marked in African ranids and astylosternines as well as in

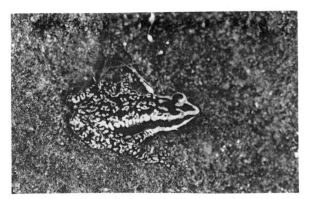

Fig. 23.1. *Atelopus crucier*. (Photo Mus. Nat. Hist., Univ. of Kansas, or J.K. Langhammer.)

Neotropical leptodactylines. The African ranines include the big *Euphlyctis occipitalis* related to the asiatic *E. tigerina*, a few species of the genus *Rana*, *Aubria subsigillata* which is more aquatic than terrestrial, and the large genus *Ptychadena* with common forms like *P. mascareniensis bibroni* and rare and secretive species like *P. christyi*. The Phrynobatrachinae comprise small frogs belonging to the genera *Dimorphognatus*, *Phrynobatrachus*, *Phrynodon*. Some of them, the smallest, probably manage to depend little on water, because they are often found far from any swamp; the aquatic habitat of the West African *Petropedetes* is mainly running water.

In the South American tropical forests, the same ecological niches are occupied by a host of leptodactylid frogs. The most similar to the ranids are the leptodactylines, but apart from being unrelated they differ from them conspicuously by their lack of webs and their floating "spume nests" in which the eggs develop. This habit has been interpreted as an adaptation to arid environments, but obviously it is far from being harmful in the rain forest. Some big species, like *Leptodactylus pentodactylus*, are more or less the ecological equivalents of *Euphlyctis occipitalis*, which small species like those of the *L. fuscus* group are surprisingly similar to *Ptychadena* species; their foam nests are hidden in small cavities, a still better adaptation which, again, seems a luxury in wet forests. Still smaller frogs like *Physalaemus* can be very similar to the African *Phrynobatrachus*.

The Atlantic forest in southeastern Brazil is especially rich in terrestrial frogs which belong to relatively primitive groups: the Elosiini which have still a normal aquatic tadpole; *Thoropa* establishes itself (adults and tadpoles) in an interphase of streaming stones and the other genera of the subfamily Grypiscinae, which lay eggs in damp places, have short-lived tadpoles that most often metamorphose in situ without any aquatic stage, a step towards the direct development of the Eleutherodactylinae.

The richest part of the African forest (Cameroon area) is also inhabited by somewhat primitive frogs, like *Petropedetes* or *Cardioglossa* (the only arthroleptine that has kept a larval stage) and the subfamily Astylosterninae, including the famous hairy frog *Trichobatrachus* whose tadpoles are adapted to strongly running water.

Tortoises

In both continents, two closely related species dwell in the rain forest: *Geochelone denticulata* and *G. carbonaria* in South America, *Kinixys homeana* and *K. erosa* in Africa.

Lizards

The dominant families in both continents are vicariant: Iguanidae and Teiidae in South America, the Agamidae and Lacertidae in Africa. But the ecological equivalents of the middle-sized and large Teiidae, like *Ameiva* and *Tupinambis* are, respectively, the African Gerrhosaurinae and Varanidae. The skinks (genus *Mabuya*) are present in both continents, but considerably more numerous in Africa (Fig. 23.2).

Snakes

The terrestrial rain-forest snakes are numerous: the Boidae are represented by *Boa* and *Epicrates* in South America, by *Python sebae* in Africa. In both continents, the terrestrial rain-forest Colubridae

Fig. 23.3. *Clelia clelia*. (Photo Mus. Nat. Hist., Univ. of Kansas.)

include about a dozen genera, among them snake-eaters [*Clelia* in South America (Fig. 23.3), *Mehelya* in Africa], frog-eaters (*Xenodon* in South America, *Geodipsas* in Africa), but egg-eaters like *Dasypeltis* and *Oophilositum* seem to be an African privilege.

Most venomous snakes are terrestrial. The coral snakes (*Micrurus*) are numerous and diverse in South America and are mimicked by some harmless and similarly colored Colubridae (*Oxyrhopus* and *Erythrolamprus* spp.). The African genus *Elapsoidea* is somewhat similar, although unrelated. The African cobra (*Naja melanoleuca*) has no imitator in the New World unless the huge *Lachesis muta* could be so considered. Other Crotalidae, like numerous *Bothrops* species, are the neotropical equivalents of African adders like *Causus* and *Bitis*, but those are not so dangerous, *Causus* because its venom is not very potent, *Bitis* because of its sluggishness (Fig. 23.4).

Fossorial zone

The fossorial zone is not clearly distinct from the ordinary terrestrial zone. Some terrestrial species just like to hide below dead leaves, in holes they find or between stones, whereas others are active burrowers, boring their way through the ground. While the zone is not so heavily occupied in forest as in savanna, presumably because the main incentive of such adaptation is drought which is uncommon in forests, not a few forest species acquired burrowing habits, but they are less common in amphibians than in reptiles.

Fig. 23.2. *Mabuya maculilabris*. (Photo J.L. Perret.)

Fig. 23.4. *Bitis nasicornis*. (Photo R.F. Laurent.)

Amphibians

However, a group of amphibians is almost exclusively fossorial: the caecilians. They are rather numerous in South America, mainly genera *Caecilia* and *Siphonops* but rare in the Zaïre forest; [genera *Geotrypetes* (Fig. 23.5) and *Herpele*]. Although many forest terrestrial frogs and toads may be considered mildly fossorial, since they readily take advantage of any hiding place to conceal themselves, few are really adapted to digging and less so than their savanna counterparts. For instance in Africa the forest species, *Arthroleptis variabilis* and *Hemisus olivaceus* have smaller internal metatarsal tubercles (which are used as spades) than *Arthroleptis stenodactylus* and *Hemisus guineenses*, which have to dig into harder soils. In the Amazonian forest some *Eleutherodactylus* species are ecological vicariants of *Arthroleptis*, whereas quite an array of Microhylids (*Cteno-*

phryne, Otophryne) are acting the role of *Hemisus olivaceus* and *H. perreti* in Africa. Besides, the escuerzos (*Ceratophrys* and *Proceratophrys*) make the group of burrowers more important in the Neotropics than in Africa.

Lizards

Fossorial reptiles are more common, which seems paradoxical since they need, much less than amphibians, protection against drought. The explanation might be that reptiles, being better equipped to burrow because of their hard skin, have intrinsically a stronger propensity to invade this adaptive zone; in other words, what is a retreat for amphibians (although once they are in the trend, they make the best of it) is a conquest for the reptiles. The best burrowers among reptiles are obviously the amphisbaenians. They are well represented in both continents (but not elsewhere) by about 30 species of *Amphisbaena* (Fig. 23.6) contrasting with a few species of *Cynisca* and *Zygaspis* in Africa. Similarly the shovel-snouted species of *Leposternon* of South America are more diverse than their African equivalents, the genus *Monopeltis*.

The burrowing lizards in Africa are specialized skinks like some short-legged species of *Panaspis* (Fig. 23.7) and legless *Melanoseps* and *Feylinia* which is also almost eyeless. The same niche is occupied in the Amazon by the dozen species of the legless *Gymnophthalmus*, *Bachia* and one *Ophiodes* species in the southeastern Atlantic forest of Brazil.

Fig. 23.5. *Geotrypetes seraphini*. (Photo J.L. Perret.)

Fig. 23.6. *Amphisbaena fuliginosa varia*. (Photo Mus. Nat. Hist., Univ. of Kansas.)

Fig. 23.7. *Panaspis breviceps.* (Photo J.L. Perret.)

Snakes

Burrowing snakes are still more numerous. On both sides of the Atlantic one finds the nearly blind Typhlopidae, again more diverse in South America than in Africa (Fig. 23.8) and the Leptotyphlopidae — which however, are only savanna dwellers in Africa. In the Congo forest, a boid *Calabaria reinhardti* is also a burrower which is not paralleled in America unless one so considers *Anilius scytale*.

Most of the preceding fossorial reptiles are relatively microphagous (small soil arthropods — mainly ants and termites); they are themselves the usual prey of burrowing colubrids and venomous snakes, but they belong to different groups in each continent. In South America, we find the aglyphous *Atractus*, the rear-fanged *Apostolepis* and *Elapomorphus* and the poisonous coral snakes *Micrurus* (Fig. 23.9). In Africa, their ecological niche is filled by the genus *Polemon*, similar to *Elapomorphus*, the elapid *Elapsoidea* and *Atrac-*

Fig. 23.8. *Typhlops congestus.* (Photo J.L. Perret.)

Fig. 23.9. *Micrurus hippocrepis.* (Photo Mus. Nat. Hist., Univ. of Kansas.)

taspis previously considered an adder, but now seen as a member of the subfamily Aparallactinae. *Aparallactus* itself is not such a predator, it is a centipede eater, a very peculiar diet which is unknown, as far as the author knows, among Neotropical reptiles.

Aquatic zone

In spite of their being tetrapods, that is animals adapted to a terrestrial locomotion, many amphibians and reptiles have reverted to an aquatic mode of life.

Amphibians

Among amphibians the family Pipidae, present in Africa and South America, is specially notorious. The neotropical *Pipa* is famous for the eggs which develop in alveoles of the dorsal skin of the female, giving birth to metamorphosed froglets. Similar although less extremely specialized are *Protopipa* and *Hemipipa* which have kept the tadpole stage. Still less specialized are the African genera *Xenopus* and *Hymenochirus* (Fig. 23.10) whose eggs are released in water as in most other frogs. In South America, the Pseudidae, although unrelated to the Pipidae, live very much like *Xenopus*.

Besides, most amphibians are aquatic during their early life (as tadpoles) and go back often to water, at least during the breeding season. Some spend the major time of their life there, namely *Rana palmipes* and some leptodactylids in South America, whereas most ranids do so in Africa.

Fig. 23.10. *Hymenochirus boettgeri camerunensis.* (Photo J.L. Perret.)

Fig. 23.11. *Caiman fuscus.* (Photo Mus. Nat. Hist., Univ. of Kansas.)

Crocodilians

Although evolutionarily farther from the fishes, reptiles have many secondarily aquatic groups. One is the whole order of Crocodilians, with only three species in Africa (*Crocodylus cataphractus, C. niloticus* and the small *Osteolaemus tetraspis*), and twice as many in South America: *Crocodylus acutus* in the northern forest, and five Alligatorinae, including *Caiman* spp., *Melanosuchus niger* and *Paleosuchus*, in the south.

Ecologically some equivalence are obvious: the fearsome Nile crocodile is paralleled by the black caiman (*M. niger*); the narrow-snouted African crocodile has more or less the same niche as *Paleosuchus*, while the swamp-dwelling *Osteolaemus* is emulated by the genus *Caiman* (Fig. 23.11).

Turtles

Most equatorial chelonians are aquatic in both continents but again, those in the Neotropics clearly outnumber those in Africa: 22 against 6. The families are also different apart from the Pelomedusinae represented in the South American forest by *Podocnemis* (five species) and in Africa by *Pelusios* (Fig. 23.12) (four forest species).

Another sideneck turtle family radiated beautifully in tropical America: the Chelidae, with genera like *Phrynops* and *Platemys* and the strange Matamata (*Chelus*). Conversely the soft-shelled turtles of the family Trionychidae (*Cycloderma, Trionyx*) only exists in Africa. Turtles in northern origin also invaded forested South America:

Fig. 23.12. *Pelusios niger.* (Photo J.L. Perret.)

Chelydra and *Pseudemys* only in Colombia and Venezuela, *Kinosternon* in all tropical forest areas.

Lizards

A few neotropical lizards are largely aquatic. They are all Teiidae: *Crocodilurus, Neusticurus* and the snail-eater *Dracaena guyanensis*. The same niche is only partly occupied in Africa by forest monitor *Varanus niloticus ornatus*.

Snakes

Not a few snakes are also aquatic in both realms, but only South America has a predominantly water-dwelling boid, the anaconda (*Eunectes murinus*), and only Africa has aquatic poisonous snakes, two water cobras: *Boulengerina annulata* and *B. christyi*. Besides, each continent has aquatic colubrids, but again South America has about

Fig. 23.13. *Helicops angulatus.* (Photo Mus. Nat. Hist., Univ. of Kansas.)

twice as many species as Africa: *Helicops* (Fig. 23.13), *Hydrodynastes, Hydrops, Pseudoeryx* and *Tretanorhinus* in the new World, *Grayia, Helophis, Hydraethiops* and *Natriciteres* in the West African and Congo forests.

Arboreal zone

The arboreal adaptive zone is of course the forest habitat "par excellence" and the diversity and number of tree-dwellers is remarkable in both continents.

Amphibians

Even salamanders sometimes indulge in tree climbing, at least those of the neotropical genus *Bolitoglossa.*

Many ground frogs and toads, at least the smallest species, climb onto shrubs almost unwittingly, then fall because they do not have the necessary adhesive devices, and start again in a haphazard way or if they see some prey on a low small branch. But the real tree frogs belong to whole families or subfamilies, the Hylidae and Centrolenidae in South America, the Hyperoliinae and *Chiromantis* in Africa. Some do not climb very high, living only on plants growing within swamps or around them, but these are not real forest species; ecologically, they rather belong to the savanna ecosystems, which still exist in the rain forests, along the shores of rivers or lakes, around villages, in cultivated plots of land and in clearings. The true forest species live in darker parts, climbing up the trees or the creepers to a height of a few meters, often hiding in epiphytes like Bromeliaceae; some are canopy dwellers; those are generally rare in collections because they are difficult to collect.

Here too, the Neotropical fauna is richer than the African one: 179 species of tree frogs can be counted in Lynch's paper (1979) on the amphibians of the Neotropical rain forest, whereas about 80 are known from the African forest from Sierra Leone to eastern and southern Zaïre. The American tree frogs belong to four distinct groups, the Hylinae, the Phyllomedusinae and the Hemiphractinae, subfamilies of the great family Hylidae, and the family Centrolenidae. The African tree frogs also belong to two families, but only one species, *Chiromantis rufescens,* is a rhacophorid, while all others are hyperoliids. The ± 90 species of the genus *Hyla* almost cover morphologically and ecologically the whole gamut of the African Hyperoliinae. Some parallelisms are striking: small species like *Hyla minuta* or *H. nana* could very well be mistaken for *Afrixalus laevis,* while other almost black and white species like *H. leucophyllata* look astoundingly like *Afrixalus dorsalis* or *A. osorioi,* and the large Neotropical *Phrynohyas* is similar to the African *Leptopelis* (Fig. 23.14)

The most common colors in tree frogs from everywhere are bright green, obviously protective in the foliage and dirty dappled brown or gray similar to the bark of trunks and branches. Some

Fig. 23.14. *Leptopelis calcaratus.* (Photo J.L. Perret.)

species seem to overdo the resemblance by their rugose (*Osteocephalus* in South America) or even spiny skin like the African *Acanthixalus* which hides in watery holes inside hollow trees. A common color in both realms is a pale almost translucent green characteristic of the family Centrolenidae, but paralleled in Africa by many species of *Hyperolius* like *H. nasutus*, the males of *H. fusciventris* and *H. phantasticus*, and many others. Sometimes, the green color is so pervading that it also affects the bones and the eggs (*Hyperolius frontalis*) a phenomenon due to the high rate of biliverdine in the blood, as Barrio (1965) discovered in various South American tree frogs: Centrolenidae, *Hyla punctata*, *Phrynohyas venulosa*.

The similarities may also concern the nesting habits. The Phyllomedusinae are famous by the way they protect their eggs: they wrap them with a few leaves of a tree which overhangs a swamp or a pond and the tadpoles live there for a while, after which they fall into the water. The completely unrelated Rhacophorinae, and particularly the African *Chiromantis*, do the same thing, with the difference that the fertilized eggs are surrounded by empty capsules in *Phyllomedusa*, and by a spumous slime in *Chiromantis*.

The most original peculiarities are, however, not paralleled. For instance, the Neotropical rain forest harbours 'helmeted' tree frogs whose bizarrely deformed heads (*Corythomantis, Aparasphenodon*) are used to plug the holes where they take refuge. This phenomenon made possible by cephalic exostosis is named 'phragmosis'. Another privilege of South America is to have marsupial frogs. They are also tree frogs and all belong to the subfamily Hemiphractinae. In this group, the females keep the fertilized eggs on their back, exposed (*Stefania*) or hidden in a pouch (*Gastrotheca*). The eggs may be small and numerous in which case they give birth to tadpoles or they may be big and few, in which case the tadpole stage is entirely skipped and froglets hatch out.

Nothing similar happens in the African forests, but the frogs of the genus *Hyperolius* have an unique peculiarity: an inverted sexual dichromatism. Generally in fishes, lizards, birds, etc., the males are brightly colored and the females are drab, but in *Hyperolius* the reverse is true or nearly so, since some males keep the subdued color-pattern of the juveniles, while others adopt a down-toned version of the female colors.

Lizards

Many tropical lizards are arboreal, but if one compares South America with Africa in this respect, one sees that quite different groups are involved, exactly as for tree-frogs. Gekkonids are present on both sides of the Atlantic Ocean but the climbers are predominantly the northern Sphaerodactylinae in South America, while they belong to the genera *Hemidactylus* and *Lygodactylus* in Africa. Although these two genera succeeded in invading America, only more or less anthropophilous species have been involved. The gekkonine niche is actually filled in the Neotropical forests by the extremely species-rich iguanid genus *Anolis*, which have similar adhesive lamellae under the distal part of the fingers and toes. A few other Neotropical arboreal iguanids have no more peculiar adaptations than Asiatic agamids: *Basiliscus, Iguana, Polychrus* (Fig. 23.15), etc., or for that matter, the Old World genus *Agama* which is mainly terrestrial, but is not adverse to tree climbing, at least in tropical Africa. However, the most efficient arboreal lizards of Africa are the strange chameleons (Fig. 23.16) which developed some unique specializations: hands and feet converted into pliers, prehensile tail, independent eyes, protractile tongue. Still odder is the short-tailed chameleon *Rhampholeon* which, in spite of its arboreal adaptation is often encountered on the ground, lying on its side among dead leaves to which it bears a striking likeness.

Fig. 23.15. *Polychrus marmoratus*. (Photo Mus. Nat. Hist., Univ. of Kansas.)

Fig. 23.16. *Chamaeleo cristatus.* (Photo J.L. Perret.)

Even the lacertids invaded the arboreal zone in Africa with rare species like *Bedriagaia tropidopholis*, (Fig. 23.17) *Centromastix echinata* and *Holaspis guentheri* which can extend the sides of its body to the point of becoming almost circular, a feat that allows in to glide in the air for short distances. The South American teiids which gener-

ally emulate the similar lacertids failed to do so in this particular instance, probably because the iguanids and specially the genus *Anolis* filled the arboreal environment so completely in tropical America.

Snakes

The snakes perhaps radiated into the arboreal zone even more than lizards and frogs. Several groups are present both in Neotropical and African forests. The most remarkable fact about them is that three vicariant assemblages can be recognized among colubrids. Parallel evolution is generally put forward to explain this, because the colubrid radiation is much later than the separation of South America from Africa. However it must be stressed that (1) the Atlantic Ocean must have been very much narrower in Eocene and Oligocene times; (2) arboreal reptiles are the likeliest sailors on floating islands; (3) others, like two geckos (*Hemidactylus brookii* and *H. mabouia*) did just that in Pliocene times (Kluge, 1969), when the ocean was almost as wide as it is nowadays; and (4) successful establishment was very likely if the niche was empty as it probably must have been. Furthermore, parallelism could be advocated if the adaptation had occurred in only one constrained way, or else in different ways on different continents. But it happened in three distinct ways resulting in three groups present in all tropical forests (that is, in Asia as well).

There are the generally green slender snakes with large eyes and a round pupil. In Africa they are represented by genera like *Gastropyxis*, *Hapsido-*

Fig. 23.17. *Bedriagaia tropidopholis.* (Photo R.F. Laurent.)

Fig. 23.18. *Imantodes gemmistratus.* (Photo Mus Nat. Hist., Univ. of Kansas.)

phrys, *Philothamnus*, *Thrasops* etc., and their neotropical vicariants are *Chironius* and *Leptophis*.

There is the group of wideheaded back-fanged snakes with a vertical pupil: *Boiga* and *Dipsadoboa* in Africa, *Imantodes* and *Leptodeira* (Fig. 23.18) in tropical America. In their case, convergence appears likelier than in the two others.

The vinesnakes are again so similar that a parallel evolution would be surprising. They are back-fanged, definitely dangerous as proven by the death of two prominent herpetologists of this century: Prof. Robert Mertens from Frankfurt a/M and Dr. Karl Patterson Schmidt from Chicago. They are generally very slender, with a long, narrow, tapering head, horizontal pupils: *Thelotornis* in Africa, *Oxybelis* in South America, *Dryophis* in tropical Asia.

Some poisonous snakes also are arboreal. They all belong to the family Crotalidae in South America. Some *Bothrops* species unusually slender and greenish move on, among and around the twigs in neotropical forests. Their counterpart in Africa is the genus *Atheris*, also greenish[1], which proves a hazard for people gathering coffee beans in the plantations.

Elapids comprise arboreal snakes in Africa: *Pseudohaje goldii* which is a tree cobra, and the fearsome green mamba, *Dendroaspis jamesoni*, one of the deadliest snakes of the world.

It is admittedly unfortunate that the present account does not cover the Asiatic and Australo-Papuan rain forests. Information about these herpetofaunas can be gathered in several papers by R.F. Inger and his collaborators (Asia), R. Zweifel, M.T. Tyler and S.B. MacDowell (New Guinea). As

a general treatment of the fauna of the rain forest, an excellent book is that of R. Mertens (1947).

---

[1]In *Atheris squamigera*, there is also a strange orange color phase, which is far from being homochromous.

REFERENCES

Barrio, A., 1965. Cloricia fisiológica en batracios anuros. *Physis*, 25: 137–142.

Blair, W.F., 1972. *Evolution in the Genus Bufo*. Univ. of Texas Press, Austin, Tex., 459 pp.

Dixon, J.R., 1979. Origin and distribution of reptiles in lowland tropical rainforests of South America. In: W.E. Duellman (Editor), *The South American Herpetofauna: Its Origin, Evolution and Dispersal*. Monogr. Mus. Nat. Hist., Univ. of Kansas, 7: 217–240.

Duellman, W.D., 1978. The biology of an equatorial herpetofauna in Amazonian Ecuador. *Misc. Publ. Mus. Nat. Hist., Univ. of Kansas*, 65: 1–352.

Kluge, A.G., 1969. The evolution and geographical origin of the New World *Hemidactylus mabouia-brooki* complex (Gekkonidae, Sauria). *Misc. Publ. Mus. Zool., Univ. of Michigan*, 138: 1–78.

Laurent, R.F., 1972. Amphibiens. In: Explor. *Parc Nat. Virunga*, (2) 22: 1–125.

Laurent, R.F., 1973. A parallel survey of equatorial amphibians and reptiles in Africa and South America. In: B.J. Meggers, E.S. Ayensu and W.D. Duckworth (Editors), *Tropical Forest Ecosystems in Africa and South America: A Comparative Review*. Smithsonian Inst. Press, Washington, D.C., pp. 259–266.

Laurent, R.F., 1979a. Esquisse d'une phylogenèse des Anoures. *Bull. Soc. Zool. Fr.*, 104: 397–422.

Laurent, R.F., 1979b. Herpetofaunal relationships between Africa and South America. In: W.D. Duellman (Editor), *The South American Herpetofauna: Its Origin, Evolution, and Dispersal*. Monogr. Mus. Hist. Nat., Univ. of Kansas, 7: 55–72.

Lynch, J.D., 1979. The Amphibians of the lowland tropical forests. In: W.D. Duellman (Editor), *The South American Herpetofauna: Its Origin, Evolution, and Dispersal*. Monogr. Mus. Hist. Nat., Univ. of Kansas, 7: 129–216.

Mertens, R., 1948. *Die Tierwelt des tropischen Regenwaldes*. Kramer, Frankfurt, 144 pp.

Perret, J.L., 1966. Les amphibiens du Cameroun. *Zool. Jahrb. Syst.*, 8: 289–464.

Schiøtz, A., 1967. The tree frogs Rhacophoridae of West Africa. *Spolia Zool. Mus. Hauniensis*, 25: 1–346.

Chapter 24

THE SPATIAL DISTRIBUTION OF FLYING INSECTS

S.L. SUTTON

INTRODUCTION

Little is yet known on this subject. This review is as much concerned with the gaps in our knowledge as with considering the rather few publications that are available. Discussion will be confined to a consideration of the vertical and horizontal distribution of insects engaged in flight activity within the forest. It will concern itself only with "micro-spatial activity" here defined as occupying a space between forest floor and just above the tops of the tallest trees, and between tree crowns in close proximity. It deals therefore, on a horizontal scale, with distances of metres rather than kilometres. It does not consider differences between adjacent forest types, as studied, for example, by Holloway (in press) in the case of the moths of the Mulu National Park in Sarawak.

The term "tropical rain forest" as used here can be taken to cover the first two forest categories in Whitmore (1984), namely Tropical Lowland Evergreen Rain Forest and Tropical Semi-Evergreen Rain Forest.

The approach adopted is to look first at techniques of data acquisition and analysis, then consider the detailed evidence for vertical stratification between floor and canopy, the fragmentary evidence for crown-to-crown flight activity and finally to summarize current ideas concerning micro-spatial distribution of flying insects within the forest matrix.

The early history of this subject is one of anecdotal evidence dating back to the days of Bates (1863) and Wallace, concerning the relative richness of insect life in the upper canopy. Pioneering work carried out at Moraballi Creek in Guyana was summarized by Hingston (1932) in a

popular account. Murphy (1973) gives a brief glimpse of vertical stratification of insects found on Bukit Timah, Singapore. Extensive research on the flight behaviour of insects of medical importance in East Africa led, in the 1950's, to the building of a tower in Uganda which provided the foundation of the quantitative approach to vertical stratification. It could not, however, contain any element of crown-to-crown analysis, which had to wait for the advent of means of sampling a number of tree crowns simultaneously. This work has only recently begun.

Techniques of data acquisition

Owing to the heroic vertical scale on which most rain forests are constructed, the problems of access above the forest floor are considerable, and must be considered as part of the technique of study. The range of techniques available at present is briefly summarized by Mitchell (1982). Perry (1984) gives a non-technical account of his canopy rope web which is under development. The emphasis in the past has been to send up a local climber to collect specimens or to fix ropes allowing a ground based operator to trap specimens. The emphasis now is for the operator to work in the upper canopy. Cave-climbing technology has proved useful in gaining access, particularly Single Rope Technique (SRT). This allows a researcher of only average agility and expertise to work in the canopy. A line-throwing gun or crossbow is used to instal the rope. A series of ropes allows multiple access, and platforms can be built at each canopy outpost. A logical extension of this approach is to link the platforms together by aerial walkways, which can span as much as

70 m and transect a series of tree crowns. Walkways allow fairly free movement and greater flexibility for observation and placing traps than other systems. In particular they allow comparisons to be made of flight activity within tree crowns and between the crowns. Perry's rope web has similar potential but probably allows less free movement. SRT and walkways are well suited to temporary sites where observations are only going to be continued for several months. Towers, on the other hand, are only justified for longer-term studies. Being free-standing, they can be built above the emergent trees, and this is an important advantage. They can also carry heavy loads. Towers have been erected in the Mpanga and Zika forests of Uganda, at Barro Colorado Island in Panama, at Abidjan on the Ivory Coast and elsewhere, but have not always been used for entomological recording.

The need to work above the canopy, coupled with the expense and logistical difficulty of towers has led to an interest in tethered hot air balloons (Mitchell, 1982), but to my knowledge no published work has resulted from such an exercise.

Means of access have allowed vertical, horizontal or matrix studies of the forest volume using a wide variety of methods of data acquisition. Visual observation is the simplest and one of the most important. It has been particularly useful in studying the flight behaviour of butterflies (Papageorgius, 1975). Sound recordings are now coming into their own. The use of bait has always been popular, human bait being an old stand-by of medical entomologists. Decomposing prawns exert a powerful fascination for some species of butterflies, and various rotting fruits and carcases have been used in particular studies. A variant on this theme is the use of water-filled bamboos or other containers to provide oviposition sites, particularly for mosquitoes. The Centre for Disease Control trap (Penny and Arias, 1982) dissipates carbon dioxide, thereby attracting blood-feeding insects, which are further attracted by a light and then sucked in by a fan. Light, suction, sticky and water traps come in a range of designs and combinations. Details of the range are given by Southwood (1978), but not all types have been used in the rain forest. The most widely employed have been ultraviolet fluorescent tube traps [see Sutton (1979a) for a typical design].

Three particular problems are encountered with these traps. The most important is the high degree of bias they show. The trap that samples a given volume of air without bias does not exist. Suction traps are often claimed to do this, but many insects are sensitive to wind shear and/or respond effectively to displacement so that these traps tend to under-sample larger insects (personal observation). However, a switch from the use of light traps to suction traps would be a real step forward if sufficient power could be developed to make larger catches of the bigger insects.

Trap bias has led to a search for other methods of sampling, of which "fogging" with an insecticide is one (Erwin, 1983). The spectrum of insects collected by fogging is radically different from that collected by other methods. It is very good at sampling beetles, ants and other insects which are relatively heavy and not given to flight. Lepidoptera and Homoptera are probably much less well sampled, although direct comparisons of techniques have yet to be made (if indeed they are possible). Fogging has limited relevance here because many of the insects sampled seldom or never fly.

The second problem with insect traps in rain forest is the sheer size of the catch that often results. A number of studies have foundered on the volume of material, far more than was actually needed. Traps need to be designed or modified for rain forest use to introduce a modicum of inefficiency to cut the catch, although such action may increase the bias of the trap concerned. The third problem is a special case of the second. The advent of 50 sphingids (hawk moths) in a trap effectively ruins the rest of a catch, and often it is necessary to exclude the larger moths and beetles by screening devices.

Given the variable nature and degree of bias of traps, it is unwise to attempt detailed comparison between data collected by different trapping methods. The only safe course is to standardize on a trapping strategy and then to use it extensively so that internal comparisons can be made and generalizations attempted. However, even an apparently standardized trapping technique can spring surprises. UV light trap catches taken in the upper canopy during different phases of the moon can produce contrasting results, due either to differences in trap efficiency or in flight behaviour of insects. The large oriental bee *Apis dorsata* is more frequently caught on light nights than dark ones, for example (Sutton, unpublished), apparently because it flies more readily in moonlight.

A major problem affecting the processing of insect material is the high level of species diversity and low level of taxonomic knowledge available. In a situation where 90% of species collected may be undescribed (for instance, Broadhead, 1983), identification is a major problem and delimitation of species often impractical. In this situation a common approach is to define "Recognizable Taxonomic Units" (RTU) at or near the species level based on readily observed morphological characteristics (that is, those that do not involve dissection). Such an approach is probably the only way forward at present, but does rely heavily on the particular skills and perceptions of individual workers, and standardization of RTU between workers is very difficult. A further problem is that some of the most crucial ecological data may be obscured by the failure to separate species in critical genera. For instance, in a batch of trap catches taken in Brunei in 1979, 38 RTU were recognized in the critical genus *Batracomorphus* (Homoptera) (Sutton, 1983). This was shown to consist of 132 species using normal museum criteria (W.J. Knight, pers. commun., 1982). If critical genera are avoided, or treated separately, the RTU approach is probably a useful tool, however, and in many cases it is the only way open at present.

The methods that can be used to analyse data are those applicable to any data set, and those techniques most often used on insect data are summarized by Southwood (1978). His treatment of diversity indices reflects a particular point of view. A consensus does not at present exist as to which diversity index is "best". Recent papers have opted for a whole range of such expressions, with a bias towards log series α among British authors and the log normal amongst American authors. With regard to the indices of similarity a useful assessment has been published by Wolda (1981), but subsequently (Wolda, 1983) he recommended Grassle and Smith's (1976) index NESS (which was not mentioned in his 1981 paper).

Vertical stratification

Medical entomologists had been studying the vertical distribution of biting insects in rain forests for years before the erection of the high steel tower in the Mpanga forest of Uganda, but this development provided a wealth of new information, summarized in a series of 12 papers in the Transactions of the Royal Entomological Society (Vol. 113) (Haddow et al., 1961, *et seq.*). The tower was subsequently moved to Zika forest in Uganda (Haddow and Ssenkubuge, 1965). A further paper by Haddow et al. (1966) described the nocturnal flight cycle of male doryline ants. The tower was 36 m high, well clear of the main canopy and on a level with the tops of the emergent trees. Additional platforms were placed at ground level, 3, 18 and 27 m, with meteorological equipment at 2, 15 and 33 m.

Comprehensive data on biting insects were gathered and analysed, showing the prevalence of supra-canopy swarming behaviour, diurnal vertical migrations, age and oviposition differences in mosquitoes flying at different heights and much of substance besides. A feature of the project was detailed meteorological work. This will be discussed later.

Apart from the thorough work on medical insects and meteorology, brief summaries were given of work on butterflies, sphingids, Coleoptera, Ephemeroptera and Odonata, but no attempt was made at a general synthesis and the majority of insect groups were not mentioned. A tendency for diversity and abundance to be greater in the upper canopy than below, as noted by earlier observers, is not at all obvious from this series of papers, the emphasis of which lies elsewhere. An interesting point concerning mosquito catches in light traps is the suggestion that mosquitoes are only attracted to light traps when engaged in "non-specific flight activity". If this were so, and applied to other insects, it would suggest that flight activity and location as recorded by light traps is a poor indication of flight activity concerned with the substantive elements of an insect's life, such as feeding and breeding. At present evidence on this point is lacking, but cautious interpretation of data is indicated.

Limited data on vertical stratification has been collected by a number of workers primarily interested in other things — for instance Wolda (1979), who studied the seasonality of insects in Panamanian forests, and Penny and Arias (1982), who investigated the life and diversity of forest insects near Manaus in Brazil. By use of light traps at 1 and 15 m they established that many, but by no means all, flying insects were much more common at the upper level, including major groups like staphylinid beetles, and cicadellids among the Homoptera.

Broadhead and Wolda (1985) have carried out a detailed comparison of the abundance and diversity of psocids at two forest sites in Panama (Barro Colorado Island and Fortuna, Chiriqui Province). Light traps were set up at 2 and 25 m above ground level. The relationship between abundance, diversity and height proved complex and varied with season. Because these authors were able to record their results species by species rather than in terms of RTU's and because of the long-term nature of the work, this is one of the most important studies yet carried out on vertical distribution of insects in tropical forests.

A knowledge of Haddow's work and a desire to obtain quantitative data on vertical distribution led to a series of studies by the writer and his associates between 1974 and 1982. The first study, at two sites in Zaïre in semi-deciduous rain forest [= Semi-Evergreen Tropical Rain Forest of Whitmore (1984)] utilized UV light (actinic) traps and sticky traps designed especially for this project (Sutton and Hudson, 1980; Sutton, 1979b). Traps of each type were hung at four levels (1, 8, 18, 27 m) for 5 to 11 days. All insects were collected and counts made at Order or Family level. Good correspondence was found between the pattern of catches in the two types of traps, although they were sampling rather different elements of the insect fauna (see Fig. 24.1 for representative data). The top two traps (Levels 1 and 2), which were in the continuous leaf layer of the upper canopy at both sites, collected far more insects than the two below, and in the catches as a whole there was clear evidence of a falling gradient of abundance between the upper canopy and below. No attempt was made to separate the catch into RTU except for selected families of Lepidoptera, where the results clearly showed both greater abundance of individuals and greater diversity of taxa in the upper canopy (Fig. 24.2). Dry-weight biomass of all medium and small insects caught in actinic (UV light) traps was 2.7 and 2.1 times as great in the top trap as compared to the bottom. Sutton and Hudson (1980) concluded that the null hypothesis

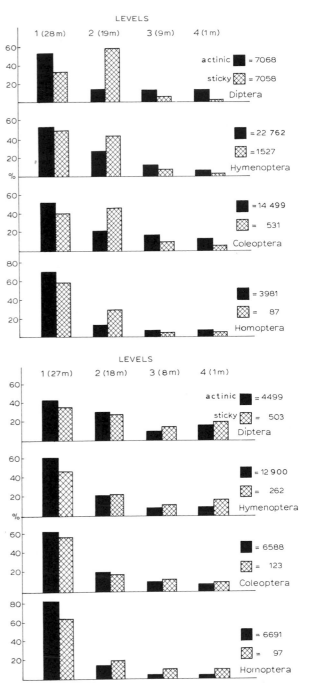

Fig. 24.1. Percentage of catch by level at two sites in semi-deciduous rain forest in Zaïre (Sutton and Hudson, 1980). (A) Weko, near Yangambi; (B) Scierie, near Kindu.

of no difference in abundance of insects between upper canopy and below had been disproved by these data, and that, arguing inductively, the upper canopy of the tropical rain forest could be expected

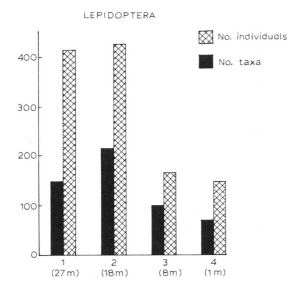

Fig. 24.2. Number of individuals and numbers of taxa (RTU) of macro-Lepidoptera caught over a five-day period in actinic traps. Scierie, Zaïre.

generally to show greater abundance of insects than below, as predicted by earlier workers on the basis of more limited observations.

Subsequent work in Brunei (Sutton, 1979b), Panama and Papua New Guinea (Sutton et al., 1983) and Sulawesi (Sutton, 1983) demonstrated the generality of this statement for most groups of insects for most localities studied. All the data were brought together for comparison in Sutton (1983). It was concluded that the gradient in abundance between floor and canopy was greatest where the ecological inversion surface (Oldeman, 1974; Richards, 1983) was relatively smooth. Irregular topography, or other factors causing this surface to be rough, made the gradient less marked.

Two groups were singled out for separation to RTU. These were the Coleoptera (excluding certain families) and the Homoptera. The work on the beetles has not yet been completed, but that on the diversity of Homoptera at different levels at sites in Panama, Brunei and Sulawesi shows a greater richness in the canopy (Sutton, 1983). In general the gradient of the number of individuals falls much more steeply with decreasing level than the gradient of number of RTU. This appears to be due to the dominant RTU in the upper canopy having a "tail" of representatives at the lower levels, giving diversity but poor numbers of individuals at these lower levels.

Using the Morishita–Horn index of similarity (Rees, 1983), it was possible to show that there was no sharp boundary between the upper-canopy taxa and those below — that is there was no sign of an upper-canopy "community" sharply differentiated from a forest-floor assemblage. That there are forest-floor specialists in all groups of insects cannot be denied, but with them are individuals of taxa which perhaps "belong" in the upper canopy and can be regarded as strays or "tourists" at lower levels. Similar results were obtained by Broadhead (1983) for psocids (and see also Rees, 1983). Given the relatively short distances involved (c. 30 m) it is perhaps remarkable that vertical stratification is so clearly marked. It certainly seems to imply some real biological significance, pace the suggestion cited above that mosquitoes are only attracted to light traps when engaged in "non-specific behaviour" (if such an activity exists).

Although no other workers have set out specifically to study vertical stratification of insects from floor to canopy in tropical rain forest, other studies (for instance, Wolda, 1979) have produced similar data. In general it is accepted that the upper canopy is considerably richer in species and individuals than the levels below, although exceptions occur [Broadhead (1983) with reference to some psocids] and the effects of topography, diversity of tree architecture, season and weather may cause local or temporary departures from the norm.

Trapping is an indirect means of investigation, requiring a level of interpretation which direct visual observation would seem not to require. Papageorgius (1975) exploited the opportunities for visual observation offered by butterflies to study flight levels in the forest in relation to colour and pattern. Using binoculars, she found that, in Peru, different coloured butterflies (particularly those making up Mullerian mimicry rings) flew at different levels. Largely transparent species flew near the ground, tiger-patterned species flew in the understorey, and species with red and yellow patterns above that. Blue butterflies flew in the upper canopy, and those coloured bright orange above the canopy. She produced a histogram to show the modal height of each type in the forest. Further work on this topic, by Dr. Keith Brown, is said to modify this scheme somewhat, but the data are not yet published. Other workers in other forest regions have not been able to reach the same conclusions, although very clearly species have well-defined flight levels. Opportunities for quantified direct observations of flight behaviour are numerous and need to be taken up.

Nothing has so far been said in detail of the vertical movements of insects on a diurnal (or other) basis between floor and upper canopy. Very little work has been done on this, and little can be said except that such movements do exist and may indeed be forcefully impressed upon the observer, in the case of mosquitoes. The paper of Haddow et al. (1961) summarizes the work on insects of medical importance to that date, and further references can be found in recent books on medical entomology. In a preliminary study, the use of suction traps at four levels at Morowali in Sulawesi indicated major changes of flight level of several species of beetles (particularly staphylinids) and other insects over 24-h periods (Rees and Sutton, unpubl.). The study of diurnal migration of insects in the forest is a major potential field of investigation.

Vertical stratification in relation to microclimate

A feature of the Uganda tower project was the detailed meteorological work mentioned earlier. This suggested that during the day strong discontinuities built up between the forest and the air above the canopy, in terms of humidity, light, wind and temperature. At night these broke down, allowing free interchange of insects at the canopy/ air interface. Profiles over 24-h periods brought out the important effect of afternoon rain on temperature regimes and saturation deficits. The meteorological findings were very largely in accord with the earlier findings of Allee (1926). The picture that builds up is of a very stable microclimate within the forest, given to much less fluctuation than the air above or in a clearing, with marked differences between the inside and the outside during the day, but not at night. For more information on the tropical rain-forest climate see the chapters by Lauer and Kira and Yoda (Ch. 2 and 3, respectively).

These observations were confirmed in all essentials by the work of Read (1977). He made a series of observations on microclimate as a background to ecological studies of insects in tropical forest, and studied net radiation balance, rainfall, evaporation, run-off and wind regime. His most interesting finding in the present context was that during the day the temperature profile from floor to canopy was isothermal or showed a weak inversion, with the canopy c. 1°C warmer than below. At night the canopy was 1 to 2°C cooler, enough to create vertical instability and air flow, which might cause vertical displacement of insects caught in the minor turbulence of updraughts and downdraughts. If at the same time the barrier at the canopy/upper air breaks down (Haddow and Corbet, 1961), then a mechanism exists for the vertical movement of small insects into the canopy and above for dispersal, or to swarm.

Read's observations, although valuable, were not linked with actual observations of insect flight activity, so that the ideas put forward were not tested.

Cachan (1964) did manage a synthesis of insect vertical distribution and microclimate, working from a 45 m tower in the forest of Banco, Abidjan, Ivory Coast on populations of scolytid beetles. Vertical stratification and seasonal abundance were the main aspects studied. He constructed eight platforms and "baited" these with cut sections of *Macrolobium* (Caesalpinaceae) tree branches from which he later collected the xylophagous beetles. Detailed work on *Platyscapulus auricomus* (Platypodidae) suggested that a negative geo-taxis causing the animals to fly to higher levels above the forest floor was countered by a need for very humid conditions, which confined them to the forest floor most of the time. He arrived at this result by calculating correlation coefficients for beetle distribution with a number of microclimate variables (it should be noted that Cachan reserves "microclimate" for the actual climate of an ecological "niche", and used "mesoclimate" for the floor-to-canopy space dimension. There is much to be said for this but I will follow the more normal convention, as defined in Lincoln et al., 1982).

Considering a range of twelve xylophages, Cachan showed very elegantly (Fig. 24.3) that each species had its own height profile. He further demonstrated that preferences for certain evaporation rates determined the species' pattern of vertical distribution. No work so thoroughly

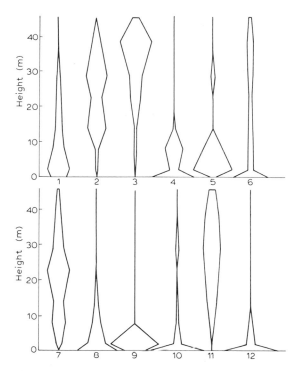

Fig. 24.3. Profiles of vertical distribution of twelve xylophage beetles near Abidjan, Ivory Coast (Cachan, 1964). *1 = Platyscapulus auricomus; 2 = P. camerunus; 3 = Xyleborus cavipennis; 4 = X. alluaudi; 5 = X. cachani; 6 = X. mascarensis; 7 = Polygraphus militaris; 8 = X. ambariusculus; 9 = Poecileps sannio; 10 = X. semigranosus; 11 = Hypothenemus eruditus; 12 = X. ambasius.*

relating microclimate to vertical stratification of members of the same insect guild has been published before or since.

A somewhat similar analysis, but on a much broader scale, was that of Rees (1983). He found that the vertical distribution of Homoptera and Heteroptera differed on rainy and dry nights, so that when it was wet relatively more bugs flew in the upper canopy as compared to the levels below. He suggested that this might be a response to predators. A study of raindrop size in relation to the sound emission frequencies of echo-locating bats raised the possiblity that rain may screen bugs of certain sizes against echo-locative predation by bats. It was notable that those bugs whose body size approximated closest to rain-drop size were the most responsive to rainy weather, as indicated by their increased numbers in traps on rainy nights.

Rees also found that on dry nights a visible

moon depressed the number of bugs caught in the upper canopy, but not below. Data for these and other insects caught during the same study (Rees and Sutton, unpubl.) showed a variety of related responses (Fig. 24.4). Nights have been divided into (1) moonlit and dry, and (2) dark and wet. Unfortunately, during the trapping period there were no dry/dark nights. Light/wet nights (that is, brief showers when the moon was up) did not occur either; so it is not possible to separate the effects of lunar illumination from rain. However, some insight into the relative importance of light and rain can be gained from general observations. A case in point is the behaviour of *Apis dorsata*. This is markedly a creature only active on dry, light nights and probably uses the moonlight for visual navigation. In Fig. 24.4D it can be seen that

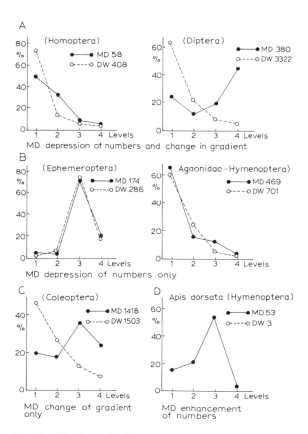

Fig. 24.4. Numbers of individuals by level of selected insect taxa on moonlit/dry nights (*MD*) and dark/wet nights (*DW*) (three nights in each case) at Morowali, east-central Sulawesi (Rees and Sutton, unpubl.). Homoptera, Diptera and Coleoptera samples include a range of species, Ephemeroptera and Agaonidae only a few.

only three were caught on dark/wet nights, whereas 53 were caught on moonlit/dry nights.

This is rather exceptional behaviour, the great majority of insects being much more common on such rainy nights. Where numbers flying on dry/light nights are adequate, it is possible to see that distribution between levels is affected too, so that catches in the upper canopy are depressed. These responses were obtained from both suction and light traps, so that the simple explanation of relatively low efficiency of actinic traps in the lighter conditions of the upper canopy is not sufficient. The effect is to shift downwards the modal flight height of these insects on dry/light nights as well as to reduce the numbers flying. This could perhaps again be seen as a response to predation.

A feature of the microclimate of almost all forests studied is the stability of the air. Even above the canopy, light winds or calm air are the norm, and the internal space of the forest is very much calmer still. It can be surmised that the vertical stratification of weakly flying insects is very much encouraged by this stability, and that tropical forests provide exceptional environments for flight activity of such insects.

However, the air is not equally stable at all levels within the forest, with some channelling of air below the upper canopy as in Sulawesi (Fig. 24.5). This may be very important in determining the micro-spatial dynamics of insects in the forest.

Variation in the numbers and diversity from tree crown to tree crown

Although there is now a certain amount of evidence about the vertical distribution of flying insects in tropical rain forest, virtually nothing has been published on horizontal distribution patterns at the microspatial level, that is from tree crown to tree crown, although a good deal of work is in progress, particularly using fogging techniques. Very limited data have been reported for one group only — the Homoptera. Wolda (1979) gave results for fogging samples from a set of five crowns of *Luehea seemannii* trees in Panama. He found a great deal of variation in the number of species present (range 11–34) in different crowns, and a great contrast in the number of individuals. One factor causing this variation was probably the

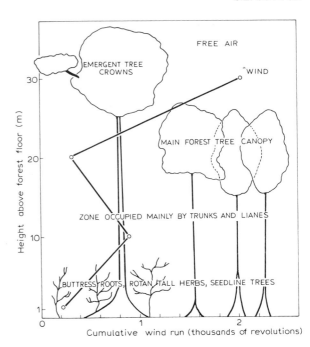

Fig. 24.5. Pattern of wind run at different levels in an alluvial lowland forest (described in Sutton, 1983) at Morowali, east-central Sulawesi, 15 February 80 to 24 March 80. (From Rees and Sutton, unpubl.)

number of species of lianes, for there was a strong correlation between species richness of Homoptera and the diversity of the woody climbers. Sutton (1983) pointed out that each tree crown in tropical forest consists of a complex of plant life rather than a single species structure. This is in great contrast to temperate forest crowns, and can be expected to increase the degree of overlap of species between tree crowns, and the diversity of insects within each crown. Unfortunately epiphytes greatly complicate attempts to discover which insects are associated with particular tree species.

Sutton (1983) also analysed similar data to those of Wolda, for Homoptera from Panama and Sulawesi, using light traps. Considerable variation was found in the numbers of individuals, with slightly smaller variation in the number of RTU. There were no greater differences between crowns of different species than between crowns of the same species. The overlap of taxa between crowns was also tested. High levels of similarity were found, due in part to an abundant delphacid. When this was removed from the reckoning, levels of similarity fell somewhat, but remained even. The overall impression that results is of a general circulation of Homoptera between crowns, rather than of discrete faunal sets, with the attendant implication that many of the insects are flying in crowns which can provide no food resource, if the insects are monophagous. In fact monophagy seems unlikely (in the absence of any evidence either way) given the high diversity of the forest trees, their dispersion (in many forests) and the apparent mobility of the flying insects. Studies of insect herbivore attack on leaves provide no strong indication of monophagy either (W. Wint, pers. commun., 1984). However, until studies of the host specificity of insect herbivores currently in progress are published, no clear statement can be made.

The picture of a cloud of insects circulating freely between and within tree crowns becomes understandable if the stable air conditions within the forest are considered. Minor vertical turbulence has been mentioned above, but wind sufficient to cause major displacement is rare in most forests. Indeed probably no other type of ecosystem enjoys such stable air conditions. This may encourage flight and allow Homoptera and other weak fliers to carry out "controlled" dispersals as well as allowing marked and stable vertical stratifications to build up as mentioned earlier.

Microspatial dynamics

Whatever the difficulties of establishing the patterns of inter-crown abundance, diversity and similarity of flying insects, one needs to gain detail in order to understand the three-dimensional or micro-spatial dynamics of the system. Studies of vertical stratification inevitably emphasize the layering of flying insects in the forest. This may be misleading. Each tree crown represents a sphere, discrete to some extent from adjacent spheres. Each sphere has a cluster of insects associated with it and each cluster contains species with greater or lesser tendencies to disperse beyond the crown. There are in addition "tourists" which are simply passing through. Species with high dispersal values create uniformity within the upper canopy, and vice versa. When more is known of the differing dispersal rates and specificity of insects in the forest, it should be possible [as suggested elsewhere (Sutton, 1983)] to model the upper canopy of the forest as a set of close-packed spheres, and to study

variation in microspatial insect distribution in relation to forest structure, diversity and microclimate. An important development in this will be to look not only at differences between tree crowns, but at the differences between inner and outer areas of crowns, and the gaps between crowns (which are particularly important in the case of emergents). Recent information on the degree of scleromorphy of leaves on different parts of the same tree (Roth, 1984) will be relevant to this study.

Such an approach can then pave the way towards an integration of spatial and temporal dynamics of flying insects in tropical rain forest, to enable one to understand more fully the role of insects in this type of ecosystem. Given the problems caused by riotous diversity and attendant taxonomic deficiencies, such an approach may not be practical. Then again, it is of great importance to establish the place of insects in these ecosystems. Necessity may yet prove the mother of invention.

REFERENCES

Allee, W.C., 1926. Measurement of environmental factors in the tropical rain-forest of Panama. *Ecology*, 7: 273–302.

Bates, H.W., 1863. *The Naturalist on the River Amazons*. Murray, London.

Broadhead, E., 1983. The assessment of faunal diversity and guild size in tropical forests with particular reference to the Psocoptera. In: S.L. Sutton, T.C. Whitmore and A.C. Chadwick (Editors), *Tropical Rain Forest: Ecology and Management*. Blackwell, Oxford, pp. 107–119.

Broadhead, E. and Wolda, H., 1985. Diversity of Psocoptera in the two tropical forests of Panama. *J. Anim. Ecol.*, 54 (3): 739–854.

Cachan, P., 1964. Analyse statistique des pullulations de Scolytoidea mycetophages en foret Sempervirente de Cote d'Ivoire. *Ann. Fac. Sci., Univ. Dakar*, 14: 5–70.

Erwin, T.L., 1983. Beetles and other insects of tropical forest canopies at Manaus, Brazil sampled by insecticidal fogging. In: S.L. Sutton, T.C. Whitmore and A.C. Chadwick (Editors), *Tropical Rain Forest: Ecology and Management*. Blackwell, Oxford, pp. 59–76.

Grassle, J.F. and Smith, W., 1976. A similarity measure sensitive to the contribution of rare species and its use in investigation of variation in marine benthic communities. *Oecologia*, 25: 13–22.

Haddow, A.J. and Corbet, P.S., 1961. Observations on certain environmental factors at different levels. *Trans. R. Entomol. Soc. London*, 113: 257–269.

Haddow, A.J. and Ssenkubuge, Y., 1965. Entomological studies from a high steel tower in Zika forest, Uganda, 1. The biting activity of mosquitos and tabanids as shown by

24 h catches. *Trans. R. Entomol. Soc. London*, 117: 215–243.

Haddow, A.J., Corbet, P.S. and Gillet, J.D., 1961. Entomological studies from a high tower in Mpanga forest, Uganda. *Trans. R. Entomol. Soc. London*, 113: 249–368.

Haddow, A.J., Yarrow, I.H.H., Lancaster, G.A. and Corbet, P.S., 1966. Nocturnal flight cycle in the males of African doryline ants (Hymenoptera: Formicidae). *Proc. R. Entomol. Soc., Ser. A*, 41: 93–132.

Hingston, R.W.G., 1932. *A Naturalist in the Guiana Forest*. Arnold, London, 384 pp.

Holloway, J.D., 1984. The larger moths of the Gunung Mulu National Park. In: A.C. Jermy and K. Kavanagh (Editors), *Gunung Mulu National Park, Sarawak. Part II*. Sarawak Mus. J., 30: 149–190.

Lincoln, R.J., Boxshall, G.A. and Clark, P.F., 1982. *A Dictionary of Ecology, Evolution and Systematics*. Cambridge Univ. Press, Cambridge, 298 pp.

Mitchell, A.W., 1982. *Reaching the Rain Forest Roof*. Leeds Philosophical and Literary Society, Leeds, 36 pp.

Murphy, D.H., 1973. Animals in the forest ecosystem. In: C.H. Chuang (Editors), *Animal Life in Singapore*. Univ. of Singapore Press, Singapore, pp. 32–44.

Oldeman, R.A.A., 1974. *L'Architecture de la Forêt Guyanaise*. Mem. ORSTROM. 73.

Papageorgius, C., 1975. Mimicry in neo-tropical butterflies. *Am. Sci.*, 63: 522–532.

Penny, N.D. and Arias, A.R., 1982. *Insects of an Amazon Forest*. Columbia Univ. Press, New York, N.Y., 269 pp.

Perry, D.R., 1984. The canopy of the tropical rain forest. *Sci. Am.*, 251(5): 114–125.

Read, R.G., 1977. Microclimate as background environment for ecological studies of insects in a tropical forest. *J. Appl. Meteorol.*, 16: 1282–1291.

Rees, C.J.C., 1983. Microclimate and flying Hemiptera fauna of a primary lowland rain forest in Sulawesi. In: S.L. Sutton, T.C. Whitmore and A.C. Chadwick (Editors), *Tropical Rain Forest: Ecology and Management*. Blackwell, Oxford, pp. 121–136.

Richards, P.W., 1983. The three dimensional structure of tropical rain forest. In: S.L. Sutton, T.C. Whitmore and A.C. Chadwick (Editors), *Tropical Rain Forest: Ecology and Management*. Blackwell, Oxford, pp. 3–10.

Roth, I., 1984. Stratification of tropical forests as seen in leaf structure. *Tasks Veget. Sci.*, 6: 1–522.

Southwood, T.R.E., 1978. *Ecological Methods*. Chapman and Hall, London, 524 pp.

Sutton, S.L., 1979a. A portable light trap for studying insects of the upper canopy. *Brunei Mus. J.*, 4(3): 156–160.

Sutton, S.L., 1979b. The vertical distribution of flying insects in the lowland rain forest of Brunei: preliminary report. *Brunei Mus. J.*, 4(3): 161–173.

Sutton, S.L., 1983. The spatial distribution of flying insects in tropical rain forests. In: S.L. Sutton, T.C. Whitmore and A.C. Chadwick (Editors), *Tropical Rain Forest: Ecology and Management*. Blackwell, Oxford, pp. 77–91.

Sutton, S.L. and Hudson, P.J., 1980. The vertical distribution of small flying insects in the lowland rain forest of Zaire. *Zool. J. Linn. Soc.*, 68: 111–123.

Sutton, S.L., Ash, C.P. and Grundy, H., 1983. The vertical distribution of flying insects in the lowland rain forests of Panama, Papua New Guinea and Brunei. *Zool. J. Linn. Soc.*, 78(3): 287–297.

Whitmore, T.C., 1984. *Tropical Rain Forests of the Far East*. Clarendon, Oxford, 2nd ed., 352 pp.

Wolda, H., 1979. Abundance and diversity of Homoptera in the canopy of a tropical forest. *Ecol. Entomol.* 4(2): 181–190.

Wolda, H., 1981. Similarity indices, sample size and diversity. *Oecologia*, 50: 296–302.

Wolda, H., 1983. Spatial and temporal variation in abundance in tropical animals. In: S.L. Sutton, T.C. Whitmore and A.C. Chadwick (Editors), *Tropical Rain Forest: Ecology and Management*. Blackwell, Oxford, pp. 93–105.

Chapter 25

MOTHS

J.D. HOLLOWAY

INTRODUCTION

Our knowledge of moths in tropical rain forest is exceedingly patchy. Observations on adult behaviour are few as most fly at night. Host-plant data are sparse with the notable exception of D.H. Janzen's seasonal forest site in Costa Rica. The taxonomy is often extremely superficial hence biogeographic and host specificity patterns may be obscured until detailed revisional work has been undertaken.

Diversity is high, with perhaps 200 000 described species worldwide, but our knowledge of the distribution of this diversity is barely more than generalities about latitudinal and altitudinal gradients (Holloway, 1987a).

The larvae of Lepidoptera are mainly plant defoliators but there are also leaf miners (several microlepidopteran families such as Nepticulidae), stem borers (for instance in Noctuidae and Pyralidae), flower feeders [Noctuidae (Nolinae), Geometridae (Larentiinae)], fruit and seed predators (mainly Microlepidoptera like Tortricidae), predators of Hemiptera (for instance Epipyropidae and *Eublemma* species in the Noctuidae), timber borers (Cossidae, Hepialidae), detritus feeders [Noctuidae (Hypeninae); among others], fungus feeders (some Tineoidea, some Noctuidae) and lichen and moss grazers [many Arctiidae (Lithosiinae)]. There are also more bizarre associations such as the pyralid moths which live in the fur of sloths in Neotropical rain forests, leaving them to oviposit on the dung when the sloths descend to the ground to defecate (Waage and Best, 1985).

It is not possible to do justice to the Lepidoptera in the full range of their trophic diversity in a short chapter. My own taxonomic experience and quan-

titative sampling efforts have been restricted to the macrolepidoptera and so the discussion presented will be biassed towards these: the superfamilies Cossoidea, Zygaenoidea, Bombycoidea (including Sphingidae), Noctuoidea and Geometroidea.

Few quantitative surveys of aspects of moth biology and distribution in tropical rain forest have been made. Janzen (1983a) has illustrated the value of an intensive, localised study of all aspects of insect biology in rain forest. I will try and present here what I hope is a complementary approach based on light-trap surveys in a range of habitats and localities in the Indo-Australian tropics and on taxonomic and biogeographic studies.

ADULT BEHAVIOUR

A light-trap survey, despite the bias inherent in the technique, can indicate some aspects of moth behaviour. The bias itself can be illuminating. Males tend to come to light in greater numbers than females in most species, though the reservoir population has the sexes in even numbers (Janzen, 1983b). Janzen suggested this may be because males are more active in mate-searching and thus are more likely to navigate with reference to distant light sources. They may also disperse more in upper layers of air (Holloway, 1967). The predominance of males in light-trap samples reflects that also seen in hill-topping behaviour and migrant swarms (Holloway, 1977) and in mud-puddling by tropical butterflies (Arms et al., 1974; Holloway, 1984a). In all these instances the common factor may be the greater mobility of males and corresponding physiological requirements (Arms et al., 1974). It would be interesting to make comparisons of sex ratios in canopy-flying versus understorey-flying species; the latter operate in a very different environment with regard to both structure and sources of illumination.

The response of moths to light also appears to be uneven through a given night, from night to night through adult life, and from species to species (Holloway, 1967; Janzen, 1983b; among others). This variability is common to moth faunas world-wide as is the tendency of fruit- and sugar-feeding species to respond relatively weakly to light. Investigation of these factors in light-trap bias will be necessary to ensure that the sort of diversity measurements discussed later reflect reality and not an artifact of the sampling technique (Holloway, 1977).

The majority of species in Old World tropical rain forests appear to fly in or above the canopy. There is a very much smaller number that come to light mainly in the understorey (Sutton, 1979, 1983; Sutton and Hudson, 1980; Holloway, 1984b). This vertical segregation is not unique to the Lepidoptera but occurs in other insect groups. Understorey flight is distributed unevenly amongst the various taxonomic groups (Holloway, 1984b). It is frequent in the Geometridae (Ennominae), Lasiocampidae, Euptero-tidae, Lymantriidae, Notodontidae and Noctuidae (Hypeninae), but has not been noted to any significant extent in other groups such as the Geometridae (Geometrinae), Arctiidae (Lithosiinae), and most subfamilies of the Noctuidae.

Examination of the groups well represented in the understorey has led me to the subjective impression that they tend on the whole to have strongly bipectinate antennae in the male whereas canopy-flying groups do not, though the Noctui-dae (Euteliinae) and Geometridae (Geometrinae) are exceptions to the latter. If this observation is confirmed by objective analysis it might reflect the different problems and solutions concerning mate location in the understorey as compared with the canopy. This explanation is more likely than one concerning the location of food resources as the Lymantriidae and the Bombycoidea families have reduced mouthparts and are not thought to feed as adults (Norris, 1936; Janzen, 1984). A comparable phenomenon is seen in the relative frequency of territoriality in understorey versus canopy butter-flies in Borneo (Holloway, 1984a).

It is unclear as yet whether understorey versus canopy flight is correlated with the level within the forest at which the larva feeds. It is likely that, as in the butterflies, many canopy-flying species descend to the understorey for oviposition and may at this time be unresponsive to light.

I have not been able to locate any observations of mud-puddling behaviour in Oriental rain-forest moths comparable to that known in butterflies, but some species such as the geometrid *Ectropis ischnadelpha* Prout have been observed to drink at water seepages (Holloway, 1976). Collenette (1934) observed large numbers of nocturnal moths to visit damp, possibly salt-rich sand and sweat soaked objects in South America. Families involved were Arctiidae, Geometridae, Noctuidae, Notodonti-dae, Pyralidae, Thyrididae, and Uraniidae. Males predominated at roughly 67% in Noctuidae but made up over 95% in all the other families.

Records of moths visiting lachrymal secretions of large mammals have been made in all tropical regions (Norris, 1936; Bänziger, 1972). In South-East Asia Bänziger observed the same species to suck at sweat, blood in wounds or at soil with urine or dung. The genera involved, such as the geometrids *Hypochrosis*, *Semiothisa* and *Zythos* (*Nobilia*) were also those taken in some numbers in carrion-baited pitfall traps by I. Hanski in the Gunung Mulu National Park. The geometrid genus *Fascellina* was recorded in the pitfall traps but has yet to be noted at lachrymal secretions by Bänziger. The pitfall material was also predomi-nantly male. Presumably this behaviour has the same physiological basis as that suggested by Arms et al. (1974) for mud puddling butterflies: the acquisition of essential salts or proteins, with sodium the trigger, not obtained during the larval stage.

SEASONALITY

Observations of seasonality in the life cycles of moths in rain forest are again sparse and usually restricted to considering peaks of adult abundance in light-trap records. For insects generally (Wolda, 1983a) and for Lepidoptera in particular (Hol-loway, 1977) the presence and coincidence of seasonal peaks would appear to be correlated with the condition of the plant food resource, such as a flush of foliage or flowers, which itself is usually correlated with climatic parameters. In areas such as parts of Borneo and New Guinea where annual rainfall is relatively evenly distributed, definite seasonal peaks coincident for many species are not readily apparent. Janzen (1983b) has suggested that, in evergreen tropical rain forest with uniform rainfall, any coincident peaking of adult insects may correspond to drier, sunnier periods. In any one locality different species associations may have different general seasonal peaks as occurs in Norfolk Island (Holloway, 1977) and New Caledonia (Holloway, 1979). We require data collected through several seasonal cycles in different types of rain forest and over transects in each locality to be able to appreciate the complete picture of the response of species associations to seasonal climatic changes. Intensive work at selected sites, such as that in progress by Tho Yow Pong in Peninsular Malaysia, will be needed to relate moth seasonality to host-plant condition.

HOST-PLANT RELATIONSHIPS

Moths are undoubtedly a very important component of the rain-forest biota, with considerable impact on plant life. D.H. Janzen (1983a, and pers. commun., 1984) has indicated that 80% of the defoliation in the deciduous rain forest in Costa Rica is by caterpillars, and 90% of these are Lepidoptera. He has suggested, following Ehrlich and Raven (1965), that plant predation by invertebrates and its degree of specificity along both taxonomic and structural lines (for instance, parts of the plant, seedling foliage versus mature crown foliage, young versus old foliage) may be one of the major contributory forces towards increasing diversity in tropical rain forest, possibly the major one. He supported this assertion with data from the forests of Costa Rica where even apparently euryphagous species are found to show stenophagy locally. This stenophagy and the close coevolutionary relationships frequently observed between moth and plant taxonomic lineages has led Janzen to suggest that species-richness of herbivores in rain forest should be at least in part dependent on the species-richness of the plants. Vane-Wright (1978) has questioned this in an analysis for the butterflies and, as will be seen later, data for moths

in the Oriental tropics also show inconsistencies with the hypothesis.

The extent to which the hypothesis might be general to tropical rain forest and the differences, basic to any theory of a driving force for greater tropical diversity, with the situation in subtropical and temperate ecosystems have yet to be gauged with any precision. To test the hypothesis that high diversity in tropical rain forests is specifically a result of herbivore pressure interacting with plant defence systems will require intensive field studies in a number of sites throughout the world akin to that undertaken by Janzen. This effect would be in addition to herbivore pressure permitting higher diversity through a differential effect on dominants.

Extensive insect/host-plant data (to the depth that negative data become reliable) are lacking for most world ecosystems except those in temperate parts of the world where a tradition of amateur entomology has accumulated records over decades or even centuries.

In temperate forests Lepidoptera specificity along plant-taxonomic lines differs widely between angiosperms and gymnosperms, being far more precise in the latter, and is not so strong as to mask a secondary component of specificity to *ecologically* associated host-plants that regularly occur together in the same biotope; presumably in the latter instance potentially euryphagous species are restricted to that biotope by some other factor (Holloway and Hebert, 1979). An analysis of Costa Rican data along similar lines might provide an interesting comparison.

A survey of the more readily accessible sources of literature on host-plants of macrolepidoptera in the Indo-Australian tropics (as listed by Holloway, 1983a, 1985a, 1986b, in press a) has revealed both the sparsity of information and also sufficient in the way of patterns and trends to indicate that the gathering of further data is a priority for the study of the interaction between Lepidoptera and rain forest. Hardly any information on structural specificity of the "canopy crown versus seedling" nature is available. There is little information on the chemical diversity of the foliage of the various plant taxa of the type beginning to be accumulated in African rain forests by Waterman (1983). The possibility of testing hypotheses of herbivore load by insecticidal fogging of selected tree crowns also holds promise, as will be seen later.

Certain families and groups within families stand out as containing a high proportion of euryphagous species (there is no information on localised stenophagy of the Costa Rican type), for example Lasiocampidae, Saturniidae, Limacodidae, Arctiidae (Arctiinae), Lymantriidae and Geometridae (Boarmiini). These are all groups that show a similar wide range of host-plant in temperate regions, even straddling at species level the major angiosperm/gymnosperm discontinuity demonstrated by Holloway and Hebert (1979).

There are other groups which have a predominance of host records from one family yet are not exclusive to it, such as relationships between the Euteliinae (Noctuidae) and the Anacardiaceae (Holloway, 1985a, 1986b, in press b) and the genus *Macroglossum* (Sphingidae) and the Rubiaceae.

The connection between some host-plant relationships and the ecology or biogeography of the lepidopteran group concerned requires further investigation in many cases. The macroglossine Sphingidae feed mainly on a small group of families such as Araceae, Convolvulaceae, Dilleniaceae, Nyctaginaceae, Rubiaceae and Vitaceae (Bell and Scott, 1937; Moulds, 1981); they are more diverse in disturbed habitats such as early regenerating forest, riparian habitats and abandoned farmland. Specialists on the family Malvaceae, such as the noctuid genera *Anomis*, *Chasmina*, *Earias*, *Paracrama* and *Xanthodes*, tend to contain a high proportion of species that range throughout the Indo-Australian tropics; both moths and plants may tend towards *r*-strategy and dispersability.

There are a number of examples of more exclusive specificity. The family Bombycidae (Holloway, in press b) appears to be restricted to the Moraceae (*Bombyx*, *Ocinara* and allies) and the Symplocaceae and Theaceae (*Andraca*, *Mustilia*), and one major lineage of the noctuid subfamily Stictopterinae is only recorded from the Guttiferae (Holloway, 1985a). The few records available for Uraniidae are mainly from the genus *Endospermum* (Euphorbiaceae). At a lower taxonomic level a group of Notodontidae (*Ambadra*, *Pydna* and allies) are feeders on monocotyledons, particularly palms and bamboos, a specificity reflected in the butterflies by sections of the Hesperiidae and the Satyrinae and Amathusiinae. The noctuid genus *Callopistria* feeds on ferns as does the family

Callidolidae and the geometrid tribe Lithini (Holloway, 1987b). *Othreis* and allied noctuid genera are virtually restricted to Menispermaceae (Bänziger, 1982). The noctuid genera *Avatha*, *Pseudathyrma* and *Serrodes* are probably related and have been recorded mainly from the Sapindaceae.

The geometrid genus *Agathia* parallels the butterfly subfamily Danainae in feeding on both Apocynaceae and Asclepiadaceae (Holloway and Sommerer, 1984). Two genera of the Notodontidae (*Cerura* and *Clostera*) tend to favour Salicaceae in north temperate areas and Flacourtiaceae in the Tropics, a switch also shown by the nymphalid genus *Phalanta* (Holloway, 1983a). In the first example the two plant families are closely related, but in the second they are not.

Examination of the Indo-Australian data also leads to the impression that some plant families, perhaps those that are known generally to synthesise insect toxins, have a more specific fauna than others, such as the Leguminosae with *Allata* and allies in the Notodontidae, and *Rhesala* and allies, *Anticarsia* and allies, *Ericeia*, *Lacera* and *Pericyma* in the Noctuidae. The Euphorbiaceae have already been noted as supporting the uraniids but may also be specific for sections of the *Parallelia/Achaea* complex in the Noctuidae and for the *Gargetta* group in the Notodontidae. Most records for *Asota* and allies (Aganainae) have been from the Moraceae, in addition to the Bombycidae already mentioned. *Diospyros* in the Ebenaceae has provided all the few records for, in the Noctuidae, the possibly related genera *Blenina* and *Labanda* and most of those for *Hypocala*.

Some plant genera seem to have a particularly diverse fauna of lepidopteran defoliators, the most notable of which is *Terminalia* (Combretaceae). It is therefore perhaps surprising to find within the noctuid subfamily Chloephorinae two genera which appear to be restricted to *Terminalia* (*Aiteta* and *Westermannia*) as well as a group of genera (*Teleclita* and allies) in the Notodontidae (Holloway, 1983a).

The Dipterocarpaceae, in view of their predominance in both diversity and biomass in South-East Asian rain forest, might be expected to support a correspondingly diverse fauna of defoliators. Their economic importance as timber trees would also suggest that sampling from them would be, if anything, greater than that from other families.

Nevertheless, records of defoliating Lepidoptera are very few; microlepidopteran seed predators are possibly more frequently recorded. The majority of records have been of euryphagous species, especially from the families with high proportions of such species mentioned earlier, such as the Lymantriidae. The only indication of a degree of preference for Dipterocarpaceae has been found in the *Lophoptera* lineage of the noctuid subfamily Stictopterinae (Holloway, 1985a) with other subgroups of this lineage recorded from the Euphorbiaceae. Again data are very sparse and the situation requires further investigation. Could the predominance of Dipterocarpaceae in lowland rain forests of South-East Asia be a reflection of success in avoiding herbivore pressure? If so, then an alternative explanation must be sought for their high taxonomic diversity.

Hegnauer (1966) reviewed chemical data for Dipterocarpaceae and indicated their richness in triterpenoid oleo-resins, a similarity with gymnosperms where dipterpenoid oleo-resins predominate (P.G. Waterman, pers. commun., 1984). It may be, therefore, that the apparent low level of defoliators on dipterocarps is because they have adopted a chemical strategy that places them on the "gymnosperm side" of the angiosperm/gymnosperm discontinuity identified by Holloway and Hebert (1979); the Lepidoptera groups recorded from dipterocarps are those with a high proportion of euryphages that straddle this major discontinuity. Dipterocarps also show relatively high acid detergent fibre levels (P.G. Waterman, pers. commun., 1984, and Ch. 29).

Data on plant defences (Waterman, 1983; and others) may also pose more questions than they answer. Waterman singled out the Guttiferae in Africa as an example of a family where sympatric members tend not to overlap in chemical defence strategy, yet we have already seen that one lineage of the noctuid subfamily Stictopterinae is specific to the family (though records of other Lepidoptera from Guttiferae are sparse in Asia and Australasia). Only half a dozen or so members of this lineage occur in Africa, compared with over twenty (over thirty if *Gyrtona* is included) in Borneo. It is not possible to assess the compatibility of these two observations as no host records for the subfamily in Africa have been located nor biochemical records for the plant family in Asia and

Australasia. There is thus no way to tell if the very much lower diversity of African stictopterines of this lineage is associated with a comparatively higher biochemical diversity in the Guttiferae.

There is both pattern and paradox in the sparse host-plant data available for macrolepidoptera in the Indo-Australian tropics. The question of whether the intensity and specificity of herbivore pressure make a positive contribution to plant diversity has yet to be answered for this major tropical region. If increased euryphagy can be taken as a mark of success for Lepidoptera in coping with chemical defences of plants, then can one consider that the concomitant response of affected plant populations to increase chemical polymorphism would lead ultimately to speciation? Some indications, such as for the Dipterocarpaceae which appear to have speciated extensively in the absence of intense herbivore pressure, are counter to this hypothesis. I shall return to this question in a later section after attempting to assess the distribution of Lepidoptera diversity in relation to forest type in Borneo.

PATTERNS OF LEPIDOPTERA DIVERSITY

Bourlière (1983), following the work of R.H. Whittaker, distinguished between alpha (community), beta (species replacement over a continuum) and gamma (the sum of communities within a broad ecosystem) diversity and suggested that several discrete communities may exist within a tropical rain-forest "landscape" which could have very different alpha diversities. This has been demonstrated for moths in a wider range of vegetation types in both New Caledonia (Holloway, 1979) and Norfolk Island (Holloway, 1977). However, in New Caledonia it was only possible to identify a single rain-forest moth association, albeit with components of beta diversity on continua, one probably successional, the other correlated with geology. It is always possible that a larger sample might reveal discontinuities.

The techniques used in these analyses contrast with the usual approach of studying the diversity of samples, and are much better suited to testing Bourlière's hypothesis of a multiplicity of communities in tropical rain forest. Individual sample diversities are likely to be the sums of the alpha diversities of overlapping communities — that is they incorporate an element of gamma diversity. But it is possible to sample from a range of forest types and use cluster analysis and ordination methods to recognise groups of species significantly associated with each other in their distributions amongst the samples; these groups are usually also associated with a particular vegetation type.

A light-trap survey I conducted in the Gunung Mulu National Park, Sarawak (Holloway, 1984), included altitude transects on limestone (Gunung Api) and siliceous-sedimentary (Gunung Mulu) mountains as well as samples from alluvial, regenerating alluvial and wet (kerangas) heath forests in the lowlands.

The four lowland forest types were studied intensively in sample plots by other workers (Proctor et al., 1983a, b): alluvial, kerangas, dipterocarp forest on Gunung Mulu and forest on the lowest slope of Gunung Api (limestone). These forest types were found to be significantly different in floristic composition (Table 25.1) and diversity. The alluvial and dipterocarp forests had the highest diversity of large trees [> 10 cm diameter

breast height (d.b.h.)] with similarly sloped cumulative species/area curves. The slope for the limestone forest was only half as steep, with that for kerangas intermediate. Small trees (< 10 cm d.b.h.) were twice the density in limestone forest compared with the other three. Lianes were five or six times as frequent in terms of density in the alluvial and limestone forests compared with the other two. Ground herbs were low in the dipterocarp and limestone forests, twice as numerous in kerangas and an order of magnitude more numerous in alluvial forest. Understorey epiphytes were twice as numerous in the kerangas than in the alluvial forest and insignificant in the other two forest types.

Evidence of herbivory in fallen leaves was greatest in the alluvial forest, followed by kerangas, dipterocarp forest and limestone forest. Phenolics in fallen leaves were highest in kerangas, lowest in alluvial forest.

Comparable data were not collected in montane forests. The lower montane forest on Gunung Mulu is floristically perhaps as rich as the dipterocarp forest, but with the families Fagaceae, Guttiferae and Myrtaceae providing the principal

TABLE 25.1

Plant families ranked in order of importance of their contribution to the tree population over 10 cm d.b.h. in four forest types in the lowlands of the Gunung Mulu National Park, Sarawak (from Proctor et al., 1983a). The upper section refers to actual numbers (families with 80 + individuals) and thus may reflect diversity. The lower section refers to percentage contribution (families with over 3%) to total basal (trunk) area and may be more closely correlated to crown size and therefore total foliage biomass (author's interpretation)

Alluvial	Limestone	Dipterocarp	Kerangas
Euphorbiaceae (97)	Dipterocarpaceae (140)	Dipterocarpaceae (114)	Guttiferae (170)
Myrtaceae (44)	Euphorbiaceae (89)	Euphorbiaceae (70)	Dipterocarpaceae (92)
Leguminosae (33)	Meliaceae (50)	Myrtaceae (65)	Myrtaceae (74)
Guttiferae (42)	Myrtaceae (47)	Sapotaceae (52)	Euphorbiaceae (65)
Ebenaceae (37)	Sapotaceae (39)	Myristicaceae (49)	Sapotaceae (38)
Dipterocarpaceae (33)	Tiliaceac (32)	Burseraceae (35)	Annonaceae (32)
Sapotaceae (30)		Guttiferae (35)	
Leguminosae (15.05)	Dipterocarpaceae (47.41)	Dipterocarpaceae (43.15)	Dipterocarpaceae (42.90)
Dipterocarpaceae (12.99)	Sapindaceae (9.54)	Leguminosae (5.12)	Guttiferae (16.96)
Euphorbiaceae (8.92)	Tiliaceae (7.75)	Sapotaceae (4.79)	Myrtaceae (11.01)
Myrtaceae (6.37)	Euphorbiaceae (5.79)	Myrtaceae (4.00)	Sapotaceae (3.34)
Lauraceae (5.46)	Myrtaceae (5.07)	Burseraceae (3.14)	
Guttiferae (5.42)	Sapotaceae (4.08)		
Sapotaceae (4.79)	Meliaceae (3.61)		
Ebenaceae (4.67)	Sterculiaceae (3.32)		

In the lower section below "Alluvial", the Sapindaceae are ranked 16th (1.34%) and the Rubiaceae and Combretaceae are unplaced (for comparison with Table 25.3 as discussed on p. 448).

dominants at lower elevations and with Flacourtiaceae and Sapotaceae increasing in importance at higher elevations (Anderson and Chai, 1983). The formation is found from roughly 800 to 1200 m.

The upper montane forest is floristically less diverse, with Guttiferae and Myrtaceae still important but joined by conifers, numerous ericaceous shrubs, and shrubs of the Gesneriaceae, Rubiaceae and Melastomataceae; Ericaceae increase in frequency with altitude and a diverse herbaceous flora occurs (Anderson and Chai, 1983).

On the limestone of Gunung Api similar montane formations occur at similar altitudes but, because of the more broken terrain, differ in appearance, tending to be more open, gnarled, with greater development of a ground flora. Further details can be found in Anderson and Chai (1983) and Collins et al. (1984).

Preliminary analyses of the moth data (Holloway, 1984b, 1985b), classifying samples according to similarity of species composition for several taxonomic subsets of the data, recorded, for most subsets, a major discontinuity between an upper montane group of samples and the rest. The lower montane samples were the next to be discriminated and there were some indications of grouping according to lowland forest type.

Assessment of sample diversity for all macrolepidoptera using the α statistic [see Wolda (1983b) for a "consumer guide" to diversity measures] indicated that diversity was highest ($\alpha = 400$) in the Mulu lower montane forest, followed by, of all lowland forest types, the floristically least diverse lowland limestone forest (Holloway, 1987a). This pattern of high diversity in lower montane and limestone forests was shown particularly by the Geometroidea but also by the Arctiidae and Noctuidae (Nolinae). The Lymantriidae and Notodontidae were best represented in the lowland limestone forest, the former being weak in montane forests. In contrast the Limacodidae were relatively more diverse in the kerangas and most noctuid subfamilies occur in the alluvial forest.

Within the Geometridae there is also differentiation along taxonomic lines, with the Larentiinae most diverse in upper montane forest, the Ennominae in lower montane forest and Geometrinae in the lowlands. The change in representation of Geometridae subfamilies with altitude is reflected by the change with latitude, and a similar altitudinal pattern is seen in the African tropics (Holloway, 1984b, 1986a, 1987a).

The difference in geometrid diversity in a few of the major Mulu survey samples is shown in Fig. 25.1 for all species with four or more

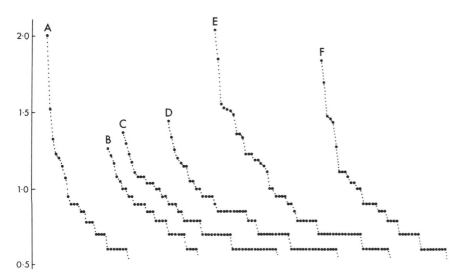

Fig. 25.1. The upper sections of rank/abundance curves for six major samples of Geometroidea from the Mulu survey. A = Mulu upper montane forest, Site 1; B = Api lower montane forest, Site 25; C = Mulu lower montane forest, Site 14; D = lowland limestone forest, Site 23; E = dipterocarp forest, Site 8; F = alluvial forest, Site 16. Logarithm of abundance (ordinate) is plotted against rank order of abundance (abscissa).

individuals; this sort of rank/abundance curve is obtained by plotting rank order against the logarithm of abundance. Generally, the shallower the curve, the greater is the diversity. As stated earlier, it is unclear whether high diversity in a sample, such as those from lower montane forest and limestone in Fig. 25.1, is due to high α diversity in an association intrinsically associated with a predominant vegetation type or due to summed (γ) diversity through the overlap of several associations.

Classification of the more abundant (10 + individuals) species of Geometroidea into associations by cluster analysis (Holloway, in prep.) enabled species representing two thirds of the individuals in the total sampled to be assigned with confidence, the rest of the individuals being those of rare species or species peripheral to the main clusters. For the Geometroidea the analysis indicated that the high diversity in the lower montane forest was an intrinsic α diversity but that there was an element of γ diversity with several associations overlapping to give the high sample diversity observed in the limestone forest. The representation of each association in each sample is given in Table 25.2. Overlap between the associations in the

samples was generally moderate and the associations reflected the discontinuities shown up in the classifications of samples.

The rank/abundance curves for the associations recognized, summed from all samples, are shown in Fig. 25.2. The diversity of the curves can roughly be assessed from their shallowness. The three montane associations are thus distinctly more diverse than the four lowland ones and, of the latter, one is associated with each of the four forest types and that for alluvial forest is somewhat more diverse. All have the truncated sigmoid form of a partially sampled log-normal distribution of abundance. The significance of the log-normal distribution is still debated (May, 1975; Holloway, 1977; Sugihara, 1980).

In the majority of these associations Ennominae predominate but Larentiinae make up one third of the upper montane association (A) and in the alluvial forest association (D) the Ennominae only contribute half the species. The subfamily Sterrhinae has its highest number of species in the lowland limestone forest but these tend to be rare and do not feature in the analysis to any great extent. The kerangas association (G) contains a group of species virtually restricted to that forma-

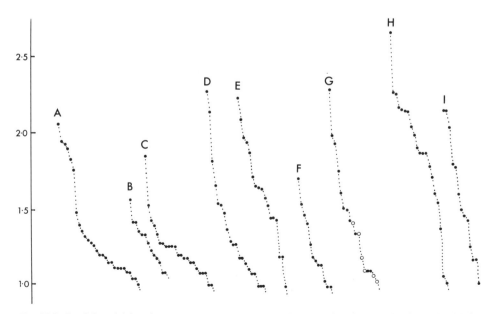

Fig. 25.2. Partial rank/abundance curves for species associations of Geometroidea from the Mulu survey and New Caledonia as described in the text. *A* = upper montane; *B* = Api lower montane; *C* = Mulu lower montane; *D* = alluvial; *E* = dipterocarp; *F* = limestone; *G* = kerangas (open circles: exclusively kerangas); *H* = New Caledonian maquis; *I* = New Caledonian forest. Axes as in Fig. 25.1.

TABLE 25.2

Percentage representation (individuals) of the various species associations recognised for the Geometroidea and Arctiidae in the eighteen most important samples made during the survey of the Gunung Mulu National Park. Individuals of rare and unassigned species are excluded

Site	Location and formation	Alt. (m)	Geometroidea							Arctiidae					
			UMF	LMF Api	LMF Mulu	Dipt	Allv	Lst	Ker	UMF	LMF Mulu	LMF Api	Low-land	Lst+ker	Ker
			28	13	23	17	20	11	17	11	24	2	26	5	2
27	G. Api UMF	1500	55	4	14	4	8		15		62			38	
26	G. Api UMF	1200	34	17	10	23	8		8	11	22	45	22		
25	G. Api LMF	900	7	53	12	7	11		9		67	23	9	1	
23	G. Api Lowland Forest	250		8	2	17	15	34	24		15		59	26	
18	Melinau Gorge, riverine, limestone	100		5		24	30	24	17		7		93		
7	Base, alluvial, some limestone	50				7	35	8	49			6	88	6	
16	As 7 but canopy outlook	70		+	+	18	67	6	9		1	+	98	1	
17	Long Melinau, regenerating alluvial (10 yr)	50		3	4	33	52	5	3				98	2	
20	Western Melinau Gorge, kerangas	150		4	5	9	5	1	76		4		37	15	44
8	G. Mulu Dipterocarp canopy	150	+	2	3	65	17	4	9		4		95	1	
11	G. Mulu Dipt. understorey	150		4	8	35	18	6	29		29		59	9	3
13	G. Mulu Dipt. understorey	500	1	3	13	35	8	1	39		68		26	6	
14	G. Mulu LMF canopy	1000	9	7	52	23	6	+	3	1	91		8		
15	G. Mulu LMF understorey	1000	7	8	52	17	8	+	8	+	93		6	1	
1	G. Mulu UMF canopy	1790	86	1	2	2	6		3	93	6		1		
2	G. Mulu UMF understorey	1790	88	1	3	1	6		1	99	1				
3	G. Mulu UMF	1780	88	+	2	2	7		1	98	2				
5	G. Mulu UMF low facies	1780	97	1		1			1	99	1				

tion (open circles) and a slightly larger group well represented in most lowland forest understorey samples but particularly common in the kerangas. A contributory factor may be the presence of the highest density of understorey epiphytes together with a well-developed ground flora, perhaps a response to the somewhat more open canopy of this formation.

In Fig. 25.2 two associations of Geometroidea from New Caledonia (Holloway, 1979) are also plotted, one (I) from rain forest and the other (H) from a shrubby maquis association where the fauna has a strong Australian character. The former curve is of low diversity, almost exponential, but the latter is of the same order of diversity as the four Mulu lowland forest curves. Values of α for all macrolepidoptera are an order of magnitude higher for Bornean lowland forest samples compared with New Caledonian ones (Holloway, in press b). Comparison of the curves for the associations suggests that gamma diversity may contribute at least in part to the higher Bornean sample diversities observed.

A similar analysis for the Arctiidae classified the commoner species into three well-defined associations: lowland, lower montane and upper montane. The family was found to be poorly represented in montane zones on the limestone Gunung Api though two species were commonest in the lower montane zone there. The lowland species were distributed fairly evenly over the samples from alluvial, limestone and dipterocarp forest with some representation in the kerangas; a few showed preference for one or other type but the analysis did not reveal any strongly specific associations. There was, however, a small group of species assigned to a separate kerangas association, and another group was found in both kerangas and limestone forest. The rank/abundance curves for the three major associations are shown in Fig. 25.3 and the percentage representation of each association in major samples shown in Table 25.2. The upper montane association is clearly distinguished, the lowland limestone sample again has indications of γ diversity, and the lower montane association on Gunung Mulu extends more strongly into the upper elevations of the dipterocarp zone than does that for the Geometroidea.

The diversity curves are striking in that they are approximately linear rather than the incomplete

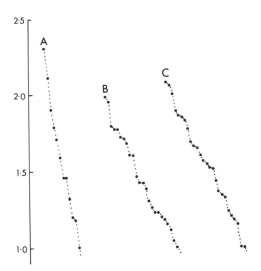

Fig. 25.3. Partial rank/abundance curves for species associations of Arctiidae from the Mulu survey. A = upper montane; B = lower montane; C = lowland. Axes as in Fig. 25.1.

log-normal sigmoids of Figs. 25.2 and 25.5. The lowland and lower montane plots are comparable in diversity, the evenness component of which might be regarded as the slope of the line, but that for the upper montane association indicates a much lower diversity.

A possible explanation is that this sort of linear plot is obtained when there is a degree of β diversity involved in the association — that is some sort of continuum. Different species may show dominance in different parts of the continuum such that the "upper tail" of the typical sigmoid curve disappears when samples of the association from across the continuum are pooled as they are in this case (though the suspected forest continuum in New Caledonia does not produce such a curve).

Plotting of rank/abundance curves for the arctiid lowland association within the three largest lowland samples tends to support this (Fig. 25.4). The curve for the alluvial forest sample (A) appears somewhat sigmoid whereas those for the dipterocarp forest (B) and limestone forest (C) still have a linear character. In each case the slope of the curve is steeper than that for the complete association from all samples pooled, indicating that extremes of abundance are reduced (evenness is increased) by the pooling. Changes in species rank order are also considerable between the three samples, averaging out at about a rank change of eight places per species in pairwise comparisons.

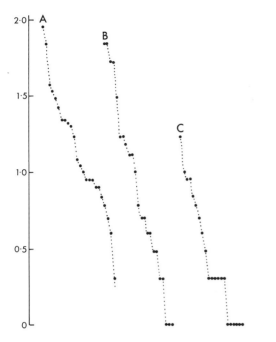

Fig. 25.4. Partial rank/abundance curves for species of the arctiid lowland association in three major lowland samples. A = alluvial, Site 16; B = dipterocarp, Site 8; C = limestone, Site 23. Axes as in Fig. 25.1.

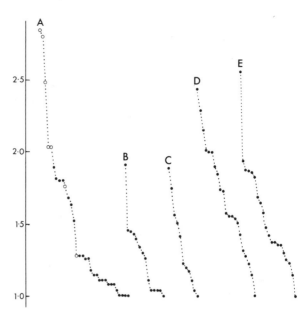

Fig. 25.5. Partial rank/abundance curves for species associations of Noctuidae from the Mulu survey. A = upper montane; B = lower montane; C = limestone; D = wide-ranging; E = lowland, mainly alluvial. Axes as in Fig. 25.1. Open circles in A are species suspected of hill-topping.

Only two species feature in the most abundant five for all three samples and only one further species has such rank in two samples.

The reason for the difference between the Arctiidae and the other two groups discussed here may lie in the dietary preferences of the family. Many Arctiinae are euryphagous and the Lithosiinae are probably either euryphagous defoliators or general moss and lichen browsers. Therefore the available resource base may appear more uniform, less discontinuous on a plant biochemical/floristic basis, leading to a continuum that may vary in response to other factors such as microclimate rather than discrete associations that reflect floristics. Once again there is a need for much more detailed information on the biological requirements of the insects and more intensive sampling programmes to investigate whether such differences are general within the tropics.

The analysis of data for the Noctuidae is still in progress but the main features are already apparent, with several associations recognised. Their rank/abundance curves are shown in Fig. 25.5. Associations are less clearly defined than in the other analyses, perhaps due to the greater mobility

of the species, and one large group (D) is recorded over a wide range of habitats from the lowlands to the upper montane zone. There is a large group (E) that was taken most abundantly in alluvial forest, less so in dipterocarp forest, a smaller group (C) associated with the limestone forest, a very small, weakly defined kerangas/understorey group (not plotted), a small lower montane assemblage (B) and a moderate upper montane one (A).

The upper montane association contains several Stictopterinae of the lineage associated with Guttiferae and several Chloephorinae of the *Carea* group of genera which are often recorded from Myrtaceae. Some of the more abundant species in this association (in *Amyna*, *Leucocosmia*, *Sasunaga*; open circles in the curve) could conceivably have been hill-topping from the lowlands, as discussed for Norfolk Island by Holloway (1977).

The species of the alluvial association are mostly from quadrifine subfamilies. Host-plant records for these species or very close relatives are distributed amongst plant families as follows: Sapindaceae (3); Euphorbiaceae, Guttiferae, Rubiaceae, Combretaceae (2); Leguminosae, Myrtaceae, Verbenaceae, Gramineae (1).

LEPIDOPTERA DIVERSITY AND PLANT DIVERSITY

It is evident from the analyses in the previous section that moth diversity in tropical rain forest is a highly complex subject and does not as yet proffer a clear indication of the extent to which herbivore diversity reflects plant diversity. In New Caledonia the evidence was strongly counter to this suggestion (Holloway, 1979). The most diverse and floristically distinctive association there had no moths that could be definitely associated with it and yielded light-trap samples of low diversity even on most favourable nights; a reason for this absence of defoliators in the Lepidoptera might be plant toxicity generated by accumulation of unusual metal ions (like, for instance, nickel) in the sap of many of the plants concerned.

The degree to which faunistic diversity might be expected to reflect floristic diversity will depend on the differential rates with which (a) plants develop toxins to enable them to escape predation, and (b) insects evolve physiological mechanisms to cope with new toxins. A one-to-one relationship would only be expected if these rates were intrinsically uniform and in balance with each other. Within such a uniform system one might expect a high degree of coevolutionary specificity as host switching and evolution of euryphagy might be limited by diffuse competition. In such a system imbalance of rate between (a) and (b) would lead to the eventual extirpation of one component, as may have happened in one plant association in New Caledonia.

In effect rates (a) and (b) are undoubtedly intrinsically variable but, because both herbivores and plant prey are successful today, are in balance on average. In such a situation one would expect to find parts of the taxonomic spectrum of each component gaining a "head start" and perhaps undergoing competitive release and some sort of explosive speciation as is seen in some island situations, other parts locally "in balance" with rates more uniform, matching and perhaps with a high degree of coevolutionary specificity, and at the other extreme a scattering of rare components with negative success rates (cf. Holloway, 1977, pp. 230–233). Such a system might well lead to the sort of relationship between plants and butterflies described by Vane-Wright (1978) where butterflies tend to be found on the larger, more diverse plant families that present greater "target areas"; he suggested that plant radiation precedes herbivore occupation rather than being "driven" by it.

Perhaps one can identify the Dipterocarpaceae with their low load of Lepidoptera defoliators as a plant group that is ahead in at least part of the contest, and the geometrid subfamily Ennominae, one of the most abundant and diverse groups in the Bornean fauna with a relatively high degree of euryphagy, as an insect group that is ahead.

There are no Bornean data to permit ranking of plant families according to how often they are favoured as moth larval pabula. The closest one might come to such a sample at present could be found in a mass of unpublished records made by T.R.D. Bell in southern India, the typescript of which is now in the British Museum (Natural History). It appears that he encouraged local people to bring him larvae and their hosts; many records refer to arboreal feeders.

The majority of records are of moth genera and species also found in Borneo. If the number of records for each plant family are totted up for Bornean taxa in Geometridae and Noctuidae they are ranked as in Table 25.3. Records collected from throughout the Indo-Australian tropics mainly in the course of agriculture and forestry practice are accumulated by the Commonwealth Institute of Entomology Lepidoptera taxonomists. These provide a similar picture but are less numerous. Records for the Bombycoidea families

TABLE 25.3

Plant families most frequently recorded as host-plants for Noctuidae and Geometridae in southern India by Bell, restricted to Lepidoptera species shared with Borneo. The numbers in brackets refer to the number of species recorded

Noctuidae	Geometridae
Leguminosae (30)	Leguminosae (10)
Combretaceae (19)	Lauraceae (10)
Menispermaceae (10)	Rubiaceae (9)
Ebenaceae (9)	Anacardiaceae (4)
Sapindaceae (8)	Myrtaceae (3)
Myrtaceae (7)	Apocynaceae (3)
Tiliaceae (7)	Melastomataceae (3)
Guttiferae (6)	
Euphorbiaceae (5)	
Anacardiaceae (5)	
Sterculiaceae (5)	
Malvaceae (5)	

with comparisons with Janzen's (1984) observations in Costa Rica may be found in Holloway (in press b).

The list from Bell's data and that for the species of the large lowland alluvial noctuid association referred to earlier bear no relationship to the rankings of these families according to their importance in Bornean rain-forest types (Table 25.1). Allowing for the fact that the Bell sample may be biassed according to human access to certain types of plant such as shrubs or saplings and that the ranking may be closer to the plant family importance ranking in southern Indian forest, it nevertheless does offer some explanation of relative moth diversities in Bornean lowland forests. For the Noctuidae (emphatically) and the Geometoidea (slightly) the alluvial forest association is the most diverse. It is this forest type that is least dominated by Dipterocarpaceae, shows most evidence of defoliation and has the highest diversity of "preferred pabula", especially Leguminosae which are particularly favoured by Noctuidae.

Another indication of the low level of Lepidoptera defoliators on Dipterocarpaceae is provided by data collected by N.E. Stork in Brunei. He collected insects from individual tree crowns by fogging them with insecticide. A preliminary sorting of the Lepidoptera larvae by I.J. Kitching has resulted in the data presented in Table 25.4.

It can be seen from these data that the non-dipterocarps have the highest defoliator load, though that on the two *Pentaspadon* crowns was mostly due to one lymantriid species. *Castanopsis* yielded the highest diversity. Within the data for the two *Shorea* species there is a strong indication of a correlation between the presence of lianes and a high defoliator load, suggesting that the larvae were feeding on the lianes rather than the tree.

Further data for a wider range of plant families from canopy fogging would be very valuable in elucidating the relationships between plant and Lepidoptera diversity, though the scope for identification of the larvae to more than a very general level is at present very much limited by the state of the taxonomy.

Bell probably did not collect much in montane forests, hence assessment of tropical Fagaceae as host-plants for Lepidoptera is not possible unless one can extrapolate to the Tropics the temperate faunistic richness associated with this family and the indications in Table 25.4. Substitution of Fagaceae for Dipterocarpaceae, greater emphasis of Myrtaceae and Guttiferae and development of a

TABLE 25.4

Numbers of Lepidoptera larvae obtained from the insecticidal fogging of ten tree crowns in alluvial rain forest in Brunei by N.E. Stork. The trees are ranked according to numbers of larvae produced

Tree	Noctuidae, Quadrifinae (semi-looper)	Lymantriidae species 1	Other Lymantriidae	"Hairy" Noctuoidea, ?mainly Arctiidae	Geometridae	Limacodidae	Others, including unidentified first instars	Total
Pentaspadon motleyi (Anacardiaceae); no lianes	6	70	3	4	–	2	13	99
Castanopsis sp. (Fagaceae); no lianes	24	–	29	5	4	2	31	95
Pentaspadon motleyi; several lianes	17	30	4	8	–	2	24	85
Shorea johorensis (= *leptoclados*) (Dipterocarpaceae); large lianes present	18	–	3	7	–	1	33	62
S. johorensis; large lianes present	16	–	4	9	5	–	18	52
Unidentified; no lianes	32	–	4	5	–	1	6	48
Shorea macrophylla; epiphytes, ferns, some lianes	7	–	2	8	6	1	18	42
S. macrophylla; one small liane	4	1	2	2	2	–	29	40
S. johorensis; no lianes	4	–	3	1	2	1	4	15
S. johorensis; no lianes	2	–	2	2	–	–	6	12

shrub layer that includes Rubiaceae and Melastomataceae may mean the lower, and to some extent the upper, montane forests provide a greater resource base for defoliating Lepidoptera which leads to greater alpha diversity.

There may be another reason for greater α diversity in the tropical montane forests of Borneo. Firstly, the centres of species richness for a majority of butterfly genera, and probably also moth genera, are outside the tropics in the northeastern Himalaya (Holloway, 1969, 1974). Secondly, during the glaciations the altitudinal vegetational zones on mountains in the Indo-Australian tropics may have been depressed by from 500 to 1000 m (Flenley, 1979), bringing the Bornean lower montane forest almost down to the lowlands and possibly restricting the dipterocarp-dominated forest to refugia. If this occurred, then the relatively high diversity in montane forests could be explained in terms of the relative areas of the two broad habitat types in South-East Asia in the recent past.

Much more effort is needed to survey habitat preference, delimit associations and obtain host-plant records for Lepidoptera in order to provide a firm basis for testing the conjecture presented in this paper.

ZOOGEOGRAPHY

In both Africa and South America the tropical rain forest exists on a large continental area with, excepting the Andes, a relatively old cratonic landscape broken up by the basins of large, mature rivers. In both there has been a recent succession of arid and pluvial periods. In arid periods the forest is thought to have retreated to refugia, small areas where a wetter climate favoured its persistence, and from where it expands again in pluvials to coalesce over the equatorial tropics as a whole. In such circumstances one might expect the evolution of polytypic genera with groups of localised species distributed in a one to one relationship with the refugia. The phyletic relationships within such species groups might be expected to show a common pattern that reflects the course of fragmentation of a more or less continuous tract of forest into refugia isolated from each other by varying distances and over varying lengths of time.

Such a hypothesis is open to testing by the methods of vicariance biogeography (Nelson and Platnick, 1981), as may be illustrated by the two groups of heliconiine butterflies studied by Turner (1983).

Even during pluvial periods with tropical rain forest extensive, its quality may vary throughout its extent and the expansion of species from the refugia may be only partial. The refugia might therefore be expected to exhibit greater alpha diversity at their permanent centres than in peripheral, recolonised localities. Light-trap sampling of moths along a transect from the recolonised periphery to the presumed permanent centre of a refugial system might enable this to be tested.

In the Indo-Australian tropics the situation is much more complicated as most of the landscape is of extreme relief: young mountain systems deeply dissected by vigorous streams and rivers. The central and eastern part is fragmented into numerous islands of which the tectonic history has not yet been satisfactorily resolved; indeed zoogeographic data may be useful in weighing up rival theories of island arc tectonics (Holloway, in press a). Superimposed on this geological complexity are the effects of recent climatic fluctuations, seen both in the exposure of continental shelves such as the Sunda and Sahul to unite groups of islands with each other and with the cratonic mainlands, and in the depression and elevation of vegetation belts mentioned earlier.

I have tried over the past decade and a half to address some aspects of this complexity in studies of Lepidoptera zoogeography: general patterns of faunistic similarity and discontinuity (Holloway and Jardine, 1968); identification of common patterns of distribution in species and, with assessment of centres of richness, genera (Holloway, 1969, 1973, 1974, 1979); the zoogeography of montane faunas (Holloway, 1970, 1986a); the relationships of species within genera to each other and to alternative hypotheses of past geography (Holloway, 1973, 1979, 1982, 1983b, 1984c, in press a). Despite recent writings of the vicariance and panbiogeographic schools I find no reason to alter my concept of the development of the rain-forest biota of the Indo-Australian tropics in terms of colonisation of newly emergent island groups by elements from the South-East Asian mainland and, to a variably lesser extent, from geologically older areas of Australasia (Australia, New Caledonia, probably southeastern New Guinea and possibly, in a very minor way, Fiji). The predominantly west to east dispersal of plants and animals implied by this is apparent even in distribution patterns that are probably of relatively recent origin (Holloway, 1982, 1985a). Indeed the vicariance and panbiogeographic methodologies may provide additional means for examining the colonialist hypothesis (Holloway, 1983, 1984c).

Very few animal groups, let alone Lepidoptera taxa, have been analysed in sufficient, essentially cladistic detail (Holloway, 1982; Duffels, 1983) to provide a good sample of patterns for the Indo-Australian tropics. Frequently encountered, but geographically contradictory distribution patterns (or perhaps Croizatian tracks) might, if one were able to establish a time sequence for their origin, provide a series of snapshots of past geography in terms of area relationships. There are indications that some groups may reflect the evolution of Melanesia as two island arcs, now partially convergent and, in New Guinea, fused (Holloway, 1979, 1984c; Duffels, 1983). Others may indicate, in more recent times, a route of colonisation for Polynesia from Melanesia that excludes Fiji (Robinson, 1975; Holloway, 1983b).

Groups indicating a relationship between the Philippines, Sulawesi and the Lesser Sundas, reviewed by Holloway (1984c, in press a), need further investigation to establish the historical relationships of Sulawesi, itself probably geologically heterogeneous, with lands to the east and west. Has the island been a main route for faunal exchange, a cross-roads or a side track? For montane faunas it may have been a main route (Holloway, 1970) but the situation for lowland taxa is not so clear (Holloway and Jardine, 1968; Holloway, 1973, in press a).

The large island of New Guinea has a moth fauna that has exhibited a high degree of endemic speciation of taxa that appear to have been derived partly from the northwest and partly from within Australasia. A large number of these species complexes have all their members brightly coloured, though often their closest relatives are Asian, much more drab and nocturnal. Presumably they are day-flying but more information on their biology is needed. Many of these groups appear to belong to mimicry rings and are drawn from a wide range of moth families. Mimicry and mimicry complexes involving moths elsewhere in the Indo-Australian tropics are far less frequent and are found most particularly in the Zygaenidae (Chalcosiinae). The situation in New Guinea begins to approach in complexity that observed in parts of the Neotropical rain forest (Papageorgis, 1975). The taxonomic relationships of these colourful groups are only just beginning to be elucidated (Holloway, 1984c) and the field behaviour has yet to be studied, but the phenomenon could provide a fascinating example of parallel evolution of a rather complex biological phenomenon or at least its intensification. What are the factors in common between the Neotropical forests and those in New Guinea?

MOTHS AS INDICATORS

Moths provide one of the most accessible faunistic components of tropical rain forest in terms of the geographical breadth of material available, the degree to which it has been worked taxonomically and the ease with which large samples can be obtained and quantified. More work is needed on the effects of bias in the light-trapping technique: for example what is the effect of moon phase on the shape of the rank/abundance curve in samples for a species association? But elucidation of the bias, if any, is unlikely to alter the picture presented here of the degree of specificity between moth associations and vegetation zones and the relevance of the floristics of the vegetation to the species that are found there. Much more information is needed on the host-plants of Lepidoptera species and this can best be achieved by workers stationed for a long period in the tropics rather than by ephemeral expeditions.

Once the relationship between moth associations and vegetation in any area has been established then it may be possible to monitor changes in that vegetation due to climatic fluctuations or the activities of man by sampling the moth population periodically. On Norfolk Island a relationship between departure of rainfall from the monthly mean and the equitability component in the diversity of a moth association has been discovered (Holloway, 1977, 1983c) but records from other areas are needed to test whether this effect is general. A monitoring technique of this nature might also be valuable in the sort of experimental approach being pioneered by Lovejoy et al. (1983) in their investigations of ecosystem decay in isolates of rain forest of different size in Amazonia; the work is directed at discovering the minimal critical size of reserve necessary to maintain tropical rain forest at close to its characteristic diversity.

ACKNOWLEDGEMENTS

I would like to thank the Royal Geographical Society, the Sarawak Government and all those connected with the Gunung Mulu Expedition for facilitating my field programme there. This programme was financed by a Government Scientific Investigations Grant, administered by the Royal Society.

I am very grateful to N.E. Stork and I.J. Kitching for allowing me to publish the data on Lepidoptera larvae from tree crown fogging, and to L.M. Cook for help in computing the Mulu data. R.I. Vane-Wright and T.C. Whitmore kindly read through an earlier draft of this paper and provided some useful comments.

REFERENCES

Anderson, J.A.R. and Chai, P.P.K., 1983 (dated 1982). Vegetation. In: A.C. Jermy and K.P. Kavanagh (Editors), Gunung Mulu National Park, Sarawak. Sarawak Mus. J., Special Issue 2 (Part I), 30: 195–223.

Arms, K., Feeny, P. and Lederhouse, R.C., 1974. Sodium: stimulus for puddling behaviour by tiger swallowtail butterflies, Papilio glaucus. Science, 185: 372–374.

Bänziger, H., 1972. Biologie der lacriphagen Lepidopteren in Thailand und Malaya. Rev. Suisse Zool., 79: 2181–2269.

Bänziger, H., 1982. Fruit-piercing moths (Lep., Noctuidae) in Thailand: a general survey and some new perspectives. Mitt. Schweiz. Entomol. Ges., 55: 213–240.

Bell, T.R.D. and Scott, F.B., 1937. Sphingidae. Moths Vol. V. In: R.B.S. Sewell (Editor), The Fauna of British India Including Ceylon and Burma. Taylor and Francis, London, pp. 1–537.

Bourlière, F., 1983. Animal species diversity in tropical forests. In: F.B. Golley (Editor), Tropical Rain Forest Ecosystems, Structure and Function. (Ecosystems of the World, 14A) Elsevier, Amsterdam, pp. 77–91.

Collenette, C.L., 1934. On the sexes of some South American moths attracted to light, human perspiration and damp sand. Entomologist, 67: 81–84.

Collins, N.M., Holloway, J.D. and Proctor, J., 1984. Notes on

the ascent and natural history of Gunung Api, a limestone mountain in Sarawak. Sarawak Mus. J., 33.54 (NS): 219–234.

Duffels, J.P., 1983. Distribution patterns of Oriental Cicadoidea (Homoptera) east of Wallace's Line and plate tectonics. GeoJournal, 7: 491–498.

Ehrlich, P.R. and Raven, P.H., 1965. Butterflies and plants: a study in coevolution. Evolution, 18: 586–608.

Flenley, J.R., 1979. The Equatorial Rain Forest: a Geological History. Butterworths, London, 162 pp.

Hegnauer, R., 1966. Chemotaxonomie der Pflanzen, Vol. 4. Birkhäuser, Basel.

Holloway, J.D., 1967. Studies and suggestions on the behaviour of moths at light. Proc. South London Entomol. Nat. Hist. Soc., 1967: 31–45.

Holloway, J.D., 1969. A numerical investigation of the biogeography of the butterfly fauna of India, and its relation to continental drift. Biol. J. Linn. Soc., 1: 373–385.

Holloway, J.D., 1970. The biogeographical analysis of a transect sample of the moth fauna of Mt. Kinabalu, Sabah, using numerical methods. Biol. J. Linn. Soc., 2: 259–286.

Holloway, J.D., 1973. The taxonomy of four groups of butterflies (Lepidoptera) in relation to general patterns of butterfly distribution in the Indo-Australian area. Trans. R. Entomol. Soc. London, 125: 125–176.

Holloway, J.D., 1974. The biogeography of Indian butterflies. In: M.S. Mani (Editor), Ecology and Biogeography in India. Junk, The Hague, pp. 473–499.

Holloway, J.D., 1976. Moths of Borneo with Special Reference to Mt. Kinabalu. Malayan Nature Society, Kuala Lumpur.

Holloway, J.D., 1977. The Lepidoptera of Norfolk Island, their Biogeography and Ecology. (Series Entomologica, 13) Junk, The Hague, pp. 1–291.

Holloway, J.D., 1979. A Survey of the Lepidoptera, Biogeography and Ecology of New Caledonia. (Series Entomologica, 15) Junk, The Hague, pp. 1–588.

Holloway, J.D., 1982. Mobile organisms in a geologically complex area: Lepidoptera in the Indo-Australian tropics. Zool. J. Linn. Soc., 76: 353–373.

Holloway, J.D., 1983a. The moths of Borneo: Family Notodontidae. Malay. Nat. J., 37: 1–107.

Holloway, J.D., 1983b. The biogeography of the macrolepidoptera of south-eastern Polynesia. GeoJournal, 7: 517–525.

Holloway, J.D., 1983c. Insect surveys — an approach to environmental monitoring. Atti XII Congresso Nazionale Italiano di Entomologia, Roma, 1980, 1: 239–261.

Holloway, J.D., 1984a. Notes on the butterflies of the Gunung Mulu National Park. In: A.C. Jermy and K.P. Kavanagh (Editors), Gunung Mulu National Park, Sarawak, Part II. Sarawak Mus. J., 30: 89–131.

Holloway, J.D., 1984b. The larger moths of the Gunung Mulu National Park; a preliminary assessment of their distribution, ecology, and potential as environmental indicators. In: A.C. Jermy and K.P. Kavanagh (Editors), Gunung Mulu National Park, Sarawak, Part II. Sarawak Mus. J., 30: 149–190.

Holloway, J.D., 1984c. Lepidoptera and the Melanesian Arcs. In: F.J. Radovsky, P.H. Raven and S.H. Sohmer (Editors), Biogeography of the Tropical Pacific. Bishop Mus., Spec. Publ., 72: 129–169.

Holloway, J.D., 1985a. The moths of Borneo: Family Noctuidae: Subfamilies Euteliinae, Stictopterinae, Plusiinae and Pantheinae. *Malay. Nat. J.*, 38: 157–317.

Holloway, J.D., 1985b. Moths as indicator organisms for categorising rain forest and monitoring changes and regeneration processes. In: A.C. Chadwick and S.L. Sutton (Editors), *Tropical Rain-Forest: The Leeds Symposium.* Spec. Publ., Leeds. Philos. Lit. Soc., pp. 235–242.

Holloway, J.D., 1986a. Origins of lepidopteran faunas in high mountains of the Indo-Australian tropics. In: M. Monasterio and F. Vuilleumier (Editors), *High Altitude Tropical Biogeography*. Oxford Univ. Press, New York, N.Y., pp. 533–556.

Holloway, J.D., 1986b. The moths of Borneo: key to families; families Cossidae, Metarbelidae, Ratardidae, Dudgeoneidae, Epipyropidae and Limacodidae. *Malay. Nat. J.*, 40: 1–166.

Holloway, J.D. 1987a. Macrolepidoptera diversity in the Indo-Australian tropics: geographic biotropic and taxonomic variations. *Biol. J. Linn. Soc.*, 30: 325–341.

Holloway, J.D., 1987b. Bracken-feeding Geometridae in the genus *Idiodes* Guenée, 1857, and allied taxa in the tribe Lithini (Lepidoptera). *Tinea*, 12 (suppl.): 242–248.

Holloway, J.D., in press a. Lepidoptera patterns involving Sulawesi: what do they indicate of the past geography? In: T.C. Whitmore (Editor), *Biogeographical Evolution of the Malay Archipelago*. Oxford Univ. Press, London.

Holloway, J.D., in press b. *The moths of Borneo: Superfamily Bombycoidea: families Lasiocampidae, Eupterotidae, Bombycidae, Brahmaeidae, Saturniidae, Sphingidae*. Southdene, Kuala Lumpur, 200 pp.

Holloway, J.D. and Hebert, P.D.N., 1979. Ecological and taxonomic trends in macrolepidopteran host plant selection. *Biol. J. Linn. Soc.*, 11: 229–251.

Holloway, J.D. and Jardine, N., 1968. Two approaches to zoogeography: a study based on the distributions of butterflies, birds and bats in the Indo-Australian area. *Proc. Linn. Soc. London*, 179: 153–188.

Holloway, J.D. and Sommerer, M.D., 1984. Spolia Sumatrensia: three new Geometrinae. *Heterocera Sumatrana*, 2: 20–25.

Janzen, D.H., 1983a. Food webs: who eats what, why, how, and with what effects in a tropical forest? In: F.B. Golley (Editor), *Tropical Rain Forest Ecosystems, Structure and Function*. (Ecosystems of the World, 14A) Elsevier, Amsterdam, pp. 167–182.

Janzen, D.H., 1983b. Insects: Introduction. In: D.H. Janzen (Editor), *Costa Rican Natural History*. Univ. of Chicago Press, Chicago, Ill., pp. 619–645.

Janzen, D.H., 1984. Two ways to be a tropical big moth: Santa Rosa saturniids and sphingids. Oxford Surv. *Evol. Biol.*, 1: 85–140.

Lovejoy, T.E., Bierregaard, R.O., Rankin, J. and Schubart, H.O.R., 1983. Ecological dynamics of tropical forest fragments. In: S.L. Sutton, T.C. Whitmore and A.C. Chadwick (Editors), *Tropical Rain Forest: Ecology and Management*. Blackwell, Oxford, pp. 377–384.

May, R.M., 1975. Patterns of species abundance and diversity. In: M.L. Cody and J.M. Diamond (Editors), *Ecology and Evolution of Communities*. Harvard Univ. Press,

Cambridge, Mass., pp. 81–120.

Moulds, M.S., 1981. Larval food plants of hawk moths (Lepidoptera: Sphingidae) affecting commercial crops in Australia. *Gen. Appl. Entomol.*, 13: 69–80.

Nelson, G. and Platnick, N., 1981. *Systematics and Biogeography, Cladistics and Vicariance*. Columbia Univ. Press, New York, N.Y.

Norris, M.J., 1936. The feeding habits of the adult Lepidoptera Heteroneura. *Trans. R. Entomol. Soc. London*, 85: 61–91.

Papageorgis, C., 1975. Mimicry in Neotropical butterflies. *Am. Sci.*, 63: 522–532.

Proctor, J., Anderson, J.M., Chai, P. and Vallack, H.W., 1983a. Ecological studies in four contrasting lowland forests in Gunung Mulu National Park, Sarawak, I. Forest environment, structure and floristics. *J. Ecol.*, 71: 237–260.

Proctor, J., Anderson, J.M., Fogden, S.C.L. and Vallack, H.W., 1983b. Ecological studies in four contrasting lowland forests in Gunung Mulu National Park, Sarawak, II. Litterfall, litter standing crop and preliminary observations on herbivory. *J. Ecol.*, 71: 261–283.

Robinson, G.S., 1975. *Macrolepidoptera of Fiji and Rotuma, a Taxonomic and Geographic Study*. Classey, Faringdon, 422 pp.

Sugihara, G., 1980. Minimal community structure: an explanation of species abundance patterns. *Am. Nat.*, 116: 770–787.

Sutton, S.L., 1979. The vertical distribution of flying insects in the lowland rain forest of Brunei: preliminary report. *Brunei Mus. J.*, 1979: 161–173.

Sutton, S.L., 1983. The spatial distribution of flying insects in tropical rain forests. In: S.L. Sutton, T.C. Whitmore and A.C. Chadwick (Editors), *Tropical Rain Forest: Ecology and Management*. Blackwell, Oxford, pp. 77–91.

Sutton, S.L. and Hudson, P.J., 1980. The vertical distribution of small flying insects in the lowland rain forest of Zaire. *Zool. J. Linn. Soc.*, 68: 111–123.

Turner, J.R.G., 1983. Mimetic butterflies and punctuated equilibria: some old light on a new paradigm. *Biol. J. Linn. Soc.*, 20: 277–300.

Vane-Wright, R.I., 1978. Ecological and behavioural origins of diversity in butterflies. In: L.A. Mound and N. Waloff (Editors), *Diversity of Insect Faunas*. Symp. R. Entomol. Soc. London, 9: 56–70.

Waage, J.K. and Best, R.C., 1985. Arthropod associates of Sloths. In: G.G. Montgomery (Editor), *The Evolution and Ecology of Armadillos, Sloths and Vermilinguas*. Smithsonian Institution Press, Washington, D.C., pp. 297–311.

Waterman, P.G., 1983. Distribution of secondary metabolites in rain forest plants: towards an understanding of cause and effect. In: S.L. Sutton, T.C. Whitmore and A.C. Chadwick (Editors), *Tropical Rain Forest: Ecology and Management*. Blackwell, Oxford, pp. 167–179.

Whitmore, T.C., 1982. Wallace's Line: a result of plate tectonics. *Ann. M. Bot. Gard.*, 69: 668–675.

Wolda, H., 1983a. Spatial and temporal variation in abundance in tropical animals. In: S.L. Sutton, T.C. Whitmore and A.C. Chadwick (Editors), *Tropical Rain Forest: Ecology and Management*. Blackwell, Oxford, pp. 93–105.

Wolda, H., 1983b. Diversity, diversity indices and tropical cockroaches. *Oecologia*, 58: 290–298.

Chapter 26

TERMITES

N.M. COLLINS

INTRODUCTION

In rain forests termites (Isoptera) are abundant but secretive insects, usually concealing and protecting themselves in the soil or in nests and foraging galleries. Most species live underground or inside dead wood, but a few build bizarre mounds and arboreal nests unlike any other constructions in the animal kingdom. Their ability to feed on dead plant materials makes them an extremely important component of the forest (Golley, 1983).

Termites are eusocial insects with colonies of a few hundred to a maximum of seven million individuals (Spragg and Paton, 1980). One reproductive king and queen, or sometimes several pairs, are tended by sterile workers and soldiers. Queens of more advanced termites can lay up to 30 000 eggs per day. Flying reproductives are released for the short nuptial flight which precedes the founding of new colonies. Good introductions to termites may be found in Harris (1961) and Wilson (1971), while research on the biology, behaviour, physiology and ecology of termites has been summarized by Krishna and Weesner (1969, 1970), Lee and Wood (1971), Brian (1978) and Hermann (1979–1982). None of these specifically consider termites in rain forests, but all give information about forest species.

Tropical rain forests are the stronghold of the Isoptera. There are 2331 described species worldwide (Wood and Johnson, 1984), with more found in rain forest than in any other biome. Faunistic information is available for all the rain-forest blocks. Queensland, Australia, has only four common species and these, plus the termites of Madagascar and Oceania (including New Guinea)

have not been studied since the reviews in Krishna and Weesner (1970). The discussion that follows will therefore be restricted to the three continental rain-forest blocks of the Neotropics, the Afrotropics and the Orient.

ZOOGEOGRAPHY AND FAUNISTICS

In the Isoptera, important evolutionary advances have developed on two main fronts: (1) entering into mutualistic associations with Protozoa, bacteria and fungi, thereby acquiring the capacity to fix atmospheric nitrogen and improve digestion and assimilation of plant materials; and (2) methods of defence, including anatomical and morphological adaptations of soldiers and workers and development of the capacity to build protective structures (Table 26.1).

There are seven living families of termites (Grassé, 1949), all of which had evolved and dispersed to the major tropical areas by late Mesozoic times (Emerson, 1952). Six of these families are known collectively as the "lower termites" and have mutualistic Protozoa living in their hindguts (Table 26.1). These flagellates are vital to the termites since without them they are unable to digest the cellulose that is a major component of their diet (Breznak, 1982). In addition to Protozoa, all families that have been studied can fix atmospheric nitrogen by virtue of facultative, anaerobic bacteria in the hindgut (Table 26.1) (Breznak, 1982; Collins, 1983a).

The Mastotermitidae, Termopsidae and Hodotermitidae do not occur in rain forest. The Serritermitidae includes only one little-known species found in wooded savannas in Brazil (Emerson and Krishna, 1975).

TABLE 26.1

The nomenclature of termites, with estimated numbers of living genera and described species (after Grassé, 1949; Wood and Johnson, 1986), their mutualistic associations (after Breznak, 1982), and their main defensive strategies (after Deligne et al., 1981)

Families	Number of genera									Number of species	Mutualistic associations	Primary defences
	total	Afr	Mal	Neo	Ori	Oce	Aus	Nea	Pal			
Lower termites												
Mastotermitidae	1	0	0	0	0	0	1	0	0	1	Protozoa, bacteria	Simple nests, mandibulate soldiers, salivary glands
Kalotermitidae	21	9	19	12	9	6	8	8	4	350	Protozoa, bacteria	Simple nests, mandibulate (biting, reaping) and phragmotic soldiers
Termopsidae	5	2	0	1	2	0	2	1	0	17	Protozoa, bacteria	Simple nests, mandibulate (biting) soldiers
Hodotermitidae	3	2	0	0	1	0	0	0	3	17	Protozoa, bacteria (?)	Simple or complex nests, mandibulate (biting) soldiers
Rhinotermitidae	14	4	4	7	10	3	4	3	3	206	Protozoa, bacteria	Simple nests, mandibulate soldiers (1/2 castes), frontal glands
Serritermitidae	1	0	0	1	0	0	0	0	0	1	Protozoa, bacteria (?)	Simple nest, mandibulate soldiers, soldier gut ruptures
Higher termites												
Termitidae												
Apicotermitinae	40	32	0	4	6	0	0	1	0	169	Bacteria	Simple nests, mandibulate (reaping) and phragmotic soldiers, worker gut ruptures
Termitinae	71	36	4	18	18	3	10	2	4	639	Bacteria	Simple or complex nests, mandibulate (reaping or snapping) soldiers, soldier gut ruptures (*Globitermes*), frontal glands
Macrotermitinae	13	11	1	0	5	0	0	0	0	288	Fungi, bacteria	Complex nests, mandibulate (reaping) soldiers (1/2 castes), salivary glands, labral glands (?)
Nasutitermitinae	67	12	4	25	23	3	6	1	0	543	Bacteria	Simple or complex nests, nasute soldiers, frontal gland, chemical defence
Totals	236									2231		

The Kalotermitidae (dry wood termites; for instance, *Glyptotermes*, *Kalotermes*, *Neotermes*) are often difficult to find, but probably occur in small numbers in all rain forests. They are virtually confined to dead limbs and trunks in the canopy, perhaps as a result of competitive exclusion by the more advanced Termitidae. They may also be found on the forest floor after tree-falls.

The most important family of lower termites in rain forests is the Rhinotermitidae (damp wood termites), which probably evolved in the Oriental region (Emerson, 1955). They feed mainly in standing or fallen trunks and limbs. *Coptotermes* and *Heterotermes* are tropicopolitan, the latter introduced in modern times to Ethiopia from Central America (Bouillon, 1970). *Parrhinotermes* and *Schedorhinotermes* are important in the Indo-malayan forests, the latter having reached Africa but not Madagascar. *Dolichorhinotermes* and *Rhinotermes* are widespread in the Neotropics.

Over 73% of termite species are in the higher termite family Termitidae (Table 26.1) and in terms of species richness and population density they predominate in all tropical rain forests (Table 26.2). The family probably arose from rhinotermitid ancestors and is divided into four subfamilies (Sands, 1972), each with specialist feeding and defensive strategies. The evolution and dispersal of these subfamilies during the Cretaceous and Tertiary eras has been an important formative factor in the nature of present forest faunas (Emerson, 1955). At least three of the subfamilies had differentiated by mid-Cretaceous, before the Old and New World tropics were separated (Emerson and Krishna, 1975), but in terms of genera the present-day distribution of the subfamilies between continents is very uneven (see below).

The Termitidae do not harbour unusual Protozoa, but use either anaerobic bacterial cultures in their hindguts, or mutualistic fungi grown on their faeces (Macrotermitinae only), to assist their digestive processes. Representatives of the Termitinae and the Nasutitermitinae have been shown to harbour nitrogen-fixing bacteria, but the Macrotermitinae do not appear to have this capacity. The Apicotermitinae have not yet been investigated (Breznak, 1982; Collins, 1983a).

The soil-feeding subfamily Apicotermitinae probably has an Afrotropical origin, but it is absent from Madagascar (Table 26.1). There are two branches based on *Apicotermes* and *Anoplotermes* (Sands, 1972), the latter including the soldierless termites, a significant component of both forest and savanna soils (Sands, 1972; Mathews, 1977; Wood et al., 1982). Their taxonomy is difficult; the Afrotropical soldierless termites have been revised and divided between sixteen new genera (Sands, 1972) and the Neotropical *Anoplotermes* awaits similar treatment (Mathews, 1977). *Ruptitermes* from Brazil is unusual in feeding in the open on leaf litter and lichens (Mathews, 1977; Mill, 1982a). In the Orient the soldierless termites are represented only by one questionable record from India (Roonwal, 1970; Krishna, 1970). Six other genera (with the soldier caste) from the *Anoplotermes* branch are to be found, but they are all rare on the mainland and absent from the South-East Asian islands. The fourteen genera in the Apicotermes branch are all Afrotropical (Sands, 1972; Collins, 1977b) and confined to rain forest, living in soil or very rotten wood and feeding on soil.

The second subfamily of the Termitidae, the Termitinae (sensu Sands, 1972), includes both wood-feeding and soil-feeding species that are important components of rain-forest faunas. The wood-feeding branch is primitive and formerly constituted a separate subfamily, the Amitermitinae, now reduced to synonymy with the Termitinae (Sands, 1972). With seven genera endemic to the Orient, their origin may lie there, but this is far from clearly established (Krishna, 1970). Two large genera, *Amitermes* and *Microcerotermes*, are tropicopolitan, and a number of smaller genera are endemic to the Afrotropics (e.g. *Cephalotermes*), the Neotropics (e.g. *Cylindrotermes*) and the Orient (e.g. *Globitermes*) (Krishna, 1970). The predominantly soil-feeding branch of the Termitinae probably evolved during the Cretaceous from wood-feeding ancestors in tropical Africa (Emerson, 1955). The genera fall into two groups, one with biting mandibles in the soldier (for instance, *Cubitermes*, *Noditermes*, *Procubitermes*) and the other with snapping mandibles (for instance, *Dicuspiditermes*, *Neocapritermes*, *Procapritermes*, *Termes*). The former is believed to be more primitive and has diverged widely in Africa, but failed to reach South America or the Orient. The group with snapping mandibles has diverged widely in all regions.

TABLE 26.2.

Taxonomic composition and diet structure of termite communities from various tropical forests, with a savanna community for comparison

Locality	Type of vegetation	Author	Lat.	Long.	Annual rainfall (mm)	Number of species feeding on[1]				Number of species						Total
						grass and grass litter	fresh wood and leaf litter	rotten wood and leaf litter	soil	Kalotermitidae	Rhinotermitidae	Termitinae	Apicotermitinae	Macrotermitinae	Nasutitermitinae	
Mokwa, Nigeria	Woodland in Southern Guinea savanna	Collins (1977c) Wood et al. (1977)	9°N	5°E	1175	7	11	4	9	0	1	9	3	11	7	31
Rabba, Nigeria	Riparian forest in savanna	Wood et al. (1982)	9°N	5°E	1100	0	7	7	19	0	2	14	7	7	3	33
Ibadan, Nigeria	Semi-deciduous forest	Wood et al. (1982)	7.5°N	4°E	1270	0	9	8	14	0	2	9	6	9	5	31
Douala-Edea, Cameroon	Lowland rain forest	Collins (1977a)	3.5°N	10°E	3000	0	5	7	31	0	1	25	9	5	3	43
Pasoh Forest, Pen. Malaysia	Lowland dipterocarp rain forest	Abe (1978)	3°N	102°E	2000	0	12	31	14	0	6	19	0	12	20	57
Gunung Mulu, Sarawak	Lowland dipterocarp rain forest	Collins (1979b)	4°N	115°E	5000	0	12[2]	29	18	2	12	23	0	3	19	59
Mato Grosso, Brazil	Riparian forest in cerrado	Mathews (1977, tables 22–28)	13°S	52°N	1300	0	6[3]	14	21	2	2	9	4	0	24	41
Anavilhanas, Amazonas, Brazil	Lowland rain forest	Mill (1982a, b)	2.5°S	61°W	2000	0	9[3]	28	6	1	6	12	4	0	20	43

[1] Species are listed only under their principal food source. Kalotermitidae, *Coptotermes, Heterotermes,* Macrotermitinae = fresh litter; Rhinotermitidae (except *Coptotermes, Heterotermes*), Termitinae, *Termes, Microcerotermes, Amitermes, Nasutitermes* = rotten litter.
[2] Includes three species of *Hospitalitermes,* which feed on lichens and mosses.
[3] Including *Ruptitermes* and *Constrictotermes,* which can take dry leaves and lichens.

The third subfamily of the Termitidae, the Macrotermitinae, is restricted to the Old World and probably has its origin in the Afrotropics (Emerson, 1955). Macrotermitinae have a mutualistic relationship with basidiomycete fungi of the genus *Termitomyces*, which grow upon combs built by the termites from their faeces. Other termites use their faeces to build nests and galleries, but the Macrotermitinae use only soil and saliva (Noirot, 1970). The combs are dynamic structures which the worker termites build up on one side and consume from the other. During the turnover time of one or two months the fungus breaks down the faecal material, degrading complex polysaccharides and concentrating nitrogenous and other nutrients through respiratory loss of organic carbon (Collins, 1983a). As a result of this mechanism the colonies of macrotermitine termites tend to have considerably higher weight-specific consumption rates than other termites, and a correspondingly greater impact on decomposition processes (Collins, 1981, 1983b). Of the thirteen genera (Krishna, 1970; Ruelle, 1978), eight are found only in the Afrotropics, two only in the Orient and three are shared (*Macrotermes*, *Microtermes* and *Odontotermes*). The presence and importance of these termites in rain forest is highly variable and will be discussed in more detail below. They feed on dead wood and leaves, often in a relatively fresh condition, being enabled to do so by the action of their mutualistic fungi. Most other termites require the action of free-living fungi to make their food palatable.

The fourth subfamily, the Nasutitermitinae, is the largest and in many respects the most specialized. The group probably has its origins in the Neotropics, where the primitive genera *Cornitermes*, *Paracornitermes*, *Procornitermes* and *Syntermes* are confined. These have retained the biting mandibles in the soldier caste, but in the other 63 known genera these are partially or wholly redundant because of the development of a defensive nasus, or snout, from which irritating, sticky and topically poisonous fluids may be ejected (Prestwich, 1983a, b). It has been postulated from a morphological standpoint that the nasute soldier evolved independently along two phyletic lines (Krishna, 1970). This theory has been brought into question by recent analyses of the chemistry of the defensive secretions (Prestwich, 1983b). The most

advanced members of each supposed line, *Nasutitermes* and *Subulitermes*, have been found to produce identical diterpenes, a capacity unlikely to have evolved independently along parallel lines (Prestwich and Collins, 1981).

Nasutes are an important element of the rain forest in all biogeographical realms, but are particularly prevalent in the Neotropics, where the Macrotermitinae and the *Apicotermes* branch of the Apicotermitinae are absent, and in the Orient, where the Apicotermitinae are rare and the Termitinae have a limited diversity. This is clearly demonstrated in the analysis of communities shown in Table 26.2, and in the nesting locations illustrated in Fig. 26.2. Their feeding habits are extremely catholic, ranging from organic remnants and humus utilized by *Subulitermes* and its relatives, through rotten wood (*Armitermes*, *Bulbitermes*, *Nasutitermes*) and rotten leaves (*Havilanditermes*, *Longipeditermes*) to dry leaves (*Ruptitermes*), lichens and mosses (*Hospitalitermes*).

ADAPTATIONS OF TERMITES TO CLIMATIC FACTORS

The world distribution of termites is constrained primarily by temperature and moisture. Temperature denies the survival of termites below the 49°F (9.4°C) annual isothermal line (Emerson, 1955), which lies at a maximum of about 50° of latitude. In fact, very few termite species extend beyond 45°, and the vast majority are confined within the 24° Tropics of Cancer and Capricorn. This is illustrated in Fig. 26.1 which demonstrates that the richest sites for termites are in equatorial rain forests, where up to 59 species may occur in a single locality. A similar figure using different data is given by Lepage (1983).

Diurnal and seasonal variations in ground temperatures in lowland equatorial rain forest are smaller and more equable than in any other terrestrial biome. In tropical savannas some termite genera build huge mounds that maintain a virtually independent microclimate (Noirot, 1970; Lee and Wood, 1971). In rain forests such protection is not needed and the generally small nests have temperatures that follow the fluctuations in air temperature, with only slight homeostasis. African species that conform to this general-

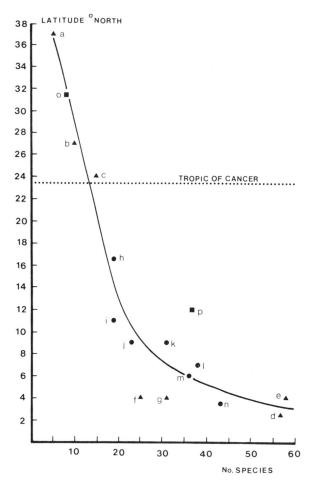

Fig. 26.1. The number of termite species at world-wide latitudes north of the Equator. Datum points refer to collections from individual ecosystems and vegetation types except for the four most northerly collections, which are complete for the regions indicated. Data from South-East Asia (triangles) (*a*) Japanese Islands (*b*) Ryukyu Islands (*c*) Formosa (*d*) dipterocarp forest, West Malaysia (*e*) dipterocarp forest, Sarawak (*f*) kerangas forest, Sarawak (*g*) alluvial forest, Sarawak. Data from Africa (circles) (*h*) sahel savanna, Senegal (*i*) Northern Guinea savanna, Nigeria (*j*) Southern Guinea savanna, Nigeria (*k*) riparian forest, Nigeria (*l*) semi-deciduous forest, Nigeria (*m*) derived savanna, Ivory Coast (*n*) rain forest, Cameroon. Data from the Americas (squares) (*o*) Arizona desert, U.S.A. (*p*) riparian forest, Brazil (full references for data are given by Collins, 1983b).

ization include *Cubitermes fungifaber* (Sjöstedt), *C. gaigei* (Emerson), *C. heghi* Sjöstedt and *Procubitermes arboricola* (Sjöstedt) in Cameroon (Collins, 1977a) and *Cubitermes fungifaber*, *Thoracotermes brevinotus* Silvestri and *Nasutitermes arborum* (Smeathman) in Ivory Coast (Noirot, 1970) (Fig. 26.2). One exception is *Cephalotermes*

rectangularis (Sjöstedt), builder of a bulky and complex three-layered nest up to 80 cm high that maintains nest temperatures 4° to 6°C higher than the outside air (Collins, 1977a).

There is no evidence that temperatures in lowland rain forest control foraging activity, although direct sunlight could adversely affect canopy species, and possibly species that forage in open columns, like *Hospitalitermes*, *Havilanditermes* and *Longipeditermes* in South-East Asia. Low temperatures restrict the distribution of termites at higher altitudes, even in forested equatorial regions. In the rain forests of Gunung (Mt.) Mulu in Sarawak, 58 species were found in lowland forest, ten species in montane forests above 1000 m and none above 1860 m (Collins, 1980a, 1984).

In rain forests the frequent excess of water can cause difficulties in nesting and foraging. The direct effects of heavy rainfall include disruption and inhibition of exposed foraging columns, such as those of the nocturnal *Rhynchotermes* and *Velocitermes* in South America (Mathews, 1977), and *Hospitalitermes*, *Longipeditermes* and *Macrotermes carbonarius* Hagen in South-East Asia (Collins, 1979a). Free-standing nests and those attached to tree trunks are vulnerable to heavy storms and stem flow, respectively, and some species have developed devices for minimizing the impact. In African forests *Cubitermes fungifaber* and *C. gaigei* build one or more caps to the nest, giving the appearance of huge mushrooms (Noirot, 1970; Collins, 1977a). Tree-side nests of *C. subarquatus* (Sjöstedt), *C. intercalatus* Silvestri and *C. heghi* build tiers of semicircular roofs, up to 15 or more reaching 2 to 3 m up the trunk (Emerson, 1928, 1938, 1949; Noirot, 1970; Collins, 1977a). *Procubitermes* species plaster up to 40 chevrons of mud onto the tree trunk in an effort to divert stem flow away from the nest (Emerson, 1928, 1938, 1949; Collins, 1977a). Some nests of *Constrictotermes*, built on tree trunks at heights of up to 4 m, may also shed rain by means of a series of roofs and chevron-shaped mud structures (Emerson, 1938). Arguably the globular, arboreal nests of Oriental *Bulbitermes* and certain Neotropical *Nasutitermes* assist non-erosive flow of rain water. *Amitermes* and *Microcerotermes* build tree-side carton nests covered irregularly with small hanging protuberances that shed rain, thus conserving nest material (Emerson, 1938).

Flooding rivers in Gunung Mulu National Park, Sarawak, caused great reduction in termite populations and species richness. Only 31 species were found in dipterocarp forest on an alluvial plain, compared to 59 species in freely draining soils above the flood levels (Collins, 1979b, 1984). Similarly at Anavilhanas in Brazil, seasonally inundated forest (*igapó*) contained only 12 species, compared with 43 species in forest on *terra firme* (Mill, 1982b).

DISTRIBUTION OF TERMITES WITHIN RAIN FOREST

The complex three-dimensional structure of lowland rain forest offers a greater variety of nesting and feeding sites for termites than any other biome. Figure 26.2 is a diagrammatic illustration of the nesting locations of termite genera collected in three lowland rain-forest localities on different continents. Broad comparisons may be made between them, but each is probably incomplete and influenced to different extents by local ecological conditions.

With the exception of unusual genera such as *Hospitalitermes*, which can feed on living lichens, few termites feed in the forest canopy. Dead boughs may be occupied by primitive Kalotermitidae like *Glyptotermes* and *Neotermes*, but this is the only group of termites that need have no contact with the forest floor. Similarly, the zone between the canopy and the soil contains few nesting sites, although some species, such as *Bulbitermes*, *Lacessititermes* and *Nasutitermes*, build nests high up on branches and trunks. In the Brazilian and Malaysian forests there are more such arboreal nesting Nasutitermitinae than in the Cameroon forest. The bases and boles of trees are also used for support by a number of genera, for instance *Constrictotermes* in Brazil, *Procubitermes* in Cameroon and *Termes* in all three sites.

In rain forest the soil interface is indistinct and soil invertebrates such as earthworms and termites can be found feeding in the soil-like debris of epiphytes many metres high up on tree trunks and boughs. Compared with the distribution of termite nesting sites in savannas, those in forests are greatly extended vertically. Genera that tend to build subterranean nests in savanna, such as *Amitermes* and *Microcerotermes*, may be found

nesting in free-standing mounds or on the sides of trees in forest. Large mounds are built by forest-dwelling *Macrotermes* species in Malaysia, *Cephalotermes* in Cameroon and *Armitermes* in Brazil. Builders of small mounds are mainly Nasutitermitinae in Brazil (e.g. *Rotunditermes*) and soil-feeding Termitinae in Cameroon (e.g. *Cubitermes*) and Malaysia (e.g. *Dicuspiditermes*). Recolonization of old mounds is important in Cameroun, where 31 species of termites have been found secondarily occupying almost a third of the nests of the main dozen or so mound-building species (Collins, 1980a). These termitariophiles are also common in Brazil (Mathews, 1977), but less frequent in Malaysia (Collins, 1984).

TAXONOMIC COMPOSITION OF TERMITE COMMUNITIES

An understanding of the breadth of resource exploitation by termites requires analysis of thorough collections from defined habitats. Josens (1983, table 23.1) analysed African savanna communities in an earlier volume in this series. Table 26.2 takes one savanna community for comparison and continues in a similar format, taking examples from riparian, semi-deciduous and evergreen rain forests in the Oriental, Neotropical and Afrotropical regions. All four lowland evergreen rain-forest communities that have been studied are included, but less rich communities in poorly drained and podzolic rain-forest soils, montane and deciduous forests studied by Mathews (1977), Collins (1979b, 1984), Mill (1982a, b) and Salick et al. (1983) have not been included.

The species richness of the communities shown in Table 26.2 increases with the combined effects of decreasing latitude and increasing rainfall and complexity of vegetation. The four lowland rain-forest sites are broadly similar in terms of richness and contain more species (43–59) than the riparian and semi-deciduous forests (31–41), or the African savanna sites (19–31) (Josens, 1983, excluding derived savanna). The proportion of these faunas contributed by the subfamilies of the Termitidae is variable, as would be expected from biogeographical considerations. The Nasutitermitinae are more important in the Oriental (19–20 species), and particularly the Neotropical (20–24 species), than in the Afrotropical (3–5 species) sites. The Macrotermitinae become less important with low latitude and high rainfall and are absent from the Neotropical sites. The Apicotermitinae are absent from the Oriental sites, but the *Apicotermes* branch is well represented in the Cameroon site (Collins, 1977b). There are more species of Termitinae in the Oriental (19–23) and Afrotropical (9–25) sites than in the Neotropical (9–12) sites. An interesting observation is the greater number of Rhinotermitidae in the Oriental sites (6–12), the presumed centre of origin of the family, than in the Afrotropical (1–2) or the Neotropical (2–6) sites. The Kalotermitidae are few in all areas, but probably more widespread than the data imply.

DIETARY PATTERNS IN TERMITE COMMUNITIES

The wider range of foodstuffs and of feeding sites in rain forest permits more specialized feeding habits as well as a greater diversity of species. For example, although leaves are taken opportunistically by *Macrotermes bellicosus* (Smeathman) and other species in African savannas, forest species such as *Macrotermes carbonarius*, *Longipeditermes longipes* (Haviland) and *Havilanditermes atripennis* (Haviland) feed on little else (Collins, 1984). Similarly, lichens are incidentally consumed by *Odontotermes* foraging on tree bark in savanna in Kenya (Collins, 1983a), but *Hospitalitermes* in Asian forests, and *Constricototermes* and *Ruptitermes* in South American forests, all use lichens as

an important dietary component (Collins, 1979a; Mathews, 1977).

Most species will take food from at least two sources and in rain forest, where practically all dead wood is rotten to some extent, and the division between rotten litter and soil organic matter is difficult to assess, the boundaries become particularly vague. Different authors might list *Microcerotermes* as a fresh wood-feeder or rotten wood-feeder, *Termes* as a rotten wood-feeder or soil-feeder. In Table 26.2 the divisions into dietary categories are on a slightly different basis to that of Josens (1983) and Wood et al. (1982). Each species has been allotted only to its principal food in an attempt to achieve greater comparability, albeit at a cost of some artificiality in the categories. These principal food sources are also indicated in Fig. 26.2, which shows representative genera from the regions.

Grass and grass litter: with the exception of bamboos, Gramineae are virtually absent from rain forests and the lack of grass-feeding species is an expected deviation from the savanna pattern.

Fresh wood and leaf litter: this is an important resource in the savanna community but less common in forests where decay sets in very quickly under conditions of high temperature and humidity. This food source therefore attracts a much smaller proportion of the total community in forest than in savanna, although the actual numbers of species are broadly similar. The Macrotermitinae are the Old World specialists on fresh litter and in the rather dry forests of Pasoh in

---

Fig. 26.2. The spatial distribution of termite nests in lowland evergreen rain forests in three sites in the Neotropics, Orient and Afrotropics. Principal foodstuffs are indicated by [1]fresh litter, [2]lichens and mosses, [3]rotten litter, [4]soil.

Brazil: Anavilhanas, Amazonas: 24 genera (Mill, 1982a, b). Kalotermitidae: *Neotermes*[1]. Rhinotermitidae: *Coptotermes*[1], *Dolichorhinotermes*[3], *Heterotermes*[1], *Rhinotermes*[3]. Termitidae, Apicotermitinae: *Anoplotermes*[4], *Grigiotermes*[4], *Ruptitermes*[2]. Termitinae: *Amitermes*[3], *Cavitermes*[4], *Cylindrotermes*[3], *Genuotermes*[4], *Microcerotermes*[3], *Neocapritermes*[4], *Spinitermes*[4], *Termes*[3]. Nasutitermitinae: *Armitermes*[3], *Constrictotermes*[2], *Labiotermes*[4], *Nasutitermes*[3] *Rotunditermes*[3], *Subulitermes*[4] *Syntermes*[1], *Triangulariodotermes*[3].

Sarawak: Gunung Mulu: 30 genera (Collins 1984). Kalotermitidae: *Glyptotermes*[1], *Neotermes*[1]. Rhinotermitidae: *Coptotermes*[1], *Heterotermes*[1], *Parrhinotermes*[3], *Schedorhinotermes*[3]. Termitidae, Termitinae: *Amitermes*[3], *Dicuspiditermes*[4], *Globitermes*[3], *Homallotermes*[4], *Labritermes*[4], *Microcerotermes*[3], *Pericapritermes*[4], *Procapritermes*[4], *Prohamitermes*[3], *Protohamitermes*[3], *Termes*[3]. Macrotermitinae: *Macrotermes*[1], *Odontotermes*[1]. Nasutitermitinae: *Bulbitermes*[3], *Ceylonitermes*[4], *Havilanditermes*[3], *Hirtitermes*[3], *Hospitalitermes*[2], *Lacessititermes*[3], *Longipeditermes*[3], *Nasutitermes*[3], *Oriensubulitermes*[4], plus two unidentified genera[3].

Cameroon: Douala-Edea, Sanaga-Maritime: 32 genera (Collins, 1977a). Rhinotermitidae: *Schedorhinotermes*[3]. Termitidae, Apicotermitinae: *Anenteotermes*[4], *Apicotermes*[4], *Astalotermes*[4], *Coxotermes*[4], *Phoxotermes*[4], *Machadotermes*[4]. Termitinae: *Apilitermes*[4], *Cephalotermes*[3], *Crenetermes*[4], *Cubitermes*[4], *Euchilotermes*[4], *Fastigitermes*[4], *Foraminitermes*[4], *Furculitermes*[4], *Microcerotermes*[3], *Noditermes*[4], *Ophiotermes*[4], *Orthotermes*[4], *Pericapritermes*[4], *Procubitermes*[4], *Promirotermes*[4], *Profastigitermes*[4], *Termes*[3], *Thoracotermes*[4], *Unguitermes*[4]. Macrotermitinae: *Microtermes*[1], *Odontotermes*[1], *Pseudocanthotermes*[1], *Protermes*[1], *Sphaerotermes*[1]. Nasutitermitinae: *Nasutitermes*[3].

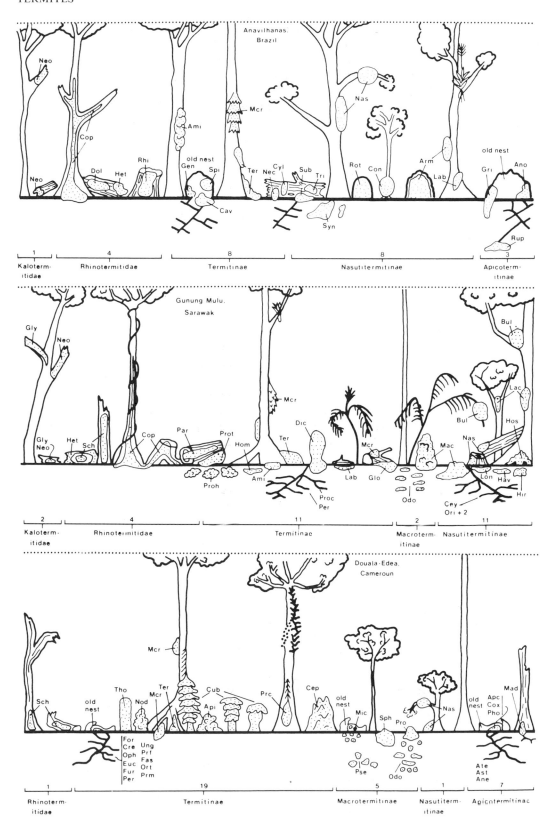

Anavilhanas, Brazil

1	4	8	8	3
Kaloterm-itidae	Rhinotermitidae	Termitinae	Nasutitermitinae	Apicoterm-itinae

Gunung Mulu, Sarawak

2	4	11	2	11
Kaloterm-itidae	Rhinotermitidae	Termitinae	Macroterm-itinae	Nasutitermitinae

Douala-Edea, Cameroun

1	19	5	1	7
Rhinoterm-itidae	Termitinae	Macrotermitinae	Nasutiterm-itinae	Apicotermitinae

West Malaysia *Macrotermes carbonarius* and *M. malaccensis* (Haviland) are important consumers of leaf and wood litter, respectively (Abe, 1979, 1980; Matsumoto and Abe, 1979). Although they are still present in wetter forests, such as Mulu, their populations decline (see below). In the New World forests *Syntermes* specializes in attacking fresh leaf litter (Mill, 1982a). Both the Orient and the Neotropics have lichen-feeders included in this category.

Rotten wood and leaf litter: all forests have more rotten wood-feeders than the savanna, where this resource is comparatively scarce. They are particularly diverse in Malaysia, where the Rhinotermitidae are very active, and at Anavilhanas in Brazil, where *Nasutitermes* (nine species) and a variety of Termitinae and Rhinotermitidae are found in rotten wood.

Soil: data from the Afrotropical sites indicate a general trend of increasing diversity of soil-feeders from savannas to forests. This may be partly an ecological effect of increasing levels of organic matter in forest sites, but it is facilitated and accentuated by zoogeographical and evolutionary factors. As indicated above, soil-feeding Apicotermitinae and Termitinae have diverged widely in Africa. In the Malaysian sites there is a greater diversity of rotten litter-feeders than soil-feeders. Again this is largely due to zoogeographical factors. Both the Apicotermitinae and the more primitive members of the soil-feeding branch of the Termitinae (with biting mandibles) are absent from these sites (although one genus, *Euhamitermes*, does occur in Peninsular Malaysia). The soil-feeders in these sites are Termitinae from the soil-feeding branch with snapping mandibles, or Nasutitermitinae from the *Subulitermes* group.

In the Brazilian forests the soil-feeders are mainly Nasutitermitinae, with a few species of Apicotermitinae. The latter may be under-represented because of the need for taxonomic revision. The apparent decline in the proportion of soil feeders in the rain forest compared to the riparian forest is unexplained. More data are required from this region.

ECOLOGICAL IMPACT OF TERMITES

Termites have an impact on rain-forest ecosystems in three main ways, with a fourth possibility poorly understood. They are: (1) feeding on plant material, often of a very poor quality; (2) reproducing and providing material for predatory food chains; (3) physically translocating and chemically altering soils through their building activities; and (4) fixing atmospheric nitrogen. All of these factors are related to the abundance and biomass of termites in forests, measurement of which is fundamental to a greater understanding of termite ecology.

Populations and biomass

The data presented in Table 26.3 are highly variable in terms of the type of forest and the extent of sampling. The forests listed include lowland rain forests of various types, montane forests and riparian forests. Termites are distributed in soil, wood and epigeal or arboreal nests, each requiring a separate sampling procedure. All the forests listed have been sampled for subterranean populations and most for above-ground nests. Termites are known to have a substantial impact on the removal of dead wood (Abe, 1980), but populations in trunks and limbs are very difficult to sample; only Collins (1983b) has made estimates, and these were crude. Nevertheless, comparison of the data permits a few basic observations. Maximum abundance and biomass are in the region of 4000 m^{-2} and 10 g m^{-2}, respectively, levels which, as Wood et al. (1982) have observed, closely resemble the levels found in savanna ecosystems. However, when the various taxa in Table 26.3 are examined and their feeding habits considered, differences between savanna and forest, and between different types of forest become apparent. The Sarawak sites show that termite populations decrease with rising altitude or poor drainage (alluvial site), but may be relatively high in nutrient-poor podzolic soils with a high organic content (kerangas site). Comparison between the Pasoh and Mulu dipterocarp sites show how variable populations may be. The fungus-growing Macrotermitinae are co-dominant in Pasoh but virtually absent in Mulu. Termitinae and Nasutitermitinae soil populations were broadly similar in the two sites (Abe, 1979; Collins, 1983b), and the higher total populations shown in Table 26.3 are due mainly to more numerous epigeal and arboreal nests at Pasoh. The reason for

TABLE 26.3

The abundance and biomass of termites in tropical forests

Localities	Populations estimated[1] g m^{-2}			Numbers m^{-2}						Biomass g m^{-2} (w.w.)	Author
	S	N	W	Rhino-termit-idae	Term-itinae	Apico-term-itinae	Macro-term-itinae	Nasuti-term-itinae	Total		
Malaysia, Pasoh:											
dipterocarp forest	+	+	−	n.d.	1280–1730	0	934–984	943–1093	3160–3810	8.69–10.13	Abe (1979)
Sarawak, Mulu:											
dipterocarp forest	+	+	+	293	612	0	5	617	1527	2.4	Collins (1983b)
alluvial forest	+	+	+	96	103	0	21	170	390	0.72	Collins (1983b)
kerangas forest	+	+	+	600	1127	0	0	544	2271	4.1	Collins (1983b)
lower montane forest	+	−	−	0	33	0	0	5	38	0.09	Collins (1980b)
upper montane forest (1310–1860 m)	+	−	−	0	10–286	0	0	9–182	99–295	0.01–0.78	Collins (1980b)
upper montane forest (1970–2376 m)	+	−	−	0	0	0	0	0	0	0	Collins (1980b)
Trinidad, rain forest	+	−	−	n.d.	n.d.	n.d.	n.d.	n.d.	4450	n.d.	Strickland (1944)
Surinam forests:											
Dirkshoop	+	−	−	n.d.	n.d.	n.d.	n.d.	n.d.	0–310	n.d.	Van der Drift (1963)
Boven Sarakreek	+	−	−	n.d.	n.d.	n.d.	n.d.	n.d.	940–1420	n.d.	Van der Drift (1963)
Nigeria, riparian forest	+	+	−	0	1533	754[2]	249[3]	110	2646	6.9	Wood et al. (1982)
Zaire, riparian forest	+	+	−	n.d.	n.d.	n.d.	n.d.	n.d.	1000	11.0[4]	Maldague (1964)

[1]S = subterranean populations, N = populations in nests on or near ground, W = populations in wood. Accessible arboreal nests are included in N; canopy populations have never been estimated but are generally believed to be low.
[2]Including unidentified species
[3]Not including mound populations of *Macrotermes subhyalinus*, perhaps another 158 m^{-2} (Wood et al., 1982).
[4]This estimated biomass is generally considered to be an exaggeration.

this is obscure, particularly since the species compositions of the two sites were broadly similar in these two subfamilies (Collins, 1984).

No thorough studies of termite populations have been made in South America. The examples quoted from Trinidad and Surinam were part of general studies of soil fauna and too few samples were used accurately to assess the very clumped distribution of soil termites. The results are only quoted to indicate that termite populations in Neotropical soils are in the same order of magnitude as those found in the Orient.

The Afrotropical studies lack a true rain-forest site, but the riparian forest data from Nigeria indicate that the soil-feeding Apicotermitinae and rotten wood or soil-feeding Termitinae become more numerous, at the expense of the fresh litter-feeding Macrotermitinae so characteristic of the savannas (Wood et al., 1982). Almost 90% of the total population consisted of soil-feeders. Similarly at the Zaire site, one soil-feeder, *Cubitermes fungifaber*, comprised over 30% of the total population. To judge from the abundance of soil-feeding species and their mounds in Cameroon (Collins, 1977a, 1980a), the African rain forests may prove to have similar proportions and population levels of soil-feeders.

Some perspective on the significance of termites may be obtained by comparing their biomass levels with other groups of animals. All studies of tropical rain forests have indicated that the biomass of the decomposer fauna greatly exceeds that of the herbivores and predators. Analyses from the Oriental region show that termites comprise a larger component of the soil fauna than any other group (with ants invariably in second place), and by far the largest component of the decomposer soil fauna (Collins, 1980b, 1983b; Kondoh et al., 1980). In Malaysia termites dominate the soil macrofauna in terms of both abundance and biomass (Collins, 1980b). Biomass values for various vertebrate groups in comparable Malaysian forests are far lower than for termites. In Peninsular Malaysia the range of primate biomass was 0.23 to 0.75 g m^{-2} (Marsh and Wilson, 1981), in Semengoh forest near Kuching the total bird biomass was 0.12 g m^{-2} (Fogden, 1977) and in the alluvial forest at Mulu the understorey bird biomass was 0.05 g m^{-2} while the "trappable" mammal biomass was 0.73 g m^{-2} (Labang and Medway, 1979). To judge from the patchy data available, total mammal and bird biomass in forests may lie in the range 1 to 3 g (w.w.) m^{-2}.

Consumption

No measurements of total consumption of organic matter and humus by termites have been made in any rain forest and quantitative estimates have been achieved for only three rain-forest species, *Hospitalitermes umbrinus* (Collins, 1979a), *Longipeditermes longipes* (Haviland) and *Macro-*

termes carbonarius (Matsumoto and Abe, 1979). Studies in tropical savannas are more advanced and these, coupled with laboratory experiments, have provided estimates of feeding rates for all the major taxonomic groups except the Termitinae. The Macrotermitinae have consumption rates 2 to 6 times higher than other groups. Using estimates of consumption rates broadly supported by these data Collins (1983a) has calculated consumption by termite communities in Malaysia and Salick et al. (1983) have made similar estimates for Venezuelan sites (Table 26.4). The differences between the two Malaysian localities are quite striking. The Mulu fauna consumes 7 to 35 g m^{-2} yr^{-1} depending upon the soil conditions, but at Pasoh termites take 155 to 173 g m^{-2} yr^{-1}. Clearly the main difference is due to the voracious Macrotermitinae (Table 26.4), abundant at Pasoh but very rare at Mulu (Table 26.3). The Pasoh consumption data resemble very closely the 188 g m^{-2} yr^{-1} consumed by termites at Mokwa in the southern Guinea savanna of Nigeria (Collins, 1981), where the fauna was also dominated by the Macrotermitinae. The role of termites in consuming litter depends to a large extent on the proportions of the different groups in the fauna. Data from Old World sites indicate that in general high rainfall (or

TABLE 26.4

Calculated consumption rates for rain forest termite communities in Malaysia (after Collins, 1983b) and Venezuela (after Salick et al., 1983)

	Consumption of organic matter (g m^{-2} yr^{-1})					% of annual litter production
	Rhino-termi-tinae	Termi-tinae	Macro-termi-tinae	Nasuti-termi-tinae	All termites	
Sarawak, Mulu						
dipterocarp forest	6.4	11.2	0.7	1.7	20.0	2.1
alluvial forest	2.1	1.9	2.9	0.5	7.4[1]	0.6[1]
kerangas forest	13.1	20.7	0	1.5	35.3	3.4
Pen. Malaysia, Pasoh						
dipterocarp forest	n.d.	23.8– 31.3	129.4– 138.4	2.2– 3.5	155.4– 173.2	14.7– 16.3
Venezuela, Rio Negro						
laterite soil					59±80	5
podzolic soil					21±75	3
bana soil					32±92	n.d.

[1]Figures of 11.0 and 0.9 in Collins (1983b) are misprints.

groundwater availability) may encourage free-living fungal activity and soil-feeding termite groups, and discourage the fungus-growing Macrotermitinae (Wood et al., 1982; Collins, 1983b). In this event, the termite faunas of the wetter forests (such as Mulu) may take a smaller proportion of litter input, even though populations may be high. The situation in the Venezuelan sites, where Macrotermitinae are absent, appears to be very similar to the wetter forests of South-East Asia.

Relatively little is known about the ecological impact of soil-feeding termites but considerable advances of our knowledge of their digestive processes have recently been made. Studies on *Cubitermes* and *Procubitermes* have demonstrated in detail the structure and function of the alimentary canal in soil-feeding Termitinae (Bignell et al., 1983). In the hindgut, alkaline hydrolysis of organic and humic material is an important prerequisite to efficient digestion by the bacterial symbionts. Because of the lack of ecological work, the precise nature of the food of soil-feeders is unknown, as are consumption rates and assimilation efficiencies. The single study of the feeding rates of *Cubitermes* (Okwakol, 1980) has given a lead in methodology, but may have over-estimated consumption. The suggested deleterious impact of *Cubitermes* on soil organic matter is certainly open to question (Collins, 1983b). There is a great need for further study of soil-feeding termites. They offer the opportunity to study some of the most fundamental ecological processes in rain-forest soils.

The weight of organic matter actually consumed by termites is only one aspect of their impact on decomposition. Processing or translocating organic matter without actually consuming it may also be significant. Termites do not consume whole trees, but they may assist tree-fall, thereby creating access for other decomposer organisms. It is known that termites nest and feed inside tree trunks, sometimes to a height of 10 m or more (Becker, 1972; Abe and Matsumoto, 1979). Recently, one species at least, *Microcerotermes dubius* (Haviland), has been implicated in conjunction with fungal pathogens as a cause of tree falls and gap formation in virgin forest (Tho, 1982). Comminution as well as consumption of leaf litter may be an important impact of foraging by leaf-

feeding termites at Pasoh (Collins, 1983b). Abe (1980, 1982) has demonstrated that Macrotermitinae at Pasoh encourage microbial decay by increasing the surface area of woody litter available to microbes, and by importing microorganisms with the soil they use for building.

Production

No quantitative estimates of termite production have been made in any rain-forest ecosystem. Production : biomass ratios for a wide range of invertebrates, including termites, is about 3:1, although production by the Macrotermitinae may be 2 to 4 times higher. Erring on the conservative side and using this lower figure for all groups, the biomass figures in Table 26.3 imply the potential for production of up to about 30 g m^{-2} yr^{-1} (300 kg ha^{-1} yr^{-1}). In terms of weight this is approximately equivalent to the production of one cow per hectare and in a steady-state population the biomass would be lost annually to predatory and decomposer food chains. In view of this, it is perhaps not surprising that termites support an army of specialized and opportunistic predators, from ants to anteaters, that attack termite nests, alate swarms and foraging columns anywhere from underground burrows to the forest canopy. For further information on termite predation the reader should refer to the recent review by Deligne et al. (1981).

Building

All termites except the Macrotermitinae use some or all of their faeces in building nests or foraging galleries. As these are abandoned and decompose, the components are recycled. Wood-feeding species produce carton, a woody substance with low nutrient concentrations and high levels of lignin and other undigested components. Nests made from carton support low populations of bacteria and are slow to decay (Lee and Wood, 1971). The soil-feeding termites of the Apicotermitinae, Termitinae and Nasutitermitinae all build their nests from faeces augmented with soil and saliva. It has often been observed that abandoned, or even occupied, nests are taken over by plant roots (Mathews, 1977; among others). In both Nigerian riverine forest and Venezuelan nutrient-poor forests nests formed fertile patches of significance in determining the availability of nutrients to germinating seedlings (Salick et al., 1983; Anderson and Wood, 1984). The nests contained higher concentrations of carbon, nitrogen, phosphorous, potassium and other elements than the soil. In the Venezuelan sites nests were abandoned at a rate of 165 ± 66 nests ha^{-1} yr^{-1} providing abundant microsites for tree seedling establishment. Similarly, in 1.8 ha of Cameroon rain forest, 150 out of 417 epigeal nests examined were empty, 110 being nests of *Cubitermes fungifaber* (Collins, 1980a). If these contain the high nutrient levels found in *Cubitermes severus* mounds (Anderson and Wood, 1984) then they are also good germination sites.

The role of termites in the mixing of soil profiles is not clear. As might be expected, subterranean termite populations are characteristically found in the organic layers of soil profiles. In Pasoh, Malaysia, termites were mainly found in the 0 to 15 cm layer, and were rare below 25 cm (Abe and Matsumsoto, 1979). There was evidence of stratification, with Termitinae mainly in the 0 to 10 cm layer, Nasutitermitinae in the 5 to 10 cm layer and the Macrotermitinae at 15 to 20 cm. In Nigerian riparian forest most termites were also in the 0 to 25 cm layer (Wood et al., 1982). *Pericapritermes* and *Eutermellus* were exceptional in also foraging in deeper layers, and a number of species moved downwards in the dry season.

Nitrogen fixation

Estimates of nitrogen fixation rates by termites vary widely and although many rain forest species are now known to have this capacity, there are insufficient data to calculate the impact of a whole termite community on the nitrogen cycle of a forest. Data on nitrogen fixation have been reviewed by Breznak (1982) and Collins (1983a). No insects other than termites and the cockroach *Cryptocercus punctulatus* Scudder have been shown to fix nitrogen and this is an interesting field for further study.

EFFECTS OF DEFORESTATION ON TERMITE COMMUNITIES

Deforestation affects termites by destroying nesting sites, reducing the input and changing the

nature of plant litter, increasing the severity of the microclimate and reducing the levels of soil organic matter by causing rapid oxidation. These factors inevitably cause a drastic reduction in species richness of termite communities. During limited periods of collecting at Sawai in Sarawak, Collins (1980c) found twenty-five species in virgin dipterocarp forest, twelve species in selectively felled forest and only six species in a clear-felled and burnt-over area on which one rice crop had been grown. Similarly in Nigeria only eight species were found in an area of sugar cane adjacent to a riparian forest where 33 species occurred (Wood et al., 1982). The abundance of termites in these sites was 2646 m^{-2} (6.9 g m^{-2}) and 1151 m^{-2} (5.38 g m^{-2}), respectively.

The groups most seriously affected by deforestation are those that lose their foodstuffs (for instance, soil-feeders and rotten wood-feeders), those that forage in open columns and lose the shelter of the forest canopy, and those that build simple nests that are poorly protected from extremes of microclimate. This includes most rain forest species. Concomitant with a general downward trend in species richness is the development of large populations of certain pre-adapted or generalist species that may become pests of agriculture or silviculture. The Macrotermitinae, a group that can survive because of their fungus-growing habit and can cause serious pest infestations, were least affected by clearance at Sawai in Sarawak (Collins, 1980c). In the Nigerian riparian site *Amitermes evuncifer*, a pest of root crops, increased its populations from very rare to 832 m^{-2} (Wood et al., 1982).

CONCLUSIONS

Rain forests support the largest known termite communities, with up to 59 species recorded in small (<5 ha) plots (Fig. 26.1). Most species are in the family Termitidae, but the Rhinotermitidae are also well represented (Table 26.2). The Kalotermitidae are scarce in rain forests, but are the only group that can live in the canopy with no connection to the soil, a pre-adaptation that makes them successful in mangrove forests. Most termites live and nest in or on the soil, or within a few metres of its surface (Fig. 26.2).

The evolution and dispersal of the subfamilies of the Termitidae have been decisive factors in the present nature of forest termite faunas. Evolution has tended to promote the occupation of similar feeding and nesting niches by termites in the three main forest blocks, but because of ancient dispersal patterns the genera which occupy them are, with the exception of a few tropicopolitan genera, quite different. For example, treeside nests with rain-shedding devices are built by *Procubitermes* (Termitinae) in Africa and *Constrictotermes* (Nasutitermitinae) in South America, although they are in different subfamilies. Similarly, both the South American *Ruptitermes* (Apicotermitinae) and the Oriental *Hospitalitermes* (Nasutitermitinae) have developed the unusual habit of feeding on lichens.

Although the various communities are similar in their feeding and nesting habits, dispersal and evolutionary mechanisms have caused disparity in emphasis. For example, rain forest soils tend to have a higher content of organic matter than savanna soils, encouraging the soil-feeding habit, but some faunas have been better placed to take advantage of this fact than others. In African forests the soil-feeding termites are a prevalent proportion of the termite fauna, partly because the Apicotermitinae and soil-feeding Termitinae have their origins there. In South America the Nasutitermitinae have less thoroughly occupied this niche and both there and in the Orient there is a greater proportion of species utilizing rotten wood (Table 26.2).

Data on populations and biomass are few, but indicate that levels are within the range found in savannas (Table 26.3). The ecological impact of these populations is understood even less, but it seems that the taxonomic composition of the community is important. The Macrotermitinae consume more than other groups and have greater impact in removing litter (Table 26.4).

Consumption of litter is not the only impact of termites on the forest ecosystem. They also comminute litter and thereby speed up bacterial and fungal decay. By causing large, overmature trees to fall they facilitate their breakdown and replacement by young stock. Termite nests, particularly abandoned ones, are an important source of nutrients for seedlings. Termites themselves are an important source of food for a wide variety of forest animals. These and other aspects of the ecological role of termites in rain forest require further study if their full impact is to be understood.

ACKNOWLEDGEMENTS

I should like to thank A.E. Mill for comments on the manuscript and M.M. Collins for the line drawings.

REFERENCES

Abe, T., 1978. Studies on the distribution and ecological role of termites in a lowland rain forest of West Malaysia (1). Faunal composition, size, colouration and nest of termites in Pasoh Forest Reserve. *Kontyu*, 46: 273–290.

Abe, T., 1979. Studies on the distribution and ecological role of termites in a lowland rain forest of West Malaysia (2). Food and feeding habits of termites in Pasoh Forest Reserve. *Jpn. J. Ecol.*, 29: 121–135.

Abe, T., 1980. Studies on the distribution and ecological role of termites in a lowland rain forest of West Malaysia (4). The role of termites in the process of wood decomposition in Pasoh Forest Reserve. *Rev. Ecol. Biol. Sol*, 17: 23–40.

Abe, T., 1982. Ecological role of termites in a tropical rain forest. In: M.D. Breed, C.D. Michener and H.E. Evans (Editors), *The Biology of Social Insects*. Westview Press, Boulder, Colo., pp. 71–75.

Abe, T. and Matsumoto, T., 1979. Studies on the distribution and ecological role of termites in a lowland rain forest of West Malaysia (3). Distribution and abundance of termites in Pasoh Forest Reserve. *Jpn. J. Ecol.*, 29: 337–351.

Anderson, J.M. and Wood, T.G., 1984. Mound composition and soil modification by two soil-feeding termites (Termitinae, Termitidae) in Nigerian riparian forest. *Pedobiologia*, 26: 77–82.

Becker, G., 1972. Termiten im Regenwald des Magdalenen-stromtals in Kolumbien, *Z. Angew. Entomol.*, 71: 431–441.

Bignell, D.E., Oskarsson, H., Anderson, J.M., Ineson, P. and Wood, T.G., 1983. Structure, microbial associations and function of the so-called "mixed segment" of the gut in two soil-feeding termites, *Procubitermes aburiensis* and *Cubitermes severus* (Termitidae, Termitinae). *J. Zool.*, 201: 445–480.

Bouillon, A., 1970. Termites of the Ethiopian region. In: K. Krishna and F.M. Weesner (Editors), *Biology of Termites, Vol. 2*. Academic Press, New York, N.Y., pp. 154–280.

Breznak, J.A., 1982. Intestinal microbiota of termites and other xylophagous insects. *Ann. Rev. Microbiol.*, 36: 323–343.

Brian, M.V. (Editor), 1978. *Production Ecology of Ants and Termites*. Cambridge Univ. Press, Cambridge, 409 pp.

Collins, N.M., 1977a. Oxford Expedition to the Edea–Marienberg Forest Reserve, United Republic of Cameroun, 1973. *Bull. Oxford Univ. Explor. Club*, 3: 5–15.

Collins, N.M., 1977b. Two new termites from the United Republic of Cameroun. *Syst. Entomol.*, 2. 95–104.

Collins, N.M., 1977c. *The population ecology and energetics of Macrotermes bellicosus (Smeathnon) isoptera.* Ph.D. thesis, Univ. of London, London, 339 pp.

Collins, N.M., 1979a. Observations on the foraging activity of *Hospitalitermes umbrinus* (Haviland), (Isoptera: Termitidae) in the Gunung Mulu National Park, Sarawak. *Ecol. Entomol.*, 4: 231–238.

Collins, N.M., 1979b. A comparison of the soil macrofauna of three lowland forest types in Sarawak. *Sarawak Mus. J.*, 27: 267–281.

Collins, N.M., 1980a. Inhabitation of epigeal termite (Isoptera) nests by secondary termites in Cameroun rain forest. *Sociobiology*, 5: 47–54.

Collins, N.M., 1980b. The distribution of soil macrofauna on the West Ridge of Gunung (Mt.) Mulu, Sarawak. *Oecologia*, 44: 263–275.

Collins, N.M., 1980c. The effect of logging on termite (Isoptera) diversity and decomposition processes in lowland dipterocarp forests. In: J.I. Furtado (Editor), *Tropical Ecology and Development*. Int. Society of Tropical Ecology, Kuala Lumpur, pp. 113–121.

Collins, N.M., 1981. The role of termites in the decomposition of wood and leaf litter in the southern Guinea savanna of Nigeria. *Oecologia*, 51: 389–399.

Collins, N.M., 1983a. The utilization of nitrogen resources by termites (Isoptera). In: J.A. Lee, S. McNeill and I.H. Rorison (Editors), *Nitrogen as an Ecological Factor*. The 22nd Symp. of the British Ecological Society, Blackwell, Oxford, pp. 381–412.

Collins, N.M., 1983b. Termite populations and their role in litter removal in Malaysian rain forests. In: S.L. Sutton, T.C. Whitmore and A.C. Chadwick (Editors), *Tropical Rain Forest: Ecology and Management*. Blackwell, Oxford, pp. 311–325.

Collins, N.M., 1984. The termites (Isoptera) of the Gunung Mulu National Park, with a key to the genera known from Sarawak. *Sarawak Mus. J.*, 30: 65–87.

Deligne, J., Quennedey, A. and Blum, M.S., 1981. The enemies and defense mechanisms of termites. In: H.R. Hermann (Editor), *Social Insects. Vol. 2*. Academic Press, New York, N.Y., pp. 1–76.

Emerson, A.E., 1928. Termites of the Belgian Congo and the Cameroon. *Bull. Am. Mus. Nat. Hist.*, 57: 401–574.

Emerson, A.E., 1938. Termite nests — a study of the phylogeny of behaviour. *Ecol. Monogr.*, 8: 247–284.

Emerson, A.E., 1949. Termite studies in the Belgian Congo. *I.R.S.A.C. Deuxième Rapport Annuel*, pp. 149–159.

Emerson, A.E., 1952. The biogeography of termites. *Bull. Am. Mus. Nat. Hist.*, 99: 217–225.

Emerson, A.E., 1955. Geographical origins and dispersion of termite genera. *Fieldiana, Zool.*, 37: 465–521.

Emerson, A.E. and Krishna, K., 1975. The termite family Serritermitidae. *Am. Mus. Novit.*, 2570: 1–31.

Fogden, M.P.L., 1977. A census of a bird community in tropical rain forest in Sarawak. *Sarawak Mus. J.*, 24: 251–267.

Golley, F.B., 1983. Decomposition. In: F.B. Golley (Editor), *Tropical Rain Forest Ecosystems*. (Ecosystems of the World, 14A) Elsevier, Amsterdam, pp. 157–166.

Grassé, P.P., 1949. Ordre des Isoptères ou Termites. In: P.P. Grassé (Editor), *Traité de Zoologie Vol. 9*, Masson, Paris, pp. 408–544.

Harris, W.V., 1961. *Termites, their Recognition and Control*. Longmans, London, 187 pp.

Hermann, H.R. (Editor), 1979–1982. *Social Insects. Vols. 1–4*. Academic Press, New York, N.Y., 1772 pp.

Josens, G., 1983. The soil fauna of tropical savannas. III. The termites. In: F.B. Golley (Editor), *Tropical Rain Forest Ecosystems*. (Ecosystems of the World, 14A) Elsevier, Amsterdam, pp. 505–524.

Kondoh, M., Watanabe, S., Chiba, S., Abe, T., Shiba, M. and Saito, S., 1980. Studies on the productivity of soil animals in Pasoh Forest Reserve, West Malaysia V. Seasonal change in the density and biomass of soil macrofauna: Oligochaeta, Hirudinea and Arthropoda. *Mem. Shiraume Gakuen College*, 16: 1–26.

Krishna, K.R., 1970. Taxonomy, phylogeny and distribution of termites. In: K. Krishna and F.M. Weesner (Editor), *Biology of Termites, Vol. 2*. Academic Press, New York, N.Y., 127–152.

Krishna, K.R. and Weesner, F.M., 1969, 1970. *Biology of Termites*. Academic Press, New York, N.Y., 2 vols., 643 + 598 pp.

Labang, D. and Medway, Lord, 1979. Preliminary assessments of the diversity and density of wild mammals, man and birds in alluvial forest in the Gunung Mulu National Park, Sarawak. In: A.G. Marshall (Editor), *The Abundance of Animals in Malesian Rain Forests*. Univ. of Hull, Hull, pp. 53–62.

Lee, K.E. and Wood, T.G., 1971. *Termites and Soils*. Academic Press, New York, N.Y., 251 pp.

Lepage, M., 1983. Structure et dynamique des peuplements de termites tropicaux. *Acta Oecol./Oecol. Generalis*, 4: 65–87.

Maldague, M.E., 1964. Importance des populations de termites dans les sols équatoriaux. *Trans. 8th Int. Congress of Soil Science, Bucharest*, 3: 743–751.

Marsh, C.W. and Wilson, W.L., 1981. *A Survey of Primates in Peninsular Malaysian Forests*. Final Report for the Malaysian Primates Research Programme, Univ. Kebangsaan Malaysia and Univ. of Cambridge.

Mathews, A.G.A., 1977. *Studies on Termites from the Mato Grosso State, Brazil*. Academia Brasileira de Ciencias, Rio de Janeiro, 267 pp.

Matsumoto, T. and Abe, T., 1979. The role of termites in an equatorial rain forest ecosystem of West Malaysia. II. Leaf litter consumption on the forest floor. *Oecologia*, 38: 261–274.

Mill, A.E., 1982a. Studies on termites (Isoptera) and observations on their ant predators (Hymenoptera: Formicidae) in the Amazon Basin. *Rev. Bras. Entomol.*, 26: 253–260.

Mill, A.E., 1982b. Populacoes de térmitas (Insecta: Isoptera) em quatro habitats no baixo rio Negro. *Acta Amazon.*, 12: 53–60.

Noirot, C., 1970. The nests of termites. In: K. Krishna and F.M. Weesner (Editors), *Biology of Termites. Vol. 1*. Academic Press, New York, N.Y., pp. 73–126.

Okwakol, M.J.N., 1980. Estimation of soil and organic matter consumption by termites of the genus *Cubitermes*. *Afr. J. Ecol.*, 18: 127–131.

Prestwich, G.D., 1983a. The chemical defenses of termites. *Sci. Am.*, August: 78–87.

Prestwich, G.D., 1983b. Chemical systematics of termite exocrine secretions. *Annu. Rev. Ecol. Syst.*, 14: 287–311.

Prestwich, G.D. and Collins, M.S., 1981. Chemotaxonomy of *Subulitermes* and *Nasutitermes* termite soldier defense secretions. Evidence against the hypothesis of diphyletic evolution of the Nasutitermitinae. *Biochem. Syst. Ecol.*, 9: 83–88.

Roonwall, M.L., 1970. Termites of the Oriental region. In: K. Krishnan and F.M. Weesner (Editors), *Biology of Termites, Vol. 2*. Academic Press, New York, N.Y., pp. 315–391.

Ruelle, J.E., 1978. *Megaprotermes*, a new genus of the subfamily Macrotermitinae (Isoptera). *J. Entomol. Soc. S. Afr.*, 41: 17–23.

Salick, J., Herrera, R. and Jordan, C.F., 1983. Termitaria: nutrient patchiness in nutrient deficient rainforests. *Biotropica*, 15: 1–7.

Sands, W.A., 1972. The soldierless termites of Africa (Isoptera: Termitidae). *Bull. Br. Mus. Nat. Hist. (Entomology)*, *Suppl.*, 4: 172 pp.

Spragg, W.T. and Paton, R., 1980. Tracing, trophallaxis and population measurement of colonies of subterranean termites (Isoptera) using a radioactive tracer. *Ann. Entomol. Soc. Am.*, 73: 708–714.

Strickland, A.H., 1944. The arthropod fauna of some tropical soils. *Trop. Agric.*, 21: 107–114.

Tho, Y.P., 1982. Gap formation by the termite *Microcerotermes dubius* in lowland forests of Peninsular Malaysia. *Malay. For.*, 45: 184–192.

Van der Drift, J., 1963. A comparative study of the soil fauna in forests and cultivated land on sandy soils in Suriname. *Stud. Fauna Suriname Guyanas*, 6(19): 1–42.

Wilson, E.O., 1971. *The Insect Societies*. Belknap, Harvard Univ. Press, Cambridge, Mass., 548 pp.

Wood, T.G. and Johnson, R.A., 1986. The biology, physiology and ecology of termites. In: S.B. Vinson (Editor), *Economic Impact and Control of Social Insects*. Praeger, New York, N.Y., pp. 1–68.

Wood, T.G., Johnson, R.A., Ohiagu, C.E., Collins, N.M. and Longhurst, C.E., 1977. *Ecology and Importance of Termites in Crops and Pastures in Northern Nigeria*. Project Report 1973–6, COPR, London, 131 pp.

Wood, T.G., Johnson, R.A., Bacchus, S., Shittu, M.O. and Anderson, J.M., 1982. Abundance and distribution of termites (Isoptera) in a riparian forest in the southern Guinea savanna vegetation zone of Nigeria. *Biotropica*, 14: 25–39.

Chapter 27

LEAF-CUTTING ANTS

J.M. CHERRETT

INTRODUCTION

Leaf-cutting ants are a subgroup of the fungus-growing ants (family Formicidae, subfamily Myrmicinae, tribe Attini) comprising those species with workers large and strong enough to cut pieces out of living leaves. This effectively restricts them to the genera *Acromyrmex* with 24 species and *Atta* with 15 species, although the tribe as a whole consists of approximately 190 species in 12 genera (Weber, 1972).

A characteristic feature of the tribe is that all its members culture fungi which they eat, although the substrate used to culture the fungus varies from the leaf particles cut by the leaf-cutting ant genera, to the insect faeces, fragments of rotting wood and flowers, and insect carcasses collected by some of the smaller species. Anatomically, there are no clear relationships with other groups of ants and, as a consequence, the origins of the tribe and of its fungus-growing habit are speculative. Garling (1979) has reviewed the hypotheses of how the ant–fungus mutualism originated. Von Ihering (1894) suggested that attine ancestors were harvesting ants which brought seeds back to their nest. Fungi grew on these seeds, and the ants increasingly ate this fungus growth and eventually cultured it. Forel (1902) proposed that the fungi originally grew on insect excrement, especially the faeces of wood-boring beetles living in the rotten wood in which the ants nested, and Weber (1958) modified this by suggesting that the fungus originally grew on refuse from the ant colony itself. In either case, the ants eventually came to eat and culture the fungus. The use of living plant material by leaf-cutting ants was seen by Forel and Weber as a late development, which is supported by the advanced nature of leaf-cutting ant societies. Garling (1979), however, considered that the fungus may originally have been an ectomycorrhizal fungus rather than a saprophytic one, and so was associated with living plant material from the start. The initial contact with the ants would have been via the plant root systems which hang down into the nest's underground chambers. In this scenario, the ants began to cover the roots with substrate into which the fungus grew, and its transference from living root to living leaf tissue could have occurred at an earlier stage in the evolution of the fungus-growing habit.

DISTRIBUTION AND DENSITY

The tribe Attini is restricted to the New World, where members are found between approximately 40°N and 44°S of the Equator. The leaf-cutting ants have a narrower distribution of approximately 33°N and 44°S, *Acromyrmex* having a slightly wider latitudinal range than *Atta*. Wilson (1971) drew attention to the replacement of the Attini in the Old World tropics, by the Macrotermitinae (fungus-growing termites) which do not occur in the New World. This mutually exclusive distribution of the two fungus-culturing social insects might, he suggested, be a result of the competitive exclusion of one group by the other, or might simply be an accidental outcome of geographic separation. He was inclined to the latter view, as it is not clear why the ants should have succeeded competitively in the New World over a wide range of habitats, whilst the Macrotermitinae succeeded in the Old World. Leaf-cutting ants and fungus-growing termites would not, of course, compete for

473

TABLE 27.1

The mainland geographical distribution of leaf-cutting ants by countries (sources in footnote)

Country (Left to right in order of most northerly part)

Species	U.S.A.	Mexico	Belize	Guatemala	Honduras	Nicaragua	El Salvador	Colombia	Venezuela	Costa Rica	Panama	Guyana	Surinam	French Guiana	Brazil	Ecuador	Peru	Bolivia	Paraguay	Argentina	Uruguay
Acromyrmex — cutting dicotyledonous leaves																					
A. ambiguus															A				D	A	C
A. aspersus															A		A			A	
A. coronatus								L	E	L	L				A	L	G	A	D	C	C
A. crassispinus															A				A	A	
A. disciger															A				D		
A. hispidus															A		O	O	C	L	C
A. hystrix									A			A			A		G	L	A	A	A
A. laticeps															A			A	A	A	A
A. lundi															A			G		A	
A. niger															A						
A. octospinosus		A	C	A	C	C		A	A	A	A	A	A	A	A	A	G	A	A	A	
A. rugosus								A							A		F		A	A	G
A. subterraneus									E			A		A	A		A				
A. versicolor	L	L																			
Acromyrmex — cutting monocotyledonous leaves																					
A. heyeri															A				D	A	A
A. landolti								A	A			N		K	A		O	O	A		
A. striatus															A			A	D	A	A
A. diazi															Q						
Acromyrmex — miscellaneous cutting habits[1]																					
A. gallardoi																				G	
A. lobicornis															A			A	A	A	
A. mesopotamicus																				L	
A. nobilis															A						
A. pulvereus																		I		L	
A. sylvestrii																				H	G
Total	1	2	1	1	1	1	0	4	5	2	2	4	1	3	19	2	8	10	13	17	9
Atta — cutting dicotyledonous leaves[2]																					
A. cephalotes		B	C	B	C	B		B	B	B	B	B	B	P	B	B	B	B			
A. colombica		B	B	B				B	B	B	B				B						

										Total	Grand total
A. mexicana	B	B	C	M	M			B		2	3
A. opaciceps	B	B						B		3	5
A. robusta								B		2	3
A. saltensis						B	B	B		3	4
A. sexdens						B	B	B	B	2	3
A. silvai							B	R	B	1	2
A. texana	B	M									
Atta — cutting monocotyledonous leaves										4	8
A. bisphaerica								B		9	9
A. capiguara								B	D	5	5
A. vollenweideri							G	B	B	5	5
Atta — miscellaneous cutting habits[1]										7	7
A. goiana								B		3	3
A. laevigata							B	B	B	5	5
Total	2	3	2	3	2	1		10		29	
Grand total	3	5	3	4	3	2				20	11

A: Gonçalves (1961) (primary reference); B: Borgmeier (1959) (primary reference); C: Cherrett and Peregrine (1976); D: Fowler and Robinson (1979a); E: Gonçalves (1982a); F: Kelderman (1978); G: Kempf (1972); H: Kusnezov (1949); I: Marcus (1949); J: Mariconi (1970); K: Pastel et al. (1980); L: Santschi (1925); M: Smith (1963); N: Weber (1946); O: Wille (1952); P: Blanche (1961); Q: Gonçalves (1982b); R: Gonçalves (1984).

[1] Includes species which cut both mono and dicotyledonous plants, and species where information is not available.

[2] *Atta insularis* Guérin, a species cutting dicotyledons, is restricted to the island of Cuba and so is not included.

resources, as the former utilize living leaves, whilst the latter take dead plant material. If the New World distribution of the leaf-cutting ants is a result of their evolution in geographic isolation from the Old World, then there is no obvious reason why they should not become a dominant group in Africa or Asia if introduced. Some spread of their distribution in the Caribbean to the islands of Carriacou and Guadeloupe has occurred (Cherrett, 1968a).

Their site of origin in the New World is also a matter of debate. Weber (1972, 1982) considered that they evolved in the moist lowland tropics of northern South America, probably in the Amazon basin, and on this view the habit of cutting broad-leafed dicotyledonous vegetation would have preceded the grass-cutting habit. Fowler (1982), however, considered that leaf-cutting ants originated in savannas in the subtropical southern regions, and that the grass cutters were therefore the more primitive. Species richness in both *Acromyrmex* and *Atta* increases towards the South American subtropics, Argentina, Bolivia, Paraguay and Uruguay being particularly rich for their size (Table 27.1). Certainly the southern tropics are much richer in leaf-cutting ant species than the northern ones, but within the southern tropics the greater present-day diversity in the region of southern Brazil and northern Argentina may simply reflect the greater diversity of natural vegetation types to be found there when compared with the Amazon basin. Among those species whose habits are known rather few are predominantly grass cutters (3 *Acromyrmex* and 3 *Atta*) compared with the number which predominantly cut dicotyledonous leaves (14 and 9 respectively).

Fowler (1982) suggested that, in grass-cutting ants, the reduced metathoracic leg/mandible ratio, and the much simpler procedure for preparing the substrate on which the fungus is cultured were evidence of a more primitive condition, although the reasons behind these contentions were not developed. It is possible, however, that both features are a specialized response to the tough siliceous grass blades. Uvarov (1966) recognized two broadly different types of mandibles in locusts, depending upon whether the species lived on grasses or on other plants, the former having squat blunt mandibles which hardly overlapped. A similar situation seems to exist in *Atta* and *Acromyrmex*.

For both genera, Cherrett (unpubl.) compared grass cutters with leaf cutters, measuring the mandible and head sizes of ten individuals. The significance of the differences observed was assessed using t or d tests as appropriate. In both cases, grass cutters had significantly ($P<0.01$) smaller, more squat mandibles with fewer teeth (larger ratios of head width to mandible length and smaller ratios of mandible length to mandible width). This agrees with Weber (1982), who noted that the subgenus *Moellerius*, in which all the grass-cutting *Acromyrmex* are found, possessed short, stout mandibles.

If grass leaves are difficult to cut then they would not be so finely prepared for the fungus garden as the softer dicotyledonous leaves which are often chewed to pulp. This may then appear to be a more primitive stage in the evolution of fungus culture. Accordingly, the site of evolution of leaf-cutting ants is not at present resolved.

With 37 species occupying such a wide geographic range, and having radiated to exploit both dicotyledons and monocotyledons, leaf-cutting ants are found in many habitats ranging from deserts to swamp forests, and from subtropical grasslands to tropical rain forest.

Members of the genus *Atta* build large nests several metres deep, $250 \, m^2$ or more in surface area, and containing several million ants (Fig. 27.1). The occurrence and distribution of such nests in tropical forests have therefore attracted attention, and the species most frequently reported are *A. colombica* from Central America and the northernmost part of South America (Lugo et al., 1973; Rockwood, 1976; Weber, 1982), *A. cephalotes* from Central and South America (Cherrett, 1968b) and to some extent *A. sexdens* from South America, although this species favours secondary forest and agricultural areas (Cherrett, 1981). Very little information has been published on the density and distribution of *Atta* nests within rain forest; it is presumed that nests cannot be built in swamp forests or where the water table is high, and in the Bush Bush Forest Reserve in Trinidad *A. cephalotes* nests are very superficial, and restricted to a low island in the Nariva Swamp (Worth, 1967). Comparative data are needed on *Atta* densities in the various forest types, especially in some single-dominant forests. Table 27.2 assembles density estimates from a variety of

Fig. 27.1. Medium-sized nest of *Atta cephalotes* in Trinidad.

TABLE 27.2

Estimates of *Atta* nest densities in some tropical and subtropical forests

Atta species	Forest type	Location	Density (ha^{-1})	Author
NATURAL FORESTS				
A. cephalotes	*Quercus oleoides* dry forest	Costa Rica	1.0	Rockwood (1973)
A. cephalotes	*Scheelea rostrata* moist forest	Costa Rica	1.8	Rockwood (1973)
A. cephalotes, A. colombica	Evergreen wet forest	Costa Rica	2.5	Rockwood (1973)
A. cephalotes	Evergreen wet forest	Costa Rica	1.7	Dix (In Rockwood 1973)
A. cephalotes, A. colombica	Evergreen wet forest	Costa Rica	1.8	Dix (In Rockwood 1973)
A. cephalotes	Lowland evergreen rain forest	Trinidad	0.6	Cherrett (1968a)
A. cephalotes	Lowland evergreen rain forest	Bahia, Brazil	3.0	Leston (1978)
Atta spp.	Lowland evergreen rain forest	Pará, Brazil	1 to 18	Ribeiro and Woessner (1979)
PLANTATIONS				
Atta spp.	*Gmelina* and *Pinus*	Pará, Brazil	2 to 30	Ribeiro and Woessner (1979)
A. laevigata, A. sexdens	*Eucalyptus* and *Pinus*	São Paulo, Brazil	4.0	Amante (1972)

natural and planted tropical and subtropical forests, but these are likely to be high estimates, as they are from areas with sufficient nests to attact research workers, or to have attracted attention through the damage caused. As Jonkman (1979) showed from aerial surveys of 80 000 km^2 of grassland in Paraguay, the grass-cutting ant *Atta vollenweideri* was restricted to a few main areas comprising only 10% of the total surveyed. Within these, however, nest densities reached a maximum of 4.5 ha^{-1} with a mean of 0.2 ha^{-1}.

Members of the genus *Acromyrmex* build small nests rarely exceeding one or two square metres in surface area, and containing only tens of thousands of ants (Lewis, 1975). It is not uncommon for these nests to be built in detritus which has lodged high up in tree forks or in holes in trunks, and so members of this genus can also be found in more swampy areas. As the nests are inconspicuous however, virtually nothing is known about their distribution and density in tropical forests. Rodrigues (1966) studying Amazonian forests recorded nest densities of *Acromyrmex coronatus* and *A. hystrix* from 0.9 to 16.8 ha^{-1}. *A. hystrix* was the commoner species (83% of all nests found), and the most favoured single nest location was between 0.2 and 11.0 m up the trunks of trees. Cherrett (1968a) did not find any *A. octospinosus* nests in the 8 ha of lowland evergreen rain forest he searched in Trinidad, although they were very common in nearby cultivated land. However, he attributed this in part to the inconspicuous nature of the nests, as he did catch foraging workers in pitfall traps, and subsequently (Reed and Cherrett, unpubl.) an *A. octospinosus* nest was found within the foraging area of an *Atta cephalotes* nest in forest in the Arima Valley, Trinidad. Leston (1978) recorded *Acromyrmex* damage in his reserve plot in lowland evergreen rain forest in Bahia, Brazil, although the nest was not within the experimental area. Mendes Filho (1979) has cited *Acromyrmex* spp. nest densities of 200 ha^{-1} in *Eucalyptus* forest, which is comparable with the maximum *A. octospinosus* nest density of 153 ha^{-1} recorded by Lewis (1975) for young cocoa plantations in Trinidad.

DEFOLIATING ACTIVITIES

Periodicity

Large *Atta* nests are spectacular defoliators, and the sight of columns of workers, sometimes 15 cm wide, with each ant carrying a fragment of leaf or flower, moving down the tree trunk and along cleared trails over the forest litter at 1.3 m min^{-1} is a remarkable sight. Large nests may have up to ten trails coming into them at any one time (Fig. 27.2).

Fig. 27.2. Trail of *Atta cephalotes* workers with cut leaves descending a forest tree in Trinidad. Note the smallest caste workers (minims) riding back on the cut leaf pieces.

Defoliating activity has marked daily rhythms, and at the northern and southern limits of *Atta* distribution these are largely determined by climatic factors. Thus *Atta texana* in Louisiana, and *Atta sexdens* in Paraguay can only forage in the heat of the day during the winter months, becoming more nocturnal in the summer (Moser, 1967; Fowler and Robinson, 1979b). In tropical forests where the seasons are much more equable, the timing of the rhythmic pattern is less clear, some workers describing *Atta cephalotes* as a nocturnal forager (Beebe, 1921; Weber, 1941, 1946; Cherrett, 1968b) whilst others observed it to be diurnal (Lutz, 1929; Hodgson, 1955). To complicate matters, Cherrett (1968b) found two adjacent colonies of *Acromyrmex octospinosus* in Trinidad, one of which was diurnal, whilst the other was nocturnal. Lewis et al. (1974a, b), in a comprehensive study of the foraging activity of *Atta cephalotes* in Trinidad, concluded that there was a marked daily rhythm for any given colony, but that activity might begin at dusk (the most common), at dawn, or at some intermediate time. At any one time, some colonies might be on the day and others on the night "shift", and from time to time any given colony might change from one pattern to another, after some days of intermediate activity. They eventually found a colony where one trail was diurnal, and another nocturnal! Not surprisingly, no relation could be found between foraging and climatic factors. Lewis et al. (1974a) suggested that *A. cephalotes* was normally a nocturnal forager, but that at times of heavy demand for protein, as when large quantities of brood were developing, the workers became diurnal to harvest leaves rich in carbohydrates and proteins resulting from active photosynthesis during the day. The colony with one diurnal and one nocturnal trail was explained by postulating that they served two different groups of underground fungus chambers, only one group of which was rich in brood. As Lewis et al. (1974a) showed that less time is spent foraging during the day than at night, and that smaller quantities of leaves are brought in, it is not obvious that the higher protein content compensates for the smaller harvest, nor why the ants do not spend longer on the night shift until the necessary amount of protein has been obtained. Further studies are required to test this intriguing hypothesis. Hubbell and Wiemer (1983) have demonstrated that the ants can distinguish between sun and shade leaves, of both the old and young leaves of the three tree species tested. Littledyke (1977), however, was unable to show any preference for leaves of *Vicia faba* which had been kept in darkness for the previous 24 h compared with those in the light.

Amount of leaves taken

Lugo et al. (1973) collected data from twelve studies of the input of leaves to *Atta* nests in forests. These covered three ant species, four countries, nests of varying sizes, and observation periods from 4 h to 77 months. Estimates of the leaf input to the nest varied from 13 to 290 g h^{-1} (dry weight) and a mean figure of 62 g h^{-1} was quoted. If one assumes a mean density of 1.7 nests ha^{-1} (Table 27.2), this would mean that the ants are taking into the nest the equivalent of 0.253 g m^{-2} day^{-1}, or assuming an energy content of 4.25 kcal g^{-1} of leaf tissue (Lugo et al., 1973), 1.075 kcal m^{-2} day^{-1} (4.5 kJ m^{-2} day^{-1}). As the ants do not succeed in bringing back to the nest every leaf fragment they cut, their impact as forest defoliators could be greater.

No simultaneous estimates of leaf standing crop or of production were made in the forests where the ant studies were conducted, but data are available from the U.S. Atomic Energy Commission study of the El Verde tropical rain forest in the Luquillo Mountains of Puerto Rico (Odum, 1970). As no leaf-cutting ants occur in Puerto Rico, the figures provide background information without ant depredations. Gross photosynthesis was estimated at 131.2 kcal m^{-2} day^{-1} (549.3 kJ) and leaf production which was assumed to be the same as leaf fall plus herbivore consumption was estimated at 6.24 kcal m^{-2} day^{-1} (26.1 kJ). On average, holes made by herbivores occupied 7% of the leaf area. This suggests that leaf-cutting ants may have been harvesting 0.8% of the gross productivity of the vegetation, or more significantly 17% of the production of leaves. Anderson and Swift (1983) cite two other estimates of leaf fall in tropical lowland moist forests in the New World. Corrected for a 7% herbivore loss, these are 8.72 kcal m^{-2} day^{-1} (36.6 kJ) in Panama and 7.60 kcal m^{-2} day^{-1} (31.8 kJ) in Manaus, Brazil. Here, the ant impact would be somewhat reduced — to 12 and 14% of leaf production, respectively. When these figures are compared with the 7% loss attributed to all leaf herbivores in the El Verde forest, it provides some justification for their descriptions as "dominant invertebrates" (Wheeler, 1907) and "prevalent herbivores" (Wilson, 1982). Wint (1983) has suggested that as much as 80% of the apparent leaf damage seen in Panama rain forests may be caused by *Atta* spp., and this compares well with 72%, the calculated proportion if the average amount of damage were to occur in the El Verde forest.

The rain forests in which these colonies are found are renowned for their plant and animal diversity. There are several hypotheses to explain this, but for phytophagous insects a higher plant diversity will itself produce a higher animal diversity, unless the plant feeders become more polyphagous. In fact, plant-feeding insects in the tropics may well specialize on a narrower range of host plants than they do in temperate regions, in response to increased competition from other herbivores, and to the high levels of secondary metabolites in the long-lived "apparent" rain-forest vegetation which serve to defend the plants against herbivore attack (Waterman, 1983). As an example of this process, Janzen (1975) cited the 111 species of bruchids in Costa Rica, 102 (92%) of which were monophagous. In asking how one or two species of *Atta* are able to crop up to 17% of leaf production, their ability to exploit a wide range of plant species is a key issue.

Plant species attacked

Atta spp. show an impressive degree of polyphagy when foraging for leaf material in mixed rain forests. During a 10-week study in Wallaba forest in Guyana, Cherret (1968b) noted that one nest of *A. cephalotes* attacked 36 out of the 72 tree species growing in the vicinity (50%). When comparable efforts were used, however, this became 23 out of 28 available species (82%). Rockwood (1976), in an 11-month study in Costa Rica, recorded that a colony in evergreen oak forest (*Quercus oleoides*) cut 77% of the plant species growing in the area, and that an *A. colombica* colony in evergreen riparian forest cut 67%. The remaining four colonies studied (two *A. cephalotes* and two *A. colombica*) cut between 49 and 60% of all woody species within their territory. In the laboratory, Hubbell and Wiemer (1983) found that *A. cephalotes* picked up leaf discs from 34 out of 37 plant species (92%) selected at random out of 150 tree and shrub species known to occur in the Santa Rosa National Park forest in Costa Rica.

It is unusual for an insect to exploit such a wide range of plants from many different families as a direct or indirect source of food. This degree of polyphagy is more commonly associated with larger animals, such as howler monkeys (*Alouatta*), which ate 64% of the tree species available in a tropical forest (Rockwood and Glander, 1979). Mammals often eat small amounts of many plant species, and frequently employ gut microorganisms to detoxify the secondary plant metabolites (Janzen, 1975). Cherret (1980) has suggested that detoxification is also an important reason why leaf-cutting ants culture a fungus.

All the arguments so far employed to demonstrate the dominance and polyphagy of *Atta* spp. in rain forests apply with equal force to the fungus *Attamyces bromatificus* which they culture. As Quinlan and Cherret (1977) pointed out, it is equally unusual for a fungus using fresh leaves as a resource to attack such a wide range of plant species, as a parasitic way of life (the only way to get living leaves) normally imposes specialization. Only saprophytic species living on dead, nutritionally inferior, material are normally so polyphagous. Cherret (1980) maintained that two organisms of very different physical and physiological make-up, an ant and a fungus, had formed an "unholy alliance" to break down plant defences, the fungus neutralizing some of the plant's insect-defence mechanisms, and the ant breaking through some of its fungus-defence ones. As a result of this co-evolved ecological breakthrough, both have achieved, through polyphagy, a degree of dominance in diverse rain-forest vegetation which neither could have done alone.

As with all polyphagous animals, it is to be expected that the ants would prefer some plant species to others even within the list of exploited species, and Hubbell and Wiemer (1983) have shown in laboratory tests that the form this preference takes is that of a geometric relation between the number of leaf discs of a particular plant species taken and the acceptability of that species when ranked in order. There are many reasons why *Atta* spp. may prefer some leaves to others:

(1) Leaves may contain chemicals which act as attractants or repellents, and both were demonstrated in the laboratory for *Atta cephalotes* and *Acromyrmex octospinosus* using a moving air

olfactometer (Littledyke and Cherrett, 1978). There are no data on the distance at which these may operate in the field.

(2) Leaves may contain chemicals which act on contact as cutting stimulants or inhibitors. Both were demonstrated in privet leaves for *Atta cephalotes*, and their actions could be simulated with sucrose or quinine sulphate solutions (Barrer and Cherrett, 1972).

As the ants ingest sap from leaves both when cutting them, and during the process of preparing them as substrate for their fungus (Littledyke and Cherrett, 1976), and as sap forms the principal energy source for the colony (Quinlan and Cherrett, 1979) there are several reasons why the ants should react positively or negatively to chemicals within the leaves. They may be toxic or reduce digestibility for the ants, or for their fungus, or for both, or they may be of nutritional value. Hubbell and Wiemer (1983) isolated an ant repellent, caryophyllene epoxide, from *Hymenaea courbaril*

and showed it to be a potent fungicide, which could be the reason why the ants have evolved to find it repellent. Quinlan and Cherrett (1978) mixed baits with chemicals which inhibited growth of the ant fungus, but in only one out of four cases did this inhibit pick-up of the bait by the ants either immediately, or after a learning period.

(3) Leaves may have cuticular barriers to prevent the release of volatile attractants (Littledyke and Cherrett 1978): they may be tough and so inhibit cutting (Cherrett, 1972a; Waller, 1982a, b) (Fig. 27.3) or they may contain latex which oozes from the cut leaf, makes the ants mandibles sticky and inhibits further attack (Stradling, 1978). Stradling showed that species containing latex in a Guyana rain forest were significantly less attacked than species without latex.

(4) The leaves of one species of tree may not have been encountered for some time, and the "novelty effect" of a new leaf type can stimulate foraging, and, for a while, raise that leaf type's

Fig. 27.3. *Atta cephalotes* worker cutting leaves of a forest tree in Trinidad. Note the unsuccessful cuts, and the plant juice which has oozed onto the surface of the leaf.

position in the preference hierarchy (Cherrett, 1972b).

What is perhaps more surprising than the degree of selectivity shown is how and why *Atta* remains so polyphagous, and thus probably exploits some sub-optimal substrate.

Impact on the vegetation

There are records of trees in natural forests being killed as a result of repeated defoliations by leaf-cutting ants (Rockwood, 1975; Leston, 1978), although this is an uncommon phenomenon. Indeed, there are no immediately obvious differences in tree density or species composition between rain forests on the mainland where the ants abound, and on some of the Caribbean islands such as Puerto Rico or Dominica where they are absent. By contrast, the presence or absence of leaf-cutting ants in many forest plantations of exotic trees is very obvious, and Cherrett (1986) has collated some figures for losses to forestry and to orchard crops. It seems likely that in many areas *Eucalyptus* spp., *Pinus caribaea*, *Gmelina arborea* and *Citrus* spp. could not be grown without measures to control leaf-cutting ants. As *Atta cephalotes* is known to kill virtually all of the trees in a citrus plantation by repeated defoliation within seven years of control being abandoned (Cherrett and Jutsum, 1983), it raises the interesting question of why this herbivorous combination of polyphagous ant and fungus which has broken through so many of the conventional plant defences does not similarly damage its natural rain-forest habitat. As Thomas Belt (1874) in his classic book "The Naturalist in Nicaragua" put it, "What forests can stand before such invaders? How is it that vegetation is not eaten off the face of the earth?".

Belt thought that the long period of co-evolution of leaf-cutting and South American rain forest vegetation had developed specific defences in the native trees which limited ant exploitation and protected the forest. He pointed to the susceptibility of exotic crop plants, and concluded "…we can easily understand that trees and vegetables introduced from foreign lands where these ants are unknown could not have acquired, excepting accidentally, and without any reference to the ants, any protection against their attacks, and now they are most eagerly sought by them". Mechanical

defences which operate to prevent leaf cutting, and so are not susceptible to the combined ant/fungus assault would be obvious examples, and leaf latex and defensive ant faunas which prevent the leaf-cutters from attacking the tree (Cherrett and Jutsum, 1983) spring to mind. It will be interesting to see if these defences are commoner in New World rain forests where the ants are found, than in comparable Old World forests where they are not. If there is no difference it may imply that leaf-cutting ants are not such an important selective force as they appear to be.

Atta nests in rain forests are large, and remain in one place for a long time, perhaps 20 years or more. If plant resistance was the only factor involved in protecting forests, the least resistant trees nearest to the nest would be defoliated repeatedly year after year until they were killed, leaving an increasingly large zone around the nest consisting only of species unpalatable to the ants. There is no evidence that this happens, and Cherrett (1983) has argued that, for a species such as *Atta cephalotes* which may not begin to produce reproductives until the colony is 5 or 6 years old, foraging in this manner would not be an optimal long-term strategy. He has therefore advanced the theory (Cherrett, 1968b, 1983) that the ants adopt a conservational foraging pattern which maintains vegetation resources in the vicinity of the nest throughout its reproductive life span. Shepherd (1982) accepts that the foraging pattern effectively exploits resources over the lifetime of the colony, but does not accept that this is a prudent or conservational strategy. However as the nest may be reproducing up to 20 years after its foundation, behaviour which allows individual trees to go on being exploited for that length of time in effect conserves the vegetation indefinitely. Four mechanisms help achieve this:

(1) By scouting principally from the ends of the existing branched trunk trails rather than from the nest itself (Shepherd, 1982), grazing pressure is to some extent equalized over the whole foraging area, although at the expense of greatly increased retrieval costs when the ants exploit a tree which is not the nearest suitable one to the nest. This reduces the danger that trees near to the nest may be killed.

(2) The area foraged increases as the nest grows, maintaining the number of individual ants supported per unit of foraging area within long-term sustainable limits.

(3) The foraging territory is defended at considerable cost against exploitation by other conspecific colonies, and fighting has been frequently observed.

(4) Overgrazing on preferred plant species is minimized by retaining the maximum degree of polyphagy. This is accomplished through the chance element in tree discovery, especially when coupled with seasonally changing palatability; through the influence of individual scouts each with its own idiosyncratic preferences; and through the marked preference already noted for novel materials. The cost of this polyphagy must be the utilization of some suboptimal plant material.

As Cherrett (1968b, 1983) pointed out, these behaviours and the values of their parameters (the proportion of effort put into scouting, the lengths which trails may attain, the degree of aggressiveness to conspecifics, the thresholds of plant acceptability and their relation to novelty) were set by natural selection in *Atta cephalotes*. Their values represent a balance between the short-term advantages of obtaining as high a quality of resource from as near to the nest as possible with the minimum expenditure on defence, and the long-term advantages of using the resource in such a way as to enable the maximum effort to be put into reproduction between years five and twenty. If the parameters were set for rain forest, it is no surprise that they are no longer optimal when man cuts it down and replaces it with a monoculture of citrus, cocoa or *Pinus caribaea* having a much lower foliage density, and where a proportion of the habitat's productivity goes into grass production which *Atta cephalotes* cannot exploit. The result is widespread destruction.

This interpretation is controversial. The key behavioural observation is that *Atta* seems to travel much further to cut leaves than it needs to do, as other apparently suitable vegetation is available closer to the nest. Cherrett (1968b) working on *Atta cephalotes* and Shepherd (1982) working on *Atta colombica*, both in rain forest, found that most cutting occurred about 50 m from the nest. Other interpretations of this phenomenon are:

(1) That all the specimens nearer than the one being exploited are defended by other ant species (Leston, 1978). This will undoubtedly be a partial explanation, but often trees nearer to the nest are

cut a few days after ones further away, and it is unlikely that their defensive ants have just deserted them.

(2) That a clumped food source requires trails and an area-restricted search to locate it, the increased distance walked when retrieving the leaves presumably being offset by the effort saved in finding them (Fowler and Stiles, 1980). Whilst this may be true of the individual ant locating the piece of leaf it has been recruited to cut, it is not so obviously true of the colony locating trees which are random or only weakly aggregated.

(3) That walking over uncleared trails, and clearing them, are energetically costly, and it may be cheaper to go further on a cleared trail (Shepherd, 1982; Cherrett, 1983). However, it is not obvious that finding a new tree, and clearing a trail to it, is energetically cheaper if you start from the end of an existing trail, rather than from the nest itself. In the former case, the cost of maintaining the original trail must be included.

(4) In the event of competition from other colonies it may be energetically cheaper to go further for leaves, than to risk conflict in a disputed area near to the nest (Shepherd, 1982). This is possible, but as Rockwood (1973) has found that *Atta* nests in forests tend to be regularly distributed, border conflicts become more likely the further an ant gets from its nest.

EFFECTS ON SOIL AND NUTRIENT CYCLING

Mature *Atta* nests are formidable structures. Jonkman (1977) excavated a nest of *Atta vollenweideri* in the Chaco of Paraguay which was 35 m² in surface area, reached a depth of nearly 5 m and contained some 3000 chambers of total volume 5 m³. Stahel and Geijskes (1939) excavated a nest of *Atta cephalotes* in Surinam 256 m² in surface area and containing 283 chambers. Another nest had 592 chambers. As soil excavated from underground chambers and tunnels is brought to the surface by the workers where it is dumped, it represents a substantial disturbance of the soil profile. Weber (1972) claimed that this was important in transferring soil mineral nutrients to the upper layers where they may be more available to plant roots. Alvarado et al. (1981) noted disturbance by leaf-cutting ants in 85% of the 27 soil profiles they studied within an area of 2.5 ha in Costa Rica, although only 1% of the aboveground disturbed area was active. The main effects noted were the transport of material from the AB and B horizons to the soil surface, producing a new A1 horizon, and the filling of some subsoil chambers with plant material. The organic refuse which remains, after the fungus has extracted what nutrients it can from the chewed-up leaves originally supplied, is dumped by *Atta colombica* on the soil surface (Lugo et al., 1973; Haines, 1975). Other species including *A. cephalotes* dump the refuse in underground chambers. In *A. vollenweideri* these are large, specially constructed for refuse, and may be several metres underground. As Haines (1975) pointed out, *Atta* collects organic material in the form of living leaves from a large area, and the refuse, rich nitrogen, phosphorus, potassium, magnesium and calcium, is dumped at a specific point. Other herbivores tend to scatter it when they defaecate. He showed that the surface dumps of *A. colombica* stimulated the production of small-diameter tree roots in the vicinity, and these in turn removed water from the organic pile so efficiently that woody seedlings were inhibited from growing on it. The effects of the more usual dumping of refuse deep underground on the availability of nutrients to trees has not been studied. Haines (1975) specifically mentioned that *A. colombica* frequently dropped its rubbish into water when it was available, and where this is free flowing, the loss of nutrients through run-off must be enhanced. The structure of the nest, and the many deep tunnels dug by the ants, must affect local drainage and aeration, whilst the piles of loose earth on the surface are open to water erosion; but the overall implications of this for nutrient cycling in the forest as a whole are by no means clear.

RELATIONS WITH OTHER ANIMALS

Atta nests contain large numbers of workers. Lewis et al. (1974a) estimated that a medium-sized nest of *A. cephalotes* contained 651 000 ants, Jonkman (1980) that an average adult nest of *A. vollenweideri* contained 4 to 7 million, and, using data from Martin et al. (1967), Weber (1982) calculated that a nest of *A. colombica* must have had 2.5 to 5 million ants. Such large populations present a significant resource to be exploited by

predators, parasites and pathogens, whilst the complex nest structure provides a variety of niches for commensals. As the ants consume so much vegetation, they are also potential competitors with other herbivores for these resources.

Weber (1972, 1982) listed 111 organisms found associated with nests of leaf-cutting ants; 41 (37%) were predators, ranging from large, non-specific ones such as edentate anteaters and domestic fowl to more specific small arthropod predators such as 25 species of phorid flies, the larvae of which feed as parasitoids on the ant workers. Thirty-three (30%) were just listed in the literature as being found in the nest, and although some may have had close relationships with the ants others may have wandered in by chance. Eighteen (16%) were found in the refuse chambers, either exploiting the detritus directly, or feeding on other decomposers. Waller (1980) has shown how some inhabitants of refuse chambers, such as the milichiid fly *Pholeomyia texensis*, gain access to the nest by riding in on leaf fragments cut by the workers. Nine organisms were phoretic on the ants themselves, and two were fungus feeders exploiting the ants' fungus gardens. Some of the organisms are undoubtedly dependent upon leaf-cutting ants for their existence, and are only found in ant-infested forests. Others are facultative, and would remain part of the forest fauna even in their absence.

The role of leaf-cutting ants as competitors with other organisms will modify the normal forest fauna more directly. No studies seem to have been made on the fate of existing invertebrate defoliators when leaf-cutting ants attack a tree. Some may be able to deter the ants from cutting the leaves they are eating, but if not, and they cannot escape, they will either be removed with the leaves or left on the defoliated plant. However, some other ant species which do not utilize the leaves directly, but tend Homoptera which live on them, defend the plant and deter attack by leaf-cutting ants. Eberhard and Kafury (1974) suggested that *Azteca trigona* might deter leaf-cutters, and Leston (1978) showed that *Dolichoderus attelaboides* chemically repulsed individuals of *Atta cephalotes*, or lifted them clear of the trunk and dropped them to the ground. Finally, Jutsum et al. (1981) demonstrated experimentally that *Azteca* on citrus trees encourages populations of the soft green scale (*Coccus viridis*) and a stem coccid (*Toumeyella sp.* n) on trees in which it nests, and also prevented *Atta cephalotes* from gaining access to the tree. When the *Azteca* were killed with a poison bait, the tree was rapidly defoliated, the leaf scales being removed with the leaves, whilst the stem scales then died. The ant *Dolichoderus bidens* also protected citrus from *Atta*, but seemed capable only of defending the area immediately around its leaf nests, whilst the rest of the tree was stripped of leaves. Ants defending trees against *Atta* attack did not seem capable of sustaining the defence in the long term. As already noted, within seven years of ant control being abandoned, few citrus trees were still alive. Presumably, once a tree is stripped and its Homoptera have gone, it is no longer worth defending so momentary lapses in vigilance can have major consequences. It was noticeable that *Atta* damage could be found even on well-defended trees, where they touched undefended trees, so enabling the leaf-cutters to gain access to peripheral areas of the tree without having to ascend the usually well-defended trunk. Also, as *Azteca* is polydomous with several linked nests in adjacent trees, it is likely that *Atta* will succeed in invading a satellite tree if the defensive effort there is reduced for any reason. Experimental studies like this on the defensive ant mosaic in rain forests now need to be undertaken.

A second area for potential competition between ants and other animals is for the resources in the fungus gardens. Quinlan and Cherrett (1978) compared the acceptability of the ant fungus (*Attamyces bromatificus*) with the acceptability of eleven other common fungi to five temperate fungivores. All preferred the ant fungus, and it was concluded that it must contain few or no chemical defence mechanisms against fungivores. In the absence of leaf-cutting ants, other fungivores such as woodlice, diplopods and Collembola rapidly invaded fungus gardens, but in their presence these were attacked and physically prevented from feeding. In the field, it was observed that fungus gardens of *Acromyrmex octospinosus* were immediately invaded by millipedes once poison bait had begun to affect the activity of the leaf-cutting ant workers, but before they were dead.

CONCLUSIONS

Leaf-cutting ants are important herbivores in the New World rain forests. It should be possible to judge how important they are by the incidence of those defence mechanisms, such as latex and defensive ant faunas, which are effective in preventing attack by this powerful combination of ant and fungus. To do this will involve comparing the floras of comparable Old and New World rain forests and of rain forests on Caribbean islands with and without leaf-cutters. To admit the importance of the ants as herbivores in rain forests is also to admit the importance of their fungus as a dominant rain-forest organism.

As important herbivores, all the arguments about the role of phytophagous insects as regulators of forest primary production (Mattson and Addy, 1975) apply to the ants and their fungus, and Weber (1976) has claimed that by acting as pruners, and inducing further flushing on the part of the trees, they accelerate the green plant to fungus saprophyte stage. The significance of these effects are, however, more difficult to ascertain. A heavy herbivore load and more rapid recycling of minerals may increase the opportunities for loss to the system through leaching. Overgrazing of pastures can do this, and dumping of detritus in streams by *Atta colombica* could certainly exacerbate the problem. Also, as Janzen (1979) has pointed out, a tree stripped of its leaves by a herbivore may well respond with a period of rapid growth and repair, thus increasing foliage productivity in the short term. This does not however necessarily increase the fitness of the plant, which may have had to use resources that would otherwise have gone into reproduction. Conversely, insect pruning, which may increase flowering and fruiting in a way analogous to human pruning of fruit trees to increase yield, may divert resources from growth, which in the competitive conditions of a rain forest may fatally handicap the attacked plant in competing for light. At the present state of our knowledge, charts showing the impact of leaf-cutting ants, such as those produced by Weber (1982), must remain speculative.

There is of course ample scope for long-term ecological experiments. Eliminating all nests of leaf-cutting ants in sections of forest, and then noting how the vegetation changes over the subsequent years when compared with forest areas where the ants remain, is a long overdue experiment which would help replace speculation with data.

ACKNOWLEDGEMENTS

I am grateful for stimulating discussions over the years with the members of the leaf-cutting ant research group in Bangor. The British Overseas Development Administration provided financial support for many of the studies discussed.

REFERENCES

Alvarado, A., Berish, C.W. and Peralta, F., 1981. Leaf-cutter ant (*Atta cephalotes*): influence on the morphology of andepts in Costa Rica. *Soil Sci. Soc. Am. J.*, 45: 790–794.

Amante, E., 1972. *Influência de alguns fatores microclimaticos sôbre a formiga saúva Atta laevigata (F. Smith, 1858), Atta sexdens rubropilosa Forel, 1908, Atta bisphaerica Forel, 1908 e Atta capiguara Gonçalves, 1944 (Hymenoptera, Formicidae), em formigueiros localizados no estado de São Paulo.* Doct. Thesis, Univ. of São Paulo (Piracicaba), 175 pp.

Anderson, J.M. and Swift, M.J., 1983. Decomposition in tropical forests. In: S.L. Sutton, T.C. Whitmore and A.C. Chadwick (Editors), *Tropical Rain Forest: Ecology and Management.* Blackwell, Oxford, pp. 287–309.

Barrer, P.M. and Cherrett, J.M., 1972. Some factors affecting the site and pattern of leaf-cutting activity in the ant *Atta cephalotes* L. *J. Entomol., Ser. A*, 47: 15–27.

Beebe, W., 1921. *Edge of the Jungle.* Holt, New York, N.Y., 303 pp.

Belt, T., 1874. *The Naturalist in Nicaragua.* Bumpus, London, 306 pp.

Blanche, D., 1961. *La Fourmi-Manioc.* Ministère de l'Agriculture, Service de la Protection des Végétaux, Editions SEP, Paris.

Borgmeier, T., 1959. Revision der Gattung *Atta* Fabricius (Hym. Formicidae). *Stud. Entomol.*, 2: 321–390.

Cherrett, J.M., 1968a. Some aspects of the distribution of pest species of leaf-cutting ants in the Caribbean. *Proc. Am. Soc. Horticult. Sci., Trop. Region*, 12: 295–310.

Cherrett, J.M., 1968b. The foraging behaviour of *Atta cephalotes* L. (Hymenoptera, Formicidae). I. Foraging pattern and plant species attacked in tropical rain forest. *J. Anim. Ecol.*, 37: 387–403.

Cherrett, J.M., 1972a. Some factors involved in the selection of vegetable substrate by *Atta cephalotes* (L.) (Hymenoptera: Formicidae) in tropical rain forest. *J. Anim. Ecol.*, 41: 647–660.

Cherrett, J.M., 1972b. Chemical aspects of plant attack by leaf-cutting ants. In: J.B. Harborne (Editor), *Phytochemical Ecology*, Annu. Proc. Phytochem. Soc., 8, Academic Press, London, pp. 13–24.

Cherrett, J.M., 1980. Possible reasons for the mutualism between leaf-cutting ants (Hymenoptera: Formicidae) and their fungus. *Biol.–Ecol. Méditerr.*, 7: 113–122.

Cherrett, J.M., 1981. The interaction of wild vegetation and crops in leaf-cutting ant attack. In: J.M. Thresh (Editor).

Pests, Pathogens and Vegetation. Pitman, Boston, Mass., pp. 315–325.

Cherrett, J.M., 1983. Resource conservation by the leaf-cutting ant *Atta cephalotes* in tropical rain forest. In: S.L. Sutton, T.C. Whitmore and A.C. Chadwick (Editors), *Tropical Rain Forest: Ecology and Management.* Blackwell, Oxford, pp. 253–263.

Cherrett, J.M., 1986. The economic importance and control of leaf-cutting ants. In: S.B. Vinson (Editor), *Economic Impact and Control of Social Insects.* Praeger, New York, N.Y., pp. 165–192.

Cherrett, J.M. and Jutsum, A.R., 1983. The effects of some ant species, especially *Atta cephalotes* (L.). *Acromyrmex octospinosus* (Reich) and *Azteca* sp. (Hym. Form.) on citrus growing in Trinidad. In: P. Jaisson (Editor), *Social Insects in the Tropics.* Proc. 1st Int. Symp. organised by the International Union for the Study of Social Insects and the Sociedad Mexicana de Entomologia, Univ. Paris-Nord, 2: 155–163.

Cherrett, J.M. and Peregrine, D.J., 1976. A review of the status of leaf-cutting ants and their control. *Ann. Appl. Biol.*, 84: 124–128.

Eberhard, G. and Kafury, O., 1974. *La Ecologia de la Hormiga Azteca trigona, una Possible Defensa Contra las Arrieras.* Mem. II, Congreso de la Sociedad Colombiana de Entomologia, Cali, pp. 33–37.

Forel, A., 1902. Beispiele phylogenetischer Wirkungen und Rückwirkungen bei den Instinkten und dem Körperbau der Ameisen als Belege für die Evolutionslehre und die psychophysiologische Identitätslehre. *J. Psychol. Neurol.*, 1: 99–110.

Fowler, H.G., 1982. Evolution of the foraging behaviour of leaf-cutting ants (*Atta* and *Acromyrmex*). In: M.D. Breed, C.D. Michener and H.E. Evans (Editors), *The Biology of Social Insects.* Proc. 9th Congress of the Int. Union for the Study of Social Insects, Boulder, Colo., West View Press, Boulder, Colo., p. 33.

Fowler, H.G. and Robinson, S.W., 1979a. Field identification and relative pest status of Paraguayan leaf-cutting ants. *Turrialba*, 29: 11–16.

Fowler, H.G. and Robinson, S.W., 1979b. Foraging by *Atta sexdens* (Formicidae: Attini): seasonal patterns, caste and efficiency. *Ecol. Entomol.*, 4: 239–247.

Fowler, H.G. and Stiles, E.W., 1980. Conservative resource management by leaf-cutting ants? The role of foraging territories and trails, and environmental patchiness. *Sociobiology*, 5: 25–41.

Garling, L., 1979. Origin of ant-fungus mutualism: a new hypothesis. Biotropica, 11: 284–291.

Gonçalves, C.R., 1961. O gênero *Acromyrmex* no Brasil (Hym. Formicidae). *Stud. Entomol.*, 4: 113–180.

Gonçalves, C.R., 1982a. *Acromyrmex subterraneus* Forel 1893 y *A. coronatus* (Fabricius 1804), especies de hormigas nuevas para Venezuela. *Newslett. Attini, Private Publ.*, 12: p. 5.

Gonçalves, C.R., 1982b. Discricao de *Acromyrmex diasi*; uma nova especie de formiga cortadeira de folhas (Hym. Formicidae). *Rev. Bras. Biol.*, 42: 485–487.

Gonçalves, C.R., 1984. *Atta silvai*; nova especie de formiga sauva (Hymenoptera; Formicidae). *Arq. Univ. Fed. Rur. Rio de Janeiro*, 5: 173–178.

Haines, B., 1975. Impact of leaf-cutting ants on vegetation development at Barro Colorado Island. In: F.B. Golley and E. Medina (Editors), *Tropical Ecological Systems: Trends in Terrestrial, and Aquatic Research*. Springer, New York, N.Y., pp. 99–111.

Hodgson, E.S., 1955. An ecological study of the behaviour of the leaf-cutting ant *Atta cephalotes*. Ecology, 36: 293–304.

Hubbell, S.P. and Wiemer, D.F., 1983. Host plant selection by an Attine ant. In: P. Jaisson (Editor), *Social Insects in the Tropics*. Proc. 1st Int. Symp. organised by the Int. Union for the Study of Social Insects and the Sociedad Mexicana de Entomologia, Univ. Paris-Nord, 2: 133–154.

Janzen, D.H., 1975. *Ecology of Plants in the Tropics*. Edward Arnold, London, 66 pp.

Janzen, D.H., 1979. New horizons in the biology of plant defences. In: G.A. Rosenthal and D.H. Janzen (Editors), *Herbivores, their Interaction with Secondary Plant Metabolites*. Academic Press, New York, pp. 331–350.

Jonkman, J.C.M., 1977. *Biology and ecology of Atta vollenweideri Forel 1893 and its impact in Paraguayan pastures*. Thesis, Universiteitsbibliotheek, Leiden.

Jonkman, J.C.M., 1979. Distribution and densities of nests of the leaf-cutting ant *Atta vollenweideri* Forel, 1893 in Paraguay. *Z. Angew. Entomol.*, 88: 27–43.

Jonkman, J.C.M., 1980. Average vegetative requirement, colony size and estimated impact of *Atta vollenweideri* on cattle-raising in Paraguay. *Z. Angew. Entomol.*, 89: 135–143.

Jutsum, A.R., Cherrett, J.M. and Fisher, M., 1981. Interactions between the fauna of citrus trees in Trinidad and the ants *Atta cephalotes* and *Azteca* sp. *J. Appl. Ecol.*, 18: 187–195.

Kelderman, W., 1978. *Control of the Grass-Cutting Ant Acromyrmex landolti*. Proyecto Coperholta, Peru, Rep. No. 2 (Cyclostyled).

Kempf, W.W., 1972. Catálogo abreviado das Formigas da Região Neotropical (Hym. Formicidae). *Stud. Entomol.*, 15: 1–344.

Kusnezov, N., 1949. Sobre la reproducion de las Formas sexuales en *Solenopsis patagonica* (Emery) (Formicidae). *Acta Zool. Lilloana*, 8: 281–290.

Leston, D., 1978. A Neotropical ant mosaic. *Ann. Entomol. Soc. Am.*, 71: 649–653.

Lewis, T., 1975. Colony size, density and distribution of the leaf-cutting ant, *Acromyrmex octospinosus* (Reich) in cultivated fields. *Trans. R. Entomol. Soc. London*. 127: 51–64.

Lewis, T., Pollard, G.V. and Dibley, G.C., 1974a. Rhythmic foraging in the leaf-cutting ant *Atta cephalotes* (L.) (Formicidae:Attini). *J. Anim. Ecol.*, 43: 129–141.

Lewis, T., Pollard, G.V. and Dibley, G.C., 1974b. Microenvironmental factors affecting diel patterns of foraging in the leaf-cutting ant *Atta cephalotes* (L.) (Formicidae: Attini) *J. Anim. Ecol.*, 43: 143–153.

Littledyke, M., 1977. *Studies on the foraging and feeding behaviour of leaf-cutting ants of the genera Atta and Acromyrmex*. Unpubl. Ph.D. thesis, Univ. of Wales, Bangor.

Littledyke, M. and Cherrett, J.M., 1976. Direct ingestion of plant sap from cut leaves by the leaf-cutting ants *Atta cephalotes* (L.) and *Acromyrmex octospinosus* (Reich) (Formicidae, Attini). *Bull. Entomol. Res.*, 66: 205–217.

Littledyke, M. and Cherrett, J.M., 1978. Olfactory responses of the leaf-cutting ants *Atta cephalotes* (L.) and *Acromyrmex octospinosus* (Reich) (Hymenoptera: Formicidae) in the laboratory. *Bull. Entomol. Res.*, 68: 273–282.

Lugo, A.E., Farnworth, E.G., Pool, D., Jerez, P. and Kaufman, G., 1973. The impact of the leaf cutter ant *Atta colombica* on the energy flow of a tropical wet forest. *Ecology*, 54: 1292–1301.

Lutz, F.E., 1929. Observations on leaf-cutting ants. *Am. Mus. Novit.*, 388: 1–21.

Marcus, H., 1949. Supplementary notes on polymorphy and castration in *Acromyrmex sylvestri*. Cochabamba, *Folia Univ.*, 2: 23–27.

Mariconi, F.A.M., 1970. *As Saùvas*. Editôra Agronômica "Ceres", São Paulo, 167 pp.

Martin, M.M., Carls, G.A., Hutchins, R.F.N., MacConnell, J.C., Martin, J.S. and Steiner, O.D., 1967. Observations on *Atta colombica tonsipes* (Hymenoptera: Formicidae). *Ann. Entomol. Soc. Am.*, 60: 1329–1330.

Mattson, W.J. and Addy, N.D., 1975. Phytophagous insects as regulators of forest primary production. *Science*, 190: 515–522.

Mendes Filho, J.M., 1979. Tecnicas de combate as formigas. *Piracicaba, I.P.E.F., Circ. Tech.*, 75: 14 pp.

Moser, J.C., 1967. Trails of the leafcutters. *Nat. Hist.*, 76: 32–35.

Odum, H.T. (Editor), 1970. *A Tropical Rain Forest. A Study of Irradiation and Ecology at El Verde, Puerto Rico*. Office of Information Services, U.S. Atomic Energy Commission, 3 vols.

Pastel, J., Papa, J. and Kermarrec, A., 1980. Presence d'*Acromyrmex moellerius landolti* (Hymenoptera, Myrmicinae) en Guyane française. *Caribb. Plant Protect.*, 9: p. 2.

Quinlan, R.J. and Cherrett, J.M., 1977. The role of substrate preparation in the symbiosis between the leaf-cutting ant *Acromyrmex octospinosus* (Reich) and its food fungus. *Ecol. Entomol.*, 2: 161–170.

Quinlan, R.J. and Cherrett, J.M., 1978. Aspects of the symbiosis of the leaf-cutting ant *Acromyrmex octospinosus* (Reich) and its food fungus. *Ecol. Entomol.*, 3: 221–230.

Quinlan, R.J. and Cherrett, J.M., 1979. The role of fungus in the diet of the leaf-cutting ant *Atta cephalotes* (L.). *Ecol. Entomol.*, 4: 151–160.

Ribeiro, G.T. and Woessner, R.A., 1979. Teste de eficiência com seis (6) sauvicidas no control de saúvas (*Atta* spp.) na Jari, Pará, Brasil. *An. Soc. Entomol. Brasil.* 8: 77–84.

Rockwood, L.L., 1973. Distribution, density, and dispersion of two species of *Atta* (Hymenoptera: Formicidae) in Guanacaste province, Costa Rica. *J. Anim. Ecol.*, 42: 803–817.

Rockwood, L.L., 1975. The effects of seasonality on foraging in two species of leaf-cutting ants (*Atta*) in Guanacaste Province, Costa Rica. *Biotropica*, 7: 176–193.

Rockwood, L.L., 1976. Plant selection and foraging patterns in two species of leaf-cutting ants (*Atta*). *Ecology*, 57: 48–61.

Rockwood, L.L. and Glander, K.E., 1979. Howling monkeys and leaf-cutting ants: comparative foraging in a tropical deciduous forest. *Biotropica*, 11: 1–10.

Rodrigues, M.G., 1966. *Ecologia das Formigas Cortadeiras do Gênero Acromyrmex da Mata Amazônica.* Annual Report, Ministerio da Agricultura D.P.E.A. Instituto de Pesquisas e Experimentação Agropecuárias do norte Belém, Pará, Brasil.

Santschi, F., 1925. Revision du genre *Acromyrmex* Mayr. *Rev. Suisse Zool.*, 31: 355–398.

Shepherd, J.D., 1982. Trunk trails and the searching strategy of a leaf-cutter ant, *Atta colombica. Behav. Ecol. Sociobiol.*, 11: 77–84.

Smith, M.R., 1963. Notes on the leaf-cutting ants *Atta* spp. of the United States and Mexico. *Proc. Entomol. Soc. Wash.*, 65: 299–302.

Stahel, G. and Geijskes, D.C., 1939. Ueber den Bau der Nester von *Atta cephalotes* L. und *Atta sexdens* L. (Hym., Formicidae). *Rev. Entomol.*, 10: 27–78.

Stradling, D.J. 1978. The influence of size on foraging in the ant *Atta cephalotes*, and the effect of some plant defence mechanisms. *J. Anim. Ecol.*, 47: 173–188.

Uvarov, B., 1966. *Grasshoppers and Locusts, a Handbook of General Acridology. Vol. 1.* Cambridge Univ. Press, Cambridge, 481 pp.

Von Ihering, H., 1894. Die Ameisen von Rio Grande do Sul. *Berl. Entomol. Z.*, 39: 321–446.

Waller, D.A., 1980. Leaf-cutting ants and leaf-riding flies. *Ecol. Entomol.*, 5: 305–306.

Waller, D.A., 1982a. Leaf-cutting ants and avoided plants: Defenses against *Atta texana* attack. *Oecologia*, 52: 400–403.

Waller, D.A., 1982b. Leaf-cutting ants and live oak: the role of leaf toughness in seasonal and intraspecific host choice. *Entomol. Experiment. appl.*, 32: 146–150.

Waterman, P.G., 1983. Distribution of secondary metabolites in rain forest plants: towards an understanding of cause and effect. In: S.L. Sutton, T.C. Whitmore and A.C. Chadwick (Editors), *Tropical Rain Forest: Ecology and Management.* Blackwell, Oxford, pp. 167–179.

Weber, N.A., 1941. The biology of the fungus-growing ants VII. The Barro Colorado Island, Canal Zone, species. *Rev. Entomol.*, 12: 93–130.

Weber, N.A., 1946. Biology of the fungus-growing ants IX. The British Guiana species. *Rev. Entomol.*, 17: 114–172.

Weber, N.A., 1958. Evolution in fungus-growing ants. *Proc. 10th Int. Congress of Entomology*, 2: 459–473.

Weber, N.A., 1972. Gardening ants the attines. *Mem. Am. Philos. Soc.*, 92: 146 pp.

Weber, N.A., 1976. A ten-year laboratory colony of *Atta cephalotes.* Ann. Entomol. Soc. Am., 69: 825–829.

Weber, N.A., 1982. Fungus ants. In: H.R. Hermann (Editor), *Social Insects. Vol. 4.* Academic Press, London, pp. 255–363.

Wheeler, W.M., 1907. The fungus-growing ants of North America. *Bull. Am. Mus. Nat. Hist.*, 23: 669–807.

Wille, J.E., 1952. *Entomologia Agricola del Peru.* Ministerio de Agriculture, Lima, 468 pp.

Wilson, E.O., 1971. *The Insect Societies.* Belknap, Cambridge, Mass., 548 pp.

Wilson, E.O., 1982. Of insects and man. In: M.D. Breed, C.D. Michener and H.E. Evans (Editors), *The Biology of Social Insects.* Proc. 9th Congress of the Int. Union for the Study of Social Insects, Boulder, Colo., Westview Press, Boulder, Colo., pp. 1–3.

Wint, G.R.W., 1983. Leaf damage in tropical rain forest canopies. In: S.L. Sutton, T.C. Whitmore and A.C. Chadwick (Editors), *Tropical Rain Forest: Ecology and Management.* Blackwell, Oxford, pp. 229–239.

Worth, C.B., 1967. *A Naturalist in Trinidad.* Lippincott, New York, N.Y., 291 pp.

Chapter 28

DUNG BEETLES

I. HANSKI

INTRODUCTION

The ecology of dung- and carrion-associated beetles is constrained by the environment in much the same way in tropical forests as in other biomes. Their food, in the case of coprophagous (dung-feeding) and necrophagous (carrion-feeding) species, or their feeding stations, in the case of predators, parasitoids, mould-feeders, etc., are scattered in space: problems of locating the microhabitat must be solved. More than that, this must be done quickly — there is intense competition for high-quality, defenceless remains of animals as well as the food of the insect predators. The "First come, first served" principle — the so-called priority effect — is very true for these insects.

Patchiness and temporariness are the key characteristics of the dung and carrion microhabitats. Natural selection has undoubtedly shaped the species to become better in using these kaleidoscopic resources. Patchiness and temporariness have important consequences beyond the population level, by contributing to variation in species composition and timing of events in single pieces of carrion and dung. Such variation increases the chances that many species may co-occur in the same locality (community) though depending on the same resources (Horn and MacArthur, 1972; Slatkin, 1974; Levin, 1978; Hanski, 1981a, b, 1983a). The rate of exploitation of dung and carrion by beetles and by insects in general may be expected to be exceptionally high in tropical forests, due to continuously high temperatures and sufficient humidity. The high rate of removal of dung and carrion makes the priority effect (Hanski and Kuusela, 1977) referred to above of especial

importance, and enhances the temporariness of the microhabitat. On the other hand, lack of marked seasonality in many tropical forests allows continuous reproduction, and excludes seasonal adaptations as a means of coexistence (Hanski and Kuusela, 1980).

How much dung and carrion are available to insects in tropical rain forests? Assuming that animal production provides a useful index, figures presented by Whittaker (1975) suggest that of the forest biomes, tropical forests have the largest available amounts of dung and carrion, two to three times higher than temperate deciduous forests. The difference may be even greater. Herbivore biomass was 4 to 6 kg ha^{-1} in mixed forests in Czechoslovakia (Turček, 1969), while figures up to 30–50 kg ha^{-1} have been published for tropical forests (Odum et al., 1970; Fittkau and Klinge, 1973; Montgomery and Sunquist, 1975). For further discussion see Eisenberg (1980).

The highest mammal biomasses, and presumably the highest availability of dung and carrion, are found in tropical grasslands (250 kg ha^{-1} in African savannas according to Owen, 1983). Scarabaeinae — the archetypal dung beetles — have their highest number of species and individuals, as well as their presumed evolutionary home, in tropical grasslands (Halffter and Matthews, 1966), but many species have made the shift to tropical forests. Cambefort (1984) for example reports 201 species from savannas and 85 species from forests in the Ivory Coast. Cambefort (1984) has also estimated that, in West African (Guinean) savanna, dung beetles bury one metric ton of dung per hectare per year, while in forest the dung burial rate is ten times lower.

Of the numerous families of beetles associated

with dung [see, for instance, Valiela (1969, 1974) and Koskela and Hanski (1977)] and carrion (see Kuusisto, 1933; Fuller, 1934; Reed, 1958; Payne and Crossley, 1966; Payne and King, 1969), little ecological information has been published for tropical rain forests [see, however, Cornaby (1974) and Young (1978)] excepting, to some extent, Scarabaeinae (references throughout this chapter). Much of what is known remains unpublished in the form of "field lore acquired by the collector through years of experience" (Halffter and Matthews, 1966, p. 4).

ASSEMBLAGE OF DUNG AND CARRION BEETLES IN TROPICAL FORESTS

The only locality in tropical rain forests where all groups of beetles associated with dung and carrion have been collected, most of them sorted to species, and named and described as far as possible (Hanski, 1981, 1983b; Hammond, unpubl.; Hanski and Hammond, 1986; Krikken, unpubl.), is the Gunung Mulu National Park in Sarawak (Hanbury-Tenison and Jermy, 1979; Hanbury-Tenison, 1980; Anderson et al., 1982). This study has revealed more than 300 species of dung and carrion

insects and covers a range of habitats from three lowland forest types to upper montane tropical rain forest. It would be unwise to generalize these results to tropical rain forests of other regions, but a first reference point can now be established.

Figure 28.1 summarizes the distribution and abundance of 11 families and subfamilies in the six main forest types. There are two strictly necrophagous groups, Hybosorinae (Scarabaeidae) and Silphidae, represented by 4 and 1 large species, respectively (adult Hybosorinae are necrophagous, but the biology of their larvae is unknown). The silphid *Nicrophorus podagricus* occurs exclusively at altitudes above 1400 m, in upper montane tropical rain forest, with three necrophagous flies of similarly northern temperate affinities (*Lucilia*, *Calliphora*). Generally, *Nicrophorus* is restricted to montane forests in the Southeast Asian tropics, but in Sulawesi *N. distinctus* occurs in the lowland forests, up to 1500 m, at which altitude it is replaced by another, undescribed species of *Nicrophorus* (Hanski, unpubl.).

Forest over limestone in Mulu has soils only 11 cm in depth on average (Proctor et al., 1983), perhaps too shallow to allow normal nesting behaviour of many Scarabaeinae. Mammals are probably scarce in this forest type. In fact, no

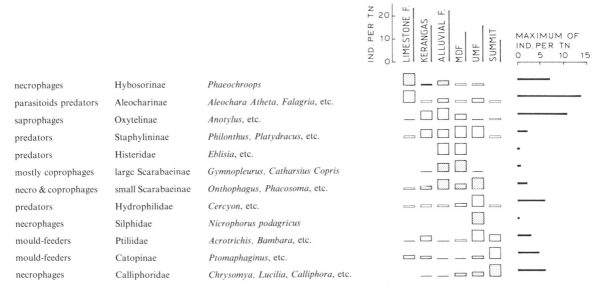

Fig. 28.1. Abundances of the main beetle taxa associated with dung and carrion in six forest types in Mulu, Sarawak. The maximum abundance of each taxon has been scaled to unity; the histogram on the right gives this maximum abundance in terms of individuals per 100 trap-nights. The upper histogram gives the same measure of abundance in the pooled material. The different shadings identify different trophic groups. (Data from Hanski, 1983b; Hanski and Hammond, 1986.)

species of Scarabaeinae was abundant in forest over limestone, but the necrophagous *Phaeochroops gilleti* (Hybosorinae) was strikingly abundant. Another group well represented here was Aleocharinae (Staphylinidae), again strongly dominated by a single, probably parasitic species (Peter Hammond, pers. comm.). Forest over limestone had exceptionally high moth diversity (Holloway, 1984), but it appears that the carrion community consisted, at the time of sampling, of essentially two species of beetles. Not all species assemblages in tropical rain forests are complex!

Many of the smaller Scarabaeinae are necrophagous while most of the larger species use both dung and carrion (Hanski, 1983b; this will be discussed in detail below). The large species and most of the smaller ones were confined to the lowlands, where dung and carrion are more abundant (cf. distribution of mammals and birds; Anderson et al., 1982), but two small species (*Onthophagus* sp. n. and *Phacosoma* sp. n.) were remarkably abundant in upper montane tropical rain forest, at altitudes between 1300 and 2000 m, where they co-occurred with the silphid *N. podagricus*, three predatory staphylinids (*Philonthus*), several predatory Hydrophilidae, some abundant mould-feeding Ptiliidae and Catopinae, and some probably parasitic Aleocharinae (Fig. 28.1). The upper montane tropical rain forest has a relatively simple community consisting of several abundant but few rare species.

Predatory beetles in the family Histeridae were represented by three relatively common lowland species. In the tropical rain forests of some other regions Histeridae are more numerous, both in species and in individuals (for instance, West Africa: Hanski, unpubl.; Panama: Young, 1978). The most prominent predator group was the Staphylinidae, as in temperate dung and carrion communities (Kuusisto, 1933; Koskela and Hanski, 1977).

One group of beetles remains to be mentioned, the Oxytelinae (Staphylinidae), a group of small-sized and very numerous saprophagous species. Most of them are found in the lowlands (Fig. 28.1).

Carrion and dung communities naturally include a host of insects other than beetles, particularly flies, of which only the Calliphoridae (carrion flies) are included in Fig. 28.1. Knowledge about the ecology of other groups is nearly a complete

blank. Poulson (unpubl.) lists Sepsidae, Micropezidae and Otitidae as feeding on dung on Barro Colorado Island, Panama, and in Mulu in Sarawak, Sphaeroceridae, Muscidae and Phoridae were abundant on carrion (Hanski, unpubl.). Cornaby (1974) has studied carrion insects in two contrasting tropical forests in Costa Rica. He recorded more than 170 species representing 49 families, among which larvae of Calliphoridae and Sarcophagidae, ants and dung beetles were most numerous. Phoretic and predatory mites are as prevalent in tropical forests as they are in temperate dung and carrion communities.

NATURAL HISTORY OF DUNG BEETLES (SCARABAEINAE)

Little or nothing is known about the natural history of beetles other than Scarabaeinae associated with dung and carrion in tropical forests. This section is restricted to the Scarabaeinae, and the term "dung beetle" is here used in reference to this subfamily only.

Foraging behaviour

Dung beetles locate their resource — dung, carrion or (less commonly) rotting vegetable matter — by smell. *Megathoposoma candezei*, a large Neotropical forest species, is able to locate a food source from a distance of 50 to 75 m (Wille et al., 1974). Beetles generally pursue a zig-zag flight pattern, moving upwind, a metre or less above the ground level, and land on or close to the source of the odour (Halffter and Matthews, 1966; Howden and Young, 1981; Peck and Forsyth, 1982; Hanski, unpubl.). Little is known about possible sex pheromones, though their existence has been suspected in *Canthon cyanellus* (Halffter and Edmonds, 1982, citing work by Bellés and Favila, 1983) and in *Kheper nigroaeneus* (Tribe, 1975; not a species of tropical rain forest). Poulson (1979) believes that odours act as sexual attractants only at very short distances in dung beetles of the tropical rain forests.

Other types of foraging behaviour are less common but interesting as special adaptations to the tropical rain forests. The following examples come mostly from Barro Colorado Island,

Panama, a locality exceptionally well studied even in terms of dung beetles (Young, 1978; Poulson unpubl.; Howden and Young, 1981).

Canthon angustatus is a yellowish-brown, shining dung beetle 4.5 to 6.5 mm long, one of the most abundant ones on Barro Colorado Island (Howden and Young, 1981). It occurs only in those areas of lowland moist forest where the howler monkey *Alouatta palliata* is found, whose faeces *C. angustatus* appears to prefer. The first beetles to arrive at dung are usually able to land on the food but later ones — perhaps after failing to locate the source of the odour — often land on leaf surfaces (Howden and Young, 1981).

Perching on leaves, with the antennae outstretched, waiting for fresh odour currents, is a common foraging method amongst dung beetles of the Neotropical forests (Halffter and Matthews, 1966; Howden and Nealis, 1978), but to what extent it occurs elsewhere is less clear. Walter (1980) specifically mentioned not having seen dung beetles perching on leaves in Zaïre, while Cambefort (1984) has positive observations for 8 out of 85 species in the Ivory Coast. In Sarawak, dung beetles were hardly seen on leaves, but in Sulawesi several small species of *Onthophagus* regularly perch on leaves, usually *c*. 50 cm above the ground (Hanski, unpubl.). The most frequent perching scarab, *O. fuscostriatus*, is a dung specialist, probably dependent on faeces of the Celebes monkey *Macaca nigra* in the same way as *C. angustatus* in Panama specializes on those of the howler monkey.

Howden and Nealis (1978), working in Ecuador, found that small species (particularly *Canthidium*) tend to perch more frequently and closer to the ground than larger species; this was also found in Sulawesi (Hanski, unpubl.). They suggested that small food sources might be best detected by perching near the ground in favourable areas. Perching may also have other causes than foraging (Gill, 1984; Young, 1984).

Canthon angustatus and another congeneric species, *C. subhyalinus*, have evolved the ultimate behaviour pattern for locating food in the three-dimensional space of a tropical rain forest (Howden and Young, 1981). Howler monkey faeces, placed at the top of a 23 m tower was approached first at a height of only 15 to 60 cm above the ground, and then, from the base of the tower, by vertical flight up to the top of the tower. These two

species are able to form and roll primate faeces adhering to leaf surfaces. The beetle remains attached to the ball as it falls to the forest floor, managing to land on top of it (Howden and Young, 1981). Walter (1982) found five species foraging in the canopy in Gabon, but Cambefort (1984) caught none in the Ivory Coast. In Sulawesi, one *Onthophagus* species was trapped *only* in the canopy (Hanski, unpubl.). Its biology remains unknown.

Once a beetle has arrived at the food it either feeds on it directly, buries it without transport, or transports it overland with or without formation of a ball. Halffter and Matthews (1966, pp. 93–121) have presented a comprehensive discussion on feeding and related behaviour. Unfortunately, relatively few direct observations have been made in tropical rain forest, especially outside tropical America [important Neotropical works are Young (1978), Poulson (unpubl.) and Peck and Forsyth (1982)]. Rolling and other forms of food transport are a means by which a beetle can secure a portion of the resources for its exclusive use; additionally, rolling behaviour facilitates pair bonding (Halffter et al., 1974).

Breeding

Most dung beetles feed for a relatively long period of time, up to several months, after emergence from the nest; this is necessary for the full development of the gonads and eggs (Halffter and Matthews, 1966). The long pre-reproductive feeding period is a cost that the offspring must pay for the relatively small amount of food brought into the nest by the breeding pair of beetles, which themselves are often severely resource-limited because of intense competition (see below).

Feeding is followed by breeding, with its more-or-less complicated nesting behaviour, excellently described and analysed in a recent book by Halffter and Edmonds (1982) (see also Halffter and Matthews, 1966; Halffter, 1977). They classify the various types of nesting behaviour into seven groups or patterns, diagnosed on the basis of the form of larval provision, nest location and complexity, disposition of brood masses or balls in the nest, manipulation of larval provision, outer surfaces of brood balls, location of egg chamber, male–female cooperation, and brood care. This list may give a feeling for the complexity and diversity in the nesting habits of Scarabaeinae. Even a brief discussion is outside the scope of this paper, and the interested reader should consult Halffter and Edmonds (1982). The following examples are not typical but are of interest as probable adaptations to the conditions of tropical rain forest.

"*Megathoposoma candezei* is a typical dung beetle of the tropical rain forest, never found in open places" (Wille, 1973). It is a large beetle, up to 3 cm in length. Some 15 individuals may occur per hectare at suitable sites in Costa Rica (Wille, 1973; Wille et al., 1974) — this is one of the few attempts to estimate dung beetle density in tropical rain forests. The life cycle (from egg to adult) is about six months (Wille et al., 1974), longer than in many smaller species (30 to 50 days according to Halffter and Matthews, 1966). *Megathoposoma candezei* coats food balls with mud, and buries them in superficial chambers (Wille, 1973), a common trait in forest dung beetles but uncommon in species of open grassland, which have deep burrows (Halffter and Matthews, 1966), presumably because of the more seasonal and less humid climate in grasslands.

The tribe Scarabaeini of ball-rollers has an Australian endemic genus *Cephalodesmius* with three flightless species restricted to the rain forests of southeastern Queensland. Monteith and Storey (1981) have published an excellent account of their unusual biology.

The three species are all common where they occur. At one site *C. armiger* reached 20 000 to 50 000 individuals per hectare, a fantastic figure for a dung beetle 12 to 15 mm in length (Fig. 28.2). In fact, the local supply of dung and carrion falls short of supporting such a biomass of beetles. But *Cephalodesmius* has a unique solution: although dung is occasionally collected, transported to burrows and presumably consumed, the main food source is leaves and other plant material, which are collected mostly by the male and dragged into feeding and breeding burrows (Fig. 28.2), where the female processes the plant material into a plastic, dung-like material.

The life history of *Cephalodesmius* has other unique features. The generation length is one year, with little overlap between the generations (the Queensland rain forest is seasonal). The newly emerged beetles are active on the ground surface in

Fig. 28.2. (Upper) Foraging male of *Cephalodesmius armiger* carrying a dead leaf backwards towards its burrow. (Lower) Foraging male of *C. armiger* with two specimens of a phoretic staphylinid beetle (*Anotylus* sp.) clinging to its dorsum. The staphylinid breeds in the brood mass in burrows of *C. armiger*. (From Monteith and Storey, 1981.)

late summer, and they copulate out of the breeding context — a unique feature in Scarabaeinae. Copulation at this stage is probably a part of mate selection and pair bonding. *Cephalodesmius* has a monogamous breeding system with a life-long pair bond. Feeding burrows are constructed by a mated pair of beetles, but breeding does not commence before next summer.

In August – September the pair converts the feeding burrow into a brood burrow. The female makes four or five small brood balls from the material brought in by the male, and lays an egg in each. Unlike all other Scarabaeinae, the brood balls are too small to provide food for the entire larval development. The parent beetles cooperate during larval growth in progressive provisioning of the larval brood balls, apparently guided by a stridulating larva, another fascinating detail.

The brood nests of *Cephalodesmius* are inhabited by at least four species of mites, one springtail, two staphylinid beetles (*Anotylus* and *Oxytelus*) and a sphaerocerid fly, with more or less complex trophic and phoretic relationships with *Cephalodesmius* (Fig. 28.2).

The nesting behaviour of dung beetles has evolved along two main lines: some species bury dung in preformed burrows at the food source (tribes Onthophagini, Oniticellini, Onitini and Coprini), whilst others make dung or carrion balls and transport them away to be buried at a distance from the food source (Scarabaeini). This classification leaves out the tribe Eurysternini, with the single Neotropical genus *Eurysternus* of tropical forests. The following account of their extraordinary breeding biology is based on Halffter et al. (1980) and Halffter and Edmonds (1982).

Eurysternus feeds directly from the food source without making balls for as long as 200 days. The species have longer lifespans than most Scarabaeinae, in some cases over two years. The beginning of the breeding period is signalled by ball-making by the female. Tens of balls may be constructed at this stage, termed the "nuptial feast" by Halffter et al. (1980). Once the nuptial feast has begun, the female is joined by a male; if not, the nuptial feast is interrupted. Ball-making here functions, in part at least, as an attractant for a male.

Although some of the balls constructed during the nuptial feast may be used as brood balls, most are either simply abandoned or consumed. Why should the female expend such a great effort in constructing balls during the nuptial feast? Halffter et al. (1980) suggest that frantic ball-making at this stage may help in fierce competition for excrement in tropical forests. Ball-making also brings the female and the male together.

The next stage is even more intriguing than the nuptial feast. Halffter and Edmonds (1982) described "experimental nesting" in *E. balachowskyi* as follows:

"Next, as in *E. magnus*, a crater is dug beneath some balls and others are pushed into it; three balls are provided with eggs and are partially covered with soil. Parental brooding occurs, especially by the female, but with a difference from *magnus*: at a certain moment, either the female or male attacks a part of the balls containing eggs while both continue to care for the others. A few days later, the female or male destroys the remaining brood balls and they both abandon the nest. Some brood balls may accidentally survive this ovicidal frenzy and their larvae live to complete development. After a direct feeding period in dung the above activities are repeated, perhaps several times, with resulting abandonment of the craters with partially consumed balls."

In the final stage of nesting, the female *E. balachowskyi* chooses two brood balls, places them on a flat surface so that the balls touch each other, digs a furrow around them and covers them with soil. The furrow is made deeper until the balls are elevated with a minimum of support from untouched soil beneath them (Fig. 28.3). The female cares for this nest for about 40 days. After a month of feeding directly in the dung, the female begins once again to manufacture balls.

Eurysternus appears to defy theories of "reproductive effort" by its seemingly pointless construction of "extra" balls and destruction of its own

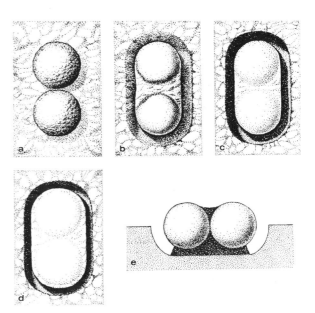

Fig. 28.3. *Eurysternus balachowskyi*. (a–d) Stages in the formation of the definitive nest as seen from above; two brood balls are united with soil and surrounded by a groove. (e) Completed nest as seen from the side. (From Halffter et al., 1980.)

progeny. Halffter et al. (1980) attributed the anomalous breeding behaviour to a lack of coordination between internal regulators of nesting behaviour and those of ovarial function. They also observed that "when several females engaged in the nuptial feast occur in the same terrarium, a strong competition for space ensures. Each female tries to isolate her balls from other females, which may attack and eat them". Actual fights occur. Perhaps the seemingly maladaptive behaviour in experimental nesting stems from uncertainty as to whose eggs the brood balls actually contain? Perhaps the very special final nest construction (Fig. 28.3) ensures that other females have no chance of secretly laying eggs in the brood balls? It would be crucial to know what happens in the tropical forests where *Eurysternus* live; what are the ecological conditions under which this unusual breeding behaviour has evolved?

COMPETITION FOR DUNG AND CARRION IS FIERCE IN TROPICAL FORESTS

The relationship between organisms and their food resources is fundamental in ecology. In particular, ecologists often ask whether populations are food-limited. If several species utilizing partly or entirely the same resources are thus affected, the species are competing with each other.

Ecologists have become critical about questions relating to interspecific competition (see Annales Zoologici Fennici vol. 19, no. 4, 1982; American Naturalist vol. 122, no. 5, 1983) and especially its role in the evolution of coexisting species (Connell, 1980). Are differences in the "niches" of coexisting competitors attributable to coevolution? The current approach is to demand strong, experimental evidence for on-going competition, and to dismiss past competition if infered from community structure. Recent work has not only demonstrated present-day competition to be common [see reviews by Schoener (1983) and Connell (1983)], but also built a good case that interspecific competition has structured certain communities of lizards (Roughgarden et al., 1983) and birds (Schluter and Grant, 1984).

Though no study on competition in dung and carrion beetles has provided incontrovertible evidence, it would be inexcusable to ignore competi-

tion here. Dung and carrion beetles of the tropical rain forest live in an extremely competitive world. How can this statement be justified?

Observation 1: Exploitative competition. Beetles arrive fast, literally in minutes, to freshly deposited human faeces, the most attractive food source, and remove it fast. Though several authors have been impressed by this (Ohaus, 1900; Halffter and Matthews, 1966; Wille, 1973; Howden and Young, 1981; Hanski, 1983b), only Peck and Forsyth (1982) have presented quantitative figures (from an Ecuadorian rain forest). The first beetles usually arrived within 1 min, and always within 5 min, during the day. Small and abundant species usually arrived first, while the largest species, *Oxysternon conspicillatus*, never discovered the dung in less than 5 min. Arrival rates were up to 150 beetles during the first hour, and up to 30 individuals of *Canthon angustatus*, the main ball-roller, could be seen cutting balls at one time on a single piece of dung. During the day or evening, 200 g of human faeces were invariably buried in less than two hours.

Human faeces remain highly attractive to beetles for several days [Howden and Nealis (1975); Peck and Forsyth (1982); Hanski, unpubl.; see Young (1978) for carrion]. In view of the observed high removal rates this practically proves that exploitative competition occurs. On Barro Colorado Island, Panama, necrophagous scarabs are clearly more abundant in the wet season, when carrion availability is higher than in the dry season (Young, 1978).

The behaviour of manufacturing dung or carrion balls and transporting them away from the food source, though not especially prominent in forest species (see Cambefort, 1984), has probably evolved because of competition (Halffter et al., 1974). Young (1976, 1978) has even maintained that some ball-rollers will consume food in situ in the absence of competitors, and will make and roll balls when competitors become abundant on the food source.

Elephant dung in West African forests is not removed as fast as in savannas (Y. Cambefort, pers. commun., 1984). Possibly elephant droppings represent such large and exceptional resource concentrations with respect to the average availability of dung in forests that the numbers of beetles are insufficient to remove the droppings efficiently.

Carrion-associated beetles face severe competition from vertebrate scavengers (on large carcasses), calliphorid flies and ants (Cornaby, 1974; Hanski, unpubl.).

Observation 2: Interference competition. Young (1978) and Peck and Forsyth (1982) in Panamanian and Ecuadorian tropical forests respectively, have observed direct interference competition in dung beetles, involving attempts at food stealing. Both intraspecific and interspecific competition has been observed. Peck and Forsyth (1982) found larger species to be superior competitors, while Young (1978) observed and experimentally confirmed a linear dominance hierarchy with ball-rollers competitively superior to the others. *Canthon septemmaculatus* routinely robs food balls from other ball-rolling species (Young, 1978; Howden and Young, 1981).

Young (1978) reported a high incidence of kleptoparasitism from Barro Colorado Island, competitively inferior small species consuming food balls, and possible eggs and young larvae, of the host species.

A form of interspecific competition mediated by olfactory communication has been observed by Young in Panama (reported by Howden and Young, 1981). When *Canthon angustatus* individuals were active at monkey droppings, individuals of its main competitor, *Canthon lamprimus*, surrounded the faecal material at a distance of *c*. 15 cm, and remained at this distance until most *C. angustatus* individuals left the site. Laboratory experiments proved that *C. angustatus* is a superior competitor in one-to-one confrontations.

Observation 3: Competition between necrophagous beetles and flies. Necrophagous beetles were abundant in lowland forests in Sarawak, where carrion flies (Calliphoridae) were found to be scarce (Hanski, 1981c), apparently because their chances of breeding were limited. In a similar lowland forest in Liberia, on the contrary, necrophagous beetles were much scarcer and carrion flies were more abundant by one or two orders of magnitude than in Sarawak (Hanski, unpubl.). Carrion flies were abundant but necrophagous beetles were scarce in two tropical forests in Costa Rica in the dry season (Cornaby, 1974). Scarabaeinae were absent in upper montane tropical rain forest in Mulu, Sarawak, and again carrion flies appeared to have benefited from their absence

(Hanski, 1981c, 1983b). Carrion flies were the main decomposers of a dog carcass in a montane forest in Costa Rica (Jiron and Cartin, 1981).

The above competition hypothesis is meant to work with small carcasses. Beetles are unable to remove large carcasses fast enough to prevent flies breeding (Young, 1978), and hence in regions where mammals are abundant, but vertebrate scavengers not especially effective, carrion flies can be abundant in spite of competition from beetles. Sulawesi is a possible example (Hanski, unpubl.).

Bellés and Favila (1983) have described a chemical component in the competition between carrion flies and an American necrophagous forest scarab, *Canthon cyanellus*. The male *C. cyanellus* (but not the female) secretes a chemical substance from pores in the 7th abdominal sternite onto the surface of food balls. Bellés and Favila (1983) showed experimentally that balls thus treated are discriminated against by *Calliphora* larvae.

Observation 4: Density compensation. Islands and isolated "habitat islands" usually have fewer species than comparable mainland areas (MacArthur and Wilson, 1967). The montane tropical rain forest on Gunung Mulu is a habitat island with a reduced species number (Hanski, 1983b), but the species have dense populations (Fig. 28.4).

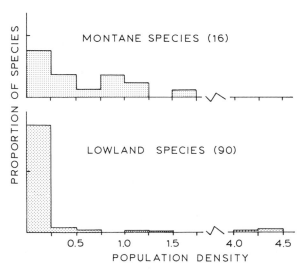

Fig. 28.4. Densities of montane and lowland species of Scarabaeidae, Staphylininae, Oxytelinae and Silphidae in Mulu, Sarawak (individuals per trap-night). Montane forests have few species but montane populations tend to be denser than lowland ones, $\chi^2 = 21.3$, $P > 0.001$. (Data from Hanski, 1983b; Hanski and Hammond, 1986.)

This can be explained by the competition theory (for example, MacArthur, 1972; Case et al., 1979): because there are few species there are more resources per species than in lowland forests, hence the montane populations can be denser. This assumes equal resource availability in the two habitats, which is hardly true; but here the difference is in the direction of higher resource availability in the lowland forests (Anderson et al., 1982), making the "natural experiment" conservative.

One more observation may be recollected. The Australian saprophagous dung beetle *Cephalodesmius* has up to 50 000 beetles per hectare, which must be a higher density than any "true" dung beetle of the same size could achieve in tropical forests. Peck and Forsyth (1982) marked a sample of 2178 individuals representing the whole dung beetle assemblage in an Ecuadorian rain forest, and obtained an estimate of 2000 beetles per hectare. The most abundant species had below 1000 individuals per hectare. This is further indirect evidence for food limitation in dung and carrion beetles of tropical forests. It may be added that predation and even parasitism appear to be minor mortality factors in dung beetles (Ritcher, 1958; Young, 1978).

Taking competition for granted, what can one learn about its consequences from existing data on dung and carrion beetles of tropical rain forests? The following sections discuss ecological diversification and abundance relations, but do not answer this question satisfactorily, because factors other than competition must affect community structure.

Perhaps because of competition, the most abundant species are often relatively more abundant than their temperate counterparts (Hanski, 1983b; see also next section). Caswell (1976) has argued that strong interspecific interactions, presumed to prevail in tropical forests, should indeed increase dominance, not decrease it, as has commonly been believed (MacArthur, 1969).

Are the dung and carrion beetle communities of tropical rain forests saturated with species? The answer is of course not known, but observations indicating good ecological segregation and tight "species packing" (Hanski, 1983b; see also below) suggest that these communities may be saturated as far as the numbers of abundant species are concerned.

The rest of this section gives two examples of the kinds of patterns which many ecologists would attribute to interspecific competition but which could be due to other causes as well.

Two abundant, small Scarabaeinae, *Phacosoma* sp. n. and *Onthophagus* sp. n., were collected along a transect line through homogeneous upper montane tropical rain forest, situated on a level ridge at an altitude of 1700 m on Gunung Mulu, Sarawak. Abundances of the two species were negatively correlated between the trapping sites (Fig. 28.5; for further details see Hanski, 1983b). It is difficult to explain this result by environmental factors, as high density patches of the two species were intermingled with each other.

Another example is the distribution of *Platydracus aeneipennis* and five species of *Philonthus*, all predatory Staphylininae, on the same mountain. These species show two series of displacements along an elevational gradient, consisting of three large species (>4 mg dry wt.) and four smaller ones (<3 mg dry wt.) (Fig. 28.6). These beetles most likely prey upon eggs and maggots of calliphorid flies, which in Mulu were scarce in the lowlands but abundant in montane forests (Hanski, 1981c). Such an elevational pattern seems

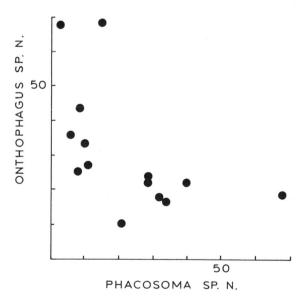

Fig. 28.5. Abundances of two small scarabs, *Onthophagus* sp. n. and *Phacosoma* sp. n., at 14 sites in homogeneous upper montane tropical rain forest at an altitude of 1700 m on Gunung Mulu, Sarawak. The two species show negative association between the sites, $\chi^2 = 14.0$, $P < 0.001$. (Data from Hanski, 1983b.)

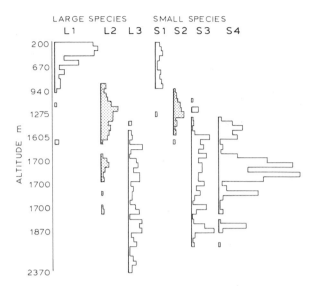

Fig. 28.6. Abundances of seven predatory staphylinids along a mountain slope (Gunung Mulu, Sarawak) from an altitude of 200 to 2370 m (summit). There are three large species (L1–3) and four smaller ones (S1–4) (L1 is *Platydracus aeneipennis*, the others are undescribed species of *Philonthus*). Note the parallel series of elevational replacements in the large and small species; abundances of the "middle-species" have been shaded. (Data from Hanski, 1983b; see discussion by Hanski and Hammond, 1986.)

difficult to explain without ascribing some role to interspecific competition, especially because the lower and upper elevational limits of these species do not agree well with those of other carrion insects (Hanski, 1983c).

ECOLOGICAL DIVERSIFICATION: FOOD, TIME AND SPACE

Ecological segregation amongst species at the same trophic level usually involves, in one way or another, the food they eat, the time when they are active, or the place where they occur [Schoener (1974); for a study on dung-inhabiting beetles in the temperate zone see Hanski and Koskela (1979)]. I shall consider some aspects of each below.

Feeding specializations

Before discussing the major adaptations, coprophagy and necrophagy, it is appropriate to mention less common feeding specializations largely or

entirely restricted to tropical forests. Tens, if not hundreds of species in tropical forests throughout the world are saprophagous, attracted to fallen fruits and other soft, decaying vegetable matter. Many species are copro-saprophagous, and several euryphagous forest species are attracted to rotting fungi — for example *Onthophagus batillifer* in Sarawak (Hanski, 1983b). Halffter and Matthews (1966, pp. 34–41) have presented a comprehensive discussion with numerous examples.

Canthon virens, an Amazonian species, has evolved the extraordinary feeding specialization of attacking ants of the genus *Atta* (Navajas, 1950; Halffter and Matthews, 1966). Brood balls are made of the abdominal contents of ovigerous females.

Scarabaeinae are believed to have evolved in tropical grasslands, where practically all the species are coprophagous (Halffter and Matthews, 1966), utilizing the often vast amounts of dung from large herbivores available there. Moving to tropical forests from grasslands, one observes a nearly complete change in species composition (Halffter and Matthews, 1966; Howden and Nealis, 1975; Janzen, 1983; Cambefort, 1984), and a tendency in many species to shift to necrophagy. This change in food selection is more evident in tropical America (Halffter and Matthews, 1966) and South-East Asia (Hanski, 1983b) than in Africa (Cambefort, 1982, 1984) (Fig. 28.7). Halffter and Matthews (1966)

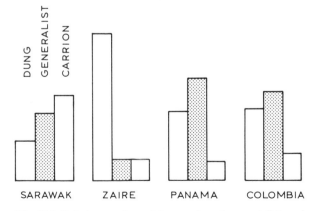

Fig. 28.7. Relative numbers of dung and carrion specialists and food generalists among Scarabaeidae in Sarawak, Zaïre, Panama and Colombia. There are significantly fewer carrion specialists and food generalists in Africa than in the South-East Asian and Neotropical forests. [Data from and analysis in Hanski (1983b) but correcting the proportions of the Panamanian species from Howden and Young (1981).]

attributed the shift to necrophagy in many South American Scarabaeinae to the absence of large herds of herbivorous mammals, predominance of forests, relative scarcity of mammals even inside tropical American forests, and to the relative unimportance of other necrophagous insects in South America. The first three observations apply to South-East Asian tropical forests, but the last one does not; adult Hybosorinae (Scarabaeidae) are superabundant carrion specialists in many parts of South-East Asia (Hanski, 1983b: Borneo; Hanski, unpubl.: Sulawesi; H. Räisänen, pers. commun., 1984: Sumatra).

Why are many Scarabaeinae of tropical rain forests euryphagous generalists, feeding on both dung and carrion, or even on decomposing fruits? The temperate species show a greater degree of specialization. This is in contrast to the idea that tropical forests have many narrowly specialized species (see, for instance, MacArthur, 1972, p. 216; Pianka, 1974, pp. 238–241; Pielou, 1975, pp. 135–136).

The question concerns the evolution of feeding habits as well as foraging ecology. Carrion and dung are not the same, even in tropical forests, hence individual beetles need to make decisions about food selection. In Sarawak, most species were attracted to both dung and carrion, but in varying proportions (Hanski, 1983b). The optimal foraging theory (see Krebs and Davies, 1981) predicts specialization to occur when the preferred food items are sufficiently abundant. It seems reasonable to assume that low food availability amplified by intense competition makes the generalist strategy advantageous in many tropical forests [see Beaver, (1979, 1984) for bark and ambrosia beetles]. This creates a selection pressure towards copro-necrophagy in the originally coprophagous Scarabaeinae. Here interspecific competition does not increase specialization, as in many other systems (for instance MacArthur, 1972), but decreases it, because of extreme patchiness of the habitat. Competition may nonetheless have contributed to some cases of specialization — for example, scarabs feeding exclusively on faecal material from reptiles and amphibians (Young, 1981), or scarabs associated with living sloths (see below).

If resources were more abundant one would expect more specialization. Elephants are still relatively abundant in some African forests, and they produce a distinct and abundant resource for dung beetles. In a forest in the Ivory Coast, many species, including some of the largest ones, are entirely or almost restricted to elephant dung (Cambefort, 1984).

Seasonality

Seasonality of insects in tropical forests is often conspicuous (see Owen, 1971; Janzen, 1973; Wolda, 1978a, b; and especially Wolda, 1983). If a tentative conclusion may be drawn from the scanty data that are available, seasonality appears less pronounced in dung and carrion beetles than in many other insects. There is a natural reason for such a difference: availability of dung and carrion shows less seasonal variation than the availability of many other resources.

Peck and Forsyth (1982) observed no marked seasonality in an Ecuadorian rain forest with no severe dry season, and Hanski (unpubl.) found no seasonality in the dung beetles in North Sulawesi. In a more seasonal forest on Barro Colorado Island, Panama, most species of Scarabaeinae occur throughout the year (31%) or more abundantly in the wet season (41%); 15% occur only in the wet season, 10% occur more abundantly in the dry season, and one or two species appear to be restricted to the dry season (Howden and Young, 1981). In forests in the Ivory Coast, scarab numbers followed bimonthly rainfall records rather closely (Cambefort, 1984). In a deciduous Costa Rican forest with a six-month dry season dung beetle activity is markedly seasonal (Janzen, 1983). Undoubtedly, the more seasonal the environment, the more seasonal is the occurrence of dung and carrion beetles. In African savannas dung beetles are extremely seasonal (Kingston, 1977).

Many species are most abundant in particular phases of the wet season (Howden and Young, 1981), but how seasonal reproduction is in various types of tropical forests remains to be studied.

Diurnal versus nocturnal activity

It is occasionally assumed (for instance, Southwood, 1978) that a difference in diel[1] activity

---

[1]The word "diel" relates to the period of 24 hours, and is distinguished here from "diurnal", which refers to the hours of day-light. Thus, one can speak of a diel rhythm involving diurnal activity.

patterns between syntopic, competing species makes their coexistence easier. This is not automatically true because diurnal and nocturnal species may well compete for the same resources. To what extent they do so depends on the dynamics of the resources. (On the other hand, differences in diel activity patterns may decrease spatial covariance, and thus decrease competition in some cases; Otronen and Hanski, 1983.) Dung and carrion beetles of tropical forests are an extreme case: food patches are often consumed within hours, which means that resources available to nocturnal species may be depleted before the time of activity of diurnal species and vice versa [but see Cambefort (1984) for elephant dung in West African forests].

This extreme priority effect may explain why many tropical forests have two well-differentiated species assemblages of dung and carrion beetles, the nocturnal and diurnal communities (in open areas most Scarabaeinae are diurnal according to Halffter and Matthews, 1966; but see Cambefort, 1984). The best studied example comes again from Barro Colorado Island, Panama (Howden and Young, 1981).

Amongst 39 more abundant species out of the total of 59 Scarabaeinae, 17 species are nocturnal, another 17 species are diurnal, and 5 species appear to be active both by night and day. In reality the times of activity may be much more restricted (but this is not different from temperate species; Koskela, 1979). *Canthon angustatus* is active on Barro Colorado Island mostly from 0600 to 1000 h, and from 1500 to 1800 h, which are the defecation periods of the howler monkey, the most important dung-producer on the island (Howden and Young, 1981).

Figure 28.8 is a construction of the Barro Colorado Island species assemblage of Scarabaeinae, indicating a rather similar composition of the diurnal and nocturnal guilds in terms of food selection, size, and food removal technique. In fact, in pair-wise comparisons between seasonality (previous section), diel activity, food selection, size and food removal technique, no significant deviations from the expectation were detected, though Fig. 28.8 shows that diurnal dung specialists tend to be small (this is definitely the case in Ivory Coast; Cambefort, 1984). Not shown in Fig. 28.8 are seasonal shifts in food selection — for instance, *Canthon aequinoctialis* and *Ateuchus candezei*

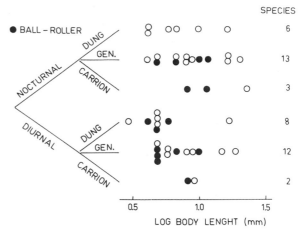

Fig. 28.8. Community structure of Scarabaeinae on Barro Colorado Island, Panama, with respect to diel activity, food selection, food removal technique and body size. (Data from Howden and Young, 1981; see also Young, 1978.)

mostly use dung in the dry season but both dung and carrion in the wet season (Howden and Young, 1981).

Figure 28.8 suggests that dung and carrion beetles partition resources along the time-of-day axis. In the Ivory Coast, 27 forest species were diurnal while 42 species were nocturnal (Cambefort, 1984). Halffter and Matthews (1966) believed that most Scarabaeinae in tropical forests were nocturnal. Such a bias could perhaps be expected on the basis of the mainly nocturnal activity of mammals in the tropical rain forests, but more data are needed, especially as an "exceptional" community has recently been discovered: in the monsoon forests in North Sulawesi, the great majority of dung and carrion beetles are diurnal, only *Copris* (most species) and *Phaeochrous emarginatus* (Hybosorinae) being nocturnal (Hanski, unpubl.).

If differences in diel activity are even partly caused by competition, one would expect the same species to behave differently in radically different competitive situations. Regional differences in diel activity may in fact occur. Wille (1973) found *Megathoposoma candezei* to be diurnal in Costa Rica, whereas a Mexican population studied by Halffter and Martinez (1966) was nocturnal.

Forest-type selection

Tropical forests include an enormous variety of forest types in environments varying in seasonality, annual precipitation, soil, etc. (Whitmore, 1975; Richards, 1979). Different kinds of forests are inhabited by animal communities which are at least partly different. In this section I describe forest type "selection" in dung and carrion beetles within a relatively small area, some tens of square kilometres, in Gunung Mulu National Park, Sarawak, with a remarkable range of forest types including three kinds of lowland forests and several montane forest types on two kinds of bedrock, sandstone and limestone. Figure 28.1 and the text associated with it broadly described where the main taxa could be found most abundantly; here I return to forest-type selection at the species level.

Scarabaeinae and Hybosorinae were abundant in two types of lowland forest, alluvial and mixed dipterocarp forest, while relatively few species were montane (Fig. 28.1). Nonetheless, the three genera richest in species differed dramatically in forest-type selection. The genus *Onthophagus* with 38 species shows practically no segregation — that is, interspecific differences; the four species of *Phaeochroops* show clear differences but also substantial overlap; while the five species of *Phacosoma* show absolutely no spatial overlap (Table 28.1).

Phaeochroops appears to exemplify classical resource partitioning along the forest-type axis. These are large and often extremely abundant species (adults necrophagous), among which competition is certainly to be expected. Their forest-type selection appears to stem from simple re-

TABLE 28.1

Phacosoma, Phaeochroops and *Onthophagus*: numbers of individuals trapped in five forest types in Mulu, Sarawak (from Hanski, 1983b)

Genera species	Tropical heath forest	Forest over limestone	Alluvial forest	Lower montane rain forest	Upper montane rain forest
Phacosoma					
dytiscoides Bouc.	22	–	–	–	–
sp. n. G	–	12	–	–	–
sp. n. A	–	–	22	–	–
sp. n. F	–	–	–	95	–
sp. n. B	–	–	–	–	16
Phaeochroops					
gigas Arrow	29	3	16	–	–
gilleti Beud.	9	692	913	19	–
silphoides Fair.	–	–	43	–	–
acuticollis Arrow	–	–	–	7	113
Onthophagus					
sp. n. K	11	–	10	–	–
sp. n. F	18	1	57	–	–
mentaveiensis Bouc.	3	–	193	–	–
rudis Sharp	2	–	73	1	–
deflexicollis Lansb.	1	1	84	8	–
aurifex Har.	–	–	20	–	–
dux Sharp	–	–	139	–	–
sp. n. J	–	–	40	–	–
sp. n. G	–	–	11	–	–
semicupreus Har.	–	–	57	–	–
vulpes Har.	–	–	32	–	–
batillifer Har.	–	–	57	–	–
sarawacus Har.	–	–	69	6	–
sp. n. C	4	–	88	88	195
sp. n. H	–	–	–	1	507

Note the differences in the degree of habitat segregation in the three genera. Only common species of *Onthophagus* are included but the rare species do not change the picture.

source competition, though naturally other causes of habitat selection may contribute, especially as the larval biology is unknown.

The species of *Phacosoma* are necrophagous, or necro-coprophagous, but they are less abundant and smaller than *Phaeochroops*. Resource competition may not play such an important role in this genus as in *Phaeochroops*. The strictly non-overlapping distribution in Mulu (Table 28.1) suggests that these five closely related species (J. Krikken, pers. commun., 1984) lack effective premating reproductive barriers; selection penalizes interspecific contact because of hybridization and low hybrid fitness. *Phacosoma* presents intriguing speciation problems.

The species of *Onthophagus* finally are an entirely different story. It is difficult to imagine that competition would not affect them at all, yet there is very little forest-type segregation (Table 28.1). The key question is why resource competition leads to forest-type segregation in one group of species (*Phaeochroops*) but not in another (*Onthophagus*). The difference in species number may provide a clue (*Onthophagus* 38 vs. *Phaeochroops* 4). It seems that the species of *Phaeochroops* are poorly adapted to coexist, therefore new species can be fitted to the regional community only through a process of habitat segregation. The species of *Onthophagus* appear good at coexisting (for largely unknown reasons), therefore selection pressures work on something other than pushing species to less favourable forest types (alluvial forest and mixed dipterocarp forest have the highest resource availability for dung and carrion beetles; Anderson et al., 1982).

Figure 28.6 demonstrated extensive habitat segregation along an elevational gradient in Staphylininae, on which basis one might expect extensive forest-type segregation in the lowland Staphylininae, but this is not the case (Hanski and Hammond, 1986). The lowland guild of Staphylininae consists of only one very abundant and many rare species (see p. 490).

Oxytelinae are saprophagous, relatively small Staphylinidae that are generally abundant in dung and carrion communities. In Mulu, there were 30 species, most of which occurred in the lowland forests. Intriguingly, the most abundant species of all, an undescribed *Anotylus* (species B in Hanski and Hammond, 1986), which was exceedingly abundant in kerangas and mixed dipterocarp forest, was entirely absent from alluvial forest, where a large number of related and abundant species occurred. It may be significant that *Anotylus* B is a generalist in respect of microhabitat (and perhaps food), while many of the alluvial forest oxytelinids are specialists. One is tempted to conjecture that the many specialist species in alluvial forest competitively exclude *Anotylus* B (Hanski and Hammond, 1986), especially because this kind of distribution was unique in dung and carrion beetles.

In conclusion, several factors may cause restricted forest type selection. Interspecific competition is probably one of them, but competition is not a sufficient cause of habitat segregation in a guild of competing species (cf. *Onthophagus*).

Extreme specializations

Several species of Scarabaeinae have been collected from living three-toed sloths *Bradypus tridactylus* (Ratcliffe, 1980; Howden and Young, 1981): *Pedaridium bradyporum* in Costa Rica, *Uroxys gorgon* in Colombia and Panama, *U. metagorgon* in Panama, and *U. besti* and *Trichillum adisi* in the vicinity of Manaus, Brazil. The following account of their largely unknown biology is based on that of Ratcliffe (1980).

Sloths descend from trees to defecate once a week and bury their faeces in a shallow hole excavated by the hind feet. Burying the dung is curious in itself; another mystery is that no dung beetles are attracted to traps baited with sloth dung [but see Howden and Young (1981) for *U. gorgon*]. It is not known where the larvae of the abovementioned species develop. Ratcliffe (1980) is of the opinion that the beetles are not parasitic, merely phoretic.

How do disembarked beetles find a sloth again? It is even more difficult to understand what beetles riding on sloths in seasonally flooded forests do, where sloths defecate into the water. Do the scarabs wait up the trees for 2 to 5 months while the forest is flooded? What do they feed on — dung of other arboreal mammals and birds? And again, where do the larvae develop? There is the possibility that at least some of these species (especially *Trichillum*) are necrophagous or saprophagous (Ratcliffe, 1980).

SPECIES RICHNESS AND ABUNDANCE RELATIONS

Local scale

An ecologist trapping dung and carrion beetles in a tropical forest may expect to find a local species assemblage of the kind presented in Fig. 28.9 for three localities. Typically, some 20 species may be captured at one point (trapping site) in a short period of time with moderate effort; if sample size is increased or many sites and/or forest types are studied, more species will naturally be encountered (Table 28.2). One or two large species may be expected, but most species are relatively small (Fig. 28.9) — in the Ivory Coast, for example, generally somewhat smaller than savanna species (Cambefort, 1984). Small isolates of tropical forest have lower species richness and may lack large species (Table 28.2) — *Dichotomius*

carolinus colonicus, the biggest Panamanian species in Fig. 28.9, is lacking from Barro Colorado Island. Howden and Nealis (1975) found reduced species richness (10 species) and small species in an annually flooded area in Colombia, where only small "islands" of high ground escaped flooding.

Dung and carrion beetles are suitable for studies on convergence at the community level (see, for instance, Orians and Paine, 1983) and diffuse competitive coevolution in general (Roughgarden, 1983). Present data are insufficient for drawing conclusions on these matters, except that size distributions appear reasonably similar in the three species assemblages in Fig. 28.9, though taxonomically the Panamanian species stand apart from the African and South-East Asian faunas. A more detailed comparison should take into account the size of the mammals present in the region. For instance, elephant dung in West African (Cambe-

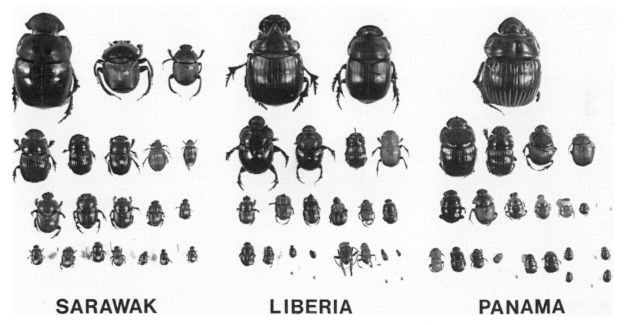

Fig. 28.9. A local assemblage of abundant and relatively abundant species of Scarabaeidae associated with dung and carrion from Sarawak (lowland mixed dipterocarp forest), Liberia and Barro Colorado Island, Panama (the largest species does not occur on the island but is found on the nearby mainland). The species are (from left to right and from top to bottom): Sarawak: *Catharsius molossus, Gymnopleurus maurus, G. striatus, Copris agnus, C. doriae, C. ramosiceps, Phaeochroops gilleti, P. silphoides, Onthophagus sarawacus, O. dux, O. aurifex, O. orientalis, O. obscurior, O. mentaveiensis, Onthophagus* sp. n., *O. semicupreus, O. rudis, O. batillifer, Onthophagus* sp. n., *O. deflexicollis*; Liberia: *Heliocopris dianae, Catharsius gorilla, Diastellopalpus pluton, D. noctis,* indet., *Pseudopedaria grossa, Onthophagus semiviridis, O. liberianus, O. rufopygus, O. bartosi, Onthophagus* sp. 1, *O. foulliouxi, O. picatus, Onthophagus* sp. 2, indet., indet., *Neosisyphus angulicollis, Sisyphus gazanus, Aphodius* sp. 1, *Aphodius* sp. 2; Panama: *Dichotomius satanas colonicus, Copris lugubris, Phanaeus pyrois, Deltochilum pseudoparile, Canthon aequinoctialis, C. septemmaculatus, C. cyanellus sallei, C. angustatus, C. moniliatus, C. lamprimus, Eurysternus plebejus, Onthophagus stockwelli, O. acuminatus, O. coscineus, Ateuchus candezei, Canthidium haroldi, C. aurifex, C. planovultum, Uroxys platypyga, U. micros*.

fort, 1984) and Sumatran (H. Räisänen, pers. commun., 1984) forests is exploited by a guild of large, specialist dung beetles.

Quantitative trapping data have been published for only three localities: Gunung Mulu in Sarawak (Hanski, 1983b), Leticia, Amazonas, in Colombia (Howden and Nealis, 1975), and Pinchincha Province in Ecuador (Peck and Forsyth, 1982). Although the data are limited (Table 28.2) some instructive observations may be made.

Species richness is higher in Colombia than in Sarawak, which is to be expected because of the enormously larger forest area, and hence greater species pool, in South America than in Borneo. Cambefort (1984) has collected 78 species from a lowland forest in the Ivory Coast, where species richness appears comparable to that in Colombia, though quantitative comparisons cannot be made with the published results. The Ecuadorian site was a small (80 ha) isolate of primary forest surrounded by areas of variously disturbed habitat (Peck and Forsyth, 1982). The small area most likely explains the low species number at this site.

Howden and Nealis (1975) trapped at one site in Colombia in 1972 and 1974 with roughly similar results, though in 1972 the most abundant species was relatively more abundant than in 1974 (42 vs.

20%). Another site 7 km away gave similar results. Species number is naturally higher if several bait types are used in trapping instead of only one.

A closer analysis of the Sarawakian and Colombian samples revealed relatively even distributions of abundances amongst the species, as compared with the log-series distribution (Hanski, 1983b). There are some notable exceptions, however, one species occasionally being much more abundant than the others (Table 28.2). I shall return to this question below.

Thirty species of saprophagous Oxytelinae were trapped in Mulu, Sarawak (Hanski and Hammond, 1986), and their abundance distribution was found to be bimodal (Fig. 28.10), which is an unusual result [Williams (1964); see Hanski and Koskela (1977) and Hanski (1983b) for examples among dung and carrion beetles]. Possibly some of the rare species do not feed on carrion, and are hence caught in small numbers only. If this is the cause of the bimodal distribution, the corresponding food webs seem to be structured into little connected guilds (cf. Pimm, 1982). Alternatively, there are many genuinely rare species, and species tend to cluster into "abundant" and "rare" ones for reasons of population dynamics such as Hanski (1982), for instance, envisaged.

TABLE 28.2

Species richness of dung and carrion beetles (Scarabaeidae) in Sarawak, Colombia and Ecuador

| Locality | Sample size | Species number | Expected number[1] | | Maximum relative abundance (%) |
			mean	SD	
Sarawak[3]					
alluvial forest[2]	1631	33	25.4	1.8	54
mixed DF	615	33	31.2	1.2	15
Colombia[4]					
site 1, 1972	1486	53	42.8	2.1	42
site 2, 1974	466	47	46.8	0.5	20
site 2	851	51	44.6	2.0	19
site 1[2]	453	38	38.0		47
Ecuador[5]					
80-ha preserve	10911	27	13.6	1.6	37

[1]Rarefaction, $n = 453$ — see Simberloff (1979).
[2]Only carrion-baited traps were used in trapping.
[3]Data from Hanski (1983b).
[4]Data from Howden and Nealis (1975).
[5]Data from Peck and Forsyth (1982).

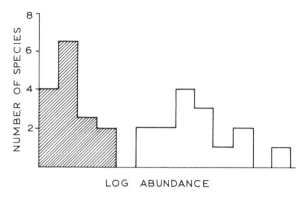

Fig. 28.10. Abundance distribution of Oxytelinae (Staphylinidae) in Mulu, Sarawak. Note bimodality; rare species have been shaded. (From Hanski and Hammond, 1986.)

Figure 28.11 gives the abundance distribution of Staphylininae, predators of carrion-fly eggs, maggots and adults. This distribution is unimodal, most species being rare. A comparison with a northern temperate community from Finland (Fig. 28.11) shows no difference in species richness (analysis by Hanski and Hammond, 1986). The most abundant species was relatively more abundant in Sarawak than in Finland, but the tropical forest community has also many very rare species, yielding a markedly uneven abundance distribution. The montane community of Staphylininae in Sarawak, however, is again entirely different, consisting of relatively few but abundant species [see Figs. 28.4 and 28.6, and Hanski and Hammond, 1986].

Caswell (1976) concluded from his "neutral" model analysis of abundance relations of birds, trees and foliage insects that tropical communities tend to have higher, not lower, dominance than temperate communities. He argued that in the stable physical conditions of tropical forests, specialists may invade communities, thus increasing species richness but, because such specialists would often remain rare, decreasing the evenness of the abundance distribution. Interspecific competition may further enhance abundance differences in tropical forests. Whatever is the explanation, in Sarawak several superdominants were present (Hanski, 1983b; Hanski and Hammond, 1986): *Platydracus aeneipennis* among large predatory staphylinids (*c.* 80% of individuals in lowlands); *Anotylus* sp. n. B of Hanski and Hammond (1986) in saprophagous staphylinids (*c.* 90% in several

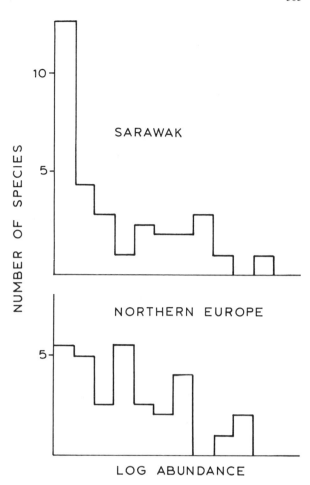

Fig. 28.11. Abundance distributions of Staphylininae in Sarawak and in southern Finland (the latter species were collected from cow dung). Note the less even distribution in the tropical forest, Sarawak. (From Hanski and Hammond, 1986.)

forest types); *Phaeochroops gilleti* among necrophagous scarabs (54% in alluvial forest and 98% in forest over limestone), and an unidentified aleocharin, probably a parasitoid, which was exceedingly abundant in forest over limestone. Superdominance was thus observed in predators, parasitoids, saprophagous and necrophagous species, but not in coprophagous species. The most abundant species in Howden and Nealis's (1975) study was a generalist, while Peck and Forsyth (1982) used only traps baited with human faeces (Table 28.2).

The only solid conclusion one can draw from these limited data is that, for little understood reasons, some dung and carrion beetles are at least occasionally extremely abundant in tropical forests.

Abundance relations on mountain tops

A striking fact about the montane populations on Gunung Mulu in Sarawak was their density: 10 out of 16 montane populations in Scarabaeinae, Hybosorinae, Staphylininae, Oxytelinae and Silphidae had relative density greater than 0.25 individuals per trap-night, while most lowland populations in the same taxa were sparse, density being less than 0.25 beetles per trap-night (Fig. 28.4; the difference is significant, $\chi^2 = 21.3$, $P < 0.001$).

The summit of Gunung Mulu is small and isolated, and the upper montane forest on the mountain is a habitat island, where a rare species may become extinct without being replaced. Common species are left behind. Some of the species may be endemic to this single mountain top, for example a wingless species of *Onthophagus* (Hanski, 1983b).

It is important to note however that some lowland species too were very abundant, especially three species of Oxytelinae, with remarkably similar density of 4 to 5 beetles per trap-night (Fig. 28.4).

Other tropical mountains have endemic species of Scarabaeinae, especially on islands. See Vinson (1951) for *Nesosisyphus* on Mauritius, and Matthews (1965) for canthonines on Puerto Rico.

Patterns on regional scale

Regional diversity may increase with increasing local diversities but also with increasing difference in species composition between neighbouring areas. Perhaps the clearest example of this is seen on mountain slopes; in Mulu in Sarawak no species occurred from lowlands to above 1500 m altitude (Table 28.3).

Table 28.3 gives support to the idea that closely related species often replace each other along a habitat gradient. There are some 10 replacements by congeners in Table 28.3, while the expected value under the null hypothesis, obtained with a randomization technique (Hanski, 1983b), is 4.2 ± 1.5 (standard deviation) replacements. This suggests that interspecific interactions of one kind or another partly determine the occurrence of species in different forest types (for further discussion see Hanski, 1983b).

Figure 28.12 depicts the profile of Gunung Mulu, and gives the numbers of species and individuals of Scarabaeidae and Staphylinidae (exclusive of Aleocharinae) associated with dung and carrion along the trapping transect. Trends in point diversity (number of species per trapping site) are remarkably similar in the two groups of beetles in spite of the major difference in their biology. Tropical heath forest (kerangas) has few species compared with the other lowland forest types, and species richness begins to decline in both groups at an altitude of 200 m. This contrasts with high species richness of moths, for instance, at mid-altitudes, reported for New Guinea (Hebert, 1980)

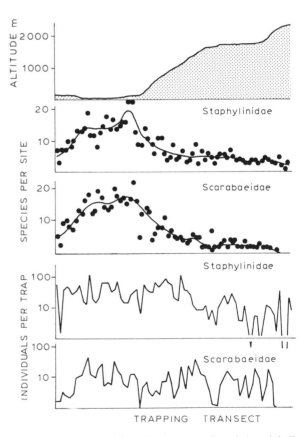

Fig. 28.12. Numbers of species (per trapping site) and individuals (per trap) in Scarabaeidae and Staphylinidae (exclusive of Aleocharinae) along an elevational gradient in Sarawak (Gunung Mulu). Five or ten traps were operated per site. The uppermost panel shows the mountain profile and gives the altitudes. Note logarithmic transformation of abundance. Numbers were low in tropical heath forest (the extreme left on the transect) but high in the other lowland forest types (alluvial and mixed dipterocarp forests). (From Hanski, 1983b; Hanski and Hammond, 1986.)

TABLE 28.3

Elevational occurrence of 22 common carrion-associated beetles and flies on Gunung Mulu, Sarawak. The table gives the numbers trapped at 57 sites (rows). Forest type abbreviations are: MDF = mixed dipterocarp forest, LMF = lower montane rain forest, and UMF = upper montane rain forest. *Onthophagus* and *Phacosoma* belong to Scarabaeinae, *Phaeochroops* to Scarabaeidae: Hybosorinae, *Nicrophorus* to Silphidae, *Anotylus* to Staphylinidae: Oxytelinae, *Platydracus* and *Philonthus* to Staphylininae, and the flies *Lucilia* and *Calliphora* belong to Calliphoridae (from Hanski, 1983b)

Forest type	Altitude (m)	Onthophagus sp. C	Onthophagus sp. H	Phacosoma sp. C	Phacosoma sp. A	Phacosoma sp. F	Phacosoma sp. B	Phaeochroops gilleti	Phaeochroops acuticollis	Nicrophorus podagricus	Anotylus sp. 12	Anotylus sp. 28	Anotylus sp. 11	Platydracus aeneipennis	Philonthus sp. 82	Philonthus sp. 81	Philonthus sp. 86	Philonthus sp. 85	Philonthus sp. 84	Philonthus sp. 83	Lucilia porphyrina	Calliphora atripalpis	Calliphora fulviceps
MDF	90	1												117			5						
MDF	100			1		5								79			1						
MDF	105			1		11								75			1						
MDF	110	26		2		4					4			132			3						
MDF	130	13		5							122			74			10						
MDF	150	15		11							264			22			3						
MDF	150	1									39			1									
MDF	200	5			4						379			41			4						
MDF	300	4			2						218			46			5						
MDF	350	2			1	5					159			42			7						
MDF	500					3					108	1		9			3				4		
MDF	585	2				2					231			25			1				3		
MDF	670	1			1	2					177	3		4			1				2		
MDF	715	8			2	5					239			10			5				1		
MDF	765	9			3	2					310			4			4						
LMF	860	10			52	4					254			5			6				1		
LMF	895	8			6	5					207	9		5	4		8				6		
LMF	940	4			2	1					62	4		1	2			1			1		
LMF	1020	4			5	5					36	21			5			3			1		
LMF	1070	52			26	2					409	45		6	6			4		1	1		
LMF	1130	9	1			2			7		54	69		1	10			7			7		
UMF	1220	36						1	61		98				18				8	7			
UMF	1275	28	4					1	14		105	1			12		1		11		11		
UMF	1320	96	10	9				13	28		35				12		2	1	2			10	
UMF	1420	32	24	29				1	9	1			2		7	3			3	2		14	26
UMF	1460	3	22	29					1	1	2				9				1	1		25	8
UMF	1510		22	40							6		1	3	8	3			2	3		14	2
UMF	1605	10	21								5				6	4			19	20	4		
UMF	1640	4	10									1	3	1	1			1	9	1	13	1	
UMF	1650	3													16				13	4	4	2	
UMF	1650	1	4												2				7	2			
UMF	1700	13	9										3		1	1			16	20			
UMF	1700	36	6							5					5	9			7	52		1	
UMF	1700	68	3							12		1			7	10			11	79			
UMF	1700	44	8							1					3	5			11	31		3	
UMF	1700	25	8							3		6	9		1	13			7	87			
UMF	1700	27	11							4				2	13				7	47		5	
UMF	1700	9	2												2				13	3		3	
UMF	1700	11	11							2		1			4				5	8	1	2	
UMF	1700	18	32							2					4				9	42	1	1	
UMF	1700	1	9												4				3	4		2	
UMF	1700	4	17							2					1				1	1			
UMF	1700	19	68							5					1	8			16	1			
UMF	1700	17	33							7					2	12			5	4		1	
UMF	1750	1	6												1				1			1	
UMF	1750	12	5												14				2	1	1		
UMF	1810	69	15							6			1		12				14	29			
UMF	1870	33	10							2			1		15				24	4	1		
UMF	2000									1			24		3	3							
UMF	2080	1								1					6				1			5	1
UMF	2120												165		9				2	1		4	2
UMF	2180												2		1								
UMF	2200														1							1	1
UMF	2240												90		5							5	1
UMF	2310												18		9								8
UMF	2365												1		4							16	2
UMF	2370									4					4							18	5

and for Mount Kinabalu and Gunung Mulu in Borneo (Holloway, 1970, 1979). The situation with dung and carrion beetles may be different in more extensive mountain ranges.

Pooled abundance of Staphylinidae fluctuated within the same limits from the lowlands up to an altitude of c. 1200 m, suggesting density compensation (see above, p. 490). Abundance fluctuations were greater in scarabs but even the upper montane community with only two species (Fig. 28.5) had relatively high pooled abundance.

Cambefort (1984) has presented interesting results from four forest localities in West Africa, ranging from moist lowland forest through mesic (semideciduous) to xeric forests towards the north, away from the equator. The number of forest-inhabiting Scarabaeinae declined from 78 to 25 to 5, but the number of savanna species penetrating into forest increased from 0 to 10 to 38. The clear distinction between forest and grassland species in regions of true rain forest appears to break down in regions where small woodlands are scattered in savanna.

Cambefort (1984) has also classified the forest dung beetles (Scarabaeinae) occurring in the Ivory Coast into six geographical range classes. More than half of the species are distributed throughout the African evergreen tropical rain forests, while 10% occur even more widely in most or all forest zones in Africa. Thirty per cent of the species are confined to a smaller or larger part of the West African rain-forest region.

CONCLUDING REMARKS

Are tropical forests exceptionally rich in species of dung and carrion beetles? Data permitting a tentative answer to this question come primarily from Sarawak (Hanski, 1983b; Hanski and Hammond, 1986) and southern Finland (Hanski and Koskela, 1977, 1978; Hanski, 1980). As far as predatory species of Staphylinidae and Histeridae are concerned, the answer is "No". On the other hand, tropical forests have more coprophagous, necrophagous and, generally, saprophagous species of Scarabaeidae and Staphylinidae, as well as species in other families, than temperate forest communities. But even here the increase in species number is modest (c. twofold), nowhere near the increase in the number of herbivorous insects.

Resource availability appears to explain these main trends in species number. Predators are to a great extent dependent upon fly eggs, maggots and even adults, which are not especially abundant in many tropical forests. But tropical forests have higher production of dung and carrion than temperate forests, hence coprophagous and necrophagous species may be expected to be more numerous in the tropics. In the case of Scarabaeinae it may be important that the subfamily has evolved in the tropics (Halffter and Matthews, 1966).

It seems to me, though I cannot prove this claim here, that dung and carrion insects in tropical forests exemplify equilibrium assemblages of species, strongly affected by interspecific competition. Temperate assemblages of species associated with dung and carrion represent communities which are less stable, characterized by great short-term and long-term fluctuations in abundance. Unfortunately, not a single study has examined the temporal dynamics of dung and carrion beetles in tropical forests. Folivorous insects in tropical forests have been studied especially by Wolda (1977, 1978a, b, 1979, 1980, 1982, 1983; Wolda and Galindo, 1981), who has found no difference in temporal stability as compared with temperate environments. I therefore make the risky prediction that dung and carrion insects show a different pattern in this respect.

This chapter cannot be concluded without commenting on what happens to the beetles when forest is cleared or becomes fragmented. In Colombia, a forest clearing had only six species, whereas 60 species were recorded in undisturbed forest (Howden and Nealis, 1975). Moreover, four of the six species on the clearing were not found in the forest. Forest clearing eliminates the native forest fauna of dung and carrion beetles and their place is taken by a smaller group of eurytopic species associated with human activity. (The situation is different in regions of the forest – savanna interface, but even there a loss of forest species is inevitable.)

What happens if an isolate of previously more extensive tropical forest is preserved? What is perhaps the only trustworthy law in ecology predicts that species number will decline (MacArthur and Wilson, 1967; for experiments on tropical rain forest see Lovejoy et al., 1984). This appears to have happened in the plot of tropical rain forest (measuring 80 ha) studied in Ecuador by Peck and Forsyth (1982). They trapped 16720 Scarabaeinae representing only 31 species, while the "standard" species richness in a large sample is 50 to 70. Large species with small populations are likely to become extinct in isolated preserves. *Deltochilum gibbosum panamensis*, a species larger than any dung or carrion beetle on Barro Colorado Island, was collected from the nearby mainland (Young, 1978). Excessive hunting of vertebrate populations, commonplace in many regions of the tropical rain forest, obviously has an adverse effect on dung and carrion beetles; species number may be expected to decrease and again especially large species are vulnerable and may become extinct. No good comparative study yet exists to show this unhappy course of events.

REFERENCES

Anderson, J.A.R., Jermy, A.C. and Lord Cranbrook, 1982. *Gunung Mulu National Park. A Management and Development Plan.* Royal Geographic Society, London, 345 pp.

Beaver, R.A., 1979. Host specificity of temperate and tropical animals. *Nature*, 281: 139–141.

Beaver, R.A., 1984. Insect exploitation of ephemeral habitats. *S. Pac. J. Nat. Sci.*, 6: 3–47.

Bellés, X. and Favila, M.E., 1983. Protection chimique du nid chez Canthon cyanellus cyanellus LeConte (Col. Scarabaeidae). *Bull. Soc. Entomol. Fr.*, 88: 602–607.

Cambefort, Y., 1982. Les Coléoptères Scarabaeidae S.Str. de Lamto (Côte-d'Ivoire): structure des peuplements et rôle dans l'écosystème. *Ann. Soc. Entomol. Fr. (N.S.)*, 18: 433–459.

Cambefort, Y., 1984. *Étude Écologique des Coléoptères Scarabaeidae de Côte d'Ivoire.* Travaux des Chercheurs de la Station de LAMTO, 3, Univ. d'Abidjan, 294 pp.

Case, T.J., Gilpin, M.E. and Diamond, J.M., 1979. Overexploitation, interference competition, and excess density compensation in insular faunas. *Am. Nat.*, 113: 843–854.

Caswell, H., 1976. Community structure: a neutral model analysis. *Ecol. Monogr.*, 46: 327–354.

Connell, J.H., 1980. Diversity and the coevolution of competitors, or the ghost of competition past. *Oikos*, 35: 131–138.

Connell, J.H., 1983. On the prevalence and relative importance of interspecific competition: evidence from field experiments. *Am. Nat.*, 122: 661–696.

Cornaby, B.W., 1974. Carrion reduction by animals in contrasting tropical habitats. *Biotropica*, 6: 51–63.

Eisenberg, J.F., 1980. The density and biomass of tropical mammals. In: M.E. Soulé and B.A. Wilcox (Editors), *Conservation Biology.* Sinauer, Sunderland, Mass., pp. 35–56.

Fittkau, E.J. and Klinge, H., 1973. On the biomass and trophic structure of the Central Amazonian rain forest ecosystem. *Biotropica*, 5: 2–14.

Fuller, M.E., 1934. The insect inhabitants of carrion: study in animal ecology. *Counc. Sci. Ind. Res., Aust. Bull.*, 195: 62 pp.

Gill, B.D., 1984. Flight Activity, Foraging Behaviour, and Community Structure among Neotropical Scarabaeinae. *17th Int. Congress Entomol.*, Hamburg, p. 318.

Halffter, G., 1977. Evolution of nidification in the Scarabaeinae. *Quaest. Entomol.*, 13: 231–253.

Halffter, G. and Edmonds, W.D., 1982. *The Nesting Behavior of Dung Beetles (Scarabaeinae).* Instituto de Ecologia, Mexico, D.F., 176 pp.

Halffter, G. and Martinez, A., 1966. Revision monografica de los Canthonina americanos. *Rev. Soc. Hist. Nat.*, 27: 89–177.

Halffter, G. and Matthews, E.G., 1966. *The Natural History of Dung Beetles of the Subfamily Scarabaeinae (Coleoptera, Scarabaeidae).* Folia Entomol. Mex. 12–14, 312 pp.

Halffter, G., Halffter, V. and Lopez, I.G., 1974. Phanaeus behaviour: food transportation and bisexual cooperation. *Environ. Entomol.*, 3: 341–345.

Halffter, G., Halffter, V. and Huerta, C., 1980. Mating and nesting behavior of Eurysternus (Coleoptera: Scarabaeinae). *Quaest. Ent.*, 16: 599–620.

Hanbury-Tenison, R., 1980. *Mulu. The Rain Forest.* Weidenfeld and Nicolson, London, 176 pp.

Hanbury-Tenison, A.R. and Jermy, A.C., 1979. The RGS Expedition to Gunung Mulu, Sarawak 1977–78. *Geogr. J.*, 145: 175–191.

Hanski, I., 1980. Spatial patterns and movements in coprophagous beetles. *Oikos*, 34: 293–310.

Hanski, I., 1981a. Exploitative competition in transient habitat patches. In: D.G. Chapman and V.F. Gallucci (Editors), *Quantitative population dynamics.* (Statistical Ecology Series 13) Int. Coop. Publishing House, Md., pp. 25–38.

Hanski, I., 1981b. Coexistence of competitors in patchy environment with and without predation. *Oikos*, 37: 306–312.

Hanski, I., 1981c. Carrion flies (Calliphoridae) in tropical rain forests in Sarawak, South-East Asia. *Sarawak Mus. J.*, 29: 191–200.

Hanski, I., 1982. Dynamics of regional distribution: the core and satellite species hypothesis. *Oikos*, 38: 210–221.

Hanski, I., 1983a. Coexistence of competitors in patchy environment. *Ecology*, 64: 493–500.

Hanski, I., 1983b. Distributional ecology and abundance of dung and carrion-feeding beetles (Scarabaeidae) in tropical rain forest in Sarawak, Borneo. *Acta Zool. Fenn.*, 167: 45 pp.

Hanski, I. and Hammond, P., 1986. Assemblages of carrion and dung Staphylinidae in tropical rain forests in Sarawak, Borneo. *Ann. Entomol. Fenn.*, 52: 1–19.

Hanski, I. and Koskela, H., 1977. Niche relations among dung-inhabiting beetles. *Oecologia*, 28: 203–231.

Hanski, I. and Koskela, H., 1978. Stability, abundance and niche width in the beetle community inhabiting cow dung. *Oikos*, 31: 290–298.

Hanski, I. and Koskela, H., 1979. Resource partitioning in six guilds of dung-inhabiting beetles (Coleoptera). *Ann. Entomol. Fenn.*, 45: 1–12.

Hanski, I. and Kuusela, S., 1977. An experiment on competition and diversity in the carrion fly community. *Ann. Entomol. Fenn.*, 43: 108–115.

Hanski, I. and Kuusela, S., 1980. The structure of carrion fly communities: differences in breeding seasons. *Ann. Zool. Fenn.*, 17: 185–190.

Hebert, P.D.N., 1980. Moth communities in montane Papua New Guinea. *J. Anim. Ecol.*, 49: 593–602.

Holloway, J.D., 1970. The biogeographical analysis of a transect sample of the moth fauna of Mt. Kinabalu, Sabah, using numerical methods. *Biol. J. Linn. Soc.*, 2: 259–286.

Holloway, J.D., 1979. Ecological and zoogeographical implications of lepidopteran fauna. *R. Geogr. Soc. Symp.* (unpubl.).

Holloway, J.D., 1984. The larger moths of the Gunung Mulu National Park; a preliminary assessment of their distribution ecology, and potential as environmental indicators. *Sarawak Mus. J.*, 51: 149–190.

Horn, H.S. and MacArthur, R.H., 1972. Competition among fugitive species in a harlequin environment. *Ecology*, 53: 749–752.

Howden, H.F. and Nealis, V.G., 1975. Effects of clearing in a tropical rain forest on the composition of coprophagous scarab beetle fauna (Coleoptera). *Biotropica*, 7: 77–83.

Howden, H.F. and Nealis, V.G., 1978. Observations on height of perching in some tropical dung beetles (Scarabaeidae). *Biotropica*, 10: 43–46.

Howden, H.F. and Young, O.P., 1981. Panamanian Scarabaeinae: taxonomy, distribution and habits (Coleoptera, Scarabaeidae). *Contrib. Am. Entomol. Inst.*, 18: 204 pp.

Janzen, D.H., 1973. Sweep samples of tropical foliage insects: effects of season, vegetation type, elevation, time of day, and insularity. *Ecology*, 54: 687–708.

Janzen, D.H., 1983. Seasonal changes in abundance of large nocturnal dung beetles (Scarabaeidae) in a Costa Rican deciduous forest and adjacent horse pasture. *Oikos*, 41: 274–283.

Jiron, L.F. and Cartin, V.M., 1981. Insect succession in the decomposition of a mammal in Costa Rica. *J. N.Y. Entomol. Soc.*, 89: 158–165.

Kingston, T.J., 1977. *Natural manuring by elephants in the Tsavo Natural Park, Kenya*. D.Ph. thesis, Univ. of Oxford, Oxford, 204 pp.

Koskela, H., 1979. Patterns of diel flight activity in dung-inhabiting beetles: an ecological analysis. *Oikos*, 33: 419–439.

Koskela, H. and Hanski, I., 1977. Structure and succession in a beetle community inhabiting cow dung. *Ann. Zool. Fenn.*, 14: 204–223.

Krebs, J.R. and Davies, N.B., 1981. *An Introduction to Behavioural Ecology*. Blackwell, Oxford, 292 pp.

Kuusisto, I., 1933. *Tutkimuksia Raadoilla Elävistä Kovakuoriaisista Turun Ruissalossa*. Diss., Univ. of Turku, Turku, 180 pp.

Levin, S.A., 1978. Population models and community structure in heterogeneous environments. In: S.A. Levin (Editor), *Populations and Communities. Vol. II*. Study in Mathematical Biology. Mathematical Association of America, Washington, D.C., pp. 439–478.

Lovejoy, T.E., Rankin, J.M., Bierregaard Jr., R.O., Brown Jr., S.B., Emmons, L.H. and Van der Voort, M.E., 1984. Ecosystem decay of Amazon forest remnants. In: M.H. Nitecki (Editor), *Extinctions*. Univ. of Chicago Press, Chicago, Ill., pp. 295–326.

MacArthur, R.H., 1969. Patterns of communities in the tropics. *Biol. J. Linn. Soc.*, 1: 19–30.

MacArthur, R.H., 1972. *Geographical Ecology*. Harper and Row, New York, N.Y., 269 pp.

MacArthur, R.H. and Wilson, E.O., 1967. *The Theory of Island Biogeography*. Princeton Univ. Press, Princeton, N.J., 203 pp.

Matthews, E.G., 1965. The taxonomy, geographical distribution, and feeding habits of the canthonines of Puerto Rico (Coleoptera, Scarabaeidae). *Trans. Am. Entomol. Soc.*, 91: 431–465.

Monteith, G.H. and Storey, R.I., 1981. The biology of Cephalodesmius, a genus of dung beetles which synthesizes "dung" from plant material (Coleoptera: Scarabaeidae: Scarabaeinae). *Mem. Queensl. Mus.*, 20: 253–271.

Montgomery, G.G. and Sunquist, M.E., 1975. Impact of sloths on neotropical forest energy flow and nutrient cycling. In: F.B. Golley and E. Medina (Editors), *Tropical Ecological Systems*. Springer, Berlin, pp. 69–98.

Navajas, E., 1950. Manifestaçoes de predatismo em Scarabaeidae do Brasil e alguns datos bionémicos de Canthon virens (Mannh.) (Col. Scarabaeidae). *Ciénc. Cult.*, 2: 284–285.

Odum, H.T., Abbott, W., Selander, R.K., Golley, F.B. and Wilson, R.F., 1970. Estimates of chlorophyll and biomass of the Tobomuco Forest of Puerto Rico. In: H.T. Odum and R.F. Pigeon (Editors), *A Tropical Rain Forest: A Study of Irradiation and Ecology at El Verde, Puerto Rico*. U.S. Atomic Energy Commission, Washington, D.C., pp. 3–18.

Ohaus, F., 1900. Bericht über eine entomologische Reise nach Central-brasilien. *Stettiner Ent. Z.*, 60: 164–191, 193–274.

Orians, G.H. and Paine, R., 1983. Convergent evolution at the community level. In: D.J. Futuyma and M. Slatkin (Editors), *Coevolution*. Sinauer, Sunderland, Mass., pp. 431–458.

Otronen, M. and Hanski, I., 1983. Movement patterns in Sphaeridium: differences between species, sexes, and feeding and breeding individuals. *J. Anim. Ecol.*, 52: 663–680.

Owen, D.F., 1971. *Tropical Butterflies*. Clarendon, Oxford, 214 pp.

Owen, D.F., 1983. The abundance and biomass of forest animals. In: F.B. Golley (Editor), *Tropical Rain Forest Ecosystems*. (Ecosystems of the World, 14A) Elsevier, Amsterdam, pp. 93–100.

Payne, J.A. and Crossley Jr., D.A., 1966. *Animal Species Associated with Pig Carrion*. Publ. No. 153, Rad. Ecol. Sect., Oak Ridge Natl. Lab., 70 pp.

Payne, J.A. and King, E.W., 1969. Coleoptera associated with pig carrion. *Entomol. Mon. Mag.*, 105: 224–232.

Peck, S.B. and Forsyth, A., 1982. Composition, structure and comparative behaviour in a guild of Ecuadorian rain forest dung beetles (Coleoptera, Scarabaeidae). *Can. J. Zool.*, 60: 1624–1634.

Pianka, E.R., 1974. *Evolutionary Ecology*. Harper and Row, New York, N.Y., 356 pp.

Pielou, E.C., 1975. *Ecological Diversity*. Wiley, New York, N.Y., 165 pp.

Pimm, S.L., 1982. *Food Webs*. Chapman and Hall, London, 219 pp.

Proctor, J., Anderson, J.M., Chai, P. and Vallack, H.W., 1983. Ecological studies in four contrasting lowland rain forests in Gunung Mulu. I. Forest environment structure and floristics. *J. Ecol.*, 71: 237–260.

Ratcliffe, B.S., 1980. New species of Coprini (Coleoptera: Scarabaeidae: Scarabaeinae) taken from the pelage of three-toed sloths (Bradypus tridactylus L.) (Edentata: Bradypodidae) in Central Amazonia with a brief commentary on scarab–sloth relationships. *Coleopt. Bull.*, 34: 337–350.

Reed, H.B., 1958. A study of dog carcass communities in Tennessee with special reference to the insects. *Am. Midl. Nat.*, 59: 213–245.

Richards, P.W., 1979. *The Tropical Rain Forest*. Cambridge Univ. Press, Cambridge, 450 pp.

Ritcher, P.O., 1958. Biology of Scarabaeidae. *Annu. Rev. Entomol.*, 3: 311–334.

Roughgarden, J., 1983. Coevolution between competitors. In: D.J. Futuyma and M. Slatkin (Editors), *Coevolution*. Sinauer, Sunderland, Mass., pp. 383–403.

Roughgarden, J., Heckel, D. and Fuentes, E., 1983. Coevolutionary theory and the biogeography and community structure of Anolis. In: R. Huey, E. Pianka and T. Schoener (Editors), *Lizard Ecology*. Harvard Univ. Press, Cambridge, Mass., pp. 371–410.

Schluter, D. and Grant, P., 1984. Determinants of morphological patterns in communities of Darwin's finches. *Am. Nat.*, 123: 175–196.

Schoener, T.W., 1974. Resource partitioning in ecological communities. *Science*, 185: 27–39.

Schoener, T.W., 1983. Field experiments on interspecific competition. *Am. Nat.*, 122: 240–285.

Simberloff, D., 1979. Rarefaction as a distribution-free method of expressing and estimating diversity. In: J.F. Grassle, G.P. Patil, W. Smith and C. Taillie (Editors), *Ecological Diversity in Theory and Practice*. (Statistical Ecology Series 6) Int. Cooper. Publishing House, Md., pp. 159–176.

Slatkin, M., 1974. Competition and regional coexistence. *Ecology*, 55: 128–134.

Southwood, T.R.E., 1978. The components of diversity. In: L.A. Mound and N. Waloff (Editors), *Diversity of Insect Faunas*. Symp. R. Entomol. Soc. London, 9: 19–40.

Tribe, G.D., 1975. Pheromone release by dung beetles (Coleoptera: Scarabaeidae). *S. Afr. J. Sci.*, 71: 277–278.

Turček, F.J., 1969. Large mammal secondary production in European broad leaved and mixed forests: some results and methods of recent research. *Biologia (Bratislava)*, 24: 173–181.

Valiela, I., 1969. The arthropod fauna of bovine dung in central New York and sources on its natural history. *J. N.Y. Entomol. Soc.*, 77: 210–220.

Valiela, I., 1974. Composition, food webs and population limitation in dung arthropod communities during invasion

and succession. *Am. Midl. Nat.*, 92: 370–385.

Vinson, J., 1951. Le cas des Sysiphes Mauricieus. *Proc. R. Soc. Arts Sci. Mauritius*, 1: 105–122.

Walter, P., 1980. Comportement de recherche et d'exploitation d'une masse stercorale chez quelques coprophages afrotropicaux (Coleopt. Scarabaeidae). *Ann. Soc. Entomol. Fr. (N.S.)*, 16: 307–323.

Walter, P., 1982. Contribution á la connaissance des Scarabéides coprophages du Gabon. I. Trois espèces nouvelles de la région de Mahokon (Coleoptera). *Rev. Fr. Entomol. (N.S.)*, 4: 167–171.

Whitmore, T.C., 1975. *Tropical Rain Forests of the Far East*. Clarendon, Oxford, 282 pp.

Whittaker, R.H., 1975. *Communities and Ecosystems*. MacMillan, New York, N.Y., 385 pp.

Wille, A., 1973. Coleoptera: Scarabaeidae. Observations on the behaviour of a tropical rain forest dung beetle, Megathoposoma candezei (Harold). *Rev. Biol. Trop.*, 21: 41–57.

Wille, A., Fuentes, G., Orozco, E. and Soleis, E., 1974. Additional observations on the behaviour of a tropical forest dung beetle, Megathoposoma candezei (Coleoptera: Scarabaeidae). *Rev. Biol. Trop.*, 22: 129–133.

Williams, C.B., 1964. *Patterns in the Balance of Nature*. Academic Press, London, 324 pp.

Wolda, H., 1977. Fluctuations in abundance of some Homoptera in a neotropical forest. *Geo-Eco-Trop.*, 1: 229–257.

Wolda, H., 1978a. Fluctuations in abundance of tropical insects. *Am. Nat.*, 112: 1017–1045.

Wolda, H., 1978b. Seasonal fluctuations in rainfall, food and abundance of tropical insects. *J. Anim. Ecol.*, 47: 369–381.

Wolda, H., 1979. Abundance and diversity of Homoptera in the canopy of a tropical forest. *Ecol. Entomol.*, 4: 181–190.

Wolda, H., 1980. Seasonality of tropical insects. I. Leafhoppers (Homoptera) in Las Cumbres, Panama. *J. Anim. Ecol.*, 49: 277–290.

Wolda, H., 1982. Seasonality of Homoptera on Barro Colorado Island. In: E.G. Leigh, A.S. Rand and D.M. Windsor (Editors), *The Ecology of a Tropical Forest: Seasonal Rhythms and Long-Term Changes*. Smithsonian Press, Washington, D.C., pp. 319–330.

Wolda, H., 1983. Spatial and temporal variation in abundance in tropical animals. In: S.L. Sutton, T.C. Whitmore and A.C. Chadwick (Editors), *Tropical Rain Forest: Ecology and Management*. Blackwell, Oxford, pp. 93–106.

Wolda, H. and Galindo, P., 1981. Population fluctuations of mosquitos in the non-seasonal tropics. *Ecol. Entomol.*, 6: 99–106.

Young, O.P., 1976. Ball-rolling behaviour and competition in a neotropical forest dung beetle. *15th Int. Congress Entomol., Washington, D.C.* (cited in Young, 1978).

Young, O.P., 1978. *Resource partitioning in a Neotropical scarab guild*. D.Ph. thesis, Univ. of Maryland, College Park, Md., 227 pp.

Young, O.P., 1981. The attraction of neotropical Scarabaeinae (Coleoptera, Scarabaeidae) to reptile and amphibian fecal material. *Coleopt. Bull.*, 35: 345–348.

Young, O.P., 1984. Perching of neotropical dung beetles on leaf surfaces: an example of behavioural thermoregulation? *Biotropica*, 16: 324–327.

Chapter 29

HERBIVORY AND SECONDARY COMPOUNDS IN RAIN-FOREST PLANTS

P.G. WATERMAN and D. McKEY

INTRODUCTION

All plants probably contain compounds of the heterogeneous group generally referred to as plant secondary metabolites. These compounds contrast with a plant's primary metabolites by their high structural diversity and limited distribution, many being restricted to only a few species, and by the absence of any clearly defined role in the metabolic processes of the plant. The view is now widely held that the functions of these compounds lie in interactions with other organisms, and there is a great deal of evidence to support this. One obvious interactive role concerns attraction, of pollinators to flowers (Vogel, 1983) and of seed-dispersal agents to fruits (Herrera, 1982; Janzen, 1983a). Another possible role is that of allelopathy, wherein competition is limited by prevention of the growth of other plants nearby. That allelopathy exists there is little doubt; unfortunately, well-documented examples are rare, and the importance of this role as a factor selecting for the production of secondary metabolites remains unclear (Newman, 1983). Langenheim (1984) has reviewed existing studies of allelopathy in wet tropical forests.

Many secondary metabolites are thought to function in defence of the plant against enemies (herbivores and pathogens), with some perhaps having an ancillary role in modifying nutrient-cycling processes to the benefit of the plant producing them. This chapter deals with these anti-herbivore defences. We attempt to summarize what is presently known about the distribution of secondary metabolites in tropical rain-forest vegetation. We then examine these data in the light of current hypotheses about distribution of anti-

herbivore defences within and among plant species, and suggest kinds of studies that would add most to the existing very fragmentary knowledge in this area.

A plant, as a food source, is more than its chemistry; chemical and other features of the host plant interact with numerous other factors in the biology of herbivores. For example, the role that herbivore predators play in aiding escape of the plant from herbivory are probably crucial (Lawton and McNeill, 1979; Price et al., 1980). While it is impossible here to review adequately all aspects of herbivore biology in tropical rain forests, it is also impossible to discuss plant secondary chemistry in isolation from other factors. Our approach here is somewhat eclectic. We discuss nutrient chemistry of plants and the interactions of chemical defences with phenological and other defences (for instance, the interactions between herbivores and their enemies) where this seems appropriate.

Despite the enormous efforts that have been made by organic chemists, phytochemists and chemical taxonomists, and the considerable resulting literature on the structure and occurrence of secondary metabolites, the data base from which the ecologist works in interpreting the distribution of secondary metabolites in tropical rain-forest plants must still be regarded as totally inadequate. Firstly, the data have been gathered by researchers with very varied sets of aims. Phytochemical surveys for sources of biologically active compounds, or aimed at the detection of particular groups of compounds, yield information that for the ecologist's purpose is very incomplete. Secondly, a good balance has yet to be struck between community studies and detailed investigations of particular plant species. Our own investigations have been in the nature of broad comparative community studies, with the goal of characterizing the profile of secondary metabolites in different rain-forest communities, and relating this information to food selection by, and population biology of, Old World primates (McKey et al., 1978; Oates et al., 1980; McKey et al., 1981; Waterman, 1984). While this approach has also yielded information contributing to an understanding of the biology of specialist and generalist insect herbivores (Janzen and Waterman, 1984), it is clear that more intensive studies of plant chemistry are required if the interactions of a particular plant with its suite of herbivores are to be understood in depth. Intensive studies of a focal plant are as yet rare, that on *Hymenaea* spp. (Caesalpiniaceae) by Langenheim and her co-workers standing out in this respect.

Several misconceptions are frequently met in this field, reflecting the multidisciplinary input. What is obvious to one group of specialists is often misunderstood by another. The following seem worthy of comment:

(1) In the chemical literature tables of (+) and (−) values, for alkaloids for example, can often be misleading. A (−) reaction is generally correct but there are many compounds that will give false (+) reactions. To ensure correct identification, those materials that give a (+) must be treated further and then re-examined (Gartlan et al., 1980).

(2) Secondary metabolites occur in all plants (although perhaps not necessarily in all parts of a plant) and must be confronted by most, if not all, herbivores. Their presence and importance to herbivores is *not* a rare occurrence and is not limited to extreme sites.

(3) The chemical literature on the distribution of secondary plant metabolites is highly canalized. Plants have often been examined for only one group of metabolites; others are often thrown away unstudied! For example, reports of alkaloid occurrence in a plant may channel future investigators of this plant to examine it for alkaloids only. Most studies deal only with one part of the plant; other parts of that plant can have a very different profile of metabolites. When using the phytochemical literature it is always necessary to remember that one may have blinkered vision!

(4) Information on toxicity of compounds can often be very misleading. Different compounds,

even those closely related chemically, can exhibit a widely different spectrum of biological activity, both in terms of their effects and the organisms on which those effects are most pronounced. Toxicity tests carried out by intra-venous injection need not show any relationship to toxicity on ingestion. There is no such thing as *the* protein/tannin interaction. Different tannins interact with different proteins to different degrees, and the strength and persistence of these interactions varies with pH. There are, in fact, a whole range of different tannin/protein interactions; these are generally reversible, and can be nullified by processes that occur in many herbivores.

(5) Herbivore damage to a plant's fitness is not the same as visually perceived "damage". Factors other than the area of leaf removed must be considered in determining the impact of folivory, such as the part of the leaf lost, the time at which it is lost, and the longevity of the leaf.

(6) Crawley (1983, p. 14) attempted to predict herbivore biomass on the basis of net primary production. However, it is also possible similarly to make predictions regarding the quantity and type of investment plants will make in particular classes of defence compounds, and these levels of investment by the vegetation in defence chemistry seem to be accurate predictors of biomass of certain large herbivores. However, correlations between net productivity and herbivore biomass cannot be interpreted as meaning that one can forget about chemical defences.

(7) Attempts to explain feeding preferences in terms either of maximizing nutrient intake or of avoiding high levels of defence compounds (Crawley, 1983, p. 166) are generally unsound. Feeding preferences in most cases will be balanced by the interaction of these factors and their interactions in turn with other variables not directly arising from plant chemistry.

PATTERNS OF SECONDARY METABOLITE DISTRIBUTION

Most recent work on patterns of plant defence chemistry attempts to relate defence characteristics to patterns of life history, phenology and spatial distribution of the plant concerned, within the general framework of the "apparency" hypothesis of Feeny (1976) and the general hypotheses related to the roles of different types of secondary metabolites by Rhoades and Cates (1976) and Rhoades (1979).

Feeny (1976) and Rhoades and Cates (1976) independently arrived at similar hypotheses to explain the distribution of different classes of secondary compounds among plants. Using Feeny's (1976) terminology, some plants can be regarded as highly apparent to herbivores — that is, because they are long-lived and/or separated by only short distances in space and time from conspecifics, they are likely to be found by specialist herbivores. Such plants, it is argued, must be chemically and/or mechanically defended against both generalist and specialist herbivores. Other plants are relatively unapparent; their short lifespan and spatial and temporal separation from conspecifics make them less likely to be found by specialists. On the assumption that they will achieve "escape in space and time" from specialist herbivores, such plants must be defended chemically only against generalist herbivores. Different parts of the same plant, owing to differences in phenology, will differ in their apparency. Feeny extended the argument to predict what kinds of defence chemicals best suited each circumstance. Apparent plants and plant parts it was argued will possess "quantitative" defences (tannins, lignin, low nutrient levels), which pose an effective barrier against all herbivores, whether specialist or generalist. Unapparent plants or plant parts on the other hand will possess "qualitative" defences (small toxic molecules, such as alkaloids), which are highly effective against non-adapted generalists but which are relatively easily overcome by specialist herbivores. Thus unapparent plants protect themselves chemically against generalists, and escape specialists in space and time.

These hypotheses, and recent criticisms of them, provide a framework for discussion of the work reviewed here. We begin by summarizing the results of studies comparing different communities, then proceed to analysis of patterns within communities. Finally we examine variation between individuals, and the distribution of anti-herbivore defences within individual plants.

Differences between communities

The first systematic comparison of the defence chemistry of two rain-forest communities dealt with the leaf chemistry of the tree flora in the Douala–Edea Forest Reserve in west Cameroon and the Kibale Forest in Uganda. These studies, which incorporated data from species making up over 85% of the total tree biomass at each site, revealed that the leaves of trees at Douala–Edea accumulated higher levels of condensed tannins and other phenolics (McKey et al., 1978; Gartlan et al., 1980) than leaves of trees from Kibale, had lower levels of minerals and nitrogen (Waterman et al., 1980), and were more fibrous and less digestible (Waterman et al., 1980; Choo et al., 1981). In Kibale fewer of the common tree species appeared to be defended by condensed tannins, but a significantly greater percentage were sources of alkaloids. These results were interpreted to mean that Douala–Edea tree species, growing on sandy, highly acidic, nutrient-poor soils, invested a greater part of their resources in the generation of defensive compounds, and were more likely to have quantitative defence phenotypes. The findings for Douala–Edea agree with the chemical profile predicted by Janzen (1974) for climax vegetation on a nutrient-deficient site. By contrast, nitrogen-based defences, such as alkaloids, were considered to be favoured at Kibale because (a) nitrogen is less likely to be limiting in this comparatively nutrient-rich site; and (b) allocation of large amounts of photosynthate to the formation of defence compounds, in the face of the more intense vegetative competition expected when nutrient availability is high, would appreciably lower fitness. It was argued that polyphenols and defences based on fibre and lignin were more important in Douala–Edea species not only because low productivity demands high investment in defences, but also because such carbohydrate-rich defences are relatively cheaper when plants are limited by nitrogen and mineral nutrients rather than by energy.

Subsequent studies on other tropical areas in southern India (Oates et al., 1980), Costa Rica (Janzen and Waterman, 1984) and sites in South-East Asia (Waterman et al., submitted) have added to this initial investigation in important ways. Firstly, they have highlighted the generally high levels of quantitative defence compounds in leaves of rain-forest trees (Table 29.1), and it now seems possible to regard Kibale as having exceptionally low investment in these materials rather than to consider Douala–Edea as a site of particularly

TABLE 29.1

Comparison of composition (% dry wt.) of mature foliage from different rain forest sites

Site	Number of species	Total phenol	Condensed tannin (CT)	Acid detergent fibre (ADF)	Cellulase digestibility	Nitrogen (N)	$\dfrac{6.25N}{ADF+CT}$	$\dfrac{6.25N}{ADF}$
Barro Colorado[1]	24[2]	10.10	4.80	37.40	–	2.20	0.33	0.37
Douala–Edea[3]	38	7.31	5.41	47.03	33.63	1.96	0.23	0.26
Kakachi[4]	13	6.52	5.83	40.55	31.60	1.84	0.25	0.38
Kibale[3,5]	14[6]	3.64	2.65	36.21	50.69	2.73	0.44	0.47
Kibale[3,5]	44	4.00	5.84	35.40	51.30	2.68	0.41	0.47
Kuala Lompat[7]	37	4.30	4.90	46.20	39.60	2.10	0.26	0.28
Santa Rosa[8]	78	6.20	5.62	41.00	–	–	–	–
Sepilok[7]	42	6.00	9.60	58.15	29.30	1.60	0.15	0.17
Visoke[9]	21	5.01	1.08	35.45	56.45	2.48	0.43	0.44
Zanzibar[10]	15	6.29	3.27	47.10	41.10	1.55	0.19	0.21

[1]Central American lowland forest (Coley, 1983a). [2]Climax species only used. [3]Cameroon lowland rain forest (Waterman et al., 1980; Choo et al., 1981; Ross, unpubl.). [4]South Indian upland rain forest (Oates et al., 1980). [5]Kibale, upland rain forest (Waterman, unpubl. results). [6]Common species only [see McKey et al. (1978) for list]. [7]South-East Asian lowland rain forest (Waterman et al., submitted). [8]Costa Rican deciduous forest (Janzen and Waterman, 1984). [9]Afro-alpine vegetation (Waterman et al., 1983). [10]Coastal rain forest with strong South-East Asian floristic element (Omari and Waterman, unpubl.).

heavy investment. Furthermore, the availability of considerable additional data from Kibale, including many rarer species with high levels of condensed tannins, shows that the average phenolic content is similar to that at other sites. By contrast, the average content of fibre and lignin for Kibale is still low, and the nitrogen level high.

Secondly, studies on digestibility (Waterman et al., 1980; Choo et al., 1981) and food selection by generalist herbivores (Oates et al., 1980; McKey et al., 1981; Davies et al., submitted) have implicated fibre rather than polyphenolics as the most important component of quantitative defence systems. Fibre, and perhaps specifically lignin, appear generally more important than tannins both in influence on herbivores and in the input of resources involved; as in other studies of that period, it would appear that our early work probably gave tannins more emphasis than they deserved.

Thirdly, data on the feeding behaviour and population density of colobine monkeys in several of these sites indicates the overall importance of chemical defences in determining patterns of food selection and carrying capacity. We found (McKey et al., 1981) a strong positive correlation between (1) the ratio of protein content to fibre [6.25N/

ADF] and combined totals of fibre and condensed tannin [6.25N/(ADF+CT) of Table 29.1] in mature leaves of different tree species, and (2) use of these species by black colobus (*Colobus satanas*). Subsequent studies of vegetation from other sites where colobine monkeys occur (Kibale, Kakachi, Kuala Lompat, Sepilok, Zanzibar; Table 29.1) have shown that it is possible to predict colobine biomass, estimated from census data, from the average value of this ratio for mature leaves of common species at these sites (Waterman et al., submitted). Of the measures involved, the influence of the condensed tannin is marginal and variable and use of the simpler ratio appears more reliable. It is important to realize that relationship holds true despite the fact that in most cases mature leaves form a relatively minor part of the diet. We suspect that this correlation exists for at least three reasons:

(a) The ratio used, involving the available protein in mature leaves and the metabolites that limit the rate to which it can be obtained, reflects the extent to which these herbivores are forced to avoid mature leaves and to rely on young leaves, seeds and fruits; these are less abundant and more patchily distributed in space and time, and consequently allow only a low density of herbivores.

This estimator of food quality does not take into account the presence of toxic secondary metabolites which would also be deterrent. However for the ruminant-like colobines, which have a gut microflora capable of detoxifying some of these, this omission does not confound the relationship.

(b) In some sites, carrying capacity may be determined by "bottle-neck" seasons when young leaves and other high-quality items are unavailable and the monkeys are restricted to mature leaves. At such times, feeding is highly selective, and directed primarily to species whose mature leaves are relatively rich in nutrients and low in components which reduce digestibility. The scarcity of such mature leaves may thus limit colobine biomass.

(c) Plants whose mature leaves are heavily defended are likely to defend other parts heavily as well. In sites characterized by heavily-defended mature leaves, more species may produce young leaves, seeds, etc., that are also heavily defended. Furthermore, to the extent that high investment in defence of mature leaves reflects low productivity, production of young leaves, flowers, and seeds and fruits will be lower in sites where the mature leaves are highly defended.

Patterns within a community

Hypotheses put forward by Feeny (1976) and by Rhoades and Cates (1976) predict that chemical-defence phenotypes will vary between plant species within the community, and will differ in various features of life history and vegetative strategy — for instance, quantitative defences will be more important in species of the climax phase, and in the foliage of evergreen species when compared to deciduous species. To what extent are these predictions supported by observations? Also, to what extent does existing information on the chemical defences of different species within the community enable one to understand patterns of food selection by generalist herbivores? What are the implications for the biology of specialist herbivores on different kinds of host plants?

Our studies in several rain-forest sites have shown sharp differences in the defence phenotypes of different tree species within single communities. In all sites studied there is a distinctive separation between some species with mature leaves rich in tannins but lacking alkaloids and others in which the converse is true (Table 29.2). These two classes of compound are found together in leaves much more rarely than would be expected by chance (Gartlan et al., 1980; Janzen and Waterman, 1984). A similar observation specifically concerning the distribution of these compounds in the Apocynaceae had been made in the last century (Greshoff, 1890). A major reason for this dichotomy would seem to lie in the ability of tannins and alkaloids to interact to form insoluble complexes, in which the biological activity of each is negated.

However, this may not be the whole story. Other differences exist between tannin-rich and alkaloid-containing mature leaves. Where data are available, mature leaves containing alkaloids seem on average to be less fibrous and to contain a higher proportion of nitrogen than mature leaves rich in tannins. Whatever the reason, there does seem to exist, among tree species in tropical rain forests, a

TABLE 29.2

Condensed tannin (% dry wt.) in mature leaves of alkaloid-positive and alkaloid-negative species from three tropical forests (Gartlan et al., 1980; Janzen and Waterman, 1984)

Site	Alkaloid-positive		Alkaloid-negative	
	number of species	condensed tannin	number of species	condensed tannin
Douala–Edea, Cameroon	11	2.38	59	6.66
Kibale, Uganda	10	0.54	10	6.32
Santa Rosa, Costa Rica	18	4.51	40	13.03

tendency for some species to produce leaves protected primarily by small toxic molecules (the "qualitative" defences of Feeny, 1976), while other species produce leaves characterized by large amounts of big molecules with potential for reducing digestibility, such as tannins and lignin, and by other "quantitative" defences such as low content of nutrients and of water.

There is some evidence for the ecological significance of such between-species variation in gross defence phenotypes. Although this evidence comes from studies of tropical deciduous forests, we feel it has great relevance for herbivore biology in rain forests. Studies on the host-plant relationship and larval biology of moths of the Saturniidae and Sphingidae in Santa Rosa National Park, Costa Rica (Janzen and Waterman, 1984) show that saturniids are less host-specific than sphingids and tend to select as host plants species with leaves which are relatively rich in condensed tannins (and, perhaps, other phenolics), relatively fibrous and lower in water content, but which tend to lack alkaloids or other toxins (Table 29.3). Sphingids, on the other hand, are more host-specific and are more likely to be found on plants containing alkaloids or other types of qualitative defence compounds [for

instance, *Annona reticulata* (Annonaceae), which contains alkaloids and diterpenes]. Their host plants tend to contain less fibre and condensed tannins and more moisture than host plants of most saturniids. Larval development of sphingids tends to be much faster than for saturniids.

These results support the notion that quantitative defences may be difficult to counteract, whereas toxin-based defences are effective only against generalists (Feeny, 1976; Rhoades and Cates, 1976).

Current hypotheses also make predictions about features of life-history and vegetative strategy that make it more likely that one or the other of these gross chemical defence phenotypes will be selected for. Data from our own studies do not permit adequate tests of these predictions, though the patterns are certainly suggestive. For example, in the Santa Rosa site where a large element of the flora is deciduous, leaves of evergreen trees are in general richer in fibre and tannins than those of deciduous species (Table 29.4), a finding consistent with the hypotheses mentioned above (p. 514). Data from Coley's (1981, 1983a) study on Barro Colorado which allows separation of species with a leaf life-span of less than 10 months from those in

TABLE 29.3

Composition of the foliage of food plants of larvae of the Sphingidae and Saturniidae of the Santa Rosa National Park, Costa Rica (Janzen and Waterman, 1984)

(a) Total phenol (TP), condensed tannin (CT) and acid detergent fibre (ADF) (% of dry matter)

Leaf age	Measure	Host plants of Saturniidae			Host plants of Sphingidae		
		species number	mean %	standard deviation	species number	mean %	standard deviation
Young leaves	TP	19	15.64	5.73	15	11.47	4.02
	CT	19	17.04	11.14	15	6.57	6.72
	ADF	19	38.33	6.28	15	35.29	10.17
Old leaves	TP	23	14.40	4.31	13	11.17	3.57
	CT	23	15.82	8.65	13	8.31	6.87
	ADF	23	43.79	5.63	13	36.89	8.30
	MOISTURE	23	51.64	4.56	13	55.26	4.72

(b) Alkaloids and latex

	total species	species alkaloids	containing latex
Host plants of Saturniidae	25	2	0
Host plants of Sphingidae	19	7	5

TABLE 29.4

Comparison of levels of total phenol (TP), condensed tannin (CT), acid detergent fibre (ADF) and nitrogen (N) (% dry wt.), in the young and mature foliage of evergreen and deciduous species from Santa Rosa National Park, Costa Rica (Janzen and Waterman, 1984) and Barro Colorado Island (Coley, 1980)

| | Deciduous species | | | | Evergreen species | | | |
| | young leaves | | mature leaves | | young leaves | | mature leaves | |
	SRNP[1]	BCI[2]	SRNP[1]	BCI[2]	SRNP[1]	BCI[2]	SRNP[1]	BCI[2]
Species number	49	22	47	22	12	18	15	18
Total phenol	12.9	13.1	12.4	8.0	15.8	14.7	19.0	10.5
Condensed tannin	10.0	3.7	10.1	1.9	9.5	11.0	13.7	5.2
Acid detergent fibre	35.6	27.8	38.9	28.9	44.1	32.6	44.5	40.0
Nitrogen	–	3.2	–	2.5	–	3.3	–	2.1

[1]Santa Rosa National Park, Costa Rica (Janzen and Waterman, 1984).
[2]Barro Colorado Island, Panama (Coley, 1980).
Deciduous species are taken as those with leaf life-span of less than 10 months, evergreen as greater than 20 months.

which the leaves persist more than 20 months show a similar pattern (Table 29.4).

Coley's (1983a) study was the first tropical investigation designed to test predictions about the distribution of anti-herbivore defences among ecologically different groups of species within a community. In order to test predictions of Feeny (1976) and Rhoades and Cates (1976) concerning the distribution of anti-herbivore defences in relation to successional states she compared defence characteristics and rates of herbivory sustained by foliage of gap-colonizing and shade-tolerant tree species. She found that mature leaves of colonizers were less tough, had lower concentra-

tions of fibre and phenolics, more nitrogen and moisture, and were shorter-lived than mature leaves of climax species (Table 29.5). Gap-colonizers also grew faster. The mature leaves of colonizers were found to be grazed at six times the rate of climax species; leaf toughness, fibre and nutritive quality were the factors most strongly related to herbivory.

These findings are consistent with expectations based on current hypotheses, but some predictions were not supported by Coley's study. For example, in density-manipulation experiments she could find no evidence that colonizers were more likely to escape discovery, as would be anticipated from the

TABLE 29.5

Comparison of composition (% dry wt.) in the young and mature foliage of climax and colonizer species from Barro Colorado Island (data from Coley, 1983a)

| | Young leaves | | Mature leaves | |
	colonizers	climax species	colonizers	climax species
Number of species	22	24	22	24
Total phenol	12.7	19.2	7.7	10.1
Condensed tannin	3.4	9.7	1.7	4.8
Acid detergent fibre	27.5	31.5	29.5	37.5
Lignin	17.0	19.5	17.6	23.4
Nitrogen	3.2	3.3	2.5	2.2
Water	74	76	70	62

apparency model (Feeny, 1976; see p. 514). The observed differences seemed to be primarily due to the ability of the colonizers to "tolerate high rates of herbivory because of cheaper leaves and faster growth rates." Her study supported the prediction of Janzen (1974) that for equal absolute amounts of tissue removed by herbivores the reduction in fitness will be lower for faster growing plants, selecting for lower defences than in slower growing plants. If this is correct, then differences in the potential growth rates of different species should be reflected by differences in typical rates of herbivory. This is confirmed by Coley (1983a) who found, for a set of 46 species, that maximum growth rate was strongly positively correlated with susceptibility to grazing.

This relationship leads one to expect other patterns in the distribution of anti-herbivore defences between species differing in life-form and vegetative strategy. For example, lianes as a class are characterized by rapid growth. We predict that leaves of lianes will relatively often be characterized by low contents of tannins and fibre, and may perhaps contain more toxins of low molecular weight than leaves of trees from the same site.

The rain-forest understorey should also be an inhospitable place for folivores. In this low-energy environment the cost of losing leaves will be high, leading to selection for highly effective defences. Insect densities are low in the forest understorey (Janzen, 1973c); folivorous mammals concentrate their activity in forest edges, light gaps and secondary forest (Feer, 1979); and many terrestrial mammalian herbivores feed mostly on fruits produced by the canopy. For example, many of the small antelopes of African forests (Gautier-Hion et al., 1980), and even the forest elephant (Alexandre, 1978), are largely frugivorous. By contrast, the herb layer of an energy-rich montane rain forest in Africa (Visoke, Table 29.1) is characterized by a paucity of secondary compounds, low fibre and high levels of digestibility and nitrogen content (Waterman et al., 1983). By similar reasoning, one might expect epiphytes to be among the most adequately defended plants of rain-forest vegetation. In this respect it is noteworthy that the recent study of the slow-growing epiphytic climbers of the genus *Hoya* by Baas (1983) confirmed that they exhibited a considerable range of secondary compounds. Root-climbers, plants such as some Ara-

ceae that begin life as epiphytes and then send roots to the ground, and other forms morphologically intermediate between the true woody lianes and epiphytes, may also exhibit intermediate patterns of defence chemistry.

Such differences in defence phenotypes among species within a community will be reflected in differences in the structure of the herbivore fauna of these plants, if the saturniid/sphingid study (Janzen and Waterman, 1984) is any basis for generalization. It can also be expected that differences in development time, as found in that study, will influence the interaction of insects with their natural enemies. Maybe not only the structure of the herbivore fauna, but also the entire food web based on a plant is partly determined by the plant's chemical-defence phenotype.

Recent criticisms of defence theory

Coley's (1983a) results are consistent with much of the defence theory developed following the ideas put forward by Feeny (1976) and by Rhoades and Cates (1976), but she found no evidence for the importance of apparency. Fox (1981) has made a more general criticism of defence theory and the apparency hypothesis in particular, and elements of this critique are relevant to our discussion. Fox's critique has three major targets: (a) the reliance of defence theory on arguments based on comparison of metabolic costs; (b) the dichotomy envisaged between qualitative and quantitative defences; and (c) the supposition of stepwise co-evolution between plants and herbivores.

Fox (1981) has questioned the view that qualitative defences (based on small amounts of specific toxins) are inherently less expensive metabolically than quantitative defences (based on relatively large amounts of digestibility-reducing compounds). We agree. Large amounts of polyphenol and lignin may cost more to produce than small amounts of alkaloids in a site relatively rich in nutrients and under conditions of competition for light, but the reverse may be true in a site where nutrients are more limiting than light (Gartlan et al., 1980; Bryant et al., 1983). Fox (1981) also pointed out that cost estimates based on the concentration present fail to take account of higher maintenance costs imposed by turnover of toxins. We concur. Turnover of secondary metabolites is a widespread phenomenon (Barz and Koster, 1981) and can sometimes be very rapid (for instance, half-lives of 10–20 h). Under such circumstances tannins and lignins may be cheaper in long-lived leaves because their once-and-for-all synthesis may have a lower overall cost. By contrast, the continuous generation of a toxin at a low concentration and its reclamation by degradation or transport may be cost-effective in short-lived leaves (McKey, 1979). The point made by Fox (1981) that sweeping generalizations about costs of various chemical-defence strategies are premature, and that such costs are difficult to quantify, is clearly true; but the fact that the costs are difficult to quantify does not make them less important. In cases where rough calculations of costs have been made [Mooney and Gulmon (1982), and references therein], this approach seems promising. We see no way to avoid consideration of costs in evolutionary ecology. Like "fitness", the concept seems troublesome but necessary.

A second feature of the apparency hypothesis criticised by Fox (1981) concerns the dichotomy in effectiveness between qualitative defences envisaged as being all or none and quantitative as being dose-dependent. A dichotomy often proves to be an artificial simplification of a more complex underlying pattern. If it simplifies reality without distorting it, a dichotomy can have heuristic value. The distinction of qualitative and quantitative defences has had such heuristic value, we feel. The differences in growth rate and larval development times between sphingids and saturniids discussed above suggests that defence theory can correctly predict differences in effectiveness of defences. Fox's (1981) contribution here is to point out that tannins in particular have been overemphasized as quantitative defences Fox cites a number of studies (and see Zucker, 1983) showing that tannins are not absolutely effective defences against all herbivores, that some herbivores have ways of circumventing them, and that there is more diversity in tannin/protein interactions than envisaged in the original hypotheses of Feeny (1976) and Rhoades and Cates (1976). Indeed, it has recently been reported (Martin and Martin, 1984; Martin et al., 1987) that many, perhaps all, insects contain in their gut surface-active substances able to inhibit the formation of tannin/protein complexes. Bile salts have similarly been implicated in the inhibition of tannin/protein complex formation under conditions existing in the mammalian gut (Mole and Waterman, 1985, 1987). Whilst it still remains possible that tannins can inhibit proteolysis under conditions found in the guts of both insect and mammalian herbivores, widespread mechanisms for the reduction or inhibition of this effect must now be considered probable. Although these recent findings point to a less important role for tannins relative to the other chemical factors grouped under the general heading of quantitative defences (fibre, nutrient and water content) we feel they do not weaken the basic hypothesis that plants show strategies in chemical-defence phenotypes along a continuum whose extremes differ in the ways originally postulated for qualitative and quantitative defences.

The third point made by Fox (1981) is that defence theory implies stepwise co-evolution, but that in fact this will only apply to unapparent plants; the argument is developed as follows. Unapparent plants, often small herbs, are likely to interact with fewer herbivores than apparent species, because herbivore species richness is low on architecturally simple plants with short life cycles (Lawton, 1983). Fox (1981) did not address the question of whether other unapparent plants (e.g. patchily distributed larger plants) also have herbivore faunas of lower species richness. Because an unapparent plant is interacting with few herbivore species and it is presumed that those herbivores will be largely specialists, Fox argued that there is the potential for strong reciprocal evolutionary interactions. The most likely defence to be selected in such circumstances is, Fox suggested, one specific in its action against that particular herbivore and capable of conferring defence at low cost. Under such conditions stepwise co-evolution is anticipated. A possible example of such a system with strong reciprocal interactions between a plant and a few specialist herbivores is that of *Passiflora* and *Heliconius* (Futuyma, 1983).

We see a major problem with this hypothesis. It may be misguided to think that the herbivores currently attacking a plant are the ones that have shaped its defence phenotype (Janzen, 1981a). *Heliconius* breached some of the chemical defences of *Passiflora*; in consequence, the plant has evolved novel defences, many of them non-chemical. The question then becomes, why are these chemical defences maintained despite the fact that they are ineffective against *Heliconius*? We suspect they are maintained by selection pressures arising from herbivores which are not *Passiflora* specialists against individuals lacking these defences. In this sense *Passiflora* is not interacting just with the guild of herbivore species found on typical individuals. One can ask the same question in many other cases: why do many species of Brassicaceae persist in producing glucosinolates, and many legumes form non-protein amino-acids, when these substances do not deter specialists? Our interpretation of the function of specific toxins differs from that of Fox (1981). Fox equates specificity of physiological action with selective effects on specific herbivores. We feel, however, that specificity in mode of physiological action is a prerequisite for acute toxicity (McKey, 1979), and that many toxins are excellent broad-spectrum defences by virtue of their focused action on critical physiological processes that are widespread in herbivores and pathogens. Fox sees toxins as being maintained as defence against specialists while we see them as being maintained largely against generalists which would include the plant in their repertoire in the absence of the toxin. While we feel that stepwise co-evolution has occurred in many of these systems, this is not the *cause* of these toxins but rather an *effect* of the fact that these plants contain toxins which have enforced specialization, allowing strong reciprocal evolutionary interaction. We believe that these compounds owe their existence in large part to the same kind of "diffuse coevolution" with a great variety of herbivores that Fox (1981) envisaged as being largely restricted to "apparent" plants.

Distribution of defences within individual plants

The allocation of secondary compounds and other anti-herbivore defences to various parts of the plant should be influenced by several factors (McKey, 1979). The cost of herbivory on different plant parts, in terms of the reduction of plant fitness, may vary, leading to preferential allocation of defences to tissues of greatest value. Differences may also be qualitative. Different secondary metabolites may be suited to defence of different plant parts, because these compounds may be suited to the physiological, energetic and nutrient-related constraints to which the different organs are subject, and because each plant part is attacked by a particular collection of herbivores with particular susceptibilities. The distribution of benzophenanthridine alkaloids appears to offer a good example of this last point; these extremely fungitoxic alkaloids are concentrated in the root bark of some Rutaceae and Berberidaceae (references cited by McKey, 1979). On the other hand, if the plant evolves a compound effective against a broad spectrum of herbivores and pathogens, it may be accumulated in all parts of the plant. *Garcinia mannii* (Clusiaceae), from Cameroon, may offer an example. All the vegetative parts of this species, except the wood and the fruit, contain very large amounts of a biflavonoid, manniflavanone (Crichton and Waterman, 1979; Gartlan et al., 1980), but only traces of the phenolics typical of sympatric species of this genus. It might be considered that uniform chemical defence throughout a plant could allow a herbivore to attack all organs once it is on the plant. However, many other factors (nutritional status, morphology, phenology) restrict most herbivores to a single plant part. An organ may achieve more escape by being chemically different from analogous parts of other plants than by being chemically different from other parts of the same plant (Janzen, 1973b).

Young and mature leaves

Many insect folivores in tropical rain forests are restricted to young leaves of their host plants. Generalist herbivores, including colobine monkeys (McKey et al., 1981), howler monkeys (Milton, 1979), and *Atta* leaf-cutter ants (Rockwood and Glander, 1979; Waller, 1982), generally prefer young to mature leaves. What are the reasons for these preferences?

A number of studies have compared the nutrient and quantitative defence chemistry of young and mature leaves of tropical-forest plants (see, for example, Milton, 1979; Oates et al., 1980; Waterman et al., 1980; Choo et al., 1981; Coley, 1983a). In all of these studies there has been a discernible (and not surprising) trend toward lower nitrogen content and higher content of fibre and lignin in the mature leaf. The most striking finding about chemical defences of young leaves that has emerged in recent work on tropical rain-forest plants is that they usually appear to be richer in extractable polyphenols than are the mature leaves of the same species (Gartlan et al., 1980; Oates et al., 1980; Becker, 1981; Crankshaw and Langenheim, 1981; Coley, 1983a), in contrast with earlier findings in some temperate-zone species (Feeny, 1976; Rhoades and Cates, 1976). Crankshaw and Langenheim (1981) suggested that the latter pattern is associated with the seasonality of herbivore pressure faced by temperate-zone trees; but some recent studies have shown young leaves to be richer in polyphenols in some temperate-zone species as well (Fox, 1981; Ottosson and Anderson, 1983). Becker and Martin (1982) have demonstrated that the higher concentration of polyphenols in young leaves of *Shorea* spp. appears to be reflected in greater protein-precipitating capacity in extracts of young leaves. However, studies of digestibility of leaf dry-matter from a number of rain forests (Oates et al., 1980; Waterman et al., 1980; Choo et al., 1981; Waterman, unpubl.) together with a wealth of data for agricultural plants have shown that the greater dry weight concentrations of tannin sometimes found in young leaves do not generally prevent young leaves having a greater dry-matter digestibility than mature leaves. The implication of these findings is that polyphenols appear in many cases to be allocated to the leaf early in its life-history and that they are then passively diluted as the leaf ages. Alternatively, as suggested by Gartlan et al. (1980) they may simply be easier to extract from the young leaf. Some other secondary metabolites often considered to be quantitative defences have also been shown to occur in greatest amounts in the young leaf — for instance, the sesquiterpene resin of *Hymenaea* (Crankshaw and Langenheim, 1981). The observation made by Lowman and Box (1983) that, in Australian rain-forest trees, toughness and chemical toxicity most often increased as leaves aged is probably true for all rain-forest floras.

Nearly all studies of tropical plants carried out to date have failed to produce examples of another pattern seen in some earlier work; the allocation of different defence chemicals to leaves of different ages (Dement and Mooney, 1974; Lawton, 1976). The finding of Baas (1983) that ageing leaves of *Hoya* species show an accumulation of seco-triterpenes in their leaf waxes, whereas young leaves contain only normal triterpenes, may be an exception or may indicate the passive oxidation of

the triterpene nucleus with time. However, very few species of tropical plants have yet been investigated for such gross changes in defence repertoire with leaf maturation.

Phenological defences of young leaves

It has been postulated that patchy spatial and temporal distribution of young leaves enables them to avoid herbivory (McKey, 1974) in a manner analogous to the case of seeds and seed predators (Janzen, 1971, 1978b). The availability of "phenological defences" may influence a plant's tactics in the evolution of chemical defences of young leaves.

An individual young leaf is a temporary resource. The consequences of this fact for herbivores depend on properties of the plant, such as the length of time a young leaf is available, the period during which young leaves are continuously available on an individual plant, the length of time gaps between such periods, and the degree of synchrony between individual plants. The consequences also depend on properties of the herbivore, such as its mobility, and its host specificity (in terms of species and plant parts to which it is restricted).

Direct escape in space and time may be achieved by production of young leaves in a manner that reduces the rate at which they are found by herbivores, or that results in the local satiation of populations of the herbivores eating them. Escape in space and time may also be achieved indirectly in that the patchy spatial and temporal distribution may reduce the individual and/or population growth rates of the herbivore, or increase its susceptibility to natural enemies. For example, Auerbach and Strong (1981) believed that the extremely slow larval development of the rolled-leaf beetle *Chelobasis perplexa* [Chrysomelidae (Hispinae)] was ultimately caused by the patchy spatiotemporal distribution of the young leaves on which these insects feed. They argued that slow growth may have resulted from the evolution of low metabolic rates serving as a mechanism for resisting starvation between periods of young-leaf availability.

Coley (1983a, b) attempted to test ideas about the role of patchiness in space and time in the escape of young leaves from herbivores. She argued that if species which produce young leaves synchronously within and between individuals, with gaps separating these bursts of production, are by this means escaping herbivores, this should be mirrored by greater variation between individuals in losses of young leaves by herbivory than in species whose production of young leaves is more continuous. This did not hold for the species she studied, and she concluded that synchronous production of young leaves does not result in escape from herbivores. We find this result interesting, but not adequate as a test of the hypothesis. Alternative explanations for her results are possible. For example, if young leaves of a plant are attacked by a single herbivore species, a relatively even distribution of damage could indicate that individuals are not escaping in time. If the damage is caused by five different herbivore species, then a relatively even distribution of damage could mean the same thing, but it could also mean that each plant has escaped by chance a different subset of the five herbivores, and that damage to each would be greater if leaf production were less synchronous and each plant escaped none of the five. Additionally, Coley's (1983a, b) interpretation is based on comparison of species which differ in many traits other than phenology of leaf production. We feel that adequate tests of the role of phenology in permitting young leaves to escape herbivory will only come when a plant population and each of the suite of herbivores attacking it are studied in detail, as Augspurger (1981) has done for the role of reproductive synchrony of *Hybanthus* (Violaceae) in escaping seed predators.

One fact leads us to believe that there is still very much to learn about the anti-herbivore defences of young leaves: the enormous variety in patterns of growth and development of leaves among plants of tropical forests. Leaves may be produced synchronously at intervals, or continuously. Growth and development of a leaf may proceed basipetally, centripetally, or acropetally. Expansion may be rapid and precede the major period of dry-matter accumulation and of lignification, or these processes may occur concurrently. Leaf development times may vary greatly between species. What is the significance of this variety? We believe that a large part of it is related to different ways of protecting young leaves, and that the chemical, phenological, and biotic defences (for instance, ant-guards; McKey, in press a, b) of young leaves can only be understood when they are considered in this comprehensive context of the developmental

biology of leaves. We predict that in the near future the framework employed in current studies to account for young-leaf defences will be seen as hopelessly simplistic, at least for rain-forest species.

Bark and wood

Janzen (1981b) has argued that seeds are probably the most thoroughly protected of all plant parts, and pointed out that many are defended by a range of compounds, including very active toxins, digestion-inhibitors of several kinds and, often, a mechanical protective layer as well. We would suggest that the bark of trees offers strong competition for the "title" of most defended part of a tropical tree. Studies on species from African rain forests reveal a range of different types of toxin and polyphenolics as well as high levels of fibre and lignification that often reduce percentage digestibility to single-figure values. Examples of the diversity of bark chemistry are legion, and the reader is invited to scan through any copy of *Phytochemistry* to illustrate the point, or to consider the vast array of compounds listed in recent reviews of the Annonaceae (Leboeuf et al., 1982) or the families of the Rutales (Waterman and Grundon, 1983). Most trees have only one main trunk, and the importance of protecting the transport systems and wood is clearly reflected in the allocation of high concentrations of defence chemicals to stem bark. The strategies adopted by herbivores to overcome bark defences can be complex, as is illustrated by Raffa and Berryman (1983) for conifers and associated bark beetles. To date, there do not seem to be any comparable data available for bark herbivores on rain-forest plants. By contrast the wood is often a relatively poorly defended section of the plant [for comparative data on bark and wood of Ebenaceae and Clusiaceae see Gartlan et al. (1980) and Waterman and Hussain (1983)].

Root bark is also often a rich source of secondary compounds, but the significance of these in the interaction of tropical rain-forest plants with soil-dwelling herbivores and pathogens remains virtually unexplored.

Reproductive tissues and seeds
Very little is known about flower chemistry in relation to defence against herbivores. Chemical

data available from general surveys (Waterman, 1984) suggest that chemical profiles of mature flowers are generally comparable to those of leaves, although nutrient levels, particularly at the bud stage, are often very high. Flowers offering rewards for pollinators possess a variety of mechanical defences against nectar exploitation by non-pollinators, but the role of chemicals in defence of floral rewards (either in surrounding tissues or in nectar or pollen itself) has not been widely examined. Baker et al. (1978) have pointed out the existence of uncommon amino acids and other secondary compounds in floral nectar, and have suggested they may function in defence of this reward.

Little need be said here about the defence chemistry of fruits and seeds, as various aspects of this problem have recently been thoroughly reviewed, both in general (Janzen, 1978a, b, 1983a) and particularly with respect to the role of chemical defences in mature fruit in warding off microbial and fungal attack (Janzen, 1977) and in focusing seed dispersal through a limited number of dispersal agents (Herrera, 1982; Howe and Smallwood, 1982). Recent work on seeds of rainforest trees (Lee, 1979), not cited by Janzen, supports his contention that lectins and other toxic proteins are widespread as seed defences, and reinforces the supposition that seed defences are often drawn from the subset of compounds that might also act as nitrogen and energy reserves for the seedling (McKey, 1979).

Janzen (1978b), pointing out that tannins apparently are not transported into seedlings as such, nor converted and transported in some other form, predicted that they would be mainly found in large seeds in which dispersal systems set less stringent demands for a compact, nutrient-rich packet. This prediction is supported by studies so far. *Mora megistosperma* (Caesalpiniaceae) produces what is possibly the world's largest dicotyledonous seed, which is water-dispersed and very rich in tannins (Waterman, unpubl.). The most tannin-rich seeds in the Douala–Edea Forest Reserve, Cameroon, are those of *Strephonema* spp. (Combretaceae). The seeds of *S. pseudocola* are the largest of any plant in the Reserve, and those of *S. mannii* are large and water-dispersed. Seeds of *S. pseudocola* fall to the ground and are seldom removed from beneath the parent. They lack a fleshy fruit and have no obvious dispersal agent.

The anti-herbivore chemistry of seeds (and of other nutrient-storage tissues such as tubers) has a potential source of complexity lacking in vegetative organs such as leaves with high metabolic activity: there are a greater variety of ways in which a package of stored nutrients can be constructed than there are of constructing a metabolically active leaf (McKey et al., 1981). Qualitative variation in nutrient content probably plays a much greater role in the interaction of seeds with seed predators than is the case for interactions between herbivores and leaves. Photosynthesis requires a fixed set of enzymes and co-enzymes and results in a fixed set of products, so that qualitative variation in nutrient content among leaves of various species is probably minimal (Waterman, 1984b). Seeds on the other hand provide a great contrast; they may be capable of photosynthesis (Janzen, 1982), they may contain a balanced mixture of energy, nitrogen, and mineral nutrients, or they may consist largely of energy stores which are available to mycorrhizae in exchange for mineral nutrients upon germination. Their nitrogen reserves may be in the form of proteins or free amino acids and, if the latter, may consist of a mixture, or have a single amino acid predominating, to be converted to the others after germination. Energy reserves may be in the form of lipids, starch, or other polysaccharides such as hemicellulose. All of these reserves may be in the form of non-toxic molecules mixed with various toxins, or they may be toxic themselves. Current investigations have only scratched the surface of the problem of explaining the variety of nutrient-composition patterns in seeds.

Intraspecific variation in content of secondary compounds

Janzen (1973a) suggested that a species would benefit from maximizing the distinctness of its defence repertoire from those of species which are in close proximity. There is now some evidence to support this; variation between sympatric species that are taxonomically closely related is generally high (Cates and Rhoades, 1977; Waterman et al., 1978; Gottlieb and Kubitzki, 1981; Waterman, 1983, 1986). The same arguments are likely to hold for variation within a species, so that offspring varying in defence chemistry from their parent(s) may be at an advantage. Temporal unpredictability may lead to situations where only those offspring which differ in this respect from their parents survive in the changed environment. Spatial heterogeneity may lead to one defence phenotype performing better in one microhabitat, while another performs better under other conditions. On the other hand, variability among the individuals in a population may be adaptive in itself, and be maintained by frequency-dependent selection. For example, when host-specific herbivores whose effectiveness in colonizing individuals of the host plant is governed by the density of the host or the distance between host plants, then it may be advantageous to a plant to be unlike its conspecific neighbours.

Genetic component of variation

Levin (1975) and Janzen (1983b) have stressed the importance of recombination and sexual reproduction for tropical plants faced with ever-evolving biotic challenges. As Janzen (1983b) stated, few tropical trees can afford to isolate themselves from the solutions to biotic challenges found by their conspecifics. Although recent studies indicate that even within the humid tropics there exists ecogeographic variation in tree breeding systems (Primack and Tomlinson, 1980), the bulk of available information points to the prevalence of open genetic systems and widespread outcrossing in tropical trees (Bawa, 1974; Levin, 1975; Arroyo, 1976).

The predominance of outcrossing and high rates of recombination would be expected to have effects on variation in secondary compounds and other anti-herbivore defences — all the more so since herbivores are one of the major challenges faced by tropical plants. Depending on the selective environment, high recombination rate might have one of two genetic consequences: (a) it might allow rapid replacement of one genotype by another, favoured as a result of its defence phenotype; or (b) it might result in the maintenance of genetically based variability in secondary metabolism. Of these two possibilities, the chances of observing the second in ecological time are better.

The only well-studied case of intrapopulation variation in the defence chemistry of a tropical rain-forest plant appears to show a type of frequency-dependent selection. Langenheim and her co-workers [Langenheim and Stubblebine (1983), Langenheim (1984) and references therein] have studied variation in production of sesquiterpene resins in the leaves of Hymenaea spp. (Caesalpiniaceae) in the Neotropics. They have established that resin composition varies little with environmental conditions, and is therefore under tight genetic control (Langenheim et al., 1978, 1980; Arrhenius and Langenheim, 1983; Langenheim and Hall, 1983; Langenheim and Stubblebine, 1983). Genetically based variation in resin composition gave at least six compositional types (Fig. 29.1); the variation appeared to be discontinuous, with few intermediates between these types. They also found that the different compositional types exhibited differential inhibitory effects on herbivores. Intrapopulation variation in sesquiterpenes for Hymenaea has proved to be greatest in the rain forests of central Amazonia and lowest in savanna sites. Langenheim and her co-workers have proposed that herbivore selection pressure may be greater in rain-forest sites. Comparison of sesquiterpene chemistry of the mother plant and its progeny indicate how this intrapopulation variation might be maintained. The parent characterized by one compositional type produces outcrossed seedlings of a variety of compositional types, and after several years only juveniles with different compositional types to the parent have survived. Langenheim and her co-workers suggest that seedlings with resin composition similar to the parent are destroyed by the local concentration of insect herbivores genetically adapted or physiologically conditioned to the resin type of the parent (Langenheim and Stubblebine, 1983). This example, if confirmed, is analogous to that of Pinus ponderosa, in which adaptation of herbivores to an individual tree interacts with frequency-dependent selection in the same way (Edmunds and Alstad, 1978).

Aside from the work on Hymenaea and other resin-producing leguminous trees (summarized in detail by Langenheim, 1984) the only other study of which we are aware addressing the possibility of genetically based variation of secondary metabolites in tropical plants is that of Janzen et al. (1980), who have studied seasonally consistent differences between plants in hydrogen cyanide production by Acacia farnesiana (Mimosaceae) in a highly seasonal site in Costa Rica. In this case it is not clear

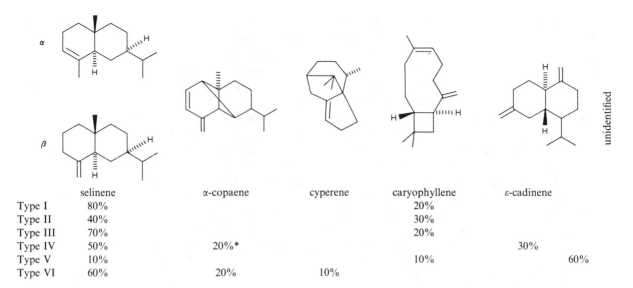

	selinene	α-copaene	cyperene	caryophyllene	ε-cadinene	
Type I	80%			20%		
Type II	40%			30%		
Type III	70%			20%		
Type IV	50%	20%*			30%	
Type V	10%			10%	60%	
Type VI	60%	20%	10%			

Fig. 29.1. Six types of leaf in *Hymenaea* characterized by differences in quantitative proportions of major sesquiterpenes (Langenheim et al., 1980). The asterisk indicates β-form copaene.

whether the variation involved is genetically or environmentally based.

The variation shown by Janzen et al. is simply in quantity of a particular compound, while that shown by Langenheim et al. is simply of the relative proportions of various compounds in qualitatively similar mixtures. We know of no study that documents polymorphism in secondary metabolite production within a population of a rain-forest plant comparable to those documented for *Lotus* and *Trifolium* spp. in Europe (Jones et al., 1978) or *Duboisia* spp. in Australia (Trease and Evans, 1978). Studies of the production of condensed tannins by foliage of numerous rain-forest trees shows the expected variability, but very few cases which suggest that there might be tannin-rich and tannin-free forms (Gartlan et al., 1980; Waterman, unpubl.). However, the behaviour of some herbivores in tropical forests certainly suggests that such qualitative differences may exist. Howler monkeys (Glander, 1978) and leaf-cutter ants (Hubbell et al., 1983; Cherrett, Ch. 27) feed repeatedly on the same set of individuals of some tree species, while avoiding completely some other individuals of the same species.

Geographical (interpopulation) variation in secondary chemistry has been shown for several rain-forest plants. *Hymenaea courbaril* growing in Puerto Rico, where a major seed predator (*Rhinochenus* beetles: Curculionidae) is absent, produces

much lower concentrations of sesquiterpene resin in its fruits than does the species in mainland parts of its range (Janzen, 1975). Secondary compounds in the bark or seeds from a large number of Cameroon rain-forest species have been studied by one of us (P.G.W.). In several cases comparison of the compounds isolated with others reported from elsewhere in the range of that species has revealed qualitative variation between the populations — for instance *Xylopia aethiopica* (Hasan et al., 1982; see Fig. 29.2), *Greenwayodendron (Polyalthia) suaveolens* (Waterman, 1985) (both Annonaceae), and *Mammea africana* (Crichton and Waterman, 1978) (Clusiaceae). Langenheim (1984) has presented further examples of geographical variation in secondary chemistry. The significance of these differences is completely unknown.

Environmental component of variation

There is rather little information on environmentally based variation between individuals in secondary chemistry (or any other components of food quality for herbivores) within tropical-forest populations. Judging from data for temperate-zone plants, quantities of secondary compounds accumulated, and the overall composition of mixtures of these compounds, could be influenced in complex ways by soil quality, light intensity and moisture stress.

Once again the *Hymenaea* studies of Langen-

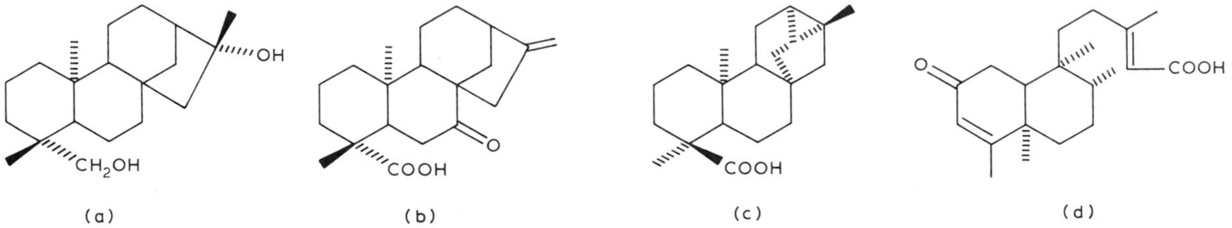

Fig. 29.2. Diterpenes isolated from *Xylopia aethiopica* in western Africa. (a) and (b) from Nigerian material (Hasan et al., 1982), (b) and (d) from Cameroonian material (Hasan et al., 1982), and (c) from Sierra Leone (Faulkner et al., 1985).

heim and her co-workers is the most detailed and informative. They have found that physical environmental factors (light intensity, temperature, moisture and photoperiod) had negligible effects on the composition of sesquiterpene leaf resins (Crankshaw and Langenheim, 1981; Langenheim and Stubblebine, 1983). Total sesquiterpene concentration was not influenced by variation in moisture availability, but increased light intensity significantly increased resin yield.

Similar studies of *Barteria fistulosa* (Passifloraceae) in Cameroon (Waterman et al., 1984) showed that mature leaves of this species growing in highly insolated sites in light gaps accumulated significantly higher concentrations of condensed tannins and other phenolics than did those of individuals growing in semi-shaded conditions. Increased tannin content was associated with lower cellulose digestibility and reduced nitrogen content in leaves from light gaps (Table 29.6), indicating that the variation observed could have significance for herbivores. Further studies carried out on four rain-forest species in Sierra Leone (Mole et al., 1987) have confirmed that there is correlation between incident light intensity and foliar phenolics, even between branches on the same individual.

Increased production of phenolic compounds with increasing light intensity has been demonstrated in a number of plants [Bryant et al. (1983), Waterman et al. (1984) and references therein], and we anticipate that this pattern is probably widespread in tropical plants. The existence of such variation raises new questions for the ecologist and plant biochemist. Can such variation be explained by mechanical arguments implicating tannins and other aromatic non-nitrogenous compounds as "sinks" for excess photosynthate (Phillips and Henshaw, 1977)? Or does this represent an adaptive response whereby (a) more of a defence compound is generated when production becomes cheaper, or (b) the plant varies its defence phenotype according to the herbivore load of its particular microhabitat (Waterman et al., 1984)? These observations, taken in conjunction with comments by Bryant et al. (1983), suggest a dichotomy: phenolics and some other carbon-based metabolites are light(energy)-dependent defence systems, whereas others, notably nitrogen-based metabolites, are nutrient-dependent. These arguments have been developed by Coley et al. (1985) as a "resource allocation" hypothesis. This appears to offer a promising framework from which an explanation of the distribution of

TABLE 29.6

Comparison of composition (% dry wt.) of mature leaves from individuals of *Barteria fistulosa* growing in light gaps and under canopy shade in the Douala–Edea Forest Reserve, Cameroon (Waterman et al., 1984)

	Number of trees	Total phenol	Condensed tannin (CT)	Acid detergent fibre (ADF)	Cellulase digestibility	Nitrogen (N)	6.25N / (ADF+CT)	6.25N / ADF
Semi-shaded	11	5.39	11.96	45.59	35.04	1.94	0.214	0.23
Full sun	15	8.46	19.10	45.90	28.24	1.68	0.163	0.27

secondary metabolites within and between species can be developed.

Induced defences as a component of intraspecific variation

Induction of anti-herbivore defences as a response of plants to herbivore attack has received much attention in the past five years, all so far concentrated on temperate-zone plants (for example, see Haukioja, 1980). Induction of defences may have a variety of functions other than the intuitively obvious one of enabling the plant to avoid investment in defences until they are needed. As pointed out by Janzen (1979, 1983c) and by Edwards and Wratten (1983), local wound-induced responses may function to disperse grazing in such a way that its effect on plant fitness is minimized: the insect spreads its attention over the whole tree rather than defoliating a branch whose position could then be occupied by a branch from a neighbouring tree. Furthermore, an unpredictable mosaic of vegetation of variable food quality created by local wound-induced responses could increase the frequency with which herbivores are forced to make hazardous moves from one patch of food to another (Edwards and Wratten, 1983; Schultz, 1983). It is even possible, as suggested by Whitham and Slobodchikoff (1981), that individual plants may undergo somatic mutations that could enhance chemical diversity within the lifespan of an individual plant.

Finally, fluctuation in herbivore populations could cause selection of plants which generate defence compounds only when they are required. Compounds produced de novo in response to fungal attack (phytoalexins) are not uncommon (Harborne and Ingham, 1978). Janzen (1981a, 1983c) has pointed out that spatial and temporal unpredictability is characteristic of herbivore attack in the tropics as well as in the temperate zone, and this is borne out by the large year-to-year variation in populations of tropical insects (Wolda, 1978a, b, 1983). Although few studies of wound-induced responses concern tropical plants (Carroll and Hoffmann, 1980) we believe that investigation will show that they are as widespread here as in other ecosystems.

SOME COMMENTS ON THE DIVERSITY OF THE CHEMICAL-DEFENCE REPERTOIRE OF INDIVIDUAL PLANTS

Much work points to the advantage accruing to plants that maintain a variety of chemical defences (Feeny, 1976; Rhoades and Cates, 1976; Cates and Rhoades, 1977; Janzen, 1981b). While the within-plant diversity of toxin-based systems has been emphasized (Cates and Rhoades, 1977), it is becoming increasingly clear that there are probably considerable differences in quantitative defences as well (Zucker, 1983), and that a plant's "tannin" may represent a mix of compounds with different properties. At least three kinds of advantages have been proposed for multi-barrelled chemical-defence systems (McKey, 1979): (1) synergistic effects; (2) differential effects of different compounds on different herbivore species; and (3) the greater difficulty faced by the herbivore in evolving resistance to a variety of compounds simultaneously (Pimental and Belotti, 1976). A complex mixture of defences is thus more stable against counter-adaptation than a single kind of defence would be, leading to "gene conservation" as envisaged by Atsatt and O'Dowd (1976) as opposed to unstable, evolutionarily dynamic "gene-for-gene" co-evolution. All these advantages should be especially important to plants in herbivore-rich tropical forests.

How is this diversity produced? The most obvious way is the maintenance of a number of different secondary metabolic pathways, as has clearly been demonstrated to occur in many species (see, for example, Waterman and Grundon, 1983). While a single plant part can have a variety of active pathways, there are some selective factors acting to restrict the distribution of particular compounds to particular plant parts. If in fact some secondary compounds are restricted to particular plant parts, this could have interesting consequences, in view of a fundamental asymmetry in the interaction between a tropical tree and its herbivores. While the tree interacts with a number of herbivores on its various parts and selection integrates their effects (Janzen, 1973b), each herbivore interacts with and experiences the defence repertoire of only a small part of the tree (McKey and Waterman, in prep.).

Consider a seed predator that has evolved counter-adaptations to the seed defence of its host. One potential response of the plant is the evolution of a new chemical defence. An alternative response, and one that might evolve more quickly, is selection for a mutation that leads to expression in the seeds of an enzyme system already actively producing secondary compounds in other parts of the plant.

While emphasis has been placed on the maintenance by the plant of a diversity of secondary metabolic pathways, we suspect that another design feature of chemical-defence systems has gone unnoticed. We suggest that the relatively low substrate specificity of some enzymes of secondary metabolism may lead to a diversity of secondary metabolites from a single metabolic pathway. That this is generally the case is supported by the common occurrence of a range of related compounds rather than one single product of a reaction sequence, leading to a metabolic grid of products of the type outlined by Cornforth (1972) and Waller and Dermer (1981). In other words, secondary metabolism may be constructed in such a way that the plant produces a maximum of phenotypic (chemical) diversity from a minimum of genetic information. A small number of enzymes, some of them specific for the putting together of different structural types of secondary metabolites, and the remainder general for the reactions modifying these structural types, could together generate a wide spectrum of secondary metabolites.

Ironically, the low substrate specificity of some enzymes of secondary metabolism, whose function may be viewed as maximizing individual adaptability, may also be the source of qualitatively new steps in the evolution of new pathways for secondary metabolism (cf. Gottlieb, 1982). Many novelties in the evolution of defence compounds seem to have developed by the adaptation of pre-existing mechanisms to new combinations of precursors (McKey, 1980). The relatively low substrate specificity of some enzymes of secondary metabolism, together with the interchange of substrates between pathways, may have been all that was necessary for the apparent "quantum leaps" in secondary chemistry. This hypothesis is supported by the recent report (Wink and Witte, 1983) that quinolizidine alkaloids can be formed from normal substrates in normally alkaloid-free

plants from a number of families not known to produce these alkaloids, implying that the necessary enzymes and genetic material are present, but are either not "switched on", or are being fed other substrates.

POTENTIAL IMPACT OF SOME PHENOLIC SECONDARY METABOLITES IN FOREST SOILS

The floor of the forest receives a "rain" of litter in the form of senescent leaves, twigs, bark, fruit, flower remains, herbivore frass, etc. The following comments will deal with leaf litter, which is the dominant litter component and the best-characterized chemically, but the potential contribution of other plant parts should be remembered. Leaf fall in the predominantly evergreen tropical rain forests occurs throughout the year, the degree of seasonality being dependent on the importance of deciduous trees and on the patterns of rainfall. Estimates from a number of tropical rain forests (Procter et al., 1983b) show litter fall, in terms of dry matter, ranging from 3440 to 15 300 kg ha^{-1} yr^{-1}.

Leaf senescence is preceded by withdrawal of nutrients from the leaf (Chabot and Hicks, 1982); it is estimated that about half of the nitrogen and one third of the phosphorus are returned to the parent tree. Similarly, there is considerable evidence indicating the withdrawal of some classes of secondary metabolites, such as alkaloids (McKey, 1979), although others, notably among the phenolics, often appear to be lost with the leaf. This certainly seems to be true for the condensed tannins. In a northern temperate oak–pine climax forest, Rice and Pancholy (1974) estimated the "tannin-fall" in the leaf litter at 84.78 kg ha^{-1} yr^{-1}. No figures exist for tropical rain forests; but, given a medium-low value of 5000 kg ha^{-1} yr^{-1} for leaf litter, and an averaged phenol/tannin content of 4% dry weight in the senescing leaf, then an input of 200 kg ha^{-1} yr^{-1} of phenolics does not seem to be unreasonable. To that figure must be added further phenolics that derive from other phenol-rich litter such as some fruits and barks, and from the leaching of phenolics from still living foliage.

What is the fate of these phenolic compounds in the soil? Rice and Pancholy (1974) showed that for a number of temperate-zone sites tannin levels in the soil were considerably in excess of the computed input levels, thus indicating that a large proportion is retained rather than being quickly leached out, despite the water-solubility of these compounds.

To what extent do phenolic compounds accumulate in soils beneath tropical rain-forest vegetation? The rapid rates of litter decomposition typical of evergreen tropical rain forest, and the rapid leaching imposed by high rainfall, may reduce build-up in comparison to temperate-zone sites. However, according to Janzen's (1974) hypothesis, the highest tannin production may occur in acid, nutrient-poor rain-forest sites where the impoverished soil biota is least capable of degrading phenolic compounds. If Janzen's hypothesis is correct, there may be ecogeographic variation among tropical rain forests in the extent of accumulation of phenolics in soil, and in some sites, such as tropical heath forests, the accumulation may be extensive.

What effects might these phenolics have on soil chemistry and biology? Janzen (1974) documents many deleterious effects of phenolic compounds on soil biota, as well as on aquatic organisms living in the "blackwater" rivers that result from leaching of these phenol-rich soils. Potential types of deleterious activity include the following:

(a) Inhibiting the activity of litter detritivores (isopods, etc.). According to Cameron and La Point (1978), tannins in the leaves of *Sapium sebiferum* reduce the activity of both terrestrial and aquatic isopod detritivores and thereby slow the rate at which decomposition is initiated. These findings were not supported by Neuhauser and Hartenstein (1978), who stated that "our data show there is no correlation between phenolic content of leaves and [isopod/millipede] feeding preference". Toxic plant metabolites in *Melia azedarach* leaves (probably limonoids) are also reported to have an adverse effect on the efficiency of isopods (Merriam, 1971).

(b) Fungistatic activity. The mixed hydrolysable and condensed tannins of oak leaf litter are reported to be inhibitory to a range of fungi, including a number of species considered to be of particular importance in decomposition (Harrison, 1971).

(c) Inhibition of nitrification. Studies by Rice and Pancholy (1973) showed that condensed and hydrolysable tannins present in concentrations of 2 ppm were capable of completely inhibiting the ability of *Nitrosomonas* to convert NH_4^+ to NO_3^- for periods of at least three weeks. Similar inhibitory effects, although less pronounced, were observed for *Nitrobacter*. Populations of both these nitrifying bacteria were found to be lowest in areas of climax temperate forest where there was a large "tannin-fall". Jordan et al. (1979) confirmed that, in South American rain forest, populations of *Nitrosomonas* were relatively low, and nitrogen was present almost entirely in the NH_4^+ form.

(d) The build-up of phenolics will have severe implications for soil chemistry. It will certainly enhance soil acidity, and this may reduce the availability of some mineral nutrients, such as phosphorus. Rice and Pancholy (1973) suggested that tannins are held in complexes in the soil by bonding with the peptide linkages of humus proteins. This suggestion is in line with well-known tannin/protein interactions, particularly at the low pH characteristic of many tropical soils. That this does indeed happen is supported by a recent report (Sivapalan, 1982) showing that a high content of polyphenolic residues in decomposing plant material enhances the quantity of humic matter in the soil, leading to the incorporation of a greater proportion of total soil nitrogen in the humic portion. However, other binding interactions are possible and should not be overlooked, particularly the formation of simple protein/tannin complexes or of chelates with metal ions such as iron and aluminium.

All the above evidence clearly points to continuing biological activity by post-senescence leaf polyphenolics acting in a number of ways leading to the retention of nitrogen in the soil, either by slowing down its rate of release from decomposing tissue or by preventing its conversion to the NO_3^- form in which it is easily leached out of the soil. The penalty that is paid for this is in increasing humus and humic-acid-bound nitrogen, and in increasing soil acidity. This increasing acidity may in itself inhibit nitrifying bacteria (Jordan et al., 1979).

A specific association between acidic mor soils and enhanced production of foliar polyphenols in temperate plants has long been known (Handley, 1961; Davies et al., 1964). Its ecological implications in tropical-forest environments have been explored by Janzen (1974), who suggested that there was an association between nutrient-poor (acid) soils and polyphenol production, and that this was a closed system, with increasing soil acidity and decreasing nutrient availability leading to an ever greater emphasis on the production of phenolic secondary compounds. That there is a relationship between soil acidity and nutrient availability in a rain-forest site and the production of polyphenols by the vegetation there has some experimental support (Waterman, 1983). However, studies on this topic have been few and the number of conflicting arguments remains large.

In extreme cases, Janzen (1974) has envisaged the outcome of this process as an ecosystem dominated by a very slow-growing flora of species rich in secondary compounds, with long-lived, scleromorphic foliage; the heath forests ("blackwater river forests") of Borneo are cited as an extreme example. In such forests, high levels of chemical investment and leaf toughness will, Janzen argued, lead in turn to a lowering of levels of herbivory and a depauperate herbivore fauna. It has recently been confirmed (Anderson et al., 1983; Proctor et al., 1983a, b) that heath forest on Gunung Mulu, Sarawak, does produce a litter relatively rich in phenols, and with less nitrogen at litter-fall than is found in senescent foliage from other rain-forest types on Gunung Mulu. However, Procter et al. (1983b) could not confirm that levels of herbivory were reduced in heath forest compared to the other forest types. Unfortunately their data on herbivory, derived from computation of area removed from the leaf by herbivory measured after senescence, takes no account of leaf longevity, which Janzen anticipated would be greater in forests of this type.

It seems established that the input of considerable amounts of biologically active polyphenolics does have important implications for nutrient cycling in an ecosystem, and may play a considerable role in shaping that ecosystem. Foliar nitrogen can be tied up in the humic fraction of the soil, and the acidity generated can lead to the loss of other nutrients, or at least make their uptake difficult. On the other hand, the presence of the humic fraction seems greatly to reduce nitrification, and hence loss of nitrogen from the system, and by concentrating available nutrients in the surface layers of the soil acts as a focus for nutrient recapture by the plants.

The effects of this phenol burden are generally held to be totally negative. Janzen (1974) postulated that selection among individual plants for highly effective chemical defences in nutrient-poor sites has, ironically, resulted in long-term accumulation of phenolics that further reduce the capacity of the soil to supply nutrients to plants. Because this negative effect is long-term and occurs at the level of the community, it is not responsive to selection at the level of the individual.

We suggest that the accumulation of phenolics in the soil beneath a tree may confer at least short-term direct advantages to that individual, and that the dropping of phenolic-rich leaf litter might thus be a trait maintained by selection at the level of the individual plant. We suggest that tannins in leaf litter may, by the various mechanisms discussed above, reduce the rate of loss of nitrogen. To the extent that the leaves drop into an area of soil inhabited by the root system of the same tree this advantage could result in positive selection for the trait.

Negative effects of soil phenolics on soil biology and chemistry and on plant growth are better documented, but positive effects are also possible. While we are not completely convinced of our hypothesis that phenolics accumulating in the soil beneath a tree may result in a net advantage for that tree, we feel that this point is worthy of consideration. The above discussion has considered only polyphenolics. It should be pointed out that many other secondary metabolites, such as resins and triterpenes, have the chemical stability required for relatively long-term persistence in the soil. Virtually nothing is known of the fate of these compounds, and studies on them would seem to be a particularly profitable area for research.

REFERENCES

Alexandre, D., 1978. Le rôle disséminateur des éléphants en forêt de Tai, Cote d'Ivoire. *Terre Vie*, 31: 47–72.

Anderson, J.M., Proctor, J. and Vallack, H.W., 1983. Ecological studies in four contrasting lowland rain forests in Gunung Mulu National Park, Sarawak. III. Decomposition processes and nutrient losses from leaf litter. *J. Ecol.*, 71: 503–527.

Arrhenius, S.P. and Langenheim, J.H., 1983. Inhibitor effects of *Hymenaea* and *Copaifera* leaf resins on the leaf fungus *Pestalotia subcuticularis*. *Biochem. Syst. Ecol.*, 11: 361–366.

Arroyo, M.T.K., 1976. Geitonogamy in animal pollinated tropical angiosperms: a stimulus for the evolution of self-incompatibility. *Taxon*, 25: 543–548.

Atsatt, P.R. and O'Dowd, D.J., 1976. Plant defense guilds. *Science*, 193: 24–29.

Auerbach, M.J. and Strong Jr., D.R., 1981. Nutritional ecology of *Heliconia* herbivores: experiments with plant fertilization and alternative hosts. *Ecol. Monogr.*, 51: 63–83.

Augspurger, C.K., 1981. Reproductive synchrony of a tropical shrub: experimental studies on effects of pollinators and seed predators on *Hybanthus prunifolius* (Violaceae). *Ecology*, 62: 775–788.

Baas, W.J., 1983. *Triterpenoids in latex and leaf wax of some Hoya species*. Diss., Univ. of Utrecht, Utrecht.

Baker, H.G., Opler, P.A. and Baker, I., 1978. A comparison of the amino acid complements of floral and extrafloral nectars. *Bot. Gaz.*, 139: 322–332.

Barz, W. and Koster, J., 1981. Turnover and degradation of secondary (natural) compounds. In: E.E. Conn (Editor), *The Biochemistry of Plants, Vol. 7*. Academic Press, London, pp. 35–84.

Bawa, K.S., 1974. Breeding systems of tree species of a lowland tropical community. *Evolution*, 28: 85–92.

Becker, P., 1981. Potential physical and chemical defenses of *Shorea* seedling leaves against insects. *Malay. For.*, 44: 346–356.

Becker, P. and Martin, J.S., 1982. Protein-precipitating capacity of tannins in *Shorea* (Dipterocarpaceae) seedling leaves. *J. Chem. Ecol.*, 8: 1353–1367.

Bryant, J.P., Chapin III, F.S. and Klein, D.R., 1983. Carbon/nutrient balance of boreal plants in relation to vertebrate herbivory. *Oikos*, 40: 357–368.

Cameron, G.N. and La Point, T.W., 1978. Effects of tannins on the decomposition of Chinese tallow leaves by terrestrial and aquatic invertebrates. *Oecologia*, 32: 349–366.

Carroll, C.R. and Hoffman, C.A., 1980. Chemical feeding deterrent mobilised in response to insect herbivory and counteradaptation by *Epilachna tredecemnotata*. *Science*, 209: 414–416.

Cates, R.G. and Rhoades, D.F., 1977. Patterns in the production of antiherbivore chemical defenses in plant communities. *Biochem. Syst. Ecol.*, 5: 185–193.

Chabot, B.F. and Hicks, D.J., 1982. The ecology of leaf life spans. *Annu. Rev. Ecol. Syst.*, 13: 229–259.

Choo, G.M., Waterman, P.G., McKey, D. and Gartlan, J.S., 1981. A simple enzyme assay for dry matter digestibility and its value in studying food selection by generalist herbivores. *Oecologia*, 49: 170–178.

Coley, P.D., 1981. *Ecological and evolutionary responses of tropical trees to herbivory: a quantitative analysis of grazing damage, plant defenses and growth rates*. Diss., Univ. of Chicago, Chicago, Ill.

Coley, P.D., 1983a. Herbivory and defensive characteristics of tree species in a lowland tropical forest. *Ecol. Monogr.*, 53: 209–233.

Coley, P.D., 1983b. Intraspecific variation in herbivory on two tropical tree species. *Ecology*, 64: 426–433.

Coley, P.D., Bryant, J.P. and Chapin III, F.S., 1985. Resource availability and plant antiherbivore defenses. *Science*, 230: 895–899.

Cornforth, J.W., 1972. The logic of working with enzymes. *Chem. Soc. Rev.*, 2: 1–20.

Crankshaw, D.R. and Langenheim, J.H., 1981. Variation in terpenes and phenolics through leaf development in *Hymenaea* and its possible significance to herbivory. *Biochem. Syst. Ecol.*, 9: 115–124.

Crawley, M.J., 1983. *Herbivory. The Dynamics of Animal–Plant Interactions*. Blackwell, Oxford, 437 pp.

Crichton, E.G. and Waterman, P.G., 1978. Dihydromammea C/OB: a new coumarin from the seed of *Mammea africana*. *Phytochemistry*, 17: 1783–1786.

Crichton, E.G. and Waterman, P.G., 1979. Manniflavanone, a new 3,8-linked flavanone dimer from the stem bark of *Garcinia mannii*. *Phytochemistry*, 18: 1553–1557.

Davies, A.G., Bennett, E.L. and Waterman, P.G., submitted. Food selection by two south-east Asian colobine monkeys (*Presbytis rubicunda* and *Presbytis melalophos*) in relation to plant chemistry. *Biol. J. Linn. Soc.*

Davies, R.I., Coulson, C.B. and Lewis, D.A., 1964. Polyphenols in plant, humus and soil. IV. Factors leading to increase in biosynthesis of polyphenol in leaves and their relationships to mull and mor formation. *J. Soil Sci.*, 15: 310–318.

Dement, W.A. and Mooney, H.A., 1974. Seasonal variation in the production of tannins and cyanogenic glycosides in the chaparral shrub, *Heteromeles arbutifolia*. *Oecologia*, 15: 65–76.

Edmunds, G.F. and Alstad, D.N., 1978. Coevolution in insect herbivores and conifers. *Science*, 199: 941–945.

Edwards, P.J. and Wratten, S.D., 1983. Wound induced defences in plants and their consequences for patterns of insect grazing. *Oecologia*, 59: 88–93.

Faulkner, D.F., Lebby, V. and Waterman, P.G., 1985. Further diterpenes from the stem bark of *Xylopia aethiopica*. *Planta Med.*, 354–355.

Feeny, P., 1976. Plant apparency and chemical defense. *Recent Adv. Phytochem.*, 10: 1–40.

Feer, F., 1979. Observations écologiques sur le néotrage de Bates (*Neotragus batesi* de Winton, 1903, Artiodactyle, Ruminant, bovide) du nord-est du Gabon. *Terre Vie*, 33: 159–239.

Fox, L.R., 1981. Defense and dynamics in plant–herbivore systems. *Am. Zool.*, 21: 853–864.

Futuyma, D.J., 1983. Evolutionary interactions among herbivorous insects and plants. In: D.J. Futuyma and M. Slatkin (Editors), *Coevolution*. Sinauer, Sunderland, Mass., pp. 207–231.

Gartlan, J.S., McKey, D., Waterman, P.G., Mbi, C.N. and Struhsaker, T.T., 1980. A comparative study of the phytochemistry of two African rain forests. *Biochem. Syst. Ecol.*, 8: 401–422.

Gautier-Hion, A., Emmons, L.H. and Dubost, G., 1980. A comparison of the diets of three major groups of primary consumers of Gabon (primates, squirrels and ruminants). *Oecologia*, 45: 182–189.

Glander, K.E., 1978. Howling monkey feeding behaviour and plant secondary compounds: a study of strategies. In: G.G. Montgomery (Editor), *The Ecology of Arboreal Folivores*.

Smithsonian Institute Press, Washington, D.C., pp. 561–574.

Gottlieb, O.R., 1982. *Micromolecular Evolution. An Essay into a Novel Botanical Discipline.* Springer, Berlin, 165 pp.

Gottlieb, O.R. and Kubitzki, K., 1981. Chemogeography of *Aniba* (Lauraceae). *Plant. Syst. Evol.*, 137: 281–289.

Greshoff, M., 1890. Overzicht der Nederlands-Indische alcaloid-houdende Apocynaceae. *Meded. Planten, Batavia*, 7: 45–69.

Handley, W.R.C., 1961. Further evidence for the importance of residual leaf protein complexes in litter decomposition and the supply of nitrogen for plant growth. *Plant Soil*, 15: 37–73.

Harborne, J.B. and Ingham, J.L., 1978. Biochemical aspects of the coevolution of higher plants and their fungal parasites. In: J.B. Harborne (Editor), *Biochemical Aspects of Plant and Animal Coevolution.* Academic Press, London, pp. 343–405.

Harrison, A.F., 1971. The inhibitory effect of oak leaf litter tannins on the growth of fungi, in relation to litter decomposition. *Soil Biol. Biochem.*, 3: 167–172.

Hasan, C.M., Healey, T.M. and Waterman, P.G., 1982. Kolavane and kaurane diterpenes from the stem bark of *Xylopia aethiopica. Phytochemistry*, 21: 1365–1368.

Haukioja, E., 1980. On the role of plant defences in the fluctuation of herbivore populations. *Oikos*, 35: 202–213.

Herrera, C.M., 1982. Defense of ripe fruit from pests: its significance in relation to plant–disperser interactions. *Am. Nat.*, 120: 218–241.

Howe, H.F. and Smallwood, J., 1982. Ecology of seed dispersal. *Annu. Rev. Ecol. Syst.*, 13: 201–218.

Hubbell, S.P., Wiemer, D.F. and Adejare, A., 1983. An antifungal terpenoid defends a neotropical tree (*Hymenaea*) against attack by a fungus-growing ant (*Atta*). *Oecologia*, 60: 321–327.

Janzen, D.H., 1971. Seed predation by animals. *Annu. Rev. Syst. Ecol.*, 2: 465–492.

Janzen, D.H., 1973a. Community structure of secondary compounds in plants. *Pure Appl. Chem.*, 34: 529–538.

Janzen, D.H., 1973b. Host plants as islands. II. Competition in evolutionary and contemporary time. *Am. Nat.*, 107: 786–790.

Janzen, D.H., 1973c. Sweep samples of tropical foliage insects: description of study sites, with data on species abundance and size distribution. *Ecology*, 54: 659–686.

Janzen, D.H., 1974. Tropical blackwater rivers, animals, and mast fruiting by the Dipterocarpaceae. *Biotropica*, 6: 69–103.

Janzen, D.H., 1975. Behaviour of *Hymenaea courbaril* when its predispersal seed predator is absent. *Science*, 189: 145–147.

Janzen, D.H., 1977. Why fruits rot, seeds mold, and meat spoils. *Am. Nat.*, 111: 691–713.

Janzen, D.H., 1978a. Seeding patterns of tropical trees. In: P.B. Tomlinson and M.H. Zimmerman (Editors), *Tropical Trees as Living Systems.* Cambridge Univ. Press, New York, N.Y., pp. 83–128.

Janzen, D.H., 1978b. The ecology and evolutionary biology of seed chemistry as relates to seed predation. In: J.B. Harborne (Editor), *Biochemical Aspects of Plant and*

Animal Coevolution. Academic Press, London, pp. 163–206.

Janzen, D.H., 1979. New horizons in the biology of plant defenses. In: G.A. Rosenthal and D.H. Janzen (Editors), *Herbivores, their Interaction with Secondary Plant Metabolites.* Academic Press, New York, N.Y., pp. 331–350.

Janzen, D.H., 1981a. Patterns of herbivory in a tropical deciduous forest. *Biotropica*, 13: 271–282.

Janzen, D.H., 1981b. Lectins and plant–herbivore interactions. *Recent Adv. Phytochem.*, 15: 241–258.

Janzen, D.H., 1982. Ecological distribution of chlorophyllous developing embryos among perennial plants in a tropical deciduous forest. *Biotropica*, 14: 232–236.

Janzen, D.H., 1983a. Physiological ecology of fruits and their seeds. In: O.L. Lange, P.S. Nobel, C.B. Osmond and H. Ziegler (Editors), *Physiological Plant Ecology, III.* Springer, Berlin, pp. 625–655.

Janzen, D.H., 1983b. Insects. In: D.H. Janzen (Editor), *Costa Rican Natural History.* Univ. of Chicago Press, Chicago, Ill., pp. 619–645.

Janzen, D.H., 1983c. Food webs: who eats what, why, how, and with what effects in a tropical forest. In: F.B. Golley (Editor), *Tropical Rain Forest Ecosystems, A. Structure and Function.* (Ecosystems of the World, 14A) Elsevier, Amsterdam, pp. 167–182.

Janzen, D.H. and Waterman, P.G., 1984. A seasonal census of phenolics, fibre and alkaloids in foliage of forest trees in Costa Rica: some factors influencing their distribution and relation to host selection by Sphingidae and Saturniidae. *Biol. J. Linn. Soc.*, 21: 439–454.

Janzen, D.H., Doerner, S.T. and Conn, E.E., 1980. Seasonal constancy of intra-population variation of HCN content of Costa Rican *Acacia farnesiana* foliage. *Phytochemistry*, 19: 2022–2023.

Jones, D.A., Keymer, R.J. and Ellis, W.M., 1978. Cyanogenesis in plants and animal feeding. In: J.B. Harborne (Editor), *Biochemical Aspects of Plant and Animal Coevolution.* Academic Press, London, pp. 21–34.

Jordan, C.F., Todd, R.L. and Escalante, G., 1979. Nitrogen conservation in a tropical rain forest. *Oecologia*, 39: 123–128.

Langenheim, J.H., 1984. The roles of plant secondary chemicals in wet tropical ecosystems. In: E. Medina, H.A. Mooney and C. Vasques-Yanes (Editors), *Physiological Ecology of Plants in the Wet Tropics.* Junk, The Hague, pp. 189–208.

Langenheim, J.H. and Hall, G.D., 1983. Sesquiterpene deterrence of a leaf-tying lepidopteran, *Stenoma ferrocanella*, on *Hymenaea stigonocarpa* in central Brazil. *Biochem. Syst. Ecol.*, 11: 29–36.

Langenheim, J.H. and Stubblebine, W.H., 1983. Variation in leaf resin composition between parent tree and progeny in *Hymenaea*: implications for herbivory in the humid tropics. *Biochem. Syst. Ecol.*, 11: 97–106.

Langenheim, J.H., Stubblebine, W.H., Lincoln, D.E. and Foster, C.E., 1978. Implications of variation in resin composition among organs, tissues and populations of the tropical legume *Hymenaea. Biochem. Syst. Ecol.*, 6: 299–313.

Langenheim, J.H., Foster, C.E. and McGinley, R.B., 1980. Inhibitory effects of different quantitative compositions of

Hymenaea leaf resins on a generalist herbivore, *Spodoptera exiqua. Biochem. Syst. Ecol.,* 8: 385–396.

Lawton, J.H., 1976. The structure of the arthropod community on bracken. *Bot. J. Linn. Soc.,* 73: 187–216.

Lawton, J.H., 1983. Plant architecture and the diversity of phytophagous insects. *Annu. Rev. Entomol.,* 28: 23–39.

Lawton, J.H. and McNeill, S., 1979. Between the devil and the deep blue sea: on the problem of being a herbivore. In: R.M. Anderson, B.D. Turner and L.R. Taylor (Editors), *Population Dynamics.* Blackwell, Oxford, pp. 223–244.

Leboeuf, M., Cavé, A., Bhaumik, P.K., Mukherjee, B. and Mukherjee, R., 1982. The phytochemistry of the Annonaceae. *Phytochemistry,* 21: 2783–2813.

Lee, D.W., 1979. Biological activity of seed proteins in Malesian legumes. *Biotropica,* 11: 214–218.

Levin, D.A., 1975. Pest pressure and recombination systems in plants. *Am. Nat.,* 109: 437–451.

Lowman, M.D. and Box, J.D., 1983. Variation in leaf toughness and phenolic content among five species of Australian rain forest trees. *Aust. J. Ecol.,* 8: 17–25.

Martin, J.S., Martin, M.M. and Bernays, E.A., 1987. Failure of tannic acid to inhibit digestion or reduce digestibility of plant protein in gut fluids of insect herbivores: implications for theories of plant defense. *J. Chem. Ecol.,* 13: 605–621.

Martin, M.M. and Martin, J.S., 1984. Surfactants: their role in preventing the precipitation of proteins by tannins in insect guts. *Oecologia,* 61: 342–345.

McKey, D., 1974. Adaptive patterns in alkaloid physiology. *Am. Nat.,* 108: 305–320.

McKey, D., 1979. The distribution of secondary compounds within plants. In: G.A. Rosenthal and D.H. Janzen (Editors), *Herbivores, their Interaction with Secondary Plant Compounds.* Academic Press, New York, N.Y., pp. 56–133.

McKey, D., 1980. The evolution of novel alkaloid types: a mechanism for the rapid phenotypic evolution of secondary compounds. *Am. Nat.,* 115: 754–759.

McKey, D., in press a. Interactions between ants and leguminous plants. In: J. Zarucchi and C. Stirton (Editors), *Advances in Legume Biology.* Ann. M. Bot. Gard.

McKey, D., in press b. *Promising New Directions in the Study of Ante–Plant Mutualisms.* Proc. XIV Int. Botanical Congress, Berlin. Willdenowia.

McKey, D., Waterman, P.G., Mbi, C.N., Gartlan, J.S. and Struhsaker, T.T., 1978. Phenolic content of vegetation in two tropical rain forests: ecological implications. *Science,* 202: 61–64.

McKey, D., Gartlan, J.S., Waterman, P.G. and Choo, G.M., 1981. Food selection by black colobus monkeys (*Colobus satanas*) in relation to plant chemistry. *Biol. J. Linn. Soc.,* 16: 115–146.

Merriam, H.G., 1971. Sensitivity of terrestrial isopod population (*Armadillidium*) to food quality differences. *Can. J. Zool.,* 49: 667–674.

Milton, K., 1979. Factors influencing leaf choice by howler monkeys: a test of some hypotheses of food selection by generalist herbivores. *Am. Nat.,* 114: 362–378.

Mole, S. and Waterman, P.G., 1985. Stimulatory effects of tannics and cholic acid on the tryptic hydrolysis of proteins: ecological implications. *J. Chem. Ecol.,* 11: 1323–1332.

Mole, S. and Waterman, P.G., 1987. Tannins as anti-feedants to mammalian herbivores — still an open question? In: G.R. Waller (Editor), *Allelochemicals: Role in Agriculture and Forestry.* American Chemical Society, Washington, D.C., pp. 572–587.

Mole, S., Ross, J.A.M. and Waterman, P.G., 1987. Light induced variation in phenolic levels in foliage of rain-forest plants. I. Chemical changes. *J. Chem. Ecol.* (in press).

Mooney, H.A. and Gulmon, S.L., 1982. Constraints of leaf structure and function in reference to herbivory. *BioScience,* 32: 198–206.

Neuhauser, E.F. and Hartenstein, R., 1978. Phenolic content and palatability of leaves and wood to soil isopods and diplopods. *Pedobiologia,* 18: 99–109.

Newman, E.I., 1983. Interactions between plants. In: O.L. Lange, P.S. Nobel, C.B. Osmond and H. Ziegler (Editors), *Physiological Plant Ecology, III.* Springer, Berlin, pp. 679–710.

Oates, J.F., Waterman, P.G. and Choo, G.M., 1980. Food selection by the South Indian Leaf-monkey, *Presbytis johnii,* in relation to leaf chemistry. *Oecologia.* 45: 45–56.

Ottosson, J.G. and Anderson, J.M., 1983. Seasonal and interspecific variation in the biochemical composition of some British fern species and their effects on *Spodoptera littoralis* larvae. *Biol. J. Linn. Soc.,* 19: 305–320.

Phillips, R. and Henshaw, G.G., 1977. The regulation of synthesis of phenolics in stationary phase cell cultures in *Acer pseudoplatanus* L. *J. Exper. Bot.,* 28: 785–794.

Pimental, D. and Bellotti, A.C., 1976. Parasite–host population systems and genetic stability. *Am. Nat.,* 110: 877–888.

Price, P.W., Bouton, C.E., Gross, P., McPheron, B.A., Thompson, J.N. and Weis, A.E., 1980. Interactions among three trophic levels: influence of plants on interactions between insect herbivores and natural enemies. *Annu. Rev. Ecol. Syst.,* 11: 41–65.

Primack, R.B. and Tomlinson, P.B., 1980. Variation in tropical forest breeding systems. *Biotropica,* 12: 229–231.

Proctor, J., Anderson, J.M., Chai, P. and Vallack, H.W., 1983a. Ecological studies in four contrasting lowland rain forests in Gunung Mulu National Park, Sarawak. I. Forest environment, structure and floristics. *J. Ecol.,* 71: 237–260.

Proctor, J., Anderson, J.M., Fogden, S.C.L. and Vallack, H.W., 1983b. Ecological studies in four contrasting lowland rain forests in Gunung Mulu National Park, Sarawak. II. Litterfall, litter standing crop and preliminary observations on herbivory. *J. Ecol.,* 71: 261–283.

Raffa, K.F. and Berryman, A.A., 1983. The role of host plant resistance in the colonization behavior and ecology of bark beetles (Coleoptera: Scolytidae). *Ecol. Monogr.,* 53: 27–49.

Rhoades, D.F., 1979. Evolution of plant chemical defense against herbivores. In: G.A. Rosenthal and D.H. Janzen (Editors), *Herbivores, their Interaction with Secondary Plant Metabolites.* Academic Press, New York, N.Y., pp. 3–54.

Rhoades, D.F. and Cates, R.G., 1976. Toward a general theory of plant antiherbivors chemistry. *Recent Adv. Phytochem.,* 10: 168–213.

Rice, E.L. and Pancholy, S.K., 1974. Inhibition of nitrification by climax ecosystems. II. Additional evidence and possible role of tannins. *Am. J. Bot.*, 60: 691–702.

Rockwood, L.L. and Glander, K.E., 1979. Howling monkeys and leaf-cutting ants: comparative foraging in a tropical deciduous forest. *Biotropica*, 11: 1–10.

Schultz, J.C., 1983. Impact of variable plant defensive chemistry on susceptibility of insects to natural enemies. In: P.A. Hedin (Editor), *Plant Resistance to Insects*. American Chemical Society, Washington, D.C., pp. 37–54.

Sivapalan, K., 1982. Humification of polyphenol-rich plant residues. *Soil Biol. Biochem.*, 14: 309–310.

Trease, G.E. and Evans, W.C., 1978. *Pharmacognosy*. Balliere Tindall, London, 11th ed., pp. 672–673.

Vogel, S., 1983. Ecophysiology of zoophilic pollination. In: O.L. Lange, P.S. Nobel, C.B. Osmond and H. Ziegler (Editors), *Physiological Plant Ecology, III*. Springer, Berlin, pp. 560–624.

Waller, D.A., 1982. Leaf-cutting ants and avoided plants: defences against *Atta texana* attack. *Oecologia*, 52: 400–403.

Waller, G.R. and Dermer, O.C., 1981. Enzymology of alkaloid metabolism in plants and microorganisms. In: E.E. Conn (Editor), *The Biochemistry of Plants, Vol. 7*. Academic Press, New York. pp. 317–402.

Waterman, P.G., 1983. Distribution of secondary compounds in rain forest plants: toward an understanding of cause and effect. In: S.L. Sutton, T.C. Whitmore and A.C. Chadwick (Editors), *Tropical Rain Forest: Ecology and Management*. Blackwell, Oxford, pp. 167–179.

Waterman, P.G., 1984. Food acquisition and processing by primates as a function of plant chemistry. In: D.J. Chivers (Editor), *Food Acquisition and Processing by Primates*. Plenum, New York, N.Y., pp. 177–211.

Waterman, P.G., 1985. Indolosesquiterpenes. In: S.W. Pelletier (Editor), *The Alkaloids: Chemical and Biological Perspectives*. Wiley, New York, N.Y., pp. 91–112.

Waterman, P.G., 1986. A phytochemist in the African rain-forest. *Phytochemistry*, 25: 3–17.

Waterman, P.G. and Grundon, M.F. (Editors), 1983. *Chemistry and Chemical Taxonomy in the Rutales*. Academic Press, London, 464 pp.

Waterman, P.G. and Hussain, R.A., 1983. Systematic significance of xanthones, benzophenones and biflavonoids in *Garcinia*. *Biochem. Syst. Ecol.*, 11: 21–28.

Waterman, P.G., Meshal, I.A., Hall, J.B. and Swaine, M.D., 1978. Biochemical systematics and ecology of the Toddalioideae in the central part of the west African forest zone. *Biochem. Syst. Ecol.*, 6: 239–245.

Waterman, P.G., Mbi, C.N., McKey, D. and Gartlan, J.S., 1980. African rain forest vegetation and rumen microbes: phenolic compounds as correlates of digestibility. *Oecologia*, 47: 22–33.

Waterman, P.G., Choo, G.M., Vedder, A.L. and Watts, D., 1983. Digestibility, digestion-inhibitors and nutrients in herbaceous foliage and green stems from an African montane flora and comparison with other tropical flora. *Oecologia*, 60: 244–249.

Waterman, P.G., Ross, J.A.M. and McKey, D., 1984. Factors affecting levels of some phenolic compounds, digestibility and nitrogen content of the mature leaves of *Barteria fistulosa* (Passifloraceae). *J. Chem. Ecol.*, 10: 387–401.

Waterman, P.G., Bennett, E.L., Davies, A.G. and Ross. J.A.M., submitted. A comparison of the floristics and leaf chemistry of two Malaysian rain-forests and the influence of leaf chemistry on populations of colobine monkeys in the Old World. *Biol. J. Linn. Soc.*

Whitham, T.G. and Slobodchikoff, C.N., 1981. Evolution by individuals, plant–herbivore interactions, and mosaics of genetic variability: the adaptive significance of somatic mutations in plants. *Oecologia*, 49: 287–292.

Wink, M. and Witte, L., 1983. Evidence for a wide-spread occurrence of the genes of quinolizidine alkaloid biosynthesis. *FEBS Lett.*, 159: 196–200.

Wolda, H., 1978a. Seasonal fluctuations in rainfall, food and abundance of tropical insects. *J. Anim. Ecol.*, 47: 369–381.

Wolda, H., 1978b. Fluctuations in abundance of tropical insects. *Am. Nat.*, 112: 1017–1045.

Wolda, H., 1983. "Long-term" stability of tropical insect populations. *Res. Popul. Ecol. Suppl.*, 3: 112–126.

Zucker, W.V., 1983. Tannins: does structure determine function? An ecological perspective. *Am. Nat.*, 121: 335–365.

Chapter 30

MYCORRHIZAS

D. JOSEPH BAGYARAJ

INTRODUCTION

In 1842 Vittadini proposed that "tree rootlets are nourished by certain fungal mycelia which mantle them", as observed by him more than a decade earlier. This hypothesis was elaborated to a theory of mutualistic symbiosis by Frank (1885), who named the fungus – root organ as "mycorrhiza". The concept of fungus – root symbiosis has since been a subject of extensive research. Earlier mycorrhiza research was concerned primarily with temperate host species, and has been reviewed by Harley (1969), Mosse (1973), and others. However, interest in the mycorrhizal associations of tropical plants began in the same year that the term "mycorrhiza" was coined, when Treub (1885) recorded the vesicular arbuscular mycorrhizal association on sugar-cane in Java.

The first extensive survey of the occurrence of mycorrhizal associations in tropical plants was carried out in 1896 by Janse in Java. He studied the bryophytes, vascular cryptogams, gymnosperms, monocotyledons, and 38 species of woody dicotyledons. He found that 69 of the 75 species so examined, including all the woody dicotyledons, had characteristic endotrophic mycorrhizal associations. Despite this promising start, further interest was rather sporadic and the next extensive survey of mycorrhizal associations in the tropics was made fifty years later by Johnston (1949). He examined 93 species, including 13 species of forest trees, and observed that 80, including all the forest trees, possessed endotrophic mycorrhizal associations. Tropical rain-forest ecologists, familiar with Janse's study, saw great significance in the fact that a large proportion of rain-forest plants contained mycorrhizal fungi. They realized that rain-forest soils were, generally speaking, extremely poor in plant nutrients and that the apparent richness of plant life in these forests was mainly due to the tightly closed cycle of nutrients (Farnworth and Golley, 1973; Walter, 1973). Richards (1952), in his book on tropical rain forests, mentioned that the role of mycorrhizas in these ecosystems was little understood — that nothing could be said with certainty regarding their importance, although they might have striking ecological significance. The number of scientists working on mycorrhizas in the tropics has been on the increase in the past twenty years. An international conference held at Kumasi, Ghana, in 1978 (Mikola, 1980), wholly devoted to tropical mycorrhizas, demonstrated the trend and the increasing concern for mycorrhizal studies in the tropics. Some mycorrhiza specialists, reviewing the role of mycorrhizas in the tropics, have emphasized their importance in tropical rain forests (Janos, 1980b, 1983; Redhead, 1980).

TYPES OF MYCORRHIZAS

There are mainly five different types of mycorrhizas (Lewis, 1975): (1) Ectomycorrhizas; (2) vesicular arbuscular mycorrhizas; (3) eriocoid mycorrhizas; (4) orchidaceous mycorrhizas; and (5) arbutoid mycorrhizas. In tropical rain forests vesicular arbuscular mycorrhizal associations predominate, followed by ectomycorrhizas and orchid mycorrhizas (Redhead, 1968; Janos, 1983). In this review, only the vesicular arbuscular and ectomycorrhiza types are dealt with in some detail. Orchid mycorrhizas are excluded from this review because they would need much more room. They do not have as much relevance to improved forest productivity as the former two types; however, they are essential to the ecology of epiphytic members of the family, which predominate in the tropical rain forest.

Vesicular arbuscular mycorrhizas

Vesicular arbuscular mycorrhizas, probably evolved with the Devonian land flora (Nicolson, 1975), are now formed by most angiosperms, gymnosperms and ferns (Baylis, 1975; Trappe, 1977). According to Gerdemann (1975), it is easier to list plant families that do not form such mycorrhizas than to list those that do. Families not forming vesicular arbuscular mycorrhizas include Betulaceae, Commelinaceae, Ericaceae, Fumariaceae, Orchidaceae, Pinaceae and Urticaceae. Families which rarely form mycorrhizas of this type include Brassicaceae, Chenopodiaceae, Cyperaceae and Polygonaceae. Families which form both ectomycorrhizas and vesicular arbuscular mycorrhizas include Caesalpiniaceae, Fagaceae, Juglandiaceae, Myrtaceae, Salicaceae and Tiliaceae (Gerdemann, 1975). In addition to the widespread distribution of vesicular arbuscular mycorrhizas throughout the plant kingdom, the association is geographically ubiquitous, occurring in plants from the arctic to the tropical regions over a broad ecological range, from aquatic to desert environments (Mosse et al., 1981). These mycorrhizas are formed by non-septate zygomycetous fungi belonging to the genera *Acaulospora, Gigaspora, Glomus* and *Sclerocystis* in the family Endogonaceae of the order Mucorales. At present, over 107 species of fungi forming vesicular arbuscular mycorrhizas have been described (Hall, 1984). Many are cosmopolitan in distribution, but some may be strictly tropical like *Acaulospora foveata* and *A. tuberculata* (Janos and Trappe, 1982). The vesicular arbuscular endophytes are not host-specific, although evidence is growing that certain endophytes may form preferential associations with certain host plants (Mosse, 1977).

The fungi forming vesicular arbuscular mycorrhizas have the largest known resting spores of any fungi, their size ranging up to 600 μm. These spores can be isolated from soil by the wet sieving and decantation method (Gerdemann and Nicolson, 1963). A root system colonized by these fungi does not show any morphological variations from the normal root system. Hence the status of a root system in this respect can only be known after staining the roots with trypan blue (Phillips and Hayman, 1970). The presence of vesicles and arbuscules is the diagnostic criterion for identifying a vesicular arbuscular mycorrhizal fungus in a root (Figs. 30.1A, B and 30.2).

Most infection by the fungi forming vesicular arbuscular mycorrhizas in tropical rain forests is transmitted from root to root. This is possible even in mixed forests, because these fungi are not very host-specific (Janos, 1980b). Their spores, being large, are not wind-dispersed, although they may be disseminated with soil transported by wind or water. Earthworms, ants, birds, crickets, grasshoppers and wasps (Gerdemann and Trappe, 1974; McIlveen and Cole, 1976) can transport spores with soil; but, because of the small amounts of soil carried, these are insignificant vectors. Small mammals like mice, rats, lemmings, voles, shrews, pikas and others which eat sporocarps may be the principal long-distance vectors of the fungi forming vesicular arbuscular mycorrhizas. The spores pass through their digestive tract intact and, when defecated, are effective inocula (Maser et al., 1978; Rothwell and Holt, 1978: Emmons, 1982). Since these fungi are obligate symbionts, they cannot grow without host roots (Mosse, 1973). Perhaps the broad host ranges of these fungi compensate for poor dispersal.

It is a well-established fact that vesicular arbuscular mycorrhizas improve plant growth (Mosse, 1973; Tinker, 1982; Abbott and Robson, 1982; Hayman, 1983). Janos (1975) found that mycorrhizal inoculation almost doubled the growth of three tropical rain-forest trees in Costa Rica — *Inga oerstediana, Vitex cooperi* and an unidentified species of the Euphorbiaceae. Redhead (1975) in Nigeria found that inoculated seedlings of *Khaya grandifolia* produced six times more dry matter compared to uninoculated ones. The main effect of these mycorrhizas in improving plant growth is through improved uptake of nutrients, especially phosphorus, due to the exploration by the external hyphae of the soil beyond the root-hair zone where phosphorus is depleted (Gray and Gerdemann, 1969; Gerdemann, 1975). Hyphae are also known to absorb phosphorus from lower concentrations than can be used by non-mycorrhizal roots (Howeler et al., 1981).

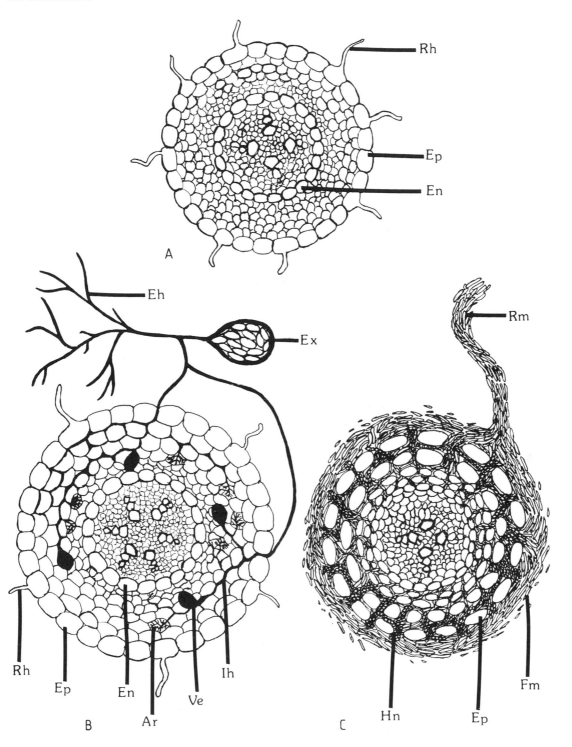

Fig. 30.1. Diagrammatic representation of the transverse section of a (A) non-mycorrhizal, (B) vesicular arbuscular mycorrhizal, and (C) ectomycorrhizal root. *Ar* = arbuscule, *Eh* = external hyphae, *En* = endodermis, *Ep* = epidermis, *Ex* = extramatrical chlamydospores, *Fm* = fungal mantle, *Hn* = hartig net, *Ih* = internal hyphae, *Rh* = root hair, *Rm* = rhizomorph, *Ve* = vesicle.

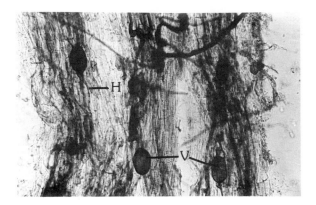

Fig. 30.2. Vesicular arbuscular mycorrhizal colonization of the root of *Atrocarpus heterophyllus*, a tropical rain-forest tree, showing vesicles (*V*) and hyphae (*H*).

Experiments with phosphate labelled with ^{32}P indicate that the hyphae of vesicular arbuscular mycorrhizas obtain their extra phosphate from the labile pool rather than by dissolving insoluble phosphate (Raj et al., 1981). The better utilization of sparingly soluble rock phosphate is explained by the hyphae making closer physical contact with the particle surface where the ions are dissociating (Hayman, 1983). These fungi produce phosphatases (Macdonald and Lewis, 1978) which allow utilization of organic phosphorus, especially under humid tropical conditions where hyphae can be in close contact with finely divided litter, and where acid soil reaction reduces the sorption of organic phosphates on soil surfaces (Tinker, 1975). Vesicular arbuscular mycorrhizas have also been reported to improve the uptake of the minor elements zinc and copper (La Rue et al., 1975; Krishna et al., 1982) and water (Nelson and Safir, 1982). They also produce plant hormones (Allen et al., 1982), increase the activity of nitrogen-fixing organisms in the root zone, and reduce the severity of disease caused by root pathogens (Bagyaraj, 1984; Subba Rao et al., 1985; Manjunath and Bagyaraj, 1986).

Ectomycorrhizas

Ectomycorrhizas are most common among tree species in the families Betulaceae, Fagaceae, Pinaceae, Salicaceae and Tiliaceae, as well as in some members of Caesalpiniaceae, Juglandaceae and Rosaceae (Meyer, 1973). The fungal partner in an ectomycorrhizas most frequently, belongs to the Basidiomycetes (Marx, 1972). Structurally the ectomycorrhizas can be distinguished by the presence of a thick fungal mantle or sheath (20–40 μm in diameter) around the feeder roots (Hatch and Doak, 1933). From the mantle fungal strands radiate outside into the soil, thus enhancing the absorption area of the root surface. The hyphae also penetrate through the epidermis into the intercellular spaces of the cortical cells forming an inter-connecting network known as the "Hartig net" (Fig. 30.1C). Ectomycorrhizal roots are generally short, swollen and dichotomously branched, with distinctive colours of either white, black, orange, yellow or olive green. Strict host specificity is rare (Lange, 1923), and one plant may form mycorrhizas with several fungi simultaneously (Dominik, 1959). A fungus may be specific to one host genus (Molina, 1979), although a wider host range and a broad geographical range is normal (Marx, 1977). Most of the ectomycorrhizal fungi produce small, wind-dispersed spores which are widely distributed.

Ectomycorrhizas greatly stimulate plant growth and nutrient uptake, especially in soils of low to moderate fertility (Bowen, 1973). Ectomycorrhizas stimulate phosphorous uptake from soluble and insoluble sources in the soil (Malajczuk et al., 1975), in which the acid phosphatases bound to the surface and sheath (Ho and Zak, 1979) may be important. Ectomycorrhizal infection also increases the uptake and translocation of calcium, zinc, sodium and some other alkali metals (Bowen et al., 1974). Many ectomycorrhizal fungi offer protection against soil-borne plant pathogens (Marx, 1972; Kais and Snow, 1979). Ectomycorrhizal fungi are also known to play a role in the degradation of cellulose and humic material (Todd, 1979). These fungi can be cultured on laboratory media, and considerable work has been done on the production of inoculum and methods of inoculation for forest nurseries (Marx et al., 1982).

Information on ectomycorrhizas in tropical rain forests is limited. In the lowland humid tropics ectomycorrhizas are a regular feature of Dipterocarpaceae, Fagaceae and Pinaceae, and are often found in members of Caesalpiniaceae (Janos, 1980a; Redhead, 1980). In addition, they have also been observed in species of Euphorbiaceae (Horak, 1977; Redhead, 1980), Fabaceae (Edmisten, 1970;

St. John and Uhl, 1986), Gnetaceae (Horak, 1977; St. John, 1980a), Myrtaceae (Thomazini, 1974; Horak, 1977; Shamsuddin, 1979), Nyctaginaceae (Janos, 1980a; St. John, 1980a; Pegler and Fiard, 1979); Polygonaceae (Kreisel, 1971; Janos, 1980a) and Sapindaceae (Singer and Morello, 1960; Alexander, 1981). Ectomycorrhizal fungi in the tropical rain forests, as elsewhere, are predominantly Basidiomycetes (Singh, 1966; Singer and Araujo, 1979; Ivory, 1980), although Ascomycetes like *Cenococcum* spp. may also be involved (de Alwis and Abenayake, 1980). Some of the ectomycorrhizal fungal species are strictly tropical (Horak, 1977), while some are ubiquitous (Malloch et al., 1980). Restriction of species to the tropics has probably resulted from adaptation to high soil temperatures or high moisture regimes (Bowen and Theodorou, 1973), or from host specificity. Redhead (1974), studying *Brachystegia eurycoma*, the commonest species of Cacsalpiniaceae in the lowland rain forest of Nigeria, found the tree to be associated with more than one species of fungus. Inoculation studies done on the two distinct mycorrhizas showed that both the fungi improved plant growth. Redhead (1980) also found that indigenous ectomycorrhizal fungi of two Nigerian caesalpinioid legumes would not form mycorrhizas with an introduced pine, nor would an ectomycorrhizal fungus of pine produce mycorrhizas on the legumes.

OCCURRENCE OF MYCORRHIZAS IN TROPICAL RAIN FORESTS

The surveys conducted so far in tropical rain forests indicate that most of plant species are mycorrhizal and the great majority of these form vesicular arbuscular mycorrhizas. Janse (1896) sampled plants of a mid-elevation forest in Java, and found only the vesicular arbuscular type of association. Johnston (1949) observed vesicular arbuscular mycorrhizas in all 13 forest species surveyed in Trinidad. Redhead (1968) investigated the incidence of mycorrhizal associations in 51 tree species indigenous to the lowland rain forests of Nigeria, and also in 15 exotic tree species. All the exotic species and 44 of the indigenous species were found to have vesicular arbuscular mycorrhizal associations, and 3 indigenous species had ectotro-

phic associations. Only very young plants or those from newly cleared and burnt nurseries lacked mycorrhizas. Edmisten (1970), examining mycorrhizas in sectioned roots, reported that, out of 32 principal forest species in Puerto Rico, only 6 were ectomycorrhizal and 9 non-mycorrhizal. His results need confirmation, as it is difficult to observe vesicular arbuscular mycorrhizas in sectioned roots.

Shamsuddin (1979) reported that out of about 200 species of Malaysian forest trees, only one lacked mycorrhizas. All 40 species of Dipterocarpaceae thus examined, some Fagaceae, Myrtaceae and Pinaceae had ectomycorrhizas. De Alwis and Abeynayake (1980), examining 63 forest species of Sri Lanka, observed mycorrhizas in 59 species. All the dipterocarp species so examined had ectomycorrhizas. St. John and Uhl (1986) found all the 12 forest and 10 early-successional species from 17 families examined in Venezuela to be mycorrhizal. Most of them had vesicular arbuscular mycorrhizal associations, except three leguminous species which had ectomycorrhizas. The report of St. John (1980a), based on a survey conducted near Manaus, Brazil is contradictory to most of the earlier reports. He found that 36% of 86 species examined were non-mycorrhizal. However, he found only 3 species out of 86 with ectomycorrhiza, agreeing with the low numbers of ectomycorrhizal species, usually encountered in tropical rain forests.

Where ectomycorrhizal species do occur in rain forest, they are often locally abundant or clumped, either as pioneer or gap-colonizing species or as dominants of mature communities (Janos, 1983). Effective colonization by ectomycorrhizal species was suggested because of their more effective dispersal mechanisms compared to the fungi of vesicular arbuscular mycorrhizas (Janos, 1980a).

Some tropical species have been reported to be colonized by both vesicular arbuscular and ectomycorrhizal fungi, for instance *Hopea* (Shamsuddin, 1979), *Casuarina* (National Research Council, 1983), *Eperua purpurea* (St. John and Uhl, 1986) and *Eucalyptus* (personal observation). *Glycoxylon inophyllum* was found to have vesicular arbuscular mycorrhizas by St. John (1980b), while it was found to be ectomycorrhizal by Singer and Araujo (1979). Study of such species could reveal the relative ecological importance of each type, comparing the costs and benefits of vesicular arbuscular associations with those of ectomycorrhizas.

DEPENDENCE ON MYCORRHIZAS

In a series of pot experiments with seedlings of 32 species of lowland tropical plants, Janos (1975, 1977, 1980b) found that vesicular arbuscular mycorrhizas improved the growth of 28 species to varying degrees, while the rest were unable to grow without mycorrhizal fungi. Plants can be grouped into three categories, based on their dependence on mycorrhizas: (1) non-mycorrhizal; (2) facultative mycotrophs; and (3) obligate mycotrophs.

Non-mycorrhizal plants are those which grow normally without forming mycorrhizas, even under infertile conditions. The growth of these plants is not affected by mycorrhizal inoculation (Janos, 1975). Species of the Aizoaceae, Amaranthaceae, Brassicaceae, Caryophyllaceae, Chenopodiaceae, Commelinaceae, Cyperaceae, Fumariaceae, Juncaceae, Nyctaginaceae, Phytolaccaceae, Polygonaceae, Portulaceae and Urticaceae do not usually form mycorrhizas (Gerdemann, 1968). Non-mycorrhizal plants usually have well-developed root systems with highly branched fine roots, as well as numerous root hairs. Some of them, like *Banksia*, *Hakea*, *Personia*, and *Viminaria*, produce proteoid roots (Pathmaranee, 1974; Lamont, 1982; Janos, 1983). Non-mycorrhizal species may secrete organic acids, thereby utilizing the bound forms of phosphorus (Tinker, 1975; Graustein et al., 1977), or have tissues with low mineral requirements, or have slow growth rates or durable tissues which compensate for the limited nutrient supply. Nonmycorrhizal species reject mycorrhizal association either because it is incompatible with their physiology, or in order to favour their persistence in competition with mycotrophic species (Janos, 1980b). They are the only species which are effective competitors on infertile soils in the absence of mycorrhizal fungi.

Facultative mycotrophs are those plant species which are able to grow without mycorrhizas, but in which mycorrhizal colonization improves growth. In fertile soil, facultatively mycotrophic species reject mycorrhizas which are of no benefit for mineral nutrient uptake (Bowen, 1980). They also produce fine roots as well as profuse root hairs (Baylis, 1975; St. John, 1980c). They may root more deeply (St. John, 1980a), have higher root/shoot ratios (Azcon and Ocampo, 1981) or lower total mineral requirements (Janos, 1980b) than

obligate mycotrophs. Some facultatively mycotrophic species are able to take up minerals from relatively low substrate concentrations when uninfected, and may fail to support much infection.

Obligate mycotrophs are those which can neither grow nor survive without mycorrhizas. Janos (1980a) defined them as species which would not survive to reproductive maturity at the fertility levels encountered in the natural habitats, if not colonized by mycorrhizal fungi. Obligate mycotrophs do not respond to fertilizer applications (Vozzo and Hacskaylo, 1971), suggesting therein obligate dependence on mycorrhizas for nutrition. Obligately mycotrophic tree species tend to have large seeds (Janos, 1980b), which favour the persistence of uninfected seedlings and the formation of large pre-infection root systems, maximizing the probability of infection. Obligate mycotrophs have coarse hairless roots. They are often light-demanding, partly because of the energy requirements of mycorrhizal association. Thus, under shade mycorrhizas become a liability; but they are still retained because of their importance to seedling growth when canopy gaps open. Tree species of the mature forest canopy and subcanopy tend to be obligately mycotrophic, while many pioneer and early-successional species are facultatively mycotrophic or non-mycorrhizal (Janos, 1980b). Mineral nutrient availability, especially of phosphorus, and the type of mycorrhizal fungi in different habitats, are probably the primary selective factors which produced different degrees of dependence on mycorrhizas.

THE IMPACT OF MYCORRHIZAL FUNGI ON PLANT COMMUNITY COMPOSITION

The varied dependence of different plant species on different types of mycorrhizas can influence the composition of both seral and mature plant communities. Although there is a lack of host specificity among fungi producing vesicular arbuscular mycorrhizas, host preferences have been recorded (Mosse, 1977). Thus, the species of mycorrhizal fungus present can influence the competitive abilities of plant species. In the absence of mycorrhizal fungi, only the species which do not need mycorrhizas will be able to grow. Therefore, non-mycorrhizal species are most likely to dominate plant communities on poor soils, with no or few mycorrhizal fungi. Even if mycorrhizas form slowly, the growth lag of mycotrophic plants before infection can confer a competitive advantage on non-mycorrhizal plants. On fertile soils, the facultative mycotrophs can also occur in the absence of mycorrhizal fungi. Regardless of the availability of mycorrhizal fungi, facultatively mycotrophic species are those most likely to dominate plant communities on fertile soils.

Obligately mycotrophic species are most likely to dominate plant communities on poor soils with abundant mycorrhizal propagules. They are probably better competitors than facultative mycotrophs on infertile soils, because the adaptations of facultative mycotrophs for mineral uptake, without mycorrhiza, are redundant. For example, the hyphae can reach much farther beyond the zone of phosphorus depletion than root hairs (Janos, 1980a). Most of the plants dependent on mycorrhizas, in tropical rain forests, do not have root hairs (Baylis, 1975; Janos, 1977). Species obligately dependent on vesicular arbuscular mycorrhizas probably have similar mineral-uptake characteristics within a habitat because there are few fungal species available for this type of association compared to the large number of host species (Janos, 1975). Consequently, the great species-richness of tropical forests in which vesicular arbuscular mycorrhizal associations predominate is unlikely to reflect niche differentiation with respect to mineral uptake. In mixed plots of nine tropical tree species, including three which were non-mycorrhizal, three facultative mycotrophs, and three which were strongly mycorrhiza-dependent, the seedling survival of the last group was increased by vesicular arbuscular mycorrhizas (Stark and Jordan, 1978; Janos, 1983). This experiment suggested that vesicular arbuscular mycorrhizas reduce differences in competitive ability among the species, and thereby contribute to the high within-habitat species diversity characteristic of most tropical forests. Species diversity in mature tropical forests is correlated with the presence of different types of mycorrhizas. Several monospecific stands in the tropics are known to be ectomycorrhizal (Connell, 1978). Perhaps, as Baylis (1975) suggested, optimal ectomycorrhizal associations assist a species to dominance. Mono-

specific stands are frequently formed on infertile soils (Richards, 1952) where the decomposing ability of the ectomycorrhizal fungi could be highly advantageous. The role of mycorrhizal fungi in direct nutrient cycling, occurring in tropical rain forests, has been discussed by Janos (1983).

Non-mycorrhizal species and some ectomycorrhizal species may have the demographic characteristics of pioneer or fugitive species because non-mycorrhizal plants can quickly establish without awaiting infection, and ectomycorrhizal inoculum can build up very rapidly. Obligate mycotrophs probably are the best competitors under mature forest conditions. Janos (1980a) has given a detailed account of how obligate mycotrophs could replace non-mycorrhizal and facultatively mycotrophic seral species during tropical succession.

THE IMPACT OF PLANT-COMMUNITY COMPOSITION ON MYCORRHIZAL FUNGI

Mycorrhizal fungi are likely to be affected by plant-community composition (Janos, 1980a; Kormanik et al., 1980). Baylis (1962) observed that soil from the rooting zone of a tree which bore abundant mycorrhizas readily infected seedlings, although soil from beneath a species that is rarely infected did not. The vesicular arbuscular mycorrhizal populations in tropical rain forests may rapidly respond to the proportion of mycotrophic plants in a community because the fungi cannot live without hosts, and there are few spores in tropical rain-forest soils (Janos, 1975). The lower spore production is probably associated with the ability of the fungus to spread by hyphal growth from root to root, and thus save the energy needed for sporulation. In the absence of suitable hosts, the vesicular arbuscular mycorrhizal fungi probably persist only as spores. When many spores are produced, as in cut-over areas, they are often subject to intensive predation or parasitism because they are large and rich in lipids (Janos, 1975).

Frequent or extensive disturbance can favour non-mycorrhizal or ectomycorrhizal species, which are effective colonizers. Non-mycorrhizal species reduce mycorrhizal fungus populations indirectly by not sustaining mycorrhizal infection. In addition, some non-mycorrhizal species can have a direct antagonistic chemical effect on the fungi (Hayman et al., 1975). The amounts of mycorrhizal fungus in the soil will thus be low where non-mycorrhizal plants dominate the communities, and in fertile soils where facultative mycotrophs are dominant. High populations of mycorrhizal fungi are expected in stands of facultative mycotrophs on infertile soils or where obligate mycotrophic plants are dominant. There are reports to show that in field crops the soil type has a greater influence on the vesicular arbuscular mycorrhizal fungi than the plant system has (Sreeramulu and Bagyaraj, 1986). Extending this analogy to the rain-forest situation, a fungal species forming vesicular arbuscular mycorrhizas probably dominates in a certain soil because of its ability to outgrow other species in that environment rather than because of selection by a host, although hosts could favour particular fungus species indirectly through modification of the soil environment. Instead of plants determining the distribution of these mycorrhizal fungi, however, it is more likely that the distribution of fungus species might influence the composition of the plant community.

REFERENCES

Abbott, L.K. and Robson, A.D., 1982. The role of vesicular–arbuscular mycorrhizal fungi in agriculture and the selection of fungi for incoculation. *Aust. J. Agric. Res.*, 33: 389–408.

Alexander, I.J., 1981. Mycorrhizas in the Sapindaceae. *Program and Abstracts, Fifth North American Conf. on Mycorrhizae, Univ. of Laval, Que.*, pp. 60.

Allen, M.F., Moore Jr., T.S. and Christensen, M., 1982. Phytohormone changes in *Bouteloua gracilis* infected by vesicular–arbuscular mycorrhizae II. Altered levels of gibberellin-like substances and abscisic acid in the host plant. *Can. J. Bot.*, 60: 468–471.

Azcon, R. and Ocampo, J.A., 1981. Factors affecting the Vesicular–arbuscular infection and mycorrhizal dependency of thirteen wheat cultivars. *New Phytol.*, 87: 677–685.

Bagyaraj, D.J., 1984. Biological interactions with VA mycorrhizal fungi. In: C.L. Powell and D.J. Bagyaraj (Editors), *VA Mycorrhiza*. CRC Press, Boca Raton, Fla., pp. 131–153.

Baylis, G.T.S., 1962. *Rhizophagus*. The Catholic symbiont. *Aust. J. Sci.*, 25: 195–209.

Baylis, G.T.S., 1975. The magnolioid mycorrhiza and mycotrophy in root systems derived from it. In: F.E. Sanders, B. Mosse and P.B. Tinker (Editors) *Endomycorrhizas*. Academic Press, New York, N.Y., pp. 373–390.

Bowen, G.D., 1973. Mineral nutrition of ectomycorrhizae In:

G.C. Marks and T.T. Kozlowski (Editors), *Ectomycorrhizae: Their Ecology and Physiology*. Academic Press, New York, N.Y., pp. 151–205.

Bowen, G.D., 1980. Mycorrhizal roles in tropical plants and ecosystems. In: P. Mikola (Editor), *Tropical Mycorrhiza Research*. Clarendon, Oxford, pp. 165–190.

Bowen, G.D. and Theodorou, C., 1973. Growth of ectomycorrhizal fungi around seeds and roots. In: G.C. Marks and T.T. Kozlowski (Editors), *Ectomycorrhizae*. Academic Press, New York, N.Y., pp. 107–150.

Bowen, G.D., Skinner, M.F. and Bevege, D.I., 1974. Zinc uptake by mycorrhizal and uninfected roots of *Pinus radiata* and *Araucaria cunninghamii*. *Soil Biol. Biochem.*, 6: 141–144.

Connell, J.H., 1978. Diversity in tropical rain forests and coral reefs. *Science*, 199: 1302–1310.

De Alwis, D.P. and Abeynayake, K., 1980. A survey of mycorrhiza in some forest trees of Sri Lanka. In: P. Mikola (Editor), *Tropical Mycorrhiza Research*. Clarendon, Oxford, pp. 146–153.

Dominik, T., 1959. Development dynamics of mycorrhizae formed by *Pinus silvestris* and *Boletus lutens* in arable soils. *Pr. Szczecin. Towar. Nauk.*, 1: 1–30.

Edmisten, J., 1970. Survey of mycorrhiza and root nodules in the El Verde forest. In: H.T. Odum and R.F. Pigeon (Editors), *A Tropical Rain Forest*. U.S. Atomic Energy Commission, Oak Ridge, Tenn., pp. 15–20.

Emmons, L.H., 1982. Ecology of *Proechimys* (Rodential, Echimyidae) in southeastern Peru. *Trop. Ecol.*, 3: 280–290.

Farnworth, E.G. and Golley, F.B., 1973. *Fragile Ecosystems*. Springer, New York, N.Y., 258 pp.

Frank, A.B., 1885. Ueber die auf Wurzelsymbiose beruhende Ernährung gewisser Bäume durch unterirdische Pilze. *Ber. Dtsch. Bot. Ges.*, 3: 128–145.

Gerdemann, J.W., 1968. Vesicular–arbuscular mycorrhiza and plant growth. *Annu. Rev. Phytopathol.*, 6: 397–418.

Gerdemann, J.W., 1975. Vesicular–arbuscular mycorrhizae. In: J.G. Torrey and D.T. Clarkson (Editors), *The Development and Function of Roots*. Academic Press, New York, N.Y., pp. 576–591.

Gerdemann, J.W. and Nicholson, T.H., 1963. Spores of mycorrhizal *Endogone* species extracted from soil by wet-sieving and decanting. *Trans. Br. Mycol. Soc.*, 46: 235–244.

Gerdemann, J.W. and Trappe, J.M., 1974. The Endogonaceae in the Pacific Northwest. *Mycologia Mem.*, 5: 1–76.

Graustein, W.C., Cromack, K. and Sollins, P., 1977. Calcium oxalate: its occurrence in soils and effect on nutrient and geochemical cycles. *Science*, 198: 1252–1254.

Gray, L.E. and Gerdemann, J.W., 1969. Uptake of phosphorus^{32} by vesicular arbuscular mycorrhizae. *Plant Soil*, 30: 415–422.

Hall, I.R., 1984. Taxonomy of VA mycorrhizal fungi. In: C.L. Powell and D.J. Bagyaraj (Editors). *VA Mycorrhiza*. CRC Press, Boca Raton, Fla., pp. 57–112.

Harley, J.L., 1969. *The Biology of Mycorrhiza*. Leonard Hill, London, 2nd ed., 334 pp.

Hatch, A.B. and Doak, K.D., 1933. Mycorrhizal and other features of the root system of *Pinus. J. Arnold Arbor., Harvard Univ.*, 14: 85–99.

Hayman, D.S., 1983. The physiology of vesicular–arbuscular endomycorrhizal symbiosis. *Can. J. Bot.*, 61: 944–963.

Hayman, D.S., Johnson, A.M. and Ruddlesdin, I., 1975. The influence of phosphate and crop species on *Endogone* spores and vesicular–arbuscular mycorrhiza under field conditions. *Plant soil*, 43: 489–495.

Ho, I. and Zak, B., 1979. Acid phosphatase activity of six ectomycorrhizal fungi. *Can. J. Bot.*, 79: 1203–1205.

Horak, E., 1977. Biogeography of native ectomycorrhizae. Agarics in the Southern Hemisphere. In: *Abstracts Second Int. Mycological Conf., Univ. of South Florida, Tampa, Fla.*, 305 pp.

Howeler, R.H., Edwards, D.G. and Asher, C.J., 1981. Application of the flowing solution culture techniques to studies involving mycorrhizas. *Plant Soil*, 59: 179–183.

Ivory, M.H., 1980. Ectomycorrhizal fungi of lowland tropical pines in natural forests and exotic plantations. In: P. Mikola (Editor), *Tropical Mycorrhiza Research*. Clarendon, Oxford, pp. 110–117.

Janos, D.P., 1975. Effects of vesicular–arbuscular mycorrhizae on lowland tropical rain forest trees. In: F.E. Sanders, B. Mosse and P.B. Tinker (Editors), *Endomycorrhizas*. Academic Press, New York, N.Y., pp. 437–446.

Janos, D.P., 1977. Vesicular–arbuscular mycorrhizae affect the growth of *Bactris gasipaes*. *Principes*, 21: 12–18.

Janos, D.P., 1980a. Mycorrhizae influence tropical succession. *Biotropica*, 12 (Suppl.): 56–64.

Janos, D.P., 1980b. Vesicular–arbuscular mycorrhizae affect lowland tropical rain forest growth. *Ecology*, 61: 151–162.

Janos, D.P., 1983. Tropical Mycorrhizas. In: S.L. Sutton, T.C. Whitmore and A.C. Chadwick (Editors), *Tropical Rain Forest: Ecology and Management*. Blackwell, Oxford, pp. 327–345.

Janos, D.P. and Trappe, J.M., 1982. Two new *Acaulospora* species from tropical America. *Mycotaxon*, 15: 515–522.

Janse, J.M., 1896. Les endophytes radicaux de quelques plantes javanaises. *Ann. Jard. Bot. Buitenzorg*, 14: 53–212.

Johnston, A., 1949. Vesicular–arbuscular mycorrhiza in Sea Island cotton and other tropical plants. *Trop. Agric.*, 26: 118–121.

Kais, A.G. and Snow, G.A., 1979. Interaction of long leak Pine ectomycorrhizae, benlate and brown-spot needle blight. In: C.P.P. Reid (Editor), *Fourth North American Conf. on Mycorrhizae, Colorado State Univ., Fort Collins, Colo.*

Kormanik, P.P., Bryan, W.C. and Schultz, R.C., 1980. Increasing endomycorrhizal fungus inoculum in forest nursery soil with cover crops. *South. J. Appl. For.*, 4: 151–153.

Kreisel, H., 1971. Ectotrophe Mykorrhiza bei *Coccoloba uvifera* in Kuba. *Biol. Rundsch.*, 9: 97–98.

Krishna, K.R., Bagyaraj, D.J. and Rai, P.V., 1982. Response of groundnut to VA mycorrhizal inoculation in black clayey soil. *Ind. J. Microbiol.*, 22: 206–208.

Lamont, B., 1982. Mechanisms for enhancing nutrient uptake in plants, with particular reference to mediterranean south Africa and Western Australia. *Bot. Rev.*, 48: 597–689.

Lange, J.E., 1923. Studies in the agarics of Denmark, Part I. *Dan. Bot. Ark.*, 4: 1–52.

La Rue, J.H., McClellan, W.D. and Peacock, W.L., 1975. Mycorrhizal fungi and Peach nursery nutrition. *Calif. Agric.*, 29: 6–7.

Lewis, D.H., 1975. Comparative aspects of the carbon nutrition of mycorrhizas. In: F.E. Sanders, B. Mosse and P.B. Tinker (Editors), *Endomycorrhizas*. Academic Press, New York, N.Y., pp. 119–148.

Macdonald, R.M. and Lewis, M., 1978. The occurrence of some acid phosphatases and dehydrogenases in the vesicular–arbuscular mycorrhizal fungus, *Glomus mosseae*. *New Phytol.*, 80: 135–141.

Malajczuk, N., McComb, A.J. and Longeragan, J.F., 1975. Phosphorus uptake and growth of mycorrhizal and uninfected seedlings of *Eucalyptus calophylla* R. Br. *Aust. J. Bot.*, 23: 231–238.

Malloch, D.W., Pirozynski, K.A. and Raven, P.H., 1980. Ecological and evolutionary significance of mycorrhizal symbioses in vascular plants (a review). *Proc. Natl. Acad. Sci.*, 77: 2113–2118.

Manjunath, A. and Bagyaraj, D.J., 1986. Response of black-gram, chickpea and mungbean to vesicular–arbuscular mycorrhizal inoculation in an unsterile soil. *Trop. Agric.*, 63: 33–35.

Marx, D.H., 1972. Ectomycorrhizae as biological deterrents to pathogenic root infections. *Annu. Rev. Phytopathol.*, 10: 429–454.

Marx, D.H., 1977. Tree host range and world distribution of the ectomycorrhizal fungus *Pisolithus tinctorius*. *Can J. Microbiol.*, 23: 217–223.

Marx, D.H., Ruehle, J.L., Kenney, D.S., Cordell, C.E., Riffle, J.W., Molina, R.J., Pawuk, W.H., Navratil, S., Tinus, R.W. and Goodwin, O.C., 1982. Commercial vegetative inoculum of *Pisolithus tinctorius* and inoculation techniques for development of ectomycorrhizae on container grown tree seedlings. *For. Sci.*, 28: 373–400.

Maser, C., Trappe, J.M. and Nussbaum, R.A., 1978. Fungal–Small mammal interrelationships with emphasis on Oregon coniferous forests. *Ecology*, 59: 799–809.

McIlveen, W.D. and Cole Jr., H., 1976. Spore dispersal of Endogonaceae by worms, ants, wasps and birds. *Can. J. Bot.*, 54: 1486–1489.

Meyer, F.H., 1973. Distribution of ectomycorrhizae in native and man-made forests. In: G.C. Marks and T.T. Kozlowski (Editors), *Ectomycorrhizae. Their Ecology and Physiology*. Academic Press, New York, N.Y., pp. 79–105.

Mikola, P. (Editor), 1980. *Tropical Mycorrhiza Research*. Clarendon, Oxford, 270 pp.

Molina, R., 1979. Pure culture synthesis and host specificity of red alder mycorrhizae. *Can. J. Bot.*, 57: 1223–1228.

Mosse, B., 1973. Advances in the study of vesicular–arbuscular mycorrhiza. *Annu. Rev. Phytopathol.*, 11: 171–196.

Mosse, B., 1977. The role of mycorrhiza in legume nutrition on marginal soils. In: J.M. Vincent, A.S. Whitney and J. Bose (Editors), *Exploiting the Legume–Rhizobium Symbiosis in Tropical Agriculture*. College of Tropical Agriculture, Univ. of Hawaii, Misc. Publ., 145: pp. 275–292.

Mosse, B., Stribley, D.P. and Le Tacon, F., 1981. Ecology of mycorrhizae and mycorrhizal fungi. *Adv. Microbial Ecol.*, 5: 137–210.

National Research Council, 1983. *Innovations in Tropical Reforestation VI. Casuarinas*. National Academy Press, Washington, D.C., 118 pp.

Nelson, C.E. and Safir, G.R., 1982. Increased drought tolerance of mycorrhizal onion plants caused by improved phosphorus nutrition. *Planta*, 154: 407–413.

Nicolson, T.H., 1975. Evolution of vesicular-arbuscular mycorrhizas. In: F.E. Sanders, B. Mosse and P.B. Tinker (Editors), *Endomycorrhizas*. Academic Press, New York, N.Y., pp. 25–34.

Pathmaranee, N., 1974. *Observations on proteoid roots*. M.Sc. Thesis, Univ. of Sydney, N.S.W.

Pegler, D.N. and Fiard, T.P., 1979. Taxonomy and ecology of *Lactarius* (Agaricales) in the Lesser Antilles (West Indies). *Kew Bull.*, 33: 601–628.

Phillips, J.M. and Hayman, D.S., 1970. Improved procedures for clearing roots and staining parasitic and vesicular–arbuscular mycorrhizal fungi for rapid assessment of infection. *Trans. Mycol. Soc.*, 51: 377–387.

Raj, J., Bagyaraj, D.J. and Manjunath, A., 1981. Influence of soil inoculation with vesicular–arbuscular mycorrhiza and a phosphate dissolving bacterium on plant growth and ^{32}P uptake. *Soil Biol. Biochem.*, 13: 105–108.

Redhead, J.F., 1968. Mycorrhizal associations in some Nigerian forest trees. *Trans. Br. Mycol. Soc.*, 51: 377–387.

Redhead, J.F., 1974. *Aspects of the biology of mycorrhizal associations occurring on tree species in Nigeria*. Ph.D. Thesis, Univ. of Ibadan, Ibadan.

Redhead, J.F., 1975. Endotrophic mycorrhizas in Nigeria. Some aspects of the ecology of the endotrophic mycorrhizal association of *Khaya grandifolia* C. DC. In: F.E. Sanders, B. Mosse and P.B. Tinker (Editors), *Endomycorrhizas*. Academic Press, New York, N.Y., pp. 447–459.

Redhead, J.F., 1980. Mycorrhiza in natural tropical forests. In: P. Mikola (Editor), *Tropical Mycorrhiza Research*. Clarendon, Oxford, pp. 127–142.

Richards, P.W., 1952. *The Tropical Rain Forest*. Cambridge Univ. Press, Cambridge, 450 pp.

Rothwell, F.M. and Holt, C., 1978. Vesicular–arbuscular mycorrhizae established with *Glomus fasciculatus* spores isolated from the feces of cricetine mice. *U.S. Forest Service Research Note* NE-259, 4 pp.

Shamsuddin, M.N., 1979. Mycorrhizas of tropical forest trees. In: J. Furtado (Editor), *Abstracts Fifth Int. Symp. on Tropical Ecology, Univ. of Malaya, Kuala Lumpur*, 173 pp.

Singer, R. and Araujo, I. de J. da S., 1979. Litter decomposition and ectomycorrhiza in amazonian forests. *Acta Amazon.*, 9: 25–41.

Singer, R. and Morello, J.H., 1960. Ectotrophic forest tree mycorrhizac and forest communities. *Ecology*, 41: 549–551.

Singh, K.G., 1966. Ectotrophic mycorrhiza in equatorial rain forests. *Malay. For.*, 29: 13–18.

Sreeramulu, K.R. and Bagyaraj, D.J., 1986. Field response of chilli to VA mycorrhiza on black clayey soil. *Plant Soil.*, 93: 299–302.

Stark, N.M. and Jordan, C.F., 1978. Nutrient retention by the root mat of an Amazonian rain forest. *Ecology*, 59: 434–437.

St. John, T.V., 1980a. A survey of mycorrhizal infection in an Amazonian rain forest. *Acta Amazon.*, 10: 527–533.

St. John, T.V., 1980b. Uma lista de especies de plantas tropicais brasileiras naturalmente infectadas commicorriza vesicular–arbuscular. *Acta Amazon.*, 10: 229–234.

St. John, T.V., 1980c. Root size, root hairs and mycorrhizal infection. A re-examination of Baylis's hypothesis with tropical trees. *New Phytol.*, 84: 483–487.

St. John, T.V. and Uhl, C., 1986. Mycorrhizae at San Carlos de Rio Negro, Venezuela. *Acta Cient. Venezol.* (in press).

Subba Rao, N.S., Tilak, K.V.B.R. and Singh, C.S., 1985. Effect of combined inoculation of *Azospirillum brasilense* and vesicular–arbuscular mycorrhiza on pearl millet (*Pennisetum americanum*). *Plant Soil*, 84: 287–291.

Thomazini, L.I., 1974. Mycorrhiza in plants of the "Cerrado". *Plant Soil*, 41: 707–711.

Tinker, P.B., 1975. The soil chemistry of phosphorus and mycorrhizal effects on plant growth. In: F.E. Sanders, B. Mosse and P.B. Tinker (Editors), *Endomycorrhizas*. Academic Press, New York, N.Y., pp. 353–371.

Tinker, P.B., 1982. Mycorrhizas: The present position. In: *Whither Soil Research*. Trans. 12th Int. Congress of Soil Science, New Delhi, pp. 150–166.

Todd, A.W., 1979. Decomposition of selected soil organic matter components by douglas fir ectomycorrhizal associations. In: C.P.P. Reid (Editor), *Fourth North American Conf. on Mycorrhiza, Colorado State Univ., Fort Collins, Colo.*

Trappe, J.M., 1977. Selection of fungi for ectomycorrhizal inoculation in nurseries. *Annu. Rev. Phytopathol.*, 15: 203–222.

Treub, M., 1885. Onderzoekingen over sereh-zeck suikerriet. *Meded. Plant Tuinb. Batavia II.*

Vittadini, C., 1842. *Monographia Lycoperdineorum*. Augustae Taurinorum, Torino, 93 pp.

Vozzo, J.A. and Hacskaylo, E., 1971. Inoculation of *Pinus caribaea* with ectomycorrhizal fungi in Puerto Rico. *For. Sci.*, 17: 239–245.

Walter, H., 1973. *Vegetation of the Earth*. Springer, New York, N.Y., 274 pp.

Chapter 31

DECOMPOSITION

M.J. SWIFT and J.M. ANDERSON

DECOMPOSITION AS AN ECOSYSTEM CONCEPT

Ecosystems may conveniently be subdivided into three major components: the plant subsystem, the grazing subsystem, and the decomposer subsystem. These three components are distinct in their internal trophic structure and physiological characteristics and have often been studied in isolation. The functioning of the three subsystems is however highly interdependent. The temporal and spatial patterns of flux, and the relative partitioning of energy and matter between the subsystems, is indeed one of the major features of distinction between ecosystem types. It is furthermore generally true that for any given type of ecosystem the decomposer subsystem will have received by far the least detailed attention of the three subsystems, and generalizations concerning it are correspondingly more difficult to make. This is particularly true of tropical ecosystems.

Nonetheless, a number of attributes of the decomposer subsystem are commonly used as descriptive features when attempts are made to distinguish the specific character of ecosystem types. A frequently used attribute in this respect is the "turnover coefficient", k, given by the equation, $k = F/X$, where F is the annual input of organic matter (that is, usually the above-ground transfer of litter between plant and decomposer subsystems) and X the mean annual standing crop (the nett accumulation of plant litter at the soil surface). Another well-quoted characteristic is the "nett accumulation of organic matter". This does not necessarily correspond to the value X in the previous equation — indeed it has been interpreted in a number of ways. It may be taken as referring to the humus content of soil or to embrace both

that and the partially degraded litter at the surface. In this chapter the former interpretation is taken.

As a result of comparative investigations, two broad generalizations about tropical forest ecosystems are common in the literature; (1) that the rate of turnover (decomposition) of organic matter is higher than that in other ecosystem types; and (2) that the organic matter content of the soil is lower than that of other ecosystem types. Furthermore it has been suggested or implied that these two features are reciprocally related, in that a high decomposition rate is assumed to result in a diminished extent of accumulation of organic matter in the soil.

In recent years a number of authors have reviewed aspects of decomposition in tropical forests and other ecosystems, and concluded that neither generalization can be sustained on present evidence — and, moreover, that the link between the two features is far from simple (Schlesinger, 1977; Swift et al., 1979; Sanchez et al., 1982; Anderson and Swift, 1983; Golley, 1983). The current difficulty in characterizing ecosystem types in terms of their decomposition processes derives from three inter-related problems: the lack of a clear conceptual framework within which to describe the structure and function of the decomposer subsystem; the variation in methods of study, leading to low comparability of data sets; and the scarcity of intensive studies, leading to incompleteness in data sets and poor cover of the range of different forest types.

The objective in this review will not be to re-examine these aspects but to concentrate on a description of the internal components of the decomposer subsystems of tropical forests and their functional inter-relationships. Wherever possible comparisons will be made across forests of differing characteristics, but the major aim will be to provide a simple conceptual framework that will stimulate interest in the study of the decomposer subsystem as a unified concept within tropical forest ecosystems.

A GENERAL MODEL OF DECOMPOSITION

There is no single study of decomposition processes in tropical forest that can serve to illustrate all the major features of the subsystem, so we have drawn on data from a relatively limited number of studies, in particular those described in Tables 31.1 and 31.2. In selecting these for particular concentration the main criterion has been compatibility of data. Nonetheless comparability is limited as will be clear from the detailed considerations given in later sections. The inclusion of experiments into the time-course of decomposition by use of the litter-bag technique has been taken as the minimum level of comparison, this being regarded as a more suitable basic index of decomposition than the turnover coefficient or soil "respiration" (Anderson and Swift, 1983).

The data sets nonetheless cover a wide range of forest types, thus enabling a broad comparative view to be taken. Variations in the rate and pattern of decomposition may derive from a variety of factors. The analysis of these is aided by viewing them from within a general structure. In Fig. 31.1 a simplified version of a generalized model of decomposition is given, derived from the proposals of Swift et al. (1979). The model pictures the change of state of units of organic matter (termed *resources*) in three distinct micro-habitats of the forest; the canopy, the litter layer and the soil. The fluxes (*dk1* to *dk4*) are changes in the physical and chemical nature of the resource over any given period of time. These changes include; (1) mineralization of the resource material (transfers to sinks *M1* to *M4*): this type of transformation includes enzymatic conversion of organic carbon to carbon dioxide or protein nitrogen to ammonium ions; (2) synthesis of humus (transfers to *H1*, freshly synthesized humus); (3) removal by emigration of decomposer organisms or by leaching (not shown explicitly in the diagram). The resource material

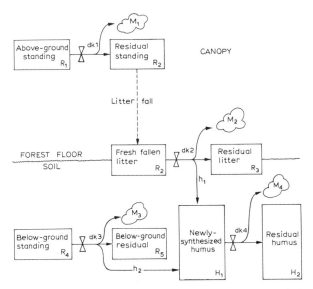

Fig. 31.1. A generalized model of decomposition in tropical forest (see text for explanation).

remaining after the processes of decomposition is shown as residual (*R2*, *R3*, *R5* and *H2*), but it should be noted that in any succeeding period of time these residual fractions will themselves be subject to similar transformations until such time as all material is transferred to either *M* or *H*.

Each of the decomposition fluxes is under the control of a set of regulating factors, indicated by the valve symbol on the flux arrow. These factors may conveniently be placed in one of three categories (Swift et al., 1979): the influence of the physical environment (*P*); the influence of the resource quality (*Q*); and the influence of the community of decomposer organisms (*O*). These features are highly interactive, and might even be said to have a hierarchy of action; macro-*P* > micro-*P* > *Q* > *O*, where *P* and *Q* can be described as exerting their influence on decomposition through their effect on the decomposer organisms; but it is convenient to consider them individually as a means of extracting the major factors determining observed patterns of decomposition in tropical forests.

ENVIRONMENTAL INFLUENCE ON DECOMPOSITION

Climate

The warm wet climate of tropical forest regions explains the generally high levels of turnover of

TABLE 31.1

Characteristics of tropical rain-forest sites in which the selected decomposition studies have been carried out

Sites and locations	Altitude (m)	Annual rainfall (mm)	Dry season (months < 100 mm)	Mean monthly temp. (range, °C)	Soil description	Soil pH[1]	Soil organic matter[1,2] (% d.w.)	Soil carbon[1] (% d.w.)
Sarawak, Gunung Mulu, 4°N[3]								
Alluvial forest	50	5090	0–1	26–28	Gray-brown silty Clay loam	4.4	20	12
Dipterocarp forest	200–250	5110	0–1	26–28	Red-yellow podzolic	4.1	19	11
Heath forest	170	5700	0–1	26–28	Humus podzol	3.6	54	29
Limestone forest	300	5700	0–1	26–28	Shallow peaty	3.6	82	42
Panama, Barro Colorado Island 9°N[4]								
Zetek 6 forest	150	2725	3–4	23–27	Brown-red sandy clay	6.4	–	8
Nigeria, IITA, Ibadan, 7°30'N[5]								
5 yr regrowth thicket	150	1500	5	24–31	Sandy loam	6.7	–	2.5
Brazil, Manaus, 3°S[6]								
Igapo (blackwater inundation forest)	44	2100	3–4	27–29	Clay/organic sediment	6.2[9]	–	–
Jamaica, Blue Mountains, 18°N[7]								
Mor ridge forest	1615	2500	1–2	9–24	–	3.0	96	47
Mull ridge forest	1600	2500	1–2	8–23	–	3.6	73	29
Wet slope forest	1575	2500	1–2	10–23	–	4.1	14	4
Gap forest	1575	2500	1–2	10–22	–	4.3	21	9
New Guinea, Marafunga, 6°S[8]								
Ridge forest	2480	4000	0–1	8–18	Humic brown clay	5.5–6.3	–	8–10
Valley forest	4440	4000	0–1	8–18	Humic brown clay	5.5–6.3	–	–

[1]0–100 mm.
[2]loss on ignition.
[3]Proctor et al., 1983a; Anderson et al., 1983.
[4]Healey and Swift (unpubl.); Haines and Foster, 1977.
[5]Perfect et al., 1979; Swift et al., 1981.
[6]Irmler, 1975; Irmler and Furch, 1979a.
[7]Tanner, 1977, 1980, 1981.
[8]Edwards and Grubb, 1977; Edwards, 1977.
[9]inundation water.

TABLE 31.2

Decomposition and turnover of leaf litter in six tropical forest sites

Location	Weight loss (%)				K_L
	Period of exposure (months)				
	1	3	6	12	
Panama[1]	13–53	34–98	85–100	–	2.6
Sarawak[2]	7–30	25–52	30–90	–	1.4–1.8[3]
Nigeria[4]	20–70	52–92	–	–	1.3
Brazil[5]	5–30	8–50	–	–	–
New Guinea[6]	2–12	5–40	16–65	26–87	1.0–1.4[7]
Jamaica[8]	–	11–17	11–19	21–40	0.5–0.7[9]

Details of the sites and references are given in Table 31.1. Data for weight loss are for leaf litter in litter bags with a mesh size of 10 mm except where indicated. In all cases the bags were placed on the forest floor. Except where otherwise indicated (fresh) the litter was obtained after fall and the range of values indicates differences between the slowest decaying sample and the fastest decaying sample in the same site. The litter turnover coefficient (K_L) is in all cases derived from the ratio of total leaf fall in one year to the mean standing crop of leaf litter in that year, the range being for different sites.

[1]Range = five species; [2]Range = mixed litter and two species on three sites; [3]Range = three sites; [4]Range = fresh mixed leaves in two years; [5]Range = Igapo site mixed litter (low) vs. single species (varzea) (high); [6]Range = six species; [7]Range = three sites; [8]Range = four species on three sites, 2-mm bags; [9]Range = four sites.

plant litter on the forest floor (Table 31.2). Meentmeyer (1985) showed that there was good correlation between the actual evapotranspiration (AET) and k at seventeen sites worldwide. The relationship was exponential (Fig. 31.2), indicating that the differences in rate between the tropical sites were on the whole proportionately greater than those between the sites at colder latitudes. The reasons for this are unclear, but indicate that climatic regulation is not straightforwardly expressed.

Climatic variables only set the broad limits to the rate of decomposition. Differences between sites with broadly similar AET may be attributable to environmental or other factors operating at finer scales of resolution in space or time.

This is illustrated by the data for leaf litter decay given in Table 31.2. The ranking of turnover coefficients broadly follows the expected pattern in relation to the climatic differences between the sites; for instance the highest rates of decomposi-

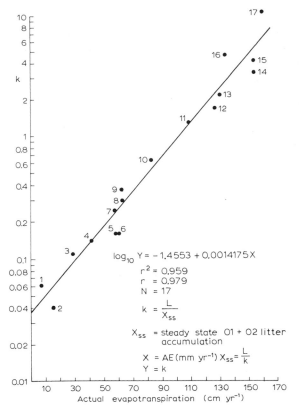

Fig. 31.2. Relationship between decomposition and actual evapotranspiration for seventeen sites (after Meentmeyer, 1985). Sites 10 to 17 are tropical forest. The rate of decomposition is expressed as the Litter Turnover Coefficient K where $K = L/X_{ss}$ (L = Annual Litter Fall and X_{ss} = mean annual accumulation of 01 and 02 litter); the independent variable is Actual Evapotranspiration (AET). The relationship between k (y) and AET (X) is given by $\log_{10} Y = 1.45 + 0.0014X$ ($r = 0.98$, $n = 17$).

tion are found in the lowland forests of Panama and Sarawak, the lowest in the cooler montane areas of Jamaica and New Guinea. The k values are broadly but not exactly, paralleled by the maximum rates of initial weight loss (that is, after three to six months) from litter bags. But there are a number of anomalies in each set of data which point to the influence of other factors. For instance the rate of leaf decay in the Nigerian site is very high in contrast to the low value of k. This may reflect the effect of two factors: firstly an environmental one in which the litter bag experiment shows the response to only the wet season whilst the turnover figure incorporates the effect of the extensive and severe dry period characteristic of this site which is at the margin of the West African forest zone. Secondly it should be noted that the leaves used in the litter bag experiment were taken directly from the tree, rather than being collected as fallen litter. This probably results in them being of higher quality (that is, in particular containing a higher content of nitrogen and phosphorus and of leachable and readily decomposable constituents such as sugars) than "natural" litters which commonly have a significant proportion of such materials re-absorbed into the plant before litter fall (Swift et al., 1979, and see below).

Micro-environmental effects

Environmental factors such as temperature and moisture operate at the scale of the individual organism. The range of size of decomposer organisms determines significant fluctuations in these factors within scales varying from microns and seconds (for instance, flushes of bacterial growth in response to input of high-quality resources) to metres and decades (for instance, the decay of a tree trunk by the combined activity of fungi in situ and foraging termites). Variations of ecosystem significance can perhaps best be summarized at a level somewhere between that of the decomposer and of the forest it inhabits.

Stratification of the forest environment occurs in both vertical and horizontal planes. There is little information on decomposition within the rainforest canopy. It is probable that extensive canopy decay of wood is common in rain-forest, but there is little quantitative information to substantiate this. Healey and Swift (unpubl. data) showed that the mean weight loss of small branch wood at litter fall in the Barro Colorado Forest, Panama was 43%, but individual logs varied from 5 to 80% decay. Similarly Edwards (1977) found losses ranging from 36% for twigs of less than 50 mm in diameter to 61% for branches greater than 200 mm in the montane forest in New Guinea. Most of the decay in the canopy is microbial; the branches in the Panamanian sample showed only infrequent attack by termites and other invertebrates (Swift and Boddy, 1984). Although there is greater termite activity in the canopy in other forests (Pasoh, Malaysia, and others) the contribution to overall energy flow is not generally very significant (Abe, 1979, 1980).

Leaf decomposition in the canopy is probably less substantial, though it has been rarely measured; Edwards (1977) did, however, estimate the loss of material (presumed to be by reabsorption into the standing tree) from leaves prior to abscission in the New Guinea forest as about 10% of dry weight on average. Leaching of both inorganic and organic constituents from senescent leaves may also constitute a significant flux from canopy to ground, particularly in leaves with protracted senescence.

Each of these processes is influenced by variation in the micro-environment at different strata in the canopy. There is now accumulating a body of information on the ecology of invertebrates (mainly herbivores and their predators) in the canopies of tropical forests, largely as a result of the employment of canopy walkways (Sutton et al., 1983; see also, Ch. 24, this volume). In some instances this also includes measurements of the physical environment (Rees, 1983). The development of these techniques offers a good opportunity to explore the characteristics of decomposition in the canopy.

The fall of litter to the forest floor represents a dramatic change in environment for the decomposer organism in situ on a decaying resource. Very surprisingly this easily documented feature has attracted little study, but there are some potentially interesting interactions. This is particularly so when the interaction of seasonal (phenological) and spatial effects is considered. Differences in leaf phenology (between tree species or at different points in the canopy within the same species) mean that the opportunities for initial colonization of senescent leaves on the tree may arise under different environmental conditions, with a resultant selective effect determining the character of the colonizing microflora and fauna. The period of time between initial colonization and fall may also vary, so that resources colonized under the same conditions may be subjected to widely different environmental transitions at litter fall, thus imposing a second selective effect. An even wider spectrum of permutations may occur with branches which have a much less strongly seasonal pattern of input to the decomposer subsystem. The high diversity of composition of the component ("unit") communities of the decomposer subsystem is partly a product of this variability in microenvironment over space and time (Swift, 1976,

1984). The structural complexity of the tropical forest canopy is such as to make it likely that this diversity will find its highest level in this biome, but there is as yet no evidence to support this notion (see, however, p. 557).

Moving to the lowest stratum, the subterranean environment, diurnal and seasonal fluctuations in such factors as temperature and moisture are damped down, an effect which is enhanced with depth (see Ch. 3, this volume). In consequence, the environment of decomposing roots and of litter buried by the activity of soil animals is quite different to that of surface material of the same quality. Regrettably there seem to have been no studies of subterranean decay in tropical forests, but Swift et al. (unpubl. data) showed, for a crop ecosystem derived from tropical forest in Nigeria, that the rate of decomposition of cowpea stems buried 100 mm in the soil was nearly twice as fast as that at the soil surface. Within the shade of the forest, however, the differences between surface and depth are likely to be less extreme.

Variations in microenvironment which may affect the pattern of decomposition are also present on a horizontal scale. A major characteristic of tropical forest is the diversity of tree species and the variations between them in the pattern of their leaf fall with time (see, for instance, Medway, 1972). This may result, at any given time, in a mosaic structure of the cover of leaf litter at the soil surface (Heatwole, 1961). This means, inter alia, that the micro-environment at the surface of the ground may vary markedly over a few metres — from a deep mat of moist leaves to an exposed area of bare soil. At a slightly larger scale, tree-falls impose another mosaic of varying environment. The area of ground covered by the stem itself, the mat of leaves and other fine litter that it brings down with it, and the area dominated by the stump will each have different decay characteristics — determined by both environmental and quality factors — which may persist for many years. The effect of these micro-environmental discontinuities may be such as to create corresponding discontinuities in the physical and chemical properties of the underlying soil. The possibility that this type of effect could influence the pattern of tree regeneration is an intriguing hypothesis, which might have some relevance to the mechanism of maintenance of plant species diversity in tropical forest.

Seasonal effects

The data given in Table 31.1 indicate that all the sites show some seasonal variation in rainfall pattern. In some sites the dry season is sufficiently long and severe to result in desiccation of the leaf litter at the soil surface (for instance, Nigeria and Panama), thus effectively inhibiting decomposition for that period of the year; in other sites the humidity and soil moisture levels remain high all the year except for a few weeks, so that moisture is never effectively limiting (Sarawak, Jamaica and New Guinea). The igapo and varzea sites in Brazil have the added interesting seasonal dimension of inundation during the rainy season. In all cases the input of fine litter, and particularly leaf litter which constitutes between 75 and 90% of the total, also displays a seasonal trend. The time of major input broadly corresponds with the dry period. This is most clearly seen in the strongly seasonal environments of Nigeria and Panama (Fig. 31.3), but a similar association of high litter input with periods of relatively lower rainfall was also observed in the two montane sites (Edwards, 1977; Tanner, 1980). In the much wetter lowland forests of Sarawak, litter fall is high throughout the year (Proctor et al., 1983b), but there is a peak which coincides with a time of relatively higher rainfall. It is possible that this is a physical rather than a physiological effect. In the Brazilian inundation forest, peak litter fall corresponds with the submergence period (Adis et al., 1979), in contrast with the nearby terra firme forests, where litter fall is associated with the drier season (Klinge and Rodrigues, 1968; Franken et al., 1979). Rather different physiological adaptations are presumably operating in these two instances.

In the sites with severe dry seasons, deposition of litter on the forest floor during the dry season, coupled with inhibition of the decomposition rate due to desiccation of the litter layer, results in an accumulation of litter at the soil surface (Fig. 31.3b). The onset of moist conditions after the first rains is the trigger which initiates decomposition in the mat of organic matter (Fig. 31.4). This combination of effects may have considerable significance for nutrient cycling in these ecosystems. High-quality leaf litter loses a considerable amount of its more mobile nutrient elements very early in the decomposition process (Fig. 31.5a).

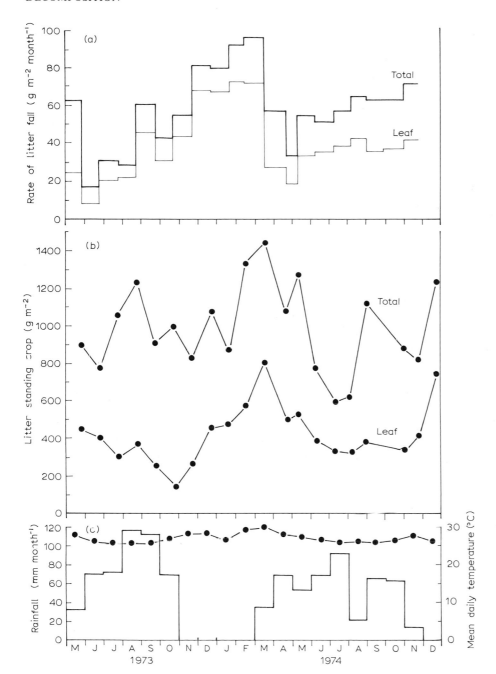

Fig. 31.3. The relationship between litter dynamics and seasonal rainfall in secondary forest, Ibadan, Nigeria (Swift et al., 1981). (a) Litter fall; (b) litter standing crop; (c) rainfall and temperature.

One may note, however, that in other litter of lower quality, immobilization of major elements may persist to the late stages of decomposition (Fig. 31.5b). The heavy leaching effect of the first rains on a rapidly decomposing mat of leaf litter can result in the release of a substantial pulse of soluble nutrients within the first few weeks of the rainy season (Fig. 31.6). Even in seasonal environments, however, there are often marked phenological differences between tree species (Medway, 1972); although most species drop their litter in response to moisture stress during the dry season, litter fall in a

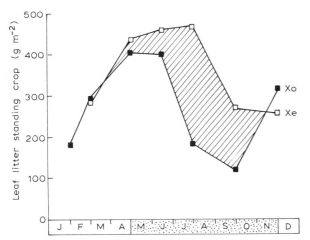

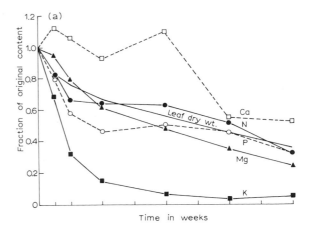

Fig. 31.4. The relationship of decomposition to climate. The observed change in standing crop of the leaf litter in the Panamanian forest during the year (*Xo*) is shown together with the theoretical line for the standing crop (*Xe*) if there was no decomposition, that is, by addition of the monthly observed leaf litterfall to the initial standing crop for the month. The shaded area thus shows the estimated amount of leaf litter decomposed during each period between observations. Months with rainfall greater than 100 mm are shown stippled. (Healey and Swift, unpubl., in Swift et al., 1979.)

significant minority of species may coincide with the wettest part of the year (see, for instance, Haines and Foster, 1977; Proctor et al., 1983b), thus spreading the period of nutrient release.

In the seasonal, but substantially evergreen, terra firme forests near Manaus, Klinge (1973, 1977) showed that, whilst the main peak of litter fall occurred in the dry season, moisture was not sufficiently limiting to inhibit decomposition. The differences between seasons were also probably diminished in this system by the fact that litter falling in the rainy part of the year was of generally lower quality (particularly with regard to nutrient concentration) than dry-season litter. Thus in these forests nutrient release also has a seasonal maximum, but in this case it coincides with the dry season.

Rainfall and litter fall was more evenly distributed throughout the year in the Mulu forests, Sarawak (Proctor et al., 1983b) with maximum litter fall occurring during the period of highest rainfall. Conditions for decomposition appeared to be generally favourable, except for occasional periods of one or two weeks without rain, and hence nutrient release apparently shows no strongly seasonal pattern (Anderson et al., 1983).

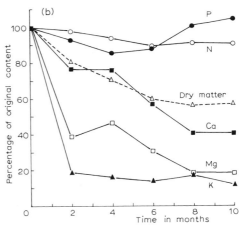

Fig. 31.5. Patterns of nutrient-element retention and release in decomposing leaf litter. (a) mixed fresh leaves in secondary forest, Nigeria (Swift et al., 1979); (b) mixed leaf litter, Sarawak (Anderson et al., 1983). In both cases the litter was put out on the forest floor in fine mesh bags. Note the differences in the rate of decomposition as well as the patterns of nutrient release.

A final permutation of the effects of seasonal climate can again be illustrated by reference to the data from Nigeria in Table 31.2. The extent of weight loss of identical samples of litter after three months was much lower in 1973 than in 1974. The explanation advanced for this discrepancy was that the onset of the rainy season in the former year was much delayed, resulting in an initial period in which virtually no decomposition took place.

In summary it may be concluded that the seasonal pattern of the rainfall in tropical forest may have a very sensitive regulating influence on the time at which substantial pulses of nutrients become available to the plants. This major feature of ecosystem dynamics deserves a great deal more

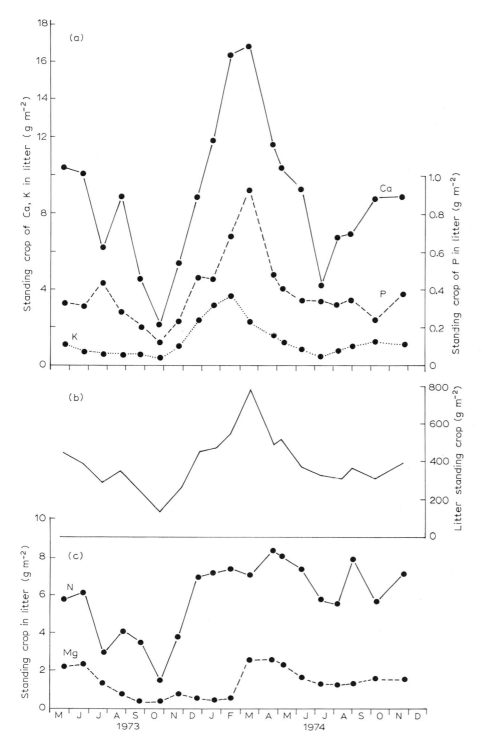

Fig. 31.6. Changes in the standing crop of nutrient elements in the leaf litter with season in secondary forest in Nigeria (Swift et al., 1981). (a) Standing crop of Ca (continuous line), P (pecked line) and K (dotted line); (b) total leaf litter; (c) N (continuous solid line) and Mg (pecked line). Compare the positioning of peaks and troughs of the individual elements with that of the leaf standing crop in (b). The relationship to seasonal climate can be seen by comparison with Fig. 31.3.

detailed investigation; in particular it is important to ascertain how decomposition seasonality matches with that of primary production. Leaf flush and reproduction are commonly triggered by moisture stress in tropical environments, but there is enormous variation both between and even within species at the same site. At an ecosystem level, in consequence, it is difficult to determine whether there is any correspondence between, for instance, the access of nutrients from decomposition and the flushing of vegetation. It is important that these features be investigated at more appropriate scales, influenced by the phenology of individual trees. In this respect the sequence of events in tree-gaps may be of particular interest (see p. 552). At this scale the seasonal patterns of rainfall in tropical forests may have sensitive regulatory effects which serve to couple the activities of the plant and the decomposition subsystems.

Edaphic factors

The relationship between tropical forests and their soils is discussed by Sanchez in Ch. 4. The underlying soil may influence the pattern of decomposition processes of a forest in a number of ways, direct or indirect.

The direct influences are those in which the physical factors of the soil environment affect the rate of decay of buried organic materials. This would apply most significantly to roots; but, as already acknowledged, this is a subject that has been totally ignored in tropical forest studies. This is a serious omission as dead roots, and root exudates, may represent an input to the decomposer system of equal magnitude to that of above-ground litter fall. The rate of decay of buried litter may be affected by the pH of the soil, its organic content and nutrient status, and its physical character (for instance, moisture availability as determined by the particulate structure).

These influences may extend to effects on surface litter. This can be demonstrated where the same litter type (or a standard substrate such as cellulose) is exposed under identical experimental conditions at the surface of soils of varying characteristics. For instance, Tanner (1981) demonstrated a clear difference between the rate of decomposition in two montane forest sites for eight different species of tree leaf litter irrespective of origin (Table 31.3). The slower rate of decomposition at the Mor site is associated with the much greater accumulation of humus at this site, and attendant on this a lower pH, a higher cation exchange capacity and a greater water-holding capacity (Table 31.1). The higher levels of raw organic matter in the soil may be regarded as a product rather than a determinant of the slow decomposition rates. Nonetheless the initial cause of the differences in the two sites, including those in productivity, remain uncertain (Grubb, 1977).

That interpretation of the relationships between

TABLE 31.3

Weight loss of leaf litter in 2-mm mesh bags on the forest floor of two montane forest sites in Jamaica (Tanner, 1981)

Species of litter	Site of origin	Weight loss after 383 days (%) Site of decomposition	
		Mull	Mor
Alchornea latifolia	Mor	69	52[1]
	Mull	66	46[1]
Clethra occidentalis	Mull	41	34[1]
Clusia havetioides	Mor	33	22[1]
Cyrilla racemiflora	Mor	46	28[1]
	Mull	38	27[1]
Hedyosmum arborescens	Mull	64	47[1]
Lyonia octandra	Mor	40	31[1]
Podocarpus urbanii	Mull	47	40
Vaccinnium meridionale	Mor	35	29

[1]Significant difference between values in adjacent columns ($P < 5\%$).

rates of litter decomposition and humus accumulation is not straightforward is shown by the results of Anderson et al. (1983) for forests in Sarawak. Weight losses from mixed leaf litter in fine mesh bags over ten months were significantly higher in heath forest on a well-developed humus podsol (54.8%) than from litter in alluvial forest (41.3%), on an oxisol. The hypothesis put forward in this case was that the high water-holding capacity of the soil organic matter in the heath forest buffered the moisture content in the surface litter layers, thereby maintaining optimum conditions for leaf litter decomposition throughout the year. On the other hand the same high water table inhibited the later stages of decomposition (that is, of litter residues, faeces of invertebrates, etc.), thus enabling the development of an organic soil. These conditions seem characteristic of the "peaty" soils of the area (Tie et al., 1979).

Indirectly, the soil type may influence decomposition via the composition of the decomposer community and the resource quality of the plant litter input. The composition of the decomposer community is affected by variations in the physical structure of the soil such as the clay content, pore space, moisture holding capacity, etc. It is also important to note that the spectrum of resource quality of plants growing on soils of different types may vary, and thus affect the decomposition characteristics of the site. The interaction of these effects can only be unravelled by experimentation which removes the influence of the quality factors (for instance, as in the experiments quoted above where identical litter samples are exposed in different sites). An illustration of the difficulty of interpretation that occurs in the absence of such controls is given by the example of decomposition in the two types of inundation forest near Manaus (Table 31.2). The rate of decomposition of litter in the igapo site was only half that in the varzea (Irmler and Furch, 1979a, b). This may be attributed to the difference in nutrient status of the soil, that in the varzea being much higher than in the igapo; or equally convincingly it can be interpreted as due to the difference in the resource quality of the litter at the two sites, the leaves at the igapo site having a lower initial content of most macro-nutrient elements than those in the varzea forest.

In some instances the soil type may influence the whole structure of the decomposition subsystem. On the very infertile soils of large tracts of the Amazon basin, the trees form a dense root mat above the surface of the mineral soil (Klinge, 1973). Decomposition is described as being a process of "direct nutrient cycling" because inorganic nutrients released from litter during decomposition do not enter the mineral soil pool before being taken up by plant roots (Herrera et al., 1978a, b; Stark and Jordan, 1978). In this situation, the mycorrhizal system of the roots is envisaged as having a direct interface with the decomposer system. Although the low nutrient status of the soil is here pictured as having a primary determining effect on the way in which decomposition takes place in these forests, the direct influence of the soil microenvironment, through factors such as pH, is correspondingly diminished because of the spatial separation of decomposer system from mineral soil.

THE INFLUENCE OF RESOURCE QUALITY ON DECOMPOSITION PROCESSES

Resource quality (Q) is defined as the set of intrinsic features of a unit (piece) of organic matter (resource) which influence its rate of decomposition (Swift et al., 1979). These features include the degree of lignification, the composition in terms of essential macro- and micro-nutrient elements, the content of soluble organic molecules, and the presence of stimulatory or allelopathic molecules at biologically significant concentrations. As with the physical environment the influence of these factors on decomposition is indirect, in the sense that they are exerted through their regulatory influence on the activity of the decomposer organisms. Resource quality factors exert their influence at a different scale of resolution, however — a "fine-tuning" of the rate of decomposition within limits imposed by the physical environment. It is because of the profound influence of Q that generalization of decomposition rates on the basis of climatic variables alone is not justified.

The turnover coefficients for five major constituents of litter fall in the Sarawak and Panama forest are shown in Table 31.4. A striking feature is that whereas the values of k for leaves and fruits (that is, high-Q resources) are high compared with values typically obtained from temperate forests, the values for low-Q resources such as branches are

TABLE 31.4

Turnover coefficients (K_L) of different above-ground litter components from one-year studies in Sarawak and Panama (see Table 31.1 for references and details of sites)

	Reproductive material	Leaves	Palm fronds	Twigs (<20 mm)	Branches (>20 mm)
Panama	9.8	2.6	1.6	0.5	0.15
Sarawak[1]	9.1	1.6	–	1.1	0.3

[1]Mean of four sites.

no different. This again illustrates the complex way in which Q and P interact to determine the overall rate of decomposition.

The characterization of branches as "low" and leaves as "high" quality resources can be substantiated on the criteria given earlier; branches have higher lignin contents, are harder, and have lower nutrient and higher polyphenol concentrations than leaves. They are also more massive, although it has never been clearly established that mass *per se* affects the decomposition rate. It is not easy to determine which of these factors is the most significant in determining the differences in decay pattern.

The turnover coefficient gives a constant for the decomposition of the total leaf litter at a site. This value is a weighted mean of the spectrum of species-specific decomposition rates of the different leaves. For example, the experiments of Tanner (1981) reported in Table 31.3 demonstrate marked differences in decay rate between tree leaf species decomposing in the same montane environment in Jamaica. The full range of fifteen species tested shows annual weight losses ranging from 17 to 96%; Edwards (1977) found a comparable range, although for six species only, in New Guinea (Table 31.2). Time-course experiments show the differences between leaf types even more vividly, as illustrated in Fig. 31.7 for two species of leaf litter in the Barro Colorado forest. Weight losses over the full period of the rainy season are shown for litter enclosed in bags of three mesh sizes (see below). The weight losses over the first month for all mesh types are over three times higher in *Gustavia* than in *Anarcardium*. This can probably be attributed to a much larger component of soluble (leachable) materials in the former. Losses in the second month are also greater in *Gustavia* but over the remaining period the rate of loss in weight is actually higher in *Anacardium*, particularly in the coarse mesh bags. This demonstrates

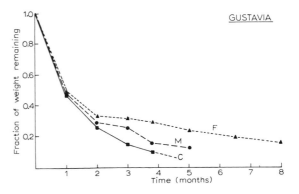

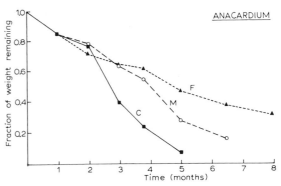

Fig. 31.7. Patterns of weight loss from litter bags of two leaf species in Panama: *Gustavia superba* (H.B.K.) Berg., and *Anacardium excelsum* (Bert. & Bulb.) Skeels. c = coarse mesh (10 mm); m = medium mesh (2 mm); F = fine mesh (80 μm) bags, respectively. (Healey and Swift, unpubl. data.)

how the relative quality of a resource may change with time as decomposition proceeds. In this case it is probable that the significant effect is on the one hand the rapid depletion of readily decomposed substances from the *Gustavia* leaves, leaving after two months a relatively low-Q residue; whereas in the case of *Anacardium* the initial effect during the first two months of slow decay is to raise the quality. This may be due to an increase in palatability to soil fauna following destruction or removal of allelopathic substances.

Unfortunately, in none of these examples is there the hard evidence to link supposed features of resource quality to effects on the decomposer organisms. Anderson et al. (1983) analysed the leaf litter used in their decomposition experiments in Sarawak. *Ficus* leaves had higher nutrient concentrations and a lower content of polyphenols than *Parashorea*, the lignin contents being almost identical. Despite this apparent difference in quality however, little difference in the decay characteristics of the two species was noted from a total of six time-course experiments involving two mesh sizes and three sites.

Details are now emerging of the wide range of potentially allelopathic secondary metabolites to be found in the leaves of tropical forest trees (Waterman, 1983, and Ch. 29, this volume). One very striking feature of this is the high level of specificity (Janzen and Waterman, 1984). Whilst interest in these compounds has been largely directed towards their role in controlling herbivore activity, the significance to ecosystem function may be even greater in relation to their effects on decomposers.

The importance of Q as a regulator of decomposition processes lies in the supposition that it may play a much more direct role than the physical environment in controlling the pattern of nutrient release and the synthesis of humus molecules. This is illustrated by comparison of the two graphs for leaf litter dynamics in Fig. 31.4. The rapidly decomposing litter of the Nigerian regrowth thicket shows an early release pattern for all the nutrient elements, whereas the slower rate of decomposition of the Sarawak litter is correlated with immobilization of nitrogen and phosphorus. Once again there is no evidence to link any features of Q to the observed differences, but this only serves to emphasize the importance of adopting an experimental approach to the unravelling of decomposition processes in tropical forests.

THE DECOMPOSER COMMUNITY OF TROPICAL FORESTS

Biologically mediated processes of decomposition and nutrient release

The significance of decomposition processes for ecosystem functioning lies in the end effects of mineralization and humification. These processes are to a considerable degree biologically mediated. The active biota is a diverse community of micro-organisms and invertebrate animals. The trophic structure of this decomposer community has proved difficult to determine, but the relative importance of different components of the community can be deduced from the results of exclusion experiments with litter bags of differing mesh size. The time-course data in Fig. 31.7 illustrate this approach. The fine mesh bags were constructed of material with pores less than 100 μm in diameter. They thus excluded from contact with the litter all organisms except bacteria, fungi, Protozoa and the smallest of the invertebrate fauna. The rate of weight loss from two months onward is much slower in these bags than in those of medium (2 mm) and coarse (10 mm) mesh which permitted access to fauna of varying body size. The losses in the fine mesh bags can be attributed to leaching plus microbial catabolism, whilst those in the larger sizes will additionally include consumption and export by the animals and comminution by feeding activity to a particle size lower than the mesh diameter. Whilst such interpretation is necessarily crude, it can be hypothesized that intervention by the mesofauna and macrofauna results in a 60 to 80% increase in weight loss over that due to the microflora and microfauna in *Anacardium* within five months of the initiation of decay. The effect on *Gustavia*, with its very rapid initial loss (attributable to leaching), is less marked. It is noticeable that in both species the rate of decomposition over the first two months is virtually identical irrespective of mesh size. The weight losses during this period can be attributed to a combination of physical leaching and microbial catabolism; animal intervention is only noticeable subsequent to this.

Modern concepts of decomposition processes suggest that micro-organisms, particularly fungi, are largely responsible for the primary processes of decomposition, particularly the catabolism of the macromolecules (polysaccharides, lignin, etc.) of plant litter; during this process some mineralization of nitrogen and other elements may occur, but generally speaking the early stages of decomposition are characterized by microbial immobilization of these elements, particularly in low-Q materials (see Fig. 31.5b). The decomposer fauna intervene later in the process, often following an increase in the palatability of the resource due to the action of the microflora. In many cases the animals may feed directly on the microflora. This type of interaction between microtroph and microbe has been experimentally demonstrated as one of the major features stimulating nutrient release from decomposing litter (Swift, 1977; Anderson et al., 1981; Anderson and Ineson, 1984; Seastedt, 1984).

It remains for the same phenomena to be explicitly demonstrated for tropical-forest biota involved in litter decomposition, though higher losses of nutrients than of mass in coarse-mesh as contrasted with fine-mesh bags were suggested by

Anderson et al. (1983) as evidence for the fauna reducing microbial immobilization of nutrients during the initial states of litter decomposition in Sarawak. But while these litter-bag exclusion experiments may be used to partition the role of the soil and litter biota in decomposition in very broad terms, the determination of specific roles for individual groups, let alone species, has proved elusive. Although there is now accumulating a substantial body of data on the populations and biomass of the soil and litter fauna in tropical forests (Table 31.5), very little is known about the part that these animals play in decomposition

TABLE 31.5

Soil and litter macrofauna in three sites[1] in Sarawak (Collins, 1980b; Anderson et al., 1983)

	Alluvial forest	Dipterocarp forest	Heath forest
Weight loss (%) of mixed litter after 10 months			
Coarse mesh	57	51	54
Fine mesh	41	44	55
Animal biomass (mg wet weight m^{-2})			
ANNELIDA			
Hirudinea (Gnathobdellida)	12	1	E[2]
Oligochaeta (Megascolecidae and Moniligastridae)	1003	645	389
MOLLUSCA			
Pulmonata	19	0	18
CRUSTACEA			
Isopoda	31	31	34
(Decapoda)	(710)	(0)	(0)
MYRIAPODA			
Diplopoda	110	11	73
Chilopoda	79	370	313
Symphyla	10	10	5
ARACHNIDA (mainly Araneae)	128	171	109
INSECTA			
Diplura	43	48	33
Blattodea	162	121	598
Isoptera	522	1818	3579
Coleoptera	361	494	1433
Formicidae	134	527	353
Orthoptera	61	29	86
Others	64	244	145
Total	2739[3]	4520	7168

[1] See Table 31.1.
[2] Not estimated.
[3] Excluding crabs.

processes. Furthermore it should be noted that quantitative information on the micro-organisms is limited. In contrast, a number of summaries of energy flows in temperate ecosystems have concluded that all but a minor component of the energy fixed by primary production is eventually channelled through heterotrophic processing by the microflora, with the fungi playing a major role (Heal and MacLean, 1975; Swift et al., 1979; Swift, 1982; among others). A similar synthetic approach to energy partitioning in the savanna ecosystem of the Serengeti Plains (Phillipson, 1973) showed that nearly 70% of above-ground primary production was respired by micro-organisms. There is, a priori, no reason to believe that tropical forests function greatly differently in this respect to these other terrestrial ecosystems. Ecosystems with high levels of termite activity, such as Pasoh (Matsumoto and Abe, 1979) or the Guinea Forest Savanna in Nigeria (Collins, 1981), may, however, merit special consideration in respect of energy and nutrient fluxes through saprotrophic invertebrates.

Little is known of the mechanisms of humus synthesis and decomposition in tropical forest soils; but, as the instability of humus in tropical soils is believed to be a determinant of the low sustainable fertility under cultivation, clearly this is a feature of high priority in research. Conclusions drawn from the study of temperate soils implicate fungi in both the synthesis and breakdown of humus molecules; it is unclear whether tropical soils are likely to differ in these respects.

The soil and litter microflora

It was argued earlier that fungi are the major agents of primary decomposition of plant litters. Regrettably little is known of the quantitative ecology of these organisms in tropical forest. A substantial amount of floristic information is accumulating, particularly for the macrofungi (Basidiomycetes and Ascomycetes) from wood and leaf litter. It should be possible eventually to derive some biogeographical generalizations from these data, but this has not yet been attempted. The same applies to the more limited information that is accruing for the microfungi from soil.

Although there has been much theoretical speculation in recent years, there is still no coherent testable set of hypotheses linking micro-bial community structure with their role in decomposition. In other words, it has not proved possible to predict the pattern of decomposition process from knowledge of the composition of the fungal or bacterial community. Current theory suggests that microbial niches are determined by features operating at the level of micro-environment and chemical substrate rather than those that would be expressed at the major ecosystem level (Swift, 1976, 1984). If this is so, the major determinant of differences between ecosystems and tropical forest types is differences in the spectrum of resource quality. Parasitic micro-organisms often show a very specific relationship with their host. It would be expected therefore that there should be a high degree of endemism in this ecological group in species-diverse ecosystems such as rain forests. The decomposer fungi also exhibit a degree of this specific relationship with the resources they inhabit (Swift, 1976, 1982), although others are very "generalist" in their distribution. Investigation of this type of relationship in the tropical-forest ecosystems for either parasites or decomposers remains to be carried out.

One structural feature of decomposer communities that has attracted a lot of attention from fungal ecologists is the so-called "fungal succession"; it has been demonstrated for a wide range of resource types that, as decomposition proceeds, there is a parallel change in the sequence of the fungi inhabiting the resource. Within the extensive literature reviewing this phenomenon there is not a single example recorded from tropical forest (Hudson, 1968; Hayes, 1979; Wicklow and Carroll, 1981). Recently, however, this lack of interest in decomposer fungi of tropical forest has been relieved by the publication by Rambelli et al. (1983) of a preliminary account of the microfungi from the litter and soil of the Tai National Forest, Ivory Coast. Whilst the study is again largely floristic in nature, the data have been collected in such a way that it will be possible to link the information with other studies in progress at the same site. The authors isolated over 170 species of Hyphomycetes from the litter and over 250 from the top 50 mm of underlying soil. Dematiaceous forms were dominant in the former and hyaline mycelia in the latter. This is probably the most comprehensive study of its kind in a tropical environment, and although it would be foolish to argue from a single study it is of interest to note that the number of species is greater than the highest recorded for temperate deciduous forest (Novack and Whittingham, 1968; Swift, 1976). Perhaps the record of tropical forest for diversity is going to be maintained in this habitat also.

This study again reveals the difficulties surrounding investigation of the decomposer microflora. The list of fungi, because of the methods used, inevitably excludes all but a very few of the Basidiomycetes and Ascomycetes; yet it is probably these enzymatically well-endowed organisms that are the major contributors to energy flow in the litter environment (Frankland, 1982; Swift, 1982).

Whereas existing knowledge of the decomposer fungi in tropical forest is deficient in all respects beyond that of systematics, that of other significant groups (the saprotrophic Bacteria, Actinomycetes, Myxomycetes and Protozoa for instance) is effectively non-existent. The microbiology of tropical-forest soils remains virtually an unexplored field of investigation.

The soil and litter fauna

As already observed, little difference could be found in the rate of decomposition of litter at the three sites studied by Anderson et al. (1983) in Sarawak. Nonetheless the structure of the animal communities of the litter layer and underlying soil at those sites did show some considerable differences (Table 31.5). The alluvial forest had a greater biomass than the other sites of macrofauna which in other ecosystem types are often implicated with litter processing — that is, millipedes and earthworms. Furthermore, Collins (1980a) has suggested that the populations of terrestrial crabs found exclusively in this site may also be important in litter comminution and removal. On the other hand the heath forest had the greatest biomass of other macrofauna such as cockroaches and gryllids, as well as of potentially important mesofauna such as termites and beetles. The differences in animal population structure thus seem insignificant as far as overall decomposition rates are concerned. It is possible to hypothesise that the greater abundance of one group compensates for the absence of another, either by fulfilling the same role (occupying the same niche) or by promoting an alternative pathway of decomposition.

There have been few comprehensive studies of the full range of potentially significant decomposer fauna; among those that do exist, sampling methods are often so variable that the comparability among different groups is difficult to ascertain (see, for instance, Kitazawa, 1971).

The inundation forest sites in Brazil have been intensively studied, however (Irmler, 1975, 1979; Beck, 1976; Adis, 1981) and are of particular interest because of the presence of an aquatic (benthic) as well as terrestrial fauna. Beck (1976) has described the migration of the terrestrial component to and from the neighbouring terra firme in response to the movement of the flood waters. Irmler and Furch (1979b) have described the role of one macro-invertebrate, the cockroach *Epilampra irmleri*, in leaf-litter breakdown. They estimated that this animal may be responsible for the consumption of nearly 6% of the annual leaf-litter input of the inundation forests. This is one of the few examples where a specific decomposer role has been established and quantitatively examined. Equivalent importance is often assigned to various of the other groups listed in Table 31.5, but without concrete evidence. Two groups in particular are often thought to be of significance in the breakdown of tropical-forest litter, the termites among the mesofauna and the earthworms among the macrofauna.

Although the decay of utility timbers by termites has been a subject of intensive study in many parts of the tropics, much less is known of their role as decomposers in natural ecosystems. Broadly speaking, they appear to occupy two distinct niches in this respect: as primary decomposers of plant litter above the soil; and as processors of humus within the soil (see also Ch. 4, this volume). Whilst it is probable that primary decomposition of leaf and wood by termites is a feature of all tropical forests, the quantitative significance of this function appears to vary from site to site. Abe (1979) reported that termites (mainly the fungus-growing Macrotermitinae) removed 32% of the leaf-litter input in the Pasoh Forest Reserve in peninsular Malaysia. Termites are also reported as the major processors of woody resources at the same site, removing up to 80% of the weight of small branches within eighteen months (Abe, 1980). In nearby Sarawak, however, humus feeders (Termitinae) dominated the termite fauna, although rotten-wood feeders seem occasionally to be locally dominant (Collins, 1980b). The direct role of termites in decomposition is therefore suggested as being relatively minor.

The same situation seems to pertain in the riparian forests of Nigeria (Wood et al., 1982) although again humus-feeding species are abundant. It is interesting to note the contrast with the adjacent savanna, where fungus-growing termites take more than 70% of the woody input (Collins, 1981). Nor is there any indication of a major role of the termites in wood decay in the Barro Colorado Forest in Panama. Healey and Swift (unpubl.) found that only 10% of branches at litter fall and 25% in the litter had any signs of termite attack and in most cases only superficial feeding was recorded. From analysis of the published differences in activity of termites in forests, Collins (Ch. 26) suggests that litter processing by termites may be limited by high rainfall or a high water table.

Foraging termites comminute dead wood or leaf litter and carry the particulate organic matter back to the nest. In the nest, wood is digested by the joint action of termite and symbiotic microflora resulting in a dissipation of carbon, but a concentration, by continuing immobilization, of nitrogen and other elements. This has led to speculation concerning the effects of termites on the ecosystems they occupy in terms of the availability of nutrients to other components (Wood and Sands, 1978; Collins, 1983a, b). The impact of termites on nutrient fluxes has not been calculated for Pasoh or for any other rain-forest ecosystem with high levels of termite activity. But the estimates for the Guinea savanna, that most of the nitrogen in above-ground litter production was converted into termite tissues, indicates an upper threshold of effect in tropical systems (Collins, 1983a, b). It is possible to argue that this concentration of nutrients into the termite nests could result in significant depletion of other nutrient pools, and ultimately have a direct regulatory effect on primary production, initially in the removal of nutrients and later in the return through alate death and decay. This fresh "pulse" of nutrient entry could be regarded as analogous to the climatically controlled seasonal pulse of wetter forests.

The humus-feeding activities of termites are even less well understood than their roles as primary decomposers. About 50% of extant termite species are humus feeders and they are particularly abundant in the humid forests of Africa and South America. For example, Wood et al. (1982) recorded termite population densities in a riparian forest in Nigeria as being 2646 m^{-2}, comprising 33 species; of these, 20 species and 90% of the individuals were humus feeders. The calculation that these termites turned over 30% of the top 25 cm of the soil profile per annum, coupled with the demonstration that the faecal mounds of some species contained up to 76 times more available phosphorus than the surrounding soil (Wood, Johnson and Anderson, 1983; Anderson and Wood, 1984), gives some indication of the potential importance of these termites in forest nutrient cycles. Parodoxically, even less is known about the ecology of humus feeders than the other trophic groups of termites.

In many parts of the tropics termites and earthworms may occupy analogous niches within the decomposer subsystem, and their occasionally inverse distribution patterns is perhaps an indication of this. This proposition can be pressed further by suggesting that earthworms have similar roles in decomposition to those of termites — that is, as litter processors and as soil feeders.

In temperate forests of relatively neutral pH, earthworms are major processors of leaf litter either by direct comminution or by removing litter to lower horizons (Edwards and Lofty, 1977). Oligochaete populations and biomass in tropical forests rarely reach the same levels as those in temperate areas, but they can nonetheless be locally abundant. Considerable doubt exists, however, as to whether these tropical groups play the same direct roles in litter decomposition as the Lumbricidae characteristic of the temperate biomes, but humus-feeding (endogeic) forms may be of greater significance (Lavelle, 1983). These earthworms live permanently at depth, and their populations have almost certainly been underestimated. Since 5 to 36 times their own weight of soil is passed through the gut each day (Lavelle, 1984), it is probable that they have a substantial influence on all aspects of the soil they inhabit — physical, chemical and biological. Although only a low proportion of the soil ingested by these earthworms is generally deposited on the soil surface (depending upon the trophic structure of the worm community in a particular habitat), the production of casts can be as high as 100 to 300 t ha^{-1} yr^{-1} (Lavelle, 1984). Lee (1983) has given data for casting activity from a number of sites, which clearly demonstrates the profound pedological effect that it must have. Worm casts have been shown to have higher content of organic matter and mineral nutrients than surrounding soil (Nye, 1955; Lee, 1967; Cook et al., 1980), which may be associated with an enhanced level of microbial activity; Russell-Smith and Swift (unpublished data) found that leaf litter and filter-paper cellulose decomposed more quickly when covered with worm-cast soil than under unprocessed soil from the same Nigerian forest. Nye (1955) has graphically described how the forest floor in many parts of West Africa is covered by a dense population of worm casts. It is tempting to conclude that in these areas the processes of decomposition are to a large extent regulated by earthworm activity, even though the direct influence may be low. It is also interesting to note that the role of termites in litter breakdown in the same forest soils is thought to be relatively minor.

CONCLUSIONS

The significance of the decomposition sub-system lies in its function as the driving force of nutrient cycles within ecosystems. Decomposition is the exact antithesis of primary production, the heterotrophically driven process of mineralization matching the fixation processes of the autotrophs. It is now generally established that aggrading or climax ecosystems are highly conservative of nitrogen and phosphorus, and low amounts of these elements are lost from the system under undisturbed conditions (Bolin and Cook, 1983; among others). But ecosystem types differ in their internal patterns, particularly in the relationship between the size of the nutrient pool and the rapidity of its turnover through production and decomposition (Jordan and Herrera, 1981). Ecosystems such as rain forests which have a high organic productivity must also evolve mechanisms for satisfying the demand of the vegetation for available mineral nutrients. This might be achieved by the development of what Vitousek (1984) has

called "efficient within-stand cycling". A strategy of this kind may be achieved by an increased economy in fixation — less nutrient required per unit of carbon fixed — and/or by conserving the proportion of mineral nutrients shed at litter fall. On sites with low nutrient availability, tree species tend to translocate nitrogen and phosphorus more efficiently before leaf abscission than under conditions of high nutrient availability (Loveless, 1962; Bryant et al., 1983). The relationship between mass of litter produced and nutrient concentrations in the litter can therefore be seen as an index of the "efficiency" with which the system is able to sustain productivity in relation to the nutrient supply (Vitousek, 1982). The Amazonian terra firme forests have this type of adaptation, a large proportion of mineral nutrients being reabsorbed into the tree before litter fall (Klinge, 1977). As described by Herrera et al. (1978a) and Fittkau (1983), this represents part of an overall "strategy" of nutrient conservation, which is an adaptation to the occupation of leached acidic soils which are very deficient in nutrient reserves. Associated with the nutrient conservation are other features such as rapid litter turnover rates, suppression of nitrification (Jordan et al., 1979), and the "direct cycling" of nutrients from soil to plant (that is, tight coupling of the decomposition processes with those of uptake by the plant) that has been described earlier. In this system a major part of the nutrient capital is locked up in the plant biomass and there is correspondingly a low standing crop of organically bound nutrient in litter and soil. This spectrum of characteristics is sometimes assumed to be characteristic of tropical rain forest in general.

As the foregoing discussion indicates, however, this is by no means the case. Vitousek (1984) has analysed the efficiency of within-stand nutrient cycling for a wide range of tropical forests. He showed that the data sets for tropical forests were basically an extension of the trends set for nitrogen cycling in temperate and boreal forests, but that the efficiency of phosphorus cycling was higher in tropical forests on oligotrophic sites. Melillo and Gosz (1983) have similarly concluded that rain-forest productivity is closely linked to phosphorus availability — a phenomenon related to the ancient and highly weathered nature of many tropical soils where phosphorus is strongly bound in organic and inorganic fractions (Walker and Syers, 1976). In contrast to the Amazonian forests, the soils and vegetation of the Mulu forests of Sarawak contributed some of the lowest ratios of dry mass to phosphorus in Vitousek's (1984) analysis; this is associated with the production of low-Q resources, which decompose slowly (Anderson et al., 1983). These differences are further consistent with the predictions made from consideration of plant growth strategies in different nutrient environments (Mooney, 1972; Grime, 1977; Bryant et al., 1982).

The reviews of Sanchez et al. (1982) and Anderson and Swift (1983) have made the point that large standing crops of organic matter in litter or soil are not unusual in tropical forests. With high reserves of nutrients in the litter or soil a low fractional rate of nutrient return may still suffice to supply plant demand. In this case the amount of nutrient returned annually may be the same as in forests with more rapid cycling, but the mean residence time of an atom in the litter and soil will be longer. It is apparent then that there are a number of potential strategies for ensuring the return of sufficient nutrient to satisfy the productive demand of a tropical forest; which strategy is found in a particular forest will depend on climate and soil type.

Such general statements on the functioning of rain forests at the ecosystem level mask important difference in the responses of individual species and trees to the varying conditions within the system. For example, while mixed litter in alluvial forest at Mulu decomposed slowly in comparison with litter in many other rain forests, litter of high quality from species such as *Ficus* and *Parashorea*, actually decomposed relatively rapidly. Thus, while the site may be characterized as generally oligotrophic in terms of phosphorus availability and "phosphorus use efficiency", it is a mosaic of patches of high and low resource quality, with associated differences in rates of nutrient cycling. This pattern is determined by the distribution and phenology of the different tree species.

Many tropical tree species show clumped distributions, rather than being randomly distributed as is generally supposed (Poore, 1968; Hubbell and Foster, 1983). On an oligotrophic site in the Cameroon, Gartlan et al. (1986) showed a very strong correlation between available phosphorus in the soil and such patterns of tree species distribution. Patches of low phosphorus availability were dominated by Caesalpiniaceae, the mycorrhizal infections of which may give them a competitive advantage. It is interesting to speculate whether such patches are maintained by the vegetation through the decomposition characteristics and nutrient status of their leaves. In contrast, however, Baillie and Ashton (1983) found no correlation between vegetation species mosaics at a small (40 m) scale in dipterocarp forest on a more eutrophic soil. At broader scales of analysis, opportunities to determine such relationships might be lost (Newberry and Proctor, 1984).

Patterns in nutrient cycling occur in time as well as space, and temporal phenomena should be considered at small as well as large scales.

The efficiency of nutrient return to the plant from decomposing litter and organic matter is dependent on a synchronization of the time of nutrient release (availability) with that of demand by the plant. In some forests this may be achieved by means of a single large pulse of nutrient being made available early in the rainy season, corresponding to the time of maximum flush in the vegetation. In some seasonal forests there is a close correlation of release patterns with the same environmental triggers that control productivity; the onset of decomposition is regulated by the pattern of rainfall, and in particular by the intensity of seasonality. Thus the initiation of nutrient release and the period of time over which it extends may be primarily determined by the character of the transition between dry and wet seasons. This may be sufficient to account for differences in nutrient-cycling patterns between forests at different positions along the climatic spectrum for the type. Rand and Rand (1977) have shown how variable the onset of rain may be when compared from year to year in tropical areas. Adaptation to this variability may be a major feature of many tropical-forest systems; it may also be that the resilience of the system in relation to the stresses imposed by disturbance is at its weakest during the crucial period around the onset of rains.

In other systems, however, the efficiency of coupling may be enhanced by lengthening the period over which nutrient release occurs. Such a strategy might be thought to give greater stability to the nutrient cycles, and may be more characteristic of forest types in non-seasonal environments. Resource quality has been identified as a major regulating factor for nutrient release from decomposing plant litter. The high diversity of vegetational composition and structure of tropical forest results in the production, at litter fall, of a diverse input of organic materials. As these resources also commonly contain a wide spectrum of secondary metabolites, this presents an enormous diversity of resource types to the decomposer community. It may be hypothesized that the immediate consequence of this is a widened range of decomposition rates, which will lengthen the period over which nutrient release takes place. It should also have the effect of producing a high diversity in the decomposer biota, including a high degree of equivalence in the role played by different decomposers on apparently identical resources.

Temporal and spatial variations converge when consideration is given to the processes of gap formation and regeneration in the forest vegetation. Much attention has been given to the relationship of the physical environment to the latter process, but disturbance to nutrient fluxes within the system can also be seen as a potential factor influencing species replacement in gaps, and decomposition processes play a part in regulating these influences.

There is considerable evidence that vegetation regrowth after disturbance is influenced by microclimatic conditions affecting seed germination, seedling survival and tree growth (Whitmore, 1975; Hartshorn, 1980; Putz, 1983). But one may speculate that the process of gap formation and the change in soil temperature and moisture regimes which occur on the forest floor when the canopy is removed also provide a soil nutrient regime for regrowth vegetation different to that under undisturbed forest cover. The fall of a tree deposits an enormous amount of litter on the surface of the soil within the gap it creates. One component of this is high in resource quality and will decompose very rapidly, releasing substantial amounts of nutrients very soon after tree fall. Some of this nutrient will be available to the early colonizers of the gap, but will be competed for by the immobilization tendencies of the low-quality resources still present on the forest floor — that is, the fallen stems and branches. These woody materials, high in carbohydrate but low in nutrient content, tend

to "suck in" nutrient from the surrounding environment during the early stages of decay (Swift, 1977; Heal et al., 1982). As decomposition proceeds, however, this nutrient will once again be released to the soil to supply the needs of the plants in the later stages of succession. Adaptation to these fluctuations in nutrient availability may be one of the features leading to success in the process of colonization, and Janos (1980) has pointed out that the nature of mycorrhizal infection may also be of great significance here.

Furthermore, the changed quality and quantity of litter inputs from the regrowth vegetation will itself reflect and reinforce these changes in nutrient availability and physical environment within the colonization area. For instance, Coley (1983) has shown in Costa Rica that gap-colonizing species have less fibre, higher nitrogen and lower phenolic concentrations than shade-tolerant trees. Other studies have shown differences in leaf chemistry between colonizing species and mature-phase species and between sun and shade leaves in the same species (for instance, Newberry and De Foresta, 1985). It is well established that such differences will bring about variations in decomposition rate and, by implication, the pattern of nutrient release (Heath and Arnold, 1966; King and Heath, 1967), adding a further dimension to the pattern of events during re-closure of a tree-gap (Whitmore, 1982).

Thus the over-riding conclusion of this consideration of decomposition processes in tropical rain forests is the difficulty of either characterizing the biome in these terms or of making general distinctions between forest types. This difficulty derives, at least in part, from the absence of information on the variation between and within forest sites, and on those factors which are the main determinants of decomposition rate — the patterns of environment at various scales in space and time, the spectrum of resource qualities and the qualitative and quantitative nature of the decomposer community.

REFERENCES

Abe, T., 1979. Studies on the distribution and ecological role of termites in a lowland rain forest of West Malaysia. (2) Food and feeding habits of termites in Pasoh Forest Reserve. *Jpn. J. Ecol.*, 29: 121–135.
Abe, T., 1980. Studies on the distribution and ecological role of

termites in a lowland rain forest of West Malaysia. (4) The role of termites in the process of wood decomposition in Pasoh Forest Reserve. *Rev. Ecol. Biol. Sol.*, 17: 23–40.

Adis, J., 1981. Comparative ecological studies of the terrestrial arthropod fauna of Central Amazonian inundation forests. *Amazoniana*, 7: 87–173.

Adis, J., Furch, K. and Irmer, U., 1979. Litter production of a Central Amazonian black water inundation forest. *Trop. Ecol.*, 20: 236–245.

Anderson, J.M. and Ineson, P., 1984. Interactions between microorganisms and soil invertebrates in nutrient flux pathways of forest ecosystems. In: J.M. Anderson, A.D.M. Rayner and D.W.H. Walton (Editors), *Invertebrate–Microbial Interactions*. British Mycological Symposium 6, Cambridge Univ. Press, Cambridge, pp. 59–88.

Anderson, J.M. and Swift, M.J., 1983. Decomposition in tropical forest. In: S.L. Sutton, T.C. Whitmore and A.C. Chadwick (Editors), *Tropical Rain Forest: Ecology and Management*. Blackwell, Oxford, pp. 287–299.

Anderson, J.M. and Wood, T.G., 1984. Mound composition and soil modification by two soil-feeding termites (Termitinae: Termitidae) in a riparian Nigerian forest. *Pedobiologia*, 26: 77–82.

Anderson, J.M., Proctor, J. and Vallack, H.W., 1983. Ecological studies in four contrasting lowland rain forests in Gunung Mulu National Park, Sarawak. III. Decomposition processes and nutrient losses from leaf litter. *J. Ecol.*, 71: 503–528.

Anderson, J.V., Coleman, D.C. and Cole, C.V., 1981. Effects of saprotrophic grazing on net mineralisation. In: F.E. Clark and T. Rosswall (Editors), *Terrestrial Nitrogen Cycles*. Ecol. Bull (Stockholm), 33: 201–217.

Baillie, I.C. and Ashton, P.S., 1983. Some soil aspects of the nutrient cycle in mixed Dipterocarp forests in Sarawak. In: S.L. Sutton, T.C. Whitmore and A.C. Chadwick (Editors), *Tropical Rain Forest: Ecology and Management*. Blackwell, Oxford, pp. 347–356.

Beck, L., 1976. Zum Massenwechsel der Makro-Arthropodenfauna des Bodens in Ueberschwemmungswäldern des zentralen Amazonasgebietes. *Amazoniana*, 6: 1–20.

Bolin, B. and Cook, R.B., 1983. *The Major Biogeochemical Cycles and their Interactions*. (SCOPE 21) Wiley, New York, N.Y.

Bryant, J.P., Chapin III, F.S. and Klein, D.R., 1983. Carbon-nutrient balance of boreal plants in relation to vertebrate herbivory. *Oikos*, 40: 357–368.

Coley, P.D., 1983. Herbivory and defensive characteristics of tree species in lowland rainforest. *Ecol. Monogr.*, 53: 209–233.

Collins, N.M., 1980a. The habits and populations of terrestrial crabs (Brachyura: Gecarcinucoidea and Grapsoidea) in the Gunung Mulu National Park, Sarawak. *Zool. Meded.*, 55: 81–85.

Collins, N.M., 1980b. The distribution of soil macrofauna on the West range of Gunung (Mount) Mulu, Sarawak. *Oecologia*, 44: 263–275.

Collins, N.M., 1981. The role of termites in the decomposition of wood and leaf litter in the Southern Guinea Savanna of Nigeria. *Oecologia*, 51: 389–399.

Collins, N.M., 1983a. The utilisation of nitrogen resources by

termites (Isoptera) In: J.A. Lee, S. McNeill and I.H. Rorison (Editors), *Nitrogen as an Ecological Factor*. 22nd Symp. Brit. Ecol. Soc., Blackwell, Oxford, pp. 381–412.

Collins, N.M., 1983b. Termite populations and their role in litter removal in Malaysian rain forests. In: S.L. Sutton, T.C. Whitmore and A.C. Chadwick (Editors), *Tropical Rain Forest: Ecology and Management*. Blackwell, Oxford, pp. 311–325.

Cook, A.G., Critchley, B.R., Critchley, U., Perfect, T.J. and Yeadon, R., 1980. Effects of cultivation and DDT on earthworm activity in a forest soil in the humid sub-tropics. *J. Appl. Ecol.*, 17: 21–31.

Edwards, C.A. and Lofty, J.R., 1977. *Biology of Earthworms*. Chapman and Hall, London, 2nd ed., 333 pp.

Edwards, P.J., 1977. Studies of mineral cycling in a montane rain forest in New Guinea II. The production and disappearance of litter. *J. Ecol.*, 65: 971–992.

Edwards, P.J. and Grubb, P.J., 1977. Studies of mineral cycling in a montane rain forest in New Guinea I. The distribution of organic matter in the vegetation and soil. *J. Ecol.*, 65: 943–969.

Fittkau, E.J., 1983. Flow of nutrients in a large open system: the basis of life in Amazonia. *Environ. Supp.*, 5: 41–49.

Franken, M., Irmler, U. and Klinge, H., 1979. Litterfall in inundation, riverine and terra firme forests of Central Amazonia. *Trop. Ecol.*, 20: 225–235.

Frankland, J.C., 1982. Biomass and nutrient cycling by decomposer basidiomycetes. In: J.C. Frankland, J.N. Hedger and M.J. Swift (Editors), *Decomposer Basidiomycetes: Their Biology and Ecology*. Cambridge Univ. Press, Cambridge, pp. 241–262.

Gartlan, J.S., Newberry, D. McC., Thomas, D.W. and Waterman, P.G., 1985. Studies on the rain forest vegetation of Cameroun I. The role of phosphorus in species distribution in Korup Forest Reserve. *Vegetatio*, 65: 131–148.

Golley, F.B., 1983. Decomposition. In: F.B. Golley (Editor), *Tropical Rain Forest Ecosystems*. (Ecosystems of the World, 14A) Elsevier, Amsterdam, pp. 157–166.

Grime, J.P., 1977. Evidence for the existence of three primary strategies in plants and its relevance to ecological and evolutionary theory. *Am. Nat.*, 111: 1169–1194.

Grubb, P.J., 1977. Controls of forest growth and distribution on wet tropical mountains with particular reference to mineral nutrition. *Annu. Rev. Ecol. Syst.*, 8: 83–107.

Haines, B. and Foster, R.G., 1977. Energy flow through litter in a Panamanian forest. *J. Ecol.*, 65: 147–155.

Hartshorn, G.S., 1980. Neotropical forest dynamics. *Biotropica*, 12 (suppl.): 23–30.

Hayes, A.J., 1979. The microbiology of plant litter decomposition. *Sci. Progr. (Oxford)*, 66: 25–42.

Heal, O.W. and Maclean Jr., S.F., 1975. Comparative productivity in ecosystems — secondary productivity. In: W.H. van Dobben and R.H. Lowe-McConnell (Editors), *Unifying Concepts in Ecology*. Junk, The Hague, pp. 89–108.

Heal, O.W., Swift, M.J. and Anderson, J.M., 1982. Nitrogen cycling in United Kingdom forests: the relevance of basic ecological research. *Philos. Trans. R. Soc. London, Ser. B*, 296: 427–444.

Heath, G.W. and Arnold, M.K., 1966. Studies in leaf-litter

breakdown. II Breakdown rate of "sun" and "shade" leaves. *Pedobiologia*, 6: 238–243.

Heatwole, H., 1961. Analysis of the forest floor habitat with a structural classification of the litter of L layer. *Ecol. Monogr.*, 31: 267–283.

Herrera, R., Jordan, C.F., Klinge, H. and Medina, E., 1978a. Amazon ecosystems. Their structure and functioning with particular emphasis on nutrients. *Interciencia*, 3: 223–232.

Herrera, R., Merida, T., Stark, N. and Jordan, C.F., 1978b. Direct phosphorus transfer from leaf litter to roots. *Naturwissenschaften*, 65: 208–209.

Hubbell, S.R. and Foster, R.B., 1983. Diversity of canopy trees in a neotropical forest and implications for conservation. In: S.L. Sutton, T.C. Whitmore and A.C. Chadwick (Editors), *Tropical Rain Forest: Ecology and Management*. Blackwell, Oxford, pp. 25–41.

Hudson, H.J., 1968. The ecology of fungi on plant remains above the soil. *New Phytol.*, 67: 837–874.

Irmler, U., 1975. Ecological studies of the aquatic soil invertebrates in three inundation forests of Central Amazonia. *Amazoniana*, 5: 337–409.

Irmler, U., 1979. Considerations on structure and function of the "Central Amazonian Inundation Forest Ecosystem" with particular emphasis on selected soil animals. *Oecologia*, 43: 1–18.

Irmler, U. and Furch, K., 1979a. Weight, energy and nutrient changes during the decomposition of leaves in the emersion phase of Central-Amazonian inundation forests. *Pedobiologia*, 20: 118–130.

Irmler, U. and Furch, K., 1979b. Production, energy and nutrient turnover of the cockroach *Epilampra irmleri* Rocha e Silva & Aguiar, in Central-Amazonian inundation forests. *Amazoniana*, 6: 497–520.

Janos, D.P., 1980. Mycorrhiza influence in tropical succession. *Biotropica*, 12 (suppl.): 56–95.

Janzen, D.H. and Waterman, P.G., 1984. A seasonal census of phenolics, fibre and alkaloids in foliage of forest trees in Costa Rica: some factors influencing their distribution and relation to host selection by Sphingidae and Saturniidae. *Biol. J. Linn. Soc.*, 21: 439–454.

Jordan, C.F. and Herrera, R., 1981. Tropical rain forests: are nutrients really critical? *Am. Nat.*, 117: 167–180.

Jordan, C.F., Todd, R.L. and Escalante, G., 1979. Nitrogen conservation in a tropical rainforest. *Oecologia*, 39: 123–128.

King, H.G.C. and Heath, G.W., 1967. The chemical analysis of small samples of leaf material and the relationship between the disappearance and composition of leaves. *Pedobiologia*, 7: 192–197.

Kitazawa, Y., 1971. Biological regionality of the soil fauna and its function in forest ecosystem types. In: P. Duvigneaud (Editor), *Productivity of Forest Ecosystems*. Proc. Brussels Symp. Conserv., 4: 485–498.

Klinge, H., 1973. Biomasa y materia orgánica del suelo en el ecosistema de la pluriselva centro-amazónica. *Acta Cient. Venez.*, 24: 174–181.

Klinge, H., 1977. Preliminary data on nutrient release from decomposing leaf litter in a neotropical rain forest. *Amazoniana*, 6: 193–202.

Klinge, H. and Rodrigues, W.A., 1968. Litter production in an area of Amazonian Terra Firme forest. Part I. Litter-fall, organic carbon and total nitrogen contents of litter. *Amazoniana*, 1: 287–302.

Lavelle, P., 1983. The structure of earthworm communities. In: J.E. Satchell (Editor), *Earthworm Ecology: From Darwin to Vermiculture*. Chapman and Hall, London, pp. 449–466.

Lavelle, P., 1984. The soil system in the humid tropics. *Biol. Int.*, 9: 2–17.

Lee, K.E., 1967. Microrelief features in a humid tropical lowland area, New Guinea, and their relation to earthworm activity. *Aust. J. Soil Res.*, 5: 263–274.

Lee, K.E., 1983. Earthworms of tropical regions — some aspects of the ecology and relationships with soils. In: J.E. Satchell (Editor), *Earthworm Ecology: From Darwin to Vermiculture*. Chapman and Hall, London, pp. 179–194.

Loveless, A.R., 1962. Further evidence to support a nutritional interpretation of sclerophylly. *Ann. Bot. (London) New Ser.*, 26: 551–561.

Matsumoto, T. and Abe, T., 1979. The role of termites in the equatorial rain forest system of West Malaysia. (2) Leaf litter consumption on the forest floor. *Oecologia*, 38: 261–274.

Medway, Lord, 1972. Phenology of a tropical rain forest in Malaya. *Biol. J. Linn. Soc.*, 4: 117–146.

Meentmeyer, V., 1985. Climatic control of litter dynamics in tropical forests. In: K.C. Misra (Editor), *Jubilee Symp. Int. Society of Tropical Ecology*. Bhopal (in press).

Melillo, J.M. and Gosz, J.R., 1983. Interactions of biogeochemical cycles in forest ecosystems. In: B. Bolin and R.B. Cook (Editors), *The Major Biogeochemical Cycles and their Interactions*. Wiley, New York, N.Y., pp. 177–222.

Mooney, H.A., 1972. The carbon balance of plants. *Annu. Rev. Ecol. Syst.*, 3: 315–346.

Newberry, D. McC. and De Foresta, H., 1985. Herbivory and defence in pioneer, gap and understorey trees of tropical rainforest in French Guiana. *Biotropica*, 17: 238–244.

Newberry, D. McC. and Proctor, J., 1984. Ecological studies in four contrasting lowland rain forests in Gunung Mulu National Park, Sarawak IV, Associations between tree distribution and soil factors. *J. Ecol.*, 72: 475–493.

Novack, R.O. and Whittingham, W.F., 1968. Soil and litter microfungi of a maple-elm-ash floodplain community. *Mycologia*, 60: 776–787.

Nye, P.H., 1955. Some soil-forming processes in the humid tropics. IV. The action of the soil fauna. *J. Soil Sci.*, 6: 73–83.

Perfect, T.J., Cook, A.G., Critchley, B.R., Critchley, U., Davies, A., Moore, R.L., Russell-Smith, A.R., Swift, M.J. and Yeadon, R., 1979. The effect of DDT contamination on the productivity of a cultivated forest soil in the sub-humid tropics. *J. Appl. Ecol.*, 16: 705–721.

Phillipson, J., 1973. The biological efficiency of protein production by grazing and other land-based systems. In: J.G.W. Jones (Editor), *The Biological Efficiency of Protein Production*. Cambridge Univ. Press, Cambridge, pp. 217–235.

Poore, M.E.D., 1968. Studies in Malaysian rain forest. I. The forest on Triassic sediments in Jenka Forest Reserve. *J. Ecol.*, 56: 143–196.

Proctor, J., Anderson, J.M., Chari, P. and Vallack, H.W.,

1983a. Ecological studies in four contrasting lowland rain forests in Gunung Mulu National Park, Sarawak. I. Forest environment, structure and floristics. *J. Ecol.*, 71: 237–260.

Proctor, J., Anderson, J.M., Fogden, S.C.L. and Vallack, H.W., 1983b. Ecological studies in four contrasting lowland rain forests in Gunung Mulu National Park, Sarawak. II. Litterfall, litter standing crop and preliminary observations on herbivory. *J. Ecol.*, 71: 261–283.

Putz, F.F., 1983. Treefall pits and mounds, buried seeds and the importance of soil disturbance to pioneer trees on Barro Colorado Island, Panama. *Ecology*, 64: 1069–1074.

Rambelli, A., Persiani, A.M., Maggi, O., Lunghini, D., Onofri, S., Riess, S., Dowgiallo, G. and Puppi, G., 1983. *Comparative Studies on Microfungi in Tropical Ecosystems: Mycological Studies in South-western Ivory Coast Forests.* Report No. 1, MAB, UNESCO, Rome.

Rand, W. and Rand, S., 1977. The rainfall of Barro Colorado Island, Panama. *Act. 4 Symp. Int. Ecol. Trop.*, 1: 31–50.

Rees, C.J.C. 1983. Microclimate and the flying Hemipteran fauna of a primary lowland rain forest in Sulavesi. In: S.L. Sutton, T.C. Whitmore and A.C. Chadwick (Editors), *Tropical Rain Forest: Ecology and Management.* Blackwell, Oxford, pp. 121–136.

Sanchez, P.A., Gichuru, M.P. and Katz, L.B., 1982. Organic Matter in Major Soils of the Tropical and Temperate Regions. *Proc. 12th Int. Congress Soil Sci., New Delhi*, pp. 99–114.

Schlesinger, W.H., 1977. The carbon balance in terrestrial detritus. *Annu. Rev. Ecol. Syst.*, 8: 51–82.

Seastedt, T.R., 1984. The role of microarthropods in decomposition and mineralisation processes. *Annu. Rev. Entomol.*, 29: 25–46.

Stark, N.M. and Jordan, C., 1978. Nutrient retention by the root mat of an Amazonian rain forest. *Ecology*, 59: 434–437.

Sutton, S.L., Ash, C.P. and Grundy, A., 1983. The vertical distribution of flying insects in the lowland rain forest of Panama, Papua New Guinea and Brunei. *Zool. J. Linn. Soc.*, 78: 287–297.

Swift, M.J., 1976. Species diversity and the structure of microbial communities. In: J.M. Anderson and A. MacFadyen (Editors), *The Role of Aquatic and Terrestrial Organisms in Decomposition Processes.* Blackwell, Oxford, pp. 185–222.

Swift, M.J., 1977. The role of fungi and animals in the immobilisation and release of nutrient elements from decomposing branch-wood. In: U. Lohm and T. Persson (Editors), *Soil Organisms as Components of Ecosystems.* Proc. 6th Int. Coll. Soil Zool., Ecol. Bull. (Stockholm), 25: 193–202.

Swift, M.J., 1982. The basidiomycete role in forest ecosystems. In: J.C. Frankland, J.N. Hedger and M.J. Swift (Editors), *Decomposer Basidiomycetes: Their Biology and Ecology.* Cambridge Univ. Press, Cambridge, pp. 307–338.

Swift, M.J., 1984. Microbial diversity and decomposer niches. In: M.J. Klug and C.A. Reddy (Editors), *Current Perspec-tives in Microbial Ecology.* American Society for Microbiology, Washington, D.C., pp. 8–16.

Swift, M.J. and Boddy, L., 1984. Animal–microbial interactions in wood decomposition. In: J.M. Anderson, A.D.M. Rayner and D.W.H. Walton (Editors), *Invertebrate Microbial Interactions.* British Mycological Society Symp. 6, Cambridge Univ. Press, Cambridge, pp. 89–132.

Swift, M.J., Heal, O.W. and Anderson, J.M., 1979. *Decomposition in Terrestrial Ecosystems.* Blackwell, Oxford, 372 pp.

Swift, M.J., Russell-Smith, A. and Perfect, T.J., 1981. Decomposition and mineral-nutrient dynamics of plant litter in a regenerating bush-fallow in sub-humid tropical Nigeria. *J. Ecol.*, 69: 981–995.

Tanner, E.V.J., 1977. Four montane forests of Jamaica: a quantitative characterisation of the floristics, the soils and the foliar mineral levels and a discussion of the interrelations. *J. Ecol.*, 65: 883–918.

Tanner, E.V.J., 1980. Litterfall in montane rain forests of Jamaica and its relation to climate. *J. Ecol.*, 68: 833–848.

Tanner, E.V.J., 1981. The decomposition of leaf litter in Jamaican montane rain forests. *J. Ecol.*, 69: 263–276.

Tie, Y.L., Baillie, I.C., Phang, M.S. and Lim, C.P., 1979. *Soils of Gunung Mulu National Park.* Department of Agriculture, Sarawak.

Vitousek, P.M., 1982. Nutrient cycling and nutrient use efficiency. *Am. Nat.*, 119: 553–572.

Vitousek, P.M., 1984. Litterfall, nutrient cycling and nutrient limitation in tropical forests. *Ecology*, 65: 285–298.

Walker, T.W. and Syers, J.K., 1976. The fate of phosphorus during pedogenesis, *Geoderma*, 15: 1–19.

Waterman, P.G., 1983. Distribution of secondary metabolites in rain forest plants: towards an understanding of cause and effect. In: S.L. Sutton, T.C. Whitmore and A.C. Chadwick (Editors), *Tropical Rainforest: Ecology and Management.* Blackwell, Oxford, pp. 167–180.

Whitmore, T.C., 1975. *Tropical Rain Forests of the Far East.* Clarendon, Oxford, 282 pp.

Whitmore, T.C., 1982. On pattern and process in forests. In: E.I. Newman (Editor), *The Plant Community as a Working Mechanism.* Blackwell, Oxford, pp. 45–59.

Wicklow, D.T. and Carroll, G.C., 1981. *The Fungal Community: Its Organisation and Role in the Ecosystems.* Dekker, New York, N.Y., 710 pp.

Wood, T.G. and Sands, W.A., 1978. The role of termites in ecosystems. In: M.V. Brian (Editor), *Production Ecology of Ants and Termites.* Cambridge Univ. Press, Cambridge, pp. 245–292.

Wood, T.G., Johnson, R.A., Bacchus, S., Shittu, M.O. and Anderson, J.M., 1982. Abundance and distribution of termites (Isoptera) in a Riparian Forest in the Southern Guinea Savanna Vegetation Zone in Nigeria. *Biotropica*, 14: 25–39.

Wood, T.G., Johnson, R.A., and Anderson, J.M., 1983. Modification of soils in Nigerian savanna by soil-feeding *Cubitermes* (Isoptera: Termitidae). *Soil Biol. Biochem.*, 15: 575–579.

Chapter 32

DECOMPOSITION IN TROPICAL RAIN FORESTS COMPARED WITH OTHER PARTS OF THE WORLD

G. ESSER and H. LIETH

INTRODUCTION

The speed of decomposition of dead material in forests is seldom measured. It is obvious, however, that it differs widely among different forest types worldwide, and does so also in the tropics. Because of its importance, several attempts have been made to derive mathematical models to determine decay rates from environmental and biological parameters. In this volume the approaches of Meentemeyer (Ch. 31) have been used extensively. Recent assessment by Esser et al. (1982) have largely expanded our knowledge of global decomposition patterns, including those in the various tropical forest types.

We have therefore included a second paper on decomposition in this volume. This paper compares the decomposition of tropical rain-forest material in comparison to that in other biomes because only in this way one can fully understand the immensely faster decay under certain moist tropical conditions.

In ecosystems the standing crop of phytomass (P) (biomass and necromass) is balanced by the net primary productivity (NPP), the consumption by phytophages (E) and the amount of dead phytomass decomposed (LD):

$$\Delta P = NPP - E - LD \qquad (1)$$

In terrestrial systems consumption of phytophages is normally less than 5% (sometimes as low as 1%) of NPP so that by far the major part of the organic material produced is finally decomposed by the foodwebs of soil organisms such as animals, fungi, or micro-organisms. If steady-state conditions are assumed ($\Delta P = 0$), the amount of decomposed

material more or less equals the net primary productivity or fluctuates around its mean value.

The amount of material decomposed over a time period t_0 to t depends on the amount of dead material present (L) and the decomposition constant k for a given geographical location:

$$LD = L \left[1 - e^{-k(t-t_0)}\right] \qquad (2)$$

The decomposition constant k depends on the vector of environmental parameters of a given location such as temperature (T), precipitation (Pp), and others, and material parameters such as "woody" or "herbaceous".

$$k = f(T, Pp, w, h, \ldots) \qquad (3)$$

It is well known that in tropical rain-forest ecosystems the decomposition constant k is high except during times of low precipitation (dry month). Since net primary productivity (that is, the flux into the phytomass pool) is also high, the litter pool may nevertheless reach considerable amounts, at least during certain periods of the year. In this paper we analyse decomposition data from tropical rain-forest ecosystems in comparison with data from other regions of the world.

DATA ANALYSIS

Basically two different data sources were exploited to derive litter depletion rates — namely, measured rates and calculated rates. The values actually measured were inhomogenous because different methods were applied. Some problems of these methods are discussed by Edwards (1977).

We are now beginning a more detailed analysis of all litter decomposition studies.

Many authors calculate the depletion rate from measured litter production and litter pool data. The depletion rate (or depletion constant) is usually calculated by:

$$D = \frac{LP}{L_{OLD}} \cdot 100$$

in the case of continuous litter fall, and:

$$D = \frac{LP}{LP + L_{OLD}} \cdot 100$$

in the case of seasonal, discrete annual litter fall (see Jenny et al., 1949; Olson, 1963), where D is the annual depletion rate in percent, LP is the annual litter production and L_{OLD} is the minimum amount of litter on the ground just before litter fall begins.

These equations may lead to errors, especially when LP is large in comparison to L_{OLD} (Nye, 1961). Further errors of the method rise from the difficulties in separating the litter on the ground into herbaceous and woody material, and separating the litter fraction from organic material already decomposed like moder, mull, or peat.

Either method thus determines litter depletion rather than litter decomposition to inorganic compounds like carbon dioxide, water, and minerals, since it includes leaching of partly decomposed organic material as well as erosion processes by water, wind, and animal transport.

To make results of the various authors comparable we defined a depletion rate (D) (percent per year depletion of a given litter pool) as:

$$D = \frac{100}{2t_{1/2}} \tag{4}$$

with the half-life $t_{1/2} = \frac{\ln 2}{k}$

Thus the depletion constant k of eq. 2 is expressed by the depletion rate D:

$$k = \frac{2\ln 2}{100} D \tag{5}$$

Litter depletion data extracted from the literature (80 data points for herbaceous material and 13 data points for woody material) have been used to construct a regression model. Different

measurements at one geographical location were averaged to one value before incorporation into the regression procedure.

In Table 32.1, results of depletion of various materials under tropical humid conditions are compared with results from other tropical climates.

For the analysis of the data distribution with respect to temperature and precipitation, litter depletion values for herbaceous material were classified in temperature classes. Additional artificial data points were created by the logical assumption that for zero precipitation the depletion rate is also zero.

The data in Table 32.1 show highest depletion values over 400% at temperatures above 20°C and at precipitation values around 2000 mm. Higher precipitation seems to suppress litter depletion. The fact that an optimum precipitation level exists for litter decay is supported by the shift of the optimum range with temperature. When the initial decay rates are separated in blocks of 10°C the precipitation level for the maximal depletion rate declines with temperature (Fig. 32.1). The maximal depletion occurs in the lowest temperature class at 800 mm average annual precipitation, in the 10 to 20° class at 1500 mm, and in the 20 to 30° class at 1800 mm. The maximum values are 88, 182 and 465%, respectively, suggesting an exponential correlation with temperature (Fig. 32.2).

According to the data analysis it was assumed that: (1) depletion rates follow mean annual temperature as an exponential function; and (2) depletion rates related to average annual precipitation give an optimum function with sigmoid shaped ascent and descent.

A pair of equations was fitted to either woody and herbaceous litter depletion rates by Marquardt's least-squares method (Marquardt, 1963) (eqs. 6–11).

It was assumed that the lower depletion value calculated from either the temperature or precipitation equation predicts the average depletion rate for a given weather station. Thus our depletion model rests on the following system of equations (which is a parameterization of eqs. 3 and 5).

Depletion of woody material:

$$D_W = \min|D_{WT}, D_{WPp}| \tag{6}$$
$$D_{WT} = 2.67\, e^{0.0522\,(T+31.63)} - 2.51 \tag{7}$$

TABLE 32.1

Litter depletion data for fresh litter

Location	Mean annual temp. (°C)	Mean annual precipitation (mm)	D	Material	Reference
Australia Charleville grassland	21.0	501	50	leaves	Christie, 1979
Australia eucalyptus forest	20.5	1959	49	litter	Rogers and Westman, 1977
Columbia Calima rain forest	26.6	9123	169	litter	Jenny et al., 1949
Chinchina lawn	22.0	2770	120	leaves alfalfa medicago	Jenny et al., 1949
Chinchina tropical mountain forest	21.0	2770	113	leaves alfalfa medicago	Jenny et al., 1949
Chinchina mountain forest	21.0	2800	61	litter	Jenny et al., 1949
Costa Rica Diamantes lawn, forest	24.4	3007	181	leaves alfalfa medicago	Jenny et al., 1949
Turrialba mountain forest plantation	22.8	1870	161	leaves alfalfa medicago	Jenny et al., 1949
Ghana Kade semi-deciduous forest	25.9	1818	465	leaves	Nye, 1961
Guatemala Lago de Izabal humid successional forest	27.0	2400	325	leaves	Ewel, 1976
Jamaica Blue Mountains lower mountain rain forest	15.5	3115	68	leaves	Tanner, 1980
Blue Mountains lower mountain rain forest	15.6	1745	50	leaves	Tanner, 1980
Blue Mountains upper mountain rain forest	15.5	1745	46	leaves	Tanner, 1980
New Guinea Bismarck Range mountain forest	13.0	4000	123	leaves	Edwards, 1977
Bismarck Range mountain forest	13.0	4000	48	leaves	Edwards, 1977
Bismarck Range mountain forest	13.0	4000	71	wood	Edwards, 1977
Nigeria Olokemeji humid semi-deciduous rain forest	27.4	1327	269	leaves	Hopkins, 1966
Olokemeji humid semi-deciduous forest	27.4	1327	82	wood	Hopkins, 1966

TABLE 32.1 (*continued*)

Location	Mean annual temp. (°C)	Mean annual precipitation (mm)	*D*	Material	Reference
Olokemeji successional savanna	27.5	1268	220	leaves	Hopkins, 1966
Olokemeji successional savanna	27.5	1268	96	wood	Hopkins, 1966
Omo (Akilla) primeval evergreen rain forest	26.7	1787	236	leaves	Hopkins, 1966
Omo (Akilla) primeval evergreen rain forest	26.7	1787	20	wood	Hopkins, 1966
Ibadan seasonal rain forest	26.4	1230	273	litter	Madge, 1965
Puerto Rico subtropical dry forest	25.8	929	37	leaves	Lugo et al., 1978
subtropical dry forest	25.8	929	32	leaves	Lugo et al., 1978
subtropical dry forest	25.8	929	27	leaves	Lugo et al., 1978
subtropical dry forest	25.8	929	43	litter	Lugo et al., 1978
subtropical dry forest	25.8	929	33	litter	Lugo et al., 1978
subtropical dry forest	25.8	929	20	wood	Lugo et al., 1978
subtropical dry forest	25.8	929	15	wood	Lugo et al., 1978
El Verde mountain rain forest	19.5	3000	80	leaves	Wiegert and Murphy, 1970
El Verde mountain rain forest	19.5	3000	66	leaves	Wiegert and Murphy, 1970
El Verde mountain rain forest	19.5	3000	59	leaves	Wiegert and Murphy, 1970
El Verde mountain rain forest	19.5	3000	52	leaves	Wiegert and Murphy, 1970
El Verde mountain rain forest	19.5	3000	29	leaves	Wiegert and Murphy, 1970
Thailand Mt. Inthanon evergreen gallery forest	25.5	1409	866	litter	Ogawa et al., 1961
Mt. Inthanon temperate evergreen forest	19.5	1500	192	litter	Ogawa et al., 1961
Mt. Inthanon mixed savanna forest	27.0	1500	116	litter	Ogawa et al., 1961
Mt. Inthanon dipterocarp. – savanna forest	25.0	1500	85	litter	Ogawa et al., 1961
Mt. Inthanon Eragrostis grassland	21.4	1409	187	litter	Ogawa et al., 1961
Mt. Inthanon *Themeda* grassland	21.4	1409	74	litter	Ogawa et al., 1961

TABLE 32.1 (*continued*)

Location	Mean annual temp. (°C)	Mean annual precipitation (mm)	D	Material	Reference
Trinidad Northern Range seasonal rain forest	26.0	1800	175	leaves	Cornforth, 1970
Northern Range seasonal rain forest	26.0	1800	164	leaves	Cornforth, 1970
Zaire Lubumbashi Muhulu forest	20.3	1273	140	litter	Malaisse et al., 1970
Lubumbashi Miombo woodland	20.3	1273	111	litter	Malaisse et al., 1972

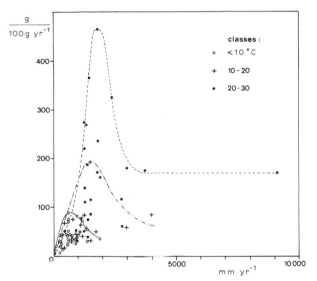

Fig. 32.1. Depletion rates of herbaceous litter separated in temperature blocks. The maxima of the three "Nyquist" lines shift with increasing temperature range to higher values of precipitation.

$$D_{WPp} = \left(\frac{27.8}{0.021 + e^{8.53 - 0.0095\,Pp}} + 712 \right)$$

$$\times \left(\frac{0.126}{1.51 + e^{0.003\,Pp - 4.65}} + 0.05 \right) \cdot 0.5(1 - e^{-0.001\,Pp})$$

$$(8)$$

Depletion of herbaceous material:

$$D_H = \min|D_{HT}, D_{HPp}| \qquad (9)$$
$$D_{HT} = 7.67\,e^{0.0926\,(T + 6.41)} + 17.06 \qquad (10)$$

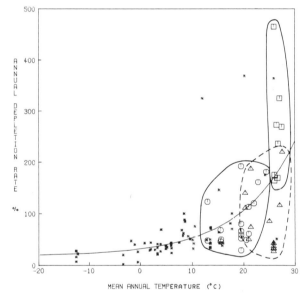

MEAN ANNUAL TEMPERATURE (°C)

Fig. 32.2. Influence of mean annual temperature (T) on depletion rates of fresh herbaceous litter (D_H). The rates are in % of the reported litter pool per year. The regression curve is calculated from the running means of 5°C classes by Marquardt's least-squares method. Values higher than 100% indicate depletion times shorter than 1 year. Squares: tropical rain-forest data; triangles: tropical savanna data; circles: tropical mountain forest data; stars: data from other regions.

$$D_{HPp} = \left(\frac{50}{0.0215 + e^{4.2 - 0.0053\,Pp}} + 670 \right)$$

$$\times \left(\frac{0.094}{0.7 + e^{0.0023\,Pp - 5.05}} + 0.076 \right) 0.64(1 - e^{-0.001\,Pp})$$

$$(11)$$

where D_W is depletion rate of woody material (percent of litter per year),

D_H is depletion rate of herbaceous material (percent per year),

T is mean annual temperature (°C), and

Pp is average annual precipitation (mm).

Other relevant data to verify the above results are data for soil organic carbon. This data pool is completely independent for it has been elaborated from soil-profile analyses published by FAO–Unesco (1974).

In Fig. 32.3 the percentage of soil organic carbon (according to FAO, 1974) of various soil profiles in the tropics (mean annual temperature above 20°C) is plotted against the average annual precipitation. The function that envelopes the carbon data has a maximum near 1800 mm of precipitation where the litter depletion is at its maximum (Fig. 32.1). This indicates that levels of soil organic carbon develop independently from those for the litter pool.

As a result it can be concluded that the data pools for "depletion rates" (Table 32.1) and "soil organic carbon" (Fig. 32.5) are consistent. The highest rates for litter depletion appear in the

moderate humid tropics near 1800 mm annual precipitation, which corresponds for example to large parts of central Amazonia and the Congo Basin. Higher and lower precipitation (that is, perhumid or moderately arid regions) reduce the depletion as does decreasing temperature.

In contrast, soil organic carbon in the mineral soil layers (A, B and C horizon) seems to be related to the decomposed amount of litter on ground.

LITTER-POOL MODEL

For the construction of a litter-pool model, the following assumptions were made:

(1) The vegetation is in a steady state, that is, changes in pool size are negligible within the period of investigation.

(2) Vegetation is in a natural state without agriculture, forestry or other influence of man.

(3) No harvesting of phytomass by men or herbivores occurs.

With these assumptions litter production is equal to the amount of decomposed litter (weight loss), and may be written:

$$NPP = NPP_W + NPP_H = LP_W + LP_H = LD_W + LD_H \qquad (12)$$

where:

NPP is net primary productivity,

NPP_W is share of woody material of total NPP,

NPP_H is share of herbaceous material of total NPP,

LP_W is litter production woody material,

LP_H is litter production herbaceous material,

LD_W is amount of woody litter decomposed, and

LD_H is amount of herbaceous litter decomposed.

The model was executed for a global set of 2433 grid elements of a 2.5° grid which covers the land areas except Antarctica. The basic data for mean annual temperature and average annual precipitation were elaborated from NCAR-Tape (1983), Walter and Lieth (1960), and Müller (1980, 1982). The data were recalculated for the mean elevation of each grid element.

The computed pattern of decomposition rates for woody material is plotted in Fig. 32.4. Obviously, rates higher than 50% per year initial decomposition of fresh woody material only occur

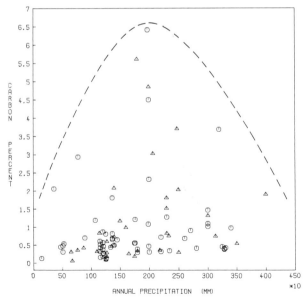

Fig. 32.3. Percentage of organic carbon (weighted means in A, B and C horizons) in various tropical soil profiles with mean annual temperatures above 20°C (data from FAO–Unesco, 1974). Triangles: soil under natural vegetation; circles: soil of cultivated areas.

Fig. 32.4. Global distribution of decomposition rates of woody litter (trunks, branches, twigs, large roots, etc.) as calculated by eqs. 6 to 8 in g 100 g^{-1} yr^{-1}. The map is based on a set of climatic data (mean annual temperature and average annual precipitation) for a $2.5°$ grid. Each plot sign represents the mean value of the related grid element.

Fig. 32.5. The litter pools shown on the map were calculated for woody and herbaceous material separately and then joined together to generate the map. High litter pool sizes are either due to high production of litter, or low depletion rates, or large share of slower decomposing wood on total litter production. The total amount of the global litter pool as presented by this map amounts to 168×10^9 t dry matter.

in humid tropical lowlands. Low temperatures in tropical mountain areas as well as seasonal dryness in semi-humid tropics strongly reduce decomposition.

For the calculation of the *NPP* we use the Hamburg Model which takes soil fertility into account, as well as temperature and precipitation (Esser et al., 1982; Esser, 1985). The partition factors herbaceous/woody used are published in the references cited and in Esser (1984).

The amount of litter decomposed either woody or herbaceous is connected to the litter pools and the depletion rates by eqs. 2, 5, and 6 to 11. The litter pool results are mapped in Fig. 32.5.

In tropical regions litter pools appear generally low. Comparatively high values are found in zones with semi-humid to moderately arid climates where productivity is seasonally high but decomposition is somewhat suppressed by a dry period when leaves are shed (see also Bourlière and Hadley, 1983). Such areas are, for example, the Caatinga in Brazil, the Gran Chaco (at least its northern part) in Argentina and Paraguay, and the savanna regions south of the Sahara and in Australia.

The model as used here does not consider human influences through burning, grazing, forest clearing, and agriculture which may reduce net primary productivity considerably, mainly in semi-humid and semi-arid regions. In semi-arid regions litter may be transported by wind and water which is also not considered here. Thus litter pools in those regions may be lower than proposed in Fig. 32.5.

REFERENCES

Bourlière, F. and Hadley, M., 1983. Present-day savannas: An overview. In: F. Bourlière (Editor), *Tropical Savannas*. (Ecosystems of the World, 13) Elsevier, Amsterdam, pp. 1–17.

Christie, E.K., 1979. Ecosystem processes in semiarid grasslands. II. Litter production, decomposition and nutrient dynamics. *Aust. J. Agric. Res.*, 30: 29–42.

Cornforth, I.S., 1970. Leaf-fall in a tropical rain forest. *J. Appl. Ecol.*, 7: 603–608.

Edwards, P.J., 1977. Studies of mineral cycling in a mountain rain forest in New Guinea. II. The production and disappearance of litter. *J. Ecol.*, 65: 971–992.

Esser, G., 1984. The significance of biospheric carbon pools and fluxes for atmospheric CO_2: A proposed model structure. *Progr. Biometeorol.*, 3: 253–294.

Esser, G., 1986. Der Kohlenstoff-Haushalt der Biosphäre, Struktur und erste Ergebnisse des Osnabrücker Biosphären Modells. *Veröff. Naturforsch. Ges. Emden 1814*, N.F., 7: 160 pp.

Esser, G., Aselmann, I. and Lieth, H., 1982. Modelling the carbon reservoir in the system compartment "litter". *Mitt. Geol. Paläontol. Inst. Univ. Hamburg, SCOPE/UNEP Sonderb.*, 52: 39–58.

Ewel, J.J., 1976. Litterfall and leaf decomposition in a tropical forest succession in eastern Guatemala. *J. Ecol.*, 64: 971–992.

FAO–Unesco, 1974. *Soil Map of the World, Vols. I–X.* Paris.

Hopkins, B., 1966. Vegetation of the Olokemeji forest reserve Nigeria. IV. The litter and soil with special reference to their seasonal changes. *J. Ecol.*, 54: 687–703.

Jenny, H., Gessel, S.P. and Bingham, F.T., 1949. Comparative study of decomposition rates of organic matter in temperate and tropical regions. *Soil Sci.*, 68: 417–432.

Lieth, H. and Whittaker, R.H. (Editors), 1975. *Primary Productivity of the Biosphere*. Springer, New York, N.Y., 339 pp.

Lugo, A.E., Gonzalez-Liboy, J.A., Cintron, B. and Dugger, K., 1978. Structure, productivity, and transpiration of a subtropical dry forest in Puerto Rico. *Biotropica*, 10: 278–291.

Madge, D.S., 1965. Leaf fall and litter disappearance in a tropical forest. *Pedobiologia*, 5: 273–288.

Malaisse, F., Malaisse-Mousset, M. and Bulaimu, J., 1970. Contribution à l'étude de l'écosystème forêt dense sèche (muhulu), Note 1: Phénologie de la défoliation. *Trav. Serv. Sylv. Pisc. Univ. Off. Congo Lubumbashi*, 9: 1–11.

Malaisse, F., Alexandre, J., Freson, R., Goffinet, G. and Malaisse-Mousset, M., 1972. The Miombo ecosystem: A preliminary study. In: F. Golley and P. Golley (Editors), *Tropical Ecology*. Univ. Georgia Press, Athens, Ga., pp. 363–405.

Marquardt, D.W., 1963. An algorithm for least-squares estimation of non-linear parameters. *J. Soc. Ind. Appl. Math.*, 2: 431–441.

Müller, M.J., 1980. *Handbuch ausgewählter Klimastationen der Erde*. Forschungsstelle Bodenerosion Mertesdorf, Univ. Trier, 2nd ed., 346 pp.

Müller, M.J., 1982. *Selected Climatic Data for a Global Set of Standard Stations for Vegetation Science*. (Tasks for Vegetation Science, 5) Junk, The Hague, 306 pp.

NCAR, National Center for Atmospheric Research, 1983. *TD-9645 Tape Documentation (Climatic Data Research)*. Boulder, Colo.

Nye, P.H., 1961. Organic matter and nutrient cycles under moist tropical forest. *Plant Soil*, 13: 333–346.

Ogawa, H., Yoda, K. and Kira, T., 1961. A preliminary survey on the vegetation of Thailand. *Nature Life South-East Asia*, 1: 21–157.

Olson, J.S., 1963. Energy storage and the balance of producers and decomposers in ecological systems. *Ecology*, 44: 322–331.

Rogers, R.W. and Westmann, W.E., 1977. Seasonal nutrient dynamics of litter in a subtropical Eucalypt forest, North Stradbroke Island. *Aust. J. Bot.*, 25: 47–58.

Tanner, E.V.J., 1980. Studies on the biomass and productivity in a series of montane rain forests in Jamaica. *J. Ecol.*, 68: 573–588.

Walter, H. and Lieth, H., 1960. *Klimadiagramm Weltatlas.* Fischer, Jena.

Wiegert, R.G. and Murphy, P., 1970. Effect of season, species and location on the disappearance rate of leaf litter in a Puerto Rican rain forest. In: H.T. Odum (Editor), *A Tropical Rain Forest*. Clearinghouse for Federal Scientific and Technical Inf., National Bureau of Standards, Oak Ridge, Tenn., pp. 101–104.

Chapter 33

THE EXPLOITATION OF THE AFRICAN RAIN FOREST AND MAN'S IMPACT[1]

R.M. LAWTON

INTRODUCTION

This chapter is confined to a discussion on the exploitation of the Guineo-Congolian rain forest as defined by White (1983), disregarding the montane forests. Most of the forest occurs below an altitude of 1000 m. The forest canopy is at least 30 m high, with some trees attaining a height of 50 to 60 m. Lianes or climbers are a feature of the forest. General descriptions of the various forest types are given by Hamilton (Ch. 8) and White (1983).

During January and February a hot desiccating wind, known as the harmattan, blows from the Sahara and reaches the rain forest of West Africa. The humidity within the forest forces the harmattan to rise. Further east in the Zaïre basin a dry wind from the Ethiopian Highlands blows over the rain forest, but this wind is not as severe as the harmattan. The forest plays a protective role in mitigating the effects of the dry hot winds that blow from the arid regions.

METHODS OF EXPLOITATION

The principal methods of exploitation are as follows: (1) the exploitation of timber wealth of the forest for export; (2) clearing patches of forest for the cultivation of subsistent agricultural crops; (3) the replacement of the natural forest with economic tree crops; and (4) the collection of minor forest resources of importance to the local population.

THE HISTORY OF THE EXPLOITATION FOR TIMBER

For nearly a century the valuable timber trees of the forest have been exploited for export. The main species include the African mahoganies, for instance species of the genera *Khaya* and *Entandrophragma*, and other valuable timbers, such as *Aucoumea klaineana*, *Chlorophora excelsa*, *Pericopsis elata*, *Terminalia ivorensis*, *T. superba*, and *Triplochiton scleroxylon*. Recently many more species are being utilized (Oseni and Abayomi, 1972; Lawton, 1978; Hall and Swaine, 1981).

Timber concessions were made by the tribal "owners" of the forest, granting a lease of timber rights over a specified area to a large timber firm. A payment was made for the concession, and royalties were paid for each tree that was felled and utilized (Logan, 1947). The trees were felled by axe (Fig. 33.1) and were sometimes converted into sawn timber by gangs of pit-sawyers (Fig. 33.2) in the forest. Alternatively the logs were manually hauled on a sled along an extraction path (Figs. 33.3 and 33.4) for a distance of anything up to 2.4 km, to the nearest track where they could be loaded on to a lorry for transportation to the railhead, or for floating down a river. Manual exploitation and extraction was in use up to about 30 to 40 years ago (Logan, 1947) and, although it was expensive, only the accessible parts of the forest were exploited and a minimum amount of disturbance and damage was caused.

With the advent of mechanical methods, bulldozers are used to clear extraction routes and heavy caterpillar tractors haul the logs out to lorry-loading sites. The axe has been replaced by the chain saw, so it is now much easier and quicker to fell trees and clear areas of forest. Much more disturbance, destruction and compaction of the soil is caused by mechanical methods than by the

_____
[1]Chapter completed in 1984.

Fig. 33.1. Felling of mahogany by axe (Ghana, Gold Coast).

Fig. 33.2. Pit-sawing in the high forest (Ghana, Gold Coast).

former manual methods, and of course machinery can penetrate and open up any part of the forest.

Most countries have a written statement of forest policy and forest legislation. During the colonial era forest reserves were established under the protection of the forest law, and many of them are still maintained. The timber concessions that covered land outside the forest estate (forest reserves), have now been largely exploited for their timber wealth, and the construction of extraction routes have opened them up for other forms of land-use.

The large timber trees that were measured half a century ago in the Akure Forest Reserve, in Nigeria (Jones, 1948; Lawton, 1978), where eleven specimens of *Entandrophragma cylindricum* with girths of over 366 cm were recorded, or some of the many examples of large trees given by Taylor (1960), such as a specimen of *E. cylindricum* felled in Bobiri Forest Reserve, Ghana, with a girth of nearly 400 cm at the felling point, a merchantable bole of 25 m and a total height of 57 m, or the trees enumerated by Pierlot (1966) in the forests of Zaïre, are now extremely rare.

Timber exploitation may have led to the loss of some of the valuable genotypes that produced such large trees. It is therefore necessary to initiate a plant breeding programme to select the best genotypes from the existing growing stock. Successful methods of tissue culture have been developed for tropical forest trees, particularly *Triplochiton scleroxylon* and *Terminalia* spp. (Longman et al., 1977).

THE MANAGEMENT OF THE FOREST

There is a prevalent view that tropical forests are too difficult to manage, and therefore their timber wealth should be exploited and they should eventually be converted to other forms of land-use. Certainly much of the forest land outside the forest reserves will be required for the production of food and other crops, but the forest reserves must be managed for the production of a sustained yield of valuable timber trees and not treated as a wasting

Fig. 33.3. Manual haulage. The log is hauled on a crude sled (Ghana, Gold Coast; Logan, 1947).

Fig. 33.4. The extraction path of corrugated poles for manual haulage. (Ghana, Gold Coast; Logan, 1947).

asset. The forests are part of the renewable capital wealth of tropical Africa. Fortunately there are signs that there is a renewed interest in the management, ecology and regeneration of tropical forest (Kio, 1976; Aweto, 1981a, b, c; Swaine and Hall, 1983), and every effort should be made to encourage this trend.

Natural regeneration

Where the stocking of natural timber trees is more than one per hectare, it may be possible to obtain natural regeneration. It will be necessary to acquire a knowledge of the autecology of the timber species and the dynamic ecology of patterns within the natural forest, and then to use this knowledge to manipulate the canopy in order to obtain natural regeneration of the valuable timber species (Lawton, 1981).

Such knowledge can only be acquired by intensive field observations. In the 1920s and 30s some silvicultural experiments were carried out by Kennedy (1935) in Nigeria. An area of c. 0.8 ha was cleared around the stumps of exploited trees, but regeneration failed to colonize the gaps. It was decided to attempt to establish natural regeneration around mature trees that were still below the exploitable girth limit (240 cm). The selected trees were kept under observation until they were seen to be in flower. The undergrowth, climbers, and some of the understorey trees were then cut, opening up a gap of c. 0.8 ha. The felled material was removed from the vicinity of the parent tree

and left to dry a little before burning. The direction of the prevailing wind was noted during seed-fall, and the gap was enlarged to provide a natural seed bed. The experiment was successful; natural regeneration of *Triplochiton scleroxylon*, a light-demander, was obtained. This species was in seed just before the harmattan, the dry wind that blows from the north, and the young seedlings required light overhead shade to protect them from desiccation. The herbaceous ground flora of the forest provided protection from the harmattan, and after the harmattan had ceased the herbaceous plants were removed by weeding. The seedlings of *T. scleroxylon* were thinned to a density of 1 per square metre, and later a second thinning reduced the density to 1 per four square metres. Where natural regeneration had failed, seed or transplants were dibbled into the gaps.

The silvicultural experiments by Kennedy (1935), and similar ones by MacGregor (1934), were successful partly because they were based on a detailed knowledge of a particular forest stand, and on field observations and supervision.

As large areas of forest were exploited in the 1940s, it became impossible to apply intensive methods of management, so it was decided to try the Tropical Shelterwood System (TSS) in West Africa. The aim of the TSS is to open the canopy and establish natural regeneration of the desired species before exploitation. The objective is to let sufficient light on to the forest floor to obtain regeneration, but not to encourage a dense growth of lianes and weeds. Lianes or climbers, particularly *Acacia pinnata* and *A. ataxacantha*, are light-demanders and quickly colonize gaps. They may form part of the natural succession back to high forest (Jones, 1950, 1956). A gradual opening up of the canopy may favour tree growth at the expense of climbers.

A series of operations was laid down and amended in the light of this experience (Lancaster, 1961). Treatment started with cutting of climbers six years before exploitation. This was followed by a gradual removal of understorey trees by poisoning, and a second cutting of climbers. Weeding or freeing any natural regeneration followed. After exploitation there was a series of cleaning and weeding operations. Details are given in reviews by Baur (1964) and Neil (1981). In some forests TSS has been successful; Gutzwiller (1956) reported satisfactory regeneration of *Mansonia altissima* and *Entandophragma* spp. seven years after TSS treatment in the Bobiri Forest Reserve, Ghana, but there also were many failures. Competition from fast-growing climbers and weed growth suppressed regeneration. The TSS has now been abandoned in most countries.

It is unsatisfactory to apply a routine system of management to a forest that requires individual and intensive management techniques. The forest is floristically diverse and has a complex structure; each stand is unique. Seasonal climatic factors may vary, so management prescriptions must be flexible. Some computer programmes have been designed to assist in the management of tropical forests, but how can a computer programme predict the chance availability of seed to colonize a gap in the forest canopy following exploitation, or predict an infestation of pests that may destroy the seed of a forest dominant in a particular season? Only foresters working in the field can tackle these problems.

A modified selection system has been practised in Ghana (Baidoe, 1970, 1972). The aim is to increase the survival rate and growth of immature valuable timber trees. Only forests with a stocking of *c*. 22 immature (200 cm girth) merchantable trees per hectare are treated. Climbers and unwanted trees are felled to free the valuable species from competition. The forest is exploited on a 15-year felling cycle, but there is no provision for the establishment of natural regeneration under the selection system, and the system has now been abandoned (Hall and Swaine, 1981).

It is possible that natural regeneration may occur without any treatment. Onyeagocha (1962) reported a high stocking of valuable timber trees 40 years after exploitation in the Benin forest of Nigeria; however, there were also areas of climber tangles in this forest.

Artificial regeneration

Where the forest is poorly stocked with immature timber trees, it will be necessary to enrich it by some form of artificial regeneration. Line planting has been tried, but the young trees were either destroyed by browsing animals, or suppressed by weeds or shade. Rarely has the method succeeded.

A modification of the Anderson group method (Anderson, 1951) was tried at Yangambi in Zaïre (Dawkins, 1955). A sample plot of 5×5 m was completely cleared and planted or sown at a spacing of 1×1 m. The central nine plants in the group of twenty-five were kept free of weeds and climbers, and the edge of the group was weeded for the first few years. Eventually one of the central trees will become dominant and occupy the gap. The system has been successful; the groups were revisited in 1975, and well-grown timber trees were found in many of them (R. Pierlot, pers. commun., 1975). The size of the gap, or group, can be modified according to the structure of the natural forest. The system simulates the natural gaps that occur in the canopy when a mature or over-mature tree dies. Skorupa and Kasenene (1984) have studied the pattern of natural treefall in Uganda, and have suggested how their observations could be applied to the management of tropical forests.

Agri-silviculture or the taungya system has been practised for many years in West Africa. A farmer, or group of farmers, or a village, is allocated a block of forest in a forest reserve, for clearing and cultivation. As soon as the area is cleared the Forestry Department plants out saplings of valuable timber trees during the period of cultivation, which may cover two, three or more years. Once the trees are established and their crowns begin to form a light canopy, cultivation will cease, and the cultivator will be allocated another block. The system works well where there is a shortage of land for cultivation outside the forest reserves. The cultivators are then prepared to accept the conditions laid down by the Forestry Department.

Bananas or plantains are a good nurse crop for trees, so are maize and sorghum, but root crops like cassava, yams and sweet potatoes are unsatisfactory because harvesting may damage the tree roots. The light-demanders *Terminalia ivorensis*, *T. superba* and *Triplochiton scleroxylon*, will colonize fallow land following cultivation, and they are ideal species for raising under the taungya system. In Zaïre *T. superba* has been successfully raised in banana taungyas (Dawkins, 1955). The development of the taungya system in Nigeria has been reviewed by Olawoye (1975).

Young saplings of the African mahoganies, *Khaya* spp. and *Entandrophragma* spp., require light shade, but once they become large saplings, 3 to 4 m tall, they require freedom from overhead shade (Jones, 1956). They can be raised under the taungya system, particularly if plantains are used as the agricultural crop. If the mahoganies are given sufficient light they will grow rapidly through the middle-girth classes and reach the canopy — for instance, *E. cylindricum*, at Sapoba in Nigeria, reached girths of 122 to 125 cm in 16 years, and *Khaya ivorensis* attained girths of 267 to 305 cm in about 36 years (Onyeagocha, 1962).

Some timber trees can be grown as a plantation crop, particularly the light-demanders, such as *Chlorophora excelsa*, *Terminalia ivorensis*, *T. superba* and *Triplochiton scleroxylon*, but they should be grown at a wide spacing so that the natural secondary forest species can colonize the spaces between them. Monocultures may not thrive in the tropical forest environment. They are vulnerable to pests and diseases. In Ghana, monocultures of *Terminalia ivorensis* began to die before they reached the age of 30 years (Ofosu-Asiedu and Cannon, 1976), and research by CTFT and Orstom has shown that a leaf extract from *T. ivorensis* inhibits nitrogen mineralization in the soil (UNESCO, 1978, p. 457). This suggests that some species must be grown in mixed stands, but others, like the pioneer colonizers *Musanga cecropioides* and *Trema orientalis*, will grow naturally in pure stands (compare Hall and Swaine, 1981).

The valuable timber tree *Aucoumea klaineana* will grow in pure plantations; it occurs in dense natural stands following cultivation. It has been established on well-chosen sites in Gabon (Catinot, 1978). The silvicultural treatment for the establishment of *A. klaineana* plantations following logging operations is given by Catinot: (1) suppression of all trees less than 35 to 40 cm diameter at breast height; (2) progressive destruction of all other trees by girdling or poisoning; (3) planting of *A. klaineana* at 4 × 4 m (or 5 × 4 m); (4) manual weeding 2 to 3 times a year for 5 to 6 years so that natural secondary forest regrowth is allowed to surround the young trees but not to overtop them; (5) thinning in one or two operations at 10 to 12 years, leaving 100 to 120 stems per hectare; and (6) harvesting at 45 to 50 years when the trees will have a diameter of 70 to 75 cm.

THE EXPLOITATION OF THE FOREST FOR THE CULTIVATION OF AGRICULTURAL CROPS

In the past when the human population was low, only small patches of forest about one hectare in extent were felled by axe and cultivated for subsistence agricultural crops. The patches were cultivated for one or two years, and then abandoned because the competition from luxuriant weeds and climbers made it too difficult to continue to cultivate. It was easier to clear a new patch than to try to compete with the weed growth. Under this system of shifting cultivation the abandoned land was rapidly recolonized by forest species.

Secondary forest regrowth, or forest fallow, restores the organic matter content, mineral nutrients and structure to the soil. Even after as short a period as ten years under forest fallow, the organic matter content of the top 10 cm of soil is 78% of the organic matter content of a natural forest soil (Aweto, 1981b). Unfortunately, due to the ever increasing human population pressure, particularly the increase in large urban communities, there is a great demand for the production of food. Land is only allowed to rest under natural forest fallow for a period of 5 to 7 years in parts of Nigeria. This period is too short to restore soil fertility, therefore the agricultural yields decline. So, more forest needs to be cleared, and the introduction of the chain saw, that has now replaced the axe, makes it easier and quicker to clear the forest.

In some cases planted fallow crops are introduced to restore soil fertility and structure. Leguminous crops like cowpea (*Vigna unguiculata*), pigeon pea (*Cajanus indicus*), or the winged

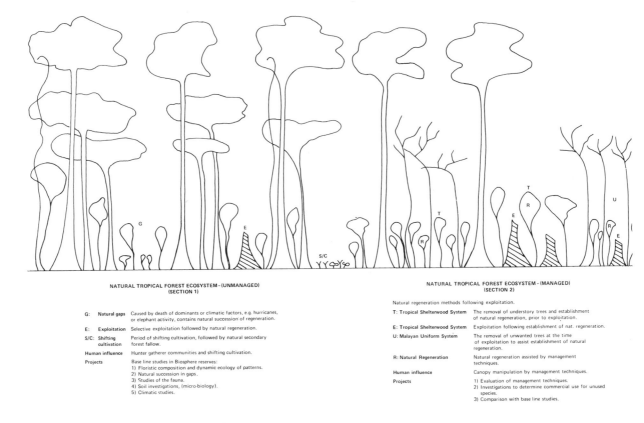

Fig. 33.5. MAB Project 1: Schematic diagram illustrating scientific content (biosphere reserves sited throughout the profile for comparative studies).

bean (*Psophocarpus tetragonolobus*), will restore organic matter and add nitrogen to the soil, as well as providing an edible crop.

It has been suggested that the tree *Gmelina arborea* should be grown as a fallow crop; it would also provide timber and fuel during the fallow phase (Kio, 1972). *Cassia siamea* has been grown as a fuel crop, and could form part of an agricultural cycle. Trees grown as agricultural fallow, even if they are used as a source of fuel, should not be considered as part of the forest estate which must be reserved for the production of commercially valuable timber trees.

Good yields of maize have been obtained from the same site for a number of years by the use of mulching with crop residues and weeds, and minimum or zero tillage (Rockwood and Lal, 1974). It is recommended that mulching techniques should form part of the agricultural system in the humid tropics.

Monocultures are susceptible to attacks by pests

and diseases. It has been demonstrated that multiple or mixed cropping will reduce the incidence of attacks by pests and diseases (Bradfield, 1969). Therefore a combination of mulching and mixed cropping is recommended, and if this can be combined with a satisfactory agricultural fallow crop, preferably a leguminous crop, then this should take the pressure off the demand for more forest land for the production of food crops.

THE REPLACEMENT OF THE FOREST BY ECONOMIC TREE CROPS

Following the opening up of the forest for timber extraction, the cultivators move in quickly and establish cacao (*Theobroma cacao*) plantations. In fact they have been known to move in before the contractors have had time to remove all the timber, and they then claim compensation for any young cacao plants damaged during timber extraction. The cacao plants are raised with food

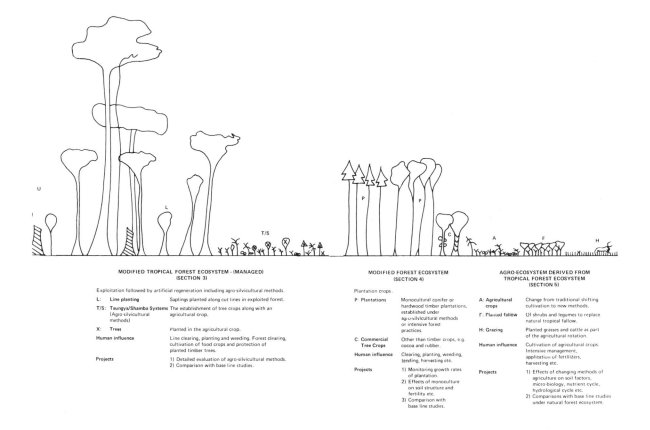

The following information appears below the figure:

MODIFIED TROPICAL FOREST ECOSYSTEM - (MANAGED)
(SECTION 3)

Exploitation followed by artificial regeneration including agro-silvicultural methods.

L:	Line planting	Saplings planted along cut lines in exploited forest.
T/S:	Taungya/Shamba Systems (Agro-silvicultural methods)	The establishment of tree crops along with an agricultural crop.
X:	Trees	Planted in the agricultural crop.
	Human influence	Line clearing, planting and weeding. Forest clearing, cultivation of food crops and protection of planted timber trees.
	Projects	1) Detailed evaluation of agro-silvicultural methods. 2) Comparison with base line studies.

MODIFIED FOREST ECOSYSTEM
(SECTION 4)

Plantation crops.

P:	Plantations	Monocultural conifer or hardwood timber plantations, established under agro-silvicultural methods or intensive forest practices.
C:	Commercial Tree Crops	Other than timber crops, e.g. cocoa and rubber.
	Human influence	Clearing, planting, weeding, tending, harvesting etc.
	Projects	1) Monitoring growth rates of plantation. 2) Effects of monoculture on soil structure and fertility etc. 3) Comparison with base line studies.

AGRO-ECOSYSTEM DERIVED FROM
TROPICAL FOREST ECOSYSTEM
(SECTION 5)

A:	Agricultural crops	Change from traditional shifting cultivation to new methods.
F:	Planted fallow	Of shrubs and legumes to replace natural tropical fallow.
H:	Grazing	Planted grasses and cattle as part of the agricultural rotation.
	Human influence	Cultivation of agricultural crops. Intensive management, application of fertilizers, harvesting etc.
	Projects	1) Effects of changing methods of agriculture on soil factors, micro-biology, nutrient cycle, hydrological cycle etc. 2) Comparisons with base line studies under natural forest ecosystem.

crops in a form of the taungya system. Cacao plantations grown under light forest shade are healthier than those that are grown where the forest has been completely removed.

The oil palm (*Elaeis guineensis*) is grown in large plantations, particularly in Nigeria. Kola (*Cola acuminata*) and *Citrus* spp. are grown on a smaller scale. *Gmelina arborea*, *Cassia siamea* and *Eucalyptus* spp. are grown as plantations to meet the demand for fuel, either as firewood or charcoal, by the expanding human population.

All this land has been taken out of the natural forest ecosystem, and out of the agricultural cycle, but it does of course provide an economic crop for the benefit of the local population. So, in fact, does the timber wealth of the forest.

THE COLLECTION OF MINOR FOREST RESOURCES

Although the tropical forest existed long before the present inhabitants moved into the region, the forest has become part of the national heritage and culture of the people. The forest is in fact part of the world heritage, and the present-day inhabitants are really the guardians, who should ensure that the forest is maintained in perpetuity for the benefit of future generations. This does not mean that it should not be utilized; of course it must be utilized, but it must not be destroyed.

The forest is an important source of protein for the local population in the form of small mammals, snails and caterpillars. The giant or pouched rat (*Cricetomys gambianus*), a forest species, is now being raised successfully in Nigeria for consumption (Ajayi, 1974a, b). Leaves, fruits, fungi, honey, gums, resins, drugs, dyes and medicine are obtained from the natural forest. All these natural resources are taken for granted by the local population, and their value is often only appreciated when they become scarce or are unobtainable. It is clear that the destruction of the forest leads to a lowering of the quality of life of the local population.

HUMAN IMPACT ON THE FOREST

The impact of human activities on tropical forest ecosystems, with particular reference to increasing human population pressure, is the theme of the UNESCO Man and the Biosphere Programme (MAB) Project No. 1, "Ecological effects of increasing human activities on tropical and subtropical forest ecosystems". The scientific content of the project is clearly illustrated in a schematic diagram (Fig. 33.5), reproduced from UNESCO-MAB report series No. 16 (1974).

It is recommended that biosphere reserves should be created in areas of natural tropical forest, and the following base-line studies should be undertaken: (1) a detailed study of the floristic composition of the forest, with particular reference to dynamic ecology and patterns within the forest ecosystem; (2) investigations into the succession and natural regeneration in gaps within the forest canopy following timber extraction, or death of the canopy dominants through natural or other causes; (3) a study of the natural fauna of the forest; (4) a study of the physical and chemical properties of the soil, including an investigation of the soil micro-fauna or flora, with particular reference to the dynamic ecology of earthworms, termites, mites, other arthropods, fungi, bacteria, etc. and their role in the nutrient cycle; and (5) a study of the climate and the micro-climate of the forest environment, including the hydrological cycle. The baseline studies are discussed in MAB report series No. 16.

The impact of various management techniques following exploitation for timber, or the conversion of the forest to other forms of land-use (modified ecosystems) — conversion to agricultural systems, or to monoculture tree crops — can then be compared with the baseline studies. The results of the comparative studies can be used to guide the future management of the tropical forests.

There are a number of social, political, economic and ecological factors which must be considered. An area of natural forest is traditionally considered to be a piece of land available for development. If the wishes of the local community are considered, it is almost certain that the remaining areas of natural forest will ultimately be cleared and converted to agricultural land, just as the natural woodland has been cleared in the temperate regions of the world. But climatic conditions are such that as much as possible of the forest cover should be maintained in the humid tropics.

The reason is that apart from timber wealth the forest is of ecological importance: water catchments, particularly in hilly country, must remain under forest cover in order to check soil erosion following the heavy tropical storms. The physical presence of the forest checks surface run-off, and enables the rain water to penetrate the soil and to feed the water table.

The forest also provides protection from the desiccating winds of the harmattan, without which it would be difficult to grow crops like cacao, or some other agricultural crops.

Certainly the increase in human population is bound to lead to an increasing demand for agricultural land. It is therefore necessary to increase the productivity of the existing agricultural land derived from the forest, by the introduction of the improved methods of agriculture that have already been discussed.

To safeguard the remaining patches of forest the central government must have control over the forest estate, regardless of whether it is state-owned or tribally owned. This control may lead to unpopularity and there is a risk that the forest may be used for political gain, — that is, forest areas could be released for cultivation in return for political support. However, since the forest is part of the renewable natural wealth of the country, it should be above the sphere of party politics.

ACKNOWLEDGEMENTS

I wish to thank the Director of the Land Resources Development Centre for permission to use the facilities provided by the library, also the Editor of the Commonwealth Forestry Association for permission to use Mr. Logan's photographs (Figs. 33.3 and 33.4). UNESCO kindly gave permission for the reproduction of Fig. 33.5 from UNESCO-MAB Report No. 16.

REFERENCES

Ajayi, S.S., 1974a. Giant rats for meat and some taboos. *Oryx*, 12: 379–380.
Ajayi, S.S., 1974b. Caging and breeding the African giant rat (*Cricetomys gambianus*). *J. Inst. Anim. Tech.*, 25: 75–81.

Anderson, M.L., 1951. Space group planting and irregularity in stand structure. *Emp. For. Rev.*, 30(4): 328–341.

Aweto, A.O., 1981a. Secondary succession and soil fertility restoration in south-western Nigeria. I. Succession. *J. Ecol.*, 69: 600–607.

Aweto, A.O., 1981b. Secondary succession and soil fertility restoration in south-western Nigeria. II. Soil fertility restoration. *J. Ecol.*, 69: 609–614.

Aweto, A.O., 1981c. Secondary succession and soil fertility restoration in south-western Nigeria. III. Soil and vegetation inter-relationships. *J. Ecol.*, 69: 951–963.

Baidoe, J.F., 1970. The selection system as practised in Ghana. *Com. For. Rev.*, 49: 159–165.

Baidoe, J.F., 1972. The management of the natural forests of Ghana. In: *7th World Forestry Congress* (Buenos Aires, Argentina). Congrès Forestier Mondial, 1/4 E, pp. 2510–2516.

Baur, G.N., 1964. *The Ecological Basis of Rain Forest Management*. André Mayer Fellowship 1961/62, FAO, Rome, p. 499.

Bradfield, R., 1969. *Intensive Multiple Cropping*. Los Baños Int. Rice Research Inst., Multigr., Manila.

Catinot, R., 1978. The forest ecosystems of Gabon: an overview. In: *Tropical Forest Ecosystems. A State of Knowledge Report*. UNESCO/UNEP/FAO, pp. 575–579.

Dawkins, C.H., 1955. INEAC in the "Forêt-Dense", impressions of the high forest research in the Congo. *Emp. For. Rev.*, 34: 55–60.

Gutzwiller, R., 1956. Principales pratiques silvicoles en vue de la production de bois d'oeuvre en forêt dense équatoriale. *J. For. Suisse*, 3: 1–20.

Hall, J.B. and Swaine, M.D., 1981. *Distribution and ecology of vascular plants in a tropical rain forest. Forest Vegetation in Ghana*. Junk, The Hague, p. 383.

Jones, A.P.D., 1948. *The Natural Forest Inviolate Plot*. Nigerian Forest Department, Ibadan, 33 pp.

Jones, E.W., 1950. Some aspects of natural regeneration in the Benin Rain Forest. *Emp. For. Rev.*, 29: 108–124.

Jones, E.W., 1956. Ecological studies on the rain forest of southern Nigeria. IV. The plateau forest of the Okomu Forest Reserve. *J. Ecol.*, 44: 83–117.

Kennedy, J.D., 1935. The group method of natural regeneration in the rain forest at Sapoba, Southern Nigeria. *Emp. For. Rev.*, 14: 19–24.

Kio, P.R.O., 1972. Shifting cultivation and multiple use of forest land in Nigeria. *Com. For. Rev.*, 51: 144–148.

Kio, P.R.O., 1976. What future for natural regeneration of tropical high forest? An appraisal with examples from Nigeria and Uganda. *Com. For. Rev.*, 55: 309–318.

Lancaster, P.C., 1961. *History of T.S.S.* Department of Forest Research, Nigeria, Tech. Note 12, p. 11.

Lawton, R.M., 1978. The management and regeneration of some Nigerian high forest ecosystems. In: *Tropical Forest Ecosystems. A State of Knowledge Report*. UNESCO/UNEP/FAO, pp. 580–588.

Lawton, R.M., 1981. Dynamics of forest ecosystems in relationship to their utilization; subtropical and tropical regions. *Inst. Land Reclam. Improv., Publ.*, 28: 31–47.

Logan, W.E.M., 1947. Timber exploitation in the Gold Coast. *Emp. For. Rev.*, 26: 20–53.

Longman, K.A., Leakey, R.R.B., Howland, P. and Bowen, M.R., 1977. *Physiological Approaches for Utilizing and Conserving the Genetic Resources of Tropical Trees*. Third World Consultation on Forest Tree Breeding, Canberra, A.C.T., FAO/IUFRO, pp. 1043–1054.

MacGregor, W.D., 1934. Silviculture of the mixed deciduous forest of Nigeria. *Oxf. For. Mem.*, 18: 108 pp.

Neil, P.E., 1981. Problems and opportunities in tropical rain forest management. *Commonw. For. Inst., Occas. Pap.*, 16: p. 127.

Ofosu-Asiedu, A. and Cannon, P., 1976. *Terminalia ivorensis* in decline in Ghana. *PANS*, 22: 239–242.

Olawoye, O.O., 1975. The agri-silvicultural system in Nigeria. *Com. For. Rev.*, 54: 229–236.

Onyeagocha, S.C., 1962. *The Development of the System of Natural Regeneration in Malaya Compared with Nigeria*. C.F.I., Oxford, Special Study (unpubl.).

Oseni, A.M. and Abayomi, G.O., 1975. Development trends of Nigerian silvicultural practice. *Niger. Forest. Inf. Bull.*, 24: 16 pp.

Pierlot, R., 1966. Structure et composition de forêts denses d'Afrique Centrale, spécialement celles du Kivu. *Acad. R. Sci. Outre-Mer, N.S.*, XVI(4): p. 367.

Rockwood, W.G. and Lal, R., 1974. Mulch tillage; a technique for soil and water conservation in the tropics. *PANS*, 17: 77–79.

Skorupa, J.P. and Kasenene, J.M., 1984. Tropical forest management: can rates of natural treefalls help guide us? *Oryx*, 18: 96–101.

Swaine, M.D. and Hall, G.B., 1983. Early succession on cleared forest land in Ghana. *J. Ecol.*, 71: 601–627.

Taylor, C.G., 1960. *Synecology and Silviculture in Ghana*. Nelson, Edinburgh, 418 pp.

UNESCO, 1978. *Tropical Forest Ecosystems. A State of Knowledge*. UNESCO/UNEP/FAO, Nat. Resour. Res., 14: 683 pp.

UNESCO-MAB, 1974. *International Working Group on Project 1: Ecological Effects of Increasing Human Activities on Tropical and Sub-tropical Ecosystems*. MAB Report Series, 16: 96 pp.

White, F., 1983. The vegetation of Africa. A descriptive memoir to accompany the UNESCO/AET FAT/UNSO vegetation map of Africa. *Nat. Resour. Res.*, 20: 356 pp.

Chapter 34

EXPLOITATION IN SOUTHEAST ASIA

K. KARTAWINATA, T.C. JESSUP and A.P. VAYDA

INTRODUCTION

Intensified exploitation of tropical rain forests has created problems of widespread resource depletion and environmental degradation. At low intensities of exploitation, as were characteristic of the extraction of forest products in Southeast Asia before the Second World War, forest management can be lax without leading to resource depletion or other environmental problems. Harvesting rates remain well below the reproductive capacity of most exploited populations, and side-effects of harvesting, such as damage to the surrounding stand caused by logging, are scattered and localized. This situation is still characteristic of some remote and isolated regions of Southeast Asia — for example, in parts of the New Guinea highlands and the far interior of Kalimantan (Borneo) — but elsewhere, particularly in lowland dipterocarp forests, the exploitation of timber and other forest products during the last 20 years has been far more intensive and has been carried out over a much greater area than at any time in the past. Mechanized logging, which replaced smaller-scale manual logging in much of Indonesia in the 1970's, employs bulldozers and other heavy equipment to fell and haul timber, and requires networks of roads for access to the forest and to transport logs. Minor forest products such as rattan have also been exploited more heavily during this period than previously. Collectors and traders of minor forest products operate on a smaller scale than that of timber companies, but they too, responding to increased commercial demand for forest products, have adopted new technologies — notably that of outboard motors, with which small craft can penetrate farther and faster into remote, up-river

areas (Peluso, 1983b). Collectors also use logging roads to reach forests far from navigable streams. Similarly, pioneer farmers of pepper, coffee, and other cash crops use roads both for initial access to forested land and, subsequently, to transport their crops to market. Pioneer farmers, who need to clear forest from the land, as well as itinerant woodcutters who also work close to roads for the same reasons, have both made increasing use of chain-saws in the last 20 years — another instance of technical innovation in response to commercial opportunity in developing rural areas[1].

Depletion and degradation of rain forests are partly consequences of intensification per se, as some of the detrimental effects of harvesting forest products and of forest clearing are made more severe simply by an increase in the rates of these activities. Environmental problems are exacerbated, however, by new methods of harvesting and extraction, particularly those of mechanized logging, which we shall examine in detail. Attempts to deal with these problems include restrictions on the intensity of forest exploitation and on the use of

---

[1]Compare these innovations — outboard motors and chainsaws — with their cousins in the family of miniaturized internal combustion engines, the motorcycles and scooters that have replaced bicycles throughout large parts of Indonesia, Malaysia, and other countries of Southeast Asia. Japan has been a leader in developing this technology, as well as a principal consumer of timber from Southeast Asia. This internal-combustion "revolution", in the context of rising demand for forest products and forested land, is also comparable to an earlier technological transition among shifting cultivators, that from stone to iron tools, which made possible a tremendous gain in the efficiency of tree-felling, canoe-making, and the construction of houses and granaries. See Freeman (1970) for a discussion of the importance of iron tools for shifting cultivators in Borneo.

particularly destructive methods. Such restrictions and, sometimes, outright prohibitions have been applied in areas designated as parks, nature reserves, and other types of protected forest. In 1980, these comprised about 7 million ha (around 5%) of insular Southeast Asia's closed, broadleaf forest (FAO, 1980, table 1a), although there are considerable problems of enforcement and reserve management. Another approach, which in our view should be complementary to that of establishing reserves, is to seek more appropriate methods of exploitation — appropriate, that is, to the ecology of rain-forest species, including those which are not directly exploited but which may suffer the effects of human disturbance. Unfortunately, there is as yet scant empirical evidence that sustainable methods can be implemented at or near the high intensities of exploitation which have been stimulated by commercial demand in recent years. This article, therefore, focuses not on solutions but rather on problems and on methods for identifying problems. We describe several types of exploitation currently employed in the rain forests of Southeast Asia, and deal with some environmental problems associated with these types. This is not done in a pessimistic spirit, however, since the search for sustainable methods of rain-forest exploitation needs to proceed from the identification of relevant environmental problems. We believe that solutions to these will come, not in the form of perfect technical "fixes" that avoid all adverse effects, but rather as strategies to minimize and localize those effects through a combination of suitable technology, application of ecological knowledge, and some degree of non-technological control over forest exploitation.

The area we cover is insular Southeast Asia, or Malesia, comprising the Philippines, Malaysia, Singapore, Brunei, Indonesia, and Papua New Guinea. The countries of mainland Southeast Asia are excluded, as they contain little tropical rain forest. Our own research experience leads us to focus mainly on Indonesia.

We consider three categories of exploitation: logging, rattan collection, and shifting cultivation. All are economically important in Southeast Asia, and all have had increasingly widespread and deleterious effects in the last few decades. We first describe an example of "traditional" (that is, non-mechanized) logging, from the remote Apo Kayan

region of the Indonesian province of East Kalimantan on the island of Borneo. Timber cutting in the Apo Kayan is still largely for local use, and employs means that must have been more widespread in Borneo in pre-industrial times. It is far less environmentally destructive than modern commercial logging in lowland dipterocarp forests, which is a subject we also consider. We then turn to rattan collection, drawing especially on the work of Dransfield (1979, 1981), who has considered the relation of rattan biology to methods of management and conservation. The last section is a discussion of some aspects of shifting cultivation. More is known about the effects of shifting cultivation, at least at the scale of individual fields, than about the ecology of logging or the collection of minor forest products. Rather than recapitulate the literature on shifting cultivation, we refer interested readers to reviews by Padoch and Vayda (1983), Sanchez (1976, ch. 10), and Whitmore (1984, ch. 20). We shall, however, discuss some larger-scale features of shifting cultivation, particularly the interdigitated distribution of fields and "patches" of secondary and primary forest, which we feel have been neglected. This leads us to our concluding section, in which we compare human exploitation with natural disturbances and make methodological suggestions about such comparisons.

LOGGING

Traditional logging in the Apo Kayan

The Apo Kayan is a highland plateau in the interior of East Kalimantan and is inhabited by several thousand Kenyah, Kayan, and Punan people, most of whom practise shifting cultivation. The various forest products exploited for local use include timber, rattan and other minor forest products, fish, and game. A few valuable products — notably aloes wood (*Aquilaria* spp., Thymelaeaceae) and bezoars (gallstones of certain monkeys and porcupines) — are collected principally for commercial trade. Most, including timber, are harvested mainly or solely for local use. There have been no large-scale commercial logging or other enterprises such as those in the lowlands. The difficulty of transporting logs down-river (a large proportion reportedly were lost or damaged in rapids) or over mountainous terrain, together with the availability of alternative sources of timber elsewhere, has so far limited commercial logging in the Apo Kayan to one or two small-scale ventures. However, men from the Apo Kayan travel to the lowlands of Sarawak and Indonesian Kalimantan to work as loggers. Some have brought chain-saws back to the Apo Kayan, but the scarcity of fuel greatly curtails their use in that remote region.

Jessup's investigation of traditional logging in the Apo Kayan (Jessup, 1983; Vayda et al., 1985), summarized here, included studies of timber-tree selection, felling, on-site preparation, transport out of the forest, and uses of various kinds of wood. He also measured gaps created by felling, and compared them with nearby natural tree-fall gaps.

Uses of trees

Trees are felled in the Apo Kayan in order to obtain wood, sago, and, in some cases, fruit or latex. Fruit, latex, and resins are usually harvested or tapped without felling whole trees, however.[1] Some timber, mainly for decay-resistant posts, is taken from the heartwood of dead, already fallen trees in primary forest [species of *Eugenia* (Myrtaceae), and an unidentified tree called *merang* in the Kenyah language] and from partially burned logs in old fields (*Castanopsis* sp.: Fagaceae). Firewood is collected from residual logs in old fields and cut from live trees in secondary and primary forests close to villages. (Firewood cutting is not a major cause of deforestation in sparsely populated East Kalimantan.)

Apart from shifting cultivation, timber — that is, wood used in the construction and repair of such durable structures as houses, bridges, and boats — accounts for the majority of medium and large trees (those with diameter greater than about 30 cm) felled in the Apo Kayan. Commonly exploited families of timber trees include Fagaceae, especially the genera *Lithocarpus* and *Castanopsis*, and Myrtaceae, especially *Eugenia*; these are relatively abundant in the lower montane forest

(*c.* 800–1000 m elevation) near the Apo Kayan village of Sungai Barang, where Jessup did most of his research. Dipterocarpaceae and the extremely durable *Eusideroxylon zwageri* (Borneo ironwood: Lauraceae) are valued, and they are used where they occur, but they are less abundant than in the lowlands. Other useful genera of timber trees in the Apo Kayan are *Agathis* (Araucariaceae), *Podocarpus* (Podocarpaceae), and *Cratoxylon* (Hypericaceae).

The Kenyah and Kayan people of the Apo Kayan, like many other shifting cultivators in Borneo and some other parts of Southeast Asia, live in large, wooden longhouses (Fig. 34.1) in stable village communities. Village groups do move occasionally, but most reside at a site for decades, sometimes for more than a century. Longhouses, some occupied by dozens of families and stretching well over 100 m, are constructed of massive wood columns, floorboards, and beams in addition to numerous smaller parts such as wood or leaf shingles and rattan bindings. Each part of a house — and of canoes and bridges, the other major uses of timber — has its own requirements of strength, weight, resilience, resistance to decay, and durability against weathering. These varied requirements are met by exploiting a variety of species and sizes of trees in primary and secondary forests. Primary-forest species and large trees generally are harder and more durable than secondary-forest species and smaller trees. However, the latter are often more common or more accessible, their softer woods are more easily worked, and in any case they are acceptable for a number of uses. Large primary-forest trees are the only ones acceptable for some purposes, however, particularly where strength and durability are needed — for example, in a canoe hull or a longhouse column.

The availability of timber (and other forest products such as rattan and game) has been an important consideration in the selection of village sites in the Apo Kayan. An established village maintains a reserve of intact old-growth or primary forest to provide a ready supply of forest products. No shifting cultivation is practised within reserves, which tend to be situated on less fertile soils than those which are cultivated.

Traditional methods of felling

Most felling in the Apo Kayan is still done with axes; chain-saws are used occasionally where fuel is

---

[1]According to Corner (1952), trees of *Palaguium* (Sapotaceae) in Sarawak were seriously depleted during the 19th century by the practice of felling them to obtain gutta percha, a latex then used to insulate submarine cables.

Fig. 34.1. The exterior and interior of a longhouse.

Fig. 34.2. Traditional tree-felling.

available. Here we describe the traditional, axe-using methods[1]. Trees less than about 30 cm diameter at breast height can be felled by a single man, but large trees require several men working as a team. If a tree to be felled is buttressed (as many are in primary forest), a platform is built so that the axe-men can cut above the buttresses (Fig. 34.2). The direction in which the tree is to be felled is determined and, if necessary, neighboring trees that might cause "hang-ups" are felled in advance. Lianas linking a tree to its neighbors also can "hang up" a falling tree. Such trees are therefore cut part-way through before the main tree is felled so that the weight of the latter as it

falls will snap the linked trees and bring them down together. Timber is prepared at the felling site; only the final product — beams, boards, shingles, or other pieces — has to be carried from the forest. If a large, heavy piece of timber is needed, as for a longhouse column or the hull of a big cargo canoe, it is prepared close by a river and floated downstream (lashed to canoes for buoyancy if it is a "sinker") to where it will be used.

Environmental effects of traditional logging

Jessup measured the area and determined the cause of gaps in a one-hectare plot in primary forest near Sungai Barang[2]. People from the village had been felling trees in the reserve for about 40 years, and earlier inhabitants exploited the forest as well. The plot was situated on a broad ridge, at about 900 m elevation, and included the upper slopes on either side of the ridge-top. Gaps

---

[1]Steel axe heads are obtained by Apo Kayan men in the lowlands of Sarawak and East Kalimantan. In former times, during the 19th century and earlier, Kenyah and Kayan smiths made their own steel tools from local ore. Their excellent cutlass blades were traded throughout Borneo (Harrison and O'Connor, 1969).

---

[2]Jessup also measured gaps in a 40-year-old secondary forest, but these are not discussed here (see Vayda et al., 1985).

of 20 m² or more were measured, including all openings in the main canopy [that is, regardless of whether or not "building phase" vegetation (cf. Whitmore, 1984) had begun to fill them]. There were 20 such gaps in the plot. Jessup at first intended to classify gaps simply as those caused by felling and those caused by natural tree-falls. However, most of the gaps that showed some evidence of felling (determined from stumps) also were affected by apparently natural tree-falls — that is, falls of trees that had snapped, tipped up at the roots, or suffered crown damage. It could not be determined, in most cases, whether the "natural" tree-falls occurred before, during, or after felling but there seems to be a considerable amount of interaction or overlap of various gap-forming processes.

Felling was at least a partial cause of 11 (55%) of the gaps. Only one gap (5%) was made by felling alone; all others showed some evidence of snapped or tipped-up trees or of crown damage as a cause of the gaps. The total area in gaps and the average sizes of gaps are shown in Table 34.1. There is not much difference between the sizes of natural gaps and of those caused at least partially by felling, considering that the range in size for all gaps in the plot was from 22 to 509 m². Apparently, the traditional felling methods employed in the Apo Kayan do not create gaps much larger than those made by natural tree-falls alone. Furthermore, there was no apparent difference between felling and non-felling gaps in damage to soil, understory vegetation, and neighboring trees. On the other hand, observations of felling at nearby sites, as described in the preceding paragraph, revealed trampling of seedlings and cutting of seedlings and saplings (many of which resprout, however). These

disturbances may affect the species composition of gap-phase vegetation. Finally, the overall rate of felling during the last 40 years (estimated from the numbers of large and medium timber trees used in Sungai Barang houses, bridges, and canoes) has probably been less than the rate of natural tree-falls in the forest reserve. However, logging is selective and some preferred species may have been depleted locally.

Depletion of timber and old-growth forest by cutting and clearing has occurred in some parts of the Apo Kayan where local population densities were high in the past and where neighboring settlements or extensive secondary forest restricted villagers' access to primary forest. One response to local shortages of timber has been to use other materials, such as palm-leaf thatch from the sago palm (*Eugeissona utilis*) in place of wooden shingles. Another response by some groups has been to resettle closer to primary forest, both in the lowlands and in sparsely inhabited highland areas. [The reasons for moving, however, are many, and access to forest products is only one of them (Jessup, 1981).] Competition for forest resources leading to their depletion is now more of a problem in lowland areas, where the effects of local use are exacerbated by intensive commercial exploitation, than it is in the less populous and more isolated Apo Kayan.

Commercial logging

Before the Second World War, logging in the forests of Southeast Asia was relatively light and limited primarily to the extraction of heavy and durable woods. However, by the late 1930's, due to increasing demand for timber and the introduction of medium-powered sawmills, many softer and less durable species were logged also. In the Philippines, the mechanization of logging occurred earlier than in other countries in the region. By the mid-1920s it was already well developed, although manual and animal methods were still used (Nicholson, 1979). After the war, the increase of mechanized logging operations was considerable, and was particularly spectacular in recent years in Indonesia, where large-scale modern logging began only in 1969 (Soedjarwo, 1978; cf. Bruenig, Ch. 35 of this volume). The late 1960's and 1970's were marked by a rapid increase in demand for tropical

TABLE 34.1

Total area and size of gaps caused at least partially by human felling, and of gaps with no evidence of felling (that is, those caused solely by natural tree-falls)

	Gaps with felling	Gaps with no felling
Number per ha	11	9
Total area (m²)	1655.5	1122.3
Size: mean (m²)	150.5	124.7
median (m²)	152	94

Data from FAO (1980).

hardwood logs and wood products. This spurred a major timber boom in Southeast Asia, where the exceptional richness of commercially valuable tree species in lowland dipterocarp forests, especially in Borneo, Sumatra, and Malaya (Peninsular Malaysia), has led to more intensive (and more destructive) logging than in tropical forests elsewhere (FAO, 1980). Indonesia was in a particularly good position to take advantage of the timber boom. The Indonesian government, recognizing the vast and relatively unexploited timber resources of the country, encouraged investment by foreign and multinational timber companies in mechanized logging and, later, in wood processing (Manning, 1971; Habir, 1983).

The *banjir kap* method

One aspect of the Indonesian development program was to ban the use of the existing labor-intensive method of logging known as *banjir kap*. In the *banjir kap* ("log flood") method, logs were hauled manually, or in some areas with the help of draft animals, from felling sites to nearby rivers, where the logs were left to be carried to downstream collection points during periods of high water. Due to the absence of heavy machinery, damage to the forest during felling and extraction was less than that done by mechanized logging. Furthermore, few if any logging roads were built into the forest, so that access to forest land and its value for purposes of development and speculation were not thereby increased. And last, logs with a specific gravity greater than that of water (known as "sinkers") could not easily be transported by river, so species with dense wood (for instance, *Shorea laevis*) were exploited less than now.

In 1971, soon after the start of the timber boom, the Indonesian government banned non-mechanized logging on the grounds that it does more damage to logs than does mechanized extraction. The use of roads in areas where there are rapids also reduces damage to and losses of logs. Another reason for the outlawing of the *banjir kap* method may have been pressure both from medium-scale mechanized timber companies which were finding it difficult to obtain cheap local labor and from the large multinational companies which were losing their control over the price of logs (Magenda, 1981).

Uniform and selective logging systems

Two types of mechanized logging systems have been developed in Southeast Asia. These are the Malayan Uniform System (MUS) and the Selective Logging System (SLS) (see Bruenig, Ch. 35). The MUS is a monocyclic system, where all commercial trees are removed in a single operation and the cutting cycle is about the same as the rotation age of the trees (Whitmore, 1984, ch. 10). It was developed and used in Malaya and is, in essence, "the removal in one operation of all economic crops from areas that have been shown by sampling to carry an adequate stocking of regeneration". This is to be "followed immediately by a poison girdling of all the remaining uneconomic canopy and all smaller trees down to about 5 to 15 cm diameter, excepting commercial species of good form" (Anon., 1963; Nicholson, 1979). This treatment thus favors faster-growing species at the expense of the slow-growing and heavier hardwoods. Because of the severe damage to the forest that results from this logging method, a large portion of the future crop depends on the seedlings present at the time of logging rather than on advanced growth. This method is effective and easily employed in lowland forests with gentle terrain, but it is apparently not as successful in steep terrain with difficult access, which is where logging operations have shifted in recent years as lowland forests have been converted to agricultural land. Since seedling regeneration is frequently lacking or inadequate, and rehabilitation work is difficult and costly in hill forests with steep terrain, the MUS is not applicable. The SLS, which is also known in Malaysia as the Selective Management System (SMS), has therefore been adopted (Nor and Baharuddin, 1983).

The MUS has been employed not only in Peninsular Malaysia, but also in Sabah and Sarawak (East Malaysia, in Borneo). In Sabah, it was slightly modified by attention to the importance of advanced growth for intermediate yields, and by the reduction of logging damage by abandoning poison-girdling treatment of the logged forests (Chai and Udarbe, 1977; Nicholson, 1979). In Sarawak, the MUS has been successfully used in exploiting swamp forests.

The SLS is a polycyclic system, in which commercial trees are removed more than once in a continuing series of felling cycles which are shorter than the rotation age of the trees. It has been employed in the Philippines and Indonesia. In contrast to the MUS, the SLS relies heavily on advanced growth. The original version, developed in the Philippines, is known also as the Philippine Selective Logging System. The system entails the following procedures: (1) 5% sampling of the forest to be logged; (2) marking a certain percentage (50–60%) of healthy young commercial trees 15 to 17 cm diameter to be left as "core" trees, undamaged by logging; (3) felling all commercial trees over 75 cm diameter, plus 70% of the trees from 55 to 75 cm; and (4) undertaking an inventory of the residual trees (a 100% count) after logging to determine the condition and number of residual trees (Anon., 1965; Nicholson, 1979). The Indonesian Selective Felling System is similar to the Philippine version of the SLS, but differs in the size limits of the trees to be felled and in the criteria used to determine the number of trees to be left as core trees. It is designed especially for use in mixed dipterocarp forests with a normal diameter distribution. It involves the following operations (Soerianegara, 1970; Soerianegara and Kartawinata, 1983): (1) taking a stand inventory and marking trees to be cut and healthy trees to be left as core trees, one year before felling; (2) selective felling of trees above certain diameter limits; (3) taking an inventory of the residual stand one year after felling; (4) removing weeds, cutting lianas, carrying out enrichment planting of commercial tree species in poor sections of logged areas, and planting open ground — all two years after felling; and (5) again removing weeds, restocking, and thinning overly dense regeneration, five years after felling. The number and size of core trees to be left in the residual stands are determined by the felling diameter limits (30–50 cm) and cutting cycles (25–40 years). The number ranges from 25 to 40 trees and the size from 20 to 30 cm, based on the assumption that tree diameters increase by 0.5–1.0 cm per year, so that after one cutting cycle the core trees will have reached or exceeded the felling diameter limit. If a forest is dominated by dipterocarps and has a concentration of large-diameter trees, thus diverging from the normal diameter distribution, and if commercial seedling regeneration is adequate (more than 40%), a method of "clear-felling with natural regeneration" — essentially the MUS — is appropriate. If,

however, a forest is poorly stocked (less than 25 m^3 ha^{-1} of commercial species), it can be converted into a more productive forest by employing a method known as "clear-felling with replanting" (Soerianegara and Kartawinata, 1983). This method can be applied also in secondary forest.

Until now, only selective logging has been practised by holders in Indonesia of forest concessions, though not in conformity with the Indonesian selective felling system described above. In fact, step 1 and steps 3 to 5 are completely ignored; selective cutting is done with no consideration of the condition of the forest, and relogging is frequently carried out in a shorter time than that of the specified cutting cycles. The condition of logged-over forest, therefore, is not as good as should be expected.

The MUS and SLS both rely on natural regeneration of desired species. Fox (1976) stresses that successful natural regeneration is constrained by various factors, some of which are environmental (light, water, soil, disturbance, biotic interactions), some "intrinsic" (population structure, growth rate, phenology), and some related to management (logging methods, use of fire, availability of manpower). Nicholson (1979) stated that either the MUS or SLS may be applicable, depending on the stand structure just before logging. According to Ashton (1980), however, a sound ecological basis for selective logging has never been established, and it will rarely be successful in mixed dipterocarp forests. Its drawback is the high mortality due both to natural causes and exploitation; about a third of the residual young trees undamaged by the exploitation process will die before maturity. Other important considerations include differences in the growth rates of trees upon which the cutting cycles depend. With reference to the Selective Management System mentioned above, but with applicability also to the SLS, Awang (1982) rightly argued that too many unknowns about the forest bear on the exploitation system. The composition, structure, and dynamics of natural forests, the types and extent of tree damage and environmental disturbances that the forests can bear, and the silvics of species that can satisfy the adequate stocking requirement and their effects on silvicultural practices, are little known. This points to the need for more comprehensive research (see, for instance,

Ashton, 1980; Ewel and Conde, 1980; Kartawinata, 1981; Awang, 1982; Baharuddin, 1982) before the SLS or other selective logging systems can be well employed.

The environmental impacts of mechanized logging

Because of its relatively low intensity and use of less intrusive technology, traditional tree-felling has milder effects than mechanized logging. The effects of the former are more similar to those of natural tree-falls where the frequency, size, and number of gaps are small and the soil, seedlings and saplings, and surrounding trees are disturbed relatively little. Even with the use of gasoline-fueled chain-saws and draft animals to skid logs, the damage to residual trees is less than in fully mechanized logging in which bulldozers, skidders, and heavy-duty trucks are employed (Kartawinata and Vayda, 1984). In mechanized selective logging, trees are felled and cut into logs with gasoline-fueled chain-saws, and dragged to loading points by tractors. The logs are then transported to log-ponds or log-yards by heavy-duty trucks. Bulldozers and steam rollers are employed to construct a network of logging roads to facilitate log transportation.

The use of the SLS results in large canopy openings and great damage, and in the MUS these are even greater (see also Bruenig, Ch. 35). Large gaps in the canopy favor the growth of light-demanding, fast-growing and light-wood pioneer species, including light timber species that behave like pioneers (for instance *Shorea* spp.). The larger gaps in the MUS result in greater exposure of residual tree crowns to light and space, which in turn results in better tree forms than in the SLS (Whitmore, 1984). The major proportion of the residual stand, after some years of regrowth, consists of gap and building phases. Figures 34.3 and 34.4 show the canopy conditions in a two-hectare plot of residual stand five years after selective logging, in which 20 trees were extracted

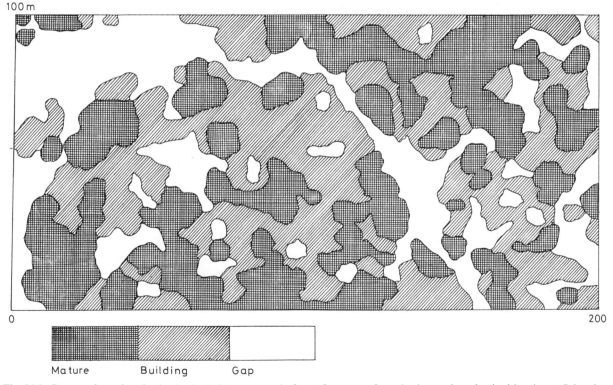

Fig. 34.3. Canopy phases in a lowland mixed dipterocarp rain forest five years after selective, and mechanized logging at Sekundur, northern Sumatra, Indonesia. A long, narrow, diagonal gap is in the tractor path. Other gaps are remaining open area with low regrowth resulting from felling of trees with DBH > 50 cm, and existing small gaps before logging. The extensive area of building phase represents the regrowth in the area affected by tree-felling, and natural gaps formed before logging. (After Abdulhadi et al., 1985.)

Fig. 34.4. A profile diagram of a lowland mixed dipterocarp rain forest five years after selective and mechanized logging at Sekundur, northern Sumatra, Indonesia. The diagram was made within the two-hectare block shown in Fig. 34.3. Note the wide gaps with a low developing sapling layer (shaded black). (After Abdulhadi et al., 1985.)

(Abdulhadi et al., 1985). The mature phase constitutes only 38%, whereas the building and gap phases are 31% each.

Consequences of mechanized logging (both MUS and SLS) have been reviewed (Meijer, 1973; Nicholson, 1979; Ewel and Conde, 1980; Kartawinata, 1981) and discussed in various symposia (Soeparto ct al., 1978; Hallé et al., 1981; Awang et al., 1983; among others). Findings may be summarized by considering the impact of mechanized logging on each of the following: vegetation, fauna, and soil and water [see Kartawinata (1981) and references cited therein].

Vegetation. Felling operations and log extraction both damage the vegetation, but most of the damage is due to the extraction process. Felling breaks the crowns and stems of saplings and trees, peels off bark, and crushes seedlings under the crown and boles of felled trees. The extent of damage is related to the size of individual trees and the number of trees removed per unit area. Residual trees of smaller diameters suffer most. Relogging of exploited forest, long before it is appropriate in the cutting cycle, is practised by

many concessionaires and has caused more destruction of residual stands. Its effect is to retard succession and recovery, and to make the forest poorer in desirable timber species. Ponding due to the blocking of natural drainage results in a rise of water level and the death of trees and other woody species. This particularly affects dipterocarp seedlings, which are vulnerable to flooding (Fox, 1976). The flooded area may be small and localized or, if logging has been extensive, very substantial.

Much of an exploited forest is occupied by skid trails, haul roads, and log-yards. These may comprise 14 to 50% of the ground in the exploited forest. This bare area is invaded by pioneer species which almost always become dominant within a short period of time. Only a few species of desirable timber can grow here. In poorer sites, such as "kerangas" (heath) forest on white sand soil, the vegetation recovery is very slow and the growth is less vigorous. In many instances, climbers invade bare ground also and overgrow residual trees, whose own growth often is thereby suppressed.

Logging operations result in microclimatic changes. Changes in light, humidity, temperature, and wind directly affect the growth of residual trees, saplings, and seedlings, as well as that of new seedlings. Because the gaps caused by mechanized logging are much larger than most natural tree-fall gaps in primary forest, the changes can be deleterious to organisms adapted to the less severe regime of natural disturbances. Soil desiccation — caused by a high rate of evapotranspiration — may prevent seed germination, and may result also in the death of established seedlings. Crown dieback, sun-scalding of trunk and branches, water stress, and insect attacks, all of which can lead to the death of residual trees, are observed in logged forest as a result of microclimatic changes. Light is considered the most important of the altered factors. With an increase in light levels brought about by large canopy openings, the growth of saplings of some primary forest species, previously arrested, is renewed, and that of some seedlings is increased; but they must compete with secondary-forest species which respond even more vigorously to the higher light intensity.

The recovery of a logged area to conditions similar to unlogged forest is very slow. It has been experimentally shown that forest recovery depends on the size of gaps (Kramer, 1928, 1933; Whitmore, 1982, 1984). The time required for succession to primary or "climax" forest is estimated to be at least 250 years (Riswan, 1982); the recovery of bare areas in logged forest may be at least of the same order of magnitude.

The current exploitation of primary forest which has a high species diversity will lead to genetic erosion and the loss of species. Selective logging is in fact a process of "creaming" or "high-grading" the best trees of the commercial species, in particular those of dipterocarps (*Dipterocarpus*, *Dryobalanops* and *Shorea*) that currently have a good market value. The individuals left to provide seeds for future crops are thus mostly undesirable, smaller, and genetically inferior. The possible loss of species is an even more serious problem. This is especially true considering the fact that most tropical forest species have low densities (only a few individuals per unit area). It is suspected, therefore, that the loss of species goes hand in hand with the loss of individuals. Many species are still unknown to science, and may have economic potential other than for timber. Bruenig (1983, p. 9), however, has doubted "the reality of genetic

erosion in selective logging, especially after only one or a few rotations" and argued that "utilization of all species and clear felling are much more suspected to cause genetic loss of species rather than genetic erosion".

Animals. The most profound effect of selective logging on forest animals, especially arboreal mammals, is the destruction of habitats, resulting in a disruption of the availability of resources to a degree beyond their extreme natural fluctuations (Johns, 1985). Browsing animals, however, are less adversely affected, and to an extent their habitats are improved by the lush growth of pioneer and secondary-forest species in logged-over forest. The effects of logging operations on primates vary with the primate species and the degree of disturbance. The likelihood of a primate species decreasing in numbers may be correlated with its ability to adapt to changes in distribution and abundance of food in regenerating forest (Johns, 1985). Progressive destruction of primary forest results in the progressive elimination of native small mammals, until in clear-cut forest only introduced species of rats may survive. Birds, especially those living in the upper canopy, are likely to be seriously disturbed by logging, but some species require mature trees for nesting and need a large area of relatively undisturbed forest to maintain breeding populations. However, colonizing birds which preferentially feed in disturbed forest increase in number following selective logging (Johns, 1985). There are no data yet concerning the effect of logging on insects, but it is presumed to be even more serious than that on other animals, since insects tend to be more specialized environmentally than other taxa (Price, 1980). Even a single tree provides insects with a large number of distinct habitats. Certain groups of insects and certain tree species — dipterocarps, for instance — have intimate and interdependent relationships, so that the elimination of either will affect the life of the other (see Ashton, 1983, and Ch. 11).

Soil and water. The process of skidding, hauling, and yarding is the primary cause of the opening up of the ground surface, which can affect as much as 50% of the overall surface area. The degree of damage and its effects depend on the nature of soils, topography, the intensity and methods of exploitation, and the size and quantity of equipment used. The most obvious physical effect is erosion, which takes place mostly along compacted roads and skid trails. It is attributed to the decrease and stoppage of water infiltration, leading to an increase in surface runoff. In fully forested areas, runoff is less than in those which are only partially forested; this is because the closed canopy and multilayered vegetation of the forest partially intercept rainfall. When the canopy is opened, the amount of rain reaching the soil surface increases, while the removal of ground vegetation cover results in the development of a dense rill network on slopes, especially on clay soils.

Studies on the effects of logging and other types of forest clearing on water yields and quality are almost absent. However, available data indicate that sediment yield in deforested areas is considerably higher than in forests. The highest values have been recorded where clear-cutting is followed by certain kinds of cropping, such as unterraced pepper plantations. In logged areas sediment load in the low-flow period is 2 to 3 times higher than in unlogged forest, while during storm flow it can be from 5 to as much as 20 times higher, depending on the condition of the forests.

The nutrient status of the soil is significantly affected by mechanized logging activities. The cation exchange capacity (CEC) of tropical forest soils is largely attributable to colloidal organic matter derived from the above-ground biomass. Clearing lowland primary forest has been shown to lower the organic matter (hence CEC) and nutrient content of the soil, although after several years of secondary forest growth they return to or even surpass their original levels (Riswan, 1982). However, in a very poor, white-sand podzol (kerangas soil), the return is extremely slow, concomitant with the very slow recovery of vegetation (Riswan, 1982). Litter production is higher and the rate of litter decomposition slower in primary forest than in the secondary forest which develops within a selectively logged stand. The faster decomposition in the latter apparently is related to higher soil temperature. Most importantly, mycorrhizal fungi, on which many tropical forest trees (especially dipterocarps) depend for nutrient uptake, are severely affected by even slight increases in soil temperature, soil compaction, and soil desiccation (Smits, 1983).

RATTAN COLLECTION

Minor forest products

Rattan and other so-called "minor" forest products are minor now mainly because timber has overtaken them as the major forest product of tropical countries. In Indonesia, for example, the predominance of timber over other forest products is very recent (Jacobs, 1982). In the 1930's, the value of non-timber products exported from the outer islands of the (then) Dutch East Indies (mainly rattan, resins, camphor, and tanning bark) still exceeded that of timber by a considerable margin (Van den Koppel, 1945, p. 221). By 1985, the proportion of non-timber products had fallen to 4 or 5% of forest-product exports. But even as the proportion of non-timber products has declined, demand and rates of harvesting of some of these products, such as rattan, have increased to the point where many species are threatened with extinction by over-exploitation (Dransfield, 1981; Peluso, 1983a). Furthermore, minor forest products and species of little commercial value are lost as their forest habitats are degraded by heavy logging and cleared for farms, plantations, ranches, and other types of land-use (Myers, 1980; FAO, 1980; Jacobs, 1982; Kartawinata and Vayda, 1984). We consider rattan as an example of minor forest products.

Rattan has long been collected and traded throughout Southeast Asia, but it is now exploited more heavily than ever before. Since the late 1960's, demand for rattan has surged ahead of supply to such an extent that natural stocks are either threatened with depletion or, in some areas, have already been exhausted (Dransfield, 1981). Even 50 years ago, Burkill (1966, pp. 1904–1905) remarked on the problem of increasing over-exploitation of rattan in Malaya. As natural stocks of rattan are depleted and prices rise, stems of immature plants and of species formerly not sought after are increasingly collected (Dransfield, 1981; Peluso, 1983a, b). Dransfield (1981, p. 184) observed: "It appears now that no species can be classed as useless — a worrying fact for the rattan conservationist." In fact, it is extremely difficult to identify all the species subsumed under a particular commercial class of rattan, although certain "elite" species are preferred. Other less desirable species are probably included in the same class as an elite species, but sorted into grades of lower quality (Whitmore, 1973).

Biological context of rattan exploitation

The geographic distribution of rattans (Arecaceae: Lepidocaryoideae) corresponds closely to that of the dipterocarps (Corner, 1966), a family of trees which not only is dominant in the lowland forests of Southeast Asia but also is the major source of the region's commercial timber. For this reason, and because logging activities affect the collection of rattan, the management and conservation of rattans and dipterocarps are closely intertwined.

Rattans growing in lowland primary forest, where most collecting is done, reach to the top of the canopy, 45 to 60 m above the ground. They climb by means of sharp, barbed spines and a twisting habit of growth. Due to coiling and sagging, the stems commonly attain a length of 60 to 90 m and a weight great enough to snap tree branches (Whitmore, 1973). Corner (1966, p. 221) described the arduous and sometimes dangerous task of rattan collection, or "pulling" (Fig. 34.5):

"Dead and living limbs, clumps of epiphytes with their biting ants, wasp-nests, and other upper debris tumble down and, if the crown of the rattan should be dislodged, it flops with its cruel whips flaring. The crown of old stems is generally too securely fixed to be dislodged. The puller is content with the loose coils or the younger stems not so firmly established. The last part of the stem is, in any case, too fresh and sappy to be of use, but it does provide a bud which, if bitter, is generally edible. During the pulling, the puller pauses to clean off the dead leaves in order to get a new grip. When as much stem as possible has been pulled down, it is coiled up and carried back on the shoulder to the village".

Thick-stemmed rattans (the source of "cane") must be processed by boiling in oil to remove natural gums and resins. If this is not done within 15 days, the cane will be spoiled. Slender rattans are coiled and dried in or near the collection areas before being sold. Their stems are later split to make the strips and cores used by manufacturers.

Rattan species vary in their light requirements. Some only grow up into the forest canopy when light becomes available from a tree-fall gap or other opening. *Calamus manan*, which is probably typical of most species, seems to exploit small

Fig. 34.5. Pulling rattan.

openings in primary forest. Some species grow in dense shade, while others grow in large openings or secondary forests, where light levels are high (Dransfield, 1979). Logging and shifting cultivation both disrupt the canopy of primary forest, increasing light levels and thus affecting rattans as well as other forest species.

The growth form of a rattan species determines its response to cutting and, therefore, to both collecting and attempts at cultivation (Dransfield, 1979, 1981). Species with multiple (clumped) stems regenerate from the base after cutting, but single-stemmed (solitary) species do not. The solitary habit of *C. manan*, a valuable cane species, has led to its depletion because of its inability to regenerate after cutting. Depletion and a high demand for good-quality cane have in turn led collectors to cut immature plants. This means that fewer seed-producing, mature plants are available to restock the species, a vicious cycle that may end in extinction. Probably because of the inability of the single-stemmed species to regenerate, only species with multiple stems (such as *C. caesius*) are at all widely cultivated.

Growth rates vary both within and between species of rattan. Data are available for only a few species, and some of these are from plantations of cultivated rattan, which may differ significantly from rattans in the forest. Maximum reported rates of stem growth range from 1.2 to 3 m yr^{-1} for *C. manan*, and up to 4 or 5 m yr^{-1} for *C. caesius* and *C. trachycoleus* respectively (Dransfield, 1981). In central Kalimantan, the time required for cultivated rattan (*C. caesius* and *C. trachycoleus*) to reach a harvestable size is variously reported as 7 to 10 or 7 to 15 years (Dransfield, 1979; Kuswara, 1982). Wong (1983), with data from Malaysian trials, reckoned that 12 to 15 years was required to grow a crop of *C. manan*. Rattans growing in the forest probably do not often achieve a maximum rate of growth, so that sustainable harvest rotations for natural stocks must be considerably longer than those cited above. Under present conditions, however, immature plants are frequently harvested.

It is difficult to protect wild rattan populations, even in strict nature reserves. However, commercial pressures to collect wild rattans may be reduced by encouraging the cultivation of "elite" species (Dransfield, 1981). Unfortunately, *C. manan*, one of the most valuable, is difficult to cultivate because of its solitary habit.

SHIFTING CULTIVATION AND DEFORESTATION

Shifting cultivation has been identified as an important cause of tropical deforestation or forest conversion (see, for instance, Myers, 1980; Lanly, 1982). It is often associated, particularly in Southeast Asia, with logging and logging roads[1]. A

---

[1] "Shifting cultivation in the wake of logging" is cited by the FAO (1980) authors as the major cause of deforestation in tropical Asia. "Shifting cultivation" may well be a misnomer in this statement. In our research in East Kalimantan, we found that what had been called "shifting cultivation in the wake of logging" included forest clearing for the establishment of gardens of such perennial crops as pepper; these gardens were maintained for ten or more years (Kartawinata and Vayda, 1984).

recent survey of tropical forest resources (FAO, 1980; Lanly, 1982) found that deforestation in tropical Asia was most widespread in logged-over forests, where 59% of the region's deforestation occurred. "Deforestation" is used by the FAO authors in a rather strict sense to refer only to the actual removal of closed forest cover. It is distinct from "degradation", which is defined as "other, less radical alterations of tree populations", including logging (Lanly, 1982, p. 74). The susceptibility of logged-over forest to shifting cultivation is attributed to its greater accessibility (due in large part to the existence of logging roads), gentle slopes (suitable for shifting cultivation as well as for logging), and relative ease of clearing (since some of the larger trees have already been removed). The association of logging and subsequent clearing is especially strong in the lowland dipterocarp forests of insular Southeast Asia, which are richer in commercially valuable species and therefore more intensively logged than other tropical rain forests.

Extent of deforestation and forested areas

The FAO's estimates of the magnitude of deforestation in the region, from all causes, provide a quantitative context for what has been said about shifting cultivation. The average annual rate of deforestation from 1976 through 1980 in insular Southeast Asia, which accounted for nearly half of all deforestation in tropical Asia as a whole, was 880 000 ha or 0.60% of the total area in closed broad-leaved forests in 1976 (FAO, 1980, pp. 78–83 and *passim*). Of the area deforested annually in tropical Asia as a whole, 49% is attributable to shifting cultivation, according to the FAO study (Lanly, 1982, p. 83).

"Areas of natural woody vegetation", estimated as at the end of 1980, covered 198 000 000 ha in insular Southeast Asia, 77% of the total land area, and 40 000 000 ha or 86% of the total area in Papua New Guinea (FAO, 1980, table 1f). "Natural woody vegetation" includes closed broad-leaved forests, both logged and unlogged; coniferous forests; shrub formations; open woodlands; and woody fallows derived from shifting cultivation. We have regrouped the FAO data to show, in Table 34.2, the estimated area in each of the following categories:

TABLE 34.2

Areas of natural vegetation in insular Southeast Asia as of 1980 (in ha $\times 10^3$)

Country	Intact forest	Logged forest	Fallows	Open and shrub	Total
Brunei	306	17	237	0	560
Indonesia	79 075	34 820	17 360	26 900	158 155
Malaysia	12 972	8023	4825	0	25 820
Philippines	5620	3890	3520	0	13 030
Papua New Guinea	33 995	235	1445	4030	39 705
Total	131 968	46 985	27 387	30 930	237 270

Data from FAO (1981).

Intact forest: that which has neither been cleared in the last 20 to 30 years nor logged in the last 60 to 80 years (these being the time frames for which determinations could be made, according to the FAO authors). Intact forest includes closed broad-leaved and coniferous formations in what the FAO classifies as "undisturbed productive" forests (which can be logged but have not been logged for 60 years or more) as well as "unproductive" forests (which cannot be logged because of difficult terrain or other physical factors or because they are legally restricted — for instance, as reserves).

Logged forest: including areas managed under a silvicultural system or, more commonly, areas of unmanaged logging and logged-over forests. Managed forest accounts for 2 500 000 ha in Malaysia (mostly in Sarawak), 40 000 ha in Indonesia, and none of the areas in other countries of the region (FAO, 1980, table 1a).

Fallows: vegetation affected by shifting cultivation. This is presumed to be mainly secondary forest less than about 20 to 30 years old, but it is interspersed with patches of older forest, shrubs and grasses, fields and settlements. Such patches cannot be distinguished at the level of resolution of the FAO study — an important point, which we shall discuss below. In Table 34.2, we have combined closed, or forest, fallows with fallows of open formations occurring in Indonesia (3 900 000 ha) and Papua New Guinea (65 000 ha) (FAO, 1980, Table 1f).

Open and shrub formations: including woody vegetation that is not strictly forest (because the dominant layer is lower than about 7 m, or the canopy is open and there is a continuous understory of grass). Open woodlands occur in

Indonesia and Papua New Guinea, mainly where there is a monsoon (seasonally dry) climate and where site conditions or human interference prevent the development of a closed canopy (FAO, 1980, p. 372 and *passim*). Most (23.9 million ha) of the shrublands in the region occur in Indonesia, where they are called *belukar*. (Another 85 000 ha are in Papua New Guinea.) Shrub formations are created, in many if not all cases, by repeated clearing and burning (FAO, 1980, p. 43).

Internal heterogeneity of forest "fallow"

We believe that the estimates of the FAO authors are imprecise, as well as misleading in some respects, because the authors were unable to make the following important distinctions: (1) whether the forests cut by shifting cultivators are true old-growth or primary forests, or secondary forests more than about 20 to 30 years old (Lanly, 1982, p. 10); and (2) whether patches of old-growth or primary forest exist within areas designated as "fallow" or "forest fallow". (In addition to this imprecision, there are inaccuracies in the estimates of areas in each forest type, as provided by government agencies in the tropical countries surveyed.)[1] Given the deficiencies of the data, no qualitative difference can be detected between shifting cultivation in primary forest — such as that studied by Colfer (1982) in lowland East Kalimantan — and that in secondary forest more than 20 to 30 years old, as was found to be common in the Apo Kayan region of East

_____

[1] Our criticism reflects shortcomings in the available data rather than in the work of the FAO authors.

Kalimantan (Jessup, 1981). The majority of shifting cultivators, in fact, farm in secondary forest that is, on average, less than 20 years old (Vasey, 1979). This type of forest is classified by the FAO authors as "forest fallow". However, imprecision again enters, here due to an inability to distinguish between secondary forest of this age and other types of vegetation, including patches of primary and old-growth forest, which occur within the area designated as "forest fallow". Old-growth patches are often left in areas where shifting cultivation is practised (Fig. 34.6) (Clarke, 1976; Jessup, 1981; Vayda et al., 1985). Such patches can provide fields and young secondary communities with seed sources of primary-forest and late-successional species. They cover ridge-tops and steep slopes where such sites are left uncleared, not necessarily from an intention by the cultivators to conserve but because those sites are less fertile or more difficult to cultivate than others. It is important to recognize that "integral" shifting cultivators (those for whom shifting cultivation is a way of life and who are experienced in its practice) are effectively more environmentally conservative than "marginal" shifting cultivators (those for whom shifting cultivation is not a major activity) and novice farmers. The latter groups, especially if they take up shifting cultivation as colonists in a new and unfamiliar environment, tend to be more destructive in their farming practices (Watters, 1971; Sanchez, 1976). The distinction between different kinds of shifting cultivators and their practices is not always clear in the FAO report.

EXPLOITATION AS DISTURBANCE

In order to predict or assess the environmental effects of human activities such as shifting cultivation and logging, we must know something about the "background" rates and distributions of natural disturbances; about the adaptations and responses of organisms to disturbances; and about the stability of ecosystems into which human exploitation has only come recently — and industrial technologies much more recently — on an evolutionary time-scale (Covich, 1978). On the other hand, human activities even in prehistoric times have had profound effects in some tropical forests, as in the spread of grasslands and secondary forests in New Guinea and the Philippines (Walker, 1970; Flenley, 1979); thus, the detection and reconstruction of "natural" states is difficult if not impossible in many cases (Fosberg, 1960). Non-agricultural activities, such as the scattered felling of trees, fishing, hunting, and collecting, have had relatively subtle but possible widespread effects on forest structure and species composition for a longer time than agriculture (Alcorn, 1981; Padoch and Vayda, 1983). However, these activities have been studied relatively little, and their long-term, cumulative effects on forests cannot be distinguished from those of natural disturbances.

The direct and secondary effects of human activities can interact with those of natural phenomena, including long-term and widespread processes of climate and ecological succession as well as localized disturbance events. People's activities may either exacerbate or ameliorate the disruptive effects of natural disturbances. For instance,

Fig. 34.6. Old-growth forest patches within shifting cultivation.

timber cutting, forest clearing, and burning all seem to have contributed to the disastrous effects of the severe drought and subsequent forest fires during 1982 and 1983 in East Kalimantan. The primary cause of the drought itself was an abnormally strong El Niño–Southern Oscillation event (Leighton, 1984), but its effects on forests and other ecosystems in the region appear to have been compounded by the effects of logging and shifting cultivation (Mackie, 1984). On the other hand, many so-called "integral" shifting cultivators (those for whom the necessary skills and knowledge are closely bound to their whole way of life) take conservative measures to protect their environment, including the preparation of fire-breaks and other practices to inhibit the spread of fire (Clarke, 1976).

A disturbance-regime context for exploitation

Human activities such as shifting cultivation and tree felling create patches comparable to those made by natural disturbances (Jessup, 1983; Bazzaz, 1983; Vayda et al., 1985), which are known to play an important role in governing forest structure and growth cycles (Pickett, 1982; Whitmore, 1984). Using the concept of a "disturbance regime" (Pickett, 1982; Godron and Forman, 1983) we can analyze spatial and temporal patterns of disturbance caused by human activities in the same way as the patterns with natural causes. A disturbance

regime consists of information about the temporal frequency of disturbance, the size of patches created by disturbances, and the rate of change (recovery or succession) of patches. Other parameters, such as the spatial distribution of patches, their shape and internal structure, and interactions between patches, can also be included. Successional patches made by human activities and those created by natural phenomena can be defined and measured using the same parameters, thus permitting direct comparisons of their effects on organisms and ecosystems. Our own research (Vayda et al., 1985) provides examples of this approach, which we would like to see developed further.[1]

We have already indicated the importance of considering age differences between fields, old fields, and patches of secondary and primary forest within a landscape where shifting cultivation is practised. The age distribution of patches and their relative positions are determined by the frequency with which farmers clear and re-clear field sites (not only the average frequency but its variance as well), and the criteria which they use to select sites. Since those criteria often include floristic indicators (such as species composition and vegetation structure) and soil characteristics, both of which vary with the local history of cultivation, the cumulative effects of farmers' decisions and activities become quite complex over a number of generations (Fig. 34.6). This is somewhat analogous to the cumulative effect of interactions between the history of natural disturbances and species' responses to disturbance in a forest landscape.

Fig. 34.7. Patches of trees within fields.

[1]Our research was done in the Apo Kayan, where there is no mechanized logging. Nor are there any large-scale government or commercial projects, such as extensive land-clearing and colonization schemes, the construction of roads and dams, or the development of oil-palm plantations, all of which have disturbed huge sections of lowland forest elsewhere in Southeast Asia (FAO, 1980). However, we believe that these, too, are comparable to natural disturbances; that is, they can be measured and analyzed according to the parameters of a suitably defined disturbance regime. This is not to say that they are similar to common natural disturbances, such as those which cause tree-fall gaps, but rather that they can be included in a comprehensive analytical framework. On the other hand, the effects of some rare natural disturbances of great magnitude may actually be similar to those of some large-scale human activities. These might include, for example, volcanic eruptions (White, 1975; Foster, 1980) and freak wind-storms (Whitmore, 1984).

Forest structure and species composition are partly determined by the disturbance regime, but the effects of disturbances are mediated, in turn, by the size, distribution, and biological responses of organisms. (For example, the pattern of tree-fall gaps in a forest depends in part on the population densities, individual sizes, and mechanical properties of trees.)

The size and shape of swiddens (shifting cultivation fields) may be expected to be critical factors for forest recovery after cultivation, because both of these parameters can affect the distance seeds must travel from sources at the edge of clearings to the interior. If the edge of a swidden is bounded by forest, there may also be a moderating effect on microclimate there, which could affect seed germination and seedling growth. The distance from interior to edge is less, on the average, in fields with an irregular shape, which have a greater ratio of perimeter to area than fields which are more nearly circular. Field size by itself may therefore be less critical than expected if larger fields, by virtue of their shapes, maintain a center-to-edge distance characteristic of smaller but more symmetrical fields. This is indeed the case for swiddens in the Apo Kayan, studied by Jessup and Mackie (Vayda et al., 1985), where farmers adjust the shape of their fields to conform to local topography. Swidden borders follow the contours of hills and ridges, and fields are linked end-to-end along streams and narrow valleys, with strips and patches of forest left intact on the steeper slopes, hilltops, and ridge-tops. Smaller patches of trees are also left within fields, on rocky outcrops and other non-arable spots (Fig. 34.7).

From their studies of disturbances in the Apo Kayan, Jessup and Mackie were able to conclude that the a priori distinction between natural phenomena and human activities as a cause of disturbance does not correspond to any clear distinction according to measurable parameters such as the size of patches or the severity of disturbance (cf. Bazzaz, 1983). Even some complex, internal features of disturbance patches show similarities that cut across the "natural versus man-made" division. For example, tree-falls caused by human felling are structurally similar to those caused naturally by the snapping of trees, but they are different from natural "tip-ups", where trees turn over, exposing roots and mineral

soil.[1] Swiddens cleared by felling not surprisingly show internal structural similarities to the felling and "snap" gaps. However, the size of fields more closely approximates that of some large, natural landslides. The eroded, upper slope of a two-year-old landslide showed little evidence of recovery towards secondary forest, indicating that a severe disturbance had occurred. This was in contrast to old fields (fallow swiddens) of a similar age and size, which contained many forest species as seedlings and stump sprouts despite the fact that they had been burned and cultivated. Man-made and natural disturbances are not distinct classes, if what we have defined as disturbance regime parameters, rather than an anthropocentric view of their causes, are the criteria of classification.

ACKNOWLEDGEMENTS

We thank Cynthia Mackie of Rutgers University for her part in the East Kalimantan research cited in this chapter. For support of the research, we thank the U.S. Forest Service, and, for their help and cooperation, the Indonesian Institute of Sciences (LIPI) and Rutgers University.

REFERENCES

Abdulhadi, R., Kartawinata, K. and Sukardjo, S., 1981. Effects of mechanized logging in the lowland dipterocarp forest at Lempake, East Kalimantan. *Malay. For.*, 44: 407–418.

Abdulhadi, R., Mirmanto, E. and Kartawinata, K., 1985. *A Lowland Dipterocarp Forest in Sekundur, North Sumatra: Five Years after Mechanized Logging.* Paper presented at the Third Round Table Dipterocarp Conf., Samarinda, Indonesia, 16–23 April.

Alcorn, J.B., 1981. Huastec non-crop resource management: implication for historic rain forest management. *Human Ecol.*, 9: 395–417.

Anonymous, 1963. *Manual of Malayan Silviculture for Inland*

---

[1] In "snap gaps", as in felling gaps and swiddens, stumps and their root systems remain intact. Many later resprout, some even after burning (Nakano, 1978; Kartawinata et al., 1980; Riswan, 1982; Vayda et al., 1985). A "tip-up", on the other hand, leaves an exposed root plate and exposed mineral soil, which may provide germination sites for species different from those which colonize snap and felling gaps (Bazzaz and Pickett, 1980; Brokaw, 1985). Soil is even more severely disturbed by landslides, which expose subsoil and sometimes even bedrock (Veblen and Ashton, 1978; Garwood et al., 1979; Vayda et al., 1985).

Forests. Malayan Forest Records No. 23.

Anonymous, 1965. *Handbook of Selective Logging*. Bureau of Forestry, Manila, Philippines.

Ashton, P.S., 1980. Biological and ecological principles for the utilization of dipterocarp species. *BioIndonesia*, 7: 43–54.

Ashton, P.S., 1982. Dipterocarpaceae. In: C.G.G.J. van Steenis (Editor), *Flora Malesiana, Ser. I, Vol. 9*. Nijhoff, The Hague, pp. 237–552.

Awang, K., 1982. Current and future forestry research in view of recent developments in Malaysian forestry. In: *Proc. Workshop on Ecological Basis for Rational Resource Utilization in the Humid Tropics of Southeast Asia, Serdang, Malaysia*, pp. 62–69.

Awang, K., Lai, F.S., Lee, S.S. and Derus, D.R.M. (Editors), 1983. *Proc. Workshop on Hydrological Impacts of Forestry, Univ. Pertanian Malaysia, Serdang, Malaysia*.

Bazzaz, F.A., 1983. Characteristics of populations in relation to disturbance in natural and man-modified ecosystems. In: H.A. Mooney and M. Godron (Editors), *Disturbance and Ecosystems: Components of Response*. Springer, Berlin.

Bazzaz, F.A. and Pickett, S.T.A., 1980. Physiological ecology of tropical successions: a comparative review. *Annu. Rev. Ecol. Syst.*, 11: 287–310.

Brokaw, N.V.L., 1985. Treefalls, regrowth, and community structure in tropical forests. In: S.T.A. Pickett and P.S. White (Editors), *The Ecology of Natural Disturbance and Patch Dynamics*. Academic Press, New York, N.Y., in press.

Bruenig, E.F., 1983. *Deforestation and its Ecological Implications for the Rain Forests in Southeast Asia*. Paper presented at the IUCN Int. Symposium on the Future of Tropical Rainforests in Southeast Asia, Kepong, Malaysia, 1–2 September 1983.

Burkill, I.H., 1966. *A Dictionary of Economic Products of the Malay Peninsula*. 2 vols., 2nd ed., Ministry of Agriculture and Cooperatives, Kuala Lumpur.

Chai, D.N.P. and Udarbe, M.P., 1977. The effectiveness of current silvicultural practices in Sabah. *Malay. For.*, 40(1): 27–35.

Clarke, W.C., 1976. Maintenance of agriculture and human habitats within the tropical forest ecosystem. *Human Ecol.*, 4: 247–259.

Colfer, C.J.P., 1982. *Kenyah Dayak Tree Cutting in Context*. Unpublished final report for the MAB's Project on Interactions Between People and Forests in East Kalimantan, Indonesia.

Corner, E.J.H., 1952. *Wayside Trees of Malaya*. Government Printer, Singapore, 2nd ed.

Corner, E.J.H., 1966. *The Natural History of Palms*. Univ. of California Press, Berkeley, Calif.

Covich, A.P., 1978. A reassessment of ecological stability in the Maya area: evidence from lake studies of early agricultural impacts on biotic communities. In: P.D. Harrison and B.L. Turner (Editors), *Pre-Hispanic Maya Agriculture*. Univ. of New Mexico Press, Albuquerque, N.M.

Dransfield, J., 1979. *A Manual of the Rattans of the Malay Peninsula*. Malayan Forest Records No. 29.

Dransfield, J., 1981. The biology of Asiatic rattans in relation to the rattan trade and conservation. In: H. Synghe (Editor), *The Biological Aspects of Rare Plant Conservation*. Wiley, New York, N.Y.

Ewel, J. and Conde, L.F., 1980. Potential ecological impacts of increased intensity of tropical forest utilization. *BIOTROP, Spec. Publ.*, 11.

FAO, 1980. *Forest Resources of Tropical Asia*. Technical Report No. 3 of the Tropical Resources Assessment Project, FAO, Rome.

Flenley, J.R., 1979. *The Equatorial Rain Forest: A Geological History*. Butterworth, London.

Fosberg, 1960. Nature and detection of plant communities resulting from activities of early man. In: *Symp. on the Humid Tropics Vegetation, Goroka, Territory of Papua and New Guinea, September 1960, UNESCO, Paris*, pp. 251–262.

Foster, R.B., 1980. Heterogeneity and disturbance in tropical vegetation. In: M.E. Soule and B. Wilcox (Editors), *Conservation Biology: An Evolutionary-Ecological Perspective*. Sinauer, Sunderland, Mass.

Fox, J.E.D., 1976. Constraints on the natural regeneration of tropical moist forest. *For. Ecol. Manage.*, 1: 37–65.

Freeman, D., 1979. *Report on the Iban*. (London School of Economics Monographs on Social Anthropology, 41) Athlone, London.

Garwood, N.C., Janos, D.P. and Brokaw, N.V.L., 1979. Earthquake caused landslides: a major disturbance to tropical forests. *Science*, 205: 997–999.

Godron, M. and Forman, R.T.T., 1983. Landscape modification and changing ecological characteristics. In: H.A. Mooney and M. Godron (Editors), *Disturbance and Ecosystems: Components of Response*. Springer, Berlin, pp. 12–28.

Habir, M., 1983. Timber: It all depends on how supply is nurtured. *Far East. Econ. Rev.*, 121(33): 52–53.

Hallé, F. and six others (Editors), 1981. *Forest Regeneration in Southeast Asia*. Proc. BIOTROP Symp. on Forest Regeneration in Southeast Asia. BIOTROP, Spec. Publ., 13.

Harrison, T. and O'Connor, S.J., 1967. *Excavations of the Prehistoric Iron Industry in West Borneo. Vol. 2: Associated Artifacts and Ideas*. Southeast Asia Program, Department of Asian Studies, Cornell Univ., Ithaca, N.Y.

Jacobs, M., 1982. The study of minor forest products. *Flora Males. Bull.*, 35: 3768–3782.

Jessup, T.C., 1981. Why do Apo Kayan shifting cultivators move? *Borneo Res. Bull.*, 13(1): 16–32.

Jessup, T.C., 1983. *Interactions Between People and Forest in Apo Kayan*. Final Report on the Project on Interactions Between People and Forest in East Kalimantan, Indonesia. Man and the Biosphere Program (manuscript).

Johns, A.D., 1985. Selective logging and wildlife conservation in tropical rain forest: problems and recommendations. *Biol. Conserv.*, 31: 355–375.

Kartawinata, K., 1981. The environmental consequences of tree removal from forests in Indonesia. In: V.H. Sutlive, N. Althuser and M.D. Zamora (Editors), *Where Have All the Flowers Gone? Deforestation in the Third World*. Stud. Third World Soc., Publ. 13: 191–214.

Kartawinata, K. and Vayda, A.P., 1984. Forest conversion in East Kalimantan, Indonesia: the activities and impacts of timber companies, shifting cultivators, migrant pepper farmers and others. In: F. di Castri, F.W.G. Baker and M.

Hadley (Editors), *Ecology in Practice: 1. Ecosystem Management.* Tycooly, Dublin, and UNESCO, Paris, pp. 98–126.

Kartawinata, K., Riswan, S. and Soedjito, H., 1980. The floristic change after disturbances in lowland dipterocarp forest in East Kalimantan, Indonesia. In: J.I. Furtado (Editor), *Tropical Ecology and Development.* Int. Society for Tropical Ecology, Kuala Lumpur, pp. 47–54.

Kartawinata, K., Adisoemarto, S., Riswan, S. and Vayda, A.P., 1981. The impact of man on a tropical forest in Indonesia. *Ambio,* 10: 115–119.

Kartawinata, K. and eight others, 1983. *Suksesi sekunder dan perubahan ekologi lainnya di hutan tropika setelah perusakan oleh manusia di Kalimantan Timur (Secondary successions and other ecological changes in a tropical forest after human disturbance in East Kalimantan).* Lembaga Biologi Nasional – LIPI, Bogor, and Panitia Program MAB Indonesia, Jakarta.

Kramer, K., 1926. Onderzoek naar de natuurlijke verjonging in den uitkap in Preanger gebergte-bosch. *Meded. Proefstn. Boschw., Bogor,* 14.

Kramer, K., 1933. De natuurlijke verjonging in het Goenoeng Gede complex. *Tectona,* 26: 156–185.

Kuswara, T., 1982. Budidaya rotan di Kalimantan Tengah. (Cultivation of rattans in Central Kalimantan). *Bul. Kebun Raya (Bogor),* 5: 85–90. English summary in *Rattan Information Centre Bulletin (Kepong),* 2: 6–7 (1983).

Lanly, J.P., 1982. *Tropical Forest Resources.* FAO Forestry Paper 30. (Technical Report of the Tropical Forest Resources Assessment Project). FAO, Rome.

Leighton, M., 1984. *The El Niño Southern Oscillation Event in Southeast Asia: Effects of Drought and Fire in a Tropical Forest in eastern Borneo.* Paper presented at the Meetings for American Association for Advancement of Science, 24–29 May 1984, New York.

Mackie, C., 1984. The lesson behind East Kalimantan's forest fires. *Borneo Res. Bull.,* 16: 63–74.

Magenda, B., 1981. *East Kalimantan: the fail of a dependent aristocracy.* Ph.D. Thesis, Cornell Univ., Ithaca, N.Y. (manuscript).

Manning, C., 1971. The timber boom, with special reference to East Kalimantan. *Bull. Indon. Econ. Stud.,* 7(3): 30–60.

Meijer, W., 1973. Devastation and regeneration of lowland dipterocarp forests in Southeast Asia. *Bioscience,* 23(9): 528–533.

Myers, N., 1980. *Conversion of Tropical Moist Forests.* National Academy of Sciences, Washington, D.C.

Nakano, K., 1978. An ecological study of swidden agriculture at a village in Northern Thailand. *Southeast Asian Stud.,* 16(3): 411–416.

Nicholson, D.I., 1979. *The Effects of Logging and Treatment on the Mixed Dipterocarp Forests of Southeast Asia.* FAO, Rome.

Nor, S.M. and Baharuddin, J., 1983. *Silvicultural Practices in Peninsular Malaysia.* Paper presented at the IUCN Int. Symp. on Future of Tropical Rainforests in Southeast Asia, Forest Research Institute, Kepong, Malaysia, 1–2 September 1983.

Padoch, C. and Vayda, A.P., 1983. Patterns of resources use and human settlements in tropical forests. In: F.B. Golley

(Editor), *Tropical Rain Forest Ecosystems: Structure and Function.* (Ecosystems of the World, 14A) Elsevier, Amsterdam, pp. 301–313.

Peluso, N.L., 1983a. Networking in the commons. *Indonesia,* 35: 95–108.

Peluso, N.L., 1983b. *Market and merchants: the forest products trade of East Kalimantan in historical perspective.* M.Sc. Thesis, Cornell Univ., Ithaca, N.Y.

Pickett, S.T.A., 1980. Non-equilibrium coexistence in plants. *Bull. Torrey Bot. Club,* 107: 238–248.

Pickett, S.T.A., 1982. Differential adaptation of tropical tree species to canopy gaps and its role in canopy dynamics. *Trop. Ecol.,* 24(1): 68–84.

Poore, M.E.D., 1968. Studies in Malayan rain forest. I. Triassic sediments in Jengka Forest Reserve. *J. Ecol.,* 56: 143–196.

Price, P.W., 1980. *Evolutionary Biology of Parasites.* Princeton Univ. Press, Princeton, N.J.

Riswan, S., 1982. *Ecological studies of primary, secondary, and experimentally cleared mixed dipterocarp forest and kerangas forest in East Kalimantan.* Ph.D. Thesis, Univ. of Aberdeen, Aberdeen.

Sanchez, P.A., 1976. *Properties and Management of Soils in the Tropics.* Wiley, New York.

Smits, W.Th.M., 1983. Dipterocarps and mycorhiza: an ecological adaptation and a factor in forest regeneration. *Flora Malesiana Bull.,* 36: 3926–3937.

Soedjarwo, 1978. Keynote address. In: *Symp. on the Long-Term Effects of Logging in Southeast Asia.* BIOTROP Spec. Publ. 3: 11.

Soerianegara, I., 1970. The silvicultural systems for the tropical forests in Indonesia. *Rimba Indon.,* 15.

Soerianegara, I. and Kartawinata, K., 1983. *Silvicultural Management of the Logged Natural Dipterocarp Forest in Indonesia.* Paper presented at the IUCN Int. Symp. on Future of Tropical Rainforests in Southeast Asia, Kepong, Malaysia, 1–2 September 1983.

Spencer, J.E., 1966. *Shifting Cultivation in Southeast Asia.* Univ. of California Press, Berkeley, Calif.

Van den Koppel, C., 1945. Forestry in the Outer Provinces of the Netherlands Indies. In: P. Honig and F. Verdoorn (Editors), *Science and Scientists in the Netherlands East Indies, Surinam and Curacao.* New York, N.Y.

Vasey, D.E., 1979. Population and agricultural intensity in the humid tropic. *Human Ecol.,* 7: 269–283.

Vayda, A.P., Colfer, C.J.P. and Brotokusumo, M., 1980. Interactions between people and forests in East Kalimantan. *Impact Sci. Soc.,* 30: 179–190.

Vayda, A.P., Jessup, T.C. and Mackie, C., 1985. *Shifting Cultivation and Patch Dynamics in an Upland Forest in East Kalimantan,* Indonesia. Final Report to the U.S. Forest Service for the U.S.–Indonesian MAB Project (manuscript).

Veblen, T.T. and Ashton, D.H., 1978. Catastrophic influences on the vegetation of the Valdevian Andes, Chile. *Vegetatio,* 36: 149–167.

Walker, D., 1970. The changing vegetation of the montane tropics. *Search,* 217–221.

Watters, R.F., 1971. *Shifting Cultivation in Latin America.* FAO Forestry Development Paper No. 17, FAO, Rome.

White, K.J., 1975. *The Effects of Natural Phenomena on the Forest Environment*. President's address to the Papua New Guinea Scientific Society, 26 March 1975.

Whitmore, T.C., 1973. *Palms of Malaya*. Oxford Univ. Press, London.

Whitmore, T.C., 1984. On patterns and process in forests. In: E.I. Newman (Editor), *The Plant Community as a Working Mechanism*. Blackwell, Oxford, pp. 44–136.

Wong, K.M., 1983. Rattans: Cane for the world. *Wallaceana*, December 1983, pp. 19–20.

Chapter 35

USE AND MISUSE OF TROPICAL RAIN FORESTS

E.F. BRUENIG

EARLY HISTORY OF NATIVE FOREST USE

The complexity and diversity of the tropical rain forest (Fig. 35.1) and its even climate provided varied and rich diet, shelter and tranquillity needed for the evolution of man from arboreal man-ape to terrestrial hominid. Excessive brain capacity and low physical specialization helped early man out of paradisiacal existence into his modern role as an external disturbance factor. Terrestrial life and cultural development gradually lead to ever more aggressive attitudes toward the environment. Initially, early man hardly affected the structure and functioning of the tropical rain-forest ecosystem. Locally, certain plant species might have been exterminated by over-use, or enriched by dispersal of propagules or removal of competitors. This remained more or less accidental, however, and had only very localized effects. In time, man's impact became more profound and intentional. Consequently, forest structure and functions were changed, but not seriously perturbed. Basically, the rain-forest ecosystems remained intact. Important food plants, such as sago-producing palms (Fig. 35.2), fruit-producing trees and medicinal plants were purposely aggregated and tended in convenient places. Eventually, the forest garden, a kind of Garden of Eden, emerged. These jungle gardens on good soils of easy access required little maintenance and hardly any hard work. So they could be run by the women while males remained more addicted to roaming the landscape for protein-rich food and adventure. These forest gardens as a land-use system persist in the form of individual home gardens or communal village gardens which are widespread in the humid tropics, and especially well developed and sophisticated in Southeast Asia (Fig. 35.3).

When man had learned to handle fire and axe, he was ready for the conquest of the drier, more open and more easily cleared and burned deciduous tropical forests. Only in the deciduous, seasonally dry forest could the technique of clearing and burning for field cropping be developed. The smaller understorey trees could be felled easily even with primitive stone axes. The large heavy-wooded emergents shed their leaves during the dry season, allowing the slash to dry. In contrast, emergents in the evergreen rain forest remain in leaf and would have to be felled to assure sufficient drying of the slash. This would have needed, and still needs, a highly developed technology, especially improved axes and felling techniques. Even today, the work load for felling primary rain forest and the uncertainties of obtaining a good burn are harassing problems for the shifting cultivators.

The exodus into the deciduous and dry forests initiated the first agricultural revolution and led to profound social changes. The new capability to grow annual field crops, the technical skills and physical strength required to clear, use and defend the land, gave the men a new and more vital role than in the previous paradisiacal existence in the rain forest. Here, only few people remained and persisted in the original subsistence form of existence as gatherers and hunters. Later, "secondary primitives" returned from the savannas to the rain forest under pressure from more aggressive or culturally superior groups. They continue to live even now in the forest in the reacquired role as integrated hunters, scavengers and collectors.

The main human onslaught on the predominantly evergreen moist to wet tropical forests is

Fig. 35.1. Internal structure of a mature stage in the medium successional phase (B stage, phase 3 in Fig. 35.6) species-rich, complex, mesophyll, pristine Mixed Dipterocarp forest on ultisol soil. The forest offers multiple benefits to man: timber and camphor from the large *Dryobalanops beccarii* tree, Malacca cane and leaves from climbing and terrestrial palms to build his shelters and huts, starchy, fatty and protein-rich fruits, pharmaceuticals, fibre, dyes, spices, game, fish and spiritual abode. Selang Forest Reserve, Sarawak.

Fig. 35.2. Sago is one of the forest products which have been exploited from natural forests since time immemorial. Forest dwellers used it as staple food, their settled descendants produce sago flour in village industries for sale at home and for export. In the course of exploitation and tending, forest sago palm stands may if well managed become enriched to almost pure stands. On rich alluvial wetland and fresh-water swamps such stands can produce a sustained yield without detriment to the soil. Nomadic forest dwellers still depend on sustained production of sago and other forest produce for their livelihood. Tatau river, Sarawak.

more recent. It came with the backlash migration from the deciduous and drier biomes. These migrations were slow and gradual, and continue to this day. An example is the spread of the Iban in Borneo during the last 500 years. The migrations were usually initiated by many interacting factors, such as climatic changes, population increases and land shortage, and by political events such as the rise and shift of centres of power and harassment by wars of conquest. The implements and techniques of those who moved back were now quite different and sufficiently perfected to cope with the dense, tall rain forests. Better stone, bronze and finally iron axes and efficient felling techniques made the big trees an easier prey and thereby slash-

and-burn crop culture became practical. This development gained momentum during the last few centuries, and a great variety of local forms of shifting cultivation techniques developed. A dramatic boom in forest destruction by shifting cultivation is happening since the Second World War.

Under the original systems of shifting cultivation virgin forest was felled and burned, the land was cropped 2 or 3 times, sometimes with an intermittent fallow year, then committed to fallow. Freshly cleared forest land was added annually, while land on which cropping was completed entered the fallow cycle. The labour of felling the large emergents of the tropical rain forest being extremely heavy, and the drying of the thick stems and branches very uncertain in wet years, the farmers tended to reduce labour and risk by farming parts of the fallow land as early as possible. This naturally shortened the fallow, thus hastening the progress of site degradation. Finally, all virgin forest in reasonable walking distance was

Fig. 35.3. The complex, near-natural forest structure of a permanent, sustained combination of trees, shrubs and herbaceous plants. This crop-type resembles the ancient and traditional jungle family or communal garden which is particularly widespread throughout Southeast Asia. *A* = shelter trees producing timber and fruit; *B* = intermediate-storey multi-purpose trees; *C* = understorey trees and shrubs; *D* = condiments, tubers and other bottom shade plants; *L* = lianas (such as pepper, vanilla). The two pictures represent the state of the garden at 50 years' interval of time.

consumed. Successive crop–fallow rotations reduced regenerating efficiency of the fallow and increased degradation of the soil; in the end after several rotations, weeds and pest would have increased and productivity declined so much that subsistence was no longer possible. In response, the whole or parts of the village began to shift in stages to a new site with fresh forested land, leaving deforested and degraded land behind, which might recover over centuries unless a fire disclimax arrested succession (Fig. 35.16).

The vicious circle of degradation in the tropical slash-and-burn fallow system is not primarily caused by nutrient deficiency and loss. Deterioration is due to feed-backs between increased light, weed growth, fire, inadequate fallow, build-up of pests and diseases, distance from homestead to field, reduced fallow periods and increased population densities. The combined synergistic effects eventually lead to fire-arrested types of vegetation and degraded soil conditions, which to restore is beyond the technological abilities of the native farmer. In the past, the answer to this problem was migration into pristine forest lands (shifting cultivation in the true sense). With new political barriers arising and increasing population densities this option becomes less and less available. Permanent deforestation and site degradation has acquired a scale in recent decades which is threatening the very survival of the tropical rain-forest biome.

This modern slash-and-burn cultivation is exotic to the rain forest and in every respect fundamentally different from the ancient rain-forest garden of the early food gatherers and the modern home or village garden of settled cultivators. The two land-use systems are ecologically and evolutionarily almost diagonally opposed. The forest and home garden developed in the rain forest as an autochthonous, adapted and self-regulating sustained ecosystem. The slash-and-burn rotational and migratory field cropping is an exogenous, predatory and non-sustainable system, exploitative and wasteful of land, and ecologically not adapted to humid tropical site conditions. It is merely a question of time, population density, soil quality and topography how quickly deterioration progresses toward eventual collapse of the system. Practicable alternatives on average sites and soils in the humid tropical biome are systems which combine the elements of the ancient forest garden with those of field cropping in the form of mixed farming systems. On less favourable sites and soils, adapted and sustainable land use is possible only by means of natural protective and productive forest and forest garden types of agroforestry. Intensive cultivation of annual crops will have to remain restricted to irrigated and/or terraced fields on very favourable soils, applying advanced techniques of soil management (Sanchez and Cochrane, 1980; Cochrane and Sanchez, 1983; Bruenig, 1984) (Fig. 35.4).

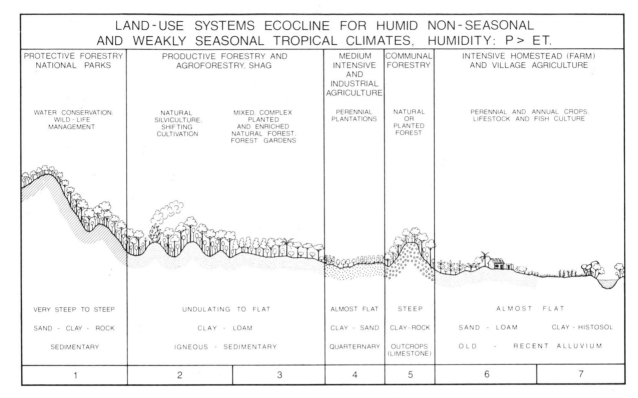

Fig. 35.4. Example of the integration of forestry and agriculture in accordance with site and soil, infrastructure, accessibility and the need to maintain adequate environmental conditions at landscape unit level. *1* = absolute protective forestry sites, ulti-oxisols on steep slopes and spodosols on gentle dip-slopes; *2* and *3* = relative forest sites, system choice depending on landform, physiography, soil type; typical region of currently continuing shifting cultivation which should be abandoned in favour of more adapted forms of agriculture and agroforestry as soon as possible; *4* = almost flat sites with good soil conditions, fully suited to agriculture but usually too distant for intensive cultivation; *5* = absolute forest site for protective and productive communal forestry; *6* = high productivity sites, as in *4*, but better access and therefore more intensive agriculture possible; *7* = very high production potential for irrigated agriculture, but trees planted around houses and in shelterbelts for soil and climatic protection, maintenance of broad river-bank protective forest strips essential for ecological stability on land and in the river.

DEFORESTATION

Deforestation is the complete clearing of the land of trees and shrubs, and subsequent conversion of the land to agricultural or other non-silvicultural uses. Deforestation for agriculture has build-in multiplier effects. The problems, difficulties and delimitation of deforestation and reforestation are discussed by Kartawinata et al. (Ch. 34, this volume). With the present rate of population increase, deforestation and degradation have spread throughout the tropical rain-forest biome by two processes. Firstly, the unescapable degradation of the "shifting agriculture" system in all respects leads eventually to arrested fire disclimaxes with little capacity for succession back to forest. Secondly, settled rain-fed field agriculture depends on maintaining nutrients, humus, microbial life and soil structure. This requires inputs of fertilizers and organic matter. There is no alternative under native farming systems but to import ash, litter, fodder and top-soil from the surrounding land. This will continue until the productivity of surrounding forests and lands is exhausted and destroyed. Consequently, the agricultural fields degrade to useless wasteland overgrown by weeds, which to reclaim is beyond the technical capabilities of the local farmers. The present regional and global deforestation rates in the tropical humid forest area have been assessed reasonably reliably, and as well as possible under the circumstances, by FAO (1982b, table 5 and fig. 1). The pathways of global deforestation are reproduced in Fig. 35.5. The area of natural tropical rain forest will be

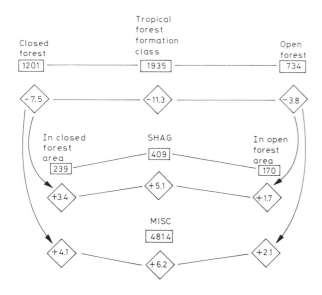

Fig. 35.5. Pathways and net amounts (in million hectares) of deforestation in tropical humid closed forest and subhumid/semi-arid open forest formation subclasses. Squares = area of category in 1980 (somewhat larger than estimated in Table 35.1); diamonds = annual rate of change 1981–1985; SHAG – shifting cultivation, including secondary fallow vegetation; MISC = a mixture of other categories, such as settled agriculture, forest tree plantations, scrub, grasslands, desertified and desert land, etc. (Source: FAO, 1982a, fig. 1, p. 86, and 1982b, fig. 1, p. 22.)

halved by 2050 and the rates of forest destruction will not nearly be compensated by the establishment of tree plantations (Table 35.1). The area and the annual area increase of agriculture and forestry plantations are insignificant in relation to the annual forest loss by slash-and-burn shifting cultivation.

Timber and fuel-wood harvesting in the humid tropical forests make little direct contribution to deforestation. Well-planned and cautiously executed selective timber exploitation will not destroy the viability and regenerative vigour of the mixed rain-forest ecosystem. It is careless working and excessively heavy and over-mechanized logging and particularly slash-and-burn agriculture which causes degradation and lasting deforestation, especially on fragile, oligotrophic soils (Bruenig, 1974). Indirectly, timber logging contributes by providing easy access to fresh and semi-cleared virgin land for landless farmers. This is particularly so in Africa and Southeast Asia, but less in America where the old single-species creaming and river-scratching practices of timber logging still prevail, except along the new highways of the Amazonia network.

In conclusion, tropical deforestation is the result

TABLE 35.1

Forecast of changes in the world area of natural tropical forests

Tropical closed and open forest formations subclass	Forest area (in 10^6 km²; optimistic scenario) in the years:			
	1965	1980	2000	2050
Predominantly evergreen per-humid forests	5.5	4.4	3.7	2.7
Predominantly deciduous humid forests	7.5	6.5	5.9	4.8
Predominantly deciduous semi-arid forests	7.5	6.5	5.5	4.5
Sum (optimistic)	20.5	17.4	15.1	12.0
(pessimistic)	20.5	16.0	12.5	8.0
Man-made forest plantations	0.06	0.12	0.25	0.50
Agricultural tree plantations	0.23	0.26	0.28	0.35

Both open and closed forest (but excluding agricultural tree fallow) are included, the former composing about one-third of the total, mainly in the semi-arid zone. It is assumed that non-destructive utilization and improvements of agriculture to replace shifting cultivation and control soil deterioration are successfully introduced (optimistic scenario with <0.6% deforestatation rate), or that present political attitudes and bureaucratic ineptitude obtain (pessimistic scenario, >0.6% deforestation rate). The increases of man-made forestry and agriculture are based on the assumption of effective implementation of development policies.

of agricultural expansion. Logging does not defor-
est directly. The globally logged pristine forest
area, almost exclusively in the humid tropical
forests is estimated at between 4 and 5×10^6
hectares annually, FAO estimates a rate of
4.3×10^6 ha (FAO, 1982b, p. 18) which regenerate
unless they are cleared and burnt. Slash-and-burn
agriculture consumes at least 11 000 000 ha of
forest annually, of which a small proportion is
previously logged forest. Clearing for pasture has
consumed many millions of hectares of forest, but
the practice will diminish on average soils because
it is proving to be unsustainable. The dramatic
decline of forest area during the post-war period is
illustrated by the vegetation maps of Malesia by
Van Steenis (1958) and Whitmore (1984).

GROWING STOCK STRUCTURE AND FOREST FUNCTIONS

The tropical rain forest appears at first sight to
be a homogeneous "green desert". In reality, it is a
complex mixture of very heterogeneous soils,
landforms, tree associations and phases of regeneration, growth and decay. Consequently, timber
harvesting does not cover tracts of forests evenly.
Logging operations focus on easily accessible areas
in which the volume of growing stock and the kind
and quality of timber are technically most acceptable and commercially attractive. These conditions
may be correlated with certain site and soil types.
Examples are the agglomerations of commercial
dipterocarp species especially along the ridge crests
in lowland dipterocarp forest, or of *Dryobalanops
fusca* or *Agathis borneensis* on medium-deep to
very deep spodosol soils in kerangas forest in
Borneo. In the peat-swamp forest of Borneo,
certain stages of the primary peat-swamp forest
succession carry consociations dominated by single
gregarious species which regenerate profusely, if
only episodically successfully, and maintain themselves as long as peat and drainage conditions
remain adequate for their survival. Examples are
the commercially valuable species *Shorea albida*
and *Dryobalanops rappa*. While such forests regenerate adequately under a regime of constant small-
to medium-scale catastrophes (Fig. 35.6), regeneration after wholesale logging is unreliable, and
chances depend on episodic mass fruiting and the

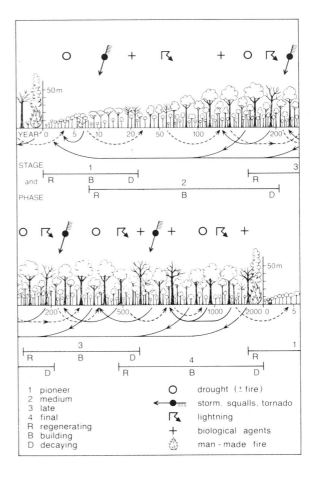

Fig. 35.6. Hypothetical scheme of the dynamics of natural
primary and secondary succession, and exemplary illustration
of the reactions induced by disturbance from natural agents or
by logging or silvicultural treatment. The hypothetical complete
sequence of natural succession includes four successional stages
with the phases: R = regeneration, B = building and maturing,
and D = decay. The arrows indicate advance or regression of
phasic development and succession as a result of weak, small-
scale (broken arrows) or destructive large-scale disturbances or
catastrophes. The most common stages in primary forest are *2*
and *3*; stage *1* only occurs after rare die-backs, fire or other
collapses, or after large-scale complete logging. Stage *4* is hardly
ever reached and usually only occupies small patches which
escaped natural or man-made disturbances. The dynamic
changes initiated by exploitative or silvicultural manipulation
of the primary forest are dependent on the intensity and area
scale of the interference.

These catastrophes are essential components of the regulatory mechanisms which keep the forest structurally adapted and
dynamic, preventing conditions of unstable stagnation with
excessive negentropy accumulation and moribund senescence
(for instance in stage *4*).

physiological state of the seedlings. Fires, such as those which raged through the peat-swamps of Kalimantan in 1982/83, may destroy forest and peat to such an extent that many centuries will be needed to restore the forest (see also Whitmore, Ch. 10).

Similar self-maintaining single-species consociations are known from Africa and America. In Africa, *Tetraberlinia tubmanniana* forms dense stands of merchantable timber on bottom lands and sandy-loamy upland soils in the evergreen forest belt of Liberia and Sierra Leone. In America, dense stands of merchantable timber are formed by several species of *Eperua* (Caesalpiniaceae) on several types of rather unfavourable spodosols and ultisols in the Rio Negro and Orinoco basins and in Surinam.

Contrasting with these self-maintaining stands of gregarious species are those in which high frequency and dominance are ephemeral and associated with certain seral stages of secondary succession. Examples are the relativly high growing-stock volumes of medium-light wooded large timber trees in certain seral stages of old secondary rain forest in West Africa which were the source of export timber to Europe, but regenerate poorly after exploitation (see also Lawton, Ch. 33).

In addition to this variation in the species composition and structure of growing stock, there is variation of timber quality in relation to site and successional stage. Early successional stages contain a higher proportion of specics with light to medium-light wood than late stages which contain a large proportion of trees giving very heavy, naturally durable, timber. Decay phases (Fig. 35.6, D-phases) contain particularly large proportions of defective, hollow trees.

As a result of this heterogeneity, the amount of merchantable growing stock of species which are considered commercial under current market conditions varies widely. Merchantable volumes of commercial species may represent as much as 80 to 90% of the growing stock, or even more. Examples are the single-species consociations dominated by *Dryobalanops rappa*, *Shorea albida* or *Eperua* spp. mentioned earlier. These cases are rare, their commercial value is high, and its realization by complete exploitation is often destructive.

The proportion of merchantable growing stock of commercial species is on average around 50 to 70% in lowland Mixed Dipterocarp forest. Few merchantable timber types are produced by groups of species in various genera of the dipterocarps (such as *Dipterocarpus*, *Parashorea*, *Pentacme* and *Shorea*) which tend to gregariousness and produce stocking levels between 50 and 150 m^3 ha^{-1}. Actual volumes cut and removed are influenced by the condition of the growing stock, marketing intensity and market potentials, kind and quality of local processing facilities, and the quality of management and supervision. On average 40 to over 100 m^3 ha^{-1} are extracted from lowland Mixed Dipterocarp forest. Very high volumes are removed from Bornean peat-swamps where more than 500 m^3 ha^{-1} of saw and veneer logs may be extracted from the Alan Bunga forest consociation.

Particularly the cutting of high-quality export logs of preferred species is not only selective of individual trees, but also of stands in certain seral stages of forest development or on certain types of soil and site. Logged-over forest is, therefore, irregularly patchy, which accentuates the natural patchiness of the forest. Usually, D-phases (Fig. 35.6) remain untouched, while B-phases are more or less clear-felled. The overmature patches remain to become more senile, while vigorous patches are thrown back to the early R-phases of the same or the previous successional stage. Continued selective logging without subsequent intensive silvicultural treatment of relict trees and patches, therefore, will eventually result in a very unbalanced and unfavourable pattern of forest structure. The increment of the residual forest will be correspondingly varied and patchy. The increased patchiness may, however, favourably affect habitat diversity, and retention of old relict trees may improve the biotope value of the logged-over forest land for certain bird and mammal species. Prospects for expanding the range of commercial species by promoting individual lesser-known species are generally poor, because their growing stock volumes are too low for individual marketing.

On the domestic market, increasing demands and diminishing virgin forest timber resource is causing a general trend, very acutely in many tropical countries such as Malaysia, Brunei and most African and Central American countries, to accept almost any tree species on the market provided the timber is of sufficient size and is neither poisonous nor technologically extremely unfavourable. In rural areas, timber and fuel-wood harvesting by natives for their own use is highly selective. For each purpose certain timber species with specific properties are traditionally preferred. These traditions are one of the obstacles to local marketing of lesser-known species.

Growing-stock conditions are very different in most rain forests in Africa and America. On average sites, the dominance of single species or of species groups producing similar timber types is much rarer; and usually, where it occurs, volumes are much lower. In West Africa, much of the timber currently exported originates from late seral secondary forest. Growing-stock volumes and quality are even less favourable in the geo-chemically disadvantaged Amazon and Orinoco basins. The proportion of timber volume which is currently merchantable is low, and much less than in the dipterocarp forests of Southeast Asia. The interaction of growing stock and export market conditions in Africa and America cause the removal rates per hectare to be generally lower, and it would be difficult to raise them to Southeast Asian levels except for supply of a growing domestic market.

Variation of structure and physiognomy of natural tropical rain forest is closely associated with site and soil conditions, in a manner which can be interpreted as adaptation to the physical and chemical environment (Bruenig, 1962a, b). The structural changes by carefully executed SIS/TPI (see Fig. 35.12) are short-term and the crop physiognomy is hardly affected. Clear felling causes drastic reduction of biomass density and is followed by the development of regrowth which has a more uniform and, on soils with sufficient moisture supply, more mesophytic canopy (see Fig. 35.6, stage 1). On oligotrophic xeric soils the regrowth remains as sclerophytic and xeromorphic as the mother stand.

The decreases in aerodynamic roughness and biomass density have most profound effects on the stand functions. Simplification of the canopy reduces the rates of interception of energy and matter. Consequently, the rates of intake, turn-over and output of energy and matter and the intensity of cycling processes are similarly reduced. By contrast, light reflection, direct through-flow of water and lateral wind-speeds are increased. At the same time, floristic and structural diversity, but usually not species richness (Queensland Department of Forestry, 1983), are reduced. Replacement by man-made crop types accentuates these ecologically most important changes (Fig. 35.7). In cropping and land-use planning these effects must be considered, but are usually overlooked (Bruenig and Sander, 1983; Bruenig, 1984).

TIMBER TRADE AND CONSUMPTION

Exploitation of tropical forests for fuel-wood, fibres, bark, wax, resin, oil, medicines, dyes and other essential or luxury items for domestic use and export has a history as long as human civilization. Tropical timbers found their way from equatorial Africa and southern Asia to Egypt and Europe many thousands of years ago (Gonggryp, 1942). Chinese junks crossed the South China Sea to the northern Bornean coast at least 1000 years ago, when during the Tang dynasty belian (*Eusideroxylon* spp., the Bornean ironwood), rhinoceros horn, bird nests and camphor were bartered for pottery, beads and delicacies (Fig. 35.8) (see also Kartawinata et al., Ch. 34). Similarly, ebony and the luxury woods have been exploited for local use, especially by nobility, but also found their way into international trade channels in Asia and Africa and to Europe. These traditional trade channels existed long before the western conquest of the world. One may assume that similar trade patterns existed in tropical America within the Aztec, Maya and Inca empires in pre-Columbian times. The humid forests of the colonial empires supplied Europe first with small amounts of highly valued cabinet woods, but eventually, especially toward the end of the colonial era, with increasing volumes of round and converted wood for mass production. An example is the export of peeler logs and veneers from West Africa. But, on the whole, the round-wood equivalents of imports of products of the wood-working industry, including paper and board, from the industrial countries into the tropics exceeded the exports of timber from the tropics.

The annual volume of commercial timber presently extracted from the productive natural broad-leaved forests of the tropics is estimated to be on

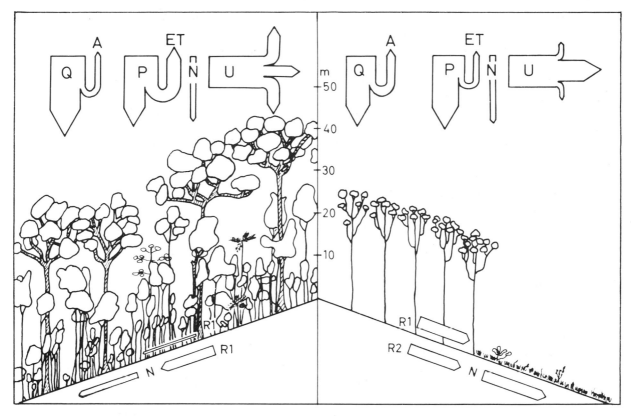

Fig. 35.7. The changes in structure following primary forest conversion to tree plantations, agriculture, pasture or waste land. The corresponding changes of functions are illustrated by the arrows. The relative intensity of processes is indicated by the width of the arrows. A change of major ecological significance is the reduced aerodynamic roughness z_0 of the canopy as a result of lower stature and smoother surface. This is associated with lower rates of interception, evaporation and transpiration of water, and less deviation of the lateral wind-flow and therefore less air-mixing. Also, the ecosystem is organisationally, architecturally and floristically less diverse and therefore the biotope diversity and the ecological value of the ecosystem is reduced.

Q = solar radiation; A = reflected solar radiation (albedo), P = precipitation; ET = evapotranspiration; N = minerals; U = wind flow; $R1$ = surface runoff; $R2$ = water loss through percolation.

average about 110 000 000 m³ of hardwood logs, together with 15 000 000 m³ of softwood logs from coniferous forests (Table 35.4). About two-thirds of the hardwood logs come from closed primary forest, the rest mainly from relogged forest, and much less from open forests. Only 15% of the softwood harvest comes from pristine forest (FAO, 1982b, p. 18). These removals are only a tiny fraction of the gross volume of growing stock. The 125 000 000 m³ removals are somewhere around 0.1% of the estimated global growing stock of the tropical forests and the 4 300 000 ha area from which they are harvested annually is less than 0.3% of the present closed forest area (Tables 35.1, 35.2, and Fig. 35.5).

The amounts of timber cut, removed and sold on the domestic market are as difficult to assess as the amounts removed for immediate local consumption for building, farm implements and boats. Even more difficult to assess are the amounts removed from primary and secondary forests for local fuel-wood consumption.

A large proportion of the population in the developing countries depends on wood for fuel. The Earth Scan programme of the International Institute for Environment and Development estimated in 1984 that at least 100 000 000 people suffer from acute want of fire-wood, while for 1 300 000 000 people the supply is deficient. The FAO (1982b, p. 24) estimated that about 2 000 000 000 people in the tropical countries suffer from fuel shortages. Total removals of fuel-

Fig. 35.8. Native entrepreneurs have creamed rain forest for highly valued timber since time immemorial, mainly by felling and manually extracting saw-timber, poles and shingles and in special workshops making coffins of naturally durable Bornean ironwood (belian, *Eusideroxylon zwageri*) which have been exported to China for at least 1000 years. This form of harvesting, conversion and marketing is fully adapted and integrated with the ecological and socio-economic environment. It causes no more disturbance in the forest than natural catastrophes and is highly flexible and adaptable to market conditions. Ulu Rambugan, Sarawak.

wood and timber for local consumption will certainly be many times the statistically recorded commercial removals of saw and veneer logs for the home and export markets (Table 35.3). The fairly high density of rural and total population per hectare of forested land (Table 35.4) and their high growth rates support the assumption of the widespread existence of an already critical supply situation. The situation will gradually worsen, particularly in dry areas which are already poorly forested. Supply situations which are locally critical, from the economic and social points of view, exist in the humid tropics in governmental resettlement schemes, usually badly planned, designed and executed, as well as in some urban agglomerations.

Keeping the difficulties and uncertainties of assessment in mind, the best available estimate of global consumption of wood from tropical forests is between 1.3 and 1.5 billion m³. Of this about 85% is used as fuel and charcoal, and 10% as timber, within the countries of origin. Only a small amount of the removals, between 50 000 000 and 60 000 000 m³ roundwood equivalents, is exported, almost half of this from Southeast Asia to Japan.

The least known but probably by far the largest amount of wood is consumed each year by agriculture. Wood is burnt to exterminate weeds, pests and diseases and to provide fertilizing ash to permanently and intermittently cultivated fields. The amount of wood consumed in the burn and

TABLE 35.2

Total gross volumes of forest growing stock in tropical forests (in 10^9 m³) in 1980

Continent*	Broad-leaved forest, closed			Broadleaved forest open productive	Coniferous forest	Grand total
	productive	unproductive	total			
America	77.5	12.2	89.7	7.8	1.9	99.4
Africa	38.8	6.2	44.9	4.7	0.1	49.7
Asia	30.7	13.1	43.8	0.4	1.1	45.3
Total	146.9	31.5	178.3	12.9	3.1	193.3

The data cover 76 countries representing 97% of the tropical land surface (listed in FAO, 1982a, p. 33). Data from FAO (1982b, table 4, p. 17; see also 1982a, fig. 4c, p. 66, for very slightly deviating figures).

TABLE 35.3

Annual statistically recorded legal removal of saw and veneer logs in 75 tropical countries (10^6 m^3)[1]

Region	1961–65	1966–70	1971–75	1976–79	1976–79[2] (%)
America (23 countries)	22.4	26.4	32.3	42.4	33.4 (78.8)
Africa (37 countries)	10.3	13.7	15.8	16.7	15.5 (92.8)
Asia (15 countries)	32.1	47.0	65.3	80.0	76.3 (95.4)
Sum					
— coniferous	11.5	14.6	17.4	23.7	14.9 (62.8)
— broadleaved	53.5	72.5	95.9	115.4	110.3 (95.6)
Total	64.7	87.1	113.3	139.1	125.2 (90.0)

[1]Same countries as Table 35.2, less Bhutan.
[2]Estimated proportion which has originated from natural (more or less primary, pristine virgin) forest.
Data abstracted from FAO (1982a, p. 59).

TABLE 35.4

Population densities per hectare in 1980 in tropical regions

Region	Total population				Rural population			
	per hectare of			annual growth rate	per hectare of			annual growth rate
	total area	arable land	forest area		total area	arable land	forest area	
America	0.19	2.96	0.36	2.89	0.07	0.95	0.13	0.93
Africa	0.16	2.46	0.49	2.95	0.11	1.76	0.34	2.09
Asia	1.34	4.42	3.75	2.48	0.85	2.86	2.39	1.53
Total tropics	0.40	3.62	1.00	2.63	0.24	2.19	0.60	1.58

Abstracted from FAO (1982a, p. 34 and 1982b, table 7, p. 26).

the amount left unburned to decompose in the course of time may be as much as 2 000 000 000 tons dry matter annually in the humid tropics alone, but is certainly not less than 1 000 000 000 tons dry matter or approximately 1.5 billion m^3 wood and bark. Of the total consumption of wood in the tropics, therefore, about 50% is for agriculture, 43% for fuel, 5% for domestic timber supply, and only about 2% for export.

Other traditional products, such as resins from dipterocarp and coniferous species, incense wood, fruits (more commonly from gap size forest gar

dens and old secondary forest), medicinal substances, latexes, plants and animals, continue to be exploited, but their impact on rain-forest structure and functioning is small. Serious damage may occur only at the species level by local extermination through careless exploitation and overuse.

FOREST MANAGEMENT PLANNING AND CONTROL

Neil (1981, pp. 37–122), elaborating on a suggestion by H.C. Dawkins (pers. commun.), distinguishes five phases of development of the management of tropical rain forests: (1) before 1850: premanagement; (2) 1850–1900: Indo-Burman (Franco-Teutonic); (3) 1900–1950: Afro-Malaysian; (4) 1950–1980: pantropical exploitative; and (5) 1980–onward: new phase (system-oriented).

The management of tropical rain forests has spread from its early beginnings in the dry deciduous and moist deciduous forests of India and Burma to all countries where this complex ecosystem exists (Neil, 1981, p. 105). But even now, only a small portion of the tropical rain forests has been covered by management plans, and even less has benefited from implementation of such plans. With due regard to the unreliability of the data base, the information given by FAO (1982b, table 2 and p. 15) on the basis of a world-wide review clearly indicates that proper management in the tropical rain forest is currently almost non-existent. Of the total area of productive tropical broad-leaved forest (approx. 8 600 000 km²) about 20% have already been logged in some way or other, but only about 4% are covered by management plans, and may be considered to be subject to some form of planned and regulated management at a scale other than experimental. These managed tropical forests are almost exclusively in India and Malaysia. These countries both have a long tradition of working plans and silvicultural management.

Orderly forest management in India and Burma followed in the wake of an "orgy of destruction" to supply land and timber for the development of the tea industry and agriculture, and for the building of railways during the 19th century (Trevor and Smythies, 1923). A serious timber shortage in the middle of that century led to the establishment of a forest administration in India and the appointment of Dr. Brandis (later Sir Richard Brandis), on transfer from Burma, as its head. A vigorous forest policy was subsequently implemented (Schlich, 1922). Forests were demarcated and gazetted as permanent forests, and the first formal working plans were prepared and implemented between 1860 and 1865 by foresters trained in France and Germany. This was the beginning of orderly tropical forest management and silviculture, which soon spread to Malaya and eventually to many other tropical countries.

Development of forest management in the humid tropical forest in Africa began later and followed a different course. The original deciduous forests had been converted to savannahs in prehistoric times. Also, many of the more accessible evergreen forests had been modified by slash-and-burn agriculture, but eventually reverted to old secondary and semi-secondary forest. Emphasis of early colonial forest policies at the turn of the century was consequently on enrichment planting or afforestation. The evergreen rain forest received litle attention until after the first World War, when large quantities of medium-light hardwoods began to be exported from West Africa to Europe. However, in spite of over-cutting and resource exhaustion, and inherent difficulties in the regeneration of seral forests, little was done in practice to regulate harvesting and to manage the forests as a renewable resource instead of exploiting them as a wasting asset (see also Lawton, Ch. 33).

In Africa, management procedures for tropical evergreen moist forest were first codified for Uganda by Dawkins (1958). In Asia, codification of management planning and control procedures for Sarawak were partly framed on these procedures and on the management procedures in Britain (Bruenig, 1961, 1965). The principles and procedures of silvicultural management of Malesian tropical rain forest were described in great detail and variety in the now classic Manual of Malayan Silviculture (Wyatt-Smith, 1963).

Reservation programmes for communal and village forests were initiated in many tropical countries. For example in Sarawak, now part of Malaysia, an extensive communal forest programme was initiated between the two World Wars and revived in the fifties. Similar developments happened in the thirties in some parts of India and Africa, mainly to ensure fire-wood supplies, but activities experienced a lapse after the Second World War. More recently, interest and activities have revived, especially in India, after the advocacy of the ancient concept of "social forestry" at the 8th World Forestry Congress in Jakarta in 1978. The main objectives still are to ensure supply of fuel-wood, timber, fruits and other forest products to the villages, but also to improve and safeguard environmental conditions.

The control of forested land and the utilization of forests in former times were traditionally the customary right of the native people. These rights and activities were adapted to local conditions and needs and, except for the growing menace of deforestation, worked well for the benefit of the people and the forests (Figs. 35.9 and 35.10). These rights and activities are being progressively pruned and reduced by governments in favour of investing full authority over the forest lands and their resources in the state. This development has its origin in the colonial period, but was not confined to colonies, and rapidly gained momentum during the post-colonial period. It was driven both by the inherent urge of state bureaucracies to assume and centralize control of resources and their utilization, and by the recent rush of politicians and entrepreneurs to secure a share in the rapidly rising commercial value of tropical timber. The result in many cases has been acceleration of the destructive

Fig. 35.10. The traditional *kuda-kuda* system of extraction is labour-intensive and ecologically adapted. It can be, and has been, technically improved to relieve labour from excessive strains and danger. Heavy logging machinery, however, is no acceptable alternative on the fragile tropical soils.

Fig. 35.9. Structure of selectively logged high-stature noto-/microphyll bindang (*Agathis borneensis*) Kerangas forest on medium-deep sandy spodosol soil. The traditional manual *kuda-kuda* extraction and careful felling keeps forest and soil ecologically and economically fully functional and productive. The gap in the rear is hardly more disturbing than a lightning or wind gap. Nyaban Forest Reserve, Sarawak.

impact of man on the forest (Fig. 35.11). The erosion of native customary rights and traditions also has had disruptive social consequences. The overall result has been a shift away from activities aiming at the conservation and prudent use of the forest resource towards mere fiscal control and unsustainable exploitation of the resource. Often, this fiscal control concerns mainly the collection of revenue and collecting of export fees. As a side effect, such fiscal measures conferred some aspect of respectability and authorization on an unrestrainedly destructive waste of resources for the sake of short-term profits at inordinately high social costs.

In tropical America, management began in Trinidad where a formal working plan with 25 ha annual coupe and 60 years rotation was introduced with a shelter-wood system in the Arena Forest Reserve during the thirties and fifties of this

Fig. 35.11. Selective logging of a few species for export employs fewer people but needs imported expensive and heavy machinery. It results in ruthless approaches to site and forest which causes forest destruction, soil degradation and erosion, and in lasting changes of ecosystem structure and functioning. Often, logging road sides, spar tree locations and skid roads remain open or under secondary scrub for years or decades.

century (Neil, 1981). Almost simultaneously, planned management was introduced in the evergreen forests in Mount Luquillo in Puerto Rico (Wadsworth, 1951/1952). Somewhat later, management to sustain timber yields developed in Surinam (De Graaf, 1982, 1984); but for the rest of tropical America, the time had not yet come to introduce planned and sustained management into practice. Pure exploitation of the evergeen rain forest prevails in most countries to this day.

HISTORY OF SILVICULTURE

Like the emergence of slash-and-burn agriculture in the seasonally dry zone, the development of silvicultural systems using natural regeneration in the tropics began in the moist deciduous forest. The seasonal changes provide improved conditions of light and nutrient supply to the regeneration when the top-canopy trees are bare but the understorey in leaf. As a result, natural regeneration is much easier than in the predominantly evergreen rain-forest biome. The history of rain-forest silviculture began with experimental treatments in Malaya at the turn of this century. Adapting European concepts, attempts were made to promote natural regeneration by manipulating the understorey, removing palms, lianas and unwanted trees. Successes were rare and spurious. Manipulation of the understorey alone does not alter the microclimate sufficiently for the regeneration of top-canopy species to benefit enough for rapid development. This also applies to the shelter-wood system, in which the top canopy is very cautiously opened and emphasis laid on understorey manipulation, and which consequently benefits shade-bearers more than the more desirable light-demanders. Eventually, these exotic approaches were replaced by ecologically better adapted indigenous concepts and treatment procedures. Observation of successful regeneration in areas of large-scale storm throws after the Krakatoa outbreak in 1883 and after very heavy logging by Japanese forces during the Second World War paved the way for the development of the more radical Malayan Uniform System (MUS) (Fig. 35.12). An exhaustive description of the history, ecological basis and the procedures of Malayan silviculture is given in the Manual of

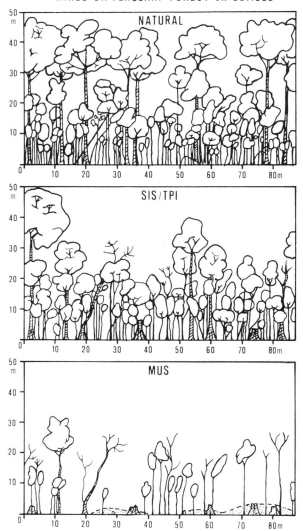

MIXED DIPTEROCARP FOREST ON ULTISOL

Fig. 35.12. Tropical rain-forest structure after heavy, complete logging of commercial stock and after selective logging. The diagrams show the effect of the Malayan Uniform System (MUS = harvesting of all merchantable trees followed by poison-girdling of undesirables) and of the Philippine Selective Logging *cum* Improvement System [SIS = harvesting of all trees marked for felling, and light poison-girdling of competitors, later adapted for application in Kalimantan as Tebang, Pileh Indonesia (TPI)] in a lowland Mixed Dipterocarp forest of the species-rich, complex Meranti-Keruing type in Malaysia. Regeneration in the MUS dotted.

Malayan Silviculture (Wyatt-Smith, 1963). Later developments were influenced by the loss of lowland forests to agriculture and the consequent need to develop methods which are suitable for the less easily regenerating hill forests with a general tendency to more cautious and lighter logging and supplementary planting.

While MUS emerged in Malaya, a most notable development took place during the sixties and seventies in the Philippines and Indonesia. The unorganized, unsystematic creaming practices were gradually replaced by silvicultural management systems of selective logging. These systems were codified as Selection Improvement System (SIS) of natural regeneration in the Philippines (Bureau of Forestry, 1965). In a slightly simplified form the system was recently adopted in Indonesia as Tebang Pileh Indonesia (TPI) (Direktorat Jenderal Kehutanan, 1980). The salient features of the SIS/TPI in distinction to the MUS are illustrated in Fig. 35.12 which depicts the profile structure for the time after harvest and first silvicultural treatment (see also Kartawinata et al., Ch. 34).

The large-scale export-oriented timber operations which developed in South-East Asia during the fifties exploited a range of timber species groups, such as Meranti or Lauan, representing between 20 and 50% of the growing stock, or only about 15 to 30% of the biomass above ground, but caused excessive damage by careless operating, over-mechanization and excessively heavy machinery. Small-scale domestic operators are both more selective of timber species and qualities and more adaptable and diversified with respect to conversion and marketing. Their operations at best are a light selective cut with low level of mechanization resembling natural gap formation, stimulating rather than damaging natural regeneration. Adverse ecological effects from the operations of small local operators may accrue in two cases. These are the re-logging of the felling areas of large companies, usually illegal, and the clear-felling of forests dominated by one species. In the first case, excessive damage is done to crop and soil, in the second case heavy felling damage, sudden exposure of seedlings and the marked periodicity of regeneration make natural regeneration hazardous if not impossible. An example of the latter is the exploitation of the primary successional stages or phasic communities of Alan and Alan Bunga forest in the peatswamp forests of Sarawak (Bruenig, 1969a, b; Fig. 35.13).

In Africa, natural silviculture began almost as early as in Malaya with trials of natural regeneration in Nigeria about 1900. During the twenties

Fig. 35.13. Logs extracted by a small local saw-mill from the Alan Association and the Alan Bunga consociation of the phasic community sequences in peat-swamp forests in Sarawak. Such sawmills, labour-intensive in their logging and conversion activities, are flexible in supplying specialized assortments to a diverse and variable market, in contrast to the big export-orientated national and international companies. Poor-quality and defective logs and lesser-known species also find better outlets through small companies into local or regional markets.

silvicultural activities in the mostly old to very old secondary, mainly semi-evergreen or deciduous, closed forests of Nigeria received new impulses from foresters transferred from Malaya. They introduced the Regeneration Improvement System and the Tropical Shelterwood System. Line planting was not attempted. Experimental plantations were established as early as 1900. Later also combinations of tree planting with agricultural field crops were introduced from Burma to reduce establishment and weeding costs. However, the viability of this technique in the tropical rain forest depends on high land demand and low living standards. In Nigeria, as in most other humid tropical countries, population pressure on the land during pre-war days remained too small to stimulate and sustain activities in agroforestry. Conditions changed dramatically during the post-war period in this respect, and combinations of tree planting with field crops as a silvicultural technique and as an integrated agricultural system became a more practicable proposition.

Planting to assist natural regeneration has been practised in MUS and SIS, but the feasibility of such investments and their ecological and socio-economic value and success still remain doubtful. Afforestation as well as enrichment planting into existing vegetation developed much earlier and maintained greater importance in Africa, especially in francophone countries. A review of methods is given by Catinot (1965). The ecological and economic feasibility of enrichment planting of quick-growing, light-demanding, desirable species into natural forest before or after logging remains open to doubt, particularly in view of the high expenses, chiefly caused by the need for intensive tending following planting, which is needed to control competition in favour of the planted trees.

While francophone African foresters, as also previously German foresters, were preoccupied with planting procedures, the ecological and economic feasibility of natural regeneration, especially of the commercially valuable Meliaceae, continues to be a matter of controversy. However, in practice little was done effectively to regenerate forests while the big boom in forest exploitation depleted the West African forests of growing stock. In the Belgian Congo (now Zaïre), systematic silviculture, mostly enrichment and pure planting, commenced shortly before the Second World War on a small scale and with inconclusive success. Trials with the European Shelterwood System in the thirties seemed successful, but subsequent comparison with untreated areas revealed no significant differences in seedling density (see also Lawton, Ch. 33).

In humid tropical America, natural forest silviculture has only recently been introduced on an experimental scale, notable by Dutch scientists in Surinam (De Graaf, 1982, 1984, 1986), French scientists in Guyana (Schmitt, 1984) and British foresters in Trinidad and Tobago, where high population pressure stimulated silviculture in the mostly secondary semi-natural forests. After unsuccessful first trials with planting after clearing and burning, shelter-wood systems were developed, using natural regeneration and enrichment plantings in varying proportions. Pitt (1961) reviewed purely experimental silvicultural activities in the Brazilian Amazon and suggested improvements. Subsequent actions under FAO sponsorship remained experimental, as in FAO projects in

Venezuela. Implementation of natural silviculture in practical management has yet to come to the Amazon and Orinoco basins, while replacement of natural forest by large-scale plantations has yet to prove its ecological and economic viability as a sustainable land-use option. A concise review of the state and development of tropical silviculture is given by Lamprecht (1986).

FEASIBILITY OF NATURAL SILVICULTURE

One set of problems has caused and still causes concern and disagreement among tropical silviculturists: "What kind of crop are we to grow? Which species should we consider acceptable? What are the criteria of sustained yield?". The verdict on the feasibility of natural regeneration of tropical rain forests depends on the answers to these vital questions. The complexity of the problem and the time-scale of forest production require a comprehensive approach and a long-term view of the ecological, technological, economical and socio-political interdependencies. The narrower the outlook and the definition of the production goal, the fewer species will be acceptable, and the less likely is natural regeneration to be able to meet the goal. But also, the less adaptable and flexible will be the silvicultural approach, whether it is natural regeneration, assisted natural regeneration, mixed or monocultural plantation. The question is to what extent it is feasible and justifiable to: (1) insist that natural regeneration should produce a crop which contains the same species mix and merchantable volumes and sizes as the original virgin forest; (2) restrict the list of acceptable species to those which currently happen to be commercial and merchantable; and (3) accept the heavy investment needed to establish a narrowly specified crop of trees.

In these respects, arguments on the feasibility and adequacy of natural regeneration for sustained production are commonly far removed from reality. The indeterministic and dynamic nature of the forest and of the economy are ignored. Instead, rigid and dogmatic, largely backward-looking guide-lines and species lists, and narrow optimizing concepts, are adopted and applied to decide options for an unpredictable future.

Instead, sustained natural silviculture of tropical rain forest should be based on the principle of choosing the option which has the highest likelihood of proving the least wrong. This option is the alternative which has the highest capacity for survival, self-regulation and adaptation in a changing environment. The silvicultural system which is most likely to meet these requirements is characterized by: (1) broad optimization to maintain the capacity to supply a wide range of products and functions; (2) diversity of structure and functions which maintains adequate levels of self-regulation and functioning of the soil–vegetation–atmosphere system; (3) function orientation instead of narrow product orientation; and (4) low input requirements for silviculture and management.

In this way, economically and ecologically attractive forestry is a feasible proposition on the bulk of less favourable humid tropical soils. That these sites become available to forestry, however, requires that agriculture is consolidated and successfully developed in order to reduce its demands on the land resources and to stop further destruction of forests and forest land.

An important advantage of low-cost, broadly optimized natural silviculture for long-term development planning is that is spreads risk over many species and functional pathways. In contrast to plantation monoculture, it produces flexible, adaptable and resistant stands which effectively buffer the effects of ecological, economic and social perturbations, thus economically balancing the effects of their possibly lower volume increments. De Graaf (1982) considered natural silviculture with a cautious girth-limit selection system and low-cost silvicultural treatment to be economically viable even at the very low annual increment of about 1 m^3 ha^{-1} at 20 yrs cutting cycle on poor, acid sand in the Mapane forest in Surinam.

Potential timber yields from natural silviculture of mixed forests are usually underestimated, while yield expectations from monocultural tree plantations are usually excessively optimistic. Common mistakes are to confuse potential net biological productivity of above-ground woody matter with realizable net merchantable wood production. The two may differ by a factor of 2 as a result of climatic variation, pests, diseases and abiotic damage. In plantations, additional effects of poor genetic stock and poor management may increase the ratio to 3:1 or more. The potentials and limitations in the production of timber from humid tropical trees and forests have been critically discussed by Dawkins (1959, 1963). Kio (1983) concluded from his earlier research that the frequently quoted rate of 2 to 3 m³ ha⁻¹ annual increment in natural silviculture may be increased to 10 m³ ha⁻¹ by improvement of silvicultural techniques after cautious logging. Substantial increases of the yield from the first cut in primary rain forest could be achieved by adequate planning of roads and skid-ways, orderly felling progress, careful and directional cutting, and systematic pre-planned skidding and transport. Not only is the output of timber per hectare increased, but the reduction of damage to the soil and the residual stand leads to more rapid recovery and higher increments in the subsequent rotation, and thus makes natural silviculture an economically more attractive and competitive option.

Bruenig (1965) assumed that sustainable annual timber increments would be between 2.4 and 7 m³ ha⁻¹ in naturally regenerated lowland dipterocarp forest (Table 35.5). Taking these figures as a reasonable, rather conservative approximation, very simple linear programming showed that natural regeneration is feasible, but that the allocation of resources to achieve optimum use of land and capital is made by a combination of natural regeneration and planting. After first logging the largest portion of the forest land should be naturally regenerated at low cost, and a minor portion, selecting the naturally most productive soils and the ecologically and economically most suitable sites, should be planted at high cost

TABLE 35.5

Estimated realizable mean annual increment (m³ ha⁻¹) of export-quality saw-log and veneer timber of presently commercial species in two types of Mixed Dipterocarp forest (MDF) in peninsular Malaysia and one type in Mindanao

Forest type	Silvicultural system	
	MUS R = 70 years	SIS R = 30 years
Single-species dominated MDF, Malaya	7	2.4
Meranti–Kerning MDF, Malaya Mixed MDF,	7	3.5
Mindanao	7	3.8

with high-yield species. Still higher economic and environmental benefits accrue from establishing plantations on deforested land outside the forest area. The logged forest area is first completely regenerated naturally and the remaining money then used to plant suitable areas on deforested land outside. If the choice is only between natural, silvicultural systems, the decision between MUS and SIS/TPI depends on the original growing-stock structure and the possibility of reducing logging damage to the residual stand and the soil. The comparative analysis of the financial criteria "annual forest rent" = net cash flow, "opportunity costs" and "net discounted revenues" showed that creaming under the SIS in Mindanao with no prescribed limitation of the annual felling area gave the highest net return in cash to the logging company but a low cut per hectare and a low subsequent increment. The system requires much more land for the same volume yield than the MUS, and high social costs are incurred for keeping timber stock which is below the girth limit but actually merchantable for another 30 to 40 years at considerable risk of damage and mortality (Fig. 35.14). Under Malayan conditions, the highest net return per hectare and for the whole annual felling area, under volume yield control, accrues from the MUS. It is therefore understandable if companies prefer the SIS in Mindanao and the MUS in Malaya, if exploitation is controlled by the logging capacity of the company and by the market capacity to absorb timber, and not by annual felling area and working plan prescription. In contrast, if a ceiling is prescribed for the annual volume yield but no area limit, the highest annual net cash return to the company is obtained by application of the SIS/TPI system, even if the cut per hectare is fairly low (for instance, below 20 m³ ha⁻¹), because of the high minimum diameter limit, and therefore higher unit price and lower extraction costs of the timber (Bruenig, 1972).

UTILITY AND USE OPTIONS

The utility of rain forest to man lies mainly in two areas: environmental preservation and wood production. The environmental aspects have recently been reviewed by the author (Bruenig, 1983) and mainly concern the consequences of deforesta-

Fig. 35.14. The nightmare of tropical timber men: defective and hollow trees, especially in decay stages of succession and in some site-related phasic forest communities. Hollow tree in Mixed Dipterocarp forest, Rejang Valley, Sarawak.

tion (Fig. 35.15). Environmental and ecological consequences of technically high-standard and cautious wood harvesting, and subsequent adapted silvicultural management, may be disruptive, especially for animals. However, effects are locally restricted to a few, successive annual coupes, accumulating to at most 10 to 15% of the management area, and are ephemeral and repaired rapidly by regrowth. Soil protection, habitat value and species diversity are quickly restored (Queensland Department of Forestry, 1983). Somewhat more time is needed to replenish nutrient stocks if logging was heavy and careless, or if fire occurred. This may require from a few to many decades depending on the soil, the kind of vegetation and the elements concerned (Bruenig, 1983; Bruenig and Sander, 1983). The general trend of changes following conversion of virgin rain forest to

plantations or to fields or grassland is illustrated in Figs. 35.7, 35.15, 35.17 and 35.18.

Full protection for environmental reasons is required in a minor part of the rain-forest area. This applies to steep ground and sensitive catchment areas, which may perhaps cover 10% of the rain-forest area in Africa and America, possibly 20 to 25% in Asia. On these sites any timber harvesting should be excluded, but non-timber products could still be collected. The areas would primarily serve as nature and biosphere reserves for nature conservation, scientific research, and ecosystem and environmental monitoring, and as genetic reservoirs (Fig. 35.16). The impacts of mechanized logging of various kinds and intensities (complete to selective) on soil, growing stock and natural regeneration, the characteristics of the silvicultural systems developed in the various parts of the tropics, and the ecological and economic feasibility of natural silviculture have recently been critically reviewed by Neil (1981).

Long-term demand and consumption trends for the tropical countries and the world at large indicate increases in the demand for timber and, in the tropics, for fuel-wood. World-wide wood production and supply will balance with demands about the middle of the 21st Century, but regionally serious deficits in supply of timber and fuel-wood will develop. The fuel-wood deficit in the semi-arid lands will continue to increase, expand and become critical to human survival in these areas, because vegetation destruction and land devastation will continue, while the scope for afforestation is limited by lack of water and by excessive grazing pressures. In conclusion, the tropical rain forest as the largest and most productive forest resource world-wide and in the tropics will have to play a major role in meeting the domestic and regional demands for wood.

In accordance with this, Baur (1964) in a review of the state of the art of tropical silvicultural management, declared as important aims of forest policy: (1) maintenance of environmental conditions; (2) adequate fuel-wood supplies, "but this is likely to be a diminishing demand" (in 1985 still rising!); (3) provision of saw-logs, pulp and paper for local consumption; and (4) provision of timber for export.

Wood production in the productive rain forest area which is likely to survive the present period of

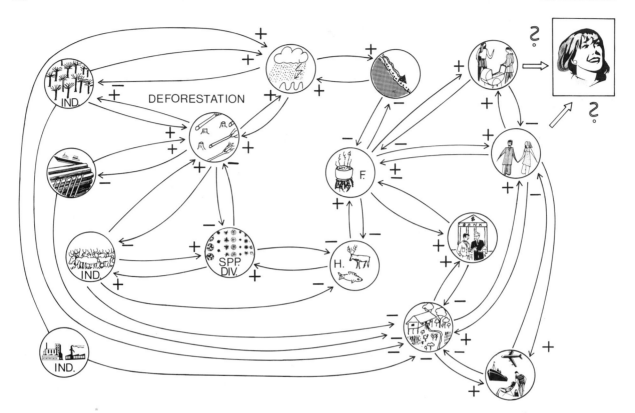

Fig. 35.15. Network of feed-back loops between sectors which are affected by activities which finally result in deforestation. Deforestation releases land for agricultural and forestry industrial plantations and industrial meat growing, but also increases variations and extremes of climate and soil deterioration, while fuel-wood availability declines. More produce is supplied to the timber industry and export market in the short term until resource exhaustion and productivity declines take effect. The natural species diversity and supplies of customary home-grown foods (H = game, fish) dwindle and feeding habits change (F.). These changes and employment in industry, together with effects of tourism and information media change customary ways of life, increase dependence on credit systems, affect social habits and demographic dynamics and finally the happiness of people. + changes in quality, quantity or activity in one sector affects the other sector in the same direction; − changes in one sector induce changes into the opposite direction in the other sector. Closed loops with positive signs dominating tend to build-up through positive feedback, those with more negative than positive signs are balanced through self-regulation.

destruction (Table 35.1) should therefore be kept at the highest level compatible with ecology and economy. This means basically maintenance of productivity of tropical rain-forest vegetation, soils and sites at the lowest possible micro-economic and social cost, and the avoidance of further destruction and degradation by careless timber logging and by agricultural expansion into sites which are neither needed, nor suitable (Fig. 35.16).

The importance of tropical rain forest as a source of plant species for cultivation is well illustrated by such crops as rubber (*Hevea brasiliensis*), oil palm, sago palm, pepper, vanille, nutmeg, cloves, cocoa and many fruit trees. The natural forest continues to serve as a source of

genetic material for improving cultivars or for introducing new crops. The value of this function is difficult to assess. Particularly in recent years the potential value of this gen-pool as reservoir of pharmaceutical plants has been very highly rated. But in reality discovery of commercially successful new drugs is rare and when it occurs, substitution by synthetics is quick to come. The traditional value of tropical forest as a source of fruits, foods, medicines, fats, resins, condiments and other forest products for local consumption, and in bumper crop years for export, will continue to be important and could be increased by breeding, improvement of the natural crop and development of artificial agroforestry management systems.

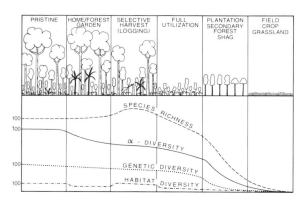

Fig. 35.17. The tendency of trend of change of structural and floristic features of humid tropical vegetation in relation to intensity of human interference. Shown are natural pristine forest; natural forest modified by aboriginal hunters and gatherers to favour useful species of trees, palms, shrubs and herbs which has evolved into the traditional forest home or village garden; natural forest selectively logged and managed under a sustained silvicultural system, for instance a well-applied selection forest system; regeneration of natural forest after full utilization and poison-girdling in a uniform system with natural or assisted regeneration, for example Malayan Uniform System; planted tree monoculture or secondary pioneer forest after clearing and burning; annual or perennial field crops, like rice, sugarcane or pasture. α = diversity expresses the evenness of the proportions the species contribute to the number of individuals in the stand, for example by the McIntosh or information indexes of diversity (Bruenig, 1987).

Fig. 35.16. Shifting cultivation with or without prior timber exploitation eventually will inevitably lead to degradation of vegetation and soil. Degraded and eroding land in the very sparsely populated upper reaches of the Ulu Ai, Batang Lupar, Sarawak. Difficult terrain forces people to keep distances to the field short, which means short fallow periods, and intrusion of fire during burning into adjacent fallows, which accelerates the vicious circle of degradation to final collapse of the ecological and socio-economic systems. The end stage is a lallang (*Imperata cylindrica*) fire disclimax. Sites and fragile soils as on the photograph should be kept permanently under protective or carefully managed productive forest (compare Fig. 35.4).

ASSESSMENT OF FOREST RESOURCE POTENTIAL AND LONG-TERM PLANNING

The scientific knowledge necessary to assess the potentials and dangers of rain-forest use, and to design cropping plans and long-term management concepts has been provided in recent decades by applied and pure research, building on more than two centuries of taxonomic study and almost half a century of ecological exploration and research in tropical rain forests.

Forest inventory for policy formulation and preparation of working plans were introduced to the tropical rain forests during the late 19th Century and the first half of this century by colonial forest officers, foremost and most successfully in India, Malaya and East Africa. Integrated soil/site/growing-stock assessments by combined aerial and ground surveys were developed after the Second World War in some areas. In Sarawak, such comprehensive surveys provided the data base for the preparation of "Management Unit Working Plans" and for "Regional Development Plans" which aimed at integration of forestry and agricultural development in regions (Bruenig, 1961, 1963, 1965). Similar procedures were adopted by other countries throughout the tropics. A comprehensive description of the methods is given by Loetsch and Haller (1964) and Loetsch et al. (1973).

Tropical forest and site classification for planning purposes must cope with great heterogeneity of vegetation and site conditions, and the uncertainty of any prediction due to the nature of the

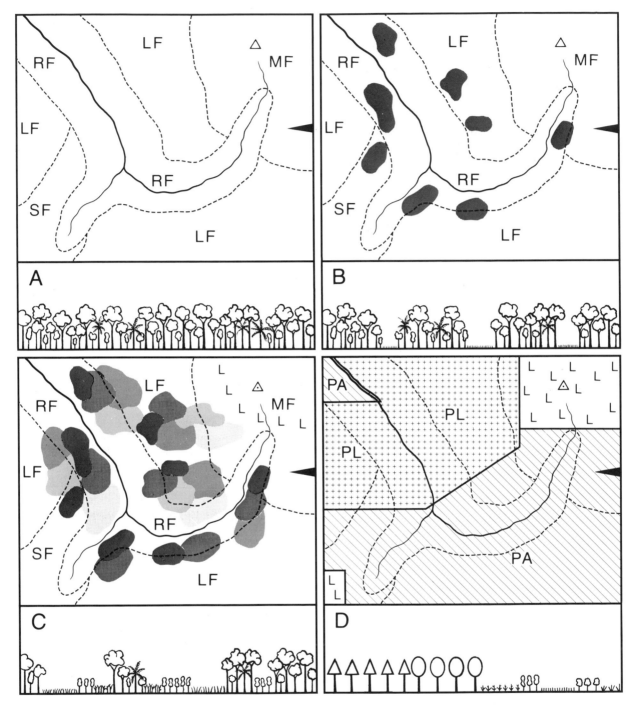

Fig. 35.18. The notorious trend of degradation and simplification of the humid tropical landscape as a result of ecologically and socio-economically non-adapted land-use development. The effect on diversity is illustrated in Fig. 35.17. (A) Pristine humid tropical forest, with riparian forest (*RF*), lowland mixed forest (*LF*), freshwater swamp forest (*SF*), montane forest (*MF*); (B) Beginning of slash-and-burn rotational agriculture (shifting cultivation) by eight farmers. (C) Five years later the cleared area has extended and tends to coalesce in a leopard-skin pattern, logging has started in the remaining hill forest. (D) The final stage of replacement of forest by permanent forms of rainfed and irrigated agriculture (*PA*), unproductive grassland and scrub, plantations (*PL*), remaining forest is restricted to inaccessible or unproductive sites and has been exploited for commercial timbers. The position of the profile transects are indicated by the arrows at the right edge of the maps.

complex dynamic forest ecosystems and the socio-economic system (Bruenig et al., 1975; Bruenig, 1976). Another problem is the notorious failure in most forest surveys to collect ecologically meaningful data (Bruenig, 1976). Ross (1984) described a simple but fairly comprehensive method of forest and land evaluation in connection with resettlement programmes in Indonesia. A general review of the situation in tropical land-value assessment is given by Carpenter (1981). The largest and most ambitious project for land assessment in rain forests and humid tropical lands has been the RADAM project in Brazil. This survey of Amazonia has produced a wealth of information on the natural resources and provides a suitable base for the more rational development of land use which among others was suggested at the 1st Symposium on Humid Tropics in Belem by Pandolfo (1984) — see also Prance (Ch. 6).

A most vexing and critical problem of great practical significance is the uncertainty of assessing and predicting the post-logging yield potential of natural rain forest by means of stand and soil features before logging. The assessment of soil conditions before logging and of the quantity, quality and commercial value of the growing stock is relatively easy. But forest increment and yield after logging and under silvicultural management systems are most difficult to predict because: (1) net primary productivity is poorly, if at all, correlated with the amount and structure of biomass stocking of the virgin growing stock; (2) physical and chemical soil conditions and site climate not only are naturally heterogeneous and variable, but also are changed by logging and the effects on productivity are as yet poorly understood; (3) any forest tract is a mosaic of small groups to large (several hectares) stands of trees which are more uniform within than between themselves, which differ by age, past history and present vigour, and which therefore react unpredictably differently to logging and silvicultural treatment; (4) any individual residual tree is in a specific state of vigour, health and growth potential as a result of its history which cannot be assessed with any reliability from its present outward appearance; (5) social position and crown characteristics of trees relate poorly to future performance; and (6) the new crop after heavy logging (for instance, MUS) may be very different

from the mother stand in species composition and proportions, and its long-term development is difficult to predict.

Particularly disconcerting is the presently inadequate understanding of the ecological and economic significance of species richness and species diversity, or vice versa evenness of species mixture, in general and to silviculture and management in particular. Our state of knowledge simply does not permit to assess with any certainty, except in general biocybernetic terms, and with any precision the ecological and economic utility of species richness, even of complex mixture patterns and structural complexity. Forest practitioners generally agree that species-rich and complex stands have ecological advantages, but usually consider them economically less attractive. As a result, the great potential of natural regeneration is not appreciated and simpler crops are preferred. Conservationists, on the other hand, believe that any reduction of the high levels of richness and complexity of humid tropical forests impairs the functioning and viability of the pristine ecosystem, that any human interference causes stress and lasting damage. The problem is that we do not know enough to judge whether the richness of species and structure of the pristine forest is luxury, whether it can be reduced without harm or whether it is essential to provide the capability of restoration or substitution after destruction of parts of the system. Episodic extreme natural events and die-backs related to synergisms between climate, soil-changes and ageing (Bruenig, 1986b) may cause failures or loss of parts of the system which requires immediate restitution or substitution.

Human impacts change species richness and structural features. The general trends of change in the humid tropical forest and landscape towards simplification and deforestation is illustrated in Figs. 35.16, 35.17 and 35.18. As a result. buffering capacity, adaptability, flexibility and capacity for self-regulation of the forest and landscape ecosystems are reduced. How much and where the critical thresholds are ecologically, economically and environmentally, is yet unknown. To escape into conventional narrow goal-oriented planning by rigid and specific prescriptions may work well for very short time spans, but will not do for the typically wide time horizons of forest and land-use planning. Planning at this time scale requires the application of more sophisticated methods of systems and a sensitivity analysis and the recognition of biocybernetic principles at all natural, economic and social ecosystems (Bruenig et al., 1986). Such methods have in recent years been developed for planning at the system levels of forest stands, forest business and management unit and region. Some of these are described by Grossmann (1979) and the Man and the Biosphere programme (MAB, 1982, 1983; Vester, 1980).

OBSTACLES TO RATIONAL FOREST CONSERVATION AND MANAGEMENT

The obstacles to conservation and to the rational and sustained use and management of tropical rain forests are mainly political. Since the fifties, third world politicians have increasingly shifted priority away from agricultural development to urbanization, industrialization, armament, war-making and political power struggles. The consequences are a decline of agricultural production. Food surplus has turned to food deficiency in many tropical countries. Spreading malnutrition is causing bad health, lowered manual working capacity and mental decline, and this in turn reduces agricultural productivity of the land and increases the need for new land. All this is amplified by the effects of low food prices as a result of price control and foreign food aid, misguided governmental agricultural policies, bureaucratic and ideological hindrances and personal greed. As a result of accelerated land degradation and neglect of agriculture, forest destruction has increased. In the humid tropics plantations and rangeland development are insignificant in comparison to shifting cultivation as a cause of rain-forest destruction and land degradation. Exceptions are some parts of peninsular Malaysia, Vietnam, Central America and the fringe of Amazonia.

Another important political obstacle to forestry stabilization and development is insecurity of land tenure, which restrains timber companies from necessary investments and the adoption of sustained management. Timber companies are increasingly owned by nationals, often politicians, members of government or government agencies. The combined effect of insecurity, power and greed

is that forests are not managed but mined, and that careless logging continues to cause excessive loss and damage to timber, forest stands and soils. These negative trends are amplified universally by the restrictive and stifling governmental bureaucracies which adversely affect economic activities in all fields, but particularly in forestry.

The importance of the political sector was clearly recognized by an international seminar in Malaysia in 1984 which came to the conclusion that the proposed technical strategies of rain-forest conservation and management can only be successfully implemented with greater political, professional and private industry commitments as well as government investment incentives. This puts the finger squarely on the core problem: failure of the political sector to provide conditions which are conducive to cautious resource use and conservation and to sustained forest management instead of cut-and-run destructive timber mining.

At the natural and technical ecosystem levels, major obstacles to improvements are: (1) lack of understanding of the potentials and misjudging the risks and uncertainties of natural regeneration, leading either to total rejection of natural silvicultural management or to expensive but ineffective inputs into excessive, silvicultural treatments and planting; (2) narrow optimization of crop types to yield a narrowly defined product, especially in the case of assisted regeneration and monoculture plantations; (3) inability to recognize that forests, forestry and economy as systems are largely non-deterministic in behaviour and unpredictable in development, and linear forecasts are therefore apt to mislead into failure and catastrophe; (4) misjudgement of long-term requirements and of ecological, economic and social side effects of forestry projects and failure to make long-term provisions accordingly; (5) failure to recognize and appropriately apply available technology to forest exploitation and management; and (6) inadequate interchange of information between scientific research, applied research, technology development, forestry practice and the general public, administrators and politicians.

Underlying all this is ignorance and neglect of the properties of complex dynamic ecosystems and of their behaviour in a variable environment. Systems dynamics are not understood, sensitive interactions are not realized, the conditions of dynamic ecological, economic and social systems, and the basic requirements for dynamic stability and survivability are not known or purposely ignored. Particularly at higher socio-political levels, the interrelationships between natural, economical and social ecosystems are not recognized, not understood or purposely ignored, and available knowledge is not utilized — sometimes even straightforwardly rejected. In conclusion, application of knowledge, implementation of plans and improvement of forestry practice are not so much problems of scientific knowledge and technical practicability, as of public awareness, and political responsibility and goodwill.

REFERENCES

Baur, G.N., 1964. *Ecological Basis of Rainforest Management.* Forestry Commission of N.S.W., Government Printer, Sydney, N.S.W., 499 pp.

Bruenig, E.F., 1961. *Forest Working Plans Code.* Sarawak Forest Dep., Government Printer, Kuching (pages unnumbered).

Bruenig, E.F., 1963. The history of forest inventories in Sarawak. *Malay. For.*, 26: 141–159.

Bruenig, E.F., 1965. The management of forest estates through working plans. *Malay. For.*, 28: 46–55.

Bruenig, E.F., 1969a. Stand structure, physiognomy and environmental factors in some lowland forests in Sarawak. Abstracts 11th Int. Botanical Congress, Seattle, Wash., *Trop. Ecol.* (1970), II, I: 26–43.

Bruenig. E.F., 1969b. Forest classification in Sarawak. *Malay. Forest.*, 32 (2): 143–179.

Bruenig, E.F., 1972. The decision between alternative silvicultural process in production planning. In: *Silvics and Silvicultural Management in Humid Tropical Forests.* Manuscript and lecture script, Hamburg, 36 pp.

Bruenig. E.F., 1974. *Ecological Studies in the Kerangas Forests of Sarawak and Brunei.* Borneo Literature Bureau for the Forest Dept., Sarawak, Kuching, 237 pp.

Bruenig, E.F., 1976. Classifying for mapping of Kerangas and peatswamp forest as example of primary forest types in Sarawak (Borneo). In: P.S. Ashton (Editor) *The Classification and Mapping of Southeast Asian Ecosystems.* Dept. of Geography, Univ. of Hull, Hull, Misc. Ser., 17: 57–75.

Bruenig, E.F., 1985. Deforestation and its ecological implications for the rainforests of Southeast Asia. *Environmentalist*, 5 (suppl.): 17–35.

Bruenig, E.F., 1986a. *Forestry and Agroforestry System Designs for Sustained Production in Tropical Landscapes.* Proc. 1st Symp. on Humid Tropics, Belem, EMBRAPA/CPATU, II: 217–228.

Bruenig, E.F., 1986b. The forest ecosystem: tropical and boreal. *Ambio*, 16 (2–3): 68–79.

Bruenig, E.F., 1987. *Tropical forest areas as a source of*

biological diversity. European Conference, Biological Diversity — A Challenge to Science, the Economy and Society, Dublin (in press).

Bruenig, E.F. and Sander, N., 1983. Ecosystem structure and functioning: some interactions of relevance to agroforestry. In: P.A. Huxlex (Editor), *Plant Research in Agroforestry.* Proc. of a consultative meeting, ICRAF, Nairobi, pp. 221–247.

Bruenig, E.F., Von Buch, M.-W., Heuveldop, J. and Panzer, K., 1975. Stratification of tropical moist forest for land use planning. *Mitt. Bundesforschungs anst. Forst-Holzwirtsch.*, 109: 2–57.

Bruenig, E.F., Bossel, H., Elpel, K.P., Grossmann, W.D., Schneider, T.W., Wan Zhu-hao and Yu Zuo-yue, 1986. *Ecologic–Socioeconomic System Analysis and Simulation: A Guide for Application of System Analysis to the Conservation, Utilization and Development of Tropical and Subtropical Land Resources in China.* National MAB-Committee, Bonn, Mitt. No. 24, and German Foundation for International Development (DSE), Feldafing, DOK 1381, SE 78-059086 ox, 388 pp.

Bureau of Forestry, 1965. *Handbook of Selective Logging.* Bureau of Forestry, Manila, 1st ed., 264 pp.

Carpenter, R.A. (Editor), 1981. *Assessing Tropical Forest Lands. Their Suitability for Sustainable Uses.* (Natural Resources and the Environment Series, 3) Tycooly International Publishing, Honolulu, Hawaii, 337 pp.

Catinot, R., 1965. Sylviculture en forêt dense africaine. *Rev. Bois For. Trop.*, 100: 5–18; 101: 3–16; 102: 3–16; 103: 3–16; 104: 17–29.

Cochrane, T.T. and Sanchez, P.D., 1983. Land resources, soils and their management in the Amazon region: a state of knowledge report. In: *Amazonia, Agriculture and Land Use Research.* Proc. Int. Conf. sponsored by Rockefeller Foundation, GTZ, CIAT, NCSU, ICRAF. CIAT Series 03E-3(82), Univ. of Missouri, Columbia, Mo., pp. 137–209.

Dawkins, H.C., 1958. *The Management of Natural Tropical High Forest with Special Reference to Uganda.* Inst. Paper No. 34, Imperial Forestry Institute, Oxford, 155 pp.

Dawkins, H.C., 1959. The volume increment of natural tropical high-forest and limitations on its improvement. *Emp. For. Rev.*, 38, 96: 175–180.

Dawkins, H.C., 1963. *The Productivity of Tropical High Forest Trees and their Reaction to Controllable Environment.* D.Ph. Thesis, Univ. of Oxford, Oxford.

De Graaf, N.R., 1982. Sustained timber production in the tropical rainforest of Surinam. In: J.F. Wienk and H.A. de Wit (Editors), *Management of Low Fertility Acid Soils of the American Humid Tropics.* Inst. Interamericano de Cooperación para la Agricultura (IICA), San José, Costa Rica, pp. 179–189.

De Graaf, N.R., 1984. *Silviculture and Management of Tropical Rainforest in Surinam.* Proc. 1st Symp. on Humid Tropics, Belem, EMBRAPA/CPATU, II: 233–235.

De Graaf, N.R., 1986. *A silvicultural system for natural regeneration of tropical rainforest in Suriname.* Ph.D. thesis, Agricultural Univ. Wageningen, 250 pp.

Direktorat Jenderal Indonesia, 1980. *Pedoman Tebang Pileh Indonesia.* Directorate General of Forests, Jakarta.

FAO, 1982a. *Tropical Forest Resources.* FAO Forestry Paper 30, Rome, 106 pp.

FAO, 1982b. *Conservation and Development of Tropical Forest Resources.* FAO Forestry Paper 37, Rome, 122 pp.

Gonggryp, J.W., 1942. Die Holzzufuhr aus den Tropen nach Europa. *Intersylva.* 2: 232–247.

Grossmann, W.D., 1979. Meta-analysis of the importance of forestry in a region (I). The dynamic meta-model (II). In: S. Adisoemarto and E.F. Brünig (Editors), *Trans. 2nd Int. MAB–IUFRO Workshop on Tropical Rainforest Ecosystem Research, Jakarta,* Chair of World Forestry, Hamburg, Special Report 2, pp. 186–214 (I); pp. 215–235 (II).

Kio, P.R.O., 1983. Management potentials of the tropical high forest with special reference to Nigeria. In: S.L. Sutton, T.C. Whitmore and A.C. Chadwick (Editors), *Tropical Rainforest: Ecology and Management.* Blackwell, Oxford, pp. 445–463.

Lamprecht, H., 1986. *Waldbau in den Tropen.* Parey, Hamburg, 318 pp.

Loetsch, F. and Haller, K.E., 1964. *Forest Inventory, Vol. I.* BLV, München, 436 pp.

Loetsch, F., Zoehrer, F. and Haller, K.E., 1973. *Forest Inventory, Vol. II.* BLV, München, 469 pp.

MAB, 1982, 1983. *Mitteilungen des Deutschen Nationalkomitees für das UNESCO-Programm "Mensch und Biosphaere".* Nr. 10: 3rd MAB/IUFRO Workshop, 1982. No. 11: MAB-Seminar, 1982. No. 12: Interactions between ecological, economic and social systems. No. 14: Modelling, 1983. Nos. 16 and 17: Ecosystem research and modelling, MAB 6, 1983. No. 19: International Seminar "Influence of man on mountain ecosystems in the Alpine National Park Berchtesgaden". Obtainable from: MAB-Kontaktstelle, Melbweg 42, D-5320 Bonn 1.

Neil, P.E., 1981. *Problems and Opportunities in Tropical Rainforest Management.* (C.F.I. Occasional Paper Nr. 16) Univ. of Oxford, Oxford, 176 pp.

Pandolfo, C., 1984. *Perspectivas do uso Continuo dos Recursos Naturais da Amazonia.* Proc. 1st Symp. on Humid Tropics, Belem, EMBRAPA/CPATU, I: 126–135.

Pitt, C.J.W., 1961. *Application of Silvicultural Methods to some Forests* of the Amazon. BRA/FO Rep. No. 1337, FAO, Rome, 137 pp.

Queensland Department of Forestry, 1983. *Rainforest Research in Queensland.* (Position Paper) Government Printer, Brisbane, Qld., 52 pp.

Ross, M.S., 1984. *A Method for Selecting Agricultural Land from Production and Conversion Forests in Indonesia.* (C.F.I. Occasional Paper 22) Univ. of Oxford, Oxford, 183 pp.

Sanchez, P.A. and Cochrane, T.T., 1980. Soil constraints in relation to major farming systems of tropical America. In: *Priorities for Alleviating Soil-Related Constraints to Food Production in the Tropics.* Proceedings Seminar, Los Banos, International Rice Research Institute, pp. 107–139. *See also*: M.J. Swift, (Editor), 1984. *Soil Biological Processes and Tropical Soil Fertility.* Biology International IUBS, Paris, Special Issue, 5: 38 pp.

Schlich, Sir W.M., 1922. *Forestry Policy in the British Empire.* Bradbury, Agnew & Co., London, 342 pp.

Schmitt, L., 1984. *A Review of Exploitation and Improvements in Natural Forest Stands in Guyana.* Proc. 1st Symp. on Humid Tropics, Belem, EMPRAPA/CPATU, II: 229–232.

Shrivastava, P.B.L., Abdul Manap Ahmad, Kamis Awang, Ashari Muktar, Razali Abdul Kader, Freezaillah Che'Yom, Lee Su See, 1983. *Tropical Forests, Source of Energy Through Optimization and Diversification.* Penerbit Univ. Pertanian Malaysia, Serdang, 397 pp.

Sutton, S.L., Whitmore, T.C. and Chadwick, A.C., 1983. *Tropical Rainforest: Ecology and Management.* Blackwell, Oxford, 498 pp.

Trevor, C.G. and Smythies, E.A., 1923. *Practical Forest Management.* Government Press, Allahabad, 288 pp.

UNESCO, 1978. *Tropical Forest Ecosystems.* A state of knowledge report prepared by UNESCO, UNEP, FAO. Natural Resources Research XIV, UNESCO, Paris, 683 pp.

Van Steenis, C.G.G.J., 1958. *Vegetation Map of Malaysia, 1:5 000 000, with Commentary.* Unesco Humid Tropics Research Project, Paris, 8 pp.

Vester, F., 1980. *Sensitivity Model.* Regionale Planungsgemein-schaft. Umland Verband, Frankfurt, 284 pp.

Wadsworth, F.H., 1951/1952. Forest management in the Luquillo Mountains. I. The setting. *Caribb. For.,* 12: 93–114; II. Planning for multiple land use. *Caribb. For.,* 13: 49–61; III. Selection of products and silvicultural policies. *Caribb. For.,* 13; 93–119.

Whitmore, T.C., 1984. A vegetation map of Malesia at a scale of 1:5 million. *J. Biogeogr.,* 11; 461–471 and map.

Wyatt-Smith, J., 1963. *Manual of Malayan Silviculture for Inland Forest. Parts I–III.* Malayan Forest Record No. 23, Forest Research Institute, Kepong.

AUTHOR INDEX[1]

---

[1]Page references to text are in roman type, to bibliographic entries in italics.

SYSTEMATIC INDEX

GENERAL INDEX

Papua New Guinea (*see also* New Guinea), 243, 250, 431, 592, 603, 604
Para (Brazil), 120, 122, 126–128, 477
Paraguana, Peninsula de (Venezuela), 115
Paraguay, 2, 4, 474, 476, 477, 579
parakeets, 222, 403
parallel evolution of Lepidoptera in different continents, 451
Paramaribo (Surinam), 18
paramo, 19, 102, 114, 318
parasitism (*see also* epiparasitism, kleptoparasitism), 134, 135, 308, 361, 484, 497
"paratropical rain-forest", 196
Paria, Golfo de (Venezuela), 112, 119
Parima, Serra (Brazil), 113
parrots (Psittacidae), 403, 411
Pascoe River (Queensland, Australia), 249
Pasoh (Malaya): forest microclimate, 55–69
–: mass flowering of dipterocarps, 226
–, termites in, 458, 462, 464, 465, 467, 468, 561
passerines, 404
patchiness generated by disturbance, 148, 606, 607
pathogens in ant colonies, 484
Pattani (Thailand), 198
patua (*Jessenia bataua*), 123
peat, 203, 207, 210
– bogs, 207
– swamp forest, 203, 214, 215, 616, 617
Pegu Yoma (Burma), 195
Peninsular Malaysia *see* Malaya, 231
pepper, 591, 601, 613
peridotites in New Caledonia, 287
periodic water stress, 109, 208
periodically flooded forests in America, 104, 119–122
periodicity of activity in leaf-cutting ants, 478
–– fruiting, 391
Perlis (Malaya), 222
permanent swamp forest in America, 104, 119
Pernambuco (Brazil), 112
Peru (*see also* Neotropics)
–: bamboo forest, 125
–: birds, 405–407
–, butterfly behaviour in, 431
–: forests, 112, 114, 115
–:–, losses of, 2
–: *igapo* forest, 121
–: mangrove forest, 119
–: pollination of epiphytes, 147
–: pteridophytes, 329–331
–: soils, 11, 78, 82
–: species diversity, 110
–: swamp forest, 120
Pes-caprae association, 214
pH *see* soil acidity
phenolic compounds (*see also* tannina)

–– as defences against herbivores, 515, 516, 518, 519, 522, 528, 530–532
––: effects on soil biota, 531, 532
–– in evergreen vs deciduous trees, 519
–– in fallen leaves, 442
–– in soils, 530–532
phenology, 221, 223, 513, 514, 522–524, 556
Philippines (*see also* Malesia; Southeast Asia)
–: climate, 33
–: dipterocarps, 231
–: epiphytes, 263, 268
–: forest area, 604, 605
–:– exploitation, 592, 595, 597
–:– types, 223
–: Lepidoptera, 451
–: phytogeography, 263
–: pteridophytes, 263, 331, 332
–: rodents, 383, 386, 396
–: Selective Improvement System of forest management, 625
–: Selective Logging System of forest management, 597
–: shifting cultivation, 604
–: soils, 75, 78
phoresis, 478, 484, 493
phorophytes (*see also* epiphytes), 133, 150, 151
phosphorus (*see also* nutrients)
– availability affected by soil acidity, 531
–, ecosystem storage of, 85
– fixation as constraint to plant growth, 84–86
– in epiphytes, 150
– in river waters, 95
– in soils, 76, 77, 79, 81
– release from litter, 554, 555
– uptake dependent on mycorrhizas, 538
– withdrawal from senescent leaves, 530
photography, aerial, 213
photoperiod, 528
photosynthesis, 56, 141, 273, 344
–: "idling" by stomatal closure, 273
– of canopy, 68, 69
–, rates of, 151
photosynthetic pathways (*see also* C_3; crassulacean acid metabolism), 138, 139, 141
––: measurements of δC_{13}, 141, 274
photosynthetically active radiation, 56
phytoalexins, 529
phytochemistry (*see also* leaf composition; secondary compounds), 357
phytochoria (*see also* floristics; phytogeography), 157
– in Africa, 157
–– the Neotropics, 99, 102, 103
phytogeography (*see also* distribution maps; floristics)
– of Africa, 157–160
–– Australia, 248, 249
–– bryophytes, 311, 312

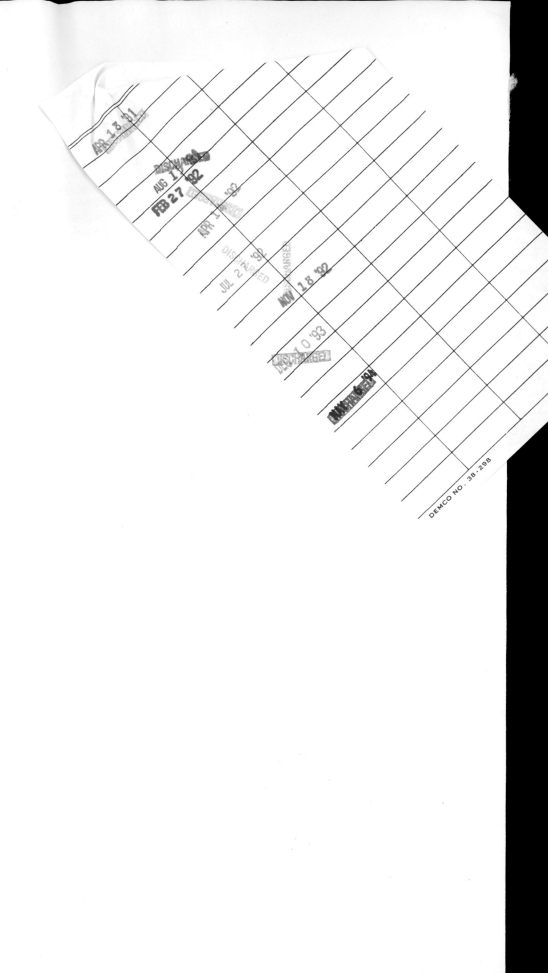

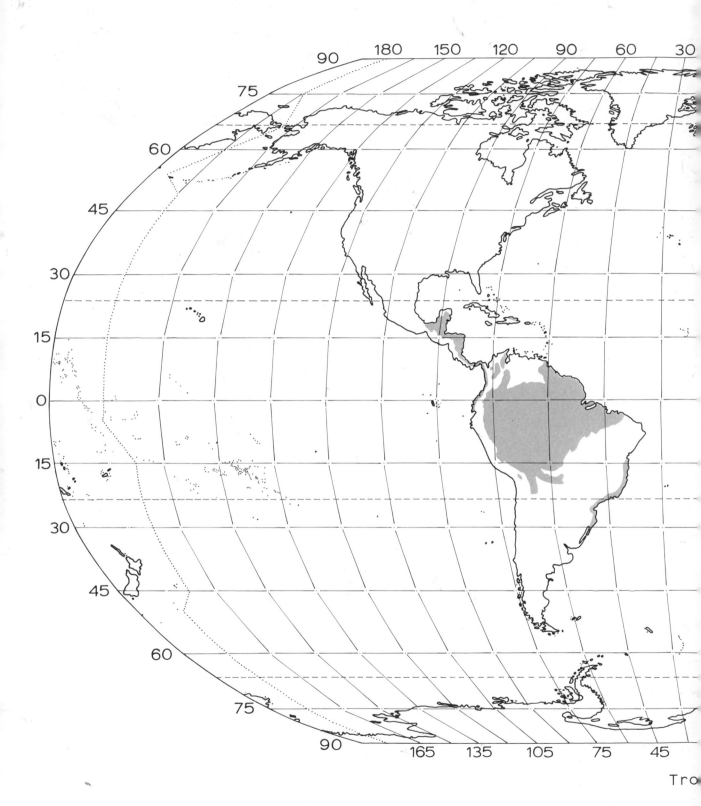

90 180 150 120 90 60 30
75
60
45
30
15
0
15
30
45
60
75
90 165 135 105 75 45

Tro